T0336653

Meta–Heuristics Optimization Algorithms in Engineering, Business, Economics, and Finance

Pandian Vasant
PETRONAS University of Technology, Malaysia

Managing Director:	Lindsay Johnston
Editorial Director:	Joel Gamon
Book Production Manager:	Jennifer Romanchak
Publishing Systems Analyst:	Adrienne Freeland
Development Editor:	Hannah Abelbeck
Assistant Acquisitions Editor:	Kayla Wolfe
Typesetter:	Nicole Sparano
Cover Design:	Nick Newcomer

Published in the United States of America by
Information Science Reference (an imprint of IGI Global)
701 E. Chocolate Avenue
Hershey PA 17033
Tel: 717-533-8845
Fax: 717-533-8661
E-mail: cust@igi-global.com
Web site: http://www.igi-global.com

Library of Congress Cataloging-in-Publication Data

Meta-heuristics optimization algorithms in engineering, business, economics, and finance / Pandian Vasant, editor.
    p. cm.
  Summary: "This book explores the emerging study of meta-heuristics optimization algorithms and methods and their role in innovated real world practical applications"-- Provided by publisher.
  Includes bibliographical references and index.
  ISBN 978-1-4666-2086-5 (hardcover) -- ISBN 978-1-4666-2087-2 (ebook) -- ISBN 978-1-4666-2088-9 (print & perpetual access) 1. Heuristic programming. 2. Heuristic algorithms. 3. Mathematical optimization--Industrial applications. I. Vasant, Pandian.
  T57.84.M48 2013
  006.3--dc23
                    2012013145

British Cataloguing in Publication Data
A Cataloguing in Publication record for this book is available from the British Library.

All work contributed to this book is new, previously-unpublished material. The views expressed in this book are those of the authors, but not necessarily of the publisher.

Table of Contents

Detailed Table of Contents

Chapter 1

Dieu Ngoc Vo, Ho Chi Minh City University of Technology, Vietnam
Peter Schegner, Institute of Electrical Power Systems and High Voltage Engineering, Germany
& Dresden University of Technology, Germany

This chapter proposes a newly improved particle swarm optimization (IPSO) method for solving optimal power flow (OPF) problem. The proposed IPSO is the particle swarm optimization with constriction factor and the particle's velocity guided by a pseudo-gradient. The pseudo-gradient is to determine the direction for the particles so that they can quickly move to optimal solution. The proposed method has been tested on benchmark functions, the IEEE 14-bus, IEEE 30-bus, IEEE 57-bus, and IEEE-118 bus systems, in which the IEEE 30-bus system is tested with different objective functions including quadratic function, valve point effects, and multiple fuels. The test results have shown that the proposed method can efficiently obtain better total costs than the conventional PSO method. Therefore, the proposed IPSO could be a useful method for implementation in the OPF problem.

Chapter 2

Petr Dostál, Brno University of Technology, Institute of Informatics, Czech Republic

Optimization methods have had successful applications in business, economics, and finance. Nowadays the new theories of soft computing are used for these purposes. The applications in business, economics, and finance have specific features in comparison with others. The processes are focused on private corporate attempts at money making or decreasing expenses; therefore the details of applications, successful or not, are not published very often. The optimization methods help in decentralization of decision-making processes to be standardized, reproduced, and documented. The optimization plays very important roles especially in business because it helps to reduce costs that can lead to higher profits and to success in the competitive fight.

Chapter 3

P. Vasant, University Technology Petronas, Malaysia

This chapter outlines an introduction to real-world industrial problem for product-mix selection involving eight variables and twenty one constraints with fuzzy technological coefficients, and thereafter, a formulation for an optimization approach to solve the problem. This problem occurs in production planning in which a decision maker plays a pivotal role in making decision under fuzzy environment. Decision-maker should be aware of his/her level of satisfaction as well as degree of fuzziness while making the product-mix decision. Thus, a thorough analysis is performed on a modified S-curve membership function for the fuzziness patterns and fuzzy sensitivity solution is found from the various optimization methodologies. An evolutionary algorithm is proposed to capture the optimal solutions respect to the vagueness factor and level of satisfaction. The near global optimal solution for objective function is obtained by hybrid meta-heuristics optimization algorithms such as line search, genetic algorithms, and simulated annealing.

Chapter 4

Ata Allah Taleizadeh, Iran University of Science and Technology, Iran
Leopoldo Eduardo Cárdenas-Barrón, Tecnológico de Monterrey, México

Recently, metaheuristic algorithms (MHAs) have gained noteworthy attention for their abilities to solve difficult optimization problems in engineering, business, economics, finance, and other fields. This chapter introduces some applications of MHAs in supply chain management (SCM) problems. For example, consider a multi-product multi-constraint SCM problem in which demands for each product are not deterministic, the lead-time varies linearly with regard to the lot-size and partial backordering of shortages are assumed. Thus, since the main goal is to determine the re-order point, the order quantity and number of shipments under the total cost of the whole chain is minimized. In this chapter, the authors concentrate on MHAs such as harmony search (HS), particle swarm optimization (PSO), genetic algorithm (GA), firefly algorithm (FA), and simulated annealing (SA) for solving the following four supply chain models: single-vendor single-buyer (SBSV), multi-buyers single-vendor (MBSV), multi-buyers multi-vendors (MBMV) and multi-objective multi-buyers multi-vendors (MOMBMV). These models typically are in any supply chain. For illustrative purposes, a numerical example is solved in each model.

Chapter 5

Jana Ries, University of Portsmouth, UK
Patrick Beullens, University of Southampton, UK
Yang Wang, Beijing University of Technology, China

Meta-heuristics are of significant interest to decision-makers due to the capability of finding good solutions for complex problems within a reasonable amount of computational time. These methods are further known to perform according to how their algorithm-specific parameters are set. As most practitioners aim for an off-the-shelf approach when using meta-heuristics, they require an easy applicable strategy to calibrate its parameters and use it. This chapter addresses the so-called Parameter Setting Problem (PSP) and presents new developments for the Instance-specific Parameter Tuning Strategy (IPTS). The IPTS presented only requires the end user to specify its preference regarding the trade-off between running time and solution quality by setting one parameter p ($0 \leq p \leq 1$), and automatically returns a good set of algorithm-specific parameter values for each individual instance based on the calculation of a set of problem instance characteristics. The IPTS does not require any modification of the particular meta-heuristic being used. It aims to combine advantages of the Parameter Tuning Strategy (PTS) and the Parameter Control Strategy (PCS), the two major approaches to the PSP. The chapter outlines the advantages of an IPTS and shows in more detail two ways in which an IPTS can be designed. The first design approach requires expert-based knowledge of the meta-heuristic's performance in relation to the problem at hand. The second, automated approach does not require explicit knowledge of the meta-heuristic used. Both designs use a fuzzy logic system to obtain parameter values. Results are presented for an IPTS designed to solve instances of the Travelling Salesman Problem (TSP) with the meta-heuristic Guided Local Search (GLS).

#### Chapter 6

The location–allocation problems are a class of complicated optimization problems that requires finding sites for m facilities and to simultaneously allocate n customers to those facilities to minimize the total transportation costs. Indeed, these problems, belonging to the class NP-hard, have a lot of local optima solutions. In this chapter, three hybrid meta-heuristics: genetic algorithm, variable neighborhood search and particle swarm optimization, and a hybrid local search approaches are studied. These are investigated to solve the uncapacitated continuous location-allocation problem (multi-source Weber problem). In this regard, alternate location allocation and exchange heuristics are used to find the local optima of the problem within the framework of hybrid algorithms. In addition, some large-scale problems are employed to measure the effectiveness and efficiency of hybrid algorithms. Obtained results from these heuristics are compared with local search methods and with each other. The experimental results show that the hybrid meta-heuristics produce much better solutions to solve large-scale problems. Moreover, the results of two non-parametric statistical tests detected a significant difference in hybrid algorithms such that the hybrid variable neighborhood search and particle swarm optimization algorithm outperform the others.

#### Chapter 7

This chapter considers the problem of understanding the relationship between company stock returns and earnings components, namely accruals and cash flows. The problem is of interest, because earnings are a key output of the accounting process, and investors have been shown to depend heavily on earnings in their valuation models. This chapter offers an elucidation on the application of a nascent data analysis technique, the Classification and Ranking Belief Simplex (CaRBS) and a recent development of it, called RCaRBS, in the returns-earnings relationship problem previously described. The approach underpinning the CaRBS technique is closely associated with uncertain reasoning, with methodological rudiments based on the Dempster-Shafer theory of evidence. With the analysis approach formed as a constrained optimisation problem, details on the employment of the evolutionary computation based technique trigonometric differential evolution are also presented. Alongside the presentation of results, in terms of model fit and variable contribution, based on a CaRBS classification-type analysis, a secondary analysis is performed using a development RCaRBS, which is able to perform multivariate regression-type analysis. Comparisons are made between the results from the two different types of analysis, as well as briefly with more traditional forms of analysis, namely binary logistic regression and multivariate linear regression. Where appropriate, numerical details in the construction of results from both CaRBS and RCaRBS are presented, as well emphasis on the graphical elucidation of findings.

Chapter 8

Lihua Jiang, Northeastern University, China

Mingcong Deng, Tokyo University of Agriculture and Technology, Japan

Considering the noise effect during the navigation of a two wheeled mobile robot, SVM and LS-SVM based control schemes are discussed under the measured information with uncertainty, and in the different environments. The noise effect is defined as uncertainty in the measured data. One of them focuses on using a potential function and constructing a plane surface for avoiding the local minima in the static environments, where the controller is based on Lyapunov function candidate. Another one addresses to use a potential function and to define a new detouring virtual force for escaping from the local minima in the dynamic environments. Stability of the control system can be guaranteed. However, the motion control of the mobile robot would be affected by the noise effect. The SVM and LS-SVM for function estimation are used for estimating the parameter in the proposed controllers. With the estimated parameter, the noise effect during the navigation of the mobile robot can be reduced.

Chapter 9

Fatima Ghedjati, Laboratoire CReSTIC-Reims (Centre de Recherche en STIC), IUT de
Reims-Châlons-Charleville, France

Safa Khalouli, Laboratoire CReSTIC-Reims (Centre de Recherche en STIC), IUT de
Reims-Châlons-Charleville, France

In this chapter the authors address a hybrid flow shop scheduling problem considering the minimization of the makespan in addition to the sum of earliness and tardiness penalties. This problem is proven to be NP-hard, and consequently the development of heuristic and meta-heuristic approaches to solve it is well justified. So, to deal with this problem, the authors propose a method which consists on the one hand, on using a meta-heuristic based on ant colony optimization algorithm to generate feasible solutions and, on the other hand, on using an aggregation multi-criteria method based on fuzzy logic to assist the decision-maker to express his preferences according to the considered objective functions. The aggregation method uses the Choquet integral. This latter allows to take into account the interactions between the different criteria. Experiments based on randomly generated instances were conducted to test the effectiveness of the approach.

Chapter 10

Alberto García-Villoria, Institute of Industrial and Control Engineering (IOC),
Universitat Politècnica de Catalunya (UPC), Spain

Albert Corominas, Institute of Industrial and Control Engineering (IOC),
Universitat Politècnica de Catalunya (UPC), Spain

Rafael Pastor, Institute of Industrial and Control Engineering (IOC),
Universitat Politècnica de Catalunya (UPC), Spain

Metaheuristics are a powerful tool for solving hard optimisation problems. Moreover, metaheuristic hybrid optimisation techniques can be applied to develop an improved metaheuristic algorithm for a given problem. It is known that some metaheuristics perform better than others for each problem. However, there is a lack of theoretical basis to explain why a metaheuristic performs well (or bad) when solving a problem, and there is not a general guide to design specific hybrid metaheuristics. In this chapter, the authors describe the response time variability problem (RTVP), which is an NP-hard combinatorial optimisation problem that appears in a wide range of engineering and business applications. They show how to solve this problem by means of metaheuristics and how to design specific hybrid metaheuristics for the RTVP. This may be useful to managers, engineers, researchers, and scientists to deal with other types of optimisation problems.

Chapter 11

Ata Allah Taleizadeh, Iran University of Science and Technology, Iran
Leopoldo Eduardo Cárdenas-Barrón, Tecnológico de Monterrey, México

The hybrid metaheuristics algorithms (HMHAs) have gained a considerable attention for their capability to solve difficult problems in different fields of science. This chapter introduces some applications of HMHAs in solving inventory theory problems. Three basic inventory problems, joint replenishment EOQ problem, newsboy problem, and stochastic review problem, in certain and uncertain environments such as stochastic, rough, and fuzzy environments with six different applications, are considered. Several HMHAs such as genetic algorithm (GA), simulated annealing (SA), particle swarm optimization (PSO), harmony search (HS), variable neighborhood search (VNS), and bees colony optimization (BCO) methods are used to solve the inventory problems. The proposed metaheuristics algorithms also are combined with fuzzy simulation, rough simulation, Pareto selecting and goal programming approaches. The computational performance of all of them, on solving these three optimization problems, is compared together.

Chapter 12

H. Bevrani, University of Kurdistan, Iran
F. Habibi, University of Kurdistan, Iran
S. Shokoohi, University of Kurdistan, Iran

The increasing need for electrical energy, limited fossil fuel reserves, and the increasing concerns with environmental issues call for fast development in the area of distributed generations (DGs) and renewable energy sources (RESs). A Microgrid (MG) as one of the newest concepts in the power systems consists of several DGs and RESs that provides electrical and heat power for local loads. Increasing in number of MGs and nonlinearity/complexity due to entry of MGs to the power systems, classical and nonflexible control structures may not represent desirable performance over a wide range of operating conditions. Therefore, more flexible and intelligent optimal approaches are needed. Following the advent of optimization/intelligent methods, such as artificial neural networks (ANNs), some new potentials and powerful solutions for MG control problems such as frequency control synthesis have arisen. The present chapter addresses an ANN-based optimal approach scheduling of the droop coefficients for the purpose of frequency regulation in the MGs.

Chapter 13

Hindriyanto Dwi Purnomo, Chung Yuan Christian University, Taiwan
*   & Satya Wacana Christian University, Indonesia*
Hui-Ming Wee, Chung Yuan Christian University, Taiwan

A new metaheuristic algorithm is proposed. The algorithm integrates the information sharing as well as the evolution operators in the swarm intelligence algorithm and evolutionary algorithm respectively. The basic soccer player movement is used as the analogy to describe the algorithm. The new method has two basic operators; the move off and the move forward. The proposed method elaborates the reproduction process in evolutionary algorithm with the powerful information sharing in the swarm intelligence algorithm. Examples of implementations are provided for continuous and discrete problems. The experiment results reveal that the proposed method has the potential to become a powerful optimization method. As a new method, the proposed algorithm can be enhanced in many different ways such as investigating the parameter setting, elaborating more aspects of the soccer player movement as well as implementing the proposed method to solve various optimization problems.

Chapter 14

Igor Litvinchev, Nuevo Leon State University - UANL, Mexico
Miguel Mata, Nuevo Leon State University - UANL, Mexico
Lucero Ozuna, Nuevo Leon State University - UANL, Mexico
Jania Saucedo, Nuevo Leon State University - UANL, Mexico
Socorro Rangel, São Paulo State University - UNESP, Brazil

In the two-stage capacitated facility location problem, a single product is produced at some plants in order to satisfy customer demands. The product is transported from these plants to some depots and then to the customers. The capacities of the plants and depots are limited. The aim is to select cost minimizing locations from a set of potential plants and depots. This cost includes fixed cost associated with opening plants and depots, and variable cost associated with both transportation stages. In this work two different mixed integer linear programming formulations are considered for the problem. Several Lagrangian relaxations are analyzed and compared, a Lagrangian heuristic producing feasible solutions is presented. The results of a computational study are reported.

Chapter 15

Laiq Khan, COMSATS Institute of Information Technology, Pakistan
Rabiah Badar, COMSATS Institute of Information Technology, Pakistan
Sidra Mumtaz, COMSATS Institute of Information Technology, Pakistan

This work explores the potential of Music-Inspired Harmony Search (MIHS), meta-heuristic technique, in the area of power system for Generator Maintenance Scheduling (GMS). MIHS has been used to generate optimal preventive maintenance schedule for generators to maintain reliable and economical power system operation taking into account the maintenance window, load and crew constraints. The robustness of the algorithm has been evaluated for five different case studies: 8-units test system, 13-units test system, 21-units test system, 62-units test system, and 136-units test system of Water and Power Development Authority (WAPDA) Pakistan. As per previous practice, WAPDA used to use manual scheduling based on hit-and-trial. The simulations have been carried out in MATLAB®. Based on its comparison with Genetic Algorithm (GA), it has been found that MIHS has fast convergence rate and optimal schedule for all the test systems satisfying the stated constraints.

A metaheuristic is conventionally described as an iterative generation process which guides a servient heuristic by combining intelligently different concepts for exploring and exploiting the search space, learning strategies are used to structure information in order to find efficiently near-optimal solutions. In the literature, usage of metaheuristic in engineering problems is increasing in a rapid manner. In this study; a survey of the most important metaheuristics from a conceptual point of view is given. Background knowledge for each metaheuristics is presented. The publications are classified with respect to the used metaheuristic techniques and application areas. Advantages and disadvantages of metaheuristics can be found in this chapter. Future directions of metaheuristics are also mentioned.

Clustering and outlier detection are important data mining areas. Online clustering and outlier detection generally work with continuous data streams generated at a rapid rate and have many practical applications, such as network instruction detection and online fraud detection. This chapter first reviews related background of online clustering and outlier detection. Then, an incremental clustering and outlier detection method for market-basket data is proposed and presented in details. This proposed method consists of two phases: weighted affinity measure clustering (WC clustering) and outlier detection. Specifically, given a data set, the WC clustering phase analyzes the data set and groups data items into clusters. Then, outlier detection phase examines each newly arrived transaction against the item clusters formed in WC clustering phase, and determines whether the new transaction is an outlier. Periodically, the newly collected transactions are analyzed using WC clustering to produce an updated set of clusters, against which transactions arrived afterwards are examined. The process is carried out continuously and incrementally. Finally, the future research trends on online data mining are explored at the end of the chapter.

#### Chapter 18

This chapter presents a Discrete Multi-objective Particle Swarm Optimization (MOPSO) algorithm that determines the optimal order of activities execution within a design project that minimizes project total iterative time and cost. Numerical Design Structure Matrix (DSM) was used to model project activities' execution order along with their interactions providing a base for calculating the objective functions. Algorithm performance was tested on a hypothetical project data and results showed its ability to reach Pareto fronts on different sets of objective functions.

N.I. Voropai, Energy Systems Institute of the Siberian Branch of the Russian Academy of Sciences, Russia

A. Z. Gamm, Energy Systems Institute of the Siberian Branch of the Russian Academy of Sciences, Russia

A. M. Glazunova, Energy Systems Institute of the Siberian Branch of the Russian Academy of Sciences, Russia

P. V. Etingov, Energy Systems Institute of the Siberian Branch of the Russian Academy of Sciences, Russia

I. N. Kolosok, Energy Systems Institute of the Siberian Branch of the Russian Academy of Sciences, Russia

E. S. Korkina, Energy Systems Institute of the Siberian Branch of the Russian Academy of Sciences, Russia

V. G. Kurbatsky, Energy Systems Institute of the Siberian Branch of the Russian Academy of Sciences, Russia

D. N. Sidorov, Energy Systems Institute of the Siberian Branch of the Russian Academy of Sciences, Russia

V. A. Spiryaev, Energy Systems Institute of the Siberian Branch of the Russian Academy of Sciences, Russia

N. V. Tomin, Energy Systems Institute of the Siberian Branch of the Russian Academy of Sciences, Russia

R. A. Zaika, Energy Systems Institute of the Siberian Branch of the Russian Academy of Sciences, Russia

B. Bat-Undraal, Mongolian University of Science and Technology, Mongolia

Optimization of solutions on expansion of electric power systems (EPS) and their control plays a crucial part in ensuring efficiency of the power industry, reliability of electric power supply to consumers and power quality. Until recently, this goal was accomplished by applying classical and modern methods of linear and nonlinear programming. In some complicated cases, however, these methods turn out to be rather inefficient. Meta-heuristic optimization algorithms often make it possible to successfully cope with arising difficulties. State estimation (SE) is used to calculate current operating conditions of EPS using the SCADA measurements of state variables (voltages, currents etc.). To solve the SE problem, the Energy Systems Institute of Siberian Branch of Russian Academy of Sciences (ESI of SB RAS) has devised a method based on test equations (TE), i.e. on the steady state equations that contain only measured parameters. Here, a technique for EPS SE using genetic algorithms (GA) is suggested. SE is the main tool for EPS monitoring. The quality of SE results determines largely the EPS control efficiency. An algorithm for exclusion of wrong SE calculations is described. The algorithm using artificial neural networks (ANN) is based on the analysis of results of the calculation performed solving the SE problem with different combinations of constants. The proposed procedure is checked on real data.

Since late in the 20th century, various heuristic and metaheuristic optimization methods have been developed to obtain superior results and optimize models more efficiently. Some have been inspired by natural events and swarm behaviors. In this chapter, the authors illustrate empirical applications of the gravitational search algorithm (GSA) as a new optimization algorithm based on the law of gravity and mass interactions to optimize closed-loop logistics network. To achieve these aims, the need for a green supply chain will be discussed, and the related drivers and pressures motivate us to develop a mathematical model to optimize total cost in a closed-loop logistic for gathering automobile alternators at the end of their life cycle. Finally, optimizing total costs in a logistic network is solved using GSA in MATLAB software. To express GSA capabilities, a genetic algorithm (GA), as a common and standard metaheuristic algorithm, is compared. The obtained results confirm GSA's performance and its ability to solve complicated network problems in closed-loop supply chain and logistics.

Foreword

Optimization has become a *key technology* in all areas on academicals life and its practical use in real life. In fact, contributions of modern Optimization range from science, engineering, economics, the sectors of finance, energy, environment and ecology to social sciences and emerging *"new frontiers,"* "hard" and "soft" ones combined, with all their challenges. *Optimization* has served and and will further serve *(i)* to represent reality in terms of mathematics and in a way which gives access to modern algorithmical methods and the power of high-performance computers, and *(ii)* to give decision aid to persons and institutions in responsibility for the world of tomorrow. In this respect, *Optimization* has been and will further be witnessing the wealth of life, and survey and select chances for improvements in the technical and economical fields of life, and for improvements of living conditions on earth, in all quantitative and qualitative aspects and respects.

In these years, in addition to the *Calculus* based traditions of *Optimization* which originate from mathematics, physics and mechanics and which are more model-based, *Engineering* has contributed a lot to *Optimization*, too, namely, via *Heuristics* and *Meta-Heuristics*. These approaches are often inspired by nature, especially, by *Biology*, e.g., by *Genetics* and *Population Dynamics*. Herewith, they are often *model-free*, and they aim at learning from nature. By this view and ability to learn and, eventually, to benefit from the "success stories" of nature, *Heuristics* and *Meta Heuristics* have become surprisingly successful. It is subject of present and future research to further rigorously compare the model-free and model-based approaches and to combine, or hybridize, these two traditions fruitfully.

The present book now is a scientific "festival" of *Meta-Heuristics* in *Optimization*, especially, from the applied perspectives of engineering, business, economics and finance. Herewith, it represents state-of-the-art and modern developments as well; by this, the new book establishes a basis for further exchange, the establishment of theoretical foundations and results, by *Optimizers* of different academicals backgrounds, and for joint efforts towards premium science and important applications - for the sake of mankind. Cordial thanks for the editors and publishers of this book who supported and encouraged that future potential and opportunity.

Gerhard-Wilhelm Weber
Institute of Applied Mathematics, METU, Turkey

Gerhard-Wilhelm Weber *is a Professor at IAM, METU, Ankara, Turkey. His research in on optimization and control (continuous and discrete), OR, financial mathematics, on life, bio, and human sciences, dynamical systems, data mining, statistical learning, inverse problems, environment, and development; he is involved into the organization of scientific life internationally. G.-W. Weber received both his Diploma and Doctorate in Mathematics, and Economics / Business Administration, at Aachen University of Technology (RWTH Aachen), and his Habilitation (second Doctorate) at Darmstadt University of Technology*

(TU Darmstadt). He held Professorships by proxy at University of Cologne, Germany, and Chemnitz University of Technology, Germany, before he worked at Cologne Bioinformatics Center and then, in 2003, went to Ankara. At IAM, METU, he is in the Programs of Financial Mathematics, Actuarial Sciences and Scientific Computing, he is Assistant to the Director of IAM and a member of three further graduate schools and institutes of METU. Further, he has affiliations at University of Siegen (Germany), University of Ballarat (Australia), University of Aveiro (Portugal), Malaysia University of Technology and University of North Sumatra (Indonesia). He has served in several national and international projects. Gerhard-Wilhelm Weber is (co-) author of more than 200 publications, e.g., papers and books, he has been member in the Editorial Boards of approximately 15 journals. G.-W. Weber has received a number of awards, calls and distinctions.

Preface

Since the beginning of the modern industrial revolution, optimization techniques have become one of the most important decision making areas concerning industrial, economics, business and financial systems. Modern optimization also plays an important role in service centered operations, and has recently received much more attention with the development of engineering and financial systems. The failure of engineering and financial systems due to uncertainties in fuzzy environment and the cause for natural disaster and manmade chaotic problems possibly can be handled by an advanced modern optimization techniques. In this book, great emphasis is given to the possibility of handling and tackling the man made disastrous human error problems with high level of satisfaction.

A great emphasis in these book chapters is given to newly develop meta-heuristic hybrid optimization (MHHO) techniques. These optimization methodologies are based on a mathematical framework that was developed by logicians, engineers, analysts, financiers, economists and computer scientists to study the intrinsic difficulty of algorithms and problems. It has proven very useful for real world practical problem solving in engineering, economics and financial systems.

The objective of the book is to explore the emerging meta-heuristics optimization algorithms and methods in engineering, business, economic, and financial sectors and their novel, original, creative, and innovative real world practical applications.

The prospective audience of the book "Meta-Heuristic Hybrid Optimization Algorithms for Engineering, Business, Economics, and Finance," is decision makers, managers, engineers, researchers, scientists, financiers, economists, as well as industrialists.

This book contains 20 outstanding chapters in the research area of meta-heuristics optimization algorithms in engineering, business, economics, and finance. Brief discussions on all the chapters are as follow:

Chapter 1 proposes a newly improved particle swarm optimization (IPSO) method for solving optimal power flow (OPF) problem. The proposed IPSO is the particle swarm optimization with constriction factor and the particle's velocity guided by a pseudo-gradient. The pseudo-gradient is to determine the direction for the particles so that they can quickly move to optimal solution. The proposed method has been tested on benchmark functions, the IEEE 14-bus, IEEE 30-bus, IEEE 57-bus, and IEEE-118 bus systems, in which the IEEE 30-bus system is tested with different objective functions including quadratic function, valve point effects, and multiple fuels. The test results have shown that the proposed method can efficiently obtain better total costs than the conventional PSO method. Therefore, the proposed IPSO could be a useful method for implementation in the OPF problem.

Chapter 2 provides a thorough analysis on the issue of optimization techniques for the business leaders in decision making process. Optimization methods have had successful applications in business, economics, and finance. Nowadays the new theories of soft computing are used for these purposes. The applications in business, economics, and finance have specific features in comparison with others. The processes are focused on private corporate attempts at money making or decreasing expenses; therefore the details of applications, successful or not, are not published very often. The optimization methods help in decentralization of decision-making processes to be standardized, reproduced, and documented. The optimization plays very important roles especially in business because it helps to reduce costs that can lead to higher profits and to success in the competitive fight.

Chapter 3 outlines an introduction to real-world industrial problem for product-mix selection involving eight variables and twenty one constraints with fuzzy technological coefficients and thereafter, a formulation for an optimization approach to solve the problem. This problem occurs in production planning in which a decision maker plays a pivotal role in making decision under fuzzy environment. Decision-maker should be aware of his/her level of satisfaction as well as degree of fuzziness while making the product-mix decision. Thus, a thorough analysis performed on a modified S-curve membership function for the fuzziness patterns and fuzzy sensitivity solution found from the various optimization methodologies. An evolutionary algorithm is proposed to capture the optimal solutions respect to vagueness factor and level of satisfaction. The near global optimal solution for objective function is obtained by hybrid meta-heuristics optimization algorithms such as line search, genetic algorithms and simulated annealing.

In chapter 4, the authors concentrate on MHAs such as Harmony Search (HS), Particle Swarm Optimization (PSO), Genetic Algorithm (GA), Firefly Algorithm (FA), and Simulated Annealing (SA) for solving the following four supply chain models: single-vendor single-buyer (SBSV), multi-buyers single vendor (MBSV), multi-buyers multi-vendors (MBMV) and multi-objective multi-buyers multi-vendors (MOMBMV). Recently, Meta-Heuristic Algorithms (MHAs) have gained noteworthy attention for their abilities to solve difficult optimization problems in engineering, business, economics, finance, and other fields. This chapter introduces some applications of MHAs in Supply Chain Management (SCM) problems. For example, consider a multi-product multi-constraint SCM problem in which demands for each product are not deterministic, the lead-time varies linearly with regard to the lot-size and partial backordering of shortages are assumed. Thus, the main goal is to determine the re-order point, the order quantity, and number of shipments under the total cost of the whole chain is minimized.

Chapter 5 reveals the significance contribution of Meta-heuristics to decision-makers due to the capability of finding good solutions for complex problems within a reasonable amount of computational time. These methods are further known to perform according to how their algorithm-specific parameters are set. As most practitioners aim for an off-the-shelf approach when using meta-heuristics, they require an easy applicable strategy to calibrate its parameters and use it. This chapter addresses the so-called Parameter Setting Problem (PSP) and presents new developments for the Instance-specific Parameter Tuning Strategy (IPTS). The IPTS does not require any modification of the particular meta-heuristic being used. It aims to combine advantages of the Parameter Tuning Strategy (PTS) and the Parameter Control Strategy (PCS), the two major approaches to the PSP. The chapter outlines the advantages of an IPTS and shows in more detail two ways in which an IPTS can be designed. The designs use a fuzzy logic system to obtain parameter values. Results are presented for an IPTS designed to solve instances of the Traveling Salesman Problem (TSP) with the meta-heuristic Guided Local Search (GLS).

In chapter 6, some hybrid heuristics including: genetic algorithm, variable neighborhood search, and particle swarm optimization approaches are investigated to solve the Euclidean uncapacitated location-allocation problem. The continuous location–allocation problems are a class of complicated optimization problems that requires finding sites for m facilities and to simultaneously allocate n customers to those facilities to minimize the total transportation costs. This problem is NP-hard and has a lot of local optima solutions. In addition, local optima of the problem are obtained by two local search heuristics that exist in the literature. These local search algorithms are combined with mentioned meta-heuristic algorithms to construct efficient hybrid approaches. Some large-scale problems are used to measure the effectiveness and efficiency of the proposed algorithms. The experimental results show that the hybrid meta-heuristics produce good solutions, is more efficient than the classical meta-heuristics and confirm the superiority of the hybrid meta-heuristic algorithms.

Chapter 7 considers the problem of understanding the relationship between company stock returns and earnings components, namely accruals and cash flows. The problem is of interest because earnings are a key output of the accounting process and investors have been shown to depend heavily on earnings in their valuation models. This chapter offers an elucidation on the application of a nascent data analysis technique, the Classification and Ranking Belief Simplex (CaRBS) and a recent development of it, called RCaRBS, in the returns-earnings relationship problem previously described. The approach underpinning the CaRBS technique is closely associated with uncertain reasoning, with methodological rudiments based on the Dempster-Shafer theory of evidence. With the analysis approach formed as a constrained optimization problem, details on the employment of the evolutionary computation based technique trigonometric differential evolution are also presented.

Chapter 8 provides an excellent application of support vector machine based mobile robot motion control. Considering the noise effect during the navigation of a two wheeled mobile robot, SVM, and LS-SVM based control schemes are discussed under the measured information with uncertainty, and in the different environments. The noise effect is defined as uncertainty in the measured data. One of them focuses on using a potential function and constructing a plane surface for avoiding the local minima in the static environments, where the controller is based on Lyapunov function candidate. Another one addresses to use a potential function and to define a new detouring virtual force for escaping from the local minima in the dynamic environments. Stability of the control system can be guaranteed. However, the motion control of the mobile robot would be affected by the noise effect. The SVM and LS-SVM for function estimation are used for estimating the parameter in the proposed controllers. With the estimated parameter, the noise effect during the navigation of the mobile robot can be reduced.

In chapter 9 the authors address a multi-criteria hybrid flow shop scheduling problem considering the minimization of the makespan in addition to the sum of earliness and tardiness penalties. This problem is proven to be NP-hard, and consequently the development of heuristic and meta-heuristic approaches to solve it are well justified. So, to deal with this problem, authors propose an hybrid method which consists on the one hand, to use a meta-heuristic based on ant colony optimization algorithm to generate feasible solutions and, on the other hand, an aggregation multi-criteria method based on fuzzy logic is used to assist the decision-maker to express his preferences according to the considered objective functions. The aggregation method uses the Choquet integral. This latter allows them to take into account the interactions between the different criteria. Experiments based on randomly generated instances were conducted to test the effectiveness of the novel techniques.

Chapter 10 innovates the novel contribution of meta-heuristics algorithms. Meta-heuristics are a powerful tool for solving hard optimisation problems. Moreover, meta-heuristic hybrid optimisation techniques can be applied to develop an improved meta-heuristic algorithm for a given problem. It is known that some meta-heuristics perform better than others for each problem. However, there is a lack of theoretical basis to explain why a meta-heuristic performs well (or bad) when solving a problem and there is not a general guide to design specific hybrid meta-heuristics. In this chapter, the authors describe the response time variability problem (RTVP), which is an NP-hard combinatorial optimisation problem that appears in a wide range of engineering and business applications. They show how to solve this problem by means of meta-heuristics and how to design specific hybrid meta-heuristics for the RTVP. This may be useful to managers, engineers, researchers, and scientists to deal with other types of optimisation problems.

In chapter 11, the authors provide several HMHAs for different problems; using different Meta-heuristic algorithms such as genetic algorithm (GA), simulated annealing (SA), particle swarm optimization (PSO), Harmony Search (HS), and Bees Colony Optimization (BCO) methods. In recent years, hybrid Meta-heuristic algorithms (HMHA) have gained significant attentions for their abilities to solve difficult problems in engineering. This proposal introduces the applications of HMHA in inventory management problems. Three specific inventory problems in certain and uncertain environments such as stochastic, rough and fuzzy environments with six different applications will be considered: joint replenishment EOQ problem, newsboy problem, and stochastic review problem. Also several HMHAs for different problems; using different Meta-heuristic algorithms such as genetic algorithm (GA), simulated annealing (SA), particle swarm optimization (PSO), Harmony Search (HS), and Bees Colony Optimization (BCO) methods will be used. The proposed Meta-heuristic algorithms will be combined with fuzzy simulation, rough simulation, Pareto selecting and goal programming approaches. The computational performance of all of them, on solving these three optimization problems will be compared together.

Chapter 12 describes the novel application of ANN in the research area of Microgrid. The increasing need for electrical energy, limited fossil fuel reserves and the increasing concerns with environmental issues, call for fast development in the area of distributed generations (DGs) and renewable energy sources (RESs). A Microgrid (MG) as one of the newest concepts in the power systems consists of several DGs and RESs that provides electrical and heat power for local loads. Increasing in number of MGs and nonlinearity/complexity due to entry of MGs to the power systems, classical and nonflexible control structures may not represent desirable performance over a wide range of operating conditions. Therefore, more flexible and intelligent optimal approaches are needed. Following the advent of optimization/intelligent methods, such as artificial neural networks (ANNs), some new potentials and powerful solutions for MG control problems such as frequency control synthesis have arisen. This chapter addresses an ANN-based optimal approach scheduling of the droop coefficients for the purpose of frequency regulation in the MGs.

A new metaheuristic algorithm is proposed in Chapter 13. The algorithm integrates the information sharing as well as the evolution operators in the swarm intelligence algorithm and evolutionary algorithm respectively. The basic soccer player movement is used as the analogy to describe the algorithm. The new method has two basic operators; the *move off* and the *move forward*. The proposed method elaborates the reproduction process in evolutionary algorithm with the powerful information sharing in the swarm intelligence algorithm. Examples of implementations are provided for continuous and discrete problems. The experiment results reveal that the proposed method has the potential to become a powerful optimization method. As a new method, the proposed algorithm can be enhanced in many different ways such as investigating the parameter setting, elaborating more aspects of the soccer player movement as well as implementing the proposed method to solve various optimization problems.

In chapter 14 the two-stage capacitated facility location problem a single product is produced at some plants in order to satisfy customer demands. The product is transported from these plants to some depots and then to the customers. The capacities of the plants and depots are limited. The aim is to select cost minimizing locations from a set of potential plants and depots. This cost includes fixed cost associated with opening plants and depots, and variable cost associated with both transportation stages. In this work two different mixed integer linear programming formulations are considered for the problem. Several Lagrangian relaxations are analyzed and compared, and a Lagrangian heuristic producing feasible solutions is presented. The results of a computational study are reported.

Chapter 15 explores the potential of Music-Inspired Harmony Search (MIHS), meta-heuristic technique, in the area of power system for Generator Maintenance Scheduling (GMS). MIHS has been used to generate optimal preventive maintenance schedule for generators to maintain reliable and economical power system operation taking into account the maintenance window, load and crew constraints. The robustness of the algorithm has been evaluated for five different case studies: 8-units test system, 13-units test system, 21-units test system, 62-units test system, and 136-units test system of Water and Power Development Authority (WAPDA) Pakistan. As per previous practice, WAPDA used to use manual scheduling based on hit-and-trial. The simulations have been carried out in MATLAB®. Based on its comparison with Genetic Algorithm (GA) it has been found that MIHS has fast convergence rate and optimal schedule for all the test systems satisfying the stated constraints.

Chapter 16 basically enlightens the literature review on the development of meta-heuristics techniques. A meta-heuristic is conventionally described as an iterative generation process which guides a servient heuristic by combining intelligently different concepts for exploring and exploiting the search space, learning strategies are used to structure information in order to find efficiently near-optimal solutions. In the literature, usage of meta-heuristic in engineering problems is increasing in a rapid manner. In this study; a survey of the most important meta-heuristics from a conceptual point of view is given. Background knowledge for each meta-heuristics is presented. The publications are classified with respect to the used meta-heuristic techniques and application areas. Advantages and disadvantages of meta-heuristics can be found in this chapter. Future directions of meta-heuristics are also mentioned

Chapter 17 explains the important of an online clustering and an outlier detection. Clustering and outlier detection are important data mining areas. Online clustering and outlier detection generally works with continuous data streams generated at a rapid rate and has many practical applications, such as network instruction detection and online fraud detection. This chapter reviews related background of online clustering and outlier detection. Then, an incremental clustering and outlier detection method for market-basket data is proposed and presented in details. This proposed method consists of two phases: weighted affinity measure clustering (WC clustering) and outlier detection. Specifically, given a data set, the WC clustering phase analyzes the data set and groups data items into clusters. Then, outlier detection phase examines each newly arrived transaction against the item clusters formed in WC clustering phase, and determines whether the new transaction is an outlier.

Chapter 18 presents a discrete Multi-Objective Particle Swarm Optimization (MOPSO) algorithm that determines the optimal order of activities execution within a design project that minimizes project total iterative time and cost. Numerical Design Structure Matrix (DSM) was used to model project activities' execution order along with their interactions providing a base for calculating the objective functions. Algorithm performance was tested on a hypothetical project data and results showed its ability to reach Pareto fronts on different sets of objective functions.

Chapter 19 exploits the vast knowledge of meta-heuristics algorithms in the research area of electric power systems. Recently the considered area of using meta-heuristic algorithms has attracted increasing attention of experts in different spheres, in particular in EPS. The known meta-heuristic methods of modeling and optimization are improved and the new ones are devised both in terms of specific features of concrete problems to be solved. This area is an important constituent of artificial intelligence approaches to solving important applied problems and in many cases demonstrates efficiency of the used methods as against the classical methods of mathematical programming and operations research. The results presented in this chapter for EPS confirm the formulated concept.

Chapter 20 describes a significance contribution of novel technique such as GSA for logistic network. Since late of 20th century until today, various heuristic and meta-heuristic optimization methods have been developed to obtain superior results and optimize models more efficiently. Some of them inspire natural events and swarm behaviors. In this paper, authors try to illustrate empirical application of gravitational search algorithm (GSA) as a new optimization algorithm based on the law of gravity and mass interactions to optimize a closed-loop logistics network. For this, the authors have discussed on necessity of green supply chain, drivers and pressures regarding this matter a mathematical model is developed to optimize total cost in closed-loop logistic for gathering automobile alternators in end of their cycle life. Finally, optimizing total cost in-logistic network is solved-using GSA in MATLAB software.

The editor of this text sincerely thanks all the contributors for their wonderful and invaluable experiential contributions in making this book a global reference for the engineers, scientist, practitioners, economist, financiers, researchers, and managers in the area of hybrid meta-heuristics optimization and its applications.

Pandian Vasant
PETRONAS University of Technology, Malaysia

Acknowledgment

We would like to take this wonderful opportunity to sincerely thank the following friends and colleagues of us for their marvelous help and unlimited support of book chapters of the manuscript. Their fabulous feedback, ideas, constructive comments and suggestions for the improvement of the overall outstanding quality of the book chapters are gratefully acknowledged.

Patrick Beullens, *University of Southampton, UK*

Petr Dostál, *Institute of Informatics, Czech Republic*

Vo Ngoc Dieu, *Asian Institute of Technology, Thailand*

Baoying Wang, *Waynesburg University, USA*

Jana Ries, *University of Portsmouth, UK*

Malcolm J. Beynon, *Cardiff University, UK*

Mark A. Clatworthy, *Cardiff University, UK*

Efren Mezura-Montes, *Laboratorio Nacional de Informatica, Mexico*

Alberto García, *Universitat Politecnica de Catalunya, Spain*

Leopoldo E. Cárdenas-Barrón, *Instituto Tecnológico y de Estudios, Mexico*

Furthermore, we sincerely thank the group of IGI Global at Hershey PA, USA, for their great help and excellent support on this book chapter's project. In particular, special thank go to Ms. Jan Travers, Mrs. Myla Merkel, and Ms. Hannah Abelbeck of IGI Global for their great cooperation.

Last but not least, we sincerely express our sincere thanks and appreciation to members of IGI Global for their great support.

P. Vasant
PETRONAS University of Technology, Malaysia
March 2012

Chapter 1
An Improved Particle Swarm Optimization for Optimal Power Flow

Dieu Ngoc Vo
Ho Chi Minh City University of Technology, Vietnam

Peter Schegner
Institute of Electrical Power Systems and High Voltage Engineering, Germany
& Dresden University of Technology, Germany

ABSTRACT

This chapter proposes a newly improved particle swarm optimization (IPSO) method for solving optimal power flow (OPF) problem. The proposed IPSO is the particle swarm optimization with constriction factor and the particle's velocity guided by a pseudo-gradient. The pseudo-gradient is to determine the direction for the particles so that they can quickly move to optimal solution. The proposed method has been tested on benchmark functions, the IEEE 14-bus, IEEE 30-bus, IEEE 57-bus, and IEEE-118 bus systems, in which the IEEE 30-bus system is tested with different objective functions including quadratic function, valve point effects, and multiple fuels. The test results have shown that the proposed method can efficiently obtain better total costs than the conventional PSO method. Therefore, the proposed IPSO could be a useful method for implementation in the OPF problem.

INTRODUCTION

The objective of an optimal power flow (OPF) problem is to find the steady state operation point of generators in the system so as their total generation cost is minimized while satisfying various generator and system constraints such as generator's real and reactive power, bus volt-age, transformer tap, switchable capacitor bank, and transmission line capacity limits. In the OPF problem, the controllable variables usually determined are real power output of generators, voltage magnitude at generation buses, injected reactive power at compensation buses, and transformer tap settings. Traditionally, mathematical programming techniques can effectively deal with

DOI: 10.4018/978-1-4666-2086-5.ch001

the problem. However, due to the incorporation of FACTS devices to systems, valve point effects or multiple fuels to generators recently, the OPF problem becomes more complicated and the mathematical programming techniques are not a proper selection. Therefore, it requires more powerful search methods for a better implementation. Due to its importance, the OPF problem has been widely studied in the world (Happ & Wirgau, 1981; Huneault, & Galiana, 1991; Momoh, Adapa & El-Hawary, 1999a; Adapa & El-Hawary, 1993b; Pandya & Joshi, 2008).

The OPF problem has been solved by several conventional methods such as gradient-based method (Wood & Wollenberg, 1996), linear programming (LP) (Abou El-Ela & Abido, 1992; Mota-Palomino & Quintana, 1986), non-linear programming (NLP) (Dommel & Tinny, 1968; Pudjianto, Ahmed, & Strbac, 2002), quadratic programming (QP) (Burchett, Happ & Vierath, 1984; Granelli & Montagna, 2000), Newton-based methods (Sun *et al.*, 1984; Santos & da Costa, 1995; Lo & Meng, 2004), semidefinite programming (Bai *et al.*, 2008), and interior point method (IPM) (Yan & Quintana, 1999; Wang & Liu, 2005; Capitanescu *et al.*, 2007). Generally, the conventional methods can find the optimal solution for an optimization problem with a very short time. However, the main drawback of these methods is that they are difficult to deal with non-convex optimization problems with non-differentiable objective. Moreover, these methods are also very difficult for dealing with large-scale problems due to large search space. Meta-heuristic search methods recently developed have shown that they have capability to deal with this complicated problem. Several meta-heuristic search methods have been also widely applied for solving the OPF problem such as genetic algorithm (GA) (Lai & Ma, 1997; Wu, Cao & Wen, 1998; Osman, Abo-Sinna & Mousa, 2004), simulated annealing (SA) (Roa-Sepulveda & Pavez-Lazo, 2003), tabu search (TS) (Abido, 2002), evolutionary programming (EP) (Wu & Ma, 1995; Yuryevich & Wong, 1999), particle swarm optimisation (PSO) (Abido, 2001), and differential evolution (DE) (Cai, Chung & Wong, 2008). These meta-heuristic search methods can overcome the main drawback from the conventional methods with the problem not required to be differentiable. However, the optimal solutions obtained by these methods for optimization problems are near optimum and quality of the solutions is not high when they deal with large-scale problems; that is the obtained solutions may be local optimums with long computational time. In addition, the hybrid methods have also developed for solving OPF problem such as hybrid TS/SA (Ongsakul & Bhasaputra, 2002), hybrid GA-IPM (Yan *et al.*, 2006), hybrid differential evolution (Li, Zhao & Chen, 2010), and hybrid of fuzzy and PSO (Liand *et al.*, 2011). The purpose of the hybrid methods is to utilize the advantages of the element methods integrated in it for obtaining better optimal solutions. Although the hybrid method can be better than the single methods in finding optimal solution they can be slower the single methods due to combination of many single methods. Moreover, the hybrid methods are also usually more complex than the single methods.

In this chapter, a newly improved particle swarm optimization (IPSO) method is proposed for solving optimal power flow (OPF) problem. The proposed IPSO is the particle swarm optimization with constriction factor and the particle's velocity guided by a pseudo-gradient. The pseudo-gradient is to determine the direction for the particles so that they can quickly move to optimal solution. The proposed method has been tested on benchmark functions, the IEEE 14-bus, IEEE 30-bus, IEEE 57-bus, and IEEE-118 bus systems, in which the IEEE 30-bus system is tested with different objective functions including quadratic function, valve point effects, and multiple fuels. The results from the proposed IPSO are also validated by comparing to those from the conventional PSO.

IMPROVED PARTICLE SWARM OPTIMIZATION FOR OPTIMAL POWER FLOW

Problems Formulation

In the OPF problem, the considered variables include control variables and state variables. The control variables include real power injected at generation buses excluding the slack bus, voltage at generation buses, tap ratio of transformers, and reactive power injected by capacitor banks. The state variables include power generation at the slack bus, voltage at load buses, reactive power output of generators, and power flow in transmission lines. In addition, the OPF problem also includes equality constraints which are power flow equations and inequality constraints which are limits control variables and state variables. Generally, the OPF problem can be formulated as a constrained optimization as follows:

$$\text{Min } f(x, u) \tag{1}$$

subject to

$$g(x, u) = 0 \tag{2}$$

$$h(x, u) \leq 0 \tag{3}$$

where f is the objective function to be minimized, g is the set of equality constraints, and h is the set of inequality constraints.

In this problem formulation, the used parameters and variables are defined as follows:

- a_i, b_i, c_i: Fuel cost coefficients of generating unit i
- e_i, f_i: Fuel cost coefficients of generating unit i considering valve point effects
- a_{ik}, b_{ik}, c_{ik}: Fuel cost coefficients of generating unit i corresponding to fuel k
- G_{ij}, B_{ij}: Transfer conductance and susceptance between bus i and bus j, respectively

- N_b: Number of buses
- N_c: Number of switchable capacitors
- N_d: Number of load buses
- N_g: Number of generating units
- N_l: Number of transmission lines
- N_t: Number of transformer with tap changing
- n_i: Number of fuels for unit i
- P_{di}, Q_{di}: Real and reactive power demands at bus i, respectively
- P_{gi}, Q_{gi}: Real and reactive power outputs of generating unit i, respectively
- Q_{ci}: Reactive power compensation source at bus i
- S_{ij}, S_{ji}: Apparent power flow from bus i to bus j and from bus j to bus i
- S_l: Maximum apparent power flow in transmission line l connecting between buses i and j
- T_k: Tap-setting of transformer branch k
- V_{gi}, V_{li}: Voltage magnitude at generation bus i and load bus i, respectively
- V_i, δ_i: Voltage magnitude and angle at bus i, respectively

The detailed OPF problem is formulated as follows:

$$\text{Min } \sum_{i=1}^{N_g} F_i(P_{gi}) \tag{4}$$

where the fuel cost function $F_i(P_{gi})$ of generating unit i can be expressed in one of the forms as follows:

- **Quadratic Function:** The fuel cost of each thermal generator is represented as a quadratic function of its power output.

$$F_i(P_{gi}) = a_i + b_i P_{gi} + c_i P_{gi}^2 \tag{5}$$

- **Valve Point Effects:** The effect of valve points in boilers of thermal generating units is represented by a sinusoidal component added to the quadratic function.

$$F_i(P_{gi}) = a_i + b_i P_{gi} + c_i P_{gi}^2 + \left| e_i \times \sin(f_i \times (P_{gi,\min} - P_{gi})) \right| \tag{6}$$

- **Multiple Fuels:** A generator may have different fuels where each fuel is represented by a piecewise quadratic function (Box 1).

Subject to the equality and inequality constraints:

A. **Real and Reactive Power Flow Equations:** At each bus, the real and reactive power balance should be satisfied (see Box 2 and 3).

B. **Limits at Generation Buses:** The real power, reactive power, and voltage at generation buses should be within between their lower and upper bounds.

$$P_{gi,\min} \leq P_{gi} \leq P_{gi,\max}; \; i = 1,...,N_g \tag{10}$$

$$Q_{gi,\min} \leq Q_{gi} \leq Q_{gi,\max}; \; i = 1,...,N_g \tag{11}$$

$$V_{gi,\min} \leq V_{gi} \leq V_{gi,\max}; \; i = 1,...,N_g \tag{12}$$

C. **Capacity Limits for Switchable Shunt Capacitor Banks:** At var sources by switch-

Box 1.

$$F_i(P_{gi}) = \begin{cases} a_{i1} + b_{i1} P_{gi} + c_{i1} P_{gi}^2, \text{ fuel } 1, \; P_{gi,\min} \leq P_{gi} \leq P_{gi1} \\ ... \\ a_{ik} + b_{ik} P_{gi} + c_{ik} P_{gi}^2, \text{ fuel } k, \; P_{gik\text{-}1} \leq P_{gi} \leq P_{gik} \\ ... \\ a_{in_i} + b_{in_i} P_{gi} + c_{in_i} P_{gi}^2, \text{ fuel } n_i, \; P_{gn_i-1} \leq P_{gi} \leq P_{gi,\max} \end{cases} \tag{7}$$

Box 2.

$$P_{gi} - P_{di} = V_i \sum_{j=1}^{N_b} V_j \left[G_{ij} \cos(\delta_i - \delta_j) + B_{ij} \sin(\delta_i - \delta_j) \right]; \; i = 1,...,N_b \tag{8}$$

Box 3.

$$Q_{gi} + Q_{ci} - Q_{di} = V_i \sum_{j=1}^{N_b} V_j \left[G_{ij} \sin(\delta_i - \delta_j) - B_{ij} \cos(\delta_i - \delta_j) \right]; \; i = 1,...,N_b \tag{9}$$

able capacitors their power output should be within their lower and upper limits.

$$Q_{ci,\min} \leq Q_{ci} \leq Q_{ci,\max}; \quad i = 1, ..., N_c \qquad (13)$$

D. **Transformer Tap Settings Constraints:** The tap settings of each transformer should be also within their lower and upper bounds.

$$T_{k,\min} \leq T_k \leq T_{k,\max}; \quad k = 1, ..., N_t \qquad (14)$$

E. **Security Constraints:** The voltage at load buses and power flow in transmission lines should not exceed their limits.

$$V_{li,\min} \leq V_{li} \leq V_{li,\max}; \quad i = 1, ..., N_d \qquad (15)$$

$$S_l \leq S_{l,\max}; \quad l = 1, ..., N_l \qquad (16)$$

$$S_l = \max\{| S_{ij} |, | S_{ji} |\} \qquad (17)$$

The shapes of different fuel cost functions are depicted in Figures 1, 2, and 3.

From the problem formulation, u is the set of control variables (independent variables) including real power output of generators at generation buses except the slack bus P_{gi} with $i = 2, ..., N_g$, voltage at generation buses V_{gi} with $i = 1, ..., N_g$, transformer tap settings T_k with $k = 1, ..., N_t$, and reactive power output from switchable capacitor banks Q_{ci} with $i = 1, ..., N_c$. Therefore, the vector of control variables u can be expressed as seen in Box 4.

The vector of state variables (dependent variables) x includes the real power output of generator at the slack bus P_{gl}, voltage at load buses V_{li} with $i = 1, ..., N_d$, reactive power output of generators Q_{gi} with $i = 1, ..., N_g$, and the apparent power flow in transmission lines Sl with $l = 1, ..., N_l$. The vector x can be expressed in Box 5.

In this problem, there are many control variables which have effects on the final result such

Figure 1. Fuel cost function of generating units in quadratic function

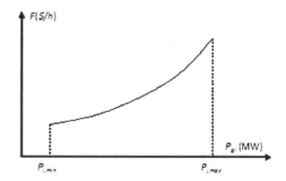

Figure 2. Fuel cost function of generating units with valve point effects

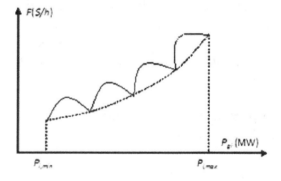

Figure 3. Fuel cost function of generating units with multiple fuels

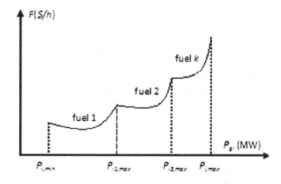

as bus voltage, transformer tap changer, generator reactive power, and switchable capacitor banks. In fact, the lower and upper limits of these vari-

Box 4.

$$u = \{P_{g2}, \ ..., \ P_{gN_g}, \ V_{g1}, \ ..., \ V_{gN_g}, \ T_1, \ ..., \ T_{N_t}, \ Q_{c1}, \ ..., \ Q_{cN_c}\}^{\ T} \qquad (18)$$

Box 5.

$$x = \{P_{g1}, \ Q_{g1}, \ ..., \ Q_{gN_g}, \ V_{l1}, \ ..., \ V_{lN_d}, \ S_{l1}, \ ..., \ S_{lN_l}\}^{\ T} \qquad (19)$$

ables have great effects on optimal solution. For instance, the case with higher maximum limits of these variables will provide better optimal solution than the case with lower maximum limits of them. Therefore, if different limits of these variables are used, different optimal solutions can be obtained.

Proposed Particle Swarm Optimization

Conventional Particle Swarm Optimization

Particle swarm optimization (PSO) is a population based method for solving optimization problems. The PSO method was developed by Kennedy and Eberhart in 1995 (Kennedy & Eberhart, 1995), inspired by social behavior from the movement of a bird flock or a fish school searching for food. The scenario of inspiration for this method is described as follows. A flock of birds is searching food in a certain area where there is only one piece of food being searched. Although the birds do not know where exactly the food is, they know how far the food is. The best strategy for finding the food is to follow the bird which is nearest to the food. PSO learned ideas from the scenario and implemented it for solving optimization problems. For implementation of PSO, each single bird which

also referred as a particle represents a candidate solution in the search space and the population which is also referred as the swarm represents a set of candidate solutions. For evaluation of candidate solutions, a fitness function associated with each particle is used and the evaluation is performed for every iteration.

Similar to other evolutionary computation techniques such as genetic algorithm (GA) and evolutionary programming (EP), PSO is also initialized with a population of random solutions and searches for optima by updating generations. However, PSO has no evolution operators such as crossover and mutation like GA and EP. In PSO, the potential solutions represented by particles fly through the search space of the problem based on their current best velocity and position. Compared to other meta-heuristic methods, the advantages of PSO are that it is easy to be implemented and there are few parameters to adjust.

PSO is a meta-heuristic method which makes few or no assumptions about the problem being considered and can deal with large-scale problems with very large spaces of candidate solutions. Moreover, PSO does not use the gradient of the problem being considered like many other classic optimization methods such as gradient search and Newton methods. Therefore, PSO does not need the problem being optimized to be differentiable.

PSO solves an optimization problem by having a population of candidate solutions or particles and move these particles in the search space of the problem using simple mathematical formulae over the particle's position and velocity. In each iteration, every particle is updated based on the two best values. The first one (local best) is the best solution that the particle achieves so far and the last one (global best) is the best solution that the population achieves so far.

Considering an *n*-dimension optimization problem with objective as follows:

$$\text{Min } f(x) \tag{20}$$

$$x_{min} \leq x \leq x_{max} \tag{21}$$

where $x = [x_1, x_2, ..., x_n]^T$ is a vector of *n* independent variables, and x_{max} and x_{min} are vectors of maximum and minimum limits for variables.

For implementation of PSO, a population of particles is used for searching the optimal solution for the problem. Suppose that there are *np* particles in the population, the position and velocity vectors of particle *d* are represented by $x_d = [x_{1d}, x_{2d}, ..., x_{nd}]^T$ and $v_d = [v_{1d}, v_{2d}, ..., v_{nd}]^T$, $d = 1, ..., np$, respectively, where x_d is the position of particle *d* representing a candidate solution and v_d is the velocity of particle *d*.

For evaluation of best solution for each particle and for the population, a fitness function is set to the objective function of the problem and every particle is associated with a fitness function. The best position of particle *d* is based on a comparison of the value of its fitness function at the current iteration and the value of best previous fitness function. The best position of the population is based on a comparison of values of fitness function from all particles. The best previous position of particle *d* is represented by $pbest_d = [p_{1d}, p_{2d}, ..., p_{nd}]^T$, $d = 1, ..., n$ and the best particle in the population represented by $gbest = [g_1, g_2, ..., g_n]^T$.

Suppose that at the current iteration *k* the best position of each particle and the population are obtained, the velocity and position of each particle in the next iteration (*k*+1) for evaluation of the fitness function are updated as follows:

$$\begin{aligned} v_{id}^{(k+1)} = v_{id}^{(k)} &+ c_1 \times rand_1 \\ &\times \left(pbest_{id}^{(k)} - x_{id}^{(k)}\right) \\ &+ c_2 \times rand_2 \times \left(gbest_i^{(k)} - x_{id}^{(k)}\right) \end{aligned} \tag{22}$$

$$x_{id}^{(k+1)} = x_{id}^{(k)} + v_{id}^{(k+1)} \tag{23}$$

where the constants c_1 and c_2 are cognitive and social parameters, respectively and $rand_1$ and $rand_2$ are the random values in [0, 1].

The upper and lower bounds for the position of each element in a particle x_{id} are limited by the maximum and minimum limits of the variable represented by the particle, respectively. The velocity of each particle is limited in the range $[-v_{id,max}, v_{id,max}]$ for $i = 1, ..., n$ and $d = 1, ..., np$, where the maximum and minimum velocities of element *i* belonging to particle *d* in the search space is determined by:

$$v_{id,max} = R \times (x_{id,max} - x_{id,min}) \tag{24}$$

$$v_{id,min} = -v_{id,max} \tag{25}$$

where *R* is the velocity limit coefficient, usually selected in the range [0.1, 0.25].

The procedure of PSO is described as follows:

```
Select parameters
Initialize position and velocity for
each particle
Evaluate fitness function for each
particle's position
Set the initial position of each par-
ticle to its best position pbest
```

```
Set the particle's position with the
best fitness function to global best
gbest
While <Termination criteria not met>
        Calculate new velocity for
each particle
            Update new position for each
particle
            Evaluate fitness function
for each particle
                If the fitness value
is better than the best fitness value
in history, set the current parti-
cle's position as the new pbest_d
                Otherwise, the par-
ticle's position corresponding to the
best fitness value in history is set
to the new pbest_d
            Choose the particle's posi-
tion corresponding to the best fit-
ness value of all particles as the
new gbest
End
```

The global best *gbest* is selected as the optimal solution

Concept of Pseudo-Gradient

Suppose that the objective function (20) in the *n*-dimension optimization problem is differentiable, the conventional gradient *g(x)* of the objective function *f(x)* is defined as an *n*-dimension vector whose components are the partial derivatives of *f(x)* as follows:

$$g(x) = \left[\frac{\partial f}{\partial x_1}, \ \frac{\partial f}{\partial x_2}, \ ..., \ \frac{\partial f}{\partial x_n} \right]^T \qquad (26)$$

This gradient is always indicates the maximum rate of change direction of the objective function at a point in the search space. However, for the non-differentiable objective functions, the con-ventional is not applicable. Therefore, there is a need for gradient approach for these non-convex functions and pseudo-gradient is a solution.

The pseudo-gradient is to determine the search direction for each individual in population based methods when dealing with non-convex optimiza-tion problems with non-differentiable objective function (Pham & Jin, 1995). The advantage of the pseudo-gradient is that it can provide a good direction in the search space of a problem without requiring the objective function to be differen-tiable. Therefore, the pseudo-gradient method is suitably implemented in the meta-heuristic search methods for solving non-convex problems with multiple minima.

For a non-convex *n*-dimension optimization problem with non-differentiable objective function *f(x)* where $x = [x_1, x_2, ..., x_n]$ as in (20), a pseudo-gradient $g_p(x)$ for the objective function is defined as follows (Wen *et al.*, 2003):

Supposed that $x_k = [x_{k1}, x_{k2}, ..., x_{kn}]$ is a point in the search space of the problem and it moves to another point x_l. There are two abilities for this movement by considering the value of the objec-tive function at these two points.

1. If $f(x_l) < f(x_k)$, the direction from x_k to x_l is defined as the *positive direction*. The pseudo-gradient at point x_l is determined by:

$$g_p(x_l) = \left[\delta(x_{l1}), \ \delta(x_{l2}), \ ..., \ \delta(x_{ln}) \right]^T \qquad (27)$$

where $\delta(x_{li})$ is the direction indicator of element x_i moving from point k to point l defined by:

$$\delta(x_{li}) = \begin{cases} 1 & \text{if } x_{li} > x_{ki} \\ 0 & \text{if } x_{li} = x_{ki} \\ -1 & \text{if } x_{li} < x_{ki} \end{cases} \qquad (28)$$

2. If $f(x_l) \geq f(x_k)$, the direction from x_k to x_l is defined as the *negative direction*. The pseudo-gradient at point x_l is determined by:

$$g_p(x_l) = 0 \qquad (29)$$

Based on the definition, the pseudo-gradient can also indicate a good direction for the non-differentiable function similar to the conventional gradient in the search space based on the two last points. From the definition, if the value of the pseudo-gradient $g_p(x_l) \neq 0$, it implies that a better solution for the objective function could be found in the next step based on the direction indicated by the pseudo-gradient $g_p(x_l)$ at point l. Otherwise, the search direction at this point should be changed due to no improvement of the objective function in this direction.

Improved Particle Swarm Optimization

The IPSO here is the PSO with constriction factor enhanced by the pseudo-gradient for speeding up its convergence process. The purpose of the pseudo-gradient is to guide the movement of particles in positive direction so that they can quickly move to the optimization.

In the PSO with constriction factor (Clerc & Kennedy, 2002), the velocity of particles is determined in Box 6 and 7.

In this case, the factor φ has an effect on the convergence characteristic of the system and must be greater than 4.0 to guarantee stability. However, as the value of φ increases, the constriction C decreases producing diversification which leads to slower response. The typical value of φ is 4.1 (i.e. $c_1 = c_2 = 2.05$).

For implementation of the pseudo-gradient in PSO, the two considered points corresponding to x_k and x_l in search space of the pseudo-gradient are the particle's position at iterations k and $k+1$ those are $x^{(k)}$ and $x^{(k+1)}$, respectively. Therefore, the updated position for particles in (23) is rewritten (see Box 8).

In (32), if the obtained pseudo-gradient is non-zero, the particle is moving to the right direction and speeded up to move to the optimal solu-tion in the search space by its enhanced velocity; otherwise the particle's position is normally updated as in (23). In fact, the proposed IPSO is the conventional PSO but for those particles moving on the right direction indicated by the pseudo-gradient their velocity is enhanced by the pseudo-gradient so that they can quickly move to the optimal solution. Therefore, the IPSO is more effective than the conventional PSO in solving optimization problems.

The procedure of IPSO is described as follows:

```
Select parameters
Initialize position and velocity for
each particle
Evaluate fitness function for each
particle's position
Set the initial position of each par-
ticle to its best position pbest_d
Set the particle's position with the
best fitness function to global best
gbest
Set the pseudo-gradient associated
with each particle to zero
While <Termination criteria not met>
       Calculate new velocity for
each particle
       Update new position for each
particle considering pseudo-gradient
       Evaluate fitness function
for each particle
          If the fitness value
is better than the best fitness value
in history, set the current parti-
cle's position as the new pbest_d
          Otherwise, the par-
ticle's position corresponding to the
best fitness value in history is set
to the new pbest_d
       Choose the particle's posi-
tion corresponding to the best fit-
ness value of all particles as the
new gbest
       Calculate the pseudo-gradi-
```

Box 6.

$$v_{id}^{(k+1)} = C \times \begin{bmatrix} v_{id}^{(k)} + c_1 \times rand_1 \times \left(pbest_{id}^{(k)} - x_{id}^{(k)} \right) \\ +c_2 \times rand_2 \times \left(gbest_i^{(k)} - x_{id}^{(k)} \right) \end{bmatrix} \qquad (30)$$

Box 7.

$$C = \frac{2}{\left| 2 - \varphi - \sqrt{\varphi^2 - 4\varphi} \right|}; \text{ where } \varphi = c_1 + c_2, \ \varphi > 4 \qquad (31)$$

Box 8.

$$x_{id}^{(k+1)} = \begin{cases} x_{id}^{(k)} + \delta(x_{id}^{(k+1)}) \times \left| v_{id}^{(k+1)} \right| & \text{if } g_p(x_{id}^{(k+1)}) \neq 0 \\ x_{id}^{(k)} + v_{id}^{(k+1)} & \text{otherwise} \end{cases} \qquad (32)$$

```
ent for each particle based on their
two latest points
End
```

The global best *gbest* is selected as the optimal solution

Implementation of Improved Particle Swarm Optimization

For implementation of the proposed IPSO to the OPF problem, each particle position representing the control variables is defined in Box 9.

Where x_d is the position of particle d and *NP* is the number of particle in the swarm.

The position and velocity of particles are initialized within their limits given by:

$$x_d^{(0)} = x_{d,\min} + rand_3 \times (x_{d,\max} - x_{d,\min}) \qquad (34)$$

$$v_d^{(0)} = v_{d,\min} + rand_4 \times (v_{d,\max} - v_{d,\min}) \qquad (35)$$

where $rand_3$ and $rand_4$ are random values in [0, 1], $x_{d,max}$ and $x_{d,min}$ are the upper and lower limit vectors of variables in (33), and $v_{d,max}$ and $v_{d,min}$ are the upper and lower limit vectors of particle's velocity calculated in (24) and (25).

During the iterative process, the position and velocity of particles are always adjusted in their limits after being calculated in each iteration as follows:

$$v_d^{new} = \min \left\{ v_{d,\max}, \max \left\{ v_{d,\min}, v_d \right\} \right\} \qquad (36)$$

$$x_d^{new} = \min \left\{ x_{d,\max}, \max \left\{ x_{d,\min}, x_d \right\} \right\} \qquad (37)$$

The fitness function to be minimized in IPSO for the problem is based on the problem objective function and dependent variables including real power generation at the slack bus, reactive power outputs at the generation buses, load bus voltages, and apparent power flow in transmission lines. The fitness function is defined as follows:

Box 9.

$$x_d = \{P_{g2d}, \ ..., \ P_{gN_gd}, \ V_{g1d}, \ ..., \ V_{gN_gd}, \ T_{1d}, \ ..., \ T_{N_td}, \ Q_{c1d}, \ ..., \ Q_{cN_cd}\}^T$$
$$d = 1, \ ..., \ NP$$

(33)

$$FT = f(x, u)$$
$$+ K_q \sum_{i=1}^{N_g} \left(Q_{gi} - Q_{gi}^{\lim}\right)^2$$
$$+ K_v \sum_{i=1}^{N_d} \left(V_{li} - V_{li}^{\lim}\right)^2$$
$$+ K_s \sum_{l=1}^{N_l} \left(S_l - S_{l,\max}\right)^2$$

(38)

where K_q, K_v, and K_s are penalty factors for reactive power generations, load bus voltages, and power flow in transmission lines, respectively.

The limits of the dependent variables in (38) are generally determined based on their calculated values as follows:

$$x^{\lim} = \begin{cases} x_{\max} & if \ x > x_{\max} \\ x_{\min} & if \ x < x_{\min} \\ x & otherwise \end{cases}$$

(39)

where x and x^{lim} respectively represent the calculated value and limits of Q_{gi}, V_{li}, or S_l.

The overall procedure of the proposed IPSO for solving the OPF problem is addressed as follows:

Step 1: Choose the controlling parameters for IPSO including number of particles NP, maximum number of iterations IT_{max}, cognitive and social acceleration factors c_1 and c_2, limit factor for maximum velocity R, and penalty factors K_q, K_v, and K_s for constraints.

Step 2: Generate NP particles for control variables within their limits including initial particle's position $x^{(0)}_{id}$ representing vector of control variables in (33) and velocity $v^{(0)}_{id}$ as in (34)

and (35), where $i = 1, \ ..., \ 2*N_g + N_t + N_c$ and $d = 1, \ ..., \ NP$.

Step 3: For each particle, calculate value of the dependent variables based on power flow solution and evaluate the fitness function F_{pbestd} in (38). Determine the global best value of fitness function $F_{gbest} = \min(F_{pbestd})$.

Step 4: Set $pbest_d$ to the initial position $x^{(0)}_{id}$ for each particle and $gbest$ to the position of the particle corresponding to F_{pbestd}.

Step 5: Set the pseudo-gradient associated with particles to zero. Set iteration counter $k = 1$.

Step 6: Calculate new velocity $v^{(k)}_{id}$ and update position $x^{(k)}_{id}$ for each particle using (30) and (32), respectively. Note that the obtained position and velocity of particles should be limited in their lower and upper bounds given by (36) and (37).

Step 7: Solve power flow based on the newly obtained value of position for each particle.

Step 8: Evaluate fitness function FT_d in (38) for each particle with the newly obtained position. Compare the calculated FT_d to $F^{(k-1)}_{pbestd}$ to obtain the best fitness function up to the current iteration $F^{(k)}_{pbestd}$.

Step 9: Pick up the position $pbest^{(k)}_d$ corresponding to $F^{(k)}_{pbestd}$ for each particle and determine the new global best fitness function $F^{(k)}_{pbestd}$ and the corresponding position $gbest^{(k)}_i$.

Step 10: Calculate the new pseudo-gradient for each particle based on its two latest positions corresponding to $x^{(k)}_{id}$ and $x^{(k-1)}_{id}$.

Step 11: If $k < IT_{max}$, $k = k + 1$ and return to Step 6. Otherwise, stop.

A flowchart for overall procedure of the proposed method for solving the OPF problem is also depicted in Figure 4.

Numerical Results

The proposed IPSO method has been tested on benchmark functions, the IEEE systems including 14, 30, 57, and 118 buses, in which all three types of objective function are considered for the 30-bus system and quadratic cost function is considered for the other systems. Some data for these systems from (Dabbagchi & Christie, 1993; Zimmerman, Murillo-Sánchez & Thomas, 2011) is given in Appendix.

In all test systems, the upper and lower voltage limits are set to 1.1 pu and 0.95 pu, respectively and the upper and lower limits of transformer tap changers are set to 1.1 pu and 0.9 pu, respectively. The transformer taps and switchable capacitor banks are discrete with a changing step of 0.01 pu and 0.1 MVAr, respectively. More data for each system will be given in each case. In this chapter, the power flow solutions for these systems are obtained from Matpower toolbox (Zimmerman, Murillo-Sánchez & Thomas, 2011).

To compare results and demonstrate the efficiency of the proposed IPSO, the conventional PSO is also implemented for solving the problem with different systems. The algorithms of the PSO methods are coded in Matlab platform and run on a 2.1 GHz with 2 GB of RAM PC. The control parameters of the PSO methods for all test systems are selected as follows: the cognitive and social parameters are set to 2.0 ($c_1 = c_2 = 2.0$) for conventional PSO and 2.05 for IPSO ($c_1 = c_2 = 2.05$), the velocity limit coefficient is set to 0.1 ($R = 0.1$), the maximum number of iterations IT_{max} is set to 2000 for benchmark functions, 250 for the IEEE 118-bus system and 200 for the other systems; the number of particles NP is set to 20 for benchmark functions, 10 for the IEEE 14 and 30-bus systems with quadratic cost function, 15 for

Figure 4. Flowchart of IPSO for solving OPF problem

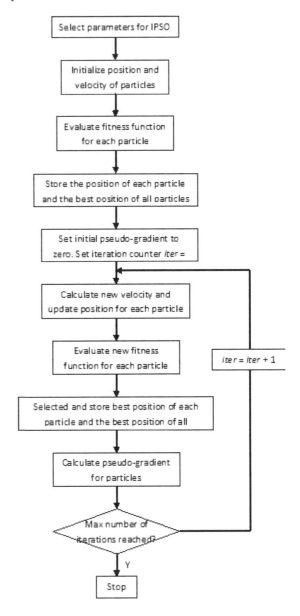

the IEEE 30-bus system with valve point effects and multiple fuels, 25 for the IEEE 57-bus system, and 40 for the IEEE 118-bus system. All penalty factors in the fitness function are set to 10^6. For each test case, the PSO methods are performed 50 independent runs. The obtained results for the systems include minimum total cost, average total cost, maximum total cost, standard deviation, and computational time.

Benchmark Functions

The proposed IPSO method is firstly tested on benchmark functions and the obtained results from the IPSO are compared to those from the conventional PSO to show the improvement from the proposed method. The tested benchmark functions include sphere or De Jong's function *F1* (De Jong, 1975), Rosenbrock function or De Jong's function *F2* (Rosenbrock, 1960), Rastrigin function (Rastrigin, 1974), Ackley function (Ackley, 1987), and Griewangk function (Bäck, Fogel & Michalewicz, 1997). These functions are given in Table 1 with dimension of 30.

The results obtained by the IPSO and PSO methods for the benchmark functions at the same conditions are given in Table 2. As observed from the table, the minimum, average, maximum, and standard deviation of objective function values

from the proposed IPSO are better than those from the conventional PSO except the standard deviation for Rastrigin and Ackley functions. For a better evaluation of improvement of the proposed IPSO over the conventional PSO, a relative improvement from the two methods is shown in Table 3, in which the improvement from the proposed IPSO over the conventional PSO is defined in Box 10.

With the relative improvement, it is indicated that the proposed IPSO is much more efficient than the conventional PSO for the benchmark functions with the improvement ranging from 11% to 100% for minimum, maximum, average, and standard deviation of objective function. That means the proposed IPSO can obtain better minimum, maximum, average, and standard deviation values than the conventional PSO method, or in other words the solution quality of the IPSO is higher than that of the PSO method.

Table 1. Definition of benchmark functions

No.	Function	Definition	Domain
1	Sphere	$$f_1 = \sum_{i=1}^{N} x_i^2$$	$x_i \in [-5.12, 5.12]$ $N = 30$
2	Rosenbrock	$$f_2 = \sum_{i=1}^{N-1} \left[100\left(x_{i+1} - x_i^2\right)^2 + \left(x_i - 1\right)^2 \right]$$	$x_i \in [-2.048, 2.048]$ $N = 30$
3	Rastrigin	$$f_3 = \sum_{i=1}^{N} \left[10 + x_i^2 - 10\cos(2\pi x_i) \right]$$	$x_i \in [-5.12, 5.12]$ $N = 30$
4	Ackley	$$f_4 = 20 + e - 20\exp\left(-0.2\sqrt{\frac{1}{N}\sum_{i=1}^{N} x_i^2}\right) - \exp\left(\frac{1}{N}\sum_{i=1}^{N}\cos(2\pi x_i)\right)$$	$x_i \in [-30, 30]$ $N = 30$
5	Griewangk	$$f_5 = 1 + \sum_{i=1}^{N} \frac{x_i^2}{4000} - \prod_{i=1}^{N} \cos\frac{x_i}{\sqrt{i}}$$	$x_i \in [-600, 600]$ $N = 30$

Table 2. Results for benchmark functions

Function	PSO				IPSO			
	Min	Average	Max	Std. dev.	Min	Average	Max	Std. dev.
Sphere	1.2371	2.0084	2.5271	0.2503	0.0000	0.0000	0.0000	0.0000
Rosenbrock	164.5722	274.0592	484.9986	55.1995	18.5334	27.3332	79.1474	10.667
Rastrigin	155.0607	186.6998	217.3017	14.6072	28.8538	61.0733	101.4856	18.8259
Ackley	1.9090	2.3688	2.6444	0.1573	0.0000	0.0300	1.5017	0.2102
Griewangk	0.0469	0.0958	0.2300	0.024	0.0000	0.0193	0.0982	0.0213

Table 3. Improvements of proposed IPSO over PSO method for benchmark functions

Function	Min (%)	Average (%)	Max (%)	Std. dev. (%)
Sphere	100	100	100	100
Rosenbrock	88.7	90.0	83.7	80.7
Rastrigin	81.4	67.3	53.3	-28.8
Ackley	100	98.7	43.2	-33.6
Griewangk	100	79.9	57.3	11.3

Box 10.

$$\text{IPSO Improvement } (\%) = \frac{\text{Value of PSO - Value of IPSO}}{\text{Value of PSO}} \times 100\% \qquad (40)$$

IEEE 14-Bus System

The test system has 14 buses as in Figure 5 consisting of 5 generation buses, 15 load buses, and 20 branches. The generators are located at buses 1, 2, 3, 6, and 8 and 3 transformers are located at branches 8, 9, and 10. The system has one switchable capacitor bank located at bus 9. For implementation in OPF problem, the system has 13 control variables including real power output of 4 generators except the generator at the slack bus, voltage at 5 generation buses, tap changer of 3 transformers, and reactive power output of one switchable capacitor bank.

The data of generators connected to generation buses including fuel cost coefficients, maximum and minimum real power outputs, and maximum and minimum reactive power outputs is given in Table 4. The maximum power flow limits of transmission lines are given in Table 5. The upper and lower bounds for the capacitor bank are 19 MVAr and 0 MVAr, respectively. The other bus and branch data can be found in Appendix.

The results including minimum total cost, average total cost, maximum total cost, standard deviation, and computational time obtained by the PSO methods for the systems are given in Table 6. The optimal solutions for the system by the PSO methods are given in Table 7 and the convergence characteristic of the fitness function of the IPSO method is given in Figure 6. The history of 50 runs from the proposed IPSO method for this system is given in Figure 7. For this system, the IPSO can obtain less minimum total cost than the

Figure 5. The IEEE 14-bus system

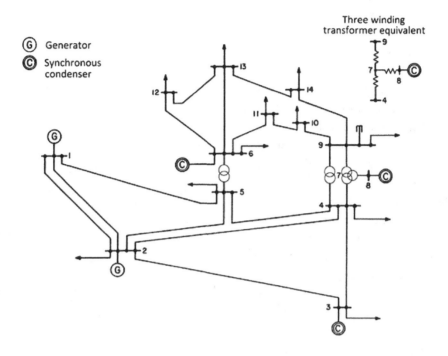

Table 4. Unit data for the IEEE 14-bus system

No.	Bus no.	a_i ($/h)	b_i ($/MWh)	c_i ($/MW²h)	$P_{gi,min}$ (MW)	$P_{gi,max}$ (MW)	$Q_{gi,min}$ (MVAr)	$Q_{gi,max}$ (MVAr)
1	1	0	16	0.0252	50	200	-50	100
2	2	0	14	0.1400	20	80	-40	50
3	3	0	8	0.5000	15	50	0	40
4	6	0	26	0.0667	10	30	-6	24
5	8	0	24	0.2000	10	35	-6	24

Table 5. Maximum power flow limits of transmission lines of the IEEE 14-bus system

Line	1	2	3	4	5	6	7	8	9	10
$S_{l,max}$ (MVA)	120	65	36	65	50	63	45	55	32	45
Line	11	12	13	14	15	16	17	18	19	20
$S_{l,max}$ (MVA)	18	32	32	32	32	32	18	12	12	12

Table 6. Results for the IEEE 14-bus system

Method	Min cost ($/h)	Average cost ($/h)	Max cost ($/h)	Standard deviation ($/h)	CPU time (s)	Min cost relative improvement (%)
PSO	6170.5506	6304.3850	6356.1970	32.1178	8.814	-
IPSO	6165.6388	6303.5894	6785.2294	92.0220	8.900	0.0008

conventional PSO while the computational times are approximately together.

IEEE 30-Bus System

The test system comprises 30 buses as in Figure 8 with 6 generation buses, 24 load buses, and 41 branches. The generators are connected at buses 1, 2, 5, 8, 11, and 13 and 4 transformers are located at branches 11, 12, 15, and 36. The system has 2 switchable capacitor bank located at buses 10 and 24. The number of control variables for the system is 17 including real power output of 5 generators except the generator at the slack bus, voltage at 6 generation buses, tap changer of 4 transformers, and reactive power output of 2 switchable capacitor banks.

For this system, three types of fuel cost function are considered including quadratic cost function, valve point effects, and multiple fuels. The unit data and capacitor limits are given in Tables 8 and 9. The coefficients for the three types of fuel cost functions are given in Tables 10, 11, and 12 and the maximum capacity of transmission

Table 7. Optimal solutions for the IEEE 14-bus system

	PSO	**IPSO**
P_{g1} (MW)	161.4592	154.7555
P_{g2} (MW)	20.0000	20.0000
P_{g3} (MW)	50.0000	50.0000
P_{g6} (MW)	10.0000	30.0000
P_{g8} (MW)	23.5941	10.0000
V_{g1} (pu)	1.1000	1.1000
V_{g2} (pu)	1.0804	1.0979
V_{g3} (pu)	1.0544	1.0734
V_{g6} (pu)	1.1000	1.0686
V_{g8} (pu)	1.0756	1.0354
T_8 (pu)	1.06	1.10
T_9 (pu)	1.01	1.06
T_{10} (pu)	0.94	1.00
Q_{c9} (MVAr)	8.8	19.00

line limits is given in Table 13. For the cases with valve point effects and multiple fuels, only units 1 and 2 are affected and the other units have the same data as in the case with quadratic fuel cost

Figure 6. Convergence characteristic for the IEEE 14-bus system

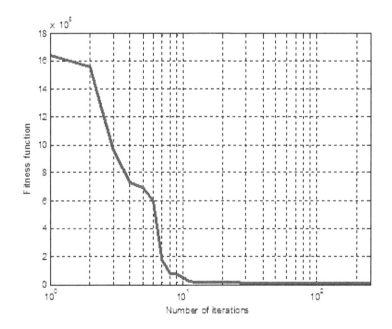

Figure 7. History of 50 runs by IPSO for the IEEE 14 bus system

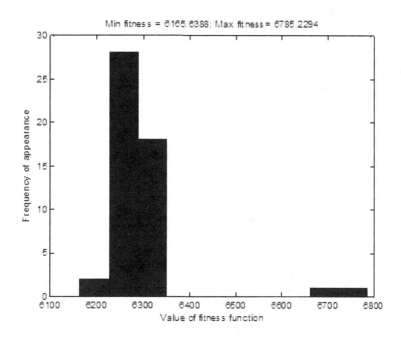

Figure 8. The IEEE 30-bus system

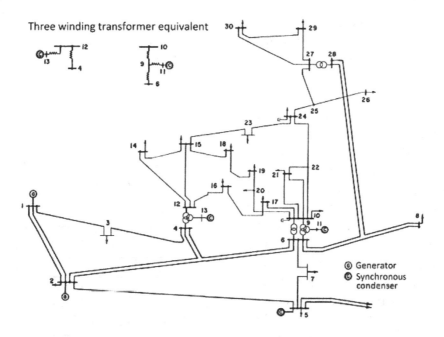

function. The nonconvex data of generators in the system is also given in (Ongsakul & Tantimaporn, 2006). The other bus and branch data can be found in Appendix.

The results including minimum total cost, average total cost, maximum total cost, standard deviation, and computational time obtained by the PSO methods for this system with different types of fuel cost functions are given in Table 14. The optimal solutions by the PSO methods for three types of fuel cost function are given in Tables 15, 16, and 17. The convergence characteristic and history of 50 runs by the IPSO method for the system with different fuel cost functions are also given in Figures 9, 10, 11, 12, 13, and 14. For all the considered cases as in Table 14, the minimum total costs from the IPSO method is slightly less those from the conventional PSO while the computational times from the two methods are approximately.

IEEE 57-Bus System

This system has 57 buses including 7 generation buses, 50 load buses, and 80 branches. The generators are located at buses 1, 2, 3, 6, 8, 9, and 12 and 15 transformers are located at branches 19, 20, 31, 37, 41, 46, 54, 58, 59, 65, 66, 71, 73, 76, and 80. The system has also 3 switchable capacitor bank installed at buses 18, 25, and 53. For dealing with this system, there 31 control variables to be handled including real power output of 6 generators except the generator at the slack bus, voltage at 7 generation buses, tap changer of 15 transformers, and reactive power output of 3 switchable capacitor banks.

For this system, only fuel cost in quadratic function is considered. The unit data and capacitor limits are given in Tables 18 and 19, respectively. The capacity limits of transmission lines of the system are given in Table 20. The other bus and branch data can be found in (Zimmerman,

Table 8. Unit data for the IEEE 30-bus system

No.	Bus no.	$P_{gi,min}$ (MW)	$P_{gi,max}$ (MW)	$Q_{gi,min}$ (MVAr)	$Q_{gi,max}$ (MVAr)
1	1	50	200	-20	200
2	2	20	80	-20	100
3	5	15	50	-15	80
4	8	10	35	-15	60
5	11	10	30	-10	50
6	13	12	40	-15	60

Table 9. Capacitor limits for the IEEE 30-bus system

No.	Bus no.	$Q_{ci,min}$ (MVAr)	$Q_{ci,max}$ (MVAr)
1	10	0	19
2	24	0	4.3

Table 10. Coefficients of quadratic fuel function for the IEEE 30-bus system

Unit no.	a_i ($/h)	b_i ($/MWh)	c_i ($/MW²h)
1	0	2.00	0.00375
2	0	1.75	0.01750
3	0	1.00	0.06250
4	0	3.25	0.00834
5	0	3.00	0.02500
6	0	3.00	0.02500

Table 11. Coefficients with valve point effects for the IEEE 30-bus system

Unit no.	a_i ($/h)	b_i ($/MWh)	c_i ($/MW²h)	e_i ($/h)	f_i ($/MWh)
1	150	2.00	0.00160	50	0.063
2	25	2.50	0.01000	40	0.098
3	0	1.00	0.06250	0	0
4	0	3.25	0.00834	0	0
5	0	3.00	0.02500	0	0
6	0	3.00	0.02500	0	0

Table 12. Coefficients with multiple fuels for the IEEE 30-bus system

Unit no.	Fuel	a_i ($/h)	b_i ($/MWh)	c_i ($/MW²h)	$P_{gi,min}$ (MW)	$P_{gi,max}$ (MW)
1	1	55.0	0.70	0.0050	50	140
	2	82.5	1.05	0.0075	140	200
2	1	40.0	0.30	0.0100	20	55
	2	80.0	0.60	0.0200	55	80
3	1	0	1.00	0.06250	15	50
4	1	0	3.25	0.00834	10	35
5	1	0	3.00	0.02500	10	30
6	1	0	3.00	0.02500	12	40

Table 13. Maximum power flow limits of transmission lines of the IEEE 30-bus system

Line	1	2	3	4	5	6	7	8	9	10	11	12	13	14
$S_{l,max}$ (MVA)	130	130	65	130	130	65	90	130	130	32	65	32	65	65
Line	15	16	17	18	19	20	21	22	23	24	25	26	27	28
$S_{l,max}$ (MVA)	65	65	32	32	32	16	16	16	16	32	32	32	32	32
Line	29	30	31	32	33	34	35	36	37	38	39	40	41	
$S_{l,max}$ (MVA)	32	16	16	16	16	16	16	65	16	16	16	32	32	

Table 14. Results for the IEEE 30-bus system with different objectives

	Quadratic fuel cost function		Valve point loading effects		Piecewise fuel cost function	
	PSO	IPSO	PSO	IPSO	PSO	IPSO
Min cost ($/h)	799.6711	799.3416	923.2104	920.5000	651.3529	646.0920
Average cost ($/h)	803.8198	800.4159	963.7260	958.2597	764.3423	725.8512
Max cost ($/h)	890.6728	813.7888	1041.6531	1070.5610	864.3829	853.1506
Std. deviation ($/h)	13.6535	2.7278	22.8178	22.2073	60.4999	65.0607
CPU time (s)	10.856	10.894	16.019	16.089	16.203	16.378
Min cost relative improvement (%)	-	0.0004	-	0.003	-	0.008

Murillo-Sánchez & Thomas, 2011; Dabbagchi & Christie, 1993).

The results including minimum total cost, average total cost, maximum total cost, standard deviation, and computational time obtained by the PSO methods for this system are given in Table 21. The optimal solutions by the PSO methods for the system are given in Table 22 and the convergence characteristic and history of 50 runs by the IPSO method for the system is given in Figures 15 and 16. For this system, the IPSO method can obtain better minimum total cost than the conventional PSO method. For the computational time, the difference between two methods is not considerable.

Table 15. Optimal solutions with quadratic fuel function for the IEEE 30-bus system

	PSO	IPSO
P_{g1} (MW)	175.1820	177.0906
P_{g2} (MW)	49.2678	48.6662
P_{g5} (MW)	21.7230	21.3156
P_{g8} (MW)	22.0514	21.1555
P_{g11} (MW)	11.8301	11.8729
P_{g13} (MW)	12.0000	12.0000
V_{g1} (pu)	1.1000	1.1000
V_{g2} (pu)	1.0800	1.0876
V_{g5} (pu)	1.0531	1.0611
V_{g8} (pu)	1.0651	1.0687
V_{g11} (pu)	1.1000	1.1000
V_{g13} (pu)	1.1000	1.1000
T_{11} (pu)	0.9600	1.07
T_{12} (pu)	1.0200	0.90
T_{15} (pu)	1.0200	0.99
T_{36} (pu)	0.9700	0.96
Q_{c10} (MVAr)	10.1000	19.00
Q_{c24} (MVAr)	4.3000	4.30

Table 16. Optimal solutions with valve point effects for the IEEE 30-bus system

	PSO	IPSO
P_{g1} (MW)	199.0960	199.5933
P_{g2} (MW)	50.5988	49.4497
P_{g5} (MW)	15.0000	15.0000
P_{g8} (MW)	10.0000	10.0000
P_{g11} (MW)	10.0000	10.0000
P_{g13} (MW)	12.0000	12.0000
V_{g1} (pu)	1.0190	1.0757
V_{g2} (pu)	0.9951	1.0507
V_{g5} (pu)	1.0062	0.9754
V_{g8} (pu)	0.9756	1.0136
V_{g11} (pu)	1.0228	0.9500
V_{g13} (pu)	1.0325	1.1000
T_{11} (pu)	0.90	1.1000
T_{12} (pu)	1.02	0.99
T_{15} (pu)	1.10	0.99
T_{36} (pu)	0.90	0.94
Q_{c10} (MVAr)	8.0	9.50
Q_{c24} (MVAr)	1.4	2.10

IEEE 118-Bus System

This system has 118 buses including 54 generation buses, 64 load buses, and 186 branches. In addition, the system has also 9 transformers are located at branches 8, 32, 36, 51, 93, 95, 102, 107, and 127 and 14 switchable capacitor bank located at buses 5, 34, 37, 44, 45, 46, 48, 74, 79, 82, 105, 107, and 110. For implementation of the IPSO to this system, there 131 control variables to be handled including real power output of 54 generators except the generator at the slack bus, voltage at 54 generation buses, tap changer of 9 transformers, and reactive power output of 14 switchable capacitor banks.

Only fuel cost in quadratic function is considered for this system. The unit data, capacitor limits, and transmission limits are given in Tables 23, 24, and 25, respectively. The other bus and branch data can be found in (Dabbagchi & Christie, 1993; Zimmerman, Murillo-Sánchez & Thomas, 2011).

The results including minimum total cost, average total cost, maximum total cost, standard deviation, and computational time obtained by the PSO methods for this system are given in Table 26. The optimal solutions by the PSO methods for the system are given in Table 27 and the convergence characteristic and the history of 50 runs by the IPSO method for the system is given in Figures 17 and 18. For this system, the IPSO method can also obtain better minimum total cost than the conventional PSO method with nearly the same computational time.

Constructive Discussion

In the numerical results, the proposed IPSO method has been tested on benchmark function

Table 17. Optimal solutions with multiple fuels for the IEEE 30-bus system

	PSO	IPSO
P_{g1} (MW)	139.8154	139.9917
P_{g2} (MW)	54.5544	54.9866
P_{g5} (MW)	27.1596	24.4612
P_{g8} (MW)	25.7023	34.7469
P_{g11} (MW)	21.5202	18.8175
P_{g13} (MW)	21.5277	16.9983
V_{g1} (pu)	1.1000	1.0988
V_{g2} (pu)	1.0908	1.0841
V_{g5} (pu)	1.0608	1.0608
V_{g8} (pu)	1.0691	1.0760
V_{g11} (pu)	1.0416	1.0826
V_{g13} (pu)	1.0367	1.0977
T_{11} (pu)	1.0100	1.03
T_{12} (pu)	1.0000	1.10
T_{15} (pu)	0.9700	1.07
T_{36} (pu)	0.9500	0.99
Q_{c10} (MVAr)	3.5000	15.40
Q_{c24} (MVAr)	0.4000	3.40

and the IEEE systems and the obtained results have been compared to those from the conventional PSO method to show the efficiency of the proposed methods. In fact, there are not many parameters to be selected for the implemented methods. The parameters for the IPSO method include maximum number of iterations, number of particles, velocity limit factor, cognitive and social parameters, and penalty factors. The principle for selection of these parameters as follows:

Maximum Number of Iterations: This parameter is usually selected based on the processing problem. For the simple problems the maximum number of iterations can be much less than for the problems with multiple minima. The larger number of iterations is used, the more ability to find the global solution is obtained. However, the maximum number of iterations is not the key parameter for obtaining the optimal final solution since large number of iterations does not the global solution is found. Therefore, the maximum number of iterations is usually selected corresponding to the number of particles so that the optimal solu-

Figure 9. Convergence characteristic with quadratic fuel function for the IEEE 30-bus system

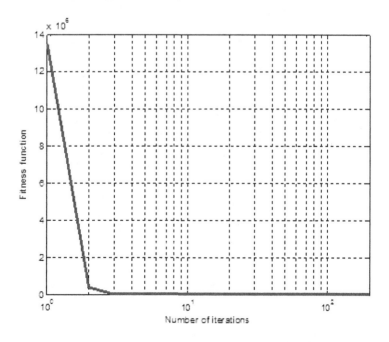

Figure 10. History of 50 runs by IPSO for the IEEE 30 bus system with quadratic fuel function

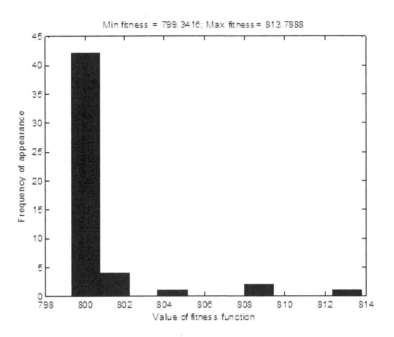

Figure 11. Convergence characteristic with valve point effects for the IEEE 30-bus system

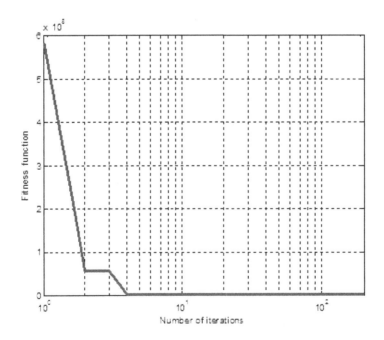

Figure 12. History of 50 runs by IPSO for the IEEE 30 bus system with valve point effects

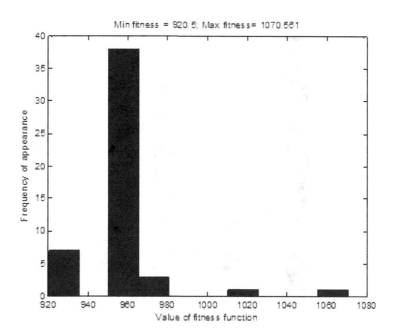

Figure 13. Convergence characteristic with multiple fuels for the IEEE 30-bus system

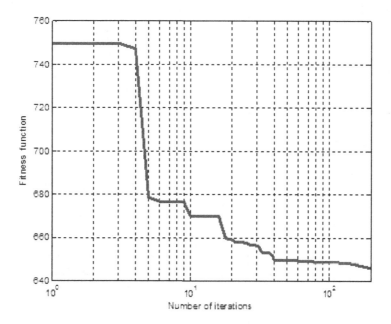

Figure 14. History of 50 runs by IPSO for the IEEE 30 bus system with quadratic fuel function

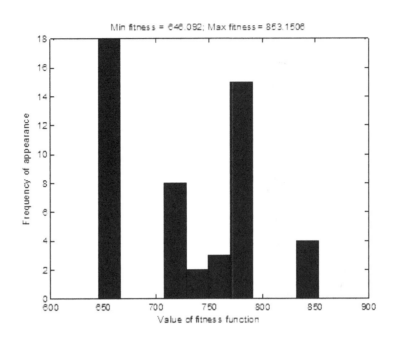

Table 18. Unit data for the IEEE 57-bus system

No.	Bus no.	a_i ($/h)	b_i ($/MWh)	c_i ($/MW²h)	$P_{gi,min}$ (MW)	$P_{gi,max}$ (MW)	$Q_{gi,min}$ (MVAr)	$Q_{gi,max}$ (MVAr)
1	1	0	20	0.0775795	0	575.88	-140	200
2	2	0	40	0.0100	0	100.00	-17	50
3	3	0	20	0.2500	0	140.00	-10	60
4	6	0	40	0.0100	0	100.00	-8	25
5	8	0	20	0.0222222	0	550.00	-140	200
6	9	0	40	0.0100	0	100.00	-3	9
7	12	0	20	0.0322581	0	410.00	-150	155

Table 19. Capacitor limits for the IEEE 57-bus system

No.	Bus no.	$Q_{ci,min}$ (MVAr)	$Q_{ci,max}$ (MVAr)
1	18	0	10.0
2	25	0	5.9
3	53	0	6.3

Table 20. Maximum power flow limits of transmission lines of the IEEE 47-bus system

Line	1	2	3	4	5	6	7	8	9-13	14	15	16-80
$S_{l,max}$ (MVA)	150	85	100	100	50	40	100	200	50	100	200	100

Table 21. Results for the IEEE 57-bus system

Method	Min cost ($/h)	Average cost ($/h)	Max cost ($/h)	Std. deviation ($/h)	CPU time (s)	Min cost relative improvement (%)
PSO	42109.7231	44688.4203	49320.6668	1786.3245	8.814	-
IPSO	41688.5004	42032.7064	44748.0342	551.9334	8.900	0.01

Table 22. Optimal solutions for the IEEE 57-bus system

	PSO	IPSO		PSO	IPSO
P_{g1} (MW)	139.1571	145.3988	T_{31} (pu)	1.00	1.02
P_{g2} (MW)	100.0000	79.0190	T_{37} (pu)	1.05	1.01
P_{g3} (MW)	75.8451	42.6999	T_{41} (pu)	0.99	0.96
P_{g6} (MW)	38.4932	75.4517	T_{46} (pu)	0.92	0.95
P_{g8} (MW)	455.5600	459.2791	T_{54} (pu)	0.99	0.95
P_{g9} (MW)	100.0000	99.5688	T_{58} (pu)	0.99	0.94
P_{g12} (MW)	360.2540	364.5374	T_{59} (pu)	0.95	0.95
V_{g1} (pu)	1.0399	1.0606	T_{65} (pu)	0.98	0.95
V_{g2} (pu)	1.0319	1.0575	T_{66} (pu)	1.02	0.91
V_{g3} (pu)	1.0378	1.0546	T_{71} (pu)	0.90	0.96
V_{g6} (pu)	1.0621	1.0608	T_{73} (pu)	1.00	1.00
V_{g8} (pu)	1.1000	1.0712	T_{76} (pu)	1.01	1.03
V_{g9} (pu)	1.0369	1.0447	T_{80} (pu)	0.97	0.96
V_{g12} (pu)	0.9892	1.0548	Q_{c18} (MVAr)	3.5	5.00
T_{19} (pu)	1.02	1.01	Q_{c25} (MVAr)	3.0	4.50
T_{20} (pu)	1.04	0.98	Q_{c53} (MVAr)	3.3	3.20

tion is found with a sufficient computational time. For the IEEE systems, the maximum number of iterations of IPSO is selected from 200 to 250 while the maximum number of iterations for the benchmark functions is up to 2000 since the benchmark functions contain multiple minima and the proposed method need more iteration to obtain the optimal solution. For the optimization problems in engineering, the maximum number of iterations of the IPSO from 200 to 500 is appropriate.

Number of Particles: This parameter is usually selected based on the scale of the processing problem. The number of particles is few for small scale problems and it increases for larger scale problems. The more number of particles is used,

Figure 15. Convergence characteristic for the IEEE 57-bus system

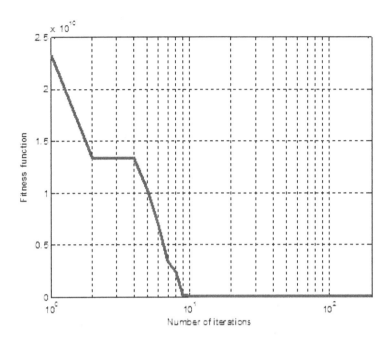

Figure 16. History of 50 runs by IPSO for the IEEE 57 bus system

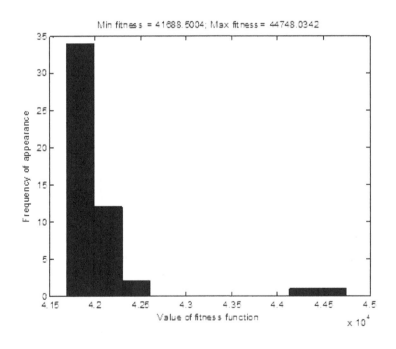

Table 23. Unit data for the IEEE 118-bus system

No.	Bus no.	a_i ($/h)	b_i ($/MWh)	c_i ($/MW²h)	$P_{gi,min}$ (MW)	$P_{gi,max}$ (MW)	$Q_{gi,min}$ (MVAr)	$Q_{gi,max}$ (MVAr)
1	1	0	40	0.01	0	100	-5	15
2	4	0	40	0.01	0	100	-300	300
3	6	0	40	0.01	0	100	-13	50
4	8	0	40	0.01	0	100	-300	300
5	10	0	20	0.0222222	0	550	-147	200
6	12	0	20	0.117647	0	185	-35	120
7	15	0	40	0.01	0	100	-10	30
8	18	0	40	0.01	0	100	-16	50
9	19	0	40	0.01	0	100	-8	24
10	24	0	40	0.01	0	100	-300	300
11	25	0	20	0.0454545	0	320	-47	140
12	26	0	20	0.0318471	0	414	-1000	1000
13	27	0	40	0.01	0	100	-300	300
14	31	0	20	1.42857	0	107	-300	300
15	32	0	40	0.01	0	100	-14	42
16	34	0	40	0.01	0	100	-8	24
17	36	0	40	0.01	0	100	-8	24
18	40	0	40	0.01	0	100	-300	300
19	42	0	40	0.01	0	100	-300	300
20	46	0	20	0.526316	0	119	-100	100
21	49	0	20	0.0490196	0	304	-85	210
22	54	0	20	0.208333	0	148	-300	300
23	55	0	40	0.01	0	100	-8	23
24	56	0	40	0.01	0	100	-8	15
25	59	0	20	0.0645161	0	255	-60	180
26	61	0	20	0.0625	0	260	-100	300
27	62	0	40	0.01	0	100	-20	20
28	65	0	20	0.0255754	0	491	-67	200
29	66	0	20	0.0255102	0	492	-67	200
30	69	0	20	0.0193648	0	805.2	-300	300
31	70	0	40	0.01	0	100	-10	32
32	72	0	40	0.01	0	100	-100	100
33	73	0	40	0.01	0	100	-100	100
34	74	0	40	0.01	0	100	-6	9
35	76	0	40	0.01	0	100	-8	23
36	77	0	40	0.01	0	100	-20	70
37	80	0	20	0.0209644	0	577	-165	280

Table 24. Capacitor limits for the IEEE 118bus system

No.	1	2	3	4	5	6	7
Bus no.	5	34	37	44	45	46	48
$Q_{ci,min}$ (MVAr)	-40	0	-25	0	0	0	0
$Q_{ci,max}$ (MVAr)	0	14	0	10	10	10	15
No.	8	9	10	11	12	13	14
Bus no.	74	79	82	83	105	107	110
$Q_{ci,min}$ (MVAr)	0	0	0	0	0	0	0
$Q_{ci,max}$ (MVAr)	12	20	20	10	20	6	6

Table 25. Maximum power flow limits of transmission lines of the IEEE 118-bus system

$S_{l,max}$ (MVA)	Line
100	1, 2, 6, 12-18, 34-35, 40, 42, 46-47, 49, 57-58, 62-64, 72-88, 91-92, 100-103, 113, 121, 128, 130, 132, 143, 146-147, 156-162, 169-173, 175-176, 180-182, 184
130	4-5, 10-11, 19-20, 22-23, 39, 43, 52-53, 55-56, 59-61, 65-71, 89, 105-106, 118, 122, 125, 129, 131, 133-136, 140, 144-145, 148-155, 164-168, 174, 177-179, 185-186
200	3, 21, 137-139
300	24-29, 33, 41, 44-45, 48, 50, 90, 93-95, 98-99, 108-112, 114-117, 119-120, 123-124, 126-127, 141-142, 163
600	30-32, 36-38, 51, 54, 96-97, 104, 106-107
650	7-9

the better solution is obtained. However, large number of particles will lead to long computational time. Moreover, large number of particles does not guarantee to obtain the optimal solution. In the benchmark functions, the number of particles is 20 due to the size of the problem is not large with 30 variables while in the IEEE systems the number of particles for the 14 and 30 bus systems is 10 with 13 and 17 variables, respectively, for the 57 bus systems is 25 with 31 variables, and

for the 118 bus systems is 40 with 131 variables. As observed, the relative between the variables and number of particles is low for small scale and high for large scale problems. Moreover, for the complex problems with multiple minima, more particles are needed for searching the optimal solution. For the engineering problems, the number of particles about from 10 to 50 is sufficient.

Velocity Limit Factor: This parameter has also effect on the final solution. It limits the velocity of particles in search space. If this factor is large, the optimal solution may be ignored. In contrary, the convergence process is slow for the small value of this factor. Therefore, this factor should be appropriately tuned for different problems. In all test cases, the velocity limit factor of the IPSO is set to 0.1 of difference between maximum and minimum values of corresponding variables. For the simple problem, the value of velocity limit factor can be chosen higher than 0.1 for faster convergence. For the complex problem with multiple minima, this value can be chosen less than 0.1 for obtaining better solution. The trade off between final solution and computational time can be decided by this factor.

Cognitive and Social Parameters: These parameters are usually fixed for different problems. In the proposed IPSO, the value of these parameters is set to 2.05 for all cases. The best value of the parameters can be found in the literature and the suggested values are not much different. Therefore, these parameters can be easily fixed at a constant in advance.

Penalty Factors: These factors associated with constraints are usually used in fitness function of metaheuristic search methods. The objective of these factors is to force variables not to violate their limits. In the numerical results by the IPSO, the penalty factors for all constraints are set to 10^6. In fact, it is very easy to choose these factors since they do not affect much on the final solution as long as they are large enough to provide a penalty to objective of the problem. The value of

Table 26. Results for the IEEE 118-bus system

Method	Min cost ($/h)	Average cost ($/h)	Max cost ($/h)	Std. deviation ($/h)	CPU time (s)	Min cost relative improvement (%)
PSO	145520.0109	158596.1725	184686.8248	9454.4231	132.233	-
IPSO	139604.1326	152204.2608	170022.9726	6344.7031	132.884	0.041

Table 27. Optimal solutions for the IEEE 118-bus system

	PSO	IPSO		PSO	IPSO		PSO	IPSO
P_{g1} (MW)	30.2147	23.4126	P_{g100} (MW)	135.8797	0.0000	V_{g76} (MW)	1.0196	0.9806
P_{g4} (MW)	86.3352	11.6750	P_{g103} (MW)	43.2253	17.4823	V_{g77} (MW)	1.0318	1.0214
P_{g6} (MW)	74.9686	55.4040	P_{g104} (MW)	22.5970	34.5793	V_{g80} (MW)	1.0446	1.0402
P_{g8} (MW)	44.3628	68.5871	P_{g105} (MW)	11.2821	56.6906	V_{g85} (MW)	1.0182	1.0227
P_{g10} (MW)	211.5380	114.8891	P_{g107} (MW)	69.6140	60.2901	V_{g87} (MW)	1.0194	1.0459
P_{g12} (MW)	46.7205	78.1779	P_{g110} (MW)	51.6372	16.0941	V_{g89} (MW)	0.9999	1.0466
P_{g15} (MW)	26.5197	74.6340	P_{g111} (MW)	85.7078	28.2028	V_{g90} (MW)	1.0550	1.1000
P_{g18} (MW)	75.0588	53.6459	P_{g112} (MW)	53.5860	98.4069	V_{g91} (MW)	1.0257	1.0468
P_{g19} (MW)	4.9868	64.8017	P_{g113} (MW)	56.9731	23.6525	V_{g92} (MW)	1.0063	1.0291
P_{g24} (MW)	36.0602	81.1971	P_{g116} (MW)	96.6802	2.0373	V_{g99} (MW)	1.0450	0.9979
P_{g25} (MW)	185.3162	194.3389	V_{g1} (MW)	1.0079	1.0113	V_{g100} (MW)	1.0259	1.0083
P_{g26} (MW)	31.0660	245.3122	V_{g4} (MW)	1.0547	1.0289	V_{g103} (MW)	1.0409	1.0063
P_{g27} (MW)	81.2534	70.0608	V_{g6} (MW)	1.0396	1.0318	V_{g104} (MW)	0.9873	1.0057
P_{g31} (MW)	31.7628	0.0000	V_{g8} (MW)	1.0375	1.0636	V_{g105} (MW)	0.9861	1.0128
P_{g32} (MW)	73.8507	43.4626	V_{g10} (MW)	1.0978	1.0912	V_{g107} (MW)	1.0086	1.0829
P_{g34} (MW)	66.1806	59.9564	V_{g12} (MW)	1.0337	1.0315	V_{g110} (MW)	1.0563	0.9903
P_{g36} (MW)	0.0000	42.1412	V_{g15} (MW)	1.0167	1.0314	V_{g111} (MW)	1.0747	0.9527
P_{g40} (MW)	29.2314	49.3408	V_{g18} (MW)	0.9882	1.0294	V_{g112} (MW)	1.0700	1.0258

these factor can be set to 10^4 to 10^6 is sufficient for many problems.

FUTURE RESEARCH DIRECTIONS

The IPSO method is a simple improvement for the PSO method with constriction factor. The IPSO method is actually more effective than the conventional PSO for the considered OPF with different test systems. Therefore, the proposed IPSO can be also implemented for other convex or non-convex optimization problems not only for engineering but also for other fields such as business, economics, and finance. Moreover, the different improvements of PSO can be combined with the pseudo-gradient which can lead to powerful search methods for optimization problems.

CONCLUSION

In this chapter, the proposed IPSO has been effectively implemented for solving OPF problem. The proposed IPSO method is a simple improvement from the PSO method with constriction

Figure 17. Convergence characteristic for the IEEE 118-bus system

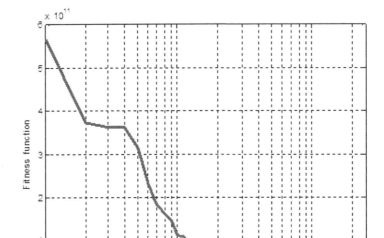

Figure 18. History of 50 runs by IPSO for the IEEE 118 bus system

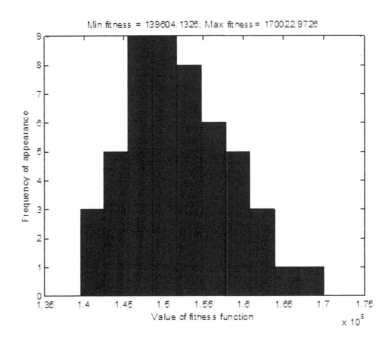

factor by integrating the pseudo-gradient in to particle's velocity to enhance its search capability. The advantage of the pseudo-gradient is that it is useful for non-differentiable functions with the same function as the conventional gradient for differentiable functions. With the combination, the IPSO method can obtain better solution than the conventional PSO via the test results from benchmark functions, the IEEE 14, 30, 57, and 118 bus systems. Therefore, the proposed IPSO could be also favorable for other optimization problems in engineering as well as other fields.

REFERENCES

Abido, M. A. (2001). Optimal power flow using particles warm optimization. *International Journal of Electrical Power & Energy Systems, 24*(7), 563–571. doi:10.1016/S0142-0615(01)00067-9

Abido, M. A. (2002). Optimal power flow using tabu search algorithm. *Electric Power and Components Systems, 30*(5), 469–483. doi:10.1080/15325000252888425

Abou El-Ela, A. A., & Abido, M. A. (1992). Optimal operation strategy for reactive power control modelling. *Simulation and Control. Part A, 41*(3), 19–40.

Ackley, D. (1987). An empirical study of bit vector function optimization. *Genetic Algorithms and Simulated Annealing*, 170-215.

Bäck, T., Fogel, D., & Michalewicz, Z. (1997). *Handbook of evolutionary computation.* Bristol, UK: Institute of Physics Publishing Ltd. doi:10.1887/0750308958

Bai, X., Wei, H., Fujisawa, K., & Wang, Y. (2008). Semidefinite programming for optimal power flow problems. *International Journal of Electrical Power & Energy Systems, 30*(6–7), 383–392. doi:10.1016/j.ijepes.2007.12.003

Burchett, R. C., Happ, H. H., & Vierath, D. R. (1984). Quadratically convergent optimal power flow. *IEEE Transactions on Power Apparatus and Systems, PAS-103*(11), 3267–3276. doi:10.1109/TPAS.1984.318568

Cai, H. R., Chung, C. Y., & Wong, K. P. (2008). Application of differential evolution algorithm for transient stability constrained optimal power flow. *IEEE Transactions on Power Systems, 23*(2), 719–728. doi:10.1109/TPWRS.2008.919241

Capitanescu, F., Glavic, M., Ernst, D., & Wehenkel, L. (2007). Interior-point based algorithms for the solution of optimal power flow problems. *Electric Power Systems Research, 77*(5–6), 508–517. doi:10.1016/j.epsr.2006.05.003

Clerc, M., & Kennedy, J. (2002). The particle swarm - Explosion, stability, and convergence in a multidimensional complex space. *IEEE Transactions on Evolutionary Computation, 6*(1), 58–73. doi:10.1109/4235.985692

Dabbagchi, I., & Christie, R. (1993). *Power systems test case archive.* University of Washington. Retrieved February 20, 2011, from http://www.ee.washington.edu/research/pstca/

De Jong, K. D. (1975). *An analysis of the behavior of a class of genetic adaptive systems.* PhD dissertation, Department of Computer and Communication Sciences, University of Michigan.

Dommel, H., & Tinny, W. (1968). Optimal power flow solution. *IEEE Transactions on Power Apparatus and Systems, PAS-87*(10), 1866–1876. doi:10.1109/TPAS.1968.292150

Granelli, G. P., & Montagna, M. (2000). Security-constrained economic dispatch using dual quadratic programming. *Electric Power Systems Research, 56*, 71–80. doi:10.1016/S0378-7796(00)00097-3

Happ, H. H., & Wirgau, K. A. (1981). A review of the optimal power flow. *Journal of the Franklin Institute*, *312*(3-4), 231–264. doi:10.1016/0016-0032(81)90063-6

Huneault, M., & Galiana, F. D. (1991). A survey of the optimal power flow literature. *IEEE Transactions on Power Systems*, *6*(2), 762–770. doi:10.1109/59.76723

Kennedy, J., & Eberhart, R. (1995). Particle swarm optimization. *Proceedings of the IEEE Conference Neural Networks* (ICNN'95), Perth, Australia, 1995, Vol. IV, (pp. 1942-1948).

Lai, L. L., & Ma, J. T. (1997). Improved genetic algorithms for optimal power)ow under both normal and contingent operation states. *International Journal of Electrical Power & Energy Systems*, *19*(5), 287–292. doi:10.1016/S0142-0615(96)00051-8

Li, C., Zhao, H., & Chen, T. (2010). The hybrid differential evolution algorithm for optimal power flow based on simulated annealing and tabu search. *International Conference on Management and Service Science* (MASS) (pp. 1-7).

Liang, R.-H., Tsai, S.-R., Chen, Y.-T., & Tseng, W.-T. (2011). Optimal power flow by a fuzzy based hybrid particle swarm optimization approach. *Electric Power Systems Research*, *81*(7), 1466–1474. doi:10.1016/j.epsr.2011.02.011

Lo, K. L., & Meng, Z. J. (2004). Newton-like method for line outage simulation. *IEE Proceedings -General Transmissions and Distributions*, *151*(2), 225-231.

Momoh, J. A., Adapa, R., & El-Hawary, M. E. (1999a). A review of selected optimal power flow literature to 1993- I. Nonlinear and quadratic programming approaches. *IEEE Transactions on Power Systems*, *14*(1), 96–104. doi:10.1109/59.744492

Momoh, J. A., Adapa, R., & El-Hawary, M. E. (1999b). A review of selected optimal power flow literature to 1993. II. Newton, linear programming and interior point methods. *IEEE Transactions on Power Systems*, *14*(1), 105–111. doi:10.1109/59.744495

Mota-Palomino, R., & Quintana, V. H. (1986). Sparse reactive power scheduling by a penalty-function linear programming technique. *IEEE Transactions on Power Systems*, *1*(3), 31–39. doi:10.1109/TPWRS.1986.4334951

Ongsakul, W., & Bhasaputra, P. (2002). Optimal power flow with FACTS devices by hybrid TS/SA approach. *International Journal of Electrical Power & Energy Systems*, *24*(10), 851–857. doi:10.1016/S0142-0615(02)00006-6

Ongsakul, W., & Tantimaporn, T. (2006). Optimal power flow by improved evolutionary programming. *Electric Power Components and Systems*, *34*(1), 79–95. doi:10.1080/15325000691001458

Osman, M. S., Abo-Sinna, M. A., & Mousa, A. A. (2004). A solution to the optimal power flow using genetic algorithm. *Applied Mathematics and Computation*, *155*(2), 391–405. doi:10.1016/S0096-3003(03)00785-9

Pandya, K. S., & Joshi, S. K. (2008). A survey of optimal power flow methods. *Journal of Theoretical and Applied Information Technology*, *4*(5), 450–458.

Pham, D. T., & Jin, G. (1995). Genetic algorithm using gradient-like reproduction operator. *Electronics Letters*, *31*(18), 1558–1559. doi:10.1049/el:19951092

Pudjianto, D., Ahmed, S., & Strbac, G. (2002). Allocation of VAR support using LP and NLP based optimal power flows. *IEE Proceedings. Generation, Transmission and Distribution*, *149*(4), 377–383. doi:10.1049/ip-gtd:20020200

Rastrigin, L. A. (1974). Extremal control systems. In *Theoretical Foundations of Engineering Cybernetics Series*. Moscow, Russia: Nauka, Russian.

Roa-Sepulveda, C. A., & Pavez-Lazo, B. J. (2003). A solution to the optimal power flow using simulated annealing. *International Journal of Electrical Power & Energy Systems, 25*(1), 47–57. doi:10.1016/S0142-0615(02)00020-0

Rosenbrock, H. H. (1960). An automatic method for finding the greatest or least value of a function. *The Computer Journal, 3*, 175–184. doi:10.1093/comjnl/3.3.175

Santos, A. Jr, & da Costa, G. R. M. (1995). Optimal power)ow solution by Newton's method applied to an augmented Lagrangian function. *IEE Proceedings. Generation, Transmission and Distribution, 142*(1), 33–36. doi:10.1049/ip-gtd:19951586

Sun, D. I., Ashley, B., Brewer, B., Hughes, A., & Tinney, W. F. (1984). Optimal power flow by Newton approach. *IEEE Transactions on Power Apparatus and Systems, PAS-103*(10), 2864–2875. doi:10.1109/TPAS.1984.318284

Wang, M., & Liu, S. (2005). A trust region interior point algorithm for optimal power low problems. *International Journal of Electrical Power & Energy Systems, 27*(4), 293–300. doi:10.1016/j.ijepes.2004.12.001

Wen, J. Y., Wu, Q. H., Jiang, L., & Cheng, S. J. (2003). Pseudo-gradient based evolutionary programming. *Electronics Letters, 39*(7), 631–632. doi:10.1049/el:20030404

Wood, A. J., & Wollenberg, B. F. (1996). *Power generation operation and control*. New York, NY: Wiley.

Wu, Q. H., Cao, Y. J., & Wen, J. Y. (1998). Optimal reactive power dispatch using an adaptive genetic algorithm. *International Journal of Electrical Power & Energy Systems, 20*(8), 563–569. doi:10.1016/S0142-0615(98)00016-7

Wu, Q. H., & Ma, J. T. (1995). Power system optimal reactive dispatch using evolutionary programming. *IEEE Transactions on Power Systems, 10*(3), 1243–1249. doi:10.1109/59.466531

Yan, W., Liu, F., Chung, C. Y., & Wong, K. P. (2006). A hybrid genetic algorithm–interior point method for optimal reactive power flow. *IEEE Transactions on Power Systems, 21*(3), 1163–1169. doi:10.1109/TPWRS.2006.879262

Yan, X., & Quintana, V. H. (1999). Improving an interior point based OPF by dynamic adjustments of step sizes and tolerances. *IEEE Transactions on Power Systems, 14*(2), 709–717. doi:10.1109/59.761902

Yuryevich, J., & Wong, K. P. (1999). Evolutionary programming based optimal power)ow algorithm. *IEEE Transactions on Power Systems, 14*(4), 1245–1250. doi:10.1109/59.801880

Zimmerman, R. D., Murillo-Sánchez, C. E., & Thomas, R. J. (2011). MATPOWER steady-state operations, planning and analysis tools for power systems research and education. *IEEE Transactions on Power Systems, 26*(1), 12–19. doi:10.1109/TPWRS.2010.2051168

ADDITIONAL READING

Abou El Ela, A. A., Abido, M. A., & Spea, S. R. (2010). Optimal power flow using differential evolution algorithm. *Electric Power Systems Research, 80*(7), 878–885. doi:10.1016/j.epsr.2009.12.018

AlRashidi, M. R., & El-Hawary, M. E. (2009). Applications of computational intelligence techniques for solving the revived optimal power flow problem. *Electric Power Systems Research, 79*(4), 694–702. doi:10.1016/j.epsr.2008.10.004

Amjady, N., & Sharifzadeh, H. (2011). Security constrained optimal power flow considering detailed generator model by a new robust differential evolution algorithm. *Electric Power Systems Research, 81*(2), 740–749. doi:10.1016/j.epsr.2010.11.005

Azadani, E. N., Hosseinian, S. H., Divshali, P. H., & Vahidi, B. (2011). Stability constrained optimal power flow in deregulated power systems. *Electric Power Components and Systems, 39*(8), 713–732. doi:10.1080/15325008.2010.541409

Bhattacharya, A., & Chattopadhyay, P. K. (2011). Application of biogeography-based optimisation to solve different optimal power flow problems. *IET Generation. Transmission & Distribution, 5*(1), 70–80.

Bhattacharya, K., Bollen, M. H. J., & Daalder, J. E. (2001). *Operation of restructured power systems*. New York, NY: Springer-Verlag. doi:10.1007/978-1-4615-1465-7

Capitanescu, F., Martinez Ramos, J. L., Panciatici, P., Kirschen, D., Marano Marcolini, A., Platbrood, L., & Wehenkel, L. (2011). State-of-the-art, challenges, and future trends in security constrained optimal power flow. *Electric Power Systems Research, 81*(8), 1731–1741. doi:10.1016/j.epsr.2011.04.003

Capitanescu, F., & Wehenkel, L. (2010). Optimal power flow computations with a limited number of controls allowed to move. *IEEE Transactions on Power Systems, 25*(1), 586–587. doi:10.1109/TPWRS.2009.2036461

Carpinelli, G., Lauria, D., & Varilone, P. (2006). Voltage stability analysis in unbalanced power systems by optimal power flow. *IEE Proceedings. Generation, Transmission and Distribution, 153*(3), 261–268. doi:10.1049/ip-gtd:20050011

Chakrabarti, A., & Halder, S. (2010). *Power system analysis: Operation and control* (3rd ed.). New Delhi, India: PHI Learning Private Limited.

Chandy, K. M., Low, S. H., Topcu, U., & Huan, X. (2010). A simple optimal power flow model with energy storage. *The 49th IEEE Conference on Decision and Control* (CDC) (pp. 1051 - 1057).

Condren, J., Gedra, T. W., & Damrongkulkamjorn, P. (2006). Optimal power flow with expected security costs. *IEEE Transactions on Power Systems, 21*(2), 541–547. doi:10.1109/TPWRS.2006.873114

de Carvalho, E. P., dos Santos Júnior, A., & Ma, T. F. (2008). Reduced gradient method combined with augmented Lagrangian and barrier for the optimal power flow problem. *Applied Mathematics and Computation, 200*(2), 529–536. doi:10.1016/j.amc.2007.11.025

El Metwally, M. M., El Emary, A. A., El Bendary, F. M., & Mosaad, M. I. (2008). Optimal power flow using evolutionary programming techniques. *The 12th International Middle-East Power System Conference* (MEPCON) (pp. 260-264).

Glover, D. J., Sarma, M. S., Overbye, T., & Learning, C. (2010). *Power system analysis and design* (5th ed.). Stamford.

Guo, C., & Chiang, H.-D. (2010). A new model of phase shifter for its efficient integration in interior point optimal power flow. *European Transactions on Electrical Power, 20*(4), 505–517.

Gutierrez-Martinez, V. J., Cañizares, C. A., Fuerte-Esquivel, C. R., & Pizano-Martinez, A., & Xueping Gu. (2011). Neural-network security-boundary constrained optimal power flow. *IEEE Transactions on Power Systems*, *26*(1), 63–72. doi:10.1109/TPWRS.2010.2050344

Hazra, J., & Sinha, A. K. (2011). A multi-objective optimal power flow using particle swarm optimization. *European Transactions on Electrical Power*, *21*(1), 1028–1045. doi:10.1002/etep.494

Honorio, L. M., da Silva, A. M. L., Barbosa, D. A., & Delboni, L. F. N. (2010). Solving optimal power flow problems using a probabilistic α-constrained evolutionary approach. *IET Generation. Transmission & Distribution*, *4*(6), 674–682.

Jabr, R. A. (2008). Optimal power flow using an extended conic quadratic formulation. *IEEE Transactions on Power Systems*, *23*(3), 1000–1008. doi:10.1109/TPWRS.2008.926439

Jabr, R. A., & Pal, B. C. (2009). Intermittent wind generation in optimal power flow dispatching. *IET Generation. Transmission & Distribution*, *3*(1), 66–74.

Kothari, D. P., & Dhillon, J. S. (2006). *Power system optimization*. New Delhi, India: Prentice Hall of India Private Limited.

Lavaei, J., & Low, S. H. (2012). Zero duality gap in optimal power flow problem. *IEEE Transactions on Power Systems*, *27*(1), 92–107. doi:10.1109/TPWRS.2011.2160974

Lee, K. Y., & El-Sharkawi, M. A. (2008). *Modern heuristic optimization techniques: Theory and applications to power systems*. New Jersey: Wiley-IEEE Press.

Li, C., Zhao, H., & Chen, T. (2010). The hybrid differential evolution algorithm for optimal power flow based on simulated annealing and tabu search. *International Conference on Management and Service Science* (pp. 1-7).

Lin, W.-M., Huang, C.-H., & Zhan, T.-S. (2008). A hybrid current-power optimal power flow technique. *IEEE Transactions on Power Systems*, *23*(1), 177–185. doi:10.1109/TP-WRS.2007.913301

Mahdad, B., Srairi, K., & Bouktir, T. (2010). Optimal power flow for large-scale power system with shunt FACTS using efficient parallel GA. *International Journal of Electrical Power & Energy Systems*, *32*(5), 507–517. doi:10.1016/j.ijepes.2009.09.013

Mo, N., Zou, Z. Y., Chan, K. W., & Pong, T. Y. G. (2007). Transient stability constrained optimal power flow using particle swarm optimization. *IET Generation. Transmission & Distribution*, *1*(3), 476–483.

Nguyen, T. T., Nguyen, V. L., & Karimishad, A. (2011). Transient stability-constrained optimal power flow for online dispatch and nodal price evaluation in power systems with flexible AC transmission system devices. *IET Generation. Transmission & Distribution*, *5*(3), 332–346.

Niknam, T., Narimani, M. R., Aghaei, J., & Tabatabaei, S. (2011). Modified honey bee mating optimisation to solve dynamic optimal power flow considering generator constraints. *IET Generation. Transmission & Distribution*, *5*(10), 989–1002.

Oñate, Y. P., Ramirez, J. M., & Coello, C. A. (2009). An optimal power flow plus transmission costs solution. *Electric Power Systems Research*, *79*(8), 1240–1246. doi:10.1016/j.epsr.2009.03.005

Onate Yumbla, P. E., Ramirez, J. M., & Coello Coello, C. A. (2008). Optimal power flow subject to security constraints solved with a particle swarm optimizer. *IEEE Transactions on Power Systems*, *23*(1), 33–40. doi:10.1109/TPWRS.2007.913196

Pizano-Martinez, A., Fuerte-Esquivel, C. R., & Ruiz-Vega, D. (2011). A New practical approach to transient stability-constrained optimal power flow. *IEEE Transactions on Power Systems, 26*(3), 1686–1696. doi:10.1109/TPWRS.2010.2095045

Rau, N. S. (2003). *Optimization principles: Practical applications to the operation and markets of the electric power industry*. US: IEEE Press.

Rebennack, S., Pardalos, P. M., & Pereira, M. V. F. (2010). *Handbook of power systems II*. Berlin, Germany: Springer-Verlag.

Riffonneau, Y., Bacha, S., Barruel, F., & Ploix, S. (2011). Optimal power flow management for grid connected PV systems with batteries. *IEEE Trans. Sustainable Energy, 2*(3), 309–320. doi:10.1109/TSTE.2011.2114901

Roy, P. K., Ghoshal, S. P., & Thakur, S. S. (2010). Multi-objective optimal power flow using biogeography-based optimization. *Electric Power Components and Systems, 38*(12), 1406–1426. doi:10.1080/15325001003735176

Roy, P. K., Ghoshal, S. P., & Thakur, S. S. (2010). Biogeography based optimization for multi-constraint optimal power flow with emission and non-smooth cost function. *Expert Systems with Applications, 37*(12), 8221–8228. doi:10.1016/j.eswa.2010.05.064

Selvan, M. P. (2009). Object-oriented optimal power flow: A new approach based on design patterns. *Electric Power Components and Systems, 38*(2), 197–211. doi:10.1080/15325000903273361

Sinsupan, N., Uthen Leeton, U., & Kulworawanichpong, T. (2010). Application of harmony search to optimal power flow problems. *International Conference on Advances in Energy Engineering* (ICAEE) (pp. 219-222).

Sivanagaraju, S., & Sreenivasan, G. (2010). *Power system operation and control. New Delhi, India: Dorling Kindersley*. India: Pvt. Ltd.

Sivasubramani, S., & Swarup, K. S. (2011). Sequential quadratic programming based differential evolution algorithm for optimal power flow problem. *IET Generation. Transmission & Distribution, 5*(11), 1149–1154.

Sousa, A. A., Torres, G. L., & Cañizares, C. A. (2011). Robust optimal power flow solution using trust region and interior-point methods. *IEEE Transactions on Power Systems, 26*(2), 487–499. doi:10.1109/TPWRS.2010.2068568

Thitithamrongchai, C., & Eua-Arporn, B. (2008). Security-constrained optimal power flow: A parallel self-adaptive differential evolution approach. *Electric Power Components and Systems, 36*(3), 280–298. doi:10.1080/15325000701603942

Todorovski, M., & Rajicic, D. (2006). An initialization procedure in solving optimal power flow by genetic algorithm. *IEEE Transactions on Power Systems, 21*(2), 480–487. doi:10.1109/TPWRS.2006.873120

Tong, X., Wu, F. F., & Qi, L. (2007). On the convergence of decoupled optimal power flow methods. *Numerical Functional Analysis and Optimization, 28*(3-4), 467–485. doi:10.1080/01630560701250135

Uturbey, W., & Costa, A. S. (2007). Dynamic optimal power flow approach to account for consumer response in short term hydrothermal coordination studies. *IET Generation. Transmission & Distribution, 1*(3), 414–421.

Verbic, G., & Canizares, C. A. (2006). Probabilistic optimal power flow in electricity markets based on a two-point estimate method. *IEEE Transactions on Power Systems*, *21*(4), 1883–1893. doi:10.1109/TPWRS.2006.881146

Xia, Y., & Chan, K. W. (2006). Dynamic constrained optimal power flow using semi-infinite programming. *IEEE Transactions on Power Systems*, *21*(3), 1455–1457. doi:10.1109/TPWRS.2006.879241

Zhu, J. (2009). *Optimization of power system operation*. New Jersey: Wiley. doi:10.1002/9780470466971

KEY TERMS AND DEFINITIONS

Fuel Cost Function: The operation characteristic of a thermal generating unit is usually represented as a nonlinear function where the operating cost is a function of unit's power output. The nonlinear function is referred as the fuel cost function whose coefficients reflects the kind of matter used to produce steam by heating boiler.

Multiple Fuels: A thermal generating unit may use different types of fuel such as coal, oil, or gas where each type of fuel is represented by a nonlinear function. The fuel cost function of a thermal generating unit with multiple fuels is a non-convex function representing the characteristics of all fuels available for the unit.

Optimal Power Flow: The optimal power flow is to determine the operating point of generators in a power system so as their total cost is minimized satisfying various generator and system constraints such as generator's real and reactive power, bus voltage, transformer tap, switchable capacitor bank, and transmission line capacity limits.

Particle Swarm Optimization: An algorithm is widely used for solving optimization problems. The algorithm was developed by J. Kennedy and R. Eberhart in 1995 inspired from the movement of a flock of bird or school of fish searching for food.

Power Flow: The power flow or load flow is to determine voltage angle and magnitude information at each bus in a power system for specified load demand and real power and voltage of generators. Based on the obtained information, real and reactive power flow in each transmission line and generator reactive power output can be calculated.

Pseudo-Gradient: Pseudo gradient method is used for determining the search direction of individuals in population based methods when dealing with non-differentiable problems. The pseudo-gradient method is based on the two latest points to determine the direction for the next search.

Valve Point Effects: In practical operation conditions, boilers of thermal generating units may have valve points for controlling their power outputs by taking into consideration of ripples in the heat-rate curves of the boilers. Therefore, the fuel cost function of a thermal generating unit with valve point effect is usually a non-convex and non-smooth function.

APPENDIX

Data for the IEEE 14-bus system is given in Tables 28 and 29.

Data for the IEEE 30-bus system is given in Tables 30 and 31.

Table 28. Load demand for the IEEE 14-bus system

Bus no.	P_{di} **(MW)**	Q_{di} **(MVAr)**
2	21.7	12.7
3	94.2	19.0
4	47.8	-3.9
5	7.6	1.6
6	11.2	7.5
9	29.5	16.6
10	9.0	5.8
11	3.5	1.8
12	6.1	1.6
13	13.5	5.8
14	14.9	5.0

Table 29. Branch data for the IEEE 14-bus system

No.	From bus	To bus	R **(pu)**	X **(pu)**	B **(pu)**	Tap ratio
1	1	2	0.01938	0.05917	0.0528	1
2	1	5	0.05403	0.22304	0.0492	1
3	2	3	0.04699	0.19797	0.0438	1
4	2	4	0.05811	0.17632	0.0374	1
5	2	5	0.05695	0.17388	0.034	1
6	3	4	0.06701	0.17103	0.0346	1
7	4	5	0.01335	0.04211	0.0128	1
8	4	7	0.00	0.20912	0.00	0.978
9	4	9	0.00	0.55618	0.00	0.969
10	5	6	0.00	0.25202	0.00	0.932
11	6	11	0.09498	0.1989	0.00	1
12	6	12	0.12291	0.25581	0.00	1
13	6	13	0.06615	0.13027	0.00	1
14	7	8	0.00	0.17615	0.00	1
15	7	9	0.00	0.11001	0.00	1
16	9	10	0.03181	0.08450	0.00	1
17	9	14	0.12711	0.27038	0.00	1
18	10	11	0.08205	0.19207	0.00	1
19	12	13	0.22092	0.19988	0.00	1
20	13	14	0.17093	0.34802	0.00	1

Table 30. Load demand for the IEEE 30-bus system

Bus no.	P_{di} (MW)	Q_{di} (MVAr)
2	21.7	12.7
3	2.4	1.2
4	7.6	1.6
5	94.2	19
7	22.8	10.9
8	30	30
10	5.8	2
12	11.2	7.5
14	6.2	1.6
15	8.2	2.5
16	3.5	1.8
17	9	5.8
18	3.2	0.9
19	9.5	3.4
20	2.2	0.7
21	17.5	11.2
23	3.2	1.6
24	8.7	6.7
26	3.5	2.3
29	2.4	0.9
30	10.6	1.9

Table 31. Branch data for the IEEE 30-bus system

No.	From bus	To bus	R (pu)	X (pu)	B (pu)	Tap ratio
1	1	2	0.0192	0.0575	0.0528	1
2	1	3	0.0452	0.1652	0.0408	1
3	2	4	0.057	0.1737	0.0368	1
4	3	4	0.0132	0.0379	0.0084	1
5	2	5	0.0472	0.1983	0.0418	1
6	2	6	0.0581	0.1763	0.0374	1
7	4	6	0.0119	0.0414	0.009	1
8	5	7	0.046	0.116	0.0204	1
9	6	7	0.0267	0.082	0.017	1
10	6	8	0.012	0.042	0.009	1
11	6	9	0	0.208	0	0.978
12	6	10	0	0.556	0	0.969
13	9	11	0	0.208	0	1
14	9	10	0	0.11	0	1
15	4	12	0	0.256	0	0.932
16	12	13	0	0.14	0	1
17	12	14	0.1231	0.2559	0	1
18	12	15	0.0662	0.1304	0	1
19	12	16	0.0945	0.1987	0	1
20	14	15	0.221	0.1997	0	1
21	16	17	0.0524	0.1923	0	1
22	15	18	0.1073	0.2185	0	1
23	18	19	0.0639	0.1292	0	1
24	19	20	0.034	0.068	0	1
25	10	20	0.0936	0.209	0	1
26	10	17	0.0324	0.0845	0	1
27	10	21	0.0348	0.0749	0	1
28	10	22	0.0727	0.1499	0	1
29	21	22	0.0116	0.0236	0	1
30	15	23	0.1	0.202	0	1
31	22	24	0.115	0.179	0	1
32	23	24	0.132	0.27	0	1
33	24	25	0.1885	0.3292	0	1
34	25	26	0.2544	0.38	0	1
35	25	27	0.1093	0.2087	0	1
36	28	27	0	0.396	0	0.968
37	27	29	0.2198	0.4153	0	1
38	27	30	0.3202	0.6027	0	1
39	9	30	0.2399	0.4533	0	1
40	8	28	0.0636	0.2	0.0428	1
41	6	28	0.0169	0.0599	0.013	1

Chapter 2
The Use of Soft Computing for Optimization in Business, Economics, and Finance

Petr Dostál
Brno University of Technology, Institute of Informatics, Czech Republic

ABSTRACT

Optimization methods have had successful applications in business, economics, and finance. Nowadays the new theories of soft computing are used for these purposes. The applications in business, economics, and finance have specific features in comparison with others. The processes are focused on private corporate attempts at money making or decreasing expenses; therefore the details of applications, successful or not, are not published very often. The optimization methods help in decentralization of decision-making processes to be standardized, reproduced, and documented. The optimization plays very important roles especially in business because it helps to reduce costs that can lead to higher profits and to success in the competitive fight.

1. INTRODUCTION

There are various optimization methods appropriate to use in business and economics: classical ones and methods using soft computing such as fuzzy logic, neural networks, genetic algorithms, and the theory of chaos.

Soft computing differs from conventional (hard) computing in that, unlike hard computing, it is tolerant of imprecision, uncertainty, partial truth, and approximation. In effect, the role model for soft computing is the human mind. The guiding principle of soft computing is: Exploit the tolerance for imprecision, uncertainty, partial truth, and approximation to achieve tractability, robustness and low solution cost. The basic ideas underlying soft computing in its current incarnation have links to many earlier influences, among them

DOI: 10.4018/978-1-4666-2086-5.ch002

Zadeh's 1965 paper on fuzzy sets. The inclusion of neural computing and genetic computing in soft computing came at a later point.

At this juncture, the principal constituents of Soft Computing (SC) are Fuzzy Logic (FL), Neural Computing (NC), Evolutionary Computation (EC) Machine Learning (ML) and Probabilistic Reasoning (PR), with the latter subsuming belief networks, chaos theory and parts of learning theory. What is important to note is that soft computing is not a melange. Rather, it is a partnership in which each of the partners contributes a distinct methodology for addressing problems in its domain. In this perspective, the principal constituent methodologies in SC are complementary rather than competitive. Furthermore, soft computing may be viewed as a foundation component for the emerging field of conceptual intelligence.

The mentioned applications in this chapter are as follows:

- Risk investment
- Risk management (loans, mortgages, direct mailing)
- Optimization of number of objects (devices, stock)
- Prediction of time series
- Journey optimization
- Description of economic phenomena (stock market).

The program MATLAB® with Fuzzy Logic, Neural Network, and Global Optimization Toolbox is used. The fields of applications of optimization methods in business, economics, and finance cover a wide area of applications.

2. FUZZY LOGIC

2.1 Fundamentals of Fuzzy Logic

In classical logic, a theory defines a set as a collection having certain definite properties. Any element belongs to the set or not according to clear-cut rules; membership in the set has only the two values 0 or 1. Later, the theory of fuzzy logic was created by Zadeh in 1965. Fuzzy logic defines a variable degree to which an element x belongs to the set. The degree of membership in the set is denoted $\mu(x)$; it can take on any value in the range from 1 to 0, where 0 means absolute non-membership and 1 full membership. The use of degrees of membership corresponds better to what happens in the world of our experience. Fuzzy logic measures the certainty or uncertainty of how much the element belongs to the set. People make analogous decisions in the fields of mental and physical behaviour. By means of fuzzy logic, it is possible to find the solution of a given task better than by classical methods.

The fuzzy logic system consists of three fundamental steps: fuzzification, fuzzy inference, and defuzzification. See Figure 1.

The first step (fuzzification) means the transformation of ordinary language into numerical values. For variable risk, for example, the linguistic values can be no, very low, low, medium, high, and very high risk. The variable usually has from three to seven attributes (terms). The degree of membership of attributes is expressed by mathematical functions. There are many shapes of membership functions. For example, for mf_1, $P = [0\ 0\ 3]$; mf_2, $P = [2\ 4\ 6]$; mf_3, $P = [4\ 6\ 7\ 9]$; mf_4, $P = [8\ 10\ 10]$; and so forth. See Figure 2.

Figure 1 Decision making solved by means of fuzzy logic

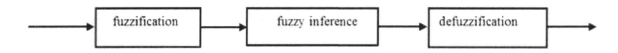

The types of membership functions that are used in practice are for example Λ and Π. There are many other types of standard membership functions on the list including spline ones. The attribute and membership functions concern input and output variables.

The second step (fuzzy inference) defines the system behaviour by means of the rules such as <IF>, <THEN>, <WITH>. The conditional clauses create this rule, which evaluates the input variables. These conditional clauses have the form

$$<IF> I_1 \text{ is } mf_a <OR> I_2 \text{ is } mf_b \ldots <OR> I_{N-1} \text{ is } mf_y$$
$$<OR> I_N \text{ is } mf_z <THEN> O_1 \text{ is } mf_{O1} <WITH> s.$$

The written conditional clause could be described by words: If the input I_1 is mf_a or I_2 is mf_b or ... or I_{N-1} is mf_y or I_N is mf_z then O_1 is mf_{O1} with the weight s, where the value s is in the range <0–1>. These rules must be set up and then they may be used for further processing.

The fuzzy rules represent the expert systems. Each combination of attribute values that inputs into the system and occurs in the condition <IF>, <THEN>, <WITH> represents one rule. Next it is necessary to determine the degree of supports for each rule; it is the weight of the rule in the system. It is possible to change the weight rules during the process of optimization of the system.

For the part of rules behind <IF>, it is necessary to find the corresponding attribute behind the part <THEN>. These rules are created by experts. The <AND > could be instead <OR >.

The third step (defuzzification) means the transformation of numerical values to linguistic ones. The linguistic values can be, for example, for variable *Risk* very low, low, medium, high, and very high. The purpose of defuzzification is the transformation of fuzzy values of an output variable so as to present verbally the results of a fuzzy calculation. During the consecutive entry of data the model with fuzzy logic works as an automat. There can be a lot of variables on the input.

The chapter is focused on applications. The fuzzy theory is described in books such as (Altroc 1996), (Dostál 2011), (Chen et al. 2004), (Chen et al. 2007), (Kazabov and Kozma 1998), (Klir and Yuan 1995), (Li et al. 2006), (The MathWorks 2010b).

2.2 Applications of Fuzzy Logic

Example 2.1: The Fuzzy Logic Toolbox enables setting up rules by means of neural networks using the command *Anfis*. The setup of fuzzy rules in the program environment MATLAB with the help of neural networks is presented for a case study, where the program creates the fuzzy rules

Figure 2. The types of membership functions Λ and Π

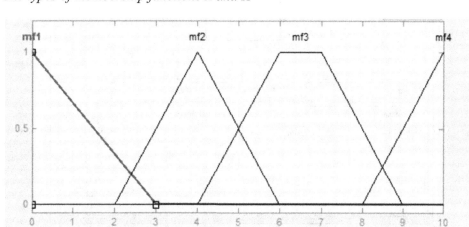

by means of neural networks. The inputs and outputs are defined by Table 1, presenting the logical operation <AND>. We demonstrate four states. The first state represent the fact that the political risk is high (0) and economic risk is high (0) and it leads to state of output of no investment (0). The second state represent the fact that the political risk is high (0) and economic risk is low (1) and it leads to state of output of no investment (0). The third state represent the fact that the political risk is low (1) and economic risk is high (0) and it leads to state of output of no investment (0). The fourth state represent the fact that the political risk is low (1) and economic risk is low (1) and it leads to state of investment (1).

The text file *Risk.dat* is created with the mentioned data at first. See Table 2.

The commands *fuzzy* and *File-New FIS-Sugeno* create a fuzzy model in the MATLAB environment, then there follow commands *Edit-Add Variable-Input* that add the second input. The fuzzy model is saved in *IR.fis* file. See Figure 3.

Table 1. The input and output values

State	Risk Po	Rick Ec	Investment
Order	Input1	Input2	Output
1	0 (H)	0 (H)	0 (N)
2	0 (H)	1 (L)	0 (N)
3	1 (L)	0 (H)	0 (N)
4	1 (L)	1 (L)	1 (Y)

Table 2. Input and output values

0	0	0
0	1	0
1	0	0
1	1	1

The command *Edit-Anfis* opens the editor. The choice of menu *Type-Training* and *From-file* and command *Load-Data* read the file *Risk.dat*. See Figure 4.

Figure 3. Fuzzy model

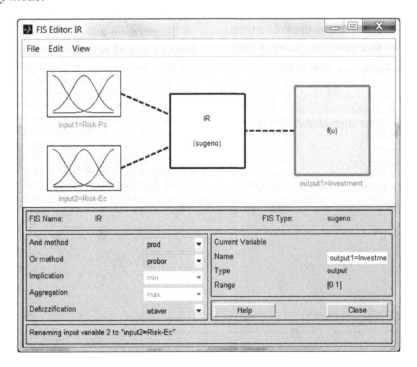

The Fuzzy Interface System is generated from the command *FIS* with the option *Grid partition*. It is set up with the numbers of two membership functions for both inputs *Number of MF's [2 2]*, then the Gaussian membership function is set up from the commands *MF Type gaussmf* and linear type *MF Type – linear*. The return is done by the *OK* menu. See Figure 5.

The values for training of neural networks create the rules chosen by options *Optim. Method-Hybrid*, *Error Tolerance* 0, and the number of *Epoch*s 20. The process of training starts with the command *Train Now*. It is desirable to watch the error training. See Figure 6.

The command *Structure* shows the created neural network used for generation of rules. See Figure 7.

The command *Test FIS – Training data* enables comparing trained data with the real ones, possibly with testing and checking data. See Figure 8.

The dependence of outputs on input can be displayed by standard commands. See Figure 9. The surface reflects the proper generation of rules.

It is possible to display the generated rules. See Figure 10.

The command *Rules* enables the verification of created rules. See Figure 11.

The presented case study describes the methodology of creation of rules by means of neural networks using the data from databases. The problem could involve complicated tasks, where a large number of rules are created. If the rules could not describe the solved problem successfully, the displayed surface shows "disturbances". In the case of wrong generalization, the trained model does not correspond with new data.

The advantage of the use of fuzzy logic in comparison with classical methods is in the fact that vague terms could be processed by fuzzy decision making model. This example presents risk of investment. More inputs are generally used.

Figure 4. Reading of data and their display

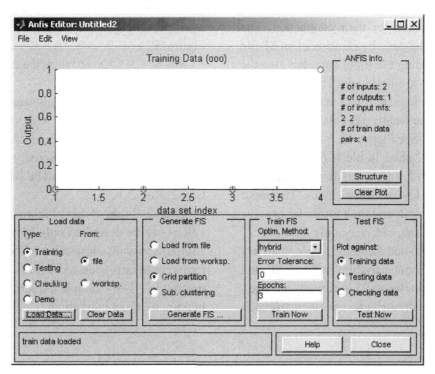

Figure 5. The setup of membership functions

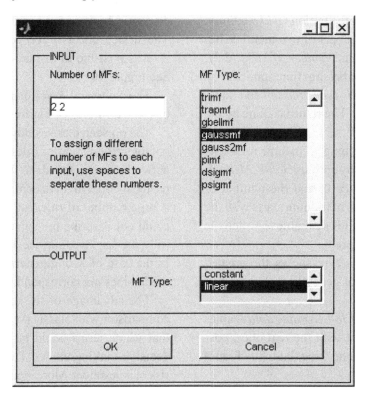

Example 2.2: There are situations when more rule boxes are necessary for using the decision-making process and for their connection. The connection can be done by creation of an M-file that enables reading the input data, but also the transfer of results to other blocks. The case presents the use of fuzzy logic at direct mailing, whether the client visit personally, sent him a letter or not to speak to him. See Figure 12.

The input variables in block B_1 and their attributes are *Loan I_{1a}* (none, small, medium, high) and *Salary I_{1b}* (low, medium, high). The input variables in block B_2 and their attributes are *Age I_{2a}* (young, medium, old, very old), *Children I_{2b}* (no, a few, many) and *State I_{2c}* (single, married, divorced). The input variables in block B_F and their attributes are *Place I_3* (big city, city, village). The rule blocks with attributes are *Finance* (excel-

lent, good, bad), *Personality* (unsuitable, suitable, good, excellent); and output *Mailing* (inactivity, mail, personally). See Figure 13, Figure 14, and Figure 15.

The M-file *BF.m* provides the calculation. See Box 1, Prog. 2.1.

The results of the calculation are presented by inputs I_{1a}, I_{1b}, I_{2a}, I_{2b}, I_{2c}, I_3 with values 0, 1, and 0.5. The results are the attributes Inactivity (client will not be spoken), or Personally (client will be visited), or Mail (a letter will be sent to him). See Box 2, Res. 2.1.

The advantage of fuzzy logic is in the use when values can be described only by vague terms in comparison with classical methods. The vague terms could be processed by fuzzy decision making model. The example presents the decision making in direct marketing.

Box 1. Prog. 2.1: M-file BF.m

```
clear all
B1v = readfis('B1.fis');
UdajB1 = input('Input values in the form [I1a; I1b]: ');
VyhB1 = evalfis(UdajB1, B1v);
B2v = readfis('B2.fis');
UdajB2 = input('Input values in the form [I2a;I2b;I2c]: ');
VyhB2 = evalfis(UdajB2, B2v);
BFv = readfis('BF.fis');
UdajBF(3)=input('Input values in the form [I3]: ');
UdajBF(1) = VyhB1;
UdajBF(2) = VyhB2;
VyhBF = evalfis(UdajBF, BFv);
if VyhBF<0.5 'Inactivity'
    elseif VyhBF<0.8 'Mail'
    else 'Personally'
end
fuzzy(BFv)
mfedit(BFv)
ruleedit(BFv)
surfview(BFv)
ruleview(BFv)
```

3. NEURAL NETWORKS

3.1 Principles of Neural Networks

The history of the development of neural networks started in the first half of the twentieth century. The first publications were by McCulloch. Later Pitts worked on the simplest model of a neuron, and after that Rosenblatt created a functional perception that solves only problems involving areas that are linearly separable. When the multi-layer network was discovered by Rumelhart, then Hinton and Williams created back-propagation methods for multi-layer networks. A great boom of neural network applications has been ongoing since the mid-1970s.

The neural network model represents the thinking of the human brains. The model is described as a "black box." It is not possible to know the inside structure of the system in detail. We make only a few suppositions about the inner structure of the system. It is simulated by a "black box" that enables us to describe the behaviour of the system by the function that performs transformation of input and output. It is suitable to use neural networks in cases where the influences on searched phenomena are random and deterministic relations are very complicated. In these cases we are not able to separate and analytically identify them. They are suitable for simulation of complicated and often irreversible strategic decision making. The biological neuron can be presented in a simple way that consists of many inputs (dendrites), body (soma), and one output (axon) as shown in Figure 16. The inputs are processed by neurons. The output information is spread by the axon to terminals that are called "synapses." The synapsis communicates with the dendrites of other neurons.

Figure 6. Anfis editor – error training

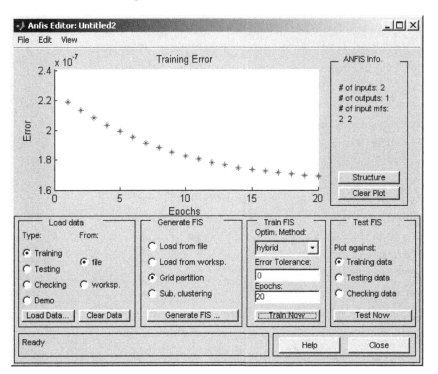

Figure 7. Created neural network

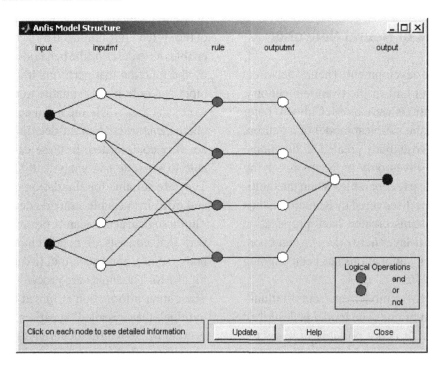

Figure 8. Evaluation of training

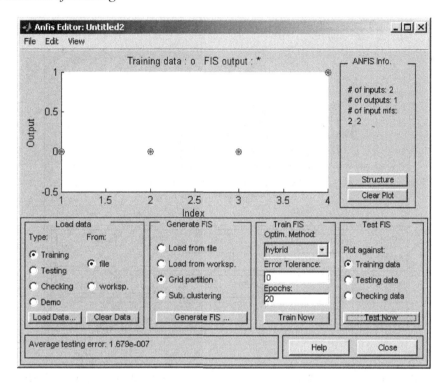

The history of the development of neural networks started in the first half of the twentieth century. The first publications were by McCulloch. Later Pitts worked on the simplest model of a neuron, and after that Rosenblatt created a functional perception that solves only problems involving areas that are linearly separable. When the multilayer network was discovered by Rumelhart, then Hinton and Williams created back-propagation methods for multi-layer networks. A great boom of neural network applications has been ongoing since the mid-1970s.

The neural network works in two phases. In the first phase the network presents a model of a complicated system as a "curious pupil"; it tries to set up parameters so as to best correspond to the topology of neural networks. In the second phase, the neural network becomes an "expert" to produce the outputs based on the knowledge obtained in the first phase. During the building up of a neural network, the layers of the network must be defined (input, hidden, output); single input and output neurons specified, and the method of connecting the neurons among them identified (the setup of transfer functions among neurons).

The simplest neural network is called a "perceptron." It may have an input of R variables p_1, p_2, p_3, . . ., p_R. These variables are multiplied by weight coefficients w_1, w_2, w_3, . . ., w_R. The threshold value b influences the output; it increases the value of sum just about this value. The formula is

$$a = w_1 * p_1 + w_2 * p_2 + w_3 * p_3 + \cdots + w_R * p_R \sum_{i=1}^{R} w_i p_i + b.$$

Figure 17 shows the single-layer neural network: perceptron.

The most important MATLAB functions are hardlim $n=0$ for $a<0$ and $n=1$ for $a\geq0$, purelin $n=a$, logsig $n=1/(1+e^{-a})$ and tansig $n=(e^a-e^{-a}) / (e^a+e^{-a})$. See Figure 18.

Figure 9. Dependence of output on inputs

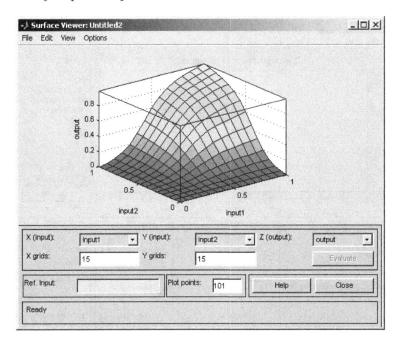

The simplest transfer function is hardlim, when output value is equal 1 or 0, according to whether the value a is less than 0 or equal and bigger than 0. With this function the transformation gives us standardized values. The function logsig has values in the interval from 0 to 1. The function tansig has values in the interval from −1 to 1. The output values could achieve high values in case of not using such or similar transfer functions, which is the problem especially of multi-layer neural networks. The value b is the so called threshold value that increases the value of sum (sum of inputs x weight coefficient) just about this value.

Figure 19 presents a multi-layer network with input layer, hidden layers, and output layer. For perception and multi-layer networks it is possible to write the equation in the matrix form $n = f(w * p + b)$.

The back-propagation method is used for calculation of weights of neural networks. It consists of two steps. First, it is necessary to make a calculation of outputs on the basis of inputs and weights (forward step). Next it is necessary to calculate the error E as a square difference of calculated output n and expected output o over all outputs, using an equation in the form $E = \Sigma (n_i - o_i)^2$. The value E is used for the backward calculation of weight (backward step). The process is repeated till the values of E converge to an acceptable value (the problem of learning is an optimization task, in which the error function E is a fitness function that must be minimized).

The chapter is focused on applications. The fuzzy theory is described in books such as (Altroc 1996), (Azoff 1994), (Bose and Liang,1996), (Dostál 2011), (Gately 1996), (Hagan and Demuth 1996), (Chen et al. 2004), (Kazabov and Kozma 1998), (The MathWorks 2010c).

3.1 Applications of Neural Networks

Example 3.1: There are many tasks from business, economics, and finance where clustering helps to

Figure 10. Generated rules

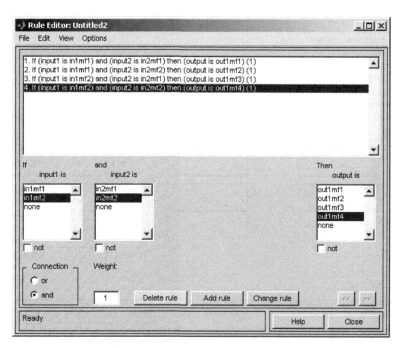

make correct decision making. The Kohonen neural network can be used for these purposes. This example describes the method of calculation, how the program is created, and how the case study is applied. The algorithm is as follows:

A. Setup of the number of input variables n according to the structure of input pattern and determination of a number N of efficient neurons according to condition $L \leq n/(4\log N)$, where L is the number of patterns to be recognized by the network

B. Setup of initial values that are selected as random values in the range $<-0.5;0.5>$

C. Setup of the shape and radius of initial environs of the winning neuron $NE(t_o)$; at first it is a maximum, then it is decreased step by step to be $R_c(t) = 1$

D. The use of the first learning pattern x_1 and foundation of the winning neuron is done in such a way that the Euclidean distance of its weighted vector w_j from x_1 is the smallest. The calculation is done according to the formula $D_j = \sum_{i=1}^{n}\left(x_i\left(t\right) - w_{ji}\left(t\right)\right)^2 \rightarrow \min$ for j=1, 2, ..., N. The ideal case is the situation when $\min_j D_j \rightarrow 0$

E. The adaptation of weighted coefficients is done according to the formula $w_{ji}\left(t+1\right) = w_{ji}\left(t\right) + \alpha\left(t\right)\left(x_i(t) - w_{ji}\left(t\right)\right)$ for $j \in NE_c(t)$ and $w_{ji}(t+1)=w_{ji}(t)$, for $j \notin NE_c(t)$.

The teaching is continued until the weighted coefficients do not change if a random pattern from the collection of learning patterns is used.

The example presents the objects recorded in MS Excel format in *DC.xls* file. See Table 3. This task is solved by the program *NNC.m*. See Box 3, Prog. 3.1.

The program is started using the command *NNC* in the MATLAB program environment. It is necessary to set up the number of clusters, in our example 4 and number epochs 1000. During the process of calculation the data are dynamically displayed in a three-dimensional graph.

Figure 11. Verification of rules

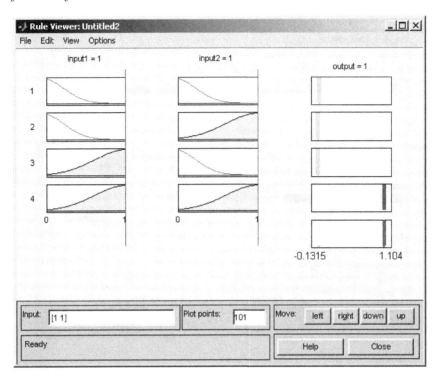

When the calculation is finished the input parameters and the results of the calculation are presented in the display. See Box 4, Res. 3.1.

The results are presented by coordinates of clusters and assignment of objects to the clusters. The two and three-dimensional stem graph is drawn. See Figure 20 and Figure 21. The task solves the problem of minimizing the costs of constructions of transmitters of mobile network.

The advantage of neural network theory is in successful use of clustering problems that are used quite often in economy and finance.

Example 3.2: The Neural Network Toolbox of MATLAB contains a special toolbox for prediction of time series, which is quite often used in the business and economics. This example presents the prediction of time series from history created by the number of sold products recorded in *D.xls* file. The menu is called from workspace using the command *ntstool*. At first, it is necessary to setup the type of neural network. The Nonlinear

Autoregressive Model (*NAR*) was chosen. See Figure 22.

Then it is necessary to click on button *Next* and download the data from the *D.xls* file. When the data are downloaded, the window is closed using the command *Finish*. See Figure 23.

After the data have been selected, as in Figure 24, the command *Next* opens a window for the setup of *Training, Validation,* and *Testing*. The default value can be used or it could be changed. See Figure 25.

The command *Next* enables the setup of the network architecture represented by *Number of Hidden Neurons* and *Number of Delays*. The default value can be used or it could be changed. See Figure 26. The commands *Next* and *Train* start training the neural network. See Figure 27.

The process of training is displayed in the window and after the process of training it is possible to evaluate the graph to determine whether the correct training was done, for example performance *Performance*. See Figure 28. It is possible to evaluate the mean square error *MSE* and fit of prediction. See Figure 29. The process of training may be repeated several times using the command *Retrain*.

When the results of training correspond to the required demands, the output has to be saved as a variable, for example *output*. See Figure 30.

Saved data sets could be used for evaluation, for example to display them at workplace or transferring data into MS Excel. The graph is presented in Figure 31. The graph presents history of 120 days of selling products and its prediction for next 30 days to help to set up a plan of production.

The script could be saved any time in an M-file using the menu *Advanced Script*. See Box 5, Prog. 3.2.

The advantage of neural network theory for prediction is in their abilities of description of nonlinear economic and financial time series. The disadvantage is, that neural network is like a black box. The prediction of time series fails when time series have a random course.

4. GENETIC ALGORITHMS

4.1 Principles of Genetic Algorithms

Genetic algorithms are used in studies where exact solution by systematic searching would be extremely slow, which is well suited for solving complicated problems. Genetic processes in nature were discovered in the nineteenth century by Mendel and developed by Darwin. The computer realization of genetic algorithms discovered in the 1970s, is connected with the names of J. Holland and Goldberg. Recently there has been considerable expansion of genetic algorithms in the spheres of economic applications and the decision making of firms and companies.

Let us mention a few terms that are used in the branch of genetics: chromosomes, selection, crossover, mutation, population, parents, and offspring. The chromosomes consist of genes (bits). Every gene inherits one or several bits and its position in chromosomes. We say that the chromosomes have locus. The information coded in chromosomes consists of phenotypes. Most of the implementations of genetic algorithm work with the original representation of chromosomes is binary representation: 0 and 1. A chromosome is represented by a binary string, e.g. 0101. These binary strings mostly represent coded decimal

Figure 12. Connection of rule blocks

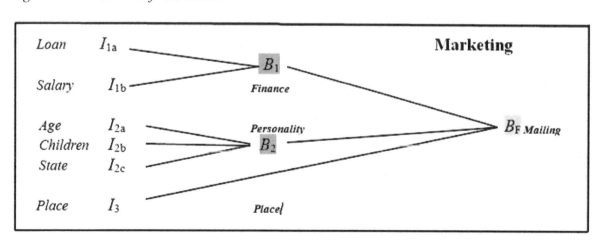

Figure 13. Box B$_F$

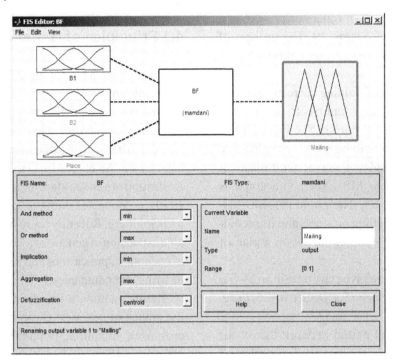

numbers. The operators of selection, crossover, and mutation are most often used in genetic algorithms. The diagram is then chained, where the permitted symbol occurs in at least one position (in case of binary representation it is 0 or 1). For the handling of chromosomes, several genetic operators have been proposed. The most used operators are selection, crossover, and mutation.

The process of selection involves the choice of chromosomes that become parents. The fitness of the parents plays an important role in the process of selection. The process of selection is presented in Table 4 when the number 7 (binary

Box 2. Res. 2.1: Results

```
Input values in the form [I1a; I1b]: [0;0]
Input values in the form [I2a; I2b; I2c]: [0;0;0]
Input values in the form [I3]: [0]
ans =Inactivity
Input values in the form [I1a; I1b]: [1;1]
Input values in the form [I2a; I2b; I2c]: [1;1;1]
Input values in the form [I3]: [1]
ans =Personally
Input values in the form [I1a; I1b]: [0.5;0.5]
Input values in the form [I2a; I2b; I2c]: [0.5;0.5;0.5]
Input values in the form [I3]: [0.5]
ans =Mail
```

Figure 14. Box B₁

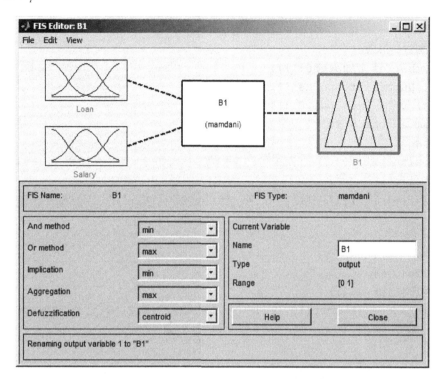

Figure 15. Box B₂

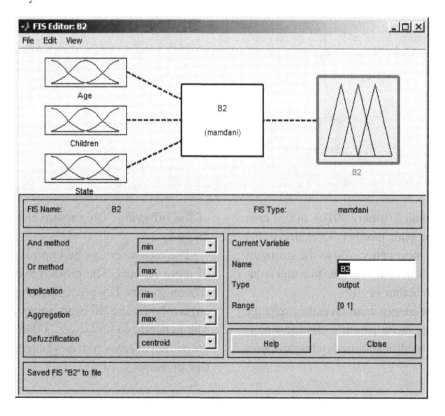

Box 3. Prog. 3.1: M-file NNC.m

```
clear all;
P=(xlsread('DCN','Data'))';
num=input('Number of clusters:');
epochs=input('Number of epochs:');
net=newc([0 1; 0 1; 0 1],num,0.1);
net.trainParam.epochs = 1;
for k=1:epochs
    net = train(net,P);
    w = net.IW{1};
    stem3(w(:,1),w(:,2),w(:,3),'sr','MarkerFaceColor','b','MarkerSize',10)
    grid on;
    hold on
    Q=P';
    for i=1:size(Q,1)
        for j=1:(size(w,1))
            distances(j)=sqrt((Q(i,1)-w(j,1))^2+(Q(i,2)-w(j,2))^2+(Q(i,3)-
w(j,3))^2);
        end
        [min_distance(i),assignment(i)]=min(distances);
    end
for i=1:size(Q,1)
    stem3(Q(i,1),Q(i,2),Q(i,3),'sr','MarkerFaceColor',[assignment(i)/
num,assignment(i)/num,
    assignment(i)/num],'MarkerSize',10)
    xlabel('x');ylabel('y');zlabel('z');
    end
    figure(gcf)
    hold off
end
total_distance=sum(min_distance)
Q;w;assignment
```

0111) is bigger than 2 (binary 0010). In this case the chromosome with number 7 (binary 0111) progresses to the next generation as the strongest specimen (it leads in computations to better solutions and thus to higher profit).

The process of crossover involves the exchange of part of two or more parent's chromosomes, which causes the modification of the chromosomes of the offspring. The crossover is presented in Table 5.

The crossover can be improved by selection of more parents. The crossover can have more crossing points. This process is called a multi-point cross when more division points are generated. The generalized crossover is done according to the pattern of zeros and ones generated by alternative divisions.

Figure 16. The biological neuron

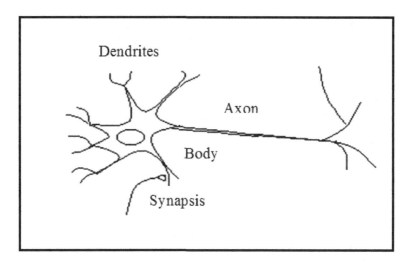

Figure 17. Perceptron

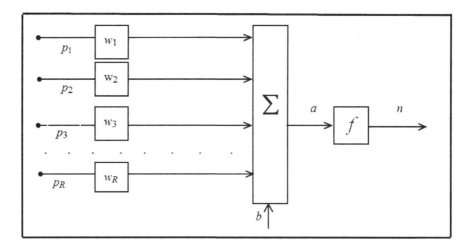

Figure 18. Transfer functions hardlim, purelin, logsig, and tansig

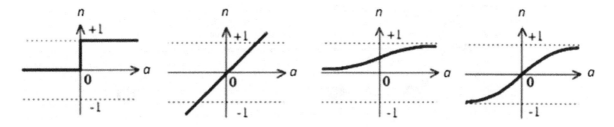

Box 4. Res. 3.1: Input parameters and results of calculation

```
Number of clusters: 4
Number of epochs: 500
Total distance =           5.3141
w =    0.3211     0.8013     4.4506
       0.8308     0.4471     2.1745
       0.4488     0.5221     3.5027
       0.4905     0.6905     2.0824
Assignment =        4     2     2     3
2      1      4     3     3     4     3     1
2      1      2
```

The process of mutation involves the modification of chromosomes. The modification is done by random change of some bit. The mutation is not frequent. The mutation is presented in Table 6.

The genetic algorithms work in such a way that the population of chromosomes is created at first. Then the population is changed by means of genetic operators until it is found that the parents are the same (the value of fitness function does not change after some number of iterations). The process of reproduction repeats. Each epoch of population (one generation) represents three steps: selection, crossover, and mutation. See Figure 32.

Note: A fitness function is a function that prescribes the optimality of a solution and correlates closely with the algorithm's goal (for example maximum profit or minimum costs in business.)

When the genetic algorithm is applied to a problem in the decision making of firms (whose decisions are not reversible), each chromosome codes some solution of the problem (thus a chromosome is a genotype and the corresponding solution is a phenotype). Chromosomes with higher fitness functions in genetic algorithms are preferred. The higher the value of the fitness function during the process of iteration, the better the solution of the

Figure 19. The diagram of multi-layer network

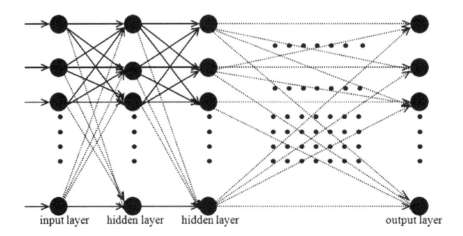

Table 3. Coordinates of objects

Number	Object	Coordinates of objects		
		x_1	x_2	x_3
1	Praha	37	72	191
2	Brno	72	30	194
3	Ostrava	100	57	215
4	Plzen	18	60	354
5	Olomouc	83	42	209
6	Liberec	47	100	402
7	Hradec Kralove	59	76	231
8	Ceské Budejovice	36	24	391
9	Usti nad Labem	30	99	326
10	Pardubice	64	67	229
11	Zlin	89	32	330
12	Kladno	30	74	451
13	Opava	94	59	255
14	Jihlava	8	81	525

economic problem. The commercially sold programs do not demand knowledge of binary algebra.

For processes where optimization is required, it is possible to use not only genetic algorithms but also ant colony, particle swarms, bee hive colony algorithms, and others.

The chapter is focused on applications. The genetic algorithm theory is described in books such as (Davis 1991), (Dostál 2011), (Chen et al. 2005), (The MathWorks 2010d).

4.2 Applications of Genetic Algorithms

Example 4.1: Cluster analysis problems can be solved by means of genetic algorithms to solve economic problems. The aim of a genetic algorithm as an optimization task is to divide a set of N existing objects into M groups. Each object is characterized by the values of K variables of a K-dimensional vector. The aim is to divide the objects into groups so that the variability inside

groups is minimized. The sequence of steps is as follows:

Let $\{x_i; i = 1, 2, \ldots, N\}$ be a set of N objects. Let x_{il} denote the value of the lth variable for the ith object. Let us define for $i = 1, 2, \ldots, N$ and $j = 1, 2, \ldots, M$ and the weights

$$w_{ij} = \begin{cases} 1 & \text{if the ith object is a part of the jth group} \\ 0 & \text{otherwise} \end{cases}$$

The matrix $W = [w_{ij}]$ has the following properties:

$$w_{ij} \in \{0; 1\} \ and \ \sum_{j=1}^{M} w_{ij} = 1$$

Let the centroid of the jth group $c_j = [c_{j1}, c_{j2}, \ldots, c_{jK}]$ be calculated so that each of its elements is the weighted arithmetic mean of relevant values, i.e.

$$c_{jl} = \frac{\sum_{i=1}^{N} w_{ij} x_{il}}{\sum_{i=1}^{N} w_{ij}}$$

The inner stability of the jth group is defined as

$$S^{(j)}(W) = \sum_{i=1}^{N} w_{ij} \sum_{l=1}^{K} (x_{il} - c_{jl})^2$$

and its total inner group variance as

$$S(W) = \sum_{j=1}^{M} S^{(j)} = \sum_{j=1}^{M} \sum_{i=1}^{N} w_{ij} \sum_{l=1}^{K} (x_{il} - c_{jl})^2$$

The distances between an object and a centroid can be calculated in this case by means of common Euclidean distances

$$D_E(x_p, x_q) = \sqrt{\sum_{l=1}^{K} (x_{pl} - x_{ql})^2} = \left\| x_p - x_q \right\|$$

Box 5. Prog. 3.2: M-file Pred.m

```
targetSeries = tonndata(data,false,false);
feedbackDelays = 1:2;
hiddenLayerSize = 10;
net = narnet(feedbackDelays,hiddenLayerSize);
net.inputs{1}.processFcns = {'removeconstantrows','mapminmax'};
[inputs,inputStates,layerStates,targets] = preparets(net,{},{},targetSeries);
net.divideFcn = 'dividerand';
net.divideMode = 'time';
net.divideParam.trainRatio = 70/100;
net.divideParam.valRatio = 15/100;
net.divideParam.testRatio = 15/100;
net.trainFcn = 'trainlm';
net.performFcn = 'mse';
net.plotFcns = {'plotperform','plottrainstate','plotresponse', ...
 'ploterrcorr', 'plotinerrcorr'};
[net,tr] = train(net,inputs,targets,inputStates,layerStates);
outputs = net(inputs,inputStates,layerStates);
errors = gsubtract(targets,outputs);
performance = perform(net,targets,outputs)
trainTargets = gmultiply(targets,tr.trainMask);
valTargets = gmultiply(targets,tr.valMask);
testTargets = gmultiply(targets,tr.testMask);
trainPerformance = perform(net,trainTargets,outputs)
valPerformance = perform(net,valTargets,outputs)
testPerformance = perform(net,testTargets,outputs)
view(net)
netc = closeloop(net);
[xc,xic,aic,tc] = preparets(netc,{},{},targetSeries);
yc = netc(xc,xic,aic)
perfc = perform(net,tc,yc)
nets = removedelay(net);
[xs,xis,ais,ts] = preparets(nets,{},{},targetSeries);
ys = nets(xs,xis,ais);
closedLoopPerformance = perform(net,tc,yc)
```

Table 4. Selection

Population I.		Population II.
0111	>	0010
7	>	2

Table 5. Crossover

Parents	Offspring
1/**001**	1/**100**
1/**100**	**1/001**

Figure 20. Two-dimensional graph – 4 clusters

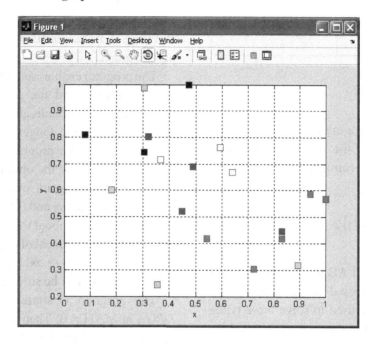

Figure 21. Three-dimensional graph – 4 clusters

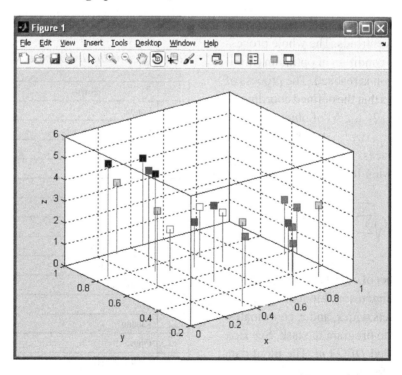

Table 6. Mutation

Before	After
1001	0101

The aim is to find a matrix $W^* = [w_{*ij}]$ that minimizes the sum of the squares of distances in groups from their centroids (over all M centroids), i.e.

$$S\left(W^*\right) = \min_W \left\{S(W)\right\}.$$

The software MATLAB and its Global Optimization Toolbox are used for the software applications that can be used to solve these types of problems. The input data are represented by coordinates x_1, x_2, . . ., x_K that characterize the objects. It is possible to define any number of groups. The fitness function is the sum of squares of distances between the objects and centroids. The coordinates of centroids c_{j1}, c_{j2}, . . ., c_{jK} ($j = 1, 2, . . ., M$) are changed. The calculation assigns the objects to their centroids. The whole process is repeated until the condition of optimum (minimum) fitness function is reached. The process of optimization ensures that the defined coordinates x_{i1}, x_{i2}, . . ., x_{iK} ($i = 1, 2, . . ., N$) of objects and assigned coordinates c_{j1}, c_{j2}, . . ., c_{jK} of groups have the minimum distances. The fitness function is expressed by following formula

$$f_{\min} = \sum_{i=1}^{N} \min_{j \in (1,2,...,M)} \left(\sqrt{\sum_{l=1}^{K} (x_{il} - c_{jl})^2}\right),$$

where N is the number of objects, M the number of groups, and K the dimension. Input data are represented by 15 objects with x_1 and x_2 coordinates.

It is convenient to program the task. See Box 6, the Prog. 4.1 called *DPGA.m*. The input data are in an MS Excel format file *DP.xls* which cor-

responds to Table 7. The Prog. 4.2 *Group.m* (Box 7) is used for calculation of Euclidean distances and Prog. 4.3 *Draw.m* (Box 8) is used for drawing the graph.

The program enables setting up the number of required groups and the population size. The larger the number of individuals the more precise the solution but the longer the duration of the calculation. Next, the program sets up the options for optimization and the optimization command *ga* is called. The program involves the calculation of the fitness function and fills the variables with data that inform us about the coordinates of centroids and the assignment of objects to groups and display them. Two- (z axis is zero) or three-dimensional tasks can be solved.

The program is started by the command *DPGA* in MATLAB. Then it is necessary to set up the requested number of groups, e.g. *Number of groups* = 4 and *Population size* = 1000. When the calculation is terminated, the input parameters and results of calculation are displayed on the screen. The results are presented by coordinates of centroids and assignment of places to groups. See

Table 7. Coordinates of places

	Town	x_1	x_2
1	Prague	37	72
2	Brno	72	30
3	Ostrava	100	57
4	Plzen	18	60
5	Olomouc	83	42
6	Liberec	47	100
7	Hradec Kralove	59	76
8	Ceske Budejovice	36	24
9	Usti nad Labem	30	99
10	Pardubice	64	67
11	Zlin	89	32
12	Kladno	90	74
13	Opava	94	59
14	Karlovy Vary	8	81
15	Jihlava	54	42

Box 6. Prog. 4.1: M-file DPGA.m

```
function DPGA
global LOCATION;
num=input('Number of groups:');
num=3*num;
PopSize=input('Population size:');
FitnessFcn = @Group;
numberOfVariables = num;
LOCATION=(xlsread('DP','Coordinates'))
my_plot = @(Options,state,flag) Draw(Options,state,flag,LOCATION,num);
Options = gaoptimset('PlotFcns',my_plot,'PopInitRange',[0;300],'PopulationSize
',PopSize);
[x,fval] = ga(FitnessFcn,numberOfVariables,Options);
assign=zeros(1,size(LOCATION,1));
for i=1:size(LOCATION,1)
    distances=zeros(num/3,1);
    for j=1:(size(x,2)/3)
        distances(j)=sqrt((LOCATION(i,1)-x(j))^2+(LOCATION(i,2)-
        x(size(x,2)/3+j))^2+(LOCATION(i,3)-x(2*size(x,2)/3+j))^2);
    end
    [min_distance,assign(i)]=min(distances);
end
assign;fval
xy=zeros(num/3,3);
for i=1:(num/3)
    xy(i,1)=x(1,i);
    xy(i,2)=x(1,num/3+i);
    xy(i,3)=x(1,2*num/3+i);
end
```

Box 7. Prog. 4.2: M-file Group.m

```
function z=Group(x)
global LOCATION
z=0;
for i=1:size(LOCATION,1)
    for j=1:(size(x,2)/3)
        distances(j)=sqrt((LOCATION(i,1)-x(j))^2+(LOCATION(i,2)-
        x(size(x,2)/3+j))^2+(LOCATION(i,3)-x(2*size(x,2)/3+j))^2);
    end
    min_distance=min(distances);
    z=z+min_distance;
end
```

Figure 22. Choice of neural network

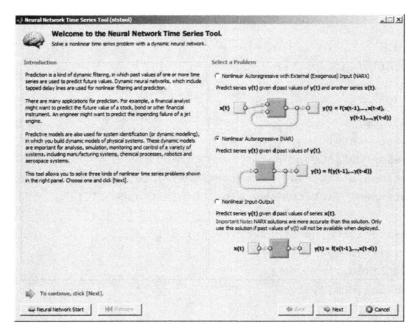

Box 9, Res. 4.1. Figure 33 presents the graph and Figure 34 its application in a geographical map.

The advantage of genetic algorithm theory is that enables to solve practical application that belongs to hard difficult problems to solve. The genetic algorithms outperformed classical meth-ods in speed of calculation to find one of the best solutions.

Example 4.2: This example shows that the program environment MATLAB with the Global Optimization Toolbox may also be used to solve the travelling salesman problem. The coordinates

Figure 23. Download of data

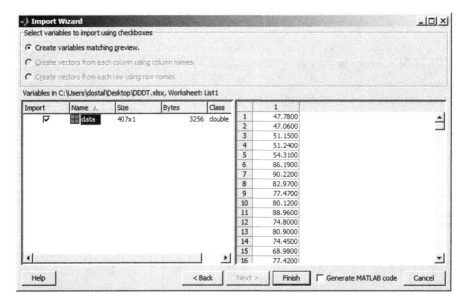

Figure 24. Select of data

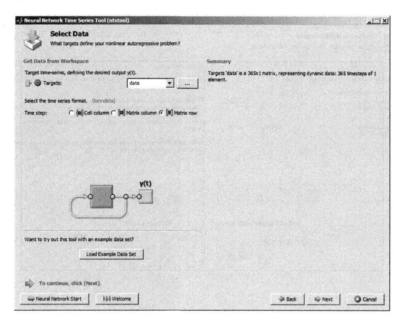

of the visited towns x_p and y_p must be set up. The aim of the task is to find the shortest tour under the condition of visiting each town only once. The challenge is that when the number of towns is high it is not possible to use exhaustive algorithms to search all combinations. The use of genetic algorithms shortens the calculation time. It finds one of the best solutions very quickly. The problem is

Figure 25. Setup of parameters

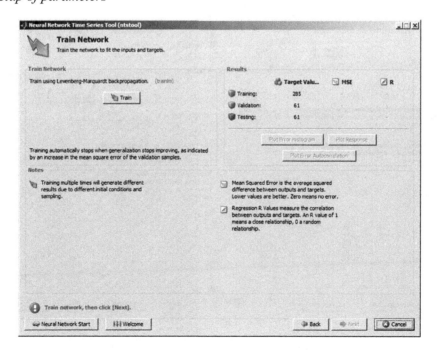

Figure 26. Set of network

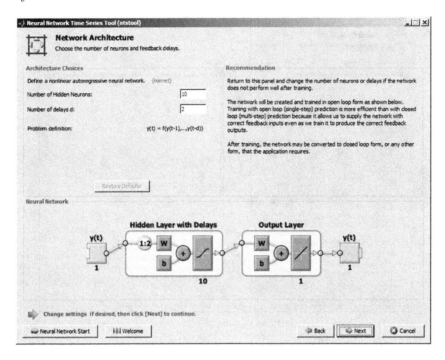

Figure 27. Process of training

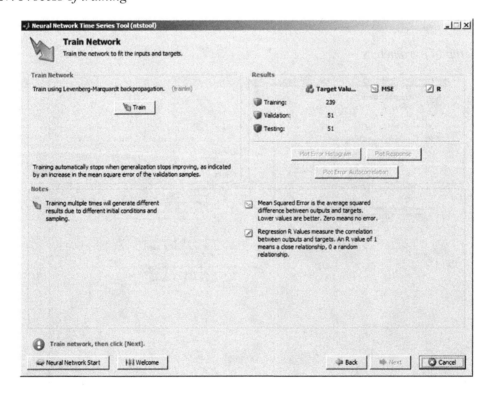

Box 8. Prog. 4.3: M-file Draw.m

```
function state = Draw(Options,state,flag,LOCATION,num)
[unused,i] = min(state.Score);
x=state.Population(i,:);
for i=1:size(LOCATION,1)
    for j=1:(size(x,2)/3)
        distances(j)=sqrt((LOCATION(i,1)-x(j))^2+(LOCATION(i,2)-
        x(size(x,2)/3+j))^2+(LOCATION(i,3)-x(2*size(x,2)/3+j))^2);
    end
   [min_distance,assign(i)]=min(distances);
end
for i=1:size(LOCATION,1)
   view(2)
   plot3(LOCATION(i,1),LOCATION(i,2),LOCATION(i,3),'sr','MarkerFaceColor',[3*(
assign(i))/
   num,3*(assign(i))/num,3*(assign(i))/num],'MarkerSize',10);
   xlabel('x');ylabel('y');zlabel('z');
   grid on;
   hold on;
end
view(2)
plot3(x(1:size(x,2)/3),x((size(x,2)/3+1):2*size(x,2)/3),x(2*size(x,2)/3+1:size
(x,2)),'sr','MarkerFace
Color','b','MarkerSize',10); hold off;
```

programmed in the MATLAB environment. See Box 10, Prog. 4.4.

The variables *xx* and *yy* are the coordinates of contour of Czech Republic. The command *save* saves the coordinates of contour. The number of cities is set up to 15. The variable locations is setup by coordinates of towns. Next two commands *for* closed using the command *end* create two cycles that calculate the distances between each pair of towns. The setup of vectors of pairs

Box 9. Res. 4.1: Coordinates of centroids and location of places

```
Number of groups: 4
Population size:1000
assign =    1     4     4     1     4     2     2     3     1     2     4
1     4     1     3
  fval = 212.7160
  xy =   29.3064    71.9184     0.0947
          58.5215    76.3774     0.9532
          48.6974    39.3067    -2.7503
          85.3377    39.9134    -0.2225
```

Figure 28. The process of training

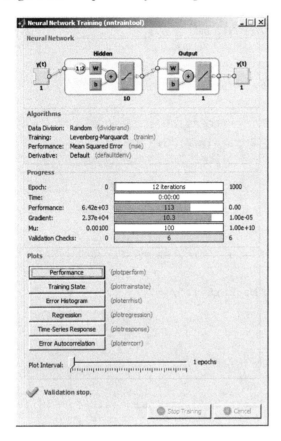

of towns x_1, y_1 and x_2, y_2 are saved to variable distances and the distances between towns are calculated by the Pythagorean Theorem as the hypotenuse of coordinates of two points. The cycles fill up only lower left matrix; the next command does this for the upper right one. Thus the cross matrix of distances among towns is set up. The last commands solve the optimization. The program calculates the fitness function *FitnessFcn*, defined by the M-file as a function called *TSMfit(x, distances)*, with parameters of the number of towns and distances between towns. The resulting value of the function is the total tour distance around the towns for the searched combination. The function *TSM_plot1* is placed in the M-file with name *M_plot1(state,locations)* with parameters *options*, *state* a *flag*. The command *gaoptimset* sets up variable *option* obtaining parameters of calculation of optimization by means of the genetic algorithms. It is necessary to do the setup if the default values are not used. The type of population *PopulationType* is set up as *custom*; the range *PopInitRange* as the dimension [1;cit-

Figure 29. Process of retraining

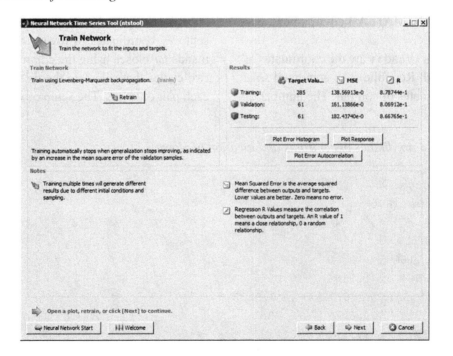

Box 10. Prog. 4.4: M-file TSM.m

```
xx=[0 5 11 95 88 103 103 116 120 130 133 159 170 178 165 190 200 195 218 230
226 236 244 255 265 267 280 267 250 238 222 200 193 192 178 168 112 97 90 87
70 26 18 7 10 4 0];yy=[106 45 84 89 62 148 113 36 146 99 47 110 87 120 62];
yy=[ 133 124 132 162 171 163 155 157 169 165 152 143 145 136 129 107 117 128
116 120 107 96 102 93 93 80 66 65 48 30 21 22 8 15 22 16 37 11 15   8 12 65 66
90 101 110 133];
save('tsm.mat','xx','yy');
cities=15;
locations(:,1)=[93  183 253 46 210 120 150 90 77 162 226 77 238 20 137];
locations(:,2)=[106 45 84 89 62 148 113 36 146 99 47 110 87 120 62];
for count1=1:cities,
    for count2=1:count1,
        x1 = locations(count1,1);
        y1 = locations(count1,2);
        x2 = locations(count2,1);
        y2 = locations(count2,2);
        distances(count1,count2)=sqrt((x1-x2)^2+(y1-y2)^2);
        distances(count2,count1)=distances(count1,count2);
    end;
end;
FitnessFcn = @(x) TSMfit(x,distances);
TSM_plot = @(options,state,flag) TSM_plot1(state,locations);
options = gaoptimset('PopulationType', 'custom','PopInitRange',[1;cities],'Cre
ationFcn',@TSMcre_p, 'CrossoverFcn',@TSMcro_p, 'MutationFcn',@TSMmut_p, 'Plot-
Fcn', TSM_plot, 'Generations',500, 'PopulationSize',60, 'StallGenLimit',200,'V
ectorized','on');
numberOfVariables = cities;
[x,fval,reason,output] = ga(FitnessFcn,numberOfVariables,options);
fval
reason
```

ies]; the population function *CreationFcn* as @*TSMcre_p*; the crossover function *CrossoverFcn* as @*TSMcro_p*; the mutation function *Mutation-Fcn* as @*TSMmut_p*; the drawing function *Plot-Fcn* as *TSM_plot*; the number of generations *Generation* as value 500; the population size *PopulationSize* as value 60; the termination of the calculation after constancy of 200 generations as *StallGenLimit*; and the fact that the calculation

of fitness function will be done by vector and that the value *Vectorized* is set up as *on*.

The next-to-last command sets up the variable *numberOfVariables* as the number of generated towns. The last command provides the optimization. The key command is *ga* with the parameters of the fitness function *FitnessFcn*, number of towns *numberOfVariables*, and the setup parameters of optimization *options*. The output variable *x* is a

Figure 30. Saving the data

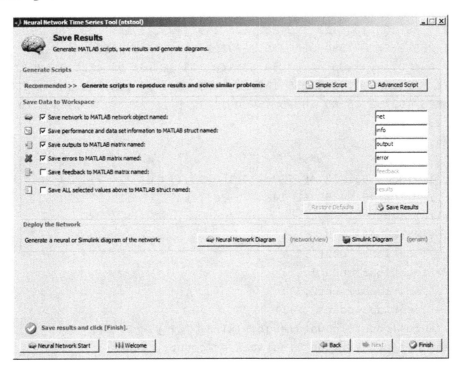

Figure 31. Historical and predicted data of time series

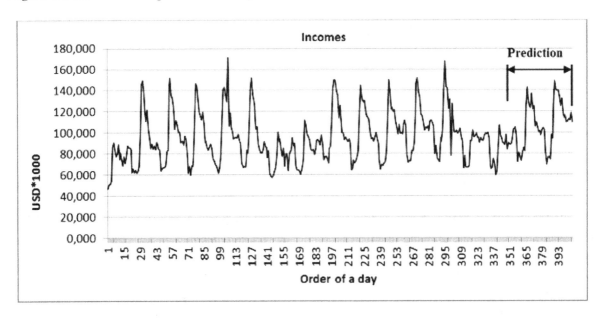

Figure 32. The reproduction process

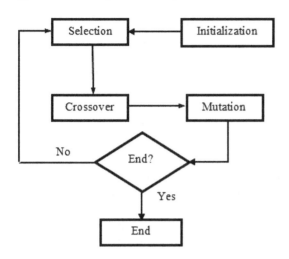

value *reason* provides information about program termination; and the variable *output* provides information about the calculation of each generation.

Writing out the variable *options* presents the setup of the parameters of optimization. See Box 11, Res. 4.2.

The command *zeros* sets up the variable *scores* to be zero. Two cycle commands *for* closed by commands *end* provide the calculation of the total tour for the given combination using the cross table *distances* of distances between towns. The command *size* returns the values of dimension of matrix in the size $m \times n$. The command *length* returns the value of the greatest dimension.

The function *TSM_plot1* is defined by an M-file. See Box 13, Prog. 4.6.

The command *persistent* ensures that the named variables are local. The command *load* downloads from *tsm.mat* file the coordinates of

vector of command of visited towns; *fval* is a value of the fitness function pepresented by the value of the shortest tour fulfilling the conditions; the

Figure 33. Places and their centroids

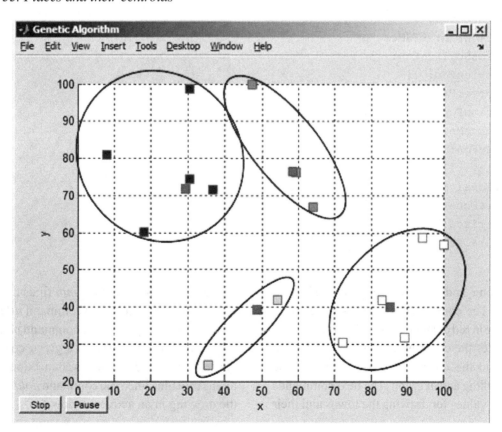

Box 11. Res. 4.2: Setup options

```
PopulationType: 'custom'
PopInitRange: [2x1 double]
PopulationSize: 60
EliteCount: []
CrossoverFraction: []
ParetoFraction: []
MigrationDirection: []
MigrationInterval: []
 MigrationFraction: []
 Generations: 500
 TimeLimit: []
 FitnessLimit: []
 StallGenLimit: 200
 StallTimeLimit: []
 TolFun: []
 TolCon: []
 InitialPopulation: []
 InitialScores: []
 InitialPenalty: []
 PenaltyFactor: []
 PlotInterval: []
 CreationFcn: @TSMcre_p
 FitnessScalingFcn: []
 SelectionFcn: []
 CrossoverFcn: @TSMcro_p
 MutationFcn: @TSMmut_p
 DistanceMeasureFcn: []
 HybridFcn: []
 Display: []
 PlotFcns: @(options,state,flag)TSM_plot1(state,locations)
 OutputFcns: []
 Vectorized: 'on'
 UseParallel: []
```

the polygon x_x and y_y that were saved by the *TSM.m* program. The command *plot* draws the contour of the state in red colour *Color, red*. The command *axis* defines the coordinates of the graph [0 300 0 200] and the command *hold on* enables the drawing of the actual graph. The next commands set up the values for drawing the towns and their connections. The command *min* finds the smallest value of the matrix. The command *title* writes out the title of the graph. The command *plot* draws the coordinates of towns in a green colour and the next command *plot* draws connections among towns by a blue line. The command *holds off* ends the drawing in an active window.

Figure 34. Geographical map

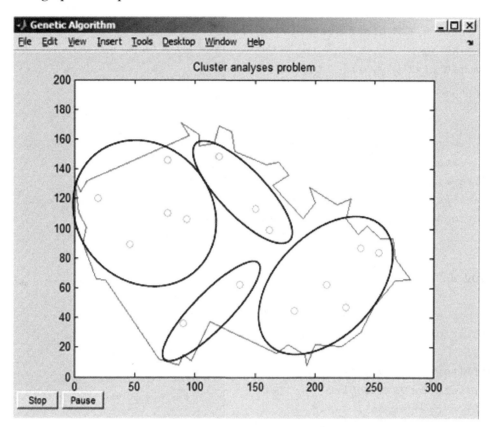

Box 12. Prog. 4.5: M-file TSMfit.m

The function *TSMfit* is defined by an M-file. See Prog. 4.5.

```
function scores = TSMfit(x,distances)
scores = zeros(size(x,1),1);
for j = 1:size(x,1)
    p = x{j};
    f = distances(p(end),p(1));
    for i = 2:length(p)
        f = f + distances(p(i-1),p(i));
    end
    scores(j) = f;
end
```

Box 13. Prog. 4.6: M-file TSM-plot1.m

```
function state = TSM_plot1(state,locations)
persistent xx yy
load('tsm.mat','xx','yy');
plot(xx,yy,'Color','red');
axis([0 300 0 200]);
hold on
[unused,i] = min(state.Score);
genotype = state.Population{i};
title ('Travel salesman problem')
plot(locations(:,1),locations(:,2),'go');
plot(locations(genotype,1),locations(genotype,2));
hold off
```

Box 14. Prog. 4.7: M-file TSMcre_p.m

```
function pop = TSMcre_p(NVARS,FitnessFcn,options)
totalPopulationSize = sum(options.PopulationSize);
n = NVARS;
pop = cell(totalPopulationSize,1);
for i = 1:totalPopulationSize
    pop{i} = randperm(n);
end
```

Box 15. Prog. 4.8: M-file TSMcro_p.m

```
function xoverKids  = TSMcro_p(parents,options,NVARS, . . .
FitnessFcn,thisScore,thisPopulation)
nKids = length(parents)/2;
xoverKids = cell(nKids,1); % Normally zeros(nKids,NVARS);
index = 1;
for i=1:nKids
    parent = thisPopulation{parents(index)};
    index = index + 2;
    p1 = ceil((length(parent) -1) * rand);
    p2 = p1 + ceil((length(parent) - p1- 1) * rand);
    child = parent;
    child(p1:p2) = fliplr(child(p1:p2));
    xoverKids{i} = child; % Normally, xoverKids(i,:);
end
```

Box 15. Prog. 4.9: M-file TSMmut_p.m

```
function mutationChildren = TSMmut_p(parents, options,NVARS, . . .
FitnessFcn, state, thisScore,thisPopulation,mutationRate)
mutationChildren = cell(length(parents),1);
for i=1:length(parents)
    parent = thisPopulation{parents(i)};
    p = ceil(length(parent) * rand(1,2));
    child = parent;
    child(p(1)) = parent(p(2));
    child(p(2)) = parent(p(1));
    mutationChildren{i} = child; % Normally mutationChildren(i,:)
end
```

Box 16, Res. 4.3: Input and results of calculation

```
Optimization terminated: average change in the fitness value less than op-
tions.TolFun.
fval =     639.4138
reason = 1
```

Figure 35. Tour before optimization

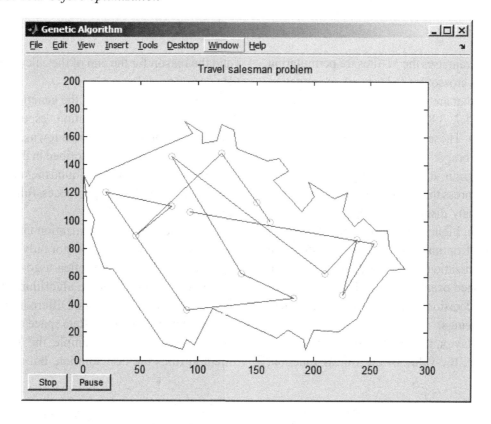

Table 8. The comparison of optimization methods

Method	Time [sec]	Fit. F.	No. of attempts	Min
1. Exhaustive	426.21405	2.6274	1x	Y
2. Back Tracking	21.54944	2.6274	1x	Y
3. Random Search	0.01945	3.43841	20x	N
4. Greedy	0.02030	2.6274	1x	Y
5. Hill Climbing	0.00543	2.6274	10x	Y
6. Simulated Annealing	0.01638	2.91421	20x	N
7. Tabu Search	0.38592	2.6272	2x	Y
8. Ant Colony	1.0983	2.6274	1x	Y
9. Genetic Search	1.33721	2.65847	5x	Y
10. Particle Swarms	1.75342	2.62739	3x	Y
11. DNA Genetic Search	21.1449	2.62739	3x	Y
12. Bee Hive Colony	0.02345	2.674	1x	Y

Box 17. Prog. 5.1: M-file MP.m

```
y=zeros
for  i = 1:99;
   y(i+1)=y(i)/(1+0.3*3*rand)+(10*rand-y(i));
end
plot(y); title ('Chaos'); xlabel ('P_t'); ylabel ('P_{t+1}')
```

The program uses the M-files for permutation (*TSMcre_p*), crossover (*TSMcro_p*), and mutation *TSMmut_p* that are part of the MATLAB library. See Progs. 4.7, 4.8, and 4.9 (Box 14, Box 15, and Box 16). These M-files are described in the MATLAB library.

The program starts by writing *TSM* on the display and press the command *Enter*. The graph is continuously displayed during the process of optimization. Figure 35 presents the graph at the beginning of optimization and Figure 36 at the end of optimization. The shortest tour is found. The mentioned example should be automated as a part of a decision-making tool not dependent on human beings.

The display on the screen presents the end of optimization, the value of the fitness function,

and the reason for the end of the calculation. See Box 16, Res. 4.3.

The advantage of using the genetic algorithm is in the speed of calculation, especially with increasing numbers of visited towns. Note: It is empirically proved and described in the literature that the genetic algorithms found the suboptimum near to the global optimum successfully and very quickly.

Example 4.3: The optimization task could be solved by various methods, not only by genetic algorithms that are quite often used in business and public services. Some algorithms can give better solutions than others. Different results are obtained when the entire state space of solutions is not searched. For example the Exhaustive method finds the best solution, but the calcula-

Box 18. Prog. 5.2: M-file BS.m

```
h=0.1;
alfa=1;
omega=0.45;
beta=0.988;
x(1)=0;
y(1)=1;
%y(2)=0.895;
dy(1)=-1;
ddy=beta*sin(omega*0)-alfa*((y(1)^2)-1)*dy(1)-(y(1)^2);
y(2)=y(1)+h*dy(1)+((h^2)*ddy)/2;
hold on;
for i=2:1000
    x(i)=x(i-1)+h;
    y(i+1)=((2*(h^2)*beta*sin(omega*x(i))-y(i)*(2*(h^2)-4)-y(i-1)*(2-
    h*alfa*(y(i)^2)+h*alfa)))/(2+h*alfa*(y(i)^2)-h*alfa);
    dy(i)=(y(i+1)-y(i-1))/(2*h);
end
yy=y(1:1000)
plot(yy,dy);
```

Figure 36. Tour after optimization

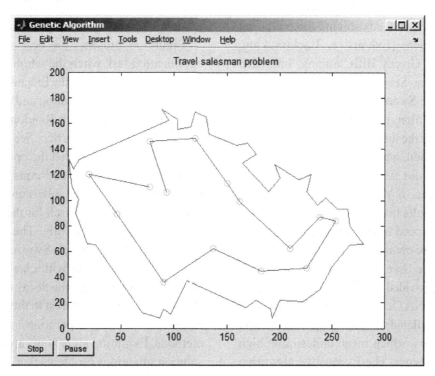

Figure 37. Graph from exhaustive methods

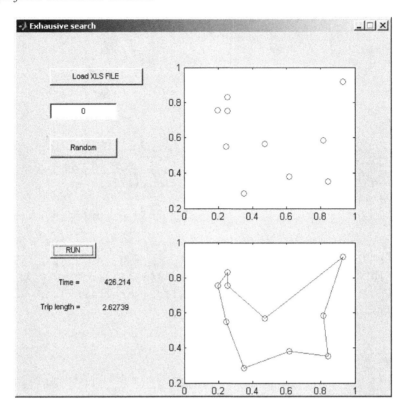

tions could last weeks. The present example compares twelve methods solving the travelling salesman problem (Exhausive, Backtracking, RandomSearch, Greedy, Hill Climbing, Simulated Annealing, Tabu Search, Ant Colony, Genetic Search, Particle Swarms, DNA Genetic Search, and Bee Hive Colony). Ten places were used and it was measured the time of calculation, the value of fitness function, and number of attempts that were necessary for finding the minimum value, which in this case is Yes. See Table 8.

The best results from the point of view of fitness function, speed of calculation, and number of attempts were obtained using the Greedy, Ant Colony, and Bee Hive Colony algorithms. Good results were provided by Tabu Search, Particle Swarms, and DNA Genetic Search. The Random Search and Simulated Annealing algorithm found the longest tours, which mean undesirable high expenses of the tour. The Exhaustive algorithm

search had the highest calculation time, but it found the global minimum for this problem.

Figure 37 presents the best solution of the optimization task when the whole state space of solution was searched by the Exhaustive algorithm. The worst time of calculation and the worst solution were obtained using Random Search, with results not usable in practice. See Figure 38.

We should mention that the optimization processes have their pros and cons. Their virtues include the fact that they solve complicated problems very easily and search for the maximum or minimum very successfully. The Genetic algorithm, Ant Colony, Particle Swarm, and Bee Hive Colony, in comparison with classical searching algorithms, search for the local extreme better (finding the solution nearest to the optimum) and require fewer math operations than the other methods. Evolution algorithms are useful for the solution of various problems that must be solved

Figure 38. Graph from random search methods

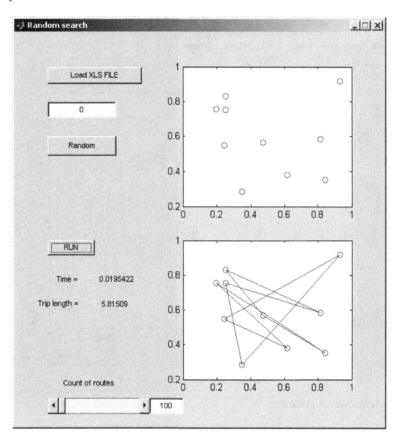

in decision making in business, economics, and finance.

Optimization methods based on evolutionary algorithms solves successfully difficult problems such as travel salesman problem, especially with increasing number of cities. Some methods give better results and some give worse results. The use of various methods must be tested and the best one to be use in practice.

5 THEORY OF CHAOS

5.1 Fundamentals of Chaos

An early proponent of chaos theory was Henri Poincaré. In the 1880s, while studying the three-body problem, he found that there can be orbits which are nonperiodic, and yet not forever increasing nor approaching a fixed point. Later studies, also on the topic of nonlinear differential equations, were carried out by G.D. Birkhoff and A. N. Kolmogorov. An early pioneer of the theory was Edward Lorenz whose interest in chaos came about accidentally through his work on weather prediction in 1961. Lorenz's discovery, which gave its name to Lorenz attractors, showed that even detailed atmospheric modelling cannot in general make long-term weather predictions. Mandelbrot described both the "Noah effect" and the "Joseph effect". In 1975 Mandelbrot published The Fractal Geometry of Nature, which became a classic of chaos theory. The same year, James Gleick published Chaos: Making a New Science, which became a best-seller and introduced the general principles of chaos theory.

Figure 39. The graph of function P_{t+1} with parameter a = 0.3

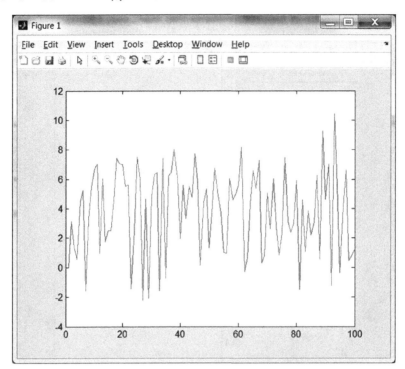

Figure 40. Graph of chaotic attractor

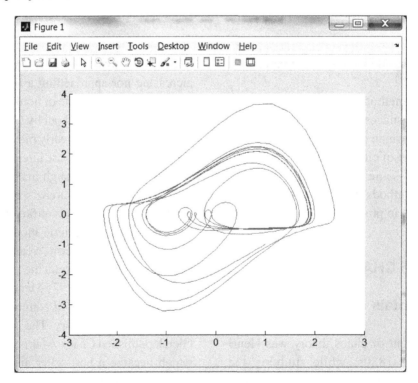

The theory of chaos came into being in solution of technical problems, where it describes the behaviour of nonlinear systems that have some hidden order, but still behave like systems controlled by chance. A linear model can describe a real system only if it is linear. If this is not fulfilled, then such models can simulate the real system only under ideal conditions, only for a short time. If a system is a nonlinear dynamic, a deterministic system it can generate not only the permanent trends and cycles, but it can also include random-looking behaviour. Processes of such behaviour are present in the economy.

In this respect we can talk about two categories that are in opposition to each other: order and randomness. Chaos is something in between. It involves some degree of order. Some phenomena can appear random, but after the study of these phenomena some inner order can be discovered that governs these phenomena. For example, the movement of people at a railway station can appear accidental, but in fact it is behaviour with order controlled by the arrival and departure of trains. Also, the economy can exist in states of various degrees of order, chaos, and randomness. The behaviour of an economy is influenced quite often by natural disasters, political changes, etc.

In connection with chaos it is possible to speak about a so-called attractor, which represents an equilibrium position. An attractor is a condition towards which a dynamical system evolves over time. That is, points that get close enough to the attractor remain close even if slightly disturbed. Geometrically, an attractor can be a point, a curve, or even a complicated set with a fractal structure known as a chaotic attractor.

The geometrical explanation of an attractor could be done with the help of a pendulum. The attractor can be:

- **Point**: The stability is represented geometrically by a point. For example, when a pendulum is displaced, its final equilib-

rium position is reached when movement ceases.
- **Cycle**: The balance is represented geometrically by a limited cycle. For example, when a pendulum is moving with constant energy (potential energy plus kinetic energy = const.), its equilibrium position is reached when movement is cyclical.
- **Chaotic**: It is represented geometrically by order underlying the apparent chaos. For example, when the pendulum is driven by random energy, then the equilibrium position will be represented by a movement in zone (no point or cycle).

The chapter is focused on applications. The chaos theory is described in books such as (Barnsley 1993), (Dostál 2011), (Gleick 1996), (Peters 1994), (Peters 1996), (Trippi 1995), (The MathWorks 2010a).

5.1 Applications of Chaos

Example 5.1: The complicated behaviour in economy could be illustrated by the equation in the form

$$P_{t+1} = \frac{P_t}{1 + a\sigma_t} + (V_t - P_t) \, ,$$

where P_{t+1} simulates the market price of the share, σ_t is the volatility of yield of share, a is a coefficient of market aversion against risk, V_t is fundamental "inner" value of share in time t, $V_t - P_t$ is the response of market on the change of inner value. The initial values (P_0, σ_0, V_0) could be different in the same way as the coefficients of market aversion against risk. If the value $\sigma = 0$ and market is neutral to risk $a = 0$, then $P_{t+1} = V_t$. Figure 39 presents graphically the course of P_{t+1} dependence on time with aversion to risk $a = 0.3$, $V_t = 10 *$ rand and $\sigma = 3*$rand. The course of the curve reminds one of real values of time series of shares, commodities, currency ratios, and values of indices on the stock market. The simulation is presented on Figure 39 and program on Prog. 5.1 (Box 17).

The theory of chaos can describe and explain some economic phenomena. This example presents possible behaviour on the stock market.

Example 5.2: The business cycle could be simulated by a van der Pol differential equation in the form

$$x^{II} + \alpha \left(x^2 - 1 \right) x^{I} + x = \beta \sin(\omega t)$$

where x denotes an economic variable such as production, the $x^{\square}$ denotes productivity with respect to time t, α is an endogenous damping parameter, β.

β denotes the driver amplitude and ω denotes the driver frequency. The dependence of $x^{\square} = f(x)$ is presented in Figure 40 and corresponds to behaviour of chaotic attractors ($\alpha = 1$, $\omega = 0.45$, $\beta = 0.988$). See the Prog. 5.2 (Box 18).

There is no evidence that economic systems have point or cycle attractors. Their attractors behave chaotically. Nevertheless, in case of the displacement of an economic system from balance, the system tries to get into an equilibrium position (for example, the displacement of economy of some states). Therefore the prediction of the behaviour of economic development is restricted by contemporary knowledge, and the longer range predictions are uncertain. The theory of chaos could describe some economic and financial phenomena. The research is done very intensively.

FUTURE RESEARCH DIRECTIONS

The use of soft computing finds its place in the field of business, economics, and finance among other methods. It is done by successful applications in practice where especially vague terms, uncertainty imprecision, uncertainty, vagueness, semi-truth, approximations and non-linear behaviour with noise are frequent phenomena. The future research must be directed to build-up the models for complex decision making processes. The future trends that are expected from the soft computing technologies, which may satisfy these needs, are as follows: new fuzzy, neural networks, genetic algorithms models and their combinations. The future research will be focused in various applications to support decision making to be quicker and more precise because processed amount of data are increasing exponentially. More and more decision making will be done by automatic systems without influence of human being. These automatic decision systems must be designed to be robust and avoiding failures.

The future research of soft computing applications in business, economics, and finance will be focussed especially on improvement in these fields: data mining, data analyses, mortgage loan applications, loan pre-screening processes, client financial risk, client asset allocation, marketing, manufacturing at economic optimum, searching for faulty or fraudulent audits or suspicious financial transactions, predictive optimal supply-chain, predictive intelligent security, protection credit card fraud, time forecasting, time series prediction, prediction of thrift failures, new product pricing, customer classification, investment management and risk control, investment advising, detection of financial crisis, flow shop scheduling, solution of travelling salesman problem, etc.

The development of quick, more precise, part-time or fully automated decision making systems where soft computing methods will be used they will save time, decrease wrong decisions, avoiding human failures, reduce costs that can lead to higher profit, or decrease expenses in business and they can help to compete successfully.

CONCLUSION

The business, economic and financial applications have specific features in comparison with others. The processes are focused on optimizing income or profit, or decreasing expenses. Therefore, such applications, both successful and unsuccessful, are not published very often because of secrecy in the highly competitive environments among firms and institutions. The advanced decision methods can help in decentralization of decision-making processes to become standardized, reproduced, and documented. The advanced decision-making methods play very important roles in companies because they help to reduce costs that can lead to higher profit and they can help to compete successfully, or decrease expenses in institutions. The decision-making processes in business are very complicated because they include political, social, psychological, economic, financial, and other factors. Many variables are difficult to measure; they may be characterized by imprecision, uncertainty, vagueness, semi-truth, approximations, and so forth.

The use of the theories mentioned above is in the sphere of analyses and simulation. Except the applications such as risk investment, risk management, optimization, prediction of time series, journey optimization, description of phenomena it could be many other applications it could be mentioned mortgage loan risk evaluation, direct mailing decision making, stock market decision, stock trading decision, decision making evaluation, client risk evaluation, supplier risk evaluation, etc.

The use of these computing methods can lead to higher quality of analyses and simulations that can be used for decision-making and control processes in business, economy, financial areas, or the public sector.

REFERENCES

Aliev, A., & Aliev, R. (2002). *Soft computing and its applications*. World Scientific Publishing.

Altroc, C. (1996). *Fuzzy logic & neurofuzzy applications in business & finance*. USA: Prentice Hall.

Azoff, E. M. (1994). *Neural network time series forecasting of financial markets*. USA: John Wiley.

Barnsley, M. F. (1993). *Fractals everywhere*. USA: Academic Press Professional.

Bose, K., & Liang, P. (1996). *Neural networks, fundamentals with graphs, algorithms and applications*. USA: McGraw-Hill.

Chen, G. (2000). *Controlling chaos and bifurcations in engineering systems*. China: CRC Press.

Chen, P., Jain, L., & Tai, C. (2005). *Computational economics: A perspective from computational intelligence*. Hershey, PA: Idea Group Publishing. doi:10.4018/978-1-59140-649-5

Chen, S., Wang, P., & Wen, T. (2004). *Computational intelligence in economics and finance*. New York, NY: Springer.

Chen, S., Wang, P., & Wen, T. (2007). *Computational intelligence in economics and finance (Vol. II)*. New York, NY: Springer. doi:10.1007/978-3-540-72821-4

Davis, L. (1991). *Handbook of genetic algorithms*. USA: Int. Thomson Com. Press.

Dostál, P. (2008). *Advanced economic analyses*. Brno, Czech Republic: VUT – FP.

Dostál, P. (2011). *Advanced decision making in business and public services*. Brno, Czech Republic: CERM.

Ehlers, F. J. (2004). *Cybernetic analysis for stock and futures*. USA: John Wiley.

Franses, P. H. (2001). *Time series models for business and economic forecasting*. UK: Cambridge University Press.

Gately, E. (1996). *Neural networks for financial forecasting*. USA: John Wiley.

Gleick, J. (1996). *Chaos*. USA: Ando Publishing.

Hagan, T., & Demuth, B. (1996). *Neural network design*. USA: PWS Publishing.

Hanselman, D., & Littlefield, B. (2005). *Mastering MATLAB 7*. USA: Prentice Hall.

Kazabov, K., & Kozma, R. (1998). *Neuro-fuzzy techniques for intelligent information systems*. Germany: Physica-Verlag.

Klir, G. J., & Yuan, B. (1995). *Fuzzy sets and fuzzy logic, theory and applications*. New Jersey, USA: Prentice Hall.

Li, Z., Halong, W. A., & Chen, G. (2006). *Integration of fuzzy logic and chaos theory*. New York, NY: Springer. doi:10.1007/3-540-32502-6

Peters, E. E. (1994). *Fractal market analysis—Applying chaos theory to investment & economics*. USA: John Wiley.

Peters, E. E. (1996). *Chaos and order in the capital markets: A new view of cycles, prices*. USA: Wiley Finance Edition.

The MathWorks. (2010a). *MATLAB – User's guide*. The MathWorks.

The MathWorks. (2010b). *MATLAB – Fuzzy logic toolbox - User's guide*. The MathWorks.

The MathWorks. (2010c). *MATLAB – Neural network toolbox - User's guide*. The MathWorks.

The MathWorks. (2010d). *MATLAB – Global optimization toolbox - User's guide*. The MathWorks.

Trippi, R. R. (1995). *Chaos & nonlinear dynamics in the financial markets*. USA: Irwin Professional Publishing.

ADDITIONAL READING

Ahn, H., Kyoung, K., & Han, I. (2006). Hybrid genetic algorithms and case-based reasoning systems for customer classification. *Expert Systems: International Journal of Knowledge Engineering and Neural Networks*, 23(3), 127–144. doi:10.1111/j.1468-0394.2006.00329.x

Bernice, C. (1997). *The edge of chaos—Financial booms, bubbles, crashes and chaos*. UK: John Wiley.

Bojadziev, G., & Bojadziev, M. (2007). *Fuzzy logic for business, finance, and management*, 2nd ed. World Scientific Publishing Co. Pte. Ltd.

Chian, A., Borotto, F. A., Rempel, E. L., & Rogers, C. (2005). Attractor merging crisis in chaotic business cycles. *Chaos, Solitons, and Fractals*, 24(3), 869–875. doi:10.1016/j.chaos.2004.09.080

Comunale, Ch., Rosner, R., & Sexton, T. (2010). The auditor's assessment of fraud risk: A fuzzy logic approach. *Journal of Forensic & Investigative Accounting*, 3(1), 149–194.

Delgado, M. C. Pegalajar, M. C., Cuéllar, & M. P. (2006). Memetic evolutionary training for recurrent neural networks: An application to time-series prediction. *Expert Systems: International Journal of Knowledge Engineering and Neural Networks*, 23(2), 99–115. doi:10.1111/j.1468-0394.2006.00327.x

Feng, S., Xu, L., Tang, C., & Yang, S. (2003). An intelligent agent with layered architecture for operating systems resource management. *Expert Systems: International Journal of Knowledge Engineering and Neural Networks*, 20(4), 171–178. doi:10.1111/1468-0394.00241

Hamad, A., Sanugi, B., & Salleh, S. (2011). *Neural network and scheduling: Neural network and job scheduling problems*. Lambert Academic Publishing.

Hand, D., & Mannila, H. (2001). *Principles of data mining*. USA: The MIT Press.

Herbst, F. (1992). *Analysing and forecasting futures prices*. USA: John Wiley.

Jiao, J., & Zhang, Y. (2010). Product portfolio identification based on association rule mining. *CAD Computer Aided Design, 37*(2), 149–172. doi:10.1016/j.cad.2004.05.006

Joo, K. O., Kim, T. Y., & Kim, C. (2006). An early warning system for detection of financial crisis using financial market volatility. *Expert Systems: International Journal of Knowledge Engineering and Neural Networks, 23*(2), 83–98. doi:10.1111/j.1468-0394.2006.00326.x

Joseph, K., Wintoki, M., & Zhang, Z. (2011). Forecasting abnormal stock returns and trading volume using investor sentiment: Evidence from online search. *International Journal of Forecasting, 27*, 116–1127. doi:10.1016/j.ijforecast.2010.11.001

Kuo, I., Shi-Jinn Horng, S., Kao, T., Lin, S., Lee, C., Chen, Y., & Terano, T. (2010). A hybrid swarm intelligence algorithm for the travelling salesman problem. *Expert Systems: International Journal of Knowledge Engineering and Neural Networks, 27*(3), 166–179. doi:10.1111/j.1468-0394.2010.00517.x

Li, E. Y. (1994). Artificial neural networks and their business applications. *Information & Management, 27*(5), 303–313. doi:10.1016/0378-7206(94)90024-8

Liebowitz, J., Krishnamurthy, V., Rodens, I., Houston, C., Baek, S., Liebowitz, A., & Potter, W. (1997). Intelligent scheduling with generically used expert scheduling system: Development and testing results. *Expert Systems: International Journal of Knowledge Engineering and Neural Networks, 14*(3), 119–128. doi:10.1111/1468-0394.00048

Liebowitz, J., Rodens, I., Zeide, J., & Suen, C. (2000). Developing a neural network approach for intelligent scheduling in generically used expert scheduling system. *Expert Systems: International Journal of Knowledge Engineering and Neural Networks, 17*(4), 185–190. doi:10.1111/1468-0394.00140

Manolas, D. A., Efthimeros, G. A., & Tsahalis, D. T. (2001). Available technologies and their optimal operating conditions for the process industry. *Expert Systems: International Journal of Knowledge Engineering and Neural Networks, 18*(3), 124–130. doi:10.1111/1468-0394.00165

Nikolopoulos, C., & Fellrath, P. (1994). A hybrid expert system for investment advising. *Expert Systems: International Journal of Knowledge Engineering and Neural Networks, 11*(4), 245–250. doi:10.1111/j.1468-0394.1994.tb00332.x

Rud, O. (2001). *Data mining cookbook: Modeling data for marketing, risk and customer relationship management*. USA: John Wiley.

Trif, S. (2011). Using genetic algorithms in secured business intelligence mobile applications. *Informatica Economica, 15*(1).

Tsai, C., Tsai, Ch. W., & Tseng, C. (2003). A new and efficient ant-based heuristic method for solving the traveling salesman problem. *Expert Systems: International Journal of Knowledge Engineering and Neural Networks, 20*(4), 179–186. doi:10.1111/1468-0394.00242

Wang, H. (2005). Flexible flow shop scheduling: Optimum, heuristics and artificial intelligence solutions. *Expert Systems: International Journal of Knowledge Engineering and Neural Networks, 22*(2), 78–85. doi:10.1111/j.1468-0394.2005.00297.x

Weigend, A. (1993). *Time series prediction: Forecasting the future and understanding the past*. Massachusetts: Addison-Wesley.

Wong, B., Bodnovich, K., & Selvi, Y. (1994). A bibliography of neural network business applications research. *Expert Systems: International Journal of Knowledge Engineering and Neural Networks, 12*(3), 253–261. doi:10.1111/j.1468-0394.1995.tb00114.x

Yamada, T., & Nakano, R. (1997). Genetic algorithms for job-shop scheduling problems . In *Proceedings of Modern Heuristic for Decision Support* (pp. 67–81). London: Unicom.

Yu, K., Luo, Z., Chou, C., Chen, C., & Zhou, J. (2007). In Enokido, T. (Ed.), *A fuzzy neural network based scheduling algorithm for job assignment on computational grids* (*Vol. 4658*, pp. 533–542). Lecture Notes in Computer Science Heidelberg, Germany: Springer. doi:10.1007/978-3-540-74573-0_55

Zhang, G. P. (2004). *Neural networks in business forecasting*. Hershey, PA: Idea Group Publishing.

KEY TERMS AND DEFINITIONS

Artificial Neural Network: A mathematical model or computational model that is inspired by the structure and/or functional aspects of biological neural networks.

Business: The state of being busy either as an individual or society as a whole, doing commercially viable and profitable work.

Economic: Economics is the social science that analyses the production, distribution, and consumption of goods and services.

Finance: The management of money or "funds" management.

Fuzzy Logic: Deals with reasoning that is approximate rather than fixed and exact.

Genetic Algorithm: An evolutionary algorithm-based methodology inspired by biological evolution to find computer programs that perform a user-defined task.

Optimization: The act of rendering optimal.

Soft Computing: Soft computing is a term applied to a field within computer science which is characterized by the use of inexact solutions to computationally-hard tasks.

Chapter 3

Hybrid Linear Search, Genetic Algorithms, and Simulated Annealing for Fuzzy Non-Linear Industrial Production Planning Problems

P. Vasant
University Technology Petronas, Malaysia

ABSTRACT

This chapter outlines an introduction to real-world industrial problem for product-mix selection involving eight variables and twenty one constraints with fuzzy technological coefficients, and thereafter, a formulation for an optimization approach to solve the problem. This problem occurs in production planning in which a decision maker plays a pivotal role in making decision under fuzzy environment. Decision-maker should be aware of his/her level of satisfaction as well as degree of fuzziness while making the product-mix decision. Thus, a thorough analysis is performed on a modified S-curve membership function for the fuzziness patterns and fuzzy sensitivity solution is found from the various optimization methodologies. An evolutionary algorithm is proposed to capture the optimal solutions respect to the vagueness factor and level of satisfaction. The near global optimal solution for objective function is obtained by hybrid meta-heuristics optimization algorithms such as line search, genetic algorithms, and simulated annealing.

INTRODUCTION

It is well known that optimization problems arise in a variety of situations. Particular interesting are those concerning management problems as decision makers who usually state their data in a vague way such as "high profits", "low cost", "average revenue", etc. Because of this vagueness, managers prefer to have not just one solution but a set of them so that the most suitable solution can be applied according to the state of existing decision of the production process at a given time without increasing delay. In these situations, fuzzy optimization is an ideal methodology since it al-

DOI: 10.4018/978-1-4666-2086-5.ch003

lows us to represent the underlying uncertainty of the optimization problem while finding optimal solutions that reflect such uncertainty. Once the uncertainty has been solved, the obtained solutions are then applied to possible instances. This allows us to obtain a model of the behavior of the solutions based on the uncertainty of the optimization problem.

Fuzzy constrained optimization problems have been extensively studied since the years of seventies. In the linear case, the first approaches to solve the so-called fuzzy linear programming problem appeared in Bellman and Zadeh (1970). Since then, important contributions for solving different linear models have been made and these models have been the subject of a substantial amount of work. In the nonlinear case (Ramik and Vlach, 2002) the situation is quite different, as there is a wide variety of specific and both practically and theoretically relevant nonlinear problems with each having a different solution method.

In this chapter, a real-life industrial problem for product mix selection involving 21 constraints and eight bound constraints has been considered. This problem occurs in production planning, in which a decision-maker plays a pivotal role in making decision under a highly fuzzy environment (Vasant, Bhattacharya, Sarkar and Mukherjee, 2007; Vasant, Barsoum, Kahraman and Dimirovski, 2007). Decision maker should be aware of his/her level-of satisfaction as well as the degree of fuzziness while making the product mix decision. Thus, we have analyzed the problem using the sigmoidal membership function, fuzziness patterns and fuzzy sensitivity of the solution. Vasant (2006) considered a linear case of the problem and solved it by using a linear programming iterative method which is repeatedly applied for different degrees of satisfaction values. In this research, a non linear case of the problem is considered and a various optimization approaches are proposed in order to capture solutions for different levels of satisfaction with a single and multiple run of the algorithm. These various optimization approaches have been proposed by Liang (2008), Sanchez, Jimenez and Vasant (2007), Turabieh, Sheta and Vasant (2007), Bhattacharya, Abraham, Vasant and Grosan (2007), Bhattacharya, Vasant, Sarkar and Mukherjee (2006) and Jim´enez, G´omez-Skarmeta and S´anchez (2004) within a soft computing optimization general context. The detail on the nonlinear case study will be provided in the following section.

Line Search (LS)

In this chapter, the line search method in solving industrial production planning problems is focused. The main advantage of this method is its ability to locate the near global optimal solutions for the fitness function with its strong criteria of global convergence. The line search method used fmincon approach from MATLAB computational toolbox. FMINCON is a gradient-based method that has been designed to work on problems where the objective and constraint functions are both continuous and have continuous first derivatives. The function with continuous first and second derivatives is suitable for the optimization process because the algorithm uses gradient-based methods. FMINCON uses a sequential quadratic programming (SQP) method. In this method, the function solves a quadratic programming (QP) of sub-problem at each iteration. A line search is performed using a merit function similar to that proposed by Powel (1983). The QP sub-problem is solved using an active set strategy similar to that described in (Powel, 1983). A full description of this algorithm can be found in Constrained Optimization in Standard Algorithms (Powel, 1983).

Genetic Algorithms

Since the late 1980s, there has been a growing interest in Genetic Algorithms (GAs) - stochastic optimization algorithms based on the principles of natural (Darwinian) evolution. These algorithms have been used widely for parameter optimization, classification and learning. More recently, production planning has been emerged as an application. A detailed introduction to GA's can be found in Goldberg (1989). One of the earliest reported applications of GA's to production was reported by Davis (1985). It is a characteristic of the robust optimization process that once good solutions have been formed their features will be carried forward into better solutions and lead ultimately to optimal solutions. It is in the nature of the GA that new solutions are formed from the features of known good solutions. Therefore, it follows that GA's are particularly attractive for production planning. Compared with other optimization methods, GA's are suitable for traversing large search spaces since they can do this relatively rapidly and because the mutation operator diverts the method away from local minima which will tend to become more common as the search space increases in size. Suitability for large search spaces is a useful advantage when dealing with production of increasing size since the solution space grows very rapidly, especially when such features compound this as alternative profit production optimization. It is important that these large search spaces are traversed as rapidly as possible to enable the practical and useful implementation of automated production optimization. If the optimization is done quickly, production managers can try out 'what-if' scenarios and detailed optimization analysis besides being able to react to 'crises' as soon as possible. Traditional approaches to production planning optimization such as mathematical programming and 'branch and bound' are computationally very slow in such a massive search space. The author has found that the key advantage of a GA is that it provides a 'general purpose' solution to the optimization problem with the peculiarities of any particular example being accounted for in the fitness function without disturbing the logic of the standard optimization (GA) routine. This means that it is a relatively straight forward and convenient to adapt the software implementation of the method to meet the needs of particular applications.

Some of the advantages of GA over classical optimization methods include (Deb, 2001):

1. GA is less susceptible to the complexity of the problem at hand than non-evolutionary methods;

2. It deals with multiple solutions in one run; hence it is useful to achieve solutions rapidly in the presence of a large number of parameters.

3. It allows the exploration of multiple local optima.

4. In the case of the existence of multiple conflicting criteria, the Pareto front contains the set of optimum solutions. As GA can deal simultaneously with a set of possible solutions it allows finding several members of the Pareto front in a single run instead of having to perform separate runs as in the case of traditional mathematical programming techniques.

5. GA is less susceptible to the shape and discontinuity of the Pareto front, whereas these two issues are a real concern for other programming techniques.

6. GA has been successfully applied to various optimization problems that include a large number of parameters, multiple criteria, and complex criteria relationships.

In its pure form, GA does not readily provide away to utilize human knowledge and subjective opinion. Interactive evolutionary computation (IEC) has been motivated by the need to entrain knowledge and subjectivity into evolutionary optimization (Takagi, 2001); where qualitative evaluation of evolutionary outcomes is vital such as the fields of art and design. The narrower definition of IEC involves a GA where a human evaluator of a built-in fitness evaluation function assigns fitness values to population members instead. Parmee (2003) suggested a broader definition of IEC as the optimization of a target system based on the human-machine interface. IEC allows both the uni-dimensional and multi-dimensional qualitative objectives to be handled by outsourcing them to the user. IEC also promotes problem reformulation as changes are easily incorporated. The lack of necessity to hard-code qualitative influences makes the IEC extremely versatile in handling changing definitions of uni- and multi-dimensionally qualitative objectives since no effort for reconfiguration is necessary. When the user is allowed to input individuals to the population or modify the existing ones as well as gain information about the search space from the system, the IEC becomes a two-way informative process.

Simulated Annealing

Constrained non linear Optimization Problems (COP) often takes place in many practical applications such as construction planning, industrial process optimization, manufacturing optimization systems and so on. These problems are challenging in terms of identifying feasible solutions when constraints are linear and the objective functions are non linear. Therefore, finding the location of the global optimum in the non-linear COP is more difficult as compared to linear bound-constrained global optimization problems. This research proposes a Hybrid Simulated Annealing method (HSA), for solving the general COP. HSA has features that it addresses both feasibility and optimality issues and here, it is supported by a local search procedure of gradient based method (LS). In this research, the work for four versions of HSA has been developed.

Many important real world problems can be expressed in terms of a set of linear constraints with nonlinear objective function that restrict the domain over which a given performance criterion is optimized (Floudas and Pardalos, 1990).

Derivative methods that attempt to solve non-linear problem might be trapped in infeasible sub-spaces if the combined topology of the constraints is too rugged. The same problem exists in the discovery of global optima in non-convex bound-constrained global optimization problems. The constrained optimization problems have augmented complexity as compared to bound-constrained problems due to the restrictions imposed by highly non-linear relationships among variables.

Here, we adopt the Simulated Annealing (SA) approach to solve the constrained optimization problems. SA is a black box stochastic algorithm that generates a sequence of random solutions converging to a global optimum. SA employs a slow annealing process that accepts worse solutions more easily in the beginning stages of the search as compared to later phases (Kirkpatrick, Gelatt and Vechi, 1983). Using this feature, SA escapes from local optima and overcomes the difficulties encountered by derivative based numerical methods. A convergence proof for SA in the real domain is provided by Dekkers and Aarts (1991). Various SA implementations exist in the literature for bound-constrained global optimization problems (Hedar and Fukushima, 2004). Ozdamar and Demirhan (2000) provide an extensive computational survey that reflects the performance of stochastic approaches including different SA algorithms and clustering methods on a large number of bound constrained test functions.

As Hedar and Fukushima (2005) mention in their report (the authors of Filter SA combined with local search), publications concerning the implementation of SA in the constrained optimization problems are quite scarce. Some successful special case SA applications for constrained engineering problems exist in the literature (Wong and Wong, 1997). Yet, general constraint handling methods are not discussed and tested extensively as they have been in the Genetic Algorithms (GA) field.

Various penalty constraint handling methods such as static, dynamic or adaptive penalties are proposed and discussed more frequently in the GA literature (Deb, 2000). Penalty methods convert a constrained optimization problem into an unconstrained problem where a penalty term reflecting the degree of infeasibility of the solution is added to the objective function. In static penalty functions (Morales and Quezada, 1998; Coello, 2000), the penalty parameter is constant throughout the search whereas in dynamic ones this parameter changes with the run time of the search (Joines and Houck, 1994; Kazarlis and Petridis, 1998). Static penalty functions suffer from the difficulty of determining the optimal magnitude of the penalty parameter which, if too large, may prevent the search from exploring infeasible regions. On the other hand, a too small parameter may result in failure to identify feasible solutions. Dynamic penalty functions overcome this obstacle though they are sensitive to certain parameters too related to run time (Michalewicz, 1995). A review of different penalty methods used in GAs and a discussion on their advantages and disadvantages can be found in Yeniay (2005).

Wah and Wang (2000) avoid parametric problems in penalty functions by introducing a penalty method where pure SA is applied in its standard algorithmic form with features derived from discrete Lagrangian theory. This method is called Constrained SA (CSA). The novelty in this work is that although the authors work with a penalty augmented objective function, they utilize SA to perturb the Lagrangian parameters as well as the solution coordinates. Their algorithm adopts an ascending approach for the Lagrangian parameters where increased penalty parameters are accepted with probability one while decreased ones are accepted with an annealing probability. In this manner, they apply a descending exploration for solution coordinates and an ascending one for penalty parameters to achieve feasibility of constraints.

However, when penalty methods are adopted by SA, a key problem arises. SA generates a sequence of solutions where each solution is derived by perturbing the previous one. Since the probability of acceptance of worse solutions typically depends on the difference in the objective function of two consecutive solutions, a feasible solution that is an immediate successor to an infeasible one might be accepted right away because it does not

have a penalty term in its assessment criterion. Even if the objective function value of a worse feasible solution is larger than its infeasible predecessor's, it can dominate the penalty term in the predecessor solution and be accepted. Hence, a feasible solution might be accepted even if it does not fare well in the range of feasible solutions obtained so far. Similarly, if an infeasible solution succeeds a feasible one, it is less likely that it will be accepted because its probability of acceptance might be too small due to the penalty term. Such situations encountered while generating a sequence of convergent solutions may cause the search to be trapped in feasible regions where there are only local stationary points. Though CSA eliminates parametric issues in penalties, they still use the augmented objective function and still suffer from this drawback.

Recently, Hedar and Fukushima (2005) apply diversified multi-start SA to achieve a better exploration in both the feasible and infeasible regions. They propose to keep a set of starting solutions (diversification set) as initiators of multi-start SA. A ranking procedure is applied to the elements of this set using Pareto optimality concepts related to feasibility and optimality. This ranking strategy differentiates solutions with regard to non-dominance in constraint violation and in the objective function value. A trial solution is compared with the best-ranked solution in this set and accepted according to its deterioration in objective function or total infeasibility, whichever is the maximum. Thus the augmented objective function becomes a dual criteria function consisting of infeasibility and objective function. The diversification set is updated with new non-dominated solutions encountered during the exploration process. The authors call this algorithm Filter SA (FSA).

In this research, we adopt a simple and easy way to use scheme to deal with the feasibility issue in constrained optimization. First, we adapt the proposed GAs in a Hybrid SA framework (HAS). HSA permits both diversification (exploration in infeasible regions) and intensification (hillclimbing in the immediate neighborhood of a worse solution) during the search. Furthermore, we integrate HSA with gradient based local search method (Zhou and Tits, 1996) as a supportive exploration tool.

HSA is a hybrid hill-climb-SA approach that is more stringent in accepting worse solutions. HAS is allowed to accept a non-improving solution probabilistically only if a consecutive number of moves have already resulted in non-improving solutions.

This strategy is also linked to the activation of the local search of gradient based approach. HSA activates local search probabilistically whenever a feasible solution better than the last feasible solution is found. Line search is also activated at the later stages of the search when a worse solution is accepted. Upon activation, the line search takes current solution in HSA as a starting point and carries out a numerical search to converge to an existing nearby stationary point (if it exists).

PROBLEM STATEMENT

Due to limitations in resources for manufacturing a product and the need to satisfy certain conditions in manufacturing and demand, a problem of fuzziness occurs in industrial systems. This problem occurs also in chocolate manufacturing when deciding a mixed selection of raw materials to produce varieties of products. This is referred here to as the product-mix selection problem (Tabucanon, 1996).

There are a number of products to be manufactured by mixing different raw materials and using several varieties of processing. There are limitations in resources of raw materials and facility usage for the varieties of processing. The raw materials and facilities usage required for manufacturing each product are expressed by means of fuzzy coefficients. There are also some constraints imposed by marketing department such as product-mix requirement, main product

line requirement and lower and upper limit of demand for each product. It is necessary to obtain maximum profit with certain degree of satisfaction of the decision-maker.

Fuzzy Constrained Optimization Problem

The firm Chocoman Inc. manufactures 8 different kinds of chocolate products. Input variable x_i represents the amount of manufactured product in 10^3 units.

The function to be maximized is the total profit obtained calculated as the summation of profit obtained with each product and taken into account their coefficients. Table 1 shows the profit coefficients (c_i), (d_i) and (e_i) for each product I (c_i, d_i and e_i are the technological coefficients given in Equation (6)).

There are 8 raw materials to be mixed in different proportions and 9 processes (facilities) to be utilized. Therefore, there are 17 constraints with fuzzy coefficients separated in two sets such as raw material availability and facility capacity. These constraints are inevitable for each material and facility that is based on the material consumption, facility usage and the resource availability. Table 2 shows fuzzy coefficients $\tilde{a}ij$ represented by (a_{ij}^l, a_{ij}^h), for required materials and facility usage j for manufacturing each product i and non fuzzy coefficients b_j for availability of material or facility j as given in Table 4.

Additionally, the following constraints were established by the sales department of Chocoman Inc.:

1. Main product line requirement. The total sales from candy and wafer products should not exceed 15% of the total revenues from the chocolate bar products. Table 3 show the values of sales/revenues (r_i) for each product i.

Table 1. Profit coefficients c_i, d_i and e_i (profit function in US $ per 10^3 units)

Product (x_i)	Synonym	c_i	d_i	e_i
x_1 = Milk chocolate, 250g	MC 250	$c_1 = 180$	$d_1 = 0.18$	$e_1 = 0.01$
x_2 = Milk chocolate, 100g	MC 100	$c_2 = 83$	$d_2 = 0.16$	$e_2 = 0.13$
x_3 = Crunchy chocolate, 250g	CC 250	$c_3 = 153$	$d_3 = 0.15$	$e_3 = 0.14$
x_4 = Crunchy chocolate, 100g	CC 100	$c_4 = 72$	$d_4 = 0.14$	$e_4 = 0.12$
x_5 = Chocolate with nuts, 250g	CN 250	$c_5 = 130$	$d_5 = 0.13$	$e_5 = 0.15$
x_6 = Chocolate with nuts, 100g	CN 100	$c_6 = 70$	$d_6 = 0.14$	$e_6 = 0.17$
x_7 = Chocolate candy	CANDY	$c_7 = 208$	$d_7 = 0.21$	$e_7 = 0.18$
x_8 = Chocolate wafer	WAFER	$c_8 = 83$	$d_8 = 0.17$	$e_8 = 0.16$

Table 2. Raw material and facility usage required (per 10^3 units) ($\tilde{a}_{ij} = [a^l_{ij}, a^h_{ij}]$) and availability ($b_j$)

Material or Facility	MC 250	MC 100	CC 250	CC100	CN250	CN100	Candy	Wafer
Cocoa (kg)	[66, 109]	[26, 44]	[56,9]	[22,37]	[37,62]	[15,25]	[45, 75]	[9, 21]
Milk (kg)	[47, 78]	[19, 31]	[37,6]	[15,25]	[37,62]	[15,25]	22, 37]	[9, 21]
Nuts (kg)	[0, 0]	[0, 0]	[28,4]	[11,19]	[56,94]	[22,37]	[0, 0]	[0, 0]
Cons. sugar (kg)	[75, 125]	[30, 50]	[66,109]	[26,44]	[56,94]	[22,37]	[157,262]	[18,30]
Flour (kg)	[0, 0]	[0, 0]	[0, 0]	[0, 0]	[0, 0]	[0, 0]	[0, 0]	[54,90]
Alum. foil (ft²)	[375,625]	[0, 0]	[375,625]	[0, 0]	[0, 0]	[0, 0]	[0, 0]	[187,312]
Paper (ft²)	[337,562]	[0, 0]	[337,563]	[0, 0]	[337,562]	[0, 0]	[0, 0]	[0, 0]
Plastic (ft²)	[45, 75]	[95, 150]	[45, 75]	[90,150]	[45,75]	[90, 150]	[1200,200]	[187,312]
Cooking(ton-hours)	[0.4, 0.6]	[0.1, 0.2]	[0.3, 0.5]	[0.1, 0.2]	[0.3,0.4]	[0.1, 0.2]	[0.4, 0.7]	[0.1,0.12]
Mixing (ton-hours)	[0, 0]	[0, 0]	0.1, 0.2]	[0.04,0.07]	[0.2, 0.3]	[0.07, 0.12]	[0, 0]	[0, 0]
Forming(ton-hours)	[0.6, 0.9]	[0.2, 0.4]	[0.6, 0.9]	[0.2, 0.4]	[0.6, 0.9]	[0.2, 0.4]	[0.7, 1.1]	[0.3, 0.4]
Grinding(ton-hours)	[0, 0]	[0, 0]	[0.2, 0.3]	[0.07, 0.12]	[0, 0]	[0, 0]	[0, 0]	[0, 0]
Wafer making (ton-hours)	[0, 0]	[0, 0]	[0, 0]	[0, 0]	[0, 0]	[0, 0]	[0, 0]	[0.2, 0.4]
Cutting (hours)	[0.07,0.2]	[0.07,0.12]	[0.07,0.12]	[0.07, 0.12]	[0.07, 0.12]	[0.07, 0.12]	[0.15, 0.25]	[0, 0]
Packaging1 (hours)	[0.2, 0.3]	[0, 0]	[0.2, 0.3]	[0, 0]	[0.2, 0.3]	[0, 0]	[0, 0]	[0, 0]
Packaging2 (hours)	[0.04,0.6]	[0.2, 0.4]	[0.04, 0.06]	[0.2, 0.4]	[0.04, 0.06]	[0.2, 0.4]	[1.9, 3.1]	[0.1, 0.2]
Labour (hours)	[0.2, 0.4]	[0.2, 0.4]	[0.2, 0.4]	[0.2, 0.4]	[0.2, 0.4]	[0.2, 0.4]	[1.9, 3.1]	[1.9, 3.1]

2. Product mix requirements. Large-sized products (250 g) of each type should not exceed 60% of the small-sized product (100 g).

Finally, the lower limit of demand for each product i is 0 in all cases, while the upper limit (u_l) is shown in Table 3.

Membership Function for Technological Coefficients

The modified S-curve membership function proposed by Vasant (2006) is considered. For a value x, the degree of satisfaction $\mu_{\tilde{a}_{ij}}(x)$ for

fuzzy coefficient $\tilde{a}ij$ is given by the membership function given in Equation (1) in Box 1.

Given a level of satisfaction value μ, the crisp value $a_{ij}\big|_{\mu}$ for fuzzy coefficient $\tilde{a}ij$ can be calculated using Equation (2) in Box 2.

The value α determines the shape of the membership function, while B and C values can be calculated from α, given in Equations (3) and (4).

$$C = -\frac{0.998}{(0.999 - 0.001e^{\alpha}} \tag{3}$$

$$B = 0.999(1 + C) \tag{4}$$

Box 1.

$$\mu_{\tilde{a}_{ij}}(x) = \begin{cases} 1.000 & x < a_{ij}^{l} \\ 0.999 & x = a_{ij}^{l} \\ \dfrac{B}{1 + Ce^{\alpha\left(\dfrac{x - a_{ij}^{l}}{a_{ij}^{h} - a_{ij}^{l}}\right)}} & a_{ij}^{l} < x < a_{ij}^{h} \\ 0.0001 & x = a_{ij}^{h} \\ 0.000 & x > a_{ij}^{h} \end{cases} \tag{1}$$

Box 2.

$$\tilde{a}_{ij}\big|_{\mu} = a_{ij}^{l} + \left(\frac{a_{ij}^{h} - a_{ij}^{l}}{\alpha}\right)\ln\frac{1}{C}\left(\frac{B}{\mu} - 1\right) \tag{2}$$

If we wish a level of satisfaction value $\mu = 0.5$, the crisp value $a_{ij}\big|_{0.5}$ is in the middle of the interval $[a_{ij}^l, a_{ij}^h]$, that is:

$$\tilde{a}_{ij}\Big|_{0.5} = \frac{a_{ij}^l + a_{ij}^h}{2} \qquad (5)$$

then, $\alpha = 13.81350956$ (Vasant, 2006).

Problem Formulation

Optimization techniques are primarily used in production planning problems in order to achieve optimal profit, which maximizes certain objective function by satisfying a number of constraints. The first step in an optimal production planning problems is to formulate the underlying nonlinear programming (NLP) problem by writing the mathematical functions relating to the objective and constraints.

Given a degree of satisfaction value μ, the fuzzy constrained optimization problem can be formulated (Jim´enez, Cadenas, S´anchez, Gmez-Skarmeta and Verdegay, 2006; Vasant, 2010) as the non linear constrained optimization problem shown below.

Maximize $\sum_{i=1}^{8} (c_i x_i - d_i x_i^2 - e_i x_i^3)$

Subject to Equation (6) in Box 3.

$$\sum_{i=7}^{8} r_i x_i - 0.15 \sum_{i=1}^{6} r_i x_i \leq 0$$

$$x_1 - 0.6x_2 \leq 0$$

$$x_3 - 0.6x_4 \leq 0$$

$$x_5 - 0.6x_6 \leq 0$$

$$0 \leq x_i \leq u_i, \quad i = 1, 2, ..., 8$$

In the non-linear programming problem, the variable vector x represents a set of variables x_i, $i = 1, 2,..., 8$. The above optimization problem contains eight continuous variables and twenty one inequality constraints. A test point x_i satisfying constrains is called feasible, otherwise, it is infeasible. The set satisfying constrains is called the feasible domain. The aim of the optimization is to maximize the total production profit for the industrial production planning problems. The formulation of the new non-linear cubic function for this particular problem has been referred to Lin (2007) and Chaudari (2007). The cubic objective function has twenty four coefficients for eight decision variables. This problem considered one of the most challenging problems in the research area of industrial production planning.

RESULTS AND DISCUSSION

Hybrid Line Search and Genetic Algorithms (HLSGA)

In this section, the simulation and computational results on the hybridization techniques of

Box 3.

$$\sum_{i=1}^{8} \left[a_{ij}^l + \left(\frac{a_{ij}^h - a_{ij}^l}{\alpha} \right) \ln \frac{1}{C} \left(\frac{B}{\mu} - 1 \right) \right] x_i - b_j \leq 0, \quad j = 1, 2, ..., 17 \qquad (6)$$

Table 3. Demand (u_k) and revenues/sales (r_k) in US $ per 10^3 units

Product (x_k)	Synonym	Demand (u_k)	Revenues/Sales (r_k)
x_1 = Milk chocolate, 250g	MC 250	$u_1 = 500$	$r_1 = 375$
x_2 = Milk chocolate, 100g	MC 100	$u_2 = 800$	$r_2 = 150$
x_3 = Crunchy chocolate, 250g	CC 250	$u_3 = 400$	$r_3 = 400$
x_4 = Crunchy chocolate, 100g	CC 100	$u_4 = 600$	$r_4 = 160$
x_5 = Chocolate with nuts, 250g	CN 250	$u_5 = 300$	$r_5 = 420$
x_6 = Chocolate with nuts, 100g	CN 100	$u_6 = 500$	$r_6 = 175$
x_7 = Chocolate candy	CANDY	$u_7 = 200$	$r_7 = 400$
x_8 = Chocolate wafer	WAFER	$u_8 = 400$	$r_8 = 150$

Table 4. Raw material availability (b_j)

Material or Facility	Availability
Cocoa (kg)	100000
Milk (kg)	120000
Nuts (kg)	60000
Cons. sugar (kg)	200000
Flour (kg)	20000
Alum. foil (ft²)	500000
Paper (ft²)	500000
Plastic (ft²)	500000
Cooking (ton-hours)	1000
Mixing (ton-hours)	200
Forming (ton-hours)	1500
Grinding (ton-hours)	200
Wafer making (ton-hours)	100
Cutting (hours)	400
Packaging 1 (hours)	400
Packaging 2 (hours)	1200
Labour (hours)	1000

merging LS and GA presented for the industrial production planning problems is propounded. LS techniques are utilized for the searching of best initial points to start the optimization process and GA techniques are used for finding the best global close to the optimal solutions. GAs are in a class of biologically motivated optimization methods that evolve a population of individuals where individuals who are more fit have a higher possibility of surviving into subsequent generations. Line search method is a type of gradient-based method that uses derivative of objective function and constraints for the continuous functions. It is suggested that this hybrid method would be a good candidate to find best near global optimal value for the fitness function and feasible solution for the decision variables as well as a reasonable computational CPU time.

The genetic algorithm (GA) is an approach that mimics biological processes in evolving optimal or near optimal solutions to problems. In this section, a practical application to challenging industrial problems of production planning has been investigated to exploit the full potential of GA to look for the promising global optimal solution.

Algorithms:

1. **Initialization**: Generate an initial population. Initialize parameters and define fitness function.
2. **Crossover**: Perform crossover using arithmetic crossover.
3. **Mutation**: Perform mutation using adaptive feasible.
4. **Selection**: Evaluate the fitness of each individual in the population. Choose N best chromosomes to form the next generation.
5. **Termination Criteria**: If stopping criteria are satisfied, then the algorithm terminates. Otherwise, select the next generation and go to Step 2.
6. Output the best solutions.

Notation used for the non-linear optimization problem:

μ = Degree of possibility
γ = Level of satisfaction
α = Vagueness factor
f = objective function or fitness function
x_i = Decision variables
Time in seconds = CPU (s)

Simulation and Computational Analysis

The hybrid algorithm of LS and GA in the program is as follows:

```
Step 1: Start
  Line search
Step 2: Genetic algorithms
Step 3: End
Parameter setting for GA:
Population type: double vector
Population size: 20
Elite count: 2
Crossover fraction: 0.8
Migration direction: forward
Generation: 100
Time limit: Infinite
Fitness limit: Infinite
Creation function: uniform
Fitness scaling: rank
Selection function: stochastic uni-
form
Crossover: Scattered
Mutation: Gaussian
```

Figure 1 depicts the simulation result for the optimal solution of objective function at α = 13.813. The optimal value for objective function is 200116.4 at γ − 0.99.

Table 5 indicates the feasible solution for the decision variables with γ = 0.001 to γ = 0.99 and objective function values at α = 13.813.

Form Table 5, it is observed that the average CPU time for running LS and GA is 0.3443 s and 0.3446 s, respectively. Even though the best optimal objective function value is same as that from LS method alone but the superiority of the hybrid LS and GA method lies on the computational CPU time supremacy. The total CPU time for running LS and GA for γ = 0.001 to γ = 0.99 is 3.7874 s and 3.7907 s, respectively. This CPU time is extremely lower than that for LS method alone and Hybrid GA with LS method. This is the major contribution of the novel techniques of GA in helping LS to achieve the best optimal objective function value of 200116.4 with the average CPU time of 0.3446 s. However, the major drawback of the HLSGA techniques is on the inability of obtaining non-zero solution for the decision variable x_8 for γ = 0.001 to γ = 0.90. There is a possibility of obtaining non-zero solution for the decision variable x_8 at γ = 41.

Figure 2 depicts the objective function values versus feasible solution of decision variables at α = 12.813. Unfortunately, there is no improvement in the feasible values for the decision variables compared to LS method alone and hybrid GA with LS. This is the major set back of incorporating GA with LS in this hybridization approach. Moreover, similar tragedy occurs for the hybrid GA with LS approach. These techniques fail to produce a productive solution for the decision variable x_8 while they are capable to produce a reasonable best solution for x_2 and x_4 feasible decision variables.

Figure 3 depicts the simulation and computational results for the objective function respect to α and γ via 3D mesh plot. The total CPU time for running this result is 7.61 seconds. This CPU time is extremely lower than that for LS (alone) techniques and hybrid GA with LS techniques. Computational efficiency is one of the novel characteristic of GA techniques when it is incorporated in the hybridization process. This is one of major achievement in these research case studies.

Figure 1. Objective value versus γ

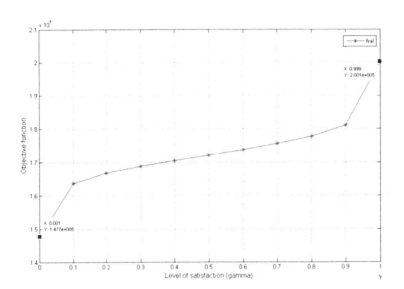

Table 5. Optimal value for objective function

γ	x_1	x_2	x_3	x_4	x_5	x_6	x_7	x_8	f	$LS_t(s)$	$GA_t(s)$
0.001	246.8	411.4	205.7	342.8	134.3	223.9	120.6	0.00	147712.9	2.8205	2.8210
0.1	284.8	474.7	239.2	398.7	148.8	248.0	150.4	0.00	163731.6	0.5864	0.5869
0.2	292.5	487.6	246.1	410.1	151.8	253.0	156.7	0.00	166763.3	0.0303	0.0306
0.3	297.9	496.5	250.8	418.0	153.8	256.4	161.2	0.00	168830.5	0.0267	0.0269
0.4	302.5	504.1	254.8	424.7	155.6	259.3	165.1	0.00	170548.7	0.0286	0.0289
0.5	306.8	511.7	258.6	431.0	157.2	262.1	168.8	0.00	172146.4	0.0795	0.0797
0.6	311.2	518.6	262.5	437.5	158.9	264.9	172.6	0.00	173763.9	0.0264	0.0267
0.7	316.1	526.9	266.9	444.8	160.8	268.1	176.9	0.00	175548.3	0.0559	0.0562
0.8	322.4	537.4	272.4	454.1	163.3	272.1	182.4	0.00	177754.9	0.0277	0.0279
0.9	332.3	553.9	281.2	468.6	167.1	278.5	191.3	0.00	181132.7	0.0679	0.0682
0.99	414.3	690.6	354.0	590.0	200.0	333.4	200.0	54.5	200116.4	0.0375	0.0377

$LS_t(s)$: CPU time for LS technique and $GA_t(s)$: CPU time for GA technique

Table 6 describes the superiority of computational efficiency in finding the best optimal objective function respect to α = 1 to α = 41 at γ = 0.99 respect to CPU time. This lowest CPU time reveals the major significant contribution of superb techniques of GA in these research findings. The findings also indicate that GA is the best quality approach in terms of CPU time concern in this research work.

The strength of GA in this hybridization process lies in the great contribution of computational efficiency of CPU time. This is clearly indicated in Table 6. The average CPU time for running LS and GA for α = 1 to α = 41 at γ = 0.99 is 0.0553 s and 0.0555 s, respectively. In fact, GA has contributed to its own CPU running time as well as the great help in CPU running time for LS techniques. The major contribution of LS is

Figure 2. Objective value versus decision variables

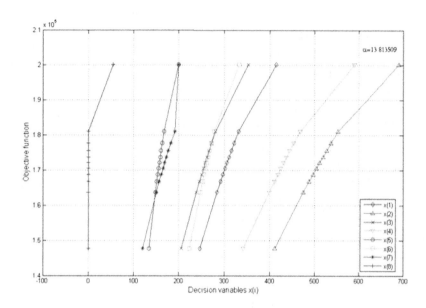

Figure 3. Objective value versus α and γ

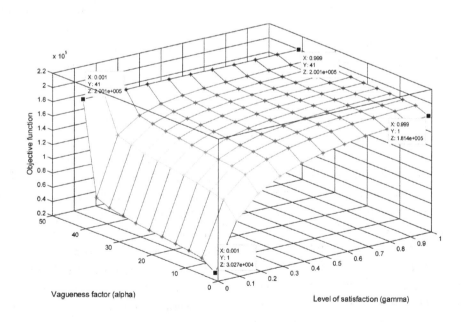

Table 6. Best CPU time for objective function at $\gamma = 0.99$

α	f	*LS CPU time (s)*	*GA CPU time (s)*
1	200116.44	0.03104	0.03129
5	200116.44	0.05659	0.05685
9	200116.44	0.02970	0.02995
13	200116.44	0.15890	0.15917
17	200116.44	0.01922	0.01947
21	200116.44	0.02525	0.02550
25	200116.44	0.02510	0.02535
29	200116.44	0.18363	0.18389
33	200116.44	0.02599	0.02625
37	200116.44	0.02660	0.02685
41	200116.44	0.02620	0.02645

in finding the benchmark solution for the best near global optimal value for the cubic objective function of industrial production planning problems. On the other hand, the great contribution of GA is on the quality of computational efficiency and robust convergence computing CPU time in this particular hybridization approach.

Hybrid Line Search and Simulated Annealing (HLSSA)

In this discussion, a novel optimization technique of simulated annealing is merged in the hybridization with line search approach. The main reason for incorporating SA in this hybridization process is that it is very easy to be implemented with few lines of algorithmic code, SA can conveniently handle continuous optimization problems, and lastly SA can possibly provide high quality solution for the objective function and outstanding computational efficiency in running CPU time. Thus, the features of SA, which has been described, make SA a very useful tool for the operational research practitioner, especially in industrial engineering.

A Hybrid Gradient Based Simulated Annealing Algorithm:

```
1. Generate x(0) randomly and evalu-
ate f(x(0)). Set k = 0.

2. Solve for the local maximum of
f(x) via a gradient-based minimiza-
tion method with x(k) as the ini-
tial guess to give x(k*) such that
f(x(k*)) - f(x(k)) ≤ ε , where ε  is
                        k           k
a positive parameter.

3. Start from x(k*), execute N simu-
lating annealing iterations until a
point x(k+1) is obtained such that
f(x(k+1)) - f(x(k*)) ≤ -δ  for some
                          k
positive parameters δ .
                       k

4. Set k = k + 1. Return to Step 2
until convergence.
```

In Step 3 of the algorithm, the simulated annealing iterations compose of three key steps, namely:

1. The generation of the next trial point in the solution space via random perturbations,
2. A choice of a probability distribution to govern the acceptance of uphill steps,
3. An annealing schedule.

In this research, following Kirkpatrick, Gelatt and Vechi (1983) and Cerny (1985), the fast annealing is used. The annealing schedule is determined by the parameters including the cooling speed α; the number of cooling steps N_c; the number of random perturbations for each temperature N; and the initial temperature T. The choices of these parameters are provided below. The algorithm for simulated algorithm can be implemented as follows:

Initiation. Select α, N_c, N, and initial T. Evaluate f(x (k*)).

Cooling:

A. Let j be the cooling step. Set j = 1.
B. If $j \in (1,\ldots, N_c)$
    1. i = random (1, 2, 3)

    Depending on the outcome of i, within the set Ω, re-generate randomly one of the followings: one element of *x*, or m $\in$ random $\{1,\ldots,n\}$ elements of *x*, or the whole vector of *x*. This gives $x = \tilde{x}$.

    Calculate $D = f(\tilde{x}) - f(x)$. If $D < -\delta k$ or random $[0, 1] < T\,e^{-\frac{D}{T}}$, then $x = \tilde{x}$.

    2. Set j: = j + 1 and return to (i) until N perturbations are executed.
C. Set T: = αT and j = j + 1. Return to Step (b) until N_c cooling steps are executed.

Experimental Results

The hybrid algorithm for LS and SA in the program is as follows:

```
Step 1: Start
  Line search
Step 2: Simulated Annealing
Step 3: End
Parameter setting for SA:
Annealing Fcn: @annealing fast
TemperatureFcn: @temperature exp
Acceptance Fcn: @acceptance sa
TolFun: 1.0000e-006
Stall Iter Limit: '500*number of
variables'
Max Fun Evals: '3000*number of vari-
ables'
Time Limit: Inf
Max Iter: Inf
Objective Limit: Inf
```

```
InitialTemperature: 100
ReannealInterval: 100
Data Type: 'double'
Stopping Conditions for the SA Algo-
rithm
```

The simulated annealing algorithms use the following conditions for stopping criteria:

- **Tol Fun**: The algorithm runs until the average change in value of the objective function in Stall Iter Lim iterations is less than Tol Fun. The default value is 1e-6.
- **Max Iter**: The algorithm stops if the number of iterations exceeds this maximum number of iterations. One can specify the maximum number of iterations as a positive integer or Inf. Inf is the default.
- **Max Fun Eval**: Specifies the maximum number of evaluations of the objective function. The algorithm stops if the number of function evaluations exceeds the specified maximum number limit of function evaluations. The allowed maximum is 3000*number of variables.
- **Time Limit**: Specifies the maximum time in seconds that the algorithm runs before stopping.
- **Objective Limit**: The algorithm stops if the best objective function value is less than or equal to the value of Objective Limit.

Figure 4 depicts the best optimal objective function values respect to eight decision variables for $\alpha = 13.813$. The best value for objective function is 200116.4 obtained at $\gamma = 0.99$. The total CPU time for running this simulation results is 1.60 seconds for $\gamma = 0.001$ to $\gamma = 0.99$.

Table 7 describes the experimental results for the simulation and computational of eight decision variables with optimal objective function and

Figure 4. Objective value versus decision variables

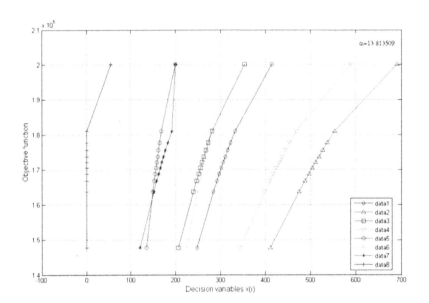

Table 7. Optimal value for Objective Function

γ	x_1	x_2	x_3	x_4	x_5	x_6	x_7	x_8	f	LS_t (s)	SA_t (s)
0.001	246.8	411.4	205.7	342.8	134.3	223.9	120.6	0.00	147712.9	0.2269	0.2273
0.1	284.8	474.7	239.2	398.7	148.8	248.0	150.4	0.00	163731.6	0.0606	0.0608
0.2	292.5	487.6	246.1	410.1	151.8	253.0	156.7	0.00	166763.3	0.0638	0.0640
0.3	297.9	496.5	250.8	418.0	153.8	256.4	161.2	0.00	168830.5	0.0258	0.0261
0.4	302.5	504.1	254.8	424.7	155.6	259.3	165.1	0.00	170548.7	0.0285	0.0287
0.5	306.8	511.7	258.6	431.0	157.2	262.1	168.8	0.00	172146.4	0.0272	0.0275
0.6	311.2	518.6	262.5	437.5	158.9	264.9	172.6	0.00	173763.9	0.0425	0.0427
0.7	316.1	526.9	266.9	444.8	160.8	268.1	176.9	0.00	175548.3	0.0244	0.0246
0.8	322.4	537.4	272.4	454.1	163.3	272.1	182.4	0.00	177754.9	0.0563	0.0565
0.9	332.3	553.9	281.2	468.6	167.1	278.5	191.3	0.00	181132.7	0.0308	0.0311
0.99	414.3	690.6	354.0	590.0	200.0	333.4	200.0	54.5	200116.4	0.0852	0.0855

$LS_t(s)$: CPU time for LS technique and $SA_t(s)$: CPU time for SA technique

CPU time. The average CPU time for running LS and SA techniques is 0.0611 s and 0.0613 s, respectively. This CPU time far better than the CPU time obtained by hybrid LS with GA techniques. The main reason for this great achievement in the computational efficiency is due to fast convergence rate of SA approach. In this case, the SA algorithm has helped the LS techniques to achieve a tremendous computational CPU time. These hybrid optimization techniques of LS with SA work extremely well in terms of the computational time. This is the major contribution of the SA optimization approach in solving a non-linear optimization problem of industrial production planning. On the other hand, this hybrid approach could not able to solve the productive decision variable x_8 while they have produced a very high productive solution for the decision variables x_2 and x_4.

Figure 5 depicts the simulation and computational results for objective function respect to α = 1 to α = 41 and γ = 0.001 to γ = 0.99. CPU time for running this simulation and computational results is 8.08 seconds.

Table 8 reports a very important findings of simulation and computational results for the objective function value respect to CPU time for LS and SA techniques at γ = 0.99.

The average CPU time for running LS and SA techniques for α = 1 to α = 41 at γ = 0.99 is 0.04107 s and 0.04132 s, respectively. This result completely outperforms against the CPU running time for the hybrid approach of LS with GA. It has

Figure 5. Objective value versus γ

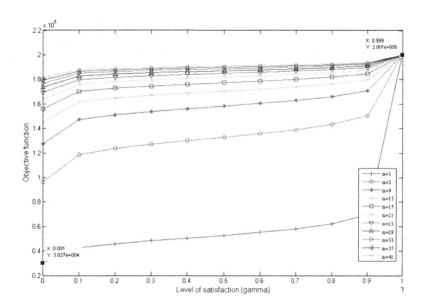

Table 8. Best CPU time for objective function at γ = 0.99

α	f	LS CPU time (s)	SA CPU time (s)
1	200116.44	0.04347	0.04372
5	200116.44	0.02914	0.02939
9	200116.44	0.02400	0.02424
13	200116.44	0.07037	0.07062
17	200116.44	0.02493	0.02518
21	200116.44	0.02458	0.02482
25	200116.44	0.08689	0.08714
29	200116.44	0.02496	0.02521
33	200116.44	0.06627	0.06653
37	200116.44	0.02568	0.02593
41	200116.44	0.03151	0.03176

shown clearly that the main strength of SA techniques is on the superiority of computational time of CPU. Again, it has proven that the SA technique has helped tremendously LS techniques in reducing the computational time for LS as well. This is one of the great contributions of SA techniques in this research.

Figure 6 exhibits the outcome for the objective function respect to α and γ. The CPU time for running this simulation results is 7.53 seconds. This CPU time is far better than that from LS (alone) CPU time and slightly improved compared to that from hybrid LS and GA approach.

In conclusion, it is highly recommended that SA technique is one of best options to be considered for the hybrid optimization techniques in terms of computational efficiency (CPU time), particularly in this research work.

FUTURE RESEARCH DIRECTIONS

The integration of LS, GA, and SA with other emerging technologies such ant colony optimization (ACO), particle swarm optimization (PSO), and artificial immune system (AIS) could be another challenging research area. The combination of these emerging technologies may not only involve GA and SA as a helper to these three but also could result in the emerging technologies being able to assist GA and SA applications. Different combinations may offer us a fruitful result in intelligent optimization systems.

Overall, the knowledge generated from hybrid evolutionary and heuristic optimization over the last three decades has now become mature. The prospect of applying hybrid intelligent optimization techniques for practical applications is overwhelming. A considerable growth in the application of hybrid intelligent optimization, particularly in the field of industrial engineering, is anticipated in the near future.

Figure 6. 3D mesh plot for objective value versus α and γ

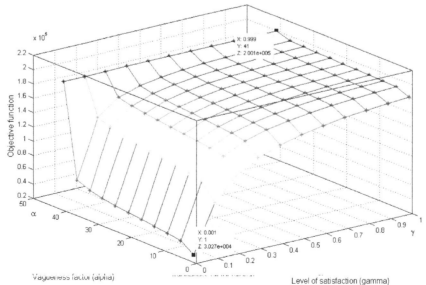

To the best of author's knowledge, this research work is among the first to apply hybrid line search with GA, hybrid line search with SA and hybrid line search with SA to the industrial production planning problems. Furthermore, in this research work there are not any global solutions available at this moment. Therefore, the further work includes solving other types of nonlinear and complex multi-objective problems arising in the real world situation, by considering other meta-heuristic techniques such as hybrid tabu search with ant colony and particle swarm optimization. In particular, construction-planning problems, product mix problem, inventory models (discount, demand and variable replenishment), design of electrical networks, mechanical components, and facility location in optimization are formulated in crisp, fuzzy or fuzzy-stochastic environment.

CONCLUSION

In this chapter, a very famous and important problem in industrial engineering called as production planning has been provided. The new research work in this chapter is on the formulation of the non-linear cubic function as an objective (fitness function) for the industrial production planning problems. This new type of non-linear cubic function was not considered in the past. This non-linear problem will be solved by other types of hybrid and non-hybrid techniques from the research areas of soft computing and classical optimization. A performance analysis table will be constructed to select the best techniques for the optimal solution on the objective (fitness) function value, feasible decision variable and computational CPU time. This is the first time that these three major criteria have been considered and investigated thoroughly in this research problem.

REFERENCES

Bellman, R. E., & Zadeh, L. A. (1970). Decision making in a fuzzy environment. *Management Science*, *17*, 141–164. doi:10.1287/mnsc.17.4.B141

Bhattacharya, A., Abraham, A., Vasant, P., & Grosan, C. (2007). Meta-learning evolutionary artificial neural network for selecting FMS under disparate level-of-satisfaction of decision maker. *International Journal of Innovative Computing, Information and Control. Special Issue on Innovative Computing Methods of Management Engineering*, *3*(1), 131–140.

Bhattacharya, A., Vasant, P., Sarkar, B., & Mukherjee, S. K. (2006). A fully fuzzified, intelligent theory-of-constraints. *Product-Mix Decision. International Journal of Production Research*, *46*(3), 789–815. doi:10.1080/00207540600823187

Chaudhuri, K. (2007, March). *Personal communication*.

Coello, C. A. C. (2000). Use of a self-adaptive penalty approach for engineering optimization problems. *Computers in Industry*, *41*, 113–127. doi:10.1016/S0166-3615(99)00046-9

Davis, L. (1985). Job shop scheduling with genetic algorithms. In *Proceedings of the 1st International Conference on Genetic Algorithms*. Lawrence Erlbaum.

Deb, K. (2000). An efficient constraint handling method for genetic algorithms. *Computer Methods in Applied Mechanics and Engineering*, *186*, 311–338. doi:10.1016/S0045-7825(99)00389-8

Deb, K. (2001). *Multi-objective optimization using evolutionary algorithms*. New York, NY: John Wiley & Sons.

Dekkers, A., & Aarts, E. (1991). Global optimization and simulated annealing. *Mathematical Programming*, *50*, 367–393. doi:10.1007/BF01594945

Floudas, C. A., & Pardalos, P. M. (1990). Lecture Notes in Computer Science: *Vol. 455. A collection of test problems for constrained global optimization algorithms*. Springer-Verlag.

Goldberg, D. E. (1989). *Genetic algorithms in search optimization and machine learning*. Toronto, Canada: Addison Wesley.

Hedar, A. R., & Fukushima, M. (2004). Heuristic pattern search and its hybridization with simulated annealing for nonlinear global optimization. *Optimization Methods and Software*, *19*, 291–308. doi:10.1080/1055678031000164518 9

Hedar, A. R., & Fukushima, M. (2005). Derivative-free filter simulated annealing method for constrained continuous global optimization. *Journal of Global Optimization*, *35*(4).

Jimenez, F., Cadenas, J. M., Sanchez, G., Gmez-Skarmeta, A. F., & Verdegay, J. L. (2006). Multi-objective evolutionary computation and fuzzy optimization. *International Journal of Approximate Reasoning*, *43*, 59–75. doi:10.1016/j.ijar.2006.02.001

Jimenez, F., Gomez-Skarmeta, A. F., & Sanchez, G. (2004). *Nonlinear optimization with fuzzy constraints by multi-objective evolutionary algorithms* (pp. 713–722). Advances in Soft Computing, Computational Intelligence, Theory and Applications. doi:10.1007/3-540-31182-3_66

Joines, J., & Houck, C. (1994). On the use of non-stationary penalty functions to solve non linear constrained optimization problems with gas. *Proceedings of the First IEEE International Conference on Evolutionary Computation* (pp. 579-584). IEEE Press.

Kazarlis, S., & Petridis, V. (1998). Varying fitness functions in genetic algorithms: studying the rate of increase in the dynamic penalty terms. *Proceedings of the 5th International Conference on Parallel Problem Solving from Nature* (pp. 211-220). Berlin, Germany: Springer Verlag.

Kirkpatrick, A., Gelatt, C. D. Jr, & Vechi, M. P. (1983). Optimization by simulated annealing. *Science*, *220*, 671–680. doi:10.1126/science.220.4598.671

Liang, T. F. (2008). Interactive multi-objective transportation planning decisions using fuzzy linear programming. *Asia Pacific Journal of Operational Research*, *25*(1), 11–31. doi:10.1142/S0217595908001602

Lin, F. T. (2007, March). *Personal communication*.

Michalewicz, Z. (1995). Genetic algorithms, numerical optimization, and constraints. In *Proceedings of the Sixth International Conference on Genetic Algorithms* (pp. 151–158). Morgan Kaufmann.

Morales, K. A., & Quezada, C. C. (1998). A universal eclectic genetic algorithm for constrained optimization. In *Proceedings 6th European Congress on Intelligent Techniques & Soft Computing, EUFIT'98*, (pp. 518–522).

Ozdamar, L., & Demirhan, M. (2000). Experiments with new stochastic global optimization search techniques. *Computers and OR*, *27*, 841–865. doi:10.1016/S0305-0548(99)00054-4

Parmee, I. C. (2003). Poor-definition, uncertainty and human factors—A case for interactive evolutionary problem reformulation. *Proceedings of the 3rd IEC Workshop of the Genetic and Evolutionary Computation Conference*.

Powell, M. J. D. (1983). Variable metric methods for constrained optimization. In Bachem, A., Grotschel, M., & Korte, B. (Eds.), *Mathematical programming: The state of the art* (pp. 288–311). Springer Verlag. doi:10.1007/978-3-642-68874-4_12

Ramik, J., & Vlach, M. (2002). Fuzzy mathematical programming: A unified approach based on fuzzy relations. *Fuzzy Optimization and Decision Making, 1*, 335–346. doi:10.1023/A:1020978428453

Sanchez, G., Jimenez, F., & Vasant, P. (2007). Fuzzy optimization with multi-objective evolutionary algorithms: A case study. *Proceedings of the 2007 IEEE Symposium on Computational Intelligence in Multi-criteria Decision Making* (pp. 58-64). Honolulu, Hawaii.

Tabucanon, T. T. (1996). Multi objective programming for industrial engineers. In Avriel, M., & Golany, B. (Eds.), *Mathematical programming for industrial engineers* (pp. 487–542). New York, NY: Marcel Dekker, Inc.

Takagi, H. (2001). Interactive evolutionary computation: Fusion of the capabilities of EC computation and human evaluations. *Proceedings of the IEEE, 89*(9), 1275–1296. doi:10.1109/5.949485

Turabieh, H., Sheta, A., & Vasant, P. (2007). Hybrid optimization genetic algorithm (HOGA) with interactive evolution to solve constraint optimization problems for production systems. *International Journal of Computational Science, 1*(4), 395–406.

Vasant, P. (2006). Fuzzy production planning and its application to decision making. *Journal of Intelligent Manufacturing, 17*(1), 5–12. doi:10.1007/s10845-005-5509-x

Vasant, P. (2010). Hybrid simulated annealing and genetic algorithms for industrial production management problems. *International Journal of Computational Methods, 7*(2), 279–297. doi:10.1142/S0219876210002209

Vasant, P., Barsoum, N., Kahraman, C., & Dimirovski, G. (2007). Application of fuzzy optimization in forecasting and planning of construction industry. In Vrakas, D., & Vlahavas, I. (Eds.), *Artificial intelligent for advanced problem solving technique* (pp. 254–265). Hershey, PA: IGI Global. doi:10.4018/978-1-59904-705-8.ch010

Vasant, P., Bhattacharya, A., Sarkar, B., & Mukherjee, S. K. (2007). Detection of level of satisfaction and fuzziness patterns for MCDM model with modified flexible S-curve MF. *Applied Soft Computing, 7*, 1044–1054. doi:10.1016/j.asoc.2006.10.005

Wah, B. W., & Wang, T. (2000). Tuning strategies in constrained simulated annealing for nonlinear global optimization. *International Journal of Artificial Intelligence Tools, 9*, 3–25. doi:10.1142/S0218213000000033

Wong, K. P., & Wong, S. Y. W. (1997). Hybrid genetic/simulated annealing approach to short-term multiple-fuel-constrained generation scheduling. *IEEE Transactions on Power Systems, 12*, 776–784. doi:10.1109/59.589681

Yeniay, O. (2005). Penalty function methods for constrained optimization with genetic algorithms. *Mathematical and Computational Applications, 10*, 45–56.

Zhou, J. L., & Tits, A. L. (1996). An SQP Algorithm for finely discretized continuous minimax problems and other minimax problems with many objective functions. *SIAM Journal on Optimization, 6*, 461–487. doi:10.1137/0806025

ADDITIONAL READING

Bhattacharya, A., & Vasant, P. (2007). Soft-sensing of level of satisfaction in TOC product-mix decision heuristic using robust fuzzy-LP. *European Journal of Operational Research, 177*(1), 55–70. doi:10.1016/j.ejor.2005.11.017

Bilgehan, M. (2011). Comparison of ANFIS and NN models - With a study in critical buckling load estimation. *Applied Soft Computing Journal*, *11*(4), 3779–3791. doi:10.1016/j.asoc.2011.02.011

Chou, C.-C., Liu, L.-J., Huang, S.-F., Yih, J.-M., & Han, T.-C. An evaluation of airline service quality using the fuzzy weighted SERVQUAL method. *Applied Soft Computing Journal, 11*(2), 2117-2128.

Elamvazuthi, I., Vasant, P., & Ganesan, T. (2010). Fuzzy linear programming using modified logistic membership function. [IREACO]. *International Review of Automatic Control*, *3*(4), 370–377.

Ganesan, T., Vasant, P., & Elamvazuthi, I. (2011). Optimization of non linear geological structure mapping using hybrid neuro-genetic techniques. *Mathematical and Computer Modelling*, *54*, 2913–2922. doi:10.1016/j.mcm.2011.07.012

Liang, T.-F., & Cheng, H.-W. (2011). Multiobjective aggregate production planning decisions using two-phase fuzzy goal programming method. *Journal of Industrial and Management Optimization, 7*(2), 365–383. doi:10.3934/jimo.2011.7.365

Liang, T.-F., Cheng, H.-W., Chen, P.-Y., & Shen, K.-H. (2011). Application of fuzzy sets to aggregate production planning with multiproducts and multitime periods. *IEEE Transactions on Fuzzy Systems*, *19*(3), 465–477. doi:10.1109/TFUZZ.2011.2114668

Madronero, M. D., Peidro, D., & Vasant, P. (2010). Vendor selection problem by using an interactive fuzzy multi-objective approach with modified s-curve membership functions. *Computers & Mathematics with Applications (Oxford, England)*, *60*, 1038–1048. doi:10.1016/j.camwa.2010.03.060

Peidro, D., & Vasant, P. (2011). Transportation planning with modified s-curve membership functions using an interactive fuzzy multi-objective approach. *Applied Soft Computing, 11*, 2656–2663. doi:10.1016/j.asoc.2010.10.014

Susanto, S., & Bhattacharya, A. (2011). Compromise fuzzy multi-objective linear programming (CFMOLP) heuristic for product-mix determination. *Computers & Industrial Engineering, 61*(3), 582–590. doi:10.1016/j.cie.2011.04.013

Vasant, P. (2006). Fuzzy decision making of profit function in production planning using S-curve membership function. *Computers & Industrial Engineering, 51*(4), 715–725. doi:10.1016/j.cie.2006.08.017

Vasant, P. (2010). Hybrid simulated annealing and genetic algorithms for industrial production management problems. *International Journal of Computational Methods*, *7*(2), 279–297. doi:10.1142/S0219876210002209

Vasant, P. (2011). Hybrid MADS and GA techniques for industrial production systems. *Archives of Control Sciences, 21*(3), 227–240. doi:10.2478/v10170-010-0045-0

Vasant, P., & Barsoum, N. (2009). Hybrid genetic algorithms and line search method for industrial production planning with non-linear fitness function. *Engineering Applications of Artificial Intelligence, 22*, 767–777. doi:10.1016/j.engappai.2009.03.010

Vasant, P., & Barsoum, N. (2010). Hybrid pattern search and simulated annealing for fuzzy production planning problems. *Computers & Mathematics with Applications (Oxford, England)*, *60*, 1058–1067. doi:10.1016/j.camwa.2010.03.063

Vasant, P., Bhattacharya, A., Sarkar, B., & Mukherjee, S. K. (2007). Detection of level of satisfaction and fuzziness patterns for MCDM model with modified flexible S-curve MF. *Applied Soft Computing Journal*, *7*(3), 1044–1054. doi:10.1016/j.asoc.2006.10.005

Vasant, P., Elamvazuthi, I., Ganesan, T., & Webb, J. F. (2010). Iterative fuzzy optimization approach for crude oil refinery industry. *Scientific Annals of Computer Science*, *8*(2), 262–280.

Vasant, P., Elamvazuthi, I., & Webb, J. F. (2010). Fuzzy technique for optimization of objective function with uncertain resource variables and technological coefficients. *International Journal of Modeling, Simulation, and Scientific Computing*, *1*(3), 349–367. doi:10.1142/S1793962310000225

Vasant, P., Ganesan, T., Elamvazuthi, I., & Webb, J. F. (2011). Fuzzy linear programming for the production planning: The case of textile firm. *International Review on Modelling and Simulations*, *4*(2), 961–970.

Vasant, P. M. (2003). Application of fuzzy linear programming in production planning. *Fuzzy Optimization and Decision Making*, *2*(3), 229–241. doi:10.1023/A:1025094504415

KEY TERMS AND DEFINITIONS

Fuzzy Environment: An uncertain environment in which the decision making process is almost not possible to achieve precisely.

Genetic Algorithms (GA): stochastic optimization algorithms are based on the principles of natural evolution.

Line Search (LS): The line search method uses fmincon approach from MATLAB computational toolbox. FMINCON is a gradient-based method that is designed to work on problems where the objective and constraint functions are both continuous and have continuous first derivatives.

Membership Function (MF): A function represents the degree of uncertainty in between the values 0 and 1.

Simulated Annealing (SA): SA is a black box stochastic algorithm that generates a sequence of random solutions converging to a global optimum.

Uncertainty: An activity in which the result is not surely available and difficult to be measured by any quantitative methodology.

Vagueness Factor: A measurement tool is to compute the uncertainty in any activity.

Chapter 4
Metaheuristic Algorithms for Supply Chain Management Problems

Ata Allah Taleizadeh
Iran University of Science and Technology, Iran

Leopoldo Eduardo Cárdenas-Barrón
Tecnológico de Monterrey, México

ABSTRACT

Recently, metaheuristic algorithms (MHAs) have gained noteworthy attention for their abilities to solve difficult optimization problems in engineering, business, economics, finance, and other fields. This chapter introduces some applications of MHAs in supply chain management (SCM) problems. For example, consider a multi-product multi-constraint SCM problem in which demands for each product are not deterministic, the lead-time varies linearly with regard to the lot-size and partial backordering of shortages are assumed. Thus, since the main goal is to determine the re-order point, the order quantity and number of shipments under the total cost of the whole chain is minimized. In this chapter, the authors concentrate on MHAs such as harmony search (HS), particle swarm optimization (PSO), genetic algorithm (GA), firefly algorithm (FA), and simulated annealing (SA) for solving the following four supply chain models: single-vendor single-buyer (SBSV), multi-buyers single-vendor (MBSV), multi-buyers multi-vendors (MBMV) and multi-objective multi-buyers multi-vendors (MOMBMV). These models typically are in any supply chain. For illustrative purposes, a numerical example is solved in each model.

DOI: 10.4018/978-1-4666-2086-5.ch004

INTRODUCTION

Always the companies have tried to design an effective and efficient business model where the main goal is to satisfy client needs better than competitors. Obviously, the success is determined by the design of systems that actually create and/or add value and with this the companies can be innovative. In nowadays companies should have always deliveries of products and services on time, with high quality, and at minimum cost. Those are some of the main issues that any client demands. As mangers attempt to accomplish these matters they often find that the enterprise lacks of needed resources and skills. Therefore, the managers are beginning to look more proactively beyond of the companies' walls to contemplate how resources of both suppliers and clients can be used to create and/or add value. Fawcett et al. (2007) mention that the efforts to align goals, share resources and collaborate across company boundaries are the essence and the challenge of the supply chain management.

A typical supply chain has several members and those are involved, directly or indirectly, in satisfying a customer request. The supply chain includes manufacturer, suppliers, transporters, warehouses, retailers, and even costumers themselves. In any organization (i.e. a manufacturer), its supply chain management should involve all functions from receiving until filling a costumer request.

According to Chopra and Meindl (2007) these functions are, but are not limited to, new product development, marketing, operations, distributions, finance and customer services.

This chapter will review four practical SCM problems. All of these problems involve uncertain demands for each product and variable delivery time due to the vendor. Some constraints such as budget, space and service level limitations are considered in the proposed models. These models are varied on the number of buyers, number of vendors and the nature of objective function.

The first one considers the simple chain which is the multi-product multi-constraint single-buyer single-vendor (SBSV). The second one deals with the multi-buyers single-vendor chain (MBSV). The third one contains a more complex chain which is comprised of multi-buyers multi-vendors (MBMV). Finally, the fourth model contains the previous one and considers three different objective functions: minimizing the total whole chain cost, minimizing lead-time and maximizing service level (MOMBMV). For most problems of practical dimensions, even though for the simple model SVSB, these models contains a large number of variables, making hard to find the optimal solution.

In the next section we will prepare a brief explanation about what we will discuss in this chapter.

BACKGROUND ON SUPPLY CHAIN

Supply chain management (SCM) has been an important research topic in the field of operations research over last two decades, and it has established into a notion that covers strategic, tactical and operational management issues.

In recent years, the companies realize a more effective and efficient management of inventories across the whole supply chain through a better coordination and more cooperation. In this direction, they are in the joint benefit of all members involved. For this reason, the joint single-buyer single-vendor (SBSV), which the simplest form of SCM problem, has received an extensive attention in the literature. Perhaps, Goyal (1977) was the first researcher in introducing the basic single-buyer single-vendor integrated inventory model. Later, Banerjee (1986) considers that the vendor plays the role of a manufacturer with a finite production rate and uses lot-sizing policy to satisfy buyer's requests as separate batches. Hill (1999) develops a SBSV with an unequal shipment policy and concludes that using shipment sizes which can be increased by a fixed factor in the beginning and then remaining constant after a well-specified number of shipments is an optimal policy for SBSV problem. Hariga and Ben-Daya (1999) develop a SBSV in which reorder point, order quantity, and lead time are the decision variables. Hsiao and Lin (2005) also investigate a SBSV where the vendor holds a monopolistic status and he or she not only owns cost information about the retailer but also has the decision making right of the lead time. For other instances of the SBSV we can refer to Goyal (1988), Goyal and Gupta (1989), and Lu (1995), just to name a few.

In the case of multi-buyers single-vendor (MBSV) supply chain problem we can refer to following researches. For example, Siajadi et al. (2006) investigate a joint replenishment policy in MBSV problem. Wee and Yang (2007) present an optimal pricing and replenishment policies for the MBSV. Centralized and decentralized adaptive inventory models for one supplier and multiple retailers are investigated by Kim et al. (2005). Su et al. (2008) develop a supply chain problem in which facilities produce raw material or final products that are shipped to other buyers. Heydari et al. (2009) study lead time variability in a serial connected supply chain considering four levels.

While both of the SBSV and MBSV supply chain problems have received a substantial attention in the literature, there is little (or no) effort in the literature for the multi-buyers multi-vendors (MBMV) problem. The best instance for this case can be found in the research work of Taleizadeh et al. (2011a). Their model deals with a multi-product multi-constraint MBMV supply chain problem with uncertain demand.

Many other researchers have studied the multi-objective optimization problems. Sabri and Beamon (2000) develop an integrated multi-objective model which considers simultaneously strategic and operational supply chain planning. Chen and Lee (2004) propose a multi-stage, multi-product, and multi-period scheduling model to deal with multi-objective with uncertain demands

rate and product prices. Altiparmak et al. (2006) present a SCM model to minimize the total cost and to maximize the service level and capacity utilization of the supply chain. Cárdenas-Barrón (2007) develops and optimizes a multi-stage supply chain with multiple buyers in each stage. Roghanian et al. (2007) develop a two-objective model to minimize the holding and the transportation cost in a supply chain problem. Xu and Zhao (2008) focus on the development of a fuzzy rough multi-objective decision-making model to maximize the profit and minimize the loss in the supply chain. Other researches on multi-objective problems can be found in Daniel and Rajendran (2005), Chern and Hsieh (2007), Azaron et al. (2008), and Sakall (2010).

BACKGROUND ON METAHEURISTIC ALGORITHMS

Since the proposed models are an integer nonlinear programming type, or multi objective integer nonlinear type, in order to solve them we will use some MHAs such as HS, PSO, GA, FA and SA techniques. These techniques are relatively new approaches to optimize supply chain models. One of the most important defining characteristic of MHAs is its capability to solve complex optimization problems. Different approaches for optimizing of an unconstrained optimization function of the basic inventory models can be found in Cárdenas-Barrón (2011). Now, we explain briefly each of the MHAs below. Basically, we present their origins and the main concepts in which they are based.

Harmony Search Algorithm (HS)

The HS algorithm is inspired in the act of musical groups. The HS algorithm was presented such as an analogy with music improvisation process where musicians in a band continue to polish their pitches to obtain a better harmony (see for instance Geem, 2001). There is a match among musical groups and HS algorithm. According to the similarity of improvisation and optimization processes, a fantastic harmony is the optimal global solution, the aesthetic is given by the objective function value, the pitches of instruments are the values for the decision variables, and each practice is equivalent to an each iteration of the algorithm. In order to solve the proposed examples we have used the harmony search of Taleizadeh et al. (2011b,c). The main steps of HS optimization algorithm include initialization (both parameter initialization and harmony memory initialization), new harmony generation and harmony memory (HM) update. For detailed information readers can see the related references such as Taleizadeh et al. (2011b) and Taleizadeh et al. (2011c).

Particle Swarm Optimization (PSO)

Kennedy and Eberhart (1995) have proposed the particle swarm optimization (PSO). In PSO, a set of solutions generated in a random fashion (initial swarm) spreads in the design space in the direction of the optimal solution through a number of iterations based on large amount of information about the design space that is assimilated and shared by all members of the swarm. PSO was inspired by the ability of flocks of birds, schools of fish and herds of animals to adapt to their environment quickly, finding rich sources of food and avoiding predators by implementing an information sharing approach; with this the species develops an evolutionary benefit (for instance see Kennedy and Eberhart 2001). Basically, the PSO algorithm has three main steps; generating particle's positions and exploration velocities, updating exploration velocity and position update.

Genetic Algorithm (GA)

Holland (1975) introduced the fundamental principle of genetic algorithms (GA) in 1975. Since then, many researchers have applied this concept in several fields of study. GA was inspired by the

concept of survival of the fittest. In GA, the best solution is the winner of the genetic game and any potential solution is assumed to be a creature that is determined by different parameters in a random fashion. In other words, GA uses a directed random search to locate good solutions for complex optimization problems. GA mimics the evolution process of the species that reproduce. Therefore the GA does not operate on a unique current solution, but on a set of current solutions called population. New individuals are generated according to a mechanism called crossover that combines part of the genetic patrimony of each parent and then applies a random mutation (Taleizadeh et al. 2009b). If the new individual (called child or offspring) inherits good characteristics from his parents the probability of its survival increases. This process will continue until a well defined stopping criterion is satisfied. Then, the best individual is chosen as a near optimum solution. Interesting works on applications of GA in inventory can be read in Taleizadeh et al. (2009a,b).

Firefly Algorithm (FA)

Firefly algorithm was inspired by the social behavior of fireflies and it was introduced by Yang (2008). FA has been used in a huge diversity of applications spanning the permutation flow shop scheduling problem, codebook design of image vector quantization and financial portfolio optimization, among others. Due to the fact of its power in solving optimization problems, we have used this algorithm in supply chain problems too. According to Yang (2009), the FA is based on three idealized laws: (1) All fireflies are unisex. In other words, one firefly is attracted to other fireflies regardless of their sex. (2) The degree of attractiveness of a firefly is proportional to its brightness, thus for any two fireflies, the bright one will go towards the brighter one. The less distance between two fireflies gives more brightness and attractiveness. If no firefly is brighter, then the firefly will move randomly. (3) The brightness of a firefly is given by the objective function value. For a maximization problem, the brightness can be proportional to the objective function value. In order to have additional information about FA algorithm readers can see the works of Sayadi et al. (2010), Yang (2008) and Yang (2009).

Simulated Annealing (SA)

Simulated annealing (SA) is a local search algorithm and it was inspired in the physical annealing process studied in statistical mechanics. According to Kirkpatrick et al. (1994) the SA is an effective and efficient algorithm that produces very good solutions. The SA algorithm does an iterative neighbor generation process and follows different search directions in order to improve the objective function value. The SA algorithm allows worse neighbor solutions in a controlled way in order to jump from local optimum and find a better solution. In order to have more detailed information, the readers can see Aarts and Korst (1989), Kirkpatrick et al. (1994), and Taleizadeh et al. (2008).

SUPPLY CHAIN MANAGEMENT

It is well known that the supply chain management is a set of tools for efficiently integrate suppliers, manufactures, warehouses, and stores. Where this integration searches that the goods manufactured being distributed at the right quantities, to the right locations, and at right time in order to satisfy the service level requirements with a minimal total whole chain cost (Simchi-Levi et al. 2008). As it was mentioned previously, we want to discuss several kinds of supply chain problems which are different according to the number of buyers, vendors and objective functions. In the following subsections SBSV, MBSV, MBMV and MOMBMV supply chain models will be studied. The main assumptions, which are used in our all proposed models, are well be defined in the next sections.

Most supply chain problems in practice involve multi products and multi constraints. For example, any store manages hundreds of thousands of different products with limited resources such as space, budget, service level, number of orders, among others. Here, we consider a supply chain system with multiproduct and multi-constraint in which (r,Q) inventory control policy is used to manage the system. In this supply chain system the demand rate of each product is a random variable that follows a uniform distribution function. The lead time (the length of time since the order is placed till receiving products by buyer) is assumed that changes linearly with regard to the order quantity of each buyer ordered to the vendor. Also, partial backordering policy is allowed for each buyer. In other words, if a customer faces to the shortages then a given constant fraction of them will leave him and remain quantity will wait to give their required products. Additionally, the supply chain system includes several limitations. One of them is service level constraint for each buyer, meaning the probability of facing his customers to shortages should be less than a predefined value. Another one is warehouse capacity limitation of vendor. This constraint causes that the vendor will not be able to manufacture what much he or she desires. A budget limitation for buyer and placing orders in multiple of packets are other restrictions of the supply chain system. Obviously, these constraints affect to all decision variables. The proposed supply chain models tend to answer real world decisions that include re-order point(where the inventory level reaches to that point the buyer should place the order), order size, and number of shipments from the vendors to the buyers. The vendor inventory graph is shown in Figure 1.

Single-Buyer Single-Vendor (SBSV) Model

This section presents the SBSV supply chain problem. It should be noted that i refers to the number of products. Equations (1), (2) and (3)

Figure 1. The vendor's inventory behavior

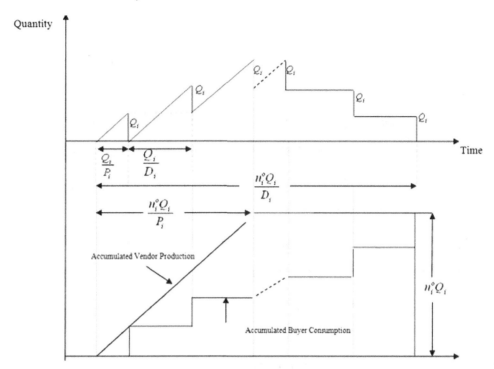

show the objective function of buyer, vendor and the whole chain respectively. The formulation of this model is due to Taleizadeh et al. (2010a) (see Box 1 and 2 for Equations (1) and (2)).

The problem is then to minimize

$$TC_1(c) = TC_1(b) + TC_1(v) \qquad (3)$$

Subject to (see Box 3 for Equation (6)):

$$\sum_{i=1}^{p} C_i n_i M_i \leq TB \qquad (4)$$

$$Q_i = n_i M_i; \\ \forall i; \ i = 1, 2, \cdots, p \qquad (5)$$

$$n_i^o, r_i, M_i \geq 0 \ Integer; \\ \forall i; \ i = 1, 2, \cdots, p \qquad (7)$$

Where the notations are:
Parameters:

- p number of products
- D_i the expected demand quantity of the buyer for i^{th} product
- $f_{D_i}(D_i)$ Probability density function of D_i. The D_i follows a uniform density function with parameters D_i^{Min} and D_i^{Max}
- A_i The ordering cost per order of the ith product
- A_i^t The buyer transportation cost per shipment of the ith product from vendor
- A_i^p The vendor production cost per setup of the ith product
- n_i Number of ith product in each packet from vendor to buyer
- h_i^b The buyer's holding cost per unit per unit time of the ith product
- h_i^v The vendor's holding cost per unit per unit time of the ith product

Box 1.

$$TC_1(b) = \sum_{i=1}^{p} \frac{D_i A_i}{n_i^o n_i M_i} + \sum_{i=1}^{p} h_i^b \left[\frac{n_i M_i}{2} + r_i - D_i \left(\frac{n_i M_i}{P_i} + \gamma_i \right) + \frac{\left(1 - \beta_i\right)\left(D_i^{Max} - r_i\right)^2}{2\left(D_i^{Max} - D_i^{Min}\right)} \right]$$
$$+ \sum_{i=1}^{p} \frac{\left(\pi_i \beta_i + \hat{\pi}_i \left(1 - \beta_i\right)\right) D_i \left(D_i^{Max} - r_i\right)^2}{2 n_i^o n_i M_i \left(D_i^{Max} - D_i^{Min}\right)} + \sum_{i=1}^{p} \frac{D_i}{n_i M_i} A_i^t \qquad (1)$$

Box 2.

$$TC_1(v) = \sum_{i=1}^{p} \frac{D_i A_i^p}{n_i^o n_i M_i} + \sum_{i=1}^{p} h_i^v \frac{n_i M_i}{2} \left[n_i^o \left(1 - \frac{D_i}{P_i} \right) - 1 + \frac{2 D_i}{P_i} \right] \qquad (2)$$

Box 3.

$$r_i \geq \left(\frac{n_i M_i}{P_i} + \gamma_i \right) \left[\left(D_i^{Max} - D_i^{Min} \right) SL_i + \left(D_i^{Min} \right) \right] \qquad \forall i; \; i = 1, 2, \cdots, p \qquad (6)$$

- γ_i A fixed delay due to transportation, production time of other products scheduled during the lead time
- P_i Production rate of the ith product $P_i > D_i$
- β_i Percentage of unsatisfied demands of the ith product that is backordered
- π_i Backordering cost per unit of the ith product
- $\hat{\pi}_i$ Shortage cost per unit of the ith product that is lost sale
- SL_i The service level lower limit for i^{th} product
- C_i The purchasing price per unit of the ith product
- TB The buyer's total available budget
- Q_i amount of the for i^{th} product ordered by the jth buyer to the vendor

Decision variables:

- n_i^o Number of shipments of the ith product from the vendor to buyer
- M_i Number of packets of the ith product ordered by the buyer to the vendor
- r_i Reorder point of the ith product for the buyer

Equation (4) imposes budget restriction for the buyer. Equation (5) shows the batch ordering constraint which forces the size of the order to be multiplier of predefined values. Equation (6) represents the service level constraint, meaning in order to be sure that SL_i percent of demand will be satisfied then the reorder point should be greater than the right hand side of the inequality. Finally Equation (7) establishes that the decision variables are nonnegative and discrete. It is important to note that the warehouse limitation for the vendor is not considered in this model. Since this mathematical model is an integer nonlinear programming type, reaching an analytical solution (if any) to the problem is difficult (Taleizadeh et al. 2010a). In order to solve it, PSO of Taleizadeh et al. (2010a), GA and SA Algorithms of Taleizadeh et al. (2010b) are employed. Below, we present the pseudo codes of the PSO, GA and SA algorithms:

The pseudo code for PSO algorithm is:

```
Repeat:
For each particle
1. Update the velocities.
2. Update the positions.
3. Evaluate its fitness value accord-
ing to the desired optimization fit-
ness
4. Update best global value and best
position of each particle over time
if necessary.
End: When the criterion is met, or
when a maximum number of iterations
is reached
```

The pseudo code for GA algorithm is:

```
1. Set the parameters P_c, P_m, and N.
2. Initialize the population random-
ly.
3. Evaluate the objective function
for all chromosomes based on objec-
tive function.
4. Select individual for mating pool.
5. Apply the crossover operation for
each pair of chromosomes with prob-
ability P_c.
6. Apply mutation operation for each
chromosome with probability P_m.
7. Replace the current population by
the resulting mating pool.
8. Evaluate the objective function.
9. If stopping criteria is met, then
stop. Otherwise, go to step 5.
```

Where P_c, P_m, and N are probability of crossover, probability of mutation and population size respectively.

The pseudo code for SA algorithm is:

```
1. Choose an initial solution i from
the group of feasible solutions S.
2. Choose the initial temperature
T_0 > 0.
3. Select the number of iterations
N(t) at each temperature.
4. Select the final temperature T_F.
5. Determine the process of the
temperature reduction until it reach-
es T_F.
6. Set the temperature exchange
counter n to zero for each tempera-
ture.
7. Create the j solution at the
neighborhood of the i solution.
8. Evaluate the objective function
f = Z at any temperature and calcu-
late Δ = f(j) − f(i).
9. Accept the solution j, if Δ < 0.
Otherwise, generate a random number
RN ~ Uniform(0,1) . If  RN < e^(−Δ/T_0) then
select the j solution.
10. Set n = n + 1. If n is equal to
N(t) then go to 12. Otherwise, go to
7.
11. Reduce the temperature. If it
reaches T_F then stop. Otherwise, go
to 6.
```

Where T_0, T_F, and $N(t)$ are initial temperature, final temperature and number of iterations at each temperature.

Table 1 shows the best values obtained for the numerical example used in Taleizadeh et al. (2010a) through the three different methods: PSO, GA and SA.

A comparison of the results in Table 1 shows that the PSO algorithm performs better than the GA and SA algorithms in terms of the objective function values. Also, Figure 2 shows the convergence path of the PSO method.

Multi-Buyer Single-Vendor (MBSV) Model

In addition to the assumptions of SBSV model, now we consider multi buyer situation. In this supply chain model the orders of each product from each buyer to vendor are placed in multiples of the batch size. Furthermore, the budget limitation is considered for each buyer. It should be noted that $i = 1, 2, ..., p$ and $i = 1, 2, ..., p$ refer to the number of products and buyers, respectively.

Equations (8), (9) and (10) show the objective function of buyer, vendor and the whole chain respectively. The formulation of this model is due to Taleizadeh et al. (2012). (refer to Box 4 for Equation (8)).

$$TC_2(v) = \sum_{j=1}^{n}\sum_{i=1}^{P} \frac{D_{ij}A_i^P}{n_{ij}^v n_i M_{ij}} + \sum_{j=1}^{n}\sum_{i=1}^{P} h_i^v \frac{n_i M_{ij}}{2}[n_{ij}^v(1-\frac{D_{ij}}{P_i})-1+\frac{2D_{ij}}{P_i}] \quad (9)$$

Thus the problem is to minimize

$$TC_2(c) = TC_2(b) + TC_2(v) \quad (10)$$

Table 1. Best results of example of SBSV case by the three different algorithms

Hybrid algorithms	Minimum cost of buyer ($)	Minimum cost of vendor ($)	Minimum cost of whole chain ($)
Particle swarm optimization	182,400	71,540	253,940
Genetic algorithm	201,152	67,220	268,372
Simulated annealing	240,620	62,660	303,280

Figure 2. Convergence path of PSO method for SBSV model

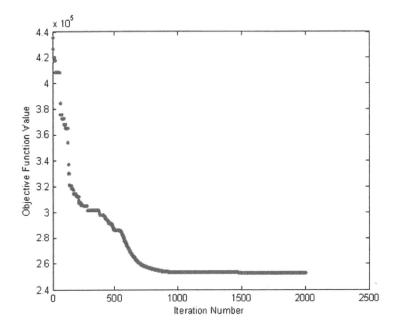

Box 4.

$$TC_2(b) = \sum_{j=1}^{n}\sum_{i=1}^{p}\frac{D_{ij}A_i}{n_{ij}^o n_i M_{ij}} + \sum_{j=1}^{n}\sum_{i=1}^{p}\frac{(\pi_{ij}\beta_{ij} + \hat{\pi}_{ij}(1-\beta_{ij}))D_{ij}(D_{ij}^{Max}-r_{ij})^2}{2n_{ij}^o n_i M_{ij}(D_{ij}^{Max}-D_{ij}^{Min})} + \sum_{j=1}^{n}\sum_{i=1}^{p}\frac{D_{ij}}{n_i M_{ij}}A_{ij}^t$$
$$+ \sum_{j=1}^{n}\sum_{i=1}^{p}h_{ij}^b[\frac{n_i M_{ij}}{2}+r_{ij}-D_{ij}(\frac{n_i M_{ij}}{P_i}+\gamma_{ij})+\frac{(1-\beta_{ij})(D_{ij}^{Max}-r_{ij})^2}{2(D_{ij}^{Max}-D_{ij}^{Min})}]$$

(8)

Subject to:

$$\sum_{i=1}^{p}C_i n_i M_{ij} \le TB_j;$$
$$\forall j; \quad j=1,2,\cdots,n$$
(11)

$$Q_{ij}=n_i M_{ij};$$
$$\forall i; \quad i=1,2,\cdots,p;$$
$$\forall j; \quad j=1,2,\cdots,n$$
(12)

$$r_{ij} \ge (\frac{n_i M_{ij}}{P_i}+\gamma_{ij})[(D_{ij}^{Max}-D_{ij}^{Min})SL_{ij}+(D_{ij}^{Min})];$$
$$\forall i; \quad i=1,2,\cdots,p \quad \forall j; \quad j=1,2,\cdots,n$$
(13)

$$\sum_{j=1}^{n}\sum_{i=1}^{p}f_i\frac{n_i M_{ij}}{2}[n_{ij}^o(1-\frac{D_{ij}}{P_i})-1+2\frac{D_{ij}}{P_i}] \le F;$$
$$\forall j; \quad j=1,2,\cdots,n$$
(14)

$$n_{ij}^o, r_{ij}, M_{ij} \ge 0 \; Integer;$$
$$\forall i; \quad i=1,2,\cdots,p;$$
$$\forall j; \quad j=1,2,\cdots,n$$
(15)

Where the nomenclature is:
Parameters:

- p number of products

- D_{ij} the expected demand quantity of the jth buyer for i^{th} product
- $f_{D_{ij}}(D_{ij})$ Probability density function of D_{ij}. The D_{ij} follows a uniform density function with parameters D_{ij}^{Min} and D_{ij}^{Max}
- A_i The ordering cost per order of the ith product
- A_{ij}^t The jth buyer's transportation cost per shipment of the ith product from vendor
- A_i^p The vendor production cost per setup of the ith product
- n_i Number of ith product in each packet from vendor to buyer
- h_{ij}^b The jth buyer's holding cost per unit per unit time of the ith product
- h_i^v The vendor's holding cost per unit per unit time of the ith product
- γ_{ij} A fixed delay due to transportation, production time of other products scheduled during the lead time
- P_i Production rate of the ith product $P_i > D_i$
- β_{ij} Percentage of unsatisfied demands of the ith product of the jth buyer that is backordered
- π_{ij} Backordering cost per unit of the ith product for the jth buyer
- $\hat{\pi}_{ij}$ Shortage cost per unit of the ith product of the jth buyer that is lost sale

- SL_{ij} the service level lower limit for ith product for jth buyer
- C_i The purchasing price per unit of the ith product
- TB_j The jth buyer's total available budget
- Q_{ij} amount of the for ith product ordered by the jth buyer to the vendor
- f_i the space required per unit of ith product
- F Total available warehouse space of the vendor

Decision variables:

- n_{ij}^o Number of shipments of the ith product from the vendor to the jth buyer
- M_{ij} Number of packets of the ith product ordered by the jth buyer to the vendor
- r_{ij} Reorder point of the ith product for the jth buyer

As same as the previous supply chain model, Equation (11) shows the budget constraint of jth buyer. Equation (12) expresses the batch ordering constraint which forces the order of jth buyer for i^{th} item to be multiplier of predefined values. Equation (13) represents the service level constraint, meaning in order to be sure that SL_{ij} percent of demand will be satisfied the reorder point of ith item for j^{th} buyer should be greater than the right hand side of the inequality. Equation (14) is the warehouse constraint of single vendor and finally Equation (15) establishes that the decision

variables are nonnegative and discrete. Again, this mathematical model is an integer nonlinear programming type. Finding the optimal solution to this type of problem by an exact method is difficult (Taleizadeh et al. 2010a). In order to solve it, PSO and GA of Taleizadeh et al. (2012) and SA of Taleizadeh et al. (2010b) are used. It should be noted the pseudo codes which we have reported before for the single-vendor single-buyer case are used for multi-buyer single-vendor case too.

Table 2 shows the best values obtained for the numerical example used form Taleizadeh et al. (2012) through the three different methods.

According to the results in Table 2 the PSO algorithm performs better than the GA and SA algorithms in terms of the objective function values. Also, Figure 3 shows the convergence path of PSO method.

Multi-Buyer Multi-Vendor (MBMV) Model

This supply chain model contains the previous one considering the multi-vendor case. In addition to the assumptions of previous one, warehouse limitation is considered for each vendor. It should be noted that $i = 1, 2, ..., p$, $j = 1, 2, ..., n$, and $k = 1, 2, ..., K$ refer to the number of products, buyers and vendors respectively.

In this case Equations (16), (17) and (18) show the objective function of buyer, vendor and whole chain respectively. The formulation of this model is due to Taleizadeh et al. (2011a) (refer to Box 5 and 6 for Equations 16 and 17).

Now, the problem is to minimize

Table 2. Best results of example of MBSV model by the three different algorithms

Hybrid algorithms	Minimum cost of buyers ($)	Minimum cost of vendor ($)	Minimum cost of whole chain ($)
Particle swarm optimization	796,660	210,350	1,007,010
Genetic algorithm	859,690	215,520	1,079,200
Simulated annealing	906,250	226,210	1,132,460

Figure 3. Convergence path of PSO method for MBSV mode

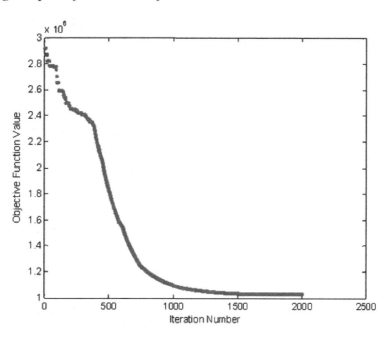

Box 5.

$$TC_3(b) = \sum_{k=1}^{K}\sum_{j=1}^{n}\sum_{i=1}^{p} \frac{D_{ijk}A_{ik}}{n_{ijk}^o n_i M_{ijk}} + \sum_{j=1}^{n}\sum_{i=1}^{p} h_{ij}^b \left[\frac{\dfrac{\sum\limits_{k=1}^{K} n_i M_{ijk}}{2} + r_{ij} - \sum\limits_{k=1}^{K} D_{ijk}\left(\dfrac{n_i M_{ijk}}{P_{ik}} + \gamma_{ijk}\right)}{} + \frac{(1-\beta_{ij})(\sum\limits_{k=1}^{K} D_{ijk}^{Max} - r_{ij})^2}{2\left(\sum\limits_{k=1}^{K}(D_{ijk}^{Max} - D_{ijk}^{Min})\right)} \right]$$

$$+ \sum_{j=1}^{n}\sum_{i=1}^{p} \frac{(\pi_{ij}\beta_{ij} + \hat{\pi}_{ij}(1-\beta_{ij}))\sum\limits_{k=1}^{K} D_{ijk}(\sum\limits_{k=1}^{K} D_{ijk}^{Max} - r_{ij})^2}{2\sum\limits_{k=1}^{K} n_{ijk}^o n_i M_{ijk}\left(\sum\limits_{k=1}^{K}(D_{ijk}^{Max} - D_{ijk}^{Min})\right)} + \sum_{k=1}^{K}\sum_{j=1}^{n}\sum_{i=1}^{p} \frac{D_{ijk}}{n_i M_{ijk}} A_{ijk}^t \qquad (16)$$

Box 6.

$$TC_3(v) = \sum_{k=1}^{K}\sum_{j=1}^{n}\sum_{i=1}^{p} \frac{D_{ijk}A_{ik}^p}{n_{ijk}^o n_i M_{ijk}} + \sum_{k=1}^{K}\sum_{j=1}^{n}\sum_{i=1}^{p} h_{ik}^v \frac{n_i M_{ijk}}{2}\left[n_{ijk}^o\left(1 - \frac{D_{ijk}}{P_{ik}}\right) - 1 + \frac{2D_{ijk}}{P_{ik}} \right] \qquad (17)$$

$$TC_3(c) = TC_3(b) + TC_3(v) \qquad (18)$$

Subject to (see Box 7 and 8 for Equations (21) and (22)):

$$\sum_{i=1}^{p} \sum_{k=1}^{K} C_i n_i M_{ijk} \leq TB_j;$$
$$\forall j; \quad j = 1, 2, \cdots, n \qquad (19)$$

$$Q_{ijk} = n_i M_{ijk};$$
$$\forall i; \quad i = 1, 2, \cdots, p;$$
$$\forall j; \quad j = 1, 2, \cdots, n; \qquad (20)$$
$$\forall k; \quad k = 1, 2, \cdots, K$$

$$n_{ijk}^o, r_{ij}, M_{ijk} \geq 0 \; Integer;$$
$$\forall i \quad i = 1, 2, \cdots, p;$$
$$\forall j; \quad j = 1, 2, \cdots, n; \qquad (23)$$
$$\forall k; \quad k = 1, 2, \cdots, K$$

Where the nomenclature is:
Parameters:

- p number of products

- D_{ijk} the expected demand quantity of the jth buyer for ith product to the kth vendor

- $f_{D_{ijk}}(D_{ijk})$ Probability density function of D_{ijk}. The D_{ijk} follows a uniform density function with parameters D_{ijk}^{Min} and D_{ijk}^{Max}

- A_{ik} The ordering cost per order of the ith product to the kth vendor

- A_{ijk}^t The jth buyer's transportation cost per shipment of the ith product from the kth vendor

- A_{ik}^p The kth vendor's production cost per setup of the ith product

- n_i Number of ith product in each packet from vendor to buyer

- h_{ij}^b The jth buyer's holding cost per unit per unit time of the ith product

- h_{ik}^v The kth vendor's holding cost per unit per unit time of the ith product

- γ_{ijk} A fixed delay due to transportation, production time of other products scheduled during the lead time

- P_{ik} Production rate of the ith product to kth vendor

- β_{ij} Percentage of unsatisfied demands of the ith product of the jth buyer that is backordered

Box 7.

$$r_{ij} \geq \left[\sum_{k=1}^{K} \left(\frac{n_i M_{ijk}}{P_{ik}} + \gamma_{ijk} \right) (D_{ijk}^{Max} - D_{ijk}^{Min}) \right] SL_{ij} + \sum_{k=1}^{K} D_{ijk}^{Min} \left(\frac{n_i M_{ijk}}{P_{ik}} + \gamma_{ijk} \right) \qquad (21)$$
$$\forall i; \quad i = 1, 2, \cdots, p \qquad \forall j; \quad j = 1, 2, \cdots, n$$

Box 8.

$$\sum_{j=1}^{n} \sum_{i=1}^{p} f_i \left(\frac{n_i M_{ijk}}{2} \left[n_{ijk}^o (1 - \frac{D_{ijk}}{P_{ik}}) - 1 + 2 \frac{D_{ijk}}{P_{ik}} \right] \right) \leq F_k; \qquad (22)$$
$$\forall k; \quad k = 1, 2, \cdots, K$$

- π_{ij} Backordering cost per unit of the ith product for the jth buyer
- $\hat{\pi}_{ij}$ Shortage cost per unit of the ith product of the jth buyer that is lost sale
- SL_{ij} the service level lower limit for ith product for jth buyer
- C_i The purchasing price per unit of the ith product
- TB_j The jth buyer's total available budget
- Q_{ijk} amount of the for ith product ordered by the jth buyer to the kth vendor
- f_i the space required per unit of ith product
- F_k Total available warehouse space of the kth vendor

Decision variables:

- n_{ijk}^o Number of shipments of the ith product from the kth vendor to the jth buyer
- M_{ijk} Number of packets of the ith product ordered by the jth buyer to the kth vendor
- r_{ij} Reorder point of the ith product for the jth buyer

Like Equation (11), Equation (19) expresses the budget constraint of jth buyer. Equation (20) shows the batch ordering constraint which forces the order of jth buyer for i^{th} item to to k^{th} vendor to be a multiplier of predefined values. The description of Equation (21) is as same as Equation (13).

Equation (22) represents the warehouse constraint of kth vendor and finally Equation (23) establishes that the decision variables are nonnegative and discrete. Like two previous supply chain models, this model is an integer nonlinear programming problem, and it is no easy to solve it by an exact method (Taleizadeh et al. 2010a). In order to solve it, HS of Taleizadeh et al. (2011a) and GA and SA of Taleizadeh et al. (2010b) are used. Also, it should be noted that GA and SA previously defined for the single-vendor single-buyer case are used for multi-buyer multi-vendor case too. Additionally, the pseudo code for HS algorithm is as follows:

```
1. Initialize both the parameters and
the HS algorithm HM.
2. Suggest a new vector X'. For each
com x'_i :
With probability HMCR, a small
change is made to x'_i.
With probability 1-HMCR, pick a new
random value within the allowable
range.
3. Pitch adjustment: For each compo-
nent x'_i :
     With probability PAR, a small
change is made to x'_i.
     With probability 1-PAR, do noth-
ing.
4. If X' is better than the worst
X^j in the memory, 1 − HMCR then
replace X^j by X'.
5. Go to step 2 until a maximum
```

Table 3. Best results of example of MBMV case by the three different algorithms

Hybrid algorithms	Minimum cost of buyers ($)	Minimum cost of vendors ($)	Minimum cost of whole chain ($)
Harmony search algorithm	1,287,022	312,300	1,599,322
Genetic algorithm	1,334,530	329,540	1,664,070
Simulated annealing	1,394,240	341,450	1,740,230

Figure 4. Convergence path of HS method for MBMV model

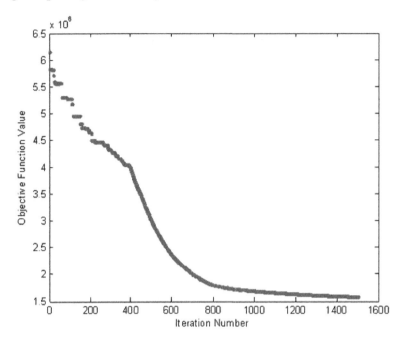

number of iterations has been reached.

Table 3 shows the best values obtained for the numerical example used form Taleizadeh et al. (2011a) through the three different methods.

Table 3 shows the HS algorithm performs better than the GA and SA algorithms in terms of the objective function values. Also Figure 4 shows the convergence path of HS method.

Multi Objective Multi-Buyer Multi-Vendor (MOMBMV) Model

In this case we will develop a multi-product multi-constraint multi-objective multi buyer and multi-vendor model. The objectives are minimizing the total whole chain cost, minimizing lead-time and maximizing the service levels. It should be noted that as same as the MBMV case $i = 1, 2, ..., p$, $j = 1, 2, ..., n$, and $k = 1, 2, ..., K$ refer to the number of products, buyers and vendors respectively. Obviously, the first objective function

which is minimizing the total cost of whole chain is the same as the Equation (18). This is shown again in Equation (24). So the lead time and service level objective functions are expressed in Equations (25) and (26) respectively.

$$TC_3(c) = TC_3(b) + TC_3(v) \qquad (24)$$

$$LT(c) = \sum_{k=1}^{K}\sum_{j=1}^{n}\sum_{i=1}^{p} \frac{n_{ijk}M_{ijk}}{P_{ijk}} \qquad (25)$$

$$SL(c) = \sum_{j=1}^{n}\sum_{i=1}^{p} \frac{r_{ij} - \sum_{k=1}^{K}\frac{D_{ijk}n_{ijk}M_{ijk}}{P_{ik}}}{\sum_{k=1}^{K}\frac{n_{ijk}M_{ijk}}{P_{ik}}\left(D_{ijk}^{Max} - D_{ijk}^{Min}\right)} \qquad (26)$$

In this supply chain model, the service level constraint shown in equation (21) is removed and is considered as an objective function shown in Equation (26). The other constraints are as same as the MBMV model. The proposed model will be solved by a novel hybrid method (a hybrid of meta goal programming (MGP) and firefly algorithm (FA)) and compared to other hybrid methods of meta goal programming with algorithms such as particle swarm optimization (PSO), genetic algorithm (GA) and simulated annealing (SA). Again, it should be noted the pseudo codes of PSO, GA and SA which we have reported before for are used also for multi-objective multi-buyer multi-vendor case. The pseudo code of the firefly algorithm is as follows:

```
Objective function f(x),
x = (x₁, x₂, ..., x_d)ᵀ
Initialize a population of fireflies
x_i (i = 1, 2, ..., n)
Define light absorption coefficient γ
While (t < Max Generation)
        for i = 1: n all n fire-
flies
        for j = 1: i all n fire-
flies
            Light intensity I_i at x_i
is determined by f(x_i)
        if I_j > I_i
            Move firefly i towards j
in all d dimensions
        end if
            Attractiveness varies with
distance r via exp −γr²
            Evaluate new solutions and
update light intensity
end for j
end for i
Rank the fireflies and find the
current best
end while
Postprocess results and visualization
```

Table 4. Best results of example of MOMBMV case by four different algorithms

Hybrid algorithms	Minimum cost of whole chain ($)	Minimum lead time	Maximum service level (Percent)
Firefly algorithm	967,579	2.8040	0.9346
Particle swarm optimization	976,550	2.8655	0.9304
Genetic algorithm	991,256	2.8480	0.9187
Simulated annealing	1,261,130	2.9085	0.9235

Table 5. Number of constraints and variables in different situations

MBMV		MBSV		SBSV		Number of
225	$3npk$	75	$3np$	15	$3p$	Total variables
5	n	5	n	1	1	Budget Constraint
75	npk	25	np	5	p	Batch order Constraint
25	np	25	np	5	p	Service Level constraint
3	k	1	1	0	0	Warehouse Constraint
108	$n(1 + p(1 + k)) + k$	56	$n(1 + 2p) + 1$	11	$2p+1$	Total Constraints

The best values obtained for the numerical example used form Taleizadeh et al. (2011e) through the four different methods are shown in Table 4. For the MOMBMV model, the results of Table 4 shows the FA method performs better than the PSO, GA and SA algorithms in terms of the objective function values.

Finally, Table 5 shows the numbers of the variables and constraints in the SBSV, MBSV and MBMV supply chain models that were dealt in this chapter based on the number of products $p=5$, the number of buyers $n=5$ and the number of vendors $k=3$.

FUTURE RESEARCH

In spite of the four supply chain models and their solutions approaches presented in this chapter, there is a need for exploring another techniques and also develop other supply chain models that support inventory decisions in more complex environments. Thus, we note some areas with potential for future research. Roughly speaking, the solutions for the numerical examples are not optimal; they are near optimal. Hence, first we suggest extend the solution method considering some other Metaheuristic algorithms such as tabu search, memetic algorithm, differential evolution, ant colony and bees colony optimization. Second, another research direction that could be considered is to solve the MOMBMV model via hybrid MHAs such hybrid method of PSO and GA or other combinations may improve the quality of results. Third, one of the limitations of the proposed supply chain models is that the four models have only two stages. Therefore, it would be useful to develop and optimize a multi-stage supply chain with multiple members in each stage. Fourth, it would be interesting to consider delay in payments or discounts, imperfect products, deteriorating items, full backordering, among others aspects.

CONCLUSION

This chapter introduces some applications of MHAs in supply chain management problems. We consider a multi-product multi-constraint SCM problem in which the demand of each product is not deterministic, lead-time varies linearly with regard to the lot-size and partial backordering shortage is assumed. The main goal is to determine the re-order point, the order quantity and number of shipments under which the whole chain total cost is minimized. Four different supply chain models including: single-vendor single-buyer (SBSV), multi-buyer single vendor (MBSV), multi-buyer multi-vendor (MBMV) and multi-objective multi-buyer multi-vendor (MOMBMV) cases are investigated. These supply chain models are non linear mixed integer programming problem of great size and complexity. Also, some MHAs such as Harmony Search (HS), Particle Swarm Optimization (PSO), Genetic Algorithm (GA), Firefly Algorithm (FA), and Simulated Annealing (SA) are used to solve one numerical example in each proposed model. For the first and second models, PSO method performs better than GA and SA techniques and for the third model HS method performs better than GA and SA algorithms. Finally, for the MOMBMV model FA obtains the best results respect to the PSO, GA and SA algorithms.

REFERENCES

Aarts, E. H. L., & Korst, J. H. M. (1989). *Simulated annealing and Boltzmann machine: A stochastic approach to computing.* Chichester, UK: John Wiley and Sons.

Altiparmak, F., Gen, M., Lin, L., & Paksoy, T. (2006). A genetic algorithm approach for multi-objective optimization of supply chain networks. *Computers & Industrial Engineering, 51*, 196–215. doi:10.1016/j.cie.2006.07.011doi:10.1016/j.cie.2006.07.011

Azaron, A., Brown, K. N., Tarim, S. A., & Modarres, M. (2008). A multi-objective stochastic programming approach for supply chain design considering risk. *International Journal of Production Economics, 116*, 129–138. doi:10.1016/j.ijpe.2008.08.002doi:10.1016/j.ijpe.2008.08.002

Banerjee, A. (1986). A joint economic lot size model for purchaser and vendor. *Decision Sciences, 17*, 292–311. doi:10.1111/j.1540-5915.1986.tb00228.xdoi:10.1111/j.1540-5915.1986.tb00228.x

Cárdenas-Barrón, L. E. (2007). Optimizing inventory decisions in a multi-stage multi-customer supply chain: A note. *Transportation Research Part E, Logistics and Transportation Review, 43*, 647–654. doi:10.1016/j.tre.2005.09.011doi:10.1016/j.tre.2005.09.011

Cárdenas-Barrón, L. E. (2011). The derivation of EOQ/EPQ inventory models with two backorders costs using analytic geometry and algebra. *Applied Mathematical Modelling, 35*, 2394–2407. doi:10.1016/j.apm.2010.11.053doi:10.1016/j.apm.2010.11.053

Chen, C. L., & Lee, W. C. (2004). Multi-objective optimization of multi-echelon supply chain networks with uncertain product demands and prices. *Computers & Chemical Engineering, 28*, 1131–1144. doi:10.1016/j.compchemeng.2003.09.014doi:10.1016/j.compchemeng.2003.09.014

Chern, C. C., & Hsieh, J. S. (2007). A heuristic algorithm for master planning that satisfies multiple objectives. *Computers & Operations Research, 34*, 3491–3513. doi:10.1016/j.cor.2006.02.022doi:10.1016/j.cor.2006.02.022

Chopra, S., & Meindl, P. (2007). *Supply chain management strategy, planning & operation* (3rd ed.). Prentice-Hall of India.

Daniel, J. S. R., & Rajendran, C. (2005). Heuristic approaches to determine base-stock levels in a serial supply chain with a single objective and with multiple objectives. *European Journal of Operational Research, 175*, 566–592. doi:10.1016/j.ejor.2005.04.039doi:10.1016/j.ejor.2005.04.039

Fawcett, S. E., Ellram, L. M., & Ogden, J. A. (2007). *Supply chain management from vision to implementation*. New Jersey, USA: Prentice-Hall.

Geem, Z. W., Kim, J. H., & Loganathan, G. V. (2001). A new heuristic optimization algorithm: Harmony search. *Simulation, 76*, 60–68. doi:10.1177/003754970107600201doi:10.1177/003754970107600201

Goyal, S. K. (1977). An integrated inventory model for a single supplier-single customer problem. *International Journal of Production Research, 15*, 107–111. doi:10.1080/00207547708943107doi:10.1080/00207547708943107

Goyal, S. K. (1988). Joint economic lot size model for purchaser and vendor: A comment. *Decision Sciences, 19*, 236–241. doi:10.1111/j.1540-5915.1988.tb00264.xdoi:10.1111/j.1540-5915.1988.tb00264.x

Goyal, S. K., & Gupta, Y. P. (1989). Integrated inventory models: The vendor–buyer coordination. *European Journal of Operational Research, 41*, 261–269. doi:10.1016/0377-2217(89)90247-6doi:10.1016/0377-2217(89)90247-6

Hariga, M., & Ben-Daya, M. (1999). Some stochastic inventory models with deterministic variable lead time. *European Journal of Operational Research*, *113*, 42–51. doi:10.1016/S0377-2217(97)00441-4doi:10.1016/S0377-2217(97)00441-4

Heydari, J., Baradaran-Kazemzadeh, R., & Chaharsooghi, S. K. (2009). A study of lead time variation impact on supply chain performance. *International Journal of Advanced Manufacturing Technology*, *40*, 1206–1215. doi:10.1007/s00170-008-1428-2doi:10.1007/s00170-008-1428-2

Hill, R. (1999). The optimal production and shipment policy for the single-vendor single-buyer integrated production–inventory problem. *International Journal of Production Research*, *37*, 2463–2475. doi:10.1080/002075499190617 doi:10.1080/002075499190617

Holland, J. H. (1975). *Adoption in neural and artificial systems*. Ann Arbor, MI: The University of Michigan Press.

Hsiao, J. M., & Lin, C. (2005). A buyer-vendor EOQ model with changeable lead time in supply chain. *International Journal of Advanced Manufacturing Technology*, *26*, 917–921. doi:10.1007/s00170-004-2063-1doi:10.1007/s00170-004-2063-1

Kennedy, J., & Eberhart, R. (1995). Particle swarm optimization. *Proceedings of the IEEE International Conference on Neural Networks*, Perth, Australia, (pp. 1942-1945).

Kennedy, J., & Eberhart, R. (2001). *Swarm intelligence*. San Diego, CA: Academic Press.

Kim, C. O., Jun, J., Baek, J. K., Smith, R. L., & Kim, Y. D. (2005). Adaptive inventory control models for supply chain management. *International Journal of Advanced Manufacturing Technology*, *26*, 1184–1192. doi:10.1007/s00170-004-2069-8doi:10.1007/s00170-004-2069-8

Kirkpatrick, S., Gelatti, C. D., & Vecchi, M. P. (1994). Optimization by simulated annealing. In H. Gutfreund & G. Tolouse (Eds.), *Advanced Series in Neurosciences, Vol. 3, Biology and computation: A physicist's choice*, (pp. 671–680).

Lu, L. (1995). A one-vendor multi-buyer integrated inventory model. *European Journal of Operational Research*, *81*, 312–323. doi:10.1016/0377-2217(93)E0253-Tdoi:10.1016/0377-2217(93)E0253-T

Roghanian, E., Sadjadi, S. J., & Aryanezhad, M. B. (2007). A probabilistic bi-level linear multi-objective programming problem to supply chain planning. *Applied Mathematics and Computation*, *188*, 786–800. doi:10.1016/j.amc.2006.10.032doi:10.1016/j.amc.2006.10.032

Sabri, E. H., & Beamon, B. M. (2000). A multi-objective approach to simultaneous strategic and operational planning in supply chain design. *Omega*, *28*, 581–598. doi:10.1016/S0305-0483(99)00080-8doi:10.1016/S0305-0483(99)00080-8

Sakall, U. S. (2010). A note on fuzzy multi-objective production/distribution planning decisions with multi-product and multi-time period in a supply chain. *Computers & Industrial Engineering*, *59*, 1010–1012. doi:10.1016/j.cie.2010.07.008doi:10.1016/j.cie.2010.07.008

Sayadi, M. K., Ramezanian, R., & Ghaffari-Nasab, N. (2010). A discrete firefly meta-heuristic with local search for makespan minimization in permutation flow shop scheduling problems. *International Journal of Industrial Engineering Computation*, *1*, 1–10. doi:10.5267/j.ijiec.2010.01.001doi:10.5267/j.ijiec.2010.01.001

Siajadi, H., Ibrahim, R. N., & Lochert, P. B. (2006). A single-vendor multiple-buyer inventory model with a multiple-shipment policy. *International Journal of Advanced Manufacturing Technology*, *27*, 1030–1037. doi:10.1007/s00170-004-2267-4doi:10.1007/s00170-004-2267-4

Simchi-Levi, D., Kaminsky, P., & Simchi-Levi, E. (2008). *Designing and managing the supply chain concepts, strategies and case studies. New York, NY*. USA: McGraw-Hill.

Su, S., Zhan, D., & Xu, X. (2008). An extended state task network formulation for integrated production-distribution planning in supply chain. *International Journal of Advanced Manufacturing Technology, 37,* 1232–1249. doi:10.1007/s00170-007-1063-3doi:10.1007/s00170-007-1063-3

Taleizadeh, A. A., Aryanezhad, M. B., & Niaki, S. T. A. (2008). Optimizing multi-product multi-constraint inventory control systems with stochastic replenishment. *Journal of Applied Sciences, 8,* 1228–1234. doi:10.3923/jas.2008.1228.1234doi:10.3923/jas.2008.1228.1234

Taleizadeh, A. A., Barzinpour, F., & Wee, H. M. (2011c). Meta-heuristic algorithms to solve the fuzzy single period problem. *Mathematical and Computer Modelling, 54,* 1273–1285. doi:10.1016/j.mcm.2011.03.038doi:10.1016/j.mcm.2011.03.038

Taleizadeh, A. A., Jolai, F., & Wee, H. M. (2011e). *Multi objective supply chain problem using a novel hybrid method of meta goal programming and firefly algorithm*. Submitted.

Taleizadeh, A. A., Niaki, S. T., & Aryanezhad, M. B. (2009a). A hybrid method of pareto, TOPSIS and genetic algorithm to optimize multi-product multi-constraint inventory control systems with random fuzzy replenishments. *Mathematical and Computer Modelling, 49,* 1044–1057. doi:10.1016/j.mcm.2008.10.013doi:10.1016/j.mcm.2008.10.013

Taleizadeh, A. A., Niaki, S. T., & Aryanezhad, M. B. (2010b). Replenish-up-to multi chance-constraint inventory control system with stochastic period lengths and total discount under fuzzy purchasing price and holding costs. *International Journal of Systems Science, 41,* 1187–1200. doi:10.1080/00207720903171761doi:10.1080/00207720903171761

Taleizadeh, A. A., Niaki, S. T., & Barzinpour, F. (2011a). Multi-buyer multi-vendor multi-product multi-constraint supply chain problem with stochastic demand and variable lead time. *Applied Mathematics and Computation, 217,* 9234–9253. doi:10.1016/j.amc.2011.04.001doi:10.1016/j.amc.2011.04.001

Taleizadeh, A. A., Niaki, S. T., & Hosseini, V. (2009b). Optimizing multi product multi constraints bi-objective newsboy problem with discount by hybrid method of goal programming and genetic algorithm. *Engineering Optimization, 41,* 437–457. doi:10.1080/03052150802582175doi:10.1080/03052150802582175

Taleizadeh, A. A., Niaki, S. T., & Makui, A. (2012). Multiproduct multiple-buyer single-vendor supply chain problem with stochastic demand, variable lead-time, and multi-chance constraint. *Expert Systems with Applications, 39,* 5338–5348. doi:10.1016/j.eswa.2011.11.001doi:10.1016/j.eswa.2011.11.001

Taleizadeh, A. A., Niaki, S. T., & Seyed-Javadi, S. M. (2011). Multi-product multi-chance-constraint stochastic inventory problem with dynamic demand and partial back-ordering: A harmony search algorithm. *Journal of Manufacturing Systems, 31*(2). doi:10.1016/j.jmsy.2011.05.006

Taleizadeh, A. A., Niaki, S. T., Shafii, N., Gha-vamizadeh Meibodi, R., & Jabbarzadeh, A. (2010a). A particle swarm optimization approach for constraint joint single buyer single vendor inventory problem with changeable lead-time and (r,Q) policy in supply chain. *International Journal of Advanced Manufacturing Technology. International Journal of Advanced Manufacturing Technology, 51*, 1209–1223. doi:10.1007/s00170-010-2689-0doi:10.1007/s00170-010-2689-0

Wee, H. M., & Yang, P. C. (2007). A mutual benefi-cial pricing strategy of an integrated vendor-buyers inventory system. *International Journal of Advanced Manufacturing Technology, 34*, 179–187. doi:10.1007/s00170-006-0581-8doi:10.1007/s00170-006-0581-8

Xu, J., & Zhao, L. (2008). A class of fuzzy rough expected value multi-objective decision making model and its application to inventory problems. *Computers & Mathematics with Applications (Oxford, England), 56*, 2107–2119. doi:10.1016/j.camwa.2008.03.040doi:10.1016/j.camwa.2008.03.040

Yang, X. S. (2008). *Nature-inspired meta-heuristic algorithms*. UK: Luniver Press.

Yang, X. S. (2009). Firefly algorithms for multi-modal optimization. In O. Watanabe & T. Zeug-mann (Eds.), *Stochastic algorithms: Foundations and applications SAGA (Vol. 5792*, pp. 169–178). *Lecture Notes in Computer Science* Berlin, Germany: Springer-Verlag. doi:10.1007/978-3-642-04944-6_14doi:10.1007/978-3-642-04944-6_14

ADDITIONAL READING

Angeline, P. J. (1998). Using selection to improve particle swarm optimization. *Proceedings of the 1998 International Conference on Evolutionary Computation*, (pp. 84–89). Piscataway, NJ: IEEE Press.

Angeline, P. J. (1998). Evolutionary optimization versus particle swarm optimization: Differences in philosophy and performance differences. In V. W. Porto, N. Saravanan, D. Waagen, & A. E. Eiben (Eds.), *Evolutionary Programming VII: Proceedings of the 7th Annual Conference on Evolutionary Programming.* Berlin, Germany: Springer-Verlag.

Cárdenas-Barrón, L. E. (2001). The economic production quantity (EPQ) with shortage derived algebraically. *International Journal of Production Economics, 70*, 289–292. doi:10.1016/S0925-5273(00)00068-2doi:10.1016/S0925-5273(00)00068-2

Cárdenas-Barrón, L. E. (2008). Optimal manufac-turing batch size with rework in a single-stage production system – A simple derivation. *Computers and Industrial Engineering Journal, 55*, 758–765. doi:10.1016/j.cie.2007.07.017doi:10.1016/j.cie.2007.07.017

Cárdenas-Barrón, L. E. (2009). Optimal order-ing policies in response to a discount offer: Extensions. *International Journal of Production Economics, 122*, 774–782. doi:10.1016/j.ijpe.2009.05.003doi:10.1016/j.ijpe.2009.05.003

Cárdenas-Barrón, L. E. (2009). Optimal order-ing policies in response to a discount offer: Corrections. *International Journal of Production Economics, 122*, 783–789. doi:10.1016/j.ijpe.2009.05.024doi:10.1016/j.ijpe.2009.05.024

Cárdenas-Barrón, L. E. (2009). On optimal batch sizing in a multi-stage production system with rework consideration. *European Journal of Operational Research, 196*, 1238–1244. doi:10.1016/j.ejor.2008.04.015doi:10.1016/j.ejor.2008.04.015

Cárdenas-Barrón, L. E. (2009). Economic production quantity with rework process at a single-stage manufacturing system with planned backorders. *Computers and Industrial Engineering Journal, 57,* 1105–1113. doi:10.1016/j.cie.2009.04.020doi:10.1016/j.cie.2009.04.020

Cárdenas-Barrón, L. E. (2010). An easy method to derive EOQ and EPQ inventory models with backorders. *Computers & Mathematics with Applications (Oxford, England), 59,* 948–952. doi:10.1016/j.camwa.2009.09.013doi:10.1016/j.camwa.2009.09.013

Cárdenas-Barrón, L. E. (In Press). A complement to A comprehensive note on: An economic order quantity with imperfect quality and quantity discounts. *Applied Mathematical Modelling,* in press. Doi: 10.1016/j.apm.2012.02.021

Cárdenas-Barrón, L. E., Smith, N. R., & Goyal, S. K. (2010). Optimal order size to take advantage of a one-time discount offer with allowed backorders. *Applied Mathematical Modelling, 34,* 1642–1652. doi:10.1016/j.apm.2009.09.013doi:10.1016/j.apm.2009.09.013

Cárdenas-Barrón, L. E., Smith, N. R., Martínez-Flores, J. L., & Rodríguez-Salvador, M. (2010). Modelling lead time effects on joint inventory and price optimization. *International Journal Logistics Economics and Globalisation, 2,* 270–291. doi:10.1504/IJLEG.2010.036304doi:10.1504/IJLEG.2010.036304

Cárdenas-Barrón, L. E., Teng, J. T., Treviño-Garza, G., Wee, H. M., & Lou, K. R. (2012). An improved algorithm and solution on an integrated production-inventory model in a three-layer supply chain. *International Journal of Production Economics, 136*(2). doi:10.1016/j.ijpe.2011.12.013doi:10.1016/j.ijpe.2011.12.013

Cárdenas-Barrón, L. E., Treviño-Garza, G., & Wee, H. M. (2012). A simple and better algorithm to solve the vendor managed inventory control system of multi-product multi-constraint economic order quantity model. *Expert Systems with Applications, 39,* 3888–3895. doi:10.1016/j.eswa.2011.09.057doi:10.1016/j.eswa.2011.09.057

Cárdenas-Barrón, L. E., Wee, H. M., & Blos, M. F. (2011). Solving the vendor-buyer integrated inventory system with arithmetic-geometric inequality. *Mathematical and Computer Modelling, 53,* 991–997. doi:10.1016/j.mcm.2010.11.056doi:10.1016/j.mcm.2010.11.056

Cárdenas-Barrón, L. E., Wee, H. M., & Teng, J. T. (2011). A supplement to "Using the EPQ for coordinated planning of a product with partial backordering and its components.". *Mathematical and Computer Modelling, 54,* 852–857. doi:10.1016/j.mcm.2011.02.038doi:10.1016/j.mcm.2011.02.038

Chung, K. J., & Cárdenas-Barrón, L. E. (In Press). The complete solution procedure for the EOQ and EPQ inventory models with linear and fixed backorder costs. *Mathematical and Computer Modelling,* in press. Doi: 10.1016/j.mcm.2011.12.051

Dorigo, M., & Stutzle, T. (2004). *Ant colony optimization.* Cambridge, MA: MIT Press.

Dueck, G., & Scheuer, T. (1990). Threshold accepting: A general purpose algorithm appearing superior to simulated annealing. *Journal of Computational Physics, 90,* 161–175. doi:10.1016/0021-9991(90)90201-Bdoi:10.1016/0021-9991(90)90201-B

Eberhart, R. C., & Shi, Y. (2000). Comparing inertia weights and constriction factors in particle swarm optimization. *Proceedings of the 2000 Congress on Evolutionary Computation,* (pp. 84–88). Piscataway, NJ: IEEE Service Center.

Eberhart, R. C., Simpson, P. K., & Dobbins, R. W. (1996). *Computational intelligence PC tools.* Boston, MA: Academic Press.

El-Sharkawi, L. (2008). *Modern heuristic optimization techniques*, 1st ed., Wiley Inter science, New Jersey, U.S.A.

García-Laguna, J., San-Jose, L. A., Cárdenas-Barrón, L. E., & Sicilia, J. (2010). The integrality of the lot size in the basic EOQ and EPQ models: Applications to other production-inventory models. *Applied Mathematics and Computation, 216*, 1660–1672. doi:10.1016/j.amc.2010.02.042doi:10.1016/j.amc.2010.02.042

Geem, Z. W. (2006). Optimal cost design of water distribution networks using harmony search. *Engineering Optimization, 38*, 259–280. doi:10.1080/03052150500467430doi:10.1080/03052150500467430

Geem, Z. W., & Hwangbo, H. (2006). *Application of harmony search to multi-objective optimization for satellite heat pipe design.* UKC AST-1.1.

Geem, Z. W., Lee, K. S., & Park, Y. (2005). Application of harmony search to vehicle routing. *American Journal of Applied Sciences, 2*, 1552–1557. doi:10.3844/ajassp.2005.1552.1557doi:10.3844/ajassp.2005.1552.1557

Gen, M., & Cheng, R. (1997). *Genetic algorithm and engineering design.* New York, NY: John Wiley & Sons.

Goyal, S. K., & Cárdenas-Barrón, L. E. (2002). Note on: Economic production quantity model for items with imperfect quality-A practical approach. *International Journal of Production Economics, 77*, 85–87. doi:10.1016/S0925-5273(01)00203-1doi:10.1016/S0925-5273(01)00203-1

Guo, Y. W., Li, W. D., Mileham, A. R., & Owen, G. W. (2008). Optimization of integrated process planning and scheduling using a particle swarm optimization approach. *International Journal of Production Research, 40*, 1–22.

Hong, S. P., & Kim, Y. H. (2009). A genetic algorithm for joint replenishment based on the exact inventory cost. *Computers & Operations Research, 36*, 167–175. doi:10.1016/j.cor.2007.08.006doi:10.1016/j.cor.2007.08.006

Jaberipour, M., & Khorram, E. (2011). A new harmony search algorithm for solving mixed-discrete engineering optimization problems. *Engineering Optimization, 43*, 507–523. doi:10.1080/0305215X.2010.499939doi:10.1080/0305215X.2010.499939

Kang, F., Li, J., & Xu, Q. (2009). Structural inverse analysis by hybrid simplex artificial bee colony algorithms. *Computers & Structures, 87*, 861–870. doi:10.1016/j.compstruc.2009.03.001doi:10.1016/j.compstruc.2009.03.001

Kaveh, A., & Ahangaran, M. (2012). Discrete cost optimization of composite floor system using social harmony search model. *Applied Soft Computing Journal, 12*, 372–381. doi:10.1016/j.asoc.2011.08.035doi:10.1016/j.asoc.2011.08.035

Kaveh, A., & Laknejadi, K. (2011). A novel hybrid charge system search and particle swarm optimization method for multi-objective optimization. *Expert Systems with Applications, 38*, 15475–15488. doi:10.1016/j.eswa.2011.06.012doi:10.1016/j.eswa.2011.06.012

Kennedy, J. (2000). Stereotyping: Improving particle swarm performance with cluster analysis. *Proceedings of the 2000 Congress on Evolutionary Computation*, (pp. 1507–1512). Piscataway, NJ: IEEE Service Center.

Kennedy, J., & Eberhart, R. C. (1997). A discrete binary version of the particle swarm algorithm. *Proceedings of the 1997 Conference on Systems, Man, and Cybernetics*, (pp. 4104–4109). Piscataway, NJ: IEEE Service Center.

Kennedy, J., & Spears, W. M. (1998). Matching algorithms to problems: An experimental test of the particle swarm and some genetic algorithms on the multimodal problem generator. *Proceedings of the 1998 International Conference on Evolutionary Computation*, (pp. 78–83). Piscataway, NJ: IEEE Service Center.

Kitano, H. (1990). Designing neural networks using genetic algorithm with graph generation system. *Complex Systems*, *4*, 461–476.

Laumanns, M., Thiele, L., Deb, K., & Zitzler, E. (2002). Combining convergence and diversity in evolutionary multi-objective optimization. *Evolutionary Computation*, *10*, 263–282. PubMed doi:10.1162/106365602760234108doi:10.1162/106365602760234108

Lee, K. S., & Geem, Z. W. (2004). A new structural optimization method based on the harmony search algorithm. *Computers & Structures*, *82*, 781–798. doi:10.1016/j.compstruc.2004.01.002 doi:10.1016/j.compstruc.2004.01.002

Man, K. F., Tang, K. S., Kwong, S., & Halang, W. A. (1997). *Genetic algorithms for control and signal processing*. London, UK: Springer Verlag.

Marinakis, Y., & Marinaki, M. (2010). A hybrid multi-swarm particle swarm optimization algorithm for the probabilistic traveling salesman problem. *Computers & Operations Research*, *37*, 432–442. doi:10.1016/j.cor.2009.03.004doi:10.1016/j.cor.2009.03.004

Melanie, M. (1996). *An introduction to genetic algorithms*. Boston, MA: Massachusetts Institute of Technology.

Pal, S., Maiti, M. K., & Maiti, M. (2009). An EPQ model with price discounted promotional demand in an imprecise planning horizon via genetic algorithm. *Computers & Industrial Engineering*, *57*, 181–187. doi:10.1016/j.cie.2008.11.016doi:10.1016/j.cie.2008.11.016

Pan, Q., Tasgetiren, M. F., & Liang, Y. C. (2008). A discrete particle swarm optimization algorithm for the no-wait flow shop scheduling problem. *Computers & Operations Research*, *35*, 2807–2839. doi:10.1016/j.cor.2006.12.030doi:10.1016/j.cor.2006.12.030

Pasandideh, S. H. R., Niaki, S. T. A., & Aryan Yeganeh, J. (2010). A parameter-tuned genetic algorithm for multi-product economic production quantity model with space constraint, discrete delivery orders and shortages. *Advances in Engineering Software*, *41*, 306–314. doi:10.1016/j.advengsoft.2009.07.001doi:10.1016/j.advengsoft.2009.07.001

Rahimi-Vahed, A. R., Mirghorbani, S. M., & Rabbani, M. (2007). A hybrid multi objective particle swarm algorithm for a mixed-model assembly line sequencing problem. *Engineering Optimization*, *39*, 877–898. doi:10.1080/03052150701512042 doi:10.1080/03052150701512042

Salman, A., Ahmad, I., & Al-Madani, S. (2003). Particle swarm optimization for fast assignment problem. *Microprocessors and Microsystems*, *26*, 363–371. doi:10.1016/S0141-9331(02)00053-4doi:10.1016/S0141-9331(02)00053-4

Sarmah, S. P., Acharya, D., & Goyal, S. K. (2008). Coordination of a single manufacturer multi-buyer supply chain with credit option. *International Journal of Production Economics*, *111*, 676–685. doi:10.1016/j.ijpe.2007.04.003doi:10.1016/j.ijpe.2007.04.003

Seeley, T. D. (1996). *The wisdom of the hive: The social physiology of honey bee colonies*. Cambridge, MA: Harvard University Press.

Sha, D. Y., & Hsu, C. (2008). A new particle swarm optimization for the open shop scheduling problem. *Computers & Operations Research*, *35*, 3243–3261. doi:10.1016/j.cor.2007.02.019doi:10.1016/j.cor.2007.02.019

Shahsavar, M., Niaki, S. T. A., & Najafi, A. A. (2010). An efficient genetic algorithm to maximize net present value of project payments under inflation and bonus–penalty policy in resource investment problem. *Advances in Engineering Software*, *41*, 1023–1030. doi:10.1016/j.advengsoft.2010.03.002doi:10.1016/j.advengsoft.2010.03.002

Shi, Y., & Eberhart, R. C. (1999). Empirical study of particle swarm optimization. *Proceedings of the 1999 Congress on Evolutionary Computation*, (pp. 1945–1950).

Smith, N. R., Limón, J., & Cárdenas-Barrón, L. E. (2009). Optimal pricing and production master planning in a multi period horizon considering capacity and inventory constraints. *Mathematical Problems in Engineering*, (932676): 1–15. doi:10.1155/2009/932676doi:10.1155/2009/932676

Taleizadeh, A. A., Cárdenas-Barrón, L. E., Biabani, J., & Nikousokhan, R. (2012). Multi products single machine EPQ model with immediate rework process. *International Journal of Industrial Engineering Computations*, *3*, 93–102. doi:10.5267/j.ijiec.2011.09.001doi:10.5267/j.ijiec.2011.09.001

Taleizadeh, A. A., & Niaki, S. T. (2009). A hybrid method of harmony search, goal programming and fuzzy simulation for bi-objectives single period problem with fuzzy cost and incremental discount. *Journal of Industrial Engineering*, *3*, 1–14.

Taleizadeh, A. A., Niaki, S. T., Aryanezhad, M. B., & Fallah Tafti, A. (2010). A genetic algorithm to optimize multi-product multi-constraint inventory control systems with stochastic replenishments and discount. *International Journal of Advanced Manufacturing Technology*, *51*, 311–323. doi:10.1007/s00170-010-2604-8doi:10.1007/s00170-010-2604-8

Taleizadeh, A. A., Niaki, S. T. A., & Aryanezhad, M. B. (2009). Multi-product multi-constraint inventory control systems with stochastic replenishment and discount under fuzzy purchasing price and holding costs. *Journal of Applied Sciences*, *6*, 1–12.

Taleizadeh, A. A., Niaki, S. T. A., & Hosseini, V. (2008). The multi-product multi-constraint newsboy problem with incremental discount and batch order. *Asian Journal of Applied Sciences*, *1*, 110–122. doi:10.3923/ajaps.2008.110.122doi:10.3923/ajaps.2008.110.122

Taleizadeh, A. A., Shavandi, H., & Haji, R. (2011). Hybrid algorithms to solve constraint single period problem with uncertain demand. [Scientia Iranica]. *International Journal of Science and Technology*, *18*, 1553–1563.

Taleizadeh, A. A., Widyadana, G. A., Wee, H. M., & Biabani, J. (2011). Multi products single machine economic production quantity model with multiple batch size. *International Journal of Industrial Engineering Computations*, *2*, 213–224. doi:10.5267/j.ijiec.2011.01.002doi:10.5267/j.ijiec.2011.01.002

Teng, J. T., Cárdenas-Barrón, L. E., & Lou, K. R. (2011). The economic lot size of the integrated vendor-buyer inventory system derived without derivatives: A simple derivation. *Applied Mathematics and Computation*, *217*, 5972–5977. doi:10.1016/j.amc.2010.12.018doi:10.1016/j.amc.2010.12.018

Teng, J. T., Cárdenas-Barrón, L. E., Lou, K. R., & Wee, H. M. (In Press). Optimal economic order quantity for buyer-distributor-vendor supply chain with backlogging derived without derivatives. *International Journal of Systems Science*, in press. Doi: 10.1080/00207721.2011.652226

Widyadana, G. A., Cárdenas-Barrón, L. E., & Wee, H. M. (2011). Economic order quantity model for deteriorating items and planned backorder level. *Mathematical and Computer Modelling*, *54*, 1569–1575. doi:10.1016/j.mcm.2011.04.028doi:10.1016/j.mcm.2011.04.028

Yapicioglu, H., Smith, A. E., & Dozier, G. (2007). Solving the semi-desirable facility location problem using bi-objective particle swarm. *European Journal of Operational Research, 177*, 733–749. doi:10.1016/j.ejor.2005.11.020doi:10.1016/j.ejor.2005.11.020

Zahara, E., & Hu, C. H. (2008). Solving constrained optimization problems with hybrid particle swarm optimization. *Engineering Optimization, 40*, 1031–1049. doi:10.1080/03052150802265870doi:10.1080/03052150802265870

KEY TERMS AND DEFINITIONS

Firefly Algorithm (FA): Firefly Algorithm (FA) was inspired by the social behavior of fireflies. This algorithm has been used in an enormous variety of applications spanning the permutation flow shop scheduling problem, codebook design of image vector quantization and financial portfolio optimization, among others.

Genetic Algorithm (GA): GA is inspired by the concept of survival of the fittest. GA uses a directed random search to locate good solutions for complex optimization problems. GA mimics the evolution process of the species that reproduce.

Goal Programming: Goal Programming (GP) was introduced as an operational research method for multi-criteria decision making and multi-objective programming problems. A new version of GP called the Meta-GP (MGP) was lately developed in which three different types of meta goals are defined.

Harmony Search (HS): The HS algorithm was inspired from the act of musical groups and it was introduced such as an analogy with music improvisation process where musicians in a band continue to polish their pitches to obtain a better harmony.

Inventory Management: Inventory theory is one of the fields where operations research has had noteworthy developments. For example, there are several mathematical models for the inventory control in use today in which the main objective is to have a good management of inventories of raw materials, spare parts and finished goods.

Lead Time: The length of time since the order is placed till receiving products by buyer.

Metaheuristic Algorithms (MHA): Metaheuristics methods were introduced to describe how works different heuristic algorithms which can be widely applied together to a set of different problems in a variety of fields. Thus, Metaheuristics should be considered as a general algorithmic structure which can be used for solving hard optimization problems with relatively few modifications to make them custom-made to a specific problem.

Order Quantity: The quantity of products of an order that is placed to the supplier.

Particle Swarm Optimization (PSO): PSO is inspired by the ability of flocks of birds, schools of fish, and herds of animals to adapt to their environment quickly, finding rich sources of food, and avoiding predators by implementing an information sharing approach; with this the species develops an evolutionary benefit.

Reorder Point: The inventory level when the buyer should place the order to the supplier.

Simulated Annealing (SA): Simulated annealing (SA) is a local search algorithm and it was inspired in the physical annealing process studied in statistical mechanics.

Supply Chain Management (SCM): Supply chain management is a set of tools for efficiently integrate suppliers, manufactures, warehouses, and stores. Where this integration searches that the goods manufactured being distributed at the right quantities, to the right locations, and at right time in order to satisfy the service level requirements with a minimal total whole chain cost.

Chapter 5
Instance-Specific Parameter Tuning for Meta-Heuristics

Jana Ries
University of Portsmouth, UK

Patrick Beullens
University of Southampton, UK

Yang Wang
Beijing University of Technology, China

ABSTRACT

Meta-heuristics are of significant interest to decision-makers due to the capability of finding good solutions for complex problems within a reasonable amount of computational time. These methods are further known to perform according to how their algorithm-specific parameters are set. As most practitioners aim for an off-the-shelf approach when using meta-heuristics, they require an easy applicable strategy to calibrate its parameters and use it. This chapter addresses the so-called Parameter Setting Problem (PSP) and presents new developments for the Instance-specific Parameter Tuning Strategy (IPTS). The IPTS presented only requires the end user to specify its preference regarding the trade-off between running time and solution quality by setting one parameter p ($0 \leq p \leq 1$), and automatically returns a good set of algorithm-specific parameter values for each individual instance based on the calculation of a set of problem instance characteristics. The IPTS does not require any modification of the particular meta-heuristic being used. It aims to combine advantages of the Parameter Tuning Strategy (PTS) and the Parameter Control Strategy (PCS), the two major approaches to the PSP. The chapter outlines the advantages of an IPTS and shows in more detail two ways in which an IPTS can be designed. The first design approach requires expert-based knowledge of the meta-heuristic's performance in relation to the problem at hand. The second, automated approach does not require explicit knowledge of the meta-heuristic used. Both designs use a fuzzy logic system to obtain parameter values. Results are presented for an IPTS designed to solve instances of the Travelling Salesman Problem (TSP) with the meta-heuristic Guided Local Search (GLS).

DOI: 10.4018/978-1-4666-2086-5.ch005

1. INTRODUCTION

Exact algorithms for combinatorial optimisation problems (COPs) guarantee that a solution - if one can be found - is optimal. In practice, however, many applications are represented by large problem instances whose optimal solution can only rarely be found in a reasonable time. Heuristic methods with practical running times, although not guaranteeing optimality, are therefore often more attractive for decision makers. Meta-heuristics, including the well-known strategies of simulated annealing, tabu search, genetic algorithms, and guided local search, are often very successful by having mechanisms in place allowing the search to escape the local optimality trap. They are known to perform according to the setting of incorporated parameters. Finding the best values for those parameters is arguably a time-consuming and tedious process. It is henceforth called the Parameter Setting Problem (PSP).

Two major approaches have emerged in the course of a decade to solve the PSP, known as the Parameter Tuning Strategy (PTS) and the Parameter Control Strategy (PCS). A PTS is based on a search for a best fixed set of parameter values for a representative set of instances of a problem. The criterion is often to maximize the average solution quality over all instances of the test set. The outcome is a single set of parameters, which is then re-used whenever new instances in the future have to be solved. A PTS does not require the modification of the meta-heuristic. A PTS is also known as an offline strategy, see Coy et al. (2001), Adenso-Diaz and Laguna (2006), and Kern (2006). A meta-heuristic is considered non-robust if instance characteristics, e.g. instance size or other structural specifics, have an impact on heuristic performance, i.e. solution quality and computational time. Hence, if the set of parameter values is fixed for all instances to be solved, performance – in form of solution quality or computational time – will be average for a set of instances. Therefore, using the same set of parameters is only disadvantageous if the

meta-heuristic is non-robust. In practice, however, this is known to be the case for most approaches considering performance values such as computational time and solution quality.

A PCS, also known as an online strategy, see Eiben et al. (1999), Smith (2008), and Jeong et al. (2009), typically starts with initial parameter values, but may update these during the run of the meta-heuristic on a particular instance. A PCS thus requires extending the code of the meta-heuristic, or at least allow for the dynamic extraction of necessary data while the meta-heuristic is running, and the capability of re-setting parameter values on the fly. A PCS works arguably well when the different instances that need solving are not a priori well known but are expected to differ significantly in their characteristics so that instance-specific tailoring of parameter values, during the meta-heuristic search process itself, pays off in solution quality or computational time.

The recently developed Instance-specific Parameter Tuning Strategy (IPTS), see Pavon et al. (2009), and Ries (2009), aims to combine advantages of PTS and PCS. An IPTS provides an initial good set of parameter values to the meta-heuristic, similar to a PTS. In addition, however, this set of parameter values is determined in function of structural information of the particular instance to be solved. The latter feature is somewhat similar to a PCS, however, instead of allowing the modification of parameter values during the runtime of the meta-heuristic, the structural information of an instance is retrieved in a pre-processing step by an IPTS algorithm that runs independently from the meta-heuristic. The meta-heuristic itself thus needs no modification. Further, it is advised to include a decision maker preference p, allowing the IPTS algorithm to return parameter values that either focus on leading to good solution quality, short computational times, or a balance between these extremes.

In this chapter, the concept of an IPTS is discussed and then applied to the case of the Travelling Salesman Problem (TSP) and Guided Local Search (GLS). Two different approaches to the design of a fuzzy IPTS system are presented. The first approach, based on Ries et al. (2012), shows the advantages of a manual design that uses expert knowledge retrieved from a statistical analysis aimed at identifying the impact of instance characteristics and algorithm-specific parameters on heuristic performance. With the aim to further automate the design of a fuzzy IPTS system, a second approach is presented that shows the value of fuzzy clustering, whereby no expert knowledge is required about the particular meta-heuristic and a statistical analysis can be avoided.

The chapter is organized as follows: An overview of parameter setting strategies including parameter control and classic parameter tuning is given in Section 2. This is followed by the introduction of the concept of instance-specific parameter tuning (IPTS) and the proposal of one particular IPTS using Fuzzy Logic in Section 3. The chapter uses the case study of the Travelling Salesman Problem and Guided Local Search to illustrate the presented IPTS. Both TSP and GLS are well-known and therefore briefly discussed in Section 4. In Section 5, the manual design of a fuzzy system for an IPTS is outlined using a statistical analysis and results presented underline the advantages of this approach in comparison to a PTS. In line with facilitating the set-up of calibration strategies such as an IPTS, Section 6 presents an automated design using fuzzy clustering to replace a statistical analysis, and corresponding results. Sections 7 and 8 provide further discussion and concluding remarks, respectively.

2. PARAMETER SETTING STRATEGIES

For decades, the re-use of well-performing parameter settings has been the main approach to calibrating a meta-heuristic in research studies. This strategy has been repeatedly criticised, see e.g. Hooker (1995), Johnson (2002), and Lokketangen (2007). The main objective of dealing with the PSP is that the intuitive approach to choosing parameter values needs to be replaced by a well-defined and algorithmic approach. In particular, Hooker suggests the consideration of instance characteristics due to the observed impact on heuristic performance. During the last decade, research into the PSP has led to two main approaches, PTS and PCS, further discussed next.

2.1 Parameter Tuning Strategies

A meta-heuristic is considered robust if it 'is less sensitive to differences in problem characteristics, data quality and parameter tuning than other approaches' (Barr et al., 1995). Hence, a robust meta-heuristic algorithm is assumed to perform well over all problem instances, disregarding instance-specific information, when using a good but fixed set of parameter values. The aim to exploit robustness has led to PTS methods that search for this good set of parameter values, then to be re-used for any future test instance. The general concept of designing and assessing the quality of a PTS involves first the optimisation of some suitably developed criterion, typically measuring average heuristic performance, across a range of instances of a test set to find one fixed set of parameter values. Subsequently, this set is then applied in an assessment phase to all instances of an evaluation test set.

Xu et al. (1998) run their experimentation on a training set of 19 instances known to be hard to solve. They apply the Friedman and Wilcoxon test in a step-by-step approach on selected values for each algorithm-specific parameter, a test which disregards any interactions between two algorithm parameters. In contrast, Coy et al. (2000) look specifically for a test set that incorporates most of the structural differences between instances in order to ensure the robustness of their best parameter setting. They point out that heuristic performance can be improved by dividing their test instances into classes according to their characteristics.

A more recent approach is CALIBRA by Adenso-Diaz & Laguna (2006). Similarly to Coy et al. (2000), it uses a fractional factorial design but applies it in combination with a local search procedure in the analysis. The authors investigate the benefits of letting the tuning method be guided by a performance measure that combines computational time and solution quality. They find that with a minor sacrifice of solution quality, computational time could be significantly reduced. Kern (2006) presents a population-based learning approach. Kern reports that the more similar the test and assessment sets of instances are in their structure, the more likely a good parameter setting is obtained. For further research, and in line with the conclusions of Coy et al. (2000), Kern suggests that his learning mechanism could possibly be improved by including problem-specific knowledge, analysing correlations between parameters, and identifying patterns. ParamILS by Hutter et al. (2008) is based on iterated local search, see Lourenco et al. (2002). These authors point out that one further direction in the field of parameter tuning should be the consideration of instance-specific information.

One important conclusion from this, and as also pointed out by Smith (2008), is that the disadvantages of a PTS include its implementation and evaluation effort, in particular when many researchers point out that one fixed parameter set does not seem to be the optimal parameter set for many future instances under investigation. The research above seems to indicate that the meta-heuristics that were studied do not appear to be that robust for the problems to which they were applied.

2.2 Parameter Control Strategies

The No Free Lunch theorem, see Wolpert and Macready (1997), states that all search algorithms are performing equally, considering their averaged performance over all possible discrete (objective) functions. At least in theory, heuristic performance can thus be improved if the algorithm is adapted to the specific problem that is considered to be solved.

Following this line of thought, some researchers have abandoned the robustness idea and have developed so-called 'online' search strategies or PCS for modifying the algorithm-specific parameters according to heuristic performance. The search mechanism for a best parameter setting is incorporated in the actual problem solving meta-heuristic strategy.

There are different ways reported in the literature for classifying this set of techniques. Eiben et al. (1999), for example, distinguish between deterministic, adaptive and self-adaptive parameter control. Deterministic strategies predefine the algorithmic approach to set a parameter without using any search feedback. In contrast, adaptive methods use feedback from the heuristic search mechanisms in order to regulate the change of the algorithmic parameter. Finally, self-adaptive strategies in evolutionary algorithms encode the parameter settings and let them undergo the algorithmic process. Hence, individuals representing improving parameter settings are more likely to survive and represent the algorithmic-parameters of the problem solving evolutionary algorithm itself.

Following the classification of Eiben et al. (1999), Jeong et al. (2009) present an adaptive parameter control strategy that incorporates a fuzzy logic controller into a simulated annealing approach for the symmetric Travelling Salesman Problem (TSP). The mechanism resets the cooling schedule based on the improvement in solution quality and the current temperature. Furthermore, it dynamically changes the number of repetitions for one set temperature value based on the solution quality improvement and the change of the temperature values. In general, an improved performance is shown compared to conventional simulated annealing. The combination of adapting two parameters compared to only controlling the temperature parameter, however, did not show a further significant improvement. Battiti (1996) introduces an adaptive parameter control strategy called reactive search for the tabu search algorithm in the context of parameter tuning. The authors implement reactive tabu search such that it sets the number of iterations for which a previously seen solution is declared tabu based on the number of repetitions. This method has evolved into a new algorithm called RASH - a self-adaptive search algorithm, see Brunato & Battiti (2008).

The majority of techniques in the area of PCS in the literature have been developed in the context of genetic algorithms. Lobo & Lima (2005), for example, present an overview of studies solely focusing on the adaptation of the parameter population size. The authors conclude that there appears to be a need to change the population size when going through the different stages of the algorithm. Hence an adaptive strategy seems to be desirable, as also portrayed by Eiben et al. (1999). Smith (2008) follows this strand of research and presents a review about self-adaptation methods for evolutionary algorithms. In particular, he focuses on self-adaptive strategies for mutation and crossover operators. While these approaches provide instance-tailored parameter settings, computational effort required increases as each instance is being tested several times for different algorithm-specific parameter combinations.

In conclusion, most implementations of a PCS adapt algorithm parameters dynamically, based on particular algorithmic or performance information. A drawback of current implementations might well be that information is not re-usable the next time an instance with similar characteristics needs to be solved. What has potentially been learned when solving one instance, is not captured and re-used when solving the next.

2.3. Multi-Objective Parameter Setting Strategies

Considering the overall aim of meta-heuristics of providing good solutions to hard problems quickly, it seems desirable to not only consider

solution quality in the search for good parameter values. Adenso-Diaz & Laguna (2006), Hutter et al. (2008), and Aine et al. (2009) have outlined that significant improvements can be achieved with respect to computational time when applying a parameter setting strategy that considers the solution quality and computational time trade-off. All authors suggest a combination of both heuristic performance measures using a fixed weight approach.

In practice, however, the importance of solution quality and computational time may change according to problem-specific preferences. For example, it may be important to solve a TSP encountered in the context of a timetable scheduling problem to the best possibly degree, sacrificing computational efforts. In contrast, a TSP encountered in a real-time (dynamic) vehicle routing application may need to provide reasonable solutions very quickly. As the designer of an IPTS for the TSP might not know a priori the final user's preference to this trade-off, the idea presented in this chapter is to let the trade-off decision be made by the final user. The algorithmic approach developed hence incorporates a single parameter p to be set by the final user, its value expressing the decision maker's particular preference with respect to the solution quality and computational time trade-off.

3. INSTANCE-SPECIFIC PARAMETER TUNING

A significant number of meta-heuristics do not appear to be robust as they show sensitivity towards changes in parameter setting and instance-specific characteristics. As Hooker (1995) suggested, efficiency of parameter setting strategies may be improved by focussing on the impact of instance characteristics. A technique that is able to retrieve instance-based information quickly and match this with a best parameter setting, may hence lead to better overall performance of the meta-heuristic. Current implementations of the

PTS do not have this feature, while the current PCS implementations do not seem to incorporate a priori learnable knowledge about the relationships between instance characteristics and good (initial) parameter values. An IPTS aims to extend the PTS by including knowledge of the instance structure when returning a set of initial parameter values. An IPTS cannot adjust parameters during run-time, however, and therefore has not got the dynamic fine-tuning capabilities of a PCS. In terms of benchmarking the performance of an IPTS, it is perhaps more natural to compare it with a PTS. An IPTS aims to overcome the burden of non-robustness encountered in a PTS while still aiming to be at least as fast as a PTS in its use, without the need to modify the meta-heuristic algorithm. The PCS, however, aims to find suitable parameter (re)setting strategies and dynamically determine stop-criteria for primarily obtaining best solution qualities, and typically requires the fine-tuning of the meta-heuristic code.

To our knowledge, the first IPTS approach was proposed by Leyton-Brown et al. (2002). The authors suggest a run-time prediction model for IPLOG's CPLEX software derived by regression analysis for the winner determination problem (WDP). It is pointed out that this instance-specific information is strongly dependent on the researcher's knowledge about the problem domain. Building on these findings, Hutter et al. (2006) have developed an approach which designs run-time prediction models for parametric algorithms using a finite set of parameter values. With respect to parameter setting, the authors suggest to select those set of parameter values that result in the lowest computational times. A practical approach has been developed by Pavon et al. (2009). Their research model uses a Bayesian case-based reasoning system that tunes parameter values before the actual meta-heuristic, a genetic algorithm, is applied. They conclude that a similar level of solution quality as in previous studies could be obtained but within a significantly reduced computational time. Ries (2009), see also Ries et

al. (2012), develops fuzzy logic based inference systems to return instance-specific parameter values for guided local search, values that can be tailored to the decision maker's preference p ($0 \leq p \leq 1$) on the trade-off between solution quality and computational time. Again, significant savings in computational time are reported while solution quality is not negatively affected.

3.1. The Concept of IPTS

Instance-specific parameter tuning strategies aim for good parameter settings based on selected structural information of the instance. When using an already designed IPTS that incorporates the specification of the user preference p ($0 \leq p \leq 1$), the user will provide an instance and his/her preferred value p as input, and by running the IPTS, invoke the programme to pass through two main stages:

1. In Stage (1), the programme will read the instance, and run a few algorithms to quantify a vector of values C of which each element represents a particular instance characteristic;
2. In Stage (2), C and p are inputs to, e.g., a fuzzy inference system (FIS) that returns a set of algorithm-specific parameter values.

Stage (1) must preferably use fast polynomial-time algorithms, as too much time lost in this stage may defeat the purpose of using an IPTS as a computational time-saving devise. The outcome of stage (2) is subsequently sent to the meta-heuristic to solve the instance under investigation (see also Figure 1). An advantage of the structure of an IPTS is that it is dislocated from the meta-heuristic. This allows users to use off-the-shelf meta-heuristics. The IPTS algorithm may run just before the meta-heuristic runs, or independently by simply returning the parameter values as output, and then allow running the meta-heuristic at some later point in time. For the designers of the IPTS,

Figure 1. Fuzzy IPTS structure

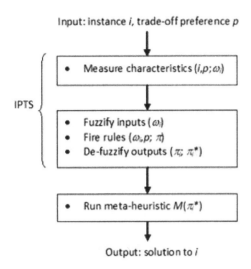

the code of the meta-heuristic does not need to be explicitly available; it may e.g. only be available as a callable routine with only the ability to set its parameter values.

It is expected that an approach by which the final user has some control over the trade-off between solution quality and computational time, without having to consider a way of calibrating the meta-heuristic, is of great benefit. A simple representation to the final user of this trade-off might be:

$$f(.) = (1-p)S(.) - pT(.) \qquad (1)$$

where p is a weight that represent the decision maker preference ($0 \leq p \leq 1$) and S(.) and T(.) are suitably calibrated functions representing solution quality and computational time, respectively. The two extreme cases are $p = 0$, for best solution quality, and $p = 1$, for shortest computational time.

3.2. IPTS Using Fuzzy Logic

The IPTS programme of stage (2) needs to incorporate the impact of changes in instance structure and algorithm-specific parameters on heuristic performance. It is impossible to gather complete knowledge about these correlations and thus design a correct programme. Hence, the authors suggest the use of fuzzy logic, a technique which copes reasonably well with uncertainties in the data and produces outputs that do not have to rely on crisp decision rules. Fuzzy logic modelling allows a clear interpretation and reasonable precision (Sugeno and Yasukawa, 1993).

Fuzzy logic has been introduced by Zadeh in 1965. It is a rule-based approach, allowing partial set membership rather than crisp set membership or non-membership. An FIS includes a set of membership functions for each input and output variable, and a rule base. A membership function describes a fuzzy set for one variable according to which crisp input data can be assigned to one or several sets with to a certain degree between 0 and 1. This process is called fuzzification. Structural instance information and a decision maker's preference represent in our case the input parameters, and their values are mapped on membership functions that are described by linguistic terms, e.g. 'small' or 'large'. The output parameters of the FIS are the algorithm-specific parameters which are also assigned with a set of membership functions. A similar process, called defuzzification, can determine a crisp value for an output parameter based on knowledge of set membership functions. Control objectives and relationships between inputs and outputs are captured in a fuzzy logic system, using a set of fuzzy rules. A fuzzy rule is described using the IF-THEN construct, for example IF a = small AND b = medium, THEN c = large, whereby a and b are inputs, and c an output. The fuzzy AND operator determines a combined degree of truth of the antecedent as the intersection (or minimum value) of all membership values of the inputs. In the presented case the centroid method is applied, returning the value corresponding to the centre of the area generated from all rules applying to that particular output.

4. CASE STUDY: TSP AND GUIDED LOCAL SEARCH

An IPTS using fuzzy logic has been developed for the TSP and Guided Local Search (GLS). The TSP is a well-known problem that has been used widely to understand and develop new approaches in combinatorial optimisation. As a component encountered in many more complex problems, such as in the area of vehicle routing, it is of theoretical interest to gain more knowledge on how relevant TSP instance characteristics are in determining meta-heuristic performance. These reasons have guided us in our subjective choice to take TSP as our case study.

There are also a number of reasons that led us to choose Guided Local Search (GLS). Amongst other meta-heuristics, it has been demonstrated to perform well for the TSP up to a few thousand vertices, and to not underperform compared to Lin-Kernighan, see Voudouris & Tsang (1999). As opposed to incorporating randomness at the heart of the meta-heuristic, such as simulated annealing or genetic algorithms, GLS is in essence a deterministic search method, which helps to simplify the analysis of the impact of instance characteristics on algorithm performance. It has a sufficient yet limited number of parameters.

4.1. Travelling Salesman Problem

The symmetric TSP calls for finding the tour of minimal length in a complete undirected graph $G = (V,E)$, visiting all vertices $V = (v_1, v_2,.., v_n)$ only once. The distance between two instance points v_i and v_j is defined by $d(v_i, v_j)$, where $d(v_i, v_j) = d(v_j, v_i)$ for $1 \leq i, j \leq n$.

For extensive overviews of the range of TSP applications, see Applegate et al. (2006) and Schmitting (1999). For a discussion on classification, further modifications, and extensions, see also Johnson and McGeoch (2002). The most commonly used distance function is the Euclidean

one. Manhattan distances, also called Taxicab distances (Stuetzle, 1998) or rectilinear distances, form another popular metric. A third well-known class are Maximum distances. Typical applications of the Euclidean metric are found in transportation, including school bus routing (Bowerman et al., 1995), postal deliveries (Irnich, 2007), meals on wheels (Bartholdi et al., 1983) and coin collection problems of payphones (Johnson & McGeoch, 2002). Manhattan distances are found in certain transportation problems within grid network cities, and order picking problems (Ratliff et al., 1983, Daniels et al., 1998). Maximum distances typically arise in machine routing problems, including drilling operations (Applegate et al., 2006), crystal art lasering (Bland and Shallcross, 1989) and storage-and-retrieval in high-rise storage systems (Kim et al., 2003).

4.2. Instance-Specific Information

In order to start designing an IPTS, instance characteristics have to be selected which may show a relevant impact on heuristic performance. In addition, one must also reflect on the computational time requirements of stage (1), as long running times encountered here would partially defeat the usefulness of the ITPS. Which instance characteristics to measure, and to what degree of accuracy, are therefore important decisions with respect to the effectiveness and efficiency of an IPTS.

Based on Johnson and McGeoch (2002), the first three instance characteristics chosen for this study are the *size* of an instance (the number of vertices), the *distance metric*, and a *measure of clustering*. In our fuzzy logic model it is assumed that the size of the instance n ($0 < n \leq 5000$ in the model) is either given or can be easily determined from the instance data file (e.g. from the size of the distance matrix). When instances are larger than 5000 vertices, the fuzzy model will take $n = 5000$.

Within this study, the focus is on instances having Manhattan or Euclidean distance metrics, or a distance metric in between. This can be formally derived when viewing Manhattan and Euclidean metrics as special cases of the 2-dimensional Minkowski metric:

$$d^s \left(v_i, v_j \right) = \left[\left(x_{vi} - x_{vj} \right)^s + \left(y_{vi} - y_{vi} \right)^s \right]^{1/s}$$

(2)

where $s = 1$ for Manhattan and $s = 2$ for Euclidean instances and (x_{vk}, y_{vk}) are the coordinates locating vertex v_k in the Euclidean plane. As the model is based on fuzzy logic, instances may have values $1 \leq s \leq 2$. In many application areas, the distance metric is typically known, and the fuzzy model therefore assumes that s can be retrieved from the data file. If s is not given, it is set at 1.5.

The level of clustering is the third characteristic of Johnson and McGeoch (2002). A formal definition of a cluster appears to be difficult, however, see Everitt et al. (2001). A cluster is seen as the set of vertices located around a chosen centre such that their distance value is smaller than their distance to any other existing cluster centre location in the area. In this study, the aim is to categorise an instance by its degree of clustering. The degree of clustering c $(0 \leq c \leq 1)$ is estimated by the calculation of the cophenetic correlation coefficient, see Everitt et al. (2001). This coefficient evaluates the hierarchical cluster tree that is created from the TSP instance coordinates and distance metric. The coefficient explains the correlation between the original and the cophenetic distances visualised in a corresponding dendogram. The closer c is to 1, the more certain the instance is clustered.

While the metric and level of clustering provide information about the distribution of the distances in an instance, an additional feature that will influence this, and is easily measurable, is arguably the shape of the overall area in which the vertices are distributed. *Shape* is therefore taken as the fourth characteristic. Within this study a ratio r is therefore introduced, that defines the smallest quadrangular area (r_x, r_y) to contain all

vertices, where $r = r_x / r_y$. Different values for r lead to various shapes of the area such as square shaped areas $(r_x = r_y, r = 1)$ or stretched rectangular areas $(r_x \gg r_y$, e.g. $r = 100)$. The range of values considered in the fuzzy model is: 1 (Square) $\leq r$ ≤ 150 (Stretched Rectangle). Any larger values of r are re-set to 150.

Finally, it is assumed some appropriate value of p is provided by the decision maker.

4.3. Guided Local Search

The meta-heuristic considered is an implementation of Guided Local Search (GLS), following closely the approaches presented in Beullens et al. (2003) and Muyldermans et al. (2005) but adapted for the symmetric TSP. At the heart lies the well-known 2-opt local search, which removes two edges in a given tour and replaces this by two other edges such that a new feasible tour is formed (Croes, 1958, Lin, 1965). The local search is embedded in GLS, a method proposed by Voudouris & Tsang (1996), and its application to TSP further described in Voudouris & Tsang (1999). GLS penalises edges in any given tour such that $d_0(v_i, v_j)$ $= d(v_i, v_j) + \lambda\, p(v_i, v_j)$, where $p(v_i, v_j)$ is the penalty parameter for the edge (v_i, v_j) and $\lambda = \alpha f(x^0)/n$; α is a parameter $(0 \leq \alpha \leq 1)$, $f(x^0)$ is the tour length of the local minimum obtained from an initial 2-opt local search using the original distance matrix, and n is the number of edges in the tour. Initially all penalty parameters are zero. At the $(k + 1)^{\text{th}}$ GLS-iteration, given solution x^k from the local search, the edge in x^k with the largest value for $d(v_i, v_j)$ $= (1 + p(v_i, v_j))$ will have its $p(v_i, v_j)$ incremented with one. The iteration continues by calling the local search algorithm to work on x^k, using the modified distances $d^0(v_i, v_j)$. The iteration is completed by evaluating the solution returned x^{k+1}, if different from x^k, against the original distances $d(v_i, v_j)$ and replacing the incumbent solution if it is better. The stopping criterion is the total number of GLS-iterations. Instead of investigating complete 2-opt neighbourhoods, only some particular 2-opt moves in the local search are investigated, using the mechanisms of neighbour lists and vertex marking. At the start of a run of a new instance, a neighbour list is constructed for every vertex v_i, containing the $(n-1)NL$ ($0 < NL \leq 1$) closest vertices, sorted in non-decreasing value of the distance to v_i. The parameter NL is specified at the start and describes the percentage of all instance points $n-1$ to be considered in a neighbour list. Only 2-opt moves are considered between an incident edge to a vertex v_i chosen from an active list AL and an incident edge to v_j chosen from v_i's neighbour list. The active list AL implements the vertex marking (do not look bits) policy, introduced by Bentley (1992). Every vertex can be either marked or unmarked. Initially, they are all marked and in AL. Searches start from marked vertices in the order in which they appear in AL (FIFO – First In First Out). When an investigated 2-opt move based on v_i from AL is unsuccessful, v_i is unmarked and removed from the AL. If the 2-opt move is successful, all of the four vertices incident to the removed edges in the tour that are unmarked and not in AL are marked and added to the end of the AL. When AL is empty, the local search terminates and returns its tour x^k to the GLS. GLS will only put the two vertices incident to the penalised edge in x^k in the AL. The combination of neighbour lists, vertex marking and GLS results in a much faster running procedure than one based on complete 2-opt neighbourhood searches without significantly affecting solution quality obtained since particularly moves that look somewhat promising (bringing vertices that are close in distance more adjacent to each other in the tour) are investigated. A starting solution is produced using a repeated nearest neighbour heuristic (rNNH). This approach applies the nearest neighbour heuristic (Rosenkrantz et al., 1977) while repeating the algorithm with each vertex as the starting vertex and choosing the best solution found. It is important to note that the GLS

implementation is a deterministic method, and thus for given values of the parameters it will always produce the same final solution. This simplifies the experimental analysis in comparison to meta-heuristics which contain random choices in their search strategy such as e.g. Simulated Annealing.

In conclusion, the implemented GLS requires the following parameters to be specified: ($0 \leq \alpha \leq 1$), NL ($0 \leq NL \leq 1$) and IT ($1 \leq IT_{max}$).

5. EXPERT-BASED IPTS DESIGN USING STATISTICAL ANALYSIS

An expert-based IPTS requires knowledge about the set of estimated instance characteristics and a decision maker preference, and the impact of changes on heuristic performance in combination with the setting of algorithm-specific parameters. In order to understand the main effects of each individual parameter on heuristic performance, and particular interactions between instance characteristics and algorithm-specific parameters, a multiple regression analysis is conducted.

5.1. Statistical Analysis

A full factorial design (Dean et al., 2001) is set up investigating seven factors, each corresponding to one of the four instance characteristics or three meta-heuristic parameters identified in the previous section. Instance size has been set at three levels (100, 500 and 1000) while all other factors are set at two levels as shown in Table 1. This results in a total of $3^1 * 2^6 = 192$ classes of combinations. In each class 6 instances have been created with a random instance generator, giving 1152 instances in the test set Φ^{TEST}.

Each instance of Φ^{TEST} is solved with respect to the combination of algorithm-specific parameters that is assigned in the factorial design, see Table 1.

Table 1. Factorial design TSP-GLS

	-1	+1
Cities *Cities on third level '0' with 500 cities	100	1000
Clustering	0 (Non-clustered)	1 (Clustered)
Distances	1 (Manhattan)	2 (Euclidean)
Ratio	1 (Square)	100 (Stretched Rectangle)
Alpha	0.2	0.4
NL-Size	0.2	0.4
GLS-Iterations	1000	100000

Solution quality S for a given instance ϕ_i and factor combination, using the meta-heuristic parameter set π, is defined in this study as:

$$S\left(\pi, \phi_i\right) = \left(f\left(\pi, \phi_i\right) - f^*_h\left(\phi_i\right)\right) / \left(f^0\left(\phi_i\right) - f^*_h\left(\phi_i\right)\right)$$

(3)

where $f(\pi, \phi_i)$ is the length of the Hamiltonian tour found for this instance and parameter set, $f^0(\phi_i)$ is the starting solution obtained from the repeated Nearest Neighbour Heuristic and $f^*_h(\phi_i)$ is an approximation for the optimal solution. In this study, $f^*_h(\phi_i)$ is set as the best found solution to the instance obtained while performing all experiments in the study. While solution quality in other studies is often measured against a lower bound solution $f^*_{lb}(\phi_i)$, based on a (relaxation) of some optimal algorithm, this is less appropriate for IPTS design. Indeed, the effectiveness of the relaxed optimal algorithm that calculates the lower bound might also be function of instance characteristics, and would then influence S. The choice of $(f^0(\phi_i) - f^*_h(\phi_i))$ as the benchmark avoids such interference, and focuses the analysis on establishing the ability of the meta-heuristic to improve its starting solution.

Experiments on each instance are conducted as follows: for each of the factors α and NL, one run is conducted for up to 3 million GLS iterations, while for any successful GLS iteration the required GLS iterations corresponding to tour length and computational time are recorded.

A multiple regression analysis has been conducted for both dependent variables - solution quality and computational time. For computational time, main model assumptions of linearity, normality and the assumption of constant variances are met, while data for solution quality show relatively more noise. The percentage of variability in the data explained by the regression model is 0.70 and 0.99 for solution quality and computational time, respectively.

The regression analysis has shown that the size of an instance n and the clustering c are both of high importance as they are affecting both solution quality and computational time. Moreover, they are part of almost all significant interaction effects of high importance. Although not affecting computational time as a single parameter, ratio r is also a crucial instance characteristic as it is part of major interaction effects mostly in combination with neighbour list size NL or clustering c. The distance information s is identified in interactions of only minor importance and is therefore considered to be of minor importance in the further analysis.

With respect to algorithm-specific parameters, the number of iterations IT has shown the expected important impact on both heuristic performance measures, which represents the well-known quality-time trade-off. Neighbour list size NL has a similar important impact on solution quality and computational time, showing significant main effects and being included in several significant interaction effects for both performance measures. The parameter α has the least impact on solution quality and only appears in interaction effects of minor importance. In contrast, α has an impact on computational time as main effect and is also of importance in interaction effects with other instance-specific parameters. Table 2 and 3 show all significant interaction effects that were detected with an impact on solution quality and computational time, respectively.

Table 2. Two-way interaction effects - Solution quality

	β	stand	p	Lower Bd. (Conf. Interval)	Upper Bd. (Conf. Interval)
c x r	0.049	0.314	0.000	0.044	0.053
c x NL	-0.036	-0.235	0.000	-0.041	-0.031
r x L	-0.035	-0.229	0.000	-0.04	-0.03
r x s	0.021	0.138	0.000	0.016	0.026
n x r	-0.024	-0.129	0.000	-0.031	-0.018
r x IT	0.016	0.105	0.000	0.011	0.021
n x IT	-0.018	-0.094	0.000	-0.024	-0.012
n x NL	0.016	0.087	0.000	0.01	0.023
c x s	-0.01	-0.068	0.000	-0.015	-0.005
n x c	-0.012	-0.065	0.000	-0.018	-0.006
s x IT	0.009	0.061	0.000	0.004	0.014
s x α	-0.009	-0.056	0.001	-0.014	-0.004
NL x IT	-0.005	-0.035	0.036	-0.01	0
c x α	0.005	0.033	0.048	0	0.01

Table 3. Two-way interaction effects - Computational time

	β	stand	p	Lower Bd. (Conf. Interval)	Upper Bd. (Conf. Interval)
n x IT	7.638	0.47	0.000	7.562	7.715
NL x IT	1.825	0.137	0.000	1.762	1.888
c x IT	1.512	0.114	0.000	1.45	1.575
n x NL	1.604	0.099	0.000	1.527	1.681
n x c	1.438	0.088	0.000	1.361	1.515
c x NL	0.56	0.042	0.000	0.497	0.622
c x r	-0.393	-0.03	0.000	-0.455	-0.33
α x IT	0.309	0.023	0.000	0.246	0.372
n x α	0.337	0.021	0.000	0.261	0.414
c x α	0.166	0.013	0.000	0.104	0.229
s x IT	0.137	0.01	0.000	0.074	0.199
s x r	0.091	0.007	0.005	0.028	0.153
r x IT	-0.087	-0.007	0.007	-0.15	-0.024
α x NL	0.066	0.005	0.039	0.003	0.129

With respect to an impact on solution quality, parameters c and r are part of the most significant interaction effects, although r has not been of importance in the context of main effects on solution quality. Additionally, instance size n, neighbour list size NL and number of iterations IT are part of most interactions, whereas α and distance metric s are less influencing. Table 3 shows that instance size n, clustering c, neighbour list size NL and number of iterations IT are the parameters involved in most significant interaction effects. It is shown that parameter combinations with IT seem to be in general of more importance compared to any other.

5.2. Fuzzy IPTS Design

With the knowledge of the impact of instance characteristics on heuristic performance, a fuzzy IPTS system can be designed to determine each algorithm-specific parameter value. A fuzzy system is characterised by a set of membership functions and a rule-base representing problem-specific knowledge. Table 4 and Table 5 list the membership functions of input and output parameters. Overall, this process uses the results of the statistical analysis within pre-determined ranges of instance characteristics, see Section 5.1, as an indication for impacts on heuristic performance.

The peak values for individual subsets are selected based on the levels chosen within the factorial design. The number of membership subsets is mainly chosen according to the number of factorial levels. With an increase of the parameter's importance, the number of membership subsets is increased.

A rule base is created by transforming main and interaction effects between instance-based information and algorithm-specific parameter obtained from the conducted regression analysis into fuzzy rules. Table 6 shows the rule base for the fuzzy ITS system.

5.3. Computational Results

Assessment of the designed FIS for ITPS has been conducted on several sets of instances derived from the random instance generator. In addition, the system has also been tested on a set Φ^{TSP} of 52 TSPLIB instances (Reinelt, 1992), with n ranging from 50 to about 1800. As these benchmark instances are well-known, and to keep the chapter within limits, we report only the performance on Φ^{TSP}. The performance of obtained algorithm parameters is compared to a fixed setting $\pi^{Fix} = (\alpha, NL, IT) = (0.3, 0.3, 200000)$. This setting of α and IT was used by Voudouris & Tsang (1999) in their paper on GLS for the TSP. An average value of $NL=0.3$ was added. Table 7, Table 8 and Table 9 show the absolute tour lengths for every instance using π^{Fix} by Voudouris & Tsang (1999) and the individual π^{Fuzzy} derived by the presented fuzzy IPTS. The solution quality is defined by calculating the excess of tour length $f(\pi^{Fuzzy}, \phi_i)$ obtained by the implemented fuzzy logic IPTS relative to the tour length $f(\pi^{Fix}, \phi_i)$ obtained by using the fixed parameter setting:

$$Excess = \left(f\left(\pi^{Fuzzy}, \phi_i\right) - f\left(\pi^{Fix}, \phi_i\right) \right) / \left(f\left(\pi^{Fix}, \phi_i\right) \right) \tag{4}$$

Computational times are reported in absolute terms (seconds), as both algorithms ran on the same computer.

Table 7, Table 8 and Table 9 show the results for $p = 0$, $p = 0.5$ and $p = 1$, respectively. If the user preference is set on saving time ($p = 1$), the excess is 0.65% on average. The average time needed is 2.30 sec, or about a factor 20 faster than a fixed parameter setting. Wanting best solution quality ($p = 0$), the excess is near zero, while time is on average slightly higher. This is mainly the result of the ITPS allocating a higher number of iterations to particular instances, in particular those of larger size. With $p = 0.5$, performance is indeed a trade-off between quality and time. The

Table 4. Input - IPTS membership functions

Parameter	Fuzzy set	Min	Med I	Med II	Max
Size n	Small	0	0	400	800
Size n	Medium	400	800	-	1200
Size n	Large	800	1200	1500	1500
Clustering c	Clustered	0	0	-	1
Clustering c	Non-Clustered	0	1	-	1
Distance c	Manhattan	0	1	-	2
Distance c	Euclidean	1	2	-	3
Ratio r	Square	0	0	10	60
Ratio r	Rectangle	10	60	-	110
Ratio r	Stretched Rectangle	60	110	150	150
DM preference p	Best SQ	0	0	-	0.5
DM preference p	Balance	0	0.5	-	1
DM preference p	Short Time	0.5	1	-	1

Table 5. Output - IPTS membership functions

Parameter	Fuzzy set	Min	Med I	Med II	Max
Penalty α	small	0.2	0.25	-	0.3
Penalty α	medium	0.25	0.3	-	0.35
Penalty α	large	0.3	0..35	-	0.4
NL-Size NL	small	0.2	0.25	-	0.3
NL-Size NL	medium	0.25	0.3	-	0.35
NL-Size NL	large	0.3	0..35	-	0.4
GLS-Iterations IT	vvvs	0	0	-	30000
GLS-Iterations IT	vvs	0	30000	-	60000
GLS-Iterations IT	vs	30000	60000	-	90000
GLS-Iterations IT	s	60000	90000	-	120000
GLS-Iterations IT	m	90000	120000	-	150000
GLS-Iterations IT	l	120000	150000	-	180000
GLS-Iterations IT	vl	150000	180000	-	210000
GLS-Iterations IT	vvl	180000	210000	240000	240000

Table 6. Rule base - Fuzzy IPTS

Input				$p = 0$ (Best SQ)			$p = 0.5$ (Balance)			$p = 1$ (Short Time)		
n	*c*	*s*	*r*	α	*NL*	*IT*	α	*NL*	*IT*	α	*NL*	*IT*
Small	Cl	Man	Square	s	l	l	s	s	vvs	s	s	vvvs
Medium	Cl	Man	Square	s	l	vl	s	s	vs	s	s	vvvs
Large	Cl	Man	Square	s	l	vl	s	s	s	s	s	vvvs
Small	Non-Cl	Man	Square	m	l	l	s	s	vvs	s	s	vvvs
Medium	Non-Cl	Man	Square	m	l	vl	s	s	vs	s	s	vvvs
Large	Non-Cl	Man	Square	m	l	vl	s	m	s	s	s	vvvs
Small	Cl	Eucl	Square	m	l	l	s	s	vs	s	s	vvvs
Medium	Cl	Eucl	Square	m	l	vl	s	s	s	s	s	vvvs
Large	Cl	Eucl	Square	m	l	vvl	s	m	m	s	s	vvvs
Small	Non-Cl	Eucl	Square	l	l	l	m	m	vs	s	s	vvvs
Medium	Non-Cl	Eucl	Square	l	l	vl	m	m	s	s	s	vvvs
Large	Non-Cl	Eucl	Square	l	l	vvl	m	m	m	s	s	vvvs
Small	Cl	Man	Rect	s	l	l	s	s	vvs	s	s	vvvs
Medium	Cl	Man	Rect	s	l	l	s	s	vs	s	s	vvvs
Large	Cl	Man	Rect	s	l	vl	s	s	s	s	s	vvvs
Small	Non-Cl	Man	Rect	m	m	l	s	s	vvs	s	s	vvvs
Medium	Non-Cl	Man	Rect	m	m	l	s	s	vs	s	s	vvvs
Large	Non-Cl	Man	Rect	m	l	vl	s	m	s	s	s	vvvs
Small	Cl	Eucl	Rect	m	l	l	s	s	vs	s	s	vvvs
Medium	Cl	Eucl	Rect	m	l	l	s	s	s	s	s	vvvs
Large	Cl	Eucl	Rect	m	l	vl	s	m	m	s	s	vvvs
Small	Non-Cl	Eucl	Rect	l	m	l	m	m	vs	s	s	vvvs
Medium	Non-Cl	Eucl	Rect	l	m	l	m	m	s	s	s	vvvs
Large	Non-Cl	Eucl	Rect	l	l	vl	m	m	m	s	s	vvvs
Small	Cl	Man	Str-Rect	s	l	m	s	s	vvs	s	s	vvvs
Medium	Cl	Man	Str-Rect	s	l	l	s	s	s	s	s	vvvs
Large	Cl	Man	Str-Rect	s	l	vl	s	s	s	s	s	vvvs

continued on following page

Table 6. Continued

Input				p = 0 (Best SQ)			p = 0.5 (Balance)			p = 1 (Short Time)		
Small	Non-Cl	Man	Str-Rect	m	m	m	s	s	vvs	s	s	vvvs
Medium	Non-Cl	Man	Str-Rect	m	m	l	sS	s	vs	s	s	vvvs
Large	Non-Cl	Man	Str-Rect	m	l	vl	s	m	s	s	s	vvvs
Small	Cl	Eucl	Str-Rect	m	l	m	s	s	vs	s	s	vvvs
Medium	Cl	Eucl	Str-Rect	m	l	l	s	s	s	s	s	vvvs
Large	Cl	Eucl	Str-Rect	m	l	vl	s	m	m	s	s	vvvs
Small	Non-Cl	Eucl	Str-Rect	l	m	m	m	m	vs	s	s	vvvs
Medium	Non-Cl	Eucl	Str-Rect	l	m	l	m	m	s	s	s	vvvs
Large	Non-Cl	Eucl	Str-Rect	l	l	vl	m	m	m	s	s	vvvs

average excess is 0.1% and therefore improved in comparison to $p = 1$ but not as good as for $p = 0$, and computational time is with an average of 22.26 sec again in between $p = 1$ and $p = 0$, and still half the time of the fixed setting.

In conclusion, the particular IPTS designed is able to exploit the strength of GLS in a more flexible manner than a fixed parameter setting approach, and shows the ability to cut computational times at little or no extra cost with respect to solution quality.

6. AUTOMATED IPTS DESIGN USING FUZZY CLUSTERING

In the design of an IPTS based on the approach introduced in the previous section clearly lies a challenge. The significant impact of structural information of an instance on heuristic performance has to be obtained through performing a statistical analysis, and these results have to be interpreted by a fuzzy design expert in setting up the FIS. This may be a valid strategy for experts that have the opportunity to invest their time in requiring extensive knowledge about the problem by setting up a (full) factorial design, and then tailoring the fuzzy logic system accordingly.

This section presents a more automated approach to the design of the fuzzy ITPS. Its advantages are in particular that membership functions and rule base are created automatically using fuzzy clustering, and hence there is no longer the need to "manually" obtain and translate knowledge on structural instance information into a rule-based system. A statistical analysis is therefore also no longer needed, and the automated approach can obtain useful information simply by provision of a large test set of representative instances, which does not necessarily need to follow the logic of a full factorial design.

6.1. Fuzzy Clustering

An FIS, incorporating a rule base and a corresponding set of membership functions, can be automatically designed using fuzzy clustering, see Wang et al.(2008). The c-means algorithm has been introduced by MacQueen (1967) and is also known as k-means or Isodata. It is distinguished

Table 7. Results: Expert-based IPTS test set Φ^{TSP} - GLS p=0 (best SQ)

TSPLIB Instance	α	NL	IT	Tour Voudouris (π^{Fix})	Tour Fuzzy (π^{Fuzzy})	Excess	Time Voudouris (π^{Fix})	Time Fuzzy(π^{Fuzzy})
a280	0.32	0.35	150000	2579	2579	0.0000	21.49	18.47
berlin52	0.31	0.35	150000	7542	7542	0.0000	3.55	2.89
bier127	0.31	0.35	150000	118282	118282	0.0000	8.94	7.50
ch130	0.33	0.35	150000	6110	6110	0.0000	9.80	8.06
ch150	0.33	0.35	150000	6528	6528	0.0000	11.67	9.48
d1291	0.33	0.35	215369	51021	50979	-0.0008	113.92	136.94
d1655	0.32	0.35	214690	62744	62669	-0.0012	149.83	175.83
d198	0.31	0.35	150000	15781	15789	0.0005	14.41	11.75
d493	0.32	0.35	159097	35015	35024	0.0003	42.16	36.42
d657	0.33	0.35	168512	48976	48960	-0.0003	56.99	51.58
dsj1000	0.32	0.35	199228	18780063	18775492	-0.0002	93.89	102.08
eil101	0.32	0.35	150000	629	629	0.0000	6.66	5.61
eil51	0.32	0.35	150000	426	426	0.0000	3.41	2.73
eil76	0.33	0.35	150000	538	538	0.0000	5.13	4.23
fl1400	0.31	0.35	216004	20522	20509	-0.0006	129.67	151.75
fl1577	0.32	0.35	215453	22309	22322	0.0006	138.86	167.99
fl417	0.31	0.35	151988	11887	11894	0.0006	33.22	28.67
kroA100	0.32	0.35	150000	21282	21282	0.0000	7.20	5.95
kroB100	0.32	0.35	150000	22141	22141	0.0000	7.09	5.89
kroB150	0.32	0.35	150000	26130	26130	0.0000	11.69	9.53
kroB200	0.33	0.35	150000	29437	29437	0.0000	16.13	13.77
kroC100	0.33	0.35	150000	20749	20749	0.0000	7.11	6.03
kroD100	0.32	0.35	150000	21294	21294	0.0000	7.31	6.03
kroE100	0.33	0.35	150000	22068	22068	0.0000	7.27	6.00
lin105	0.33	0.35	150000	14379	14379	0.0000	7.34	5.97
linhp318	0.32	0.35	150000	42029	42029	0.0000	25.78	21.22
nrw1379	0.33	0.35	214897	56785	56729	-0.0010	127.50	145.75
p654	0.31	0.35	168323	34760	34768	0.0002	57.88	52.52
pcb1173	0.33	0.35	212033	57066	56933	-0.0023	103.75	118.45
pr107	0.31	0.35	150000	44586	44586	0.0000	7.25	5.86
pr124	0.32	0.35	150000	59030	59030	0.0000	8.70	7.08
pr136	0.31	0.35	150000	96781	96772	-0.0001	9.69	7.84
pr144	0.32	0.35	150000	58537	58537	0.0000	10.27	8.28
pr152	0.32	0.35	150000	73686	73682	-0.0001	10.78	9.02
pr226	0.32	0.35	150000	80369	80369	0.0000	16.91	14.33
pr264	0.31	0.35	150000	49144	49144	0.0000	20.78	16.78
pr299	0.32	0.35	150000	48191	48195	0.0001	23.61	19.53
pr439	0.31	0.35	154139	107344	107323	-0.0002	37.31	31.45

continued on following page

Table 7. Continued

TSPLIB	α	NL	IT	Tour	Tour	Excess	Time	Time
pr76	0.32	0.35	150000	108159	108159	0.0000	5.13	4.22
rat195	0.32	0.35	150000	2323	2323	0.0000	14.14	11.55
rat99	0.33	0.35	150000	1211	1211	0.0000	6.59	5.45
rd100	0.32	0.35	150000	7910	7910	0.0000	7.19	6.00
rd400	0.33	0.35	150000	15280	15282	0.0001	35.39	28.95
rcl1304	0.33	0.35	215410	253274	253333	0.0002	120.25	142.08
rcl1323	0.33	0.35	215321	270681	270699	0.0001	121.08	141.58
rcl1889	0.33	0.35	215300	317495	318741	0.0039	195.84	230.00
ts225	0.33	0.35	150000	126643	126643	0.0000	16.78	13.78
tsp225	0.32	0.35	150000	3861	3861	0.0000	17.16	14.31
u1060	0.33	0.35	204413	224690	224599	-0.0004	93.19	102.98
u1432	0.32	0.35	214336	153126	153185	0.0004	122.50	166.33
u159	0.33	0.35	150000	42080	42080	0.0000	11.92	9.75
u1817	0.34	0.35	215876	57417	57287	-0.0023	167.56	208.66
						0.0000	44.42	48.56

between hard (or crisp) and fuzzy k-means, which consider the membership of a data point to a cluster in the classical (crisp) or fuzzy sense, respectively. Fuzzy k-means is an extension of the hard k-means clustering algorithms and has been introduced by Bezdek (1981). The algorithm is based on the idea of fuzzy membership values. Each cluster is defined as a fuzzy set and called a fuzzy cluster.

6.2. Fuzzy IPTS Design

In order to model a set of membership functions, the fuzzy c-means mechanism is applied on a given data set Φ^n of n randomly created instances with a set of input variables $a_1, a_2, .., a_A$ and a set of output variables $b_1, b_2, ..., b_B$. The algorithm generates k clusters such that each instance $j, j = 1, .., n$, with the corresponding tuple $(a_{1j}, a_{2j}, .., a_{Aj}, b_{1j}, b_{2j}, .., b_{Bj})$ is assigned to a cluster c_i. The number of clusters is derived by subtractive clustering, based on the mountain method (Yager et al., 1992). The applied fuzzy modelling design uses Gaussian membership functions. Hence, two parameters, the mean

u_i and standard deviation σ_i need to be determined for each membership function corresponding to the ith cluster. The mean value u_i is equal to the centre point of cluster c_i. Standard deviation σ_i is calculated by:

$$\sigma_i = \frac{1}{n} \sqrt{\sum \sum_{j=1}^{n} \frac{-(v_i - \bar{c})^2}{2 \ln(\mu_{ij})}} \tag{5}$$

where μ_{ij} represents the degree of membership of data point v_j being in cluster ci, and $\bar{c}$ is the centre point of cluster ci, see Wang et al. (2008). Using fuzzy c-means, the corresponding rule base is extracted from the fuzzy c-partition by applying the logical AND operator. Hence, a rule R_i ($i = 1, .., k$) is derived by combining the membership subsets of each input a_u and output b_v variable that are corresponding to the same cluster c_i. The implementation of the algorithm is done in Matlab. The following characterises the inputs needed to set-up the automated FIS design algorithm:

Table 8. Results: Expert-based IPTS test set Φ^{TSP} - GLS p=0.5 (balance)

TSPLIB Instance	α	NL	IT	Tour Voudouris (π^{Fix})	Tour Fuzzy (π^{Fuzzy})	Excess	Time Voudouris (π^{Fix})	Time Fuzzy (π^{Fuzzy})
a280	0.27	0.27	60000	2579	2579	0	21.49	6.11
berlin52	0.26	0.26	60000	7542	7542	0	3.55	1.047
bier127	0.26	0.26	60000	118282	118282	0	8.94	2.61
ch130	0.28	0.28	60000	6110	6110	0	9.8	2.828
ch150	0.28	0.28	60000	6528	6528	0	11.67	3.422
d1291	0.28	0.3	120000	51021	50973	-0.0009	113.92	67.781
d1655	0.27	0.3	120000	62744	62812	0.0011	149.83	87.86
d198	0.26	0.26	60000	15781	15795	0.0009	14.41	3.938
d493	0.27	0.27	69050	35015	35012	-0.0001	42.16	13.89
d657	0.28	0.28	78441	48976	49033	0.0012	56.99	21.578
dsj1000	0.27	0.28	105028	18780063	18774331	-0.0003	93.89	46.61
eil101	0.27	0.27	60000	629	629	0	6.66	2.047
eil51	0.27	0.27	60000	426	426	0	3.41	1
eil76	0.28	0.28	60000	538	538	0	5.13	1.547
fl1400	0.26	0.3	120000	20522	20554	0.0016	129.67	73.235
fl1577	0.27	0.3	120000	22309	22327	0.0008	138.86	80.734
fl417	0.26	0.26	61853	11887	11913	0.0022	33.22	10.079
kroA100	0.27	0.27	60000	21282	21282	0	7.2	2.141
kroB100	0.27	0.27	60000	22141	22141	0	7.09	2.11
kroB150	0.27	0.27	60000	26130	26130	0	11.69	3.453
kroB200	0.28	0.28	60000	29437	29437	0	16.13	4.86
kroC100	0.28	0.28	60000	20749	20749	0	7.11	2.141
kroD100	0.27	0.27	60000	21294	21294	0	7.31	2.187
kroE100	0.28	0.28	60000	22068	22068	0	7.27	2.187
lin105	0.28	0.28	60000	14379	14379	0	7.34	2.188
linhp318	0.27	0.27	60000	42029	42029	0	25.78	7.578
nrw1379	0.28	0.3	120000	56785	56800	0.0003	127.5	74.766
p654	0.26	0.26	78254	34760	34703	-0.0016	57.88	20.75
pcb1173	0.28	0.29	116805	57066	57038	-0.0005	103.75	58.75
pr107	0.26	0.26	60000	44586	44586	0	7.25	2.125
pr124	0.27	0.27	60000	59030	59030	0	8.7	2.579
pr136	0.26	0.26	60000	96781	96772	-0.0001	9.69	2.906
pr144	0.27	0.27	60000	58537	58537	0	10.27	2.969
pr152	0.27	0.27	60000	73686	73682	-0.0001	10.78	3.156
pr226	0.27	0.27	60000	80369	80369	0	16.91	4.906
pr264	0.26	0.26	60000	49144	51012	0.038	20.78	5.672
pr299	0.27	0.27	60000	48191	48195	0.0001	23.61	7.031
pr439	0.26	0.26	64075	107344	107316	-0.0003	37.31	11.391

continued on following page

Table 8. Continued

TSPLIB	α	NL	IT	Tour	Tour	Excess	Time	Time
pr76	0.27	0.27	60000	108159	108159	0	5.13	1.593
rat195	0.27	0.27	60000	2323	2323	0	14.14	4.203
rat99	0.28	0.28	60000	1211	1211	0	6.59	2.031
rd100	0.27	0.27	60000	7910	7910	0	7.19	2.125
rd400	0.28	0.28	60000	15280	15282	0.0001	35.39	10.312
rcl1304	0.28	0.3	120000	253274	253639	0.0014	120.25	71.219
rcl1323	0.28	0.3	120000	270681	271571	0.0033	121.08	71.906
rcl1889	0.28	0.3	120000	317495	318022	0.0017	195.84	114.797
ts225	0.28	0.28	60000	126643	126643	0	16.78	4.938
tsp225	0.27	0.27	60000	3861	3861	0	17.16	4.859
u1060	0.28	0.28	108700	224690	224715	0.0001	93.19	48.453
u1432	0.27	0.3	120000	153126	153204	0.0005	122.5	70.266
u159	0.28	0.28	60000	42080	42080	0	11.92	3.375
u1817	0.29	0.3	120000	57417	57425	0.0001	167.56	95.375
						0.001	**44.42**	**22.26**

1. **The Set of Input Parameters:** For an IPTS it consists of all investigated instance characteristics while a decision maker preference is fixed. Hence, the derived FIS is valid for one particular decision maker preference only;

2. **The Output Parameter:** Corresponds to an algorithm-specific parameter;

3. **The Type of Fuzzy Inference Method:** Which is selected to be Mamdani in this analysis;

4. **The Number of Clusters:** Can be fixed or retrieved by subtractive clustering (Chiu, 1994).

An experimental set of 300 instances Φ^{300} has been created by the random generator used in the previous section, where each instance is drawing its instance- and algorithm-specific parameters randomly from within a pre-set parameter domain as specified in Table 10. In order to assess solution quality, each instance is solved with all possible combinations of algorithm-specific parameter values for α and *NL* within the factorial design in Table 1 and *IT* = 3 million GLS iterations. The tour length of each instance is then obtained by a random set of algorithm-specific parameters in comparison to the best obtained solution by all fixed combinations which are run for 3 million GLS iterations. Solution quality of an instance ϕ_i is calculated by Equation (3). Computational times are recorded in absolute times for the corresponding random combination of all three algorithm-specific parameter values.

The set of performance data for Φ^{300} needs to be pre-processed such that all features are on a unified scale. The min-max normalisation is applied. In order to normalise the data corresponding to each input and output variables, the largest value max_i and the smallest value min_i of each parameter q_i is determined and subsequently each set of parameter values is normalised to an interval [max, min] such that:

$$q_i^{Norm} = \left(\left(q_i - min_i \right) / \left(max_i - min_i \right) \right) \times \left(max - min \right) + min. \tag{6}$$

Table 9. Results: Expert-based IPTS test set Φ^{TSP} - GLS p=1 (short computational times)

TSPLIB Instance	α	NL	IT	Tour Voudouris (η^{Fix})	Tour Fuzzy (η^{Fuzzy})	Excess	Time Voudouris (η^{Fix})	Time Fuzzy (η^{Fuzzy})
a280	0.25	0.25	10910	2579	2579	0.0000	21.49	1.17
berlin52	0.25	0.25	9883	7542	7542	0.0000	3.55	0.19
bier127	0.25	0.25	9741	118282	118361	0.0007	8.94	0.44
ch130	0.25	0.25	10892	6110	6110	0.0000	9.80	0.61
ch150	0.25	0.25	10697	6528	6546	0.0028	11.67	0.66
d1291	0.25	0.25	10152	51021	52557	0.0301	113.92	5.58
d1655	0.25	0.25	10658	62744	63818	0.0171	149.83	7.98
d198	0.25	0.25	9377	15781	15826	0.0029	14.41	0.72
d493	0.25	0.25	10587	35015	35411	0.0113	42.16	2.31
d657	0.25	0.25	10321	48976	49708	0.0149	56.99	3.13
dsj1000	0.25	0.25	11067	18780063	19029304	0.0133	93.89	5.24
eil101	0.25	0.25	11006	629	629	0.0000	6.66	0.41
eil51	0.25	0.25	10857	426	426	0.0000	3.41	0.23
eil76	0.25	0.25	10657	538	538	0.0000	5.13	0.31
fl1400	0.25	0.25	9742	20522	20731	0.0102	129.67	6.17
fl1577	0.25	0.25	10094	22309	22772	0.0208	138.86	6.88
fl417	0.25	0.25	9845	11887	12029	0.0119	33.22	1.77
kroA100	0.25	0.25	10755	21282	21282	0.0000	7.20	0.41
kroB100	0.25	0.25	10758	22141	22141	0.0000	7.09	0.44
kroB150	0.25	0.25	10371	26130	26132	0.0001	11.69	0.73
kroB200	0.25	0.25	11062	29437	29449	0.0004	16.13	0.95
kroC100	0.25	0.25	10510	20749	20749	0.0000	7.11	0.41
kroD100	0.25	0.25	10642	21294	21294	0.0000	7.31	0.45
kroE100	0.25	0.25	10708	22068	22068	0.0000	7.27	0.49
lin105	0.25	0.25	10930	14379	14379	0.0000	7.34	0.42
linhp318	0.25	0.25	10618	42029	42176	0.0035	25.78	1.66
nrw1379	0.25	0.25	10502	56785	57812	0.0181	127.50	6.08
p654	0.25	0.25	10358	34760	34735	-0.0007	57.88	2.86
pcb1173	0.25	0.25	10450	57066	58158	0.0191	103.75	5.39
pr107	0.25	0.25	9353	44586	44586	0.0000	7.25	0.34
pr124	0.25	0.25	11062	59030	59030	0.0000	8.70	0.50
pr136	0.25	0.25	9823	96781	96785	0.0000	9.69	0.61
pr144	0.25	0.25	10342	58537	58590	0.0009	10.27	0.53
pr152	0.25	0.25	9963	73686	73682	-0.0001	10.78	0.53
pr226	0.25	0.25	10120	80369	80414	0.0006	16.91	0.92
pr264	0.25	0.25	9348	49144	49235	0.0019	20.78	1.00
pr299	0.25	0.25	10090	48191	48269	0.0016	23.61	1.30

continued on following page

Table 9. Continued

TSPLIB	α	NL	IT	Tour	Tour	Excess	Time	Time
pr439	0.25	0.25	9874	107344	109687	0.0218	37.31	1.94
pr76	0.25	0.25	10625	108159	108159	0.0000	5.13	0.36
rat195	0.25	0.25	10808	2323	2323	0.0000	14.14	0.80
rat99	0.25	0.25	10974	1211	1211	0.0000	6.59	0.41
rd100	0.25	0.25	10649	7910	7910	0.0000	7.19	0.47
rd400	0.25	0.25	10952	15280	15376	0.0063	35.39	1.95
rcl1304	0.25	0.25	10124	253274	260257	0.0276	120.25	6.28
rcl1323	0.25	0.25	10185	270681	276261	0.0206	121.08	6.08
rcl1889	0.25	0.25	10200	317495	325279	0.0245	195.84	9.61
ts225	0.25	0.25	11067	126643	126643	0.0000	16.78	1.00
tsp225	0.25	0.25	10726	3861	3893	0.0083	17.16	0.98
u1060	0.25	0.25	10286	224690	228636	0.0176	93.19	4.86
u1432	0.25	0.25	10956	153126	154496	0.0089	122.50	5.70
u159	0.25	0.25	10756	42080	42080	0.0000	11.92	0.67
u1817	0.25	0.25	9815	57417	58611	0.0208	167.56	6.89
						0.0065	**44.42**	**2.27**

Table 10. Parameter domains for test set Φ^{300}

Instance-specific parameter domain			
Cities	n	100	1300
Clustering	c	0	1
Distance	s	1	2
Ratio	r	1	150
Algorithm-specific parameter domain			
Alpha	α	0.1	0.5
NL-Size	NL	0.1	0.5
GLS-Iterations	IT	1000	240000

Considering the 0-1 normalisation, Equation (5) can be simplified such that:

$$q_i^{Norm} = \left(\left(q_i - \min_i\right) / \left(\max_i - \min_i\right)\right) \quad (7)$$

In order to incorporate a decision maker preference valuing both objective variables, solution quality and computational time are normalised on a 0-1 scale and combined to one performance value f using Equation (1).

In order to build a fuzzy system, a decision maker's preference has to be chosen at this stage so that the combined heuristic performance value is calculated and the clustering is applied on the combined objective value f. Furthermore, the objective variable should be considered to be of more importance than the (independent) explanatory variables (Nakamori et al., 1994). In order to weight the objective variables solution quality and computational time with more importance, performance value f has been normalised on a larger scale than all explanatory variables. The suggested scale for the objective variable f is [1,100]. In contrast, all instance- and algorithm-specific parameters are normalised on a 0-1 scale. In order not to exceed the range of a parameter in the fuzzy system, the data is pre-processed such that if a new incoming parameter value q_i of an instance ϕ_j exceeds the particular interval, it is reset such that $q_i(\phi_j) = 0$, if $q_i \leq min_i$, and $q_i(\phi_j) = 1$ if $q_i \leq max_i$.

6.3. Computational Results

Three fuzzy systems have been designed choosing three different values for decision maker preferences p: $p = 0$ (Time), $p = 0.5$ (Balance) and $p = 1$ (SQ). All three derived systems for GLS consist of about 130 rules which is equivalent to the number of membership functions. Table 11, 12 and 13 show the results for Φ^{TSP} for values of p = 0, 0.5 and 1, respectively. The tour lengths derived from a fixed setting of parameter values π^{Fix} ($\alpha = 0.3$, $NL = 0.3$, $IT = 200000$) (Voudouris and Tsang, 1999) are compared to the solution using an instance-specific parameter setting by the automated IPTS (π^{Fuzzy_A}), see column 'Tour length Voudouris' and 'Tour length Fuzzy', respectively. Subsequently, solution quality is expressed by calculating the excess, see Equation 4. Computational times are reported in absolute terms (seconds), as both algorithms ran on the same computer.

Table 11 shows that large instances affect the average time value significantly as the corresponding parameter settings lead to larger computational times. For the automated case, the average computational time for $p = 1$ is significantly larger compared to the corresponding results in Section 5. In contrast, the solution quality value reflects that on average the tour lengths are

shorter. The designed system for parameter settings that lead to balanced solutions ($p = 0.5$), see Table 12, shows a moderate medium level of average solution quality and computational time between both other preferences. In terms of solution quality, the designed system resulted in a slight improvement on average for Φ^{TSP} while computational time is on average smaller than the expert-based system presented in Section 5. In conclusion, the average results are in a smaller range than the expert-based design with the computational time being on average larger and solution qualities on average better.

Table 14 shows an overview of the results that were obtained for the test set Φ^{TSP} for both IPTS designs presented in this chapter. For three different decision maker preferences, the table shows the average performance for Φ^{TSP} with regards to solution quality ('Excess', see Equation 4) and computational time. In comparison, the expert-based approach results in a significantly bigger range with regards to both performance measures, while the automated approach shows slightly less variation. This phenomenon is based on the concept of using insights to create the membership functions for an expert-based approach manually. Hence, the decision maker has an indirect impact on the performance variation with respect to different decision maker preference. This flexibility is not given for an automated approach as shown in Table 14. Reasons for this are suggested to be related to the initial experimental set Φ^{300}. This set consisted of 300 instances each of which has been assigned with a random set of algorithm-specific parameters. Hence, only a somewhat restricted set of combinations is used in training the IPTS. For example, it is an obvious insight that small instances could be solved with a smaller number of iterations resulting in a reasonable good solution quality whereas larger instances would require a larger number of iterations to be solved on the same level of solution quality. If in the experimental set of instances Φ^{300} the combination of very small instances and small iteration values does not ex-

Table 11. Results: Automated IPTS test set ΦTSP - GLS p=0 (best SQ)

TSPLIB Instance	α	NL	IT	Tour Voudouris (n^{Fix})	Tour Fuzzy (n^{Fuzzy_A})	Excess	Time Voudouris (n^{Fix})	Time Fuzzy (n^{Fuzzy_A})
a280	0.22	0.34	140750	2579	2579	0.0000	21.49	13.38
berlin52	0.2	0.29	183171	7542	7542	0.0000	3.55	2.83
bier127	0.18	0.26	197284	118282	118282	0.0000	8.94	7.21
ch130	0.24	0.34	144631	6110	6110	0.0000	9.80	6.58
ch150	0.24	0.34	141685	6528	6528	0.0000	11.67	7.57
d1291	0.4	0.31	139728	51021	50860	-0.0032	113.92	97.55
d1655	0.4	0.31	139654	62744	62525	-0.0035	149.83	126.29
d198	0.17	0.26	209424	15781	15787	0.0004	14.41	11.96
d493	0.22	0.34	140804	35015	35033	0.0005	42.16	26.79
d657	0.38	0.31	139790	48976	48954	-0.0004	56.99	46.86
dsj1000	0.42	0.31	139674	18780063	18761564	-0.0010	93.89	84.07
eil101	0.24	0.35	151645	629	629	0.0000	6.66	4.97
eil51	0.24	0.36	151735	426	426	0.0000	3.41	2.38
eil76	0.24	0.36	151737	538	538	0.0000	5.13	3.80
fl1400	0.39	0.31	139479	20522	20512	-0.0005	129.67	109.28
fl1577	0.4	0.31	139654	22309	22337	0.0013	138.86	120.98
fl417	0.22	0.29	164088	11887	11866	-0.0018	33.22	25.00
kroA100	0.24	0.35	151735	21282	21282	0.0000	7.20	5.22
kroB100	0.24	0.35	151735	22141	22141	0.0000	7.09	5.22
kroB150	0.21	0.31	181452	26130	26130	0.0000	11.69	9.14
kroB200	0.23	0.34	140748	29437	29437	0.0000	16.13	10.44
kroC100	0.24	0.36	151737	20749	20749	0.0000	7.11	5.25
kroD100	0.24	0.35	151735	21294	21294	0.0000	7.31	5.33
kroE100	0.24	0.36	151737	22068	22068	0.0000	7.27	5.22
lin105	0.24	0.35	151206	14379	14379	0.0000	7.34	5.28
linhp318	0.22	0.34	140831	42029	42029	0.0000	25.78	16.21
nrw1379	0.4	0.31	139654	56785	56782	-0.0001	127.50	105.52
p654	0.29	0.28	163290	34760	34746	-0.0004	57.88	49.70
pcb1173	0.42	0.31	139696	57066	56990	-0.0013	103.75	91.07
pr107	0.17	0.26	205910	44586	44586	0.0000	7.25	6.44
pr124	0.24	0.34	146793	59030	59030	0.0000	8.70	6.02
pr136	0.2	0.26	187674	96781	96772	-0.0001	9.69	8.13
pr144	0.2	0.31	183459	58537	58537	0.0000	10.27	8.36
pr152	0.2	0.31	183233	73686	73818	0.0018	10.78	8.91
pr226	0.21	0.32	173259	80369	80369	0.0000	16.91	12.57
pr264	0.17	0.26	205256	49144	49135	-0.0002	20.78	16.35
pr299	0.22	0.33	152113	48191	48191	0.0000	23.61	16.54
pr439	0.22	0.31	151761	107344	107314	-0.0003	37.31	25.21

continued on following page

Table 11. Continued

TSPLIB Instance	α	NL	IT	Tour Voudouris (n^{Fix})	Tour Fuzzy (n^{Fuzzy_A})	Excess	Time Voudouris (n^{Fix})	Time Fuzzy (n^{Fuzzy_A})
pr76	0.24	0.34	151972	108159	108159	0.0000	5.13	3.88
rat195	0.23	0.34	140728	2323	2323	0.0000	14.14	9.32
rat99	0.24	0.36	151737	1211	1211	0.0000	6.59	5.02
rd100	0.24	0.35	151735	7910	7910	0.0000	7.19	5.25
rd400	0.22	0.34	140589	15280	15284	0.0003	35.39	23.00
rcl1304	0.4	0.31	139654	253274	253380	0.0004	120.25	102.30
rcl1323	0.4	0.31	139654	270681	271250	0.0021	121.08	103.66
rcl1889	0.4	0.31	139654	317495	317844	0.0011	195.84	164.63
ts225	0.22	0.34	140748	126643	126643	0.0000	16.78	10.83
tsp225	0.22	0.34	140748	3861	3861	0.0000	17.16	11.07
u1060	0.42	0.31	139670	224690	224366	-0.0014	93.19	82.63
u1432	0.4	0.31	139654	153126	153171	0.0003	122.5	106.23
u159	0.24	0.34	141259	42080	42080	0.0000	11.92	7.47
u1817	0.4	0.31	139654	57417	57541	0.0022	167.56	140.06
						-0.0001	**44.42**	**36.44**

ist, the fuzzy clustering process will not create a cluster consisting of small sized instances and small number of iterations. Hence, the clustering would not lead to a fuzzy system considering different number of iterations for small and large instances. The sensitivity of the derived systems could therefore be improved by either narrowing the ranges of each randomly selected parameter in Φ^{300}, or by extending the number of instances in the training set to sufficiently more than 300.

The process of automating the generation of a fuzzy system based ITPS on an experimental set of test instances has led to significantly good results compared to the use of a fixed parameter setting for GLS. The results are intriguing taking into consideration that a reasonably small set of 300 randomly solved instances has been the main basis of this approach and the design can be applied to any instance with characteristics either within or close to the range of instance characteristics present within this set.

In contrast, a manual design may be able to explore the benefits of performance improvements to a larger extent, which in turn, however, requires some knowledge about the problem itself.

7. DISCUSSION

Sections 5 and Section 6 have shown two approaches for a design of an IPTS using Fuzzy Logic systems. While Section 5 uses a manual design using a statistical analysis, Section 6 introduced an automated design strategy that applied fuzzy clustering to set-up a fuzzy system.

The results have shown that the manual design allows manual tweaking to improve performance thresholds and hence, performance could be im-

Table 12. Results: Automated IPTS test set ΦTSP - GLS p=0 (balance)

TSPLIB Instance	α	NL	IT	Tour Voudouris (n^{Fix})	Tour Fuzzy (n^{Fuzzy_A})	Excess	Time Voudouris (n^{Fix})	Time Fuzzy (n^{Fuzzy_A})
a280	0.3	0.16	99012	2579	2579	0.0000	21.49	10.61
berlin52	0.28	0.17	82049	7542	7542	0.0000	3.55	1.50
bier127	0.26	0.22	115327	118282	118282	0.0000	8.94	5.05
ch130	0.28	0.16	81716	6110	6110	0.0000	9.80	4.03
ch150	0.28	0.16	81780	6528	6528	0.0000	11.67	4.74
d1291	0.29	0.23	97793	51021	51405	0.0075	113.92	56.17
d1655	0.29	0.24	97798	62744	63205	0.0073	149.83	74.53
d198	0.23	0.31	158527	15781	15784	0.0002	14.41	10.34
d493	0.34	0.26	130296	35015	35029	0.0004	42.16	30.34
d657	0.35	0.38	109231	48976	49010	0.0007	56.99	35.42
dsj1000	0.29	0.21	97514	18780063	18843434	0.0034	93.89	45.91
eil101	0.28	0.16	81671	629	629	0.0000	6.66	2.77
eil51	0.28	0.16	81666	426	426	0.0000	3.41	1.44
eil76	0.28	0.16	81666	538	538	0.0000	5.13	2.17
fl1400	0.36	0.38	124457	20522	20547	0.0012	129.67	95.25
fl1577	0.37	0.37	118915	22309	22377	0.0030	138.86	100.67
fl417	0.33	0.26	121650	11887	11874	-0.0011	33.22	23.00
kroA100	0.28	0.16	81666	21282	21282	0.0000	7.20	3.03
kroB100	0.28	0.16	81666	22141	22141	0.0000	7.09	3.08
kroB150	0.28	0.16	81780	26130	26130	0.0000	11.69	5.03
kroB200	0.28	0.16	83127	29437	29437	0.0000	16.13	7.00
kroC100	0.28	0.16	81666	20749	20749	0.0000	7.11	3.00
kroD100	0.28	0.16	81666	21294	21294	0.0000	7.31	3.05
kroE100	0.28	0.16	81666	22068	22068	0.0000	7.27	3.03
lin105	0.28	0.16	81634	14379	14379	0.0000	7.34	3.06
linhp318	0.31	0.15	102573	42029	42029	0.0000	25.78	13.91
nrw1379	0.29	0.24	97798	56785	56884	0.0017	127.50	60.50
p654	0.32	0.34	199448	34760	34759	0.0000	57.88	61.83
pcb1173	0.29	0.21	97479	57066	57019	-0.0008	103.75	48.67
pr107	0.19	0.29	193587	44586	44586	0.0000	7.25	6.09
pr124	0.28	0.16	81677	59030	59030	0.0000	8.70	3.64
pr136	0.28	0.18	86594	96781	96781	0.0000	9.69	4.28
pr144	0.28	0.16	81770	58537	58537	0.0000	10.27	4.41
pr152	0.28	0.17	82135	73686	73682	-0.0001	10.78	4.56
pr226	0.29	0.16	86678	80369	80369	0.0000	16.91	7.84
pr264	0.29	0.34	107405	49144	49135	-0.0002	20.78	11.69
pr299	0.32	0.17	115961	48191	48191	0.0000	23.61	15.30
pr439	0.33	0.26	135190	107344	107308	-0.0003	37.31	28.03

continued on following page

Table 12. Continued

TSPLIB Instance	α	NL	IT	Tour Voudouris (n^{Fix})	Tour Fuzzy (n^{Fuzzy_A})	Excess	Time Voudouris (n^{Fix})	Time Fuzzy (n^{Fuzzy_A})
pr76	0.28	0.16	81666	108159	108159	0.0000	5.13	2.27
rat195	0.28	0.15	82635	2323	2323	0.0000	14.14	5.94
rat99	0.28	0.16	81666	1211	1211	0.0000	6.59	2.81
rd100	0.28	0.16	81666	7910	7910	0.0000	7.19	3.06
rd400	0.31	0.16	108492	15280	15280	0.0000	35.39	19.44
rcl1304	0.29	0.24	97798	253274	254134	0.0034	120.25	59.20
rcl1323	0.29	0.24	97798	270681	272749	0.0076	121.08	60.86
rcl1889	0.29	0.24	97798	317495	318260	0.0024	195.84	94.61
ts225	0.29	0.15	84655	126643	126713	0.0006	16.78	7.27
tsp225	0.29	0.15	84655	3861	3861	0.0000	17.16	7.30
u1060	0.29	0.21	97555	224690	224811	0.0005	93.19	45.08
u1432	0.29	0.24	97798	153126	153303	0.0012	122.50	58.05
u159	0.28	0.16	81881	42080	42080	0.0000	11.92	4.84
u1817	0.29	0.24	97798	57417	57591	0.0030	167.56	78.28
						0.0008	44.42	24.12

proved for single decision maker preference. For example, the average computational time could be significantly reduced in comparison to the experimental results using an automated approach.

This implies that a manual design takes advantage of significant knowledge about the meta-heuristic and the particular problem. Further, the use of a statistical analysis is required to obtain an indication of the impact of particular parameter changes. Hence the final decision of fuzzy settings is dependent on the subjective judgement. This may be advantageous for research studies in the field where prior knowledge on the parameter setting problem for meta-heuristics is available. However, in practice this may only rarely be the case. Most practitioners aim for an off-the-shelf approach without any required judgement on parameter settings. Hence, a toolbox that designs the very specific fuzzy design for an application is desirable. The automated approach presented in Section 6 is a first step in this direction by using a

set of test instances to design a fuzzy IPTS tool. In contrast to the manual design, however, the range of performance values is strongly dependent on the choice of a test set.

8. CONCLUSION AND FUTURE RESEARCH

This chapter has looked at strategies towards an algorithmic approach to the Parameter Setting Problem (PSP). The instance-specific parameter tuning strategy or IPTS has been discussed in relation to PTS and PCS, and the application of a fuzzy logic-based IPTS has been illustrated for the Travelling Salesman Problem and Guided Local Search.

Two different ways of designing a fuzzy logic-based IPTS have been proposed. The first method requires the designer to have extensive knowledge of the problem and meta-heuristic under investiga-

Table 13. Results: Automated IPTS test set ΦTSP - GLS p=0 (short computational times)

TSPLIB Instance	α	NL	IT	Tour Voudouris (π^{Fix})	Tour Fuzzy (π^{Fuzzy_A})	Excess	Time Voudouris (π^{Fix})	Time Fuzzy (π^{Fuzzy_A})
a280	0.25	0.28	52266	2579	2579	0.0000	21.49	5.55
berlin52	0.26	0.23	77333	7542	7542	0.0000	3.55	1.40
bier127	0.26	0.23	79541	118282	118282	0.0000	8.94	3.57
ch130	0.24	0.29	44666	6110	6110	0.0000	9.80	2.18
ch150	0.24	0.29	44666	6528	6528	0.0000	11.67	2.59
d1291	0.29	0.23	98023	51021	51409	0.0076	113.92	58.18
d1655	0.29	0.23	97984	62744	63090	0.0055	149.83	73.10
d198	0.23	0.24	110198	15781	15781	0.0000	14.41	7.14
d493	0.25	0.24	74443	35015	35084	0.0020	42.16	15.18
d657	0.26	0.26	82050	48976	49071	0.0019	56.99	22.32
dsj1000	0.3	0.25	96838	18780063	18756968	-0.0012	93.89	46.98
eil101	0.24	0.29	45587	629	629	0.0000	6.66	1.61
eil51	0.25	0.28	51442	426	426	0.0000	3.41	0.89
eil76	0.24	0.29	45596	538	538	0.0000	5.13	1.19
fl1400	0.29	0.23	97872	20522	20653	0.0064	129.67	63.14
fl1577	0.29	0.23	97984	22309	22319	0.0004	138.86	69.42
fl417	0.26	0.23	77957	11887	11893	0.0005	33.22	13.01
kroA100	0.25	0.27	52015	21282	21282	0.0000	7.20	1.82
kroB100	0.25	0.27	52015	22141	22141	0.0000	7.09	1.84
kroB150	0.25	0.26	61214	26130	26130	0.0000	11.69	3.55
kroB200	0.24	0.29	44666	29437	29437	0.0000	16.13	3.62
kroC100	0.24	0.29	45596	20749	20749	0.0000	7.11	1.64
kroD100	0.25	0.27	52015	21294	21294	0.0000	7.31	1.92
kroE100	0.24	0.29	45596	22068	22068	0.0000	7.27	1.65
lin105	0.24	0.29	45323	14379	14379	0.0000	7.34	1.65
linhp318	0.25	0.26	61396	42029	42029	0.0000	25.78	7.81
nrw1379	0.29	0.23	97984	56785	56874	0.0016	127.50	60.46
p654	0.25	0.24	103940	34760	34728	-0.0009	57.88	27.88
pcb1173	0.29	0.23	98023	57066	56980	-0.0015	103.75	50.41
pr107	0.25	0.26	107007	44586	44586	0.0000	7.25	3.88
pr124	0.24	0.29	44666	59030	59030	0.0000	8.70	1.92
pr136	0.26	0.23	78304	96781	96772	-0.0001	9.69	3.85
pr144	0.25	0.25	62231	58537	58537	0.0000	10.27	3.10
pr152	0.26	0.23	75770	73686	73826	0.0019	10.78	4.04
pr226	0.25	0.24	71459	80369	80369	0.0000	16.91	5.98
pr264	0.25	0.24	104019	49144	52255	0.0633	20.78	10.25
pr299	0.25	0.24	72443	48191	48195	0.0001	23.61	8.61
pr439	0.26	0.23	77511	107344	107673	0.0031	37.31	14.05

continued on following page

Table 13. Continued

TSPLIB Instance	α	NL	IT	Tour Voudouris (n^{Fix})	Tour Fuzzy (n^{Fuzzy_A})	Excess	Time Voudouris (n^{Fix})	Time Fuzzy (n^{Fuzzy_A})
pr76	0.25	0.27	52015	108159	108159	0.0000	5.13	1.41
rat195	0.25	0.27	51440	2323	2323	0.0000	14.14	3.65
rat99	0.24	0.29	45596	1211	1211	0.0000	6.59	1.60
rd100	0.25	0.27	52015	7910	7910	0.0000	7.19	1.88
rd400	0.25	0.25	68238	15280	15282	0.0001	35.39	11.53
rcl1304	0.29	0.23	97984	253274	253279	0.0000	120.25	59.31
rcl1323	0.29	0.23	97984	270681	271273	0.0022	121.08	60.84
rcl1889	0.29	0.23	97984	317495	318418	0.0029	195.84	94.39
ts225	0.25	0.27	53578	126643	126713	0.0006	16.78	4.41
tsp225	0.25	0.27	53578	3861	3861	0.0000	17.16	4.54
u1060	0.29	0.23	98022	224690	224801	0.0005	93.19	46.07
u1432	0.29	0.23	97984	153126	153239	0.0007	122.50	60.03
u159	0.24	0.29	44666	42080	42080	0.0000	11.92	2.57
u1817	0.29	0.23	97984	57417	57615	0.0034	167.56	77.9
						0.0019	**44.42**	**19.95**

Table 14. Expert-based vs automated fuzzy IPTS

	Expert-based Fuzzy IPTS	Automated Fuzzy IPTS
Solution Quality ('Excess')		
p=0	0.0000	-0.0001
p=0.5	0.0010	0.0009
p=1	0.0065	0.0019
Computational Time ('seconds')		
p=0	48.56	36.44
p=0.5	22.26	24.12
p=1	2.27	19.95

tion and relies on using a combination of intuitive thinking and statistical insights for constructing membership functions and rule base of the fuzzy IPTS. A more automated approach was then presented that allows the memberships functions and rule base of a fuzzy IPTS become the output of a fuzzy clustering algorithm, which only needs the availability of a test set of instances. An IPTS as presented in this chapter has the advantage that the parameters it returns are tailored to the instance characteristics and the user-defined preference towards the solution quality and computational time trade-off. Its design is such that is can be implemented as a separate entity in a software environment without the need to modify the meta-heuristic to which it applies.

The design of an FIS-based IPTS can be approaches in yet other ways. Ries and Beullens (2011), for example, use decision trees to determine a set of rules, while allowing for the manual design of the membership functions.

An aspect that has not received that much attention in this chapter, but may be critical to the success of an IPTS design, concerns the identification of relevant instance characteristics. The presented work was largely based on those characteristics used in previous classification studies for the TSP, and has introduces only one additional parameter. This set may not be the best for TSP in combination with another meta-heuristic, or even not be the best for TSP and GLS. In general, it may be difficult to decide which characteristics are relevant for given problems and meta-heuristics. Smith-Miles and Lopes (2012) give an overview about instance difficulty for combinatorial optimisation problems, and provide a basis for a potentially more structured approach to the identification of relevant instance characteristics.

The next level of an IPTS design might be to take into consideration a set of several applicable meta-heuristics. Using the same principles as set out in this chapter, the ITPS could be designed with the additional aim of returning an output parameter that selects the best meta-heuristic (in addition to its best parameter values) to use for a particular instance and user preference. The selection of meta-heuristic is then, in principle, also guided by the best parameter configurations of all potential meta-heuristics. It seems worthwhile to investigate this approach as one potential way to implement the hyper-heuristic paradigm, see Burke et al. (2003).

REFERENCES

Adenso-Diaz, B., & Laguna, M. (2006). Fine-tuning of algorithms using fractional experimental designs and local search. *Operations Research, 54*(1), 99–114. doi:10.1287/opre.1050.0243

Applegate, D. L., Bixby, R. E., Chvatal, V., & Cook, W. J. (2006). *The travelling salesman problem - A computational study. Princeton Series in Applied Mathematics.* Princeton University Press.

Barr, R. S., Golden, B. L., Kelly, J., Stewart, W. R., & Resende, M. G. C. (1995). Guidelines for designing and reporting on computational experiments with heuristic methods. *Journal of Heuristics, 1*(1), 9–32. doi:10.1007/BF02430363

Bartholdi, J. J., Collins, R. L., Platzman, L. K., & Warden, W. H. (1983). A minimal technology routing system for meals on wheels. *Interfaces, 13*(3), 1. doi:10.1287/inte.13.3.1

Battiti, R. (1996). Reactive search: Toward self-tuning heuristics. In Rayward-Smith, I. H., Osman, I. H., Reeves, C. R., & Smith, G. D. (Eds.), *Modern heuristic search methods* (pp. 61–83). John Wiley and Sons Ltd.

Bentley, J. J. (1992). Fast algorithms for geometric traveling salesman problems. *ORSA Journal on Computing, 4*(4), 387–411. doi:10.1287/ijoc.4.4.387

Beullens, P., Muyldermans, L., Cattrysse, D., & Van Oudheusden, D. (2003). A guided local search heuristic for the capacitated arc routing problem. *European Journal of Operational Research, 147*(3), 629–643. doi:10.1016/S0377-2217(02)00334-X

Bezdek, J. C. (1981). *Pattern recognition with fuzzy objective function algorithms.* New York, NY: Plenum Press Advanced Applications in Pattern Recognition. doi:10.1007/978-1-4757-0450-1

Bowerman, R., Hall, B., & Calamai, P. (1995). A multi-objective optimization approach to urban school bus routing: Formalation and solution method. *Transportation Research Part A, Policy and Practice, 29A*(2), 17.

Brunato, M., & Battiti, R. (2008). Rash: A self-adaptive random search method. In Cotta, C., Sevaux, M., & Soerensen, K. (Eds.), *Adaptive and multilevel metaheuristics*. Berlin, Germany: Springer. doi:10.1007/978-3-540-79438-7_5

Burke, E., Kendall, G., Newall, J., Hart, E., Ross, P., & Schulenberg, S. (2003). Hyperheuristics: An emerging direction in modern search technology. *International Series in Operational Research & Management Science*, 57, 457–474. doi:10.1007/0-306-48056-5_16

Chiu, S. L. (1994). Fuzzy model identification based on cluster estimation. *Journal of Intelligent and Fuzzy Systems*, 2, 267–278.

Coy, S. P., Golden, B. L., Runger, G. C., & Wasil, E. A. (2001). Using experimental design to find effective parameter settings for heuristics. *Journal of Heuristics*, 7(1), 77–97. doi:10.1023/A:1026569813391

Croes, G. A. (1958). A method for solving traveling salesman problems. *Operations Research*, 6, 791–812. doi:10.1287/opre.6.6.791

Daniels, R. L., Rummel, J. L., & Schantz, R. (1998). A model for warehouse order picking. *European Journal of Operational Research*, 105, 1–17. doi:10.1016/S0377-2217(97)00043-X

Dean, A., Dean, A., & Voss, D. (2001). *Design and analysis of experiments*. Berlin, Germany: Springer Texts in Statistics.

Eiben, A. E., Hinterding, R., & Michalewicz, Z. (1999). Parameter control in evolutionary algorithms. *IEEE Transactions on Evolutionary Computation*, 3(2), 124–141. doi:10.1109/4235.771166

Everitt, B. S., Landau, S., & Leese, M. (2001). *Cluster analysis*. London, UK: Arnold.

Hooker, J. N. (1995). Testing heuristics: We have it all wrong. *Journal of Heuristics*, 1(1), 33–42. doi:10.1007/BF02430364

Hutter, F., Holger, H. H., Leyton-Brown, K., & Stuetzle, T. (2008). *Paramils: An automatic algorithm configuration framework*.

Irnich, S. (2007). Solution of real-world problems. *European Journal of Operational Research*, 190(1), 16.

Jeong, S.-J., Kim, K.-S., & Lee, Y.-H. (2009). The efficient search method of simulated annealing using fuzzy logic controller. *Expert Systems with Applications*, 36(3), 5. doi:10.1016/j.eswa.2008.08.020

Johnson, D. S. (2002). A theoretician's guide to the experimental analysis of algorithms. In M. H. Goldwasser, D. S. Johnson, & C. C. McGeoch, (Eds.), *Data structures, near neighbor searches, and methodology: Proceedings of the 5th and 6th DIMACS Implementation Challenges*, (pp. 215-250). Providence.

Johnson, D. S., & McGeoch, L. A. (2002). *Experimental analysis of heuristics for the STSP. The traveling salesman problem and its variations*. Kluwer Academic Publishers.

Kern, M. (2006). *Parameter adaption in heuristic search - A population-based approach*. PhD thesis, University of Essex.

Kim, B. I., Heragu, S. S., Graves, R. J., & Onge, A. S. (2003). Clustering-based order-picking sequence algorithm for an automated warehouse. *International Journal of Production Research*, 41(15), 3445–3460. doi:10.1080/0020754031000120005

Leyton-Brown, K., Nudelman, E., & Shoham, Y. (2002). Learning the empirical hardness of optimization problems: The case of combinatorial auctions. In *Principles and Practice of Constraint Programming - CP 2002*, (pp. 91 – 100).

Lin, S. (1965). Computer solutions of the travelling salesman problem. *The Bell System Technical Journal*, 44, 2245–2269.

Lobo, F. G., & Lima, C. F. (2005). A review of adaptive population sizing schemes in genetic algorithms. In *Proceedings of the 2005 Workshop on Parameter Setting in Genetic and Evolutionary Algorithms* (PSGEA 2005), part of GECCO 2005, Washington.

Lokketangen, A. (2007). The importance of being careful. *Lecture Notes in Computer Science, 4638*, 1–15. doi:10.1007/978-3-540-74446-7_1

Lorenco, H. R., Martin, O. C., & Stuetzle, T. (2002). Iterated local search. In *Handbook of metaheuristics* (pp. 321–353). Kluwer.

MacQueen, J. B. (1967). Some methods for classification and analysis of multivariate observations. In *5th Berkeley Symposium on Mathematical Statistics and Probability,* Vol. 1, (p. 281–297). Berkeley, CA: University of California Press.

Muyldermans, L., Beullens, P., Cattrysse, D., & Van Oudheusden, D. (2005). Exploring variants of 2- and 3-opt for the general routing problem. *Operations Research, 53*(6), 982–995. doi:10.1287/opre.1040.0205

Nakamori, Y., & Ryoke, M. (1994). Identification of fuzzy prediction models through hyperellipsoidal clustering. *IEEE Transactions on Systems, Man, and Cybernetics, 4*(8), 1153–1173. doi:10.1109/21.299699

Pavon, R., Diaz, F., Laza, R., & Luzon, V. (2009). Automatic parameter tuning with a bayesian case-based reasoning system. a case of study. *Expert Systems with Applications, 36*(2), 3407–3420. doi:10.1016/j.eswa.2008.02.044

Ratliff, H. D., & Rosenthal, A. S. (1983). Order-picking in a rectangular warehouse: A solvable case of the traveling salesman problem. *Operations Research, 31*(3), 507–521. doi:10.1287/opre.31.3.507

Reinelt, G. (1991). Tsplib - A traveling salesman problem library. *Journal of Computing, 3*, 376–384.

Ries, J. (2009). *Instance based flexible parameter tuning for meta-heuristics using fuzzy logic*. PhD thesis, University of Portsmouth.

Ries, J., & Beullens, P. (2011). *A semi-automated instance-based fuzzy parameter tuning strategy. Technical Report*. University of Portsmouth.

Ries, J., Beullens, P., & Salt, D. (2012). Instance-specific multi-objective parameter tuning based on fuzzy logic. *European Journal of Operational Research, 218*(2), 305–315. doi:10.1016/j.ejor.2011.10.024

Rosenkrantz, D. J., Stearns, R. E., & Lewis, P. M. II. (1977). An analysis of several heuristics for the traveling salesman problem. *SIAM Journal on Computing, 6*, 567–581. doi:10.1137/0206041

Schmitting, W. (1999). *Das Traveling Salesman Problem: Anwendung und heuristische Nutzung von Voronoi-/Delaunay-Strukturen zur Loesung euklidischer, zweidimensionaler Traveling-Salesman-Probleme*. PhD thesis, University of Duesseldorf.

Smith, J. E. (2008). Self-adaption in evolutionary aglorithms for combintorial optimisation. In Cotta, C., Sevaux, M., & Soerensen, K. (Eds.), *Adaptive and multilevel metaheuristics (Vol. 136,* pp. 31–57). Springer. doi:10.1007/978-3-540-79438-7_2

Smith-Miles, K., & Lopes, L. (2012). Measuring instance difficulty for combinatorial optimization problems. *Computers & Operations Research, 39*(5), 875–1194. doi:10.1016/j.cor.2011.07.006

Stuetzle, T. (1998). *Local search algorithms for combinatorial problems*. PhD thesis, Technische Universitaet Darmstadt.

Sugeno, M., & Yasukawa, T. (1993). A fuzzy logic based approach to qualitative modelling. *IEEE Transactions on Fuzzy Systems*, *1*(1), 7–31. doi:10.1109/TFUZZ.1993.390281

Voudouris, C., & Tsang, E. (1996). *Function optimization using guided local search. Technical report*. Department of Computer Science, University of Essex.

Voudouris, C., & Tsang, E. (1999). Guided local search and its application to the traveling salesman problem. *European Journal of Operational Research*, *113*(2), 469–499. doi:10.1016/S0377-2217(98)00099-X

Wang, Y., Liu, H., Beullens, P., & Brown, D. (2008). Travel speed prediction using fuzzy reasoning. *Lecture Notes in Artificial Intelligence*, *5314*, 446–455.

Wolpert, D. H., & Marcready, W. G. (1997). No free lunch theorems for optimization. *IEEE Transactions on Evolutionary Computation*, *1*(1), 67–82. doi:10.1109/4235.585893

Xu, J., Chiu, S. Y., & Glover, F. (1998). Fine-tuning a tabu search algorithm with statistical tests. *International Transactions in Operational Research*, *5*, 233–244. doi:10.1111/j.1475-3995.1998.tb00117.x

Yager, R. R., & Filev, D. P. (1992). *Approximate clustering via the mountain method. Technical report*. Machine Intelligence Institute, Iona College.

Zadeh, L. A. (1965). Fuzzy sets. *Information and Control*, *8*, 338–353. doi:10.1016/S0019-9958(65)90241-X

ADDITIONAL READING

Bartz-Beielstein, T., Lasarczyk, C., & Preu, M. (2005). Sequential parameter optimization. In B. McKay et al. (Eds.), *Congress on Evolutionary Computation*, Vol. 1, (pp. 773-780). Edinburgh, UK: IEEE Press.

Battiti, R. (1996). Reactive search: Toward self-tuning heuristics. In Rayward-Smith, I. H., Osman, I. H., Reeves, C. R., & Smith, G. D. (Eds.), *Modern heuristic search methods* (pp. 61–83). John Wiley and Sons Ltd.

Battiti, R., & Brunato, M. (2005). *Reactive search: Machine learning for memory-based heuristics. Technical report*. Universita Degli Studi di Trento.

Bentley, J. J. (1992). Fast algorithms for geometric traveling salesman problems. *ORSA Journal on Computing*, *4*(4), 387–411. doi:10.1287/ijoc.4.4.387

Birattari, M. (2004). *The problem of tuning metaheuristics - As seen from a machine learning perspective*. PhD thesis, Universit Libre de Bruxelles.

Bonner, R. E. (1964). On some clustering techniques. *International Business Machines Journal of Research and Development*, *8*, 22–32.

Bowerman, R., Hall, B., & Calamai, P. (1995). A multi-objective optimization approach to urban school bus routing: Formulation and solution method. *Transportation Research Part A, Policy and Practice*, *29A*(2), 17.

Cerny, V. (1985). Thermodynamical approach to the traveling salesman problem: An efficient simulation algorithm. *Journal of Optimization Theory and Applications*, *45*, 41–51. doi:10.1007/BF00940812

Cook, S. (1971). *The p vs np problem*.

Glover, F. (1989). Tabu search - part 1. *ORSA Journal on Computing, 1*(3), 190–206. doi:10.1287/ijoc.1.3.190

Hansen, P., & Mladenovic, N. (2003). Variable neighbourhood search. In Glover, F., & Knochenberger, G. (Eds.), *Handbook of metaheuristics* (pp. 145–184). New York, NY: Kluwer Academic Publisher.

Hutter, F., Hamadi, Y., Leyton-Brown, K., & Hoos, H. H. (2005). Performance prediction and automated tuning of randomized and parameteric algorithms. In 12th *International Conference on Principles and Practise of Constraint Programming (CP-06)*, (pp. 213-228).

Hutter, F., Hoos, H. H., & Stuetzle, T. (2007). Automatic algorithm configuration based on local search. In *Twenty-Second Conference on Artifical Intelligence (AAAI '07)*, (pp. 1152-1157).

Irnich, S. (2007). Solution of real-world problems. *European Journal of Operational Research, 190*(1), 16.

Jang, J. S. (1993). ANFIS: Adaptive-network-based fuzzy interference system. *IEEE Transactions on Systems, Man, and Cybernetics, 23*, 665–685. doi:10.1109/21.256541

Kosko, B. (1994). *Fuzzy thinking*. Glasgow, UK: Flamingo.

Lawler, E., Lenstra, J., Rinnooy Kan, A., & Shmoys, D. (1985). *The traveling salesman problem: A guided tour of combinatorial optimization*. New York, NY: Wiley. doi:10.2307/2582681

Leyton-Brown, K., Nudelman, E., & Shoham, Y. (2002). *Learning the empirical hardness of optimization problems: The case of combinatorial auctions* (pp. 556-572).

Lin, S., & Kernighan, B. W. (1973). An effective heuristic algorithm for the traveling-salesman problem. *Operations Research, 21*, 498–516. doi:10.1287/opre.21.2.498

Mamdani, E. H., & Assilian, S. (1975). An experiment in linguistic synthesis with a fuzzy logic controller. *International Journal of Man-Machine Studies, 7*(1), 1–13. doi:10.1016/S0020-7373(75)80002-2

Ross, T. (2004). *Fuzzy logic with engineering applications* (2nd ed.). Chichester, UK: John Wiley Sons Inc.

Sastry, K., Goldberg, D., & Kendall, G. (2005). Genetic algorithms. In Burke, E. K., & Kendall, G. (Eds.), *Search methodologies: Introductory tutorials in optimization and decision support techniques* (pp. 97–125). Springer.

Stuetzle, T. (1998). *Local search algorithms for combinatorial problems*. PhD thesis, Technische Universitaet Darmstadt.

Sugeno, M. (1985). *Industrial applications of fuzzy control*. New York, NY: Elsevier Science.

Zimmermann, H. J. (1987). *Fuzzy sets, decision making, and expert systems*. Boston, MA: Kluwer International Series in Management Science/Operations Research. doi:10.1007/978-94-009-3249-4

KEY TERMS AND DEFINITIONS

Fuzzy Logic: A rule-based approach, allowing partial set membership rather than crisp set membership or non-membership.

Guided Local Search: A meta-heuristic concept that uses a penalization strategy to overcome local optima. For the case of the Travelling

Salesman Problem, long edges in a solution are penalized to ensure its elimination for selecting shorter edges instead.

Meta-Heuristics: Solving concepts in combinatorial optimization. Due to the NP-hardness of combinatorial optimization problems, meta-heuristics incorporate mechanisms that allow escaping local optimality. While optimal solutions cannot be guaranteed, meta-heuristics allow finding good solutions in reasonable computational time.

Parameter Control: The idea of adapting algorithm-specific parameter values dynamically during the run of a meta-heuristic based on heuristic performance improvements.

Parameter Setting Problem: In the context of meta-heuristics, the Parameter Setting Problem searches for a set of parameter values that results in optimal heuristic performance for an instance.

Parameter Tuning: Describes the concept of setting algorithm-specific parameter values a priori to a meta-heuristics by choosing one fixed set of parameter values that is used for all instances in a test set.

Travelling Salesman Problem: Searches the tour of minimal length in a complete undirected graph $G = (V,E)$, visiting all vertices $V = (v_1, v_2,.., v_n)$ only once. The distance between two instance points v_i and v_j is defined by $d(v_i, v_j)$, where for the symmetric case, $d(v_i, v_j) = d(v_j, v_i)$ for $1 \leq i, j \leq n$.

Chapter 6

Investigating of Hybrid Meta-Heuristics to Solve the Large-Scale Multi-Source Weber Problems and Performance Measuring of them with Statistical Tests

Abdolsalam Ghaderi
University of Kurdistan, Iran

ABSTRACT

The location–allocation problems are a class of complicated optimization problems that requires finding sites for m facilities and to simultaneously allocate n customers to those facilities to minimize the total transportation costs. Indeed, these problems, belonging to the class NP-hard, have a lot of local optima solutions. In this chapter, three hybrid meta-heuristics: genetic algorithm, variable neighborhood search and particle swarm optimization, and a hybrid local search approaches are studied. These are investigated to solve the uncapacitated continuous location-allocation problem (multi-source Weber problem). In this regard, alternate location allocation and exchange heuristics are used to find the local optima of the problem within the framework of hybrid algorithms. In addition, some large-scale problems are employed to measure the effectiveness and efficiency of hybrid algorithms. Obtained results from these heuristics are compared with local search methods and with each other. The experimental results show that the hybrid meta-heuristics produce much better solutions to solve large-scale problems. Moreover, the results of two non-parametric statistical tests detected a significant difference in hybrid algorithms such that the hybrid variable neighborhood search and particle swarm optimization algorithm outperform the others.

DOI: 10.4018/978-1-4666-2086-5.ch006

INTRODUCTION

Facility location theory involves a wide range of problems that share certain common elements. The first paper in this field was introduced by Weber (1909). After that, significant research has been carried out and many models with different assumptions have been introduced in this area of science. The literature on facility location theory is rich, and, since Weber's work, many papers have been published that provide admirable introductions and reviews of the development in this field. One may refer to survey papers in this area such as (Klose and Drexl, 2005; Melo et al., 2009; ReVelle et al., 2008). In these survey papers, various strategies were employed to classify the facility location models based on different issues like discrete vs. continuous problems, deterministic vs. probabilistic problems, dynamic vs. static models and so on. P-median, P-center, covering location, hub location and location-allocation problems are just a few basic models in the literature that has been advocated most of research in this area of science. Various extensions of these models with emerging the real world assumptions like uncertainty in parameters, maximum available budget for investment in facilities and capacity constraints have been also proposed in the literature. Moreover, due to the high complexity of most models, different optimization approaches were presented to find the optimal or near-optimal solution.

The location-allocation problem, as a well known basic problem, is one of the toughest facility location problems that comprise of two main decisions: where to locate the central facilities (*Location*); and which subsets of the demand should be served from each facility (*Allocation*). Therefore, the objective of location-allocation problem is to locate *m* facilities and to simultaneously allocate *n* customers to those facilities to minimize the total transportation costs. *n* customers are located at fixed locations with associated discrete demands. Supply centres such as plants and warehouses may constitute the facilities while retailers and dealers

may be considered as demand points (Aras et al., 2006). These problems occur in many practical settings where facilities provide a homogeneous service, such as the location of plants, warehouses, retail outlets, and public facilities (Jabalameli and Ghaderi, 2008).

The Euclidean uncapacitated location allocation problem is also known as the Multisource Weber Problem (MWP). Under the assumption that there are no capacity constraints on the new facilities, it can be shown that the demand at each point is satisfied by the nearest facility at minimum cost. This property is known as single assignment property and could be found in (Krarup and Pruzan, 1983). In the general case, most single-facility location problems are convex, and the optimal solutions can be developed through either optimal algorithms or some heuristics (Cooper, 1964). However, multi-facility location problems are nonconvex and nonlinear, and known algorithms cannot solve large scale problems optimally. Cooper (1963) proves that the objective function of this problem is neither concave nor convex, and may contain several local minima. Hence, the multisource Weber problem falls in the realm of global optimization problems. Due to Non-deterministic Polynomial-time hard (NP-hard) nature of the problem, exact solution approaches are not able to solve the problem in realistically size and heuristic methods have been shown to be the best way to tackle the larger problems. Megiddo and Supowit (1984) represented the problem as an enumeration of the Voronoi partitions of the customer set and proved its NP-hardness. To tackle to these type of optimization models, modern heuristics such as Simulated Annealing (SA), Tabu Search (TS), Genetic Algorithm (GA), variable neighborhood search (VNS), and Ant Systems increase the chance of avoiding local optimality (Brimberg and Salhi, 2005).

Location-allocation problems are subject to various assumptions such as distance measure, capacity of facilities, and fixed cost. In the continuous version of the location-allocation problem, the objective is to generate **m** new facility sites in $\Re^2$ to serve the demands of **n** customers or fixed points in a manner that minimizes the total transportation (or service) costs. The mathematical formulation of the uncapacitated version of location allocation problem may be formulated as follows (Love et al., 1988):

$$\min \quad \sum_{i=1}^{n}\sum_{j=1}^{m}W_{ij}d(X_j,P_i) \qquad (1)$$

Subject to:

$$\sum_{j=1}^{m}W_{ij} = w_i \qquad \forall i \qquad (2)$$

$$W_{ij} \geq 0 \qquad \forall i,j \qquad (3)$$

where the following notations are used:
Indexes:

- i : Set of customers, $i = 1,2,...,n$
- j : Set of new facilities, $j = 1,2,...,m$

Decision variables:

- W_{ij} : The quantity assigned from facility j to fixed point i (Allocation variable)
- $X_j = (x_j,y_j)$: The coordinate of the new facility j (Location variable)

Parameters:

- $P_i = (a_i,b_i)$: The coordinate of a customer at fixed point i
- w_i : The demand or weight of customer i
- $d(X_j,P_i)$: The Euclidean distance from the location (coordinates) of facility j, (x_j,y_j), to the location of a customer at fixed point i, (a_i,b_i) and is calculated by the following equation.

$$\|X_j - P_i\| = \sqrt{\left(x_j - a_i\right)^2 + \left(y_j - b_i\right)^2} \qquad (4)$$

In this model, the objective function (1) minimizes the total service cost. The constraint (2) states that the demand of customer i should be serviced by opened facilities. In its most general form, the location-allocation problem may involve the determination of the following parameters (Liu et al., 1994):

1. m : The number of new facilities,
2. W : The allocation matrix, and
3. $X_j : j = 1,2,...,m$: The location of new facilities.

In this study, the number of new facilities is assumed to be known in advance.

Many extensive studies of location-allocation problem were developed after Cooper's research. This problem was solved by using exact, heuristic, metaheuristic and hybrid techniques. In the exact solution approaches, the problem needs to find a set of locations as solution without using any approximation. In these methods, solution needs to complete counting to get optimal results. Selecting m facility out of n is a location-allocation problem. To complete counting of this type of problem we need to consider all combination of m facility out of n facility. The total number of these combinations equals to:

$$\binom{n}{m} = \frac{n!}{m!(n-m)!} \qquad (5)$$

According to this formula the total number of solutions for a problem with 200 customers and 20 facilities is $1.6 * 10^{27}$. This problem is NP-hard and has many local optima. Brimberg et al. (2004) were able to obtain 272, 3008 and 3363 local optima from 10,000 random restarts of Cooper's alternating heuristic in a problem instance with n=50 and m=5, 10 and 15, respectively. The authors further observed that the worst deviations from the optimal solution were, in the respective cases, 47%, 66% and 70%. The optimal solution was obtained 690 times for $m = 5$, 34 times for $m = 10$ and only once for $m = 15$ (Brimberg et al., 2006). In addition, another interesting point that should be considered is increasing in the number of local optima exponentially with problem size. Thus, the main difficulty in solving this class of problems relates to a highly non-convex objective function and the existence of multiple local minima. Thus the main focus of most of studies was on introducing and implementing solving methods includes exact, heuristic and metaheuristic algorithms.

This chapter discusses some efficient hybrid algorithms to solve the large-scale location-allocation problem. These algorithms are constituted from meta-heuristic and local search algorithms. By meta-heuristic the solution space is searched via a specific systematic approach and local search algorithms help to find local optima for the problem. Thus, if the hybrid algorithms design well, they could be much better to solve the hard problems such as location-allocation problem. Genetic algorithm, variable neighborhood search and particle swarm optimization (PSO) are combined with two known local searches to construct these efficient hybrid meta-heuristic algorithms. The performance of these methods is compared subject to some computational results. Moreover, comparative results are analysed by using non-parametric statistical tests.

To do so, this chapter is organized as follows: Firstly, the literature review of problem is considered such that some main works in the literature are mentioned. Then, the considered hybrid algorithms to solve the problem are illustrated. The main steps of each hybrid algorithm are also given. The chapter is followed by computational testing of hybrid algorithms using some large-scale instances in the literature. Lastly, a brief summary and conclusions are provided and directions for future research are suggested.

LITERATURE REVIEW

The literature of location-allocation problem can be divided into two main categories as extensions on the basic model and solving the models. However, between these two groups, more efforts made on developing new algorithms to solve the presented models. Thus, many solving methods including exact, heuristic and metaheuristic algorithms have been proposed in the literature to solve the multisource Weber problem. A comprehensive survey of solution algorithms for the continuous location-allocation problem was carried out by Brimberg et al. (2008). They classified the heuristics developed for the problem into exact, heuristic and metaheuristic algorithms. In the following, some related works are considered.

Besides Cooper's work, which is well-known to the Alternate Location-Allocation algorithm (ALA) (Cooper, 1964), many solving methods have been proposed in the literature. These solution techniques can be classified into two major categories, namely, exact and heuristic methods.

The first category, exact methods, have been scarce in the literature and are based on branch-and-bound (Kuenne and Soland, 1972), partitioning the customers space (Ostresh, 1973), DC programming (Chen et al., 1992) and column generation(Hansen et al., 1997). Except for the case of two facilities, which can be solved with 1000 customers (Chen et al., 1992), large problems, are difficult to solve precisely. With these methods, the optimal solutions can be obtained by exact techniques; however, the size of the applied problems is limited because these methods require a great deal of computational time to achieve the optimal solutions, even on small-scale problems. The problem dimensions that were solved by these types of algorithms are small. For instance, problems with $m=5$, $n=30$ and $m=6$, $n=25$ were solved by Rosing (1992). Hansen et al. (1997) proposed a column generation approach combined with global optimization and branch-and-bound, which leads to the exact solution of instances with 287 customers and 2 to 100 facilities. These solutions have frequently been used for comparison of heuristics in the literature. He used a dual formulation which is equivalent to a concave minimization problem. Hansen et al.(1997) developed a very effective algorithm based on a bundle method in the l_1-norm that aims to stabilize solution of the dual. This algorithm could reach to the optimal solution for the problems up to size $n=1000$ and $m=100$.

The second group is heuristic methods, which include heuristic, metaheuristic and hybrid algorithms. These algorithms generate good solutions; however, they may or may not produce optimal or even near-optimal solutions. This group of methods can handle large-scale problems and has been shown to be a very good way to tackle large NP-hard problems. As mentioned before, the maximum dimension of the problem solved by exact algorithms is restricted to size $n=1000$ and $m=100$ (Hansen et al., 1997). However, Brimberg et al. (2006) were able to find good solutions for the problem in size $n=3038$ and $m=500$ in reasonable CPU time.

A heuristic based on neighborhood structure was proposed by Love and Juel (1982). Bongartz et al. (1994) introduce a projection method which solves simultaneously for location and allocation variables. Brimberg et al. (2000) compare various heuristic methods, i.e. ALA (Cooper, 1964), projection method (Bongartz et al., 1994), TS (Brimberg and Mladenovic, 1996), GA (Houck et al., 1996) and several versions of VNS. It has been found that VNS consistently gives the best results on average. An efficient variable neighborhood decomposition search (VNDS) heuristic was developed to solve the large-scale problems by Brimberg et al. (2006). They used various decomposition strategies including deterministic, random and mixed strategies. Interested readers can be refer to (Brimberg et al., 2008) for comprehensive overviews of heuristics.

Recently, hybrid algorithms methods have been increasingly used to obtain near optimal solutions for different problems. Hybrid algorithms aim to achieve better performance by exploiting the advantages of the individual pure algorithms. Hybridization has become a pervasive trend and a very promising strategy in designing and developing improved metaheuristic solution methods, in view of their heuristic nature, greater flexibility and less strict mathematical property. A hybrid metaheuristic method combines structure and efficiency advantages from different principles and approaches and often provides a highly flexible and efficient tool in solving difficult combinatorial optimization problems (Xie et al., 2011). Raidl G.R. (2006) had a survey on hybrid meta-heuristic algorithms and categorized them based on various characteristics. Blum et al. (2008) published a book about hybrid meta-heuristics that cover some of the main topics of hybrid metaheuristics. Most of the chapters in this book were devoted to the integration of metaheuristics with other techniques, namely, mathematical programming, constraint programming and various combinations of complete and incomplete search techniques. Recently, Günther et al. (2010) had a comprehensive review on a large number of different possibilities for combining traditional metaheuristic strategies with each other or with algorithmic techniques coming from other fields.

Jabalameli and Ghaderi (2008) proposed three hybrid algorithms to solve uncapacitated continuous location allocation problem that combine elements of several traditional metaheuristics (GA and VNS) and local search (LS) algorithms to find near-optimal solutions. Proposed hybrid algorithms provide some better results in comparison to the best methods in the literature (GA and VNS). In another study, Neema et al. (2011) developed two hybrid algorithms combining the GAs with different replacement procedures and a traditional local search heuristic. Computational results showed that the hybrid methods obtained much better solutions with less computational effort. Moreover, Ghaderi et al. (2011) presented an efficient hybrid PSO to solve the problem. They showed that this algorithm outperforms other heuristics in the literature. Focus of this chapter is on solving the large-scale problems with the presented hybrid algorithms in (Ghaderi et al., 2011; Jabalameli and Ghaderi, 2008).

INVESTIGATED ALGORITHMS

This section provides the background knowledge for the techniques used in this study. The best well-known local searches in the literature are used during the hybrid heuristic. In the following, algorithms and methods that used in the skeleton of hybrids procedure are described in brief. Readers could see the papers (Ghaderi et al., 2011; Jabalameli and Ghaderi, 2008) for more description.

In this study for representing the problem solutions, a real number representation are used where each solution consists of m pairs representing the sites of facilities to be located. For instance solution S is represented as follows:

$$S: \left\{ (x_1, y_1), (x_2, y_2), ..., (x_j, y_j), ..., (x_m, y_m) \right\}$$

where:

(x_j, y_j) : The location of the jth facility, $j = 1, ...,$ m. and,

$$x_j \in [\underline{a}, \overline{a}], \quad y_j \in [\underline{b}, \overline{b}]$$

Note that unlike VNS heuristic, GA and PSO algorithms are population-based and they are working on a set of solutions named population at each iterations. In each stage of the algorithms, the generated solutions must be within the scope of the solution space between

$$x_{hj} \in [\underline{a}, \overline{a}], \quad y_{hj} \in [\underline{b}, \overline{b}]$$

such that

$$\underline{a} = \min \left\{ a_i, \forall i \in n \right\} \quad and \quad \overline{a} = \max \left\{ a_i, \forall i \in n \right\}$$

$$\underline{b} = \min \left\{ b_i, \forall i \in n \right\} \quad and \quad \overline{b} = \max \left\{ b_i, \forall i \in n \right\}$$

The hth solution is denoted by

$$S^h: \quad \left[(x_{h1}, y_{h1}), (x_{h2}, y_{h2}), ..., (x_{hj}, y_{hj}), ..., (x_{hm}, y_{hm}) \right] \mapsto F_h$$

and F_h is the objective value of chromosome h.

In all studied algorithms, each initial solution is generated with the clustering method that was presented by Salhi and Gamal (2003). The motivation of using this method is due to a fact that choosing the points randomly without knowledge of the clusters may result in poor initial locations. Thus, this strategy was used to find the initial solutions in the investigated algorithms. The clustering generation approach will produce, with high probability, location points where clusters exist and roughly within the convex hull of the fixed points, as shown in Figure 1 specifically. As mentioned before, according to single assignment property, the demand at each point is satisfied by the nearest facility and nothing is gained by "splitting up" a demand and sending parts of it to different facilities. Thus, there is no need to bring allocation decisions to the solution representation and they can be found so easily.

An illustration of fixed point positions and the location of facilities is shown in Figure 1 as an example. A feasible solution generated by clustering method is also shown. As can be seen easily in the Figure 1, no points are selected to open new facilities in cells without any customers. In this approach, whatever a cell has more density, the selection probability of one or more facility points in that cell increases.

Figure 1. A representation of fixed point positions and the location of facilities for an example with a feasible solution (Ghaderi et al., 2011)

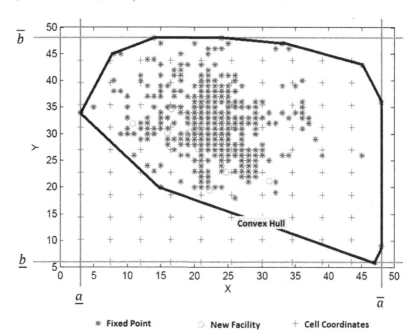

Local Searches

Local searches play a very important role in the investigated hybrid algorithms. Local search is a traditional technique to solve combinatorial search problems and has raised much interest in recent years(Michel et al., 1997). Local search algorithms move from solution to solution in the space of candidate's solutions (the search space) until a solution deemed optimal is found or a time bound is elapsed. The famous example of a local search method for location-allocation problems is alternate location allocation heuristic. In addition, exchange heuristic is another local search that able to reach the local optima of p-median problem. However, exchange heuristic outperforms the ALA algorithm to solve the problem at hand. At this study, a neighborhood of the current solution defined as the set of points obtained by a given number of facilities relocations. Three metaheuristic algorithms (GA, VNS and PSO) are combined with these local searches to construct

the hybrid heuristics. Note that most of computational requirement of the considered hybrid algorithms is belonging to implement these local search methods. During design and implementing of hybrid algorithms, different possible strategies were used to form the efficient hybrid algorithms that the best of them were given in (Ghaderi et al., 2011; Jabalameli and Ghaderi, 2008).

Alternate Location-Allocation Heuristic

This heuristic was proposed by Cooper (1964) and is a well-known local search approach that guarantees a local minimum for the problem at hand. This heuristic technique uses the property that the location and allocation phases of the problem are very easy to solve in separation. Thus, given the facility locations, each customer is simply allocated to its nearest one. Alternatively, knowing the allocation of the customers among the facilities, the problem is reduced to the solution of m independent single facility minisum problems, which because of the convexity of the objective function for normed distances are readily solved by descent methods such as the Weiszfeld procedure or etc (Brimberg et al., 2000). This process, alternating between the location and the allocation phases, is repeated until no further improvement can be made. The main steps of this algorithm can be extracted from Figure 2 without considering phase 1. The repetition of Cooper's algorithm several times is also known as the Multi-Start Alternate Location Allocation Algorithm (MALT). This method is used frequently in the literature and offers good solutions for small problems.

The optimal location of a single facility location is achieved by using the Weiszfeld procedure as follows (Weiszfeld, 1937). Let locating a facility among a set of p customers is considered. The customer i is located on location (a_i, b_i) and its demand is w_i. The iterative equation to find the optimal location, $(\bar{X}, \bar{Y})$, is given as follows. In these equations, the iteration number is given with superscript e.

$$\bar{X}^{(e)} = \frac{\sum_{j=1}^{n} \dfrac{w_j . a_j}{d(\bar{X}^{(e-1)}, P_j)}}{\sum_{j=1}^{n} \dfrac{w_j}{d(\bar{X}^{(e-1)}, P_j)}}, \qquad \bar{Y}^{(e)} = \frac{\sum_{j=1}^{n} \dfrac{w_j . b_j}{d(\bar{X}^{(e-1)}, P_j)}}{\sum_{j=1}^{n} \dfrac{w_j}{d(\bar{X}^{(e-1)}, P_j)}}$$

(6)

and the initial value of these equations calculates from:

$$\bar{X}^{(0)} = \frac{\sum_{j=1}^{n} w_j . a_j}{\sum_{j=1}^{n} w_j}, \qquad \bar{Y}^{(0)} = \frac{\sum_{j=1}^{n} w_j . b_j}{\sum_{j=1}^{n} w_j}$$

(7)

Thus, in order to obtain the optimal location of the single facility location, these values would be calculated until no significant changes observed in two successive iterations.

Exchange Heuristic (CH)

Another local search method that was proposed by Teitz and Bart (1968) is used to construct the investigated hybrid algorithms. This local search approach is used for solving location-allocation

Figure 2. The main framework of hybrid local search (ALA and CH) algorithm

---

Repeat the following operations:
  Step 0: Choose *m* facility locations by clustering method as the initial solution
  Phase 1: Do the CH algorithm:
    Step 1: Allocate each customer to its nearest facility
    Step 2: Looking for pair of facilities (one to be inserted into the current solution and another to be removed) that would lead to an improved solution if swapped
    Step 3: If this pair is found, repeat steps 1 and 2 until the stopping criteria are met; Else, there is no further improvement and the generated solution move to the phase 2 to find it's local optimum
  Phase 2: Do the Cooper's algorithm (ALA):
    Step 1: Allocate each customer to its nearest facility
    Step 2: Holding the current customer assignment fixed, relocate the facilities by solving *m* single facility location problems with Weiszfeld's method
    Step 3: Repeat steps 1 and 2 until there is no further improvement. The current solution is a local minimum
Until stopping criteria are satisfied; retain the best solution from al obtained local minima

---

problems in a discrete space (p-median problem). In each iteration, the algorithm looks for a pair of facilities (one to be inserted into the current solution and another to be removed) that would lead to an improved solution if swapped. If such a pair exists, the swap is made, and the procedure is repeated. A detailed description of this local search can be found in (Jabalameli and Ghaderi, 2008; Resende and Werneck, 2007). The experimental results showed that this algorithm is faster and achieves better results for p-median problem in comparison to the other local search methods (Resende and Werneck, 2007). The motivation behind using this approach in the problem at hand is that at the optimal solution quite often some of the locations chosen for a facility in the MWP coincide with customer's locations. This property was presented by Hansen et al. (1998). Note that the obtained solution by this heuristic is a local minimum for the p-median and a good solution for the MWP. However, the local optimum of this solution can be readily calculated by using the output of CH as input of Cooper's algorithm. At the computational results section, the performance of CH heuristic is compared with Cooper's algorithm in solving the large-scale problems.

The pseudo code of this local search can be extracted in Figure 2 without considering phase 2. In this paper, two variants of the CH method are used to construct the hybrid algorithms. In each iteration of the first method, the most profitable swap was found (Best CH or BCH). Thus, all pairs of facilities were considered, and the best of them were selected. However, in another method, the first profitable swap was selected (Fast CH or FCH). Experimental results showed that the latter method was much faster than the former; however, the generated solutions were not very different. Thus, BCH and FCH have the same framework just at the Step 2, BCH finds the best improving move among all moves whilst FCH stops after finding the first improvement move.

INVESTIGATED HYBRID ALGORITHMS

Hybrid Local Searches

The first hybrid algorithm is composed of two considered local search (Cooper and best CH) methods. Figure 2 gives the main steps of this algorithm. The initial solution is generated by clustering method. After that, BCH and Cooper's algorithms are consecutively applied on solution to find a good and local optimum solution, respectively. Note that the obtained solution by BCH is a local minimum for the p-median problem and a pretty good solution for the continuous location-allocation problem. As mentioned before, Cooper's and CH algorithms can be obtained without considering phase 1 and 2 of given pseudo code, respectively.

Hybrid Genetic Algorithm

Genetic algorithm is randomized search and optimization technique guided by the principles of evaluation and natural genetics, and has a large amount of implicit parallelism. In general, a GA contains a fixed-size population of potential solutions over the search space. These potential solutions of the search space are encoded as binary, integer, or floating-point strings and called chromosomes. The initial solution can be created randomly or based on the problem of a specific knowledge. In each iteration step, a new population is created from the preceding one using the Evaluation, Selection, Crossover and Mutation procedures (Doong et al., 2007). The above procedures are iterated for many generations until a satisfactory solution is found or a terminated criterion is met.

This algorithm was sometimes used to solve the location-allocation problem and the best version of this algorithm was proposed by Salhi and Gamal (2003). They proposed new approaches for every operator of GA and proved that their method is effective. Hybrid genetic algorithm is similar to the GA except that it does a local search on offsprings and improves their fitness. The flowchart of the hybrid GA is shown in Figure 3. As can be seen, hybrid GA starts with an initial population that each chromosome is generated by Clustering method. Then, generated solutions are evaluated with allocating the customers to their nearest facility. In order to improve the generated solutions, Cooper's local search algorithm is applied on each solution to find the local optima. The new generation is generated with mutation and crossover operators. Because of the computational requirements of considered local searches, best CH and Cooper's algorithms are implemented respectively only on the best offspring in each iteration. Finally, an approach stemmed from roulette-wheel selection procedure is used to select the solutions to the next generation. The hybrid GA cycle is repeated until the stopping criterion is reached. Interested readers could refer to (Salhi and Gamal, 2003) and (Jabalameli and Ghaderi, 2008) for additional explanation about genetic and hybrid GA algorithms, respectively. There are some parameters in the proposed framework of the hybrid GA as follows:

Figure 3. The overall flowchart of the hybrid genetic algorithm

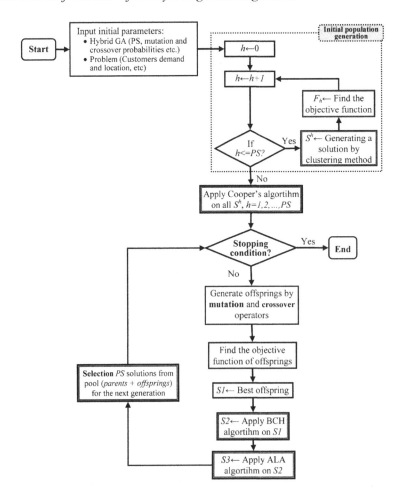

- PS : The size of population
- h : A counter for the chromosomes (solution)
- S^h : The chromosome of h
- $S1$: The best offspring of current generation
- $S2$: An improved solution after applying FCH on the best offspring of current generation
- $S3$: A local optima after applying ALA on the improved solution $(S2)$
- F_h : The objective function of solution h

Hybrid Variable Neighborhood Search

Variable neighborhood search (VNS) is a relatively new metaheuristic aimed at solving combinatorial and global optimization problems. This algorithm systematically exploits the idea of neighborhood change, both in descent to local optima and in escape from the valleys which contain them. One jumps from the current solution to a new one if and only if a better solution has been found. Thus, VNS is not a trajectory method (as SA or TS) and does not specify forbidden moves.

The VNS algorithm first appears in the literature by Mladenovic and Hansen (1997) and since then rapidly developed both in its methods and applications. Hansen et al. (2010) thoroughly surveyed an extensive bibliography about VNS from these two aspects. There are many successful applications of VNS, or its hybridizations with other algorithms in the numerous areas. Hansen et al. (2010) categorized a list of different application of VNS. Furthermore, the multi-source Weber problem was the first model in continuous space that solved by VNS in (Brimberg et al., 2000). Also, a hybrid VNS was proposed to solve the uncapacitated continuous location-allocation problem by Jabalameli and Ghaderi (2008). The main skeleton of this hybrid is shown in Figure 4.

Considered hybrid VNS is a combination of basic versions of VNS and Reduced Variable Neighborhood Search (RVNS) and two illustrated local search algorithms. The hybrid VNS proceeds as follows: The algorithm starts with an initial solution that created by clustering method. Then, the RVNS algorithm is employed to improve the initial solution. At this algorithm, unlike the basic VNS, generated solution in each iteration is not followed by a descent procedure. Hence, this algorithm aims to search the feasible region and find a good solution quickly. At the next step, the local optimum of improved solution by RVNS is obtained with Cooper's algorithm. Now, the heuristic starts from the first neighborhood of the current solution and explores increasingly distant neighborhoods until the stopping criterion is met. A neighbor with rank k^{th} of a given solution is defined as exactly k exchanges of the location of existing facilities with customer's location. Thus, all locations except one are similar in a 1-neighborhood of a given solution. Within the main loop of hybrid VNS, a best CH algorithm is implemented on each new generated neighbor. Finally, the Cooper's algorithm is performed on the best solution found. There are some parameters in the proposed framework of the hybrid VNS as follows:

- N_k : A finite set of neighborhood structures, $k = 1, 2, ..., k_{max}$
- k_{max} : The maximum number of neighborhoods
- $N_k(S)$: The set of solutions in the kth neighborhood of S
- S : Is a current solution
- $\hat{S}$: Is a new point in the kth neighborhood of S
- $\hat{S}1$: An improved solution after applying BCH algorithm on $\hat{S}$
- $\hat{S}2$: A local optima of problem after applying ALA algorithm on $\hat{S}1$
- F_s : The objective function of solution s

Figure 4. The main skeleton of the hybrid variable neighborhood search

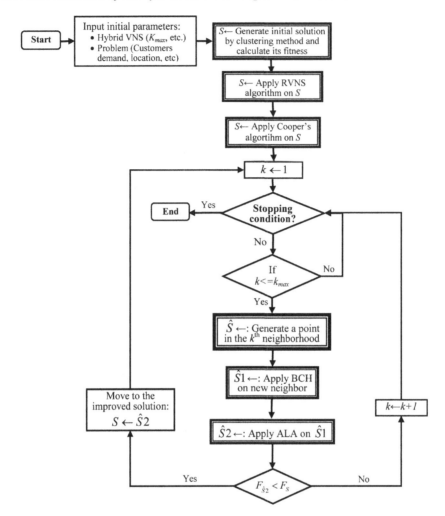

Hybrid Particle Swarm Optimization

The last discussed method is the hybrid particle swarm optimization. PSO is an evolutionary approach developed by Kennedy and Eberhat (1995). Recently, this algorithm has been considered by many research projects, including but not limited to (Andres and Lozano, 2006; Eberhart and Salhi, 2004; Eberhat and Shi, 2001; Yapicioglu et al., 2007) and some survey paper presented by (Banks et al., 2007, 2008) and (Eberhat and Shi, 2001).

The PSO algorithm has been applied successfully to a wide range of NP-complete optimization problems. The principal advantages of the PSO algorithms over other stochastic global optimization schemes like GA and SA are fewer parameters, higher convergence rate than GAs, greater ease of implementation, and significantly fewer lines of code needed for implementation on standard platforms like MATLAB and C coding languages (Noel, 2006). This algorithm was first employed to solve facility location problems in 2006 by Sevkli and Guner (2006). Then, Yapicioglu et al. (2007) proposed a bi-objective PSO for solving the facility location problem. And finally, Ghaderi et al (2011) proposed a classical and hybrid PSO to solve the location-allocation problem. In this section the main framework of this algorithm is described in brief. Interested readers could refer to this paper for more illustrations and how to set the parameters of PSO (Ghaderi et al., 2011).

The proposed Hybrid PSO algorithm combines the idea of particle swarms with the local search approach. This algorithm employs the PSO for exploration and local search methods (Cooper and CH) for exploitation. To construct the Hybrid PSO, many strategies were examined, and the best of them finally selected. The framework of the algorithm is demonstrated in Figure 5. In

addition, it should be taken into account that the solutions obtained by CH are much better than those obtained by Cooper's method. However, the computational time of algorithms is more time consuming, and Cooper's method is faster than CH. The coefficient K is located between zero and one. Numerous experiments were performed to tune the parameters in the algorithm. Experimental results showed that 0.7 is fit for parameter K (Ghaderi et al., 2011). There are some parameters in the proposed framework of the hybrid PSO as follows:

Figure 5. The flowchart of the hybrid particle swarm optimization

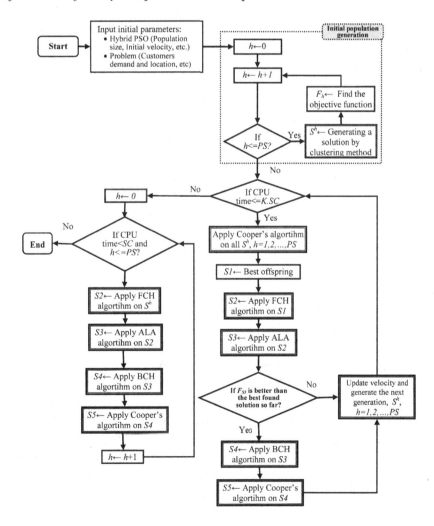

- PS : The size of population
- h : A counter for the chromosomes (solution)
- S^h : The chromosome of h
- $S1$: The best offspring of current generation
- $S2$: An improved solution after applying FCH on $S1$
- $S3$: A local optimum after applying FCH on the improved solution ($S2$)
- $S4$: An improved solution after applying BCH on $S3$
- $S5$: A local optimum after applying BCH on the improved solution ($S4$)
- F_h : The objective function of solution h
- SC : Stopping time criterion

SOLUTIONS AND RECOMMENDATIONS

In this section, empirical studies derived from the investigated methods and algorithms are presented. For this purpose, the algorithms were implemented on two well-known problems with 3038 and 5934 customers listed in the TSP library (Reinelt, 1991). These algorithms have not implemented on these large-scale instances so far. Brimberg et al. (2006) proposed different decomposition strategies that embedded in a variable neighbourhood decomposition search and solved the problem with 3038 customers. However, it is the first time that the instances with 5934 customers are solved for the uncapacitated continuous location-allocation problem. In this section, the performance of hybrid algorithms is compared with local search methods and with each other. In addition, to compare methods in equal conditions, all methods were coded in MATLAB and implemented on a dual quad core 2.66GHz Intel Xeon X5550 processors and 32GB of RAM.

A unique stopping criterion was assumed for all algorithms and defined as follows. Various algo-rithms were compared on the basis of equivalent CPU time. For this purpose, different instances of problem were involved initially by 40 runs of Cooper's alternating algorithm from gener-ated starting points with clustering method. The resulting CPU time was then used as a stopping criterion for the other heuristics. Therefore, the algorithm would terminate and the best solution found so far will be shown, if the total running CPU time exceeded the stopping criterion and; otherwise the iterations were allowed to continue. The concluded CPU time of implementing 40 runs of Cooper's algorithm is given at the forth column of Table 1.

Some tuning processes on a set of test problems were carried out by Ghaderi et al. (2011) and, Jabalameli and Ghaderi (2008), which suggests the different parameter values for each hybrid metaheuristic. In this paper, the concluded values for the problem with 1060 customers are used. The main parameters with their values in each algorithm defined as follows:

- **Hybrid GA:** Population size 6, crossover probability 0.9, mutation probability 0.4
- **Hybrid VNS:** *kmax=m*
- **Hybrid PSO:** Population size 6, initial ve-locity 0, acceleration constants 1.2

Ten and five instances in problems with 3038 and 5934 customers were solved by the considered algorithms, respectively. For the problem with 3038 customers, the number of new facilities varies from 50 to 500 with an increment of 50. For another problem, the number of new facilities varies from 50 to 250 with an increment of 50. In addition, for the instances with 3038 customers, the best known values are given in (Brimberg et al., 2006) that depicted in Table 1. However, the problem with 5934 customers was not solved in the literature. Hence, the best objective function found by considered hybrid heuristics are reported for these instances in the table.

Table 1. The instances dimensions, maximum CPU time, and best known (found) solutions

Instance	n (Customers)	m (Facilities)	Stopping criterion (CPU, seconds)	Best known or found solution
1	3038	50	1280.362607	506496.09
2	3038	100	2216.636929	351493.69
3	3038	150	2766.393813	280123.81
4	3038	200	4196.810662	236858.63
5	3038	250	4736.992205	207328.17
6	3038	300	5931.560503	185581.09
7	3038	350	4798.509639	169033.31
8	3038	400	5951.743912	155387.86
9	3038	450	7327.872413	143854.88
10	3038	500	8049.504959	134038.14
11	5934	50	14650.94936	4018893.60*
12	5934	100	19691.18254	2717848.89*
13	5934	150	25259.4604	2140105.35*
14	5934	200	34110.22705	1803085.58*
15	5934	250	34644.24344	1564692.27*
*: The best found solution in the computational experiments by considered hybrid heuristics				

All algorithms are implemented for 5 times and the average and the best found solutions are reported in Tables 2 and 3. These results are expressed as a percent deviation from the best known solutions (Table 2) or the best found solutions (Table 3). The deviation is computed as follows:

$$dev = \frac{F_{best} - F^*}{F^*} * 100\% \qquad (8)$$

where F_{best} is the total cost found by considered methods, and F^* refers to the best found solution so far in the literature. For the problem 5934, F^* is the best found solution by considered heuristics. The average results of all instances for each problem are also summarized in the last row of the tables under the overall average (AVT.)

The summary results, as described above, for the 10 instances in the problem with 3038, demonstrated in Table 2. In this table the results for different types of algorithms are given. The first two algorithms are local searches. The first

algorithm is MALT that its required CPU time employed as stopping criterion in other algorithms. The second local search is the exchange heuristic (CH). Another group of algorithms is the hybrid GA, VNS, PSO and local search algorithms. As shown in this table, CH algorithm is able to find much better results in comparison to MALT and outperforms this algorithm for all solved instances. Overall, hybrid algorithms consistently and significantly outperform these two local search methods, in terms of the objective function value. It is apparent that these two simple heuristics can reach to the local minima, whilst the meta-heuristic algorithms are used to search the all solution space with a systematically process. As can be seen, hybridization of local search methods leads to the better results for the majority of solved instances in this problem. In addition, hybrid metaheuristic algorithms reach to solutions with smaller gap than the hybrid local search. We can also observe that in these problems, hybrid VNS and hybrid PSO have the worst and the best performance on average, respectively.

Table 2. The obtained gap of local search and hybrid heuristics with the best known solution in the literature for the problem with 3038 customers

	Local Searches				Hybrid algorithms							
	MALT		CH		Local Searches		GA		VNS		PSO	
Instance	Av.	Best.	Av.	Best.	Av.	Best.	Av.	Best.	Av.	Best.	Av.	Best.
1	1.26	1.07	0.34	0.24	0.46	0.19	0.73	0.29	0.38	0.21	0.47	0.08
2	2.75	2.45	0.84	0.71	0.94	0.53	1.15	0.63	0.94	0.64	1.06	0.56
3	3.72	3.31	1.08	0.79	1.11	0.94	0.90	0.50	1.07	0.76	0.65	0.45
4	4.79	4.32	1.43	1.37	1.19	1.06	0.96	0.62	0.92	0.68	0.69	0.48
5	5.34	4.88	2.07	1.99	1.19	1.04	0.89	0.47	0.91	0.74	0.56	0.44
6	6.29	5.63	2.34	2.07	1.39	1.19	0.91	0.77	1.04	0.86	0.80	0.59
7	6.81	6.53	2.45	2.18	1.91	1.73	0.91	0.76	1.36	1.25	0.69	0.55
8	7.39	7.26	2.84	2.40	2.13	2.02	0.90	0.66	1.67	1.29	0.73	0.54
9	8.21	7.79	3.08	2.88	2.43	2.26	1.18	0.94	2.10	2.02	0.82	0.73
10	9.15	9.05	3.74	3.14	2.84	2.68	1.06	0.82	2.46	2.28	1.04	0.96
AVT.	5.57	5.23	2.02	1.78	1.56	1.36	0.96	0.65	1.29	1.07	0.75	0.54

Table 3. The obtained gap of local search and hybrid heuristics with the best solution found by heuristics for the problem with 5934 customers

	Local Searches				Hybrid algorithms							
	MALT		CH		Local Searches		GA		VNS		PSO	
Instance	Av.	Best.	Av.	Best.	Av.	Best.	Av.	Best.	Av.	Best.	Av.	Best.
11	1.12	0.85	0.77	0.65	1.02	0.21	0.87	0.53	0.17	**0.00**	0.67	0.29
12	1.93	1.64	0.89	0.78	1.03	0.26	0.61	0.20	0.07	**0.00**	0.41	0.17
13	3.42	3.03	1.21	0.93	0.86	0.67	0.94	0.31	0.16	**0.00**	0.40	0.24
14	4.09	2.91	1.08	0.99	0.93	0.72	0.77	0.31	0.18	**0.00**	0.29	0.12
15	5.11	4.51	1.17	0.89	0.33	**0.00**	0.78	0.46	0.35	0.18	0.30	0.18
AVT.	3.14	2.59	1.02	0.85	0.83	0.37	0.79	0.36	0.19	0.04	0.41	0.20

Table 3 reports the computation results obtained from experiments on the problem with 5934 fixed points. As mentioned before, there is no objective function value for this set of instances in the literature and the reported gap is the percent deviation from the best found solutions by considered algorithms. The hybrid VNS and local search methods could find the best results in 4 and 1 instances, respectively. Evidently, the performance of the MALT method is far below the CH method for all 5 instances. We also note that the CH algorithm would appear to be much less sensitive to problem dimensions, than is the MALT. We can see clearly that the solutions obtained by hybrid VNS algorithm are better than other algorithms, on average. Note that the calculated gap for the hybrid local search and GA are close together.

The level of improvement achieved with the considered heuristics is also investigated. For this purpose, the behavior of the hybrid heuristics is studied to solve the model over time. For this study, test problem 1 is selected, and its results for one run are plotted in Figure 6. As the execution time increases, the calculated GAP of the best-known solution decreases in all approaches. It is interesting to note that Hybrid LS finds the first solution at a time of 731 seconds with a gap of 1.4% that means this heuristic needs much time but reach to good solution. However, hybrid meta-heuristics start with a solution with large gap in one or couple of seconds. Hybrid algorithms improve the initial solution and reach to very good solution fast. For example, hybrid VNS improves the solution form GAP 37.72 to 0.43 in 6 iterations.

Nonparametric Statistical Tests to Compare the Performance of Hybrid Algorithms

The average gap value of some heuristics given in Tables 2 and 3 are very similar and it is difficult to select the best among these algorithms. Thus, it is necessary to perform statistical tests to evaluate if obtained differences in the average values are statistically significant. In this subsection, nonparametric statistical tests are used to compare the performance of the considered heuristics in solving the large-scale instances at uncapacitated continuous location-allocation problem. To do so,

firstly the nonparametric Friedman rank-based test is carried out to compare the performance of 4 considered hybrid algorithms. If at least one of the studied heuristics has different performance, it would be necessary to perform paired comparisons to know which methods are really different. Hence, POST HOC test is used to perform paired comparisons if needed. The nonparametric tests will be used to show significant statistical differences among the different algorithms of the study. There are some tutorials on the use of nonparametric statistical tests for comparing algorithms in the literature (e.g. Conover, 1998; Derrac et al., 2011; Taillard et al., 2008; Villegas, 2011)). The following notations are used for doing statistical tests:

- l: The number of instance
- k: The number of considered algorithms in computations
- X_{ij}: Is the obtained gap of heuristic j within instance i
- R: Rank the results of the hybrid heuristic for each instance, given 1 to the best and k to the worst

In Friedman test, the null and alternative hypotheses are defined as follows:

Figure 6. The trend of improvement of solution over time in investigated heuristics at instance 1 for one run

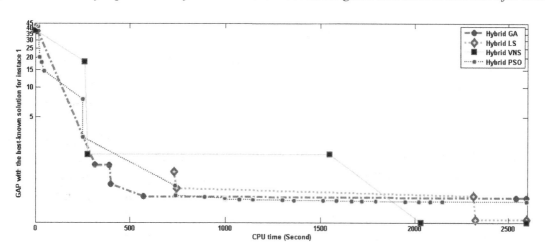

H_0: There is no significant difference between hybrid algorithms

H_1: At least one hybrid algorithms has different performance with others

To carry out the Friedman test, the following procedure should be done (Villegas, 2011):

- Rank the results of hybrid heuristics within each instance, given *1* to the best and *k* to the worst. Let $R(X_{ij})$ be the rank, from 1 to *k*, assigned to in problem *i*.
- For each algorithm *j*, calculate the following values:
  ∘ The summation of ranks R_j, $j = 1, 2, ..., k$ and, calculate A_2 as follows:

$$R_j = \sum_{i=1}^{l} R(X_{ij}) \tag{9}$$

$$A_2 = \sum_{i=1}^{l} \sum_{j=1}^{k} \left[R(X_{ij}) \right]^2 \tag{10}$$

  ∘ Total summation of squared ranks B_2

$$B_2 = \frac{1}{l} \sum_{j=1}^{k} R_j^2 \tag{11}$$

- The Friedman statistic can be computed by

$$T_2 = \frac{(l-1)[B_2 - lk(k+1)^2 / 4]}{A_2 - B_2} \tag{12}$$

- Reject the null hypothesis at the level of significance α if T_2 is greater than $1 - \alpha$ quantile of the F distribution with $k_1 = k - 1$ and $k_2 = (k-1)(l-1)$ degrees of freedom

According to described procedure to carry out the Freidman test, the rank and squared rank of hybrid heuristics with its summation are depicted in Table 4. We can observe that Hybrid PSO and LS are the best and the worst performing algorithms, respectively, in solving the problem. The values of $A_2 = 450$ and $B_2 = 408.40$ was obtained based on given formulas. Thus, we have $T_2 = 11.24$ for the test statistic. In other hand, using a table of F distribution with a level of significance $\alpha = 0.01$, we found that:

$$F_{1-\alpha, k-1, (l-1)(k-1)} = F_{0.99, 3, 42} = 4.30$$

Since $T_2 \geq F_{0.99, 3, 42}$, the null hypothesis is rejected and Freidman method detected the existence of significance difference among hybrid heuristics. Therefore, it is crucial to carry out paired comparisons to find which hybrid algorithms are really different. At the following, a POST HOC test is used for this purpose.

The following approach is used to know if heuristic *i* and *j* are considered different after the rejection of the null hypothesis with the Friedman test (Villegas, 2011). Calculate the absolute difference of the summation of the rank of heuristics *i* and *j* and declare *i* and *j* different if:

$$\left| R_i - R_j \right| \succ t_{1-\alpha/2} \left[\frac{2l(A_2 - B_2)}{(l-1)(k-1)} \right] \tag{13}$$

where, $t_{1-\alpha/2}$ is the $1 - \alpha / 2$ quantile of the t distribution with $(l-1)(k-1)$ degrees of freedom. In this study, $t_{1-\alpha/2}$ for $\alpha = 0.01$ and 42 degrees of freedom is 2.698 and the critical value for the difference is 14.70(2.698*5.451). The POST HOC analysis in Table 5 shows that there is a significant difference between some considered heuristics. Highlighted entries indicate that the heuristics are different. As can be seen from Table 5, the hybrid GA has the same performance with the hybrid VNS and LS. Hybrid PSO outperforms the hybrid LS and GA algorithm and has the same performance with Hybrid VNS.

Table 4. The rank and squared rank of hybrid heuristics with their summation

	Hybrid GA				Hybrid VNS				Hybrid PSO				Hybrid LS		
l	X_{ij}	R	R^2		X_{ij}	R	R^2		X_{ij}	R	R^2		X_{ij}	R	R^2
1	0.73	4	16		0.38	1	1		0.47	3	9		0.46	2	4
2	1.15	4	16		0.94	1	1		1.06	3	9		0.94	2	4
3	0.90	2	4		1.07	3	9		0.65	1	1		1.11	4	16
4	0.96	3	9		0.92	2	4		0.69	1	1		1.19	4	16
5	0.89	2	4		0.91	3	9		0.56	1	1		1.19	4	16
6	0.91	2	4		1.04	3	9		0.80	1	1		1.39	4	16
7	0.91	2	4		1.36	3	9		0.69	1	1		1.91	4	16
8	0.90	2	4		1.67	3	9		0.73	1	1		2.13	4	16
9	1.18	2	4		2.10	3	9		0.82	1	1		2.43	4	16
10	1.06	2	4		2.46	3	9		1.04	1	1		2.84	4	16
11	0.87	3	9		0.17	1	1		0.67	2	4		1.02	4	16
12	0.61	3	9		0.07	1	1		0.41	2	4		1.03	4	16
13	0.94	4	16		0.16	1	1		0.40	2	4		0.86	3	9
14	0.77	3	9		0.18	1	1		0.29	2	4		0.93	4	16
15	0.78	4	16		0.35	3	9		0.30	1	1		0.33	2	4
Average Rank	2.80				2.13				1.53				3.53		
R_j	**42**				**32**				**23**				**53**		
R_j^2			1764				1024				529				2809

Table 5. The results of paired comparisons for hybrid algorithms

		Hyrbid		
		VNS	PSO	LS
	GA	10	**19**	11
Hybrid	VNS			**21**
	PSO			**30**

DISCUSSION

The main body of this chapter is an algorithmic framework of integrating two effective local search and meta-heuristic algorithms. The considered hybrid meta-heuristic algorithms provide a promising way to solve a class of location-allocation problems for large-scale instances. Metaheuristic approaches and local search techniques have some advantages and disadvantages in isolation, so it is very important to exploit and combine the advantages of both in order to overcome their disadvantages. Local search algorithms generally search only in specific areas of solution space and move from a solution to a near one. These algorithms finally find the best solution in this area that is locally optimal. On the other hand, metaheuristic algorithms search all solution space and have a process to prevent from getting trapped in a local optimum. Hybrid heuristics provide more exploration and exploitation abilities, and hence, these algorithms have the potential to find good solutions and escape from local optima in comparison to the classical ones. Thus, hybrid considered algorithms use the meta-heuristic for diversification of search, and use local search component for intensification.

Conducted computational results show that the use of GA, VNS and PSO meta-heuristic algorithms combined with two efficient local searches, Cooper's and exchange heuristic in solving large-scale instances at MWP, returned much better outputs than using only classical metaheuristics or local search. Among these algorithms, hybrid PSO reach to better results on average for 15 solved instances. However, hybrid VNS outperforms the hybrid PSO for the largest solved instances.

FUTURE RESEARCH DIRECTIONS

Future research in this area might include the examination of other strategies like mathematical programming techniques and combine them, and a comparative study through extensive experimental testing for large-scale instances. The solution methods investigated in this chapter are heuristic methods on classical continuous location-allocation problem. This model has been extended subject to real assumptions in the literature and as a result some other models have been proposed. Therefore, another future research could focus on modelling issues, including the derivation of further theoretical properties, stronger problem formulations and valid inequalities, as well as heuristic approaches and hybrid heuristics that could combine the elements of heuristic methods with exact algorithms to construct efficient algorithms. In addition, other metaheuristics such as simulated annealing, tabu search, ant colony optimization, scatter search and etc could be considered to construct the hybrid algorithm for this problem or other variants of it.

CONCLUSION

In this chapter, solving one of the tightest models in facility location area by local searches and hybrid algorithms is studied. To do so, some hybrid meta-heuristic algorithms based on classical meta-heuristic and two local search algorithms for solving the large-scale instances of the uncapacitated continuous location–allocation problem (also called the MWP) have been investigated. A hybrid local search algorithm is also studied. In addition, a computational analysis was performed on fifteen instances from the literature and two statistical tests planned for the comparison purposes.

Preliminary computational results suggest that hybrid GA, VNS and PSO algorithms are capable of obtaining much better solutions on large-scale instances than local search and hybrid local search heuristics. These experimental results indicated that exchange heuristic (CH) outperforms the well known Cooper's algorithm to find the local minimum. In addition, Friedman rank-base and POST DOC nonparametric statistical tests are also carried out to compare the performance of considered hybrid algorithms. Freidman method detected the existence of significance difference among hybrid heuristics. Moreover, according to POST HOC test, hybrid PSO outperforms the hybrid LS and GA algorithm and has the same performance with Hybrid VNS. Overall, hybrid PSO and VNS have better performance than others, on average.

REFERENCES

Andres, C., & Lozano, S. (2006). A particle swarm optimization algorithm for part–machine grouping. *Robotics and Computer-integrated Manufacturing*, *22*, 468–474. doi:10.1016/j.rcim.2005.11.013

Aras, N., Ozkısacık, K. C., & Altinel, I. K. (2006). Solving the uncapacitated multi-facility Weber problem by vector quantization and self-organizing maps. *The Journal of the Operational Research Society*, *57*, 82–93. doi:10.1057/palgrave.jors.2601962

Banks, A., Vincent, J., & Anyakoha, C. (2007). A review of particle swarm optimization. Part I: background and development. *Natural Computing*, *6*(4), 467–484. doi:10.1007/s11047-007-9049-5

Banks, A., Vincent, J., & Anyakoha, C. (2008). A review of particle swarm optimization. Part II: hybridisation, combinatorial, multicriteria and constrained optimization, and indicative applications. *Natural Computing*, *7*(1), 109–124. doi:10.1007/s11047-007-9050-z

Blum, C., Roli, A., Aguilera, M., & Sampels, M. (2008). Hybrid metaheuristics: An introduction. In *Hybrid Metaheuristics* (*Vol. 114*, pp. 1–30). Berlin, Germany: Springer. doi:10.1007/978-3-540-78295-7_1

Bongartz, I., Calamai, P. H., & Conn, A. R. (1994). A projection method for l_p norm location-allocation problem. *Mathematical Programming*, *66*(1-3), 283–312. doi:10.1007/BF01581151

Brimberg, J., Hansen, P., & Mladenovic, N. (2004). *Convergence of variable neighborhood search*. Montreal, Canada.

Brimberg, J., Hansen, P., & Mladenovic, N. (2006). Decomposition strategies for large-scale continuous location–allocation problems. *IMA Journal of Management Mathematics*, *17*, 307–316. doi:10.1093/imaman/dpl002

Brimberg, J., Hansen, P., Mladenovic, N., & Salhi, S. (2008). A survey of solution methods for the continuous location-allocation problem. *International Journal of Operations Research*, *5*(1), 1–12.

Brimberg, J., Hansen, P., Mladenovic, N., & Taillard, E. D. (2000). Improvements and comparison of heuristics for solving the uncapacitated multisource Weber problem. *Operations Research*, *48*, 444–460. doi:10.1287/opre.48.3.444.12431

Brimberg, J., & Mladenovic, N. (1996). Solving the continuous location-allocation problem with Tabu search. *Studies in Locational Analysis*, *8*, 23–32.

Brimberg, J., & Salhi, S. (2005). A continuous location-allocation problem with zone-dependent fixed cost. *Annals of Operations Research*, *136*(1), 99–115. doi:10.1007/s10479-005-2041-5

Chen, P. C., Hansen, P., Jaumard, B., & Tuy, H. (1992). *Solution of the multisource Weber and conditional Weber problems by d.c. programming*.

Conover, W. (1998). *Practical nonparametric statistics*. New York, NY: Wiley.

Cooper, L. (1963). Location-allocation problem. *Operations Research*, *11*, 331–343. doi:10.1287/opre.11.3.331

Cooper, L. (1964). Heuristic methods for location-allocation problems. *SIAM Review*, *6*, 37–53. doi:10.1137/1006005

Derrac, J., García, S., Molina, D., & Herrera, F. (2011). A practical tutorial on the use of non-parametric statistical tests as a methodology for comparing evolutionary and swarm intelligence algorithms. *Swarm and Evolutionary Computation*, *1*, 3–18. doi:10.1016/j.swevo.2011.02.002

Doong, S. H., Lai, C. C., & Wu, C. H. (2007). Genetic subgradient method for solving location-allocation problems. *Applied Soft Computing*, *7*(1), 373–386. doi:10.1016/j.asoc.2005.06.008

Eberhart, R. C., & Salhi, S. (2004). Special issue on particle swarm optimization. *IEEE Transactions on Evolutionary Computation*, *8*(3), 201–203. doi:10.1109/TEVC.2004.830335

Eberhat, R. C., & Shi, Y. (2001). *Particle swarm optimization: Developments, applications and resources.* Paper presented at the IEEE Congress on Evolutionary Computation.

Ghaderi, A., Jabalameli, M. S., Barzinpour, F., & Rahmaniani, R. (2011). An efficient hybrid particle swarm optimization algorithm for solving the uncapacitated continuous location-allocation problem. *Networks and Spatial Economics*. doi:10.1007/s11067-011-9162-y

Hansen, P., Jaumard, B., & Krau, S. (1997). *A stabilized column generation algorithm for the multisource Weber problem.* University of Montreal.

Hansen, P., Mladenovic, N., & Pérez, J. A. M. (2010). Variable neighborhood search: Methods and applications. *Annals of Operations Research*, *175*(1), 367–407. doi:10.1007/s10479-009-0657-6

Hansen, P., Mladenovic, N., & Taillard, E. D. (1998). Heuristic solution of the multisource Weber problem as a P-median problem. *Operations Research Letters*, *22*, 55–62. doi:10.1016/S0167-6377(98)00004-2

Houck, C. R., Joines, J. A., & Kay, M. G. (1996). Comparison of genetic algorithms, random restart and two-opt switching for solving large location-allocation problems. *Computers & Operations Research*, *23*(6), 587–596. doi:10.1016/0305-0548(95)00063-1

Jabalameli, M. S., & Ghaderi, A. (2008). Hybrid algorithms for the uncapacitated continuous location-allocation problem. *International Journal of Advanced Manufacturing Technology*, *37*, 202–209. doi:10.1007/s00170-007-0944-9

Kennedy, J., & Eberhat, R. C. (1995). *Particle swarm optimization.* Paper presented at IEEE International Conference on Neural Networks.

Klose, A., & Drexl, A. (2005). Facility location models for distribution system design. *European Journal of Operational Research*, *162*(1), 4–29. doi:10.1016/j.ejor.2003.10.031

Krarup, J., & Pruzan, P. M. (1983). The simple plant location problem: survey and synthesis. *European Journal of Operational Research*, *12*(3), 36–81. doi:10.1016/0377-2217(83)90181-9

Kuenne, R. E., & Soland, R. M. (1972). Exact and approximate solutions to the multisource Weber problem. *Mathematical Programming*, *3*(1), 193–209. doi:10.1007/BF01584989

Liu, C. M., Kao, R. L., & Wang, A. H. (1994). Solving location-allocation problems with rectilinear distances by simulated annealing. *The Journal of the Operational Research Society*, *45*(11), 1304–1315.

Love, R. F., & Juel, H. (1982). Properties and solution methods for large location-allocation problems. *The Journal of the Operational Research Society, 33*(5), 443–452.

Love, R. F., Morris, J. G., & Wesolowsky, G. O. (1988). *Facilities layout and location: Models and methods*. New York, NY: North-Holland.

Megiddo, N., & Supowit, K. J. (1984). On the complexity of some common geometric location problems. *SIAM Journal on Computing, 13*(1), 182–196. doi:10.1137/0213014

Melo, M. T., Nickel, S., & Saldanha-da-Gama, F. (2009). Facility location and supply chain management – A review. *European Journal of Operational Research, 196*(2), 401–412. doi:10.1016/j.ejor.2008.05.007

Michel, L., & Van Hentenryck, P. (1997). LOCALIZER a modeling language for local search. *Principles and Practice of Constraint Programming-C, P97*, 237–251. doi:10.1007/BFb0017443

Mladenovic, N., & Hansen, P. (1997). Variable neighborhood search. *Computers & Operations Research, 24*(11), 1097–1100. doi:10.1016/S0305-0548(97)00031-2

Neema, M. N., Maniruzzaman, K. M., & Ohgai, A. (2011). New genetic algorithms based approaches to continuous p-median problem. *Networks and Spatial Economics, 11*(1), 83–99. doi:10.1007/s11067-008-9084-5

Noel, M. M. (2006). *Explorations in swarm algorithms: Hybrid particle swarm optimization and adaptive culture model algorithms*. The University Of Alabama At Birmingham.

Ostresh, L. M. (1973). *TWAIN - Exact solutions to the two source location-allocation problem*, (pp. 29-53). Lowa city: Department of Geography, University of Lowa.

Raidl, G. R. (2006). A unified view on hybrid metaheuristics. In Almeida, F., Blesa Aguilera, M., Blum, C., Moreno Vega, J., Pérez Pérez, M., Roli, A., & Sampels, M. (Eds.), *Hybrid metaheuristics* (*Vol. 4030*, pp. 1–12). Berlin, Germany: Springer. doi:10.1007/11890584_1

Raidl, G. R., Puchinger, J., & Blum, C. (2010). Metaheuristic hybrids. In Gendreau, M., & Potvin, J.-Y. (Eds.), *Handbook of metaheuristics* (*Vol. 146*, pp. 469–496). Springer, US. doi:10.1007/978-1-4419-1665-5_16

Reinelt, G. (1991). TSLIB-A traveling salesman library. *ORSA Journal on Computing, 3*, 376–384. doi:10.1287/ijoc.3.4.376

Resende, M. G. C., & Werneck, R. F. (2007). A fast swap-based local search procedure for location problems. *Annals of Operations Research, 150*(1), 205–230. doi:10.1007/s10479-006-0154-0

ReVelle, C. S., Eiselt, H. A., & Daskin, M. S. (2008). A bibliography for some fundamental problem categories in discrete location science. *European Journal of Operational Research, 184*(3), 817–848. doi:10.1016/j.ejor.2006.12.044

Rosing, K. E. (1992). An optimal method for solving the generalized multi-Weber problem. *European Journal of Operational Research, 58*(3), 414–426. doi:10.1016/0377-2217(92)90072-H

Salhi, S., & Gamal, M. D. H. (2003). A genetic algorithm based approach for the uncapacitated continuous location allocation problem. *Annals of Operations Research, 123*(1-4), 203–222. doi:10.1023/A:1026131531250

Sevkli, M., & Guner, A. R. (2006). *A new approach to solve uncapacitated facility location problems by particle swarm optimization*. Paper presented at the 5th International Symposium on Intelligent Manufacturing Systems.

Taillard, É. D., Waelti, P., & Zuber, J. (2008). Few statistical tests for proportions comparisons. *European Journal of Operational Research*, *185*(3), 1336–1350. doi:10.1016/j.ejor.2006.03.070

Teitz, M. B., & Bart, P. (1968). Heuristic methods for estimating the generalized vertex median of a weighted graph. *Operations Research*, *16*(5), 955–961. doi:10.1287/opre.16.5.955

Villegas, J. G. (2011). *Using nonparametric test to compare the performance of metaheuristics.* [Electronic Version]. Retrieved from www-labsticc.univ-ubs.fr/or/sites/default/files/Friedman test-24062011.pdf

Weber, A. (1909). *Uber den Standort der Industrian, (Alferd Weber's theory of the location of industries)*. University of Chicago Press.

Weiszfeld, E. (1937). Sur le point pour lequel la somme des distances de n points donnes est minimum. *Tohoku Mathematical Journal*, *43*, 355–386.

Xie, C., Turnquist, M. A., & Waller, S. T. (2011). A hybrid Lagrangian relaxation and Tabu search method for interdependent-choice network design problems. In Montoya-Torres, A. J. J., Huaccho Huatuco, L., Faulin, J., & Rodriguez-Verjan, G. (Eds.), *Hybrid algorithms for service, computing and manufacturing systems: Routing and scheduling solutions* (pp. 294–324). doi:10.4018/978-1-61350-086-6.ch013

Yapicioglu, H., Smith, A. E., & Dozier, G. (2007). Solving the semi-desirable facility location problem using bi-objective particle swarm. *European Journal of Operational Research*, *177*(2), 733–749. doi:10.1016/j.ejor.2005.11.020

ADDITIONAL READING

Arroyo, J., Santos, A., dos Santos, P., Ribeiro, W., Takahashi, R., & Deb, K. (2011). A bi-objective iterated local search heuristic with path-relinking for the p-median problem. In *Evolutionary Multicriterion optimization* (*Vol. 6576*, pp. 492–504). Berlin, Germany: Springer. doi:10.1007/978-3-642-19893-9_34

Bischoff, M., & Dachert, K. (2009). Allocation search methods for a generalized class of location-allocation problems. *European Journal of Operational Research*, *192*(3), 793–807. doi:10.1016/j.ejor.2007.10.022

Bischoff, M., & Klamroth, K. (2007). An efficient solution method for Weber problems with barriers based on genetic algorithms. *European Journal of Operational Research*, *177*, 22–41. doi:10.1016/j.ejor.2005.10.061

Blesa, M. J., Blum, C., Raidl, G., Roli, A., & Sampels, M. (2010). Hybrid metaheuristics. *Proceedings 7th International Workshop, HM 2010, Vienna, Austria, October 1-2, 2010*, (Vol. 6373). New York, NY: Springer-Verlag Inc.

Blum, C., Puchinger, J., Raidl, G., & Roli, A. (2010). A brief survey on hybrid metaheuristics. *Proceedings of BIOMA*, (pp. 3-18).

Blum, C., Puchinger, J., Raidl, G. R., & Roli, A. (2011). Hybrid metaheuristics in combinatorial optimization: A survey. *Applied Soft Computing*, *11*(6), 4135–4151. doi:10.1016/j.asoc.2011.02.032

Bouhafs, L., Hajjam, A., Koukam, A., Gabrys, B., Howlett, R., & Jain, L. (2006). *A combination of simulated annealing and ant colony system for the capacitated location-routing problem. Knowledge-Based Intelligent Information and Engineering Systems* (*Vol. 4251*, pp. 409–416). Berlin, Germany: Springer.

Brimberg, J., & Mladenovic, N. (1996). Variable neighbourhood algorithm for solving the continuous location-allocation problem. *Studies in Locational Analysis, 10*, 1–10.

Brito, J., Martinez, F., Moreno-Perez, J., & Verdegay, J. (2011). ACO-GRASP-VNS metaheuristic for VRP with fuzzy windows time constraints. *Computer Aided Systems Theory– EUROCAST 2011, 6927/2012*, (pp. 440-447).

Chen, C.-H., & Ting, C.-J. (2008). Combining Lagrangian heuristic and ant colony system to solve the single source capacitated facility location problem. *Transportation Research Part E, Logistics and Transportation Review, 44*(6), 1099–1122. doi:10.1016/j.tre.2007.09.001

Derbel, H., Jarboui, B., Hanafi, S., & Chabchoub, H. (2012). Genetic algorithm with iterated local search for solving a location-routing problem. *Expert Systems with Applications, 3*, 2865–2871. doi:10.1016/j.eswa.2011.08.146

Farahani, R. Z., & Hekmatfar, M. (2009). *Facility location: Concepts, models, algorithms and case studies*. Springer.

Francis, R. L., McGinnis, L. F. Jr, & White, J. A. (1992). *Facility layout and location: An analytical approach*. Englewood Cliffs, NJ: Prentice-Hall.

Gendreau, M., & Potvin, J. Y. (2010). *Handbook of metaheuristics* (*Vol. 146*). Springer Verlag.

Gong, D., Gen, M., Yamazaki, G., & Xu, W. (1997). Hybrid evolutionary method for capacitated location-allocation problem. *Computers & Industrial Engineering, 33*, 577–580. doi:10.1016/S0360-8352(97)00197-6

Hansen, P., & Mladenovic, N. (2001). Invited review variable neighborhood search: Principles and applications. *European Journal of Operational Research, 130*, 449–467. doi:10.1016/S0377-2217(00)00100-4

Hsieh, K. H., & Tien, F. C. (2004). Self-organizing feature maps for solving location-allocation problem with rectilinear distances. *Computers & Operations Research, 31*, 1017–1031. doi:10.1016/S0305-0548(03)00049-2

Hussin, M. S., & Stutzle, T. (2011). *High performing stochastic local search algorithms for the QAP and their performance in dependence to the instance structure and size*. Malaysia: Melacca. doi:10.1109/HIS.2011.6122094

Jiang, J. L., & Yuan, X. M. (2008). A heuristic algorithm for constrained multi-source Weber problem – The variational inequality approach. *European Journal of Operational Research, 187*(2), 357–370. doi:10.1016/j.ejor.2007.02.043

Jourdan, L., Basseur, M., & Talbi, E. G. (2009). Hybridizing exact methods and metaheuristics: A taxonomy. *European Journal of Operational Research, 199*(3), 620–629. doi:10.1016/j.ejor.2007.07.035

Landa-Torres, I., Del Ser, J., Salcedo-Sanz, S., Gil-Lopez, S., Portilla-Figueras, J. A., & Alonso-Garrido, O. (2011). A comparative study of two hybrid grouping evolutionary techniques for the capacitated P-median problem. *Computers & Operations Research, 39*(9), 2214–2222. doi:10.1016/j.cor.2011.11.004

Leitner, M., Raidl, G., Moreno-Díaz, R., Pichler, F., & Quesada-Arencibia, A. (2011). Variable neighborhood and greedy randomized adaptive search for capacitated connected facility location. In *Computer Aided Systems Theory – EUROCAST 2011* (*Vol. 6927*, pp. 295–302). Berlin, Germany: Springer. doi:10.1007/978-3-642-27549-4_38

Li, X., Zhao, Z., Zhu, X., & Wyatt, T. (2011). Covering models and optimization techniques for emergency response facility location and planning: A review. *Mathematical Methods of Operations Research, 74*(3), 281–310. doi:10.1007/s00186-011-0363-4

Li, Y., Sun, H., Zhang, C., & Li, G. (2009). *Sites selection of ATMs based on particle swarm optimization*. Paper presented at the International Conference on Information Technology and Computer Science.

Ljubic, I. (2007). A hybrid VNS for connected facility location. *Hybrid Metaheuristics, 4771/2007,* 157-169.

Lorena, L. A. N., & Senne, E. L. F. (2003). Local search heuristics for capacitated p-median problems. *Networks and Spatial Economics, 3*(4), 407–419. doi:10.1023/A:1027353520175

Lozano, M., & Garcia-Martinez, C. (2010). Hybrid metaheuristics with evolutionary algorithms specializing in intensification and diversification: Overview and progress report. *Computers & Operations Research, 37*(3), 481–497. doi:10.1016/j.cor.2009.02.010

Lozano, S., Guerrero, F., Onieva, L., & Larrañeta, J. (1998). Kohonen maps for solving a class of location-allocation problems. *European Journal of Operational Research, 108,* 106–117. doi:10.1016/S0377-2217(97)00046-5

Luis, M., Salhi, S., & Nagy, G. (2009). Region-rejection based heuristics for the capacitated multi-source Weber problem. *Computers & Operations Research, 36*(6), 2007–2017. doi:10.1016/j.cor.2008.06.012

Maniezzo, V., Stutzle, T., & Vob, S. (2009). *Matheuristics: Hybridizing metaheuristics and mathematical programming* (*Vol. 10*). Springer Verlag.

Manzour-al-Ajdad, S. M. H., Torabi, S. A., & Eshghi, K. (2012). Single-source capacitated multi-facility Weber problem-An iterative two phase heuristic algorithm. *Computers & Operations Research, 39*(7), 1465–1476. doi:10.1016/j.cor.2011.08.018

Merz, P., & Freisleben, B. (1999). *A comparison of memetic algorithms, tabu search, and ant colonies for the quadratic assignment problem.* Paper presented at the the 1999 Congress on Evolutionary Computation.

Pilotta, E. A., & Torres, G. A. (2011). A projected Weiszfeld algorithm for the box-constrained Weber location problem. *Applied Mathematics and Computation, 218*(6), 2932–2943. doi:10.1016/j.amc.2011.08.041

Plastria, F., & Elosmani, M. (2008). On the convergence of the Weiszfeld algorithm for continuous single facility location allocation problems. *Top (Madrid), 16*(2), 388–406. doi:10.1007/s11750-008-0056-1

Potluri, A., Singh, A., Panigrahi, B., Suganthan, P., Das, S., & Satapathy, S. (2011). Two hybrid meta-heuristic approaches for minimum dominating set problem. In *Swarm, Evolutionary, and Memetic Computing* (*Vol. 7077*, pp. 97–104). Berlin, Germany: Springer. doi:10.1007/978-3-642-27242-4_12

Pradeepmon, T. G., & Paul, B. (2011). A hybrid algorithm for uncapacitated facility location problems. *International Journal of Services. Economics and Management, 3*(2), 197–206.

Pullan, W. (2009). *A population based hybrid meta-heuristic for the uncapacitated facility location problem*. New York, NY, USA. doi:10.1145/1543834.1543898

Resende, M. G. C., & Werneck, R. F. (2006). A hybrid multistart heuristic for the uncapacitated facility location problem. *European Journal of Operational Research, 174*(1), 54–68. doi:10.1016/j.ejor.2005.02.046

Salcedo-Sanz, S., Xu, Y., & Yao, X. (2006). Hybrid meta-heuristics algorithms for task assignment in heterogeneous computing systems. *Computers & Operations Research, 33*(3), 820–835. doi:10.1016/j.cor.2004.08.010

Shariff, S. S. R., Moin, N. H., & Omar, M. (2012). Location allocation modeling for healthcare facility planning in Malaysia. *Computers & Industrial Engineering*. doi:10.1016/j.cie.2011.12.026

Shi, Y., & Eberhat, R. C. (1998). *Parameter selection in particle swarm optimization.* Paper presented at the Evolutionary Programming VII

Voß, S., Floudas, C. A., & Pardalos, P. M. (2009). *Metaheuristics encyclopedia of optimization* (pp. 2061–2075). Springer, US.

Wen, M., & Kang, R. (2011). Some optimal models for facility location-allocation problem with random fuzzy demands. *Applied Soft Computing*, *11*(1), 1202–1207. doi:10.1016/j.asoc.2010.02.018

Yao, Z., Lee, L. H., Jaruphongsa, W., Tan, V., & Hui, C. F. (2010). Multi-source facility location-allocation and inventory problem. *European Journal of Operational Research*, *207*(2), 750–762. doi:10.1016/j.ejor.2010.06.006

Yu, V. F., Lin, S.-W., Lee, W., & Ting, C.-J. (2010). A simulated annealing heuristic for the capacitated location routing problem. *Computers & Industrial Engineering*, *58*(2), 288–299. doi:10.1016/j.cie.2009.10.007

Zhou, J., & Liu, B. (2003). New stochastic models for capacitated location-allocation problem. *Computers & Industrial Engineering*, *45*, 111–125. doi:10.1016/S0360-8352(03)00021-4

KEY TERMS AND DEFINITIONS

Facility Location Problem: Modeling, formulation, and solution of a class of problems that can best be illustrated as locating facilities in some given spaces.

Heuristic Algorithm: Heuristic algorithm is a common technique that designed for problem solving to find the optimal or a satisfactory solution. The majority of heuristics are presented specifically for a given problem.

Hybrid Algorithm: A relatively new group of solution approaches that combined from two or more methods to overcome on disadvantages of these methods, separately.

Local Search Algorithm: Start from a candidate solution and then iteratively move to a neighbor solution in order to find a better solution.

Location Allocation Problems: A large category of facility location problems that aim at locating some new facilities among existing points and simultaneously, allocating the fixed points to opened facilities.

Metaheuristic Algorithm: An iterative process that guides and modifies the operations of subordinate heuristics to efficiently produce high quality solutions.

Non-Parametric Statistical Test: Covers techniques that do not rely on data belonging to any particular distribution. These are the techniques that do not assume that the structure of a model is fixed.

Chapter 7
Analysing the Returns–Earnings Relationship:
Dempster–Shafer Theory and Evolutionary Computation Based Analyses Using the Classification and Ranking Belief Simplex

Malcolm J. Beynon
Cardiff University, UK,

Mark Clatworthy
Cardiff University, UK,

ABSTRACT

This chapter considers the problem of understanding the relationship between company stock returns and earnings components, namely accruals and cash flows. The problem is of interest, because earnings are a key output of the accounting process, and investors have been shown to depend heavily on earnings in their valuation models. This chapter offers an elucidation on the application of a nascent data analysis technique, the Classification and Ranking Belief Simplex (CaRBS) and a recent development of it, called RCaRBS, in the returns-earnings relationship problem previously described. The approach underpinning the CaRBS technique is closely associated with uncertain reasoning, with methodological rudiments based on the Dempster-Shafer theory of evidence. With the analysis approach formed as a constrained optimisation problem, details on the employment of the evolutionary computation based technique trigonometric differential evolution are also presented. Alongside the presentation of results, in terms of model fit and variable contribution, based on a CaRBS classification-type analysis, a secondary analysis is performed using a development RCaRBS, which is able to perform multivariate regression-type analysis. Comparisons are made between the results from the two different types of analysis, as well as briefly with more traditional forms of analysis, namely binary logistic regression and multivariate linear regression. Where appropriate, numerical details in the construction of results from both CaRBS and RCaRBS are presented, as well emphasis on the graphical elucidation of findings.

DOI: 10.4018/978-1-4666-2086-5.ch007

INTRODUCTION

In this chapter we describe the employment of a nascent analysis technique, utilising Dempster-Shafer theory and evolutionary computation, to examine the relationship between stock returns and earnings components, namely accruals and cash flows. The problem is of interest because earnings are a key output of the accounting process and investors have been shown to depend heavily on earnings in their valuation models (e.g. Imam *et al.*, 2008). Recent research, however, suggests that there are differences in levels of persistence of the cash flow and accruals components of earnings (e.g. Sloan, 1996), which, *cetris paribus*, should lead to them being weighted differentially by stock markets.

The Classification and Ranking Belief Simplex (CaRBS) non-parametric soft-computing technique, introduced in Beynon (2005a, 2005b), was presented as a novel approach to data mining. The rudiments of CaRBS are based on the general methodology of Dempster-Shafer theory (DST), introduced in Dempster (1967) and Shafer (1976). It is considered one of the key mathematical approaches to uncertainty modeling (Roesmer, 2000). One consequence of the association of the CaRBS technique with DST is the ability to undertake analysis in the presence of a form of mathematical based ignorance (Safranek *et al.*, 1990; Beynon, 2005b).

The original CaRBS technique is here employed in a classification-type analysis, plus a development, termed RCARBS (Beynon *et al.*, 2010), which facilitates regression-type analysis on the same problem. The RCaRBS analysis presented in this chapter illustrates, at the technical level, how a data analysis technique based on uncertain modelling, such as CaRBS, can be developed to undertake more general types of analysis, in this case multivariate regression. The chapter also describes how the configuration mechanics of the techniques are defined as constrained optimisation problems, solved here using the evolutionary computation technique trigonometric differential evolution (TDE - Fan and Lampinen, 2003). Indeed, how the configuration processes are able to be adapted with the use of different objective functions with the TDE, depending on whether RCaRBS against CaRBS is being employed, is shown.

The rest of the chapter is organised as follows: The next section describes the methodologies employed, namely CaRBS, its development RCaRBS and TDE. This is followed by a description of the returns-earnings relationship problem that forms the basis of the analysis in this chapter. The following section presents the CaRBS and RCaRBS analyses of the returns-earnings relationship (along with logistic and linear regression results for benchmarking purposes), including the level of model fit and analysis of the contribution of the financial variables considered. Finally, future research directions and conclusions are drawn and the implications of the content of the chapter are discussed.

BACKGROUND

The Classification and Ranking Belief Simplex (CaRBS) technique was originally devised as a tool to undertake the binary classification and ranking of objects in the presence of ignorance (see Beynon, 2005a). The background discussed here surrounds the related technical issues, namely an exposition of the CaRBS technique and the development of it, called RCaRBS, which enables regression-type analyses to be performed (see Beynon *et al.*, 2010), and the power house methodology behind the necessary configuration optimisation, namely the evolutionary computation approach TDE.

The methodology underpinning the CaRBS technique is Dempster-Shafer theory (DST), introduced in Dempster (1967) and Shafer (1976), and generally acknowledged to be a mathematical approach associated with uncertainty modelling

(Roesmer, 2000). Fundamentally, DST is based on the idea of obtaining degrees of belief for one question (the equivalent of a dependent variable), from subjective probabilities describing the evidence from others (the equivalent of independent variables), and that the concordance of pieces of evidence reinforce each other. This uncertain reasoning methodology, it has been argued, is a generalization of the well-known Bayesian probability calculus (Shafer and Srivastava, 1990; Schubert, 1994).

DST is a general methodology whose fundamentals consider a finite set of p hypotheses $\Theta = \{O_1, O_2, ..., O_p\}$, called a frame of discernment. The *mass values* associated with subsets of Θ come from a function $m: 2^\Theta \rightarrow [0, 1]$ such that $m(\varnothing) = 0$ ($\varnothing$ - the empty set) and $\sum_{s \in 2^\Theta} m(s) = 1$ (2^Θ - the power set on Θ). Any proper subset s of the frame of discernment Θ, for which $m(s)$ is non-zero, is called a focal element and the associated mass value $m(s)$ represents the exact belief in the proposition depicted by s. The collection of mass values (and focal elements) associated with a single piece of evidence is called a *body of evidence* (BOE), defined $m(\cdot)$. The mass value $m(\Theta)$ assigned to the frame of discernment Θ is considered the amount of mathematical ignorance within the BOE, since it represents the level of exact belief that cannot be discerned to any proper subsets of Θ.

DST also provides a method to combine the BOEs from different pieces of evidence, using Dempster's rule of combination. This rule assumes these pieces of evidence are independent; the combination function $[m_1 \oplus m_2]: 2^\Theta \rightarrow [0, 1]$, acting on two BOEs, is then defined by (on a particular focal element s);

$$[m_1 \oplus m_2](s) = \begin{cases} 0 & s = \varnothing \\ \dfrac{\sum\limits_{s_1 \cap s_2 = x} m_1(s_1)m_2(s_2)}{1 - \sum\limits_{s_1 \cap s_2 = \varnothing} m_1(s_1)m_2(s_2)} & s \neq \varnothing \end{cases},$$

and is a mass value, where s_1 and s_2 are focal elements from the BOEs, $m_1(\cdot)$ and $m_2(\cdot)$, respectively.

The combination rule can be considered over all the elements in the power set of Θ ($s \in 2^\Theta$), to formulate the new BOE. Further, the combination rule can be used iteratively to combine the evidence contained in a number of BOEs. The denominator part of the combination rule includes $\sum\limits_{s_1 \cap s_2 = \varnothing} m_1(s_1)m_2(s_2)$, considered to measure the level of conflict in the combination process between BOEs (Murphy, 2000), and is based on the sum of the products of mass values associated with focal elements from the different BOE, which have empty intersection. For examples on the utilisation of DST, with numerical details to elucidate the full workings, see Haenni (2002) and Sentz and Ferson (2002).

The technical details of the CaRBS technique are next briefly described (see Beynon, 2005a; 2005b, for further details), with its subsequent development to undertake regression-type analyses then exposited (RCaRBS - see Beynon *et al.*, 2010). Throughout the description of the CaRBS and RCaRBS techniques, where appropriate, terminology relating to the returns-earnings relationship problem is utilised. As described later, the data set analysed relates companies' annual stock returns to certain financial variables, in this case the profit-related variables accruals and cash flow (where both variables sum to equal annual profit).

Within CaRBS, the information from one of an object's independent variables (profit-related variables - accruals and cash flow), is quantified in a BOE, generally denoted by $m_j(\cdot)$, where all assigned mass values sum to unity and there is no belief in the empty set (as stated earlier in the technical description of DST). Moreover, for a company O_j ($1 \leq j \leq n_O$) and the ith profit-related variable V_i ($1 \leq i \leq n_V$) describing it, a *profit-related* BOE, defined $m_{j,i}(\cdot)$, is made up of the mass values, $m_{j,i}(\{x\})$ and $m_{j,i}(\{\neg x\})$, which denote levels of exact belief in the association of the company to a hypothesis x (positive returns) and not-the-hypothesis $\neg x$ (not-positive or negative returns), and $m_{j,i}(\{x, \neg x\})$ the level of concomitant ignorance. In the case of $m_{j,i}(\{x, \neg x\})$, its association with the term ignorance is because this mass value is unable to be assigned specifically to either x or $\neg x$.

A profit-related BOE represents the evidence from one of a company's profit-related variables (independent variables). From Safranek *et al.* (1990), used in CaRBS, the mass values in a profit-related BOE are given by the expressions (for a profit-related variable value v);

$$m_{j,i}\left(\{x\}\right) = \frac{B_i}{1 - A_i} cf_i(v) - \frac{A_i B_i}{1 - A_i},$$

$$m_{j,i}\left(\{\neg x\}\right) = \frac{-B_i}{1 - A_i} cf_i(v) + B_i$$

and $m_{j,i}(\{x, \neg x\}) = 1 - m_{j,i}(\{x\}) - m_{j,i}(\{\neg x\})$,

where $cf_i(v) = 1/(1 + \exp(-k_i(v - \theta_i)))$, a sigmoid function similar to that used in neural networks. The assignment of values to the k_i, θ_i, A_i and B_i control variables incumbent in CaRBS confers the configuration of a CaRBS system. Importantly, in the construction of a profit-related BOE $m_{j,i}(\cdot)$, if either of the mass values $m_{j,i}(\{x\})$ or $m_{j,i}(\{\neg x\})$ are initially calculated to be negative they are set to zero, and the respective $m_{j,i}(\{x, \neg x\})$ then calculated.

Figure 1 presents, with respect to the CaRBS technique, a graphical presentation of the process from an independent profit-related variable value v to a profit-related BOE, and its subsequent representation as a single simplex coordinate in a simplex plot. The role of the simplex coordinate and simplex plot is to offer a visualisation dimension of the evidence and results from a CaRBS analysis (demonstrated later). Further, as part of the development of CaRBS to be able to perform regression-type analysis, the graphical "regres-sion" of a BOE to a single predicted returns value, as part of the RCaRBS development, is also shown (explained later).

In Figure 1, an example company's profit-related variable value v is first transformed into a confidence value $cf_i(v)$ (1*a*), from which it is de-constructed into its associated profit-related BOE $m_{j,i}(\cdot)$ (1*b*), made up of the triplet of mass values, $m_{j,i}(\{x\})$, $m_{j,i}(\{\neg x\})$ and $m_{j,i}(\{x, \neg x\})$, using the expressions given previously. Stage (1*c*) then shows a profit-related BOE $m_{j,i}(\cdot)$; $m_{j,i}(\{x\}) = v_{j,i,1}$, $m_{j,i}(\{\neg x\}) = v_{j,i,2}$ and $m_{j,i}(\{x, \neg x\}) = v_{j,i,3}$, can be represented as a simplex coordinate $(p_{j,i,v})$ in a simplex plot (equilateral triangle). That is, a point $p_{j,i,v}$ exists within an equilateral triangle such that the least distance from $p_{j,i,v}$ to each of the sides of the equilateral triangle are in the same proportions (ratios) to the values, $v_{j,i,1}$, $v_{j,i,2}$ and $v_{j,i,3}$ (see for example, Canongia Lopes, 2004; Beneš et al., 2007). In the case of a simplex plot with unit side, with vertices $(0, 0)$, $(1, 0)$ and $(0.5, 0.5\sqrt{3})$, the pj,i,v simplex coordinate (xp, yp) is given by xp $= vj,i,1 + 0.5vj,i,3$ and yp $= 0.5\sqrt{3}\, v_{j,i,3}$.

The set of profit-related BOEs $\{m_{j,i}(\cdot), i = 1, ..., n_C\}$, associated with a company O_j, found from its profit-related variable values, can be combined using Dempster's combination rule into a *firm-year* BOE, defined $m_j(\cdot)$.[1] Moreover, considering $m_{j,i}(\cdot)$ and $m_{j,k}(\cdot)$ as two independent profit-related BOEs, $[m_{j,i} \oplus m_{j,k}](\cdot)$ defines their combination (on a sequence of single focal elements), and is given here by (in terms of a newly created BOE made up of three mass values - such as $m_{j,i}(\{x\})$, $m_{j,i}(\{\neg x\})$ and $m_{j,i}(\{x, \neg x\})$) (refer to Box 1).

The ability to explicitly write out the combination of two profit-related BOEs, rather than showing the original combination rule (see background section), is due to a binary frame of discernment being considered (the hypotheses x and $\neg x$ only). This combination process is then used iteratively to combine all the profit-related BOEs describing the evidence in a company's profit-related variables' values, into its associated firm-year BOE

Figure 1. Stages in CaRBS for a single profit-related variable value v to formulate a profit-related BOE and its representation in a simplex plot, and subsequent regression to a single predicted returns value

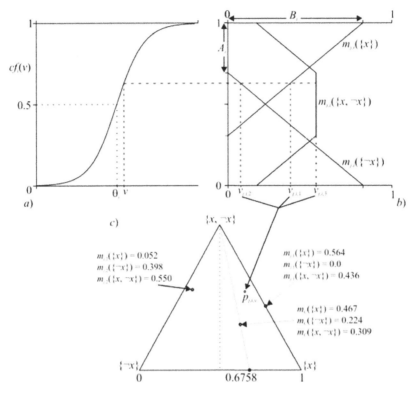

Box 1.

$$[m_{j,i} \oplus m_{j,k}](\{x\}) = \frac{m_{j,i}(\{x\})m_{j,k}(\{x\}) + m_{j,k}(\{x\})m_{j,i}(\{x, \neg x\}) + m_{j,i}(\{x\})m_{j,k}(\{x, \neg x\})}{1 - (m_{j,i}(\{\neg x\})m_{j,k}(\{x\}) + m_{j,i}(\{x\})m_{j,k}(\{\neg x\}))},$$

$$[m_{j,i} \oplus m_{j,k}](\{\neg x\}) = \frac{m_{j,i}(\{\neg x\})m_{j,k}(\{\neg x\}) + m_{j,k}(\{x, \neg x\})m_{j,i}(\{\neg x\}) + m_{j,k}(\{\neg x\})m_{j,i}(\{x, \neg x\})}{1 - (m_{j,i}(\{\neg x\})m_{j,k}(\{x\}) + m_{j,i}(\{x\})m_{j,k}(\{\neg x\}))},$$

$$[m_{j,i} \oplus m_{j,k}](\{x, \neg x\}) = 1 - [m_{j,i} \oplus m_{j,k}](\{x\}) - [m_{j,i} \oplus m_{j,k}](\{\neg x\}).$$

$m_j(\cdot)$. In the original CaRBS technique, the firm-year BOE contained the evidence that described a company's association to the considered hypotheses, namely the binary consideration of hypothesis (positive returns) and not-the-hypothesis (negative returns), and the concomitant ignorance (positive or negative returns).

To illustrate this method of combination, and to see the connection between the numerical details and the graphical interpretation of the combination process, the two example BOEs, $m_1(\cdot)$ and $m_2(\cdot)$, shown in Figure 1c, are considered. Utilising the numerical details shown in Figure 1c, see Box 2.

Box 2.

$$[m_1 \oplus m_2](\{x\}) = \frac{m_1(\{x\})m_2(\{x\}) + m_2(\{x\})m_1(\{x, \neg x\}) + m_1(\{x\})m_2(\{x, \neg x\})}{1 - (m_1(\{\neg x\})m_2(\{x\}) + m_1(\{x\})m_2(\{\neg x\}))},$$

$$= \frac{0.564 \times 0.052 + 0.052 \times 0.436 + 0.564 \times 0.550}{1 - (0.000 \times 0.052 + 0.564 \times 0.398)} = 0.467,$$

$$[m_1 \oplus m_2](\{\neg x\}) = \frac{m_1(\{\neg x\})m_2(\{\neg x\}) + m_2(\{x, \neg x\})m_1(\{\neg x\}) + m_2(\{\neg x\})m_1(\{x, \neg x\})}{1 - (m_1(\{\neg x\})m_2(\{x\}) + m_1(\{x\})m_2(\{\neg x\}))},$$

$$= \frac{0.000 \times 0.398 + 0.550 \times 0.000 + 0.398 \times 0.436}{1 - (0.000 \times 0.052 + 0.564 \times 0.398)} = 0.224,$$

$$[m_1 \oplus m_2](\{x, \neg x\}) = 1 - [m_1 \oplus m_2](\{x\}) - [m_1 \oplus m_2](\{\neg x\}),$$

$$= 1 - 0.467 - 0.224 = 0.309.$$

This combination process is graphically shown in Figure 1c, including the simplex coordinate representation of the combined BOE $m_c(\cdot)$ $(=[m_1 \oplus m_2](\cdot))$ (with evaluated simplex coordinate (0.622, 0.268)). The relative position of the $m_C(\cdot)$, to the simplex coordinates of $m_1(\cdot)$ and $m_2(\cdot)$, shows it is nearer the base line of the equilateral triangle (furthest away from the $\{x, \neg x\}$ vertex of the presented BOEs), so has less associated ignorance than each of the pieces of evidence that combined to create it (as is the case). Further, the horizontal position of $m_C(\cdot)$, nearer to the $\{x\}$ vertex than the $\{\neg x\}$ vertex, indicates the evidence in $m_C(\cdot)$ supports more the association to x than $\neg x$, due to the lesser ignorance in the evidence in $m_1(\cdot)$ than in $m_2(\cdot)$.

The CaRBS technique is governed by the values assigned to the incumbent control variables k_i, θ_i, A_i and B_i, for each profit-related variable, evaluated through a configuration process. These control variables contribute directly to the construction of the profit-related BOEs $m_{j,i}(\cdot)$, which are combined to produce the respective firm-year BOEs $m_j(\cdot)$. A CaRBS configuration process is considered a constrained optimisation problem (see later), able to be solved using an evolutionary algorithm such as Trigonometric Differential

Evolution (TDE - Storn and Price, 1997; Fan and Lampinen, 2003), the algorithm employed here.

The TDE approach to affect this stated optimisation is next briefly described, being a development on the nascent differential evolution (DE) algorithm, introduced in Storn and Price (1997). The domain of DE, and TDE, is the continuous space made up of the number of CaRBS control variables considered. For a series of control variable values they are represented as a point in this continuous space (member vector). In DE, a population of vectors is considered at each generation of the progression to an optimum solution, measured through a defined objective function (OB).

Starting with an initial population, TDE generates new vectors by adding to a third member the difference between two other members (this change subject to a crossover operator). If the resulting vector yields a lower OB value than a predetermined population member then it takes its place. This construction of a resultant vector is elucidated in Figure 2, where an example two dimensional (X_1, X_2) case is presented.

In Figure 2, the effect of the 'vector' difference between two vectors $\overrightarrow{y_{r_2}^G}$ and $\overrightarrow{y_{r_3}^G}$ on the resultant

Figure 2. Example of an OB with contour lines and process for generation of the resultant vector

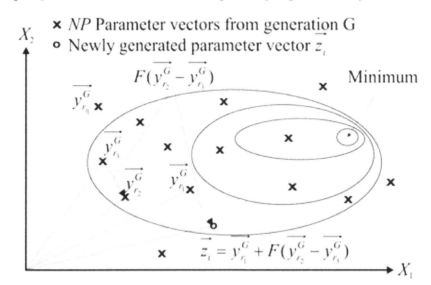

vector $\vec{z}_i$ from another vector $\vec{y}_{r_1}^G$ is elucidated (F amplification parameter). The TDE development, presented in Fan and Lampinen (2003), takes account of the associated OB values of potential solutions, to hasten the convergence to an optimum solution (the optimum assignment of values to the control variables incumbent in CaRBS). The necessary operating parameters used throughout this chapter with TDE, were (*ibid.*): amplification control $F = 0.99$, crossover constant $CR = 0.85$ and number of parameter vectors $NP = 100$.

The effectiveness of a configured CaRBS system is measured by a defined OB (used in the TDE process), whether for classification-type or regression-type analyses. With CaRBS (classification-type analyses), an objective function, defined OBC, uses the equivalence classes, $E(x)$ and $E(\neg x)$, the groups of companies known to be associated with a defined x and $\neg x$, respec-

tively. It follows, the optimum solution, based on the firm-year BOEs $m_j(\cdot)$ here, is to maximise the difference values $(m_j(\{x\}) - m_j(\{\neg x\}))$ and $(m_j(\{\neg x\}) - m_j(\{x\}))$ depending on where the considered company O_j is associated with x (in $E(x)$) or $\neg x$ (in $E(\neg x)$), respectively. The intention to maximise differences, in terms of the simplex plot representation, is to attempt to force companies associated with x and $\neg x$ to the bottom right and left vertices of a simplex plot.

Where optimisation is minimisation with lower limit zero, the OBC is given by (see Beynon, 2005*b*) (refer to Box 3).

in the limit, $0 \leq OBC \leq 1$. It is noted, maximising a difference value such as $(m_j(\{x\}) - m_j(\{\neg x\}))$ minimises classification ambiguity but only indirectly the associated ignorance.

Also demonstrated in Figure 1*c* is the development of the CaRBS technique that allows it to be

Box 3.

$$OBC = \frac{1}{4}\left(\frac{1}{|E(x)|}\sum_{O_j \in E(x)}(1 - m_j(\{x\}) + m_j(\{\neg x\})) + \frac{1}{|E(\neg x)|}\sum_{O_j \in E(\neg x)}(1 + m_j(\{x\}) - m_j(\{\neg x\}))\right)$$

considered a tool for regression-type analysis, the proposed RCaRBS development of the original CaRBS technique (Beynon *et al.*, 2010). Continuing the example above, the BOE $m_C(\cdot)$ (potentially representing a firm-year BOE), includes the evidential information to calculate the associated predicted value over the domain ranging from $\neg x$ to x (as would be found from a regression-type analysis), where each company O_j has an actual known value in this domain. Returning to Figure 1c, this predicted value is found by projecting the associated simplex coordinate for $m_C(\cdot)$ onto the base line of the simplex plot (projected using a line from the $\{x, \neg x\}$ vertex through the simplex coordinate of $m_C(\cdot)$). Representing the simplex coordinate of $m_C(\cdot)$ as (x_C, y_C), and considering an equilateral triangle of unit side (as previously), the projected value is given by $(\sqrt{3} \, x_C - y_C)/(\sqrt{3} - 2y_C)$, over a domain 0 to 1.

The projected value evaluated for each company (in our study), found this way, is considered their respective predicted value, defined Rp_j. In keeping with the use of the equilateral triangle with unit side in RCaRBS, the original company returns values (see later), are *a priori* formatted into the same 0 to 1 domain - through normalization, see Kim, 1999). For the example considered here, in Figure 1, using $m_C(\cdot)$, with $x_C = 0.622$ and $y_C = 0.268$ found previously, the projected value from the $m_C(\cdot)$ is 0.6758 (see Figure 1c). One feature of this projection is that the evaluated predicted value is devoid of an associated ignorance value (existing in the associated firm-year BOE). Importantly also, the roles played by $\{x\}$ and $\{\neg x\}$ are different to that in the original CaRBS (hypothesis and not-the-hypothesis), now they are associated with the limits on some variable term (such as a continuous returns variable - see later).

As with the original CaRBS, the required configuration of a RCaRBS system depends on the assignment of values to the incumbent control variables $(k_i, \theta_i, A_i$ and $B_i, i = 1, \ldots, n_V)$. In RCaRBS, this configuration is defined by minimizing the

error between the respective actual and predicted company returns values (through its objective function - defined OBR). The specific measure (OBR) employed will focus on using the well known sum of squares error term, see Radhakrishnan and Nandan (2005). With the companies actual returns values Rv_j ($j = 1, .., n_O$), and respective predicted returns values Rp_j ($j = 1, .., n_O$), from a RCaRBS configured system, the 'mean squared error' fit is measured by

$$OBR - \frac{1}{n_O} \sum_j (Rv_j - Rp_j)^2.$$

Stock Market Returns and Profits

A question of significant interest in the accounting and finance literature is the relationship between stock market data and accounting variables, particularly annual profits, which are arguably the most important output of the accounting system (e.g. Imam *et al.*, 2008). Making a number of simple assumptions (most notably that the change in shareholders' equity from time t to $t + 1$ is defined by profits and transactions with shareholders - the so-called 'clean surplus' relationship), it is possible to define the dividend discount model - the classical valuation of equity - in terms of shareholders' equity and accounting profits (e.g. see Peasnell, 1982). It is thus theoretically sound to posit a relationship between changes in share prices, i.e. stock returns and accounting profits, a large body of research has examined this relationship as part of a 'value relevance framework' (Easton and Harris, 1991).

The primary purpose of accounting data is to inform investors' capital allocation decisions and there is extensive evidence suggesting that investors rely heavily on earnings in valuing company securities (e.g. see Imam *et al.*, 2008, for recent evidence on the UK investment community). Since profit is an aggregate measure, however, attention is increasingly turning to the different components of profits, i.e. cash flows and accruals, to examine the extent to which these components are capable of explaining stock returns. Such decomposition permits an examination of whether investors treat these two profit-related constituents differentially due to differences in their persistence (i.e. the likelihood of current period accruals/cash flows recurring in future periods).

The data employed in the analysis is taken from *Datastream* (for stock returns at time t, R_t, defined as $(P_t - P_{t-1} + d_t)/P_{t-1}$, where P_t represents price at time t and d_t represents dividends at time t) and from *FAME* for accounting (accruals and cash flow) data. The sample comprises 3,600 observations for UK listed companies over the period 1995-2004 and accruals are defined as profit minus cash flow, where cash flow (from operations) is taken from the cash flow statement. Both variables are deflated by opening shareholders' equity.

Descriptive statistics for returns are shown in Table 1. They reveal that annual returns are around 14% with a relatively large degree of variation (coefficient of variation of 4.28). Moreover, there is a moderate degree of positive skewness, which is to be expected given the fact that returns have a lower bound of −100% due to limited liability, but no upper bound (with a maximum annual return in our sample of over 280%).

Four independent variables are hypothesised to influence levels of company returns and these are accruals, cash flows and one period change in both variables. As shown by Easton and Harris (1991) both levels and changes in profits are associated with returns; moreover, both complement one another and levels of returns explain significantly more of the variation in returns than either levels or changes alone.

Table 2 presents descriptive statistics for the independent profit-related variables considered here (used later in the CaRBS and RCaRBS analyses). On average, accruals are positive and are approximately 26% of shareholders' equity, whereas cash flows are negative and around 22% of shareholders' equity. Both changes variables

Table 1. Descriptive statistics of original companies' returns values

Independent Variable	R_t (Returns)
Min	−0.816
Max	2.826
Mean	0.137
Standard deviation	0.587
Skewness	1.771
Kurtosis	5.286
% negative	44.722%
% positive	55.028%
% zero	0.250%

Table 2. Description of company independent profit-related variable values and concomitant descriptive statistics

Independent Variable	ACC_t (Accruals)	CF_t (Cash flow)	ΔACC_t (Δ Accruals)	ΔCF_t (Δ Cash flow)
Min	−1.046	−2.215	−1.224	−1.543
Max	2.817	0.697	1.335	2.154
Mean	0.256	−0.223	0.021	0.005
Standard deviation	0.469	0.366	0.301	0.423
Skewness	2.271	−2.339	0.196	1.369
Kurtosis	11.234	10.505	7.015	9.614

ΔACC_t and ΔCF_t are positive, though in the case of cash flows, only 0.5% of equity. Interestingly, both variables expressed in levels (ACC_t and CF_t) have skewed distributions: positive in the case of accruals and negative in the case of cash flows.

CaRBS Analysis

This section undertakes a CaRBS analysis of the previously described company returns data set. The CaRBS technique, as described, is able to undertake binary classification optimisation (using the defined objective function OBC).

With the company returns value the dependent variable in this data set, to undertake a CaRBS analysis there is a need to discretise the dependent variable into two values, namely 0 and 1. The discretisation of the company returns variable here was simply based on whether each company's returns value is below (assigned 0) or equal to or above (assigned 1) the value zero. This signifies whether shareholders were worse (better) off at the end of the holding period than the beginning, as returns were negative (positive). For the company returns data set, following this discretisation, there were 1,990 and 1,610 firm-years associated with negative and positive returns, respectively. As described in the construction of the OBC objective function, the unbalanced nature of the numbers of observations associated with negative and positive returns is taken into account, and does have a negative impact in a CaRBS analysis.

Further, considering the control variables required to configure a CaRBS system, through the minimization of the respective OBC, to allow consistent domains to be placed over the control variables, the independent profit-related variables were standardised (so have zero mean and unit standard deviation). That is, during the optimisation process, finding the control variable values which minimise the OBC, having the same domains over the control variables simplifies the process of optimisation and comparison, see later.

Prior to the presentation of the CaRBS analysis of the transformed (discretised and standardised) version of the company returns data set, and to offer as a benchmark against the reported results, a binary logistic regression analysis was first performed on the data. Binary regression is often employed in accounting and finance research areas such as failure prediction (e.g. Ohlson, 1980; Lennox, 1999) and prediction of takeovers (e.g. Palepu, 1986). The details of the binary logistic regression of the transformed company returns data set are reported in Table 3.

In general, the coefficients for the profit-related variables, ACC_t, CF_t, ΔACC_t and ΔCF_t, are similar when expressed in either levels or changes,

Table 3. Binary logistic regression analysis results on company returns data set (binary dependent variable, where 1 indicates positive returns and 0 negative returns)

	B	S.E.	Wald	df	Sig.	Exp(B)
ACC_t	0.417	0.064	41.958	1	0.000	1.517
CF_t	0.461	0.065	49.967	1	0.000	1.586
ΔACC_t	0.284	0.054	27.591	1	0.000	1.328
ΔCF_t	0.269	0.054	24.438	1	0.000	1.309
Constant	0.215	0.034	39.308	1	0.000	1.239

	Predicted		
Observed	0	1	Percentage Correct
0	431	1179	26.770%
1	206	1784	89.648%
Overall Percentage			61.528%

though the coefficients for levels, ACC_t and CF_t, are higher (which is consistent with results from standard regression, e.g. Easton and Harris, 1991). When expressed in levels, the cash flow coefficient estimate is higher, with the opposite being true for the changes variables, ΔACC_t and ΔCF_t. The classification table indicates that the logistic regression is far more accurate classifying firm-years with positive returns (predicted 1), which is likely to be attributable to the relatively small proportion of zero values in the sample.

Returning to the intended CaRBS analysis of the company returns data set (transformed version), the utilisation of the objective function OBC in the configuration of the CaRBS system is to directly minimize the level of ambiguity present in the classification of the 3,600 companies to having either negative (labelled Neg $\equiv \neg$Pos) or positive (Pos) return values (below or equal to or above the returns value zero), but not the concomitant ignorance.

With the independent profit-related variables in the company returns data set standardised, it allows consistent domains to be placed over the control variables incumbent in CaRBS, here set as (for each independent variable); $-20 \leq k_i \leq 20$, $-20 \leq \theta_i \leq 20$, $0 \leq A_i \leq 1$ and $B_i \leq 0.6$ (see Beynon, 2005b). The upper bound on the B_i control variables ensures a predominance of ignorance in the evidence from individual profit-related variable values (in the concomitant profit-related BOEs), so reducing over-conflict during the combination of the pieces of evidence (combination of profit-related BOEs). As suggested previously, with the independent variables profit-related, describing different aspects of accruals and cash-flow, the associated BOEs containing the evidence from the independent variables are called *profit-related* BOEs.

The TDE method was then employed, utilising the previously defined TDE-based parameters, to identify the CaRBS based control variables to configure a CaRBS system. This was repeated (run) five times, each time converging to an optimum value (OBC value). The best, meaning minimum OBC, out of the five runs being associated with OBC = 0.435. A reason for this value being away from its lower bound of zero is related to the implicit minimum levels of ignorance associated with each profit-related BOE (fixing of the upper bounds of the B_i control variables), possibly also due to the presence of conflicting evidence from the independent profit-related variables. The resultant CaRBS associated control variables found from the best TDE run are reported in Table 4.

A brief inspection of these control variables shows the uniformity in the k_i control variable values, with all of them at the limit of 20.000, and all positive in value. This exhibits the attempt to offer most discernment between companies with negative (0) and positive (1) returns values (the dependent firm-year variable having 0 or 1 value), in the evidence from the four independent variables ACC_t, CF_t, ΔACC_t and ΔCF_t (see Figure 1 for the role played by the k_i control variable). The role of these defined control variable values is to allow the construction of profit-related BOEs and their subsequent combination to formulate a series of firm-year BOEs for the 3,600 companies considered.

Table 4. Control variable values associated with the four independent profit-related variables ACC_t, CF_t, ΔACC_t, and ΔCF_t using OBC in configuration of CaRBS system

Independent variable.	ACC_t	CF_t	ΔACC_t	ΔCF_t
k_i	20.000	20.000	20.000	20.000
θ_i	-0.349	0.315	-5.646	-0.200
A_i	0.918	0.308	0.788	0.975
B_i	0.600	0.600	0.600	0.600

The construction of a profit-related BOE is next demonstrated, considering the company O_1 and the independent profit-related variable ACC_t (Accruals). Following the description of the CaRBS technique, it starts with the evaluation of the confidence factor $cf_{ACCt}(\cdot)$ (see Figure 1a), for the company O_1, its actual value is $ACC_t = -0.020$, when standardised, it is $v = -0.588$ (see Table 4 presented later), then;

$$cf_{ACCt}(-0.588) = \frac{1}{1 + e^{-20.000(-0.588-(-0.349))}}$$
$$= \frac{1}{1 + 120.009} = 0.008,$$

using the control variables in Table 3. This confidence value is used in the expressions making up the mass values in the associated profit-related BOE $m_{1,ACCt}(\cdot)$, namely; $m_{1,ACCt}(\{Pos\})$, $m_{1,ACCt}(\{Neg\})$ and $m_{1,ACCt}(\{Pos, Neg\})$, found to be;

$$m_{1,ACCt}(\{Pos\}) = \frac{0.600}{1-0.918}0.008$$
$$-\frac{0.918 \times 0.600}{1-0.918} = 0.061$$
$$-0.675 = -6.690 < 0.000$$
$$\text{so} = 0.000,$$

$$m_{1,ACCt}\left(\{Neg\}\right) = \frac{-0.600}{1-0.918}0.008$$
$$+\ 0.600 = -0.061$$
$$+\ 0.600\ =\ 0.539,$$

$$m_{1,ACCt}\left(\{Pos,\ \neg C\}\right) =\ 1-0.000-0.539\ =\ 0.461.$$

For the company O_1, this profit-related BOE is representative of all the associated profit-related BOEs $m_{1,i}(\cdot)\ i=ACC_t, .., \Delta CF_t$, presented in Table 4 (using standardised independent variable values), making up the evidence from the four independent profit-related variables towards the binary classification of the returns values to Neg (negative) or Pos (positive) returns. Also shown are the details for the company O_{16}. These two observations, O_1 and O_{16}, are known to exhibit Neg and Pos returns (when discretised), respectively.

In Table 5, for the evidence from the profit-related variables to support correct classification of the company O_1, in this case to negative returns (Neg), it would be expected for the associated $m_{1,i}(\{Neg\})$ mass values to be larger than their respective $m_{1,i}(\{Pos\})$ mass values, which is the case for the profit-related variables, ACC_t, CF_t and ΔCF_t. Whereas, ΔACC_t offers more evidence towards the company having positive

returns ($m_{1,\Delta ACCt}(\{Pos\}) > m_{1,\Delta ACCt}(\{Neg\})$). The predominance of profit-related BOEs supporting correct classification is reflected in the evaluated final firm-year BOE $m_1(\cdot)$, produced through the combination of all the company's profit-related BOEs. That is, from Table 4, the firm-year BOE includes mass values $m_1(\{Neg\}) = 0.854 > 0.070 = m_1(\{Pos\})$, suggesting the company O_1 is more associated with negative returns (Neg), which is the correct classification in this case.

For the company O_{16}, the evidence from the profit-related variables is more towards its association with positive returns (Pos), in particular from ACC_t and ΔACC_t. It is noteworthy, the profit-related variable ΔCF_t offers only ignorance in its evidence ($m_{16,\Delta CFt}(\{Pos, Neg\}) = 1.000$), unable to offer belief based evidence specifically to $\{Pos\}$ or $\{Neg\}$. The combination of the concomitant profit-related BOEs, for company O_{16}, produces a firm-year BOE $m_{16}(\cdot)$, which from Table 4, indicates its majority association to positive returns (Pos), which is correct in this case. For further interpretation of the profit-related and firm-year BOEs associated with the companies, O_1 and O_{16}, the representations of the evaluated evidence and classification results as simplex coordinates in a simplex plot are reported in Figure 3.

Table 5. Independent profit-related variable values, profit-related BOEs and firm-year BOEs for the companies, O_1 and O_{16}, using OBC in configuration of CaRBS system

BOE	ACC_t	CF_t	ΔACC_t	ΔCF_t		Firm-year BOEs
O_1 (actual)	−0.020	−0.255	0.066	−0.214		-
O_1 (standardized)	−0.588	−0.087	0.150	−0.519		-
$m_{1,i}(\{Pos\})$	0.000	0.000	0.479	0.000		0.070
$m_{1,i}(\{Neg\})$	0.539	0.600	0.000	0.559		0.854
$m_{1,i}(\{Pos, Neg\})$	0.461	0.400	0.521	0.441		0.076
O_{16} (actual)	0.438	−0.201	0.053	−0.054		-
O_{16} (standardized)	0.388	0.059	0.108	−0.140		-
$m_{16,i}(\{Pos\})$	0.600	0.000	0.337	0.000		0.529
$m_{16,i}(\{Neg\})$	0.000	0.595	0.000	0.000		0.280
$m_{16,i}(\{Pos, Neg\})$	0.400	0.405	0.663	1.000		0.191

Figures 3*a* and 3*b*, offer a visual representation of the evidence from the four profit-related variables ACC_t, CF_t, ΔACC_t, and ΔCF_t to the classification of the companies, O_1 and O_{16}, as to whether they are more associated with negative (Neg) or positive (Pos) returns. In each simplex plot, the dashed vertical line partitions the regions in a simplex plot where either of the mass values assigned to {Neg} (to the left) and {Pos} (to the right) is the larger in a BOE (profit-related or firm-year). The grey shaded sub-regions show the domains where the profit-related BOEs can exist (restricted region due to the bounds on B_i control variables described previously).

The positions of the simplex coordinates of the profit-related BOEs allow their supporting or contradicting evidence for correct or incorrect classification of the companies to be clearly identified (compare with discussion of the construction of the profit-related BOEs associated with company O_1). For example, for company O_1, the profit-related BOEs, $m_{1,ACCt}(\cdot)$, $m_{1,CFt}(\cdot)$ and $m_{1,\Delta CFt}(\cdot)$, are supportive of its classification to being associated with negative returns, in contrast to the profit-related BOE $m_{1,\Delta ACCt}(\cdot)$ which is contradicting in its evidence. In both presented simplex plots, the simplex coordinates of the final firm-year BOEs, $m_1(\cdot)$ and $m_{16}(\cdot)$, are nearer the base lines

than those of the associated profit-related BOEs. This is solely due to the reduction of ignorance from the combination of evidence present in the profit-related BOEs (see also Table 4).

The process of positioning the classification of a company in a simplex plot, on their returns, can be undertaken for each of the 3,600 companies considered, see Figure 4.

Figures 4*a* and 4*b* partition the presentation of the companies' firm-year BOEs between those known to be more associated with negative (4*a*) or positive (4*b*) returns. Inspection of the simplex plots shows some patterns in the data, this is due to the relatively small number of profit-related variables considered, and where for some companies, a number of the profit-related variables offer only ignorance in their evidence towards the final classification evidence (see classification details of company O_{16}), so companies may be classified by evidence from only two or three profit-related variables (the rest only offering ignorant evidence). Based on their simplex coordinate firm-year BOE positions, either side of the vertical dashed lines in the simplex plots in Figure 4 (the grey shaded areas show where correct classification is), the classification accuracy of the configured CaRBS system can be found, see Table 6.

Figure 3. Simplex coordinates of profit-related and firm-year BOEs for companies, O_1 and O_{16}, using OBC in configuration of CaRBS system

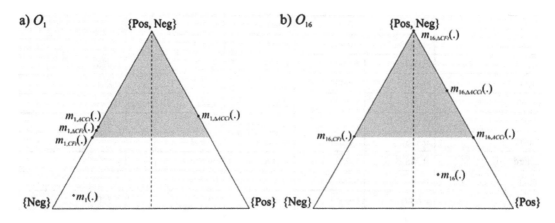

Figure 4. Simplex plot based representation of final firm-year BOEs, using OBC in configuration of CaRBS system

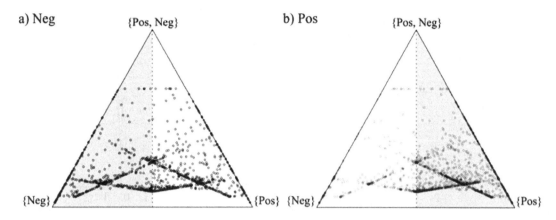

a) Neg   b) Pos

Table 6. Classification accuracy of 3,600 companies from configured CaRBS system

Observed	Predicted		
	0	1	Percentage Correct
0	751	859	46.646%
1	435	1555	78.141%
Overall Percentage			64.056%

The classification results shown in Table 5 are directly comparable with the findings in Table 3 where classification accuracy was reported for the binary logistic regression analysis undertaken on the same transformed company returns data set. The comparisons show the CaRBS analysis offers better classification accuracy with 64.056% over the binary logistic regression analysis with only 61.528%. It is noticeable that the classification of companies associated with negative returns is still an issue (as was with binary logistic regression also), with only 46.646% accuracy in the CaRBS analysis, this is shown in the simplex plot in Figure 4a, in contrast to the results for companies associated with positive returns where the 78.141% accuracy is backed up by the results in Figure 4b.

Consideration of the contribution of the individual profit-related variables can be graphically gauged, from combining stages *a* and *b* in Figure

1 (showing stages of the CaRBS system), for the profit-related variables ACC_t, CF_t, ΔACC_t and ΔCF_t, see Figure 5.

In Figure 5, each graph shows the explicit mass values which make up a profit-related BOE, based on the individual profit-related variable values from companies (here measured in terms of the number of standard deviations away from the mean - see Table 2 for descriptive statistics to consider the graphs in real value terms). Also shown at the top of each graph are points representing the companies' profit-related variable values, so aiding the reader on the distribution of the values over each variable domain.

To illustrate these graphs, the case of the profit-related variable ACC_t is considered, its contribution described in Figure 5a. As the ACC_t value increases there is little change in the mass values, with $m_{j,ACCt}(\{Neg\})$ and $m_{j,ACCt}(\{Pos, Neg\})$ both positive (and $m_{j,ACCt}(\{Pos\}) = 0$), then for a

Figure 5. Contribution graphs for profit-related variables in terms of their profit-related BOEs, for, ACC$_t$, CF$_t$, ΔACC$_t$ and ΔCF$_t$ using OBC in configuration of CaRBS system

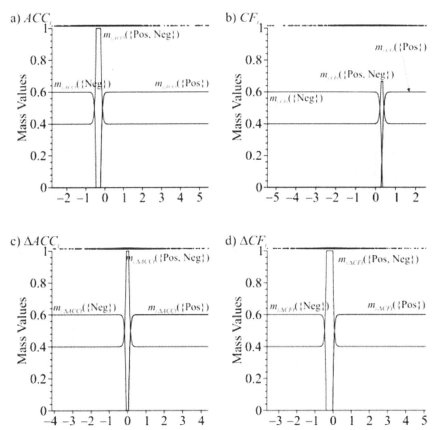

value near −1 (in standard deviations from the mean terms), there is a decrease in $m_{j,ACCt}(\{Neg\})$ and increase in $m_{j,ACCt}(\{Pos, Neg\})$, followed by a small sub-domain where $m_{j,ACCt}(\{Pos, Neg\}) = 1.000$, after which there is decrease in $m_{j,ACCt}(\{Pos, Neg\})$ and increase in $m_{j,ACCt}(\{Pos\})$. The change in the $m_{j,ACCt}(\{Neg\})$ and $m_{j,ACCt}(\{Pos\})$ values over small sub-domains of the ACC_t variable is due to the magnitude of the concomitant control variable k_{ACCt}. That is, their large value means there is only a small domain of a variable which does not associate the confidence factor $cf_t(\cdot)$ away from either 0 or 1. Further, from the graph, and sign of k_{ACCt}, the direction of contribution of this ACC_t accrual variable is positive. With $k_t = 20.000$ for each of the profit-related variables,

ACC_t, CF_t, $ΔACC_t$ and $ΔCF_t$, their contribution graphs do show similarities, namely positive, following in someway the contribution results from the logistic regression results (see Table 3).

Something worthy of note is with the profit-related variable CF_t, the $m_{j,CFt}(\{Pos, Neg\})$ mass value does not achieve the value 1.000 at any point compared to those of the other profit-related variables (this demonstrates the subtle impact of the other control variables). That is, for the profit-related variables ACC_t, $ΔACC_t$ and $ΔCF_t$, there were sub-domains of their range for which there is only ignorance in their evidential contribution, for CF_t this is not the case, instead there is an almost step-function change in the evidence contained in the profit-related BOE ($m_{j,CFt}(\cdot)$).

RCaRBS Analysis

This section undertakes a RCaRBS analysis of the company returns data set. Rather than thinking in terms of the binary classification of company returns, the original continuous returns values associated with the companies are considered. As before (in CaRBS analysis), the standardised versions of the independent profit-related variables are considered here.

To enable their analysis using RCaRBS, the company returns values are normalised over the domain 0.05 to 0.95 (just inside of the normal 0 and 1)^2, using the descriptive statistics in Table 1. The terms Neg and Pos are retained here (they are used in the CaRBS analysis), but now they subtly signify the limits of the returns values, from Neg (near 0 – meaning the lowest returns values) up to Pos (near 1 - highest returns values). Table 7 reports the descriptive statistics for the returns values' dependent variable in the RCaRBS analysis.

The differences in how the dependent variable is considered in the analysis undertaken here highlights how the CaRBS technique can be adapted for use with a continuous dependent variable, with the developed technique named RCaRBS (see Beynon *et al.*, 2010).

As in the CaRBS analysis, prior to the RCaRBS analysis, a more traditional form of analysis is first considered on the transformed (normalised and standardised) company returns data set now with normalised dependent variable, here, using ordinary least squares (OLS) regression. OLS is a standard workhorse in empirical financial accounting/capital markets research (e.g., see Easton and Harris, 1991; Charitou and Clubb, 1999; Pope and Walker, 1999). The results using OLS on the transformed company returns data set are shown in the sub-tables reported in Table 8.

Amongst the results presented in Table 8, compared to in the following RCaRBS analysis, are the residual mean squared error of 0.020 and the contribution of the independent profit-related

Table 7. Descriptive statistics of normalised companies' returns values R_t

Independent Variable	R_t (Returns)
Min	0.050
Max	0.950
Mean	0.285
Standard deviation	0.145
Skewness	1.771
Kurtosis	5.286

variables ACC_t, CF_t, ΔACC_t and ΔCF_t, here all positive in contribution and with changes ΔACC_t and ΔCF_t more strongly contributing than levels ACC_t and CF_t.

An equivalent RCaRBS nalysis is next described. The utilisation of the objective function OBR in the configuration of the RCaRBS system is to minimise the predictive error ('mean squares error'), termed here model fit, between the predicted and actual levels of company returns of the considered 3,600 companies. The same consistent domains over the control variables incumbent in CaRBS were used here, set as; $-20 \leq k_i \leq 20$, $-20 \leq \theta_i \leq 20$, $0 \leq A_i \leq 1$ and $B_i \leq 0.6$. The TDE method was again employed, using the previously defined parameters, and run five times. The best out of the five runs being associated with OBR = 0.019. This fit result is directly comparable to the linear regression result which gave a fit of 0.020 (> 0.019), hence, in terms of model fit, the RCaRBS fit is better than that found with linear regression.

The resultant control variable values found from the best TDE run, using OBR, are reported in Table 9.

A brief inspection of these results shows a lack of consistency in any of the sets of control variables across the different profit-related variables. In the case of the k_i control variable values, in particular, this is in contrast to the values consistently found in the initial CaRBS analysis (shown

Table 8. Linear regression analysis results on company returns data set (continuous dependent variable)

R	R Squared	Adjusted R Squared	Std. Error of the Estimate
0.237(a)	0.056	0.055	0.141

A. Predictors: (Constant), ACC_t, CF_t, ΔACC_t and ΔCF_t

	Sum of Squares	df	Mean Square	F	Sig.
Regression	4.239	4	1.090	53.333	0.000(a)
Residual	71.433	3595	0.020		
Total	75.672	3599			

A. Predictors: (Constant), ACC_t, CF_t, ΔACC_t and ΔCF_t
B. Dependent Variable: R_t

	Unstandardized Coefficients		Standardized Coefficients	t	Sig.
	B	Std. Error	Beta		
(Constant)	0.285	0.002		121.497	0.00000
ACC_t	0.014	0.004	0.096	3.772	0.00017
CF_t	0.015	0.004	0.100	3.912	0.00009
ΔACC_t	0.026	0.004	0.181	8.295	0.00000
ΔCF_t	0.033	0.004	0.226	10.397	0.00000

A. Dependent Variable: R_t

Table 9. Independent profit-related variable values, profit-related BOEs and firm-year BOEs for the companies, O_1 and O_{16}, using OBR in configuration of RCaRBS system

Independent variable.	ACC_t	CF_t	ΔACC_t	ΔCF_t
k_i	0.230	0.257	0.981	0.706
θ_i	−7.485	8.415	2.763	−3.278
A_i	0.127	0.102	0.828	0.832
B_i	0.387	0.600	0.418	0.347

in Table 3). However, as in the CaRBS analysis the k_i variable values are all positive showing. How these control variables impact compared to those found in the CaRBS analysis is next considered.

To show the impact of the RCaRBS analysis against that of the CaRBS analysis previously undertaken, the calculation of the ACC_t profit-related BOE is again found for the company O_1. The confidence factor $cf_{ACCt}(\cdot)$ (see Figure 1a), for the company O_1, $ACC_t = -0.020$, when standardised, it is $v = -0.588$ (see Table 9 presented later), is;

$$cf_{ACCt}\left(-0.588\right) = \frac{1}{1 + e^{-0.230(-0.588-(-7.485))}}$$

$$= \frac{1}{1 + 0.204} = 0.830,$$

using the control variables in Table 8. This confidence value is used in the expressions making up the mass values in the profit-related BOE $m_{1,ACCt}(\cdot)$, namely; $m_{1,ACCt}(\{Pos\})$, $m_{1,ACCt}(\{Neg\})$ and $m_{1,ACCt}(\{Pos, Neg\})$, found to be;

$$m_{1,ACCt}\left(\{\text{Pos}\}\right) = \frac{0.387}{1 - 0.127} 0.830$$

$$- \frac{0.127 \times 0.387}{1 - 0.127} = 0.368$$

$$- 0.056 = 0.312,$$

$$m_{1,ACCt}\left(\{\text{Neg}\}\right) = \frac{-0.387}{1 - 0.127} 0.830 + 0.387$$

$$= -0.368 + 0.387 = 0.019,$$

$$m_{1,ACCt}\left(\{\text{Pos, Neg}\}\right) = 1 - 0.312 - 0.019 = 0.669.$$

For the company O_1, again this profit-related BOE is representative of the profit-related BOEs $m_{1,j}(\cdot)$, presented in Table 9, along with those for the company O_{16}. These profit-related BOEs describe the evidential support from all the profit-related variables to a company's level of return between the limits of near 0 and 1 'normalised returns values' (O_1 and O_{16}, are known to have 0.101 and 0.290 levels of company returns 'normalised values' respectively).

In Table 10, the profit-related BOEs reported can be discussed in a similar way to those in the CaRBS analysis, where for the companies, O_1

and O_{16}, their evidence towards levels of returns should be more towards negative and positive returns, in relative terms, respectively. The final firm-year BOEs associated with the two companies are also shown in Table 7. Following the RCaRBS approach, the subsequent values found from mapping these firm-year BOEs onto the base line of a simplex plot (over a 0 to 1 domain), are, for O_1 - 0.242, and for O_{16} - 0.284 (compare with 0.101 and 0.290 respectively).

For further interpretation of the profit-related and firm-year BOEs associated with the companies, O_1 and O_{16} their representation as simplex coordinates in a simplex plot, and subsequent mapping to single predicted returns values, are reported in Figure 6.

Figures 6a and 6b, offer a visual representation of the evidence from the profit-related variables to the regression-type analysis of the companies, O_1 and O_{16}. In each simplex plot the contribution of the profit-related BOEs is shown, along with the respective firm-year BOE, and its mapping down to the base line of the simplex plot over the domain 0 to 1 (following RCaRBS). Also shown below the simplex plots are the actual levels of company returns associated with each of the two companies.

Table 10. Independent profit-related variable values, profit-related BOEs and firm-year BOEs for the companies, O_1 and O_{16}, using OBR in configuration of RCaRBS system

BOE	ACC_t	CF_t	ΔACC_t	ΔCF_t		Firm-year BOEs
O_1 (actual)	−0.020	−0.255	0.066	−0.214		-
O_1 (standardized)	−0.588	−0.087	0.150	−0.519		-
$m_{1,j}(\{\text{Pos}\})$	0.312	0.000	0.000	0.090		0.173
$m_{1,j}(\{\text{Neg}\})$	0.019	0.532	0.244	0.000		0.543
$m_{1,j}(\{\text{Pos, Neg}\})$	0.669	0.468	0.756	0.910		0.284
O_{16} (actual)	0.438	−0.201	0.053	−0.054		-
O_{16} (standardized)	0.388	0.059	0.108	−0.140		-
$m_{16,j}(\{\text{Pos}\})$	0.325	0.002	0.000	0.144		0.205
$m_{16,j}(\{\text{Neg}\})$	0.006	0.530	0.251	0.000		0.518
$m_{16,j}(\{\text{Pos, Neg}\})$	0.669	0.468	0.749	0.856		0.277

Figure 6. Simplex coordinates of profit-related and firm-year BOEs for companies, O_1 and O_{16}, using OBR in configuration of RCaRBS system

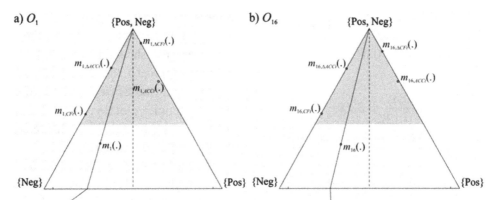

The process of positioning the predicted level of returns of a company can be undertaken for all 3,600 considered companies, see Figure 7 (top simplex plot shows firm-year BOEs of all 3,600 companies and below are the companies partitioned based on having actual levels of returns which are negative and positive - in terms of their standardised values).[3]

In Figure 7, the firm-year BOEs of the 3,600 companies are mapped to the base of the simplex plots, giving their predicted level of returns, and below them their actual levels of return. These results need to be considered with a view that the dependent variable values are heavily skewed (see Table 1), hence the predicted values are similarly skewed, see footnote 3. One feature of the results, even though the predicted values are represented along the base of the simplex plot, the firm-year BOEs have, from which the predicted values are derived, have different levels of ignorance associated with them (firm-year BOEs are at different heights in the simplex plot). The inference being that with RCaRBS you could associate different levels of ignorance with the predicted company returns values.

Consideration of the contribution of the individual profit-related variables can be graphically gauged from combining stages *a* and *b* in Figure 1, for the profit-related variables ACC_t, CF_t, ΔACC_t and ΔCF_t, see Figure 8.

The graphs in Figure 8 are only somewhat similar to those presented in Figure 5 (part of the CaRBS analysis). These graphs, in terms of direction of contribution are all positive, following the signs of the k_i values in Table 5.

One interesting facet is the similarity in the graphs for ACC_t and CF_t, and also ΔACC_t and ΔCF_t. From the OLS analysis these pairs of independent profit-related variables, ACC_t and CF_t, and also ΔACC_t and ΔCF_t, had noticeably different levels of contribution (see coefficients reported in Table 7). From Table 9, the associated k_i control variables, which are closely associated with contribution of the variables, have a similar disparity in sizes across the pairs of profit-related variables, ACC_t and CF_t, and also ΔACC_t and ΔCF_t. The graphs shown in Figure 8 confirm this variation in the way the levels, ACC_t and CF_t and changes ΔACC_t and ΔCF_t, variables contribute in the RCaRBS analysis. Moreover, they actually show two variations on their contributions, for ACC_t and CF_t their

Figure 7. Simplex plot based representation of final firm-year BOEs, and subsequent mappings, using OBR in configuration of RCaRBS system

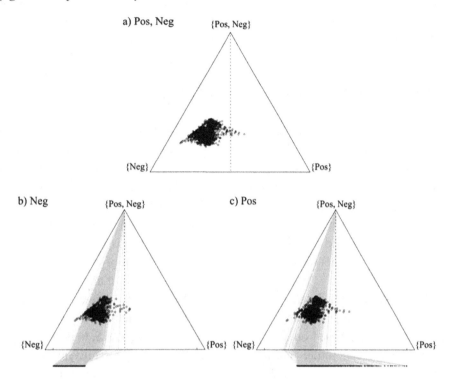

Figure 8. Contribution graphs for profit-related variables in terms of their profit-related BOEs, for, ACC$_t$, CF$_t$, ΔACC$_t$ and ΔCF$_t$ using OBR in configuration of RCaRBS system

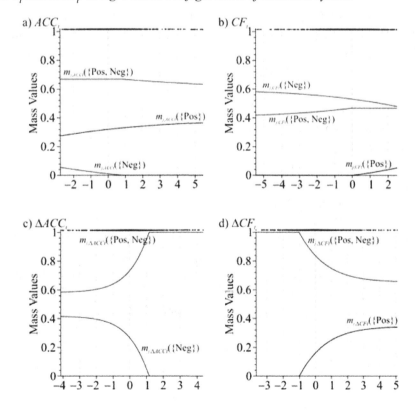

contributions change gradually over each of their respective domains, in contrast, for ΔACC_t and ΔCF_t there are parts of their domains for which there is only ignorance in their evidence.

FUTURE RESEARCH DIRECTIONS

Underlying the details in this chapter is the exposition of a nascent analysis technique CaRBS and a pertinent development RCaRBS. As nascent techniques able to undertake classification-type (CaRBS) and multivariate regression-type (RCaRBS) analyses, future research directions are both in terms of their continued technical development and practical employment in research problems.

With the CaRBS and RCaRBS techniques closely associated with uncertain reasoning, through their rudiments being based on Dempster-Shafer theory, there is the future research direction on whether they have fully utilised the developments in this theory (DST that is). That is, in the same way the understanding and use of Dempster-Shafer theory continues to develop, so these developments should be considered in relation to CaRBS and RCaRBS.

The returns-earnings relationship considered in this chapter, through the company returns data set, is one example of the typical accounting problem that could benefit from the employment of nascent analysis techniques. One possibility is the further exploration of potential non-linear relationships between returns and earning components. It was interesting to see in the contribution graphs the non-linearity across the profit related variables; clearly this is worthy of further investigation, as well as further understanding of the role played by ignorance in variables' contributions. An important feature of this type of accounting problem is the temporal dimension to the data, which is often neglected in 'pooled analysis'; it would be interesting to see how the CaRBS and RCaRBS techniques can accommodate a time-series oriented form of analysis.

CONCLUSION

Classification and Regression types of analysis are the central pillars of analysis in a wide range of research areas, including the case research area here namely in accounting and finance. With well-known techniques such as logistic and linear regression regularly employed to facilitate such analysis, it is interesting to see the place for nascent techniques which can perform the same or similar forms of analysis.

The CaRBS, technique is one such nascent technique, which itself has been developed, in the form of RCaRBS, to be able to perform classification and regression type analyses. The results shown in this chapter show that is comparable with more traditional techniques, offering a level of model fit better than the compared to logistic and linear regression techniques. There is a difference in the way the CaRBS and RCaRBS techniques offer evidence in terms of the contribution of dependent variables, when compared with the logistic and linear regression techniques. It will be interesting in the future to see how comparable such contribution based findings can be made..

REFERENCES

Beneš, O., van der Meer, J. P. M., & Konings, R. J. M. (2007). Modelling and calculation of the phase diagrams of the LiF–NaF–RbF–LaF$_3$ system. *Computer Coupling of Phase Diagrams and Thermochemistry*, *31*, 209–216. doi:10.1016/j.calphad.2006.12.004

Beynon, M. J. (2005a). A novel technique of object ranking and classification under ignorance: An application to the corporate failure risk problem. *European Journal of Operational Research, 167,* 493–517. doi:10.1016/j.ejor.2004.03.016

Beynon, M. J. (2005b). A novel approach to the credit rating problem: object classification under ignorance. *International Journal of Intelligent Systems in Accounting Finance & Management, 13,* 113–130. doi:10.1002/isaf.260

Beynon, M. J., Andrews, R. A., & Boyne, G. (2010). Evidence-based modelling of strategic fit: An introduction to RCaRBS. *European Journal of Operational Research, 207*(2), 886–896. doi:10.1016/j.ejor.2010.05.024

Canongia Lopes, J. N. (2004). On the classification and representation of ternary phase diagrams: The yin and yang of a T–x approach. *Physical Chemistry Chemical Physics, 6,* 2314–2319. doi:10.1039/b315799g

Charitou, A., & Clubb, C. (1999). Earnings, cash flows and security returns over long return intervals: Analysis and UK evidence. *Journal of Business Finance & Accounting, 26*(3-4), 283–312. doi:10.1111/1468-5957.00257

Dempster, A. P. (1967). Upper and lower probabilities induced by a multiple valued mapping. *Annals of Mathematical Statistics, 38,* 325–339. doi:10.1214/aoms/1177698950

Easton, P. D., & Harris, T. S. (1991). Earnings as an explanatory variable for returns. *Journal of Accounting Research, 29*(1), 19–36. doi:10.2307/2491026

Fan, H.-Y., & Lampinen, J. A. (2003). Trigonometric mutation operation to differential evolution. *Journal of Global Optimization, 27,* 105–129. doi:10.1023/A:1024653025686

Haenni, R. (2002). Introduction to Dempster-Shafer theory. University of Konstanz. Retrieved September 1, 2011, from http://www.iam.unibe. ch/~haenni/Homepage/TALKS/2002/ppm.pdf

Imam, S., Barker, R., & Clubb, C. (2008). The use of valuation models by UK investment analysts. *European Accounting Review, 17*(3), 503–535. doi:10.1080/09638180802016650

Kim, D. (1999). Normalization methods for input and output vectors in backpropogation neural networks. *International Journal of Computer Mathematics, 71*(2), 161–171. doi:10.1080/00207169908804800

Lennox, C. (1999). Identifying failing companies: A re-evaluation of the Logit, Probit and DA approaches. *Journal of Economics and Business, 51,* 347–364. doi:10.1016/S0148-6195(99)00009-0

Ohlson, J. (1980). Financial ratios and the probabilistic prediction of bankruptcy. *Journal of Accounting Research, 18*(1), 109–131. doi:10.2307/2490395

Palepu, K. (1986). Predicting takeover targets. *Journal of Accounting and Economics, 8,* 3–35. doi:10.1016/0165-4101(86)90008-X

Peasnell, K. (1982). Some formal connections between economic values and yields and accounting numbers. *Journal of Business Finance & Accounting,* (3): 361–381. doi:10.1111/j.1468-5957.1982. tb01001.x

Pope, P. F., & Walker, M. (1999). International differences in the timeliness and conservatism and classification of earnings. *Journal of Accounting Research, 37,* 53–87. doi:10.2307/2491345

Radhakrishnan, T., & Nandan, U. (2005). Milling force prediction using regression and neural networks. *Journal of Intelligent Manufacturing, 16,* 93–102. doi:10.1007/s10845-005-4826-4

Roesmer, C. (2000). Nonstandard analysis and Dempster-Shafer theory. *International Journal of Intelligent Systems, 15*, 117–127. doi:10.1002/(SICI)1098-111X(200002)15:2<117::AID-INT2>3.0.CO;2-2

Safranek, R. J., Gottschlich, S., & Kak, A. C. (1990). Evidence accumulation using binary frames of discernment for verification vision. *IEEE Transactions on Robotics and Automation, 6*, 405–417. doi:10.1109/70.59366

Schubert, J. (1994). *Cluster-based specification techniques in Dempster-Shafer theory for an evidential intelligence analysis of multiple target tracks*. Department of Numerical Analysis and Computer Science Royal Institute of technology, S-100 44 Stockholm, Sweden.

Sentz, K., & Ferson, S. (2002). *Combination of evidence in Dempster-Shafer theory. SANDIA Report (SAND2002-0835)*. US: Sandia National Laboratories. doi:10.2172/800792

Shafer, G., & Srivastava, R. (1990). The Bayesian and belief-function formalisms: A general perspective for auditing . In Shafer, G., & Pearl, J. (Eds.), *Readings in uncertain reasoning*. San Mateo, CA: Morgan Kaufman Publishers Inc.

Shafer, G. A. (1976). *Mathematical theory of evidence*. Princeton, NJ: Princeton University Press.

Sloan, R. G. (1996). Do stock prices fully reflect information in accruals and cash flows about future earnings? *Accounting Review, 71*(3), 289–315.

Storn, R., & Price, K. (1997). Differential evolution - A simple and efficient heuristic for global optimization over continuous spaces. *Journal of Global Optimization, 11*, 341–359. doi:10.1023/A:1008202821328

ADDITIONAL READING

Ali, M. M., & Fatti, L. P. (2006). A differential free point generation scheme in the differential evolution algorithm. *Journal of Global Optimization, 35*, 551–572. doi:10.1007/s10898-005-3767-y

Beynon, M. J., Moutinho, L., & Veloutsou, C. (2010). Supermarket choice as a gender classification problem: An expositional analysis in the presence of ignorance using CaRBS. *European Journal of Marketing, 44*(1/2), 267–290. doi:10.1108/03090561011008709

Bonissone, R. P. (1997). Soft computing: The convergence of emerging reasoning techniques. *Soft Computing, 1*, 6–18. doi:10.1007/s005000050002

Brest, J., Zumer, V., & Maucec, M. S. (2006). Self-adaptive differential evolution algorithm in constrained real-parameter optimization. *IEEE Congress on Evolutionary Computation, Vancouver*, BC, Canada, (pp. 919-927).

Callen, J. L. (2009). Shocks to shocks: A theoretical foundation for the information content of earnings. *Contemporary Accounting Research, 26*(1), 135–166. doi:10.1506/car.26.1.5

Charitou, A., & Clubb, C. (1999). Earnings, cash flows and security returns over long return intervals: Analysis and UK evidence. *Journal of Business Finance & Accounting, 26*(3/4), 283–312. doi:10.1111/1468-5957.00257

Clubb, C. (1995). An empirical study of the information content of accounting earnings, funds flow and cash flow in the UK. *Journal of Business Finance & Accounting, 22*(1), 35–52. doi:10.1111/j.1468-5957.1995.tb00670.x

Cobb, B. R., & Shenoy, P. P. (2003). A comparison of Bayesian and belief function reasoning. *Information Systems Frontiers, 5*(4), 345–358. doi:10.1023/B:ISFI.0000005650.63806.03

De Mantores, R. L. (1990). *Approximate reasoning models*. Chichester, UK: Ellis Horwood.

Dechow, P. M. (1994). Accounting earnings and cash flows as measures of firm performance: The role of accounting accruals. *Journal of Accounting and Economics*, *18*(3), 3–42. doi:10.1016/0165-4101(94)90016-7

Demirakos, E. G., Strong, N. C., & Walker, M. (2004). What valuation models do analysts use? *Accounting Horizons*, *18*(4), 221–240. doi:10.2308/acch.2004.18.4.221

Habib, A. (2007). The role of accruals and cash flows in explaining security returns: Evidence from New Zealand. *Journal of International Accounting, Auditing & Taxation*, *17*(1), 51–66. doi:10.1016/j.intaccaudtax.2008.01.003

Jones, L., Holt, C. A., & Beynon, M. J. (2008). Reduction, classification and ranking of motion analysis data: An application to osteoarthritic and normal knee function. *Computer Methods in Biomechanics and Biomedical Engineering*, *11*(1), 31–40. doi:10.1080/10255840701550956

Kaelo, P., & Ali, M. M. (2006). A numerical study of some modified differential evolution algorithms. *European Journal of Operational Research*, *169*, 1176–1184. doi:10.1016/j.ejor.2004.08.047

Kim, Z. W., & Nevatia, R. (1999). Uncertain reasoning and learning for feature grouping. *Computer Vision and Image Understanding*, *76*(3), 278–288. doi:10.1006/cviu.1999.0803

Lucas, C., & Araabi, B. N. (1999). Generalisation of the Dempster-Shafer theory: A fuzzy-valued measure. *IEEE Transactions on Fuzzy Systems*, *7*(3), 255–270. doi:10.1109/91.771083

Russell, S., & Norvig, P. (1995). *Artificial intelligence: A modern approach*. New York, NY: Prentice–Hall.

Smets, P. (1990). The combination of evidence in the transferable belief model. *IEEE Transactions on Pattern Analysis and Machine Intelligence*, *12*(5), 447–458. doi:10.1109/34.55104

Yang, J.-B., Liu, J., Wang, J., Sii, H.-S., & Wong, H.-W. (2006). Belief rule-base inference methodology using the evidential reasoning approach—RIMER. *IEEE Transactions on Systems, Man, and Cybernetics. Part A, Systems and Humans*, *36*(2), 266–285. doi:10.1109/TSMCA.2005.851270

Yuan, X., Cao, B., Yang, B., & Yuan, Y. (2008). Hydrothermal scheduling using chaotic hybrid differential evolution. *Energy Conversion and Management*, *49*, 3627–3633. doi:10.1016/j.enconman.2008.07.008

KEY TERMS AND DEFINITIONS

Accruals: The component of earnings other than cash flow from operations (scaled by beginning of period equity in our empirical analysis).

Cash-Flow: Cash flow generated from companies' operations (scaled by beginning of period equity in our empirical analysis).

Confidence Factor: A function to transform a value into a standard domain, such as between 0 and 1.

Equivalence Class: Set of objects considered the same subject to an equivalence relation (e.g. those objects classified to x).

Evolutionary Algorithm: An algorithm that incorporates aspects of natural selection or survival of the fittest.

Focal Element: A finite non-empty set of hypotheses.

Mass Values: A positive function of the level of exact belief in the associated proposition (focal element).

Objective Function: A positive function of the difference between predictions and data estimates that are chosen so as to optimize the function or criterion.

Returns: The annual returns to shareholders from holding a share, defined as change in price plus dividends, divided by opening price.

Simplex Plot: Equilateral triangle domain representation of triplets of non-negative values which sum to one.

ENDNOTES

[1]   The term firm-year is used here since the returns value to be considered is a year value, so it describes a value representing a year.

[2]   This form of normalisation means there is the possibility for predicted returns values to be outside of the know range of the actual returns values.

[3]   Since the minimum and maximum company returns values are not equidistant from 0, it means the cut-off point between negative and positive returns in normalised terms is 0.252.

Chapter 8
Support Vector Machine Based Mobile Robot Motion Control and Obstacle Avoidance

Lihua Jiang
Northeastern University, China

Mingcong Deng
Tokyo University of Agriculture and Technology, Japan

ABSTRACT

Considering the noise effect during the navigation of a two wheeled mobile robot, SVM and LS-SVM based control schemes are discussed under the measured information with uncertainty, and in the different environments. The noise effect is defined as uncertainty in the measured data. One of them focuses on using a potential function and constructing a plane surface for avoiding the local minima in the static environments, where the controller is based on Lyapunov function candidate. Another one addresses to use a potential function and to define a new detouring virtual force for escaping from the local minima in the dynamic environments. Stability of the control system can be guaranteed. However, the motion control of the mobile robot would be affected by the noise effect. The SVM and LS-SVM for function estimation are used for estimating the parameter in the proposed controllers. With the estimated parameter, the noise effect during the navigation of the mobile robot can be reduced.

INTRODUCTION

In a general way, the types of robots are divided into robot manipulators, wheeled mobile robots, aerial robots, underwater robots and humanoid robots etc. Wheeled mobile robots increasingly are applied in industrial and service robotics, particularly when flexible motion capabilities are required on reasonably smooth grounds and surfaces. In general, path planning and controller design of the mobile robot are being given much attention, which aim at enabling robots attain the goal without collision with other objects in given environments, therewith path planning has been

DOI: 10.4018/978-1-4666-2086-5.ch008

a central topic in robotics for several decades and many path planning algorithms have been presented in the literatures. In some studies of path planning and control, collision free motion of the mobile robot has been discussed while there exist obstacles.

The potential fields typically proceed optimum path planning by defining an artificial repulsive field (which acts to steer the robot away from obstacles) and an artificial attractive field (which acts to pull the robot toward the goal configuration) (Latombe, 1991). The potential field method is computationally much less expensive. It is particularly attractive because of its elegant mathematical analysis and simplicity. Therefore the research activity in this field has been increasing. The developments of constructing potential field for robot navigation are also being given much attention correspondingly (Rimon, 1992; Hwang, 1992; Louste, 2002; Ge, 2002; Luh, 2007). Usually, the potential field function is defined over the robot's space, with a global minimum at the goal. In the presence of obstacles, local minima appear in the potential field. The mobile robot may run into one of them and can not attain the goal. Therefore, the issue of local minima problem and obstacle avoidance have also been addressed by many researchers (Koren, 1991; Okuma, 2004; Mabrouk, 2008).

In fact, constructing potential fields for robot navigation are considered in given environments. The static environments are with unmoved obstacles and unmoved target (AL-Taharwa, 2008). In the static environments, Rimon (1992) has proposed a navigation function for the mobile robot path planning and control, in which the obstacles are modelled with arbitrary shapes in a generalized sphere world with simplification of the shape of the objects. At the same time, Lyapunov function candidate based methods are presented for the robot path planning (Tsuchiya, 1999; Dixon, 2000; Okuma, 2004; Deng, 2008). Okuma (2004) proposed a state feedback controller for collision avoidance of the mobile robot

by a suitable choice of the Lyapunov function. Meanwhile, Deng (2008) showed a potential field method based on Lyapunov function candidate for the case of unmoved obstacle and target in the static environments. For this case, a compensating function based on maximum point information of Lyapunov function candidate is designed for canceling the local minima and avoiding the obstacles. However, the Lyapunov compensation function is difficult to design with the moving obstacle and the moving target. In the dynamic environments, the obstacle and the target are moving and their velocities are known. In the dynamic environments, Ge (2000; 2002) introduced an artificial potential method in the dynamic environments which consist of moving target and moving obstacle. Loizou (2003) considered the navigation for the mobile robot moving amongst the moving obstacles. Luh (2007) discussed the motion planning for the mobile robot in the dynamic environments using a potential field immune network. However, in real application, the measured data is with uncertain noise, the observation information is uncertain. The uncertainty in the measured data is not considered in the mentioned methods. In general, sensing is not perfect either and does not provide an exact knowledge of the robot's current configuration during execution. Hence, a fundamental difficulty is that uncertainty exists not only at planning time, but also at execution time. The above case imposes a restriction on the existed methods. The desired control results are difficult to obtain because of uncertainty in the measured data. The need for reducing the noise effect arises because the noise would affect the motion of the mobile robot, as well as the control accuracy of the mobile robot.

On the other hand, a computational learning method based on the statistical learning theory is introduced for reducing the noise effect during the navigation of the mobile robot. Support vector machine (SVM) which is based on the idea of structural risk minimization has recently been presented for solving various classification problems and function estimation problems. SVM solves convex optimization problems, typically quadratic problem. The foundations of SVM have been developed by Vapnik and are gaining popularity due to many attractive features, and promising empirical performance (Vapnik, 1995). The formulation embodies the structural risk minimization (SRM) principle, which has been shown to be superior to traditional empirical risk minimization (ERM) principle, employed by conventional neural networks. SRM minimizes an upper bound on the expected risk, as opposed to ERM that minimizes the error on the training data. It is the difference which equips SVM with a greater ability to generalize, which is the goal in statistical learning. SVM is developed to solve the classification problem, but recently they have been extended to the domain of regression problems. Moreover, unlike other machine learning methods, the number of free parameters in the SVM does not depend explicitly on the input dimensionality of the problem, which suggests that SVM can be especially useful in problems with a large number of inputs. The generalization of SVM for estimating real-valued functions is presented in (Vapnik, 1995). SVM has been applied successfully to classification and regression tasks. These include optical character recognition (OCR) (Schölkopf, 2005), fault diagnosis (Widodo, 2007), time series prediction (Müller, 1997), handwriting recognition (Adankon, 2009), image denoising (Li, 2009), etc. In some cases, least squares support vector machines (LS-SVM) are reformulations to standard SVM. Suykens (2002) proposed LS-SVM in which the training algorithm solves a convex problem like the SVM. In LS-SVM, the cost function is a regularized least squares function with equality constraints leading to linear Karush-Kuhn-Tucker (KKT) systems for classification tasks as well as regression. In a word, the training algorithm of the LS-SVM is highly simplified. Therefore, an issue to reduce the noise effect for path planning of the mobile robot is attempted in this chapter.

THE FUNCTIONS OF SVM

Support Vector Machine (SVM) for Function Estimation and Regression

SVM for function estimation and regression is called support vector regression (SVR) (Smola, 1998; Schölkopf, 1999; Schölkopf, 2005), it is concerned with estimating a real-valued function (1) based on a finite number set of independent and identically distributed data $(\tilde{x}_i, \tilde{y}_i)(i = 1, \ldots, N)$, where d-dimensional input $\tilde{x} \in R^d$ and the output $\tilde{y} \in R$, and b is threshold.

$$f(\tilde{x}) = w \cdot \tilde{x} + b, w \in R^d, b \in R \qquad (1)$$

In Vapnik's ε-insensitive SVR, the aim is to find a function $f(\tilde{x})$ which allows error of $\tilde{y}_i$ is no more than $\varepsilon(\varepsilon \geq 0)$, and makes $\tilde{y}_i$ flatter for all the training data. Considering more interferential error, non-negative slack variables ξ_i, ξ_i^* are introduced. The optimization problem is given as follows,

$$\min \quad \frac{1}{2} \| w \|^2 + C \sum_{i=1}^{N} (\xi_i + \xi_i^*)$$

$$s.t. \begin{cases} \tilde{y}_i - w \cdot \tilde{x}_i - b \leq \varepsilon + \xi_i \\ w \cdot \tilde{x}_i + b - \tilde{y}_i \leq \varepsilon + \xi_i^* \\ \xi_i, \xi_i^* \geq 0, \quad i = 1, \cdots, N \end{cases} \qquad (2)$$

where, C is a positive constant and to control the punishment to the samples beyond error ε. Generalization to kernel-based regression estimation by introducing Lagrange multipliers, one can arrive at the following optimization problem seen in Equation (3) in Box 1.

Ultimately the regression estimation takes the form

Box 1.

$$\max_{\alpha^\dagger, \alpha^*} W(\alpha^\dagger, \alpha^*) = -\varepsilon \sum_{i=1}^{N} (\alpha_i^\dagger + \alpha_i^*) + \sum_{i=1}^{N} \tilde{y}_i (\alpha_i^\dagger - \alpha_i^*)$$
$$-\frac{1}{2} \sum_{i,j=1}^{N} (\alpha_i^\dagger - \alpha_i^*)(\alpha_j^\dagger - \alpha_j^*)(\tilde{x}_i \cdot \tilde{x}_j) \tag{3}$$

$$s.t. \quad \alpha_i^\dagger, \alpha_i^* \in [0, C], \quad \sum_{i=1}^{N} (\alpha_i^\dagger - \alpha_i^*) = 0, \quad i = 1, \cdots, N$$

$$f(\tilde{x}) = \sum_{i=1}^{N} (\alpha_i^\dagger - \alpha_i^*)(\tilde{x}_i \cdot \tilde{x})$$
$$+ b = \sum_{i=1}^{N} (\alpha_i^\dagger - \alpha_i^*) K(\tilde{x}_i, \tilde{x}) + b \tag{4}$$

where $K(\tilde{x}_i, \tilde{x}) = \langle \Phi(\tilde{x}_i), \Phi(\tilde{x}) \rangle$ is kernel function, the dot product in feature space by using a non-linear mapping Φ can be obtained by two given vectors in input space. That is, linear regression in a high dimensional space corresponding to nonlinear regression in the low dimensional input space can be realized by mapping the input vectors into a feature space. There are different kernel functions used in SVM, such as

Polynomial

$$K(\tilde{x}_i, \tilde{x}) = \langle \tilde{x}_i, \tilde{x} \rangle^d \tag{5}$$

where d is degree.

Radial basis function (Gaussian)

$$K(\tilde{x}_i, \tilde{x}) = exp(-\frac{\| \tilde{x}_i - \tilde{x} \|^2}{2\sigma^2}) \tag{6}$$

where, $\sigma > 0$.

Sigmoid

$$K(\tilde{x}_i, \tilde{x}) = tanh(\kappa \langle \tilde{x}_i, \tilde{x} \rangle + \vartheta) \tag{7}$$

where, κ is gain and ϑ is offset.

In the radial basis function case, the support vector algorithm automatically determines centers, weights, and threshold that minimizes an upper bound on the expected test error (Scholköpf, 1997). In this chapter, radial basis function (RBF) is adopted. There is an available Matlab toolbox LibSVM for SVM (Chang, 2011).

Least Squares Support Vector Machine (LS-SVM) for Function Estimation and Regression

LS-SVM for function estimation and regression is introduced. Support vector machines theory (Smola, 1998) has drawn much attention for the high generalization ability and global optimization property. Analytical solutions can be obtained by solving linear equations instead of a quadratic programming (QP) problem in LS-SVM (Suykens, 1999). The main advantage of LS-SVM is that it is computationally more efficient than the standard SVM method. Therefore, LS-SVM method for function estimation is also selected to estimate the state variables by using the measured data. LS-SVM (Suykens, 1999) is regularized for supervised approximators, which is efficient for function estimation. Only solving linear equations instead of a quadratic programming problem is needed in the optimization process, which simplifies the process to the standard SVM. Consider a given regression data set $(\tilde{x}_i, \tilde{y}_i)(i = 1, ..., N)$, where the N is the total number of training data pairs, $\tilde{x}_i \in R^N$ is the regression vector and $\tilde{y}_i \in R$ is the output. According to SVM (Schölkopf, 2005), the input space R^N is mapped into a feature space H with the nonlinear function $\Phi(\tilde{x}_i)$. In the feature space,

$$y(\tilde{x}) = w^T \Phi(\tilde{x}) + b \quad w \in \text{H}, b \in R \quad (8)$$

is taken as estimation function, where vector w and scalar b are the parameters of the model. The optimization problem is defined as follows,

$$\min_{w,e} J(w, e) = \frac{1}{2} w^T w + \gamma \frac{1}{2} \sum_{i=1}^{N} e_i^2 \quad \gamma > 0 \quad (9)$$

$$subject \ to \ \tilde{y}_i = w^T \Phi(\tilde{x}) + b + e_i, \quad i = 1, 2, ..., N \quad (10)$$

where e_i is error between actual output and predictive output of the i th data, γ is the regularization parameter which balances the estimated model's complexity and approximation accuracy. The use of kernel function to avoid carrying out $\Phi(\cdot)$ explicitly is known as the kernel trick. The LS-SVM model of the data set is given by

$$y(\tilde{x}) = \sum_{i=1}^{N} \alpha_i K(\tilde{x}_i, \tilde{x}) + b \quad (11)$$

where $\alpha_i \in R$ and $K(\tilde{x}_i, \tilde{x}) (i = 1, 2, ..., N)$ are Lagrange multipliers and kernel functions satisfying the Mercer condition respectively.

However, in standard SVM, the optimization problem is defined by Equation (12) in Box 2.

where, C is a positive constant and to control the punishment to the samples beyond the error, non-negative slack variable ξ_i is to measure the deviation of training samples. In comparison to the starandard SVM, LS-SVM simplifies the required computation by (10). In this case, training requires the solution of a linear equation set. The LS-SVM model of the data set can be given by

$$y(\tilde{x}) = \sum_{i=1}^{N} \alpha_i K(\tilde{x}_i, \tilde{x}) + b \quad (13)$$

where $\alpha_i \in R(i = 1, 2, \cdots, N)$ are Lagrange multipliers and $K(\tilde{x}_i, \tilde{x})(i = 1, 2, \cdots, N)$ is any kernel functions satisfying the Mercer condition (Smola, 1998). Analytical solutions of α_i and b can be obtained from

$$\begin{bmatrix} b \\ \alpha \end{bmatrix} = \Phi^{-1} \begin{bmatrix} 0 \\ Y \end{bmatrix} \quad (14)$$

with $Y = [\tilde{y}_1 \quad \tilde{y}_2 \cdots \tilde{y}_n]^T, \pm = [\alpha_1 \quad \alpha_2 \cdots \alpha_n]^T$ and the supposed nonsingular matrix

$$\Phi = \begin{bmatrix} 0 & 1^T \\ 1 & \Omega + \gamma^{-1} I \end{bmatrix} \quad (15)$$

Box 2.

$$\min_{w, b} J(w, b) = \frac{1}{2} w^T w + C \sum_{i=1}^{n} \xi_i$$

$$subject \ to \quad y_i [w^T \Phi(\tilde{x}_i) + b] \geq 1 - \xi \quad i = 1, 2, \cdots, N, \quad \xi_i > 0 \quad (12)$$

where $1 = [1 \quad 1 \cdots 1]^T$, I is a $N \times N$ identity matrix and Ω is a $N \times N$ symmetric matrix with the elements

$$\begin{aligned}\Omega_{ij} &= \Phi(\tilde{x}_i)^T \Phi(\tilde{x}_j) \\ &= K(\tilde{x}_i, \tilde{x}_j) \quad i, j = 1, 2, \cdots, N\end{aligned} \quad (16)$$

There is an available Matlab toolbox LS-SVMlab for LS-SVM (De Brabanter, 2011). The LS-SVMlab is built around a fast LS-SVM training and simulation algorithm. The corresponding function calls can be used for classification as well as for function estimation.

Parameters Selection of SVM

It is well known that SVM generalization performance (estimation accuracy) depends on setting of hyperparameters C, ε and the kernel parameter. The problem of optimal parameter selection is complicated because SVM model depends on these three parameters. However, the SVM parameters are usually determined based on priori knowledge or application-domain knowledge. That is, in the application of SVM, its parameters are usually determined by trial and error.

Parameter C determines the trade off between the model complexity (flatness) and the degree to which deviations larger than ε are tolerated in optimization formulation. And parameter ε controls the width of the ε-insensitive zone for fitting the training data. The value of ε can affect the number of support vectors used to construct the regression function. The bigger ε, the fewer support vectors are selected. On the other hand, bigger ε-values result in more flat estimations. ε is as accuracy parameter. That is, both C and ε affect model complexity.

These three hyperparameters C, ε and the RBF kernel parameter are choosing as follows (Cherkassky, 2004),

$$C = max(|\ \overline{y} + 3\sigma_y\ |, |\ \overline{y} - 3\sigma_y\ |) = 3\sigma_y \quad (17)$$

where $\overline{y}$ and σ_y are the mean and the standard deviation of the training outputs. In the application, for example, the training data are often scaled, so that $\overline{y} = 0$, then the proposed C is $3\sigma_y$.

To select ε of SVM regression relies on the knowledge of the standard deviation of noise. The problem is that the noise variance is not known a priori, and it needs to be estimated from training data $(\tilde{x}_i, \tilde{y}_i), (i = 1, \dots N)$. In practice, the noise variance can be estimated from the squared sum of residuals (fitting error) of the training data. The estimation formula is given by (Cherkassky, 2004)

$$\hat{\sigma}_n^2 = 1.5 \frac{1}{N} \sum_{i=1}^{N} (\tilde{y}_i - y_i^*)^2 \quad (18)$$

where, y_i^* is target value.

The width parameter σ of the RBF kernel function is appropriately selected to reflect the input range of the training data. The RBF width parameter is usually set to $(0.2 - 0.5) * range(\tilde{x})$.

In LS-SVM, function estimation is done by solving a linear set of equations instead of solving a quadratic problem. The LS-SVM formulation also involves less tuning parameters. Some researchers gave the discussions on evaluating the model of LS-SVM and tuning the hyperparameters of the model by using LS-SVM (Lendasse, 2005; Zhou, 2008).

Since the aim is to optimal selection of SVM parameters, performance evaluation with different parameters set in SVM is introduced.

Traditional performance index which is used to determine the quality of the estimation such as root mean squared error (RMSE), can be used as measure of forecasting accuracy. The RMSE is shown as follows,

$$RMSE = \sqrt{\frac{1}{N}\sum_{i=1}^{N}(\hat{y}_i - \tilde{y}_i)^2} \qquad (19)$$

where N is the number of forecasting periods, $\hat{y}_i$ is the estimation value. The smaller value of performance indices denotes the higher precision of estimation.

MODEL OF TWMR AND PATH PLANNING

Path Planning

Path planning problems generally involve computing a continuous sequence (a path) of configurations (generalized coordinates) between an initial configuration (start) and a final configuration (goal) while respecting certain constraints. Path planning of mobile robots means to generate an optimal path from a starting position to a goal position within its environments. The obstacle avoidance problems deal with identification of obstacle free trajectories between the starting point and goal point. Path planning addresses the existence of a collision-free admissible path and the computation of such a path (Laumond, 1998).

In general, classic path planning approaches include roadmaps method, cell decomposition method and potential field method (Latombe, 1991).

- **Roadmaps:** Represent the connectivity of free space by a graph, a network of one dimensional curve. It connects the initial and goal positions of the robot to the roadmap, and searches the resulting graph for a path between the initial and goal positions of the robot. There are many possible definitions of the roadmap, e.g., visibility graph, Voronoi diagram.
- **Cell Decomposition:** Decomposes the free space into simple cells and repre-

sent the connectivity of the free space by the adjacency graph of these cells. Cell is connected with region of free space, such that computing a path between any two points in the same cell is straightforward. It searches the connectivity graph for a sequence of adjacent cells connecting the initial to the goal cell and transforms the sequence of cells (if one has been produced) into a path.
- **Potential Field:** Defines a function over the free space that has a global minimum at the goal configuration and follows its steepest descent of the potential function.

In the chapter, motion control and obstacle avoidance of two wheeled mobile robot (TWMR) are discussed, the navigation functions are base on potential field methods. Consequently, the potential field is mainly introduced.

The potential field approach has been used extensively and has been addressed by many researchers because of its ability to find an optimal solution for mobile robot path planning and navigation. Potential field approaches are not based on graph search, which is different from the roadmaps approaches and cell decomposition approaches. A robot is a particle moving under the influence of an artificial potential produced by the goal (positive) and the obstacle (negative). The negative gradient of the total potential is treated as a force applied to the robot. The direction of the force is considered the most promising direction of the motion.

The potential field method is analogous to fastest descent optimization method, it can be efficient, as well as it may get trapped into local minima (Laumond, 1998). The potential field method is the popular approach used to navigate the mobile robot to the target within environments containing obstacles. Some limitations of potential field method for path planning are discussed in (Koren, 1991). For example, trap situations due to local minima, no passage between closely spaced obstacles, oscillations in the presence of obstacles and oscillations in narrow passages. That is, potential field is efficient but suffers from local minima which is not the global minimum of the total potential and makes the robot be trapped in it. Therefore, the robot can not reach target due to the local minima. The local minima remain an important cause of inefficiency of potential field method. Therefore, dealing with local minima is the major issue in designing a potential field for robot navigation. The local minima problem can be addressed at two levels (Latombe, 1991),

- Definition of the potential field function, by attempting to specify a function with no or few local minima,
- Design of a search algorithm by including appropriate techniques for escaping from local minima.

Since it is not easy to construct a potential function with no local minima in a general configuration, the second issue is more realizable (Mabrouk, 2008).

Model of Two Wheeled Mobile Robot

In this research, the controlled system is considered as a two wheeled mobile robot (Mita, 2000), the mobile robot features two differentially driven wheels and a third castor wheel at the rear to passively roll along while preventing the robot from falling over (Lavalle, 2006). Differential drive robot typically has two powered wheels, one on each side of the mobile robot and each of them is attached to its own motor. And there are other passive wheels that keep the robot from tipping over. Here, x and y are the positions of the mobile robot (the geometric center of the robot), θ is the heading angle of the mobile robot on two-dimensional Cartesian workspace, in

which global coordinates are defined. Here, velocities of the position (x, y) are $(\dot{x}, \dot{y})$. The wheels of the mobile robot roll and do not slip. Then, there exists a constraint.

$$\dot{x}sin\theta - \dot{y}cos\theta = 0 \tag{20}$$

The mobile robot system is an underactuated system, namely, it has two inputs (translational velocity and angular velocity of the mobile robot) and three outputs (position and heading angle of the mobile robot, which are state variables for the robot system). The parameters of the robot are as follows,

- (x, y): Position of the mobile robot
- θ: Heading angle of the mobile robot
- u_1: Translational velocity of the mobile robot
- u_2: Angular velocity of the mobile robot
- r: Radius of a wheel of the mobile robot
- L: Distance between both wheels of the mobile robot
- v_l, v_r: Angular velocity of left wheel and right wheel

With the above definitions on the control inputs and the state variables, the motion of the mobile robot is described by

$$\begin{bmatrix} \dot{x} \\ \dot{y} \\ \dot{\theta} \end{bmatrix} = \begin{bmatrix} \cos \theta & 0 \\ \sin \theta & 0 \\ 0 & 1 \end{bmatrix} \begin{bmatrix} u_1 \\ u_2 \end{bmatrix} \tag{21}$$

then,

$$\frac{d}{dt}\begin{bmatrix} x \\ y \\ \theta \end{bmatrix} = \begin{bmatrix} \cos \theta \\ \sin \theta \\ 0 \end{bmatrix} u_1 + \begin{bmatrix} 0 \\ 0 \\ 1 \end{bmatrix} u_2 \tag{22}$$

It can be transformed to Equation (23)

$$\frac{dz}{dt} = Bu \qquad (23)$$

where

$$z = \begin{bmatrix} x \\ y \\ \theta \end{bmatrix}, B = \begin{bmatrix} \cos\theta & 0 \\ \sin\theta & 0 \\ 0 & 1 \end{bmatrix}, u = \begin{bmatrix} u_1 \\ u_2 \end{bmatrix} \qquad (24)$$

Let D be an open subset in R^3, $z \in D$. The robot can be driven by independent two wheels (Mita, 2000), the following description makes the explanations more clear.

$$\frac{r}{2}(v_l + v_r) = u_1$$
$$\frac{r}{L}(v_l - v_r) = u_2 \qquad (25)$$

For the mobile robot, angular wheels velocities of left and right wheel v_l, v_r are written in the form of Equation (26) with r and L to establish the relationship between the speed of the robot and the speeds of two wheels.

$$\begin{bmatrix} v_l \\ v_r \end{bmatrix} = \begin{bmatrix} \dfrac{1}{r} & \dfrac{L}{2r} \\ \dfrac{1}{r} & -\dfrac{L}{2r} \end{bmatrix} \begin{bmatrix} u_1 \\ u_2 \end{bmatrix} \qquad (26)$$

The mobile robot moves when different actions are applied (Lavalle, 2006). If $v_l = v_r > 0$, then the robot moves forward in the direction that the wheels are pointing. The speed is proportional to r. Namely, translation occurs when both wheels move at the same angular velocity. If $v_l = -v_r \neq 0$,

then the robot rotates clockwise because the wheels are turning in the opposite directions. This motivates the placement of the body-frame origin at the center of the axle between the wheels. By this assignment, no translation occurs if the wheels rotate at the same rate but in the opposite directions. With the knowledge of the model of the mobile robot, problem of this research is discussed in the next section.

Problem Setup

In this chapter, considering the static environments, as well as the dynamic environments, two kinds of controllers are discussed for reducing the uncertainty of the measured data by using SVM method and LS-SVM method during the navigation of the mobile robot. The motion planning problem of the mobile robot is to plan and to control the robot motion from an initial position to a target position in a desired manner while avoiding the obstacles. Some assumptions of basic problem are given to simplify the analysis as follows (Laumond, 1998),

- Robot is a single rigid object and moving in the two-dimensional workspace,
- Dynamic properties of the robot are ignored (no temporal issues),
- Motions restricted to non-contact, the mechanical interaction between two physical objects in contact can be ignored.

It is therefore the physical motion planning problem is reduced to geometrical path planning problem based on these assumptions. It is also assumed that the obstacles are convex polygons, all of the positions information could be measured by a global camera, such as the robot position, the obstacle position and the goal position, at the same time, the velocity of the goal and the velocity of the target can be known prior. However, the measured information always accompanies noise. The noise would affect the control and the motion of the robot. SVM and LS-SVM based control schemes of the mobile robot are discussed in this chapter, SVM/LS-SVM method is used for estimating the controller parameter for reducing the noise effect for the path planning of the mobile robot, with considering the static environments and the dynamic environments. Under the observation information with uncertainties, a scheme based on the SVM method is proposed for providing reliable control information in order to control the mobile robot by using a potential function, where the potential function is based on Lyapunov function candidate.

For the local minima problem of the potential field, in the static environments, local minima avoidance is achieved by compensating the potential function with a plan surface. Namely, this flat plane is constructed to escape from the local minima for compensating the Lyapunov function candidate. In the dynamic environments, local minima problem is solved by designing the detouring virtual force, where the potential function used for the design of the controller considers the Euclidean distance information and the magnitude information of the relative velocity between the robot and the target/obstacle. In a word, the objective of this chapter is to propose the methods for reducing the uncertainty of the observation information by using SVM and LS-SVM for the path planning of the mobile robot with considering the static environments and dynamic environments, where, local minima avoidance is achieved by compensating the potential field function with a plan surface in the static environments and is achieved by designing the detouring virtual force in the dynamic environments.

CONTROLLER DESIGN IN STATIC ENVIRONMENT

Controller Design and Local Minima Compensation under the Existence of the Uncertainty in the Measured Information

For the robot system, the following controller is considered. The Lyapunov function candidate $V(z)$ is selected by satisfying the following properties.

- $V(z)$ is continuously on D,
- $V(z) \geq 0$ for $\forall z \in D$ and $V(z) = 0$ for $z = 0$,
- $\partial V(z) / \partial t < 0$ for $V(z) \in D$,
- The value of $V(z)$ is uniformly maximal on the boundary of D, $V(z)$ has a unique minimum at the origin,
- $\| z \| \to \infty \Rightarrow V(z) \to \infty$.

In Rimon's robot navigation by using artificial potential functions (Rimon, 1992), it is assumed that each obstacle i is a star shaped set and can be transformed to a disk by a certain coordinate transformation. Let the target point be the origin, the function $V(z)$ is constructed based on the method in (Rimon, 1992; Okuma, 2004), that is, the function $V(z)$ is based on the definitions of the obstacles, when there exist M isolated obstacles which are expressed by obstacle function $O_i(i = 1, \ldots, M)$ in the area that is bounded by a wall described by O_0.

$$V(z) = \frac{\hat{x}^2 + \hat{y}^2 + w\theta^2}{((\hat{x}^2 + \hat{y}^2 + w\theta^2)^\kappa + \prod_{i=0}^{M} \hat{O}_i(\hat{r}))^{1/\kappa}}$$

(27)

where

$$\underline{r} = [x, y]^T$$

$$\hat{r} = [\hat{x}, \hat{y}]^T = (1 - \sum_{i=0}^{M} s_i)\underline{r} + \sum_{i=0}^{M} s_i T$$

$$s_i(\underline{r}) = \frac{(x^2 + y^2)\prod_{j \neq i} O_j(\underline{r})}{(x^2 + y^2)\prod_{j \neq i} O_j(\underline{r}) + \lambda O_i(\underline{r})}$$

$$T_i(\underline{r}) = \frac{\rho_i(1 + O_i(\underline{r}))}{\|\underline{r} - q_i\|}[\underline{r} - q_i] + p_i$$

$$w(\hat{x}, \hat{y}) = \frac{k_w}{\hat{x}^2 + \hat{y}^2 + k_w}$$

$$\hat{O}_i(\hat{r}) = \|\hat{r} - p_i\|^2 - \rho_i^2$$

$$\hat{O}_0(\hat{r}) = \rho_0^2 - \|\hat{r} - p_0\|^2$$

and κ, λ, k_w are positive constants, p_i, ρ_i denote the center and the radius of the disk where the obstacle i is transformed to, respectively, and q_i is the center of the obstacle.

The controller based on Lyapunov function candidate is selected in order to calculate the input vector u as follows (Deng, 2008),

$$u = -(\alpha I + \hat{\beta} J) B^T \nabla V \qquad (28)$$

where

$$I = \begin{bmatrix} 1 & 0 \\ 0 & 1 \end{bmatrix}, J = \begin{bmatrix} 0 & 1 \\ -1 & 0 \end{bmatrix}, B = \begin{bmatrix} \cos\theta & 0 \\ \sin\theta & 0 \\ 0 & 1 \end{bmatrix}$$

$$\hat{\beta} = \frac{\beta}{\|B^T \nabla V\|}[-\sin\theta, \cos\theta, 0]\nabla V$$

and α and β are positive constants. The derivative of the function $V(z)$ is computed with the controller (29) as follows,

$$\dot{V} = -\alpha \|B^T \nabla V\|^2 \leq 0 \qquad (29)$$

So, $B^T \nabla V \to 0$ as $t \to \infty$ is obtained. That is, the controlled system converges to a set of points determined by $B^T \nabla V = 0$, $H = \{z \in D \mid B^T \nabla V = 0\}$. A point z_0 on this set is a stable equilibrium point of the system, if and only if it satisfied the following conditions

$$\nabla V(z_0) = 0, \quad \frac{\partial^2 V}{\partial x^2(z_0)} > 0 \qquad (30)$$

The controlled system may converge to the point when V has the local minima and satisfies the conditions in (30). The mobile robot would move into the local minimum and could not attain the goal when the mobile robot comes near to the local minimum area.

According to the position information which is obtained from the camera, V is computed in (27). The output of the controller is calculated in (28). Therefore, the input u of the controlled system is obtained. That is, for the mobile robot, the uncertainty of the observation information can affect the accuracy of the motion. Based on the above analysis, during navigation of the mobile robot, obtaining the precise position and compensating the local minima need to be considered. Therefore, during navigation of the mobile robot, the control schemes to reduce the noise effect by using SVM method and LS-SVM method are proposed.

Controller Parameter Estimation by Using SVM/LS-SVM Method

With the knowledge of the SVM/LS-SVM for function estimation and regression, the uncertainties of the measured information can be reduced by using the estimation results from the measured information. That is, the desired position information could be estimated by using the measured position information. Let (x_r, y_r, θ_r) be the position which would be estimated and (x, y, θ) be the measured position. In the training, at first, estimated functions are designed as follows,

$$\begin{cases} x_r = f(x, \theta, u_1) \\ y_r = g(y, \theta, u_1) \\ \theta_r = h(\theta, u_2) \end{cases} \qquad (31)$$

where, x, y, θ, u_1, u_2 are the features which are crucial factors for obtaining models of estimation function of the measured information. The features of the estimated functions are selected respectively, which are of considerable influential factors. The crucial factors are including translational velocity of the mobile robot, angular velocity of the mobile robot, position and heading angle of the mobile robot. That is, x position, heading angle and translational velocity of the mobile robot are the features in designing the estimated function of the x_r position. y position, heading angle and translational velocity of the mobile robot are the features in designing the estimated function of the y_r position. Heading angle and angular velocity of the mobile robot are the features in designing the estimated function of the θ_r.

Then, according to these features, the desired position models of the robot can be obtained from training data. Assuming the robot does the iteration movements for several times, the measured position information is considered as training data to estimate the models.

Finally, with the estimation models, the uncertainties of the measured information can be reduced in the application. The estimated x_r, y_r, θ_r are used as controller parameter for the design of the controller in the static environments.

Local Minima Compensation

Local minima compensation under the existence of the uncertainty in the observation information from the camera is discussed. In presence of obstacles, the local minima are avoided by compensating the $V(z)$ function. Inside the local minimum area, the ∇V is calculated by the magnitude a and the direction θ_p of gradient of the compensation plane surface (Deng, 2008). Therefore, when the mobile robot passes by the local minimum area, the control input vector u could be computed based on the ∇V by the compensation function.

The description of the compensation method is given in brief. The steps of construction the plane surface for compensating Lyapunov function candidate are described. The local minima are the minimum points of Lyapunov function candidate $V(z)$ where $z \neq 0$. In order to avoid the local minima, the compensating function constructed for substituting $V(z)$ which is regarded as the plane surface. As mentioned in the above, the simulation environment is structured in presence of the isolated obstacle. However, in the real application, it is difficult to find a decreasing compensating function along the direction of angle $\theta = 0$. z_{min} and z_{max} are selected, the compensating function $V(z)$ is designed along the direction θ_p, where the relationship between V and z should be ensured. The detailed explanations are given as follows (see Figure 1).

Firstly, some definitions are given. The local minimum adjacent neighborhood R_c is defined with radius R, and inside the neighborhood, $V(z)$ is defined as the function with constant gradient. The point where value of $V(z)$ is the largest in circumference of the local minimum neighborhood is defined as z_{max}. Make the circle with radius R_f of distance to apex of closest obstacle from the local minimum, the point where $V(z)$ becomes the smallest with respect to R_f is defined as z_{min}. V_{max} and V_{min} are defined as value of $V(z)$ at z_{max} and z_{min} respectively. There are two candidates of z_{min} in both sides of the obstacle, where one of them is selected.

Secondly, magnitude a and direction θ_p of gradient of the plane surface are defined as follows,

Figure 1. Definitions of R_c, z_{max}, z_{min} and R_f

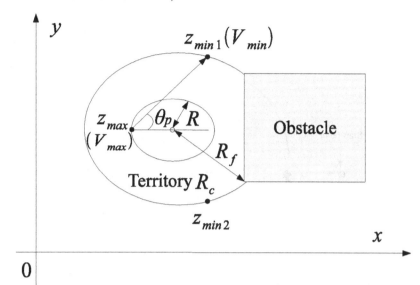

$$a = \frac{V_{max} - V_{min}}{\sqrt{(z_{max_x} - z_{min_x})^2 + (z_{max_y} - z_{min_y})^2}}$$

(32)

$$\theta_p = \tan^{-1} \frac{z_{max_y} - z_{min_y}}{z_{max_x} - z_{min_x}}$$

(33)

where, z_{max_x} is the x coordinate of z_{max}, z_{min_x} is the x coordinate of z_{min} respectively, z_{max_y}, z_{min_y} are the y coordinates of z_{max} and z_{min} respectively.

Finally, inside the local minimum area, the ∇V is calculated by the magnitude a and the direction θ_p of gradient in (32) and (33). Therefore, when the mobile robot passes by the local minimum area, the control input vector u could be computed based on the ∇V by

$$\nabla V = [\frac{\partial V}{\partial x}, \frac{\partial V}{\partial y}, \frac{\partial V}{\partial \theta}]^T = [a \cos \theta_p, a \sin \theta_p, 0]^T$$

(34)

As mentioned in the above section, the u is calculated in (28). The position z which is obtained from the camera is not in accordance with the calculating one which is the desired position. Namely, there exist measurement errors. In this case, the error should affect the motion of the mobile robot. The accurate position information of the mobile robot is desired.

Simulation Results

According to the proposed control schemes, simulations by using SVM method and LS-SVM method are shown respectively, where two kinds of simulations are shown. One is to control the mobile robot only with the local minima avoidance, where an example is illustrated. Another is to control the mobile robot under the uncertainty of observation information by using the proposed control schemes.

As shown in Figure 2, the two obstacles case is considered, it is assumed that the second obstacle appears after the mobile robot avoiding the first obstacle. The mobile robot can avoid the obstacles by using the proposed method and the plane surface for avoiding the local minimum is shown in the circle area.

Figure 2. The obtained navigation orbit in the case of two local minima

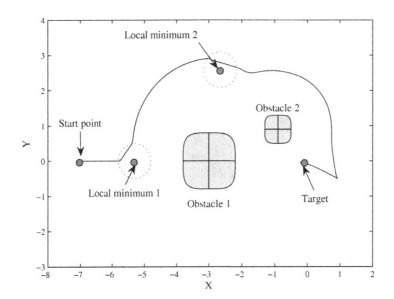

Here, the uncertain observation information is considered. At first, the reference navigation orbit without noise with considering the obstacle avoidance is obtained by using the controller (28) as shown by the dotted line in Figure 3. The effectiveness of compensating the local minimum is confirmed.

Then, in order to simulate the uncertainty in the observation information from the camera, random noise is introduced into the position of the mobile robot. For the case with the noise effect, the navigation orbit with the noise effect is shown by the solid line in Figure 3. Obviously, the noise affected the motion of the mobile robot. The movement becomes vibrate than the desired situation.

Based on the models which are obtained in (31), the prediction position of the robot can be obtained. For reducing the noise effect, support vector machine library (Chang, 2011) is used to obtain the models of the estimated position from the information with the noise. The parameters of simulation by SVM in the static environments are chosen as follows.

ε-SVM(RBF),

$$C = 30, \alpha = 0.5, \beta = 10.0, \kappa = 2, k_w = 0.2$$

The complexity and generalization performance of SVM models depend on its parameters which are (ε, C, σ). Based on the models, the prediction position of the robot can be obtained, and then, the controller (28) is designed. The navigation orbit with the noise by using the SVM method is shown by dashed line in Figure 3. That is, during the mobile robot navigation, it can be seen that the motion of the robot by using the SVM method with the nois e(see the dashed line in Figure 3) is more smooth than the one without using the SVM method with the noise (see the solid line in Figure 3)and the obtained navigation orbit by using the SVM method with the noise is closer to the reference orbit without the noise (see the dotted line in Figure 3). As a result, the motion of the mobile robot can be controlled accurately and smoothly.

For evaluating the effectiveness of the proposed scheme by using LS-SVM method, local minima problem is likely considered with static obstacle

Figure 3. The obtained navigation orbits from three kinds of cases

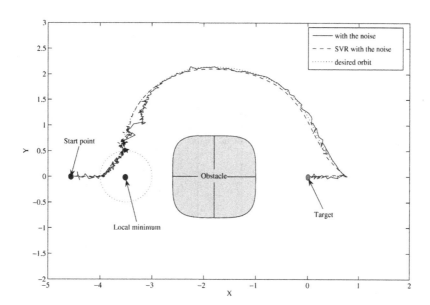

and target. The position of the obstacle is between the robot and the target. For using the proposed method, LS-SVMlab (De Brabanter, 2011) is selected to obtain the models of the estimated position information which is mixed with noise. The related arameters of simulation by LS-SVM in the static environments are set as follows.

$$\alpha = 0.5,\ \beta = 10.0,\ \kappa$$
$$= 2,\ k_w = 0.2,\ \gamma = 1000,\ \sigma^2 = 0.3$$

During the navigation of the robot, there exist random variations in the state variables x, y and θ, as they are captured by global camera. In order to simulate the measured data, random noise is introduced into the state variables. Namely, the noise brings uncertainties to the control system. The value of the noise could not be too large, otherwise it is difficult for the robot to track the navigation path. In Figure 4, the control result without the noise is shown by dashed line which is the reference result of the control system. The control result with the noise is shown by solid line in Figure 4(a). By using the proposed scheme,

the control result by reducing the noise effect is shown by solid line in Figure 4(b). The robot arrived to the target with local minimum avoidance by compensating the Lyapunov function candidate which is shown in circle areas of the Figure 4. During the mobile robot navigation, it can be seen that the motion of the robot by using the LS-SVM method with the noise (Figure 4(b)) is near to the reference result than the one without using the LS-SVM method with the noise (Figure 4(a)).

According to the distance between the desired value and the noise value of the x position and the y position and the distance between the desired value and the noise value by using LS-SVM method of the x position and the y position, the evaluation performance of the estimation is shown by the root mean squared error as follows,

- X postion:
  - Figure 4(a) RMSE=0.0587
  - Figure 4(b) RMSE=0.0201
- Y postion:
  - Figure 4(a) RMSE=0.0511
  - Figure 4(b) RMSE=0.0178

Figure 4. (a) The control result without using LS-SVM method, (b) The control result by using LS-SVM method

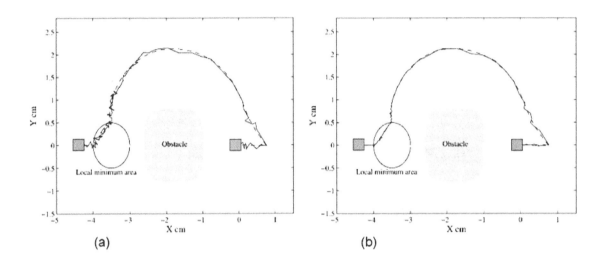

(a)   (b)

As shown in the above, the RMSE value of the estimation result without using the LS-SVM method is bigger than the estimation result by using the LS-SVM method. Namely, the control accuracy is improved. It can be seen that the desired control result of the proposed method is confirmed. By reducing the measurement noise effect, the motion control of the mobile robot becomes more accurate.

CONTROLLER DESIGN IN DYNAMIC ENVIRONMENT

Controller Design and Local Minima Avoidance under the Existence of the Uncertainty in the Measured Information

For the mobile robot system, the following controller is considered in the dynamic environments, where the control input is designed by multiplying the gradient vector of the V function.

$$u = -(\alpha I + \hat{\beta} J) B^T \nabla V \qquad (35)$$

where,

$$I = \begin{bmatrix} 1 & 0 \\ 0 & 1 \end{bmatrix}, J = \begin{bmatrix} 0 & 1 \\ -1 & 0 \end{bmatrix}, B = \begin{bmatrix} \cos \theta & 0 \\ \sin \theta & 0 \\ 0 & 1 \end{bmatrix}$$

$$\hat{\beta} = \frac{\beta}{\| B^T \nabla V \|} [-\sin \theta_r, \cos \theta_r, 0] \nabla V$$

and α, β are positive constants. Controller (35) is designed by considering the Euclidean distance information and the magnitude information of the relative velocity between the robot and the target/obstacle. That is, the distance information between the robot and the target/obstacle defined in Equation (39), (47) and (48) acted as an important part in the proposed controller. Accordingly, the correspondingly factors are determined as features which should be enhanced the estimation accuracy in (35).

By considering the Euclidean distance information and the magnitude information of the relative velocity between the robot and the target/obstacle, ∇V is designed by

$$\nabla V = \begin{bmatrix} F_{total\,x} \\ F_{total\,y} \\ 0 \end{bmatrix} \qquad (36)$$

where

$$F_{total} = F_{att} + F_{rep} + F_s \qquad (37)$$

F_{total} is integration virtual force. The definitions of attractive force F_{att} and repulsive force F_{rep} are given in (Ge, 2002), where the velocities of the robot and the target are considered.

Considering the velocities of the robot and the target, the attractive potential U_{att} is defined in Box 3.

$p = [x\ y]^T$ and $v = [v_x\ v_y]^T$ are defined in two-dimensional space, $||\cdot||$ is Euclidean norm. At time t, $p(t)$ is the position and $v(t)$ is the velocity of the robot, $p_{tar}(t)$ is the position and $v_{tar}(t)$

is the velocity of the target, α_p, α_v are scalar positive parameters, m, n are positive constants.

Attractive force F_{att} is the negative gradient of the U_{att}, when $p \neq p_{tar}$ and $v \neq v_{tar}$, $F_{att}(p, v)$ becomes Equation (39) in Box 4.

For the robot, n_{RT} is the unit vector pointing to the target, n_{VRT} is the unit vector indicating the relative velocity direction of the target. Attractive potential $U_{att}(p, v)$ has two parts, F_{att1} drives the robot near to the target, F_{att2} makes the robot to move at the same velocity of the target.

The position and the velocity of the obstacle are $p_{obs}(t), v_{obs}(t)$ respectively. The relative velocity v_{RO} from the robot to the target is $[v(t) - v_{obs}(t)]^T n_{RO}$, where, n_{RO} is a unit vector pointing from the robot to the obstacle. The repulsive potential is given in Box 5.

If $\rho_s(p, p_{obs}) < \rho_m(v_{RO})$ and $v_{RO} > 0$, U_{rep} is not defined. Where, η is a positive constant of the repulsive potential, ρ_0 is a positive constant

Box 3.

$$U_{att}(p, v) = \alpha_p \,||\, p_{tar}(t) - p(t) \,||^m \ + \alpha_v \,||\, v_{tar}(t) - v(t) \,||^n \qquad (38)$$

Box 4.

$$\begin{aligned} F_{att}(p, v) &= F_{att1}(p) + F_{att2}(v) \\ &= m\alpha_p \,||\, p_{tar}(t) - p(t) \,||^{m-1} n_{RT} + n\alpha_v \,||\, v_{tar}(t) - v(t) \,||^{n-1} n_{VRT} \end{aligned} \qquad (39)$$

Box 5.

$$U_{rep}(p, v) = \begin{cases} 0, \ if \ \rho_s(p, p_{obs}) - \rho_m(v_{RO}) \geq \rho_0 \ or \ v_{RO} \leq 0 \\ \eta(\dfrac{1}{\rho_s(p, p_{obs}) - \rho_m(v_{RO})} - \dfrac{1}{\rho_0}), \\ if \ 0 < \rho_s(p, p_{obs}) - \rho_m(v_{RO}) < \rho_0 \ and \ v_{RO} > 0 \end{cases} \qquad (40)$$

describing the influence range of the obstacle, $\rho_s(p, p_{obs})$ is the shortest distance between the robot and the obstacle, $\rho_m(v_{RO})$ is the shortest distance to the robot stop, a maximum deceleration of magnitude a_{max} is applied to the robot to reduce its velocity.

Repulsive force is defined by the negative gradient of the U_{rep} in Equation (40)

$$F_{rep}(p, v) == -\nabla_p U_{rep}(p, v) - \nabla_v U_{rep}(p, v)$$
(41)

where,

$$v_{RO}(t) = (v(t) - v_{obs}(t))^T \frac{p_{obs}(t) - p(t)}{\| p_{obs}(t) - p(t) \|}$$
(42)

The velocity and position gradients of $v_{RO}(t)$ are given as

$$\nabla_v v_{RO}(t) = n_{RO}$$
(43)

$$\nabla_p v_{RO}(t) = \frac{1}{\| p(t) - p_{obs}(t) \|} \times [v_{RO}(t) n_{RO} - (v(t) - v_{obs}(t))]$$
(44)

From the robot to the target, $v_{RO}(t) n_{RO}$ is the velocity component of $v(t) - v_{obs}(t)$. $v_{RO\perp}(t) n_{RO\perp}$ is perpendicular to $v_{RO}(t) n_{RO}$ which is given by

$$v_{RO\perp} n_{RO\perp} = v(t) - v_{obs}(t) - v_{RO}(t) n_{RO}$$
(45)

where,

$$v_{RO\perp} = \sqrt{\| v(t) - v_{obs}(t) \|^2 - v_{RO}^2(t)}$$

$$n_{RO\perp}^T n_{RO} = 1$$

Equation (44) becomes

$$\nabla_p v_{RO}(t) = -\frac{1}{\| p(t) - p_{obs}(t) \|} v_{RO\perp} n_{RO\perp}$$
(46)

Considering the safe radius r_{rob} of the robot, the distance ρ_s to the obstacle is modified by $\rho_s - r_{rob}$. With F_{rep1} and F_{rep2}, the repulsive force is described Box 6.

F_{rep1} is in the opposite direction of $v_{RO} n_{RO}$, it keeps the robot away from the obstacle. F_{rep2} is in the same direction of $v_{RO\perp} n_{RO\perp}$, it decides the moving direction of the robot.

F_s is defined as detouring force for the obstacle avoidance by

$$F_s = K_s (\| F_{rep1} \| + \| F_{rep2} \|) N_s$$
(48)

where, K_s is positive constant, N_s is the unit vector in the tangential direction of the ellipse which the obstacle is approximately expressed.

In the following, the expression of approximating the obstacle is described. Assuming that the isolated obstacle could be approximately as an ellipse (as shown in Figure 5). X_i, Y_i are local coordinates of the obstacle, (x_{oi}, y_{oi}) is position

Box 6.

$$F_{rep}(p, v) = F_{rep1} + F_{rep2} = \frac{-\eta}{(\rho_s(p, p_{obs}) - \rho_m(v_{RO}))^2} \left(1 + \frac{v_{RO}}{a_{max}}\right) n_{RO}$$

$$+ \frac{\eta v_{RO} v_{RO\perp}}{(\rho_s(p, p_{obs}) - \rho_m(v_{RO}))^2 a_{max} \rho_s(p, p_{obs})} n_{RO\perp}$$
(47)

Figure 5. Detouring force F_s

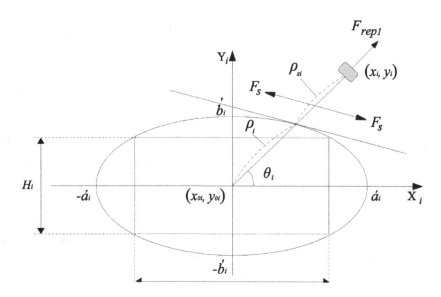

of the obstacle, (x_i, y_i) is local position of the robot and θ_i is heading angle of the robot in local coordinates. The length of inscribed ellipse of rectangle in cross and in vertical axis a_i, b_i are defined in (49) by width W_i and height H_i of the obstacle.

$$a_i = \frac{W_i}{2}, \quad b_i = \frac{H_i}{2} \tag{49}$$

The length of circumscribed ellipse of rectangle in cross and in vertical axis a_i', b_i' are given by

$$
\begin{aligned}
a_i' &= a_i \sqrt{\frac{a_i^2 + b_i^2}{a_i^2 \cos^2\varphi_i + b_i^2 \sin^2\varphi_i}} \quad, \\
b_i' &= b_i \sqrt{\frac{a_i^2 + b_i^2}{a_i^2 \cos^2\varphi_i + b_i^2 \sin^2\varphi_i}}
\end{aligned}
\tag{50}
$$

where, $\varphi_i = \tan^{-1}(\dfrac{b_i}{a_i})$. Radius of the circumscribed ellipse is given by

$$\rho_i = \sqrt{a_i'^2 \cos^2\theta_i + b_i'^2 \sin^2\theta_i} \tag{51}$$

The shortest distance between the robot and the body of obstacle ρ_{si} is given by

$$\rho_{si} = \sqrt{x_i^2 + y_i^2} - \rho_i \tag{52}$$

Then, the obstacle is approximately expressed by an ellipse.

As a result, F_s can drive the robot move on the tangential direction of the ellipse (as shown in Figure 5). The direction of F_s is divided into the direction of clockwise or the direction of anti-clockwise responding to the position of the obstacle and the target. F_s is given in proportion to repulsive force from the obstacle. The applicable range of F_s is that the robot lies on the range shown by θ^*, where the robot hits the part of the obstacle shadow in view of the target. The proposed controller includes the integration virtual force F_{total} with a detouring force F_s. In the calculation of the $F_{total}, F_{att}, F_{rep}$ and F_s, estimation results x_r, y_r and θ_r are of the parameters of controller.

The stability of the proposed controller can be guaranteed. m and n are usually chosen as $m = n = 2$, and for fast convergence of tracking errors with no oscillation, α_p and α_v are chosen such that the system has critical damping ratio (Ge, 2002).

Controller Parameter Estimation by Using SVM/LS-SVM Method

The controller is designed in the dynamic environments, local minima problem is achieved by designing the detouring virtual force, where the potential function used for the design of the controller considers the Euclidean distance information and the magnitude information of the relative velocity between the robot and the target/obstacle. The parameter estimation of the controller is described. As mentioned, the uncertainty in the observation information can be reduced by using the estimation results of the position information. The essential purpose is to reduce the noise effect of the control process, and to make the motion control of the mobile robot from an initial position to track the moving target in a desired manner while avoiding the moving obstacles. Accordingly, the design of the estimation functions differs from the estimation functions in the static environments.

The desired position information could be estimated by using the measurement position information. Let (x_r, y_r, θ_r) be the position information which would be estimated and (x, y, θ) be the measurement position information. At first, estimated functions are redesigned in Box 7.

Where, $Dis(rob, obs)$ is the shortest distance between the robot and the obstacle, $Dis(rob, tar)$ is the shortest distance between the robot and the target. x, y, θ, u_1, u_2, $Dis(rob, obs)$, $Dis(rob, tar)$ are the features which are crucial factors for obtaining the estimation models. The features of the estimated functions are selected respectively, which are of considerable influential factors and are different from the ones in the static environments. That is, x position, heading angle, translational velocity of the mobile robot, the shortest distance between the robot and the obstacle and the shortest distance between the robot and the target are the features in designing the estimated function of the x_r position. y position, heading angle, translational velocity of the mobile robot, the shortest distance between the robot and the obstacle and the shortest distance between the robot and the target are the features in designing the estimated function of the y_r position. Heading angle, angular velocity of the mobile robot, the shortest distance between the robot and the obstacle and the shortest distance between the robot and the target are the features in designing the estimated function of the θ_r.

Then, according to these features, the desired models of the mobile robot can be obtained from the training data.

Finally, with the estimation models, the uncertainty of the observation information can be reduced. The more accurate position information of the mobile robot can be obtained. The estimated x_r, y_r, θ_r are used as parameters for the design of the controller in the dynamic environments.

Box 7.

$$\begin{cases} x_r &= f(x, \theta, u_1, Dis(rob, obs), Dis(rob, tar)) \\ y_r &= g(y, \theta, u_1, Dis(rob, obs), Dis(rob, tar)) \\ \theta_r &= h(\theta, u_2, Dis(rob, obs), Dis(rob, tar)) \end{cases} \tag{53}$$

Evaluation of the SVM Method by Using Experimental Data

An experimental robot system is comprised of several systems working together as a whole. The general categories of the robot system are controller, body, sensors and communication unit. The controller is the robot's brain and controls the robot's movements. It's usually a computer of some type which is used to store information about the robot and the work environments and to store and execute programs which operate the robot. The control system contains programs, data algorithms, logic analysis and various other processing activities which enable the robot to perform. The body of the robot is related to the job it must perform. In this research, the two wheeled mobile robot is considered. Sensors are the perceptual system and measure physical quantities like distance. Sensors provide the raw information or signals that must be processed to provide meaningful information. Here, the global digital camera is equipped so the robot can have the understanding of their surrounding environments and make changes in its behavior based on the information gathered. The control system is based on H8/3048F series which is a series of high-performance microcontrollers that integrate system supporting functions together with an H8/300H CPU core.

An experiment with real robot (the two-wheel differentially-driven mobile robot) is done for testing the experimental data of the mobile robot in order to evaluate the effectiveness of SVM method. The parameters of the experimental robot are shown as follows.

- Radius of the robot: $7.5\,[cm]$
- Mass of the robot: $2.5\,[Kg]$
- Moment of inertia of the robot: $7.03125 \times 10^{-3}\,[kgm^2]$
- Radius of the wheel: $3.5\,[cm]$
- Moment of inertia of the wheel: $3.0625 \times 10^{-5}\,[kgm^2]$

In the robot field, the navigation path of the robot is designed by moving on a circle along clockwise direction. The robot moves by the velocity order from controller. In the upper part of the field, the camera is set up for measuring the position information of the robot. Then, the measured data is sent back to computer.

In Figure 6, the measured data is shown by dashed line. Obviously, it has large bias. The desired result is shown by solid line. The proposed method based on SVM is used for reducing the undesired effect. The proposed result is shown by dotted line. From Figure 6, SVM based method is successful for reducing the undesired effect in the real robot system.

Here, it mainly emphasizes that the SVM method can be applicable to the mobile robot motion control, where a basic SVM method is used. Also, the result of using the SVM method for the real robot data has been shown.

Simulation Results

For evaluating the effectiveness of the proposed controller, local minima problem is considered with the moving obstacle and the moving target in the dynamic environments. For using the proposed scheme, LibSVM (Chang, 2011) is selected to obtain the models of the estimated position and the estimated heading angle which are mixed with noise. The parameters are set as follows.

Virtual force parameter:

$$a_p = 0.08,\ a_v = 0.4,\ m = 2,\ n = 2$$

$$\eta = 0.1,\ K_s = 0.1,\ \rho_0 = 5.0,\ a_{max} = 10$$

Controller parameter:

$$\alpha = 0.8,\ \beta = 10.0,\ \varepsilon = 0.001,$$

$$\sigma^2 = 3,\ C = 1000$$

Figure 6. Comparing results by using experimental data

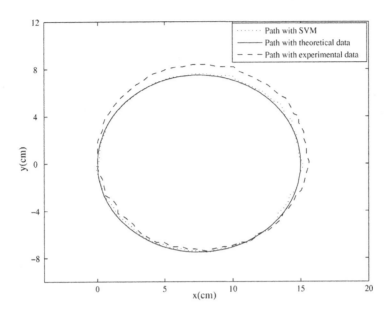

In order to simulate the measured data, random noise is introduced into x, y and θ. Namely, the noise brings the uncertainties to the control system. The case is given by considering the moving obstacle and the moving target. The robot converges to the moving target with the moving obstacle avoidance (MOA). Near by the target, the attractive force becomes smaller, so the robot takes longer time to catch the target. The robot is assumed to do iteration movement. The motion control of the robot by using the proposed method is also stable and accurate than the one without using the proposed method. Local minima avoidance by using the virtual force are achieved, where the reference results of the control system are shown by solid line (see Figures 7 and 8), the proposed control results with noise are shown by dashed line in Figure 7(a), the control results with the proposed controller are shown by dashed line (see Figure 7(b) and Figure 8). The proposed result is closer to the reference control result without the noise. The reference results of the robot system are shown by solid line (as Figures 7 and 8 shown). The result with noise by using standard SVM is shown by dashed line in Figure 7(b). It can be seen that SVM-based results are near results. In LS-SVM, function estimation is done by solving a linear set of equations instead of solving a quadratic problem in standard SVM. The LS-SVM formulation also involves less tuning parameters. The result by using LS-SVM is closer to the reference one than the result by using standard SVM (as Figure 8 shown). However, the main difference between them is the training time of the estimated model. In the similar simulation environments, 6 times training by standard SVM and LS-LSM is made as follows.

- **Standard SVM:** 11.001s, 10.875 s, 11.811s, 10.955s, 11.873s, 11.071s,
- **LS-SVM:** 7.829s, 7.703s, 7.875s, 7.859s, 7.907s, 7.938s.

Figure 7. Moving obstacle avoidance by using SVM

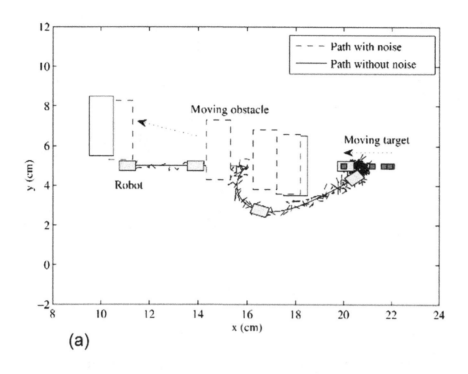

(a)

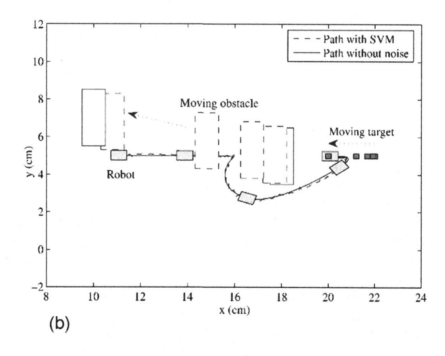

(b)

Figure 8. Moving obstacle avoidance by using LS-SVM

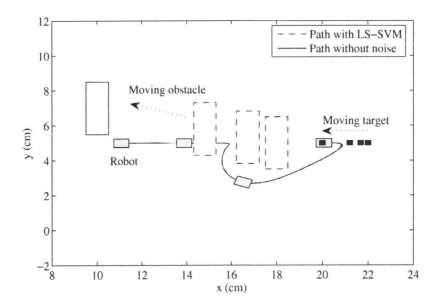

Obviously, the training time of the standard SVM is longer than the LS-SVM. That is, LS-SVM simplifies the required computation.

CONCLUSION

The research has developed two kinds of control schemes for the mobile robot motion control and obstacle avoidance with reducing the noise effect during the navigation of the mobile robot, the control schemes aim towards smooth and accurate motion for the mobile robot in different kinds of environments. SVM and LS-SVM based control scheme are considered, where the SVM method and LS-SVM method are used for reducing the noise effect of the measured data. That is, a method to drive the mobile robot to the goal position avoiding the obstacles under the uncertain measured data is proposed based on the potential field method. Stability of the control system can be guaranteed, the goal point in the state space of the controlled system becomes the only globally stable equilibrium point, and convergence to the goal point.

Simulations are given for validating of the proposed control schemes. Some kinds of cases in the static environments, as well as in the dynamic environments are illustrated to validate the effectiveness of the proposed schemes. It is shown that the motion of the mobile robot has been controlled smoothly and accurately.

On the other hand, there exit limitations of SVM on engineering application. It is mainly reflecting in the training speed and large datasets. For improving the perfomance of SVM, some research works are presented by focusing on selection of the optimal tuning parameters and simplification of the training algorithm. Improvement are obtained. In our future work, it is a further area for research to explore the synthetic with SVM and other machine learing algriothms. It is desired to improve the perfomance of SVM with the simplest and most effective.

REFERENCES

Adankon, M. M., & Cheriet, M. (2009). Model selection for the LSSVM. Application to handwriting recognition. *Pattern Recognition, 42*(12), 3264–3270. doi:10.1016/j.patcog.2008.10.023

Al-Taharwa, I., Sheta, A., & Al-Weshah, M. (2008). A mobile robot path planning using genetic algorithm in static environment. *Journal of Computer Science, 4*(4), 341–344. doi:10.3844/jcssp.2008.341.344

Chang, C. C., & Lin, C. J. (2011). *LibSVM - A library for support vector machines.* Retrieved from http://www.csie.ntu.edu.tw/~cjlin/libsvm/.

Cherkassky, V., & Ma, Y. (2004). Practical selection of SVM parameters and noise estimation for SVM regression. *Neural Networks, 17*, 113–126. doi:10.1016/S0893-6080(03)00169-2

De Brabanter, K., Karsmakers, P., Ojeda, F., Alzate, C., De Brabanter, J., & Pelckmans, K. ... Suykens, J. A. K. (2011). *The LS-SVMlab toolbox homepage.* Retrieved from http://www.esat.kuleuven.be/sista/lssvmlab/

Deng, M., Inoue, A., & Sekiguchi, K. (2008). Lyapunov function base obstacle avoidance scheme for a two wheeled mobile robot. *Journal of Control Theory and Applications, 6*(4), 399–404. doi:10.1007/s11768-008-7017-y

Dixon, W. E., Jiang, Z. P., & Dawson, D. M. (2000). Global exponential setpoint control of wheeled mobile robots: A Lyapunov approach. *Automatica, 56*(11), 1741–1746. doi:10.1016/S0005-1098(00)00099-6

Ge, S. S., & Cui, Y. J. (2000). New potential functions for mobile robot path planning. *IEEE Transactions on Robotics and Automation, 16*(5), 615–620. doi:10.1109/70.880813

Ge, S. S., & Cui, Y. J. (2002). Dynamic motion planning for mobile robots using potential field method. *Autonomous Robots, 13*(3), 207–222. doi:10.1023/A:1020564024509

Hwang, Y. K., & Ahuja, N. (1992). A potential field approach to path planning. *IEEE Transactions on Robotics and Automation, 8*(1), 23–32. doi:10.1109/70.127236

Kim, J. O., & Khosla, P. K. (1992). Real-time obstacle avoidance using harmonic potential functions. *IEEE Transactions on Robotics and Automation, 8*(3), 338–349. doi:10.1109/70.143352

Koren, Y., & Borenstein, J. (1991). Potential field methods and their inherent limitations for mobile robot navigation. In *Proceedings of the IEEE Conference on Robotics and Automation,* Sacramento, California, (pp. 1398-1404).

Latombe, J. C. (1991). *Robot motion planning.* Kluwer Academic Publishers.

Laumond, J. P. (1998). *Robot motion planning and control.* Springer. doi:10.1007/BFb0036069

LaValle, S. M. (2006). *Planning algorithms.* Cambridge University Press. doi:10.1017/CBO9780511546877

Lendasse, A., Ji, Y., Reyhani, N., & Verleysen, M. (2005). LS-SVM hyperparameter selection with a nonparametric noise estimator. *Artificial Neural Networks: Formal Models and Their Applications - ICANN 2005, 3697*, (pp. 625-630).

Li, D. (2009). Support vector regression based image denoising. *Image and Vision Computing, 27*(6), 623–627. doi:10.1016/j.imavis.2008.06.006

Loizou, S. G., Tanner, H. G., Kumar, V., & Kyriakopoulos, K. J. (2003). Closed loop navigation for mobile agents in dynamic environments. In *Proceedings of the IEEE/RSJ International Conference on Intelligent Robots and Systems,* Las Vegas, Nevada, (pp. 3769-3774).

Luh, G. C., & Liu, W. W. (2007). Motion planning for mobile robots in dynamic environments using a potential field immune network. *Proceedings of the Institution of Mechanical Engineers. Part I, Journal of Systems and Control Engineering*, *221*, 1033–1045. doi:10.1243/09596518JSCE400

Mabrouk, M. H., & McInnes, C. R. (2008). Solving the potential field local minimum problem using internal agent states. *Robotics and Autonomous Systems*, *56*, 1050–1060. doi:10.1016/j.robot.2008.09.006

Mita, T. (2000). *Introduction to nonlinear control theory - Skill control of underactuated robots*. Shokodo Co. Ltd. (In Japanese)

Müller, K. R., Smola, A. J., Rätsch, G., Schölkopf, B., Kohlmorgen, J., & Vapnik, V. (1997). Predicting time series with support vector machine. In *Proceedings of 7th International Conference on Artificial Neural Networks, Springer Lecture in Computer Science 1327*, Berlin, (pp. 999-1004).

Okuma, K., Urakudo, T., & Tada, Y. (2004) Lyapunov control of a two wheeled mobile robot in the presence of obstacles. In *Proceedings of 2004 Japan-USA Symposium on Flexible Automation*, Denver, Colorado, CD-ROM(JS-026).

Rimon, E., & Koditschek, D. E. (1992). Exact robot navigation using artificial potential functions. *IEEE Transactions on Robotics and Automation*, *8*(5), 501–518. doi:10.1109/70.163777

Schölkopf, B., Burges, C. J. C., & Smola, A. J. (1999). *Advances in kernel methods-support vector learning*. Cambridge, MA: MIT Press.

Schölkopf, B., & Smola, A. J. (2005). *Learning with kernels-support vector machines, regularization, optimization, and beyond*. London, UK: The MIT Press.

Scholköpf, B., Sung, K. K., Burges, C. J. C., Girosi, F., Niyogi, P., Poggio, T., & Vapnik, V. (1997). Comparing support vector machines with gaussian kernels to radial basis function classifiers. *IEEE Transactions on Signal Processing*, *45*(11), 2758–2765. doi:10.1109/78.650102

Smola, A. J., & Scholköpf, B. (1998). *A tutorial on support vector regression*. NeuroCOLT2 Technical Report NC-TR-98-030, Royal Holloway College, University of London, UK.

Suykens, J. A. K., Van Gestel, T., De Brabanter, J., De Moor, B., & Vandewalle, J. (2002). *Least squares support vector machines*. Singapore: World Scientific.

Suykens, J. A. K., & Vandewalle, J. (1999). Least squares support vector machine classifiers. *Neural Processing Letters*, *9*(3), 293–300. doi:10.1023/A:1018628609742

Tsuchiya, K., Urakubo, T., & Tsujita, K. (1999). Motion control of a nonholonomic system based on the Lyapunov control method. *Journal of Guidance, Control, and Dynamics*, *25*(2), 285–290. doi:10.2514/2.4880

Vapnik, V. N. (1995). *The nature of statistical learning theory*. New York, NY: Springer-Verlag.

Widodo, A., & Yang, B. S. (2007). Support vector machine in machine condition monitoring and fault diagnosis. *Mechanical Systems and Signal Processing*, *21*, 2560–2574. doi:10.1016/j.ymssp.2006.12.007

Zhou, L., Yang, H., & Liu, C. (2008). QPSO-Based hyper-parameters selection for LS-SVM regression. In *Proceedings of the 4th IEEE International Conference on Natural Computation*, Jinan, (pp. 130-133).

ADDITIONAL READING

Agirrebeitia, J., Avil`es, R., Bustos, I. F. D., & Ajuria, G. (2005). A new APF strategy for path planning in environments with obstacles. *Mechanism and Machine Theory, 40*(6), 645–658. doi:10.1016/j.mechmachtheory.2005.01.006

Alexander, J. C., & Maddocks, J. H. (1989). On the kinematics of wheeled mobile robots. *The International Journal of Robotics Research, 8*(5), 15–27. doi:10.1177/027836498900800502

Chung, T. L., Bui, T. H., Kim, S. B., & Oh, M. S. (2004). Wall-following control of a two-wheeled mobile robot. *The Korean Society of Mechanical Engineers International Journal, 18*(8), 1288–1296.

Conkur, E. S. (2005). Path planning using potential fields for highly redundant manipulators. *Robotics and Autonomous Systems, 52*, 209–228. doi:10.1016/j.robot.2005.03.005

Cristianini, N., & Shawe-Talor, J. (2005). *An introduction to support vector machines and other kernel-based learning methods*. London, UK: Cambridge University Press.

Deng, M., Saijo, N., Gomi, H., & Inoue, A. (2006). A robust real time method for estimating human multijoint arm viscoelasticity. *International Journal of Innovative Computing . Information and Control, 2*(4), 705–721.

Drew, M. (1992). Robot planning. [AAAI]. *AI Magazine: The Advancement of Artificial Intelligence, 13*(2), 55–79.

Ge, S. S., Fua, C. H., & Lim, K. W. (2004) Multi-robot formations: queues and artificial potential trenches. In *Proceedings of the IEEE International Conference on Robotics and Automation,* (pp. 3345-3350).

Gestel, T. V., Suykens, J. A. K., Baesens, B., Viaene, S., Vanthienen, J., & Dedene, G. (2004). Benchmarking least squares support vector machine classifiers. *Machine Learning, 54*, 5–32. doi:10.1023/B:MACH.0000008082.80494.e0

Gestel, T. V., Suykens, J. A. K., Baestaens, D. E., Lambrechts, A., Lanckriet, G., & Vandaele, B. (2001). Financial time series prediction using least squares support vector machines within the evidence framework. *IEEE Transactions on Neural Networks, 12*(4), 809–821. doi:10.1109/72.935093

He, X., & Chen, L. (2008) Path planning based on grid-potential fields. In *Proceedings of IEEE International Conference on Computer Science and Software Engineering*, Wuhan, China, (pp. 1114-1116).

Huang, L. (2007) A potential field approach for controlling a mobile robot to track a moving target. *The 22nd IEEE International Symposium on Intelligent Control Part of IEEE Multi-Conference on Systems and Control*, Singapore, (pp. 65-70).

Krzysztof, K. (2006). *Robot motion and control-recent developments. Lecture Notes in Control and Information Sciences, 335*. Springer.

Laumond, J. P., Sekhavat, S., & Vaisset, M. (1994) Collision-free motion planning for a nonholonomic mobile robot with trailers. *4th IFAC Symposium on Robot Control,* (pp. 171-177).

Lenoard, N. E., & Fiorelli, E. (2001). Virtual leaders, artificial potentials and coordinated control of groups. In *Proceedings of the 40th IEEE Conference on Decision and Control,* Orlando, Florida, USA, (pp. 2968-2973).

Li, Y., Guan, C., Li, H., & Chin, Z. (2008). A self-training semi-supervised SVM algorithm and its application in an EEG-based brain computer interface speller system. *Pattern Recognition Letters, 29*(9), 1285–1294. doi:10.1016/j.patrec.2008.01.030

Louste, C., & Liégeois, A. (2002). Path planning for non-holonomic vehicles: A potential viscous fluid field method. *Robotica, 20*(3), 291–298. doi:10.1017/S0263574701003691

Luo, Z., Wang, P., Li, Y., Zhang, W., Tang, W., & Xiang, M. (2008). Quantum-inspired evolutionary tuning of SVM parameters. *Progress in Natural Science, 18*(4), 475–480. doi:10.1016/j.pnsc.2007.11.012

Mester, G. (2006). Motion control of wheeled mobile robots. *The 4th Serbian-Hungarian Joint Symposium on Intelligent Systems*, (pp. 119-130).

Nof, S. Y. (1999). *Handbook of industrial robotics* (2nd ed.). New York, NY: Wiley. doi:10.1002/9780470172506

Sekhavat, S., & Chyba, M. (1999) Nonholonomic deformation of a potential field for motion planning. In *Proceedings of IEEE International Conference on Robotics and Automation*, Detroit, Michigan, (pp. 817-822).

Suykens, J. A. K., Lukas, L., & Vandewalle, J. (2000). Sparse approximation using least squares support vector machines. *IEEE International Symposium on Circuits and Systems*, (pp. II-757-II-760).

Suykens, J. A. K., Vandewalle, J., & De Moor, B. (2001). Optimal control by least squares support vector machines. *Neural Networks, 14*, 23–35. doi:10.1016/S0893-6080(00)00077-0

Takeuchi, M., Yamada, M., & Mizuno, N. (2007). Adaptive control of a twowheeled mobile robot avoiding obstacles. In *Proceedings of 7th SICE Symposium on Adaptive, Learning and Control, Tokyo*, Japan, (pp. 45-48). (In Japanese)

Tanner, H. G., Loizou, S., & Kyriakopoulos, K. J. (2001). Nonholonomic stabilization with collision avoidance for mobile robots. *Proceedings of the IEEE/RSJ International Conference on Intelligent Robots and Systems, Maul*, USA, (pp. 1220-1225).

Tsuchiya, K., Urakubo, T., & Tsujita, K. (1999). A motion control of a two-wheeled mobile robot. In *Proceedings of IEEE International Conference on Systems, Man, and Cybernetics, 5*, 690-696.

Urakubo, T., Okuma, K., & Tada, Y. (2004) Feedback control of a two wheeled mobile robot with obstacle avoidance using potential functions. In *Proceedings of IEEE/RSJ International Conference on Intelligent Robots and Systems*, Sendai, Japan, (pp. 2428-2433).

Üstün, B., Melssen, W. J., Oudenhuijzen, M., & Buydens, L. M. C. (2005). Determination of optimal support vector regression parameters by genetic algorithms and simplex optimization. *Analytiça Chimica Acta, 544*(1-2), 292–305. doi:10.1016/j.aca.2004.12.024

Wang, Y., & Chirikjian, G. S. (2000) A new potential field method for robot path planning. In *Proceedings of the IEEE International Conference on Robotics and Automation, San Francisco*, CA, (pp. 977-982).

Yang, J., Zhang, Y., & Zhu, Y. (2007). Intelligent fault diagnosis of rolling element bearing based on SVMs and fractal dimension . *Mechanical Systems and Signal Processing, 21*, 2012–2024. doi:10.1016/j.ymssp.2006.10.005

KEY TERMS AND DEFINITIONS

Controller Design in Different Environments: It relies on the controlled variables for the design of the controller in the given environments and steers the robot toward the desired set-point.

Least Squares Support Vector Machines: LS-SVM are reformulations to classical SVM. It solves a set of linear equations instead of a convex problem.

Obstacle Avoidance: It aim at enabling robots deal with identification of obstacle free trajectories between the starting point and goal point.

Path Planning: It aim at enabling robots attain the goal without collision with other objects in given environments.

Potential Field: It generate optimal path planning by artificial repulsive field to navigate the robot away from obstacles and artificial attractive field to navigate the robot toward the goal.

Support Vector Machine: It is based on the idea of structural risk minimization and is to solve convex optimization problems. SVM has been widely used for various classification and regression analysis.

Two Wheeled Mobile Robot: It can be driven by two differentially driven wheels.

Chapter 9
A Hybrid Meta-Heuristic to Solve a Multi-Criteria HFS Problem

Fatima Ghedjati
*Laboratoire CReSTIC-Reims (Centre de Recherche en STIC), IUT de Reims-Châlons-Charleville,
France*

Safa Khalouli
*Laboratoire CReSTIC-Reims (Centre de Recherche en STIC), IUT de Reims-Châlons-Charleville,
France*

ABSTRACT

In this chapter the authors address a hybrid flow shop scheduling problem considering the minimization of the makespan in addition to the sum of earliness and tardiness penalties. This problem is proven to be NP-hard, and consequently the development of heuristic and meta-heuristic approaches to solve it is well justified. So, to deal with this problem, the authors propose a method which consists on the one hand, on using a meta-heuristic based on ant colony optimization algorithm to generate feasible solutions and, on the other hand, on using an aggregation multi-criteria method based on fuzzy logic to assist the decision-maker to express his preferences according to the considered objective functions. The aggregation method uses the Choquet integral. This latter allows to take into account the interactions between the different criteria. Experiments based on randomly generated instances were conducted to test the effectiveness of the approach.

INTRODUCTION

Scheduling problems are encountered at all levels and in all sectors of activity. Most scheduling problems are very difficult to solve ((Blazewicz, Ecker, Pesch, & Schmidt, 1996)and (Graham, Lawler, & Rinnooy Kan, 1979)). That's why the majority of the problems addressed in scheduling are only evaluated by a single criterion (such as makespan, total tardiness, workloads of machines, etc) (T'kindt & Billaut, 2002). However, in the literature, many researches in scheduling show

DOI: 10.4018/978-1-4666-2086-5.ch009

that the majority of combinatorial optimization problems and especially the industrial ones involve generally simultaneous incommensurable criteria, which they can sometimes be contradictory. The combining of several criteria induces additional complexity. Optimizing multi-criteria problems seeks to optimize several components of a vector cost function (Talbi, 1999). Unlike single criterion optimization problems, there is no single optimal solution for multi-criteria problems, but a set of compromises solutions, known as Pareto-optimal solutions. These solutions are optimal in the wider sense that no other solutions in search space are superior to them when all criteria are considered (Zitzler & Thiele, 1999).

The hybrid flow shop (HFS), also called multiprocessor or flow shop with parallel machines, consists of a set of two or more processing stages (or centers) with at least one stage having two or more parallel machines. The hybrid characteristic of a flow shop is ubiquitously found in various industries. The duplication of the number of machines in some stages can introduce additional flexibility, increase the overall capacities, and avoid bottlenecks if some operations are too long. So, scheduling in HFS has a great importance from both theoretical and practical view points.

The main goal of this chapter is to present a solution methodology for solving a multi-criteria HFS problem. The considered objective is to simultaneously minimize the following criteria:

1. Minimize the completion date of all the jobs (makespan),
2. Minimize the weighted sum of the earliness and tardiness (ET) penalties.

The ET problem encompasses a category of problems with the objective to complete each job as close to its due date possible. It represents a non-regular optimization criteria based on due dates (Gupta, Krüger, Lauff, Werner, & Sotskov, 2002). This objective represents just in time (JIT) production concept (Portmann & Mouloua, 2007).

In fact, in a JIT environment, minimizing earliness would reduce inventory costs and/or deterioration of product while minimizing tardiness would reduce a late cost or the loss of customers. In this scenario both early and tardy completion of jobs is disadvantageous to manufacturers and customers. Each job has a distinct earliness or tardiness penalty weight, which represents the importance of a job production system. This multi-criteria scheduling problem is NP-hard since the simpler mono-criterion HFS problem, made up of two stages and having at least two machines available in one of the stages, with makespan criterion is already NP-hard (Gupta, 1988). In addition, earliness/tardiness criteria, with distinct due dates, usually induce NP-hard problems (Hendel & Sourd, 2007). Therefore, the development of heuristics that can give eventually optimal or near optimal solutions is well justified. For solving scheduling problem, various intelligent heuristics and meta-heuristics have become popular such as simulated annealing (SA), tabu search (TS), multi-agent system (MAS), genetic algorithm (GA) and ant colony optimization algorithm (ACO). The literature for HFS problem has adopted regular measures of performance, mainly the makespan, the sum of completion time, the tardiness. However, most of the articles that tackle ET problems deal with single machine ((Merkle & Middendorf, 2005), (M'Hallah, 2007) and (Valente & Alves, 2007)). Also, many results exist for parallel machine earliness/tardiness scheduling problems, especially when all jobs have the same due date ((Balakrishnan, Kanet, & Sridharan, 1999) and (Ventura & Kim, 2003)). However, relatively little researches have considered the ET costs in the objective function on flow and job shop environments. So, Rajendran and Alicke (Rajendran & Alicke, 2007) developed some dispatching rules to solve the flow shop ET problem with bottleneck machines. In (Valencia & Rabadi, 2003) the authors proposed a MAS approach to solve the job shop ET problem with common due date. For the job shop ET problem an ACO algorithm is presented in (Huang & Yang, 2008). To deal with the flexible job shop ET problem, a MAS scheduling method is proposed in (Wu & Weng, 2005). To our knowledge, there is a limited literature focused on the ET criteria for solving the HFS scheduling problems (Khalouli, Ghedjati, & Hamzaoui, 2010). In (Janiak, Kozan, Lichtenstein, & Oguz, 2007) three meta-heuristic approaches based on a simulated annealing SA, TS, and a hybrid SA/TS have been used to solve the HFS problem which minimizes the cost criterion consisting of the total weighted earliness, the total weighted tardiness and the total weighted waiting time. Some existing heuristic solution approaches for the classical permutation flow shop problem have been generalized for the HFS problem with controllable jobs and assignable due dates with the sum of earliness and tardiness penalties, weighted completion time of jobs and the costs of due date assignments (Gupta, Krüger, Lauff, Werner, & Sotskov, 2002).

In this chapter, we propose the development of a multi-criteria decision making methodology (Pomerol & Barba-Romero, 2000). Our purpose is to solve the proposed HFS scheduling problem by using an ACO meta-heuristic optimization and an evaluation module. This latter considers an aggregation method based on fuzzy logic to assist the decision-maker in expressing his preferences according to the considered objective functions. The aggregation method uses the Choquet integral which allows us to take into account the interactions between various criteria. The choice of ACO to solve the considered scheduling problem has the advantage of conducting at the end of the search to a population of diverse solutions. If several criteria are taken into account, this diversity is an advantage since it allows having multiple solutions. Indeed, ACO has been successfully used in solving several single criterion scheduling problems (see for example (Alaykýran, Engin, & Döyen, 2007), (Khalouli, Ghedjati, & Hamzaoui, 2008a), Khalouli, Ghedjati, & Hamzaoui, 2009). It has also been applied to multi-criteria schedul-

ing problems such as in ((Gravel, Price, & Gagné, 2002), (Khalouli, Ghedjati, & Hamzaoui, 2008b) and (Yagmahan & Yenisey, 2010).

The rest of the chapter is arranged as follows. Section 2 is dedicated to the description of the considered HFS scheduling problem. Basic definitions are presented in order to understand the multi-criteria optimization problem in section 3. In Section 4, the proposed approach to solve this problem is given. Computational results are provided in section 5 to show the efficiency of the suggested methodology. Finally, Section 6 concludes the chapter.

PROBLEM FORMULATION

The manufacturing environment of the HFS is considered as an extension of the classical flow shop. In fact, it presents a multistage production process with the property that a set of n jobs needs to be processed at all the stages in the same order, starting at stage 1 until finishing in stage S. Each stage i consists of a given number $m_i \left(m_i \geq 1 \right)$ of identical parallel machines available from time zero, and denoted $M_i = \left\{ M_{i1}, M_{i2}, ..., M_{i,m_i} \right\}$. So each job j needs several operations $O_{1j}, O_{2j}, ..., O_{Sj}$, where O_{ij} has to be processed by one machine out of a set of given machines at the ith stage during an uninterrupted p_{ij} time units (the preemption is not allowed) and can start only after the completion of the $\left(i - 1 \right)$ previous operations. Solving such a problem consists on assigning operations to machines on each stage (routing problem) and sequencing the operations assigned to the same machine (scheduling problem). Then, in order to find a feasible solution, a starting time t_{ij} and a completion time C_{ij} have to be computed for each operation O_{ij} in stage i. The completion time and the due date of a job j are denoted C_j and d_j, respectively. We assume that:

- Setting up times of machines and move times between operations are negligible;
- Machines are independent from each other;
- Jobs are independent from each other;
- At a given time, a machine can only execute one operation. It becomes available to other operations only if the operation which is processing is completed.

The objective is to find an optimal ordering through the S stages for the n jobs, by taking advantage of the multiple machines in stages, to minimize the following criteria:

- The completion time of the last job at the last stage or makespan:

$$f_1 = C_{\max} = \max_{1 \le j \le n} C_j \qquad (1)$$

- The sum of the weighted earliness/tardiness (ET) costs:

$$f_2 = \sum_{j=1}^{n} (\omega_j^E \cdot E_j + \omega_j^T \cdot T_j) \qquad (2)$$

where:

$E_j = \max(0, d_j - C_j)$ is the earliness of job j;

$T_j = \max(0, C_j - d_j)$ is the tardiness of job j;

ω_j^E is the earliness penalty weight of job j;

ω_j^T is the tardiness penalty weight of job j.

MULTI-CRITERIA OPTIMIZATION

Let $f_1, f_2, \cdots, f_{n_c}$ the n_c ($n_c \ge 2$) criterion functions of a multi-criteria optimization problem (MOP). The MOP is formally described by the following formulation:

$$\underset{x \in \Omega}{\text{minimize}} \; F(x) = \left(f_1(x), f_2(x), \cdots, f_{n_c}(x) \right) \qquad (3)$$

where Ω is a feasible solution space and $x = (x_1, x_2, \cdots, x_L)$ is a possible solution for the considered problem. In order to solve such a problem, we have to search solutions that represent a compromise between the criteria. Different heuristics and meta-heuristics have been proposed to solve the MOP. They can be classified into three categories (Talbi, 1999):

- The first consists on methods based on transforming the multi-criteria problem into a mono-criterion one. In this case the system returns a solution to the decision maker. This type of methods enables the decision maker to intervene before the resolution process by giving preference between criteria such as aggregation operator which combines a set of criteria into a single criterion function. Such approaches are known as priori approach. Among them, there are aggregation methods, E-constraint and the goal programming.
- The second category includes methods called non-Pareto. They use operators that optimize each criterion independently. These approaches enabling the decision maker to intervene during the course of the resolution process are called interactive.
- The last category contains methods known as Pareto ones. They use the Pareto dominance concept for the selection of generated solutions. These approaches enable the decision maker to intervene after the reso-

lution process. They represent posteriori approaches. Posteriori methods aim to provide the decision maker with an exhaustive set of Pareto optima, among which belongs the most satisfactory solution (i.e., the set of all non-dominated solutions in the multi-objective space). It satisfies two goals: the convergence towards the Pareto front and the obtaining of diversified solutions scattered all over the Pareto front.

In the case of our work, we focus on the first category of resolution by using an aggregation method for the conception of the decision maker support. Naturally, no aggregation method can respect all requirements. Therefore, it is necessary to decide on which requirement we are going to give up. One of the significant aspects in aggregation problems is the assigning weight to each criterion in order to give it a degree of importance. These are usually modeled by using weighted aggregation functions. The weighted arithmetic mean is the most used aggregation operators to express the preferences of the decision-maker on all the criteria (Grabisch, 1996; Marichal, 1998). They have the disadvantage of not being able to model any interaction among the criteria, since they consider their independence. The Choquet integral solves the problem of compensation between the criteria. It is considered as a weighted aggregation operator which can consider the interaction among the different criteria (Dubus, Gonzales, & Perny, 2009). Thus, to define the decision maker's preferences, we use the fuzzy integral to evaluate generated solutions. So, the solution of the problem, which takes into account the conflicting criteria, depends on the information that the decision maker can provide (T'kindt & Billaut, 2002).

Thus, a multi-criteria scheduling approach has to provide satisfactory solutions according to the preferences of the decision-maker. Thus, we developed a hybrid approach based on:

- A multi-criteria evaluation, based on the Choquet integral, which is used as the aggregation operator for computing a score. This latter takes into account the decision-maker preferences integrating the importance of each criterion independently as well as the interaction between them. So, all the criteria are reduced to only one objective.
- A meta-heuristic algorithm based on an ACO method for the resolution of the problem. The objective function is based on the Choquet integral used for criteria aggregation.

DESCRIPTION OF THE PROPOSED APPROACH

The Multi-Criteria Evaluation by Choquet Integral

In order to select the best schedule from the solutions obtained by our adapted multi-criteria ACS approach and according to the preference of the decision-maker, a fuzzy approach based on multi-criteria evaluation is used. This latter considers a Choquet integral aggregation tool, which is a fuzzy integral (Sugeno, 1977).

The Concept of Choquet Integral

The Choquet integral is a family of aggregation functions that can take into account the interactions between criteria, i.e. the redundancy or conflict between criteria. It is a sophisticated deformation of the weighted arithmetic mean model. In this latter model, a weight representing the importance of each criterion in the decision function is given. In the Choquet integral model, where criteria can be dependent, a fuzzy measure is used to define a weight on each combination of criteria and express the degree of importance for each combination. The aggregation by Choquet integral has been used in a multi-criteria scheduling in (Saad, Hammadi, Borne, & Benrejeb, 2008). In what follows, some necessary definitions related to the concept of Choquet integral, in order to introduce it, are presented according to Grabisch (Grabisch, 1996).

Definition 1: A fuzzy measure on the set $N_c = \{1, 2, \ldots, n_c\}$ of criteria is a function $\mu : F(N_C) \to [0, 1]$ satisfying:

1. $\mu(\varnothing) = 0$ and $\mu(N_C) = 1$ (boundary condition);
2. $\forall A \subset B \subset N_c \Rightarrow \mu(A) \leq \mu(B)$ (monotonicity condition).

In the context of multi-criteria aggregation, μ can be considered as the weight of importance to every subset of criteria A.

Definition 2: Let μ a fuzzy measure on the set N_c and $a = (a_1, a_2, \ldots, a_{n_c})$ the vector of criteria. The Choquet integral of a function C_μ with respect to μ is defined by:

$$C_\mu(a) = \sum_{i=1}^{n_c} \left(a_{\sigma(i)} - a_{\sigma(i-1)} \right) . \mu\left(\sigma(i), \ldots, \sigma(n_c) \right)$$

(4)

with $a_{\sigma(0)} = 0 \leq a_{\sigma(1)} \leq \cdots \leq a_{\sigma(n_c)}$.

For exemple:

$a = (a_1, a_2, a_3) = (0.9, 0.8, 0.5)$, then
$a_0 = 0 \leq a_{\sigma(1)=3} = 0.5 \leq a_{\sigma(2)=2} = 0.8 \leq a_{\sigma(3)=1} = 0.9$

Consequently:

$$C_\mu(0.9, 0.8, 0.5) = \left(a_{\sigma(1)} - a_{\sigma(0)} \right) . \mu\left(\sigma(1), \sigma(2), \sigma(3) \right)$$
$$+ \left(a_{\sigma(2)} - a_{\sigma(1)} \right) . \mu\left(\sigma(2), \sigma(3) \right)$$
$$+ \left(a_{\sigma(3)} - a_{\sigma(2)} \right) . \mu\left(\sigma(3) \right)$$

The result is:

$$C_\mu(0.9, 0.8, 0.5) = 0.5 \times \mu(3, 2, 1)$$
$$+ (0.8 - 0.5) \times \mu(2, 1)$$
$$+ (0.9 - 0.8) \times \mu(1).$$

The most common aggregation tool used in multi-criteria problem is the weighted sum, which take into account the importance of each criterion independently. In contrast, the Choquet integral is able to take into account the interactions between criteria, like the phenomenon of redundancy or synergy in addition to the importance of each criterion. Thus, we distinguish the importance of each criterion and the relative importance due to the interaction between these criteria.

The global importance of a criterion i is not determined solely by the fuzzy measure $\mu(i)$, but takes into account all measures $\mu(A)$ for a subset $A \subset N_C$ of all coalitions A for $i \in A$. Indeed, we can have almost zero suggesting that the objective i is unimportant. However we can get, by joining i to a coalition $A \subset N_C$, a value of $\mu(A \cup \{i\})$, that is greater than $\mu(A)$ suggesting the importance of criterion i in the decision. The calculation of the overall importance is based on the concept of Shapley index, derived from cooperative game theory (Grabisch, 1996).

Definition 3: The importance index or Shapley value of a criterion $i \in N_c$ with respect to $\mu(A)$, $A \subset N_c$ is defined by:

$$I_i = \sum_{A \subset N_c \setminus \{i\}} \frac{(n_c - |A| - 2)! |A|!}{(n_c - 1)!} . \left(\mu(A \cup \{i\}) - \mu(A) \right)$$

(5)

where $|A|$ is the cardinal of A.

The Shapley index is represented by the vector $\left[I_1, I_2, \cdots, I_{n_c}\right]$. This index calculates the average contribution of criterion i to all coalitions. A fundamental property of the Shapley index is that

$$\sum_{i=1}^{n_c} I_i = 1.$$

The index of interaction between criteria i and j is the average amount of synergy between i and j in the presence of a group of criteria.

Definition 4: The interaction index between two criteria $i, j \in N_c$ with respect to $\mu(A)$, $A \subset N_c$ is defined by:

$$I_{ij} = \sum_{A \subset N_c \setminus \{i\}} \frac{(n_c - |A| - 2)! |A|!}{(n_c - 1)!} \big(\mu(A \cup \{i, j\}) - \mu(A \cup \{i\}) - \mu(A \cup \{j\}) + \mu(A)\big)$$

(6)

Three situations can be considered depending on the importance of criteria i and j taken together:

- If $\mu(\{i, j\}) > \mu(\{i\}) + \mu(\{j\})$ then there is a complementarity synergy between these two criteria
- If $\mu(\{i, j\}) < \mu(\{i\}) + \mu(\{j\})$ then there is a redundancy or a negative synergy between these two criteria.
- If $\mu(\{i, j\}) = \mu(\{i\}) + \mu(\{j\})$ then the criteria are independent.

Based on the 2-additive measure (Grabisch, 1997) requiring $n_c \times (n_c + 1)/2$ coefficients represented by singletons and pairs of criteria), the Choquet integral can be expressed in terms of Shapley value and interaction index by the equation in Box 1. where $\wedge$ and $\vee$ are respectively the min and the max function, $I_i - \frac{1}{2}\sum_{i \neq j}|I_{ij}| \geq 0$ and

$$\sum_{i=1}^{n_c} I_i = 1.$$

The equation is decomposed into some conjunctive, disjunctive and additive parts corresponding respectively to positive, negative and zero synergies. So when:

- I_{ij} is positive, it implies a conjunctive behavior between criteria i and j. This indicates that the simultaneous satisfaction of these criteria is significant in the global evaluation and the satisfaction of one of the criteria will have a little effect. This represents a positive synergy between the two criteria.
- I_{ij} is negative, it implies a disjunctive behavior between criteria i and j. Thus, the satisfaction of one criterion is sufficient to have a significant effect in the global evaluation. This represents a negative synergy between the two criteria.
- I_{ij} is null, expressing the fact that the two criteria are independent and Shapley values act as a vector of weight in a weighted arithmetic average. This is the linear part of the Choquet integral.

Furthermore, the choice of the decision maker can be modeled by the interaction matrix for representing the weights of each criterion individually and their interactions as shown in Equation (8).

Box 1.

$$C_\mu(a) = \sum_{I_{i,j} \succ 0} (a_i \wedge a_j) I_{ij} + \sum_{I_{i,j} \prec 0} (a_i \vee a_j) |I_{ij}| + \sum_{i=1}^{n_c} a_i \left(I_i - \frac{1}{2}\sum_{i \neq j}|I_{ij}|\right)$$

(7)

$$I = \begin{pmatrix} I_1 & I_{12} & I_{13} & \cdots & I_{1n_c} \\ I_{12} & I_2 & I_{23} & \cdots & I_{2n_c} \\ I_{13} & I_{23} & I_3 & \cdots & I_{3n_c} \\ \vdots & \vdots & \vdots & \ddots & \vdots \\ I_{1n_c} & I_{2n_c} & I_{3n_c} & \cdots & I_{n_c} \end{pmatrix} \quad (8)$$

Illustrative Example: (Grabisch, 1996). This example considers the problem of evaluation of students in high school with respect to three subjects: mathematics (M), physics (P) and literature (L). The criteria are the marks obtained by the three students A, B and C in the three subjects (Table 1).

Usually, such an evaluation is done by a simple weighted sum, described by a linear combination of criteria $a = \left(a_1, a_2, \cdots, a_{n_c}\right)$, and presented by the following relation:

$$h_\omega(a) = \sum_{i=1}^{n_c} \omega_i \times a_i$$

when $\omega = \left[\omega_1, \omega_2, \cdots, \omega_{n_c}\right]$ is the weighted vector $\omega_i \in [0,1]$ associated to each criteria i and $\sum_{i=1}^{n_c} \omega_i = 1$.

The director establishes a weighted average based on scientific direction of the school. Then, he gives the following weights: $\omega_M = \omega_P = 3/8$ and $\omega_L = 2/8$. Consequently, we obtain $h_\omega(A) = 15.25$, $h_\omega(B) = 12.75$, and $h_\omega(C) = 14.625$. Based on this average, we notice that students are classified in this way $A \succ C \succ B$. Student A is ranked first while he has the smallest mark in literature. From this preference structure, we deduce that poor grades can be offset by good ones. Indeed, the fact of attributing importance to mathematics and physics at the expense of the literature will overestimate, by the weighted average, the

Table 1. Values of the illustrative example

		Alternatives		
		A	B	C
Criteria	M	18	10	14
	P	16	12	15
	L	10	18	15

students good in science. The director is not satisfied because, according to him, the C student is as good in science as in literature and he is better than A, which is excellent in mathematics and physics but bad in literature. The new director's preferences thus reflect the fact that:

- Scientific subjects (M, P) are the most important;
- Students, which are good in mathematics, are generally good in physics and vise versa. Therefore we must not favor them;
- Students with good scientific and literary subjects must be promoted.

The aggregation operator must consider the importance of each criterion taken alone, but must also take into account the interaction between them. To do this, the director decides to use a Choquet integral by attributing the following fuzzy measures to express the preferences described above:

- $\mu(M) = \mu(P) = 0.45$ et $\mu(L) = 0.3$ which represented that scientific subjects are more important than literature;
- $\mu(M,P) = 0.5 < \mu(M) + \mu(P)$ representing that mathematics and physics are redundant;
- $\mu(M,L) = \mu(P,L) = 0.9 > \mu(M) + \mu(L)$ to favor student equally good at scientific subjects and literature;

Applying this fuzzy measure to the three students A, B and C, we get the following result:

- For student A, knowing that his marks are classified in ascending order $L \leq P \leq M$:

$$C_{\mu}(A) = (10 - 0) \cdot \mu(\{M, P, L\})$$
$$+ (16 - 10) . \mu(\{M, P\})$$
$$+ (18 - 16) . \mu(\{M\})$$

$$C_{\mu}(A) = 10 + 6 \times 0.5 + 2 \times 0.45 = 13.9$$

- For student B, knowing that his notes are classified in ascending order $M \leq P \leq L$:

$$C_{\mu}(B) = (10 - 0) \cdot \mu(\{M, P, L\})$$
$$+ (12 - 10) . \mu(\{L, P\})$$
$$+ (18 - 12) . \mu(\{L\})$$

$$C_{\mu}(B) = 10 + 2 \times 0.9 + 6 \times 0.3 = 13.6$$

- For student C, knowing that his notes are classified in ascending order $M \leq P \leq L$:

$$C_{\mu}(C) = (14 - 0) \cdot \mu(\{M, P, L\})$$
$$+ (15 - 14) . \mu(\{L, P\})$$
$$+ (15 - 15) . \mu(\{L\})$$

$$C_{\mu}(B) = 14 + 1 \times 0.9 + 0 = 14.9$$

We notice that students are classified in this way $C \succ A \succ B$.

Ant Colony Optimization

The ant colony optimization algorithms form a class of meta-heuristic based on a natural phenomenon: the behavior of ants in their cohabitation in colonies. So, they imitate the behavior of real ants when searching for food. Some observations have shown that: although an ant has limited capacities, it can with the collaboration of other ants find the shortest path from a food source to the nest without visual cue. To perform complex tasks, a colony of ants uses a chemical substance called "pheromone", which they secrete as they move along. The pheromone provides ants the ability to communicate with each other. Being very sensitive to this substance, an ant chooses in a randomly way, the path comprising a strong concentration of this substance. Thus, when several ants cross the same space, an emergence of the shortest path is obtained. The ACO algorithms have successfully provide solutions for various hard combinatorial optimization problems, such as the traveling salesman (TSP), the vehicle routing, the quadratic assignment and the scheduling problems. They use system formed by several artificial ants. These latter not only simulate the behavior of real ants described above, but also:

1. Can apply additional problem-specific heuristic information,
2. Has a memory which is used to store the search history,
3. Can manage the deposited quantity of pheromone according to the quality of the solution; moreover it is possible to have various types of pheromone.

Each ant uses the collective experience to find a solution to the problem. A solution is built step by step and the choice made by an ant depends on the quantity of pheromone and the heuristic information. The first ACO algorithm is called ant system (AS) (Colorni, Dorigo, & Maniezzo, 1991). It has been used to solve the TSP problem. Then, AS was improved and extended. The improved versions include the ant colony system (ACS) (Dorigo & Gambardella, 1997) and the MAX-MIN ant system (MMAS) (Stützle & Hoos, 1997), etc. In the literature, different ACO approaches have been introduced for multi-criteria optimization problems. These methods mainly differ (Alaya, Solnon, & Ghedira, 2007) with respect to:

1. The number of ant colonies; In fact, one or more colonies could be used to treat each considered criteria,
2. The representation of the pheromone trails,
3. The mechanism of updating the quantity of pheromone,
4. The definition of the heuristic information.

To solve the multi-criteria scheduling HFS problem, we use an ant algorithm based on the framework of the ACS technique based on only one ant colony, to simultaneously minimize all the considered criteria.

The Proposed Algorithm

To deal with the considered HFS problem, we have, on the one hand, to solve the assignment and the sequencing sub-problems. On the other hand, we must take into account the different criteria to optimize. Our approach uses a unique ant colony to simultaneously minimize all the considered criteria.

Assignment Problem

To each repartition of the operations on the machine set, we associate an assignment. Each operation has to be assigned to a machine according to a specific technique of the scheduler generator. Indeed, if there are multiple choices (Ghedjati & Portmann, 2009), the assignment of the operations

can be done by static or dynamic rules. In case of static rules, the assignment is realized before the scheduling process and thus remains invariant along the process. In the other case, the rules use an instantaneous knowledge of the system. As a consequence, they determine the operations priorities during the process of scheduling. Each assignment is characterized by a set:

$$A = \left\{ A_{i,j,k} \in \{0,1\} \mid 1 \leq i \leq S, \ 1 \leq j \leq n, \ 1 \leq k \leq m_i \right\}$$

where

$$A_{i,j,k} = \begin{cases} 1, & \text{if } O_{ij} \text{ is assigned to } M_{ik} \\ 0, & otherwise \end{cases}$$

$$\text{and } \sum_{k=1}^{m_i} A_{i,j,k} = 1$$

To solve the assignment problem, we propose some static heuristics based on some dispatching rules (see Appendix). These heuristics determine a job-sequence for the first stage according to a dispatching rule. Then, jobs are assigned to the machines at the first stage by using the first available machine (FAM) rule. For the other stages $(1 < i \leq S)$, the first in first out (FIFO) rule is used to find the next job sequence by means of the job sequence of the previous stage. Afterwards, the jobs are assigned to the machines at the remained stages by applying the FAM rule.

Scheduling (or Sequencing) Problem

The adaptation of the ACS algorithm to the considered HFS problem requires a number of transformations. The first issue is to represent this problem with a graph model solvable by the ACS approach. We have also to choose an adequate pheromone model representation and heuristic information which can find information about the specific problem taking into account the multiple criteria. Another important point, in order to achieve feasible solutions, is to respect the precedence constraints of the problem at each construction step. This is ensured by using a restricted list (called candidate list) of all the operations that can be selected at each time. In what follows, we expose the different components of our proposed algorithm.

Disjunctive Graph

The key to apply the ACS to a new problem is to identify an appropriate representation for the problem. According to Negenman (Negenman, 2001), the HFS problem can be represented by a disjunctive graph $G = (O, C, D)$ (see Figure 1) defined as follow:

- O is the node set, consisting of all the operations O_{ij}. Two fictive nodes $(O_B^*$ and $O_E^*)$ are added to mark the beginning and the end of each job j.

- C is the set of conjunctive (directed) arcs representing the precedence relationships between the operations of the same job.
- D is the set of disjunctive (undirected) edges; each pair of operations in a stage i is related by an edge.

A feasible schedule is obtained by turning the edges of mutually disjoint cliques into arcs.

Constructive Procedure

To construct a feasible solution, each ant builds independently a sequence of operations by performing the construction step. From an existing operations subsequence, an ant k positioned on node r must choose from the candidate list L_k (which is the set of feasible successor operations that remain to be visited by the ant), the next operation y to append by using a pseudo-random rule based on the heuristic information corresponding to each considered criteria $\eta_{f_i}(r, y)$ and

Figure 1. Example of a disjunctive graph for the HFS problem

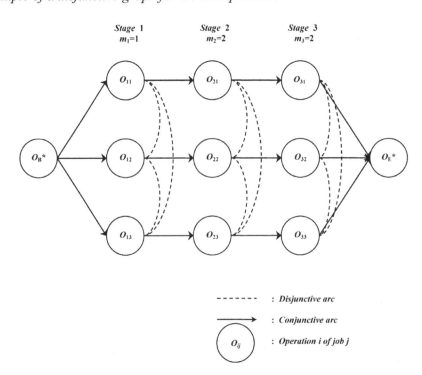

$\eta_{f_2}(r, y)$ as well as pheromone information $\tau(r, y)$. The heuristic information and the pheromone indicate the best way of visiting node y after node r considering the sub-solutions already found. In order to do that, we assume that all the considered criteria share the same pheromone trails. This rule is formally given by the following two equations in Box 2 (Dorigo & Gambardella, 1997).

where β is a parameter which determine the relative importance between τ and η. q is a random number uniformly distributed in $[0, 1]$ and q_0 a parameter that determines the relative importance between exploitation and exploration $(0 \leq q_0 \leq 1)$. Indeed, the system tends to carry out an intensification if $q \leq q_0$, and consequently the algorithm exploits more information, collected by the system. Otherwise, the system tends towards a diversification. Y is a random variable selected according to Equation (10) in Box 3 (Dorigo & Gambardella, 1997).

The procedure is repeated until all the operations are selected (see Algorithm 1). The selected operations are successively stored into a tabu list which is used to record the visited nodes of the current schedule. It is noted that the tabu list is different from the tabu search method.

Pheromone Model: Many pheromone models, for scheduling problem, are based on assigning pheromone information on every pair of operations O_{ij}, O_{hl} as shown in (Colorni, Dorigo, & Maniezzo, 1994). In this last representation, the pheromone value biases the choosing of an ant traversing two sequenced operations O_{ij} and O_{hl} regardless to the machines to which they are assigned. Other pheromone representations have been presented in literature. In the relation-learning model representation (Blum & Sampels, 2002), pheromone values are assigned to pairs of related operations: in this case two operations O_{ij}, O_{hl} are related if they have to be processed on the same machine resource. Thus, pheromone influences the relative order of operations requiring the same machine. As the aim of the considered problem is to sequence a set of operations through a set of machines, we try to influence ants into building a solution. Thus, we place the operations treated on a same machine by combining the two models exposed above. The proposed pheromone model consists on assigning a pheromone value on every pair of operations, but these values are different according to the machines to which they are assigned. In fact, in our representation, the quantity of pheromone assigned to pairs of re-

Box 2.

$$y = \begin{cases} \arg \max_{u \in L_k} \left\{ [\tau(r, u)] \cdot \left([\eta_{f_1}(r, u)]^{\beta} + [\eta_{f_2}(r, u)]^{\beta} \right) \right\}, & \text{si} \quad q \leq q_0 \\ Y, & \text{si} \quad q > q_0 \end{cases} \tag{9}$$

Box 3.

$$p_k(r, Y) = \frac{\tau(r, y) \cdot \left([\eta_{f_1}(r, y)]^{\beta} + [\eta_{f_2}(r, y)]^{\beta} \right)}{\sum_{u \in L_k} \tau(r, u) \cdot \left([\eta_{f_1}(r, u)]^{\beta} + [\eta_{f_2}(r, u)]^{\beta} \right)} \tag{10}$$

Algorithm 1. The general scheme of the proposed meta-heuristic

Initialization Set ACS parameters;
while stopping criterion not satisfied **do**
A colony of ants is initially positioned on the starting node of the graph
REPEAT
for each ant **do**
      Select next operation by applying the state transition rule;
      Apply local pheromone update to decrease the pheromone on the selected operation;
end for
until every ant has built a solution
Evaluate current solutions;
Apply global pheromone update to increase pheromone on the current best solution;
end while

lated operations is set more important than those not related. An initial quantity of pheromone is assigned to every arc connecting a pair of operations. This initial pheromone level τ_0 is assumed to be more important if operations are related.

Heuristic Information: The heuristic information finds information about the specific problem. It is used to estimate the desirability of transition from an operation O_{ij} to another operation O_{hl}. For each considered criterion, a heuristic information is proposed, to represent information related to the partial sequencing at a time. Then, for the makespan criterion, we use a heuristic based on the SPT rule (see Appendix). Likewise, for the sum of the weighted earliness/tardiness costs, another heuristic value, which specifically takes into account both the earliness and the tardiness, is proposed. This heuristic has been used essentially for solving the single machine ET problem ((Ow & Morton, 1989) and (Merkle & Middendorf, 2005)). The heuristic value $\eta_{f_2}(O_{ij}, O_{hl})$ is computed according to the following equation:

$$\eta_{f_2}\left(O_{ij}, O_{hl}\right) = \begin{cases} W_l, & \text{if } s_l \leq 0 \\ W_l - \left(s_l \times CT\right), & \text{if } 0 \leq s_l \leq 1 / CT \\ H_l, & \text{otherwise} \end{cases}$$

(11)

where:

$$W_l = \omega_l^T / p_{hl} \, ;$$

$$H_l = \omega_l^E / p_{hl} \, ;$$

$s_l = d_l - t - p_{hl}$ is the slack of job l at time t ;

$$CT = \left(H_l + W_l\right) / max\left\{0, \overline{p} - p_{hl}\right\} ;$$

$\overline{p}$ is the average processing time of all the jobs.

This dispatching rule uses a priority function reflecting the tardiness cost as its slack s_l becomes small. When the slack is large, the earliness cost dominates (Valente & Alves, 2007). The basic idea of this heuristic is to choose the next operation O_{hl} using its slack time s_l. So, for $s_l \leq 0$, the operation exceeds its due date with respect to the sum of the processing times of all the operations already scheduled. Consequently, the cost of such an operation will become higher if it is scheduled later. That is why it has to be scheduled first. In case of $0 \leq s_l \leq 1/CT$, we consider the operations that will not exceed their due date when they are scheduled next but might exceed it when they are scheduled after some other operations. Thus the priority of choosing an operation will decreases linearly as the operation slack increases. The third situation considers the operations that will be completed early.

Pheromone Updating Mechanism

As in (Dorigo & Gambardella, 1997), the mechanism of updating pheromone is used to simulate the changes in the amount of pheromone according to the new pheromone deposited by ants and pheromone evaporation. Two kinds of pheromone updating strategies are proposed.

Local Pheromone Updating Rule: In order not to influence the choice of the other ants, the local updating rule reduces the pheromone level of the visited arcs by an ant k according to equation (7). Thus, these arcs become less attractive for the other ants. Indeed, this rule is used to shuffle the tour of the other ants and avoid local optima.

$$\tau(O_{ij}, O_{hl}) = (1 - \rho_\ell).\tau(O_{ij}, O_{hl}) + \rho_\ell.\tau_0 \qquad (12)$$

where τ_0 is the initial pheromone level and ρ_g $(0 \leq \rho_g \leq 1)$ is the pheromone evaporating parameter.

Global Pheromone Updating Rule: The pheromone trail is also updated at the end of iteration. Only the best solution is globally updating. The pheromone global updating rule is defined in Box 4.

In the above equation, C_{gb} and ET_{gb} are respectively the best solution of the schedules according to the makespan and the earliness/tardiness criterion and ρ_g $(0 \leq \rho_g \leq 1)$ is the pheromone evaporating parameter of the global updating rule. The global updating rule is applied to intensify the pheromone levels on the arcs belonging to the best obtained solutions. In the case of multiple criteria, we propose to reward solutions that find the best value of each criterion, separately, in the current cycle.

Normalization and Homogenization of the Criteria Functions

For each criterion i, we calculate the criterion function f_i. In case of multi-criteria problem, the values of these criteria are often belonging to different intervals. Then, to evaluate the set of solutions generated by our adapted ACS algorithm, we propose a homogenization of the different criteria values. Thus, for each criterion, a fuzzy membership function is used (Zadeh, 1965). So, We assume that for each criterion i :

- $f_i^{\min}$ is a lower bound (for $C_{\max}$ the lower bound is calculated as in (Santos, Hunsucker, & Deal, 1995) and the lower bound of the ET costs is set equal to 0 like in (Saad, Hammadi, Borne, & Benrejeb, 2008)

- $f_i^{\max}$ is the average criterion function of the solutions obtained by some constructive heuristics using different dispatching rules (see Appendix).

Box 4.

$$\tau(O_{ij}, O_{hl}) = (1 - \rho_g).\tau(O_{ij}, O_{hl}) + \rho_g.\Delta\tau(O_{ij}, O_{hl})$$

where

$$\Delta\tau(O_{ij}, O_{hl}) = \begin{cases} 1/C_{gb}, & \text{if } (O_{ij}, O_{hl}) \in \text{best solution for the } C_{\max} \\ 1/ET_{gb}, & \text{if } (O_{ij}, O_{hl}) \in \text{best solution for the } ET \\ 0, & \text{otherwise} \end{cases}$$

$$(13)$$

The proposed membership function of the decision can be represented by Figure 2. For each feasible solution x, we associate a vector:

$$f(x) \in [f_1^{\min}(x), +\infty[\times[f_2^{\min}(x),$$
$$+ \infty[\times \cdots \times [f_{n_c}^{\min}(x), + \infty[$$

This vector represents the n_c criteria to optimize $f(x) = \left(f_1(x), f_2(x), \ldots, f_{n_c}(x)\right)^T$ (T is the transposition). For each vector, we propose a fuzzification of its components f_i according to their positions in the interval $\left[f_i^{\min}, f_i^{\max} + \varepsilon_i\right]$, where ε_i is a little positive value used to avoid the problem of dividing by zero (when $f_i^{\min} = f_i^{\max}$) and formulated by:

$$\varepsilon_i = \begin{cases} 0.01 \times f_i^{\max}, & \text{if} \quad f_i^{\min} = f_i^{\max} \\ 0, & \text{otherwise} \end{cases}$$

Two fuzzy subsets are considered: the set of good solutions denoted by G^i and the set of bad solutions denoted by B^i according to the ith criterion. The fuzzy measures of these subsets are defined by the following entities:

$$\mu_i^G(f_i(x)) = \begin{cases} 0, & \text{if} \quad f_i(x) \geq f_i^{\max} + \varepsilon_i \\ \dfrac{f_i^{\max} - f_i(x) + \varepsilon_i}{f_i^{\max} - f_i^{\min} + \varepsilon_i}, & \text{if } f_i(x) \in [f_i^{\min}, f_i^{\max} + \varepsilon_i[\\ 1, & \text{if} \quad f_i(x) \leq f_i^{\min} \end{cases}$$

$$\mu_i^B(f_i(x)) = 1 - \mu_i^G(f_i(x))$$

The quality of each solution x is determined by the vector $f^G(x)$ with homogeneous components belong to the interval $[0,1]$, where:

$$f^G(x) = (a_1, a_2, \ldots, a_{n_c})^T$$

$$a_i = \mu_i^G(f_i(x)), \forall i = 1, \ldots, n_c.$$

Figure 2: Fuzzy logic application for solving scale problem

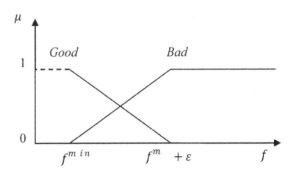

The decision-maker preferences can be expressed by linguistic variables. In this paper, we assume that the makespan is the most important criterion.

Illustration Example

Consider the HFS problem where three jobs have to be processed through three stages. The number of machines in each stage is respectively $m_1 = 1$, $m_2 = 2$ and $m_3 = 2$. The processing times are as follows: $p_{11} = 4$, $p_{21} = 6$, $p_{31} = 4$, $p_{12} = 2$, $p_{22} = 8$, $p_{32} = 2$, $p_{13} = 10$, $p_{23} = 4$ and $p_{33} = 4$. The due dates are $d_1 = 23$, $d_2 = 20$, $d_3 = 22$. We assume that $\omega_j^E = 0.5$ and $\omega_j^T = 1$ for each job l.

The importance of the criteria is defined by the strategy of the decision maker. As an example, we suppose that the criterion f_1 is the most important criterion and criterion f_2 is less important than f_1 but not negligible. The preference of the decision-maker is modeled by the following matrix:

$$I = \begin{pmatrix} 0.6 & -0.1 \\ -0.1 & 0.4 \end{pmatrix}$$

For the sharply index, $I_{f_1} = 0.6$ (respectively $I_{f_2} = 0.4$), represents the average contribution of f_1 (respectively f_2) to coalition with the other criterion. We notice that $\sum_{i=1}^{2} I_{f_i} = 0.6 + 0.4 = 1$.

The interaction measure between criteria is most informative and implies in this case a disjunctive behavior between the criteria. The satisfaction of one criterion is sufficient to have significant effect in the global evaluation. For more details on methods proposed for the determination of the matrix decision-maker preferences see Grabisch's works (Grabisch, 1996).

Four test solutions (a, b, c and d) of this example are considered. So, in Table 2, we report the obtained solutions values for each considered criteria. Then for each solution we homogenize each criterion in order to compare the proposed solutions.

Table 3 shows the homogeneous components $a_i = \mu_i^G \left(f_i \left(x \right) \right)$ belonging to the interval $[0, 1]$ for each criterion and the score C_μ calculated by the Choquet integral for each solutions. We can note that the score C_μ obtained by solution b is the best one comparing to the other.

EXPERIMENTAL DESIGN AND COMPUTATIONAL RESULTS

In this section, we present the results of a series of computational experiments conducted to evaluate the effectiveness of the considered approach. Due to the fact that no benchmark problems were found in the literature for the proposed problem, the benchmarks were randomly generated. The problem instances are represented by the number of jobs and the number of stages $(n \times S)$:

- (10×5) and (10×10)

Table 2. Criteria values

	f_1	f_2
a	24	6.5
b	20	4.5
c	22	6.5
d	26	4

Table 3. Criteria and Choquet integral values

	a_1	a_2	C_μ
a	0.21	0.23	0.25
b	1	0.46	0.91
c	0.6	0.23	0.51
d	0	0.52	0.29

- (15×5) and (15×10)
- (25×5) and (25×10)

We generate random instances with the following parameters uniformly distributed in the following ranges:

- The number of machines $m_i \in [1, 5]$
- The operation processing times $p_{ij} \in [3, 25]$;
- The due date d_j of each job j is determined by the following equation:

$$d_j = (1 + c) \times \sum_{i=1}^{E} p_{ij}$$

where $c \in [0, 1]$

- The earliness weights ω_j^E are equal to 0.5 and the tardiness weights ω_j^T are equal to 1.

We have also to determine all the parameters of our proposed ACS algorithm. Indeed, these parameters have a great impact in the quality of the solution (Dorigo & Gambardella, 1997). Some preliminary tests have been conducted to find these parameters:

$q_0 = 0.8$, $\beta = 2$, $\rho_\ell = \rho_g = 0.05$, the number of ants is assumed to be equal to 20, and the number of iterations is assumed to be equal to 500. The initial pheromone level τ_0 is set equal to 0.01, for all arcs connecting two operations, except those connecting related operations to the same machine. For these latter, we assume

that the initial pheromone level is equal to $5 \times \tau_0$. For each problem, 30 replicates are done and the best solutions of these replications are kept. The preference of the decision-maker is represented by the following interaction

matrix: $I = \begin{pmatrix} 0.6 & -0.3 \\ -0.3 & 0.4 \end{pmatrix}$.

The platform of our experiments is a personal computer with a Pentium (R) 4, 2.66 GHz, and 3 Gb of RAM. Our algorithm is coded in Java.

In Table 4, we report the solutions obtained for the considered instances. f_1 and f_2 represent the solutions of the makespan and the weighted

Table 4. Computational results

n	S	C_{max}^{LB}	f_1	f_2	C_μ	C_μ^{Heur}	CPU(s)
10	5	113	113	198.5	0.921	0.438	2.39
	5	171	173	315	0.870	0.608	2.33
	5	151	151	180	0.965	0.450	2.34
	5	151	156	308	0.735	0.719	2.42
	5	170	182	184.5	0.721	0.566	2.57
Average		**160.75**	**165.5**	**246.9**	**0.823**	**0.588**	**2.42**
10	10	223	247	275	0.699	0.598	10.30
	10	242	263	417	0.754	0.598	9.98
	10	171	228	162	0.681	0.669	10.24
	10	250	250	347.5	0.970	0.765	10.31
	10	224	232	247.5	0.864	0.689	10.17
Average		**221.75**	**243.3**	**293.5**	**0.817**	**0.680**	**10.18**
15	5	217	218	635	0.938	0.534	6.44
	5	236	240	691	0.851	0.652	6.44
	5	117	132	278	0.753	0.669	6.53
	5	252	257	938	0.894	0.668	6.43
	5	263	263	872	0.973	0.521	6.90

continued on following page

Table 4. Continued

n	S	C_{max}^{LB}	f_1	f_2	C_μ	C_μ^{Heur}	CPU(s)
Average		**217**	**223**	**694.8**	**0.868**	**0.628**	**6.58**
15	10	302	315	661	0.755	0.502	30.61
	10	284	296	790.5	0.755	0.690	31.18
	10	288	306	532.5	0.813	0.664	30.39
	10	330	346	962	0.677	0.564	29.67
	10	256	286	638	0.772	0.668	29.44
Average		**289.5**	**308.5**	**730.8**	**0.754**	**0.647**	**30.17**
25	5	230	230	1592.5	0.873	0.820	22.75
	5	370	381	2693	0.687	0.553	23.01
	5	181	207	892.5	0.714	0.713	24.68
	5	408	408	3972	0.954	0.951	23.60
	5	225	231	1334	0.871	0.832	23.18
Average		**296**	**306.8**	**2222.9**	**0.807**	**0.762**	**23.62**
25	10	465	485	3126.5	0.579	0.428	122.13
	10	424	473	2796	0.666	0.625	123.36
	10	217	306	725	0.794	0.678	120.60
	10	446	457	3758	0.819	0.646	135.48
	10	421	443	3008.5	0.638	0.313	121.52
Average		**377**	**419.8**	**2571.9**	**0.729**	**0.566**	**125.24**

earliness and tardiness costs obtained by our proposed method. C_u and C_u^{Heur} are the best scores obtained, respectively, by the Choquet integral for our proposed multi-criteria approach and the best solution of some constructive heuristics. According to the computational results, we can say that the obtained solutions are generally acceptable and satisfactory and respectful of the minimization of the makespan and the sum of earliness and tardiness of jobs. The calculation of the scores is influenced by the values of the lower bounds and the f_i^{max}, so in order to obtain good solutions, we have to choose the best values of these lowers. Our approach enables us to con-

struct solutions with good qualities in a reasonable computation time (CPU) (129 seconds (s) in the worst case). We also observe the increasing of the CPU when the problem size increases. A multi-criteria evaluation function is used to evaluate the obtained solutions.

CONCLUSION

The increase of competition has motivated the implementing of JIT production on scheduling problem to reduce process inventories and delivering goods at time. In fact, this production environment is benefic to both manufacturers and customers. The association of ET performance with the hybrid flow shop scheduling problem represents a practical production model used in real-life industries. The production goal is achieved by minimizing the early and tardy costs and completing each job as close to its due date. So, this paper addresses the problem of scheduling a multi-criteria hybrid flow shop taking in consideration this production aim by minimizing:

1. The early and tardy costs in order to complete each job as close to its due date,
2. And the completion date of all the jobs.

In order to solve such a problem, we propose an approach based on the hybridization of a multi-criteria ACS algorithm with a fuzzy logic method. Our proposed ACS technique has been applied to generate multiple schedules taking into account the different considered criteria. The evaluation of the obtained solutions is made by a multi-criteria aggregation approach based on the Choquet integral. This technique uses fuzzy logic to homogenize the different criteria functions, which belong to different integral lengths. This evaluation method is used to select the best solution satisfying the preference of the decision-maker based not only on the importance of each criterion but also on the interactions between the criteria. Due to the lack of research considering this type of problem, further work needs to be focused on solving the proposed problem with other meta-heuristics in order to compare them with the presented approach.

REFERENCES

Alaya, I., Solnon, C., & Ghedira, K. (2007). Ant colony optimization for multi-objective optimization problems. *The 19th IEEE International Conference on Tools with Artificial Intelligence,* Vol. 1, (pp. 450-457).

Alaykýran, K., Engin, O., & Döyen, A. (2007). Using ant colony optimization to solve the hybrid flow shop scheduling problems. *International Journal of Advanced Manufacturing Technology, 35*(5-6), 541–550. doi:10.1007/s00170-007-1048-2

Balakrishnan, N., Kanet, J., & Sridharan, S. (1999). Early/tardy scheduling with sequence dependent setups on uniform parallel machines. *Computers & Operations Research, 26*(2), 127–141. doi:10.1016/S0305-0548(98)00051-3

Blazewicz, J., Ecker, K. H., Pesch, E., & Schmidt, G. (1996). *Scheduling computer and manufacturing processes.* Berlin, Germany: Springer.

Blum, C., & Sampels, M. (2004). An ant colony optimization algorithm for shop scheduling problems. *Journal of Mathematical Modelling and Algorithms, 3,* 285–308. doi:10.1023/B:JMMA.0000038614.39977.6f

Colorni, A., Dorigo, M., & Maniezzo, V. (1991). Distributed optimisation by ant colonies. *Proceedings of ECAL91-First European Conference on Artificial Life,* (pp. 134-142).

Colorni, A., Dorigo, M., & Maniezzo, V. (1994). Ant system for job-shop scheduling. *Belgian Journal of Operations Research* [JORBEL]. *Statistics and Computer Science, 34*(1), 39–53.

Dorigo, M., & Gambardella, L. (1997). Ant colony system: A cooperative learning approach to the traveling salesman problem. *IEEE Transactions on Evolutionary Computation, 1*(1), 53–66. doi:10.1109/4235.585892

Dubus, J.-P., Gonzales, C., & Perny, P. (2009). *Choquet optimization using GAI networks for multiagent/multicriteria decision-making* (pp. 377–389). Algorithmic Decision Theory, Lectures Notes in Artificial Intelligence. doi:10.1007/978-3-642-04428-1_33

Ghedjati, F., & Portmann, M. (2009). Dynamic heuristic for the generalized job-shop scheduling problem. *IEEE International Conference on Systems, Man and Cybernetics (IEEE SMC'09)*, (pp. 2636-2641).

Grabisch, M. (1996). The application of fuzzy integrals in multicriteria decision-making. *European Journal of Operational Research*, *89*, 445–456. doi:10.1016/0377-2217(95)00176-X

Grabisch, M. (1997). K-ordered discrete fuzzy measures and their representation. *Fuzzy Sets and Systems*, *92*, 167–189. doi:10.1016/S0165-0114(97)00168-1

Graham, R., Lawler, E., & Rinnooy Kan, A. (1979). Optimization and approximation in deterministic sequencing and scheduling: A survey. *Annals of Discrete Mathematics*, *5*, 287–326. doi:10.1016/S0167-5060(08)70356-X

Gravel, M., Price, W., & Gagné, C. (2002). Scheduling continuous casting of aluminum using a multiple ant colony optimization metaheuristic. *European Journal of Operational Research*, *143*, 218–229. doi:10.1016/S0377-2217(01)00329-0

Gupta, J. (1988). Two-stage hybrid flowshop scheduling problem. *The Journal of the Operational Research Society*, *39*, 359–364.

Gupta, J., Krüger, K., Lauff, V., Werner, F., & Sotskov, Y. (2002). Heuristics for hybrid flow shops with controllable processing times and assignable due dates. *Computers & Operations Research*, *29*, 1417–1439. doi:10.1016/S0305-0548(01)00040-5

Hendel, Y., & Sourd, F. (2007). An improved earliness-tardiness timing algorithm. *Computers & Operations Research*, *34*, 2931–2938. doi:10.1016/j.cor.2005.11.004

Huang, R.-H., & Yang, C.-L. (2008). Ant colony system for job shop scheduling with time windows. *International Journal of Advanced Manufacturing Technology*, *39*, 151–157. doi:10.1007/s00170-007-1203-9

Janiak, A., Kozan, E., Lichtenstein, M., & Oguz, C. (2007). Metaheuristic approaches to the hybrid flow shop scheduling problem with a cost-related criterion. *International Journal of Production Economics*, *105*, 407–424. doi:10.1016/j.ijpe.2004.05.027

Khalouli, S., Ghedjati, F., & Hamzaoui, A. (2008a). Method based on ant colony system for solving the hybrid flow shop scheduling problem. *7th International Conference on Modelling, Optimization and SIMulation Systems (MOSIM'08), 2*, (pp. 1407-1416).

Khalouli, S., Ghedjati, F., & Hamzaoui, A. (2008b). Ant colony optimization for solving a bi-criteria hybrid flow shop problem. *IEEE International Conference on Systems, Man and Cybernetics (SMC)*, (pp. 1440-1445).

Khalouli, S., Ghedjati, F., & Hamzaoui, A. (2009). An integrated ant colony optimization algorithm for the hybrid flow shop scheduling problem. *International Conference on Computers & Industrial Engineering (CIE 2009)*, (pp. 554-559).

Khalouli, S., Ghedjati, F., & Hamzaoui, A. (2010). A meta-heuristic approach to solve a JIT scheduling problem in hybrid flow shop. *Engineering Applications of Artificial Intelligence*, *23*(5), 765–771. doi:10.1016/j.engappai.2010.01.008

M'Hallah, R. (2007). Minimizing total earliness and tardiness on a single machine using a hybrid heuristic. *Computers & Operations Research, 34*, 3126–3142. doi:10.1016/j.cor.2005.11.021

Marichal, J.-L. (1998). *Agregation operators for multicreteria decision aid.* Ph.D. Thesis, University of Liege, Belgium.

Merkle, D., & Middendorf, M. (2005). On solving permutation scheduling problems with ant colony optimization. *International Journal of Systems Science, 36*, 255–266. doi:10.1080/00207720500062306

Negenman, E. (2001). Local search algorithms for the multiprocessor flow shop scheduling problem. *European Journal of Operational Research, 128*(1), 147–158. doi:10.1016/S0377-2217(99)00354-9

Ow, P., & Morton, T. (1989). The single machine early/tardy problem. *Management Science, 35*(2), 177–191. doi:10.1287/mnsc.35.2.177

Pomerol, J.-C., & Barba-Romero, S. (2000). *Multicriterion decision making in management: Principles and practice.* Boston, MA: Kluwer.

Portmann, M.-C., & Mouloua, Z. (2007). A window time negotiation approach at the scheduling level inside supply chains. In *Proceedings of the 3th Multidisciplinary International Scheduling Conference: Theory and applicAtion (MISTA 2007)*, (pp. 410-417).

Rajendran, C., & Alicke, K. (2007). Dispatching in flowshops with bottleneck machines. *Computers & Industrial Engineering, 52*, 89–106. doi:10.1016/j.cie.2006.10.006

Saad, I., Hammadi, S., Borne, P., & Benrejeb, M. (2008). Choquet integral for criteria aggregation in the flexible job-shop scheduling problems. *Mathematics and Computers in Simulation, 76*, 447–462. doi:10.1016/j.matcom.2007.04.010

Santos, D., Hunsucker, J., & Deal, D. (1995). Global lower bounds for flow shops with multiple processors. *European Journal of Operational Research, 80*, 112–120. doi:10.1016/0377-2217(93)E0326-S

Stützle, T., & Hoos, H. (1997). Improvement in the ant system: Introducing min-max ant system. In *Proceedings of the International Conference on Artificial Neuronal Networks and Genetic Algorithms*, (pp. 266-274).

Sugeno, M. (1977). Fuzzy measures and fuzzy integrals: A survey . In Gupta, M. M., Saridis, G. N., & Gains, B. R. (Eds.), *Fuzzy automata and decision processes* (pp. 89–102).

T'kindt, V., & Billaut, J.-C. (2002). *Multicriteria scheduling: Theory, models and algorithms.* Berlin, Germany: Srpinger.

Talbi, E. (1999). *Métaheuristiques pour l'optimisation combinatoire multiobjectif.* Tutorial, Journées Evolutionnaires Trimestrielle.

Valencia, L., & Rabadi, G. (2003). A multiagents approach for the job shop scheduling problem with earliness and tardiness. *IEEE International Conference on Systems, Man and Cybernetics, 2*, 1217-1222.

Valente, J., & Alves, R. (2007). Heuristics for the early/tardy scheduling problem with release dates. *International Journal of Production Economics, 106*, 261–274. doi:10.1016/j.ijpe.2006.06.006

Ventura, J., & Kim, D. (2003). Parallel machine scheduling with earliness–tardiness penalties and additional resource constraints. *Computers & Operations Research, 30*(13), 1945–1958. doi:10.1016/S0305-0548(02)00118-1

Wu, Z., & Weng, M. X. (2005). Multiagent scheduling method with earliness and tardiness objectives in flexible job shops. *IEEE Transactions on Systems . Man and Cybernetics-Part B, 35,* 293–301. doi:10.1109/TSMCB.2004.842412

Yagmahan, B., & Yenisey, M. (2010). Multi-objective ant colony system algorithm for flow shop scheduling problem. *Expert Systems with Applications, 37,* 1361–1368. doi:10.1016/j.eswa.2009.06.105

Zadeh, L. (1965). Fuzzy sets. *Information and Control, 8,* 338–353. doi:10.1016/S0019-9958(65)90241-X

Zitzler, E., & Thiele, L. (1999). Multiobjective evolutionary algorithms: A comparative case study and strength Pareto approach. *IEEE Transactions on Evolutionary Computation, 3*(4), 257–271. doi:10.1109/4235.797969

APPENDIX

Dispatching Rules

- **SPT:** Select the job with the shortest processing time.
- **LPT:** Select the job with the longest processing time.
- **LWKR:** Select the job with the least work remaining.
- **MWKR:** Select the job with the most work remaining.
- **SMR:** Select the job with the shortest remaining work, excluding the operation under.
- **LMR:** Select the job with the longest remaining work, excluding the operation under.
- **EDD:** Select the job with the earliest due date d_j .
- **ODD:** Select the job with the earliest operation due date:

$$d_{ij} = d_j \times \left(\sum_{\ell=1}^{i} p_{\ell j} \right) \Big/ \left(\sum_{\ell=1}^{S} p_{\ell j} \right)$$

- **DD/BJ**(Rajendran & Alicke, 2007)**:** In this case the dispatching decision concerning a job is made with respect to the due date computed depending upon the position of the stage i, on which it is executed, relatively to the bottleneck stage g . The priority index is:

$$Z_j^1 = \left\{ \begin{array}{ll} d_{gj}, & \text{if} \quad i \leq g \\ d_j, & \text{if} \quad i > g \end{array} \right.$$

The objective of this rule is to render the jobs adhere to their operation due dates focused on either the bottleneck stage or the job due date. Then in each stage, the operations are arranged on the increasing values of Z_j^1 .

- **TPTDD/BJ (Rajendran & Alicke, 2007)]:** This rule consider in addition to the properties of the *DD/BJ* rule, the total processing time. The priority index for job j is determined by:

$$Z_j^2 = \left\{ \begin{array}{ll} d_{gj} + \sum_{\ell=i}^{g} p_{\ell j}, & \text{if} \quad i \leq g \\ d_j + \sum_{\ell=i}^{E} p_{\ell j}, & \text{if} \quad i > g \end{array} \right.$$

Then in each stage, the operations are arranged on the increasing values of Z_j^2 .

Chapter 10
Pure and Hybrid Metaheuristics for the Response Time Variability Problem[1]

Alberto García-Villoria
Institute of Industrial and Control Engineering (IOC),
Universitat Politècnica de Catalunya (UPC), Spain

Albert Corominas
Institute of Industrial and Control Engineering (IOC),
Universitat Politècnica de Catalunya (UPC), Spain

Rafael Pastor
Institute of Industrial and Control Engineering (IOC),
Universitat Politècnica de Catalunya (UPC), Spain

ABSTRACT

Metaheuristics are a powerful tool for solving hard optimisation problems. Moreover, metaheuristic hybrid optimisation techniques can be applied to develop an improved metaheuristic algorithm for a given problem. It is known that some metaheuristics perform better than others for each problem. However, there is a lack of theoretical basis to explain why a metaheuristic performs well (or bad) when solving a problem, and there is not a general guide to design specific hybrid metaheuristics. In this chapter, the authors describe the response time variability problem (RTVP), which is an NP-hard combinatorial optimisation problem that appears in a wide range of engineering and business applications. They show how to solve this problem by means of metaheuristics and how to design specific hybrid metaheuristics for the RTVP. This may be useful to managers, engineers, researchers, and scientists to deal with other types of optimisation problems.

DOI: 10.4018/978-1-4666-2086-5.ch010

1. INTRODUCTION

Since Toyota Motor Corporation popularized just-in-time (JIT) production systems, the problem of sequencing on mixed-model assembly lines has acquired high relevance. Mixed-model assembly lines are production lines that are able to produce small lots (ideally of size one) of different models with negligible costs when changing over one model to another. One of the most important JIT objectives is to get rid of all kinds of waste and inefficiency and, according to Toyota, the main waste is due to inventories. To reduce inventories, JIT production systems require producing only the necessary components in the necessary quantities at the necessary time. Because JIT is a pull production environment, the production schedule is focused on sequencing the models in the final assembly process.

The key to reduce inventories, as Monden (1983) says, is to have constant production rates and constant consumption rates of the components involved in the production process. First, the number of units of each model to be produced by the mixed-model assembly production line throughout the production period must be decided. Next, these units must be sequenced as *regularly* as possible. Regularity can be sought in the consumption of the components that arrive to the production line or in the production of the models that leave the production line. Depending on the kind of regularity desired, Kubiak (1993) classifies these sequencing problems into two categories, respectively: output rate variation (ORV) problems and production rate variation (PRV) problems.

The ORV problem concentrates on the consumption of the components needed by the models and its aim is to minimise the variations in this consumption in the production period. On the other hand, the PRV problem concentrates on the regularity of the models production. This kind of regularity is important when production needs to be adjusted to demand. Thus, according to the JIT system, it is possible to satisfy demands for a variety of models without holding large inventories or incurring large waits. Regularity in the PRV problem can be characterized in as many ways as discrepancy metrics are defined.

Miltenburg (1989) proposed four PRV metrics based on discrepancies between the real production rate and the ideal one (i.e., the one that would correspond to a constant rate of production). But other criteria can be use to measure the regularity or fairness of appearance of the models in the line (Bautista *et al.*, 1997). For instance, Inman and Bulfin (1991) considered to minimise variations with respect to ideal production due dates for each unit.

The response time variability problem (RTVP) can be considered a PRV problem in the context of mixed-model assembly lines. The metric of the RTVP is based on the regularity, for each model, of the distances between the appearances of two consecutive units of that model. The application of the RTVP is not reduced into the mixed-model assembly lines context, but also includes, among others, computer multi-threaded systems, periodic machine maintenance, waste collection and scheduling of commercials.

It is well known that metaheuristic procedures are a good technique for solving real-life scheduling, combinatorial optimisation problems, as it is the RTVP. A lot of general metaheuristics have been proposed in the literature, from which we can choose the most suitable to solve our problem. However, we cannot usually know a priori which metaheuristic is the best to solve our particular variant of the problem. In this chapter, we show how we dealt with the solution of the RTVP in our studies by means of metaheuristics. We first show how the RTVP is solved by means of several types of metaheuristics following a methodology. This methodology helps us to see which characteristics or components may help to the metaheuristics to obtain good solutions.

Then improved algorithms were developed based on new hybrid metaheuristics. It is shown that metaheuristic hybrid optimisation techniques are useful to improve the RTVP solution. We think that the steps that we followed are extendable when dealing other types of real world combinatorial optimisation problems.

The chapter is organized as follows. Section 2 describes the RTVP and explains real-life contexts in which may appear. The metaheuristics for the RTVP that we used, the followed methodology and the results of a computational experiment are shown in Section 3. Section 4 is dedicated to explain the design of the hybrid algorithms together with the results of the conducted computational experiment. Concluding remarks are given in Section 5.

2. THE RESPONSE TIME VARIABILITY PROBLEM (RTVP)

2.1. Definition

The concept of fair sequence has emerged independently from scheduling problems in industrial, computing, business, economics and other environments. The common aim of these scheduling problems, as defined by Kubiak (2004), is to build a fair sequence using n symbols, where symbol i ($i = 1,...,n$) must be copied d_i times in the sequence. The fair sequence is the one which allocates a fair share of positions to each symbol i in any subsequence. This fair or regular share of positions allocated to symbol i in a subsequence of length k is proportional to the relative importance (d_i) of symbol i with respect to the total copies of competing symbols (equal to $\sum_{i=1..n} d_i$). There is not a universal definition of fairness, as several reasonable metrics can be defined according to the specific problem considered. For a detailed introduction to fair sequences, it is recommended the book by Kubiak (2009).

The family of fair sequencing problems can be classified according to the following characteristics:

- **Cyclic vs. Non-Cyclic:** The problem is cyclic if the sequence is the same for all cycles and the distance, for each symbol i, between the first copy of i in a cycle and the last copy of i in the preceding cycle is considered.

- **Distance-Constrained vs. Not Distance-Constrained:** The problem is distance-constrained if the distance between two consecutive copies of the same symbol has an upper bound and/or a lower bound.

- **Optimality vs. Feasibility:** If the aim is to find a solution that optimises an objective function then we look for optimality. Instead, if the aim is to find a feasible solution, then we look for feasibility.

In particular, the RTVP is a fair sequencing problem which is cyclic, not distance-constrained and its aim is to optimise an objective function. It is formulated as follows (Corominas *et al.*, 2007). Let n be the number of symbols, d_i the number of copies to be sequenced of symbol i and D the total number of copies ($D = \sum_{i=1..n} d_i$). Let S be a solution of a RTVP instance represented with a circular sequence of copies ($S = s_1 s_2 \ldots s_D$), where sj is the copy sequenced in position j of sequence s. For all symbol i in which $d_i \geq 2$, let t_k^i be the distance between the positions in which copies k + 1 and k of symbol i are found (i.e. the number of positions between them, where the distance between two consecutive positions is considered equal to 1). Since the sequence is circular, position 1 comes immediately after position D; therefore, $t_{d_i}^i$ is the distance between the first copy of symbol i in a cycle and the last copy of the same symbol in the preceding cycle. Let $\bar{t}_i$ be the average or ideal distance between two consecutive copies of symbol i

$(\bar{t}_i = D/d_i)$. For all symbol i in which $d_i = 1$, t_1^i is equal to $\bar{t}_i$. The objective is to minimise the metric response time variability (RTV) which is defined by the following expression:

$$RTV = \sum_{i=1}^{n} \sum_{k=1}^{d_i} (t_k^i - \bar{t}_i)^2 \qquad (1)$$

For example, let $n = 3$ with symbols A, B and C, $d_A = 3$, $d_B = 2$ and $d_C = 2$; thus, $D = 7$, $\bar{t}_A = 7/3$, $\bar{t}_B = 7/2$ and $\bar{t}_C = 7/2$. Any sequence that contains exactly d_i times the symbol i is a feasible solution. For instance, the sequence (A, B, A, C, B, A, C) is a feasible solution, where:

$$RTV = \left[\left(2 - 7/3\right)^2 + \left(3 - 7/3\right)^2 + \left(2 - 7/3\right)^2\right]$$
$$+ \left[\left(3 - 7/2\right)^2 + \left(4 - 7/2\right)^2\right]$$
$$+ \left[\left(3 - 7/2\right)^2 + \left(4 - 7/2\right)^2\right] = 5/3$$

Note that the RTV metric is a weighted variance with weights equal to di. That is, $RTV = \sum_{i=1..n} d_i \cdot Var_i$, where $Var_i = 1/d_i \cdot \sum_{k=1..d_i} \left(t_k^i - \bar{t}_i\right)^2$. Thus, the distance between any two consecutive copies of the same symbol should be as regular as possible (ideally constant). It is worth to note that since the average distance $\bar{t}_i$ is equal to D for all symbol i such that $d_i = 1$, these symbols do not intervene in the computation of the RTV metric. That is, for all these symbols $Var_i = 0$.

2.2. Mathematical Formulation

The RTVP can be represented by the following mixed-integer linear programming (MILP) model (Corominas *et al.*, 2007).

Data:

- n number of symbols
- D number of positions in the sequence
- d_i number of copies of symbol i ($i = 1,...,n$) to be sequenced; it is assumed that $\sum_{i=1..n} d_i = D$
- $\bar{t}_i$ average distance between two consecutive copies of symbol i: $\bar{t}_i = D/d_i$ ($i = 1,...,n$)
- $G1$ set of symbols with multiple copies: $G1 = \{i : 1 \leq i \leq n \mid d_i \geq 2\}$
- UB_i upper bound on the distance between two consecutive copies of symbol i: $UB_i = D - d_i + 1$ $(\forall i \in G1)$
- E_{ik}, L_{ik} the earliest and the latest position that can be occupied by copy k of symbol i: $E_{ik} = k$ and $L_{ik} = D - d_i + k$ $(i = 1, ..., n; k = 1, ...d_i)$.
- H_{ik} set of positions that can be occupied by copy k of symbol i: $H_{ik} = \{h : E_{ik} \leq h \leq L_{ik}\}$ $(i = 1, ..., n; k = 1, ...d_i)$

Variables:

- $y_{ikh} \in \{0,1\}$ 1 if and only if copy k of symbol i is placed in position h $(i = 1, ..., n; k = 1, ...d_i, h \in H_{ik})$
- $\delta_{ik}^j \in \{0,1\}$ 1 if and only if the distances between copies k and k + 1 of symbol i is equal to j $(\forall i \in G1; k = 1, ...d_i; j = 1, ..., UB_i)$

Model:

$$[MIN]\, Z = \sum_{\forall i \in G1, k, j} j^2 \cdot \delta_{ik}^j \qquad (2)$$

$$\sum_{\forall (i,k)h \in H_{ik}} y_{ikh} = 1 \qquad (h = 1, ..., D) \qquad (3)$$

$$\sum_{h \in H_{ik}} y_{ikh} = 1, \qquad \left(i = 1, \dots, n; k = 1, \dots d_i\right)$$

(4)

$$\sum_{h \in H_{i,k+1}} h \cdot y_{i,k+1,h} - \sum_{h \in H_{ik}} h \cdot y_{ikh} = \sum_{j=1}^{UB_i} j \cdot \delta_{ik}^{j},$$

$$\left(\forall i \in G1; k = 1, \dots d_i - 1\right)$$

(5)

$$D - \sum_{h \in H_{i,d_i}} h \cdot y_{i,d_i,h} + \sum_{h \in H_{i1}} h \cdot y_{i1h} = \sum_{j=1}^{UB_i} j \cdot \delta_{i,d_i}^{j},$$

$$\left(\forall i \in G1\right)$$

(6)

$$\sum_{j=1}^{UB_i} \delta_{ik}^{j} = 1, \qquad \left(\forall i \in G1; k = 1, \dots d_i\right)$$

(7)

To minimise the objective function (Equation 2) is equivalent to minimise the response time variability (see Section 2.3); note that symbols with $d_i = 1$ $\left(i \notin G1\right)$ are not considered because their contribution to the RTV value is always equal to 0. Constraints (3) ensure that one and only one copy is sequenced in each position h. Constraints (4) ensure that each copy k of each symbol i is assigned to one and only one position of the sequence. Constraints (5) and (6) ensure that the distance between copies k and k + 1 of symbol i is equal to an integer value $j \in \left[1, UB_i\right]$. Finally, constraints (7) ensure that the distance between copies k and $k + 1$ of symbol i is obtained with one and only one integer value.

2.3. Areas of Application

When a resource must be shared between competing demands that require regular attention, it is important to schedule the access to the resource in some fair manner so that each demand receives a share of the resource that is proportional to its demand relative to the competing demands (Herrmann, 2011). The objective in the RTVP is to minimise variability in the time between the instants at which that products, clients or jobs receive the necessary resources.

In the RTVP formulation introduced in the previous subsection, a symbol represents a product, client or job that demands the resource; a position of the solution sequence represents the time slot in which the symbol sequenced has access to the resource; and the number of copies that each symbol i has to occur in the sequence (d_i) represents the number of time slots that each symbol has right to. It is assumed that all time slots are the same amount of time. Thus, we can ignore time and consider only the positions in the sequence.

This problem appears in a broad range of real world areas. As it has been introduced, the RTVP appears when sequencing in mixed-model assembly lines under the JIT production system. In this context, the RTVP can be considered a PRV problem in which the RTV metric is used. Feedback received from the manufacturing industry suggests that a good mixed-model sequence is one in which the distances between units of the same model are as regular as possible. Other metrics have been proposed in the literature for the PRV problem (Miltenburg, 1989; Inman and Bulfin, 1991). However, the drawback of these metrics is that, on the contrary of the RTVP, it takes the positions of the models with only one unit to be produced into account although the positions of these models are, in fact, irrelevant for the regularity of the sequence.

The RTVP also appears in computer multi-threaded systems (Waldspurger and Weihl, 1994 and 1995; Dong et al., 1998; Bar-Noy et al., 2002). Multithreaded systems (operating systems, network servers, media-based applications, etc.) do different tasks to attend to the requests of client programs that take place concurrently. These systems need to manage the scarce resources in order to service the requests of n clients. For example, multimedia systems must not display video frames too early or too late, because this would produce jagged motion perceptions (Kubiak, 2009). Waldspurger and Weihl, considering that resource rights could be represented by *tickets* and that each client i had a given number d_i of tickets, suggested the RTV metric to evaluate the sequence of resource rights.

Other contexts in which the RTVP can be applied are the design of sales catalogues (problem introduced in Bollapragada *et al.*, 2004), the periodic machine maintenance problem (Wei and Liu, 1983; Anily *et al.*, 1998) as well as other distance-constrained problems (e.g., see Han *et al.*, 1996).

Two case studies of the RTVP were reported in the literature. In Bollapragada *et al.* (2004), the study is motivated by the problem faced by the National Broadcasting Company (NBC) of U.S., one of the main firms in the television industry. Major advertisers buy NBC hundreds of time slots to air commercials. The advertisers ask to NBC that the airings of their commercials are evenly spaced as much as possible over the broadcast season. The problem solved finally is not the RTVP, but a non-cyclic variant. This study is continued in Brusco (2008). In Herrmann (2007), the author came up with the RTVP while he was working with a healthcare facility that needed to schedule the collection of waste from waste collection rooms throughout the building. Based on data about how often a waste collector had to visit each room and in view of the fact that different rooms require a different number of visits per shift, the facility manager wanted these visits to occur as regular as possible so that excessive waste would not accumulate in any room. For instance, if a room needed four visits per eight-hour shift, it should be ideally visited every two hours.

In some of these problems the regularity is not a property desirable by itself, but it helps to minimise costs. In fact, when the costs are proportional to the square of the distances, the problem of minimising costs and the RTVP are equivalent as follows:

$$
RTV = \sum_{i=1}^{n} \sum_{k=1}^{d_i} (t_k^i - \overline{t}_i)^2
$$

$$
= \sum_{i=1}^{n} \sum_{k=1}^{d_i} \left(t_k^i \right)^2 + \sum_{i=1}^{n} \sum_{k=1}^{d_i} \left(\overline{t}_i \right)^2
$$

$$
- \sum_{i=1}^{n} \left(2 \cdot \overline{t}_i \cdot \sum_{k=1}^{d_i} t_k^i \right) = \sum_{i=1}^{n} \sum_{k=1}^{d_i} \left(t_k^i \right)^2
$$

$$
+ \sum_{i=1}^{n} \sum_{k=1}^{d_i} \left(\overline{t}_i \right)^2 - \sum_{i=1}^{n} 2 \cdot \overline{t}_i \cdot D
$$

Since $\sum_{i=1}^{n} \sum_{k=1}^{d_i} \left(\overline{t}_i \right)^2$ and $\sum_{i=1}^{n} 2 \cdot \overline{t}_i \cdot D$ are constants, the problem of minimising RTV is equivalent to minimising $\sum_{i=1}^{n} \sum_{k=1}^{d_i} \left(t_k^i \right)^2$.

3. PURE METAHEURISTICS FOR THE RESPONSE TIME VARIABILITY PROBLEM

The RTVP is a combinatorial optimisation problem that has been proved to be NP-hard (Corominas *et al.*, 2007). However, the particular two-symbol case can be optimally solved with a polynomial algorithm proposed in Corominas *et al.* (2007). For the other cases, Corominas *et al.* (2007) proposed a MILP model whose practical limit to obtain optimal solutions is 25 copies to be sequenced. Corominas *et al.* (2010a) proposed an improved MILP model and increased the practical limit for obtaining optimal solutions from 25 to 40 copies to be sequenced.

To solve larger, real-life instances, heuristic methods have been proposed. This problem has been first time solved in Waldspurger and Weihl (1994) using a method that authors called *lottery scheduling*, which consists on generating a solution at random as follows. For each position of the sequence, a symbol to be sequenced is randomly chosen. The probability of each symbol is equal to the number of copies of this model that remain to be sequenced divided by the total number of copies that remain to be sequenced

Later, Waldspurger and Weihl (1995) used the Jefferson method of apportionment (Balinski and Young, 1982), which they renamed as the stride scheduling technique. Herrmann (2007) solved the RTVP by applying a heuristic algorithm based on the stride scheduling technique. An aggregation approach was used in Herrmann (2011). Corominas *et al.* (2007) proposed also the Jefferson method together with other four greedy heuristic algorithms and a local search method. These heuristic methods are very fast but most of the obtained solutions are not optimal or near optimal in general.

With the aim to improve the RTVP solution, we designed, coded and tested a broad range of metaheuristic-based algorithms, since metaheuristics are one of the most practical approaches for solving hard optimisation problems (Gendreau and Potvin, 2010). However, as it is pointed in the Metaheuristic Network (http://www.metaheuristics.net), "although metaheuristics are widely used techniques, the how and why they work effectively for specific problems and for others not, is still not well understood". To choose the most suitable metaheuristic, or metaheuristic components, to use when a new problem is attacked is a very interesting question that remains still open. Given the lack of guidelines, the performance assessment of a metaheuristic for solving a problem is best carried out by experimentation (Chiarandini *et al.*, 2007).

The metaheuristics that we used in our works for solving the RTVP include classical metaheuristics such as multi-start (MS) (García *et al.*, 2006; Corominas *et al.*, 2008), greedy randomized adaptive search procedure (GRASP) (García *et al.*, 2006; Corominas *et al.*, 2008), tabu search (TS) (Corominas *et al.*, 2009a and 2009b), reduced variable neighbourhood search (RVNS) (Corominas *et al.*, 2009c), simulated annealing

(SA) (Corominas *et al.*, 2010b), genetic algorithm (GA) (García-Villoria and Pastor, 2010a), particle swarm optimisation (PSO) (García *et al.*, 2006; García-Villoria and Pastor, 2009) and ant colony optimisation (ACO) (Corominas *et al.*, 2009d); and new metaheuristics such as electromagnetism-like mechanism (EM) (García-Villoria and Pastor, 2010b) and psychoclonal optimisation (PSC) (García-Villoria and Pastor, 2010c). We selected metaheuristics that perform well in several optimisation problems and, therefore, we could expect that one or more one of them perform well for the RTVP. Altogether, 10 metaheuristics were selected, and 27 algorithms based on these 10 metaheuristics were developed. In all algorithms, the stop condition is to run them for a preset time.

In most of the algorithms, one or more of the following three classical neighbourhoods were used: 1) interchanging each pair of two consecutive copies of the sequence that represents the current solution ($N1$), 2) interchanging each pair of consecutive or no-consecutive copies of the sequence ($N2$), and 3) a copy of a model i is removed from its position and inserted between a pair of consecutive positions provided that there is no another copy of i between the initial position of the copy and the position in which is inserted ($N3$).

A metaheuristic will be successful if it can provide a suitable balance between the exploration and the exploitation of the search space. The main difference between the existing metaheuristics concerns the particular way in which they try to achieve this balance (Birattari *et al.*, 2001). The metaheuristics can be classified according to different characteristics. Table 1 shows the different types of metaheuristic characteristics explained below. This classification does not correspond to all implementations of these metaheuristics, but it gives an indication of the standard method characteristics (which correspond to all algorithm implementations for the RTVP).

Table 1. Classification of the proposed metaheuristics

MS	stochastic	single-point	discontinuous	memoryless
GRASP	stochastic	single-point	discontinuous	memoryless
TS	deterministic	single-point	trajectory	memory
RVNS	stochastic	single-point	trajectory	memoryless
SA	stochastic	single-point	trajectory	memoryless
GA	stochastic	population	discontinuous	memory
PSO	stochastic	population	discontinuous	memory
ACO	stochastic	population	discontinuous	memory
EM	stochastic	population	discontinuous	memory
PSC	stochastic	population	discontinuous	memory

MS: Multi-start; GRASP: Greedy randomized adaptive search procedure; TS: Tabu search; RVNS: Reduced variable neighbourhood search; SA: Simulated annealing; GA: Genetic algorithm; PSO: Particle swarm optimisation; ACO: Ant colony optimisation; EM: Electromagnetism-like mechanism; PSC: Psychoclonal optimisation

- **Stochastic vs. Deterministic Methods:** Randomness takes part in the stochastic method design. Thus, for the same data, different executions of a stochastic method may obtain different solutions whereas a deterministic method will obtain always the same solution.

- **Population-Based vs. Single-Point Search:** Population methods work simultaneously with a population of search points whereas single-point methods works only use simultaneously one search point.

- **Trajectory vs. Discontinuous Methods:** Trajectory methods walk between neighbouring solutions whereas discontinuous methods can jump to any other solution.

- **Memory Usage vs. Memoryless Methods:** Memory usage methods use the search experience (or memory in the widest sense) to influence the exploration of the solution space whereas memoryless methods do not use any kind of memory to influence the exploration.

The MS, GRASP, TS, RVNS, SA, GA, PSO, ACO, EM and PSC based algorithms for the RTVP are explained in Sections 3.1 to 3.10, respectively.

In Section 3.11 is introduced the methodology that was followed. Finally, the results of a computational experiment are discussed in Section 3.12.

3.1. Multi-Start (MS)

The MS metaheuristic is a general scheme that consists of two phases. The first phase obtains an initial solution and the second phase improves the obtained initial solution. These two phases are applied iteratively until a stopping condition is reached. This scheme has been first used at the beginning of the 1980's (Boender *et al.*, 1982). The generation of the initial solution, how to improve them and the stop condition can go from very simple to very sophisticated. The combination of these elements gives a wide variety of multi-start methods (Glover and Kochenberger, 2003, Chapter 12).

A straightforward MS algorithm for the RTVP was proposed in García *et al.* (2006), which is based on generating, at each iteration, a random initial solution and on improving it by means of a local search procedure. The algorithm stops after it has run for a preset time. Random solutions are generated by lottery scheduling. The local search procedure is performed iteratively in the neighbourhood *N1*; the best solution in the neighbourhood is chosen; the optimisation ends when no neighbouring solution is better than the current solution.

The previous MS algorithm has the drawback that the quality of the initial solutions is usually low and the computing time required at each local search is high, specially for big RTVP instances. An easy and fast way to obtain better initial solutions without giving up the simplicity of the multi-start algorithm is proposed in Corominas *et al.* (2008). It consists in generating, at each iteration, *P* random solutions and get as the initial solution the best of them; that is, to apply the local search only to the best solution of the *P* random solutions. Thus, the only parameter of this MS algorithm to be fine-tuned is *P*. Figure 1 shows the pseudocode of this enhanced MS algorithm. Note that the algorithm shown in Figure 1 is equivalent to the algorithm proposed in García et al. (2006) when $P = 1$

3.2. Greedy Randomized Adaptive Search Procedure (GRASP)

The GRASP metaheuristic was first proposed in Feo and Resende (1989) and can be considered as a MS variant. However, the generation of the initial solutions is performed by means of a greedy strategy in which random steps are added and the choice of the elements to be included in the solution is adaptive.

Two GRASP algorithms have been proposed in the literature (García *et al.*, 2006; Corominas *et al.*, 2008) based on the MS algorithm proposed in García *et al.* (2006). In both GRASP algorithms, the random step when generating the initial solutions consists in selecting the next symbol to be sequenced from a set called candidate list. This list consist of the best symbols according to the value of an associated index and the probability of each candidate symbol is proportional to the value of its index. The index used in García *et al.* (2006) is the Webster index, which is evaluated

Figure 1. Pseudocode of the MS algorithm by Corominas et al. (2008)

---

1. Let *S** be a random solution
2. While the execution time is not reached do:
3.   Generate *P* random solutions
4.   Let *S* the best solution generated at step 3
5.   Apply the local optimisation to *S* and get *S'*
6.   If *S'* is better than *S**, then *S** := *S'*
7. Return *S**

---

as follows. Let x_{ik} be the number of copies of model *i* that have been already sequenced in the sequence of length k, $k = 0, 1, \ldots$ (assuming $x_{i0} = 0$); the value of the Webster index of model i to be sequenced in position k + 1 is $\dfrac{d_i}{\left(x_{ik} + 0.5\right)}$. On the other hand, the index used in Corominas et al. (2008) is $\dfrac{\left(k+1\right)\cdot d_i}{D} - x_{ik}$. Thus, the only parameter of the GRASP algorithms to be fine-tuned is the size of the candidate list.

The GRASP algorithm proposed in Corominas *et al.* (2008) performs, on average, better than the GRASP algorithm proposed in García *et al.* (2006).

3.3. Tabu Search (TS)

Local search methods have the great disadvantage that the local optimum found is often a fairly mediocre solution (Gendreau and Potvin, 2010, Chapter 2). To overcome this limitation, the TS metaheuristic (TS) has been proposed by Glover (1986). TS is based on applying a local search in which non-improving movements are allowed. To avoid cycling back to visited solutions, the most recent history of the search is recorded in a tabu list of tabu (forbidden) solutions. The complete tabu solutions could be recorded in the tabu list, but this may require a lot of memory, makes expensive to check whether a solution is tabu or not and, above all, does not diversify sufficiently the search. Thus, it is common to record only the last moves (transformations) performed on the current solution and forbid reverse transformations (Gendreau and Potvin, 2010, Chapter 2). The tabu lists are usually implemented as a list of fixed length with a FIFO (First In, First Out) policy. A tabu solution can be overridden if a suitable aspiration criterion is met.

Two straightforward applications of the TS classical scheme shown in Figure 2 have been proposed in the literature to solve the RTVP (Corominas *et al.*, 2009a and 2009b). The only difference between both TS algorithms is the definition of the neighbourhood. In Corominas *et al.* (2009a), the neighbourhood *N2* is used, whereas in Corominas *et al.* (2009b), the neighbourhood *N3* is used.

The elements of the two TS algorithms for the RTVP are defined as follows. The initial solution is obtained from the best solution returned by the five heuristics proposed in Corominas *et al.* (2007). As it has been said previously, the neighbourhood used in Corominas *et al.* (2009a) and in Corominas *et al.* (2009b) is *N2* and *N3*, respectively. When the neighbourhood *N2* is used, a forbidden move of the tabu list consists of two pairs of position/symbol. For instance, the move [(3, *A*), (5, *B*)] means that all solutions with the symbol *A* sequenced in position 3 and the symbol *B* sequenced in position 5 are considered tabu. And

when the neighbourhood *N3* is used, a forbidden move consists of one pair of position/symbol. The aspiration criterion is that the move produces a solution better than the best solution found in the past. Thus, the only parameter of the TS algorithms to be fine-tuned is the size of the tabu list.

The TS algorithm proposed in Corominas *et al.* (2009b) performs, on average, better than the TS algorithm proposed in Corominas *et al.* (2009a).

3.4. Reduced Variable Neighbourhood Search (RVNS)

Variable Neighbourhood Search (VNS) is a metaheuristic proposed by Mladenović and Hansen (1997). The basic idea of VNS is to apply a systematic change of neighbourhood within a local search method (Mladenović and Hansen, 1997). According to the strategies used in changing neighbourhoods and to the selection of the neighbour to be the current solution, several extensions have been proposed but most of them keep the simplicity of the basic idea (Mladenović *et al.*, 2003). VNS is based on the following three simple facts (Glover and Kochenberger, 2003, Chapter 6): 1) a local optimum with respect to one neighbourhood structure is not necessarily so with another, 2) a global optimum is a local optimum with respect to all possible neighbourhood structures, and 3) it has been observed empirically that for many

Figure 2. General scheme of TS

0. Define the neighbourhood structure *N*
1. Let *S* an initial solution and *S** := *S*
2. While the stop condition is not reached do:
3.   Let *S'* the best neighbour from *N(S)* which is non-tabu or allowed by aspiration criterion
4.   If *S'* is better than *S**, then *S** := *S'*
5.   Add the current move in the tabu list (removing its last move if the list is full)
6.   *S* := *S'*
7. Return *S**

problems local optima with respect to one or several neighbourhood structures are relatively close to each other.

In the basic VNS proposed in Mladenović and Hansen (1997) there is a local search step, which can be costly in terms of cpu time for large instances of some problems (Glover and Kochenberger, 2003, Chapter 6). Hansen and Mladenović (1998) proposed the Reduced VNS (RVNS), in which the local search step is removed. The general scheme of RVNS is shown in Figure 3.

Corominas *et al.* (2009c) proposed a RVNS algorithm for solving the RTVP because it is shown that the local search step for large RTVP instances is very costly in terms of computing time. The neighbourhood structures used are *N1*, *N2* and *N3* and the initial solution is generated at random by lottery scheduling. The original acceptance criteria used in Hansen and Mladenović (1998) is that the neighbour solution *S'* was better than the current solution *S**. However, the acceptance criteria chosen in Corominas et al. (2009c) is that the neighbour solution *S'* is better than or equal to the current solution *S*. Its aim is to facilitate escaping local optima. Thus, the RVNS algorithm has not parameters to be fin-tuned.

Note that all local optima in the neighbourhood *N2* and *N3* are always local optima with respect *N1* because the neighbourhood of a solution with respect to *N1* is a subset of its neighbourhood with respect to *N2* and *N3*. Thus, it seems that the neighbourhood *N1* is unnecessary according to the aforementioned first and second facts in which are based VNS. Corominas *et al.* (2009c) showed that although similar solutions are obtained with or without the addition of *N1* to the set of neighbourhoods, the advantage of using *N1* is that it helps to the RVNS algorithm to converge faster.

3.5. Simulated Annealing (SA)

The simulated annealing metaheuristic (SA) was proposed by Kirkpatrick *et al.* (1983) to solve complex combinatorial optimisation problems. SA can be seen as a variant of a local search procedure in which is allowed moving to a worse solution with small probability. The objective of accepting worse solutions is to avoid being trapped into a local optimum. The metaheuristic starts from an initial solution, which is initially the current solution. Then, at each iteration, a new solution from the neighbourhood of the current solution is considered. If the neighbour is not worse than the current solution, then the neighbour becomes the current solution; in the case that is worse, the neighbour can become also the current solution with a probability that depends on: (1) how worse is the neighbour, and (2) the value of a parameter called temperature, which is decreased every certain number of iterations. The general scheme of SA (when minimising the objective function) is shown in Figure 4.

Figure 3. General scheme of RVNS

```
0.  Select the set of neighbourhood structures $N_k$ ($k$=1..$kmax$), where
    $kmax$ is the number of neighbourhoods
1.  Let $S^*$ be an initial solution
2.  While the stop condition is not reached do:
3.      $k := 1$
4.      While $k \leq kmax$ do:
5.          Select a solution $S'$ at random from $N_k(S^*)$
6.          If the acceptance criterion is satisfied, then $S^* := S'$ and $k := 1$;
7.          otherwise $k := k + 1$
8.  Return $S^*$
```

Figure 4. General scheme of SA

```
Let f(S) be the objective function of the solution S to be minimised
Let N(S) the neighbourhood of solution S
Let A(t) the new temperature calculated from the temperature t
0.  Set the parameters:
         t₀ (initial temperature)
         itt (number of iterations in which the temperature is not reduced)
1.  t := t₀;
2.  S := generate the initial solution
3.  While the stop condition is not reached do:
4.       i :=0
5.       While i < itt do:
6.            S' := choose at random a solution from N(S)
7.            Δ := f(S') − f(S)
8.            If Δ ≤ 0 then S := S'
9.            If Δ > 0 then S := S' with probability exp(-Δ/t)
10.           i := i + 1
11.      t := A(t)
12. Return the best solution found
```

Corominas *et al*. (2010b) proposed a straightforward SA algorithm for solving the RTVP. The initial solution is generated at random by lottery scheduling. The neighbourhood used is *N1*. The temperature is reduced by geometric reduction (that is, $A(t) = t \cdot \alpha$, where $\alpha < 1$), which is the most popular way in the literature (Dowsland and Adenso-Díaz, 2003; Glover and Kochenberger, 2003, Chapter 10).

Thus, the SA algorithm has 3 parameters to be fine-tuned: t_0 (initial temperature), *itt* (number of iterations in which the temperature is not reduced) and α (geometric reduction factor).

3.6. Genetic Algorithm (GA)

Genetic algorithm (GA) is a population metaheuristic based on the principles of natural selection and sexual reproduction which was first proposed in Holland (1975). Since then, the number of GA applications that have been reported in the literature to solve optimisation problems has grown exponentially (Glover and Kochenberger, 2003, Chapter 3).

The classical scheme of a GA is shown in Figure 5. First an initial population of *chromosomes* is generated, each of which represents a solution of the problem. A chromosome is composed of simple elements called *genes*. A fitness function is used to evaluate the fitness of the chromosomes. Then, a new population that evolves towards better chromosomes is iteratively generated from the current one until a stop condition is reached. Figure 5 shows that the new population is obtained by the offspring of the current population, but other strategies can be followed. The key to produce better chromosomes is based on two chromosome operators called crossover and mutation. Crossover combines parent chromosomes to generate offspring chromosomes that share some features taken from each parent. The selection of the parents depends on their fitness. The aim of the crossover is to form a new population with a higher proportion of the characteristics of the good chromosomes of the previous population (Beasley *et al*., 1993). Mutation is applied to the offspring chromosomes and consists of modifications to the values of several genes selected at random. Mutation diversifies the current population, and thus prevents premature convergence (Bean, 1994).

A chromosome consists of the positions of the copies of each symbol to be sequenced. Thus, each copy has a gene associated with it and the value of each gene indicates the position of its associated copy. The building block hypothesis (Goldberg, 1989) is considered to code the chromosomes. This hypothesis states that a successful coding scheme is one that encourages the formation of *building blocks*. A building block is a list of consecutive genes that work well together. Thus, there is a building block for each symbol i formed by the genes that indicate the positions in the sequence of the copies of symbol i. The reason is that the quality of a solution depends on the response time variability for each symbol i (see Equation 1), which depends on the relative distances between the units of symbol i. For instance, $n = 3$ with symbols A, B and C, and $d_A = 3$, $d_B = 2$ and $d_C = 2$. The chromosome that code the solution (B, C, A, B, A, A, C) is $(3, 5, 6 \mid 1, 4 \mid 2, 7)$, where "|" separates the building blocks. Note that the solution space using the proposed representation is not all the space of permutations. For instance, using the same example, the chromosome $(5, 3, 6 \mid 1, 4 \mid 2, 7)$ is unfeasible because it indicates that the position of the first copy of symbol A (which is 5) is greater than the position of the second copy of symbol A (which is 3) and this is

incoherent with the definition of first copy and second copy. The initial population is initialized with P solutions generated at random by lottery scheduling. The fitness of a chromosome is the inverse of the RTV value, which is good since the fitness is used only to rank the chromosomes.

The offspring obtained by applying the classical crossover operator in a permutation search space is usually unfeasible. To solve this difficulty, García-Villoria and Pastor (2010a) proposes a variation of the partially matched crossover (PMX) operator (Goldberg and Lingle, 1985). PMX cross two parent chromosomes as follows. First, two cut points are chosen at random along the chromosomes. Next, the section between these points defines an interchange mapping. A variation of the original PMX is proposed to adapt it for the used chromosomes. The first difference is that the PMX variation selects a complete building block at random, instead of two random cut points, with the aim of ensuring the preservation of a good building block. The second difference is that a feasibility post-process is needed, as unfeasible offspring may be produced as it has been said previously. To repair the chromosome, the genes of each building block are arranged in increasing order. Figure 6 shows a complete example of the application of the PMX variation.

The proposed mutation operates as follows. Each gene has a probability p to mutate. If a gene

Figure 5. Scheme of a classical GA

```
1. Current population := generate the initial population of chromosomes
2. Evaluate the fitness of each chromosome
3. While the stop condition is not reached do:
4.      New population = Ø
5.      While new population is not full do:
6.           Select two parent chromosomes according to their fitness from the current population
7.           Apply crossover to the parents to obtain two offspring chromosomes
8.           Apply mutation to the obtained offspring chromosomes
9.           Add the generated offspring to the new population
10.     Current population = new population
11. Return the best chromosome (solution) found
```

Figure 6. Application of the PMX variation

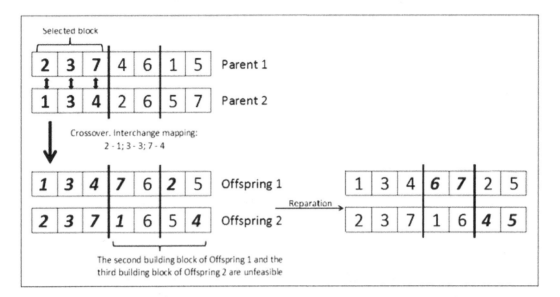

is mutated, then there is a probability of 0.5 to increase its value by one (if the value is the length of the chromosome, then its value is changed to 1) and there is a probability of 0.5 to decrease its value by one (if the value is 1, then its value is changed to the length of the chromosome). Let v and v' be the original and the new value of the mutated gene, respectively. The value of the other gene whose value is v' is changed to v. After the mutations of the chosen genes, the repairing post-process used in the proposed crossover operator is also needed.

The classical generation of the offspring population is shown in Steps 4-9 of Figure 5. It is used in García-Villoria and Pastor (2010a) together with elitist strategy and immigration. Elitist strategy, proposed in Goldberg (1989), involves copying the best chromosomes from the parent population to the offspring population. The advantage of the elitist strategy is that the best solution monotonically improves from one generation to the next (Bean, 1994). However, this strategy has the disadvantage of premature convergence of the population. To avoid this, Bean (1994) proposes the idea of immigration. This consists

of including several new chromosomes that are generated at random in the offspring population. The proportion of best parent chromosomes (*B)* and the proportion of new chromosomes (*R*) introduced into the offspring population are parameters of the algorithm. Parents are selected for the crossover as follows. One parent is chosen at random with a uniform probability from the best chromosomes population and the other parent is chosen at random with a uniform probability from the non-best population.

Thus, the GA algorithm has 4 parameters to be fine-tuned: *P* (size of the population), *p* (mutation probability), *B* (proportion of best chromosomes) and *R* (proportion of new chromosomes).

3.7. Particle Swarm Optimisation (PSO)

PSO is a population metaheuristic introduced by Kennedy and Eberhart (1995) which is based on the social behaviour of flocks of birds when they search for food. Originally, PSO was designed to work in a continuous space, although it has been successfully adapted for working in a discrete space (e.g., Secrest, 2001; Tasgetiren *et al.*, 2007). The population or swarm is composed of particles (birds), whose attributes are an *m*-dimensional real point (which represents a feasible solution) and a velocity (the vector or movement of the point in the *m*-dimensional real space). The velocity of a particle is typically a combination of three types of velocities: 1) the inertia velocity (i.e., the previous velocity of the particle); 2) the velocity to the best point found by the particle; and 3) the velocity to the best point found by the population. These components of the particles are modified iteratively by the algorithm as it searches for an optimal solution. These modifications are formalized with the following two equations:

$$v_i^{t+1} = w \cdot v_i^t + c_1 r_1 \cdot \left(p_i^t - x_i^t \right) + c_2 r_2 \cdot \left(gbest - x_i^t \right), \tag{8}$$

$$x_i^{t+1} = x_i^t + v_i^{t+1} \tag{9}$$

where *t* is the current iteration, v_i^t is the current velocity of particle i at iteration t, ω is the inertia parameter that weights the previous velocity of particle i, c1 and c2 are two parameters multiplied by two random numbers, r1 and r2 respectively, uniformly distributed in the range [0, 1], x_i^t is the current point of particle i at iteration t, $\left(p_i^t - x_i^t \right)$ is the velocity towards the best point found so far by the particle, and $\left(gbest - x_i^t \right)$ is the velocity towards the best point found so far by the whole swarm.

14 PSO algorithms have been proposed in the literature to solve the RTVP (García *et al.*, 2006; García-Villoria and Pastor, 2009). In all of them the initial population is obtained generating random solutions by lottery scheduling. Although the PSO metaheuristic was originally designed for a continuous space, all the 14 PSO algorithms were adapted to work with the sequence that represents a solution. Specifically, the operations of Equations 8 and 9 were redefined as follows. The expression $(X_2 - X_1)$, where X_2 and X_1 are two points (solutions), represents the difference between the two solutions, that is, the velocity needed to go from X_1 to X_2. This velocity consists of an ordered list of transformations (called movements) that must be applied sequentially to the particle so that its current point, X_1, changes to the other one, X_2. A movement is a pair of values (α, j). For each position *u* in the sequence (point) X_1, the algorithm determines whether the copy that is in position *u* of sequence X_1 is the same copy that is in position *u* of sequence X_2. If the copies are different, α is the copy in position *u* of X_2 and *j* is equal to position *u*. Thus, this movement denotes that to go from the sequence X_1 to the sequence X_2, the unit in position *j* must be exchanged for the unit α. The sum of a velocity plus a point gives the result of sequentially applying each movement of the velocity to the point, and the sum of two velocities is the concatenation of their own list of movements. Finally, the multiplication of a velocity by the coefficient ω, c_1 or c_2 indicates that each movement of the velocity has a probability ω, c_1 or c_2, respectively, that the movement is applied.

The best of the 14 PSO algorithms is called *DPSOpoi-c$_p$dyn* (García-Villoria and Pastor, 2009). In order to prevent a premature search convergence, *DPSOpoi-c$_p$dyn* introduces random modifications to the points of the particles after being applied Equations 8 and 9 with a frequency that changes dynamically as follows. For each position of the point (which is a sequence that represents a solution), the position has a probability cp $(0 \leq c_p \leq 1)$ of being swapped with another, randomly selected position. The parameter c_p changes dynamically according to the heterogeneity of the swarm at iteration *t* according to Equation 10:

$$c_p = e^{-K \cdot het(t)}, \tag{10}$$

where K is a parameter to be set, het(t) is a measure of the heterogeneity of the population defined as $het(t) = \dfrac{\sum_{i \in P} |v_i^t|}{D \cdot P}$, where $|v_i^t|$ is number of movements of the velocity of particle i at iteration t, D is the total number of copies to be sequenced, and P is the size of the population.

Thus, *DPSOpoi-$c_p$dyn* has 5 parameters to be fine-tuned: P (size of the population), ω (velocity inertia), c_1 and c_2 (vector weights), and K (diversity weight).

3.8. Ant Colony Optimisation (ACO)

The ACO metaheuristic was initially designed by Dorigo to solve the travelling salesman problem (Dorigo, 1992) but quickly started to be used to solve other combinatorial optimisation problems (Dorigo and Socha, 2007). ACO was initially inspired by the biological behaviour of ants but was soon modified to solve combinatorial optimisation problems more efficiently. ACO differs from real ants in the following ways (Dorigo and Socha, 2007): 1) artificial ants move through a discrete space; 2) heuristic information is also considered when the solutions are being built; 3) the pheromone update is performed only by some ants and often after a solution has been constructed; and 4) ACO may include artificial mechanisms such as local search and look-ahead.

The first step in solving a problem with ACO is to associate a graph $G = (N, E)$, called *construction graph*, with the problem. The nodes in the set N are usually components of the solution, and the artificial ants build a solution incrementally by moving from node to node along the edges of the set E. Each edge has an associated pheromone trail value and a heuristic value. The ants combine the pheromone and the heuristic information to select the next edge probabilistically. Figure 7 shows a classical scheme of the ACO metaheuristic, which consists in setting an initial value (τ_0) for each pheromone trail and then looping over the

following three components until a stop condition is reached: (1) the construction of a solution by the ants; (2) a local search from some or all the solutions (this component is optional); and (3) the update of the pheromone trail values.

The first ACO metaheuristic proposed in the literature was ant system (AS) (Dorigo, 1992). Several other variants of the ACO metaheuristic have been introduced to improve the performance of AS. All ACO metaheuristics use the scheme shown in Figure 7, but they contain different definitions for constructing solutions and updating pheromones (Steps 4 and 6 in Figure 7). For more extensive information about ACO, see the book by Dorigo and Stützle (2004).

Among the ACO variants proposed in the literature, ant colony systems (ACS) is one of the most successful ACO metaheuristics in practice (Dorigo and Blum, 2005). The step of constructing ant solutions is as follows. Given a construction graph $G = (N, E)$, each ant constructs a solution starting with an empty partial solution s^p. Then, a component from N is added to s^p at each construction step until the solution is complete. The next component to be added is determined by selecting at random an edge from the set $E(s^p)$, which is the subset of E composed of the eligible edges for the partial solution s^p. The probability that an edge e_{ij} (where i is the last component added to s^p) will be chosen is given by the Equation (11) in Box 1.

Where q is a random number distributed uniformly over [0,1], q_0 is a parameter of ACS, τ_{ij} is

Figure 7. Scheme of the ACO metaheuristic

1. Set the values of the ACO parameters
2. Initialize the pheromone trail values
3. While the stop condition is not reached do:
4.   Construct ant solutions
5.   Apply local search [optional]
6.   Update pheromones
7. Return the best solution found

Box 1.

$$p(e_{ij} \mid s^p) = \begin{cases} 1 & \text{if } q \leq q_0 \text{ and } j = \underset{k \in N \mid e_{ik} \in E(s^p)}{\arg\max} \; \tau_{ik}^{\alpha} \cdot \eta(e_{ik})^{\beta} \\[2ex] 0 & \text{if } q \leq q_0 \text{ and } j \neq \underset{k \in N \mid e_{ik} \in E(s^p)}{\arg\max} \; \tau_{ik}^{\alpha} \cdot \eta(e_{ik})^{\beta} \\[2ex] \dfrac{\tau_{ij}^{\alpha} \cdot \eta(e_{ij})^{\beta}}{\displaystyle\sum_{e_{ik} \in E(s^p)} \tau_{ik}^{\alpha} \cdot \eta(e_{ik})^{\beta}} & \text{if } q > q_0 \end{cases} \qquad (11)$$

the pheromone trail values associated with the edge e_{ij}, $\eta(e_{ij})$ is the heuristic information that indicates how desirable it is to choose the edge e_{ij}, and α and β are two positive parameters of ACS that weight the importance of the pheromone value and the heuristic information, respectively.

Pheromones are updated according to the constructed solutions (or their local optimum, if local search is applied). This component is designed to increase the pheromone trail values associated with the edges used by good solutions and to decrease the pheromone trail values associated with the edges used by bad solutions. ACS applies two pheromone updates: the offline pheromone update and the local pheromone update. The offline pheromone update is applied at the edges belonging to the best solution among all the solutions generated in the current iteration using the equation in Box 2.

$\rho \in (0,1]$ is a parameter called the evaporation rate and f is the objective function of the problem to be minimised. The local pheromone update is performed by all ants when an edge eij is chosen according to the equation $\tau_{ij} = (1 - \varphi) \cdot \tau_{ij} + \varphi \cdot \tau_0$

where $\varphi \in (0,1)$ is a parameter called the pheromone decay coefficient and τ0 is the initial value of the pheromone trails. The local update is intended to diversify the search performed by subsequent ants in the current iteration of ACS by reducing the pheromone value of the edges that are chosen by the previous ants. Note that τ_{ij} only decreases if τ_0 is smaller than the current τ_{ij}; consequently, τ_0 is usually set to a low value (Lo *et al.*, 2008).

Corominas et al. (2009d) proposed an ACS algorithm for the RTVP. The construction graph G = (N, E) is proposed as follows. The set of nodes N is the union of the sets N1 and N2, where $N_1 = \left\{ n_k^i : 1 \leq i \leq n - 1, 1 \leq k \leq d_i - 1 \right\}$ and $N_2 = \left\{ t : 1 \leq t \leq D - 1 \right\}$. Note that symbol n is not included in N1 because the positions of the copies of this symbol will be fixed when the previous symbols were sequenced. The node n_k^i belonging to N1 represents the copy k of the symbol i; the node t belonging to N2 represents a distance between two copies of the same symbol. Let $E \subset N_1 \times N_2$, where the edge $e_{ikt} = \left(n_k^i, t \right)$

Box 2.

$$\tau_{ij} = \begin{cases} (1 - \rho) \cdot \tau_{ij} + \rho \cdot \dfrac{1}{f(bs)} & \text{if } e_{ij} \text{ belong to } bs \\[2ex] \tau_{ij} & \text{otherwise} \end{cases}$$

represents that copy $k + 1$ of symbol i is sequenced at distance t of copy k of symbol i.

An ant starts to generate a solution sequence by setting copy 1 of symbol 1 to the first position of the sequence. Then, an edge has to be chosen at random from the set $E\left(s^{p}\right) = \left\{ e_{1,1,t} : 1 \le t \le D - d_1 + 1 \right\}$ using the probabilities defined by Equation 11. The choice of the edge will fix the position (let it be called p_2^1) of the second copy of symbol 1 to the value $1 + t$. Note that the highest possible position p_2^1 is $D - d_1 + 2$, so the remaining copies of symbol 1 can be sequenced at the positions $p_2^1 + 1, p_2^1 + 2, ..., D$. The ant then chooses an edge at random from the set $E\left(s^{p}\right) = \left\{ e_{1,2,t} : 1 \le t \le D - \left(d_1 - 2\right) - p_2^1 + 1 \right\}$. This process continues for copies 3, 4, ..., $d_1 - 1$ of symbol 1. The set of eligible edges when copy k of symbol 1 has been sequenced is $E\left(s^{p}\right) = \left\{ e_{1,k,t} : 1 \le t \le D - \left(d_1 - k\right) - p_k^1 + 1 \right\}$ where p_k^1 is the position at the sequence of copy k of symbol 1. When all copies of symbol 1 have been sequenced, the process is repeated for the copies of symbol 2, then symbol 3, and so on up to the penultimate symbol. The first copy of each symbol is always sequenced at the first free position in the sequence. The other copies of each symbol are sequenced in the same way as those of symbol 1, but the eligible edges must be chosen in such as way that the copies are not sequenced at an occupied position.

With respect to the heuristic information for each edge e_{ikt}, Corminas et al. (2009d) proposed to use $\eta\left(e_{ikt}\right) = \dfrac{1}{\left(t - \overline{t}_i\right)^2 + \varepsilon}$, where ε is a small value (10^{-6}) to prevent a division by zero. The authors also propose to use a local search step defined as follows. It is performed iteratively in the neighbourhood $N1$. The best solution in the neighbourhood is then chosen, and the local search

stops when a certain number of iterations (*lsiter*) are reached or when there is no any neighbour better than the current solution. The reason for using the parameter *lsiter* is that during the first iterations of the ACS algorithm usually the solutions constructed by the ants are relatively poor. Consequently, it may be very computationally expensive to apply a local search until a local optimum is found when large instances are being solved, so only a maximum of *lsiter* iterations of the ACS algorithm is allowed.

Thus, the ACS algorithm has 8 parameters to be fine-tuned: P (size of the population), q_0 (selection edge probability factor), α (pheromone weight), β (heuristic weight), τ_0 (initial pheromone trail value), ρ (evaporation rate), φ (pheromone decay coefficient) and *lsiter* (maximum local search iterations).

3.9. Electromagnetism-Like Mechanism (EM)

EM is a population metaheuristic created by Birbil and Fang (2003). It is based on an analogy with the attraction-repulsion mechanism of electromagnetism theory. Each solution of the population is considered as a point in a continuous space with an electrical charge that is measured by the objective function. This charge determines the magnitude of attraction or repulsion of the other points for applying the electromagnetism equations and EM iteratively calculates the movement of the points. Moreover, some solutions are improved by local search.

This metaheuristic works with a special class of optimisation problems with bounded variables in the following form:

$$\min \; (\max) \; f\left(x\right)$$

$$\text{subject to } x \in \Re^{m} \mid l_j \le x_j \le u_j, j = 1, ..., m$$

where f is the function that evaluates a point (which represents a solution), m is the dimension of the problem (in the case of the RTVP, m would be equal to D) and x_j is the coordinate of the jth dimension, which is lower bounded by l_j and upper bounded by u_j. The pseudocode of EM is shown in Figure 8.

The local search procedure provides the EM algorithm with a good balance between the exploration and exploitation of the feasible region. Birbil and Fang (2003) propose two possible approaches according to the points to which the local search can be applied: local search applied to all points and local search applied only to the current best point. In any case, the local search is limited to a maximum *lsiter* number of iterations.

Before calculating the total force for each point x, first its charge of each point x (q_x), which determines the intensity of attraction or repulsion of the point, is calculated as follows:

$$q_x = \exp\left(-m \frac{f(x) - f(x^{best})}{\sum\limits_{y \in CP} \left(f(y) - f(x^{best})\right)}\right)$$

Note that, unlike electrical charges, no signs are associated with the charges. The direction of a particular force between two points is determined when their objective values have been compared. Then the total force for the point x (F_x) is evaluated as follows in Box 3.

$\|y - x\|$ in Box 2 is the euclidean distance between the two points.

Finally, the point x is moved according to the next equation:

$$x = x + \lambda \frac{F_x}{\|F_x\|} (RNG)$$

where λ denotes a random number uniformly distributed between 0 and 1, $\|F_x\|$ is the norm of the force vector and RNG is a vector whose components denote the allowed feasible movement

Figure 8. General scheme of EM

1. Generate an initial population
2. While the stop condition is not reached do:
3. x^{best} := best point of the current population
4.   Apply local search
5.   Calculate for each point of the current population CP its total force vector
6.   Move each point of the current population according to their total force vectors
7. Return the best point (solution) found

Box 3.

$$F_x = \sum_{y \in CP|y \neq x} \begin{cases} (y - x)\dfrac{q_x q_y}{\|y - x\|^2} & if \quad f(y) < f(x) \quad \text{(Attraction)} \\[2ex] (x - y)\dfrac{q_x q_y}{\|y - x\|^2} & if \quad f(y) \geq f(x) \quad \text{(Repulsion)} \end{cases}$$

toward the upper bound, uj, or the lower bound, lj, of the corresponding dimension. Specifically, the jth component of RNG is $u_j - x_j$ if the jth component of F_x is greater than 0, and $x_j - l_j$ otherwise. Note that the force exerted is normalized so the feasibility is maintained (i.e., each coordinate of each point will be between l_j and u_j).

García-Villoria and Pastor (2010b) proposed a straightforward application of EM for the RTVP. Note that the operators of EM work with points of a real space as PSO does (see Section 3.7). The authors proposed to represent a solution as a D-dimensional real point using random key (Bean, 1994) as it is usual in the EM literature (e.g., Debels and Vanhoucke 2006; Chang et al. 2009). The initial population of points is obtained at random as follows. For each coordinate j of the point, a random value uniformly distributed in $[l_j, u_j]$ is generated, where $l_j = 0$ and $u_j = 1$. Finally, the local search is performed iteratively in the neighbourhood *N2* as follows; the first solution found in the neighbourhood that is better than the current solution is selected; the optimisation ends when the maximum number of iterations is reached or no neighbouring solution is better than the current solution. The local search is applied only to the best point of the current population.

Thus, the EM algorithm has 2 parameters to be fine-tuned: P (size of the population) and *Isiter* (maximum local search iterations).

3.10. Psychoclonal Optimisation (PSC)

PSC is a new population metaheuristic that was first proposed by Tiwari *et al.* (2005). According to the authors, this metaheuristic inherits its characteristics from the need hierarchy theory of Maslow (1954) and the artificial immune system, specifically the clonal selection principle (Gaspar and Collard, 2000). There are five levels of needs in Maslow's hierarchy, which in ascending order

are physiological needs, safety needs, social needs, growth needs and self-actualization needs. Clonal selection explains the response of immune systems to non-self antigens. The antibody-producing cells (lymphocytes) that are able to recognize intruding antigens are selected to proliferate by cloning. They then undergo an affinity maturation process that consists of hypermutations. The purpose of the latter is to obtain cells that produce antibodies able to improve their affinities to the non-self antigens. The worst cells undergo receptor editing: cells are deleted and replaced by new ones. The whole process continues until the self-actualization level is reached. Figure 9 shows the basic scheme of PSC.

Hypermutation is similar to the mutation operator of GA, but the difference lies in the fact that the modification rate of the hypermutation is inversely proportional to the fitness of the antibody (solution)

García-Villoria and Pastor (2010c) proposed a PSC algorithm to solve the RTVP. The affinity function of an antibody S, $f(S)$, is evaluated as $1 / (RTV(S) + \varepsilon)$, where RTV($S$) is the RTV value of the antibody S and ε is a small value (10^{-6}) to avoid a division by zero. The initial population is set with P antibodies generated at random by lottery scheduling. Iteratively, the best n antibodies according to their fitness are selected to be cloned. The number of clones that are generated for the ith best antibody (i = 1,...,n) is $\lfloor \beta \cdot P / i \rfloor$, where $\lfloor x \rfloor$ is an operator that returns the biggest integer value smaller than or equal to x, and β is a multiplying factor. Then each clone S' are submitted for hypermutation at a rate inversely proportional to their affinity value; specifically, the hypermutation rate is $\max \left(1, \left\lfloor D \cdot e^{-K \frac{f(S')}{f^*}} \right\rfloor \right)$, where K is the control factor of decay and f^* is the fitness of the best antibody of the current population. The hypermutation rate indicates how

Figure 9. General scheme of PSC

```
1. Generate an initial population of antibodies (solutions)
2. While the stop condition is not reached do:
3.     Select the best antibody and clone (replicate) them in a number proportional to their fitness
4.     Hypermutate the clones
5.     New population is formed by the best clones and by new solutions generated at random
6. Return the best antibody found
```

many simple mutations are applied to the cloned antibodies. A simple mutation consists in randomly choosing two positions of the sequence that represents the solution (antibody) and swapping them. In order to maintain the best antibodies, each original (parent) antibody remains unhypermutated. The new population is set with the $(P - d)$th best cloned or original antibodies and it is completed adding d new antibodies, which are generated at random by lottery scheduling.

Thus, the PSC algorithm has 5 parameters to be fine-tuned: P (size of the population), n (number of the best solutions to be cloned), β (multiplying factor to calculate the number of clones of a given solution), K (control factor of decay of the hypermutation rate) and d (the number of new solutions generated at random to be added to the population).

3.11. Methodology

Since metaheuristics are diverse in nature (i.e., they present very different ways to escape local optima), comparison of metaheuristics is in many ways more difficult than other algorithms comparisons (Gendreau and Potvin, 2010, p. 625).

We used a methodology that helps to compare fairly the performance of the aforementioned algorithms. This is important because it may allow us to understand the relevance of the metaheuristic components for its performance and to evaluate their contribution. Thus, we could design improved hybrid metaheuristics for the RTVP and other related problems. The methodology is defined by the following points:

- All 27 metaheuristic algorithms were applied to solve the same problem and it is used the same set of problem instances for testing the algorithms.
- The algorithms were designed and coded by the same team, so the influence of different programming skills is avoided.
- Each test instance is solved by each algorithm running it during the same amount of time. Moreover, it was used the same computing environment (i.e., computer, operating system, programming language and compiler). That allows to compare fairly their runtimes (Gendreau and Potvin, 2010, Chapter 21).
- A representative set of training instances was used to fine-tune the parameters of the algorithms instead of fine-tuning parameter on the instances used for testing. Thus, it is avoided overtraining data, which is useful for comparing metaheuristics (Gendreau and Potvin, 2010, Chapter 21). Overtraining refers to the phenomenon that the parameter values perfectly fit the tested instances, but may have a poor performance when applied to new unseen instances.
- The parameter values were set using the automatic tool called CALIBRA (Adenso-Díaz and Laguna, 2006).

Most of the metaheuristics have a set of parameters that need to be fine-tuned before the execution. This previous step, which is almost always a difficult task and requires a lot of time, is very important because the values of the parameters have usually a strong influence in the performance of algorithms. However, in the literature they are often selected using one of the following methods, which are not sufficiently thorough (Eiben *et al.*, 1999; Adenso-Díaz and Laguna, 2006): 1) "by hand", based on a small number of experiments that are not referenced; 2) using the general values recommended for a wide range of problems; 3) using the values reported to be effective in other similar problems; or 4) with no apparent explanation. On the other hand, CALIBRA was used to set the parameter values of all algorithms. It is specifically designed for fine-tuning parameters, which is based on using conjointly Taguchi's fractional factorial experimental designs and a local search procedure. CALIBRA has the advantage of being a systematic tool able to find good parameter values which needs of little human intervention and it is used in the international literature (e.g., Venditti *et al.*, 2010).

The following parameter values were found by CALIBRA for the best algorithm of each type of metaheuristic:

- **MS**: $P = 1,500$
- **GRASP:** Size of the candidate list = 3
- **TS**: Size of the tabu list = 38
- **RVNS:** It has not parameters
- **SA:** $t_0 = 13$, $itt = 1,762$ and $\alpha = 0.9875$
- **GA:** $P = 13$, $p = 0.013$, $B = 0.18$ and $R = 0.12$
- **PSO:** $P = 13$, $\omega = 0.75$, $c_1 = 0.13$, $c_2 = 0.75$ and $K = 8.70$
- **ACO:** $P = 20$, $q_0 = 0.9$, $\alpha = 1.5$, $\beta = 1.75$, $\tau_0 = 0.00013$, $\rho = 0.87$, $\varphi = 0.13$ and *lsiter* $= 50$
- **EM:** $P = 25$ and *lsiter* $= 5$
- **PSC:** $P = 25$, $n = 3$, $\beta = 1.3$, $K = 7.6$ and $d = 3$

3.12. Computational Experiment

The benchmark instances consist of 60 training instances for fine-tuning the parameters of the algorithms and 740 test instances (all instances can be found at https://www.ioc.upc.edu/EOLI/research/). These instances were grouped into four classes (from *CAT1* to *CAT4* with 15 training instances and 185 test instances in each class) according to their size. The instances were generated using the random values of D (number of copies) and n (number of symbols) shown in Table 2. For all instances and for each symbol i = 1,…,n, a random value of d_i (number of copies of symbol i) is between 1 and $\lceil (D - n + 1)/2.5 \rceil$ such that $\sum_{i=1..n} d_i = D$.

All algorithms were coded and run under Java 2 Platform Standard Edition (J2SE) 1.4.2.14 using Windows XP and all computational experiments were carried out on a 3.4 GHz Pentium IV with 1.5 GB of RAM.

Tables 3 and 4 show the average RTV values of the solutions obtained with the proposed algorithms for 50 and 1,000 computing seconds, respectively. For the sake of clarity, when there is more than one algorithm based on the same metaheuristic, only the results of the best of them are shown. We observed that 1,000 seconds is enough for the convergence of the algorithms.

We can see a wide variability between the performance of the metaheuristics; the worst RTV average (obtained with the PSO algorithm) after 1,000 seconds is around 30 times bigger than the best average (obtained with the SA algorithm). With enough time for the convergence of the al-

Table 2. Uniform distributions for generating the D and n values

	CAT1	CAT2	CAT3	CAT4
D	U(25, 50)	U(50, 100)	U(100, 200)	U(200, 500)
n	U(3, 15)	U(3, 30)	U(3, 65)	U(3, 150)

Table 3. RTV averages obtained for 50 computing seconds

	GLOBAL	CAT1	CAT2	CAT3	CAT4
MS[a]	2,106.01	11.56	38.02	154.82	8,219.65
GRASP[a]	2,308.69	13.00	60.45	270.93	8,890.37
TS[b]	210.47	10.26	22.56	73.26	735.78
RVNS[c]	63.96	10.73	23.69	51.80	169.64
SA[d]	50.87	10.26	21.67	44.57	126.98
GA[e]	186.94	11.65	29.41	84.54	622.16
PSO[f]	4,625.54	16.42	51.34	610.34	17,824.04
ACO[g]	1,651.48	10.92	36.83	504.84	6,053.31
EM[h]	3,747.05	19.14	54.54	260.79	14,653.72
PSC[i]	235.68	14.92	44.25	137.07	746.50

(a) Corominas *et al.*, 2008; (b) Corominas et al., 2009b; (c) Corominas *et al.*, 2009c; (d) Corominas *et al.*, 2010b; (e) García-Villoria and Pastor, 2010a; (f) García-Villoria and Pastor, 2009; (g) Corominas *et al.*, 2009d; (h) García-Villoria and Pastor, 2010b; (i) García-Villoria and Pastor, 2010c

Table 4. RTV averages obtained for 1,000 computing seconds

	GLOBAL	CAT1	CAT2	CAT3	CAT4
MS[a]	169.25	10.51	31.21	123.27	512.02
GRASP[a]	301.90	11.56	50.45	227.50	918.10
TS[b]	78.62	10.24	21.16	48.12	234.96
RVNS[c]	62.24	10.73	23.69	51.40	163.15
SA[d]	50.75	10.26	21.67	44.55	126.54
GA[e]	106.68	10.92	27.00	74.86	313.92
PSO[f]	1,537.34	14.35	46.55	143.96	5,944.51
ACO[g]	1,208.81	10.46	31.17	337.31	4,456.32
EM[h]	330.29	18.64	52.97	157.20	1,092.36
PSC[i]	161.60	14.90	39.90	122.38	469.23

(a) Corominas *et al.*, 2008; (b) Corominas et al., 2009b; (c) Corominas *et al.*, 2009c; (d) Corominas *et al.*, 2010b; (e) García-Villoria and Pastor, 2010a; (f) García-Villoria and Pastor, 2009; (g) Corominas *et al.*, 2009d; (h) García-Villoria and Pastor, 2010b; (i) García-Villoria and Pastor, 2010c

gorithms, there is the tendency that single-point metaheuristics (MS, GRASP, TS, RVNS and SA) perform better than population metaheuristics (GA, PSO, ACO, EM and PSC). In particular, SA, RVNS and TS outperforms all five population metaheuristics; their global RTV averages are 52.43%, 41.66% and 26.30% better, respectively, than the RTV average of the best population metaheuristic (GA). The best performance of SA, RVNS and TS is valid independently of the size of the instances (for *CAT1* to *CAT4* instances). Moreover, it is worth to mention that even, for the RTVP, two so simple metaheuristics as MS and GRASP are able to improve three sophisticated population metaheuristics (EM, ACO and PSO).

Regarding to the single-point metaheuristics, SA, RVNS and TS are trajectory methods versus MS and GRASP, which are discontinuous methods. Moreover, SA and RVNS, which are the best metaheuristics, are stochastic and memoryless versus TS, which is deterministic and uses memory. Thus, the two best metaheuristics that we tested are the ones that are stochastic, single-point, trajectory and memoryless methods.

If we compare the results obtained with 50 computing seconds (Table 3) and with 1,000 computing seconds (Table 4), we can see that SA and RVNS are also the two methods that converge faster. The improvements of the SA and RVNS results after 1,000 seconds are only 0.24% and 2.69% better with respect to the results with 50 seconds, respectively.

4. HYBRID METAHEURISTICS FOR THE RESPONSE TIME VARIABILITY PROBLEM

The main motivation of applying hybrid metaheuristic techniques was the idea that this type of algorithms may benefit from the exploitation the complementary character of different metaheuristic strategies. Thus, the combination of different concepts can be the key for high performance in solving many hard optimisation problems (Blum *et al.*, 2011).

The methodology that we followed and the analysis of the metaheuristics shown in the previous section helped to design hybrid metaheuristics by combining their main components or characteristics in order to improve the solution of the RTVP. Three metaheuristic algorithms for the RTVP based on hybridizing VNS with TS, PSO and MS, respectively, have been proposed for the RTVP (Corominas *et al.*, 2011). Moreover, we propose two new metaheuristics based on hybridizing SA with MS and VNS, respectively.

The five hybrid algorithms are explained in Sections 4.1 to 4.5, respectively, the parameter values obtained with CALIBRA are given in Section 4.6 and the computational results are discussed in Section 4.7.

4.1. TS Hybridized with VNS (TS+VNS)

In the classical TS, the current solution is moved in only one neighbourhood structure. On the other hand, Xu *et al.* (2006) and Ekşioğlu *et al.* (2008) proposed a successful hybrid metaheuristic based on applying the main TS framework but incorporating a mechanism that dynamically alters neighbourhood, which is the cornerstone of VNS. On the other hand, Corominas *et al.* (2009b and 2009c) proposed a TS and a VNS algorithms, respectively, for the RTVP, which are two of the best algorithms for solving this problem (see Table 4). Thus, it seems natural that a TS algorithm based on changing dynamically between the neighbourhoods N_1, N_2 and N_3 (the ones used in the VNS algorithm) is proposed (Corominas *et al.*, 2011). Some of the benefits of altering neighbourhood under a TS framework can be the following (Xu *et al.*, 2006): 1) different neighbourhood moves bring in various degrees of changes for the new solution, so it carries diversification effects, and 2) the computing time for finding the best neighbour in some neighbourhoods is larger than in others, but this may be effective in locating better solutions. Dynamic neighbourhood moves can better address the balance between the efficiency and effectiveness of the TS algorithm.

The mechanism of neighbourhood changing proposed in Corominas *et al.* (2011) is the following. First, the TS algorithm starts using N_1. Each move that does not improve the best solution (S^*) is counted. When a maximum number of non improvement moves is reached (max_nim_1), the next neighbourhood N_2 is used. Similarly, when max_nim_2 non improvement moves is reached using N_2, the current neighbourhood is change to N_3. Again, when max_nim_3 non improvement moves is reached using N_3, the process continues iteratively using N_1 again. The pseudocode of *TS+VNS* is shown in Figure 10.

Figure 10. Pseudocode of TS+VNS

```
0.  Set the values of the parameters max_nimₖ (k = 1..3).
3.  Let S be an initial solution and S* := S
4.  k := 1, ni := 0
5.  While the execution time is not reached do:
6.      Let S' the best solution from Nₖ(S) which is non-tabu or allowed by aspiration criterion
7.      Add the current move in the tabu list (removing its last move if the list is full)
8.      If S' is better than S*, then S* := S'
9.      Otherwise:  ni := ni + 1
10.             If ni = max_nimₖ, then k := (k mod 3) + 1 and ni := 0
11.     S := S'
12. Return S*
```

The initial solution is obtained in the same way as obtained in the original TS algorithm; that is, from the best solution returned by the five heuristics proposed in Corominas *et al.* (2007). The same aspiration criterion remains also equal; that is, that the solution (S') would better than the best solution found in the past ($S*$). With respect to the tabu list, a forbidden move of the tabu list consists of two pairs of position/symbol. For instance, the move [(3, A), (5, B)] means that all solutions with the symbol A sequenced in position 3 and the symbol B sequenced in position 5 are considered tabu. In the case of the neighbourhood N_3, if the symbol A is inserted into position 3, then the move [(3, A)] is recorded in the tabu list.

Thus, *TS+VNS* has 4 parameters to be fine-tuned: size of the tabu list, max_nim_1, max_nim_2 and max_nim_3.

4.2. PSO Hybridized with VNS (PSO+VNS)

The RVNS algorithm has the following handicap. After certain computing time the search will be trapped in a local optimum with respect to all neighbourhoods which may be not a global optimum. On the other hand, in the classical PSO the process of diversification is more taken into account than the process of intensification (Tchomté and Gourgand, 2009). Maybe this is the reason of the bad performance even of the best PSO algorithm (compared to other metaheuristic algorithms) proposed in the literature for RTVP (see Table 4). In order to overcome this shortcoming, Tasgetiren *et al.* (2007) and Anghinolfi and Paolucci (2009) proposed a hybrid PSO metaheuristic in which improve the best solution of the population at each iteration by means of a local search method and a stochastic local search method to solve the permutation flowshop problem and a single-machine tardiness problem, respectively. Since the RVNS algorithm proposed in Corominas *et al.* (2009c) is one that performs best for solving the RTVP, Corominas *et al.* (2011) proposed the same hybrid PSO scheme but using the RVNS algorithm as the improvement mechanism.

Specifically, Corominas *et al.* (2011) proposed to hybridize $DPSOpoi\text{-}c_p dyn$ with the RVNS algorithm. At each iteration, the best solution found by the swarm is improved by applying the RVNS algorithm. The stopping condition of the RVNS algorithm consists in this case on reaching a maximum number of iterations without improving the current solution. The maximum number of iterations is $\lfloor D \cdot \alpha_{pso+vns} \rfloor$, where αpso_{+vns} is a parameter of the algorithm. The scheme of *PSO+VNS* is shown in Figure 11.

Thus, *PSO+VNS* has 6 parameters to be fine-tuned: P, ω, c_1, c_2, K and $\alpha_{PSO+VNS}$.

Figure 11. Pseudocode of PSO+VNS

```
1. Initialize population
2. While the execution time is not reached do:
3.      For each particle i do:
4.          Update velocity of i according to Equation 2
5.          Update point of i according to Equation 3
6.          For each position of the point i, swap it with another position
            selected at random with a probability cₚ (Equation 4)
7.          Update best point of particle i
9.      Update best point of the population and apply the RVNS algorithm to it.
10. Return the best point (solution) found
```

4.3. MS Hybridized with VNS (MS+VNS)

Instead of using the diversification PSO mechanism (see Section 4.2), the simpler multi-start mechanism could be used. Thus, Corominas *et al*. (2011) also proposed the following hybrid metaheuristic *MS+VNS*, which embeds the RVNS algorithm in a multi-start scheme. At each iteration, a random initial solution is obtained and then is improved by means of the RVNS algorithm. As in *PSO+VNS*, the embedded RVNS algorithm stops when reaches a maximum number of iterations without improving the current solution. The maximum number of iterations is $\lfloor D \cdot \alpha_{ms+vns} \rfloor$, where D is the total number of copies to be sequenced and α_{ms+vns} is the only parameter of the algorithm to be fine-tuned. Figure 12 shows the pseudocode of *MS+VNS*.

4.4. MS Hybridized with SA (MS+SA)

Regards to SA, when the temperature is too low then the probability of accepting worse neighbour solutions is negligible. Thus, in practice, SA may be trapped in a local optimum after certain computing time. To overcome this situation, we propose the hybrid algorithm *MS+SA*, in which a multi-start diversification mechanism is incorporated to SA. *MS+SA* is equal to *MS+VNS* except that the SA is applied to improve the solutions instead of RVNS

(Step 4 in Figure 12). In this case, SA stops when it reaches a low temperature t_f. Thus, *MS+SA* has 4 parameters to be fine-tuned: t_0, *itt*, α and t_f.

It seems natural to apply a multi-start scheme (or other diversification mechanism) to SA after a certain computing time (when the temperature is very low). However, to the best of our knowledge this idea does not appear in the literature.

4.5. SA Hybridized with VNS (SA+VNS)

The two best pure metaheuristics for solving the RTVP are SA and RVNS (see Table 4). The main differences between them are that the SA allows jumping to a worst neighbour and RVNS changes dynamically the neighbourhood structure. We propose the *SA+VNS* algorithm which has the main SA scheme in which the variable neighbourhood idea is adapted as follows. At each iteration, the neighbourhood used is selected at random

Figure 12. Pseudocode of MS+VNS

```
1. Let S* be a random solution
2. While the execution time is not reached do:
3.      Let S be a random solution
4.      Apply the RVNS algorithm to S and get S'
5.      If S' is better than S*, then S* := S'
6. Return S*
```

between $N1$, $N2$ and $N3$ with probabilities p_1, p_2 and $1 - p_1 - p_2$, respectively, where $p_1 + p_2 \leq 1$. The pseudocode of SA+VNS is shown in Figure 13.

Thus, $SA+VNS$ has 5 parameters to be fine-tuned: t_0, itt, α, p_1 and p_2.

4.6. Parameter Values

The following parameter values were found by CALIBRA for the hybrid algorithms:

- $TS+VNS$: Size of the tabu list = 127, max_nim_1 = 751, max_nim_2 = 8 and max_nim_3 = 26
- $PSO+VNS$: $P = 6$, $\omega = 0.87$, $c_1 = 0.75$, $c_2 = 0.87$, $K = 27.5$ and $\alpha_{pso+vns} = 9.4$
- $MS+VNS$: $\alpha_{ms+vns} = 37.5$
- $MS+SA$: $t_0 = 25$, $t_f = 0.008$, $itt = 1,525$ and $\alpha = 0.9875$
- $SA+VNS$: $t_0 = 76$, $itt = 1,525$, $\alpha = 0.9875$, $p_1 = 0.45$ and $p_2 = 0.22$

4.7. Computational Experiment

The same methodology explained in Section 3.11 was applied for the hybrid algorithms. Tables 5 and 6 show the average RTV values of the solutions obtained with the proposed hybrid algorithms and the pure metaheuristics used in their design (which include the best metaheuristics) for 50 and 1,000 computing seconds, respectively.

The addition of variable neighbourhood mechanism to the TS and SA algorithms helps to improve their performances. The hybrid algorithm TS+VNS is able to obtain solutions 29.98% and 11.55% better, on average, than the solutions obtained with TS and RVNS, respectively, after 1,000 computing seconds. And SA+VNS obtains solutions 4.57% and 22.19% better, on average, than the solutions of SA and RVNS, respectively.

The addition of a diversification mechanism to VNS helps to obtain better hybrid metaheuristic versions. The global RTVP averages obtained with PSO+VNS and MS+VNS after 1,000 seconds are 10.25% and 11.71% better than the RVNS aver-

Figure 13. Pseudocode of SA+VNS

```
0.  Set the parameters:
         t₀ (initial temperature)
         itt (number of iterations in which the temperature is not reduced)
1.  t := t₀;
2.  S := generate the initial solution by lottery scheduling
3.  While the execution time is not reached do:
4.       i :=0
5.       While i < itt do:
6.            Let N be the neighbourhood selected at random between N₁, N₂ and N₃
                 with probabilities p₁, p₂ and 1 - p₁ - p₂, respectively
7.            S' := choose at random a solution from N(S)
8.            Δ := f(S') − f(S)
9.            If Δ ≤ 0 then S := S'
10.           If Δ > 0 then S := S' with probability exp(-Δ/t)
11.           i := i + 1
12.      t := t.α
13. Return the best solution found
```

Table 5. RTV averages obtained for 50 computing seconds

	GLOBAL	CAT1	CAT2	CAT3	CAT4
MS	2,106.01	11.56	38.02	154.82	8,219.65
TS	210.47	10.26	22.56	73.26	735.78
RVNS	63.96	10.73	23.69	51.80	169.64
SA	50.87	10.26	21.67	44.57	126.98
PSO	4,625.54	16.42	51.34	610.34	17,824.04
TS+VNS	71.57	10.38	24.00	53.99	197.90
PSO+VNS	60.03	10.47	22.42	49.37	157.86
MS+VNS	62.17	10.24	21.23	47.46	169.76
MS+SA	51.84	10.24	21.19	43.57	132.35
SA+VNS	48.97	10.26	21.54	43.62	120.45

Table 6. RTV averages obtained for 1,000 computing seconds

	GLOBAL	CAT1	CAT2	CAT3	CAT4
MS	169.25	10.51	31.21	123.27	512.02
TS	78.62	10.24	21.16	48.12	234.96
RVNS	62.24	10.73	23.69	51.40	163.15
SA	50.75	10.26	21.67	44.55	126.54
PSO	1,537.34	14.35	46.55	143.96	5,944.51
TS+VNS	55.05	10.24	22.48	47.66	139.84
PSO+VNS	55.86	10.45	22.00	46.80	144.22
MS+VNS	54.95	10.24	20.94	43.26	145.35
MS+SA	46.95	10.24	20.92	41.73	114.91
SA+VNS	48.43	10.26	21.51	43.47	118.46

age. Notice that very similar results are obtained by using the sophisticated PSO mechanism or the simple multi-start mechanism to add diversification to the search.

The best results, with 1,000 computing seconds, are obtained with the hybrid MS+SA. As in the case of the RVNS, the addition of a diversification mechanism (multi-start) helps to SA to obtain better results. MS+SA obtains solutions that are 7.49% better, on average, than SA, which is the best pure metaheuristic.

Finally, we have also solved the case study presented in Herrmann (2007), in which a real-life waste collection case is solved. This case is the only one which data is available and it has the following characteristics: $n = 14$, $d = (2, 2, 2, 2, 3, 3, 3, 3, 4, 4, 4, 4, 5, 5)$ and, therefore, $D = 46$. This example is small-sized and easy to solve (optimally solved using the MILP model presented in Corominas *et al.* (2010a)). We tried to solve it using all proposed hybrid metaheuristics and an optimal solution was returned (since there is randomness, it was solved 50 times with each algorithm, and optimal solutions were always returned).

To sum up, the analysis of the pure metaheuristics guided us to propose new hybrid metaheuristics. It was clearly useful since all hybrid metaheuristics were able to improve the performance of the metaheuristics from which they were inspired and, among them, MS+SA obtains, on average, the best solutions.\

5. CONCLUSION AND FUTURE RESEARCH DIRECTIONS

Managers, engineers and researchers have to deal with new optimisation problems or variants of known problems for their particular cases. Metaheuristics are a suitable technique to solve these types of problems. However, the theoretical basis of metaheuristics does not allow knowing which one would perform better to solve our problem. Thus, empirical evidence is necessary to determine which metaheuristic is the best for our problem. Moreover, metaheuristic hybridization techniques make possible to design improved algorithms specifically for our problem.

In this chapter we presented and solved the RTVP, which appears in a wide range of real world contexts, including engineering and business applications. This problem is a sequencing, combinatorial optimisation problem that is, in general, very hard to solve. Thus, metaheuristics are a suitable technique to solve it.

First, we select 10 metaheuristics to test on our problem. Then, we propose a methodology for a fair comparison between metaheuristics and run a computational experiment. Thus, the analysis of the obtained results helps us to design improved hybrid metaheuristics for the RTVP. A computational experiment shows that the solutions obtained with the best hybrid metaheuristic algorithm are, on average, 7.49% better than the solutions obtained with the best pure metaheuristic algorithm.

Note that other well known and powerful metaheuristics as, for instance, iterated local search, evolutionary programming, differential evolution, scatter search and path-relinking has not been included to solve the RTVP. They may also be good metaheuristics to solve the RTVP; however, since there are many of them in the literature, in practice we cannot test all existing metaheuristics.

Unfortunately, there is not a general guideline of which type of hybrid metaheuristic might work well for a certain problem (Blum *et al.*, 2011). We think that this chapter can be a useful practical example of how dealing other types of problems by means of metaheuristics and how to design specific hybrid metaheuristics.

In this chapter we have been shown hybridization between classic metaheuristics, which is a new trend to solve hard problems. Other new trend is the hybridization made by the interoperation of heuristics (or metaheuristics) and mathematical programming techniques, called matheuristics (Maniezzo *et al.*, 2009). An essential feature is the exploitation in some parts of the algorithms of features derived from the mathematical model of the problem of interest. Generally speaking, matheuristics present a so-called master-slave structure of a guiding process and an application process. Either (1) the (meta)heuristic acts at a higher level and controls the calls to the mathematical programming model or (2) the mathematical programming model acts as the master and calls and controls the use of the (meta)heuristic.

To compare the performance of different methods, we proposed and followed a methodology in order to reduce the influence of external variables. This is an important trend that has been being reflected in the literature since it allows comparing the performance of different methods more fairly. Especially, the automatic, hands-off parameter tuning of algorithms is being very relevant due to the fact that the parameter values largely influence the performance of the algorithm. For instance, an evolutionary algorithm with good parameter values can be orders of magnitude better than one with poorly chosen parameter values (Eiben and Smit, 2011).

REFERENCES

Adenso-Díaz, B., & Laguna, M. (2006). Fine-tuning of algorithms using fractional experimental designs and local search. *Operations Research, 54*, 99–114. doi:10.1287/opre.1050.0243

Anghinolfi, D., & Paolucci, M. (2009). A new discrete particle swarm optimization approach for the single-machine total weighted tardiness scheduling problem with sequence-dependent setup times. *European Journal of Operational Research, 193*, 73–85. doi:10.1016/j.ejor.2007.10.044

Anily, S., Glass, C. A., & Hassin, R. (1998). The scheduling of maintenance service. *Discrete Applied Mathematics, 82*, 27–42. doi:10.1016/S0166-218X(97)00119-4

Balinski, M. L., & Young, H. P. (Eds.). (1982). *Fair representation*. New Haven, CT: Yale University Press.

Bar-Noy, A., Nisgav, A., & Patt-Shamir, B. (2002). Nearly optimal perfectly-periodic schedules. *Distributed Computing, 15*, 207–220. doi:10.1007/s00446-002-0085-1

Bautista, J., Companys, R., & Corominas, A. (1997). Modelling and solving the production rate variation problem (PRVP). *Top (Madrid), 5*, 221–239. doi:10.1007/BF02568551

Bean, J. C. (1994). Genetic algorithms and random keys for sequencing and optimization. *ORSA Journal on Computing, 6*, 154–160. doi:10.1287/ijoc.6.2.154

Beasley, D., Bull, D. R., & Martin, R. R. (1993). An overview of genetic algorithms: Part 1, fundamentals. *University Computing, 15*, 58–69.

Birattari, M., Paquete, L., Stützle, T., & Varrentrapp, K. (2001). *Classification of metaheuristics and design of experiments for the analysis of components*. Technical Report AIDA-01-05, Darmstadt University of Technology, Germany.

Birbil, S. I., & Fang, S. C. (2003). An electromagnetism-like mechanism for global optimization. *Journal of Global Optimization, 25*, 263–282. doi:10.1023/A:1022452626305

Blum, C., Puchinger, J., Raidl, G. R., & Roli, A. (2011). Hybrid metaheuristics in combinatorial optimization: A survey. *Applied Soft Computing, 11*, 4135–4151. doi:10.1016/j.asoc.2011.02.032

Boender, C. G. E., Rinnooy, A. H. G., Stougie, L., & Timmer, G. T. (1982). A stochastic method for global optimization. *Mathematical Programming, 22*, 125–140. doi:10.1007/BF01581033

Bollapragada, S., Bussieck, M. R., & Mallik, S. (2004). Scheduling commercial videotapes in broadcast television. *Operations Research, 52*, 679–689. doi:10.1287/opre.1040.0119

Brusco, M. J. (2008). Scheduling advertising slots for television. *The Journal of the Operational Research Society, 59*, 1363–1372. doi:10.1057/palgrave.jors.2602481

Chang, P.-C., Chen, S.-H., & Fan, C.-Y. (2009). A hybrid electromagnetism-like algorithm for single machine scheduling problem. *Expert Systems with Applications, 36*, 1259–1267. doi:10.1016/j.eswa.2007.11.050

Chiarandini, M., Paquete, L., Preuss, M., & Ridge, E. (2007). *Experiments on metaheuristics: Methodological overview and open issues. Technical Report DMF-2007-03-003*. Denmark: University of Copenhagen.

Corominas, A., García-Villoria, A., & Pastor, R. (2008). Solving the response time variability problem by means of multi-start and GRASP metaheuristics. *Frontiers in Artificial Intelligence and Applications, 184*, 128–137.

Corominas, A., García-Villoria, A., & Pastor, R. (2009a). *Using tabu search for the response time variability problem*. Paper presented at the 3rd International Conference on Industrial Engineering and Industrial Management, Barcelona and Terrassa, Spain.

Corominas, A., García-Villoria, A., & Pastor, R. (2009b). *Resolución del response time variability problem mediante tabu search*. Paper presented at the 8th Evento Internacional de Matemática y Computación, Universidad de Matanzas, Cuba.

Corominas, A., García-Villoria, A., & Pastor, R. (2009c). *Solving the response time variable problem by means of a variable neighbourhood search algorithm*. Paper presented at the 13th IFAC Symposium of Information Control Problems in Manufacturing, Moscow, Russia.

Corominas, A., García-Villoria, A., & Pastor, R. (2009d). *Using an ant colony system to solve the response time variability problem*. Technical report IOC-DT-P-2009-06, Universitat Politècnica de Catalunya, Spain.

Corominas, A., García-Villoria, A., & Pastor, R. (2010b). *A new metaheuristic procedure for improving the solution of the response time variability problem*. Paper presented at the 4th International Conference on Industrial Engineering and Industrial Management, San Sebastián, Spain.

Corominas, A., García-Villoria, A., & Pastor, R. (2011). *Metaheuristic algorithms hybridized with variable neighbourhood search for solving the response time variability problem*. doi: 10.1007/s11750-011-0175-y

Corominas, A., Kubiak, W., & Moreno, N. (2007). Response time variability. *Journal of Scheduling, 10*, 97–110. doi:10.1007/s10951-006-0002-8

Corominas, A., Kubiak, W., & Pastor, R. (2010a). Mathematical programming modeling of the response time variability problem. *European Journal of Operational Research, 200*, 347–357. doi:10.1016/j.ejor.2009.01.014

Debels, D., & Vanhoucke, M. (2006). The electromagnetism meta-heuristic applied to the resource-constrained project scheduling problem. *Lecture Notes in Computer Science, 3871*, 259–270. doi:10.1007/11740698_23

Dong, L., Melhem, R., & Mosse, D. (1998). *Time slot allocation for real-time messages with negotiable distance constrains requirements*. Paper presented at the 4th IEEE Real-Time Technology and Applications Symposium, Denver, CO.

Dorigo, M. (1992). *Optimization, learning and natural algorithms*. Ph.D. Thesis. Department of Electronics, Politecnico di Milano, Italy.

Dorigo, M., & Blum, C. (2005). Ant colony optimization theory: A survey. *Theoretical Computer Science, 344*, 243–278. doi:10.1016/j.tcs.2005.05.020

Dorigo, M., & Socha, K. (2007). An introduction to ant colony optimization. In Gonzalez, T. F. (Ed.), *Handbook of approximation algorithms and metaheuristics*.

Dorigo, M., & Stützle, T. (Eds.). (2004). *Ant colony optimization*. Cambridge, MA: MIT Press. doi:10.1007/b99492

Dowsland, K. A., & Adenso-Díaz, B. (2003). Heuristic design and fundamentals of the simulated annealing. *Inteligencia Artificial, 19*, 93–102. doi:10.1023/A:1022188514489

Eiben, A. E., Hinterding, R., & Michalewicz, Z. (1999). Parameter control in evolutionary algorithms. *IEEE Transactions on Evolutionary Computation, 3*, 124–141. doi:10.1109/4235.771166

Eiben, A. E., & Smith, S. K. (2011). Parameter tuning for configuring and analyzing evolutionary algorithms. *Swarm and Evolutionary Computation, 1*, 19–31. doi:10.1016/j.swevo.2011.02.001

Ekşioğlu, B., Ekşioğlu, S. D., & Pramod, J. (2008). A tabu search algorithm for the flowshop scheduling problem with changing neighborhoods. *Computers & Industrial Engineering, 54*, 1–11. doi:10.1016/j.cie.2007.04.004

Feo, T. A., & Resende, M. G. C. (1989). A probabilistic heuristic for a computationally difficult set covering problem. *Operations Research Letters*, *8*, 67–81. doi:10.1016/0167-6377(89)90002-3

García, A., Pastor, R., & Corominas, A. (2006). Solving the response time variability problem by means of metaheuristics. *Frontiers in Artificial Intelligence and Applications*, *146*, 187–194.

García-Villoria, A., & Pastor, R. (2009). Introducing dynamic diversity in a discrete particle swarm optimization. *Computers & Operations Research*, *36*, 951–966. doi:10.1016/j.cor.2007.12.001

García-Villoria, A., & Pastor, R. (2010a). Solving the response time variability problem by means of a genetic algorithm. *European Journal of Operational Research*, *202*, 320–327. doi:10.1016/j.ejor.2009.05.024

García-Villoria, A., & Pastor, R. (2010b). Solving the response time variability problem by means of the electromagnetism-like mechanism. *International Journal of Production Research*, *48*, 6701–6714. doi:10.1080/00207540902862545

García-Villoria, A., & Pastor, R. (2010c). Solving the response time variability problem by means of a psychoclonal approach. *Journal of Heuristics*, *16*, 337–351. doi:10.1007/s10732-008-9082-2

Gaspar, A., & Collard, P. (2000). Two models of immunization for time dependent optimization. *IEEE International Conference on Systems Manufacturing and Cybernetics*, (pp. 113-118).

Gendreau, M., & Potvin, J.-Y. (Eds.). (2010). *Handbook of metaheuristics* (2nd ed.). New York, NY: Springer. doi:10.1007/978-1-4419-1665-5

Glover, F. (1986). Future paths for integer programming and links to artificial intelligence. *Computers & Operations Research*, *5*, 533–549. doi:10.1016/0305-0548(86)90048-1

Glover, F., & Kochenberger, G. A. (Eds.). (2003). *Handbook of metaheuristics*. New York, NY: Kluwer Academic Publishers.

Goldberg, D. E. (Ed.). (1989). *Genetic algorithms in search, optimization and machine learning*. Boston, MA: Addison-Wesley Longman Publishing.

Goldberg, D. E., & Lingle, R. (1985). Alleles, loci, and the traveling salesman problem. *First International Conference on Genetic Algorithms*, (pp. 154-159).

Han, C. C., Lin, K. J., & Hou, C. J. (1996). Distance-constrained scheduling and its applications in real-time systems. *IEEE Transactions on Computers*, *45*, 814–826. doi:10.1109/12.508320

Hansen, P., & Mladenović, N. (1998). An introduction to variable neighborhood search. In Voß, S., Martello, S., Osman, I. H., & Roucairo, C. (Eds.), *Meta-heuristics: Advances and trends in local search paradigms for optimization* (pp. 433–458). New York, NY: Springer.

Herrmann, J. W. (2007). *Generating cyclic fair sequences using aggregation and stride scheduling. Technical Report*. USA: University of Maryland.

Herrmann, J. W. (2011). Using aggregation to reduce response time variability in cyclic fair sequences. *Journal of Scheduling*, *14*, 39–55. doi:10.1007/s10951-009-0127-7

Holland, J. H. (1975). *Adaptation in natural and artificial systems*. Cambridge, MA: MIT Press.

Inman, R. R., & Bulfin, R. L. (1991). Sequencing JIT mix-model assembly lines. *Management Science*, *37*, 901–904. doi:10.1287/mnsc.37.7.901

Kennedy, J., & Eberhart, R. C. (1995). *Particle swarm optimization*. Paper presented at the 4th IEEE International Conference on Neural Networks, Perth, Australia.

Kirkpatrick, S., Gelatt, C. D., & Vecchi, M. P. (1983). Optimization by simulated annealing. *Science, 220*, 671–680. doi:10.1126/science.220.4598.671

Kubiak, W. (1993). Minimizing variation of production rates in just-in-time systems: A survey. *European Journal of Operational Research, 66*, 259–271. doi:10.1016/0377-2217(93)90215-9

Kubiak, W. (2004). Fair sequences. In Lenung, J. Y.-T. (Ed.), *Handbook of scheduling: Algorithms, models and performance analysis*. Boca Raton, FL: Chapman and Hall/CRC.

Kubiak, W. (Ed.). (2009). *Proportional optimization and fairness*. New York, NY: Springer.

Lo, S.-T., Chen, R.-M., Huang, Y.-M., & Wu, C.-L. (2008). Multiprocessor system scheduling with precedence and resource constraints using an enhanced and colony system. *Expert Systems with Applications, 34*, 2071–2081. doi:10.1016/j.eswa.2007.02.022

Maniezzo, V., Stützle, T., & Voß, S. (Eds.). (2009). *Matheuristics: Hybridizing metaheuristics and mathematical programming*. New York, NY: Springer Annals of Information Systems.

Maslow, A. H. (1954). *Motivation and personality*. New York, NY: Harper & Bros.

Miltenburg, J. (1989). Level schedules for mixed-model assembly lines in just-in-time production systems. *Management Science, 35*, 192–207. doi:10.1287/mnsc.35.2.192

Mladenović, N., & Hansen, P. (1997). Variable neighbourhood search. *Computers & Operations Research, 24*, 1097–1100. doi:10.1016/S0305-0548(97)00031-2

Mladenović, N., Petrović, J., Kovačević-Vujčić, V., & Čangalović, M. (2003). Solving spread spectrum radar polyphase code design problem by tabu search and variable neighbourhood search. *European Journal of Operational Research, 151*, 389–399. doi:10.1016/S0377-2217(02)00833-0

Monden, Y. (Ed.). (1983). *Toyota production systems*. Norcross, GA: Engineering & Management Press.

Secrest, B. (2001). *Travelling salesman problem for surveillance mission using PSO*. PhD thesis, Air Force Institute of Technology, Ohio, USA.

Tasgetiren, M. F., Liang, Y.-C., Sevkli, M., & Gencyilmaz, G. (2007). A particle swarm optimization algorithm for makespan and total flowtime minimization in the permutation flowshop sequencing problem. *European Journal of Operational Research, 177*, 1930–1947. doi:10.1016/j.ejor.2005.12.024

Tchomté, S. K., & Gourgand, M. (2009). Particle swarm optimization: A study of particle displacement for solving continuous and combinatorial optimization problems. *International Journal of Production Economics, 121*, 57–67. doi:10.1016/j.ijpe.2008.03.015

Tiwari, M. K., Prakash, A., Kumar, A., & Mileham, A. R. (2005). Determination of an optimal sequence using the psychoclonal algorithm. *ImechE, Part B: Journal of Engineering Manufacture, 219*, 137–149. doi:10.1243/095440505X8028

Venditti, L., Pacciarelli, D., & Meloni, C. (2010). A tabu search algorithm for scheduling pharmaceutical packaging operations. *European Journal of Operational Research, 202*, 538–546. doi:10.1016/j.ejor.2009.05.038

Waldspurger, C. A., & Weihl, W. E. (1994). *Lottery scheduling: Flexible proportional-share resource management*. Paper presented at the 1st USENIX Symposium on Operating System Design and Implementation, Monterey, CA.

Waldspurger, C. A., & Weihl, W. E. (1995). *Stride scheduling: Deterministic proportional-share resource management*. Technical Report MIT/LCS/TM-528, Massachusetts Institute of Technology, USA.

Wei, W. D., & Liu, C. L. (1983). On a periodic maintenance problem. *Operations Research Letters*, *2*, 90–93. doi:10.1016/0167-6377(83)90044-5

Xu, J., Sohoni, M., McCleery, M., & Bailey, T. G. (2006). A dynamic neighbourhood based tabu search algorithm for real-world flight instructor scheduling. *European Journal of Operational Research*, *169*, 978–993. doi:10.1016/j.ejor.2004.08.023

ADDITIONAL READING

Anghinolfi, D., Montemanni, R., Paolucci, M., & Gambardella, L. M. (2011). A hybrid particle warm optimization approach for the sequential ordering problem. *Computers & Operations Research*, *38*, 1076–1085. doi:10.1016/j.cor.2010.10.014

Baradaran, S., Ghomi, S. M. T. F., Mobini, M., & Hashemin, S. S. (2010). A hybrid scatter search approach for resource-constrained project scheduling problem in PERT-type networks. *Advances in Engineering Software*, *41*, 966–975. doi:10.1016/j.advengsoft.2010.05.010

Barr, R., Golden, B., & Kelly, J. (1995). Designing and reporting on computational experiments with heuristic methods. *Journal of Heuristics*, *1*, 9–32. doi:10.1007/BF02430363

Behnamian, J., Ghomi, S. M. T. F., & Zandieh, M. (2010). Development of a PSO–SA hybrid metaheuristic for a new comprehensive regression model to time-series forecasting. *Expert Systems with Applications*, *37*, 974–984. doi:10.1016/j.eswa.2009.05.079

Bertacco, L., Fischetti, M., & Lodi, A. (2007). A feasibility pump heuristic for general mixed-integer problems. *Discrete Optimization*, *4*, 63–76. doi:10.1016/j.disopt.2006.10.001

Birattari, M. (Ed.). (2005). *Tuning metaheuristics*. New York, NY: Springer.

Birattari, M., Yuan, Z., & Stützle, T. (2010). F-race and iterated F-race: An overview. In Bartz-Beielstein, T., Chiarandini, M., Paquete, L., & Preuss, M. (Eds.), *Experimental methods for the analysis of optimization algorithms* (pp. 311–336). New York, NY: Springer. doi:10.1007/978-3-642-02538-9_13

Blesa, M. J., Blum, C., Di Gaspero, L., Roli, A., Sampels, M., & Schaerf, A. (Eds.). (2009). *Proceedings of HM 2009 – Sixth International Workshop on Hybrid Metaheuristics, Lecture Notes in Computer Science, 5818*.

Blum, C., Aguilera, M. J. B., Roli, A., & Sampels, M. (Eds.). (2008). *Hybrid metaheuristics – An emerging approach to optimization*. New York, NY: Springer.

Blum, C., & Roli, A. (2003). Metaheuristics in combinatorial optimization: Overview and conceptual comparison. *ACM Computing Surveys*, *35*, 268–308. doi:10.1145/937503.937505

Bozejko, W., Uchronskia, M., & Mieczyslaw, W. (2010). Parallel hybrid metaheuristic for the flexible job shop problem. *Computers & Industrial Engineering*, *59*, 323–333. doi:10.1016/j.cie.2010.05.004

Burke, E., & Kendall, G. (Eds.). (2005). *Search methodologies: Introductory tutorials in optimization and decision support techniques*. New York, NY: Springer.

Chaves, A. A., & Lorena, L. A. N. (2011). Hybrid evolutionary algorithm for the capacitated centered clustering problem. *Expert Systems with Applications, 38*, 5013–5018. doi:10.1016/j.eswa.2010.09.149

Chen, P.-H., & Shahandashti, S. M. (2009). Hybrid of genetic algorithm and simulated annealing for multiple project scheduling with multiple resource constraints. *Automation in Construction, 18*, 434–443. doi:10.1016/j.autcon.2008.10.007

Cotta, C. (1998). A study of hybridisation techniques and their application to the design of evolutionary algorithms. *AI Communications, 11*, 223–224.

Dahal, K. P., & Chakpitak, N. (2007). Generator maintenance scheduling in power systems using metaheuristic-based hybrid approaches. *Electric Power Systems Research, 77*, 771–779. doi:10.1016/j.epsr.2006.06.012

Delorme, X., Gandibleux, X., & Degoutin, F. (2010). Evolutionary, constructive and hybrid procedures for the bi-objective set packing problem. *European Journal of Operational Research, 204*, 206–217. doi:10.1016/j.ejor.2009.10.014

Demeester, P., Souffriau, W., Causmaecker, P. D., & Berghe, G. V. (2010). A hybrid tabu search algorithm for automatically assigning patients to bed. *Artificial Intelligence in Medicine, 48*, 61–70. doi:10.1016/j.artmed.2009.09.001

Euchi, J., & Mraihi, R. (2012). The urban bus routing problem in the Tunisian case by the hybrid artificial ant colony algorithm. *Swarm and Evolutionary Computation, 2*, 15–24. doi:10.1016/j.swevo.2011.10.002

Fischetti, M., & Lodi, A. (2003). Local branching. *Mathematical Programming, Series B, 98*, 23–47. doi:10.1007/s10107-003-0395-5

García-Villoria, A., Salhi, S., Corominas, A., & Pastor, R. (2011). Hyper-heuristic approaches for the response time variability problem. *European Journal of Operational Research, 211*, 160–169. doi:10.1016/j.ejor.2010.12.005

Homberger, J., & Gehring, H. (2005). A two-phase hybrid metaheuristic for the vehicle routing problem with time windows. *European Journal of Operational Research, 162*, 220–238. doi:10.1016/j.ejor.2004.01.027

Hooker, J. (1995). Testing heuristics: We have it all wrong. *Journal of Heuristics, 1*, 33–42. doi:10.1007/BF02430364

Hutter, F., Hoos, H. H., Leyton-Brown, K., & Stützle, T. (2009). ParamILS: An automatic algorithm configuration framework. *Journal of Artificial Intelligence Research, 36*, 267–306.

Lau, H. C., Wan, W. C., Lim, M. K., & Halim, S. (2004). *A development framework for rapid metaheuristics hybridization*. Paper presented at the 28th Annual International Computer Software and Applications Conference, Hong Kong, China.

Leung, S. C. H., Zhang, D., Zhou, C., & Wu, T. (2012). A hybrid simulated annealing metaheuristic algorithm for the two dimensional knapsack packing problem. *Computers & Operations Research, 39*, 64–73. doi:10.1016/j.cor.2010.10.022

Liao, T. W. (2010). Two hybrid differential evolution algorithms for engineering design optimization. *Applied Soft Computing, 10*, 1188–1199. doi:10.1016/j.asoc.2010.05.007

Lozano, M., & García-Martínez, C. (2010). Hybrid metaheuristics with evolutionary algorithms specializing in intensification and diversification: Overview and progress report. *Computers & Operations Research, 37*, 481–497. doi:10.1016/j.cor.2009.02.010

Michalewicz, Z. (Ed.). (1996). *Genetic algorithms + data structures = evolution programs*. New York, NY: Springer.

Minzu, V., & Beldiman, L. (2007). Some aspects concerning the implementation of a parallel hybrid metaheuristic. *Engineering Applications of Artificial Intelligence, 20*, 993–999. doi:10.1016/j.engappai.2006.12.004

Peng, R. D. (2011). Reproducible research in computational science. *Science, 334*, 1226–1227. doi:10.1126/science.1213847

Salhi, S., & García-Villoria, A. (2011). An adaptive search for the response time variability problem. *The Journal of the Operational Research Society, 63*. doi:doi:10.1057/jors.2011.46

Shimizu, Y., Wada, T., & Yamazaki, Y. (2007). Logistics optimization using hybrid metaheuristic approach under very realistic conditions. *Computer Aided Chemical Engineering, 24*, 733–738. doi:10.1016/S1570-7946(07)80145-3

Sitarz, S. (2006). Hybrid methods in multi-criteria dynamic programming. *Applied Mathematics and Computation, 180*, 38–45. doi:10.1016/j.amc.2005.11.164

Sniedovich, M., & Voß, S. (2006). The corridor method: A dynamic programming inspired metaheuristic. *Control and Cybernetics, 35*, 551–577.

Taguchi, G., & Tokoyama, T. (1993). *Taguchi methods: Design of experiments*. ASI Press.

Tsai, C.-F., Tsai, C.-W., & Tseng, C.-C. (2004). A new hybrid heuristic approach for solving large travelling salesman problem. *Information Sciences, 166*, 67–81. doi:10.1016/j.ins.2003.11.008

Tseng, L.-Y., & Chen, S.-C. (2006). A hybrid metaheuristic for the resource-constrained project scheduling problem. *European Journal of Operational Research, 175*, 707–721. doi:10.1016/j.ejor.2005.06.014

Wang, X., & Tang, L. (2010). A hybrid metaheuristic for the prize-collecting single machine scheduling problem with sequence-dependent setup times. *Computers & Operations Research, 37*, 1624–1640. doi:10.1016/j.cor.2009.12.010

Wen, Y., Xu, H., & Yang, J. (2011). A heuristic-based hybrid genetic-variable neighbourhood search algorithm for task scheduling in heterogeneous multiprocessor system. *Information Sciences, 181*, 567–581. doi:10.1016/j.ins.2010.10.001

Zobolas, G. I., Tarantilis, C. D., & Ioannou, G. (2009). Minimizing makespan in permutation flow shop scheduling problems using a hybrid metaheuristic algorithm. *Computers & Operations Research, 36*, 1249–1267. doi:10.1016/j.cor.2008.01.007

KEY TERMS AND DEFINITIONS

Calibration of Heuristics: Most of heuristics has a set of parameters and the performance of these heuristics depends on the values of their parameters. The calibration of the heuristics refers to the action of setting the parameter values.

Combinatorial Optimisation Problem: Combinatorial optimisation problem is the problem of finding the best solution (according to a given criterion) from all feasible solutions in which the variables are discrete.

Comparison of Methods: The comparison of methods allows comparing their performance according to one or more criteria. It requires a methodology that ensures an objective comparison.

Fair Sequences: When a resource must serve many demands simultaneously, it is important to sequence the resource's activities in some fair manner, so that each demand receives a share of the resource that is proportional to its demand relative to the competing demands.

Metaheuristic Hybridization: Metaheuristic hybridization refers to the technique of merging two or more metaheuristic characteristics in a single metaheuristic in order to improve the performance of the original metaheuristic when dealing a given problem.

Metaheuristics: A metaheuristic is a top-level general strategy which guides other heuristics to search for feasible solutions in domains where the task is hard. One of their main characteristic is their ability to escape local optima. Metaheuristics are generally applied to problems for which there is no satisfactory problem-specific algorithm or heuristic.

Response Time Variability Problem: The response time variability problem is a combinatorial optimisation problem that occurs whenever products, clients, jobs, etc. need to be scheduled so as to minimise variability in the time between the instants at which they receive the necessary resources.

ENDNOTES

[1]   Supported by the Spanish Ministry of Education and Science under project DPI2007-61905, co-funded by the ERDF.

Chapter 11
Hybrid Metaheuristics Algorithms for Inventory Management Problems

Ata Allah Taleizadeh
Iran University of Science and Technology, Iran

Leopoldo Eduardo Cárdenas-Barrón
Tecnológico de Monterrey, México

ABSTRACT

The hybrid metaheuristics algorithms (HMHAs) have gained a considerable attention for their capability to solve difficult problems in different fields of science. This chapter introduces some applications of HMHAs in solving inventory theory problems. Three basic inventory problems, joint replenishment EOQ problem, newsboy problem, and stochastic review problem, in certain and uncertain environments such as stochastic, rough, and fuzzy environments with six different applications, are considered. Several HMHAs such as genetic algorithm (GA), simulated annealing (SA), particle swarm optimization (PSO), harmony search (HS), variable neighborhood search (VNS), and bees colony optimization (BCO) methods are used to solve the inventory problems. The proposed metaheuristics algorithms also are combined with fuzzy simulation, rough simulation, Pareto selecting and goal programming approaches. The computational performance of all of them, on solving these three optimization problems, is compared together.

INTRODUCTION

For as long as managers remember, companies have tried to design an effective and efficient business model where the vital goal is to satisfy customer needs better than competitors. Success depends basically on the design of processes that actually create or add value and with this one can be innovative. Companies should have always deliveries of products and services on time, with high quality, and at low cost. Those are some of the main issues that any customer demands.

Inventory is obviously a common issue in any organization. Many retail stores are stocked with a large quantity of goods. Manufacturers are also filled with huge inventory of raw materials,

DOI: 10.4018/978-1-4666-2086-5.ch011

work in process and finished goods. According to Muckstadt and Sapra (2010) manufacturers are also stored with inventories of equipment, machines, spare parts, among other things. Inventory theory is one of the fields where operations research has had noteworthy developments. For example, there are several mathematical models for the inventory control in use today in which the main objective is to have a good management of inventories of raw materials, spare parts or finished goods. Some of them are included in the most of commercial software for business solutions. Most of inventory models are developed to answer three primary questions: (1) what goods should be stored? (2) how much should be ordered when an order is placed to the vendor? and (3) when an order should be placed? The answer to these questions basically depends on the objectives of the business or even manager and the strategy used to accomplish the objectives. In actuality to answer these questions, one designs a variety of mathematical models based on a different set of assumptions concerning the way the inventory system being studied operates. Thus, the complexity of the inventory models depends on the assumptions and situation under which manager should decide about the demand, cost structure, and physical characteristic of inventory systems. It is a fact that the objective in most inventory models is to minimize costs. According to our experience, in most cases minimizing costs result in the same inventory policy as that determined by maximizing profits. This is one of the reasons why many researchers use the minimization approach instead of maximizing approach.

Typically, most inventory problems in situations of the real life involve multiple products. However, it is frequently that exist inventory models with a single product because these inventory models are capable to capture the fundamental elements of the problem. Therefore, it is not necessary to include the interaction of different products into the mathematical formulation. Furthermore multiple product inventory models are often too cumbersome to be used in practice when the variety of products is very huge. For this reason, single product inventory models are presented in the literature and are used frequently in practice. However, we will consider multi product inventory models in order to show that these models can be also implemented in practice easily.

This chapter reviews three practical inventory management problems considering certain and uncertain environments. They are: (1) joint replenishment EOQ problem, (2) newsboy problem, and (3) stochastic review problem. For each of them two different applications are provided.

The classical economic order quantity (EOQ) formula is the simplest inventory model for the cycle stock. It is well known that in the EOQ inventory model the demand, ordering and holding costs are deterministic over time. Also, the batch quantity may not be an integer, the whole batch quantity is delivered at the same time and backorders are not permissible. But we will give up all of mentioned assumptions and extend this version in two practical cases.

The newsboy problem is a classical periodic inventory management problem in which uncertainty in demand during a single period is considered. While the probability distribution of demand is known, the actual number of demand will not be known until after that the decision was made. Obviously, until the end of the period one can know the actual demand. In newsboy problem the order should be placed only in the beginning of the cycle. As it happens in the EOQ model also in the newsboy model the ordering and holding costs are deterministic over time. In this chapter we study an extended version of newsboy problem that considers fuzzy and rough environments and two different applications of the mentioned problem are proposed.

The stochastic review problem is one of the inventory management problems studied widely recently. Periodic inventory control problems are mainly developed considering two main assumptions: (1) the continuous review, where depending on the inventory level the orders can happen at any time and (2) the periodic review, where orders can only happen at the beginning of each period. Then, we relax the two assumptions aforementioned, and we assume that the periodic replenishments can randomly be placed.

BACKGROUND ON HYBRID META HEURISTICS ALGORITHMS

Metaheuristics methods were introduced to describe how work different heuristic algorithms which can be widely applied together to a set of different problems in a variety of fields. Thus, metaheuristics should be considered as a general algorithmic structure which can be used for solving hard optimization problems with relatively few modifications to make them custom-made to a specific problem. Some typical examples falling under metaheuristics methods (MHAs) are: genetic (GA) algorithm, simulated annealing (SA), particle swarm optimization (PSO), harmony search (HS), variable neighborhood search (VNS), bees colony optimization (BCO), firefly algorithm (FA), and ant colony optimization (ACO), just to name a few. According to Blum and Roli (2003) each of them has its own origins and background. Also, each one follows its own philosophies and paradigms, and sets one or more strategic ideas in the centre. Now, we explain briefly some of the MHAs below. Basically, we present their origins and the main concepts in which they are based.

Genetic Algorithms (GA): Holland (1975) introduced the fundamental principle of genetic algorithms (GA) for the first time. Since then, many academicians and researchers have applied and expanded this concept in several fields of study. GA is inspired by the concept of survival of the fittest. In GA, the best solution is the winner of the genetic game and any potential solution is assumed to be a creature that is determined by different parameters in a random fashion. In other words, GA uses a directed random search

to locate good solutions for complex optimization problems. GA mimics the evolution process of the species that reproduce. Therefore the GA does not operate on a unique current solution, but on a set of current solutions called population. New individuals (children) are generated according to a mechanism called crossover that combines part of the genetic patrimony of each parent and then applies a random. If the new individual, called child or offspring, inherits good characteristics from his parents the probability of its survival increases. This process will continue until a well-defined stopping criterion is satisfied. Then, the best child (offspring) is chosen as a near optimum solution.

Simulated Annealing (SA): Simulated annealing is a local search algorithm and it was inspired in the physical annealing process studied in statistical mechanics. According to Kirkpatrick et al. (1994) the SA is an effective and efficient algorithm that produces very good solutions. The SA algorithm does an iterative neighbor generation process and follows different search directions in order to improve the objective function value. The SA algorithm allows worse neighbor solutions in a controlled way in order to jump from local minima and find a better solution. In order to have more detailed information, the readers can see Aarts and Korst (1989), Kirkpatrick et al. (1994) and Taleizadeh et al. (2008).

Particle Swarm Optimization (PSO): Particle swarm optimization was proposed by Kennedy and Eberhart (1995). In PSO, a set of solutions generated in a random fashion (initial swarm) spreads in the design space in the direction of the optimal solution through a number of iterations (moves) based on large amount of information about the design space that is assimilated and shared by all members of the swarm. PSO is inspired by the ability of flocks of birds, schools of fish, and herds of animals to adapt to their environment quickly, finding rich sources of food, and avoiding predators by implementing an information sharing approach; with this the species develops an evolutionary benefit (for instance see Kennedy and

Eberhart 2001). Basically, the PSO algorithm has three main steps; generating particle's positions and exploration velocities, updating exploration velocity and position update.

Harmony Search Algorithm (HS): The HS algorithm was inspired from the act of musical groups and it was introduced such as an analogy with music improvisation process where musicians in a band continue to polish their pitches to obtain a better harmony (Geem, 2001). There is a similarity between musical groups and this algorithm. According to the analogy of improvisation and optimization processes, a fantastic harmony is the global optimum, the aesthetic is given by the objective function, the pitches of instruments are the values for the decision variables, and each practice is equivalent to an each iteration of the algorithm. The main steps of HS optimization algorithm include initialization (both parameter initialization and harmony memory initialization), new harmony generation and harmony memory update.

Variable Neighborhood Search (VNS): The VNS is based on a systematic change in the neighborhood within the search space. The exploration of several neighborhoods is crucial in VNS; with this the VNS is more effective and efficient and hence obtains better solutions. Basically, VNS explores distant neighborhoods of the current solution and jumps from it to a new solution if and only if a better solution is found. Obviously, the favorable characteristic of the current solution are kept and used to obtain a better neighborhood solution. Furthermore, a local search is applied repeatedly to obtain from the neighboring solutions a better solution (a local optimum). In order to have more detailed information, the readers can see Hansen and Mladenovic (2001).

Bees Colony Optimization (BCO): The BCO is inspired by bees' behavior in nature. The basic idea behind the BCO is to build a multi-agent system (colony of artificial bees) capable of solving hard combinatorial optimization problems successfully. The well-known example of bee behavior is the nectar collection and processing. Each bee targets the nectar source by following a mate who has previously found the nectar. If a bee chooses to leave the hive to get nectar, she follows one of the bee dancers to the nectar areas. Upon arrival, the foraging bee takes a load of nectar and goes back to the hive relinquishing the nectar. The bee selects for one of the above alternatives with a certain probability. Within the dance area, the bee dancers advertise different food areas (see Taleizadeh et al. 2011c). The mechanisms by which the bee decides to follow a specific dancer are not well understood, but it is considered that the recruitment among bees is always a function of the quality of the food source (Teodorovic, 2009). For more detailed information regarding BCO we refer to readers to the following research works Von Frisch 1976, Seeley 1996, Pham et al. 2006.

Firefly Algorithm (FA): Firefly algorithm was inspired by the social behavior of fireflies and it was introduced by Yang (2008). FA has been used in an enormous variety of applications spanning the permutation flow shop scheduling problem, codebook design of image vector quantization and financial portfolio optimization, among others. According to Yang (2009) the FA is based on three idealized laws: 1) All fireflies are unisex. In other words, one firefly is attracted to other fireflies regardless of their sex. 2) The degree of attractiveness of a firefly is proportional to its brightness, thus for any two fireflies, the bright one will go towards the brighter one. The less distance between two fireflies gives more brightness and attractiveness. If no firefly is brighter, then the firefly will move randomly. 3) The brightness of a firefly is given by the objective function value. For a maximization problem, the brightness can be proportional to the objective function value. In order to have additional information about FA algorithm readers can see the works of Yang (2008), Yang (2009) and Sayadi et al. (2010).

Recently, researchers have been generated a large number of combined different algorithms that basically do not fall into a unique metaheuristics category. Blum et al. (2008) state that the reason is due to the fact that these new approaches mix various algorithmic ideas, from several branches such as artificial intelligence, operations research and computer science. In the literature these approaches are usually referred to as hybrid metaheuristics.

Some researchers have been proposed general classifications for the hybrid metaheuristics algorithms (HMHAs), i.e. see the research works of Blum et al. (2011) and Jourdan et al. (2009). Here, we present briefly two general classifications for the HMHAs given in Blum et al. (2011) and Jourdan et al. (2009).

Blum et al. (2011)'s classification has five categories: (1) Hybridization of metaheuristics with heuristics or metaheuristics (HMHHMH), (2) Hybridization of metaheuristics with constraint programming (HMHCP), (3) Hybridizing metaheuristics with tree search (HMHTS), (4) Hybridization of metaheuristics with problem relaxation (HMHPR) and (5) Hybridization of metaheuristics with dynamic programming (HMHDP).

Hybridization of Metaheuristics with Heuristics or Metaheuristics (HMHHMH): In this category, the hybridization is made when one combines a metaheuristic with heuristics or other metaheuristics in order to obtain a better solution exploiting simultaneously the advantages of several algorithms.

Blum et al. (2011) state that in nowadays the hybridization of different metaheuristics is very common, particularly for solution procedures that use of local search methods within population-based methods such as genetic algorithms and particle swarm optimization technique. Certainly, evolutionary algorithms and ant colony optimization frequently are being used instead of local search procedures for improving the solutions during the search process. Indeed, this can be explained due to the fact that these heuristics or metaheuristics are good concerning to explore the search space and to identify zones with better solutions. It is well known that in initialization step, the heuristics or metaheuristics generally attempt to obtain an overall representation of the search space. After, during an exploration process the heuristics center the search on more promising zones of the search space solution. Although, heuristics or metaheuristics are usually not so effective to obtain the best solutions in the high quality zones, but they are so strong to quickly find better solutions in the vicinity of initialized solutions. It is important to remark that the population-based methods are clever in finding promising zones of the search space in which local search methods can quickly obtain the better solutions. This is the reason why the hybridization is usually successful.

Hybridization of Metaheuristics with Constraint Programming (HMHCP):This category considers the hybridization of metaheuristics with constraint programming (CP). Here, one of them is generally applied with good performance on problem classes for which the other one is not principally efficient and effective. In constraint programming basically constrained problems are modeled using the following elements: variables, domains and constraints. These elements can be mathematical or symbolic. Constraints capture well-defined parts of the problem into sub-problems.

In this approach, each constraint is used to delete values from a variable domain which do not belongs to feasible solutions. The solution process of CP is characterized by two phases: an interleaving of a propagation phase and a labeling phase. In the first phase infeasible values are removed from domain. And in the second phase an unassigned variable is selected and assign a value in its domain. It is well known that metaheuristics generally explore a search space where the states are defined by complete assignments (maybe some are possibly infeasible).On the other hand, the power of CP lies in its ability of examining a search space of partial assignments and obtaining a good solution that obviously satisfies the problem constraints.

It is important to mention that metaheuristic algorithms have been shown be effective and efficient in obtaining good solutions to hard and complex optimization problems. However, the metaheuristic algorithms are generally not very potent in tackling constrained problems. Conversely, it is well known that CP is effective and efficient in solving optimization problems. Obviously, both methods have complementary powers and then it should be interesting to try to combine them in order to explore their synergies.

Hybridizing Metaheuristics with Tree Search (HMHTS): In this category, a metaheuristic algorithm is being combined with tree search algorithm which is one of the optimization methods based on the exploring the search space of the problem. Tree search procedure considers the searching of solutions' space for a problem following a structure of a tree. A search tree is defined by a mechanism for the generation of partial solutions.

According to Blum et al. (2011), each path from the root node to one of leafs corresponds to the building of a candidate solution and the internal nodes of a tree correspond to partial solutions. The change from an inner node to one of its sub-nodes is an extension of the corresponding partial solution. The tree search techniques have approximate algorithms such as heuristics or metaheuristics. Two examples of approximate algorithms are ant colony optimization (ACO) and GRASP. Both algorithms are iterative algorithms.

One can hybridize the metaheuristics with tree search techniques as the following two examples: (1) Ant colony optimization-Branch &Bound (B&B). B&B technique makes the solution construction process of the ant colony optimization more effective and efficiently, (2) Large neighborhood search (LNS) – Mixed integer linear programming (MILP). This hybrid algorithm solves efficiently the original problem via a solution process which consists of solving sub-problems by well-known MILP solvers.

Hybridization of Metaheuristics with Problem Relaxation (HMHPR): Here, a metaheuristic al-gorithm is combined with a relaxation technique which can make simpler the model through simplifying and/or eliminating constraints or simply changing the form of objective function with the hope that the relaxed problem can be solved.

Lately, improving metaheuristic algorithms with information gained from problem relaxation has been widely used. In this hybridization technique, a relaxed version of a given problem is generated by simplifying and/or removing one or more constraints. Also it may be possible that constraints be involved as additional terms in the objective function. It is well known that problem relaxations are also amply used in several complete techniques i.e. B&B. This fact is because the optimal solution value of a relaxed problem can be considered as a bound for the optimal solution value of the original instance. Obviously, this can be used for cutting the search tree. An important type of relaxation in combinatorial optimization is changing the mixed integer programming (MIP) to linear program (LP) for which global optimal solution can be found by efficient methods such as the Simplex method.

Hybridization of Metaheuristics with dynamic Programming (HMHDP): Combining metaheuristic algorithm and dynamic programming (DP) give us as a result a practical optimization approach to solve combinatorial problems. In this approach, as the first step the given problem is separated into several sub-problems. Then, the solution to the given problem is found by combining the solutions of sub-problems into solutions to bigger sub-problems until the base problem is solved. According to Blum et al. (2011) any optimization problem must exhibit the following two properties in order to be solved by dynamic programming:

- Optimal solutions to the problem must contain optimal solutions to sub-problems.
- The space of sub-problems should be quite small. Usually, the total number of different sub-problems is polynomial in the input size.

Another classification based on cooperation is proposed by Jourdan et al. (2009). In this classification there are four categories: (1) Low-level relay hybrid (LRH), (2) Low-level teamwork hybrid (LTH), (3) High-level relay hybrid (HRH), and (4) High-level teamwork hybrid (HTH). The classification is shown in Figure 1.

This classification is made from the combinations of the following elements that involve a degree of cooperation: (1) Levels: Low-level/high-level and (2) Cooperation: Relay/teamwork.

In the low-level, the hybridization occurs when a given function of a metaheuristic is replaced by another method. On the other hand, in the high-level different algorithms are self-contained. With regard to relay, the cooperation occurs due to the fact that a set of methods is applied one after another, each one using the solution of the previous one as its input in a pipeline manner. In the teamwork, a whole cooperation between several optimization models is made.

Low-Level Relay Hybrid (LRH). In this category there is a given method that is embedded into another method. The embedded method is executed sequentially. Then, the general method depends on the solution given by the embedded method.

The LRH cooperation is regularly used when a heuristic approach is used to improve another exact method. In the cooperation among metaheuristics, the common approach is to run an evolutionary algorithm then it launches a local search in order to strengthen the search on the best solutions. In the cooperation among exact and heuristics methods, the regular approach is to design a heuristic algorithm to improve the search scheme of an exact method. In this type of cooperation, the metaheuristics always work on a problem which is different in nature of the original optimization problem. See for instance the work of Augerat et al. (1998). They developed a branch and cut algorithm (BCA) to solve a capacitated vehicle routing problem. In BCA the cutting plane generation is very important issue because this significantly determines the efficiency of the BCA. Augerat et al. (1998) mention that the linear inequality resulting from the constraint capacities are those that provide the best cutting planes. Hence they develop different metaheuristic approaches to extract a set of violated capacity constraints of the relaxed problem.

Low-Level Teamwork Hybrid (LTH): Here, also there is a given method that is embedded into another. But a specific element of a given method is replaced by the other method and the embedded method can be executed in a parallel way with the general method; with this the performance of the metaheuristics is improved a lot.

Here, the two well-known LRH cooperative classes of algorithms are memetic algorithm and genetic algorithms. Regarding the cooperation between metaheuristics and exact methods, Jourdan et al. (2009) identify the following two main types of approaches:

Figure 1. The four classes derived from the cooperation method (from Jourdan et al., 2009)

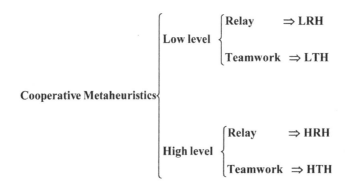

- Exact search LTH cooperation in which the exact approaches construct partial solutions and these solutions are used to define a search space for the heuristic approach. Then, the solutions found by the heuristic are studied in order to refine bounds.

- Heuristic search LTH cooperation in which the heuristic search works similar to memetic algorithms, but the genetic operator is changed by an exact search within a subspace of the global search space.

It is important to point out that the frontier between LRH and LTH categories is tinny. Jourdan et al. (2009) state that the difference basically depends on the possibility, or not, to suggest a parallel version of the proposed algorithm without applying major variations to the initial algorithm

High-Level Relay Hybrid (HRH): These metaheuristics have different methods that are self-contained and are executed in sequential fashion. Indubitably, similar to the other cooperation schemes, different types of resolution could be taking account. Nevertheless, generally speaking, the most natural approach is to design a sequential execution of a metaheuristic which is launched before an exact algorithm. The metaheuristic is built in order to provide information to the exact algorithm. For example in an exact search, the information given might be initial bounds. These bounds help to the exact algorithm to speed up the search. In the case of a heuristic search, the metaheuristic provides initial solutions to the exact search. The initial solution said to define a reduced search space to launch the exact search. For example, the search space might be reduced by defining partitions of the initial solutions, or by defining large neighborhoods around the initial solutions. Klepeis et al., (2003) suggest the cooperation between the alpha B&B algorithm and a conformational space annealing (CSA) algorithm for protein structure prediction.

High-Level Teamwork Hybrid (HTH): This category contains algorithms where self-contained procedures are executed in parallel and cooperative way. Similarly to exact methods, but here there are two different types of islands, some of which are committed to exact search, and the other ones dedicated to heuristic search. In this category, it important to mention that during the execution, the different algorithms exchange information. The main trouble is to set parameters. For example, in Nwana et al. (2005), simulated annealing and B&B are hybridized in such manner that both optimization methods work on the same problem. In some cases, the different cooperative approaches are not committed to solve instances of the same size. Consequently, to obtain a HTH cooperation, both approaches have frequently to solve different parts of the same problem in an independent way.

INVENTORY MANAGEMENT

The success of any company basically depends on its capacity to supply products and services to customers at lower cost, obviously, maximizing the benefits in an economically manner viable. For a company supplying products to its customers, one of most important issues is to provide appropriate products at an acceptable cost within a reasonable time. Several companies are facing this situation. In a company the departments such as marketing, design, finance, purchasing, sales and even manufacturing departments are working in an integrated manner in order to achieve the business goals. For any product having already located in the marketplace, one of the main activities is guarantee the continuity of supply to the consumers. Therefore, one of the tasks of inventory management is organizing the availability of products to the customers. Certainly, one needs to coordinate several activities i.e. purchasing raw materials, manufacturing and distribution in order to meet marketing needs. According to Wild (1997), the roles of inventory management includes the supply of current sales products, new products, consumables, spare parts, obsolescent items and all other supplies. Also, Wild (1997) states that a company through using its inventory will be able to support its customer service, logistic or manufacturing activities under which purchase or manufacture of the products is not able to satisfy demand.

In order to manage inventories properly, there are some classical inventory models in the literature. Three inventory models are discussed in this chapter. The first one is economic order quantity (EOQ) model; the simplest model. In the classic version of EOQ model the demand, ordering and holding costs are known and constant over time and no shortages are allowed. The second one is newsboy problem, a classical periodic inventory management problem. In the newsboy problem the demand is uncertain during a single period but the probability distribution of demand is known. The actual demand will be known until the end of the period and obviously one makes the decision on lot size before the sales period. Finally, the third one is the stochastic review problem. Typically, periodic inventory control problems are mainly studied employing two assumptions. The first one is the continuous review, where depending on the inventory level orders can happen at any time. The second one is the periodic review, where orders can only happen at the beginning of each period. As the third case we relax these two assumptions and assume that the periodic replenishments can randomly be placed. Some important definitions on fuzzy and rough environments are given in Appendix A and the notations for all mathematical models presented in this chapter are in the Appendix B.

EOQ PROBLEM

The classical economic order quantity (EOQ) formula is the simplest model for cycle stock. This inventory model was proposed in 1913 by Harris (1913). The EOQ formula also named Wilson Formula because Wilson (1934) was a consultant that implemented it in several companies. The EOQ formula has been developed through

several optimizations methods see for instance Cardenas-Barrón (2011) and Cárdenas-Barrón (2007). The discrete case of the dynamic version of EOQ was first discussed by Wagner and Whitin (1958). We use EOQ problem for two different applications as below.

Constraint Fuzzy Joint Replenishment (CFJR) Case

This case deals with a multi-product EOQ problem in which demands and costs are considered as LR fuzzy numbers and rough variables respectively while all products should be ordered together (joint replenishment). Manager is faced to several constraints such as space, budget and the number of orders per year. Also he will receive quantity discount from the supplier while a fraction of total purchasing cost should be paid before receiving products as prepayment. The mathematical model of this problem has been developed by Taleizadeh et al. (2011a) and it is shown below (see Box 1 for Equation (1)).

$$S.t: \quad \frac{1}{T}\sum_{j=1}^{P}\sum_{i=1}^{n}\hat{C}_{ij}Q_{ij} \leq W \tag{2}$$

$$\sum_{j=1}^{P}f_{j}Q_{j} \leq F \tag{3}$$

$$T \geq \frac{1}{N_{T}} \tag{4}$$

$$0 < \sum_{j=1}^{P}f_{j}m_{j} \leq \hat{f}Y_{1} \tag{5}$$

$$\hat{f}Y_{2} < \sum_{j=1}^{P}f_{j}m_{j} \leq 2\hat{f}Y_{2} \tag{6}$$
$$\vdots$$

Box 1.

$$Min : Z = \frac{1}{T}\left[A + \sum_{k=1}^{K} kA_T Y_k + \sum_{j=1}^{P}\sum_{i=1}^{n} C_{ij}^{P} Q_{ij}\right] + \left[\sum_{j=1}^{P} \frac{C_j^{h_1}\tilde{D}_j}{2}\right]T$$
$$+ \left[\sum_{j=1}^{P} C_j^c \tilde{D}_j + \sum_{j=1}^{P} C_j^{h_2}\tilde{D}_j(t_{lc} - t_0) + \sum_{j=1}^{P} C_j^{h_3}\tilde{D}_j\left[L - (t_{lc} - t_0)\right]\right]$$

(1)

$$(K-1)\hat{f}Y_k < \sum_{j=1}^{P} f_j m_j \le K\hat{f}Y_k \tag{7}$$

$$TD_j = n_j m_j \tag{8}$$

$$Q_j = Q_{1j} + Q_{2j} + \ldots + Q_{nj} \tag{9}$$

$$q_{1j}\lambda_{2j} \le Q_{1j} \le q_{1j}\lambda_{1j} \tag{10}$$

$$\left(q_{2j} - q_{1j}\right)\lambda_{3j} \le Q_{2j} \le \left(q_{2j} - q_{1j}\right)\lambda_{2j}$$
$$\vdots \tag{11}$$

$$0 \le Q_{nj} \le M\lambda_{nj} \tag{12}$$

$$Y_1 + Y_2 + \cdots + Y_k = 1 \tag{13}$$

$$\lambda_{1j} \ge \lambda_{2j} \ge \cdots \ge \lambda_{nj} \tag{14}$$

$$\lambda_{ij} = 0,1 \ ; \ Y_k = 0,1 \quad \forall k = 1,2,\cdots,K,$$
$$\forall j, \ j = 1,2,\cdots,P, \forall i, \ i = 1,2,\cdots,m \tag{15}$$

$$T \ge 0 \ ; \ m_j, Q_j \ge 0 \ \text{int}\,eger \tag{16}$$

where Equation (1) shows the objective cost function; including fixed order, holding, transportation, clearance and purchasing costs. Equations (2) and (3) show the budget and space limitations of buyers and Equation (4) indicates the maximum number of orders which can be placed during a year. Equations (5), (6), (7), (13), and (15) are used to model the transportation costs. Equation (8) shows the order quantity should be multiplied of predetermined integer value. All Equations (9), (10), (11), (12), (14), and (15) are being used to model the discount which the buyer receives from his/her vendor. Finally Equation (16) shows the decision variables which are period length and order quantity for each product must be non-negative. Additionally, the order quantity for each product and the number of packets ordered for each product must be an integer number.

The mathematical model (1)-(16) is a fuzzy integer-nonlinear-programming type. It is worth to mention that this mathematical model is hard to solve. In the other hand, the selection of an appropriate algorithm to solve any optimization problem is not an easy task. That is why in addition to a HS algorithm, a GA, as well as a PSO algorithm are developed to solve the problem at hand. A comparison study of the methods' performances can assure one of the validity of the results obtained. Therefore in order to solve the uncertain problem, a hybrid method of harmony search, fuzzy simulation and rough simulation is used. Also in order to compare the efficiency of the proposed method GA and PSO technique are used instead of HS. It should be noted that these solution methods based on Blum et al. (2011)'s classifications are a IIMHHMH type. Based on Jourdan et al. (2009)'s classifications are HTH type. Table 1 shows the best values obtained for the numerical example used form Taleizadeh et al. (2011a) through different methods.

Table 1. Best results of example of EOQ model – CFJR case

Hybrid Algorithms	Minimum Cost ($)
Hybrid method of harmony search, fuzzy and rough simulations	134,340,000
Hybrid method of particle swarm optimization, fuzzy and rough simulations	136,498,000
Hybrid method of genetic algorithm, fuzzy and rough simulations	141,100,000

A comparison of the results in Table 1 shows the hybrid method of HS algorithm performs better than the PSO and GA algorithms in terms of the objective function values. Since the best solution is derived using hybrid method of harmony search, fuzzy simulation and rough simulation, only we will focus on this method. According to Taleizadeh et al. (2011a), the procedure of estimating uncertain objective function including fuzzy and rough variables using rough and fuzzy simulation are as below;

```
Step 1: Set E=0
Step 2: Randomly generate D_jz from
α-level sets of fuzzy variables D̃_j ,
and set
```
$$\xi_z = (\xi_{1z}, \xi_{2z}, \cdots, \xi_{pz})$$
```
Step 3: Set a =
```
$Z(D_1, Q) \wedge Z(D_2, Q) \wedge \cdots \wedge Z(D_Z, Q)$, b = $Z(D_1, Q) \vee Z(D_2, Q) \vee \cdots \vee Z(D_Z, Q)$.
```
Step 4: Randomly generate r from
Uniform [a, b].
Step 5: Generate C_ijl from Δ according
to measure π .
Step 6: Generate C̄_ijl from Λ according to
measure π .
Step 7: If
```
$$r \geq 0 \text{ , then } E \leftarrow E + Cr \left\{ \frac{Z(\tilde{D}, Q, \hat{C}(\overline{\delta_i})) + Z(\tilde{D}, Q, \hat{C}(\underline{\delta_i}))}{2L} \geq r \right\}$$

.

```
Step 8: If
```
$$r < 0 \text{ , then } E \leftarrow E - Cr \left\{ \frac{Z(\tilde{D}, Q, \hat{C}(\overline{\delta_i})) + Z(\tilde{D}, Q, \hat{C}(\underline{\delta_i}))}{2L} \leq r \right\}$$

```
Step 9: Repeat the fourth to eight
steps for N times.
Step 10:
```
$$E\left[Z(\tilde{D}, Q, \hat{C})\right] = a \vee 0 + b \wedge 0 + E * \frac{b-a}{L'}.$$

In the defined procedure $Cr\{\ \}$ refers to credibility for which readers can see the works of Liu (2000) and Liu (2004) for more information regarding to credibility concept. Also, we refer to the reader to see the Appendix A in this chapter.

According to Taleizadeh et al. (2011a) the constant parameters of the HS algorithm include harmony memory size (HMS), harmony memory considering rate ($HMCR$), pitch adjusting rate (PAR), number of decision variables (N), and the maximum number of improvisations (NI). To solve the on hand model using HS, three values are considered for all parameters and the best combination is chosen. In Taleizadeh et al. (2011a) are chosen 10, 20, and 30 as different values of HMS, 0.93, 0.95, and 0.99 have been used for $HMCR$, 0.3, 0.7 and 0.9 have been utilized for PAR, 100, 500, and 1000 are chosen as different iteration numbers and because of existing only one variable, the period length, N is equal to 1.

The most important issue about the HS algorithm is the best values of HS parameters after more than one hundred runs obtained as $HMS = 10$, $HMCR = 0.7$, $PAR = 0.7$, and $NI = 100$.

In order to perform the HS algorithm, the following general steps are done.

In summary, the steps involved in the HS algorithm used in this research are:

```
1. Initialize both the parameters and
the harmony memory of the HS algo-
rithm.
2. Make a new vector X'. For each
component x'ᵢ:
With probability HMCR pick the
component from memory,
With probability 1 − HMCR pick a new
random value in the allowed range.
3. Pitch adjustment: For each compo-
nent x'ᵢ:
With probability PAR, a small change
is made to x'ᵢ.
With probability 1 − PAR do nothing.
4. If X' is better than the worst
Xʲ in the memory, then replace Xʲ
with X' by evaluating the objective
function (based on fuzzy simulation
algorithm, to estimate the uncertain
parameters).
5. Go to step 2 until a maximum
number of iterations has been
reached.
```

Also the convergence path of hybrid method of harmony search, fuzzy simulation and rough simulation is shown in Figure 2. In order to have more detailed information readers can see Taleizadeh et al. (2011a)'s research.

Constraint Fuzzy Rough Joint Replenishment (CFRJR) Case

Under normal circumstances, the parameters of inventory control problems are vague and dynamic. For example, the carrying cost of an item may be dependent on the amount in storage and the set-up cost may depend upon the total quantity to be produced in a production cycle. Moreover, the mentioned issues may have other uncertainties associated with these variables, thus resulting in fuzzy rough in nature. Similarly, goals set to maximize the allowable profit or minimize the costs are imprecise in many practical inventory problems. In these situations, fuzzy rough theory can be used to formulate the inventory models.

Figure 2. The convergence graph

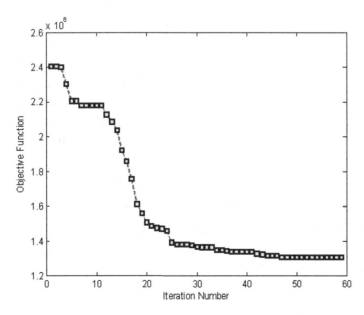

In the existing literature, few researchers have investigated the inventory models under these environments. The difference between the CFR-JR case and CFJR case are in considering the fuzzy rough demand rate, total discount strategy and shortages. So the previous problem in above lines has been developed in fuzzy rough situations by Taleizadeh et al. (2011b) and it is shown (see Box 2 for Equation (17)).

$$S.t: \quad \frac{1}{T}\sum_{j=1}^{P}\sum_{i=1}^{n}C_{ij}^{P}Y_{ij}Q_{j} \leq W \qquad (18)$$

$$\sum_{j=1}^{P}f_{j}\left(Q_{j}-b_{j}\right) \leq F \qquad (19)$$

$$T \geq \frac{1}{N_{T}} \qquad (20)$$

$$T\tilde{D}_{j} = n_{j}m_{j} \qquad (21)$$

$$\begin{aligned} Q_{j} &\geq q_{1j}Y_{2j} \\ Q_{j} &\geq q_{2j}Y_{3j} \\ &\vdots \\ Q_{j} &\geq q_{n-1,j}Y_{nj} \end{aligned} \qquad (22)$$

$$Y_{1j} + Y_{2j} + \cdots + Y_{nj} = 1 \qquad (23)$$

$$Y_{ij} = 0,1; \quad i = 1,2,...,n \quad \text{and} \quad j = 1,2,...,P \qquad (24)$$

$$T \geq 0,\, m_{j}, Q_{j}, b_{j} \geq 0 \;;\; \text{integer } j = 1,2,...,P \qquad (25)$$

where Equation (17) shows the objective cost function; including fixed order, holding, transportation, clearance, purchasing and backorders costs. Equations (18) and (19), like Equation (2) and (3), show the budget and space limitations of buyers and Equation (20) indicates the maximum number of orders which can be placed during a year. Equation (21) shows the order quantity should be multiplied of predetermined integer value. All Equations (22), (23), and (24) are being used to model the total discount which the buyer will receive from his/her vendor. Finally Equation (25) shows the decision variables which are period length, order quantity and shortage which should be non-negative. Additionally, the order quantity for each product, the backorders level, and the number of packets ordered for each product must be an integer number.

Again, the mathematical model (17)-(25) is a fuzzy rough integer-nonlinear-programming type. In order to solve it, hybrid method of bees colony optimization (BCO), fuzzy simulation and rough simulation is used. Also in order to compare the efficiency of the proposed method PSO, GA and VNS technique are used instead of BCO. It should be noted that these solution methods based on Blum et al. (2011)'s classifications are a HMHPR type. On the other hand, based on Jourdan et al. (2009)'s classification are HTH type. Table 2 shows the best values obtained for the numerical example used form Taleizadeh et al. (2011b) through different methods.

Box 2.

$$Min: Z = \frac{1}{T}\left[A + \sum_{j=1}^{P}C_{j}^{T}k_{j} + \sum_{j=1}^{P}\alpha C_{j}^{h_{2}}\tilde{D}_{j}(t_{lc} - t_{0}) + \sum_{j=1}^{P}\sum_{i=1}^{n}C_{ij}^{P}Y_{ij}q_{ij} - \sum_{j=1}^{P}C_{j}^{h_{2}}\tilde{D}_{j}t_{lc} \right]$$
$$+ \sum_{j=1}^{P}\frac{C_{j}^{h_{1}}\left(\tilde{D}_{j}T - b_{j}\right)}{2\tilde{D}_{j}T} + \sum_{j=1}^{P}\frac{C_{j}^{b}b_{j}^{2}}{2\tilde{D}_{j}T} + \sum_{j=1}^{P}\left(C_{j}^{h_{2}} + C_{j}^{c}\right)\tilde{D}_{j} \qquad (17)$$

Table 2. Best results of example of EOQ model – CFRJR case

Hybrid Algorithms	Minimum Cost ($)
Hybrid method of bees colony optimization, fuzzy and rough simulations	254,200
Hybrid method of particle swarm optimization, fuzzy and rough simulation	255,300
Hybrid method of genetic algorithm, fuzzy and rough simulations	256,500
Hybrid method of variable neighborhood search, fuzzy and rough simulation	259,400

In this case, all steps of hybrid method are done as follow;

Simulation steps:

Step 1: Set $K_i = 0$

Step 2: Generate $\underline{\delta_i}$ from Δ_i.

Step 3: Generate $\overline{\delta_i}$ from Λ_i.

Step 4: $K_i \leftarrow K_i + \dfrac{E\left[d_i(\underline{\delta})\right] + E\left[d_i(\overline{\delta})\right]}{2}$

Step 5: Repeat the second to fourth step L'' times.

Step 6: Return $D_i = \dfrac{K_i}{L''}$

Metaheuristic algorithms steps:

Step 7: Initialize the parameters of selected metaheuristic algorithm which will be used.

Step 8: Run the next steps after initialization step of selected metaheuristic algorithm.

To receive more detailed information about the simulation steps readers can see Liu (2000) and Liu (2004).

A comparison of the results in Table 2 shows the hybrid method of BCO algorithm performs better than the PSO, GA and VNS algorithms in term of the objective function values. In order to have more detailed information readers can see Taleizadeh et al. (2011b)'s research.

But since the best results are obtained from hybrid method of bees colony optimization, fuzzy simulation and rough simulation we will focus on bees colony optimization technique only. The constant parameters of the BCO algorithm include scot bees size (SBS), best randomly selected sites (M), the best sites out of M (BS), neighborhood search size (NSS), number of bees be selected randomly to be sent to BS sites (N_1). Number of bees be selected randomly to be sent to $M - BS$ sites (N_2).

To solve the on hand model using BCO, three values are considered for all parameters and the best combination is chosen. In Taleizadeh et al. (2011c) are chosen 50, 100, and 150 as different values of SBS, 25, 50, and 75 have been used for M, 5, 10 and 15 have been utilized for BS, 0.25, 0.5, and 0.75 are chosen as different values of NSS, for N_1, 30, 40 and 50 and for N_2, 15, 20 and 25 are considered.

Finally after more than two hundred runs the best combination of parameter are obtained as $SBS = 150$, $M = 75$, $BS = 10$, $NSS = 0.25$, $N_1 = 50$ and $N_2 = 15$.

In order to perform the BCO algorithm, the following general steps are done.

Step 1: Initialize population with random solutions.

Step 2. Evaluate fitness of the population.

Step 3: While (stopping criterion not met)

1. Forming new population.

2. Select sites for neighborhood search.

3. Recruit bees for selected sites (more bees for best e sites) and

```
evaluate fitnesses.
4. Select the fittest bee from each
patch.
5. Assign remaining bees to search
randomly and evaluate their fitness-
es.
End While.
```

Also the convergence path of hybrid method of bees colony optimization, fuzzy simulation and rough simulation is shown in Figure 3.

In the case of fuzzy inventory model researches, we refer to readers to see the works of Ye and Li (2011), Mandal et al. (2011), Maiti (2011), Ren et al. (2010), Roy et al. (2009) and Pirayesh and Yazdi (2010).

NEWSBOY PROBLEM

The Newsboy problem deals with situations where the demand of a product is uncertain and the ordered products that remain unsold at the end

of the cycle become obsolete. Newsboy problem have been extended in several ways, for example: under different objectives, utility functions, discount policies, multi-product and multi-constraint situations. But in this chapter we present two new extensions of newsboy problem.

Constraint Bi-Objective Multi-Product (CBOM) Case

This section presents a real-world prevalence of the multi-product, multi-constraint newsboy problem with two objectives. In this newsboy problem total and incremental quantity discounts on purchasing prices are considered. The constraints of the model are the warehouse capacity and the batch forms of the order placements. The first objective of this problem is to find the order quantities that maximize expected profit, and the second objective is maximizing the service rate. The mathematical model of this problem is given in Taleizadeh et al. (2009b) and it is shown (see Box 3 for Equation (26)).

Figure 3. Convergence path

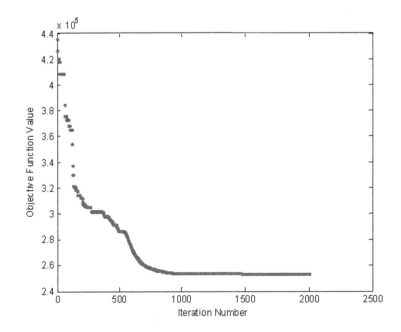

Box 3.

$$Max : Z = \sum_{j=1}^{P} \sum_{X_j=0}^{Q_j-1} P_j.X_j.f_{X_j}(x_j) + \sum_{j=1}^{P} \sum_{X_j=Q_j}^{+\infty} P_j.Q_j.f_{X_j}(x_j) - \sum_{j=1}^{P} K_j Q_j - \sum_{k=1}^{K} kAY_k$$
$$- \sum_{j=1}^{P} \sum_{i=1}^{n} C_{i_j} W_{i_j} - \sum_{j=1}^{P} \sum_{X_j=0}^{Q_j-1} \left(C_{1j}^h (Q_j - X_j) + C_{2j}^h (Q_j - X_j)^2 \right) \frac{e^{-\lambda_j} \lambda_j^{X_j}}{X_j!} \qquad (26)$$
$$- \sum_{j=1}^{P} \sum_{i=1}^{n} C_{i_j} W_{i_j} - \sum_{j=1}^{P} \sum_{X_j=0}^{Q_j-1} \left(C_{1j}^h (Q_j - X_j) + C_{2j}^h (Q_j - X_j)^2 \right) \frac{e^{-\lambda_j} \lambda_j^{X_j}}{X_j!}$$

$$Max : Z_{SR} = \frac{1}{T} \sum_{j=1}^{P} \sum_{X_j=0}^{Q_j-1} \frac{(Q_j - X_j)f_{X_j}(x_j)}{\lambda_j} \qquad (27)$$

$$S.t : \sum_{j=1}^{P} f_j m_j \leq F \qquad (28)$$

$$Q_j = n_j m_j \qquad \forall j, \qquad j = 1, 2, ..., P \qquad (29)$$

$$Q_j = \sum_{i=1}^{n} W_{i_j} \qquad \forall j, \qquad j = 1, 2, ..., P \qquad (30)$$

$$q_{1_j} \lambda_{2_j} \leq W_{1_j} \leq q_{1_j} \lambda_{1_j} \qquad \forall j, \qquad j = 1, 2, ..., P$$
$$\vdots$$
$$\qquad (31)$$

$$\left(q_{i_j} - q_{i-1_j} \right) \lambda_{i_j} \leq W_{i_j} \leq \left(q_{i_j} - q_{i-1_j} \right) \lambda_{i-1_j};$$
$$\forall i, i = 2, ..., n_j - 1 \quad \text{and} \quad \forall j, \; j = 1, 2, ..., P \qquad (32)$$

$$0 \leq W_{n_{j_j}} \leq M \lambda_{n_{j_j}} \; ; \; \forall j, \; j = 1, 2, ..., P \quad M \text{ is a}$$
big number $\qquad (33)$

$$0 < \sum_{j=1}^{P} f_j b_j \leq \hat{f} Y_1 \; (k-1) \hat{f} Y_k < \sum_{j=1}^{P} f_j b_j$$
$$\leq k \hat{f} Y_k; \; \forall k = 2, 3, \cdots, m \qquad (34)$$

$$Y_1 + Y_2 + \cdots + Y_n = 1 \qquad (36)$$

$$\lambda_{1_j} \geq \lambda_{2_j} \geq \cdots \geq \lambda_{n_{j_j}} \qquad \forall j, \qquad j = 1, 2, \cdots, P \qquad (37)$$

$$Y_k = 0, 1 \qquad \forall k, \qquad k = 1, 2, \cdots, K \qquad (38)$$

$$\lambda_{i_j} = 0, 1 \quad \forall j, \; j = 1, 2, \cdots, P$$
$$\text{and} \quad \forall i, \; i = 1, 2, \cdots, n \qquad (39)$$

$$m_j \geq 0 \text{ and integer} \quad \forall j, \quad j = 1, 2, \cdots, P \qquad (40)$$

where Equations (26) and (27) show the objective functions; maximizing profit and service level respectively. Equations (28) and (29) show the space and batch ordering limitations and Equations (30), (31), (32), (33), (37) and (39) handle the incremental discount policy. Also Equations (34), (35), (36) and (38) are some constraints which are used to transform the multi-level transportation cost to a single level as a component of profit function. Finally Equation (40) causes the number of packets becomes integer. In order to solve the above bi-objective problem, hybrid method of goal programming with genetic algorithm and hybrid method of goal programming (GP) and simulated annealing are used.

However, since the above model (26-40) has two objectives, a goal programming framework is first applied to formulate them and then a GA is employed to solve it. We refer to interested readers to see Steuer (1985) for rigorous mathematical analysis of multi-objective programming method. Several multi-objective models were formulated and solved in the nineties. For example we have the following works: Demmel and Askin(1992), Stam and Kuula (1991), Kim and Schniederjams (1993), Kalpic et al., (1995) and Nagarur et al. (1997) just to name a few studies.

In modern times, the decision makers are confronted day to day to achieving multiple conflicting objectives under complex constraints. For these challenges, the GP could be a suitable and flexible technique for decision analysis. It is important to remark that the modeling of GP does not try to maximize or minimize the objective function directly as in the case of classical linear programming. In its place GP pursues to minimize the deviations between the desired goals and the actual results to be found according to the given priorities. According to Sundaram (1978), the GP approach handles multiple goals in multiple dimensions. Moreover, Lee and Clayton (1972) mention that the distinctive characteristic of GP is that this allows for an ordinal solution. In other words, management may be unable to state the cost or utility of a goal, but often upper or lower limits may be specified for each goal. An often used generalized model for GP is proposed by Kwak et al. (1991) and it is shown below:

$$Min: Z = \sum_{i=1}^{n} w_i p_i (d_i^+ + d_i^-)$$

(41)

$$S.t: \sum_{j} a_{ij} x_{ij} + d_i^- - d_i^+ = b_i \qquad \forall i, \quad i = 1, 2, ..., m$$

(42)

$$x_{ij}, d_i^-, d_i^+ \geq 0$$

(43)

$$d_i^- . d_i^+ = 0$$

(44)

$$(i = 1, 2, ..., m; j = 1, 2, ...n)$$

(45)

where p_i is the preemptive priority level assigned to each relevant goal in rank order $(p_1 \geq p_2 \geq ... \geq p_n)$ and w_i are non-negative constants representing the relative weights assigned within a priority level to the deviational variables, d_i^+, d_i^- for each ith corresponding goal, b_i. The x_{ij} represents the decision variables and a_{ij} represents the decision variable coefficients. According to GP structure the bi-objective functions shown in Equations (26) and (27) should be replaced by;

$$Min: Z = p_1 w_1 d_1^- + p_2 w_2 d_2^-$$

(46)

and following constraints should be added to constraints set of (28) to (40) (see Box 4 for Equation (47)).

$$\frac{1}{T} \sum_{j=1}^{P} \sum_{X_j=0}^{Q_j-1} \frac{(Q_j - X_j) f_{X_j}(x_j)}{\lambda_j} + d_2^- - d_2^+ = b_2$$

(48)

$$d_1^- . d_1^+ = 0$$
$$d_2^- . d_2^+ = 0$$

(49)

$$d_1^-, d_1^+, d_2^-, d_2^+ \geq 0$$

(50)

Table 3 shows the best results obtained for the numerical example used from Taleizadeh et al. (2009b) through two different methods. A comparison of the results in Table 3 shows the hybrid method of GP and GA performs better than the GP and SA algorithms in term of the objective function values. In order to have more detailed information readers can see Taleizadeh et al. (2009b)'s research. It should be noted that these

Box 4.

$$S.t: \sum_{j=1}^{P} \sum_{X_j=0}^{Q_j-1} P_j.X_j.f_{X_j}(x_j) + \sum_{j=1}^{P} \sum_{X_j=Q_j}^{+\infty} P_j.Q_j.f_{X_j}(x_j)$$

$$- \sum_{j=1}^{P} \sum_{X_j=0}^{Q_j-1} \left(C_{1j}^h(Q_j - X_j) + C_{2j}^h(Q_j - X_j)^2 \right) \frac{e^{-\lambda_j}\lambda_j^{X_j}}{X_j!}$$

$$- \sum_{j=1}^{P} \sum_{X_j=Q_j+1}^{\infty} \left(C_{1j}^b(X_j - Q_j) + C_{2j}^b(X_j - Q_j)^2 \right) \frac{e^{-\lambda_j}\lambda_j^{X_j}}{X_j!}$$

$$- \sum_{j=1}^{P} K_j Q_j - \sum_{k=1}^{m} kAY_k - \sum_{j=1}^{P} \sum_{i=1}^{n} C_{i_j} W_{i_j} + d^-_1 - d_1^+ = b_1$$

(47)

Table 3. Best results of example of newsboy model – (CBOM) case

Hybrid Algorithms	Maximum Profit ($)	Maximum Service Level ($)
Hybrid method of goal programming and genetic algorithm	6726.21	0.7769
Hybrid method of goal programming and simulated annealing	6425.23	0.78542

solution methods based on Blum et al. (2011)'s classifications are a HMHHMH type and based on Jourdan et al. (2009)'s classification are LRH type.

In short, the steps involved in the GA algorithm used in this research are (Taleizadeh et al. 2009b):

1. Setting the parameters P_c, P_m, and N.
2. Initializing the population randomly.
3. Evaluating the objective function.
4. Selecting individual for mating pool.
5. Applying the crossover operation for each pair of chromosomes with probability P_c.
6. Applying mutation operation for each chromosome with probability P_m.
7. Replacing the current population by the resulting mating pool.
8. Evaluating the objective function.
9. If stopping criteria is met, then stop. Otherwise, go to step 5.

The constant parameters of the genetic algorithm include population size (N), possibility of crossover (P_c), and possibility of mutations (P_m). To solve the on hand model using GA, three values are considered for all parameters and the best combination is chosen. In Taleizadeh et al. (2009b) are chosen 10, 100, and 1000 as different values of N, 0.80, 0.85, and 0.90 have been used for P_c, and finally 0.01, 0.05, and 0.1 are employed as different values of the P_m nparameter.

The most important issue about the each metaheuristic algorithm is its best values. After more than one hundred runs, the best combination obtained as $N = 1000$, $P_c = 0.9$, and $P_m = 0.05$. Also the convergence path of algorithm is shown in Figure 4.

In the case of multi objective inventory management problems in which metaheuristic algorithms are used we refer to the readers to study the works of Moslemi and Zandieh (2011), Fatrias and Shimizu(2010), Liao and Hsieh (2010), Hsieh and Laio (2010) and Lee et al. (2010).

Figure 4. The convergence path of the best result

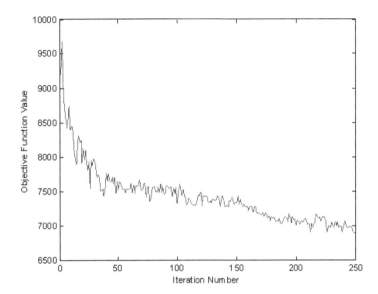

Constrained Multi-Product Fuzzy Demand (CMPFD) Case

In addition to above application of newsboy problem, now we introduce another extension, which is developed by considering the demand rate of each product as fuzzy variables. Since it is not possible to use a specific solution approach to solve the proposed model, we developed five hybrid solution approaches based on metaheuristic algorithms such as BCO, HS, PSO, GA, and SA with fuzzy Simulation. The main difference between this case (CMPFD) and previous one (CBOM) is in containing only maximizing function of profit and fuzzy demand rate. The mathematical model of this problem has been developed by Taleizadeh et al. (2011c), and it is show below;

$$Max : Z = \sum_{j=1}^{P} \left[P_j \tilde{D}_j - C_j^h (Q_j - \tilde{D}_j) \right] x_j$$
$$+ \sum_{j=1}^{P} \left[P_j Q_j - C_j^b (\tilde{D}_j - Q_j) \right] (1 - x_j)$$
$$- \sum_{j=1}^{P} \sum_{i=1}^{n} C_{ij}^P Q_{ij}^o$$

$$(51)$$

$$S.t : \quad \tilde{D}_j - M x_j < Q_j < \tilde{D}_j + M(1 - x_j);$$
$$\forall j \ , j = 1, 2, \cdots, P$$

$$(52)$$

$$\sum_{j=1}^{P} f_j m_j \leq F$$

$$(53)$$

$$\sum_{j=1}^{P} \left(\sum_{i=1}^{n} C_{ij} y_{ij} \right) Q_j \leq W$$

$$(54)$$

$$SL_j \left[\frac{1}{4} (D_{1j} + 2D_{2j} + D_{3j}) \right] \leq q_{ij} \leq u l_j;$$
$$\forall j \ , j = 1, 2, \cdots, P$$

$$(55)$$

$$Q_j = Q_{1j}^o + Q_{2j}^o + \ldots + Q_{nj}^o;$$
$$\forall j \ , j = 1, 2, \cdots, P$$

$$(56)$$

$$q_{1j} y_{2j} \leq Q_{1j}^o \leq q_{1j} y_{1j};$$
$$\forall j, \ j = 1, 2, \cdots, P$$

$$(57)$$

$$\left(q_{2j} - q_{2j}\right)y_{3j} \le Q_{2j}^o \le \left(q_{2j} - q_{1j}\right)y_{2j};$$
$$\forall j, \quad j = 1, 2, \cdots, P \tag{58}$$

$$0 \le Q_{nj}^o \le My_{nj}; \qquad \forall j, \quad j = 1, 2, \cdots, P \tag{59}$$

$$y_{1j} \ge y_{2j} \ge \cdots \ge y_{nj}; \qquad \forall j, \quad j = 1, 2, \cdots, P \tag{60}$$

$$y_{ij} = 0, 1 \quad ; \forall i = 1, 2, ..., n; \quad \forall j, \quad j = 1, 2, \cdots, P \tag{61}$$

$$x_j = 0, 1; \qquad \forall j, \quad j = 1, 2, \cdots, P \tag{62}$$

$$Q_j, m_j \ge 0 \quad , \quad \text{int } eger; \qquad \forall j, \quad j = 1, 2, \cdots, P \tag{63}$$

where Equation (51) shows the total profit objective function. It should be noted that in a moment only either positive inventory level or non-positive inventory level should exist. Therefore, Equations (52) and (62) are used to satisfy this required condition. Equations (53) and (54) show the space and budget limitations. Equation (55) shows the service level constraint and upper limit of orders together. Equations (56), (57), (58), (59), (60), and (61) handle the discount policy. Finally Equation (63) causes the number of packets and the order quantity for each product must be an integer number.

In order to solve the above proposed problem, hybrid method of BCO, HS, PSO, GA, and SA with fuzzy simulation are used.

Table 4 shows the best results obtained for the numerical example used from Taleizadeh et al. (2011c) through five different methods. A comparison of the results in Table 4 shows the hybrid method of BCO and fuzzy simulation performs better than other hybrid methods in term of the objective function values. In order to have more detailed information readers can see Taleizadeh et al. (2011c)'s research. It should be noted that these solution methods based on Blum et al. (2011)'s classifications are a HMHHMH type and based on Jourdan et al. (2009)'s classification are HTH type. Also the convergence path of hybrid method of bees colony optimization with fuzzy simulation is shown in Figure 5.

The parameter setting and steps of BCO are very similar to what we described before. So in order to shorten the length of chapter we avoid double writing something.

STOCHATIC REVIEW PROBLEM

Multi-periodic inventory control problems are mainly studied employing two assumptions. The first one is the continuous review, where depending on the inventory level orders can happen at any time. The second one is the periodic review, where orders can only happen at the beginning of each period. Here, we relax these assumptions

Table 4. Best results of example of EOQ model – CMPFD case

Hybrid Algorithms	Maximum Profit ($)
Hybrid method of bees colony optimization with fuzzy simulation,	32,231
Hybrid method of harmony search with fuzzy simulation,	31,519
Hybrid method of particle swarm optimization with fuzzy simulation,	30,945
Hybrid method of genetic algorithm with fuzzy simulation,	28,041
Hybrid method of simulated annealing with fuzzy simulation,	26,642

Figure 5. The convergence path of BCO-FS with triangular LR-fuzzy variables

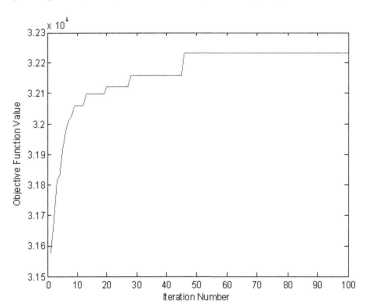

and assume that the periodic replenishments are stochastic in nature. Additionally, we consider applications in two different situations, fuzzy cost factor (FCF) and random fuzzy period length (RFPL).

Fuzzy Cost Factor (FCF) Case

Consider situation in which the periods between two replenishments of the products are independent and identically distributed random variables. Furthermore, assuming that the purchasing price are triangular fuzzy variables, the quantities of the orders are of integer-type and that there are space and service level constraints, also all units discount are considered to purchase products and a combination of back-order and lost-sales are taken into account for the shortages. The mathematical model of this problem is derived in Taleizadeh et al. 2010 and it is shown (see Box 5 for Equation (64) and Box 6 for Equation (67)).

$$S.t: \sum_{j=1}^{P} f_j R_j \leq F \qquad (65)$$

$$\frac{D_j T_{Max_j} - R_j}{D_j (T_{Max_j} - T_{Min_j})} \leq 1 - SL_j; \qquad \forall j = 1, 2, ..., P$$

$$(66)$$

$$Q_j \geq q_{j1} \lambda_{j2}; \qquad \forall j = 1, 2, ..., P$$
$$Q_j \geq q_{j2} \lambda_{j3}; \qquad \forall j = 1, 2, ..., P$$
$$\vdots \qquad \qquad \vdots \qquad (68)$$
$$Q_j \geq q_{jO-1} \lambda_{jO}; \qquad \forall j = 1, 2, ..., P$$

$$\lambda_{j1} + \lambda_{j2} + \cdots + \lambda_{jO} = 1; \qquad \forall j = 1, 2, ..., P$$
$$(69)$$

$$\lambda_{ij} = 0, 1; \qquad \forall i = 1, 2, ..., O, \quad \forall j = 1, 2, ..., P$$
$$(70)$$

$$R_j \geq 0, \ Integer; \qquad \forall j = 1, 2, ..., P$$
$$(71)$$

where Equation (64) shows the total profit ojective function. Equations (65) and (66) are the space and service level limitations. Also Equations (67),

Box 5.

$$
\begin{aligned}
Max\ Z(R_j, \tilde{C}^P_{ij}, \tilde{C}^h_j) = & \sum_{j=1}^{P} \left[\frac{\tilde{C}^h_j}{6D_j^2(T_{Max_j} - T_{Min_j})} \right] R_j^3 \\
& - \sum_{j=1}^{P} \left[\frac{(1-\beta_j)P_j + \tilde{C}^h_j T_{Max_j} + C^b_j\beta_j + (C^L_j + (\sum_{j=1}^{P}\sum_{i=1}^{T}\tilde{C}^P_{ij}\lambda_{ij}))(1-\beta_j)}{2D_j(T_{Max_j} - T_{Min_j})} \right] R_j^2 \\
& + \sum_{j=1}^{P} \left[\frac{\begin{aligned}2P_j(1-\beta_j)T_{Max_j} + \tilde{C}^h_j T_{Min_j}^2 + 2(C^b_j\beta_j + C^L_j(1-\beta_j))T_{Max_j} \\ -2(1-\beta_j)(\sum_{j=1}^{P}\sum_{i=1}^{T}\tilde{C}^P_{ij}\lambda_{ij})T_{Max_j}\end{aligned}}{2(T_{Max_j} - T_{Min_j})} \right] R_j \\
& + \sum_{j=1}^{P} \left[\frac{3(P_j - (\sum_{j=1}^{P}\sum_{i=1}^{T}\tilde{C}^P_{ij}\lambda_{ij}))D_j(\beta_j T_{Max_j}^2 - T_{Min_j}^2) - \tilde{C}^h_j T_{Min_j}^3 D_j - 3(C^b_j\beta_j + C^L_j(1-\beta_j))T_{Max_j}^2 D_j}{6(T_{Max_j} - T_{Min_j})} \right]
\end{aligned}
$$

(64)

Box 6.

$$
Q_j = \frac{(\beta_j - 1)R_j^2 + (2D_j T_{Max_j}(1-\beta_j))R_j + (\beta_j T_{Max_j}^2 - T_{Min_j}^2)D_j^2}{2D_j(T_{Max_j} - T_{Min_j})};
$$

$$
\forall j = 1, 2, ..., P
$$

(67)

Table 5. Best results of example of stochastic review model – (FCF) case

Hybrid Algorithms	Maximum Profit ($)
Hybrid method of simulated annealing and fuzzy simulation	1,016,500
Hybrid method of genetic algorithm and fuzzy simulation	998,610

(68), (69), and (70) are used to handle the discount policy. Finally Equation (71) causes the maximum level of inventory becomes integer. Since the model of this problem is a fuzzy integer nonlinear programming type and in order to solve it, a hybrid metaheuristic intelligent algorithm, combinations of two GA and SA with fuzzy simulations are

proposed. Table 5 shows the best results obtained for the numerical example used from Taleizadeh et al. (2010) through two different methods.

A comparison of the results in Table 5 shows the hybrid method of SA and fuzzy simulation performs better than another one in term of the objective function values.

In short, the steps involved in the SA algorithm used in this research are (Taleizadeh et al. 2009b):

```
1. Choosing an initial solution i
from the group of the feasible solu-
tions S.
2. Choosing the initial temperature
```
$T_0 > 0.$
```
3. Selecting the number of iterations
```
$N(t)$ `at each temperature.`
```
4. Selecting the final temperature
```
$T_F.$
```
5. Determining the process of the
temperature reduction until it reach-
es
```
$T_F.$
```
6. Setting the temperature exchange
counter n to zero for each tempera-
ture. (Balancing process).
7. Creating the j solution at the
neighborhood of the i solution.
8. Evaluating the objective function
```
$f = Z(R, \tilde{\beta}(\omega))$ `at any temperature`
```
according to algorithm 1.
9. Calculating
```
$\Delta = f(j) - f(i).$
```
10. Accepting the solution j, if
```
$\Delta < 0.$ `Otherwise, generating a ran-`
`dom number` `RN~U(0,1).`

`If` $RN < e^{\left(\frac{-\Delta}{T_0}\right)}$ `then selecting the j`
```
solution.
11. Setting
```
$n = n + 1.$ `If` n `is equal`
`to` $N(t)$ `then go to 12. Otherwise, go`
`to 7.`
```
12. Reducing the temperature. If it
reaches
```
T_F `then stop. Otherwise, go`
`to 6.`

The constant parameters of the simulated annealing algorithm include initial temperature (T_0), the coefficient of decreasing temperature function (α) ($T_s = \alpha T_{s-1}$), and number of iteration in each temperature ($N(t)$). To solve the on hand model using SA, three values are considered for all parameters and the best combination is chosen. Taleizadeh et al. (2010) are chosen 1000, 1500, and 2000 as different values of T_0, and $\alpha = 0.9$, 0.95, and 0.99 have been used. Finally 50, 100, and 200 are utilized for different values of $N(t)$. After more than one hundred runs, the best combination obtained as $T_0 = 2000$, $\alpha = 0.95$, and $N(t) = 200$. Also the convergence path of SA algorithm is shown in Figure 6.

In order to have more detailed information readers can see Taleizadeh et al. (2010)'s research. It should be noted that these solution methods based on Blum et al. (2011)'s classifications are a HMHHMH type and based on Jourdan et al. (2009)'s classification are HTH type.

In order to introduce some researches on stochastic inventory control in which metaheuristic algorithms are used, readers can see to Lopez-Garcia and Posada-Bolivar (1999), Chang et al. (2004), and Pasandideh et al. (2011).

Random Fuzzy Period Length (RFPL) Case

In addition to above application of inventory control system with stochastic period length, we want to explain another real applied inventory system when period length is random fuzzy variable. Like the previous application, decision variables are integer type and there are space and service level constraints for each product while the cost factors are deterministic. The random fuzzy mathematical model of the proposed problem is from Taleizadeh et al. 2009a (see Box 7 for Equation (72)):Where Equations (72) shows the fuzzy profit objective function and Equations (73) and (74) show the space and fuzzy service level constraints respectively. Equation (75) causes the maximum level of inventory becomes integer. In order to avoid using simulation method, Taleizadeh et al. (2009a) difuzzified the above

Figure 6. The convergence paths of the best result in uniform example

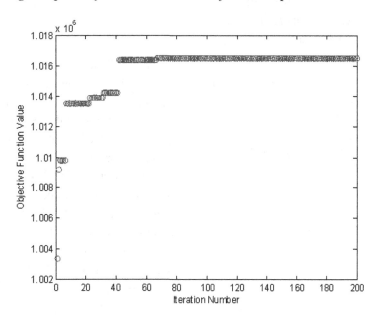

Box 7.

$$
\begin{aligned}
Max\ Z(R_j, \tilde{\theta}_j) = \sum_{j=1}^{P} & \left\{ (P_j - C_j) \left[\begin{array}{l} \int_{T_{Min_j}}^{\frac{R_j}{D_j}} \left(D_j T_j \right) f_{T_j}(t_j, \tilde{\theta}_j) dt_j \\ + \int_{\frac{R_j}{D_j}}^{T_{Max_j}} \left(R_j + \beta_j (D_j T_j - R_j) \right) f_{T_j}(t_j, \tilde{\theta}_j) dt_j \end{array} \right] \right\} \\
& - \sum_{j=1}^{P} C_j^h \left[\int_{T_{Min_j}}^{\frac{R_j}{D_j}} \left(R_j T_j - \frac{D_j T_j^{\ 2}}{2} \right) f_{T_j}(t_j, \tilde{\theta}_j) dt_j + \int_{\frac{R_j}{D_j}}^{T_{Max_j}} \frac{R_j^{\ 2}}{2D_j} f_{T_j}(t_j, \tilde{\theta}_j) dt_j \right] \\
& - \sum_{j=1}^{P} C_j^b \beta_j \left[\int_{\frac{R_j}{D_j}}^{T_{Max_j}} \left(D_j T_j - R_j \right) f_{T_j}(t_j, \tilde{\theta}_j) dt_j \right]
\end{aligned}
\tag{72}
$$

$$
S.t: \quad \sum_{j=1}^{P} f_j R_j \leq F
\tag{73}
$$

$$
\int_{\frac{R_j}{D_j}}^{T_{Max_j}} f_{T_j}(t_j) dt_j \leq 1 - SL_j; \quad \forall\ j = 1, 2, ..., P
\tag{74}
$$

$$
R_j \geq 0, Integer; \quad \forall\ j = 1, 2, ..., P
\tag{75}
$$

model and transformed the fuzzy single objective model to crisp multi objective one (see Box 8, 9, and 10 for Equations (76), (77) and (78));

$$S.t: \quad \sum_{j=1}^{P} f_j R_j \leq F \tag{79}$$

$$-(\frac{\lambda_{j1}}{D_j})R_j \leq Ln(1 - SL_j); \quad \forall j: \ j-1,2,\cdots,P \tag{80}$$

$$-(\frac{\lambda_{j2}}{D_j})R_j \leq Ln(1 - SL_j); \quad \forall j: \ j=1,2,\cdots,P \tag{81}$$

$$-(\frac{\lambda_{j3}}{D_j})R_j \leq Ln(1 - SL_j); \quad \forall j: \ j=1,2,\cdots,P \tag{82}$$

$$R_j \geq 0 \ \ \text{integer}; \qquad \forall j \quad j=1,2,...,n \tag{83}$$

The final mathematical model of this problem is multi-objective integer-nonlinear-programming type and in order to solve it, a hybrid method of Pareto selecting, TOPSIS and genetic algorithm approach is used. Table 6 shows the best results obtained for the numerical example used from Taleizadeh et al. (2009a) in which the first ten good results are ranked. In order to have more detailed information readers can see Taleizadeh et al. (2009a)'s research. It should be noted that these solution methods based on Blum et al. (2011)'s classifications are a HMHPR type and based on Jourdan et al. (2009)'s classification are HRH type.

Also parameter setting approach and steps of GA are very similar to what we described before but the best values of possibility of mutation in

Box 8.

$$Min \ Z_1 = \sum_{j=1}^{P} \left[\left[\left(\frac{C_j^h D_j}{\lambda_{1j}^2} + \frac{D_j(1-\beta_j)(P_j-C_j)+C_j^b\beta_j D_j}{\lambda_{1j}} \right) - \left(\frac{C_j^h D_j}{\lambda_{2j}^2} + \frac{D_j(1-\beta_j)(P_j-C_j)+C_j^b\beta_j D_j}{\lambda_{2j}} \right) \right] e^{\left(\frac{\lambda_{3j}}{D_j} - \frac{\lambda_{2j}}{D_j} \right) R_j} \right]$$
$$+ \sum_{i=1}^{P} \left(\frac{C_j^h}{\lambda_{1j}} - \frac{C_j^h}{\lambda_{2j}} \right) R_j + \sum_{j=1}^{P} \left(\frac{D_j(P_j-C_j)}{\lambda_{2j}} + \frac{C_j^h D_j}{\lambda_{2j}^2} \right) - \left(\frac{D_j(P_j-C_j)}{\lambda_{3j}} + \frac{C_j^h D_j}{\lambda_{3j}^2} \right) \tag{76}$$

Box 9.

$$Max \ Z_2 = \sum_{j=1}^{P} \left(-\frac{C_j^h D_j}{\lambda_{2j}^2} - \frac{D_j(1-\beta_j)(P_j-C_j)+C_j^b\beta_j D_j}{\lambda_{2j}} \right) e^{\frac{\lambda_{2j}}{D_j} R_j}$$
$$- \sum_{j=1}^{P} \frac{C_j^h}{\lambda_{2j}} R_j + \sum_{j=1}^{P} \frac{D_j(P_j-C_j)}{\lambda_{2j}} + \frac{C_j^h D_j}{\lambda_{2j}^2} \tag{77}$$

Box 10.

$$Max \ Z_3 = \sum_{i=1}^{P} \left(\frac{C_j^h D_j}{\lambda_{2j}^2} + \frac{D_j(1-\beta_j)(P_j-C_j)+C_j^b \beta_j D_j}{\lambda_{2j}} \right)$$
$$- \left(\frac{C_j^h D_j}{\lambda_{3j}^2} + \frac{D_j(1-\beta_j)(P_j-C_j)+C_j^b \beta_j D_j}{\lambda_{3j}} \right) e^{\left(\frac{\lambda_{3j}}{D_j} - \frac{\lambda_{2j}}{D_j} \right) R_j}$$

(78)

Table 6. Best results of example of stochastic review model – (RFPL) case

Objectives			TOPSIS	
Z_1	Z_2	Z_3	Score	Rank
253,980	-174,660	207,020	0.9929	1
253,840	-175,350	206,900	0.8372	2
253,710	-175,620	206,790	0.6860	3
253,700	-175,480	206,790	0.6744	4
253,700	-175,430	206,790	0.6744	4
253,690	-175,520	206,780	0.6628	5

Figure 7. The convergence path of the Pareto and GA

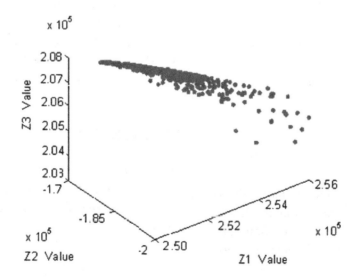

solving procedure of this problem is changed to $P_m = 0.098$. So in order to shorten the length of chapter we avoid double writing something.

Finally the convergence illustration of algorithm is shown in Figure 7. In the case of fuzzy inventory model researches we have the following works Ye and Li (2011), Mandal et al. (2011), Maiti (2011), Ren et al. (2010), Roy et al. (2009) and Pirayesh and Yazdi(2010).

FUTURE RESEARCH

In order to have some recommendations to extend the solution method considering some other Meta Heuristic algorithms such as tabu search, memetic algorithm, ant colony and bees colony optimization or considering the multi objective version of the use algorithm to solve the RFPL or CBOM cases can be useful. Also considering other hybrid MHAs such as hybrid method of PSO and GA or other combinations may improve the quality of results. On the other hand, following the solutions approaches presented in this chapter, it would be interesting to build and solve supply chain models that support inventory decisions in more complex environments. Finally, we note some areas with potential for future research. Roughly speaking, the solutions for the numerical examples are not optimal; they are near optimal. Hence, first we suggest extend the solution method considering some other metaheuristic algorithms in order to find a better solution.

CONCLUSION

In this chapter we discuss about the applications of HMHAs in inventory management problems. Three specific inventory problems in certain and uncertain environments with six different applica-

tions are described including; Joint replenishment EOQ problem, newsboy problem, and stochastic review problem. Also several HMHAs for different problems, using different metaheuristic algorithms such GA, SA, PSO, HS, and BCO are proposed to solve the mentioned problems. The proposed metaheuristic algorithms are combined with fuzzy simulation, rough simulation, Pareto selecting and goal programming approaches. Also, different numerical examples were used to show the performance of each proposed algorithm. For the first application of EOQ model, CFJR case, hybrid method of harmony search, fuzzy simulation and rough simulation performs better than other methods while for the second applications, CFRJR case, hybrid method of bees colony optimization, fuzzy simulation and rough simulation had the best results. In the first application of newsboy problem, CBOM case, hybrid method of goal programming and genetic algorithm performs better than simulated annealing algorithm and for the second applications, CMPFD case, hybrid method of bees colony optimization with fuzzy simulation had the best results. In the other hand, for the first and application of stochastic review problems, FCF case, hybrid method of simulated annealing and fuzzy simulation perform better than simulated annealing approach. Finally for the second application of stochastic review problem, RFPL case, hybrid method of Pareto selecting, TOPSIS and genetic algorithm approach is used to solve its multi objective model.

REFERENCES

Aarts, E. H. L., & Korst, J. H. M. (1989). *Simulated annealing and Boltzmann machine: A stochastic approach to computing*. Chichester, UK: John Wiley and Sons.

Augerat, P., Belenguer, J. M., Benavent, E., Corber'n, A., & Naddef, D. (1998). Separating capacity constraints in the CVRP using tabu search. *European Journal of Operational Research, 106*, 546–557. doi:10.1016/S0377-2217(97)00290-7doi:10.1016/S0377-2217(97)00290-7

Blum, C., Blesa Aguilera, M. J., Roli, A., & Sampels, M. (2008). *Hybrid meta-heuristics – An emerging approach to optimization* (*Vol. 114*). Springer Studies in Computational Intelligence.

Blum, C., Puchinger, J., Raidl, G. R., & Roli, A. (2011). Hybrid Meta-heuristics in combinatorial optimization: A survey. *Applied Soft Computing, 11*, 4135–4151. doi:10.1016/j.asoc.2011.02.032doi:10.1016/j.asoc.2011.02.032

Blum, C., & Roli, A. (2003). Metaheuristics in combinatorial optimization: Overview and conceptual comparison. *ACM Computing Surveys, 35*, 268–308. doi:10.1145/937503.937505doi:10.1145/937503.937505

Cárdenas-Barrón, L. E. (2007). Optimizing inventory decisions in a multi-stage multi-customer supply chain: A note. *Transportation Research Part E, Logistics and Transportation Review, 43*, 647–654. doi:10.1016/j.tre.2005.09.011doi:10.1016/j.tre.2005.09.011

Cardenas-Barron, L. E. (2011). The derivation of EOQ/EPQ inventory models with two backorders costs using analytic geometry and algebra. *Applied Mathematical Modelling, 35*, 2394–2407. doi:10.1016/j.apm.2010.11.053doi:10.1016/j.apm.2010.11.053

Chang, M.-S., Lin, Y.-C., & Hsueh, C.-F. (2004). Vehicle routing and scheduling problem with time windows and stochastic demand. *Transportation Research Record, 1882*, 79–87. doi:10.3141/1882-10doi:10.3141/1882-10

Demmel, J. G., & Askin, R. G. (1992). A multiple-objective decision model for the evaluation of advanced manufacturing system technologies. *Journal of Manufacturing Systems, 11*, 179–194. doi:10.1016/0278-6125(92)90004-Ydoi:10.1016/0278-6125(92)90004-Y

Fatrias, D., & Shimizu, Y. (2010). Multi-objective analysis of periodic review inventory problem with coordinated replenishment in two-echelon supply chain system through differential evolution. *Journal of Advanced Mechanical Design, Systems and Manufacturing, 4*, 637–650. doi:10.1299/jamdsm.4.637doi:10.1299/jamdsm.4.637

Geem, Z. W., Kim, J. H., & Loganathan, G. V. (2001). A new heuristic optimization algorithm: Harmony search. *Simulation, 76*, 60–68. doi:10.1177/003754970107600201doi:10.1177/003754970107600201

Hansen, P., & Mladenovic, N. (2001). Variable neighborhood search: Principles and applications. *European Journal of Operational Research, 130*, 449–467. doi:10.1016/S0377-2217(00)00100-4doi:10.1016/S0377-2217(00)00100-4

Harris, F. W. (1913). How many parts to make at once. *Factory, The Magazine of Management, 10,* 135–136, 152.

Holland, J. H. (1975). *Adoption in neural and artificial systems.* Ann Arbor, MI: The University of Michigan Press.

Hsieh, C. L., & Laio, S. H. (2010). *A multi-objective evolutionary approach for an integrated location-inventory problem in vendor-managed inventory systems.* 40th International Conference on Computers and Industrial Engineering: Soft Computing Techniques for Advanced Manufacturing and Service Systems, CIE40 2010, art. no. 5668373.

Jourdan, L., Basseur, M., & Talbi, E. G. (2009). Hybridizing exact methods and meta-heuristics: A taxonomy. *European Journal of Operational Research*, *199*, 620–629. doi:10.1016/j.ejor.2007.07.035doi:10.1016/j.ejor.2007.07.035

Kalpic, D., Mornar, V., & Baranovic, M. (1995). Case study based on a multi period multi-criteria production planning model. *International Journal of Production Economics*, *87*, 658–669.

Kennedy, J., & Eberhart, R. (1995). Particle swarm optimization. *Proceedings of the IEEE International Conference on Neural Networks*, Perth, Australia, (pp. 1942-1945).

Kennedy, J., & Eberhart, R. (2001). *Swarm intelligence*. San Diego, CA: Academic Press.

Kim, G. C., & Schniederjams, M. J. (1993). A multiple objective model for a just-in-time manufacturing system environment. *International Journal of Operations & Production Management*, *13*, 47–61. doi:10.1108/01443579310048209doi:10.1108/01443579310048209

Kirkpatrick, S., Gelatti, C. D., & Vecchi, M. P. (1994). Optimization by simulated annealing. In H. Gutfreund & G. Tolouse (Eds.), *Advanced series in neurosciences, Vol. 3, Biology and computation: A physicist's choice*, (pp. 671–680).

Klepeis, J. L., Pieja, M. J., & Floudas, C. A. (2003). Hybrid global optimization algorithms for protein structure prediction: Alternating hybrids. *Biophysical Journal*, *4*, 869–882. PubMed doi:10.1016/S0006-3495(03)74905-4doi:10.1016/S0006-3495(03)74905-4

Kwak, N. K., Schnierderjans, M. J., & Warkentin, K. S. (1991). An application of linear goal programming to the marketing distribution. *European Journal of Operational Research*, *52*, 334–344. doi:10.1016/0377-2217(91)90168-Udoi:10.1016/0377-2217(91)90168-U

Lee, J. E., Rhee, K. G., & Lee, H. H. (2010). Multi-objective hybrid genetic algorithm for reverse logistics network design of inventory systems with backordering. IEEM2010 - IEEE International Conference on Industrial Engineering and Engineering Management, art. no. 5674151, (pp. 2318-2322).

Lee, S. M., & Clayton, E. R. (1972). A goal programming model for academic resource allocation. *Management Science*, *18*, B-395–408. doi:10.1287/mnsc.18.8.B395doi:10.1287/mnsc.18.8.B395

Liao, S. H., & Hsieh, C. L. (2010). Integrated location-inventory retail supply chain design: A multi-objective evolutionary approach. *Lecture Notes in Computer Science (including subseries Lecture Notes in Artificial Intelligence and Lecture Notes in Bioinformatics) 6457 LNCS*, (pp. 533-542).

Liu, B. (2000). *Theory and practice of uncertainty programming*. Heidelberg, Germany: Springer-Verlag.

Liu, B. (2004). *Uncertainty theory*. Heidelberg, Germany: Springer-Verlag.

Liu, B., & Liu, Y. K. (2002). Expected value of fuzzy variable and fuzzy expected value models. *IEEE Transactions on Fuzzy Systems*, *10*, 445–450. doi:10.1109/TFUZZ.2002.800692doi:10.1109/TFUZZ.2002.800692

Liu, G. (2010). Rough set theory based on two universal sets and its applications. *Knowledge-Based Systems*, *23*, 110–115. doi:10.1016/j.knosys.2009.06.011doi:10.1016/j.knosys.2009.06.011

Lopez-Garcia, L., & Posada-Bolivar, A. (1999). Simulator that uses Tabu search to approach the optimal solution to stochastic inventory models. *Computers & Industrial Engineering*, *37*, 215–218. doi:10.1016/S0360-8352(99)00058-3doi:10.1016/S0360-8352(99)00058-3

Ma, J., Lu, J., & Zhang, G. (2010). Decider: A fuzzy multi-criteria group decision support system. *Knowledge-Based Systems*, *23*, 23–31. doi:10.1016/j.knosys.2009.07.006doi:10.1016/j.knosys.2009.07.006

Maiti, M. K. (2011). A fuzzy genetic algorithm with varying population size to solve an inventory model with credit-linked promotional demand in an imprecise planning horizon. *European Journal of Operational Research*, *213*, 96–106. doi:10.1016/j.ejor.2011.02.014doi:10.1016/j.ejor.2011.02.014

Mandal, S., Maity, A. K., Maity, K., Mondal, S., & Maiti, M. (2011). Multi-item multi-period optimal production problem with variable preparation time in fuzzy stochastic environment. *Applied Mathematical Modelling*, *35*, 4341–4353. doi:10.1016/j.apm.2011.03.007doi:10.1016/j.apm.2011.03.007

Moslemi, H., & Zandieh, M. (2011). Comparisons of some improving strategies on MOPSO for multi-objective (r, Q) inventory system. *Expert Systems with Applications*, *38*, 2051–12057. doi:10.1016/j.eswa.2011.01.169doi:10.1016/j.eswa.2011.01.169

Muckstadt, J. A., & Sapra, A. (2010). *Principles of inventory management* (1st ed.). New York, NY: Springer. doi:10.1007/978-0-387-68948-7doi:10.1007/978-0-387-68948-7

Nagarur, N., Vrat, P., & Duongsuwan, W. (1997). Production planning and scheduling for injection mounding of pipe fittings: A case study. *International Journal of Production Economics*, *53*, 157–170. doi:10.1016/S0925-5273(97)00109-6doi:10.1016/S0925-5273(97)00109-6

Nwana, V., Darby-Dowman, K., & Mitra, G. (2005). A co-operative parallel heuristic for mixed zero-one linear programming: Combining simulated annealing with branch and bound. *European Journal of Operational Research*, *164*, 12–23. doi:10.1016/j.ejor.2002.12.002doi:10.1016/j.ejor.2002.12.002

Pasandideh, S. H. R., Niaki, S. T. A., & Tokhmehchi, N. (2011). A parameter-tuned genetic algorithm to optimize two-echelon continuous review inventory systems. *Expert Systems with Applications*, *38*, 11708–11714. doi:10.1016/j.eswa.2011.03.056doi:10.1016/j.eswa.2011.03.056

Pawlak, Z. (1998). Rough set theory and its applications to data analysis. *Cybernetics and Systems*, *29*, 661–688. doi:10.1080/0196972981 25470doi:10.1080/019697298125470

Pham, D. T., Ghanbarzadeh, A., Koç, E., Otri, S., Rahim, S., & Zaidi, M. (2009). *The bees algorithm–A novel tool for complex optimization problems*. Cardiff, UK: Intelligent Production Machines and Systems.

Pirayesh, M., & Yazdi, M. M. (2010). Modeling (r, Q) policy in a two-level supply chain system with fuzzy demand. *International Journal of Uncertainty. Fuzziness and Knowledge-Based Systems*, *18*, 819–841. doi:10.1142/S0218488510006817doi:10.1142/S0218488510006817

Ren, M.-L., Huang, S., & Wang, B.-M. (2010). Inventory model for major equipment maintenance companies with fuzzy and discrete spare parts demands. In J. J. Z. Xitong (Ed.), Computer Integrated Manufacturing Systems, CIMS, 16, *2233-2239*.

Roy, A., Pal, S., & Maiti, M. K. (2009). A production inventory model with stock dependent demand incorporating learning and inflationary effect in a random planning horizon: A fuzzy genetic algorithm with varying population size approach. *Computers & Industrial Engineering, 57,* 1324–1335. doi:10.1016/j.cie.2009.07.008doi:10.1016/j.cie.2009.07.008

Sayadi, M. K., Ramezanian, R., & Ghaffari-Nasab, N. (2010). A discrete firefly meta-heuristic with local search for makespan minimization in permutation flow shop scheduling problems. *International Journal of Industrial Engineering Computation, 1,* 1–10. doi:10.5267/j.ijiec.2010.01.001doi:10.5267/j.ijiec.2010.01.001

Seeley, T. D. (1996). *The wisdom of the hive: The social physiology of honey bee colonies.* Cambridge, MA: Harvard University Press.

Stam, A., & Kuula, M. (1991). Selecting a flexible manufacturing system using multiple criteria analysis. *International Journal of Production Research, 29,* 803–820. doi:10.1080/00207549108930103doi:10.1080/00207549108930103

Steuer, R. E. (1985). *Multiple-criteria optimization: Theory, computation and application.* John Wiley and Sons.

Sundaram, R. M. (1978). An application of goal programming technique in metal cutting. *International Journal of Production Research, 16,* 375–382. doi:10.1080/00207547808930029doi:10.1080/00207547808930029

Taleizadeh, A. A., Aryanezhad, M. B., Wee, H. M., & Jabalameli, M. S. (2011b). *Solving economic order quantity (EOQ) Model with fuzzy rough environment, quantity discount and prepayment.* Working paper.

Taleizadeh, A. A., Barzinpour, F., & Wee, H. M. (2011c). Meta-heuristic algorithms to solve the fuzzy single period problem. *Mathematical and Computer Modelling, 54,* 1273–1285. doi:10.1016/j.mcm.2011.03.038doi:10.1016/j.mcm.2011.03.038

Taleizadeh, A. A., Niaki, S. T., & Aryanezhad, M. B. (2009a). A hybrid method of Pareto, TOPSIS and genetic algorithm to optimize multi-product multi-constraint inventory control systems with random fuzzy replenishments. *Mathematical and Computer Modelling, 49,* 1044–1057. doi:10.1016/j.mcm.2008.10.013doi:10.1016/j.mcm.2008.10.013

Taleizadeh, A. A., Niaki, S. T., & Aryanezhad, M. B. (2010). Replenish-up-to multi chance-constraint inventory control system with stochastic period lengths and total discount under fuzzy purchasing price and holding costs. *International Journal of Systems Science, 41,* 1187–1200. doi:10.1080/00207720903171761doi:10.1080/00207720903171761

Taleizadeh, A. A., Niaki, S. T., & Hosseini, V. (2009b). Optimizing multi product multi constraints bi-objective newsboy problem with discount by hybrid method of goal programming and genetic algorithm. *Engineering Optimization, 41,* 437–457. doi:10.1080/03052150802582175doi:10.1080/03052150802582175

Taleizadeh, A. A., Niaki, S. T. A., & Hosseini, V. (2008). The multi-product multi-constraint newsboy problem with incremental discount and batch order. *Asian Journal of Applied Sciences, 1,* 110–122. doi:10.3923/ajaps.2008.110.122doi:10.3923/ajaps.2008.110.122

Taleizadeh, A. A., Niaki, S. T. A., & Nikou-sokhan, R. (2011a). Constraint multi-product joint-replenishment inventory control problem using uncertain programming. *Applied Soft Computing*, *11*, 5143–5144. doi:10.1016/j.asoc.2011.05.045doi:10.1016/j.asoc.2011.05.045

Teodorovic, D. (2009). *Bees colony optimization* (pp. 39–60). Berlin, Germany: Springer.

Von Frisch, K. (1976). *Bees: Their vision, chemical senses and language*. Ithica, NY: Cornell University Press.

Wagner, H. M., & Whitin, T. M. (1958). Dynamical version of the economic lot size model. *Management Science*, *5*, 89–96. doi:10.1287/mnsc.5.1.89doi:10.1287/mnsc.5.1.89

Wild, T. (1997). *Best practice in inventory management* (1st ed.). John Wiley & Sons, Inc.

Wilson, R. H. (1934). A scientific routine for stock control. *Harvard Business Review*, *13*, 116–128.

Xu, J., & Zhao, L. (2008). A class of fuzzy rough expected value multi-objective decision making model and its application to inventory problems. *Computers & Mathematics with Applications (Oxford, England)*, *56*, 2107–2119. doi:10.1016/j.camwa.2008.03.040doi:10.1016/j.camwa.2008.03.040

Yang, X. S. (2008). *Nature-inspired meta-heuristic algorithms*. UK: Luniver Press.

Yang, X. S. (2009). Firefly algorithms for multimodal optimization. In O. Watanabe & T. Zeugmann (Eds.), *Stochastic algorithms: Foundations and applications, SAGA (Vol. 5792*, pp. 169–178). *Lecture Notes in Computer Science* Berlin, Germany: Springer-Verlag. doi:10.1007/978-3-642-04944-6_14doi:10.1007/978-3-642-04944-6_14

Ye, F., & Li, Y. (2011). A Stackelberg single-period supply chain inventory model with weighted possibilistic mean values under fuzzy environment. *Applied Soft Computing Journal*, *11*, 5519–5527. doi:10.1016/j.asoc.2011.05.007doi:10.1016/j.asoc.2011.05.007

Zhang, G., & Lu, J. (2009). A linguistic intelligent user guide for method selection in multi-objective decision support systems. *Information Science*, *179*, 2299–2308. doi:10.1016/j.ins.2009.01.043doi:10.1016/j.ins.2009.01.043

Zhang, G., Lu, J., & Dillon, T. (2007). Decentralized multi-objective bi-level decision making with fuzzy demands. *Knowledge-Based Systems*, *20*, 495–507. doi:10.1016/j.knosys.2007.01.003doi:10.1016/j.knosys.2007.01.003

ADDITIONAL READING

Abbasi, B., & Mahlooji, H. (2012). Improving response surface methodology by using artificial neural network and simulated annealing. *Expert Systems with Applications*, *39*, 3461–3468. doi:10.1016/j.eswa.2011.09.036doi:10.1016/j.eswa.2011.09.036

Abbass, H. A. (2002). The self-adaptive Pareto differential evolution algorithm. In *Congress on Evolutionary Computation (CEC'2002)*, *1*, (pp. 831–836). Piscataway, NJ: IEEE Service Center.

Abbass, H. A., & Sarker, R. (2002). The Pareto differential evolution algorithm. *International Journal of Artificial Intelligence Tools*, *11*, 531–552. doi:10.1142/S0218213002001039doi:10.1142/S0218213002001039

Afshar, M. H. (2011).Colony-mutated ant system for pipe network optimization. *Iranian Journal of Science and Technology, Transaction B: Engineering, 35,* 217-232.

Altiparmak, F., Gen, M., Lin, L., & Paksoy, T. (2006). A genetic algorithm approach for multi-objective optimization of supply chain networks. *Computers & Industrial Engineering, 51,* 196–215. doi:10.1016/j.cie.2006.07.011doi:10.1016/j.cie.2006.07.011

Angeline, P. J. (1998). Using selection to improve particle swarm optimization. *Proceedings of the 1998 International Conference on Evolutionary Computation,* (pp. 84–89). Piscataway, NJ: IEEE Press.

Angeline, P. J. (1998). Evolutionary optimization versus particle swarm optimization: Differences in philosophy and performance differences. In V. W. Porto, N. Saravanan, D. Waagen, & A. E. Eiben (Eds.), *Evolutionary Programming VII: Proceedings of the 7th Annual Conference on Evolutionary Programming.* Berlin, Germany: Springer-Verlag.

Cárdenas-Barrón, L. E. (2001). The economic production quantity (EPQ) with shortage derived algebraically. *International Journal of Production Economics, 70,* 289–292. doi:10.1016/S0925-5273(00)00068-2doi:10.1016/S0925-5273(00)00068-2

Cárdenas-Barrón, L. E. (2008). Optimal manufacturing batch size with rework in a single-stage production system – A simple derivation. *Computers and Industrial Engineering Journal, 55,* 758–765. doi:10.1016/j.cie.2007.07.017doi:10.1016/j.cie.2007.07.017

Cárdenas-Barrón, L. E. (2009). Optimal ordering policies in response to a discount offer: Extensions. *International Journal of Production Economics, 122,* 774–782. doi:10.1016/j.ijpe.2009.05.003doi:10.1016/j.ijpe.2009.05.003

Cárdenas-Barrón, L. E. (2009). Economic production quantity with rework process at a single-stage manufacturing system with planned backorders. *Computers and Industrial Engineering Journal, 57,* 1105–1113. doi:10.1016/j.cie.2009.04.020doi:10.1016/j.cie.2009.04.020

Cárdenas-Barrón, L. E. (2010). An easy method to derive EOQ and EPQ inventory models with backorders. *Computers & Mathematics with Applications (Oxford, England), 59,* 948–952. doi:10.1016/j.camwa.2009.09.013doi:10.1016/j.camwa.2009.09.013

Cárdenas-Barrón, L. E., Smith, N. R., & Goyal, S. K. (2010). Optimal order size to take advantage of a one-time discount offer with allowed backorders. *Applied Mathematical Modelling, 34,* 1642–1652. doi:10.1016/j.apm.2009.09.013doi:10.1016/j.apm.2009.09.013

Cárdenas-Barrón, L. E., Teng, J. T., Treviño-Garza, G., Wee, H. M., & Lou, K. R. (In Press). An improved algorithm and solution on an integrated production-inventory model in a three-layer supply chain. International Journal of Production Economics, in press. Doi: 10.1016/j.ijpe.2011.12.013

Cárdenas-Barrón, L. E., Treviño-Garza, G., & Wee, H. M. (2012). A simple and better algorithm to solve the vendor managed inventory control system of multi-product multi-constraint economic order quantity model. *Expert Systems with Applications, 39,* 3888–3895. doi:10.1016/j.eswa.2011.09.057doi:10.1016/j.eswa.2011.09.057

Cárdenas-Barrón, L. E., Wee, H. M., & Blos, M. F. (2011). Solving the vendor-buyer integrated inventory system with arithmetic-geometric inequality. *Mathematical and Computer Modelling, 53,* 991–997. doi:10.1016/j.mcm.2010.11.056doi:10.1016/j.mcm.2010.11.056

Chung, K. J., & Cárdenas-Barrón, L. E. (In Press). The complete solution procedure for the EOQ and EPQ inventory models with linear and fixed backorder costs. Mathematical and Computer Modelling, in press. Doi: 10.1016/j.mcm.2011.12.051

Dubois, D., & Prade, H. (1978). Operations on fuzzy numbers. *International Journal of Systems Science, 9,* 613–626. doi:10.1080/002077278089 41724doi:10.1080/00207727808941724

Dubois, D., & Prade, H. (1979). Fuzzy real algebra: Some results. *Fuzzy Sets and Systems, 2,* 327–348. doi:10.1016/0165-0114(79)90005-8doi:10.1016/0165-0114(79)90005-8

Dubois, D., & Prade, H. (1979). Operations in a fuzzy-valued logic. *Information and Control, 43,* 224–240. doi:10.1016/S0019-9958(79)90730-7doi:10.1016/S0019-9958(79)90730-7

Dubois, D., & Prade, H. (1980). *Fuzzy sets and systems: Theory and applications.* New York, NY: Academic Press.

Dubois, D., & Prade, H. (1980). Systems of linear fuzzy constraints. *Fuzzy Sets and Systems, 3,* 37–48. doi:10.1016/0165-0114(80)90004-4doi:10.1016/0165-0114(80)90004-4

Dubois, D., & Prade, H. (1981). Additions of interactive fuzzy numbers. *IEEE Transactions on Automatic Control, 26,* 926–936. doi:10.1109/TAC.1981.1102744doi:10.1109/TAC.1981.1102744

Dubois, D., & Prade, H. (1983). Ranking fuzzy numbers in the setting of possibility theory. *Information Sciences, 30,* 183–224. doi:10.1016/0020-0255(83)90025-7doi:10.1016/0020-0255(83)90025-7

Dutta, P., Chakraborty, D., & Roy, A. (2005). A single-period inventory model with fuzzy random variable demand. *Mathematical and Computer Modelling, 41,* 915–922. doi:10.1016/j.mcm.2004.08.007doi:10.1016/j.mcm.2004.08.007

Eberhart, R. C., & Shi, Y. (2000). Comparing inertia weights and constriction factors in particle swarm optimization. *Proceedings of the 2000 Congress on Evolutionary Computation,* (pp. 84–88). Piscataway, NJ: IEEE Service Center.

Eberhart, R. C., Simpson, P. K., & Dobbins, R. W. (1996). *Computational intelligence PC tools.* Boston, MA: Academic Press.

García-Laguna, J., San-Jose, L. A., Cárdenas-Barrón, L. E., & Sicilia, J. (2010). The integrality of the lot size in the basic EOQ and EPQ models: Applications to other production-inventory models. *Applied Mathematics and Computation, 216,* 1660–1672. doi:10.1016/j.amc.2010.02.042doi:10.1016/j.amc.2010.02.042

Gen, M., & Cheng, R. (1997). *Genetic algorithm and engineering design.* New York, NY: John Wiley & Sons.

Goyal, S. K., & Cárdenas-Barrón, L. E. (2002). Note on: Economic production quantity model for items with imperfect quality-a practical approach. *International Journal of Production Economics, 77,* 85–87. doi:10.1016/S0925-5273(01)00203-1doi:10.1016/S0925-5273(01)00203-1

Hosseini, S. V., Moghadasi, H., Noori, A. H., & Royani, M. B. (2009). Newsboy problem with two objectives, fuzzy costs and total discount strategy. *Journal of Applied Sciences, 9,* 1880–1888. doi:10.3923/jas.2009.1880.1888doi:10.3923/jas.2009.1880.1888

Jaberipour, M., & Khorram, E. (2011). A new harmony search algorithm for solving mixed-discrete engineering optimization problems. *Engineering Optimization, 43*, 507–523. doi:10. 1080/0305215X.2010.499939doi:10.1080/0305 215X.2010.499939

Ji, X., & Shao, Z. H. (2006). Model and algorithm for bi-level SPP problem with fuzzy demands and discounts. *Applied Mathematics and Computation, 172*, 163–174. doi:10.1016/j. amc.2005.01.139doi:10.1016/j.amc.2005.01.139

Joo, S. J., & Bong, J. Y. (1996). Construction of exact D-optimal designs by Tabu search. *Computational Statistics & Data Analysis, 21*, 181–191. doi:10.1016/0167-9473(95)00014-3doi:10.1016/0167-9473(95)00014-3

Kaveh, A., & Ahangaran, M. (2012). Discrete cost optimization of composite floor system using social harmony search model. *Applied Soft Computing Journal, 12*, 372–381. doi:10.1016/j. asoc.2011.08.035doi:10.1016/j.asoc.2011.08.035

Kaveh, A., & Laknejadi, K. (2011). A novel hybrid charge system search and particle swarm optimization method for multi-objective optimization. *Expert Systems with Applications, 38*, 15475–15488. doi:10.1016/j.eswa.2011.06.012doi:10.1016/j. eswa.2011.06.012

Kennedy, J. (2000). Stereotyping: Improving particle swarm performance with cluster analysis. *Proceedings of the 2000 Congress on Evolutionary Computation,* (pp. 1507–1512). Piscataway, NJ: IEEE Service Center.

Kennedy, J., & Eberhart, R. C. (1995). Particle swarm optimization. *Proceedings of the IEEE International Conference on Neural Networks, IV,* (pp. 1942–1948). Piscataway, NJ: IEEE Service Center.

Kennedy, J., & Eberhart, R. C. (1997). A discrete binary version of the particle swarm algorithm. *Proceedings of the 1997 Conference on Systems, Man, and Cybernetics,* (pp. 4104–4109). Piscataway, NJ: IEEE Service Center.

Kennedy, J., & Spears, W. M. (1998). Matching algorithms to problems: An experimental test of the particle swarm and some genetic algorithms on the multimodal problem generator. *Proceedings of the 1998 International Conference on Evolutionary Computation,* (pp. 78–83). Piscataway, NJ: IEEE Service Center.

Kitano, H. (1990). Designing neural networks using genetic algorithm with graph generation system. *Complex Systems, 4*, 461–476.

Laumanns, M., Thiele, L., Deb, K., & Zitzler, E. (2002). Combining convergence and diversity in evolutionary multi-objective optimization. *Evolutionary Computation, 10*, 263–282. PubMed doi:10.1162/106365602760234108d oi:10.1162/106365602760234108

Lee, K. S., & Geem, Z. W. (2004). A new structural optimization method based on the harmony search algorithm. *Computers & Structures, 82*, 781–798. doi:10.1016/j.compstruc.2004.01.002 doi:10.1016/j.compstruc.2004.01.002

Man, K. F., Tang, K. S., Kwong, S., & Halang, W. A. (1997). *Genetic algorithms for control and signal processing.* London, UK: Springer Verlag. doi:10.1007/978-1-4471-0955-6doi:10.1007/978-1-4471-0955-6

Melanie, M. (1996). *An introduction to genetic algorithms.* Boston, MA: Massachusetts Institute of Technology.

Passandideh, S. H. R., Niaki, S. T. A., & Aryan Yeganeh, J. (2010). A parameter-tuned genetic algorithm for multi-product economic production quantity model with space constraint, discrete delivery orders and shortages. *Advances in Engineering Software*, *41*, 306–314. doi:10.1016/j.advengsoft.2009.07.001doi:10.1016/j.advengsoft.2009.07.001

Rahimi-Vahed, A. R., Mirghorbani, S. M., & Rabbani, M. (2007). A hybrid multi objective particle swarm algorithm for a mixed-model assembly line sequencing problem. *Engineering Optimization*, *39*, 877–898. doi:10.1080/03052150701512042 doi:10.1080/03052150701512042

Ray, T., & Smith, W. (2006). A surrogate assisted parallel multi-objective evolutionary algorithm for robust engineering design. *Engineering Optimization*, *38*, 997–1011. doi:10.1080/0305215060088 2538doi:10.1080/03052150600882538

Rudolph, G. (1998). Evolutionary search for minimal elements in partially ordered finite sets. In V. Porto, N. Saravanan, D. Waagen, & A. Eiben (Eds.), *Evolutionary Programming VII, Proceedings of the 7th Annual Conference on Evolutionary Programming*.

Shahsavar, M., Niaki, S. T. A., & Najafi, A. A. (2010). An efficient genetic algorithm to maximize net present value of project payments under inflation and bonus–penalty policy in resource investment problem. *Advances in Engineering Software*, *41*, 1023–1030. doi:10.1016/j.advengsoft.2010.0 3.002doi:10.1016/j.advengsoft.2010.03.002

Shao, Z. H., & Ji, X. (2006). Fuzzy multi-product constraint SPP problem. *Applied Mathematics and Computation*, *180*, 7–15. doi:10.1016/j.amc.2005.11.123doi:10.1016/j.amc.2005.11.123

Taleizadeh, A. A., Aryanezhad, M. B., & Niaki, S. T. A. (2008). Optimizing multi-product multi-constraint inventory control systems with stochastic replenishment. *Journal of Applied Sciences*, *8*, 1228–1234. doi:10.3923/jas.2008.1228.1234doi:10.3923/jas.2008.1228.1234

Taleizadeh, A. A., Cárdenas-Barrón, L. E., Biabani, J., & Nikousokhan, R. (2012). Multi products single machine EPQ model with immediate rework process. *International Journal of Industrial Engineering Computations*, *3*, 93–102. doi:10.5267/j.ijiec.2011.09.001doi:10.5267/j.ijiec.2011.09.001

Taleizadeh, A. A., & Niaki, S. T. (2009). A hybrid method of harmony search, goal programming and fuzzy simulation for bi-objectives single period problem with fuzzy cost and incremental discount. *Journal of Industrial Engineering, Qazvin Islamic Azad University, 3*, 1-14.

Taleizadeh, A. A., Niaki, S. T., Aryanezhad, M. B., & Fallah Tafti, A. (2010). A genetic algorithm to optimize multi-product multi-constraint inventory control systems with stochastic replenishments and discount. *International Journal of Advanced Manufacturing Technology*, *51*, 311–323. doi:10.1007/s00170-010-2604-8doi:10.1007/s00170-010-2604-8

Taleizadeh, A. A., Niaki, S. T., & Barzinpour, F. (2011). Multi-buyer multi-vendor multi-product multi-constraint supply chain problem with stochastic demand and variable lead time. *Applied Mathematics and Computation*, *217*, 9234–9253. doi:10.1016/j.amc.2011.04.001doi:10.1016/j.amc.2011.04.001

Taleizadeh, A. A., Niaki, S. T., & Seyed-Javadi, S. M. (In Press). Multi-product multi-chance-constraint stochastic inventory problem with dynamic demand and partial back-ordering: A harmony search algorithm. *Journal of Manufacturing Systems*, in press. Doi: 10.1016/j.jmsy.2011.05.006

Taleizadeh, A. A., Niaki, S. T., Shafii, N., Gha-vamizadeh Meibodi, R., & Jabbarzadeh, A. (2010). A particle swarm optimization approach for constraint joint single buyer single vendor inventory problem with changeable lead-time and (r,Q) policy in supply chain. *International Journal of Advanced Manufacturing Technology. International Journal of Advanced Manufacturing Technology, 51,* 1209–1223. doi:10.1007/s00170-010-2689-0doi:10.1007/s00170-010-2689-0

Taleizadeh, A. A., Niaki, S. T. A., & Aryanezhad, M. B. (2009). Multi-product multi-constraint inventory control systems with stochastic replenishment and discount under fuzzy purchasing price and holding costs. *Journal of Applied Sciences, 6,* 1–12.

Taleizadeh, A. A., Niaki, S. T. A., & Hosseini, V. (2008). The multi-product multi-constraint newsboy problem with incremental discount and batch order. *Asian Journal of Applied Sciences, 1,* 110–122. doi:10.3923/ajaps.2008.110.122doi:10.3923/ajaps.2008.110.122

Taleizadeh, A. A., Niaki, S. T. A., & Makui, A. (2012). Multi-product multi-chance constraint multi-buyer single-vendor supply chain problem with stochastic demand and variable lead time. *Expert Systems with Applications, 39*(5), 5338–5348. doi:10.1016/j.eswa.2011.11.001doi:10.1016/j.eswa.2011.11.001

Taleizadeh, A. A., Shavandi, H., & Haji, R. (2011). Hybrid algorithms to solve constraint single period problem with uncertain demand. [Scientia Iranica]. *International Journal of Science and Technology, 18,* 1553–1563.

Taleizadeh, A. A., Widyadana, G. A., Wee, H. M., & Biabani, J. (2011). Multi products single machine economic production quantity model with multiple batch size. *International Journal of Industrial Engineering Computations, 2,* 213–224. doi:10.5267/j.ijiec.2011.01.002doi:10.5267/j.ijiec.2011.01.002

Teng, J. T., Cárdenas-Barrón, L. E., & Lou, K. R. (2011). The economic lot size of the integrated vendor-buyer inventory system derived without derivatives: A simple derivation. *Applied Mathematics and Computation, 217*(12), 5972–5977. doi:10.1016/j.amc.2010.12.018doi:10.1016/j.amc.2010.12.018

Teng, J. T., Cárdenas-Barrón, L. E., Lou, K. R., & Wee, H. M. (In Press). Optimal economic order quantity for buyer-distributor-vendor supply chain with backlogging derived without derivatives. *International Journal of Systems Science,* in press. Doi: 10.1080/00207721.2011.652226

Widyadana, G. A., Cárdenas-Barrón, L. E., & Wee, H. M. (2011). Economic order quantity model for deteriorating items and planned backorder level. *Mathematical and Computer Modelling, 54,* 1569–1575. doi:10.1016/j.mcm.2011.04.028doi:10.1016/j.mcm.2011.04.028

Zadeh, L. A. (1978). Fuzzy sets as a basis for a theory of possibility. *Fuzzy Sets and Systems, 1,* 3–28. doi:10.1016/0165-0114(78)90029-5doi:10.1016/0165-0114(78)90029-5

Zadeh, L. A. (1994). Fuzzy logic, neural networks and soft computing. *Communications of the ACM, 37,* 77–84. doi:10.1145/175247.175255doi:10.1145/175247.175255

Zhang, B., Zhang, G., & Lu, J. (2003). A system for solving fuzzy linear programming problems by multi-objective linear programming. *Proceedings of International Conference on Fuzzy Information Processing,* Beijing, China, (pp. 675-680).

Zimmermann, H. J. (2001). *Fuzzy set theory and its applications* (4th ed.). Boston, MA: Kluwer. doi:10.1007/978-94-010-0646-0doi:10.1007/978-94-010-0646-0

Zimmermann, H. J., & Witte, E. (1986). *Empirical research on organisational decision making.* Amsterdam, The Netherlands: North Holland.

KEY TERMS AND DEFINITIONS

Bees Colony Optimization (BCO): The BCO is inspired by bees' behavior in nature. The basic idea behind the BCO is to create a multi-agent system (colony of artificial bees) capable of solving difficult combinatorial optimization problems successfully.

Firefly Algorithm (FA): Firefly Algorithm (FA) was inspired by the social behavior of fireflies. This algorithm has been used in an enormous variety of applications spanning the permutation flow shop scheduling problem, codebook design of image vector quantization and financial portfolio optimization, among others.

Genetic Algorithm (GA): GA is inspired by the concept of survival of the fittest. GA uses a directed random search to locate good solutions for complex optimization problems. GA mimics the evolution process of the species that reproduce.

Goal Programming: Goal Programming (GP) was introduced as an operational research method for multi-criteria decision making and multi-objective programming problems. A new version of GP called the Meta-GP (MGP) was lately developed in which three different types of meta goals are defined.

Harmony Search (HS): The HS algorithm was inspired from the act of musical groups and it was introduced such as an analogy with music improvisation process where musicians in a band continue to polish their pitches to obtain a better harmony.

Hybrid Metaheuristic Algorithm: The hybridization is made when one combines a metaheuristic with heuristics or other metaheuristics in order to obtain a better solution exploiting simultaneously the advantages of several algorithms.

Inventory Management: Inventory theory is one of the fields where operations research has had noteworthy developments. For example, there are several mathematical models for the inventory control in use today in which the main objective is to have a good management of inventories of raw materials, spare parts, and finished goods.

Metaheuristic Algorithms: Metaheuristics methods were introduced to describe how works different heuristic algorithms which can be widely applied together to a set of different problems in a variety of fields. Thus, Metaheuristics should be considered as a general algorithmic structure which can be used for solving hard optimization problems with relatively few modifications to make them custom-made to a specific problem.

Particle Swarm Optimization (PSO): PSO is inspired by the ability of flocks of birds, schools of fish, and herds of animals to adapt to their environment quickly, finding rich sources of food, and avoiding predators by implementing an information sharing approach; with this the species develops an evolutionary benefit.

Simulated Annealing (SA): Simulated annealing (SA) is a local search algorithm and it was inspired in the physical annealing process studied in statistical mechanics.

Variable Neighborhood Search (VNS): The VNS is based on a systematic change in the neighborhood within the search space. Basically, VNS explores distant neighborhoods of the current solution and jumps from it to a new solution if and only if a better solution is found.

APPENDIX A: DEFINITIONS IN FUZZY AND ROUGH ENVIRONMENTS

Some Definitions of Fuzzy Environment

In this section, credibility of fuzzy event and the expected value of a fuzzy variable are defined. According to Liu (2004), the definitions of these concepts are presented in the following:

Definition 1: A Fuzzy number is of LR-Type with reference functions L (for the left), R (for the right), and scalars $\alpha > 0, \beta > 0$ with

$$
\mu(\tilde{\xi}) = \begin{cases} 1 & \tilde{\xi} \in [m, n] \\ L(\dfrac{m - \tilde{\xi}}{\alpha}) & \tilde{\xi} \leq m \\ R(\dfrac{\tilde{\xi} - n}{\beta}) & \tilde{\xi} \geq n \end{cases} \tag{A1}
$$

where $\tilde{\xi}$ is defined by $\tilde{\xi} = (m, n, \alpha, \beta)_{L-R}$. The triangular and trapezoidal fuzzy variables are specific kinds of LR-Type (Zhang et al. 2007, Ma et al. 2010, Zhang and Lu 2009).

Definition 2: Let $\tilde{\xi}$ be a fuzzy number with the membership function $\mu(\tilde{\xi})$. Then the possibility, necessity, and credibility measure of the fuzzy event $\tilde{\xi} \geq r$ can be represented, respectively, by Liu (2004):

$$
Pos\left\{\tilde{\xi} > r\right\} = \sup_{\tilde{\xi} \geq r} \mu(\tilde{\xi}) \tag{A2}
$$

$$
Nec\left\{\tilde{\xi} \geq r\right\} = 1 - \sup_{\tilde{\xi} < r} \mu(\tilde{\xi}) \tag{A3}
$$

$$
Cr\left\{\tilde{\xi} \geq r\right\} = \frac{1}{2}\left[Pos\left\{\tilde{\xi} \geq r\right\} + Nec\left\{\tilde{\xi} \geq r\right\}\right] \tag{A4}
$$

Definition 3: The expected value of a fuzzy variable $\tilde{\xi}$ is defined as (from Liu and Liu 2002)

$$
E[\tilde{\xi}] = \int_{0}^{\infty} Cr\left\{\tilde{\xi} \geq r\right\} dr - \int_{-\infty}^{0} Cr\left\{\tilde{\xi} \leq r\right\} dr \tag{A5}
$$

The expected value of a triangular fuzzy variable $\tilde{\xi} = (\xi_1, \xi_2, \xi_3)$ is:

$$E[\tilde{\xi}] = \frac{1}{4}(\xi_1 + 2\xi_2 + \xi_3) \tag{A6}$$

Definition 4: Let $\tilde{\xi}$ be a fuzzy variable, the optimistic function α is defined by Liu (2004) as:

$$\tilde{\xi}_{\text{sup}}(\alpha) = \sup\left[r \middle| Cr\left\{\tilde{\xi} \geq r\right\} \geq \alpha\right], \quad \alpha \in (0, 1] \tag{A7}$$

Definition 5: Assume the real constants $C_1, C_2, \cdots, C_k$ and the fuzzy variable function $G_1(\tilde{\xi}), G_2(\tilde{\xi}), \cdots G_k(\tilde{\xi})$ then;

$$E\left[\sum_{k=1}^{K} C_k G_k(\tilde{\xi})\right] = \sum_{k=1}^{K} C_k E(G_k(\tilde{\xi})) \tag{A8}$$

Definition 6: Assume a positive real constant K and a triangular fuzzy variable $\tilde{\xi} = (\xi_1, \xi_2, \xi_3)$, then $K.\tilde{\xi} = (K\xi_1, K\xi_2, K\xi_3)$.

Some Definitions in Rough Theory

Rough set theory, initialized by Pawlak (1998), is an excellent mathematical tool to describe vague objects. Any object from the universe is perceived through available information. If information is insufficient to describe the object exactly then a rough variable should be used. Some concepts in rough environment are introduced in this section. Referring to the studies by Liu (2004), Xu and Zhao (2008), and Liu (2010), the descriptions of these concepts are presented below:

Definition 7: Let Λ be a nonempty set, a $\sigma - A\lg ebra$ of subsets of Λ, and Δ an element in A, and π a trust measure, then $(\Lambda, \Delta, A, \pi)$ is called a rough space (see Liu 2004, Xu and Zhao 2008).

Due to a lack of information, it is difficult to determine the value of π in a real life problem. We assume all elements in Λ are equally likely to occur (according to the well-known Laplace criterion). For this case, the value of π may be taken as the cardinally of set Λ.

Definition 8: A rough variable δ is a function from rough space $(\Lambda, \Delta, A, \pi)$ to the set of real numbers. That is, for every Borel set B of $\Re$, we have $\left\{\vartheta \in \Lambda \middle| \delta(\vartheta) \in B\right\} \in A$. The lower and upper approximations of the rough variable, δ, are defined as:

$$\underline{\delta} = \left\{\delta(\vartheta) \middle| \vartheta \in \Delta\right\}, \quad \overline{\delta} = \left\{\delta(\vartheta) \middle| \vartheta \in \Lambda\right\} \tag{A9}$$

respectively.

In fact, rough variable $([a,b],[c,d])$ with $c \leq a \leq b \leq d$ is a measurable function from a rough space $(\Lambda, \Delta, A, \pi)$ to the real number, where, $\Lambda = \{\chi | c \leq \chi \leq d\}$, $\Delta = \{\chi | a \leq \chi \leq b\}$ and $\delta(\chi) = \chi$ for all $\chi \in \Lambda$ (see Liu 2004, Xu and Zhao 2008)[INSERT FIGURE 003]. It is noted that $[c,d]$ indicates the lower and upper bounds of the related variables; and $[a,b]$ are the estimated values between $[c,d]$.

For example, let $\Lambda = \{\chi | 0 \leq \chi \leq 10\}$ and $\Delta = \{\chi | 2 \leq \chi \leq 6\}$, then the function, $f(x) = x^2$, defined as $(\Lambda, \Delta, A, \pi)$, is a rough variable (see Liu 2004, Xu and Zhao 2008).

If we consider λ as a rough variable $([a,b],[c,d])$ with $c \leq a \leq b \leq d$, then its lower and upper approximations can be c and d respectively.

Some Definitions in Fuzzy Rough Theory

Fuzzy rough environment was initially defined by Liu (2004) who stated that fuzzy rough environment where a fuzzy variable has rough values. For example the triangular fuzzy variables have rough variable parameters. Since the parameters and demand of each product is fuzzy variable, demand and total cost will be fuzzy rough variables.

In this section, some concepts in fuzzy rough environment are defined. Based on Liu (2004) and Xu and Zhao (2008) works, the concepts are defined in the following:

Definition 9: A fuzzy rough variable is a function of δ from a rough space $(\Lambda, \Delta, A, \pi)$. The set of fuzzy variables $Poss\{\delta(\lambda) \in B\}$ is a measurable function of λ for any Borel set B of $\Re$ (Xu and Zhao 2008). The term $Poss\{\delta(\lambda) \in B\}$ can be determined by Equation (A2). In general, a fuzzy rough variable is a fuzzy variable having rough values.

As an example let $\delta(\lambda) = (\delta - \lambda, \delta, \delta + \lambda)$ be a triangular fuzzy rough variable in which λ is the rough variable such that $([a,b],[c,d])$ satisfy $c \leq a \leq b \leq d$. Then, we can define $\delta(\lambda) = (100 - \lambda, 100, 100 + \lambda)$; where λ may be $([2,3],[1,4])$.

The value $\delta(\lambda) = (\lambda, \lambda + 1, \lambda + 2)$ with $\lambda = ([1,2],[0,3])$ can be a fuzzy rough variable (Liu 2004). If we consider λ as a rough variable with $([a,b],[c,d])$ where $c \leq a \leq b \leq d$, then its lower and upper approximations may be c and d, respectively.

APPENDIX B: NOTATIONS

For Constraint Fuzzy Joint Replenishment (CFJR) Case

P : The number of products
K : The number of required truck
M : A very big number
α : The percent of prepayment
t_{lc} : When $(1 - \alpha)\%$ of the material purchasing cost should be paid
t_0 : When $\alpha\%$ of the material purchasing cost should be paid

$\tilde{D}_j$: The fuzzy rough annual demand of product j

n_j : The number of items in the packets of product j

$C_j^{h_1}$: The unit holding cost of the on hand inventory for product j during a period

$C_j^{h_2}$: The capital cost per unit of product j, during the period between the first and second payments

$C_j^{h_3}$: The capital cost per unit of the jth ordered product during the period after the payment of the remaining purchasing cost

$\hat{C}_{ij}$: The rough purchasing cost of the jth product in the ith discount break point

C_j^c : The clearance cost for each unit of product j

C_{ij}^P : The constant purchasing cost of product j, in the ith discount break point

q_{ij} : The ith discount break point of product j

f_j : The space required for each packet of product j

$\hat{f}$: The total available space in each truck

F : The total available space

W : The total available budget

L : The constant joint lead time for each order

A : The fixed order cost per each order

A_T : The fixed transportation cost per each shipment

Q_j : The decision variable representing the order quantity of product j

m_j : The decision variable representing the number of packets ordered for product j

T : The decision variable representing the joint cycle length

N : The number of orders in each year $\left(N = \dfrac{1}{T}\right)$

N_T : The upper limit for number of orders

For Constraint Fuzzy Rough Joint Replenishment (CFRJR) Case

P : The number of products

α : The percent of prepayment

t_{lc} : When $(1 - \alpha)\%$ of the material purchasing cost should be paid

t_0 : When $\alpha\%$ of the material purchasing cost should be paid

$\tilde{D}_j$: The fuzzy rough annual demand of product j

n_j : The number of items in the packets of product j

$C_j^{h_1}$: The unit holding cost of the on hand inventory for product j during a period

$C_j^{h_2}$: The capital cost per unit of product j, during the period between the first and second payments

C_j^b : The backordering cost for each unit of product j

C_j^c : The clearance cost for each unit of product j

C_j^T : The transportation cost for each batch of product j

C_{ij}^P : The constant purchasing cost of product j, in the ith discount break point

q_{ij} : The ith discount break point of product j

f_j : The space required for each packet of product j

k_j : The decision variable representing the number of packets ordered for product j.

F : The total available space

W : The total available budget

A : The fixed order cost per each order

Q_j : The decision variable representing the order quantity of product j

b_j : The decision variable representing the back-ordered quantity of product j

m_j : The decision variable representing the number of packets ordered for product j

T : The decision variable representing the joint cycle length

N : The number of orders in each year $(N = \dfrac{1}{T})$

N_T : The upper limit for number of orders

For Constraint Bi-Objective Multi-Product (CBOM) Case

P : The number of products

K_j : The variable transportation cost for each unit of the jth product.

M : A big number

P_j : The selling price of the jth product.

X_j : The stochastic demand of the jth product.

$f_{X_j}(x_j)$: The probability mass function of the jth product demand

λ_j : The expected demand of the jth product.

n_j : The number of items in the packets of product j

C_{i_j} : The unit purchasing cost of jth product at i^{th} break point

C_{1j}^h : The linear coefficient of the quadratic holding cost function of the jth product

C_{2j}^h : The quadratic coefficient of the quadratic holding cost function of the jth product

W_{i_j} : The decision variable representing the order quantity of jth product at i^{th} break point

C_{1j}^b : The linear coefficient of the quadratic shortage cost function of the jth product

C_{2j}^b : The quadratic coefficient of the quadratic shortage cost function of the jth product

q_{ij} : The ith discount break point of product j

f_j : The space required for each packet of product j

F : The total available space

$\hat{f}$: The capacity of a shipment

A : The fixed order cost per each order

Q_j : The decision variable representing the order quantity of product j

m_j : The decision variable representing the number of packets ordered for product j

T : The decision variable representing the joint cycle length

For Constrained Multi-Product Fuzzy Demand (CMPFD) Case

P : The number of products

ul_j : The upper limit of the order quantity for jth product.

P_j : The unit sales price for jth product

M : A big number

$\tilde{D}_j$: The fuzzy rough annual demand of product j

C_j^h : The holding cost per unit inventory at the end of the period for jth product

C_{ij} : The purchasing cost per unit of product j at ith discount point

C_j^b : The backordering cost for each unit of product j

C_{ij}^P : The constant purchasing cost of product j, in the ith discount break point

q_{ij} : The ith discount break point of product j

f_j : The space required for each packet of product j

F : Total available warehouse space

SL_j : The lower limit of the service rate for jth product

Q_j : The decision variable representing the order quantity of product j

m_j : The decision variable representing the number of packets ordered for product j

W : The total available budget

For Fuzzy Cost Factor (FCF) Case

P : The number of products

D_j : The annual constant demand of product j

n_j : The number of items in the packets of product j

$\tilde{C}_j^h$: The fuzzy holding cost for each unit of product j

$\overset{\approx}{C}_{ij}^P$: The fuzzy purchasing cost per unit of the jth product at the jth discount point

C_j^b : The backordering cost for each unit of product j

C_j^L : The lost sale cost for each unit of product j

q_{ij} : The ith discount break point of product j

f_j : The space required for each packet of product j

F : Total available warehouse space

SL_j : The lower limit of the service rate for jth product

Q_j : The decision variable representing the order quantity of product j

R_j : The inventory level of the jth product at the start of a cycle.

T_j : A random variable denoting the time-period between two replenishments (cycle length) of the jth product.

T_{Max_j} : The upper interval limit of a probability distribution for T_j.

T_{Min_j} : The lower interval limit of a probability distribution for T_j.

β_j : The percentage of unsatisfied demands of the jth product that is back-ordered.

For Random Fuzzy Period Length (RFPL) Case

P : The number of products

P_j : The sale price per unit of the jth product

λ_{ij} : The crisp form of fuzzy parameter of the exponential distribution

D_j : The annual constant demand of product j

C_j : The purchasing cost per unit of the jth product

C_j^h : The holding cost per unit inventory of the jth product in each period

C_j^b : The backordering cost for each unit of product j

f_j : The space required for each packet of product j

F : Total available warehouse space

SL_j : The lower limit of the service rate for jth product

R_j : The inventory level of the jth product at the start of a cycle.

T_j : A random variable denoting the time-period between two replenishments (cycle length) of the jth product.

T_{Max_j} : The upper interval limit of a probability distribution for T_j .

T_{Min_j} : The lower interval limit of a probability distribution for T_j .

$f_{T_j}(t_j)$: The Probability density functions of T_j with fuzzy parameter.

$\tilde{\theta}_j$: Fuzzy parameter of the probability density functions of T_j for the jth product.

β_j : The percentage of unsatisfied demands of the jth product that is back-ordered.

Chapter 12
ANN–Based Self–Tuning Frequency Control Design for an Isolated Microgrid

H. Bevrani
University of Kurdistan, Iran

F. Habibi
University of Kurdistan, Iran

S. Shokoohi
University of Kurdistan, Iran

ABSTRACT

The increasing need for electrical energy, limited fossil fuel reserves, and the increasing concerns with environmental issues call for fast development in the area of distributed generations (DGs) and renewable energy sources (RESs). A Microgrid (MG) as one of the newest concepts in the power systems consists of several DGs and RESs that provides electrical and heat power for local loads. Increasing in number of MGs and nonlinearity/complexity due to entry of MGs to the power systems, classical and nonflexible control structures may not represent desirable performance over a wide range of operating conditions. Therefore, more flexible and intelligent optimal approaches are needed. Following the advent of optimization/intelligent methods, such as artificial neural networks (ANNs), some new potentials and powerful solutions for MG control problems such as frequency control synthesis have arisen. The present chapter addresses an ANN-based optimal approach scheduling of the droop coefficients for the purpose of frequency regulation in the MGs.

DOI: 10.4018/978-1-4666-2086-5.ch012

INTRODUCTION

According to the rapid growth of energy consumption in the world, the conventional power systems are faced with problems such as environmental issues, high cost of establishing new power plants, the existing restrictions on building transmission lines and shortages of fossil fuels. To overcome these problems and due to increasing costumers demand for service with high reliability, increasing efficiency postponing construction of new transmission lines, reducing congestion in distribution feeders and reducing losses, a new concept known as distributed generation (DG) was introduced (Barker & De Mello, 2001; Willis & Scott, 2000).

A DG is a source of electrical power which is connected to distribution system and even placed directly in the consumer side (Ackermann, Andersson, & Soder, 2001). Generation units with less than ten megawatts (DGs) together with loads and storage devices may perform a Microgrid (MG) that is connected to distribution system by point of common coupling (PCC). Emerging number of MGs in power systems can change the power systems operation and control, significantly.

These changes imply a requirement for new control schemes in modern power systems. The power system is currently undergoing fundamental changes in its structure, not just with the deregulation issue and the use of competitive policies, but also to the use of new types of power production, new technologies, and rapidly increasing amounts of DG/RESs among small electric networks so called Microgrids (MGs).

Increasing in number of MGs in the power systems opens the way for looking new control strategies with a more control hierarchy/intelligence and decentralized property particularly in the field of frequency regulation. Similar to the conventional generating units, droop control is one of important control method for a MG with multiple DG units. The DG units must automatically adjust their set points using the frequency measurement to meet the overall need of the MG. But, unlike large power systems, the drooping

system is poorly regulated in MGs to support spinning reserve as an ancillary service for secondary frequency control. The main challenge is to coordinate their actions so that they can provide the regulation services.

The variability and uncertainty are two major attributes of variable renewable energy sources (RESs) in the MGs. The MG is a relatively novel concept in modern electric industry, consisting of small power systems owning the capability of performing isolated from the main network. A MG can tackle all distributed energy resources including DG, RESs, distributed energy storage systems and demand response as a unique subsystem, and offers significant control capacities on its operation. The MGs are usually based on loads fed through low/medium voltage level, mostly in distribution radial systems. Although the concept of MG is already established, the control strategies and energy management systems for MGs which cover power interchange, system stability, frequency and voltage regulation, active and reactive power control, islanding detection, grid synchronization, and system recovery are still under development.

The possibility of having numerous controllable DG units and MGs in distribution networks requires the use of intelligent, optimal, and hierarchical control schemes that enables an efficient control and management of this kind of systems. Generally for the sake of control synthesis, nonlinear systems such as MGs are approximated by reduced order dynamic models, possibly linear, that represent the simplified dominant systems' characteristics. However, these models are only valid within specific operating ranges, and a different model may be required in the case of changing operating conditions. On the other hand, due to increasing of nonlinearity and complexity of MG systems, classical and nonflexible control structures may not represent desirable performance over a wide range of operating conditions. Therefore, more flexible and intelligent approaches are needed.

The DGs used in MGs can be classified into two categories: renewable and nonrenewable resources (Puttgen, MacGregor, & Lambert, 2003). Different technologies including solar cells, wind turbines, fuel cells, and small gas turbines are used in the DG units (Ackermann, Andersson, & Soder, 2001). A MG consists of several DGs that are responsible of local power supply. Despite their many advantages, some new problems such as changes in load pattern, frequency variation, voltage fluctuations, and high frequency harmonics are composed on the power systems.

The MGs must be able to operate in both connected and disconnected modes, and continue to supply local loads in the specialized frequency and voltage values. In the present chapter, frequency stability of an islanded MG is considered. In the previous works, the conventional PI controllers are commonly used for this purpose (Díaz, González-Morán, Gómez-Aleixandre, & Diez, 2010; Fujimoto, et al., 2009; Gil & Lopes, 2007; Lee & Wang, 2008; Lopes, Moreira, & Madureira, 2006; Senjyu, et al., 2009). Due to usage of RESs like wind and photo cells, also considering variable nature of their generation and low inertia of MGs, then with a slightest disturbance, basic network parameters such as frequency and voltage may be influenced.

Therefore, existence of central and local controllers is necessary which in practice classical PI controllers are commonly used to solve this problem. Although using these controllers is economical and simpler but they do not always provide desirable choices. These controllers are tuned based on primary conditions, so if system conditions are varied from nominal operating, the conventional controllers cannot provide optimum performance. Since, the MGs are always undergoing various changes and disturbances, using evolutionary and intelligent techniques for tuning of classical controllers are useful.

The human and nature ability to control complex organisms has encouraged researchers to pattern controls on human/nature responses and neural network systems. New neural morphologies with learning and adaptive capabilities have infused new control power into the control of complex dynamic systems.

The present chapter addresses the scheduling of the droop coefficients for frequency regulation in MGs, using an ANN-based optimal approach. Following an introduction on the MG concept, the application of intelligent ANN technique on the secondary frequency control synthesis in an isolated MG is emphasized and new challenges and the related key issues are also discussed. Simulation studies are performed to illustrate the capability of the proposed optimal control approach. The resulting controllers are shown to minimize the effect of disturbances and achieve acceptable frequency regulation in the presence of various load change scenarios.

If an event occurs in the system for any reason and leads to change the output frequency, the ANN control unit senses output variations and updates PI parameters via online tuning, proportional to the variations intensity.

BACKGROUND

An introduction on the MGs and infrastructure reasons of these networks are presented in (Chowdhury, Chowdhury, & Crossley, 2009; Lasseter, et al., 2002; Lasseter, et al., 2011; Lasseter & Paigi, 2004). Based on definition introduced by the Consortium for Electric Reliability Technology Solutions (CERTS), the MG concept assumes an aggregation of the loads and microsources (MSs) operating as a single system providing both power and heat. The majority of the MSs use power electronic devices for providing the required flexibility to insure operation as a single aggregated system, and to allow a MG to present itself to the bulk power system as a single controlled unit that meets local needs for reliability and security (Lasseter, et al., 2002). The sources in the MSs and their mathematical model for simulation tasks are presented precisely in (Basak, Saha, Chowdhury, & Chowdhury, 2009; Chowdhury, et al., 2009) such as wind turbines, PV panels, diesel generators and energy storage devices including batteries and flywheels.

The advantages of the MGs as well as new challenges resulted from well known triangle policy that is environmental issues, power systems financial problems and reliability have been studied in (Chowdhury, et al., 2009; Lasseter, et al., 2002; Lasseter, et al., 2011; Lasseter & Paigi, 2004; Lasseter, 2002; Zaidi & Kupzog, 2008). Some problems and challenges on the MG operation and control are presented in (Lasseter, et al., 2002; Lasseter, et al., 2011; Lasseter & Paigi, 2004) such as challenges associated with different operating scenarios in islanding mode, protection relays, maintaining and protecting distributed energy resources, controlling voltage and system frequency in both connected and disconnected modes, as well as the role of MGs on the revised existing standards for voltage and frequency stabilities.

In context of dynamics control, (Lopes, et al., 2006) presents two control methodologies for the inverter based DGs in the presence of power electronics interfaces called single master operation (SMO) and multi master operation (MMO). In SMO, a voltage source inverter (VSI) acting as a master to provide the voltage reference when the main supply is lost and all other inverters operated in the constant active and reactive power (PQ) mode (slaves). In a multi master approach, several inverters are operating as VSI with pre-defined frequency/active power and voltage/reactive power characteristics. Existence of a communication between VSIs in MMO is necessary. In (Moreira & Lopes, 2007), the impacts of storage devices on the MG dynamics are also investigated.

In the connected mode, the MG is controlled to provide PQ mode, while in disconnected mode, the MG is controlled to maintain voltage and frequency in nominal range, independently. These controllers are usually designed based on the droop characteristics of the microsources (Díaz, et al.,

2010; Gil & Lopes, 2007; Ota, Yukita, Nakano, & Ichiyanagi, 2010; Zahnd, 2007).

In voltage stability point of view, (Karimi, Davison, & Iravani, 2010) studies an isolated MG and utilizes two methods for voltage and frequency stability: 1) an internal oscillator for frequency control, and 2) a voltage feedback signal to regulate the island voltage. As expressed in (Schauder & Mehta, 1993; Song & Nam, 1999.; Yazdani & Iravani, 2006), in connected mode, for the sake of voltage and frequency regulation, the MG uses main grid through the direct-quadrature-current control method, and voltage source converters act as a real/reactive power exchanger between the grid and the MG. But in disconnected mode, a MG operates as an autonomous system and uses the voltage source inverters. In this case, the MG frequency and voltage are controlled by local DGs and loads.

In frequency stability context, (Yuen, Oudalov, & Timbus, 2011) focused on technical aspects and economic potential of providing frequency control reserves (FCRs) with participation multiple MGs in the frequency control process. Different market scenarios like decentralized or centralized coordination approaches are investigated. Frequency stability in the MGs is mostly done by small diesel generators, PV panels and batteries. For example, (Uehara, Senjyuy, Yonaz, & Funabashi, 2010) investigates an islanded MG that contains several DGs such as wind farm, batteries and a small diesel generator. System frequency is controlled by wind farm and battery using load estimation. The loads are estimated by a disturbance observer. A robust frequency controller is designed in (Vachirasricirikul, Ngamroo, Kaitwanidvilai, & Chaiyatham, 2009) to perform a proper performance in the presence of uncertainties. Conventional and intelligent methods are used in frequency stabilizing such as (Arboleya, et al., 2010; Díaz, et al., 2010; Fujimoto, et al., 2009; Gil & Lopes, 2007; Senjyu, et al., 2009; Ota, et al., 2010; Uehara, et al., 2010; Vachirasricirikul, et al., 2009).

Power management and load sharing in the MGs are investigated in (Majumder, Ledwich, & Zare, 19th 2008; Sao & Lehn, 2008). In the connected mode, extra energy of MG is injected to the grid for supplying the common loads and in the disconnected mode local and common loads are supplied only by the MG.

Application of the Artificial Neural Networks (ANNs) in the power systems have been so far reported in the several fields like optimization, identification, control, modeling, pattern recognition, data analysis and so on. In this context, (El-Keib & Ma, 1995) studies ability of the ANNs in the voltage stability assessment. A multi-layer feed-forward ANN with error back-propagation learning is proposed for increasing voltage stability margins (VSM). Optimal selecting ANN input and effects of the ANN training pattern in different operating conditions are studied based on sensitively analysis. Modeling of the complex and nonlinear systems is another important capability of ANNs that are investigated by (Hiyama, Tokieda, Hubbi, & Andou, 1997). Dynamic load modeling and finding locations of the load in power systems are studied by ANNs with different loops. This identification can emulate season and locations of the load. Field data for ANN training pattern have been used. Generation control of interconnected power systems using intelligence approaches like Fuzzy and ANNs are considered by ((Subbaraj & Manickavasagam, 2007). Tie-line error and calculated frequency deviations are selected as input sets of the intelligent controller. The ANN controller is framed from a multi-layer perception network that is trained by sets of frequency deviations and tie-line power signals to create an intelligent controller to perform an automatic generation control (AGC) system (Bevrani & Hiyama, 2011)..

(Chu, Shoureshi, & Tenorio, 1990) investigates ANN ability for system identification. For employing ANNs in the identification process, two approaches have been considered including a Hopfield network to estimate time-varying/

time-invariant system, and an orthogonal basis functions and Fourier analysis to construct a dynamic system in terms of its Fourier coefficients.

For frequency and voltage stability preserving in the emergency conditions of the power systems, following a severe disturbance like a heavy step load and outage generating units some loads may be intentionally separated. Then under frequency load shedding (UFLS) or under voltage load shedding (UVLS) are very important issues that have direct impacts on the system stability. The ANN provides a powerful tool to design an adaptive and optimal algorithm for load shedding that is studied by (Hsu, Kang, & Chen, 2005). They focused on an ANN with back-propagation learning algorithm for network training where total generated power, total load demand and frequency decay rate are selected as the input neurons of the ANN.

MICROGRID CONCEPT AND STRUCTURE

A MG consists of clusters of load and microsources or DGs that operates as a single controllable system and provides both power and heat for its local area (Lasseter, et al., 2011). General structure of a MG is shown in Figure 1. The MG is connected to the main grid at the point of common coupling (PCC). Each microsource is usually interfaced to the MG through a power electronic converter, at the point of coupling (POC) (Bevrani & Hiyama, 2011). Two possible operating modes for a MG are grid-connected mode and islanded mode (Lasseter, et al., 2002; Lasseter, et al., 2011; Lasseter & Paigi, 2004). In the islanded operation, the MG is responsible for providing voltage and frequency stability, as well as active and reactive power balance.

The balance between generation and demand of power is one of the most important requirements of the MG management in the both grid-connected and islanded operation modes. In the grid-connected mode, the MG exchanges power to the

Figure 1. Typical structure of MG connected to the main grid

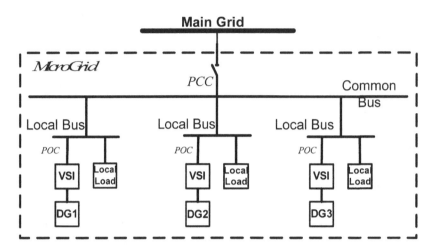

interconnected grid to make a balance, while, in the islanded mode, the MG should meet the balance for the local supply and demand using the decrease in generation or load shedding (Bevrani, et al., 2012).

Due to high diversity in generation and loads, the MGs exhibit high nonlinearities, changing dynamics, and uncertainties that may require advanced optimal/intelligent control strategies to solve. The use of more efficient control strategies would increase the performance of these systems. Since, some RESs such as wind turbines and PVs are working under turbulent and unpredictable environmental conditions, the MGs have to adapt to these variations and in this way the efficiency and reliability of MGs strongly depend on the applied control strategies (Bevrani, et al., 2012).

The MG is made of local controllable loads (LCL) and local controllable generators (LCG), so it services sensitive and insensitive loads. In fact, a MG is a complex of distributed energy resources (DERs) that work together for transferring the confident, economical, and environmental power. When MG is connected to the main grid, it can exchange energy between itself and the network. In this operation mode, MG can compensate the required power if the demand increases or it can

generate a part of main network power if the network needs a more generation. So on, if the main grid is subjected to a disturbance, the MG can prevent of voltage and frequency droops as far as possible.

If quality of electricity falls down for any reasons (due to faults, thunder storm, sudden change on load etc.), the protection systems will operate and take the MG apart from the main network and provide the requirement of local self-consumer in the islanded mode. According to the IEEE STD 1547-2003 standard (IEEE STD, 2003), islanded network is a part of main grid that has been separated from other parts, and only DGs supply it. This standard indicates that an island should be able to establish in two seconds after occurring of any incident. In this context, being islanded happens, suddenly. At the islanded operation mode, the MG has been isolated from the main network, and energy transferring to be blocked, hence most of problems of providing power like frequency and voltage fluctuation occur at this mode. Therefore, the main problems of an islanded MG are control of frequency and voltage fluctuations; and provide electric energy with high reliability, and high quality.

In islanded mode, the existence of storage devices is necessary for system stabilization, because there is no sharing power with the main grid, and there is possibility of load changing and power fluctuation. The storage devices operate based on balance between generation and consumption. The most well-known of these devices are battery energy storage system (BESS), flywheel energy storage system (FESS) and super capacitors (SCs). When generation is more than consumption, storage devices are charged and in overload times that the MG is faced with shortage of generation; their power is discharged to prevent the voltage and frequency droop.

FREQUENCY CONTROL

Frequency control synthesis and analysis in power systems has a long history and its literature is voluminous. The preliminary frequency control schemes have evolved over the past decades, and among increasing of MG systems, the interest continues in proposing new intelligent frequency control approaches with an improved ability to maintain system frequency close to the nominal value. Recently, some improvements are appeared in the area of frequency control design to cope with uncertainties, various load characteristics, changing structure, and integration of new systems such as MGs or individual energy storage devices, wind turbines, photovoltaic cells and other sources of electrical energy (Bevrani, & Hiyama, 2011).

In steady-state condition, there is a balance between production and consumption thus, frequency is stable. As described, frequency stability refers to the ability of a power system to maintain the system frequency following a severe system upset resulting in a significant imbalance between generation and load (Bevrani, 2009). It depends on the ability to maintain/restore equilibrium between system generation and load, with minimum unintentional loss of load. Instability that may result occurs in the form of sustained frequency

swing leading of generating units and/or loads (Kundur, et al., 2004).

In systems that inductance/reactance (X/R) ratio of their transmission lines is high (X/R>10), there is a linear relation between active power and frequency which any change in active power leads to frequency fluctuation in the system. According to the permanent probability of changes in generation and consumption pattern, existence of control loop for frequency stability is necessary. For this purpose, there are two main frequency control loops: primary and secondary controls.

Primary Control

If a disturbance occurs in the system, first primary control loop starts to control the frequency. This loop is embedded on the synchronous power generators like diesel generators based on active power/frequency (P/f) droop characteristic as shown in Figure 2.

If a change happens in the frequency of DG, for any reason, the effect of it can be observed on its output active power. The equation is defined by applying a linear approximation P/f control:

Figure 2. Frequency droop control characteristic

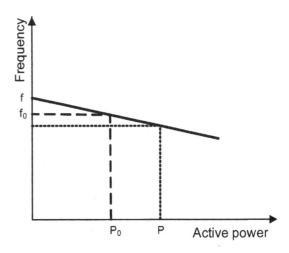

$$f - f_0 = -k_p(P - P_0) \qquad (1)$$

Here, f_0 and P0 are the rated frequency and active power of the grid, respectively. The frequency droop control characteristic is shown graphically in Figure 2. If load demand is increased, frequency drops from nominal value, this primary droop is limited to a fixed value by primary control loop.

But the steady state frequency error may not converge to zero. As shown in Figure 3, there is a steady drop in the system frequency under load deviation. If there is no primary control loop, frequency drops permanently and may lead to frequency instability, and outage of generation units from the MG.

Secondary Control

For returning the system frequency to the nominal value, and compensating the steady drop error caused by primary control, another complementary loop is used that is called secondary control. In this control loop, the conventional proportional integral (PI) controller is commonly used for eliminating the steady state error. The secondary control loop ensures that the frequency deviation of the MG is regulated towards zero after every

change in the load or supply. This control loop is also responsible for internal ancillary services. Both control loops, primary and secondary for typical synchronous generator are shown in Figure 4.

During the grid-connected operation, all DGs and inverters in the MG use the grid electrical signal as reference for frequency index. However, in islanding, they lose that reference. In this case, as has already mentioned, they may coordinate to manage the simultaneously operation using one of the following secondary control methods: i) single master operation: a master DG/inverter fixes frequency for the other units in the MG. The connected DGs are operating according to the reference given by the master. ii) multimaster operation: in this case, several DGs/inverters are controlled by means of a central controller which chooses and transmits the set points to all the generating units in the MG (Lopes, et. al, 2006).

As explained, the secondary control keeps the system frequency at nominal value by applying a simple PI controller. The PI parameters are applied to the system after initial tuning. If operational conditions are varying, it will be difficult to obtain an optimal frequency response from conventional secondary control loop. Recently, for resolving this problem, the intelligent techniques and evo-

Figure 3. System frequency with and without primary control loop

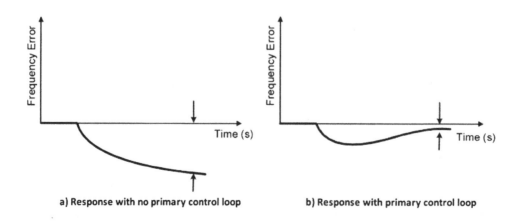

a) Response with no primary control loop   b) Response with primary control loop

Figure 4. A synchronous generator with Primary and secondary control loops

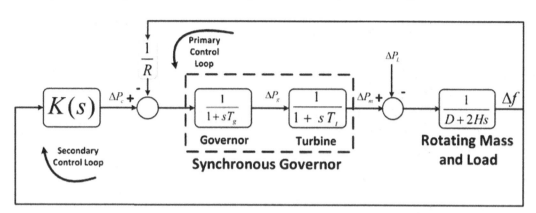

lutionary algorithms are used for online tuning of conventional controllers. In this work, an optimal algorithm based on artificial neural networks is presented to tune PI parameters.

TEST SYSTEM

Usually a part of load in the MGs is supplied by diesel engine generators (DEGs) and the rest of power is provided by other DGs such as wind turbines, photovoltaic (PV) systems, battery energy storage systems and fuel cells (FCs). Inherently, renewable sources have fluctuation in their output power. For example, as shown in Figure 5(a), the wind power is dependent on the daily wind speed, and the PV panels are only producing power during day time (Figure 5(b)).

Around noon when the sun is highest, the PV panels have maximum power production. On the other hand, often in nights production is low, and consumption is high. In this time, battery energy storage systems (BESSs) play major role to solve the power fluctuation problem. So, in day which the power production is high, the BESSs store energy as their capacity, and then participate in load peak compensation which the MG is facing with the production shortage and support the frequency stability. In this chapter, for testing the proposed control method and comparison of re-

sults, a MG similar to the network used in (Lee & Wang, 2008) is considered as shown in Figure 6(a). The equivalent frequency response model is presented in Figure 6(b). This model is presented in detail in (Lee & Wang, 2008)

As observed in Figure 6(b), the considered mathematical models for different units in the isolated MG system are first-order transfer functions. Theses mathematical models are approximated models from the actual units which for frequency studies are sufficient. However to study the MG system in the transient and short-term conditions, more accurate models are certainly needed. Mathematical models for different parts of the isolated MG system have been presented in the (Lee & Wang, 2008) as a first-order lag that are given in (2) to (6). In (2), transfer function of the wind turbine generator (WTG) is presented that variations of the mechanical power output (ΔP_w) and variations of the electrical power output (ΔP_{WTG}) are considered as denominator and numerator of transfer function of the WTG, respectively. To find a mathematical model for the PV panel, electrical power output variations (ΔP_{PV}) and changes in the sunlight flux are considered as numerator and denominator of the PV panel transfer function so that is given in (3). In (4), transfer function of the aquaelectrolyzer (AE) is presented in which electrical power output

Figure 5. a) Daily wind speed curve b) PV generation curve

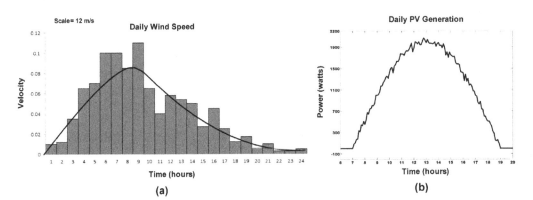

variations of the AE (ΔP_{AE}) and a fraction from electrical power output variations of the WTG, $\Delta P_{WTG}(1 - K_n)$, are considered as numerator and denominator of its transfer function. As expressed, a fraction of the generated electrical power of the WTG is used by the AE for releasing natural gases like hydrogen, which is used by the FC for producing electrical energy. Electrical power output variations of the FC (ΔP_{FC}) and ΔP_{AE} are used for expressing transfer function of the FC as numerator and denominator, respectively as given in (5). Electrical power output variations of the DEG (ΔP_{WTG}) and system frequency (Δf) are the parameters which are used to obtain a transfer function for the DEG that shown in (6).

$$G_{WTG}(s) = \frac{K_{WTG}}{1 + sT_{WTG}} = \frac{\Delta P_{WTG}}{\Delta P_W} \quad (2)$$

$$G_{PV}(s) = \frac{K_{PV}}{1 + sT_{PV}} = \frac{\Delta P_{PV}}{\Delta \Phi} \quad (3)$$

$$G_{AE} = \frac{K_{AE}}{1 + sT_{AE}} = \frac{\Delta P_{AE}}{\Delta P_{WTG}(1 - K_n)} \quad (4)$$

$$G_{FC} = \frac{K_{FC}}{1 + sT_{FC}} = \frac{\Delta P_{FC}}{\Delta P_{AE}} \quad (5)$$

$$G_{DEG} = \frac{K_{DEG}}{1 + sT_{DEG}} = \frac{\Delta P_{DEG}}{\Delta f} \quad (6)$$

In the MG which is isolated from the main grid, there are several DGs such as a small DEG, two storage energy devices (BESS and FESS), a wind farm, and a PV panel. A conventional PI controller is commonly used for frequency control in such MG system, which is usually tuned based on try and error method and experiences. Here, the response of these controllers are compared with the proposed ANN-based PI control methodology.

The P_w, P_s, ΔP_L and "f were shown in the Figure 6(b), are mechanical power output variations of the WTG, total power production of resources in the MG, load changing, and system frequency deviations, respectively. The sunlight flux variation is shown by Φ_{PV} in Figure 6(b). Parameter values of the block diagram in Figure 6(b) are given in Table 1.

ANN-BASED SELF-TUNING FREQUENCY CONTROL

ANN and Intelligent Control

Neural networks are formed by neurons. Each neuron is composed of three main parts: dendrite,

Figure 6. Test MG system: a) isolated MG, b) frequency model of the MG

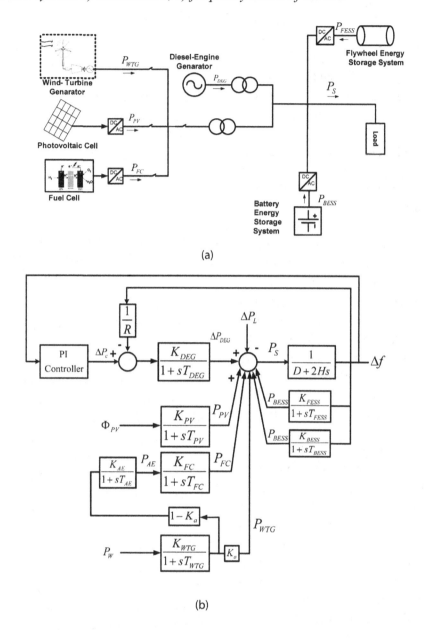

(a)

(b)

Table 1. Parameters of the isolated MG

$K_{WTG} = 1.0, \quad T_{WTG} = 1.5s$	$K_{PV} = 1.0, \quad T_{PV} = 1.8s$
$K_{AE} = 1/5, \quad T_{AE} = 0.5s$	$K_{DEG} = 1.3, \quad T_{DEG} = 2s$
$K_{FC} = 1/1, \quad T_{FC} = 4s$	$K_{BESS} = -1/3, \quad T_{BESS} = 0.1s$
$K_n = 0.6, \quad M = 0.2, \quad D = 0.012$	$K_{FESS} = -1/1, \quad T_{FESS} = 0.1s$

cell body and axon. Dendrites collect information from other neurons and send information signals to the cell body which acts as the brain of the neuron. All signals are added together and if the sum is more than a specified threshold, the neuron sends a signal to axons and this signal run an action (Gupta & al, 2003; Hagan & al, 1996; Sarangapani, 2006).

An ANN is a crude approximation for the parts of a real brain. It is a parallel computational system consisting of many simple processing elements connected together in a specific way in order to perform a particular task. The ANNs provide an important tool in optimization tasks because they are extremely powerful computational devices with capability of parallel processing, learning, generalization and fault/noise tolerating. Based on the configuration and connecting elements, there are several main applications in the ANNs such as brain modeling, financial modeling, time series prediction, control systems, and optimization.

Indeed, an ANN consists of a finite number of interconnected neurons (as described above) and acts as a massively parallel distributed processor, inspired from biological neural networks, which can store experimental knowledge and makes it available for use (Bevrani, & Hiyama, 2011). For using neural networks in optimization tasks, it is needed to have a mathematical model for the neural networks. A simplified mathematical model of a neuron is depicted in Figure 7, which shows the basic element of an ANN. It consists of three basic components including weights W_j, threshold (or bias) $,,$ and a single activation function $f(\cdot)$. The values $W_1, W_2, \ldots, W_n$ are weight factors associated with each node to determine the strength of input row vector $X^T = \begin{bmatrix} x_1 & x_2 & \cdots & x_n \end{bmatrix}$. Each input is multiplied by associated weight of the neuron connection. Depending upon the activation function, if the weight is positive, the resulted signal commonly excites the node output; whereas, for negative weights, it tends to inhibit the node output. The

Figure 7. A typical mathematical model for a neuron

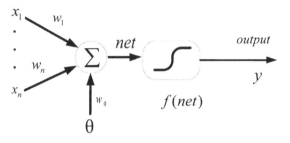

node's internal threshold θ is the magnitude offset that affects the activation of the node output y as follows (Bevrani, & Hiyama, 2011):

$$y(k) = f\left(\sum_{j=1}^{n} W_j x_j(k) + W_0, \right) \qquad (7)$$

The activation function can be selected according to the application. Tansigmoid, logsigmoid, and linear are three types of activity functions. It is noteworthy that as the threshold or bias changes, the activation functions may also shift. For many ANN training algorithms such as backpropagation, derivative of the $f(\cdot)$ is needed so that the activation function selected must be differentiable. Activity function produces neuron's output.

The neurons could be combined together and they form a layer. Layers are constituted together and make a network. Updating the weights and training of neural networks is based on two basic feedforward and feedback process. There are three methods for training the weights in feedback process: supervised, unsupervised and reinforcement learning (Gupta & al, 2003; Hagan & al, 1996; Sarangapani, 2006). Structure of these learning methods is shown in Figure 8.

In supervised learning, the output is compared with desired vector of "d", and then error vectors applied for updating the weights. There is no

Figure 8. General learning mechanisms for ANNs; (a) supervised, (b) unsupervised, and c) reinforcement learning

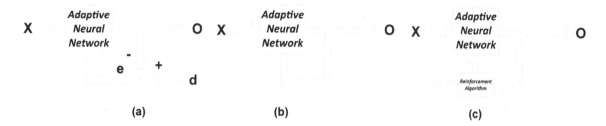

desired reference vector for reinforcement method and a revolutionary process is usually used for updating the weights. In the unsupervised learning method, updating is only based on the input data. In control structures, the supervised learning is usually used. There are several methods for supervised learning such as perceptron, widrow-hoff, correlation and back-propagation learning methods. The most employed method is the back-propagation learning.

The main objective of the intelligent control is to implement an autonomous system that could operate with increasing independence from human actions in an uncertain environment. The most common ANN-based intelligent control structures are well explained in (Bevrani, & Hiyama, 2011). In all existing structures, the control objectives could be achieved by learning from environment through a feedback mechanism. The ANN has the capability to implement this kind of learning.

Proposed Control Scheme

Schematic diagram of the proposed control scheme for the ANN-based self-tuning MG frequency control is shown in Figure 9, where the ANN unit acts as an intelligent unit for optimal tuning of classical PI control parameters, by getting input and output data based on some certain rules. In the proposed intelligent control scheme, the ANN collects information about the plant (MG) response, adjusts weights via a learning algorithm, and recommends an appropriate control signal. In

Figure 9, the ANN performs an online automatic optimal tuner for the existing PI controller. The main components of the ANN as a fine-tuner for PI controllers include a response recognition unit to monitor the controlled response and extract knowledge about the performance of the current controller gain setting, and an embedded unit to suggest suitable changes to be made in the controller gains.

The employed neural network structure for tuning the parameters of the PI controller used for frequency control (of the system given in Figure 6) is shown in Figure 10. In the ANN structure of Figure 10, twenty linear neurons are considered for network input layer; ten and two nonlinear neurons are also considered for hidden and output layers, respectively. The number of output layer's neurons is equal to the number of control parameters that must be adjusted. In Figure 10, X, W_1, and W_2 are the input vector, and weight vectors of the first and second layers, respectively.

Selection of initial conditions in an ANN-based control system is also known as an important issue. In the multi-objective control problems, some initial values may not guarantee the achievement of objectives with a satisfactory value of optimization function. The initial conditions are usually selected according to the a priori information about distributions at the already-known structure of the open-loop ANN and selected control strategy. Here, the initial quantities in the applied ANN scheme (Figure 10) are considered as follows.

Figure 9. Block diagram of the proposed control method

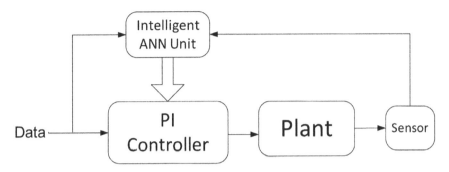

Figure 10. The ANN structure used for PI tuning

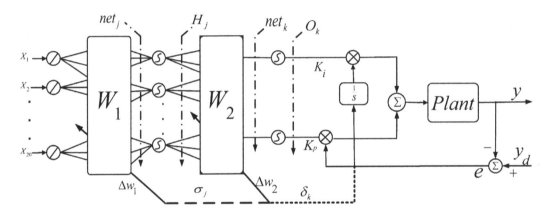

$$\begin{cases} X = \text{ones}\,(20,1) \\ W_1 = \text{rand}\,(10,20) \\ W_2 = \text{rand}\,(2,10) \end{cases} \quad (8)$$

As mentioned, linear functions are considered for the first layer, and for the second and third layers, the sigmoid functions are chosen as shown in Figure 11. In the output layer, different coefficients for sigmoid function are considered for tuning of controller parameters. The main advantage of using these nonlinear functions is in performing a smooth updating of weights.

The learning process of the applied ANN for the MG test system is to minimize the performance function given by (9), where y_d represents reference signal, y^M represents output unit and M denotes the output-layer.

$$J = \frac{1}{2}\sum_{i=1}^{n}(y_{di} - y_i^M)^2 \quad (9)$$

Implemented algorithm for updating weights is based on the back propagation learning which is described in the flowchart of Figure 12. In the feed-forward process, by using the input vector (X), the values of hidden layer output (H) and output layer result (O) are provided, and then error value (E) obtained from the process is employed to update the weights as given in (10).

$$\begin{cases} w_2(k+1) = w_2(k) + \Delta w_2 = w_2(k) + \eta \sigma H \\ w_1(k+1) = w_1(k) + \Delta w_1 = w_1(k) + \eta \delta X \end{cases} \quad (10)$$

where, the chain relations for obtaining ΔW_1 and ΔW_2 in (11) and (12) are respectively expressed step by step. All parameters which used to calculate of ΔW_1 and ΔW_2 (such as net_j, H_j, net_k, δ_k, and σ_j) can be visible in Figure 10. $\eta_1 > 0$ is a learning rate given by a small positive constant. The Net_j, net_k, H_j, δ_k and σ_j are the parameters that used for expressing relations of the ΔW_1 and ΔW_2, as described.

The learning process continues to reach the desired minimum error. This method is presented in detail in (Gupta & al, 2003; Hagan & al, 1996; Sarangapani, 2006; Bevrani & Hiyama, 2011).

For testing of the proposed control methodology for tuning the PI controller parameters, the controller is applied to the case study (Figure 6), and the results are compared with response of a conventional PI controller.

$$
\begin{cases}
\Delta W_2 = -\eta \dfrac{\partial E}{\partial w_2} \\[2mm]
\dfrac{\partial E}{\partial W_2} = \dfrac{\partial E}{\partial y} \cdot \dfrac{\partial y}{\partial u} \cdot \dfrac{\partial u}{\partial net_k} \cdot \dfrac{\partial net_k}{\partial W_2} \\[2mm]
\dfrac{\partial u}{\partial net_k} = f'(net_k) \\[2mm]
\dfrac{\partial net_k}{\partial W_2} = H_j \\[2mm]
\dfrac{\partial E}{\partial y} \cdot \dfrac{\partial y}{\partial u} \cdot \dfrac{\partial u}{\partial net_k} = \delta_k \\[2mm]
\Delta W_2 = \eta \delta_k H_j
\end{cases} \tag{11}
$$

and,

Figure 11. The considered functions for hidden and output layers

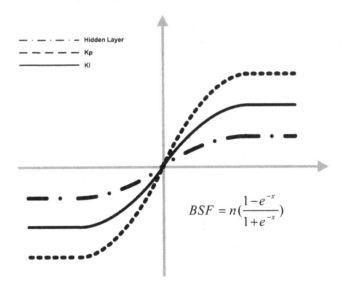

$$BSF = n \left(\frac{1 - e^{-x}}{1 + e^{-x}} \right)$$

Figure 12. Flowchart of updating weights via back-propagation learning (Bevrani, 2011)

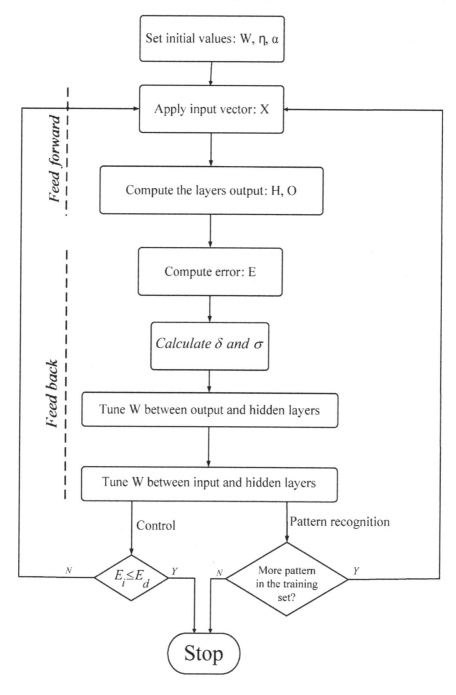

$$
\begin{cases}
\Delta W_1 = -\eta \dfrac{\partial E}{\partial w_1} \\[2mm]
\dfrac{\partial E}{\partial W_1} = \dfrac{\partial E}{\partial y} \cdot \dfrac{\partial y}{\partial u} \cdot \dfrac{\partial u}{\partial net_k} \cdot \dfrac{\partial net_k}{\partial H_j} \cdot \dfrac{\partial H_j}{\partial net_j} \cdot \dfrac{\partial net_j}{\partial w_1} \\[2mm]
\dfrac{\partial u}{\partial net_k} = f'(net_k) \\[2mm]
\dfrac{\partial net_k}{\partial H_j} = W_2 \\[2mm]
\dfrac{\partial H_j}{\partial net_j} = f'(net_j) \\[2mm]
\dfrac{\partial net_j}{\partial W_j} = X \\[2mm]
\Delta W_1 = \eta . \delta_k . f'(net_k) . W_2 . f'(net_j) . X = \eta . \sigma_j . X
\end{cases}
$$

$$(12)$$

SIMULATION RESULTS

As described in the previous sections, usually output power of the WTG and PV panel due to changing in the wind speed and in the sunlight flux is variable, and there are permanent fluctuations in the MG systems. Impacts of the WTG and PV panel output power variations on the system frequency and on the response of the different units in the MG test system are investigated as first scenario to examine the performance of proposed control strategy in comparison of the conventional PI controller.

The considered output power variations for the WTG and PV panel are shown in Figure 13. The FC and AE (Figure 6(b)) act as delay blocks or low pass filters which reduce the amplitude of high frequency noises in the WTG and PV panel output power variations, significantly. Response of the storage devices, BESS and FESS as well as system frequency response in the presence of the ANN based self-tuning PI and conventional PI controllers are shown in Figure 13.

As shown, frequency response of the proposed optimal control method is quite better than the conventional method. An important point that can be found from Figure 13 is a lower level frequency response curves related to the BESS and FESS in case of using the proposed intelligent control method. As shown by using proposed control method, amount of DEG participation in the frequency control is changed due to the action of BESS and FESS units. It reduces the BESS and FESS capacity in a long term. So, in addition to the improving of frequency stability, supplying ancillary services cost is cheaper as well.

In the second scenario, a random step load disturbance, WTG mechanical output power variations, and sunlight flux variations are simultaneously considered in the MG test system to better evaluate of the proposed closed-loop control performance. In this scenario, two main configurations for the MG test system are studied. First, is assumed that the BESS and FESS systems do not participate in the secondary frequency control issue. In the second configuration, both BESS and FESS are supporting the frequency regulation. The results for first scenario are plotted in the Figure 14(a), (b), (c), (d), and (e). The considered power fluctuations, the WTG and PV output power variations, the DEG frequency response and system frequency are shown in Figure 14(a), (b), (c), (d), and (e), respectively. As shown, only the DEG participates in the secondary frequency control process and it injects more compensating power by using the proposed intelligent control method. So, when the ANN adjusts the controller parameters, system frequency fluctuations are much more less.

In the second configuration, the BESS and FESS participate in the secondary frequency control against the considered power fluctuations. The results are shown in Figure 15 (a), (b), (c), and (d). Frequency response of the BESS and FESS systems are respectively shown in Figures 15 (a) and (b). By their participation, the DEG response according to Figure 15(c) is reduced.

Figure 13. System response for different units in the presence of power output variation of the WTGs and PV

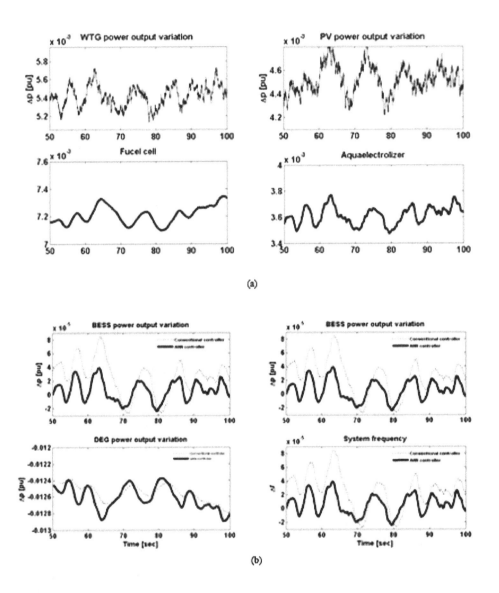

(a)

(b)

System frequency in this configuration is also shown in Figure 15(d). It can be seen that by applying the intelligent control method, amount of the BESS and FESS participation in the frequency control is less than the conventional method. This issue reduces the capacity and cost of the energy storage devices in a long term, and also reduces undershoots and overshoots amplitudes in the system frequency response, as well as the amount of DEG participation. It can be seen that, the intelligent controller shows better performance than the classical one. It should be noted the FC and AE systems have same response as shown in Figure 13 and the WTG and PV panel for the next simulations are same as those shown in Figure 14 (b) and (c).

As observed in the two considered scenarios, the step load disturbance size is greater than

Figure 14. Frequency response without the BESS and FESS participation; (a) Step load disturbances, the WTG and PV output power variations, (b) The WTG output power variation, (c) The PV power output variation, d) the DEG frequency response

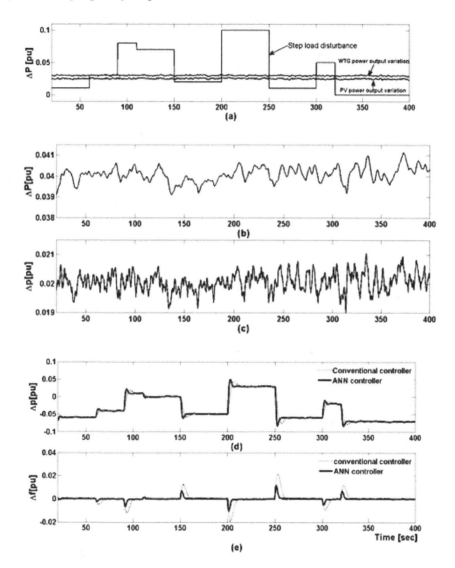

power variations of the WTG and PV systems, therefore frequency response of the MG system is often affected by these disturbances.

In order to examine the intelligent control methodology in the face of large fluctuations, a white noise as a random disturbance is applied to the MG system and the results are plotted in the Figures 16 (a), (b), (c), (d), and (e). The applied

white noise, the BESS, FESS, and DEG frequency responses to the white noise, as well as the system frequency by utilizing intelligent and classical controllers are shown in Figures 16 (a), (b), (c), (d), and (e), respectively.

The white noise amplitude changes between -0.2 pu and 0.2 pu which is considered as a severe disturbance for a small power system. Like previ-

Figure 15. Frequency response with the BESS and FESS systems participation against the power fluctuations shown in Figure 14 (a); a, b) The BESS and FESS systems frequency response, c) The DEG frequency response, d) System frequency

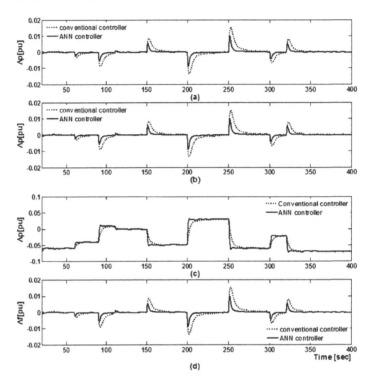

ous scenarios, the ANN-PI controller has a more favorable performance, in terms of lower settling time and fluctuations amplitude in both transient and steady state conditions.

The considered frequency response model (Figure 6(b)) for the MG system simulations was a linear frequency model and some dynamics and physical constraints are neglected. Usually, in the most frequency studies, a linear model of the actual system is considered. Here to perform a nonlinear MG system, and to approach a real system response, several nonlinear blocks, limiter and delays are added to the system frequency model as shown in Figure 17.

One of the main physical constraints in the diesel generators is due to limitation of thermal and mechanical movements that makes a rate constraint and a delay in reaction against the possible events and common disturbances. Various

filters that exist in the power system and communication channels are the main reasons for a time delay between sensing frequency deviations and applying compensating power by acting governor, turbine and generator. In addition to the time delay, rate of increasing and decreasing of the power generation is limited due to limitation of thermal and mechanical movements. So, generation rate constraint (GRC) is another important physical constraint that should be certainly considered in the nonlinear power systems. Usually, actual systems are activated for certain range of input signal. To consider this issue in the simulations and studies, dead band block is used (Bevrani, et al., 2012).

The constraints for DEG model are considered by using a more accurate model in which turbine, governor and generator dynamics are considered. As shown, output of the controller as input signal for turbine has a time delay block, turbine output has a dead band and governor has a ramping rate and a feedback signal. By these modifications in the DEG model, generation rate constraint (GRC) and physical constraints are also considered. For each BEES and FESS models, a ramping rate and a time delay block are considered. The considered time delay for different blocks is about one cycle (20 ms). To consider limitation of power production, dead band and ramping rate blocks are added to the system model.

To illustrate proposed intelligent control method performance in the nonlinear MG system, the white noise of the previous scenario is applied and the results are plotted in Figure 18 (a), (b), (c), and (d).

The frequency response of BESS, FESS, DEG, and the nonlinear system frequency are shown in Figure 18 (a), (b), (c), and (d), respectively. In comparison with the previous scenario, it can be seen that the BESS and FESS participations in the secondary frequency control are reduced due to adding the nonlinear blocks like time delay and dead band blocks.

As shown, in the nonlinear system also, the proposed intelligent controller based on adjusting the controller parameters by the ANNs shows more desirable performance than the classical controller.

Desirable performance of the proposed intelligent control methodology in comparison of the classical one is observed using several simulation test scenarios. Moreover, here to illustrate the

Figure 16. Frequency response of the MG system following a white noise; a) White noise, b, c) The BESS and the FESS systems frequency response, d) The DEG frequency response, e) The MG system frequency

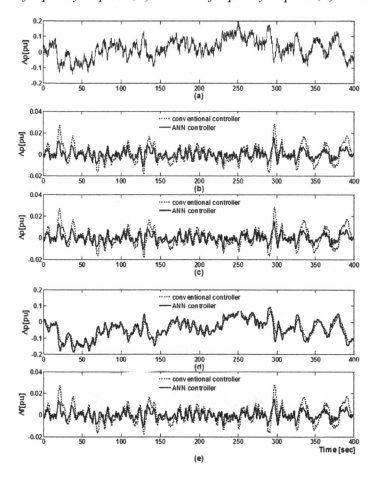

Figure 17. The nonlinear MG system

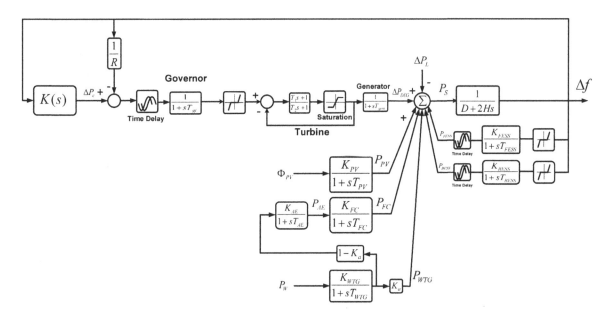

Figure 18. Frequency response of different parts of the nonlinear MG system; a, b) The BESS and FESS frequency response, c) The DEG frequency response, d) Frequency response of the MG system with several considered physical constraints

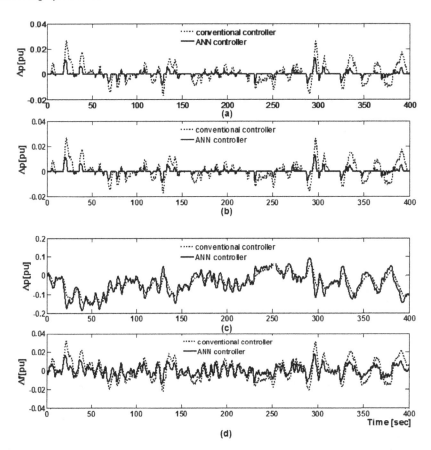

effectiveness of the designed intelligent PI controller, the following frequency deviation-based performance index is defined:

$$Index = \int_0^T |\Delta f|^2 dt \qquad (13)$$

where, $|\Delta f|$, and T are absolute value of the frequency deviations, and simulation time (400 s), respectively. The above performance index are calculated for all described simulation scenarios, and results are given in Table 2.

Scenario 1 (S-1) investigates the system response concerning the impacts of WTG and PV output power fluctuation. Scenarios S-21 and S-22 (Scenario 2) are studying the MG frequency response in the presence of random load disturbance without and with contribution of BESS and FESS units, respectively. Scenarios 3 and 4 (S-3, and S-4) examine the impacts of the white noise on the frequency response, for linear and nonlinear simulations, respectively. As shown in Table 2, calculated values for the performance index in all test scenarios using the intelligent controller is quite better than the case of using conventional controller.

FUTURE RESEARCH DIRECTIONS

In the present book chapter the WTG and FC do not participate in the secondary frequency control task. Participation of these generation units in the load frequency control by using an intelligent/optimal control approach can be considered as a future work.

CONCLUSION

This chapter presents a novel ANN-based intelligent technique for online tuning of PI parameters in a MG's frequency control loop. The impacts of DERs power fluctuation on the system frequency, and physical constraints are considered. Proper performance of the ANN based self-tuning against the conventional frequency controller is shown for output power variation and random load changes. Synthesis strategy includes enough flexibility to set a desired level of performance, and the performed nonlinear simulations show an optimal performance for the proposed control strategy. It has been demonstrated that the developed ANN-based self-tuning frequency controller provides better frequency error minimization and a proper convergence to the specified permitted bound for a MG in comparison with the traditional PI controller.

Table 2. Calculated values of the performance index (given in (13))

Controller		Conventional	ANN
S-1		0.0066	0.0009
S-2	S-21	0.0067	0.0009
	S-22	0.0038	0.0006
S-3		0.0247	0.0065
S-4		0.0410	0.0117

ACKNOWLEDGMENT

This work is supported by Department of Electrical and Computer Engineering at University of Kurdistan.

REFERENCES

Ackermann, T., Andersson, G., & Soder, L. (2001). Distributed Generation: A definition. *International Journal of Electric Power Systems Research, 57*(3), 195–204. doi:10.1016/S0378-7796(01)00101-8

Arboleya, P., Diaz, D., Guerrero, J. M., Garcia, P., Briz, F., & Gonzalez-Moran, C. (2010). An improved control scheme based in droop characteristic for microgrid converters. *Electric Power Systems Research*, (n.d), 1215–1221. doi:10.1016/j.epsr.2010.04.003

Barker, P., & De Mello, R. (2001). *Determining the impact of distributed generation on power systems. I. Radial distribution systems.* Paper presented at the IEEE Power Engineering Society Summer Meeting, Seattle, WA, USA

Basak, P., Saha, A. K., Chowdhury, S., & Chowdhury, S. P. (2009). *Microgrid: Control techniques and modeling.* Paper presented at the IEEE.

Bevrani, H. (2009). *Robust power system frequency control.* New York, NY: Springer. doi:10.1007/978-0-387-84878-5

Bevrani, H. (2011). *Artificial neural networks.* Retrieved from http://www.bevrani.com/ANN/ANN.htm

Bevrani, H., & Hiyama, T. (April 2011). Neural network based AGC design. In *Intelligent automatic generation control.* New York, NY: CRC Press (Taylor & Francis Group).

Chowdhury, S., Chowdhury, S. P., & Crossley, P. (2009). *Microgrids and active distribution networks.* London, UK: The Institution of Engineering and Technology.

Chu, S. R., Shoureshi, R., & Tenorio, M. (1990). Neural networks for system identification. *IEEE Control Systems Magazine, 10*(3), 31–35. doi:10.1109/37.55121

Díaz, G., González-Morán, C., Gómez-Aleixandre, J., & Diez, A. (2010). Scheduling of Droop coefficients for frequencyand voltage regulation in isolated microgrids. *IEEE Transactions on Power Systems, 25*(1). doi:10.1109/TPWRS.2009.2030425

El-Keib, A. A., & Ma, X. (1995). Application of artificial neural networks in voltage stability assessment. *IEEE Transactions on Power Systems, 10*(4), 1890–1896. doi:10.1109/59.476054

Fujimoto, K., Ota, T., Shimizu, Y., Ichikawa, T., Yukita, K., & Goto, Y. (2009). *Load frequency control using storage system for a micro grid.* IEEE T&D Asia. doi:10.1109/TD-ASIA.2009.5356856

Gil, N. J., & Lopes, J. A. P. (2007). *Hierarchical frequency control scheme for islanded multi-microgrids operation.* Paper presented at the PowerTech,IEEE.

Gupta, M. M., et al. (2003). *Static and dynamic neural networks: From fundamentals to advanced theory.* IEEE Press & John Wiley.

Hagan, M. T. (1996). *Neural network design.* PWS.

Hiyama, T., Tokieda, M., Hubbi, W., & Andou, H. (1997). Artificial neural network based dynamic load modeling. *IEEE Transactions on Power Systems, 12*(4), 1576–1583. doi:10.1109/59.627861

Hsu, C. T., Kang, M. S., & Chen, C. S. (2005). Design of adaptive load shedding by artificial neural networks. *IEE Proceedings. Generation, Transmission and Distribution, 152*(3), 415–421. doi:10.1049/ip-gtd:20041207

IEEESTD (2003). *IEEE standard for interconnecting distributed resources with electric power systems.* IEEE Std 1547-2003.

Karimi, H., Davison, E. J., & Iravani, R. (2010). Multivariable servomechanism controller forautonomous operation of a distributed generation unit: design and performance evaluation. *IEEE Transactions on Power Systems, 25*(2). doi:10.1109/TPWRS.2009.2031441

Kundur, P., Paserba, J., & Ajjarapu, V., Hill, Dagle, J., Stankovic, A., et al. (2004, August). Definition and classification of power system stability IEEE/CIGRE joint task force on stability terms and definitions. *IEEE Transactions on Power Systems, 19*(3), 1387–1401. doi:10.1109/TPWRS.2004.825981

Lasseter, R. H. (2002). *MicroGrids.* Paper presented at the IEEE.

Lasseter, R. H., Akhil, A., Marnay, C., Stephens, J., Dagle, J., Guttromson, R., et al. (April 2002). *The CERTS microgrid concept.* White paper for transmission reliability program, Office of Power Technologies, U.S. Dept. Energy, 1.

Lasseter, R. H., Eto, J. H., Schenkman, B., Stevens, J., Vollkommer, H., & Klapp, D. (2011). CERTS microgrid laboratory test bed. *IEEE Transactions on Power Delivery, 26*(1), 325–326. doi:10.1109/TPWRD.2010.2051819

Lasseter, R. H., & Paigi, P. (2004). *Microgrid: A conceptual solution.* Paper presented at the 35th Annul IEEE Power Elecrronics Specialisrs Conference.

Lee, D.-J., & Wang, L. (2008). Small-signal stability analysis of an autonomous hybrid renewable energy power generation/energy storage system part I: time-domain simulations. *IEEE Transactions on Energy Conversion, 23*(1), 312–315. doi:10.1109/TEC.2007.914309

Lopes, J. A. P., Moreira, C. L., & Madureira, A. G. (2006). Defining control strategies for microgrids islanded operation. *IEEE Transactions on Power Systems, 21*(2), 919–920. doi:10.1109/TPWRS.2006.873018

Majumder, R., Ledwich, A. G. G., & Zare, F. (2008, 19 March). Load sharing and power quality enhanced operation of a distributed microgrid. *IET Renewable Power Generation, 3*(2).

Moreira, C. L., & Lopes, J. A. P. (2007). *MicroGrids dynamic security assessment.* Paper presented at the IEEE.

Ota, T., Yukita, K., & Nakano, H. Y. G., & Ichiyanagi, K. (2010). *Study of load frequency control for a microgrid.* IEEE.

Puttgen, H., MacGregor, P., & Lambert, F. (2003). Distributed generation: Semantic type or the dawn of a new era. *IEEE Transactions on Power and Energy, 1*(1), 22–29. doi:10.1109/MPAE.2003.1180357

Sao, C. K., & Lehn, P. W. (2008). Control and power management of converter fed microgrids. *IEEE Transactions on Power Systems, 23*(3). doi:10.1109/TPWRS.2008.922232

Sarangapani, J. (2006). *Neural network control of nonlinear discrete-time systems.* CRC Press. doi:10.1201/9781420015454

Schauder, C., & Mehta, H. (1993, July). Vector analysis and control of advanced static VAR compensators. *Proceedings of the IEEE, 140*(Part C), 299–306.

Senjyu, T., Omine, E., Tokudome, M., Yonaha, Y., Goya, T., Yona, A., et al. (2009). *Frequency control strategy for parallel operated battery systems based on Droop characteristics by applying H∞ control theory.* Paper presented at the IEEE T&d.

Song, H., & Nam, K. (1999, Oct.). Dual current control scheme for PWMconverter under the unbalanced input voltage conditions. *IEEE Transactions on Industrial Electronics*, *46*(5), 953–959. doi:10.1109/41.793344

Subbaraj, P., & Manickavasagam, K. (2007). Generation control of interconnected power systems using computational intelligence techniques. *Generation . Transmission & Distribution, IET*, *1*(4), 557–563. doi:10.1049/iet-gtd:20060222

Uehara, A., Senjyuy, T., Yonaz, A., & Funabashi, T. (2010). A frequency control method by wind farm & battery using load estimation in isolated power system. *International Journal of Emerging Electric Power Systems Research*, *11*(2).

Vachirasricirikul, S., Ngamroo, I., Kaitwanidvilai, S., & Chaiyatham, T. (2009). *Robust frequency stabilization in a microgrid system*. IEEE T&D. doi:10.1109/TD-ASIA.2009.5356835

Willis, H., & Scott, W. E. (2000). *Distributed power generation: Planning and evaluation*. New York, NY: CRC Press.

Yazdani, A., & Iravani, R. (2006, July). A unified dynamic model and control for the voltage-sourced converter under unbalanced grid conditions. *IEEE Transactions in Power Delay*, *21*(3), 1620–1629. doi:10.1109/TPWRD.2006.874641

Yuen, C., Oudalov, A., & Timbus, A. (2011). The provision of frequency control reserves from multiple microgrids. *IEEE Transactions on Industrial Electronics*, *58*(1). doi:10.1109/TIE.2010.2041139

Zahnd, U. (February 2007). *Control strategies for load-following unbalanced microgrids islanded operation*.

Zaidi, A. A., & Kupzog, F. (December 23-24,2008). *Microgrid automation - A self-configuring approach*. Paper presented at the 12th IEEE International Multitopic Conference.

ADDITIONAL READING

Akhmatov, V., Knudsen, H., Nielsen, A. H., Pedersen, J. K., & Poulsen, N. K. (2006). Modeling and transient stability of large wind farms. *International Journal of Electrical Power & Energy Systems*, *25*, 123–144. doi:10.1016/S0142-0615(02)00017-0

Arulampalam, A., Barnes, M., Jenkins, N., & Ekanayake, J. (2006). Power quality and stability improvement of a wind farm using STATCOM supported with hybrid battery energy storage. *IEE Proceedings, Generation, Transmission and Distribution*, *153*(6), 701–710. doi:10.1049/ipgtd:20045269

Barklund, E., Pogaku, N., Prodanovic, M., Hernandez-Aramburo, C., & Green, T. C. (2008). Energy management in autonomous microgrid using stability-constrained Droop control of inverters. *IEEE Transactions on Power Electronics*, *23*(5), 2346–2352. doi:10.1109/TPEL.2008.2001910

Bevrani, H., Daneshfar, F., & Daneshmand, P. (2010). Intelligent power system frequency regulation concerning the integration of wind power units . In Wang, L. F., Singh, C., & Kusiak, A. (Eds.), *Wind power systems: Applications of computational intelligence* (pp. 407–437). Heidelberg, Germany: Springer-Verlag. doi:10.1007/978-3-642-13250-6_15

Bevrani, H., Ghosh, A., & Ledwich, G. (2010). Renewable energy sources and frequency regulation: Survey and new perspectives. *IET Renewable Power Generation*, *4*(5), 438–457. doi:10.1049/iet-rpg.2009.0049

Bevrani, H., & Hiyama, T. (2011). *Intelligent automatic generation control*. New York, NY: CRC Press.

Bevrani, H., & Tikdari, A. G. (2010). An ANN-based power system emergency control scheme in the presence of high wind power penetration . In Wang, L. F. (Eds.), *Wind power systems: Applications of computational intelligence* (pp. 215–254). Heidelberg, Germany: Springer-Verlag Series on Green Energy and Technology.

Dai, X., Zhang, K., Zhang, T., & Lu, X. (2004). ANN generalised inversion control of turbo-generator governor. *IEE Proceedings. Generation, Transmission and Distribution, 151*(3), 327–333. doi:10.1049/ip-gtd:20040380

Datta, M., Senjyu, T., Yona, A., Funabashi, T., & Kim, C.-H. (2009). A coordinated control method for leveling PV output power fluctuations of PV-diesel hybrid systems connected to isolated power utility. *IEEE Transactions on Energy Conversion, 24*(1), 153–162. doi:10.1109/TEC.2008.2008870

Demiroren, A., Zeynelgil, H. L., & Sengor, N. S. (2001, 2001). *The application of ANN technique to load-frequency control for three-area power system.* Paper presented at the Power Tech 2001 IEEE Porto.

Erlich, I., Rensch, K., & Shewarega, F. (2006). Impact of large wind power generation on frequency stability. In *Proceedings IEEE Power Engineering Society General Meeting,* Montereal, Que., Canada.

Fernandeza, L. M., Saenza, J. R., & Jurado, F. (2006). Dynamic models of wind farms with fixed speed wind turbines. *Renewable Energy, 31*(8), 1203–1230. doi:10.1016/j.renene.2005.06.011

Gilbert, M. M. (2004). *Renewable and efficient electric power systems.* Hoboken, NJ: John Wiley & Sons.

Huang, W., Lu, M., & Zhang, L. (2011). Survey on microgrid control strategies. *Energy Procedia, 12*(0), 206–212. doi:10.1016/j.egypro.2011.10.029

Jiayi, H., Chuanwen, J., & Rong, X. (2008). A review on distributed energy resources and MicroGrid. *Renewable & Sustainable Energy Reviews, 12*(9), 2472–2483. doi:10.1016/j.rser.2007.06.004

Khuntia, S. R., & Panda, S. (2012). Simulation study for automatic generation control of a multi-area power system by ANFIS approach. *Applied Soft Computing, 12*(1), 333–341. doi:10.1016/j.asoc.2011.08.039

Kook, K. S., Liu, Y., & Bang, M. J. (2008, September). Global behaviour of power system frequency in Korean power system for the application of frequency monitoring network. *IET Generation . Transmission & Distribution, 2,* 764–774.

Kundur, P. (1994). *Power system stability and control.* New York, NY: McGraw-Hill.

Lalor, G., Mullane, A., & O'Malley, M. (2005). Frequency control and wind turbine technologies. *IEEE Transactions on Power Systems, 20*(4), 1905–1913. doi:10.1109/TPWRS.2005.857393

Lidula, N. W. A., & Rajapakse, A. D. (2011). Microgrids research: A review of experimental microgrids and test systems. *Renewable & Sustainable Energy Reviews, 15*(1), 186–202. doi:10.1016/j.rser.2010.09.041

Lopes, J. A. Peças, Moreira, C. L., Madureira, A. G. (2006). Defining control strategies for analyzing microgrids islanded operation. *IEEE Transactions on Power Systems, 21,* 916–924. doi:10.1109/TPWRS.2006.873018

Lu, M.-S., Chang, C.-L., Lee, W.-J., & Wang, L. (2009). Combining the wind power generation system with energy storage equipment. *IEEE Transactions on Industry Applications, 45*(6), 2109–2115. doi:10.1109/TIA.2009.2031937

Nunes, M. V., Lopes, J. A., Zürn, H. H., Bezerra, U. H., & Almeida, R. G. (2004). Influence of the variable-speed wind generators in transient stability margin of the conventional generators integrated in electrical grids. *IEEE Transactions on Energy Conversion, 19*(4), 692–701. doi:10.1109/TEC.2004.832078

Padhy, B. P., & Tyagi, B. (2009, 27-29 December). *Artificial neural network based multi area automatic generation control scheme for a competitive electricity market environment.* Paper presented at International Conference on Power Systems, ICPS '09.

Pogaku, N., Prodanovic, M., & Green, T. C. (2007). Modeling, analysis and testing of autonomous operation of an inverter-based microgrid. *IEEE Transactions on Power Electronics, 22*(2), 613–625. doi:10.1109/TPEL.2006.890003

San Martín, J. I., Zamora, I., San Martín, J. J., Aperribay, V., & Eguia, P. (2010). Hybrid fuel cells technologies for electrical microgrids. *Electric Power Systems Research, 80*(9), 993–1005. doi:10.1016/j.epsr.2010.01.006

Shayeghi, H., & Shayanfar, H. A. (2006). Application of ANN technique based on μ-synthesis to load frequency control of interconnected power system. *International Journal of Electrical Power & Energy Systems, 28*(7), 503–511.

Shijie, C., Rujing, Z., & Lin, G. (1997). An on-line self-learning power system stabilizer using a neural network method. *IEEE Transactions on Power Systems, 12*(2), 926–931. doi:10.1109/59.589773

Tamrakar, I., Shilpakar, L., Fernandes, B., & Nilsen, R. (2007). Voltage and frequency control of parallel operated synchronous generator and induction generator with STATCOM in micro hydro scheme. *IET Generation, Transmission, and Distribution, 1*(5), 743–750. doi:10.1049/iet-gtd:20060385

Tan, W., & Xu, Z. (2009). Robust analysis and design of load frequency controller for power systems. *Electric Power Systems Research, 79*(5), 846–853. doi:10.1016/j.epsr.2008.11.005

Vaccaro, B. A., Popov, M., Villacci, D., & Terzija, V. (2011). An Integrated framework for smart microgrids modeling, monitoring, control, communication, and verification. *Proceedings of the IEEE, 99*(1), 119–132. doi:10.1109/JPROC.2010.2081651

Zamora, R., & Srivastava, A. K. (2010). Controls for microgrids with storage: Review, challenges, and research needs. *Renewable & Sustainable Energy Reviews, 14*, 2009–2018. doi:10.1016/j.rser.2010.03.019

Zeng, Z., Yang, H., & Zhao, R. (2011). Study on small signal stability of microgrids: A review and a new approach. *Renewable & Sustainable Energy Reviews, 15*(9), 4818–4828. doi:10.1016/j.rser.2011.07.069

Zeynelgil, H. L., Demiroren, A., & Sengor, N. S. (2002). The application of ANN technique to automatic generation control for multi-area power system. *International Journal of Electrical Power & Energy Systems, 24*(5), 345–354. doi:10.1016/S0142-0615(01)00049-7

KEY TERMS AND DEFINITIONS

Artificial Neural Network (ANN): ANN is a mathematical model that is inspired by the structure and/or functional aspects of biological neural networks. An ANN consists of an interconnected group of artificial neurons, and is typically defined by interconnection pattern between different layers of neurons, learning process, and the activation function.

Distributed Generation (DG): DG is defined as small-scale electricity generation by microsources such as wind turbine, diesel generator, and solar unit.

Microgrid: A microgrid is a localized grouping of small power generators, energy storage, and loads that can normally operate either connected to the main traditional centralized grid or in islanded mode. In islanded/disconnected mode, the microgrid can function autonomously.

Optimal Tuning: is Process in which one or more parameters of a controller are adjusted upwards or downwards to achieve an ultimate performance improve or desirable result.

Proportional-Integral (PI) Control: The PI control is a control loop feedback mechanism widely used in industrial control systems. A PI is the most commonly used feedback controller in power systems which attempts to minimize the error by adjusting the process control inputs. The PI controller involves two separate constant parameters, the proportional, and the integral values, denoted by P and I.

Secondary Frequency Control: is a supplementary control loop for supporting the primary control loop to remove the steady state frequency error and restore the system frequency, following a fault or disturbance.

Self-Tuning Control: A class of adaptive control, where the controller parameter(s)/gain is automatically tuned to track the control objective(s).

Chapter 13

Soccer Game Optimization:
An Innovative Integration of Evolutionary Algorithm and Swarm Intelligence Algorithm

Hindriyanto Dwi Purnomo
Chung Yuan Christian University, Taiwan & Satya Wacana Christian University, Indonesia

Hui-Ming Wee
Chung Yuan Christian University, Taiwan

ABSTRACT

A new metaheuristic algorithm is proposed. The algorithm integrates the information sharing as well as the evolution operators in the swarm intelligence algorithm and evolutionary algorithm respectively. The basic soccer player movement is used as the analogy to describe the algorithm. The new method has two basic operators; the move off and the move forward. The proposed method elaborates the reproduction process in evolutionary algorithm with the powerful information sharing in the swarm intelligence algorithm. Examples of implementations are provided for continuous and discrete problems. The experiment results reveal that the proposed method has the potential to become a powerful optimization method. As a new method, the proposed algorithm can be enhanced in many different ways such as investigating the parameter setting, elaborating more aspects of the soccer player movement as well as implementing the proposed method to solve various optimization problems.

INTRODUCTION

In the last two decades, metaheuristic algorithm has emerged as powerful optimization algorithm, especially in engineering, science, business, economic and finance. The algorithm provides a higher framework of heuristic methods to explore the search space more efficiently and effectively. The term metaheuristics was introduced by Glover (1986). The word derives from the Greek words: heuriskein and meta. Heuriskein means "discover" or *"find"* and it is generally accepted as the term for approximate methods while meta means "in upper level". Metaheuristic can be described as a

DOI: 10.4018/978-1-4666-2086-5.ch013

higher level of general methodology that provides guidance based on the heuristic search to solve various optimization problems. An important property that distinguishes between heuristic and metaheuristic algorithms is: the heuristic algorithm is problem dependent while the metaheuristics algorithm is problem independent.

A lot of successful applications of metaheuristic algorithms have been published. The metaheuristic algorithms emerge as a powerful method to solve various optimization problems (Bianchi et al., 2008; Deep et al., 2009). The method gains significant interests in research and industrial practices due to its effectiveness and general applicability. In many cases, the classical approaches based on mathematical and dynamic programming are feasible only for small size instances of problems and generally require a lot of computational efforts, therefore the metaheuristics turn up into promising alternatives to classical optimization methods (Bianchi et al., 2008). The metaheuristic algorithms exploit randomness and set of rules to produce solutions. Due to the nature of heuristic methods, the metaheuristic methods do not guarantee optimal global solutions; however, they will provide acceptable solutions for large-sized and complex problems in a reasonable time (Talbi, 2009). Compared to the exact solution, metaheuristic algorithms are more flexible in their adaptability to fit the need of various optimization problems and they do not need to put formulation of the optimization problem. However, the algorithms need considerable problem specific adaptation in order to achieve good performance (Sorensen and Glover).

Metaheuristic methods have been applied in various problems such as: logistic (Shimizu et al., 2007; Wang and Hsu., 2010,), scheduling (Zhang et al., 2011; Deng and Lin., 2011), data mining (Sorensen and Janssens, 2003; Srinivasa et al. 2007), assembly lines (Lee et al., 2001; Simaria and Vilarinho, 2009; Kim et al., 2000; Purnomo et al., 2011) and supply chain management (Silva et al., 2009; Melo et al., 2012). The

development of metaheuristic methods continually evolves to cope with the growing of optimization problems. Therefore, developing a new metaheuristic method is an important contribution to solve optimization problems in engineering and operations research. The objective of this chapter is to describe a new metaheuristic method, which combines the evolutionary algorithm and swarm intelligence concepts. The method mimics the soccer player movement during a game, and for this rationale, we name it Soccer Game Optimization (SGO). The proposed method combines the local search and global search with the use of cognitive learning as well as social learning. This chapter illustrates the work of the proposed method. Examples of continuous and discrete problems are provided in order to help understand the proposed method easily.

BACKGROUND

Metaheuristic methods are used to solve both continuous and discrete problems. In the classical method, gradient information is needed to solve the problems that have real-valued search-spaces. In the real problems, the gradient search approaches could become very difficult and even unstable. The metaheuristic methods could overcome the limitation of the conventional, computational based methods, by eliminating the need for gradient information (Lee and Geem, 2005). In combinatorial optimization, the search space is finite; however, the search space grows exponentially with the size instance of the problem. Moreover, the multidimensional combinatorial problems also suffer from the curse of dimensionality. These problems cause the enumeration based exact algorithms to have slow convergence rate or the exhaustive search for the optimal solution becomes infeasible. On the other hand, the metaheuristic algorithm does not need the gradient information and is capable of finding good solutions for realistic size instances of problems in smaller computation time. There are various studies providing evidence about the advantages of metaheuristic over the classical methods. Some of the studies are shown in Table 1.

The majority of metaheuristic algorithms are inspired from the nature behaviors and physical system. Several well known metaheuristic algorithms are Genetic Algorithm (GA) by Holland (1975), Simulated Annealing (SA) by Kirkpatrick et al. (1983), Tabu Search (TS) by Glover (1990), Ant Colony Optimization (ACO) (Dorigo and Caro, 1999) and Particle Swarm Optimization (PSO) by Kennedy and Eberhart (1995). Each of the algorithms has certain advantages and disadvantages. For example, the GA can scan a vast solution set and its parallel search reduces the possibility of local search (Lee and El-Sharkawi, 2002). But the GA can be very fast to achieve initial convergence followed by slower improvements. While the PSO has a simple concept and its conceptual search can be easily visualized. Nevertheless, it may get trapped in local optimum in heavily complex problems due to limited global search (Shi and Eberhart, 1999). The ACO has a self organizing feature which is appropriate for dynamic problems. However, it has stagnation behavior and long computational time (Hung et al., 2007).

In recent years, the combination of metaheuristic algorithms, called hybrid metaheuristics, becomes more popular. The motivation is to exploit different behaviours of metaheuristic in order to obtain better optimization algorithms. The hybridization lies on the benefit of synergy by exploiting the complementary character of different algorithms (Blum et al. 2011). There are many successful applications of hybrid metaheuristics in the literature and they can be used as guidance for developing new algorithms. The hybridization could solve more complex problems satisfactorily than single metaheuristic. Some of the applications are mentioned in Table 2.

The further development of metaheuristic algorithm will mainly fall into several areas. First, as the responses of No Free Lunch Theorem (Wolpert and Macready, 1997), novel algorithms are proposed on very specific domain. Second, in contradiction with the No Free Lunch Theorem, researchers will also propose new algorithms for broad classes of optimization problems. Third, the adaptive systems and fully intelligent algorithm are proposed to increase both, the high performance in specific case and robustness features (Chiong et al., 2009). In this paper, our research is mainly belong to the second field, which is developing a new algorithm for broad classes of optimization problems by combining two main

Table 1. Some evidence about the advantages of metaheuristics over the classical method

References	Problem	Metaheuristic methods	Exact Method	Advantages of the metaheuristic over the exact method
Lin, C.C., (2006)	Assortment problems	GA	Integer programming	Could solve large size instances problems in acceptable period of time
Cheng et al. (2009)	Large scale hydro unit load dispatch	PSO	Dynamic programming	Could solve large scale Hydro Unit Load Dispatch problem in timely manner
Sakawa, M. et al. (2001)	Operation planning of district heating	GA	Branch and bound	More efficient in terms of time
Finke et al. (2002)	Shop scheduling	TS	Mixed integer programming	Could solve large size instances problems in acceptable period of time
Bianchi et al. (2002)	Probabilistic TSP	ACO`	Branch and cut by Laporte et al. (1994)	Could solve large size instances problems

Table 2. Some successful applications of hybrid metaheuristics

References	Problem	Metaheuristic methods	Advantages
Kao Y.T, & Zahara E, 2008	Multimodal test functions	Genetic algorithm and Particle Swarm Optimization	The hybrid GAPSO approach is superior in terms of solution quality and convergence rates.
Shi, X.H et al. (2005)	6 unconstraint continuous problems	Genetic algorithm and Particle Swarm Optimization	The proposed VPGA is more efficient than standard GAs and the proposed PSO-GA hybrid algorithm (PGHA) synthesizes the merits in both PSO and GA.
Marinakis Y., Marinaki M, (2010)	Vehicle routing problem	Genetic algorithm and Particle swarm optimization	The use of an intermediate phase between the two generations, the phase of evolution of the population, will give more efficient individuals; and thus, will improve the effectiveness of the algorithm.
Juang C.F. (2004)	Recurrent network design	Genetic algorithm and Particle Swarm	The HGAPSO demonstrate the superiority over GA and PSO for temporal sequence production by FCRNN and dynamic plant control problem
Yu H., et al. (2000)	Large scale system energy integration	Genetic algorithm and simulated annealing	The GA/SA showing fast convergence and provide better results.
Chen P.H., Shahandashti S.M., (2009)	multiple project scheduling with multiple resource constraints	Genetic algorithm and simulated annealing	The GA-SA hybrid shows more advantages when the complexity of the multi-project scheduling problem (with multiple resource constraints) increases.
Katagiri et al. (2012)	*k*-minimum spanning tree problems	Tabu search and ant colony optimization	The hybrid algorithm provides better accuracy and is faster.
Lee et al. (2008)	multiple sequence alignment	Genetic algorithm and Ant colony optimization	The hybrid method performs better than the GA when the similarity of data set is low.
Kiran et al. (2012)	forecasting energy demand	Particle Swarm Optimization and Ant Colony Optimization	The hybrid model provides lower relative error and better forecast than ACO and PSO.

classes of population-based metaheuristic (evolutionary algorithm and swarm intelligence algorithm).

THE FUNDAMENTALS OF METAHEURISTICS

The metaheuristics have been greatly inspired by the natural phenomena and used the phenomena as the model or metaphor. Some of the methods mimic the biological evolution: the GA (Holland, 1975), the animals' behavior: ACO (Dorigo and Caro, 1999) and PSO (Kennedy and Eberhart, 1995); the physical processes: SA (Kirkpatrick et al., 1983); and the music improvisation: Harmony Search (HS) (Geem et al., 2001). However, there are algorithms, e.g. TS that do not mimic the natural phenomena, but rather use the problem structure to develop search strategies.

Metaheuristic methods can be single-solution based (also known as "trajectory methods") and population based metaheuristics. SA and TS are the most popular single-solution based metaheuristic methods. The GA, ACO and PSO are examples of population-based metaheuristics. There are two main families of population-based methods, namely the evolutionary algorithm and swarm intelligence algorithm. The evolution algorithm mimics the fascinating evolution, which is driven by the iterated selection and mutation. For this reason, many of its operators use the term in the evolution process such as selection, mutation, and recombination. On the other hand, the swarm intelligence mimics the colony of organism in which each individual in the colony has the ability to decide their action based on simple rules. The swarm intelligence used the cooperation approach rather than *the competition* approach which is used in evolution algorithm (Talbi, 2009). The cooperation approach requires communication mechanism among the individuals as well as learning method.

There are two important elements of metaheuristics called intensification and diversification (Talbi, 2009, Yang, 2009; Hertz and Widmer, 2003; Blum and Roli 2003). Intensification is the ability to investigate the neighborhood of a potential solution while diversification is the ability to explore the whole solution space. The intensification plays an important role in improving the potential solution during the search. It exploits the area near a potential solution found during the search in order to obtain a better solution. On the other hand, diversification is very important to avoid being trapped in local optimal solution. In other words, intensification is a local search while diversification is a global search. These two components should be laid in balance to achieve a high performance (Figure 1).

Various metaheuristic methods have different strategies in balancing the intensification and diversification, depending on their conceptual model. However, they have common similarities in their procedure: initialization, solution's manipulation and solution update (Talbi, 2009). The initialization involves problem representation and generation of the first candidate solution. Problem representation is an approach to construct and to manipulate solution, e.g. the binary representation and real number representation (Figure 2). The problem representation must fulfill the completeness, connexity and efficiency criteria. Completeness means all solution associated with the problem must be represented, connexity refers to the existence of the connection or path way between any two solutions, while efficiency means the representation can be manipulated easily (Talbi, 2009). The initial solution is usually generated randomly. For the population based metaheuristic, the spread of the initial solution can be very important in order to explore the search space as widely as possible. This could minimize the probability that search process is trapped in local optima.

Figure 1. Intensification and diversification

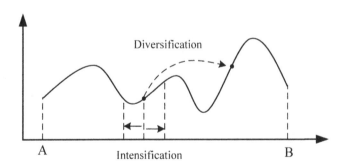

Figure 2. Problem representation

a. Binary representation   b. Real number representation

The solution's manipulation is the most important part of metaheuristic algorithms. There are various manipulation approaches among the metaheuristic algorithms that aim to balance the intensification and diversification. The differences come from different philosophy used in each metaheuristic algorithm and it distinguishes one metaheuristic algorithm from other metaheuristic algorithms.

Most metaheuristic algorithms will keep their current best solution during the search process and update it when necessary. The elitism concept is commonly used to update the current best solution, in which the best solution so far is replaced when the new candidate solution is better than the current best solution. However, there are algorithms that allow worse quality of solution to replace the current best solution, e.g. random walk in Simulated Annealing. The update strategy is important because it will drive the next search process. The random walk in Simulated Annealing is important to avoid being trapped in local optima. Some algorithms explicitly keep the 'good' solution, e.g. genetic algorithm and Particle swarm optimization, while some other keep the good 'attribute' of the solution e.g. the pheromone in Ant Colony Optimization. In the population-based metaheuristics, the update strategies will guide the rolling of the population movement. Brief overviews of several well known metaheuristic algorithms are given.

Tabu Search

Tabu Search explicitly uses the history of the search to balance the intensification and diversification. The memory is divided into short-term, medium-term and long-term memories. The short term memory, called tabu list, consists of a number of recently visited solutions/attributes. The tabu list is used to prevent the search from returning to the same visited solutions. The tabu list is updated every iteration. The length of tabu list controls the memory of the search space; the longer the list, the larger the regions to be explored (stronger diversification) and vice versa. The medium-term memory stores the elite solutions found during the search and is used to manage intensification during the search. The common features of the elite solutions will be extracted and then the search is intensified around those features. Meanwhile, the long-term memory records the information of visited solutions and then uses the record to explore unvisited areas in the search space. The long-term memory is used to manage diversification during the search (Talbi, 2009). The memories in TS are divided based on four principles: recency, frequency, quality and influence (Glover and Laguna, 1997). Recency-based memory is used to track solutions that have been visited recently. Frequency-based memory records the number of times a solution has been visited. Quality-based memory refers to the ability to determine 'good' solution during the search while influence-based memory refers to the impact of choices made during the search (which choice is the most critical one) (Glover and Laguna, 1997; Blum and Roli, 2003).

Critics on TS are mainly due to the impractical uses of tabu list as it is inefficient to manage long list of visited solutions. To overcome this problem, the tabu list stores solution attribute instead of the solution itself. However, this may result in loss of information as an attribute may represent several solutions. Therefore, several attributes or solutions in the tabu list can still be accepted under specific conditions (called aspiration criteria). In addition, if the search space is very large and has high dimensionality, the search can be trapped in local optima easily (Luke S., 2009) (see Algorithm 1).

Simulated Annealing

Simulated annealing mimics the annealing process of metals during the heat treatment. The algorithm strategy to escape local minima is conducted by allowing moves that will produce poorer quality of solution than the current solution (called random

Algorithm 1. Pseudocode of Tabu Search Algorithm

```
S = S₀; /* generate initial solution
Initialize tabu list, medium-term and long-term memory
k = 1;
While termination criteria not met
    Identify neighbor set N(S);
    Identify aspirant set T(S,k);
    Find the best admissible neighbor S'
    S = S';
    Update tabu list and aspiration condition, medium-term and long-term memory
    k = k +1;
endwhile
```

walk). The intensification and diversification are controlled by the '*cooling*' mechanism. The cooling process represents the process of finding solutions in which each iteration declares the level of annealing temperature with thermal equilibrium constant following the Boltmann distribution. After an initial solution is generated, the initial temperature T is determined. For each iteration, a solution i is randomly generated. The solution i is accepted as the new solution based on the objective values of solution $i(f(i))$, the objective values of current solution $j(f(j))$ and the current temperature T. Solution i replaces the current solution j if $f(i) < f(j)$. However, when $f(i) \geq f(j)$, solution i still can replace the current solution j according to the Boltzmann distribution function $exp\left(-\dfrac{f(i) - f(j)}{T}\right)$ (Blum and Roli, 2003). The Boltzman distribution function $exp\left(-\dfrac{f(i) - f(j)}{T}\right)$ is also called acceptance function. In the beginning of the search, the temperature T is high; therefore, the probability of random walk is also high, which means that the search has strong diversification property. During the search, the temperature T decreases and the probability of random walk will also decrease. Therefore, the diversification search will be weaker but the intensification search will be stronger (see Algorithm 2).

Evolutionary Algorithm

Evolutionary algorithms are population-based metaheuristics which are inspired by the capability of organism to evolve and to adapt with their environments. The algorithms are characterized by an initial population and a generation cycle which is presumed to evolve over the generation cycle (Chiong et al., 2009) and is based on the idea of competition (Talbi, 2009). The evolutionary algorithms adopts the biological evolution terms as their operators, such as selection, mutation and recombination or crossover. Selection operators will select 'good' individuals based on their fitness. The fitness function is commonly derived from the objective function and it represents the suitability of an individual (a potential solution)

Algorithm 2. Pseudocode of Simulated Annealing

```
S = S₀ ; /* generate initial solution
T = T₀ ; /* generate initial temperature
While termination criteria not met
    While /* non-equilibrium at fixed temperature
    Generate random neighbor solution S'
If f(S') ≤ (S)
        S = S'
    Else

    Accept S' with probability exp(- (f(S') - f(S))/T )

    Endif
    Endwhile
    Uptade (T)
endwhile
```

to the problem. Individuals with better fitness will have higher a chance to be selected. The chosen individuals (called parents) will be modified using crossover and mutation operators. Crossover recombines two or more individuals to produce new individuals (called offspring). The recombination will transmit the good characteristics of parents to the offspring. On the other hand, mutation is self-modification of an individual to produce a new individual. The mutation operation is conducted to increase the exploration capability of the algorithm. Both crossover and mutation operations play important roles to balance the intensification and diversification during the search process.

There are four areas of evolution algorithm: GA, evolution strategies (ES), evolution programming (EP) and genetic programming (GP) (Kennedy and Eberhart, 2001, Talbi, 2009). GA is the most famous metaheursitic method because this method has good performance and has been applied for various types of optimization problems, especially combinatorial problems. GA was introduced by John Holland (1975) and was then further developed by Goldberg (1989). The parent selections in genetic algorithm are commonly based on proportionate selections, ranking selection and k-tournament selection. The main operator in genetic algorithm is crossover and it becomes the main intensification mechanism in this algorithm. The recombination of two or more individuals will guide the search to the area around those individuals. On the other hand, mutation plays the role of an auxiliary operator (Zhao et al., 2007) in which low probability of perturbation is generally applied. The mutation mainly controls the diversification strategy. This self adaptation mechanism enables an individual to 'jump' from its current position to a new position regardless of its neighborhood's position. This movement is expected to detect a new promising area in the search space.

Evolutionary Strategy was originally used to solve continuous problems but later, it was also applied for discrete problems. The notation of ES is often written as $\left(\mu/\rho \,{}^+_, \lambda\right)$-ES, with μ as the population of parents, λ as the population of offspring, $+$ (comma plus) as the parent selection strategy and ρ as the number of parents who take part in producing a single offspring, $1 \leq \rho \leq \mu$ (Beyer, 1998). In ES, the parent population size and the offspring population size should be $\mu \leq \lambda$. In this algorithm, an individual is composed of decision variables and a set of parameters which guide the search, making the evolutionary algorithm have concurrent nature and self-adaptation (Talbi, 2009; Chiong et al., 2009). The primary operators in ES are selection and mutation operators, while the crossover is rarely used (Talbi, 2009; Dumitrescu et.al., 2000; Chiong et al., 2009). The mutation operator for a decision variable i is formulated as follows:

$$x_i^{'} = x_i + \sigma_i^{'} N(0,1) \qquad (1)$$

where $N(0,1)$ is a zero-mean normal distribution with standard deviation equal to 1. The major advantage of ES is in its efficiency in terms of time complexity (Talbi, 2009).

Evolutionary programming was originally used to solve discrete problems, but the algorithm is then adapted to solve continuous problems (see Algorithm 3). This algorithm shares many similarities with ES, such as its main operator is mutation and its individuals are composed of decision variables and a set of self-adaptive parameters. In EP, each individual generates an offspring. For each decision variable i, the variable will be updated as follows:

$$\sigma_i^{'} = \sigma_i \left(1 + \alpha N(0,1)\right)$$

$$x_i^{'} = x_i + \sigma_i^{'} N(0,1) \qquad (2)$$

Genetic programming is an evolutionary algorithm which is developed into a computer program. GP is motivated by the attempt to realize self evolve computer program. In this algorithm, a solution is represented by a tree. The crossover is conducted by swapping a sub-tree from two parents in order to produce two offspring. The mutation is done by removing a sub-tree and then substituting it with pseudo randomly generated tree (Chiong et al., 2009).

Harmony Search

Harmony Search is a relatively new metaheuristics which have been applied in various combinatorial problems successfully, such as design of water distribution networks (Geem, 2000), vehicle touring problem (Geem, 2005), and structural design (Degertekin, 2008). The algorithm mimics the musician's improvisation. Initially, the algorithm is used to solve combinatorial problems, but later it is also developed for continuous problems (Lee and Geem, 2005). The solution manipulation in the HS is conducted using the New Harmony improvisation, which consists of harmony memory consideration and pitch adjustment. In the harmony memory consideration, a new solution is produced by inserting each decision variable of the solution from the set of potential solution (called harmony memory) with a probability *HMCR* (Harmony Memory Consideration Rate) and from the set of available value of decision variable X_i, by a probability (1- *HMCR)*. It is generally formulated as:

Algorithm 3. Pseudocode of evolutionary algorithm

```
P = P_0 ; /* generate initial population
Evaluate (P)
While termination criteria not met
    P' = Selection (P)
    P' = Recombination(P')
    P' = Mutation (P')
    P' = Evaluate (P')
    P = update (P, P')
endwhile
```

$$x_i^{'} = \begin{cases} x_i^{'} \in \left\{ x_i^1, x_i^2, \ldots, x_i^{HMS} \right\} & \textit{with probability HMCR} \\ x_i^{'} \in X_i & \textit{with probability } (1 - HMCR) \end{cases}$$

(3)

where $y_i^{'}$ is the value of the decision variable *an HMS* is the harmony memory size. The pitch adjustment is determined to adjust the candidate value, $x_i^{'}$, obtained by the harmony consideration. The adjustment is done with the probability of HMCR × PAR, $(0 \le \text{PAR} \le 1)$, while the original candidate value, $x_i^{'}$, from HMCR is kept with the probability of HMCR × (1-PAR). The adjustment is defined as:

$$x_i^{'} = \begin{cases} x_i(k + m) \textit{ with probability} & HMCR \times PAR \\ x_i^{'} & \textit{with probability} & HMCR \times (1 = PAR) \end{cases}$$

(4)

where y_i^l is obtained in the harmony memory consideration, $x_i^l(k)$ is the kth element in X_i and *m* is the neighboring index (+1 or -1).

In the HS, adjusting the harmony memory consideration rate and pitch adjustment rate will significantly affect the intensification and diversification strategies. For the harmony memory consideration, the higher the *HMCR* the higher the probability a new solution will pick decision variable from the harmony memory (the set of candidate solution obtained during the search). This can be seen as a strong intensification strategy as the search will highly be influenced by the search history (harmony memory). On the other hand, the lower the HMCR the higher the probability a new solution will pick decision variable from X_i, which means that the search has a strong diversification strategy as the new solution has high probability to explore the search space. For the pitch adjustment, higher *PAR* will result in higher probability of disturbance, which can be considered as more exploration. Therefore, it is obvious that good combination of *HMCR* and *PAR* is critical in HS (see Algorithm 4).

Swarm Intelligence Algorithms

Swarm intelligence is an algorithm that is inspired by the collective behavior of organisms such as a flock of birds, fish schooling and ant colony. Researchers have studied how to model these collective organisms in order to understand their interaction, their development and their behavior in achieving goals. The algorithms are constructed of a population of simple and non sophisticated individuals that cooperate with one another. The swarm intelligence can be seen as a distributed system with self-organized control and cooperation. The individuals interact with other individuals but could act independently from the other individuals. The collection of individual acts will determine the behavior at the population level. According to Bonabeau et al, (1999), 'Self-organization is a set of dynamical mechanisms whereby structures appear at the global level of a system from interactions of its lower-level components.' It is obvious that communication mechanism among individuals becomes the central of the swarm intelligence algorithm. Among the swarm intelligence algorithms, PSO and the ACO are two most successful algorithms.

Algorithm 4. Pseudocode of Harmony Search

```
HM = HM_0 ; /* generate initial harmony memory
Evaluate (HM)
While termination criteria not met
    H = Ø /* initiate a new solution
    For i = 1: n /*n = decision variables
        If random ≤ HMCR /* Harmony memory consideration
            H_i =select (HM)
        Else
            H_i = random (X)
        Endif
        If random ≤ HMCR×PAR /* Pitch adjusment
            H_i = H_i (kl)
        Endif
    Endfor
    HM= update (HM, H)
endwhile
```

Particle Swarm Optimization

PSO is a metaheuristic method that mimics the social and cognitive behavior of organism (Kennedy and Eberhart, 2001). Three principles underlying the social adaptation and the cognitive learning are singled out, including evaluate, compare and imitate (Kennedy and Eberhart, 2001). Evaluate stimuli is the most ubiquitous behavior of organism and it enables them to learn. The ability to evaluate the stimuli will enable a particle (analogue with individual in evolutionary algorithm) to set a standard for measuring themselves. The particle in the population will compare themselves with their neighbors based on the critical measure and imitate their superior neighbors. The three principles could be applied in a social being in computer programs so that they can be used to solve hard problems (Kennedy and Eberhart, 2001).

In the PSO, there are two kinds of information owned by the particles, their own experiment and the information derived from the other particles. The information represents the cognitive learning and the social learning (Kennedy and Eberhart, 2001). Cognitive learning is commonly based on that particle best achievement (p_{best}). The information in the social learning can be classified into global information and local information. Global information means the information is known by all particles in the population (e.g. g_{best}) so that it connects the members of the population to one another. The local information means the information is only shared between a limited number of particles (e.g. l_{best}) and creates a neighborhood (Kennedy and Eberhart, 2001). Each particle in the population will adjust its position according to the cognitive learning and the social learning (see Algorithm 5).

A population of particles flies around in the search space during the search. Each particle is a candidate solution consisting of the decision variables x. In each iteration, the particle *i* position is updated using the following rules:

$$v_i = v_i + \varphi_1 C_1 \left(x_p - x_i \right) + \varphi_2 C_2 \left(x_g - x_i \right)$$

$$\text{(5)}$$

$$x_i = x_i + v_i \tag{6}$$

where v_i is the particle velocity in i decision space, φ_1 and φ_2 are random (0,1), C_1 and C_2 are coefficients of cognitive learning and social learning respectively, x_p is the particle best position and x_g is the global best position (best position in the population).

The particle best position x_p and global best position x_g will guide the search to a nearby position; therefore, these two components manage the intensification search. When the particle approaches the optima, the motion and randomness are reduced (Yang, X.-S. 2009). The learning coefficients, C_1 and C_2, manage the diversification search. The higher the C_1 and C_2, the further the particle steps; therefore, it can explore more areas in the search space. However, it will also reduce the convergence speed.

Algorithm 5. Pseudocode of Particle Swarm Optimization

P (x)= P$_0$; /* generate initial population
While *termination criteria not met*
   Evaluate (P(x))
   For *i = 1: n /*n = number of particle*
    Velocity update:

$$v_i = v_i + \varphi_1 C_1 \left(x_p - x_i \right) + \varphi_2 C_2 \left(x_g - x_i \right)$$

    Move to the new position:

$$x_i = x_i + v_i$$

   *particle_best*_position_update $\left(x_p, x_i \right)$
   *Global_best_position*_update $\left(x_g, x_i \right)$
   *Position_and_velocity*_update $\left(x_i, v_i \right)$,
   Endfor
endwhile

Ant Colony Optimization

The ACO is a metaheuristic method that mimics the cooperative behavior of ants (Talbi, 2009, Dorigo and Caro, 1999). The self-organizing principle underlies the basic concept of the ACO in which the complex collective behaviors emerge from the interaction among individuals that reveal a simple behavior. In the ACO, there is no predefined path to problem solving. The path is created as a result of interactions among the individuals, between the individuals and their environments as well as the behaviors of the individuals themselves (Bonabeau et al., 1999). In the real ant, the communication among the ants and between the ants and the environment is conducted via a chemical substance, called pheromones. The pheromones are used for marking the path to guide the other ants toward the food source or the nest (Dorigo and Stuzle, 2004, Talbi, 2009). The pheromones can be considered as an indirect communication mechanism. Every time an ant passes a path, it will deposit pheromones in that path; however, the pheromones will evaporate over time. The more number of ants pass a path, the higher is the pheromone level and the larger the probability that other ants will select that path. The similar communication mechanism is adopted in the ACO.

The ant colony optimization procedure is based on the mechanism of finding the best path on a weighted graph and the solution is represented by an ant moving on the graph. The initial solution is derived by moving some ants randomly to construct an initial solution. After the ants found food, they will return to their nest while laying down pheromones τ_{ij} on the path (called pheromone update). The pheromone update is given as:

$$\tau_{ij} = \tau_{ij} + \Delta_{\tau_{ij}} \tag{7}$$

The pheromone on the path will also evaporate, so that its level decreases as follow:

$$\tau_{ij} = (1 - \rho)\tau_{ij}, \forall i, j \in [1, n] \qquad (8)$$

where ρ is the evaporation rate $(0,1)$. If the path is shorter, the pheromone will evaporate fewer (because only evaporate in a short time). Therefore, its level will remain high and can better attract other ants. As a consequence, when an ant finds a good path, other ants will likely follow that path. The probability of an ant selecting a particular path is formulated as follows:

$$p_{ij} = \frac{\tau_{ij}}{\sum_{k \in S} \tau_{ik}}, \forall j \in S \qquad (9)$$

where p_{ij} is the probability of the selected path between node i and node j, and S is the list of unvisited path. During the search, the short path will tend to keep its pheromone level high so that more ants will select that path and deposit more pheromones. The positive feedback eventually leads all the ants following a single path (see Algorithm 6).

THE SOCCER GAME OPTIMIZATION

The evolutionary algorithms and swarm intelligence algorithms are currently the most widely used metaheuristic methods, due to their sophisticated performance. There is a fundamental philosophical difference between evolutionary algorithms and swarm intelligence algorithms; the evolutionary algorithms are based on competition concept while the swarm intelligence algorithms are based on the cooperation approach. The difference leads to different approaches of searching strategies. The evolutionary algorithm relies on the selection and reproduction operators. The parent selection involves randomness and there is no explicit information sharing among the individuals regarding the search direction. This

could lead to a good exploration but reduce the convergence speed. The crossover operator enables the offspring to inherit the good properties of its parents by passing the parents' elements to the offspring. On the other hand, the swarm intelligence algorithm performance relies on the information sharing mechanism among the individual. The information sharing guides the search direction which is bias to the good solution. This can lead to a fast convergence but it may suffer from being trapped in the local optima.

The main motivation of the proposed method is to integrate the reproduction mechanism and the information sharing. In both evolutionary algorithm and swarm intelligence algorithm, the intensification is generally conducted by solution movement nearby individuals while the diversification is conducted by solution movement that involves randomness. In the proposed method, the movement is based on the information from other individuals or from the past experience. These kinds of movements are observed in the soccer players' movement; and therefore, we use it as the analogy.

In a soccer game, a player tries to be in a good position so that he can dribble the ball to reach the goal. During the game, cooperation among players in a team is important. The ball moves among the players and the ball position will become the main consideration of a player's movement. Players who do not dribble the ball try to move into better positions in order to become the ball dribblers. Some of the players will move closer to the ball (called *move forward*) and some other move on to explore the soccer field (called *move off*). Besides the ball position, a player's movement is also influenced by the nearby players as well as their own experience.

The basic soccer player's movement can be associated with the optimization method. The player's effort to search a new position is similar to find the optimal solution in the optimization process. When a player moves into a new posi-

Algorithm 6. Pseudocode of Ant Colony Optimization

```
Initialize the pheromone trails
While termination criteria not met
    For i = 1: n /*n = number of ant
        Construct_solution()
        Update_pheromone_trail ()
            Evaporation ()
            Reinforcement ()
    Endfor
endwhile
```

tion, he will consider his environment (e.g. the ball position and the players nearby) as well as his own experience and this idea has been adopted in the swarm intelligence systems.

The SGO transforms the basic soccer player's movement into an optimization method by simplifying its environment and rules. The method implies a typical swarm intelligence system in which information sharing plays an important role in the movement; however, it also incorporates the basic idea of competition where each player tries to be the one who dribbles the ball. Many terms used in the method are derived from the soccer game. A team is a simultaneous set of vector solutions and each vector solution is called a player. Each player encodes a set of decision variables. The quality of a player is evaluated using the objective function. The ball dribbler represents the best solution obtained during the search process. The team, players, and decision variables can be illustrated in Figure 3.

The proposed method consists of a set of players who interact with one another. A player with the most advantageous position will dribble the ball (called ball dribbler), and this player represents the best solution so far. The ball dribbler position is shared globally, so that all players can access this information (knowing which player has the best solution). This is similar to the real soccer game where all players consider the ball dribbler position in their movements. As the game continues, the ball dribbler can pass the ball to another player or remain holding the ball. In this method,

the ball is used to point out which player is the best.

In order to control the player's movement, two main movements, called 'move off' and 'move forward', are introduced to balance the diversification and intensification. The 'move off' is mainly used to explore the solution space and it involves randomness. The movement minimizes the chance of premature convergence. The 'move forward' is mainly used to explore the solution space nearby a player. The movement is determined by the cooperation or interaction between the player and other players. The interaction describes the information sharing among them. The information sharing is divided into two types, local information and global information. Local information means the information that can only be accessed by the nearby neighboring players. For example, a player's position is only considered by other players nearby. Global information means the information that can be accessed by all players. Take for instance, the ball dribbler position is very important to every player; therefore, all players should know his position.

The SGO procedure can be described as follows:

1.   Initializing players' position and the ball dribbler

A team P_0 consists of s players $P_0 = \{X_0^1; X_0^2; \ldots; X_0^s\}$. Initially, player i position X_0^i is generated randomly. The player encodes the potential solution $X_0^i = \{x_{1,0}^i; x_{2,0}^i; \ldots; x_{n,0}^i\}$. Objective function(s) is used to evaluate the player's position and the best player is selected as the ball dribbler B_0. The initial players' position is also considered as the initial players' best position $P_b = P_0$.

2.   Players' movement

Figure 3. A team, players, and decision variables

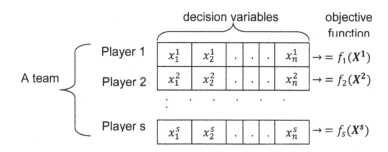

At each step, players in the team move into new positions. Each player can move into the new position by move off and move forward with certain probability (e.g. if m is the probability of move off, then 1-m is the probability of move forward). When a player selects the move off, the player explores the solution space, regardless of the ball dribbler's position, but he can still consider his knowledge by a probability c. On the other hand, when a player selects the move forward, he will move approaching the ball dribbler. But a player still has a chance to do the move off after approaching the ball.

3. The ball dribbler's and players' knowledge update

When all players have moved into their new positions, the players will be evaluated to select a candidate of the ball dribbler. If the ball dribbler candidate is better than the current ball dribbler, the ball is passed into that player. In other words, the current ball dribbler is replaced. Each player will also update their best position X_b^i. The players' movements and the process of the ball dribbler's and players' knowledge update are repeated until the stopping criteria are met.

There are various stopping criteria that can be applied to stop the search process, as are used in other metaheuristic algorithms. Some of the criteria are: the maximum number of iteration, the maximum CPU time, when there is no significant improvement after a certain number of iteration and the best solution already reach the acceptable solution.

A player's movement is strongly driven by the information sharing among the players and the player's experience. In doing so, the proposed method takes the advantages of memory usage. In order to store the player's experience, the player's best position is kept in the memory. The move off incorporates random movements in which cognitive learning is considered with a certain probability. If it is the case, perturbation is conducted on the player's best position instead of the player's current position. The move forward is conducted by considering the player's current position, the player's best position and the other players', especially the ball dribbler's position (the move forward applies the cognitive and social learning). The ball dribbler's and players' knowledge update adopts the elitism strategy in which replacement is done when the new solutions are better than the current solutions (see Algorithm 7).

The flowchart of the proposed method is shown in Figure 4.

The players' movements both *move forward* and *move off*, can be illustrated in Figure 5.

APPLICATION EXAMPLES

To illustrate the work of the proposed method, example of unconstraint continues problems and discrete problems are provided in this section.

Implementation on Continuous Problems

There are many unconstraint continuous benchmark problems in the literature (Chellapilla, 1998, Vesterstrom and Thomsen, 2004, Yao et al., 1999, Tsai et al., 2004, Deep and Thakur, 2007b). The benchmark problems can be classified into unimodal functions $(f_1 - f_7)$, multimodal functions with many local minima $(f_8 - f_{13})$ and, multimodal functions with few local minima $(f_{14} - f_{20})$. In order to assess the performance of the proposed method on unconstraint continuous problems, we compare it with the Genetic algorithm and Particle Swarm Optimization using 20 benchmark functions (Table 3).

In this paper, the move off procedure adopts the dynamical non uniform mutation that has been widely used in Genetic Algorithm, e.g. (Coello, 2000, Zhao et al., 2007, Michalewicz, 1992). The non uniform mutation improves the fine tuning capabilities by providing search in different ways as needed (e.g. exploring wider or narrower regions) over time ((Michalewicz, 1992). For the move forward, we consider the player's current position X_t^i, the player's best position X_b^i, and the ball dribbler's position B_t. Center of mass principle is implemented to calculate the player's new position and it is given by:

$$X_{t+1}^i = \frac{\alpha X_t^i + \beta X_b^i + \gamma B_t}{\alpha + \beta + \gamma} \quad (10)$$

where α, β and γ are the weight for the player's current position, the player's best position, and the ball dribbler's position respectively.

The parameters of the SGO was set as follows: team size $s = 10$, probability of *move off* the ball $m = 0.05\text{-}0.1, l = 0.05\text{-}0.3, c = 0.5, = (1 - \varphi)/2$, $\beta = (1 - \varphi)/2$ and $\gamma = \varphi$ where $Æ = 0.618$ is a golden ratio. Golden ratio is used because it has good properties in narrowing the search spaces as demonstrated in the golden section search.

For the GA, the Laplacian crossover (GA-LX) proposed by Deep and Thakur (2007a) and dynamical non uniform mutation were used as the reproduction operators. The GA parameters are conducted based on extensive experiments. The crossover rate and mutation rate were set as $CR = 0.9$ and $Pm = 0.01$ respectively. The value of location parameter for the Laplacian crossover was set to 0 as mentioned in Deep and Thakur (2007a).

The PSO parameters were set as follows: population size = 100, $v_{max} = 100$, $v_{min} = -100$, $Æ_1 = 2$, $Æ_2 = 2$ and decrement E from 0.9 to 0.4. The parameters were set following the suggestion of Clerc and Kennedy (2002). The experiments were run 30 times for each function. The number of maximum objective function evaluation was used as the stopping criterion (Table 4).

The experiment result shows that the proposed method demonstrated a good performance. It performs the best in 6 out of 7 problems for unimodal functions $(f_1 - f_7)$. In the f_1, the proposed method converges quickly in the beginning and then continues to converge more slowly while the PSO converges slowly in the beginning and then turns to converge quickly. For $f_2 - f_6$, the proposed method steadily converges faster than the other algorithms. On f_7, the GA-LX performs the best and the SGO performs almost as well. The proposed method performs the best in 4 out of 6 problems for highly multi modal functions $(f_8 - f_{13})$. At f_8, only the GA-LX can reach the optimum value. For functions f_9, f_{10}, f_{12} and f_{13}, the SGO outperforms the other algorithms while for f_{11}, the PSO reaches the closest value

Algorithm 7. Pseudocode of Soccer Game Optimization

```
P (X) = P_0 ; /* Initialize players
B = best (P(X)) /* Initialize ball dribbler
P_b (X) = P (X) /* initialize player's best position
While termination criteria not met
    For i = 1: n /*n = number of players
        If random ≤ m
            If random ≤ c
```
$$X_t^i = move\_off\left(X_b^i\right)$$
```
            Else
```
$$X_t^i = move\_off(X_{t-1}^i)$$
```
            Endif
        Else
```
$$X' = move\_forward(X_{t-1}^i, X_b^i, B)$$
```
            If random < l
```
$$X_t^i = move\_off\left(X'\right)$$
```
            Else
```
$$X_t^i = X'$$
```
            Endif
        Endif
    Endfor
    Update_ball_dribbler()
    Update_player_best_position()
endwhile
```

to the optimum. Different results are obtained for the low multi modal functions $(f_{14} - f_{20})$, where all algorithms perform approximately the same and also have similar convergence rate (Figure 6).

From the examples above, the proposed method obviously performs better for high dimensional problems $(f_1 - f_{13})$ and approximately has the same performance for low dimensional problems $(f_{14} - f_{20})$. In terms of its modality, lower rate of move off increases the convergence speed for unimodal problems. In these problems, the local optimum is equivalent with the global optima; and therefore, information sharing also speeds up the convergence rate because the search is focused nearby the good solution. For high modality problems, the *move off* mechanism plays important roles in escaping the local optima. For these problems, higher rate of *move off* often produces better results.. In addition, the proposed method seems has fast convergence

Figure 4. The flowchart of soccer games optimization

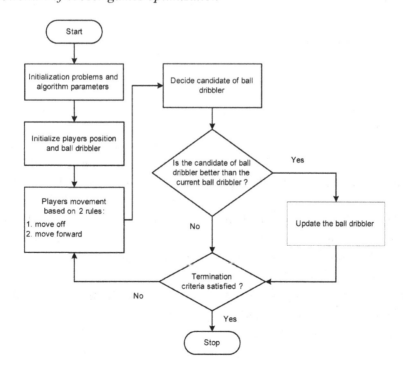

Figure 5. Illustration of the players' movements

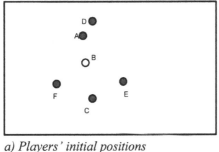

a) Players' initial positions

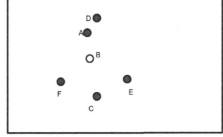

(b) Deciding the ball position-B

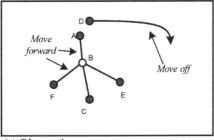

(c) Players' movements

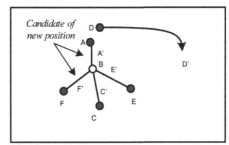

(d) Players' new positions

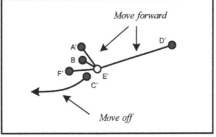

e) New ball position is updated – E'

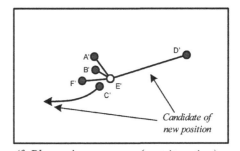

(f) Players' movements (next iteration)

speed in the beginning followed by slower convergence rate afterward.

Implementation on Two-Sided Assembly Lines Balancing Problems

We have also implemented the proposed method to solve two-sided assembly lines balancing problems (TALBP). The problems are important in manufacturing large size products such as cars and buses. The problems were firstly discussed by (Bartholdi, 1993) and then extended by many researchers such as Lee et al. (2001), Simaria and

Vilarinho (2009) and Kim et al.(2000). The assembly line is considered as pair-workstations, the left-side workstation and the right-side workstation, which are used in parallel. A pair-workstation performs different tasks simultaneously on the same individual product. The objective of the two-sided assembly lines balancing problems is to minimize the number of workstations for a given cycle time C. The configuration of two sided assembly lines is shown in Figure 7.

The notations used for the mathematical model are:

Table 3. Numerical benchmark problems

Test function	n	S	
$f_1 = \sum_i^n x_i^2$	50	$[-100, 100]^n$	0
$f_2 = \sum_{i=1}^n |x_i| + \prod_{i=2}^n |x_i|$	50	$[-10, 10]^n$	0
$f_3 = \sum_{i=1}^n \left(\sum_{j=1}^i x_j \right)^2$	50	$[-100, 100]^n$	0
$f_4 = max\left\{ |x_i|, 1 \le i \le n \right\}$	50	$[-100, 100]^n$	0
$f_5 = \sum_{i=1}^{n-1} \left[100 \left(x_{i+1} - x_i^2 \right)^2 + \left(x_i - 1 \right)^2 \right]$	50	$[-30, 30]^n$	0
$f_6 = \sum_{i=1}^n \left(\lfloor x_i + 0.5 \rfloor \right)^2$	50	$[-100, 100]^n$	0
$f_7 = \sum_{i=1}^n ix_i^4 + rand[0,1]$	50	$[-1.28, 1.28]^n$	0
$f_8 = \sum_{i=1}^n -x_i \sin\left(\sqrt{|x_i|} \right)$	50	$[-500, 500]^n$	-20949.14
$f_9 = \sum_{i=1}^n \left[x_i^2 - 10\cos\left(2\pi x_i \right) + 10 \right]$	50	$[-5.12, 5.12]^n$	0
$f_{10} = \sum_{i=1}^n -20\exp\left(-0.2\sqrt{\frac{1}{n}\sum_{i=1}^n x_i^2} \right)$ $- \exp\left(\frac{1}{n}\sum_{i=1}^n \cos\left(2\pi x_i \right) \right) + 20 + e$	50	$[-32, 32]^n$	0
$f_{11} = \frac{1}{4000}\sum_{i=1}^n x_i^2 - \prod_{i=1}^n \cos\left(\frac{x_i}{\sqrt{i}} \right) + 1$	50	$[-600, 600]^n$	0
$f_{12} = \frac{\pi}{n}\{10\sin^2\left(\pi y_i \right)$ $+ \sum_{i=1}^{n-1}\left(y_i - 1 \right)^2 \left[1 + 10\sin^2\left(\pi y_{i+1} \right) \right]$ $+ \left(y_n - 1 \right)^2\} + \sum_{i=1}^n u\left(x_i, 10, 100, 4 \right),$ $y_i = 1 + \frac{1}{4}\left(x_i + 1 \right)$ $u\left(x_i, a, k, m \right) = \begin{cases} k\left(x_i - a \right)^m & x_i > a \\ 0 & -a \le x_i \le a \\ k\left(-x_i - a \right)^m & x_i < -a \end{cases}$	50	$[-50, 50]^n$	0

continued on following page

Table 3. Continued

Test function	n	S	
$f_{13} = 0.1\{\sin^2(3\pi x_1)$ $+ \sum_{i=1}^{n-1}(x_i - 1)^2 \left[1 + \sin^2(3\pi x_{i+1})\right]$ $+ (x_n - 1)\left[1 + \sin^2(2\pi x_n)\right]\}$ $+ \sum_{i=1}^{n} u(x_i, 5, 100, 4)$	50	$[-50, 50]^n$	-1.15
$f_{14} = \left[\dfrac{1}{500} + \sum_{j=1}^{25} \dfrac{1}{j + \sum_{i=1}^{2}(x_i - a_{ij})^6}\right]^{-1}$	2	$[-65.54, 65.54]^n$	0.998
$f_{15} = \sum_{i=1}^{11}\left[a_i - \dfrac{x_1(b_i^2 + b_i x_2)}{b_i^2 + b_i x_3 + x_3}\right]^2$	4	$[-5, 5]^n$	0.0003075
$f_{16} = 4x_1^2 - 2.1x_1^4 + \dfrac{1}{3}x_1^6 + x_1 x_2 - 2x_2^2 + 4x_2^4$	2	$[-5, 5]^n$	-1.0316
$f_{17} = \left(x_2 - \dfrac{5.1}{4\pi^2}x_1^2 + \dfrac{5}{\pi}x_1 - 6\right)^2$ $+ 10\left(1 - \dfrac{1}{8\pi}\right)\cos x_1 + 10$	2	$[-15, 15]^n$	0.398
$f_{18} = [1 + (x_1 + x_2 + 1)^2 (19 - 14x_1 + 3x_1^2 - 14x_2$ $+ 6x_1 x_2 + 3x_2^2)] \times [30 + (2x_1 - 3x_2)^2$ $(18 - 32x_1 + 12x_1^2 + 48x_2 - 36x_1 x_2$ $+ 27x_2^2)]$	2	$[-2, 2]^n$	3
$f_{19} = -\sum_{i=1}^{4} c_i \exp\left[-\sum_{j=1}^{4} a_{ij}(x_j - p_{ij})^2\right]$	3	$[0, 1]^n$	-3.86
$f_{20} = -\sum_{i=1}^{4} c_i \exp\left[-\sum_{j=1}^{6} a_{ij}(x_j - p_{ij})^2\right]$	6	$[0, 1]^n$	-3.32

- WE : Workstation efficiency
- WB : The workload balance between workstations
- w : Number of workstations
- n : Number of tasks
- t_i : Processing time of task i
- t_i^s : Start time of task i
- t_i^f : Finish time of task i
- C: Cycle time

Table 4. Result for benchmark problems with 50 dimensions (mean and standard deviation of 30 runs). The best performing algorithm(s) is emphasized in boldface

f(x)	# eval	PSO		GA-LX		SGO	
		mean	stdev	mean	stdev	mean	stdev
1	500K	1.40E-17	2.64E-17	7.15E-01	1.09E-01	**1.85E-30**	3.54E-30
2	500K	3.41E+02	1.63E+02	2.87E+00	1.96E-01	**5.08E-16**	3.23E-16
3	500K	3.83E+04	1.03E+04	2.97E+04	6.20E+03	**2.93E+01**	1.08E+01
4	500K	1.50E+00	2.97E+00	7.68E-01	9.88E-02	**1.22E-03**	4.08E-04
5	500K	4.51E+03	4.84E+03	3.89E+01	3.80E+01	**2.95E+01**	3.89E+01
6	500K	3.35E+01	1.80E+01	2.83E+01	3.34E+00	**0.00E+00**	0.00E+00
7	500K	2.98E+01	2.16E+01	**1.07E-02**	2.72E-03	1.38E-02	3.24E-03
8	500K	-1.17E+04	8.36E+02	**-2.09E+04**	6.23E-03	-2.04E+04	2.62E+02
9	500K	2.97E+02	6.19E+01	2.83E+01	4.54E+00	**2.23E+00**	1.64E+00
10	500K	1.73E+01	4.10E+00	1.78E-01	1.67E-02	**6.89E-14**	1.14E-14
11	500K	**9.43E-03**	1.33E-02	5.17E-01	7.38E-02	4.82E-02	4.35E-02
12	500K	9.45E+00	1.83E+00	2.00E-03	1.21E-03	**2.40E-31**	3.67E-31
13	500K	2.78E-01	9.61E-01	-3.95E-01	2.75E-01	**-1.15E+00**	2.41E-08
14	20K	**9.98E-01**	2.00E-16	**9.98E-01**	1.14E-10	**9.98E-01**	3.02E-16
15	20K	**8.63E-04**	4.93E-03	3.30E-03	4.74E-03	4.12E-03	7.40E-03
16	20K	**-1.03E+00**	4.46E-16	**-1.03E+00**	5.58E-07	**-1.03E+00**	2.73E-14
17	20K	**3.98E-01**	0.00E+00	**3.98E-01**	3.13E-07	**3.98E-01**	4.69E-14
18	20K	**3.00E+00**	4.66E-15	**3.00E+00**	5.73E-05	**3.00E+00**	3.58E-15
19	20K	**-3.86E+00**	2.26E-15	**-3.86E+00**	7.95E-07	**-3.86E+00**	2.31E-15
20	20K	-3.27E+00	6.09E-02	**-3.28E+00**	5.83E-02	**-3.28E+00**	5.83E-02

- $\bar{d}$: Average idle time
- x_{ik} : A decision variable
- I : Set of tasks, $I = \{1, 2, \ldots, i, \ldots, n\}$
- I_L : Set of tasks that must be assigned in the left side; $I_L \in I$
- I_R : Set of tasks that must be assigned in the right side; $I_R \in I$
- I_E : Set of tasks that must be assigned in either side; $I_E \in I$
- $P(j)$: Set of immediate predecessors of task j
- LB : Lower bound

The primary objective of the TALBP is minimizing the number of workstations for a given cycle time which is equivalent to reducing the idle time as much as possible. Assembly lines with a small amount of idle time offer high efficiency. The assembly line efficiency is defined as:

$$WE = \frac{\sum_{i=1}^{n} t_i}{wC}; \quad i \in I \qquad (11)$$

Besides decreasing the idle time, the tasks should be distributed as equally as possible to balance the workload of the workstations. The distribution of the task's processing time across

Figure 6. Average best fitness curve (all the results are the mean of 30 runs)

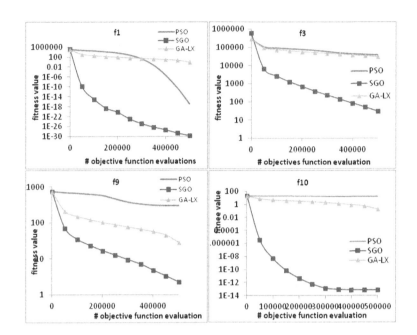

the workstations can also be done by distributing the idle time (Simaria & Vilarinho, 2009). In this paper, the standard deviation of the idle time is used to measure the distribution of tasks. Lower standard deviation means the processing time is distributed more equally. The average idle time in a workstation is given by:

$$\bar{d} = \frac{wC - \sum_{i=1}^{n} t_i}{w} \qquad (12)$$

Then, the workload balance between workstations is formulated as:

$$WB = \frac{\sqrt{\sum_{k=1}^{w} \left(C - \sum_{i=1}^{n} x_{ik} t_i - \bar{d} \right)^2}}{wC} \qquad (13)$$

Equation (11) is a maximization function while Equation (13) is a minimization function. The objective of the proposed TALBP model is defined as:

Figure 7. Two-sided assembly line

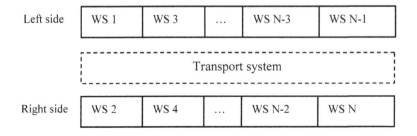

$$Maximize \quad F = \alpha WE - \beta WB \qquad (14)$$

$$subject \ to: \quad \sum_{k=1}^{w} x_{ik} = 1, \quad i \in I \qquad (15)$$

$$\sum_{k=1}^{w} \frac{2 * x_{ik}}{\mathrm{mod}(k,2)+1} = 1, \quad i \in I_L \qquad (16)$$

$$\sum_{k=1}^{w} \mathrm{mod}(k,2)x_{ik} + x_{ik} = 1, \quad i \in I_R \qquad (17)$$

$$\sum_{k=1}^{w} \left(\left\lceil \frac{k}{2} \right\rceil - 1 \right) x_{ik}C + t_i^f$$
$$\leq \sum_{k=1}^{w} \left(\frac{k}{2} - 1 \right) x_{jk}C + t_j^s, \quad for\ all\ i \in P(j) \qquad (18)$$

$$\sum_{k=1}^{w} \left(\left\lceil \frac{k}{2} \right\rceil - 1 \right) x_{ik}C + t_i^s =$$
$$\sum_{k=1}^{w} \left(\frac{k}{2} - 1 \right) x_{jk}C + t_j^s, \qquad (19)$$

$$\sum_{k=1}^{w} (k-1) x_{ik}C + t_i^f \leq \sum_{k=1}^{w} (k-1) x_{jk}C + t_j^s, \qquad (20)$$

$$\sum_{k=1}^{w} (k-1) x_{jk}C + t_j^f \leq \sum_{k=1}^{w} (k-1) x_{ik}C + t_i^s, \qquad (21)$$

$$x_{ik}.t_i^f \leq C \qquad (22)$$

$$\sum_{k=1}^{w} \frac{k}{2} x_{ik} = \sum_{k=1}^{w} \frac{k}{2} x_{jk}, \quad zoning \ \ positive \qquad (23)$$

$$\sum_{k=1}^{w} \frac{k}{2} x_{ik} \neq \sum_{k=1}^{w} \frac{k}{2} x_{jk}, \quad zoning \ \ negative \qquad (24)$$

The objective function in (14) is to minimize the number of workstation by reducing the idle time and balancing the assembly lines. Constraint (15) ensures that each task is assigned to only one workstation. Constraints (16) and (17) are the additional occurrence constraints that are needed in TALBP. Constraint (16) ensures each left-side task is assigned to the left workstation while equation (17) ensures each right-side task is assigned to the right workstation. Constraint (18) is precedence constraints. For each mated-workstation, they will be indexed in the same position by $\frac{k}{2}$. For every pair of tasks i and j such that i is an immediate predecessor of j, if they are assigned in a mated-workstation, the constraint is reduced to $t_i^f \leq t_j^s$, which means that task j can be started after task i is finished. Constraint (19) is applied to every pair of synchronous tasks in which each pair of the task must be started at the same time. Constraints (20) and (21) are applied to two tasks that do not have precedence relations. The constraints ensure that only one task is assigned in a workstation at a time. If task i is assigned earlier than j, and they are assigned in the same workstation, then constraint (20) becomes $t_i^f \leq t_j^s$. On the other hand, if task j is assigned earlier than i, and they are assigned in the same workstation, then constraint (21) becomes $t_j^f \leq t_i^s$. Constraint (22) ensures that the finished time of a task is less than

Figure 8. Problem P 9

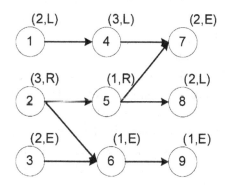

407

Table 5. Example of task assignment

Task assigned							
Left side				**Right side**			
Workstation number	Task	Start time	Finished time	Workstation number	Task	Start time	Finished time
1	1	0	2	2	2	0	3
	4	2	5		5	3	4
3	7	0	2	4	3	0	2
	8	2	4		6	2	3
					9	3	4

Figure 9. The individual representation and the sequence of the tasks

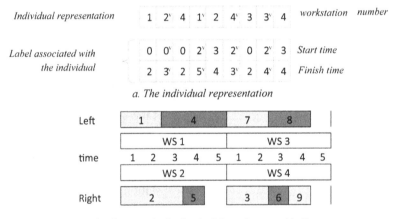

a. The individual representation

b. Illustration of task schedule in the assembly line

or equal to the cycle time. Constraints (23) and (24) are positive zoning and negative zoning respectively.

To illustrate the problem representation of the proposed method, let us consider a small-sized problem consisting of 9 tasks called P9 as shown in Figure 8. This problem can be found in Kim et al. (2000).

Suppose there are four workstations and the tasks are assigned according to Table 5, the individual representation of the example is (1 2 4 1 2 4 3 3 4). Through this representation, a workstation number will also specify the workstation side. In this paper, odd numbers represent the left workstation whereas even numbers are for the right workstation. The individual representation

and the sequence of the tasks in the assembly line can be illustrated in Figure 9.

Figure 9 (b) describes the task sequence in the assembly lines. Task 1 is assigned in the left workstation (WS 1) and task 2 is assigned in the right workstation (WS 2). Both tasks are started at the same time. Task 4 is assigned in WS 1 and is started immediately after task 1 is finished. Task 5 is assigned in WS 2 and is started immediately after task 2 is finished.

There are three parts of the proposed method that will be explained in this section: initialization, the *move off* and the *move forward*. The COMSOAL heuristic method (Arcus, 1966) is adopted for the initialization and reassigning procedure.

Initialization

The initialization steps are given as follows:

Step 1: Open the first mated-workstation. The left side workstation $wl = 1$, while the right workstation $wr = 2$. List all unassigned tasks UT.

Step 2: From UT, list all tasks in which their predecessors have been assigned (F).

Step 3: Select a task from F based on the selection rules.

Step 4: If the selected task has a specific operations direction; put the task in the appropriate side. If the finished time of the task is less than the cycle time C, put the task in that workstation; otherwise, open a new workstation based on the task's specific operations direction. If the selected task can be placed in either side, select the side in which it finishes earlier. If both sides have the same finished time, then select the side randomly.

Step 5: Remove the selected task for UT.

Step 6: If all tasks have been assigned, then stop; otherwise, go to step 2.

The selection rules in Step 3 are: (1) MAX-RPW: a task selection based on the Maximum Ranked Positional Weight, (2) MAX-TFOL: a task selection based on the Maximum Total Follower, (3) MAX-FOL: a task selection based on the Maximum number of directs Follower, (4) MAX-DUR: a task selection based on the Maximum Operation Time and (5) random selection.

The Move Off

The proposed move off is performed by reassigning tasks that starts from the randomly selected mated-workstation. Assume the selected mated-workstation $r = 1$ (the mated-workstation consists of workstation 1 and 2), then the reassignment process is started from workstation 3. Using the

Figure 10. Move off for TALBP

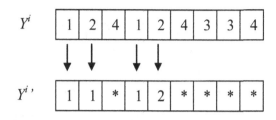

example P9 in Figure 6, the move off procedure is illustrated in Figure 10.

The procedure for the move off is described as follows:

Step 1: Generate an integer number r from [1, $w/2$] to decide the starting mated-workstation

Step 2: Copy all tasks from workstation 1 to workstation $2r$ in the Y^i to the new player position Y^i'.

Step 3: To assign the remaining task in the new player position Y^i', the reassigning procedure is performed as follows

Step 3.1: Identify all tasks that have not been assigned, UT

Step 3.2: Create a set of tasks, F, from UT such that all their predecessors have been assigned

Step 3.3: Select a task from F based on the selection rules

Step 3.4: If the selected task has a specific operation direction; put the task in the appropriate side. If the finished time of the task is less than the cycle time C, put the task in that workstation; otherwise, open a new workstation based on the task's specific operation direction. If the selected task can be placed in either side, select the side in which it finishes earlier. If both sides have the same finished time, then select the side randomly.

Step 3.5: Remove the selected task for UT

Step 3.6: If all tasks have been assigned, then stop; otherwise, go to step 3.2.

Figure 11. Move forward for TALBP

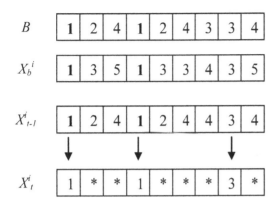

The Move Forward

In the *move* forward, the ball position B_{t-1}, the player's current position X^i_{t-1} and the player's best position X^i_b are considered to decide the player's new position. The move forward will transmit the tasks that are assigned in the same workstation in all the three positions mentioned above $(B, X^i_{t-1}$ and $X^i_b)$ while the remaining tasks will be reassigned. The *move forward* is illustrated in Figure 11.

The procedure for the move forward is described as follows:

Step 1: Copy all tasks that are assigned in the same workstation in all the B, X^i_{t-1} and X^i_b into the player's new position X^i_t.

Step 2: The reassigning procedure for the *move forward* is given as follows

Step 2.1: Identify all tasks that have not been assigned, *UT*

Step 2.2: Create a set of tasks, *F*, from *UT* such that all their predecessors have been assigned

Step 2.3: Select task *i* in *F* based on the selection rules

Step 2.4: Determine the possible earliest workstation e_i and the latest workstation l_i to define the feasible workstation *FS* for *i*.

Step 2.5: Calculate the total processing time of workstation *w* when task *i* is assigned to *w*. $e_i \leq w \leq l_i$. Task *i* is assigned to the first workstation that fulfills the cycle time and task operation direction.

Step 2.6: Remove the selected task for *UT*

Step 2.7: If all tasks have been assigned, then stop; otherwise, go to step 2.2.

The *move forward* procedure above only decides the workstation for each task. In the *move forward*, there is a chance that the player's new position X^i_t will violate the problem constraint, especially the cycle time constraint. In this case, the player's new position is set the same as the player's previous position $X^i_t = X^i_{t-1}$.

The performance of the proposed method is evaluated based on five benchmark functions: P12, P16, P24, P65 and P148 which are commonly used in the TALBP. Problems P12 and P24 can be found in Kim et al. (2000), problem P16 is mentioned in Kim et al. (2009) and problem P148 is introduced by Bartholdi (1993). The modification of P148 as in Lee et al. (2001) is used where the processing time of tasks 79 and 108 were changed from 281 to 111 and from 383 to 43. The parameter of the SGO was set with the following probability of *move off* where *m = 0.5, k = 0.3* and *l = 0.1*. The experiments were run 10 times for each problem. The number of maximum objective function evaluation for P12 was 500, P16 and P24 were 5000, P65 was 10000, and P148 was 20000.

The experiment results for the problems are given in Table 6 and Table 7.

For the small size problems, the proposed method is compared to the Mixed Integer Programming, which is an exact solution method. Columns *C* and *LB* represent the given cycle time and the lower bound respectively. The results of the experiments show that the proposed method achieves the optimal solution for all given problems.

Table 6. The result for small size problems of two-sided assembly lines balancing problems

Problem	C	LB	Mixed integer programming	SGO		
				avg	min	stdev
P12	5	5	6	6	6	0
	7	4	4	4	4	0
P16	16	6	6	6	6	0
	22	4	4	4	4	0
P24	18	8	8	8	8	0
	20	7	8	8	8	0

Table 7. Result for large size problems of two-sided assembly lines balancing problems

Problem	C	LB	2-ANTBL (Simaria & Vilarinho, 2009)			Lee et al., (2001)		SGO		
			mean	min	max	H	G	mean	min	max
P65	326	16	**17.0**	17	17	17.7	17.4	**17.0**	17	17
	381	14	**14,8**	14	15	15.7	15.0	**14.8**	14	15
	435	12	**13.0**	13	13	14.0	13.4	**13.0**	13	13
	490	11	12.0	12	12	12.1	12.0	**11.9**	11	12
	544	10	10.8	10	11	11.5	**10.6**	**10.6**	10	11
P148	204	26	**26.0**	26	26	27.8	27.0	26.2	26	27
	255	21	**21.0**	21	21	22.0	21.0	**21.0**	21	21
	306	17	18.0	18	18	19.3	18.0	**17.4**	17	18
	357	15	15.4	15	16	16.0	**15.0**	**15.0**	15	15
	408	13	**14.0**	14	14	**14.0**	**14.0**	**14.0**	13	13
	459	12	**12.0**	12	12	12.1	13.0	**12.0**	12	12
	510	11	**11.0**	11	11	12.0	**11.0**	**11.0**	11	11

For the large size problems, the proposed method is compared to heuristic rules *H* and group assignment *G* proposed by Lee et al. (2001) and the 2-ANTBAL proposed by (Simaria & Vilarinho, (2009). Columns Mean, Min and Max respectively represent the average, minimum and maximum number of workstations computed from 10 runs for each instance of the problems. The best solution for each instance problem is given in bold.

The experiment results show that the proposed method clearly outperforms the heuristic rules and group assignment procedure as it produces better solution in most problems. When compared to the 2-ANTBAL, the proposed method performs better in 4 problems, performs the same in 7 problems (mainly because the solutions are already the optimal solutions) and slightly worse in 1 problem.

DISCUSSION

As mentioned before, balancing the intensification and diversification is important as they significantly influence the performance of the metaheuristics. Intensification is useful to advance the convergence by limiting the randomness. However, when it is carried too strongly, it could lead to premature convergence as the search space is not well explored. On the other hand, when the intensification is too weak, the convergence becomes very slow. Diversification is used to ensure that the search space is explored well in an effective and efficient way. Investigating as many regions as possible in the search space can minimize the chance to be trapped in local optima. However, when diversification is too strong, it could slow down the convergence because the algorithm examines too many regions in stochastic manner. On the other hand, if the diversification is too weak, the solution may be biased in local optima (Yang, 2009).

In the SGO, the intensification is mainly controlled by the move forward operator. In the move forward, intensification is carried out using memory. In the movement, a player considers the ball dribbler's position, his current position and his experiences. It can be seen that the movement integrates the social as well as cognitive learning where a player receives information about the ball dribbler's position, his current position and his own experience (his best position). An illustration of search area for move forward is shown in Figure 12. The other operator, the move off, is basically a global search in which a player can explore the whole search space in stochastic manner. The move

off is used to maintain the diversity of potential solution and is similar to the biological mutation. Therefore, the move off is more likely a mutation in the evolution algorithm.

Based on the intensification and diversification frame, I&D frame by Blum and Roli (2003), the move off operator is not guided by the objective function. It involves randomness and may involve memory. Therefore, the operator is close to the R (randomness) and NOG (non objective guided) side, with higher diversification effect. The move forward uses memory and it is guided by the objective function (the ball dribbler selection is based on the objective function). In the frame, the move forward is close to the OG corner, which has higher intensification effect (see Figure 13).

The SGO provide a new approach in integrating the evolutionary algorithm and swarm intelligent algorithm. It differ with other hybrid algorithm such as GA-PSO, in term that the SGO operators integrates the evolution operators and the information sharing at conceptual level. The operator's mechanisms already incorporate the basic principles of evolutionary algorithms and swarm intelligence algorithms. On the other hand, the hybrid algorithms commonly only combine the algorithms at upper level; therefore, they still use the original operators of the algorithms composing it. For example, the hybrid algorithm of PSO and GA will remain using the velocity update in its operation, while the proposed algorithm

Figure 12. The local search area

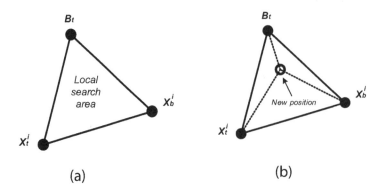

(a)   (b)

Figure 13. The move off and move forward in the I&D frame

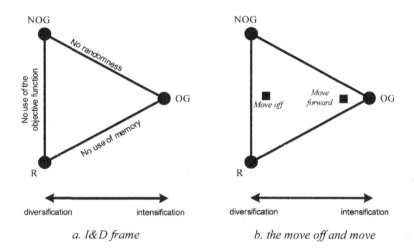

a. I&D frame   b. the move off and move

adopts the central of mass principle for its local search.

The advantages of the SGO are mainly due to the integration of evolution operators and the information sharing. The evolution operators provide flexible encoding and decoding mechanism for both continuous and discrete problem while the information sharing could drives the search process better. The flexibility of encoding mechanism can be observed in the problem example for both continuous and discrete problem. The encoding schema follows the common schema in the evolutionary algorithms. The benefit of information sharing can be observed in the example of continuous problem where the proposed method can solve the high dimensionality and high modality problems better than the GA and PSO. The information sharing can lead the search process into promising search space faster than the basic GA and PSO. From the experimental result we can see that the proposed method is a powerful optimization algorithm. However, there are several questions that need to be further investigated such as; deciding the optimal parameters tuning for particular problems and building theoretical framework.

FUTURE RESEARCH DIRECTIONS

Future research can be done to enhance the proposed method. In mimicking the soccer player movements, there are many aspects that have not been implemented and investigated in the method. For instance, the movements of a defender are usually not as aggressive as the movements of a striker, and a playmaker has more opportunities to control the flow of the ball to other players. This reveals that the individual in the population could be classified into several types in which each of them has different task priorities.

Other research can be done to investigate the sensitivity of parameter setting and the theoretical framework as well as analyze the strengths and weaknesses of the method. Some general issues are also important to be considered, such as determining factors that are needed to speed up the convergence process, increasing the effectiveness of the method and proving global optima. Another possible development is to assess the proposed method on different problems such as on constraint continuous problems, travelling salesman problems, vehicle routing problems, quadratic assignment problems, multi objective problems, dynamic problems, etc.

CONCLUSION

A new metaheuristic method has been proposed and discussed in this paper. The proposed method uses novel approach of hybrid evolutionary algorithm and swarm intelligence algorithm by integrates the evolution operators and the information sharing at conceptual level. This approach differ from commonly know hybrid algorithm which only combine the algorithms at upper level; therefore, they still use the original operators of the algorithms composing it. The proposed method has two main operators, the *move off* and the *move forward*, to balance the intensification as well as the diversification during the search process. The operators integrate the social learning and cognitive learning from the swarm intelligence as well as the evolution operators in the evolution algorithm.

The proposed method has been assessed on continuous and discrete problems. Based on the experiments, the proposed method inherit the flexible encoding and decoding mechanism in the evolutionary algorithm as well as the benefit of information sharing in swarm intelligence algorithm. Information sharing will guide the search process into promising area quickly. From the implementation and comparison result we can see that the proposed method is potentially a powerful optimization technique.

As a new method, there are still many opportunities to enhance the SGO. The proposed method is a simplification model of soccer player movements; therefore more aspects of the game can be elaborate to the method. Besides, the investigation about the sensitivity of the parameter setting and the application of the proposed method into various optimization problems will become a significant contribution in the development of the method. In addition, as there is a lack of solid theoretical framework in meta-heuristics field. This bring challenge to researchers to cope with several issues such as determine factors that are needed to speed up the convergence process for a given problem, increasing the effectiveness of the method for a specific problem and how to prove the global optima are reached by the method.

REFERENCES

Arcus, A. (1966). COMSOAL: A computer method of sequencing operations for assembly lines. *International Journal of Production Research*, *4*, 259–277. doi:10.1080/00207546508919982

Bartholdi, J. J. (1993). Balancing two-sided assembly lines: A case study. *International Journal of Production Research*, *31*, 2447–2461. doi:10.1080/00207549308956868

Beyer, H. G. (2001). *The theory of evolution strategies*. Germany: Springer.

Bianchi, L., Dorigo, M., Gambardella, L. M., & Gutjahr, W. J. (2008). A survey on metaheuristics for stochastic combinatorial optimization. *Natural Computing*, *8*(2), 239–287. doi:10.1007/s11047-008-9098-4

Blum, C., Puchinger, J., Raidl, G. R., & Roli, A. (2011). Hybrid metaheuristics in combinatorial optimization: A survey. *Applied Soft Computing*, *11*, 4135–4151. doi:10.1016/j.asoc.2011.02.032

Blum, C., & Roli, A. (2003). Metaheuristic in combinatorial optimization: Overview and conceptual comparison. *ACM Computing Surveys*, *35*(3), 268–308. doi:10.1145/937503.937505

Bonabeau, E., Dorigo, M., & Theraulaz, G. (1999). *Swarm Intelligence: From natural to artificial systems*. New York, NY: Oxford University Press.

Chellapilla, K. (1998). Combining mutation operators in evolutionary programming. *IEEE Transactions on Evolutionary Computation*, *2*, 91–96. doi:10.1109/4235.735431

Chen, P. H., & Shahandashti, S. Y. (2009). Hybrid of genetic algorithm and simulated annealing for multiple project scheduling with multiple resource constraints. *Automation in Construction, 18,* 434–443. doi:10.1016/j.autcon.2008.10.007

Cheng, C. T., Liao, S. L., Tang, Z. T., & Zhao, M. Y. (2009). Comparison of particle swarm optimization and dynamic programming for large scale hydro unit load dispatch. *Energy Conversion and Management, 50,* 3007–3014. doi:10.1016/j.enconman.2009.07.020

Chiong, R., Neri, F., & McKay, R. I. (2009). Nature that breeds solution. In Chiong, R. (Ed.), *Nature-inspired informatics for intelligent applications and knowledge discovery: Implications in business, science and engineering* (pp. 1–24). Hershey, PA: IGI Global. doi:10.4018/978-1-60566-705-8.ch001

Clerc, M., & Kennedy, J. (2002). The particle swarm—Explosion, stability, and convergence in a multidimensional complex space. *IEEE Transactions on Evolutionary Computation, 6,* 58–73. doi:10.1109/4235.985692

Coello, C. A. C. (2000). Use of a self-adaptive penalty approach for engineering optimization problems. *Computers in Industry, 41,* 113–127. doi:10.1016/S0166-3615(99)00046-9

Deep, K., & Bansal, J. C. (2009). Mean particle swarm optimization for function optimization. *International Journal of Computational Intelligence Studies, 1,* 72–92.

Deep, K., & Thakur, M. (2007a). A new crossover operator for real coded genetic algorithms. *Applied Mathematics and Computation, 188,* 895–911. doi:10.1016/j.amc.2006.10.047

Deep, K., & Thakur, M. (2007b). A new mutation operators for real coded genetic algorithms. *Applied Mathematics and Computation, 193,* 211–230. doi:10.1016/j.amc.2007.03.046

Degertekin, S. (2008). Optimum design of steel frames using harmony search algorithm. *Structural and Multidisciplinary Optimization, 36,* 393–401. doi:10.1007/s00158-007-0177-4

Deng, G. F., & Lin, W. T. (2011). Ant colony optimization-based algorithm for airline crew scheduling problem. *Expert Systems with Applications, 38,* 5787–5793. doi:10.1016/j.eswa.2010.10.053

Dorigo, M., & Caro, G. D. (1999). Ant colony optimization: A new meta-heuristic. *Proceedings of the 1999 Congress on Evolutionary Computation,* (pp. 1470-1477).

Dorigo, M., & Stuzle, T. (2004). *Ant colony optimization.* Cambridge, MA: MIT Press. doi:10.1007/b99492

Dumitrescu, D., Lazzerini, B., Jain, L. C., & Dumitrescu, A. (2000). Evolution strategies and evolutionary programming. In *Evolutionary computation* (pp. 261–281). The CRC Press International Series on Computational Intelligence.

Geem, Z. W. (2000). *Optimal design of water distribution networks using harmony search.* Unpublished doctoral dissertation, Korea University.

Geem, Z. W., Kim, J. H., & Loganathan, G. V. (2001). A new heuristic optimization algorithm: Harmony search. *Simulation, 76,* 60–68. doi:10.1177/003754970107600201

Geem, Z. W., Lee, K. S., & Park, Y. (2005). Application of harmony search to vehicle routing. *American Journal of Applied Sciences, 2*(12), 1552–1557. doi:10.3844/ajassp.2005.1552.1557

Glover, F. (1986). Future paths for integer programming and links to artificial intelligence. *Computers & Operations Research, 13*(5), 533–549. doi:10.1016/0305-0548(86)90048-1

Glover, F. (1990). Tabu search - Part II. *ORSA Journal on Computing, 2,* 4–32. doi:10.1287/ijoc.2.1.4

Glover, F., & Laguna, M. (1997). *Tabu search.* Kluwer Academic Publisher. doi:10.1007/978-1-4615-6089-0

Goldberg, D. E. (1989). *Genetic algorithms in search, optimization, and machine learning.* Addison-Wesley.

Hertz, A., & Widmer, M. (2003). Guidelines for the use of meta-heuristics in combinatorial optimization. *European Journal of Operational Research, 151,* 247–252. doi:10.1016/S0377-2217(02)00823-8

Holland, J. H. (1975). *Adaptation in natural and artificial systems.* Ann Arbor, MI: University of Michigan Press.

Hung, K.-S., Su, S.-F., & Lee, Z.-J. (2007). Improving ant colony optimization algorithms for solving traveling salesman problems. *Journal of Advanced Computational Intelligence and Intelligent Informatics, 11,* 433–442.

Kao, Y. T., & Zahara, E. (2008). A hybrid genetic algorithm and particle swarm optimization for multimodal functions. *Applied Soft Computing, 8,* 849–857. doi:10.1016/j.asoc.2007.07.002

Katagiri, H., Hayashida, T., Nishizaki, I., & Guo, Q. (2012). A hybrid algorithm based on tabu search and ant colony optimization for k-minimum spanning tree problems. *Expert Systems with Applications, 39,* 5681–5686. doi:10.1016/j.eswa.2011.11.103

Kennedy, J., & Eberhart, R. (1995). Particle swarm optimization. *Proceedings of IEEE International Conference on Neural Networks, IV,* (pp. 1942-1948).

Kennedy, J. & Eberhart, R. C. (2001). *Swarm intelligence.* Morgan Kaufmann Publisher, San Fransisco.

Kim, Y. K., Kim, Y., & Kim, Y. J. (2000). Two-sided assembly line balancing: A genetic algorithm approach. *Production Planning and Control, 11,* 44–53. doi:10.1080/095372800232478

Kim, Y. K., Song, W. S., & Kim, J. H. (2009). A mathematical model and a genetic algorithm for two-sided assembly line balancing. *Computers & Operations Research, 36*(3), 853–865. doi:10.1016/j.cor.2007.11.003

Kıran, M. S., Ozceylan, E., Gunduz, M., & Paksoy, T. (2012). A novel hybrid approach based on particle swarm optimization and ant colony algorithm to forecast energy demand of Turkey. *Energy Conversion and Management, 53,* 75–83. doi:10.1016/j.enconman.2011.08.004

Kirkpatrick, S., Gelatt, C. D. Jr, & Vecchi, M. P. (1983). Optimization by simulated annealing. *Science, 220,* 671–680. doi:10.1126/science.220.4598.671

Lee, K., & El-Sharkawi, M. A. (2002). *Modern heuristic optimization techniques with applications to power systems.* IEEE Power Engineering Society (02TP160).

Lee, K. S., & Geem, Z. W. (2005). A new meta-heuristic algorithm for continuous engineering optimization: Harmony search theory and practice. *Computer Methods in Applied Mechanics and Engineering, 194,* 3902–3933. doi:10.1016/j.cma.2004.09.007

Lee, T. O., Kim, Y., & Kim, Y. K. (2001). Two-sided assembly line balancing to maximize work relatedness and slackness. *Computers & Industrial Engineering, 40,* 273–292. doi:10.1016/S0360-8352(01)00029-8

Lee, Z. J., Su, H. F., Chuang, C. C., & Liu, K. H. (2008). Genetic algorithm with ant colony optimization (GA-ACO) for multiple sequence alignment. *Applied Soft Computing, 8*(1), 55–78. doi:10.1016/j.asoc.2006.10.012

Lin, C. C. (2006). A genetic algorithm for solving the two-dimensional assortment problem. *Computers & Industrial Engineering, 50*(1-2), 175–184. doi:10.1016/j.cie.2006.03.002

Luke, S. (2009). *Essentials of metaheuristics*. Lulu. Retrieved January 20th, 2012, from http://cs.gmu.edu/:sean/book/metaheuristics/

Marinakis, Y., & Marinaki, M. (2010). A hybrid genetic – Particle swarm optimization algorithm for the vehicle routing problem. *Expert Systems with Applications, 37*, 1446–1455. doi:10.1016/j.eswa.2009.06.085

Melo, M. T., Nickel, S., & Saldanha-da-Gama, F. (2012). A tabu search heuristic for redesigning a multi-echelon supply chain network over a planning horizon. *International Journal of Production Economics, 136*, 218–230. doi:10.1016/j.ijpe.2011.11.022

Michalewicz, Z. (1992). *Genetic algorithm + data structures = evolution programs*. Springer-Verlag.

Purnomo, H. D., Wee, H. M., & Rau, H. (2011). Two-sided assembly lines balancing with assignment restrictions. *Mathematical and Computer Modelling*, in press. Retrieved from http://dx.doi.org/10.1016/j.mcm.2011.06.010

Rechenberg, I. (1973). *Evolutions strategie: Optimierung technischer systeme nach prinzipien der biologischen evolution*. Stuttgart, Germany: Frommann-Holzboog.

Schwefel, H.-P. (1975). *Technical evolutionsstrategie und numerische optimierung*. Dissertation, University of Berlin.

Shi, X. H., Liang, Y. C., Lee, H. P., Lu, C., & Wang, L. M. (2005). An improved GA and a novel PSO-GA-based hybrid algorithm. *Information Processing Letters, 93*, 255–261. doi:10.1016/j.ipl.2004.11.003

Shi, Y. H., & Eberhart, R. C. (1999). *Empirical study of particle swarm optimization*. 1999 Congress on Evolutionary Computation, Washington DC, USA, July

Shimizu, Y., Wada, T., & Yamazaki, Y. (2007). Logistics optimization using hybrid metaheuristic approach under very realistic conditions. *Computer Aided Chemical Engineering, 24*, 733–738. doi:10.1016/S1570-7946(07)80145-3

Silva, C. A., Sousa, J. M. C., Runkler, T. A., & Costa, J. M. G. (2009). Distributed supply chain management using ant colony optimization. *European Journal of Operational Research, 199*, 349–358. doi:10.1016/j.ejor.2008.11.021

Simaria, A. S., & Vilarinho, P. M. (2009). 2-ANT-BAL: An ant colony optimisation algorithm for balancing two-sided assembly lines. *Computers & Industrial Engineering, 56*, 489–506. doi:10.1016/j.cie.2007.10.007

Sorensen, K., & Glover, F. (in press). *Metaheuristics*. Retrieved January 15th, 2012, from http://www.opttek.com/sites/default/files/Metaheuristics.pdf

Sorensen, K., & Janssens, G. K. (2003). Data mining with genetic algorithms on binary trees. *European Journal of Operational Research, 151*, 253–264. doi:10.1016/S0377-2217(02)00824-X

Srinivasa, K. G., Venugopal, K. R., & Patnaik, L. M. (2007). A self-adaptive migration model genetic algorithm for data mining applications. *Information Sciences, 177*, 4295–4313. doi:10.1016/j.ins.2007.05.008

Talbi, E.-G. (2009). *Metaheuristics, from design to implementation*. Lille, France: John Wiley & Sons.

Tsai, J.-T., Liu, T.-K., & Chou, J.-H. (2004). Hybrid taguchi-genetic algorithm for global numerical optimization. *IEEE Transactions on Evolutionary Computation, 8*, 365–377. doi:10.1109/TEVC.2004.826895

Vesterstrom, J., & Thomsen, R. (2004). A comparative study of differential evolution, particle swarm optimization, and evolutionary algorithms on numerical benchmark problems. *Congress on Evolutionary Computation, 2*, 1980–1987.

Wang, H. F., & Hsu, H. W. (2010). A closed-loop logistic model with a spanning-tree based genetic algorithm. *Computers & Operations Research, 37*, 376–389. doi:10.1016/j.cor.2009.06.001

Wolpert, D. H., & Macready, W. G. (1997). No free lunch theorems for optimization. *IEEE Transactions on Evolutionary Computation, 1*(1), 67–82. doi:10.1109/4235.585893

Yang, X.-S. (2009). *Harmony search as a metaheuristic algorithm. Music-inspired harmony search algorithm.* Heidelberg, Germany: Springer-Verlag Studies in Computational Intelligence.

Yao, X., Liu, Y., & Lin, G. (1999). Evolutionary programming made faster. *IEEE Transactions on Evolutionary Computation, 3*, 82–102. doi:10.1109/4235.771163

Yu, H., Fang, H., Yao, P., & Yuan, Y. (2000). A combined genetic algorithm:simulated annealing algorithm for large scale system energy integration. *Computers & Chemical Engineering, 24*, 2023–2035. doi:10.1016/S0098-1354(00)00601-3

Zhang, Y. H., Lei, F., & Zhi, Y. (2011). Optimization of cloud database route scheduling based on combination of genetic algorithm and ant colony algorithm. *Procedia Engineering, 15*, 3341–3345. doi:10.1016/j.proeng.2011.08.626

Zhao, X., Gao, X.-S., & Hu, Z.-C. (2007). Evolutionary programming based on non-uniform mutation. *Applied Mathematics and Computation, 192*, 1–11. doi:10.1016/j.amc.2006.06.107

ADDITIONAL READING

Atallah, M. J. (2009). *Algorithms and theory of computation handbook* (2nd ed.). CRC Press.

Back, T. (1996). *Evolutionary computation in theory and practice.* Oxford University Press.

Back, T., Fogel, D. B., & Michalewicz, Z. (1997). *Handbook of evolutionary computation.* Oxford University Press. doi:10.1887/0750308958

Back, T., Fogel, D. B., & Michalewicz, Z. (2000). *Evolutionary computation: Basic algorithms and operators.* Institute of Physics Publishing. doi:10.1887/0750306653

Blum, C., Aguilera, M. J. B., & Roli, A. (2008). *Hybrid metaheuristics: An emerging approach to optimization.* Berlin, Germany: Springer-Verlag.

Blum, C., & Merkle, D. (2008). *Swarm intelligence: Introduction and applications.* Springer.

Branke, J. (2001). *Evolutionary optimization in dynamics environment.* Springer.

Chelouah, R., & Siarry, P. (2000). A continuous genetic algorithm designed for the global optimization of multimodal functions. *Journal of Heuristics, 6*(2), 191–213. doi:10.1023/A:1009626110229

Clerc, M. (1999). The swarm and the queen: Towards a deterministic and adaptive particle swarm optimization. *IEEE Congress on Evolutionary Computation,* (pp. 1951-1957). Washington, DC.

Dasgupta, D., & Michalewicz, Z. (1997). *Evolutionary algorithms in engineering applications.* Springer.

Dean, A., & Voss, D. (1999). *Design and analysis of algorithms.* Springer.

Deb, K. (1999). Multi-objective genetic algorithms: Problem difficulties and construction of test problems. *Evolutionary Computation Journal, 7*(3), 201–230. doi:10.1162/evco.1999.7.3.205

Deb, K. (2001). *Multi-objective optimization using evolutionary algorithms.* John Wiley & Sons.

Dorigo, M., & Blum, C. (2005). Ant colony optimization theory: A survey. *Theoretical Computer Science, 344*, 243–278. doi:10.1016/j.tcs.2005.05.020

Eberhart, R. C., & Kennedy, J. (1995) A new optimizer using particle swarm theory. In *Proc. 6th International Symposium on Micro Machine and Human Science*, Nagoya, Japan, (pp. 39–43). Piscataway, NJ: IEEE Service Center.

Eiben, A. E., & Smith, J. E. (2003). *Introduction to evolutionary computing*. Springer.

Falkenauer, E. (1998). *Genetic algorithm and grouping problems*. Wiley.

Fogel, D. B. (1995). *Evolutionary computation: Toward a new philosophy of machine learning*. Piscataway, NJ: IEEE Press.

Fonseca, C. M., & Fleming, P. J. (1995). An overview of evolutionary algorithms in multiobjective optimization. *Evolutionary Computation, 3*, 1–16. doi:10.1162/evco.1995.3.1.1

Gendreau, M. (2002). An introduction to tabu search. In *Handbook of metaheuristics* (pp. 37–54). Kluwer.

Glover, F., & Kochenberger, G. A. (2003). *Handbook of metaheuristics*. The Netherlands: Kluwer's International Series.

Goldberg, D. E., Korb, B., & Deb, K. (1989). Messy genetic algorithms: Motivation, analysis and first result. *Complex Systems, 3*, 493–530.

Gutjahr, W. J. (2002). ACO algorithm with guaranteed convergence to the optimal solution. *Information Processing Letters, 82*(3), 145–153. doi:10.1016/S0020-0190(01)00258-7

Huang, M. D., Romeo, F., & Sangiocanni-Vincentelli, A. L. (1986). An efficient general cooling schedule for simulated annealing. *IEEE International Conference on Computer-Aided Design*, (pp. 381-384).

Ingber, L. (1996). Adaptive simulated annealing. *Control and Cybernetics, 25*(1), 33–54.

Jin, Y. (2005). A comprehensive survey of fitness approximation in evolutionary computation. *Soft Computing, 9*(1), 3–12. doi:10.1007/s00500-003-0328-5

Jin, Y., & Sendhoff, B. (2003). Trade-off between performance and robustness: An evolutionary multiobjective approach. In *Evolutionary Multi-Criterion Optimization, LNCS 2632*, (pp. 237-252).

Jones, T. (1995). *Evolutionary algorithms fitness landscapes and search*. Unpublished doctoral dissertation, University of Mexico, Albuquerque.

Kennedy, J. (1998). The behavior of particles. *International Conference on Evolutionary Programming VII*, (p. 1447).

Lam, J. (1988). *An efficient simulated annealing schedule*. Unpublished doctoral dissertation, Yale University.

Mitchell, M. (1996). *An introduction to genetic algorithms*. Cambridge, MA: MIT Press.

Muhlenbein, H. (1991). Evolution in time and space - The parallel genetic algorithm. In Rawlins, G. (Ed.), *Foundations of genetic algorithms* (pp. 316–337). Morgan-Kaufman.

Muhlenbein, H. (1992). How genetic algorithms really work- I: Mutation and hillclimbing. In Manner, R., & Manderick, B. (Eds.), *Parallel problem solving from nature (Vol. 2*, pp. 15–25). Amsterdam, The Netherlands: North Holland.

Preuxa, P., & Talbi, E. G. (1999). Towards hybrid evolutionary algorithms. *International Transactions in Operational Research, 6*, 557–570. doi:10.1111/j.1475-3995.1999.tb00173.x

Renders, J. M., & Flasse, S. P. (1996). Hybrid method using genetic algorithms for the global optimization. *IEEE Transactions on Systems, Man, and Cybernetics, 26*(2), 243–258. doi:10.1109/3477.485836

Rudolph, G. (1994). Convergence analysis of canonical genetic algorithms. *IEEE Transactions on Neural Networks*, 5(1), 96–101. doi:10.1109/72.265964

Shi, Y., & Eberhart, R. (1998). A modified particle swarm optimizer. *IEEE International Conference on Evolutionary Computation*, (pp. 67-73).

Socha, K., & Dorigo, M. (2008). Ant colony optimization for continuous domains. *European Journal of Operational Research*, 184, 1155–1173. doi:10.1016/j.ejor.2006.06.046

Talbi, E. G. (2002). A taxonomy of hybrid metaheuristics. *Journal of Heuristics*, 8, 541–564. doi:10.1023/A:1016540724870

Wei, L. Y., & Zhao, M. (2005). A niche hybrid genetic algorithm for global optimization of continuous multimodal functions. *Applied Mathematics and Computation*, 160(3), 649–661. doi:10.1016/j.amc.2003.11.023

Yao, X. (1999). *Evolutionary computation: Theory and applications*. Singapore: World Scientific.

KEY TERMS AND DEFINITIONS

Cognitive Learning: A term to describe the ability of individual to learn from their past experience.

Diversification: The ability to explore the whole solution space.

Evolution Operators: The operators used in the evolution algorithm, e.g. mutation, crossover.

Heuristic: The art of solving problems based on the intelligent guesswork.

Intensification: The ability to investigate the neighborhood of a potential solution.

Metahuristic: Higher level general methodologies based on the heuristic search to solve various optimization problems.

Social Learning: A term to describe the ability of individual to learn from their social environment.

Swarm Intelligence: A problem solving method based on the decentralized and self organizing agents or swarm.

Chapter 14
Two Stage Capacitated Facility Location Problem:
Lagrangian Based Heuristics

Igor Litvinchev
Nuevo Leon State University - UANL, Mexico

Miguel Mata
Nuevo Leon State University - UANL, Mexico

Lucero Ozuna
Nuevo Leon State University - UANL, Mexico

Jania Saucedo
Nuevo Leon State University - UANL, Mexico

Socorro Rangel
São Paulo State University – UNESP, Brazil

ABSTRACT

In the two-stage capacitated facility location problem, a single product is produced at some plants in order to satisfy customer demands. The product is transported from these plants to some depots and then to the customers. The capacities of the plants and depots are limited. The aim is to select cost minimizing locations from a set of potential plants and depots. This cost includes fixed cost associated with opening plants and depots, and variable cost associated with both transportation stages. In this work two different mixed integer linear programming formulations are considered for the problem. Several Lagrangian relaxations are analyzed and compared, a Lagrangian heuristic producing feasible solutions is presented. The results of a computational study are reported.

DOI: 10.4018/978-1-4666-2086-5.ch014

1. INTRODUCTION

The two-stage capacitated facility location problem can be defined as follows: a single product is produced at plants and then transported to depots, both having limited capacities. From the depots the product is transported to customers to satisfy their demands. The use of the plants/depots incurs a fixed cost, while transportation from the plants to the customers through the depots results in a variable cost. We need to identify what plants and depots to use, as well as the product flows from the plants to the depots and then to the customers such that the demands are met at a minimal cost.

Facility location problems have numerous applications and have been widely studied in the literature, see the review publications by Daskin, Snyder & Berger (2003), Klose & Drexl (2004) and Melo, Mickel & Saldanha-da-Gama (2009) and the references therein. Various applications of the facility location in supply chain optimization and management are presented in Wang (2011) and Minis et al. (2011). In Sahin & Süral (2007) the review of the hierarchical facility location models is presented focusing on applications and formulations of the problem. In what follows we focus more on solution approaches and techniques to solve facility location problems.

Various exact approaches have been proposed for the location problems. For example, Avella & Boccia (2007) presented a family of minimum knapsack inequalities of a mixed type, containing both binary and continuous (flow) variables for the capacitated problem and developed a branch and cut and price algorithm to deal with large scale instances. Klose & Drexl (2005) considered a new lower bound for the capacitated facility location problem based on partitioning the plant set and employing column generation. The use of valid inequalities in a branch-and-bound framework for capacitated facility location problem was studied in Aardal (1998). Osorio & Sánchez (2009) use a dual surrogate analysis to fix variables in the capacitated case.

Approximate approaches can be roughly divided into two large groups: metaheuristics and Lagrangian based techniques. Metaheuristic approaches to the problem like tabu search, GRASP, are discussed in Filho & Galvão (1998), Sun, Ducati and Armentano (2007) and Sun (2008). Caserta & Quiñonez (2008) studied a cross entropy-based metaheuristic algorithm for the capacitated facility location problem. An algorithm for large instances is presented in Barahona & Chudack (2005), they used a heuristic procedure that produces a feasible integer solution and used a Lagrangian relaxation to obtain a lower bound on the optimal value. Chyu & Chang (2008) presented two local-search based metaheuristics for the multisource capacitated facility location problem.

Location problems typically exhibit a rich structure that can be exploited to construct efficient solution techniques. There are various ways to divide constraints of the problem into "easy" and "complicated" ones. In other words, the problem would be an "easy" problem if the complicating constraints could be removed. A well-known way to exploit this structure is to form a Lagrangian relaxation with respect to complicating constraints. That is, the complicating constraints are relaxed and a penalty term is added to the objective function to discourage their violation. The optimal value of the Lagrangian problem, considered for fixed multipliers, provides a lower bound (for minimization problem) for the original optimal objective. The problem of finding the best, *i.e.* bound maximizing Lagrange multipliers, is called the Lagrangian dual. Lagrangian bounds are widely used as a core of many exact numerical techniques, as well as to measure the progress of the main algorithm and derive stopping criteria. In many approximate and heuristic approaches Lagrangian solution is used as a starting or a reference point to construct an approximate solution. The literature on Lagrangian relaxation is quite extensive, see, *e.g.* Lemarechal (2007), Frangioni (2005) and the references therein.

A Lagrangian based heuristic for solving the capacitated plant location problem with side constraints was presented in Sridharan (1991). Approaches and relaxations proposed in the literature for the capacitated facility location problem are compared in Cornuejols, Sridharan & Thizy (1991). Ramos & Sáenz (2005) applied the Fenchel cutting planes methodology to capacitated facility location problems and compared the results with a Lagrangian relaxation. Görtz & Klose (2009) presented a branch and bound method based on Lagrangian relaxations and subgradient optimization for solving large instances of the capacitated facility location problem.

For the two-stage uncapacitated problem a general model and dual based branch and bound solution procedure for the single echelon and two echelon uncapacitated facility location problems were presented in Gao & Robinson (1994). A linear programming based heuristic is considered in Klose (1999) for a two-stage capacitated problem with single source constraints. Liu & Zhu (2007) designed a hybrid algorithm, which integrates the approximation approach, neural network and simulated annealing to solve a capacitated fuzzy two-stage location-allocation problem. Wollenweber (2008) proposed a greedy construction heuristic and a Variable Neighborhood Descent and a Variable Neighborhood Search for the multi-stage facility location problem with staircase costs and splitting of commodities. In Landete & Marín (2009) the asymmetry inherent to the problem in plants and depots is taking into account to strengthen the formulation. Gendron & Semet (2009) presented two formulations for the problem and compared the linear relaxation of each formulation and the binary relaxation of the model.

Several Lagrangian relaxation approaches have been proposed for the two stage facility location problem. For the uncapacitated case Chardaire, Lutton & Sutter (1999) studied the effectiveness of the formulation for the two level simple plant location problem incorporating polyhedral cuts and proposed an approach combining a Lagrangian relaxation method and simulated annealing algorithm. Lu & Bostel (2005) proposed an algorithm based on Lagrangian heuristics for a 0-1 mixed integer model of a two level location problem with three types of facility to be located. In Marín (2007) a mixed integer formulation and several Lagrangian relaxations to determine lower bounds for the two stage uncapacitated facility location problem are presented.

The Lagrangian relaxation for the capacitated case was studied and numerically tested in Barros & Labbé (1994). Bloemhof et al. (1996) studied alternative model formulations of the capacitated problem obtaining lower bounds by Lagrangian relaxations of the flow-balancing constraints. They also developed heuristic procedures to obtain feasible solutions. In Marín & Pelegrín (1999) several Lagrangian relaxations for two different formulations of the two-stage problem are computationally compared. Tragantalerngsak et al. (1999) proposed a Lagrangian relaxation-based branch and bound algorithm for the two-echelon, single source, capacitated problem. A Lagrangian heuristic is proposed in Klose (2000) using relaxation of the capacity constraints for the problem with a fixed number of plants. Feasible solutions are constructed from those of the Lagrangian subproblems by applying simple reassignment procedures.

In many Lagrangian heuristics the optimal value of the Lagrangian (dual) problem is used as a dual (lower) bound for the optimal objective, while Lagrangian solution is used as a starting or reference point for a heuristic to produce a feasible solution (upper primal bound). This way the proximity of the feasible solution to the optimal one is estimated. It is assumed implicitly that the best dual bound and the corresponding Lagrangian solution produces the best primal bound by a heuristic approach. Thus, the feasible solution is constructed using heuristics (e.g., greedy approaches) based on the Lagrangian solution obtained for the optimal Lagrange multipliers corresponding to the best dual bound.

One of the core ideas of the metaheuristic approaches is recognizing the role of "near optimal" solutions. That is, instead of using for the next iteration the locally optimal solution obtained for the current iteration, near optimal solutions are also taking into account to define the next iteration. Metaheuristic approaches using this idea were successfully applied for many hard combinatorial and integer problems.

We propose to combine the use of near optimal solutions with the Lagrangian approach. We demonstrate that the best primal solution typically is generated by the Lagrangian solution which is far from optimal. That is, if we apply an iterative approach (e.g., subgradient technique) to solve the Lagrangian dual, the Lagrangian solutions corresponding to current (non optimal) multipliers result in better feasible solutions. This takes place not only for the case when we are looking for the best dual bound corresponding to a fixed relaxation. If the problem permits various Lagrangian relaxations and hence various dual bounds can be obtained for the same problem, then the best feasible solution typically corresponds to the dual bound which is far from the tightest one. The approach to recover the feasibility for non-optimal Lagrangian solutions in the course of the subgradient technique to solve the dual problem was used in Litvinchev et al (2010) for a class of the generalized assignment problems.

In this paper we consider ten Lagrangian relaxations for the two-stage capacitated facility location problem and compare numerically the quality of the dual bounds, as well as the quality of the primal bounds obtained by greedy-like heuristic. Instead of typical "relax-an-fix" strategy when the integer part of Lagrangian solution is fixed to produce a feasible solution (see, e.g., Wolsey, 1998), we fix in our heuristic a continuous part of the Lagrangian solution. We demonstrate numerically that the best feasible solution was never obtained by the best relaxation among the ten considered. Instead, we can highlight a simple decomposable relaxation that produces a poor

dual bound (and thus it has not been considered before as a promising relaxation), but results in a very tight feasible solution typically within less than 1% of the relative suboptimality. Moreover, calculating the dual bound for this relaxation (the best among Lagrangian bounds corresponding to different multipliers) we demonstrate numerically that the best feasible solution corresponds to Lagrangian multipliers that are far from optimal.

The rest of the paper is organized as follows. The next section presents two equivalent mathematical formulations for the two-stage facility location problem. Then ten Lagrangian relaxations are considered for these formulations and a heuristic procedure to get feasible solutions is presented. Computational results are reported and discussed in the following two sections. Concluding remarks are presented in the final section.

2. PROBLEM FORMULATIONS

To formally describe the problem, let $I = 1,...,n$ be the index set of potential plants, $J = 1,...,m$ the index set of potential depots and $K=1,...,k$ the index set of clients. Then, the problem can be formulated as the following mixed integer linear program (formulation A):

$$w = min \sum_i f_i y_i + \sum_j g_j z_j + \sum_{(i,j)} c_{ij} x_{ij} + \sum_{(j,k)} d_{jk} s_{jk} \tag{1}$$

$$s.t.: \quad \sum_j x_{ij} \le b_i; \quad i \in I, \tag{2}$$

$$\sum_i x_{ij} \le p_j; \quad j \in J, \tag{3}$$

$$\sum_j s_{jk} \ge q_k; \quad k \in K, \tag{4}$$

424

$$\sum_i x_{ij} \geq \sum_k s_{jk}; \quad j \in J, \tag{5}$$

$$x_{ij} \leq m_{ij} y_i; \quad i \in I, \; j \in J, \tag{6}$$

$$s_{jk} \leq l_{jk} z_j; \quad j \in J, \; k \in K, \tag{7}$$

$$x_{ij}, s_{jk} \in R^+, y_i, z_j \in \{0,1\} \tag{8}$$

In formulation A, f_i and g_j are the fixed costs associated with the installation of plant i and depot j; c_{ij} and d_{jk} are the costs of transportation from plant i to depot j and from depot j to client k, respectively; q_k is the demand of client k; while b_i and p_j are the capacities of the corresponding plant and depot. The variables in this formulation are $y_i = 1$ if plant i is installed and $y_i = 0$ otherwise, $z_j = 1$ if depot j is installed and $z_j = 0$ otherwise, x_{ij}, s_{jk} are the transportation flows between the corresponding units.

The objective function (1) minimizes the total fixed and transportation costs. Constraints (2) and (3) represent capacity limits for plants and depots, (4) is the demand constraint (for each customer, at least the demand must be met), (5) is the relaxed flow conservation constraint (the product transported from the depot must at least be transported to it from the plants), constraints (6) and (7), together with (8), assure that there is a flow only from plants and depots installed. Constants m_{ij}, l_{jk} represent the upper bounds for the respective flows, we may set, e.g., $m_{ij} = min\{b_i, p_j\}$; $l_{jk} = min\{p_j, q_k\}$. Note that by minimizing the objective (1), constraints (5) are fulfilled as equalities for an optimal solution of (1), (2), (3), (4), (5), (6), (7), and (8).

Constraints (6), (7) can be stated in a more compact form yielding an equivalent formulation of the two stage location problem (formulation B):

$$w = min \sum_i f_i y_i + \sum_j g_j z_j + \sum_{(i,j)} c_{ij} x_{ij} + \sum_{(j,k)} d_{jk} s_{jk} \tag{9}$$

$$s.t.: \quad \sum_j s_{jk} \geq q_k; \quad k \in K, \tag{10}$$

$$\sum_i x_{ij} \geq \sum_k s_{jk}; \quad j \in J, \tag{11}$$

$$\sum_j x_{ij} \leq b_i y_i; \quad i \in I, \tag{12}$$

$$\sum_i x_{ij} \leq p_j z_j; \quad j \in J, \tag{13}$$

$$x_{ij}, s_{jk} \in R^+, y_i, z_j \in \{0,1\} \tag{14}$$

Constraints (12) together with (14) assure the outflows only from plants opened, while constraints (13) together with (11) assure the flows only from and to depots opened.

Formulations A and B are equivalent in the sense that both result in the same optimal solution. However, they have different polyhedral structure of the feasible sets and thus we may expect that relaxing the same constraints may result in different values for the corresponding Lagrangian bounds.

3. LAGRANGIAN BOUNDS AND FEASIBLE LAGRANGIAN BASED SOLUTIONS

Lagrangian bounds are widely used as a core of many approximated techniques and heuristics. Most Lagrangian relaxation approaches for the capacitated facility location problem are based either on dualizing the demand constraints or the depot capacity constraints (Klose,1999).

In this section we present several Lagrangian relaxations for each formulation of the problem. These relaxations have certain decomposition properties and thus solving the Lagrangian problem is "easier" then the original one. Note that the optimal values for the formulations A, B are the same since the formulations are equivalent. For details on Lagrangian relaxation we refer the reader to Fisher (1985), Beasley (1993) and Guignard (2003).

3.1 Lagrangian Bounds

For the formulation A defined by Equations (1), (2), (3), (4), (5), (6), (7), and (8) five "decomposable" Lagrangian relaxations are considered, denoted as follows (all Lagrangian multipliers are assumed to be nonnegative):

RA1: Constraints (5), representing interconnections between the two stages, are dualized giving the Lagrangian problem:

$$w^{\mathrm{RA1}} = min \sum_i f_i y_i + \sum_j g_j z_j + \sum_{(i,j)} c_{ij} x_{ij}$$
$$+ \sum_{(j,k)} d_{jk} s_{jk} + \sum_j u_j (\sum_k s_{jk} - \sum_i x_{ij})$$

$$s.t.: \quad \sum_j x_{ij} \le b_i; \quad i \in I,$$

$$\sum_i x_{ij} \le p_j; \quad j \in J,$$

$$\sum_j s_{jk} \ge q_k; \quad k \in K,$$

$$\sum_i x_{ij} \ge \sum_k s_{jk}; \quad j \in J,$$

$$x_{ij} \le m_{ij} y_i; \quad i \in I, j \in J,$$

$$s_{jk} \le l_{jk} z_j; \quad j \in J, \ k \in K,$$

$$x_{ij}, s_{jk} \in R^+, y_i, z_j \in \{0,1\}$$

The latter decomposes into a subproblem for the first stage (plants) in variables x, y :

$$w_1^{\mathrm{RA1}} = min \sum_i f_i y_i + \sum_{(i,j)} (c_{ij} - u_j) x_{ij}$$

$$s.t.: \quad \sum_j x_{ij} \le b_i; \quad i \in I,$$

$$\sum_i x_{ij} \le p_j; \quad j \in J,$$

$$x_{ij} \le m_{ij} y_i; \quad i \in I, j \in J,$$

$$x_{ij} \in R^+, y_{ij} \in \{0,1\}$$

and a subproblem corresponding to the second stage (depots) in s, z :

$$w_2^{\mathrm{RA1}} = min \sum_j g_j z_j + \sum_{(j,k)} (d_{jk} + u_j) s_{jk}$$

$$\sum_j s_{jk} \ge q_k, k \in K$$

$$s_{jk} \le l_{jk} z_j; \quad j \in J, k \in K$$

$$s_{jk} \in R^+, z_j \in \{0,1\}$$

such that $w^{\mathrm{RA1}} = w_1^{\mathrm{RA1}} + w_2^{\mathrm{RA1}}$.

RA2: Constraints (6) are dualized giving the Lagrangian problem:

$$w^{\mathrm{RA2}} = min \sum_i f_i y_i + \sum_j g_j z_j + \sum_{(i,j)} c_{ij} x_{ij}$$
$$+ \sum_{(j,k)} d_{jk} s_{jk} + \sum_{(i,j)} u_{ij} (x_{ij} - m_{ij} y_i)$$

$$s.t.: \quad \sum_{j} x_{ij} \leq b_i; \quad i \in I,$$

$$\sum_{i} x_{ij} \leq p_j; \quad j \in J,$$

$$\sum_{j} s_{jk} \geq q_k; \quad k \in K,$$

$$\sum_{i} x_{ij} \geq \sum_{k} s_{jk}; \quad j \in J,$$

$$s_{jk} \leq l_{jk} z_j; \quad j \in J, \ k \in K,$$

$$x_{ij}, s_{jk} \in R^+, y_i, z_j \in \{0,1\}$$

The latter decomposes into $|I|$ suproblems of the form

$$w_{1i}^{\mathrm{RA2}} = min\{y_i(f_i - u_{ij} m_{ij}), \ y_i \in \{0,1\}\},$$

which can be solved analytically and a subproblem in variables x, s, z:

$$w_2^{\mathrm{RA2}} = min \sum_{j} g_j z_j + \sum_{(i,j)} c_{ij} x_{ij} + \sum_{(j,k)} d_{jk} s_{jk} + \sum_{(i,j)} u_{ij} x_{ij}$$

$$s.t.: \quad \sum_{j} x_{ij} \leq b_i; \quad i \in I,$$

$$\sum_{i} x_{ij} \leq p_j; \quad j \in J,$$

$$\sum_{j} s_{jk} \geq q_k; \quad k \in K,$$

$$\sum_{i} x_{ij} \geq \sum_{k} s_{jk}; \quad j \in J,$$

$$s_{jk} \leq l_{jk} z_j; \quad j \in J, \ k \in K,$$

$$x_{ij}, s_{jk} \in R^+, z_j \in \{0,1\} \ ,$$

such that $w^{\mathrm{RA2}} = \sum_{i} w_{1i}^{\mathrm{RA2}} + w_2^{\mathrm{RA2}}$.

RA3: Constraints (7) are dualized. Similar to RA2 we get $|J|$ subproblems in variables z and a subproblem in (x,s,y).

RA4: Constraints (2) and (4), binding with respect to index j, are dualized giving the following Lagrangian problem:

$$w^{\mathrm{RA4}} = min \sum_{i} f_i y_i + \sum_{j} g_j z_j$$
$$+ \sum_{(i,j)} c_{ij} x_{ij} + \sum_{(j,k)} d_{jk} s_{jk}$$
$$+ \sum_{i} u_i (\sum_{j} x_{ij} - b_i) + \sum_{k} v_k (q_k - \sum_{j} s_{jk})$$

$$\sum_{i} x_{ij} \leq p_j; \quad j \in J,$$

$$\sum_{i} x_{ij} \geq \sum_{k} s_{jk}; \quad j \in J,$$

$$x_{ij} \leq m_{ij} y_i; \quad i \in I, j \in J,$$

$$s_{jk} \leq l_{jk} z_j; \quad j \in J, \ k \in K,$$

$$x_{ij}, s_{jk} \in R^+, y_i, z_j \in \{0,1\} \ .$$

The Lagrangian problem then decomposes into $|J|$ independent subproblems of the form:

$$w_j^{\mathrm{RA4}} = min \sum_{i} f_i y_i + g_j z_j + \sum_{i} c_{ij} x_{ij}$$
$$+ \sum_{k} d_{jk} s_{jk} + \sum_{i} u_i x_{ij} - \sum_{k} v_k s_{jk}$$

$$\sum_{i} x_{ij} \leq p_j$$

$$\sum_{i} x_{ij} \geq \sum_{k} s_{jk}$$

$$x_{ij} \le m_{ij} y_i; \quad i \in I,$$

$$s_{jk} \le l_{jk} z_j; \quad k \in K,$$

$$x_{ij}, s_{jk} \in R^+, y_i, z_j \in \{0,1\}$$

with $w^{\mathrm{RA4}} = \sum_j w_j^{\mathrm{RA4}}$.

RA5: Constraints (3) and (5) are dualized:

$$\begin{aligned} w^{\mathrm{RA5}} = m\acute{\imath}n & \sum_i f_i y_i + \sum_j g_j z_j \\ & + \sum_{(i,j)} c_{ij} x_{ij} + \sum_{(j,k)} d_{jk} s_{jk} \\ & + \sum_j u_j (\sum_i x_{ij} - p_j) + \sum_j v_j (\sum_k s_{jk} - \sum_i x_{ij}) \end{aligned}$$

$$s.t.: \sum_j x_{ij} \le b_i; \quad i \in I,$$

$$\sum_j s_{jk} \ge q_k; \quad k \in K,$$

$$x_{ij} \le m_{ij} y_i; \quad i \in I, j \in J,$$

$$s_{jk} \le l_{jk} z_j; \quad j \in J,\ k \in K,$$

$$x_{ij}, s_{jk} \in R^+, y_i, z_j \in \{0,1\}$$

Similar to RA1 this Lagrangian problem decomposes into a subproblem corresponding to the first stage (plants):

$$w_1^{\mathrm{RA5}} = m\acute{\imath}n \sum_i f_i y_i + \sum_{(i,j)} c_{ij} x_{ij} + \sum_{(i,j)} (u_j - v_j) x_{ij}$$

$$s.t.: \sum_j x_{ij} \le b_i; \quad i \in I,$$

$$x_{ij} \le m_{ij} y_i \quad ; i \in I, j \in J,$$

$$x_{ij} \in R^+, y_i \in \{0,1\}$$

and a subproblem corresponding to the second stage (depots):

$$w_2^{\mathrm{RA5}} = m\acute{\imath}n \sum_j g_j z_j + \sum_{(j,k)} (d_{jk} + v_j) s_{jk}$$

$$\sum_j s_{jk} \ge q_k; \quad k \in K,$$

$$s_{jk} \le l_{jk} z_j; \quad j \in J,\ k \in K,$$

$$s_{jk} \in R^+, z_j \in \{0,1\} \ .$$

The Lagrangian relaxations for the formulation B defined by (9), (10), (11), (12), (13), and (14) are as follows:

RB1: Constraints (11) are dualized:

$$\begin{aligned} w^{\mathrm{RB1}} = m\acute{\imath}n & \sum_i f_i y_i + \sum_j g_j z_j + \sum_{(i,j)} c_{ij} x_{ij} \\ & + \sum_{(j,k)} d_{jk} s_{jk} + \sum_j u_j (\sum_k s_{jk} - \sum_i x_{ij}) \end{aligned}$$

$$s.t.: \sum_j s_{jk} \ge q_k; \quad k \in K,$$

$$\sum_j x_{ij} \le b_i y_i; \quad i \in I,$$

$$\sum_i x_{ij} \le p_j z_j; \quad j \in J,$$

$$x_{ij}, s_{jk} \in R^+, y_i, z_j \in \{0,1\} \ ,$$

giving two Lagrangian subproblems: a subproblem in *(x,y,z)*:

$$w_1^{\text{RB1}} = min \sum_i f_i y_i + \sum_j g_j z_j + \sum_{(i,j)} (c_{ij} - u_j) x_{ij}$$

$$\sum_j x_{ij} \leq b_i y_i; \quad i \in I,$$

$$\sum_i x_{ij} \leq p_j z_j; \quad j \in J,$$

$$x_{ij} \in R^+, y_i, z_j \in \{0,1\}$$

and a subproblem in *s*:

$$w_2^{\text{RB1}} = min \sum_{(j,k)} (d_{jk} + u_j) s_{jk}$$

$$s.t.: \sum_j s_{jk} \geq q_k; \quad k \in K,$$

$$s_{jk} \in R^+$$

The latter problem is decomposed into $|K|$ independent continuous one-dimensional knapsack problems which can be solved analytically.

RB2: Constraints (12) are dualized:

$$w^{\text{RB2}} = min \sum_i f_i y_i + \sum_j g_j z_j + \sum_{(i,j)} c_{ij} x_{ij}$$
$$+ \sum_{(j,k)} d_{jk} s_{jk} + \sum_i u_i (\sum_j x_{ij} - b_i y_i)$$

$$s.t.: \sum_j s_{jk} \geq q_k; \quad k \in K,$$

$$\sum_i x_{ij} \geq \sum_k s_{jk}; \quad j \in J,$$

$$\sum_i x_{ij} \leq p_j z_j; \quad j \in J,$$

$$x_{ij}, s_{jk} \in R^+, y_i, z_j \in \{0,1\} ,$$

resulting in $|I|$ independent subproblems of the form $w_{1i}^{\text{RB2}} = min\{y_i (f_i - u_i b_i), y_i \in \{0,1\}\}$ with only one binary variable and a subproblem in (*x; s; z*):

$$w_2^{\text{RB2}} = min \sum_i f_i y_i + \sum_j g_j z_j$$
$$+ \sum_{(i,j)} (c_{ij} + u_i) x_{ij} + \sum_{(j,k)} d_{jk} s_{jk}$$

$$s.t.: \sum_j s_{jk} \geq q_k; \quad k \in K,$$

$$\sum_i x_{ij} \geq \sum_k s_{jk}; \quad j \in J,$$

$$\sum_i x_{ij} \leq p_j z_j; \quad j \in J,$$

$$x_{ij}, s_{jk} \in R^+, z_j \in \{0,1\}$$

RB3: Constraints (13) are relaxed giving, similar to RB2, $|J|$ independent subproblems in a single variable, *z*, and a subproblem in (*x; s; y*).

RB4: Constraints (10) and (12) are dualized:

$$w^{\text{RB4}} = min \sum_i f_i y_i + \sum_j g_j z_j$$
$$+ \sum_{(i,j)} c_{ij} x_{ij} + \sum_{(j,k)} d_{jk} s_{jk}$$
$$+ \sum_k u_k (q_k - \sum_j s_{jk}) + \sum_i v_i (\sum_j x_{ij} - b_i y_i)$$

$$\sum_i x_{ij} \geq \sum_k s_{jk}; \quad j \in J,$$

$$\sum_i x_{ij} \leq p_j z_j; \quad j \in J,$$

$$x_{ij}, s_{jk} \in R^+, y_i, z_j \in \{0,1\}$$

The Lagrangian problem then decomposes into $|I|$ independent subproblems of the form $w_{1i}^{\text{RB4}} = mín\{y_i(f_i - v_i b_i),\, y_i \in \{0,1\}\}$, that can be solved analytically, and a subproblem in $(x;\, s;\, z)$:

$$w_2^{\text{RB4}} = mín \sum_j g_j z_j + \sum_{(i,j)} (c_{ij} + v_i) x_{ij}$$
$$+ \sum_{(j,k)} (d_{jk} - u_k) s_{jk}$$

$$\sum_i x_{ij} \geq \sum_k s_{jk}; \quad j \in J,$$

$$\sum_i x_{ij} \leq p_j z_j; \quad j \in J,$$

$$x_{ij}, s_{jk} \in R^+, z_j \in \{0,1\} \ .$$

The latter decomposes into $|J|$ independent subproblems of the form:

$$w_j^{\text{RB4}} = mín \ g_j z_j + \sum_i (c_{ij} + v_i) x_{ij}$$
$$+ \sum_k (d_{jk} - u_k) s_{jk}$$

$$\sum_i x_{ij} \geq \sum_k s_{jk}$$

$$\sum_i x_{ij} \leq p_j z_j$$

$$x_{ij}, s_{jk} \in R^+, z_j \in \{0,1\} \ .$$

This problem has only one binary variable and can be solved by inspection (see, e.g., Wolsey, 1998), fixing z to 0 or 1 and then solving the remaining problem with continuous variables (x,s).

RB5: Constraints (11) and (13) are dualized:

$$w^{\text{RB5}} = mín \sum_i f_i y_i + \sum_j g_j z_j$$
$$+ \sum_{(i,j)} c_{ij} x_{ij} + \sum_{(j,k)} d_{jk} s_{jk}$$
$$+ \sum_j u_j \Big(\sum_k s_{jk} - \sum_i x_{ij} \Big) + \sum_j v_j \Big(\sum_i x_{ij} - p_j z_j \Big)$$

$$s.t.: \ \sum_j s_{jk} \geq q_k; \quad k \in K,$$

$$\sum_j x_{ij} \leq b_i y_i; \quad i \in I,$$

$$x_{ij}, s_{jk} \in R^+, y_i, z_j \in \{0,1\}$$

The Lagrangian problem decomposes into three types of subproblems. We have $|J|$ independent subproblems in z of the form $w_j^{\text{RB5}} = mín\{z_j(g_j - v_j p_j),\, z_j \in \{0,1\}\}$. We also have $|K|$ independent continuous one-dimensional knapsack subproblems in s,

$$w_k^{\text{RB5}} = mín \sum_j (d_{jk} + u_j) s_{jk}$$

$$s.t.: \quad \sum_j s_{jk} \geq q_k \ ,$$

$$s_{jk} \in R^+,$$

and $|I|$ independent subproblems in x, y :

$$w_i^{\text{RB5}} = mín \ f_j y_j + \sum_i (c_{ij} - u_j + v_j) x_{ij}$$

$$\sum_j x_{ij} \leq b_i y_i$$

$$x_{ij} \in R^+, y_i \in \{0,1\}$$

The latter problem has only one binary variable and can be solved by inspection.

The problem of finding the best, *i.e.* bound maximizing lagrange multipliers, is called the Lagrangian dual. To solve the Lagrangian dual problem one can apply a constraint generation scheme (Benders method) transforming the dual problem into a large-scale linear programming problem. The main advantage of using Benders technique is that it generates two-sided estimations for the dual bound in each iteration thus producing near-optimal dual bound with guaranteed quality. Meanwhile, the computational cost of this scheme is typically high. Another popular approach to solve the dual problem is by subgradient optimization. In contrast to the Benders method, the subgradient technique does not provide the value of the bounds with the prescribed accuracy. That is, terminating iterations of the subgradient method using some stopping criteria we can expect only approximate values of the bound. We do not consider here these two well known approaches in details, referring the reader to Lasdon(1970), Wolsey (1999) and Conejo (2000) for the constraint generation (Benders) technique, and to Martin (1999) and Guignard (2003) for the subgradient scheme.

3.2 Restoring Primal Feasibility by a Greedy Heuristic

To get a feasible solution from the Lagrangian one we use a simple algorithm (Algorithm 1) to recover feasibility. This approach can be applied to a Lagrangian solution obtained by any of the ten relaxations considered in the previous section.

The main idea of the Algorithm 1 is to calculate for each plant a "saturation" indicator representing the relative usage of its capacity (step 0). Then the plant having the highest saturation is

Algorithm 1.

Let $\overline{x}_{ij}, \overline{s}_{jk}$ be a nonfeasible solution

Do $y_i = 0, \forall i, I_1 = \varnothing, I_0 = I;$

$z_j = 0, \forall j, J_1 = \varnothing, J_0 = J.$

Step 0: Do $y_i \leftarrow \dfrac{\sum\limits_j \overline{x}_{ij}}{b_i}, z_j \leftarrow \dfrac{\sum\limits_k \overline{s}_{jk}}{p_j}.$

Step 1: $i^* = \arg max \left\{ y_i \,\middle|\, i \in I_0 \right\}.$

Step 2: $y_{i^*} \leftarrow 1, I_1 \leftarrow I_1 \cup \left\{i^*\right\}, I_0 \leftarrow I_0 - \left\{i^*\right\}.$

Step 3: If $\sum\limits_{i \in I_1} b_i \geq \sum\limits_k q_k$ go to step 4 and do $y_i = 0, \forall i \in I_0$, otherwise, return to step 1.

Step 4: $j^* = \arg max \left\{ z_j \,\middle|\, j \in J_0 \right\}.$

Step 5: $z_{j^*} \leftarrow 1, J_1 \leftarrow J_1 \cup \left\{j^*\right\}, J_0 \leftarrow J_0 - \left\{j^*\right\}.$

Step 6: If $\sum\limits_{j \in J_1} p_j \geq \sum\limits_k q_k$ go to step 7 and do $z_j = 0, \forall j \in J_0$, otherwise, return to step 4.

Step 7: Fix y_i and z_j in the original problem and solve corresponding linear problem to obtain the flows.

opened (step 1). If the capacity is sufficient to satisfy the total customers' demand, the rest of the plants are closed, otherwise the plant having the next highest indicator is opened (steps 2 and 3). The depots are opened in a similar way (steps 3, 5 and 6). Fixing the binary variables obtained by this procedure, the flows are determined from the corresponding linear problem.

4. COMPUTATIONAL RESULTS

A numerical study for the two-stage capacitated facility location problem was conducted to compare the dual bounds and feasible solutions. First, the following sets of instances were generated according to the values $(I;\ J;\ K)$:

- A(3; 5; 9);
- B(5; 7; 30);
- C(7; 10; 50);
- D(10; 10; 100).

Every set contains 20 problem instances. The data were random integers generated as follows:

$$c_{ij}, d_{jk} \in U[10, 20], \quad q_k \in U[1, 10],$$
$$b_i \in \left\lceil 10\frac{J+K}{I} \right\rceil + U[0, 10], \quad p_j \in \left\lceil 10\frac{K}{J} \right\rceil + U[0, 10].$$

Two different ways to generate the fixed costs were implemented. For the first ten instances in each class the fixed costs f_i for plants were proportional to the number of depots and clients, while the fixed costs g_j for depots were proportional to the number of clients (Type 1):

$$f_i \in \left\lceil 100\frac{K+J}{I} \right\rceil + U[0, 100];$$

$$g_j \in \left\lceil 100\frac{K}{J} \right\rceil + U[0, 100]$$

For the remaining ten instances the fixed costs f_i, g_j were random integers generated independently on the number clients, plants and depots: $f_i, g_j \in U[100, 200]$ (Type 2).

The dual bounds corresponding to all Lagrangian relaxations were calculated by the subgradient technique. In each iteration of this method a feasible solution was obtained by the Algorithm 1. The best (over all iterations) feasible solution was stored. In the subgradient method the current best feasible solution was used to update the step size. If after 5 consecutive iterations of the subgradient technique the dual bound was not improved, half of the step size scaling parameter was used. The process stops if the step size scaling parameter is less than 0.0001, or if the maximum number (300) of iterations is reached. The procedure was implemented in GAMS/CPLEX 11.2 using a Sun Fire V440 terminal, connected to 4 processors Ultra SPARC III with 1602 Hhz, 1 MB of CACHE, and 8 GB of memory. For the details of the subgradient technique in the lagrangian framework see Wolsey (1999) and Martin (1999).

For all the instances we have calculated:

- z_{IP} : The value of the optimal objective of the two stage location problem.
- z_L : The value of the best Lagrangian bound.
- z_{BF} : The objective value corresponding to the best feasible solution.

The relative quality of the Lagrangian bound and of the best feasible solution was measured by

$$\varepsilon_L = \frac{z_{IP} - z_L}{z_{IP}} \times 100\% \text{ and}$$

$$\varepsilon_{BF} = \frac{z_{BF} - z_{IP}}{z_{BF}} \times 100\%,$$

respectively. Similar proximity indicators are used to measure the quality of the bounds and feasible solutions derived from all the relaxations.

The results obtained for the Type 1 instances are presented in Table 1.

The first group of columns in Table 1 represents (in %) how many times the corresponding dual bound appeared among the best 3 bounds. The second group of columns shows (in %) how many times the corresponding dual bound was the best. The indicators are presented only for the dual bounds corresponding to RB1, RB2 and RB3 since they were most frequently among the best. The last columns present indicators for the best feasible solutions obtained by the Algorithm in the course of solving the dual problem. The third group of columns in Table 1 represents (in %) how many times the corresponding feasible solution appeared among the best 3 solutions. The last group of columns shows (in %) how many times the corresponding feasible solution was the best. The indicators are presented only for the feasible solutions derived from RA2, RA3, and RB4 since they were most frequently among the best. Table 2 presents similar results for the Type 2 instances.

As can be seen from Tables 1 and 2, the bound corresponding to RB3 appears frequently among the best Lagrangian bounds. Considering the quality of the feasible solutions we may highlight RB4 which is frequently among the best and is easier to calculate than RA3. We note that relaxations giving the best dual bounds were never among those producing the best feasible solutions

In our further computational testing we concentrated in studying only relaxations RB3 and RB4 as the most promising in terms of dual and primal bound, respectively. Along with the set instances A – D we have used larger instances generated according to the values $(I; J; K)$:

- E(10; 16; 30);
- F(30; 30; 30);
- G(30; 60; 120);
- H(30; 30; 100);
- I(50; 50; 200).

Table 1. Type 1 instances

	Lagrangian relaxations							Feasible solutions					
	In the top 3 (%)			Best bound (%)				In the top 3 (%)			Best bound (%)		
Size	RB1	RB2	RB3	RB1	RB2	RB3		RA2	RA3	RB4	RA2	RA3	RB4
A	80	90	100	0	10	90		90	90	60	90	90	60
B	100	100	100	10	10	80		90	50	50	60	40	20
C	100	100	100	20	20	60		80	70	70	40	30	40
D	100	100	100	40	20	40		90	40	90	70	10	40

Table 2. Type 2 instances

		Lagrangian relaxations							Feasible solutions				
		In the top 3 (%)			Best bound (%)			In the top 3 (%)			Best bound (%)		
Size	RB1	RB2	RB3	RB1	RB2	RB3		RA2	RA3	RB4	RA2	RA3	RB4
A	70	80	40	10	0	20		70	90	90	70	90	80
B	70	80	70	10	20	60		20	90	80	10	80	50
C	90	80	50	20	40	30		20	80	90	10	60	40
D	70	80	10	40	10	0		20	90	90	20	40	50

The Tables 3, 4, 5, and 6 and 7, 8, 9, and 10 present the quality of the primal and dual bounds calculated by the subgradient technique for the relaxations RB3, RB4 respectively. The results are shown for 5 different instances for each problem size. In these Tables the first two columns present the proximity indicators for the corresponding dual bound (ε_L) and for the best (over all iterations) feasible solution (ε_{BF}) obtained by the Algorithm 1. The number in the parenthesis

in the second column indicates the iteration number corresponding to the best feasible solution. The last two columns give the proximity indicators for the feasible solution corresponding to the last (ε_{LF}) and the first iteration (ε_{FF}) of the subgradient technique. The number in parenthesis in the third column indicates the number of the last iteration. This number is omitted if the subgradient technique stops by reaching the maximum number of iterations permitted (300).

Table 3. Relaxation RB3: Type 1 instances A, B, C, and D

Size	ε_L (%)	ε_{BF} (%)	ε_{LF} (%)	ε_{FF} (%)
A1	7.46	0.00 (3)	3.32 (127)	2.74
A2	1.41	0.00 (3)	0.00 (102)	10.58
A3	3.86	0.00 (2)	0.43 (144)	4.44
A4	2.43	0.00 (12)	7.89 (168)	14.57
A5	4.37	0.00 (1)	0.00 (141)	0.00
B1	3.77	0.00 (25)	0.74 (173)	1.09
B2	2.36	0.00 (1)	0.00 (154)	0.00
B3	5.35	0.00 (21)	1.06 (157)	0.49
B4	3.38	0.00 (3)	3.47 (116)	4.05
B5	5.66	0.00 (9)	0.00 (103)	0.06
C1	4.16	0.00 (38)	0.55 (165)	0.28
C2	4.51	0.00 (34)	1.58 (171)	2.27
C3	1.09	1.33 (73)	0.02 (168)	0.94
C4	3.73	0.00 (25)	0.26 (171)	0.95
C5	2.49	0.00 (1)	0.00 (206)	0.00
D1	1.33	0.17 (18)	0.31 (167)	0.65
D2	1.23	0.00 (13)	0.19 (179)	1.16
D3	2.42	0.00 (10)	0.00 (202)	0.59
D4	3.82	0.11 (48)	0.21 (174)	1.09
D5	3.34	0.00 (1)	0.09 (204)	0.00

Table 4. Relaxation RB3: Type 1 instances E, F, G, H, and I

Size	ε_L (%)	ε_{BF} (%)	ε_{LF} (%)	ε_{FF} (%)
E1	1.08	0.02 (24)	0.94 (201)	4.20
E2	2.49	0.00 (32)	0.64 (181)	6.29
E3	1.29	0.00 (18)	0.49 (175)	7.27
E4	1.43	0.49 (34)	1.89 (200)	3.49
E5	2.63	0.59 (30)	0.56 (181)	2.61
F1	0.69	0.00 (20)	0.59 (174)	11.67
F2	0.38	0.00 (36)	1.15 (171)	12.63
F3	0.99	0.21 (35)	0.29 (191)	11.59
F4	0.56	0.59 (39)	1.61 (161)	17.41
F5	0.90	0.08 (20)	0.41 (183)	9.92
G1	0.32	0.46 (83)	0.62 (205)	5.56
G2	0.33	0.16 (79)	0.42 (208)	6.43
G3	0.46	0.35 (58)	0.36 (204)	7.20
G4	0.26	0.13 (53)	0.28 (203)	7.08
G5	0.28	0.00 (57)	0.07 (229)	6.52
H1	0.72	0.22 (113)	0.85 (239)	3.55
H2	0.59	0.09 (71)	1.86 (238)	6.26
H3	0.55	0.07 (28)	0.39 (248)	3.98
H4	0.72	0.18 (75)	0.35 (239)	3.53
H5	0.41	0.15 (54)	0.15 (204)	4.35
I1	0.25	0.28 (67)	0.50 (187)	2.81
I2	0.30	0.14 (71)	0.63 (243)	3.39
I3	0.31	0.65 (82)	0.93 (238)	3.62
I4	0.15	0.10 (99)	0.64 (240)	4.19
I5	0.29	0.09 (47)	0.12 (211)	3.29

Table 5. Relaxation RB3: Type 2 instances A, B, C, and D

Size	ε_L (%)	ε_{BF} (%)	ε_{LF} (%)	ε_{FF} (%)
A1	7.48	0.00 (9)	0.00 (138)	2.36
A2	1.12	0.00 (8)	0.00 (107)	9.57
A3	3.50	0.00 (2)	2.76 (163)	5.76
A4	3.19	0.00 (10)	6.25 (130)	9.26
A5	4.23	0.00 (1)	0.00 (178)	0.00
B1	2.58	0.00 (37)	0.44 (164)	1.82
B2	1.72	0.00 (1)	0.00 (157)	0.00
B3	2.41	0.00 (8)	0.00 (156)	2.65
B4	3.26	0.00 (25)	0.00 (147)	0.96
B5	2.83	0.00 (3)	0.18 (113)	0.75
C1	2.21	0.00 (46)	0.00 (209)	0.56
C2	0.97	1.59 (11)	2.41 (154)	2.62
C3	1.18	0.00 (35)	0.03 (165)	0.64
C4	2.48	0.00 (17)	0.00 (164)	0.43
C5	1.27	0.00 (10)	0.00 (155)	2.54
D1	1.38	0.00 (10)	0.53 (183)	1.18
D2	0.86	0.00 (27)	0.58 (170)	2.06
D3	1.87	0.00 (9)	0.00 (164)	1.04
D4	1.81	0.00 (18)	0.90 (159)	0.91
D5	1.36	0.00 (1)	0.17 (172)	0.00

Table 6. Relaxation RB3: Type 2 instances E, F, G, H, and I

Size	ε_L (%)	ε_{BF} (%)	ε_{LF} (%)	ε_{FF} (%)
E1	1.73	0.00 (37)	1.55 (185)	4.43
E2	2.01	0.16 (47)	0.53 (208)	4.34
E3	1.36	0.30 (31)	1.21 (165)	6.03
E4	1.67	0.24 (53)	0.72 (157)	3.23
E5	2.28	0.68 (22)	1.62 (179)	6.81
F1	0.77	0.62 (34)	0.67 (177)	14.05
F2	0.43	0.17 (33)	1.17 (187)	13.79
F3	1.11	0.23 (65)	0.38 (181)	12.78
F4	0.62	0.28 (26)	1.78 (184)	15.02
F5	1.01	0.09 (21)	0.09 (189)	10.49
G1	0.28	0.15 (55)	0.28 (203)	7.71
G2	0.54	0.43 (59)	0.99 (185)	7.19
G3	0.53	0.53 (83)	0.71 (172)	8.97
G4	0.46	0.04 (27)	0.49 (186)	8.42
G5	0.23	0.11 (55)	0.53 (190)	7.90
H1	0.54	0.24 (34)	0.89 (300)	2.95
H2	1.07	0.08 (40)	1.47 (135)	5.44
H3	0.53	0.05 (30)	2.09 (117)	2.37
H4	0.51	0.27 (34)	0.44 (175)	4.35
H5	0.74	0.29 (53)	1.05 (181)	3.49
I1	0.43	0.14 (50)	0.14 (201)	3.57
I2	0.48	0.06 (78)	0.34 (219)	3.26
I3	0.56	0.19 (71)	0.21 (201)	3.50
I4	0.32	0.09 (177)	0.28 (250)	3.06
I5	0.29	0.04 (125)	0.30 (185)	3.11

Table 7. Relaxation RB4: Type 1 instances A, B, C, and D

Size	ε_L (%)	ε_{BF} (%)	ε_{LF} (%)	ε_{FF} (%)
A1	13.64	0.51 (9)	4.72 (214)	10.31
A2	4.79	0.00 (29)	0.00 (166)	14.48
A3	5.33	0.43 (2)	13.46 (158)	18.41
A4	6.89	0.00 (28)	10.17 (188)	11.98
A5	19.09	0.00 (1)	0.00 (157)	0.00
B1	13.18	0.00 (137)	0.79 (212)	2.09
B2	9.09	0.00 (58)	1.62 (250)	1.44
B3	8.29	1.57 (22)	9.79 (250)	8.63
B4	5.49	0.00 (61)	6.01 (243)	6.01
B5	9.32	0.11 (21)	0.11 (252)	14.79
C1	6.68	0.00 (62)	8.28 (223)	9.95
C2	10.83	0.25 (181)	2.11 (270)	5.06
C3	6.84	0.56 (76)	2.28 (258)	4.64
C4	8.55	0.00 (27)	4.80 (237)	5.28
C5	6.47	0.00 (47)	1.49 (250)	4.34
D1	6.32	0.20 (62)	2.12 (284)	6.79
D2	6.08	0.40 (237)	4.34 (256)	4.48
D3	8.48	0.00 (67)	1.62 (277)	5.64
D4	7.29	1.91 (18)	8.18 (250)	8.45
D5	5.57	0.19 (153)	3.58 (276)	2.19

Table 8. Relaxation RB4: Type 1 instances E, F, G, H, and I

Size	ε_L (%)	ε_{BF} (%)	ε_{LF} (%)	ε_{FF} (%)
E1	4.04	2.54 (44)	9.06 (227)	13.75
E2	9.56	0.79 (71)	0.79 (205)	4.93
E3	3.71	5.76 (51)	6.83 (293)	14.73
E4	6.25	0.00 (108)	1.69 (233)	7.35
E5	7.40	0.32 (56)	8.03 (277)	8.79
F1	3.15	0.67 (133)	1.31 (257)	13.41
F2	2.94	0.00 (60)	1.14 (261)	15.65
F3	2.28	0.95 (56)	2.93 (250)	14.24
F4	2.90	0.93 (51)	2.06 (261)	13.58
F5	2.96	0.64 (32)	5.42 (277)	20.07
G1	3.33	0.61 (194)	1.12	6.94
G2	1.98	0.82 (128)	1.56	8.22
G3	1.27	0.46 (120)	2.60	8.29
G4	0.87	0.16 (260)	1.11	7.15
G5	1.51	0.70 (87)	1.87	9.14
H1	1.64	1.16 (206)	2.52	8.33
H2	2.23	0.58 (214)	2.88	8.28
H3	1.54	0.23 (240)	2.25	7.26
H4	1.47	0.58 (127)	3.49	5.37
H5	1.14	0.43 (78)	2.64	8.81
I1	1.09	0.79 (211)	1.09	6.61
I2	1.95	0.81 (207)	2.27	5.62
I3	1.59	1.41 (221)	1.81	5.28
I4	1.29	1.01 (168)	2.89	6.59
I5	1.48	0.94 (146)	1.78	5.67

Table 9. Relaxation RB4: Type 2 instances A, B, C, and D

Size	ε_L (%)	ε_{BF} (%)	ε_{LF} (%)	ε_{FF} (%)
A1	12.30	1.81 (14)	5.07 (135)	12.51
A2	2.31	0.00 (31)	0.00 (89)	14.95
A3	7.74	0.57 (5)	4.21 (138)	4.21
A4	6.39	0.00 (9)	0.00 (128)	11.63
A5	11.03	0.00 (4)	3.79 (130)	3.79
B1	6.04	0.00 (27)	0.99 (124)	3.47
B2	4.03	0.00 (17)	0.00 (135)	2.35
B3	5.93	1.26 (16)	4.73 (132)	2.66
B4	4.97	0.00 (15)	4.91 (147)	4.18
B5	4.15	0.18 (28)	0.18 (102)	8.37
C1	4.89	0.00 (36)	1.78 (118)	3.39
C2	4.43	0.35 (9)	2.81 (116)	8.22
C3	2.88	0.03 (8)	2.28 (151)	7.59
C4	4.59	0.00 (28)	6.57 (116)	8.49
C5	3.03	0.00 (28)	2.43 (118)	6.91
D1	2.89	0.00 (16)	4.26 (113)	5.30
D2	2.43	0.00 (24)	3.14 (129)	7.44
D3	3.75	0.00 (96)	5.55 (131)	9.71
D4	3.70	0.49 (1)	2.16 (130)	4.19
D5	2.07	0.00 (105)	1.75 (153)	3.79

Table 10. Relaxation RB4: Type 2 instances E, F, G, H, and I

Size	ε_L (%)	ε_{BF} (%)	ε_{LF} (%)	ε_{FF} (%)
E1	4.56	0.00 (59)	0.10 (225)	11.65
E2	5.03	0.53 (92)	0.75 (217)	7.79
E3	3.94	1.37 (49)	5.67 (231)	12.86
E4	3.47	0.52 (134)	2.05 (256)	9.14
E5	4.25	0.46 (191)	6.07 (256)	9.10
F1	2.21	0.75 (109)	1.44	13.92
F2	1.89	0.00 (53)	0.89 (235)	13.67
F3	1.88	0.03 (58)	1.17 (198)	15.48
F4	1.61	1.55 (264)	3.67	19.47
F5	1.91	0.55 (60)	1.66 (266)	13.71
G1	1.10	0.37 (240)	1.91	8.11
G2	0.99	1.18 (88)	1.58	7.63
G3	1.13	0.21 (249)	1.24	8.69
G4	0.94	0.56 (100)	1.81	7.42
G5	0.67	0.23 (194)	0.87	9.92
H1	1.04	0.46 (284)	2.02	10.28
H2	1.29	0.47 (168)	1.04	5.84
H3	1.49	0.38 (191)	1.57	8.18
H4	1.39	0.77 (284)	2.57	7.16
H5	1.73	0.73 (147)	3.93	8.83
I1	0.96	0.52 (199)	1.27	5.98
I2	0.93	0.81 (130)	2.52	6.44
I3	0.78	1.09 (196)	1.49	7.01
I4	0.73	0.92 (202)	1.57	5.94
I5	0.64	1.04 (94)	1.90	6.44

5. DISCUSSION

As can be seen from Tables 1 and 2, formulation B typically produces tighter dual bounds comparing with formulation A. Moreover, the dual bounds derived from the formulation A were never among the best three dual bounds. This takes place for all problem instances and both ways to generate the data. Concerning the quality of the Lagrangian based feasible solutions we may conclude that both formulations are similar, although the formulation A produces tighter feasible solutions more frequently. Tables 1, 2 also indicate that the relaxation RB4 seems to be promising in terms of the quality of the feasible solutions derived.

The Lagrangian problem corresponding to the relaxation RB4 is one of the simplest among all 10 relaxations considered. As the result, the quality of the dual bound is rather poor, although improves for larger instances. However, the primal bound obtained in the course of the subgradient technique is very tight. Thus RB4 can be considered as a promising relaxation to produce low cost and high quality feasible solutions.

As can be seen from Tables 3, 4, 5, 6, 7, 8, 9, and 10, the feasible solution derived from the solution of the Lagrangian dual and associated with the last iteration of the subgradient technique is not necessarily the best feasible solution. Moreover, typically $\varepsilon_{LF} > \varepsilon_{BF}$ and the best feasible solution is obtained on the early iterations of the subgradient method. Thus we may conclude that it is important to generate feasible solutions in all iterations of the subgradient technique.

Various heuristic techniques can be used to restore the feasibility of the Lagrangian solution. Usually a feasible solution is obtained only once in the course of the main algorithm, based on the optimal solution to the Lagrangian dual problem. Hence a rather sophisticated and high-cost heuristic can be implemented without raising significantly the overall cost of the solution technique. On the contrary, in our approach feasible solutions are obtained frequently, in all iterations of the subgradient technique. The main idea was to move from a single use of a costly and maybe more efficient technique to a multiple use of a low cost and maybe less efficient heuristic. Hence a low cost and simple technique was necessary to restore the feasibility. The proposed greedy heuristic meets these criteria and our computational experiment demonstrates that high quality feasible solutions can be generated.

6. FINAL REMARKS AND CONCLUSION

We considered two equivalent formulations for the two stage capacitated facility location problem. Both formulations result in the same optimal solution, but the second has fewer constraints, thus presenting different polyhedral structures of their feasible sets. For each formulation five Lagrangian relaxations were considered and compared in terms of the quality of the Lagrangian dual bounds and the proximity of the Lagrangian based feasible solutions. It turned out that relaxing the flow conservation constraints for the second formulation typically results in the tightest Lagrangian dual bound. The most surprising result concerns the case where the demand and the capacity plant constraints are relaxed for the second formulation. This relaxation provides a poor dual bound and was never considered before as a promising one, but the Lagrangian based feasible solutions are pretty good, typically within less than 1% of the relative suboptimality. Relaxing the demand and the capacity plant constraints result in a decomposable Lagrangian problem with all subproblems solved by inspection. Thus this low cost relaxation seems to be promising to form the core of the Lagrangian based heuristics.

We compared two approaches to generate a feasible Lagrangian based solution. One is to get a feasible solution by the solution of the dual problem, i.e. at the last iteration of the subgradient technique. Another approach is to generate feasible solutions in all iterations of the subgradient method and then choose the tightest. It turned out that the best (over all iterations) feasible solution was never obtained at the last iteration. That is, simply solve the Lagrangian dual and get a corresponding Lagrangian based feasible solution is not sufficient to produce a tight feasible solution. On the contrary, the population of the Lagrangian solutions generated by the subgradient technique in the course of solving the Lagrangian dual is "sufficient" to generate high quality feasible solutions.

An interesting direction for the future research is improving the heuristic used to derive the feasible solutions without increasing significantly its computational cost. For example, using in Step 0 of the Algorithm 1 saturation indicators involving more parameters of the model. Some complements in this direction are in course.

REFERENCES

Aardal, K. (1998). Capacitated facility location: Separation algorithms and computational experience. *Mathematical Programming, 81*, 149–175. doi:10.1007/BF01581103

Aardal, K., Labbe, M., Leung, J., & Queyranne, M. (1996). On the two-level uncapacitated facility location problem. *INFORMS Journal on Computing, 8*, 289–301. doi:10.1287/ijoc.8.3.289

Avella, P., & Boccia, M. (2009). A cutting plane algorithm for the capacitated facility location problem. *Computational Optimization and Applications, 43*, 39–65. doi:10.1007/s10589-007-9125-x

Avella, P., Boccia, M., & Sforza, A., A., & Vasilev, I. (2009). An effective heuristic for large-scale capacitated facility location problems. *Journal of Heuristics, 15*, 63–81. doi:10.1007/s10732-008-9078-y

Barahona, F., & Chudak, F. (2005). Near-optimal solutions to large-scale facility location problems. *Discrete Optimization, 2*, 35–50. doi:10.1016/j.disopt.2003.03.001

Barros, A., & Labbé, M. (1994). A general model for the uncapacitated facility and depot location problem. *Location Science, 2*, 173–191.

Beasley, J. E. (1993). *Lagrangian relaxation: Modern heuristic techniques for combinatorial problems*. New York, NY: John Wiley and Sons.

Bloemhof-Ruwaard, J. M., Salomon, M., & Van Wassenhove, L. N. (1996). The capacitated distribution and waste disposal problem. *European Journal of Operational Research, 88*, 490–503. doi:10.1016/0377-2217(94)00211-8

Caserta, M., & Quiñonez, E. (2009). A cross entropy-based metaheuristic algorithm for large-scale capacitated facility location problems. *The Journal of the Operational Research Society, 60*, 1439–1448. doi:10.1057/jors.2008.77

Chardaire, P., Lutton, J. L., & Sutter, A. (1999). Upper and lower bounds for the two-level simple plant location problem. *Annals of Operations Research, 86*, 117–140. doi:10.1023/A:1018942415824

Chyu, C., & Chang, W. (2008). Multi-exchange neighborhood search heuristics for the multi-source capacitated facility location problem. *IEMS, 8*, 29–36.

Conejo, A. J., Castillo, E., Mínguez, R., & García-Bertrand, R. (2006). *Decomposition techniques in mathematical programming*. Springer-Verlag.

Contreras, I. A., & Diaz, J. A. (2007). Scatter search for the single source capacitated facility location problem. *Annals of Operations Research, 157*, 73–89. doi:10.1007/s10479-007-0193-1

Cornuejols, G., Sridharan, R., & Thizy, J. M. (1991). A comparison of heuristics and relaxations for the capacitated plant location problem. *European Journal of Operational Research, 50,* 280–297. doi:10.1016/0377-2217(91)90261-S

Daskin, M., Snyder, L., & Berger, R. (2003). *Logistics systems: Design and optimization.* Springer.

Erlenkotter, D. (1978). A dual-based procedure for uncapacitated facility location. *Operations Research, 26,* 992–1009. doi:10.1287/opre.26.6.992

Filho, V. J., & Galvão, R. D. (1998). A tabu search heuristic for the concentrator location problem. *Location Sciences, 6,* 189–209. doi:10.1016/S0966-8349(98)00046-1

Fisher, M. L. (1985). An application oriented guide to Lagrangian relaxation. *Interfaces, 15,* 10–21. doi:10.1287/inte.15.2.10

Galvao, R. D. (2004). Uncapacitated facility location problems: Contributions. *Pesquisa Operacional, 24,* 7–38. doi:10.1590/S0101-74382004000100003

Gao, L., & Robinson, E. P. (1994). Uncapacitated facility location: General solution procedure and computational experience. *European Journal of Operational Research, 76,* 410–427. doi:10.1016/0377-2217(94)90277-1

Gendron, B., & Semet, F. (2009). Formulations and relaxations for a multi-echelon capacitated location-distribution problem. *Computers & Operations Research, 36,* 1335–1355. doi:10.1016/j.cor.2008.02.009

Görtz, S., & Klose, A. (2009). *A subgradient-based branch and bound algorithm for the capacitated facility location problem.* Working paper no. 2009/1, Department of Operations Research, University of Aarhus.

Guignard, M. (2003). Lagrangian relaxation. *Top (Madrid), 11,* 151–228. doi:10.1007/BF02579036

Hinojosa, Y., Puerto, J., & Fernandez, F. R. (2000). A multiperiod two-echelon multicommodity capacitated plant location problem. *European Journal of Operational Research, 123,* 271–291. doi:10.1016/S0377-2217(99)00256-8

Jia, H., Ordonez, F., & Dessouky, M. (2007). A modeling framework for facility location of medical services for large scale emergencies. *IIE Transactions, 39,* 16–29. doi:10.1080/07408170500539113

Klose, A. (1999). An LP-based heuristic for two-stage capacitated facility location problems. *The Journal of the Operational Research Society, 50,* 157–166.

Klose, A. (2000). A Lagrangian relax and cut approach for the two-stage capacitated facility location problem. *European Journal of Operational Research, 126,* 408–421. doi:10.1016/S0377-2217(99)00300-8

Klose, A., & Drexl, A. (2004). Facility location models for distribution system design. *European Journal of Operational Research, 162,* 4–29. doi:10.1016/j.ejor.2003.10.031

Klose, A., & Drexl, A. (2005). Lower bounds for the capacitated facility location problem based on column generation. *Management Science, 51,* 1689–1705. doi:10.1287/mnsc.1050.0410

Landete, M., & Marín, A. (2009). New facets for the two-stage uncapacitated facility location polytope. *Computational Optimization and Applications, 44,* 487–519. doi:10.1007/s10589-008-9165-x

Lasdon, L. S. (2002). *Optimization theory for large systems.* Boston, MA: Dover Publications.

Liao, K., & Diansheng, G. (2008). A clustering-based approach to the capacitated facility location problem. *Transactions in GIS, 12,* 323–339. doi:10.1111/j.1467-9671.2008.01105.x

Litvinchev, I., Mata, M., Rangel, S., & Saucedo, J. (2010). Lagrangian heuristic for a class of the generalized assignment problems. *Computers & Mathematics with Applications (Oxford, England)*, *60*(4), 1115–1123. doi:10.1016/j. camwa.2010.03.070

Litvinchev, I., Rangel, S., & Saucedo, J. (2010). A Lagrangian bound for many-to-many assignment problems. *Journal of Combinatorial Optimization*, *19*(3), 241–257. doi:10.1007/s10878-008-9196-3

Liu, Y., & Zhu, X. (2007). Capacitated fuzzy two-stage location-Allocation problem. *International Journal of Innovative Computing, Information, & Control*, *3*, 987–999.

Lu, Z., & Bostel, N. (2005). A facility location model for logistics systems including reverse flows: The case of remanufacturing activities. *Computers & Operations Research*, *34*, 299–323. doi:10.1016/j.cor.2005.03.002

Marín, A. (2007). Lower bounds for the two-stage uncapacitated facility location problem. *European Journal of Operational Research*, *179*, 1126–1142. doi:10.1016/j.ejor.2005.04.052

Marín, A., & Pelegrín, B. (1999). Applying Lagrangian relaxation to the solution of two-stage location problems. *Annals of Operations Research*, *86*, 179–198. doi:10.1023/A:1018998500803

Martin, R. (1999). *Large scale linear and integer optimization: A united approach*. Boston, MA: Kluwer Academic Publishers. doi:10.1007/978-1-4615-4975-8

Melo, M. T., Nickel, S., & Saldanha-da-Gama, F. (2009). Facility location and supply chain management – A review. *European Journal of Operational Research*, *196*, 401–412. doi:10.1016/j. ejor.2008.05.007

Minis, I., Zeimpekis, V., Dounias, G., & Ampazis, N. (2011). *Supply chain management: Advances and intelligent methods*. Hershey, PA: IGI Global.

Osorio, M., & Sánchez, A. (2008). A preprocessing procedure for fixing the binary variables in the capacitated facility location problem through pairing and surrogate constraint analysis. *WSEAS Transactions on Mathematics*, *8*, 583–592.

Ramos, M. T., & Sáenz, J. (2005). Solving capacitated facility location problems by Fenchel cutting planes. *The Journal of the Operational Research Society*, *56*, 297–306. doi:10.1057/palgrave.jors.2601810

Sahin, J., & Süral, H. (2007). A review of hierarchical facility location models. *Computers & Operations Research*, *34*, 2310–2331. doi:10.1016/j. cor.2005.09.005

Snyder, L. V. (2006). Facility location under uncertainty: A review. *IIE Transactions*, *38*, 14–31. doi:10.1080/07408170500216480

Sridharan, R. (1991). A Lagrangian heuristic for the capacitated plant location problem with side constraints. *The Journal of the Operational Research Society*, *42*, 579–585.

Sun, M. (2008). A tabu search heuristic procedure for the capacitated facility location problem. *Journal of Heuristics*, *18*(1), 1–28.

Sun, M., Ducati, E., & Armentano, V. (2007). Solving capacitated facility location problem using tabu search. *Proceedings of ICM 2007* (pp. 76-81).

Tragantalerngsak, S., Holt, J., & Ronnqvist, M. (2000). An exact method for the two-echelon, single-source, capacitated facility location problem. *European Journal of Operational Research*, *123*, 473–489. doi:10.1016/S0377-2217(99)00105-8

Verter, V. (2011). Uncapacitated and capacitated facility location problems. *Foundations of Location Analysis*, *155*, 25–37. doi:10.1007/978-1-4419-7572-0_2

Wang, J. (2011). *Supply chain optimization, management and integration: Emerging applications*. Hershey, PA: IGI Global.

Wang, S., Watada, J., & Pedrycz, W. (2009). Value-at-risk-based two-stage fuzzy facility location problems. *IIE Transactions on Industrial Informatics, 5*, 465–482. doi:10.1109/TII.2009.2022542

Wollenweber, J. (2008). A multi-stage facility location problem with staircase and splitting of commodities: Model, heuristic approach and application. *OR-Spektrum, 30*, 655–673. doi:10.1007/s00291-007-0114-3

Wolsey, L. A. (1998). *Integer programming*. New York, NY: John Wiley and Sons.

ADDITIONAL READING

The ideas to combine Lagrangian and Benders decomposition techniques with heuristic approaches are presented in Boschetti & Maniezzo (2009). Generating feasible solutions in intermediate iterations of the subgradient technique is used in Litvinchev & Rangel (2011) for a class of the generalized assignment problem. Various combinations of core mathematical programming approaches and metaheuristics are presented in Maniezzo et. al (2009).

The literature on Lagrangian relaxation is quite extensive. Here we refer the reader to a few pioneer and/or review papers providing a clear exposition of the subject: Everett (1963), Held & Karp (1970), Geoffrion (1974), Shapiro (1974), Fisher (1985), Beasley (1993), Lemarechal (2001), Guignard (2003). To our knowledge, the latter paper presents the most comprehensive and complete revision of the basic ideas used in Lagrangian relaxation and its applications.

Numerical techniques of non-differentiable optimization used to solve Lagrangian dual problem can be found in the references cited above. More recent approaches are presented, *e.g.*, in Barahona & Anbil (2000), Bahiense et. al (2002). Various relaxations in nonlinear integer programming are considered in Li & Sun (2006).

Bahiense, L., Maculan, N., & Sagastizabal, C. (2002). The volume algorithm revisited: Relation with bundle methods. *Mathematical Programming, 94*, 41–69. doi:10.1007/s10107-002-0357-3

Barahona, F., & Anbil, R. (2000). The volume algorithm: Producing primal solutions with a subgradient method. *Mathematical Programming, 87*, 385–399. doi:10.1007/s101070050002

Beasley, J. E. (1993). Lagrangean relaxation. In Reeves, C. R. (Ed.), *Modern heuristic techniques for combinatorial problems* (pp. 243–303). Blackwell Scientific Publications.

Boschetti, M., & Maniezzo, V. (2009). Benders decomposition, Lagrangian relaxation and metaheuristic design. *Journal of Heuristics, 15*(3), 283–312. doi:10.1007/s10732-007-9064-9

Everett, H. III. (1963). Generalized Lagrange multiplier method for solving problems of optimum allocation of resources. *Operations Research, 11*, 399–417. doi:10.1287/opre.11.3.399

Fisher, M. L. (1985). An application oriented guide to Lagrangian relaxation. *Interfaces, 15*, 10–21. doi:10.1287/inte.15.2.10

Geoffrion, A. M. (1974). Lagrangian relaxation and its uses in integer programming. *Mathematical Programming Study, 2*, 82–114. doi:10.1007/BFb0120690

Guignard, M. (2003). Lagrangian relaxation. *Top (Madrid), 11*(2), 151–228. doi:10.1007/BF02579036

Lemarechal, C. (2001). Lagrangian relaxation. In Junger, M., & Naddef, D. (Eds.), *Computational combinatorial optimization* (pp. 115–160). Springer Verlag. doi:10.1007/3-540-45586-8_4

Li, D., & Sun, X. (2006). *Nonlinear integer programming*. Springer.

Litvinchev, I., & Rangel, S. (2011). Many-to-many assignment problem: Lagrangian bounds and heuristic. In Vasant, P., Barsoum, N., & Webb, J. (Eds.), *Innovation in power, control and optimization: Emerging energy technologies* (pp. 220–247). Hershey, PA: IGI Global. doi:10.4018/978-1-61350-138-2.ch007

Maniezzo, V., Stutzle, T., & Vob, S. (Eds.). (2009). *Metaheuristics. Hybridizing metaheuristics and mathematical programming*. Springer.

Shapiro, J. F. (1974). A survey of Lagrangean techniques for discrete optimization. *Annals of Discrete Mathematics*, 5, 113–138. doi:10.1016/S0167-5060(08)70346-7

KEY TERMS AND DEFINITIONS

Lagrangian Dual Problem: Aims to find Lagrangian multipliers corresponding to the tightest Lagrangian bound.

Lagrangian Heuristic: Uses a solution to the Lagrangian (Lagrangian dual) problem as a starting or reference point in a heuristic approach.

Lagrangian Multipliers: Coefficients of the linear combination of the constraints used to form a penalty term in the Lagrangian function.

Lagrangian Relaxation Bounds: Bounds to the original optimal objective value provided by the Lagrangian problem.

Lagrangian Relaxation: Relaxation of a number of constraints together with aggregating a penalty term to the objective function to discourage their violation.

Two Stage Capacitated Location Problem: Involves location of plants and depots of limited production and storage capacities to satisfy client demands and minimize the total cost composed of the fixed cost of opening the plants and depots, and the variable cost associated with transportation of a single product from plants to depots, and from depots to customers.

Chapter 15
Generators Maintenance Scheduling Using Music–Inspired Harmony Search Algorithm

Laiq Khan
COMSATS Institute of Information Technology, Pakistan

Rabiah Badar
COMSATS Institute of Information Technology, Pakistan

Sidra Mumtaz
COMSATS Institute of Information Technology, Pakistan

ABSTRACT

This work explores the potential of Music-Inspired Harmony Search (MIHS), meta-heuristic technique, in the area of power system for Generator Maintenance Scheduling (GMS). MIHS has been used to generate optimal preventive maintenance schedule for generators to maintain reliable and economical power system operation taking into account the maintenance window, load and crew constraints. The robustness of the algorithm has been evaluated for five different case studies: 8-units test system, 13-units test system, 21-units test system, 62-units test system, and 136-units test system of Water and Power Development Authority (WAPDA) Pakistan. As per previous practice, WAPDA used to use manual scheduling based on hit-and-trial. The simulations have been carried out in MATLAB®. Based on its comparison with Genetic Algorithm (GA), it has been found that MIHS has fast convergence rate and optimal schedule for all the test systems satisfying the stated constraints.

DOI: 10.4018/978-1-4666-2086-5.ch015

1. INTRODUCTION

The advancement and expansion of modern power system has resulted into the increased number of generators. Therefore, maintenance of generating units has become inevitable for a healthy power system. For this purpose, power systems need some schedule to switch off some of its generating units for maintenance satisfying the load demand. GMS is a large-scale, nonlinear and stochastic optimization problem with many constraints and conflicting objective functions (Ben, Duffaa and Raout, 2000).

The main concern in controlling large power production systems is to make the best use of accessible resources, which require substantial planning. In the power production system, the production output of individual unit is calculated on hourly basis to fulfill the load demand. The significant aspect in power production system is to maintain units/generators following a proper schedule, so that reliability of the system can be achieved. GMS plays an important role in increasing the efficiency and effectiveness of power system. Therefore, maintenance scheduling in the power system plays a very important role in overall operations. The effectiveness of GMS is highly dependent on the target and timing of the maintenance activities.

The main aspiration of GMS is to schedule the generating units for maintenance in such an optimized way that production costs are minimized meeting certain levels of power system security and adequacy. Maintenance ensures the long life and good performance of generators. In routine maintenance, periodic inspection of generators is performed to check any buildup of contamination (dirt, oil, etc.) on the windings. If the wound components are covered with heavy concentrations of grease and grunge, the generator is disassembled and systematically cleaned. The main concern regarding the generators maintenance planning is to achieve an optimized objective function under series of constraints.

The purpose of GMS is to extend the generator's lifetime or at least the mean time to the next failure. Maintenance can be classified into two main categories (Mohammadi, Pirmoradian and Hassanpour, 2008);

- Unplanned/Corrective Maintenance (CM)
- Planned Maintenance

CM also known as run-to-failure, a generator is not maintained until it fails (Bensnard et al., 2009). This approach is suitable when the cost of failure is not important, which is perceptibly not appropriate for most transmission systems. Planned maintenance includes Predictive Maintenance (PdM) and Preventive Maintenance (PM). PdM is carried out on the basis of regular monitoring, periodic inspections and diagnostic tests.

In PM, the maintenance is performed in order to evade a failure (Saraiva et al., 2010). PM strategies are further divided into three different types;

- Time based PM
- Condition based PM
- Reliability centered PM

Time based PM is generally a traditional and costly approach, in which inspection and maintenance are performed at fixed time intervals, often, but not essentially, based on specifications. Condition based PM offers a maintenance from knowledge characterizing the generator's condition, as condition monitoring may recognize incipient failures.

Comparative to time based PM, condition based PM usually extends the interval between successive maintenances and therefore, usually incurs less cost, although it needs a vital amount of infrastructure investment to gauge, communicate, store, and utilize the essential information characterizing the state. Reliability centered PM utilizes monitoring information together with an investigation of requirements and priorities and usually results in a prioritization of maintenance responsibilities based on some catalogue or indices that reproduce generator condition. Reliability centered PM is an on-going process that determines the maintenance practices to grant the vital reliability at the minimum cost. It can help to decrease the cost of maintenance appreciably. Reliability centered PM estimates the generator's failure probability and then utilizes the prioritization of those failed generators in maintenance task.

The maintenance schedule may span over three time periods and may enhance the reliability of the power system. These time spans are long-term maintenance scheduling, mid-term maintenance scheduling and short-term maintenance scheduling.

- **Long-Term Maintenance Interval:** Spreads over the number of years. These types of models are used in electric generators in large electric production power plants.
- **Mid-Term Maintenance Interval:** Based upon one-year time. These types of models are also used in large maintenance jobs or during shutdown maintenance.
- **Short-Term Maintenance Interval:** Based upon days or weeks. In such types of models, reliability criteria of the system cannot be violated. Maintenance tasks require generator's outage, peak load (demand) of each interval, a significant amount of human attention (Crew) and earliest-latest period of each generator during which generators have to be maintained. Hence short-term PM scheduling decides the best power system performance regarding maximizing the minimum net reserves satisfying the load demand.

In case of short-term maintenance, the generator is shut down and prior to shut down all loads are disconnected, because, these loads can be damaged by low voltage. Short-term generator maintenance consists of the following steps;

- **Electrical Maintenance Section:** In this section, electrical parts of generator, which consist of rotor, stator, exciters and auxiliaries are checked and maintained.
- **Mechanical Maintenance Section:** Mechanical parts of generators such as, brakes, bearings, compressor blades, oil deflectors, oil seals, fuel nozzles, valves, quill shafts and couplings are repaired in this portion.
- **Control Panel Maintenance Section:** Control panel consists of transducers, fuel and start relays, ammeter, voltmeter, frequency meter, current transformer (CT), potential transformers (PT) etc. All these parts of generator are tested out and repaired.
- **Hardware Maintenance Section:** Cablings, wirings, AC/DC panels, air/oil filters etc. are monitored and repaired in this portion.
- **Software Maintenance Section:** Software is an application program that calculates output as a function of different variables. Supervisory Control and Data Acquisition (SCADA) is one of the application programs, which is used for monitoring and process control. This software stores backup of the system at regular intervals. Software debugging is done in this section.

Generator maintenance scheduling (GMS) is a large-scale, nonlinear and stochastic optimization problem with many constraints and conflicting objective functions (Edwin & Curtius, 1990). To solve the GMS problem, generating units are scheduled in such an optimized way so that all operational constrains are satisfied and objective function may have an optimized minimum value. To obtain optimized solution for complex GMS problem, a number of different solutions exist. They include conventional solutions including heuristic techniques or mathematical methods including integer programming, branch-and-bound techniques and dynamic programming etc (Dopazo and Merrill, 1975; Egan, Dillon and Morsztyn, 1976; Kotb, 2008; Yamayee and Sidenblad, 1983). To overcome the limitation of heuristic and mathematical methods, different meta-heuristic techniques are proposed to solve complex GMS problem. These meta-heuristic techniques are quite distinct from that of conventional methods. These include Genetic Algorithm (GA), Simulated Annealing (SA), Particle Swarm Optimization (PSO), Evolutionary Programming (EP), Tabu Search (TS) and MIHS etc.

Meta means "beyond" or "higher level" and heuristic means "to find". Generally, Meta-heuristic techniques are used to solve those problems, which don't have not appropriate problem-specific algorithm.

MIHS is a relatively new meta-heuristic technique first developed by Z. W. Geem, J. H. Kim and G. V. Loganathan in 2001 (Geem et al. 2001). MIHS is a search optimization process for optimal solution inspired by music improvisation. This harmony in music is similar to explore the optimum solution in optimization process. Music creativeness process is analogous to search process in optimization. The perfect harmony is determined by the audio aesthetic standard. This aesthetic standard depends upon the pitch, timber and amplitude of musical instruments. There is a sequence in the music notes to create the perfect harmony. Random music notes are unable to create a pleasant harmony.

The three main factors of MIHS algorithm are;

- Harmony Memory (HM)
- Pitch Adjustment (PA)
- Randomization

The best harmonies are stored in HM at rate "u_{accept}". Different notes are generated using pitch adjustment. The two important factors of PA are pitch bandwidth and pitch adjustment rate. Pitch is adjusted linearly. The last important factor of randomization is used to increase the diversity of the solution. HM and PA explores the local best solution while randomization computes the global best solution.

GMS finds out the best possible level of resources required to meet the load. These resources involve manpower, skills, spare parts, equipment and tools etc. The generators maintenance program is planned in such a way that each generator must complete its maintenance in a specified time window. The constraints, which are considered in the generators maintenance planning, are maintenance completion constraint, reliability centered PM window constraint, crew availability constraint, priority constraint and load constraint.

It is important to choose an appropriate objective function meeting all the constraints. Objective function can be either minimizing the economic cost or improving the reliability. Due to relatively small cost difference between most and least expensive maintenance schedule, it is often better to use reliability indices rather than cost minimization for objective function formulation (Dahal & Galloway, 2007). The objective function for the reliability centered PM scheduling must satisfy the following constraints;

- **Maintenance Completion Constraint:** This constraint ensures that a generator must complete its maintenance without interruption.
- **Reliability Centered Pm Window Constraint:** This constraint ensures that maintenance for each generator must be completed in a specified window.
- **Crew Availability Constraint:** Available manpower must be greater than or equal to the required manpower.
- **Priority Constraint:** This type of constraint ensures that the critical generators are maintained prior to others.
- **Load Constraint:** This type of constraint ensures that total generation must be greater than or equal to demand (load).

GMS defines the feasible generator maintenance period, duration, maintenance sequence and continual period of maintenance task. The planning to get an optimal generators maintenance schedule is expected to accomplish many goals, which include:

- The performance of generators is enhanced.
- Lifetime of each generator is extended.
- Frequency of failure of each generator is reduced.
- Maintenance cost and fuel utilization is minimized.
- The system revenues are maximized.
- System reliability level is achieved.

This chapter gives the application of MIHS, meta-heuristic approach, in terms of parameter sensitivity and optimized solutions for the GMS problem.

Rest of the chapter has been arranged as follows: section 2 gives a detailed literature review of different optimization techniques. Section 3 gives modeling of GMS problem and objective function details. Section 4 comprises introduction and the inclusion of MIHS in GMS. Section 5 gives the description of case studies used for this research and simulation results. Section 6 explores future dimensions in this field and finally section 7 concludes this research.

2. BACKGROUND

A large number of different types of optimization solution methods exist in literature to solve GMS problem. Difference between these methods is due to their computational competence, size of the problem they can solve and solution excellence of each method. These solution methods are categorized as follows:

- Mathematical techniques
- Heuristic search methods
- Expert systems

- Fuzzy approach
- Meta-heuristic techniques

The main drawback of exact mathematical methods and non-heuristic techniques is that the size of search space increases exponentially with the size of problem and becomes computationally impractical. These techniques, in their standard form, are generally unsuitable for the nonlinear objectives and constraints and several assumptions are used to solve the problem using reasonable computational resources (Miranda, Srinivasan and Proenca, 1998).

The heuristic-based techniques evaluate the problem in a specific time interval and being problem-specific techniques, they require significant operator input and may even fail to and feasible solutions (Yamayee and Sidenblad, 1983). To overcome these limitations, a number of meta-heuristic based approaches for maintenance have been studied. Some of the details of these techniques are as follows:

2.1 Mathematical Techniques

Literature survey has proved that the mathematical techniques for solving GMS are not very useful due to multidimensional nature of the problem. Mathematical techniques include dynamic programming, integer programming, mixed integer programming and branch and bound method. These methods are extensively used to solve the small size problems successfully. In case of large sized problems, these methods become inefficient due to latency. A short description of each method is given below.

2.1.1 Dynamic Programming (DP)

In DP the best possible solution is achieved by dividing the problem into different sub-stages. Each sub-stage represents a time period and consists of a number of states. These states represent the number of possible combinations of units/generators to achieve the feasible solution. The best solution of a stage is saved unless next best solution is not found and then replaces the previous best solution by current best solution. The application of DP for chronological and concurrent GMS problem is not more promising, because, it is efficient only in case of small size problems. DP limits the computational requirement of GMS. (Zurn and Quintana, 1975).

2.1.2 Integer Programming (IP) and Mixed Integer Programming (MIP)

IP is considered among one of the powerful optimization tool for solving GMS problem. It has been successfully applied to the GMS problem (Mukerji 1991; Edwin and Curtius, 1990; Satoh 1992; Chattopadhyay and Bhattacharaya, 1995).

The main disadvantage of IP is that the estimations are used for uncertainties. It also goes beyond the computer capabilities. In order to decrease the computer load of IP, MIP is used, which is a suboptimal approach. So, there is a tradeoff between computational efficiency and the optimal solution.

2.1.3 Branch and Bound (B&B) Methods

B&B method is based on the principle to divide the original problem into singular sub-problems. These singular sub-problems are easier to compute. Search space is limited by the solution achieved by each singular sub-problem. Since, the problem can be either in integer or in binary domain. In case of integer problem, each sub-problem is same as that of original problem. The only difference between them is that a certain number of integers are fixed in each sub-problem. In case of binary problem, the original problem is divided into two main sub-problems. Each sub-problem is further divided into two sub-problems and so on. This sub-division is continued until the total enumeration tree is built. B&B selects the best

node from all the active nodes in iteration and rejects all others. As B&B selects the best solution by excluding parts of solution space, therefore, this method is quite successful for medium sized GMS problems (Boardman and Meckiff, 1985).

2.2 Heuristic Search Methods

The GMS solutions provided by heuristic methods are based on trial and error concept. Each unit is considered individually. Although, heuristic methods are founded on simple and clear concepts with very less computational time, feasible solution cannot be guaranteed. A number of heuristic methods exist in the literature. The most frequently used methods are based on equalizing the risk and net reserve of whole year (Stremel, 1982; EI-Sheikhi and Billinton, 1988; Contaxis, Kavatza and Vournas, 1989).

2.3 Expert Systems (ES)

Expert systems or knowledge-based systems are more promising for solving GMS problems. The only drawback of expert systems is that sometimes rule based ES are composed of heuristic suppositions.

(Nara, Satoh and Maeda, 1997) have proposed an algorithm for optimized GMS which combines an ES with mathematical programming. In this method, a transportation problem of one-month stage length is solved to obtain a rough maintenance schedule and then this solution is modified to make it feasible by using an ES. (Lin et al., 1992) have presented a prototype knowledge based ES for solving the optimized GMS problem in Taiwan Power Corporation (TPC) system. The knowledge base in this ES, which includes generator constraints, has been built in consultation with the utility planners of TPC and is expressed by rules and logic representations. This algorithm is not applicable to other system.

2.4 Fuzzy Approach

GMS problem consists of conflicting objective functions like system maximum reliability, maximizing reserves and the minimum operation cost etc. The fuzzy approach for solving GMS problem is quite efficient. Fuzzy approach can be divided into three phases: fuzzification, inference and de-fuzzification.

Firstly, the crisp input is fuzzified by designated membership function. Inference engine is used to investigate the appropriate rules from the knowledge base. De-fuzzification gives the final output of the system. In the case of GMS objectives and constraints are also fuzzified using respective designated membership functions.

Lin et al. and Huang et al. (1992) were the first to introduce a fuzzy concept to solve the GMS by using dynamic programming combined with the fuzzy sets, so that several complicated factors and uncertainties of the maintenance scheduling, which otherwise require much more computation time, can be handled out easily. The objectives and the constraints are fuzzified by proper membership functions. The technique was applied to the TPC system having 30 generating units. The fuzzy dynamic programming is more promising to obtain a good maintenance scheduling solution as compared to other conventional techniques.

2.5 Meta-Heuristic Techniques and MIHS

Meta-heuristic techniques are used to find an efficient optimization solution within a reasonable time. These can be classified in many groups on the basis of search space and objective function. For example, on the basis of search space they can be grouped as nature inspired and non-nature inspired, population-based and local search-based, one or neighbourhood structure and memory or memory-less methods (Blum and Roli 2003). On the other hand, objective function based techniques are classified on the basis of dynamic or static

objective functions. This section gives a brief review of meta-heuristic techniques like GA, PSO and VBA alongwith MIHS.

GA is a search procedure, which is used in search problems to compute an exact and optimized solution. GA is considered as global search heuristic technique based on evolutionary biology such as inheritance, mutation, selection and crossover. GA is superb for large sized problems, which have potentially vast search space and the optimal combinations are obtained by navigating through the search space. In GA, there is a population of solutions, which is evolved by natural selection. The optimization problem is represented by chromosome and this chromosome encodes the solution parameters by a numeric string. Evaluation function is used to calculate the fitness of each solution. The fitness is measured in accordance with objective function and constraints of the problem. The fit solutions of each generation are survived to form the next generation and unfit solutions are discarded. Stochastic operators include crossover and mutation which are used to create next generation. Successive generations of the population are used to find out the optimal solution. GA is a very powerful technique to solve complex multi-objectives optimization problems, such as GMS, unit commitment, economic load dispatch etc. The three important issues while solving the optimization problem using GA are:

- Representation of optimization problem.
- Evaluation function.
- Selection criteria of new solutions.

GA is implemented on practical optimization problems. These practical optimization problems require to choose solution representation and evaluation function. The convergence of GA is improved by hybridization. In hybridization, GA is initialized with the best solution of other meta-heuristic techniques, such as PSO, VBA etc. In (Kim, Nara and Gen, 1994; Kim, Hayashi and Gen, 2004) GA is hybridized with SA and

TS to solve the maintenance problem showing improved convergence.

PSO is a population based search algorithm. It shows the social behavior of birds in a swarm. The initial intent of the particle swarm concept was to graphically simulate the graceful and unpredictable choreography of a bird flock (Kennedy & Eberhart, 1995), with the aim of discovering patterns that govern the ability of birds to fly synchronously and to suddenly change direction with regrouping in an optimal formation. This concept of birds flock introduces a simple and competent optimization algorithm.

PSO adjusts the trajectories of each particle by exploring the space of evaluation function. The movement of each particle in swarm depends upon the social psychological tendency of that particle to imitate the success of other particles. The movement of particles also depends upon the experience and knowledge of their neighbour. In this search process, the particles stochastically come back to the previous best regions in the search space. The collective behavior of particles is to explore the optimal region. In PSO algorithm, each particle represents a best possible solution.

The PSO algorithm evolves on the basis of global best and personal (local) best minima. Personal best is used to enhance the diversity in the solution worth, whereas, global best is used to accelerate the convergence of the algorithm.

Accelerated PSO check all the new locations of particles to analyze the constraints. If constraints are not satisfied in a new location, then that location is discarded and newly generated location replaces that location. This procedure is continued until all constraints are satisfied. The new solutions in which constraints are completely satisfied are then evaluated. In this way, only feasible solutions are selected and infeasible solutions are discarded.

Accelerated PSO is almost memoryless algorithm, because, it doesn't record the movement of each particle. In various studies accelerated PSO outperforms than the other conventional algorithms.

Another meta-heuristic technique named VBA was first developed by Xin-She Yang in 2005 (Xin-She, 2005). VBA is an optimization algorithm based on the intellectual behavior of honey bees. The purpose of this algorithm is to optimize multivariable functions. In order to avoid the premature convergence, VBA uses Boltzmann selection method instead of roulette wheel. VBA is inspired by the foraging behavior of the honey bees swarm. VBA presents a sort of neighbourhood search along with random search.

A swarm of bees can extend itself over long distances (more than 10 km) and in multiple directions simultaneously to exploit a large number of food sources (Frisch, 1976). In principle, flower patches with plentiful amounts of nectar or pollen that can be collected with less effort should be visited by more bees, whereas patches with less nectar or pollen should receive fewer bees (Seeley, 1996). The foraging process is done by scout bees, which are sent to explore for capable flower patches. Scout bees randomly travel from one patch to another. When they return to the hive, those scout bees that found a patch which is rated above a certain quality threshold (measured as a combination of some constituents, such as sugar content) deposit their nectar or pollen and go to the "dance floor" to perform a dance known as the "waggle dance". This mysterious dance is essential for colony communication and contains three pieces of information regarding a flower patch: the direction in which it will be found, its distance from the hive and its quality rating (or fitness) (Bonabeau, Dori, and Theraulaz, 1999). After waggle dance, the scout bees return to the flower patch with recruit bees, which are waiting inside the hive. Recruit bees gather food quickly and efficiently. Honey bees functionality to search the nectar is associated with virtual bees as follows:

- In VBA, the objective function is frequently encoded as virtual nectar.
- Efficient allocation of foraging in honey bees is equivalent to explore the possible solutions in VBA.

- Foragers evaluate the quality of food sources by waggle dance along with nectar concentration in case of honey bees is same as to evaluate the fitness function to find the optimal solutions in VBA
- No central control in case of honey bees is equivalent to decision making without global knowledge of the environment in VBA.

Due to some of initialization problems and specific mathematical requirements in the above mentioned techniques, MIHS was first introduced by Geem (2001). Due to its fast convergence and optimal performance MIHS found great applications soon after its introduction, like structural design (Lee and Geem, 2004; Geem 2009d), tour planning (Geem et al. 2005a), vehicle routing (Geem et al. 2005b), satellite heat pipe design (Geem and Hwangbo 2006), music composition (Geem and Choi 2007), Sudoku puzzle solving (Geem 2007b), dam scheduling (Geem 2007b), energy system dispatch (Vasebi et al. 2007), ground water modeling (Ayvaz 2007, 2009), ecological conservation (Geem and Williams 2008), transportation energy modeling (Ceylan et al. 2008), soil stability analysis (Cheng et al. 2008), web page clustering (Forsati et al. 2008; Mahdavi and Abolhassani 2009), timetabling (Al-Betar et al. 2008, 2010a) water network design (Geem 2009a), heat exchanger design (Fesanghary et al. 2009), image segmentation (Alia et al. 2009a,c), medical physics (Panchal, 2009), medical image (Alia et al. 2009b, 2010), RNA structure prediction (Mohsen et al. 2010) etc.

In order to improve and diversify its performance, MIHS was combined with different meta-heuristic techniques. Alia and Mandava (2011) gave a detailed review of its hybrids with other meta-heuristic techniques. MIHS, its modified versions and its hybrids with other heuristic techniques have attracted the attention of many researchers in different fields of life including scientific, technological, industrial, economic and social sectors due to its powerful optimization capability. In the field of power system, researchers have applied MIHS and its variants for cost reduction, load dispatch, combined heat and power economic dispatch, multi-stage scheduling for power system degradation, optimal power flow, optimal placement of FACTS devices for security and series-parallel power system optimization. It is used to solve multi-objective optimization problems (Geem & Hwangboo, 2006).

MIHS is based on music improvisation and does not require initial values for its decision variables.

3. GMS MODEL FORMULATION

The major concern of GMS is to provide a timetable for generators maintenance preserving system reliability, reducing the operating cost, enhancing the generator lifetime and making the system less sensitive to new installations.

The main focus of the mathematical techniques is on:

- **GMS:** Finds the sequence of scheduled outages of generators over a specified period of time in order to maintain the net reserve level.
- **Generating Unit Properties:** These involve the constraints that each generator must satisfy. All the data, used in model formulation has been taken from WAPDA power production system Pakistan.

Mathematically, the GMS test problem can be formulated as an integer-programming problem by using integer variables associated with answers to "When does maintenance start?" or alternatively by using conventional binary variables associated with answers to "When does maintenance occur?" (Dopazo and Merrill, 1975). To solve

GMS problem, firstly all the constraints must be satisfied during each interval. The following notations are used in GMS mathematical model:

- $T_{(weeks)}$ = Total number of weeks (periods) in the planning horizon
- $N_{(units)}$ = Total number of generators/units in the power production system
- $I_{(units)}$ = Set of generators indices
- ind = Index of generators
- tnd = Index of weeks
- ear_{ind} = Earliest week of generator "ind" to start maintenance
- lat_{ind} = Latest week of generator "ind" to end maintenance
- dur_{ind} = Duration of maintenance of "ind" generator
- $cap_{ind,tnd}$ = Generating capacity of generator "ind" in week "tnd"
- lod_{tnd} = Load demand for period "tnd"
- $NM_{ind,tnd}$ = Man power needed by generator "ind" at period "tnd"
- AM_{tnd} = Man power available at period "tnd"

3.1 GMS Objective Function

GMS is a challenging multi-objective constrained optimization issue. To resolve this issue, the foremost concern is the selection of objective function. The objective function could be cost based or reliability based. The operating/economic cost based objective function for GMS is used to minimize the total operational cost over the specified planning period. Economic cost comprises two components: production cost and maintenance cost. Production cost is associated with fuel cost, needed for generators to generate a certain amount of electricity. The maintenance cost is concerned with the generators maintenance tasks, when a generator is off-line.

The three main issues regarding reliability based objective function to solve GMS problem are;

- Load probability
- Expected energy
- Expected reserves

Load probability reliability based objective function, is used to minimize the sum of individual loss of the load probability during each interval. The expected energy not supplied in the power production system can be used as reliability criteria for the objective function to solve GMS problem. Net reserve is the most significant reliability criterion for solving GMS problem. The net reserve of the power production system during any time interval "t" is the sum of total capacity of all installed units, minus the peak forecasted load during that time interval and the sum of capacity of the units that are on the maintenance.

Reserve based objective function for GMS is used to maximize the minimum reserve of the system during any time period. In case, when there is a large variation in reserve margin due to either large forecasted load or a large number of units scheduled on maintenance then minimizing the sum of squares of the reserves is used to solve this problem.

3.2 Objective Function Formulation

Two types of objective functions have been considered to check the robustness of the algorithm. One is considered to optimize the reserve margin (see Box 1).

The other is to levelize the reserve margin in each generation by minimizing the sum of squares of net reserve (see Box 2).

Reserve based objective function is the most appropriate to solve the GMS problem. GMS objective function maximizes the minimum reserve margin during each generation.

Box 1.

$$\uparrow OBJ1 = \underset{U_{ind,tnd}}{Min}\left(\sum_{ind \in I_{(units)}} cap_{ind,tnd} - \sum_{ind \in I_{(units)tnd}}\left(\sum_{j \in s_{ind,tnd}} U_{ind,j}cap_{ind,j}\right) - lod_{tnd}\right) \qquad (1)$$

Box 2.

$$\downarrow OBJ2 = \underset{U_{ind,tnd}}{Min}\left\{ \sum_{tnd \in T_{(weeks)}}\left(\sum_{ind \in I_{(units)}} cap_{ind,tnd} - \sum_{ind \in I_{(units)tnd}}\left(\sum_{j \in s_{ind,tnd}} U_{ind,j}cap_{ind,j}\right) - lod_{tnd}\right)^2\right\} \qquad (2)$$

Let $T_{(weeks)ind} \subset T_{(weeks)}$ is the set of weeks when maintenance of generator "*ind*" may start.

For each unit "*ind*"; (see Box 3).

Equation (3) gives the specified time period during which a generator is maintained. If a generator is off-line for maintenance then "1" is used to represent that the generator is on maintenance whereas, "0" indicates that generator is not on maintenance (see Box 4).

For each unit '$ind \in I_{(units)}$' and '$tnd \in T_{(weeks)ind}$'. Let '$S_{ind,tnd}$' is the set of start time periods. If maintenance of a unit ind starts at week j, that unit must be maintained at period "*tnd*" (see Box 5).

The net reserve of the power production system during generators maintenance scheduling can be formulated as in Equation 6 in Box 6.

This objective function can be summarized as follows:

The term $\sum_{ind \in I_{(units)tnd}}\left(\sum_{j \in s_{ind,tnd}} U_{ind,j}cap_{ind,j}\right)$ represents that generating capacities of only those units are accumulated which are on the maintenance during time interval "tnd". The term $\sum_{ind \in I_{(units)}} cap_{ind,tnd}$ indicates the total generating capacities of all installed generators. '"lod_{tnd}"' represents the peak load during "tnd" interval.

Reserves in "tnd" interval= Total generating capacity- total generation loss due to maintenance-peak load during "tnd" interval

After completing for "$T_{(weeks)}$", one generation's net reserve is obtained by taking the minimum reserve (Khan, Mumtaz and Kamran, 2010; Yare, Venayagamoorthy and Aliyu, 2008).

3.3 Maintenance Window Constraint

This constraint guarantees that once a generator is detached from the power production system for maintenance, it completes the maintenance without any stoppage. It remains detached from the power production system until its maintenance period "dur_{ind}" is completed.

$$\sum_{tnd \in T_{(weeks)ind}} U_{ind,tnd} = 1 \qquad \forall\ ind \in I_{units} \qquad (7)$$

Equation (7) represents the maintenance window constraint.

3.4 Crew Constraint

Crew constraint states that the number of people to perform maintenance schedule for each period must be less than or equal to the available manpower (see Box 7 for Equation 8)

Box 3.

$$T_{(weeks)ind} = \left\{ tnd \in T_{(weeks)} : ear_{ind} \le tnd \le lat_{ind} - dur_{ind} + 1 \right\} \tag{3}$$

Box 4.

$$U_{ind,tnd} = \begin{cases} 1 & \text{if unit } ind \text{ starts maintenance in } tnd \text{ week} \\ 0 & \text{otherwise} \end{cases} \tag{4}$$

Box 5.

$$S_{ind,tnd} = \left\{ j \in T_{(weeks)ind} : tnd - dur_{ind} + 1 \le j \le tnd \right\} \tag{5}$$

Box 6.

$$net\_reserve = \underset{U_{ind,tnd}}{Min} \left(\sum_{ind \in I_{(units)}} cap_{ind,tnd} - \sum_{ind \in I_{(units)tnd}} \left(\sum_{j \in s_{ind,tnd}} U_{ind,j} cap_{ind,j} \right) - lod_{tnd} \right) \tag{6}$$

Box 7..

$$\sum_{ind \in I_{(units)tnd}} \sum_{j \in S_{ind,tnd}} U_{ind,j} NM_{ind,j} \le AM_{tnd}; \quad \forall \; tnd \in T_{(weeks)} \tag{8}$$

3.5 Load Constraint

Total capacity of the generating units running at any interval $"tnd"$ should not be less than the forecasted peak load at that interval. This constraint can be formulated as Equation 9 in Box 8.

Equations (3), (4), (5), (6), (7), (8), and (9) present a general mathematical model for GMS problem. The objective function given by Equa-

tion (6) calculates the reliability of the power production system. Lesser the values of objective, the reserve margin are more consistently distributed and higher reliability of the system is achieved. When the difference of reserve is large, then sum of squares of reserve is minimized.

The evaluation function for the proposed GMS solution is;

$$fx\_val = net\_reserve + w_1 * con_1 + w_2 * con_2 + w_3 * con_3 \tag{10}$$

where, "fx_val" is the fitness value and "$net\_reserve$" represents the net reserve of a particle, which is given by Equation 6.

"con_1" represents the maintenance window constraint, which is calculated by using the following equation:

$$\sum_{tnd \in T_{(weeks)ind}} U_{ind,tnd} = 1 \qquad \forall \ ind \in I_{units} \tag{11}$$

"con_2" represents the crew constraint, which is computed in Box 9.

"con_3" represents the load constraint, which is calculated by using Equation 13 in Box 10.

In Equation (10), w_1, w_2 and w_3 represent the weights of violations of con_1, con_2 and con_3 respectively.

The main purpose of the fitness function is to achieve the reliability of the power production utility by maximizing the minimum net reserves along with the satisfaction of maintenance window constraint, crew constraint and load constraint and is given by equation (2).

4. MIHS ALGORITHM

In optimization problem, the musical instruments, pitch adjustment, harmony, aesthetics and particles correspond to decision variables, value range, solution vector, objective function and iterations respectively.

During the improvisation, a musician has three possible options; selects famous music notes from memory, selects known music notes and creates new notes. In optimization process, these three choices are analogous to the use of harmony memory (HM), pitch adjustment (PA) and randomization.

Box 8.

$$\sum_{ind \in I_{(units)}} cap_{ind,tnd} - \sum_{ind \in I_{(units)tnd}} \sum_{j \in S_{ind,tnd}} U_{ind,j} cap_{ind,j} \geq lod_{tnd}; \forall \ tnd \in T_{(weeks)} \tag{9}$$

Box 9.

$$\sum_{ind \in I_{(units)tnd}} \sum_{j \in S_{ind,tnd}} U_{ind,j} NM_{ind,j} \leq AM_{tnd}; \qquad \forall \ tnd \in T_{(weeks)} \tag{12}$$

Box 10.

$$\sum_{ind \in I_{(units)}} cap_{ind,tnd} - \sum_{ind \in I_{(units)tnd}} \sum_{j \in S_{ind,tnd}} U_{ind,j} cap_{ind,j} \geq lod_{tnd} \qquad \forall \ tnd \in T_{(weeks)} \tag{13}$$

HM usage is very important, because, it guarantees that excellent harmonies are selected as new solution vectors. To make MIHS more competent, the algorithm adopts a parameter called HM accepting rate "α_{accept}". The value of "α_{accept}" lies between [0, 1]. If the value of "α_{accept}" is too small, then only few best harmonies are selected. In this case, the algorithm converges very slowly. If the value of "α_{accept}" is too large (near 1) then algorithm is unable to explore extremely good solutions (Geem, Kim and Loganathan, 2001).

Therefore, usually,

$$\alpha_{accept} = 0.7 \sim 0.95 \qquad (14)$$

PA depends upon the pitch bandwidth "$p_{bandwidth}$" and pitch adjustment rate "pa_{rate}". PA means changing the frequency to generate slightly different notes. In MIHS, pitch is adjusted linearly using the following equation;

$$h_{new} = h_{old} + p_{bandwidth} * \gamma \qquad (15)$$

where, "h_{old}" is old pitch stored in the HM and "h_{new}" is adjusted pitch. The pitch is adjusted by adding the small random amount in the old pitch. "γ" is the arbitrary number in the range of [-1, 1]. The PA rate "pa_{rate}" is used to control the degree of the adjustment. The algorithm converges quite slowly in case when the PA rate is small along narrow bandwidth, because, only a small subspace of whole space is provided to algorithm to explore optimal solution. If the PA rate is very high along with wider bandwidth, then scattered solutions around some potential optima are achieved. Thus, PA rate should be;

$$pa_{rate} = 0.1 \sim 0.5 \qquad (16)$$

The last important component of MIHS is randomization. The main aim of randomization is to increase the diversity of the solutions. Randomiza-

tion makes MIHS more promising by exploring various diverse solutions, so that global optimality is achieved. The probability of randomization is computed by using the following equation;

$$R_{prob} = 1 - \alpha_{accept} \qquad (17)$$

The PA probability is;

$$p_{prob} = \alpha_{accept} * pa_{rate} \qquad (18)$$

Two important components of MIHS are; diversification (exploration) and intensification (exploitation). PA and randomization is used to control the diversification in MIHS. Intensification ensures to accelerate the convergence by reducing the randomness and limiting diversification. Intensification is carried out by using harmony memory. To get the optimal solution, diversification and intensification is required to balance optimally.

Generally, HM and PA explores the local best solutions, while the randomization computes the global best solutions.

4.1 Harmony Search Algorithm Steps

Harmony search algorithm consists of following steps (Fesanghary *et al.*, 2008) (see Algorithm 1)

The conceptual framework of MIHS has been shown in Figure 1. MIHS is a random search optimization method in which HM plays a vital role in optimization performance by storing the past searched experiences. Figure 2 gives the detailed algorithmic flow chart of MIHS showing the sequence of operations. It is of particular importance to represent the harmony according to the optimization problem, while solving GMS problem.

Algorithm 1. Harmony search algorithm

Step 1: Initialize the optimization problem.
Step 2: Initialize Harmony Memory. HM matrix is randomly filled with solution vectors according to the size "*s*" of harmony memory. For an "*N*" dimension optimized problem $\left(h_1, h_2, \ldots, h_N\right)$ HM is initialized as follows;

$$HM = \begin{bmatrix} h_1(t), h_2(t), \ldots, h_N(t) \\ h_1(t+1), h_2(t+1), \ldots, h_N(t+1) \\ \vdots \\ h_1(t+s), h_2(t+s), \ldots, h_N(t+s) \end{bmatrix} \quad (19)$$

Step 3: A stored harmony $\left(h_1(t), h_2(t), \ldots, h_N(t)\right)$ is selected from the HM. A new harmony $\left(h_1'(t), h_2'(t), \ldots, h_N'(t)\right)$ is improvised from this selected harmony by using harmony memory accepting rate ' α_{accept} '. This new solution is further mutated using pitch adjustment rate ' pa_{rate} '. MIHS generates new solutions by fully utilizing all the HM members.
Step 4: Evaluate the fitness of new harmony. Compare the fitness of this new harmony with the fitness of old harmony. Fit harmony is placed in the HM and worst harmony is discarded thereby updating the HM with the best one.
Step 5: Repeat the step 3 and step 4, until stopping criteria is met.

Figure 1. Conceptual framework of harmony search algorithm

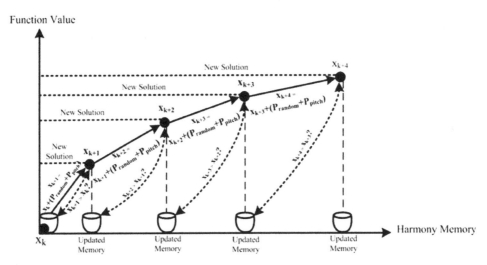

4.2 Harmony Representation

A harmony represents a complete solution for GMS problem, which consists of the maintenance start period of each generator of the power system. The size of a harmony depends upon the number of generators used in the power production system. The start week of each generator in the harmony is bounded by the earliest and latest start period (week).

A power production system consists of "*N*" number of generators, the harmony is:

$$nt_1, nt_2, \ldots, nt_i, \ldots, nt_N \quad (20)$$

where, "nt_i" is a generator bounded by;

Figure 2. HS flowchart for GMS solution

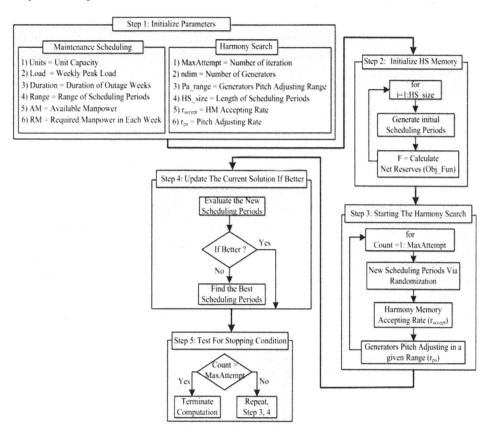

$$ear_i \leq nt_i \leq (lat_i + dur_i + 1) \qquad (21)$$

"*ear_i*" is the earliest start week, "*lat_i*" is the latest start week and "*dur_i*" is the outage duration of generator "*i*".

The fitness of every virtual harmony is calculated by evaluation function using Equation (10).

5. RESULTS AND DISCUSSION

MIHS has been investigated for five different case studies of 8-units, 13-units, 26-units and 136-units test power system. The test systems have been studied for a planning period of 6 weeks, 26 weeks, 52 weeks, 26 weeks and one year, respectively. For a time step of 110-2000, the values of different parameters of MIHS al-

gorithm have been adjusted keeping in view the facts discussed earlier in section 4, as $\alpha_{accept} = 0.95$, $pa_{rate} = 0.7$ and pitch adjustment range of 200 for MIHS size of 20-40. MATLAB® has been used as a simulation tool to generate the results. For simulation time or speed comparison the system has been simulated using Intel® dual core 2.4GHz processor with 512MB memory.

5.1 Case Study-1: 8-Units Test System

This test system comprises 8 units over a planning period of 6 weeks (Negnevisky and Kela-reva, 1999a). The maintenance outages for the generating units are scheduled to maximize the minimum net reserves as mentioned in Equation (6) satisfying all the constraints.

Figure 3 (a) shows the results for load constraint for 8-units test system showing that the available generation is much greater than the load demand and there is no need to shed the load for observed study period. RM has been shown in Figure 5 (b). Figure 3(a) and 3 (b) show that the RM will be minimum when the load demand is maximum and vice versa. There are large variations in RM. Figure 5c shows the allowed maintenance periods satisfying the window constraint.

5.2 Case Study-2: 13-Units Test System

This test system consists of 13 units over a planning period of 26 weeks (Yare, 2007). A constant system peak load 2500 MW is used. The available crew is limited to 40 in each week. The objective function used for this case study is to levelize the reserve margin in each generation by minimizing the sum of squares of net reserve, as given by equation (2).

Figure 4 (a) shows the results for load constraint for 13-units test system. RM for this system is quite satisfactory and has been shown in Figure 4 (b). Figure 4 (c) shows that the maximum available crew for this system is 40 whereas the maximum required crew is always less than 30. Figure 4 (d) gives the allowed maintenance periods satisfying the window constraint.

5.3 Case Study-3: 21-Units Test System

The test problem consists of scheduling of the maintenance of 21 generating units over a planning period of 52 weeks (Dahal et al., 2000). The test system peak load is 4739 MW. Technical staff available in each week is 20. The maintenance outages for the units were scheduled to minimize the sum of squares of reserves using equation (2) satisfying the maintenance window constraint, crew constraint and load given by Equations 7, 8 and 9 respectively.

Figure 3. 8-units test system: (a) Load constraint (b) Reserve margin (c) Window constraint

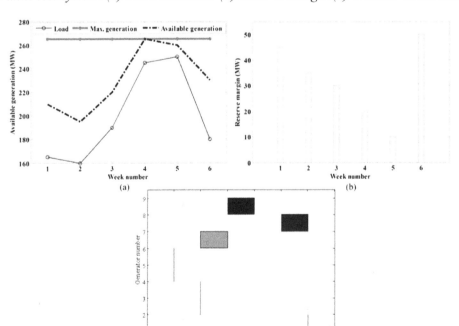

Figure 4. 13-units test system: (a) Load constraint, (b) Reserve margin,(c) Crew constraint,(d) Window constraint

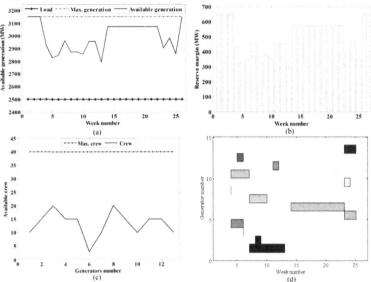

Figure 5 (a) shows the results for load constraint for 21-units test system. RM has been shown in Figure 5 (b). There are large variations in RM for 21-units test system. Figure 5 (c) shows that the maximum available crew for this system is 20 whereas the maximum required crew is always less than or equal to 20. Figure 5 (d) gives the allowed maintenance periods satisfying the window constraint.

5.4 Case Study-4: 62-Units Test System

The system consists of 62 units, which are to be maintained in 26 intervals (weeks) during a year (Negnevisky and Kelareva, 1999b). The proposed optimization approach is used to maximize the minimum net reserve and is given by Equation (7).

Figure 6 shows the results of load constraint, reserve margin, crew constraint and window constraint for 62-units test system. Figure 6 (a) shows that the maximum generation for 62-units is 2350 MW. The allowed maintenance periods have been shown in Figure 6 (c).

5.5 Case Study-5: 136-Units WAPDA Power Production System

One of the distributed and competitive power production systems is WAPDA Pakistan. WAPDA power production system was established in 1958. The massive agenda for the establishment of WAPDA was, coordinating and giving a distinct direction to the development schemes, regarding generation, transmission and distribution of electrical power. WAPDA system comprises 136 different power generators having different running costs. This system works under variation of customer demand.

The hierarchy of WAPDA power production system is divided into hydel and thermal.

Hydel power production system consists of (1) Tarbela power stations, (2) Mangla power station, (3) Ghazi Barotha power station, (4) Chashma power station and (5) Warsak power station.

Thermal power production system is further divided into independent power producers (IPPs) and generation companies (GENCOES). GENCO-1 includes four power stations, which

Figure 5. 21-units test system: (a) Load constraint,(b) Reserve margin, (c) Crew constraint, (d) Window constraint

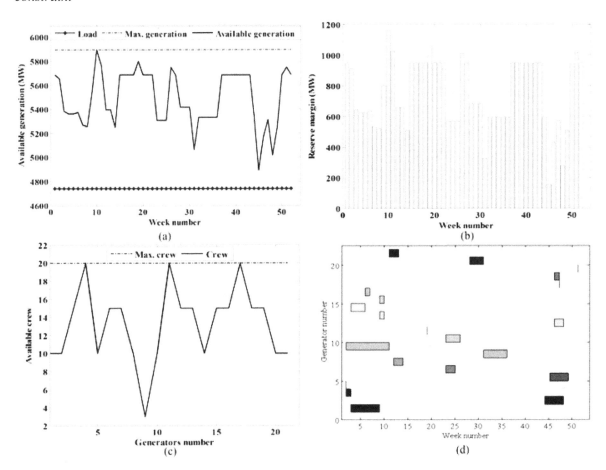

are: (6) Jamshoro, (7) Kotri, (8) Lakhra, and (9) Quetta power stations. GENCO-2 consists of (10) Guddu and (11) Sukkar Power Stations, GENCO-3 comprises of (12) Muzaffargarh, (13) Multan and (14) Gas and Steam Turbine Power Stations Faisalabad. IPPs are (15) KAPCO, (16) HUBCO, (17) KEL, (18) AES LALPIR, (19) AES PAKGEN, (20) SEPCOL, (21) HCPC, (22) UCH, (23) ROUSCH, (24) FAUJI KABIRWALA, (25) SABA POWER, (26) JAPAN POWER, (27) LIBERTY, and (28) JAGRAN.

The location of each power station, in Pakistan, has been shown in Figure 7. The production capacity of the thermal units is usually greater than that of hydel units. The electricity produced in both hydel and thermal goes to the same distribution

network and is distributed all over the country. The scheduling for the maintenance of these hydel and thermal generators of WAPDA power production system depends upon different time horizons during the 52 weeks time period (one year).

The reliability criterion of power system is achieved by maximizing the minimum net reserves by using equation (6).

Figure 8 shows the results of load constraint, reserve margin, crew constraint and window constraint for WAPDA test system. The maximum generation for 136 units is 2350 MW. Figure 8 (c) shows that the maximum available crew for WAPDA test system is 200 whereas the maximum requirement for crew is almost 110. Figure 8 (d) shows the allowed periods for which planned

Figure 6. 62-units test system: (a) Load constraint, (b) Reserve margin, (c) Window constraint

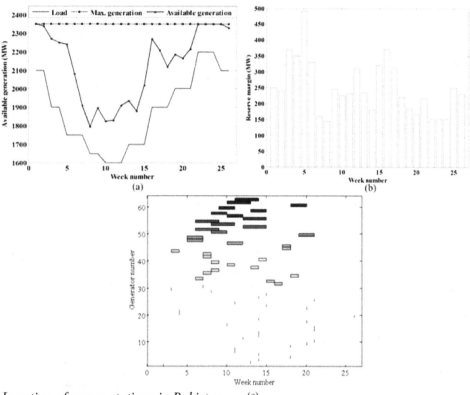

Figure 7. Location of power stations in Pakistan

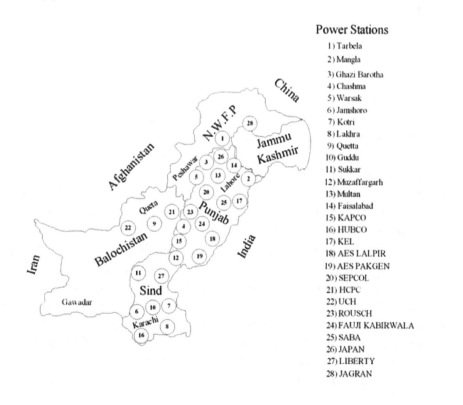

Figure 8. 136-units test system: (a) Load constraint, (b) Reserve margin, (c) Crew constraint, (d) Window constraint

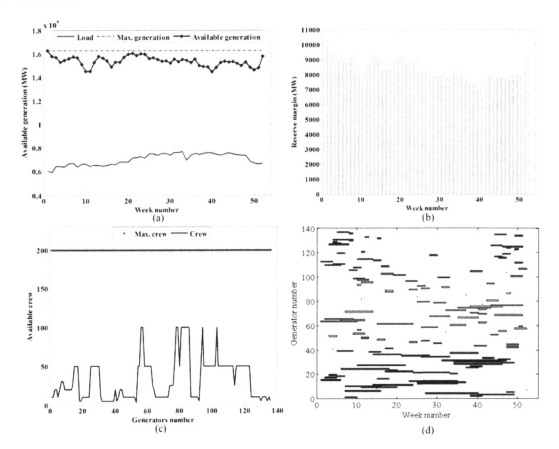

maintenance of generating units could be possible. Thermal and steam turbines could be shut down for maintenance only when the hydro plants are operating at their maximum generation. This corresponds to the months of January to April and November to December each year. The hydro plants can be scheduled for maintenance during low water level corresponding to the months of May to October. Within these months no thermal plant should be shut down for maintenance.

It is clear from Figure 8 and Figure 5 that the results are more promising in case of WAPDA test system as compared to a smaller 21-units test system. Crew margin is greater in case of 136-units test system as compared to 21-units test system, which is in accordance with the results for RM as shown in Figure 8b and Figure 5 (b). Figures

3 (a), 4 (a), 5 (a), 6 (a), 7 (a) and 8 (a) show the results for load constraint, again it can be seen that as the size of the system grows, the saved margin increases approaching the maximum generation limit.

Figure 9 shows the convergence of objective functions used for 8, 13, 21, 62 and 136 units test systems. OBJ2 has been used for case 2 and 3 and OBJ1 has been used for cases 1, 4 and 5. This is, because, the load variation for later two cases is more consistent as compared to the earlier ones as shown in Figures 3a-6a and Figure 8a. Figure 9 shows that objective function converges for almost 500 iterations in each case. These objective values were obtained with no violation of all mentioned constraint.

Figure 9. Objective function trace: (a) 13-units test system, (b) 13-units test system, (c) 21-units power system, (d) 62-units test system, (e) WAPDA power system

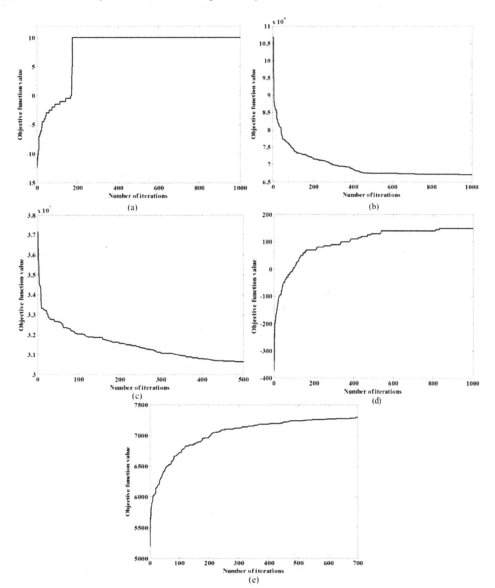

Figures 3 (b), 4 (b), 5 (b), 6 (b) and Figure 8 (b) shows that there are large variations in reserve margin for smaller size of power system whereas for large number of machines reserve margin is stable.

Finally, the results have been compared with GA. GA has been implemented using integer programming with a minimum of 500 generations and each generation consists of 20 chromosomes (population size). Table 1 gives the comparison of MIHS with GA for convergence speed and evaluation value of best solution. It is clear that MIHS is much faster than GA and hence suitable for solving GMS problem. Although, GA finds a solution with slightly better evaluation measure for all test systems as compared to MIHS, but the

Table 1. Comparison for MIHS and GA

#	Test System	No. of Iterations	Elapsed Time (sec.)		Evaluation Value of Best Solution	
			MIHS	GA	MIHS	GA
1	8-units	500	0.485	2.98	10	20
2	13-units	500	240.92	2332.24	6.55×10^6	1.1×10^6
3	21-units	500	269.02	2712.23	3.07×10^7	0.14×10^8
4	64-units	500	312.06	3150.73	145	150
5	136-units	500	403.86	4107.52	7300	7350

time taken by MIHS is quite shorter than that of GA. Tables 2 and 3 shows the optimal schedule for WAPDA power system. The power system weekly peak loads are given in Table 2. Table 3 gives the generating capacities, maintenance allowed periods, maintenance durations, available manpower and the crew needed for each generator of WAPDA. It is apparent from the above that MIHS is the best choice for GMS problems in terms of speed and quality of the solution.

6. FUTURE RESEARCH DIRECTIONS

Many variants of MIHS algorithms have been proposed in literature, each of them is tightly related to one aspect of this algorithm or the other such as parameters setting, balancing of intensification and diversification of MIHS and hybridizing it with other meta-heuristic techniques, as discussed earlier, can be used to study the optimization problem with the economic cost based objective function in addition to the objective functions used here.

Researchers have proposed a number of meta-heuristic techniques, to solve GSM problem, other than MIHS, a comparison of those techniques with MIHS on the basis of reliability index would be an interesting piece of study.

In addition to the constraints addressed in this research, geographical, material and transmission constraints could be considered to check the robustness of the algorithm.

7. CONCLUSION

This chapter presents the application of MIHS to GMS. GMS being an essential part for reliable operation of power system has been studied and discussed. A detailed literature survey along with solution methods for GMS problem has been discussed in this chapter. It has been found that analytical techniques are not much effective for multi-objective GMS problem. Heuristic search algorithms are efficient for small sized problems but they become inefficient in case of large sized problems. Expert systems become inappropriate in case when heuristic suppositions are applied on rules. Fuzzy approach can be applied to practical power systems, but cannot be generalized. Meta-heuristic optimization methods, such as genetic algorithms and particles swarm optimization seem to be more promising for large sized problems. Therefore, MIHS, meta-heuristic technique, has been proposed and successfully applied to five different case studies. Mathematical modeling for GMS incorporating each constraint and MIHS has been done. MATLAB simulation environment has been used to generate the results. MIHS has found promising results for each case by giving the optimal schedule satisfying the load, maintenance window and crew constraints, by increasing the reserve margin, for a period of one year. It has been observed that MIHS has fast convergence and low sensitivity to the parameters variation, showing that the algorithm works equally well for both small and large power systems. Finally, the proposed algorithm has been analyzed by comparing it with GA in terms of simulation speed and performance showing that MIHS is a good trade off for complexity, performance and speed.

REFERENCES

Al-Betar, M., Khader, A., & Liao, I. (2010). A harmony search with multi-pitch adjusting rate for the university course timetabling . In Geem, Z. (Ed.), *Studies in computational intelligence*. Springer. doi:10.1007/978-3-642-04317-8_13

Al-Betar, M. A., Khader, A. T., & Gani, T. A. (2008). A harmony search algorithm for university course timetabling. *7th International Conference on the Practice and Theory of Automated Timetabling* (pp. 1-12) Montreal, Canada.

Alia, O. M., & Mandava, R. (2011). The variants of harmony search algorithm: an overview. *Artificial Intelligence Review, 36*(1), 49–68. doi:10.1007/s10462-010-9201-y

Alia, O. M., Mandava, R., & Aziz, M. E. (2010). A hybrid harmony search algorithm to MRI brain segmentation. *The 9th IEEE International Conference on Cognitive Informatics, ICCI2010* (pp. 712–719). Tsinghua University, Beijing, China: IEEE.

Alia, O. M., Mandava, R., Ramachandram, D., & Aziz, M. E. (2009a). A novel image segmentation algorithm based on harmony fuzzy search algorithm. *International Conference of Soft Computing and Pattern Recognition (SOCPAR 09)* (pp. 335–340).

Alia, O. M., Mandava, R., Ramachandram, D., & Aziz, M. E. (2009b). Harmony search-based cluster initialization for fuzzy c-means segmentation of MR images. *TENCON 2009–2009 IEEE Region 10 Conference* (pp. 1–6). Singapore.

Alia, O. M., Mandava, R., Ramachandram, D., & Aziz, M. E. (2009c). Dynamic fuzzy clustering using harmony search with application to image segmentation. *IEEE International Symposium on Signal Processing and Information Technology (ISSPIT09)* (pp. 538–543).

Ayvaz, M. T. (2007). Simultaneous determination of aquifer parameters and zone structures with fuzzy c-means clustering and meta-heuristic harmony search algorithm. *Advances in Water Resources, 30*(11), 2326–2338. doi:10.1016/j.advwatres.2007.05.009

Ayvaz, M. T. (2009). Application of harmony search algorithm to the solution of groundwater management models. *Advances in Water Resources, 32*(6), 916–924. doi:10.1016/j.advwatres.2009.03.003

Ben-Daya, M., Duffaa, O. S., & Raout, A. (Eds.). (2000). *Maintenance modeling and optimization*. Boston, MA: Springer. doi:10.1007/978-1-4615-4329-9

Besnard, F., Patrikssont, M., Strombergt, A. B., Wojciechowskit, A., & Bertling, L. (2009). An optimization framework for opportunistic maintenance of offshore wind power system, 2009 IEEE Bucharest *Power Technology Conference*, (pp. 1-7). Bucharest.

Blum, C., & Roli, A. (2003). Metaheuristics in combinatorial optimization: Overview and conceptual comparison. *ACM Computing Surveys, 35*(3), 268–308. doi:10.1145/937503.937505

Boardman, J. T., & Meckiff, C. C. (1985). A branch-and-bound formulation to an electricity distribution planning problem . *IEEE Transactions in Power Applications Systems, PAS-104*(8), 2112–2118. doi:10.1109/TPAS.1985.318789

Bonabeau, E., Dorigo, M., & Theraulaz, G. (1999). *Swarm intelligence: From natural to artificial systems*. New York, NY: Oxford University Press.

Ceylan, H., Haldenbilen, S., & Baskan, O. (2008). Transport energy modeling with meta-heuristic harmony search algorithm, an application to Turkey. *Energy Policy, 36*(7), 2527–2535. doi:10.1016/j.enpol.2008.03.019

Chattopadhyay, D., & Bhattacharya, K. (1995). A systems approach to least-cost maintenance scheduling for an interconnected power system. *IEEE Transactions on Power Systems, 10*(4), 2002–2007. doi:10.1109/59.476069

Chen, L. N., & Toyoda, J. (1991). Optimal generating unit maintenance scheduling for multi area system with network constraints. *IEEE Transactions on Power Systems, 6*(3), 1168–1174. doi:10.1109/59.119262

Cheng, Y. M., Li, L., Lansivaara, T., Chi, S. C., & Sun, Y. J. (2008). An improved harmony search minimization algorithm using different slip surface generation methods for slope stability analysis. *Engineering Optimization, 40*(2), 95–115. doi:10.1080/03052150701618153

Contaxis, G. C., Kavatza, S. D., & Vournas, C. D. (1989). An interactive package for risk evaluation and maintenance scheduling. *IEEE Transactions on Power Systems, 4*(2), 389–395. doi:10.1109/59.193807

Dahal, K. P., McDonald, J. R., Burt, G. M., & Galloway, S. J. (2000). GN/SA-based hybrid techniques for the scheduling of generator maintenance in power systems. *IEEE Congress of Evolutionary Computation (CEC2000)* (pp. 567–574). San Diego.

Dopazo, J. F., & Merrill, H. M. (1975). Optimal generator maintenance scheduling using integer programming. *IEEE Transactions on Power Apparatus and Systems, PAS-94*(5), 1537–1545. doi:10.1109/T-PAS.1975.31996

Duval, P. E., & Poilpot, R. (1983). Determining maintenance schedule for thermal production units the KAPILA model. *IEEE Transactions on Power Apparatus and Systems, PAS-102*(8), 2509–2525. doi:10.1109/TPAS.1983.317751

Edwin, K. W., & Curtius, F. (1990). New maintenance scheduling method with production cast minimization via integer linear programming. *International Journal of Electrical Power & Energy Systems, 12*(3), 165–170. doi:10.1016/0142-0615(90)90029-B

Egan, G. T., Dillon, T. S., & Morsztyn, K. (1976). An experimental method of determination of optimal maintenance schedules in power systems using branch-and-bound technique. *IEEE Transactions on Systems, Man, and Cybernetics, 6*(8), 538–547. doi:10.1109/TSMC.1976.4309548

Escudero, L. F., Horton, J. M., & Scheiderich, J. E. (1980). *On maintenance scheduling for energy generators.* New York: IEEE-PES Winter Meeting.

Fesanghary, M., Damangir, E., & Soleimani, I. (2009). Design optimization of shell and tube heat exchangers using global sensitivity analysis and harmony search algorithm. *Applied Thermal Engineering, 29*(5–6), 1026–1031. doi:10.1016/j.applthermaleng.2008.05.018

Fesanghary, M., Mahdavi, M., Minary Jolandan, M., & Alizadeh, Y. (2008). Hybridizing harmony search algorithm with sequential quadratic programming for engineering optimization problems. *Computer Methods in Applied Mechanics and Engineering, 197*(33-40), pp. 3080-3091.

Forsati, R., Mahdavi, M., Kangavari, M., & Safarkhani, B. (2008). Web page clustering using harmony search optimization. *Canadian Conference on Electrical and Computer Engineering, CCECE* (pp. 1601–1604).

Frisch, K. V. (1976). *Bees: Their vision, chemical senses and language* (rev. ed.). Ithaca, NY: Cornell University Press.

Geem, Z. (2007b). Harmony search algorithm for solving sudoku. In B. Apolloni, R. J. Howlett, & L. Jain (Eds.), *11th International Conference, KES 2007 and XVII Italian Workshop on Neural Networks Conference on Knowledge-Based Intelligent Information and Engineering Systems: Part I*, (pp. 371–378). Berlin, Germany: Springer.

Geem, Z., & Choi, J. Y. (2007). Music composition using harmony search algorithm . In Giacobini, M. (Ed.), *Applications of evolutionary computing* (pp. 593–600). Berlin, Germany: Springer.

Geem, Z. W. (2009a). Particle-swarm harmony search for water network design. *Engineering Optimization*, *41*(4), 297–311. doi:10.1080/03052150802449227

Geem, Z. W. (Ed.). (2009b). *Harmony search algorithms for structural design optimization.* Berlin, Germany: Springer. doi:10.1007/978-3-642-03450-3

Geem, Z. W., & Hwangbo, H. (2006). Application of harmony search to multi-objective optimization for satellite heat pipe design. *US-Korea Conference on Science, Technology, & Entrepreneurship Teaneck* (pp 1–3). NJ, USA.

Geem, Z. W., & Hwangbo, H. (2006). Application of harmony search to multi-objective optimization for satellite heat pipe design. *US-Korea Conference on Science, Technology, & Entrepreneurship (UKC 2006)* (pp. 1–3). Teaneck, NJ: Citeseer.

Geem, Z. W., Kim, J. H., & Loganathan, G. (2001). A new heuristic optimization algorithm: Harmony search. *Simulation*, *76*(2), 60–68. doi:10.1177/003754970107600201

Geem, Z. W., Lee, K. S., & Park, Y. (2005b). Application of harmony search to vehicle routing. *American Journal of Applied Sciences*, *2*(12), 1552–1557. doi:10.3844/ajassp.2005.1552.1557

Geem, Z. W., Tseng, C. L., & Park, Y. (2005a). Harmony search for generalized orienteering problem: Best touring in China . In Wang, L., Chen, K., & Ong, Y. (Eds.), *Advances in natural computation* (pp. 741–750). Berlin, Germany: Springer. doi:10.1007/11539902_91

Geem, Z. W., & Williams, J. C. (2008). Ecological optimization using harmony search. *American Conference on Applied Mathematics*, Cambridge, Massachusetts.

Huang, C. J., Lin, C. E., & Huang, C. L. (1992). Fuzzy approach for generator maintenance scheduling. *Electric Power Systems Research*, *24*(1), 31–38. doi:10.1016/0378-7796(92)90042-Y

Kennedy, J., & Eberhart, R. C. (1995). Particle swarm optimization. *IEEE International Joint Conference on Neural Networks* (pp. 1942–1948). Piscataway, NJ.

Khan, L., Mumtaz, S., & Kamran, J. (2010). Generator maintenance scheduling using harmony search algorithm. *Journal of Engineering and Applied Sciences*, *29*(1), 99–115.

Kim, H., Hayashi, Y., & Nara, K. (1997). An algorithm for thermal unit maintenance scheduling through combined use of GA, SA and TS. *IEEE Transactions on Power Systems*, *12*(1), 329–335. doi:10.1109/59.574955

Kim, H., Nara, K., & Gen, M. (1994). A method for maintenance scheduling using GA combined with SA. *Computers & Industrial Engineering*, *27*(1-4), 477–480. doi:10.1016/0360-8352(94)90338-7

Kotb, M. F. (2008). Maintenance scheduling of generating units in electric power system. *12th International Middle-East* Power System Conference (pp. 543 – 549). Aswan.

Lee, K. S., & Geem, Z. W. (2004). A new structural optimization method based on the harmony search algorithm. *Computers & Structures*, *82*(9–10), 781–798. doi:10.1016/j.compstruc.2004.01.002

Lin, C. E., Huang, C. J., Huang, C. L., & Liang, C. C. (1992). An expert system for generator maintenance scheduling using operation index. *IEEE Transactions on Power Systems*, *7*(3), 1141–1148. doi:10.1109/59.207327

Mahdavi, M., & Abolhassani, H. (2009). Harmony k-means algorithm for document clustering. *Data Mining and Knowledge Discovery*, *18*(3), 370–391. doi:10.1007/s10618-008-0123-0

Miranda, V., Srinivasan, D., & Proenca, L. M. (1998). Evolutionary computation in power systems. *International Journal of Electrical Power & Energy Systems*, *20*(2), 89–98. doi:10.1016/S0142-0615(97)00040-9

Mohammadi, T. N., Pirmoradian, M., & Hassanpour, S. B. (2008). Implicit enumeration based 0-1 integer programming for generation maintenance scheduling. *IEEE Region 8 International Conference on Computational Technologies* in *Electrical* and *Electronics Engineering* (pp. 151–154). Novosibirsk.

Mohsen, A., Khader, A., & Ramachandram, D. (2010). An optimization algorithm based on harmony search for rna secondary structure prediction . In Geem, Z. (Ed.), *Recent advances in harmony search algorithm* (pp. 163–174). Berlin, Germany: Springer. doi:10.1007/978-3-642-04317-8_14

Momoh, J. A., Ma, X. W., & Tomsovic, K. (1995). Overview and literature survey of fuzzy set theory in power systems. *IEEE Transactions on Power Systems*, *10*(3), 1676–1690. doi:10.1109/59.466473

Mromlinski, L. R. (1985). Transportation problem as a model for optimal schedule of maintenance outages in power systems. *International Journal of Electrical Power & Energy Systems*, *7*(3), 161–164. doi:10.1016/0142-0615(85)90045-6

Mukerjee, R., Merrill, H. M., Erickson, B. W., Parker, J. H., & Friedman, R. E. (1991). Power plant maintenance scheduling optimizing economics and reliability. *IEEE Transactions on Power Systems*, *6*(2), 476–483. doi:10.1109/59.76689

Nara, K., Satoh, T., Aoki, K., & Kitagawa, M. (1991). Multi-year expansion planning for distribution systems . *IEEE Transactions on Power Systems*, *6*(3), 952–958. doi:10.1109/59.119234

Negnevisky, M., & Kelareva, G. V. (1999a). Maintenance scheduling in power systems using genetic algorithms. *International conference on Electric Power Engineering* (p. 187). Budapest, Hungary.

Negnevisky, M., & Kelareva, G. V. (1999b). Genetic algorithms for maintenance scheduling in power systems. *Australasian Universities Power Engineering Conference and IEAust Electric Energy Conference* (pp. 184-189). Darwin.

Panchal, A. (2009). Harmony search in therapeutic medical physics . In Geem, Z. (Ed.), *Music-inspired Harmony search algorithm* (pp. 189–203). Berlin, Germany: Springer. doi:10.1007/978-3-642-00185-7_12

Reed, J., Toombs, R., & Barricelli, N. A. (1967). Simulation of biological evolution and machine learning. *Journal of Theoretical Biology*, *17*(3), 319–342. doi:10.1016/0022-5193(67)90097-5

Saraiva, J. T., Pereira, M. L., Mendes, V. T., & Sousa, J. C. (2010). Preventive generation maintenance scheduling - A simulated annealing approach to use in competitive markets. 7th Mediterranean Conference and Exhibition on *Power Generation, Transmission, Distribution and Energy Conversion* (pp. 1-8), Agia Napa.

Satoh, H. (1992). A periodical maintenance scheduling of thermal and nuclear generating facilities using mixed integer programming. *Transactions of The Institute of Electrical Engineering Japan, 112-B*(l), 98–106.

Seeley, T. D. (1995). *The wisdom of the hive: The social physiology of honey bee colonies*. Cambridge, MA: Harvard University Press.

Silva, E. L., Morozowski, M., Fonseca, L. G. S., Oliveira, G. C., Melo, A. C. G., & Mello, J. C. (1995). Transmission constrained maintenance scheduling of generating units a stochastic programming approach. *IEEE Transactions on Power Systems, PWRS-10*(2), 695–701. doi:10.1109/59.387905

Stremel, J. P. (1982). Maintenance scheduling for generating system planning. *IEEE Transactions on Power Apparatus and Systems, PAS-100*(3), 1410–1419. doi:10.1109/TPAS.1981.316616

Vasebi, A., Fesanghary, M., & Bathaee, S. M. T. (2007). Combined heat and power economic dispatch by harmony search algorithm. *International Journal of Electrical Power & Energy Systems, 29*(10), 713–719. doi:10.1016/j.ijepes.2007.06.006

Xin-She, Y. (2005). Engineering optimizations via nature-inspired virtual bee algorithms . In Jose, M., & Jose, A. (Eds.), *Artificial Intelligence and Knowledge Engineering Applications: A Bioinspired Approach* (*Vol. 3562*, pp. 317–323). Lecture Notes in Computer Science Berlin, Germany: Springer. doi:10.1007/11499305_33

Yamayee, Z., & Sidenblad, K. (1983). A computationally efficient optimal maintenance scheduling method. *IEEE Transactions on Power Apparatus and Systems, PAS-102*(2), 330–338. doi:10.1109/TPAS.1983.317771

Yare, Y., & Venayagamoorthy, G. K. (2007). Optimal scheduling of generators maintenance using modified discrete particle swarm optimization. *2007 iREP Symposium- Bulk Power System Dynamics and Control- VII, Revitalizing operational reliability* (pp. 1-8). Charleston, SC, USA.

Yare, Y., Venayagamoorthy, G. K., & Aliyu, U. O. (2008). Optimal generator maintenance scheduling using a modified discrete PSO. *IET Generation, Transmission, and Distribution, 2*(6), 834–846. doi:10.1049/iet-gtd:20080030

Yellen, J., Al-Khamis, T. M., Vemuri, S., & Lemonidis, L. (1992). Decomposition approach to unit maintenance scheduling. *IEEE Transactions on Power Systems, 7*(2), 726–733. doi:10.1109/59.141779

Zurn, H. H., & Quintana, V. H. (1975). Generator maintenance scheduling via successive approximations dynamic programming. *IEEE Transactions on Power Apparatus, 94*(2), 665–671. doi:10.1109/T-PAS.1975.31894

ADDITIONAL READING

Ahmad, A., & Kothari, D. P. (2010). A review of recent advances in Generator maintenance scheduling. *Electric Machines & Power Systems, 26*(4), 373–387. doi:10.1080/07313569808955829

Angeline, P. J. (1998). Using selection to improve particle swam optimization. *IEEE Congress on Evolutionary Computations (CEC 1998)* (pp. 84-89). Anchorage, Alaska, USA.

Billinton, R., & Abdulwhab, A. (2003). Short-term generating unit maintenance scheduling in a restructured power system using a probabilistic approach. *IEE Proceeding on Generation, Transmission and Distribution, 150*(4), 463-468.

Billinton, R., & Mo, R. (2005). Composite system maintenance coordination in a deregulated environment. *IEEE Transactions on Power Systems, 20*(1), 485–492. doi:10.1109/TPWRS.2004.840449

Bonabeau, E., Dorigo, M., & Theraulaz, G. (1999). *Swarm intelligence: From natural to artificial systems.* New York, NY: Oxford University Press.

Camazine, S., Deneubourg, J., Franks, N. R., Sneyd, J., Theraula, G., & Bonabeau, E. (2003). *Self-organization in biological systems.* Princeton, NJ: Princeton University Press.

Conejo, A. J., Garcia-Bertrand, R., & Diaz-Salazar, M. (2005). Generation maintenance scheduling in restructured power systems. *IEEE Transactions on Power Systems, 20*(2), 984–992. doi:10.1109/TPWRS.2005.846078

Dahal, K. P., Aldrige, C. J., & McDonald, J. R. (1999). Generator maintenance scheduling using a genetic algorithm with a fuzzy evaluation function. *Fuzzy Sets and Systems, 102*(1), 21–29. doi:10.1016/S0165-0114(98)00199-7

Dahal, K. P., & Chakpitak, N. (2006). Generator maintenance scheduling in power systems using metaheuristic-based hybrid approaches. *Electric Power Systems Research, 77*(7), 771–779. doi:10.1016/j.epsr.2006.06.012

Dahal, K. P., & McDonald, J. R. (1997). Generator maintenance scheduling of electric power systems using genetic algorithms with integer representation. *IEE Conference on Genetic Algorithms in Engineering Systems: Innovations and Applications* (456-461). Glasgow, UK.

Dahal, K. P., McDonald, J. R., & Burt, G. M. (2000). Modern heuristic techniques for scheduling generator maintenance in power systems. *Transactions of the Institute of Measurement and Control, 22*(2), 179–194.

Egan, G. T., Dillon, T. S., & Morsztyn, K. (1976). An experimental method of determination of optimal maintenance schedules in power systems using branch-and-bound technique. *IEEE Transactions on Systems, Man, and Cybernetics, 6*(8), 538–547. doi:10.1109/TSMC.1976.4309548

El-Sharkh, M. Y., El-Keib, A. A., & Chen, H. (2003). A fuzzy evolutionary programming-based solution methodology for security-constrained generation maintenance scheduling. *Electric Power Systems Research, 67*(1), 67–72. doi:10.1016/S0378-7796(03)00076-2

Esmaeilzadeh, R., Amjadi, M., Eskandari, H., & Farrokhifar, M. (2007). Important viewpoints of maintenance scheduling in restructured power systems. *The International Conference on Computer (EUROCON)* (pp. 1621-1628). Warsaw.

Feng, C., Wang, X., & Wang, J. (2011). Iterative approach to generator maintenance schedule considering unexpected unit failures in restructured power systems. *European Transactions on Electrical Power, 21*(1), 142–154. doi:10.1002/etep.422

Feng, Y., Li, P., & Wang, H. (2011). Hydro-thermal generator maintenance scheduling accommodating both randomness and fuzziness. *International Conference on Electric Utility Deregulation and Restructuring and Power Technologies* (DRPT), (pp. 734–741).

Fetanat, A., & Shafipour, G. (2011). Generation maintenance scheduling in power systems using ant colony optimization for continuous domains based 0–1 integer programming. *Expert Systems with Applications, 38*(8), 9729–9735. doi:10.1016/j.eswa.2011.02.027

Firma, H. T., & Legey, L. F. L. (2002). Generation expansion: An iterative genetic algorithm approach. *IEEE Transactions on Power Systems, 17*(3), 901–906. doi:10.1109/TPWRS.2002.801036

Fu, Y., Li, Z., Shahidehpour, M., Zheng, T., & Litvinov, E. (2009). Coordination of midterm outage scheduling with short-term security-constrained unit commitment. *IEEE Transactions on Power Systems*, *24*(4), 1818–1830. doi:10.1109/TPWRS.2009.2030289

Geem, Z. W. (2009). *Optimal design of water distribution networks using harmony search*. Berlin, Germany: Springer. doi:10.1080/03052150500467430

Geem, Z. W. (Ed.). (2009). *Harmony search algorithms for structural design optimization*. Springer. doi:10.1007/978-3-642-03450-3

Geem, Z. W. (Ed.). (2009). *Music-inspired harmony search algorithm: Theory and applications*. Springer. doi:10.1007/978-3-642-00185-7

Geem, Z. W. (2010). *Recent advances in harmony search algorithm*. Berlin, Germany: Springer. doi:10.1007/978-3-642-04317-8

Geem, Z. W., Kim, J. H., & Loganathan, G. V. (2001). A new heuristic optimization algorithm: Harmony search. *Simulation*, *76*(2), 60–68. doi:10.1177/003754970107600201

Hu, X., & Eberhan, R. C. (2002). Adaptive particle swarm optimization: Detection and response IO dynamic systems. *IEEE Congress on Evolutionary Computation (CEC 2002)* (pp. 1666-1670). Honolulu, HI, USA.

Khan, L., Mumtaz, S., & Javed, K. (2010). Generators maintenance schedule for WAPDA system using meta-heuristic paradigms. *Australian Journal of Basic and Applied Sciences*, *4*(7), 1656–1667.

Kralj, B. L., & Petrovic, R. (1988). Optimal preventive maintenance scheduling of thermal generating units in power systems-a survey of problem formulation and solution methods. *European Journal of Operational Research*, *35*(1), 1–15. doi:10.1016/0377-2217(88)90374-8

Lei, W., Shahidehpour, M., & Tao, L. (2008). GENCO's risk-based maintenance outage scheduling. *IEEE Transactions on Power Systems*, *23*(1), 127–136. doi:10.1109/TPWRS.2007.913295

Lv, X. J., Jin, F., Lv, H. R., Tian, O. M., Yin, W. J., & Dong, J. (2011). Generation maintenance scheduling by security coordination considering transformer maintenance. Power and Energy Engineering Conference (APPEEC) (pp. 1-5). Wuhan.

Mahdavi, M., Fesanghary, M., & Damangir, E. (2007). An improved harmony search algorithm for solving optimization problems. *Applied Mathematics and Computation*, *188*(2), 1567–1579. doi:10.1016/j.amc.2006.11.033

Marwali, M. K. C., & Shahidehpour, S. M. (2000). Coordination between long-term and short-term generation scheduling with network constraints. *IEEE Transactions on Power Systems*, *15*(3), 1161–1167. doi:10.1109/59.871749

Minnda, V., & Fonscca, N. (2002) EPSO-best-of-two-world meta-heuristic applied to power system problems. *4th IEEE Congress on evolutionary computation (CEC 2002)* (pp. 1080-1085). Honolulu, HI, USA.

Oh, T., Choi, J., Cha, J., Baek, U., & Lee, K. Y. (2011). *Generator maintenance scheduling considering minimization of CO2 emissions* (pp. 1–6). IEEE Power and Energy Society.

Reihani, E., Davodi, M., Najjar, M., & Norouzizadeh, R. (2010). Reliability based generator maintenance scheduling using hybrid evolutionary approach. *IEEE Energy Conference* and *Exhibition* (EnergyCon) (pp. 847-852).

Shi, Y., & Krohling, R. A. (2002). Co-evolutionary particle swam optimization to solve min-max problems. *IEEE Congress on Evolutionary Computation (CEC 2002)* (pp. 1682-1687). Honolulu, HI, USA.

Srinivasan, D., Aik, K. C., & Malik, I. M. (2010). Generator maintenance scheduling with hybrid evolutionary algorithm. *IEEE International Conference on Probabilistic Methods Applied to Power Systems (PMAPS)* (pp. 632-637). Singapore.

Tabari, N. M., Ranjbar, A. M., & Sadati, N. (2002). Promoting the optimal maintenance schedule of generating facilities in open system. *IEEE-PES/CSEE International Conference on Power System Technology* (pp. 641-645).

Wang, Y., & Handschin, E. (2000). A new genetic algorithm for unit maintenance scheduling of power systems. *Electrical Power & Energy Systems*, *22*(5), 343–348. doi:10.1016/S0142-0615(99)00062-9

Yare, Y., & Venayagamoorthy, G. K. (2008). Comparison of DE and PSO for generator maintenance scheduling. *IEEE Swarm Intelligence Symposium* (pp. 1-8). St. Louis, MO.

Yare, Y., & Venayagamoorthy, G. K. (2010). Optimal maintenance scheduling of generators using multiple swarms-MDPSO framework. *Engineering Applications of Artificial Intelligence*, *23*(6), 895–910. doi:10.1016/j.engappai.2010.05.006

KEY TERMS AND DEFINITIONS

Generator Maintenance Scheduling: Defining a timetable for periodic dispatch of a generating unit from the system without affecting the normal system operation.

Harmony Search: Harmony search is a meta-heuristic algorithm inspired by inventiveness process of musician.

Maintenance: A combination of actions performed to retain a functional unit in its satisfactory operational condition and restore it in its working condition in case of failure.

Meta-Heuristic: Meta-heuristic is used to search feasible solution from hard task domain.

Multi-Objective Optimization: Optimizing more than one conflicting objective functions simultaneously, for given constraints.

Optimization: Minimize/maximize the objective function within the search space satisfying all the constraints to find a candidate solution.

Reliability: The probability of a system to perform a required task under certain specific conditions within a reasonable time.

Reserve Margin: The amount of unused available capacity of a power production system as percentage of total capacity.

APPENDIX

See Tables 2 and 3.

Table 2. Peak loads of WAPDA system

Interval #	Peak Load	Interval #	Peak Load	Interval #	Peak Load
1	6043	19	6796	37	7429
2	5888	20	6798	38	7510
3	6410	21	7146	39	7592
4	6440	22	7183	40	7539
5	6396	23	7251	41	7431
6	6650	24	7134	42	7352
7	6674	25	7467	43	7499
8	6408	26	7467	44	7566
9	6620	27	7351	45	7464
10	6604	28	7525	46	7401
11	6436	29	7513	47	7354
12	6550	30	7351	48	7354
13	6514	31	7584	49	6839
14	6478	32	7589	50	6701
15	6502	33	7653	51	6600
16	6631	34	6964	52	6691
17	6587	35	7364		
18	6791	36	7514		

Table 3. Data of WAPDA system

#	Power Stations	Capacity MW	Earliest Period	Latest Period	Outage Weeks	Available Manpower	Required Manpower
1	TPS GUDDU: ST-1	50	7	23	4	40	10+10+10+10
2	ST-2	75	29	45	4	40	10+10+10+10
3	ST-3	150	36	52	10	100	20+20+20+10+5+5+5
4	ST-4	150	24	50	14	150	20+20+20+20+10+10+10+5+5+5
5	CC-5 (GT7-8)	70	39	52	3	30	10+10+10
6	CC-6 (GT9-10)	65	1	20	10	100	20+20+20+10+5+5+5+5
7	GT-7	75	42	52	1	30	30
8	GT-8	80	8	21	1	30	30
9	GT-9	75	1	20	10	100	20+20+20+10+5+5+5
10	GT-10	75	1	20	10	100	20+20+20+10+5+5+5
11	GT-11	80	13	36	11	110	20+20+20+10+10+5+5+5
12	GT-12	115	16	39	11	110	20+20+20+10+10+5+5+5
13	CC-13 (GT11-12)	95	16	41	13	145	20+20+20+20+10+10+10+10+5+5+5+5+5
14	TPS JAM-SORO: ST-1	180	20	45	13	200	25+25+25+25+20+20+20+10+10+5+5+5+5
69	GT-8	77	38	52	3	20	10+5+5
70	SGT-9 (GT1,3)	105	28	43	3	20	10+5+5
71	SGT-10 (GT2,4)	99	1	18	8	50	10+10+5+5+5+5+5
72	SGT-11 (GT5,6)	86	28	46	6	35	10+5+5+5+5+5
73	SGT-12 (GT7,8)	84	38	52	3	20	10+5+5
74	GT-13	113	32	52	9	125	25+25+20+20+10+10+5+5+5
75	GT-14	115	33	52	9	125	25+25+20+20+10+5+5+5
76	SGT-15 (GT13,14)	126	33	52	9	125	25+25+20+20+10+10+5+5+5
77	HCPC	129	35	48	1	50	50
78	AES PAKGEN	350	28	48	4	250	100+50+50+50
79	AES LALPIR	350	24	40	4	250	100+50+50+50
80	SABA	125	30	46	4	120	50+25+25+20
81	ROUSCH: Half Complex	197	1	12	1	100	100
82	Half Complex	197	7	20	1	100	100

continued on following page

Table 3. Continued

#	Power Stations	Capacity MW	Earliest Period	Latest Period	Outage Weeks	Available Manpower	Required Manpower
15	ST-2	180	1	14	6	200	50+50+25 +25+25+25
16	ST-3	70	1	20	4	200	50+50+50+50
17	ST-4	170	1	15	4	200	50+50+50+50
18	GTPS KOTRI: GT-1	10	1	9	3	15	5+5+5
19	GT-2	10	1	16	3	15	5+5+5
20	GT-3	20	30	45	3	25	10+10+5
21	GT-4	20	14	36	10	65	10+5+5+5+5+5 +5+5+5
22	GT-5	20	7	27	8	50	10+10+5+5+5+5+5+5
23	GT-6	20	11	26	3	25	10+10+5
24	GT-7	40	1	19	13	65	10+10+5+5+5+5+5 +3+3+3+3
25	TPS M.GARH: ST-1	185	35	51	4	125	50+25+25+25
26	ST-2	200	35	51	4	175	50+50+50+25
27	ST-3	160	1	23	13	155	50+25+20 +10+10+5 +5+5+5+5+5
28	ST-4	245	33	52	13	155	50+25+20+10+10+5+5 +5+5+5+5+5
29	ST-5	170	40	52	4	200	50+50+50+50
30	ST-6	170	30	52	13	155	50+25+20+10+10+5+5 +5+5+5+5+5
31	NGPS MUL-TAN: ST-1	30	29	52	17	81	10+10+5 +5+5+5+5 +5+5+5+3+3 +3+3+3+3
32	ST-2	30	40	52	4	20	5+5+5+5
33	ST-4	30	26	52	4	20	5+5+5+5

#	Power Stations	Capacity MW	Earliest Period	Latest Period	Outage Weeks	Available Manpower	Required Manpower
83	Half Complex	197	16	27	1	100	100
84	Half Complex	197	24	37	1	100	100
85	Half Complex	197	33	46	1	100	100
86	Half Complex	395	38	52	2	200	100+100
87	SEPCOL: U # 1	21	15	30	3	20	10+5+5
88	U # 2	21	15	30	3	20	10+5+5
89	U # 3	21	15	30	3	20	10+5+5
90	U # 4	21	20	35	3	20	10+5+5
91	U # 5	21	20	35	3	20	10+5+5
92	U # 6	17	20	35	3	15	5+5+5
93	JAPAN	120	7	21	2	100	50+50
94	CNPP	300	30	52	3	200	100+50+50
95	TERBELA: 1	175	1	16	4	150	50+50+25+25
96	2	200	10	25	4	150	50+50+25+25
97	3	200	5	20	4	150	50+50+25+25
98	4	175	1	13	4	150	50+50+25+25
99	5	200	30	52	4	150	50+50+25+25
100	6	200	30	52	4	150	50+50+25+25
101	7	200	10	26	4	150	50+50+25+25

continued on following page

Table 3. Continued

#	Power Stations	Capacity MW	Earliest Period	Latest Period	Outage Weeks	Available Manpower	Required Manpower
34	GTPS F. ABAD: GT-1	19	20	40	8	30	5+5+5+3+3+3+3+3
35	GT-2	19	11	31	8	30	5+5+5+3+3+3+3+3
36	GT-3	19	2	22	8	30	5+5+5+3+3+3+3+3
37	GT-4	19	31	51	8	30	5+5+5+3+3+3+3+3
38	GT-5	23	2	20	4	20	5+5+5
39	GT-6	23	3	15	5	19	5+5+3+3
40	GT-7	23	2	17	1	20	20
41	GT-8	23	5	25	3	11	5+3+3
42	CC-9	42	40	52	4	30	10+10+5+5
43	SPS F. ABAD: ST-1	50	37	52	4	40	20+10+5+5
44	ST-2	50	42	52	4	40	20+10+5+5
45	KEL: U #1	15	21	36	3	20	10+5+5
46	U #2	15	15	30	3	20	10+5+5
47	U #3	15	20	35	3	20	10+5+5
48	U #4	15	5	20	3	20	10+5+5
49	U #5	10	1	13	3	20	10+5+5
50	U #6	15	2	17	3	20	10+5+5
51	U #7	15	1	9	3	20	10+5+5
52	U #8	15	41	52	3	20	10+5+5
53	STG	6	2	18	4	12	3+3+3
54	FKPCL: Full Complex	151	24	37	1	50	50

#	Power Stations	Capacity MW	Earliest Period	Latest Period	Outage Weeks	Available Manpower	Required Manpower
102	8	175	5	21	4	150	50+50+25+25
103	9	175	46	52	1	100	100
104	10	432	36	52	4	150	50+50+25+25
105	11	432	1	12	3	150	50+50+50
106	12	432	43	52	3	150	50+50+50
107	13	432	2	17	3	150	50+50+50
108	14	432	5	21	3	150	50+50+50
109	G.BAROTTHA: 1	240	1	25	5	110	50+25+20+10+5
110	2	290	1	10	4	120	50+25+25+20
111	3	290	43	52	3	125	50+50+25
112	4	290	1	14	4	120	50+25+25+20
113	5	290	2	17	3	125	50+50+25
114	MANGLA: 1	100	1	14	5	95	25+20+20+10+10
115	2	100	42	52	3	125	50+50+25
116	3	100	30	46	3	120	50+50+20
117	4	100	25	40	3	120	50+50+20
118	5	100	43	52	3	125	50+50+25
119	6	100	1	9	3	125	50+50+25
120	7	100	1	12	2	100	50+50
121	8	100	41	52	1	50	50
122	9	100	40	52	2	100	50+50

continued on following page

Table 3. Continued

#	Power Stations	Capacity MW	Earliest Period	Latest Period	Outage Weeks	Available Manpower	Required Manpower
55	Full Complex	151	37	52	3	150	50+50+50
56	LIBERTY	211	1	12	2	200	100+100
57	UCH	551	37	52	4	250	100+50+50+50
58	HUBCO: U # 1	300	22	39	5	255	50+50+50+50+25
59	U # 2	300	38	52	2	100	50+50
60	U # 3	300	33	50	5	255	50+50+50+50+25
61	U # 4	300	4	26	10	200	50+25+25+20+20+20 +20+10+5+5
62	KAPCO: GT-1	93	28	43	3	95	50+25+20
63	GT-2	52	1	20	10	97	25+20+20+10+5+5+3 +3+3
64	GT-3	81	1	18	7	49	20+10+5+5+3+3+3
65	GT-4	80	1	18	8	50	10+10+5+5+5+5+5+5
66	GT-5	78	28	46	6	35	10+5+5+5+5+5
67	GT-6	78	28	46	6	35	10+5+5+5+5+5
68	GT-7	79	33	52	8	50	10+10+5+5+5+5+5+5

#	Power Stations	Capacity MW	Earliest Period	Latest Period	Outage Weeks	Available Manpower	Required Manpower
123	10	100	30	52	2	100	50+50
124	WARSAK: 1	40	37	52	6	29	10+5+5+3+3+3
125	2	40	41	52	4	21	10+5+3+3
126	3	40	1	14	6	29	10+5+5+3+3+3
127	4	40	2	17	3	18	10+5+3
128	5	41	2	16	2	15	10+5
129	CHASHMA: 1	23	1	12	2	15	10+5
130	2	23	1	14	6	22	5+5+3+3+3+3
131	3	23	7	21	2	15	10+5
132	4	23	1	14	2	15	10+5
133	5	23	42	52	3	18	10+5+3
134	6	23	41	52	4	16	5+5+3+3
135	7	23	4	18	2	15	10+5
136	8	23	1	16	4	16	5+5+3+3

Chapter 16

Usage of Metaheuristics in Engineering:
A Literature Review

Ozlem Senvar
Marmara University, Turkey

Ebru Turanoglu
Selcuk University, Turkey

Cengiz Kahraman
Istanbul Technical University, Turkey

ABSTRACT

A metaheuristic is conventionally described as an iterative generation process which guides a servient heuristic by combining intelligently different concepts for exploring and exploiting the search space, learning strategies are used to structure information in order to find efficiently near-optimal solutions. In the literature, usage of metaheuristic in engineering problems is increasing in a rapid manner. In this study; a survey of the most important metaheuristics from a conceptual point of view is given. Background knowledge for each metaheuristics is presented. The publications are classified with respect to the used metaheuristic techniques and application areas. Advantages and disadvantages of metaheuristics can be found in this chapter. Future directions of metaheuristics are also mentioned.

1. INTRODUCTION

Metaheuristics are developed to deal with complex optimization problems where other optimization methods have failed to be either effective or efficient. These methods are known as one of the most practical approaches for solving many complex problems. This is particularly true for the many real-world problems that are combinatorial in nature. Consequently; the field of metaheuristics for the application to combinatorial optimization problems is a rapidly growing field of research. This is due to the importance of combinatorial optimization problems for the scientific as well

DOI: 10.4018/978-1-4666-2086-5.ch016

as the industrial world. The practical advantage of metaheuristics lies in both their effectiveness and general applicability (Ólafsson, 2006).

Metaheuristics are widely used for the solution of engineering problems. In the literature, some application areas are observed in ecological modeling, flow-shop scheduling, image processing, vehicle routing problem, assembly line balancing, energy forecasting, forecasting stock markets and etc. Figure 1 shows the frequencies of usage of each metaheuristic technique with respect to the publication years. From 2007 to 2011, approximately a ten times increase in the usage frequencies is observed.

Blum et al. (2011) provide a survey of some of the most important lines of hybridization. Their literature review is accompanied by the presentation of illustrative examples. They emphasize that research in metaheuristics for combinatorial optimization problems has lately experienced a noteworthy shift towards the hybridization of metaheuristics with other techniques for optimization. At the same time, the focus of research has changed from being rather algorithm-oriented to being more problem oriented.

To the best of our knowledge, there is not a recent work on the classification of the publications metaheuristics. The contribution of this chapter is to classify the publications on metaheuristics in engineering in the literature with respect to application problems and areas together with their authors.

The organization of the rest of this chapter is as follows. Section 2 summarizes metaheuristic techniques in engineering. Section 3 gives findings and discussions and the last section gives conclusions and future directions.

2. METAHEURISTIC TECHNIQUES IN ENGINEERING

In this section, metaheuristics techniques will be explained in a conceptual point of view. Additionally, a classification of each technique according to application problems and areas is presented.

2.1 Artificial Neural Networks

2.1.1 Networks

An efficient way of solving complex problems is following the lemma "divide and conquer". A complex system may be decomposed into simpler elements, in order to be able to understand it. Also simple elements may be gathered to produce a

Figure 1. Usage frequencies of each metaheuristic technique from 2007 to 2011

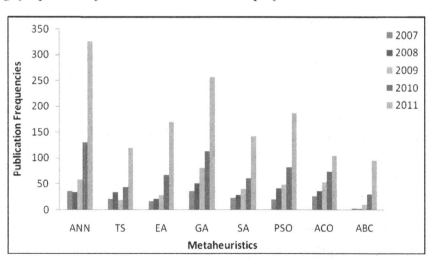

complex system (Bar-Yam, 1997). Networks are one way for achieving this. There are a large number of different types of networks, but they are all characterized by a set of nodes, and connections between nodes. The nodes can be seen as computational units. They receive inputs, and process them to obtain an output. The connections determine the information flow between nodes. They can be unidirectional, when the information flows only in one sense, and bidirectional, when the information flows in either sense. The interactions of nodes though the connections lead to a global behaviour of the network, which cannot be observed in the elements of the network. Networks are used to model a wide range of phenomena in physics, computer science, biochemistry, ethology, mathematics, sociology, economics, telecommunications, and many other areas.

2.1.2 Artificial Neural Networks (ANNs)

Artificial neural networks (ANN) have been developed as generalizations of mathematical models of biological nervous systems. In other words; ANNs, or simply neural networks (NNs), are information processing systems that roughly replicate the behavior of a human brain by emulating the operations and connectivity of biological neurons. Literally, the basic processing elements of neural networks are called artificial neurons, or simply neurons or nodes. In the literature, McCulloch and Pitts (1943) firstly introduced simplified neurons. In ANNs, network sees the nodes as artificial neurons. ANNs combine the artificial neurons in order to process information. Simply, an artificial neuron is a computational model inspired in the natural neurons.

The complexity of real neurons is highly abstracted when modeling artificial neurons. These basically consist of inputs (like synapses), which are multiplied by weights (strength of the respective signals), and then computed by a mathematical function which determines the activation of the neuron. Another function (which may be the iden-

tity) computes the output of the artificial neuron (sometimes in dependence of a certain threshold).

The signal flow from inputs $x_1, \ldots, x_n$ is considered to be unidirectional, which are indicated by arrows, as is a neuron's output signal flow (O). The neuron output signal O is expressed as follows:

$$O = f(net) = f\left(\sum_{j=1}^{n} w_j x_j\right) \tag{1}$$

where wj is the weight vector, and the function $f(net)$ is referred to as an activation (transfer) function. The variable net is defined as a scalar product of the weight and input vectors,

$$net = w^T x = w_1 x_1 + \ldots + w_n x_n \tag{2}$$

where T is the transpose of a matrix, and the output value O is simply computed as

$$O = f(net) = \begin{cases} 1, & if \ w^T x \geq 0 \\ 0, & otherwise \end{cases} \tag{3}$$

where θ is called the threshold level; and this type of node is called a linear threshold unit.

A neural network comprises the neuron and weight building blocks. The behavior of the network depends largely on the interaction between these building blocks. There are three types of neuron layers: input, hidden and output layers. Two layers of neuron communicate via a weight conection network. There are four types of weighted connections: feedforward, feedback, lateral, and time-delayed connections.

1. **Feedforward Connections:** For all the neural models, data from neurons of a lower layer are propagated forward to neurons of an upper layer via feedforward connections networks.

2. **Feedback Connections:** Feedback networks bring data from neurons of an upper layer back to neurons of a lower layer.
3. **Lateral Connections:** One typical example of a lateral network is the winners-takes-all circuit, which serves the important role of selecting the winner. In the feature map example, by allowing neurons to interact via the lateral network, a certain topological ordering relationship can be preserved. Another example is the *lateral orthogonalization network* which forces the network to extract orthogonal components.
4. **Time-Delayed Connections:** Delay elements may be incorporated into the connections to yield temporal dynamics models. They are more suitable for temporal pattern recognitions.

The synaptic connections may be fully or locally interconnected. Also, a neural network may be either a single layer feedback model or a multilayer feed-forward model. It is possible to cascade several single layer feedback neural nets to form a larger net.

The three steps in solving an ANN problem are given below:

1. Training,
2. Generalization or testing
3. Implementation.

Training is a process that network learns to recognize present pattern from input data set. Each ANN uses a set of training rules that define training method. Generalization or testing evaluates network ability in order to extract a feasible solution when the inputs are unknown to network and are not trained to network. How closely the actual output of the network matches the desired output in new situations should be examined. In the learning process the values of interconnection weights are adjusted so that the network produces a better approximation of the desired output. ANNs learn by example. They cannot be programmed to perform a specific task. The examples must be selected carefully otherwise useful time is wasted or even worse the network might be functioning incorrectly. The disadvantage is that because the network finds out how to solve the problem by itself and its operation can be unpredictable (Azadeh et al., 2011).

It is useful to understand the general network architecture. Unfortunately, general rules for determining the best architecture are not available. There are various types of artificial neural networks. Most commonly used ANN models are Multilayer Perceptron (MLP), Radial Basis Function Neural Networks (RBFNN), and Generalized Regression Neural Networks (GRNN).

ANN models can be used to infer a function from observations. This is particularly useful in applications where the complexity of the data or task makes the design of such a function by hand impractical. ANNs can be trained directly from data. ANNs can be used to extract patterns and detect trends thus it can be applied to data classification and nonlinear functional mapping. Specific application examples include process modeling, control, machine diagnosis, and real-time recognition. In addition to these, ANNs are being applied within the following broad categories:

- Robotics including directing manipulators, computer numerical control.
- Data processing including filtering, clustering, blind source separation and compression.
- Function approximation, or regression analysis, including time series prediction, fitness approximation and modeling.
- Classification, including pattern and sequence recognition, novelty detection and sequential decision making.

Some example areas of application of ANNs are listed in Table 1

2.2 Tabu Search (TS)

Difficulty in optimization problems encountered in practical settings such as telecommunications, logistics, financial planning, transportation and production has motivated in development of optimization techniques. Tabu search (TS) is a higher level heuristic algorithm for solving combinatorial optimization problems. It is an iterative improvement procedure that starts form an initial solution and attempts to determine a better solution.

The TS begins by marching to a local minima. The method records recent moves in one or more Tabu lists in order to avoid retracing the steps used,. The original intent of the list was not to prevent a previous move from being repeated, but rather to insure it was not reversed. The Tabu lists are historical in nature and form the TS memory. The role of the memory can change as the algorithm proceeds. At initialization the goal is to make a coarse examination of the solution space, known as 'diversification', but as candidate locations are identified the search is more focused to produce local optimal solutions in a process of 'intensification'. In many cases the differences between the various implementations of the Tabu method have to do with the size, variability, and adaptability of the Tabu memory to a particular problem domain. Hillier and Lieberman (2005) identify the parameters of TS as follows: local search procedure, neighborhood structure, aspiration conditions, form of tabu moves, addition of a tabu move, maximum size of tabu list, and stopping rule. Pham and Karaboga (2000) give the flowchart of TS algorithm, which is shown in Figure 2.

Hertz et al. (2005) determined the steps of TS algorithm (see Algorithm 1).

TS has traditionally been used on combinatorial optimization problems. The technique is straightforwardly applied to continuous functions by choosing a discrete encoding of the problem. TS has provided advances for solving difficult optimization problems in many domains. Many of the applications in the literature involve integer programming problems, scheduling, routing, traveling salesman and related problems. Current applications of TS span the realms of resource planning, telecommunications, financial analysis, space planning, energy distribution, molecular engineering, logistics, pattern classification, flexible manufacturing, waste management, mineral exploration, biomedical analysis, environmental conservation and scores of others. Some example areas of application of TS are listed in Table 2

Table 1. Some example areas of application of ANNs

Application Problem	Author and Year	Application Area
Modeling	Xia, 1996	Solving linear programming problems
	Dawson and Wilby, 1998	Rainfall-runoff modeling
	Lek and Guegan, 1999	Ecological modeling
Optimization	Park et al., 1991	Electric load forecasting
	Rehman and Mohandes, 2008	Estimation of global solar radiation using air temperature and relative humidity
	Yılmaz and Yuksek, 2008	Indirect Estimation of rock parameters
	Şenkal and Kuleli, 2009	Estimation of solar radiation

Figure 2. TS Procedure

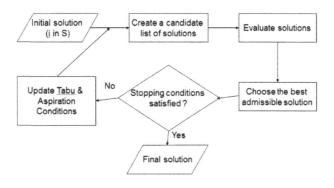

Algorithm 1. TS algorithm

Step 1: Choose an initial solution i in S. Set i* = i and k=0.
Step 2: Set k=k+1 and generate a subset V* of solution in N(i,k) such that either one of the Tabu conditions is violated or at least one of the aspiration conditions holds.
Step 3: Choose a best j in V* and set i=j.
Step 4: If f(i) < f(i*) then set i* = i.
Step 5: Update Tabu and aspiration conditions.
Step 6: If a stopping condition is met then stop. Else go to Step 2.

Table 2. Some example areas of application of TS

Application Problem	Author and Year	Application Area
Scheduling	Dodin et al., 1998	Audit scheduling
	Ben-Daya and Al-Fawzan, 1998	Flow-shop scheduling
	Geyik and Cedimoglu, 2004	Job-shop scheduling
Networking	Gallego et al., 2000	Network synthesis
	Da Silva et al.,2001	Transmission Network Expansion Planning
	Lin and Miller, 2004	Solving heat exchanger network synthesis problem
	Sun et al.,1998	Fixed charge transportation problem
Vehicle routing	Brandao, 2004	Open vehicle routing problem
	Brandao, 2006	Vehicle routing problem with backhauls

2.3 Evolutionary Algorithm (EA)

Evolutionary algorithms (EAs) are search methods that take their inspiration from natural selection and survival of the fittest in the biological world. EAs differ from more traditional optimization techniques in that they involve a search from a "population" of solutions, not from a single point. Each iteration of an EA involves a competitive selection that weeds out poor solutions. The solutions with high "fitness" are "recombined" with other solutions by swaping parts of a solution with another. Solutions are also "mutated" by making a small change to a single element of the solution. Recombination and mutation are used to generate new solutions that are biased towards regions of the space for which good solutions have already been seen. Figure 3 illustrates the EA procedure.

Figure 3. EA Procedure

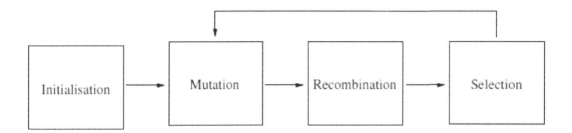

Several different types of evolutionary search methods were developed independently. These evoluationary search methods are listed below:

1. **Genetic Programming (GP):** Which evolves programs,
2. **Evolutionary Programming (EP):** Focuses on optimizing continuous functions without recombination,
3. **Evolutionary Strategies (ES):** Focuses on optimizing continuous functions with recombination,
4. **Genetic Algorithms (GAs):** Focuses on optimizing general combinatorial problems.

EAs are often viewed as a global optimization method although convergence to a global optimum is only guaranteed in a weak probabilistic sense. However, one of the strengths of EAs is that they perform well on "noisy" functions where there may be multiple local optima. EAs tend not to get "stuck" on a local minima and can often find a globally optimal solutions. EAs are well suited for a wide range of combinatorial and continuous problems, though the different variations are tailored towards specific domains:

- GPs are well suited for problems that require the determination of a function that can be simply expressed in a function form
- ESs and EPs are well suited for optimizing continuous functions

- GAs are well suited for optimizing combinatorial problems (though they have occasionally been applied to continuous problems)

The recombination operation used by EAs requires that the problem can be represented in a manner that makes combinations of two solutions likely to generate interesting solutions. Consequently selecting an appropriate representation is a challenging aspect of applying these methods.

EAs have been successfully applied to a variety of optimization problems such as wire routing, scheduling, traveling salesman, image processing, engineering design, parameter fitting, computer game playing, knapsack problems, and transportation problems. The initial formulations of GP, ES, EP and GAs considered their application to unconstrained problems. Although most research on EAs continuous to consider unconstrained problems, a variety of methods have been proposed for handling constraints. Some example areas of application of EAs are listed in Table 3

2.4 Genetic Algorithm (GA)

Holland (1975) developed genetic algorithms (GAs). GA search methods are rooted in the mechanisms of evolution and natural genetics. GAs are part of the adaptive stochastic optimization algorithms involving search and optimization. GAs provide an alternative to traditional optimization

Table 3. Some example areas of application of EAs

Application Problem	Author and Year	Application Area
Optimization	Fonseca and Fleming 1998	Multiobjective optimization and multiple constraint satisfaction
	Obayashi, 1998	Multidisciplinary design optimization of aircraft wing planform
	Handa et al., 2006	Salting route optimization (Resource minimization, Environment surveillance/protection

techniques by using directed random searches to locate optimal solutions in complex landscapes.

Genetic Algorithms are a family of computational models inspired by evolution. These algorithms encode a potential solution to a specific problem on a simple chromosome like data structure and apply recombination operators to these structures so as to preserve critical information. Genetic algorithms are often viewed as function optimizers although the range of problems to which genetic algorithms have been applied is quite broad.

The basic idea is to try to mimic a simple picture of natural selection in order to find a good algorithm. The first step is to mutate, or randomly vary, a given collection of sample programs. The second step is a selection step, which is often done through measuring against a fitness function. The process is repeated until a suitable solution is found.

The algorithm is started with a set of solutions (represented by chromosomes) called population. Solutions from one population are taken and used to form a new population. This is motivated by a hope, that the new population will be better than the old one. Solutions which are selected to form new solutions (offspring) are selected according to their fitness - the more suitable they are the more chances they have to reproduce. This is repeated until some condition (for example number of populations or improvement of the best solution) is satisfied.

Basic Genetic Algorithm Procedure is given in Algorithm 2 (reference ekle).

Some example areas of application of GAs are listed in Table 4

2.5 Differential Evolution (DE)

Differential Evolution (DE): Introduced by Storn and Price in 1996. DE is known as population-based optimisation algorithm similar to GAs using similar operators; crossover, mutation and selection. According to Karaboğa and Ökdem (2004), the main difference in constructing better solutions is that genetic algorithms rely on crossover while DE relies on mutation operation. This main operation is based on the differences of randomly

Algorithm 2.

Step 1. [**Start**] Generate random population of *n* chromosomes (suitable solutions for the problem)
Step2. [**Fitness**] Evaluate the fitness *f(x)* of each chromosome *x* in the population
Step 3. [**New population**] Create a new population by repeating following steps until the new population is complete
    1. [**Selection**] Select two parent chromosomes from a population according to their fitness (the better fitness, the bigger chance to be selected)
    2. [**Crossover**] With a crossover probability cross over the parents to form a new offspring (children). If no crossover was performed, offspring is an exact copy of parents.
    3. [**Mutation**] With a mutation probability mutate new offspring at each locus (position in chromosome).
    4. [**Accepting**] Place new offspring in a new population
Step 4. [**Replace**] Use new generated population for a further run of algorithm
Step 5. [**Test**] If the end condition is satisfied, **stop**, and return the best solution in current population
Step 6. [**Loop**] Go to step **2**

Table 4. Some example areas of application of GAs

Application Problem	Author and Year	Application Area
Estimation	Wilson and Vasudevan, 1991	Residual statics estimation
	Shin and Lee, 2002	Bankruptcy prediction modeling
Optimization	Wang, 1991	Function optimization (calibration of a conceptual rainfall-runoff model)
	Sundhararajan and Pahwa,1994	Optimal selection of capacitors for radial distribution systems
Scheduling	Lee et al.,1997	flexible flow-line scheduling with variable lot sizes
Vehicle routing	Baker and Ayechew, 2003	Vehicle routing problem

sampled pairs of solutions in the population. DE algorithm uses mutation operation as a search mechanism and selection operation to direct the search toward the prospective regions in the search space. In addition to this, the DE algorithm uses a non-uniform crossover which can take child vector parameters from one parent more often than it does from others. By using the components of the existing population members to construct trial vectors, the recombination (crossover) operator efficiently shuffles information about successful combinations, enabling the search for a better solution space. An optimization task consisting of D parameters can be represented by a D-dimensional vector. In DE, a population of NP solution vectors is randomly created at the start. This population is successfully improved by applying mutation, crossover and selection operators.

Karaboğa and Ökdem (2004) determined the main steps of the DE algorithm as follows:

```
Initialization
Evaluation
Repeat
        Mutation
        Recombination
        Evaluation
        Selection
Until (termination criteria are met)
```

DE is based on vector differences. Hence, DE is primarily suited for numerical optimization problems. DE is developed to optimise real parameter, real valued functions. DE is used for multidimensional real-valued functions but does not use the gradient of the problem being optimized, which means DE does not require for the optimization problem to be differentiable as it is required by classic optimization methods such as gradient descent and quasi-Newton methods. DE can also be used on optimization problems that are not even continuous, are noisy, change over time, etc.

Global optimization is necessary in fields such as engineering, statistics and finance. However, many practical problems have objective functions that are nondifferentiable, non-continuous, non-linear, noisy, flat, multi-dimensional or have many local minima, constraints or stochasticity. Such problems are difficult if not impossible to solve analytically. DE can be used to find approximate solutions to such problems (Table 5).

2.5 Simulated Annealing (SA)

Simulated annealing (SA) methods are methods proposed for the problem of finding, numerically, a point of the global minimum of a function defined on a subset of a k-dimensional Euclidean space. The motivation of the methods lies in the physical process of annealing, in which a solid

Table 5. Some example areas of application of DE

Application Problem	Author and Year	Application Area
Optimization	Stumberger et al., 2000	Radial active magnetic bearings
	Angira and Babu, 2006	Process synthesis and design problems
Scheduling	Onwubolu and Davendra, 2006	Scheduling flow shops
Assembly line balancing	Nearchou, 2007	Minimization of the cycle time of the line

is heated to a liquid state and, when cooled sufficiently slowly, takes up the configuration with minimal inner energy. Metropolis et al. (1953) described this process mathematically. SA uses this mathematical description for the minimization of other functions than the energy. The first results published by Kirpatrick et al. (1983), German and German (1984), Cerny (1985),

SA algorithm is a technique to find a good solution of an optimization problem using a random variation of the current solution. A worse variation is accepted as the new solution with a probability that decreases as the computation proceeds. The slower the cooling schedule, or rate of decrease, the more likely the algorithm is to find an optimal or near-optimal solution (Xinchao, 2011).

The basic elements of SA are the following:

1. A finite set S.
2. A real-valued cost function J defined on S. Let S* ⊂ S be the set of global minima of the function J, assumed to be a proper subset of S.
3. For each i∈ S, a set S(i) ⊂ S − {i}, called the set of neighbors of i.
4. For every i, a collection of positive coefficients $q_{ij}, j \in S(i)$, such that, $\sum_{j \in S(i)} q_{ij} = 1$. It is assumed that j∈ S(i) if and only if i ∈ S(j).
5. A nonincreasing function T: N → (0, ∞), called the cooling schedule. Here N is the set of positive integers, and T(t) is called the temperature at time t.
6. An initial "state" x(0)∈ S.

Given the above elements, the SA algorithm consists of a discrete-time inhomogeneous Markov chain x(t). If the current state x(t) is equal to i, choose a neighbor j of i at random; the probability that any particular j ∈ S(i) is selected is equal to q_{ij}. Once j is chosen, the next state x(t+1) is determined as follows:

```
If J(j) ≤ J(i), then x(t+1)=j.
If J(j) > J(i), then
x(t+1)=j
with probability exp[-J(j)-J(i)/T(t)]
x(t+1)=i otherwise.
```

Formally,

$$P\left[x\left(t+1\right)=j\middle|x\left(t\right)=i\right]=q_{ij}\exp$$
$$\left[-\frac{1}{T(t)}max\left\{0, J\left(j\right)-J(i)\right\}\right] \qquad (4)$$
$$if\ j \neq i, j \in S\left(i\right)$$

If j≠i and j S(i), then P[x(t+1)=j|x(t)=i]=0.

The rationale behind the SA algorithm is best understood by considering a homogeneous Markov chain $x_T(t)$ in which the temperature T(t) is held at a constant value T. Assume that the Markov chain $x_T\left(t\right)$ is irreducible and aperiodic and that $q_{ij}=q_{ji}$ for all i, j. Then $x_T\left(t\right)$ is a reversible Markov chain, and its invariant probability distribution is given by

$$\pi_T(i) = \frac{1}{Z_T} \exp\left[-\frac{J(i)}{T}\right], \qquad i \in S, \qquad (5)$$

where Z_T is a normalizing constant. It is then evident that as $T \downarrow 0$, the probability distribution π_T is concentrated on the set S* of global minima of J. This latter property remains valid if the condition $q_{ij} = q_{ji}$ is relaxed.

The probability distribution known as the Gibbs distribution plays an important role in statistical mechanics. In fact, statistical physicists have been interested in generating a sample element of S, drawn according to the probability distribution π_T. This is accomplished by simulating Markov chain $x_T(t)$ until it reaches equilibrium, and this method is known as the Metropolis algorithm (Metropolis et al., 1953). In the optimization context, it is generated an optimal element of S with high probability if it is produced a random sample according to the distribution π_T, with T very small. One difficulty with this approach is that when T is very small, the time it takes for the Markov chain $x_T(t)$ to reach equilibrium can be excessive. The SA algorithm tries to remedy this drawback by using a slowly decreasing "cooling schedule" T(t). Some example areas of application of SAs are listed in Table 6.

2.7 Swarm Intelligence (SI)

Social insects work without supervision. In fact, their teamwork is largely self-organized, and coordination arises from the different interactions among individuals in the colony. Although these interactions might be primitive (one ant merely following the trail left by another, for instance), taken together they result in efficient solutions to difficult problems (such as finding the shortest route to a food source among myriad possible paths). The collective behavior that emerges from a group of social insects has been dubbed swarm intelligence (Bonabeau and Meyer, 2001). SI indicates a recent computational and behavioral metaphor for solving distributed problems that

originally took its inspiration from the biological examples provided by social insects (ants, termites, bees, wasps) and by swarming, flocking, herding behaviors in vertebrates. Properties of SI Systems are given as follows (Blum and Roli, 2003):

- Decentralized control,
- Self organization / Emergent behavior,
- Often breaks if sufficient quantity of 'agents' are not present,
- Stigmergy,
- Use of environment to communicate e.g. pheromone markers,
- Localized communication,
- Massively parallel,
- Redundancy.

Swarm intelligence (SI) refers to a kind of problem solving ability that emerges in the interactions of simple information-processing units. The concept of swarm suggests multiplicity, stochasticity, randomness, and messiness, and the concept of intelligence suggests that the problem solving method is somehow successful. SI incorporates swarming behaviors observed in flocks of birds, schools of fish, or swarms of bees, colonies of ants, and even human social behavior, from which the intelligence is emerged (Liu et al., 2007). SI focuses on insect intelligent behaviors in order to develop some meta-heuristics which can mimic the abilities of insects in solving their problems. Interactions between insects contribute to the collective intelligence of social insect colonies and these interactions have been successfully adapted to solve scientific and real world optimization problems (Oliveira and Schirru, 2011).

Basic principles of SI are given as follows:

- **Proximity principle:** the population should be able to carry out simple space and time computations;
- **Quality principle:** the population should be able to respond to quality factors in the environment;

Table 6. Some example areas of application of SAs

Application Problem	Author and Year	Application Area
Assignment	Bos, 1993	Zoning in Forest Management with quadratic assignment
	Peng et al., 1996	Six different kinds of interchanges of facility locations
	Hasteer and Banerjee, 1997	Parallel State Assignment of Finite State Machines
	Hamam and Hindi, 2000	Assignment of program modules to processors
	Deschinkel et al., 2002	Assignment of price levels for air traffic management
	Ogura and Sato, 2006	Accurate posterioric angular assignment of protein projections
	Cheng et al., 2009	Integrated Quality of Service (QoS) routing algorithm for optical networks
	Paul, 2010	Comparison of performance of TS and SA for the quadratic assignment problem
Layout	Kouvelis et al., 1992	Machine layout in the presence of zoning constraints
	Souilah, 1995	Manufacturing systems layout design
	Braglia, 1996	Single row machine layout
	Chwif et al., 1998	Facility layout
	Wang et al., 2001	Facility layout under variable demand in Cellular Manufacturing Systems
	Hasançebi and Erbatur, 2002	Layout optimization of trusses
	Baykasoglu and Gindy, 2004	Dynamic layout
	McKendall Jr. et al., 2006	Dynamic facility layout
	Dong et al., 2009	Dynamic facility layout under dynamic business environment
	Liu et al., 2010	Two-dimensional equilibrium constraint layout
	Şahin, 2011	The bi-objective facility layout
Assembly line balancing	Özcan, 2010	Balancing stochastic two-sided assembly lines
	Cakir et al., 2011	Multi-objective optimization of a stochastic assembly line balancing
Vehicle routing	Breedam, 1995	Vehicle routing with relocating and/or exchanging stops or strings of stops between different routes
	Tavakkoli-Moghaddam et al., 2006	Capacitated vehicle routing problem with the independent route length
	Tavakkoli-Moghaddam et al., 2007	Capacitated vehicle routing problem with split service for minimizing fleet cost
	Deng et al., 2009	Soft time windows vehicle routing problem with pick-up and delivery
	Yu et al., 2010	Capacitated location routing problem
	Kuo, 2010	The time-dependent vehicle routing problem with minimizing fuel consumption
	Zarandi et al., 2011	The multi-depot capacitated location-routing problem with fuzzy travel times

continued on following page

Table 6. Continued

Application Problem	Author and Year	Application Area
Traveling salesman	Jeong and Kim, 1991	Traveling salesman problem (TSP) on SIMD machines with linear interconnections
	Chen and Zhang, 2006	Optimizing TSP from the nth-nearest-neighbor distribution
	Geng et al., 2011	Solving TSP using adaptive simulated annealing algorithm with greedy search
Scheduling	Das et al., 1990	Serial multiproduct batch processes
	Lo and Bavarian, 1992	Job scheduling on parallel machines
	Jeffcoat and Bulfin, 1993	Resource-constrained scheduling
	Gangadharan and Rajendran, 1994	Scheduling in a flowshop with bicriteria
	Zegordi et al., 1995	Minimizing makespan for flow shop scheduling
	He et al., 1996	Due-dates job-shop scheduling
	Salleh and Zomaya, 1998	Multiprocessor scheduling
	Reynolds and McKeown, 1999	A manufacturing plant scheduling
	Raaymakers and Hoogeveen, 2000	Scheduling multipurpose batch process industries with no-wait restrictions
	Liang and Wang, 2001	Main transformer ULTC and capacitors scheduling
	Kim et al., 2002	Unrelated parallel machine scheduling with setup times
	Bouleimen and Lecocq, 2003	Resource-constrained project scheduling
	Melouk et al., 2004	Single machine batch processing with non-identical job sizes
	Varadharajan and Rajendran, 2005	Flow shops scheduling
	Low, 2006	Flow shop scheduling with unrelated parallel machines
	El-Bouri et al., 2007	Job shop scheduling
	Zhang et al., 2008	Navigation scheduling for the two dams of the Three Gorges Project
	He et al., 2009	Multi-mode project payment scheduling
	Zhang and Wu, 2010	Job shop scheduling
	Saraiva et al., 2011	Generator maintenance scheduling
Optimization	Hanke and Li, 2000	Optimization of batch distillation processes
	Genovese et al., 2005	Non-smooth engineering optimization
	Suman et al., 2010	Multiobjective optimization

- **Diverse response principle:** the population should not commit its activities along excessively narrow channels;
- **Stability principle:** the population should not change its mode of behavior every time the environment changes;

- **Adaptability principle:** the population must be able to change behavior mode when it's worth the computational price.

SI proposes a new way of thinking the solution of the non-linear complex problems. Interactions between insects contribute to the collective intelligence of social insect colonies and these interactions have been successfully adapted to solve scientific and real world optimization problems (Oliveira and Schirru, 2011). Particle Swarm Optimization (Kennedy and Eberhart, 1995), Ant Colony Optimization, and Artificial Bee Colony (Karaboğa, 2005) are some of the well-known algorithms that mimic insect behavior in problem modeling and solution.

2.7.1 Particle Swarm Optimization (PSO)

Particle Swarm Optimization (PSO) is a population based stochastic optimization technique inspired by social behavior of bird flocking. PSO applies the concept of social interaction to problem solving. It was developed in 1995 by James Kennedy and Russ Eberhart. In PSO, A group of agents, "particles", are thrown into the search space. The particles communicate either directly or indirectly with one another for search directions (gradients). It is initialized with a population of random solutions and searches for optimal by updating generations. In PSO, the potential solutions (called as particles), move through the problem space by following the current optimum particles (Kuo et al., 2010). PSO is a simple but powerful search technique. It has been applied successfully to a wide variety of search and optimization problems. Its advantages and disadvantages are given.

Advantages:

- Insensitive to scaling of design variables
- Simple implementation
- Easily parallelized for concurrent processing
- Derivative free
- Very few algorithm parameters
- Very efficient global search algorithm

Disadvantages:

- Slow convergence in refined search stage (weak
- local search ability)

PSO consists of a swarm of particles. Each particle resides at a position in the search space and the fitness of each particle represents the quality of its position. The particles fly over the search space with a certain velocity. The velocity (both direction and speed) of each particle is influenced by its own best position found so far and the best solution that was found so far by its neighbors. Eventually the swarm will converge to optimal positions (Poli et al., 2007). PSO applications are given as follows:

- Training of neural networks
- Identification of Parkinson's disease
- Extraction of rules from fuzzy networks
- Image recognition
- Optimization of electric power distribution networks
- Structural optimization
- Optimal shape and sizing design
- Topology optimization
- Process biochemistry
- System identification in biomechanics

PSO is similar to a genetic algorithm (GA) in that the system is initialized with a population of random solutions. It is unlike a GA, however, in that each potential solution is also assigned a randomized velocity, and the potential solutions, called particles, are then "flown" through the problem space (Eberhart and Shi, 2001). Each particle keeps a memory of its previous best position, *pbest*, and a particle takes all the population as its topological neighbors, the best value is a global best and is called *gbest*. The PSO algorithm operates iteration by iteration and solution produced in each iteration is compared self-local best and global best of swarm. The particles try to achieve to global minimum by using global and local best information. V velocity of particle, X particle vector and N number of particle, the new position of particle is computed according to Equations (6) and (7).

$$v_i\left(t+1\right) = w.v_i\left(t\right) + c_1.rand_1.\left(pbest_i\left(t\right) - x_i\left(t\right)\right)$$
$$+ c_2.rand_2.\left(gbest_i\left(t\right) - x_i\left(t\right)\right)$$
$$(6)$$

$$x_i\left(t+1\right) = x_i\left(t\right) + v_i\left(t+1\right) \qquad \left(i = 1.....N\right)$$
$$(7)$$

where c_1 and c_2 determine the relative influence of the social and cognitive components (bias factors), $rand_1$ and $rand_2$ denote two random numbers uniformly distributed in the interval [0, 1]. w is a parameter called inertia weight used to control the impact of the previous velocities on the current one (Shi and Eberhart, 1998). In proposed PSO, inertia value of the equation changes on the each iteration (Equation 6). This change is based on the logic of decreasing from the value determined to minimum value according to inertia function. The objective is to converge the created speed by diminishing on the further iterations; hence more similar results can be obtained (Önüt et al., 2008). Inertia weight is dynamically calculated by depending on iteration number as follow:

$$w = \left(t - i\right) / t \qquad (8)$$

where t is the maximum iteration number and i is the current iteration index. In this way, while the particles approach to global minimum, velocities of particles are decreased during the iterations. According to the above explanations and equations, generic PSO algorithm is given in Table 7. Also some example areas of application of PSOs are listed in Table 8.

2.7.2 Ant Colony Optimization (ACO)

Ant colony optimization (ACO) algorithm based on the foraging behavior of ants has been first introduced by Dorigo and Gambardella (1997). The basic idea of ACO is to imitate the cooperative behavior of ant colonies. When searching for food, ants initially explore the area surrounding their nest in a random manner. As soon as an ant finds a food source, it evaluates it and carries some food back to the nest. During the return trip, the ant deposits a pheromone trail on the ground. The pheromone deposited, the amount of which may depend on the quantity and quality of the food, guides other ants to the food source (Socha and Dorigo, 2008). Quantity of pheromone on the arc is decreased in time due to evaporating. Each ant decides to a path or way according to the quantity of pheromone which has been leaved by other ants. More pheromone trail consists in short path than long path.

The first ACO algorithm developed was the ant system (AS) (Dorigo, 1992), and since then several improvement of the AS have been devised (Gambardella and Dorigo, 1995; Gambardella and Dorigo, 1996; Stützle and Hoos, 2000). The ACO algorithm is based on a computational paradigm inspired by real ant colonies and the way they function. The underlying idea was to use several constructive computational agents (simulating real ants). A dynamic memory structure incorporating information on the effectiveness of previous choices based on the obtained results, guides the construction process of each agent. The behavior

Table 7. Generic algorithm of PSO

1. Initialization *Generate random initial solutions for particles* *Determine gbest of swarm and pbest of particles* *2. For all particles* *Generate new solutions using Equations 6, 7* *3. Update global pbest and local gbest* *4. Not stopping criterion go to Step 2* *5. Stop*

Table 8. Some example areas of application of PSOs

Application Problem	Author and Year	Application Area
Training of neural networks	Chau, 2006	ANNs in stage prediction of Shing Mun River Journal of Hydrology
	Zhang et al., 2007	Back-propagation algorithm for feed forward neural network training
	Geethanjali et al., 2008	ANN-based differential protection scheme for power transformers
	Hu et al., 2010	Levenberg–Marquardt neural network
	Oh et al., 2011	Polynomial-based radial basis function neural networks (P-RBF NNs)
	Roh et al., 2010	The design methodology of radial basis function neural networks
Optimization	Perez and Behdinan, 2007	Structural design
	Jansen and Perez, 2011	Constrained structural design
	Luh et al., 2011	Continuum structural topology
	Kayhan et al., 2010	Continuous optimization
Assembly line balancing	Nearchou, 2011	Maximizing production rate and workload smoothing in assembly lines
Vehicle routing	Marinakis et al., 2010	Vehicle routing with expanding neighborhood search
	Ai and Kachitvichyanukul, 2009	Vehicle routing problem with simultaneous pickup and delivery
	MirHassani and Abolghasemi, 2011	Open vehicle routing
Travelling salesman	Shi et al., 2007	Generalized travelling salesman
	Marinakis and Marinaki, 2010	Probabilistic Traveling Salesman
Scheduling	Chuanwen and Bompard, 2005	Short term hydroelectric system scheduling in deregulated environment
	Lian et al., 2006	Permutation flowshop scheduling
	Liao et al., 2007	Flowshop scheduling
	Sha and Hsu, 2008	Open shop scheduling
	Anghinolfi and Paolucci, 2009	Single-machine total weighted tardiness scheduling
	Lin et al., 2010	Job-shop scheduling
	Tao et al., 2011	Trustworthy scheduling of a grid workflow
	Zhang et al., 2005	Resource-constrained project scheduling
	Lu et al., 2008	Resource-constrained critical path analysis
	Chen, 2011	Justification and designed mechanisms for resource-constrained project scheduling
Assignment	Salman et al., 2002	Task assignment
	Yln et al.,2006	Optimal task assignment in distributed systems

continued on following page

Table 8. Continued

Application Problem	Author and Year	Application Area
	Wang et al., 2011	Estimation of distribution for terminal assignment
	Lin et al., 2010	Efficient bi-objective personnel assignment
Energy Forecasting	Unler, 2008	Medium and long-term forecasting of energy demand
	El-Telbany and El-Karmi, 2008	Short-term forecasting of Jordanian electricity demand
	Shafie-khah et al., 2011	Price forecasting of day-ahead electricity markets
	Assareh et al., 2010	Demand estimation of oil in Iran

of each single agent is therefore inspired by the behavior of real ants.

Functioning of an ACO algorithm can be summarized as follows (Yaseen and AL-Slamy, 2008). A set of computational concurrent and asynchronous agents (a colony of ants) moves through states of the problem corresponding to partial solutions of the problem to solve. They move by applying a stochastic local decision policy based on two parameters, called trails and attractiveness. By moving, each ant incrementally constructs a solution to the problem. When an ant completes a solution, or during the construction phase, the ant evaluates the solution and modifies the trail value on the components used in its solution. This pheromone information will direct the search of the future ants.

Furthermore, an ACO algorithm includes two more mechanisms: trail evaporation and, optionally, daemon actions. Trail evaporation decreases all trail values over time, in order to avoid unlimited accumulation of trails over some component. Daemon actions can be used to implement centralized actions which cannot be performed by single ants, such as the invocation of a local optimization procedure, or the update of global information to be used to decide whether to bias the search process from a non-local perspective.

More specifically, an ant is a simple computational agent, which iteratively constructs a solution for the instance to solve. Partial problem solutions are seen as states. At the core of the ACO algorithm lies a loop, where at each iteration, each ant moves (performs a step) from a state ι to another one ψ, corresponding to a more complete partial solution. That is, at each step σ, each ant k computes a set $A_k^{\sigma(\iota)}$ of feasible expansions to its current state, and moves to one of these in probability. The probability distribution is specified as follows. For ant k, the probability $p_{\iota\psi}^k$ of moving from state ι to state ψ depends on the combination of two values:

- The attractiveness $\eta_{\iota\psi}$ of the move, as computed by some heuristic indicating the a priori desirability of that move;
- The trail level $\tau_{\iota\psi}$ of the move, indicating how proficient it has been in the past to make that particular move: it represents therefore an a posteriori indication of the desirability of that move.

Trails are updated usually when all ants have completed their solution, increasing or decreasing the level of trails corresponding to moves that were part of "good" or "bad" solutions, respectively.

2.7.2.1 Ant Colony Optimization Models

Several algorithms have been proposed in the literature following the ACO metaheuristics. Among the available ACO algorithms for NP-hard combinatorial optimization problems are Ant System, Ant Colony System, Max-Min Ant System, Rank-based Ant System, and Best-Worst Ant System. In the following, there is given a short description of these algorithms.

2.7.2.1.1 Ant System (AS)

The importance of the original Ant System (AS) resides mainly in being the prototype of a number of ant algorithms which collectively implement the ACO paradigm. AS already follows the outline presented in the previous subsection, specifying its elements as follows. The move probability distribution defines probabilities $p_{\iota\psi^k}$ to be equal to 0 for all moves which are infeasible (i.e., they are in the tabu list of ant k, that is a list containing all moves which are infeasible for ants k starting from state ι), otherwise they are computed by means of Formula (6), where α and β are user defined parameters ($0 \leq \alpha, \beta \leq 1$) (Colorni et al., 1991; Dorigo, 1992; Dorigo et al., 1991):

$$p_{\iota\psi}^k = \begin{cases} \dfrac{\tau_{\iota\psi}^\alpha + \eta_{\iota\psi}^\beta}{\displaystyle\sum_{(\iota\xi)\notin tabu_k} \left(\tau_{\iota\xi}^\alpha + \eta_{\iota\xi}^\beta\right)} & if\ (\iota\psi) \notin tabu_k \\[4mm] 0 & otherwise \end{cases} \tag{9}$$

In Formula 9, $tabu_k$ is the tabu list of ant k, while parameters α and β specify the impact of trail and attractiveness, respectively. After each iteration t of the algorithm, i.e., when all ants have completed a solution, trails are updated by means of Equation (10):

$$\tau_{\iota\psi}(\tau) = \rho\, t_{\iota\psi}(\tau - 1) + \Delta\tau_{\iota\psi} \tag{10}$$

where $\Delta\tau_{\iota\psi}$ represents the sum of the contributions of all ants that used move ($\iota\psi$) to construct their solution, $\rho, 0 \leq \rho \leq 1$, is a user-defined parameter called evaporation coefficient, and represents $\Delta\tau_{\iota\psi}$ the sum of the contributions of all ants that used move ($\iota\psi$) to construct their solution. The ants' contributions are proportional to the quality of the solutions achieved, i.e., the better solution is, and higher will be the trail contributions added to the moves it used. For example, in the case of the TSP, moves correspond to arcs of the graph, thus state ι could correspond to a path ending in node i, the state ψ to the same path but with the arc (ij) added at the end and the move would be the traversal of arc (ij). The quality of the solution of ant k would be the length L_k of the tour found by the ant and Equation (10) would become $\tau_{ij}(t) = \rho\tau_{ij}(t - 1) + \Delta_{\tau_{ij}}$, with

$$\Delta\tau_{ij} = \sum_{k=1}^{m} \Delta\tau_{ij}^k \tag{11}$$

where m is the number of ants and k $\Delta\tau_{ij}^k$ is the amount of trail laid on edge (ij) by ant k, which can be computed as

$$\Delta\tau_{ij}^k = \begin{cases} \dfrac{Q}{L_k} & if\ ant\ k\ uses\ arc\ (ij)\ in\ its\ tour \\[4mm] 0 & otherwise \end{cases} \tag{12}$$

Q is a constant parameter. The ant system simply iterates a main loop where m ants construct in parallel their solutions, thereafter updating the trail levels. The performance of the algorithm depends on the correct tuning of several parameters, namely: α, β, relative importance of trail and attractiveness, ρ, trail persistence, $\tau_{ij}(0)$, initial trail level, m, number of ants, and Q, used for defining to be of high quality solutions with low cost. The algorithm is shown in Table 9.

2.7.2.1.2 Ant Colony System (ACS)

ACS is one of the first successors of AS. AS was initially applied to the solution of the traveling salesman problem but was not able to compete against the state-of-the art algorithms in the field. On the other hand it has been merit to introduce ACO algorithms shown the potentiality of using artificial pheromone and artificial ants to drive the search of always better solutions for complex optimization problems. The next researches were motivated by two goals: the first was to improve the performance of the algorithm and the second was to investigate and better explain its behavior. Gambardella and Dorigo proposed in 1995 the Ant-Q algorithm, an extension of AS which integrates some ideas from Q-learning, and in 1996 Ant Colony System (ACS) (Gambardella and Dorigo, 1996; Dorigo and Gambardella, 1997) a simplified version of Ant-Q which maintained approximately the same level of performance, measured by algorithm complexity and by computational results. ACS introduces three major modifications into AS:

1. ACS uses a different transition rule, which is called pseudo-random-proportional rule: Let k be an ant located at a node r, $q_0 \in [0,1]$ be a parameter, and q a random value in $[0,1]$. The next node s is randomly chosen according to the following probability distribution

If $q \leq q_0$:

$$p_{rs}^k = \begin{cases} 1, & if \ s = \arg\max_{u \in N_k(r)} \left\{ \tau_{ru} * \eta_{ru}^\beta \right\}, \\ 0, & otherwise \end{cases} \tag{13}$$

else ($q > q_0$):

$$p_{rs}^k = \begin{cases} \dfrac{[\tau_{rs}]^\alpha * [\eta_{rs}]^\beta}{\sum_{u \in N_r^k} [\tau_{rs}]^\alpha * [\eta_{rs}]^\beta}, & if \ s \in N_k(r) \\ 0, & otherwise \end{cases} \tag{14}$$

Table 9. Generic algorithm of AS

1. Initialization
Initialize $\tau_{k\psi}$ and $_{k\psi}, \forall_{k\psi}$
2. Construction
For each ant k (currently in state ı) do
repeat
choose in probability the state to move into.
append the chosen move to the k-th ant's set tabu$_k$.
until ant k has completed its solution.
end for
3. Trail Update
For each ant move (ıψ) do
compute $\Delta\tau_{k\psi}$
update the trail matrix.
end for
4. Terminating condition
If not(end test) go to step 2

As can be seen, the rule has a double aim: when $q \leq q_0$, it exploits the available knowledge, choosing the best option with respect to the heuristic information and the pheromone trail. However, if $q > q_0$, it applies a controlled exploration, as done in AS. In summary, the rule establishes a trade-off between the exploration of new connections and the exploitation of the information available at that moment.

2. Only the daemon (and not the individual ants) trigger the pheromone update, i.e., an offline pheromone trail update is done. To do so, ACS only considers one single ant, the one who generated the global best solution, $S_{global-best}$.

The pheromone update is done by first evaporating the pheromone trails on all the connections used by the global-best ant (*it is important to notice that in ACS, pheromone evaporation is only applied to the connections of the solution that is also used to deposit pheromone*) as follows:

$$\tau_{rs} \leftarrow (1 - \rho) * \tau_{rs}, \quad \forall a_{rs} \in S_{global-best} \tag{15}$$

Next, the deamon deposits pheromone by the rule:

$$\tau_{rs} \leftarrow \tau_{rs} + \rho * f(C\left(S_{global-best}\right)), \ \forall a_{rs} \in S_{global-best} \tag{16}$$

Additionally, the deamon can apply a local search algorithm to improve the ants' solutions before updating the pheromone trails.

Ants apply an "online step by step pheromone trail update" that encourages the generation of different solutions to those yet found. Each time an ant travels an edge a_{rs}, it applies the rule:

$$\tau_{rs} \leftarrow \left(1 - \varphi\right) * \tau_{rs} + \varphi * \tau_0 \tag{17}$$

where $\varphi \in (0, 1]$ is a second pheromone decay parameter. As can be seen, the *online step by step update rule* includes both, pheromone evaporation and deposit. Because the amount of pheromone deposited is very small (in fact, τ_0 is the initial pheromone trail value which is chosen in such a way that, in practice, it corresponds to a lower pheromone trail limit, i.e., by the choice of the ACS pheromone update rules, no pheromone trail value can fall below τ_0), the application of this rule makes the pheromone trail on the connections traversed by an ant decrease. Hence, this results in an additional exploration technique of ACS by making the connections traversed by an ant less attractive to following ants and helps to avoid that every ant follows the same path.

2.7.2.1.3 Max-Min Ant System

Max-Min Ant System (MMAS) developed by Stützle and Hoos in 1996, is one of the best performing extensions of AS. It extends the basic AS in the following aspects:

An offline pheromone trail update is applied, similar to ACS. After all ants have constructed a solution, first every pheromone trail is evaporated:

$$\tau_{rs} \leftarrow \left(1 - \rho\right) * \tau_{rs}, \tag{18}$$

and next pheromone is deposited according to:

$$\tau_{rs} \leftarrow \tau_{rs} + \rho * f(C\left(S_{best}\right)), \quad \forall a_{rs} \in S_{best} \tag{19}$$

The best ant that is allowed to add pheromone may be the iteration-best or the global-best solution. In MMAS typically the ants' solutions are improved using local optimizers before the pheromone update.

The possible values for pheromone trails are limited to the range $\left[\tau_{min}, \tau_{max}\right]$. The chance of algorithm stagnation is thus decreased by giving each connection some, although very small, probability of being chosen. In practice, heuristics exist for setting τ_{min} and τ_{max}. First, it can be shown that, because of the pheromone evaporation, the maximal possible pheromone trail level is limited to $\tau_{max}^* = 1 / \left(\rho * C\left(S^*\right)\right)$, where S* is the optimal solution. Based on this result, the global-best solution can be used to estimate τ_{max} by replacing S* with $S_{global-best}$ in the equation for τ_{max}^*. For τ_{min} it is often enough to choose it as some constant factor lower than τ_{max}.

2. Instead of initializing the pheromones to a small amount, in MMAS the pheromone trails are initialized to an estimate of the maximum allowed pheromone trail value. This lead to an additional diversification component in the algorithm, because at the beginning the relative differences of the pheromone trails will not be very marked, which is different when initializing the pheromone trails to some very small value.

2.7.2.1.4 Rank- Based Ant System

The rank-based Ant System (AS_{rank}) is another extension of the AS proposed by Bullnheimer, Hartl and Strauss in 1997. It incorporates the idea of the ranking into the pheromone update, which is again developed offline by the daemon as follows:

The m ants are ranked according to decreasing quality of their solutions: $\left(S'_1, \ldots, S'_m\right)$, with S'_1 being the best solution built in the current generation.

1. The deamon deposits pheromone on the connections passed by the σ-1 best ant (*elitist ants*). The amount of pheromone deposited directly depends on the ant's rank and on the quality of its solution.
2. The connections crossed by the global-best solution receive an additional amount of pheromone which depends on the qulity of that solution. This pheromone deposit is considered to be the most important, hence, it receives a weight of σ.

This operation mode is put into effect by means of the following pheromone update rule, which is applied to every edge once all the pheromone trails have been evaporated:

$$\tau_{rs} \leftarrow \tau_{rs} + \sigma * \Delta\tau_{rs}^{gb} + \Delta\tau_{rs}^{rank}, \qquad (20)$$

where

$$\Delta\tau_{rs}^{gb} = \begin{cases} f\left(C\left(S_{global-best}\right)\right), & if \ a_{rs} \in S_{global-best}, \\ 0, & otherwise \end{cases}$$

$$(21)$$

2.7.2.1.5 Best-Worst Ant System

Best-Worst Ant System (BWAS) proposed by Cordon et al. in 1999, is an ACO algorithm which incorporates evolutionary computation concepts. It constitutes another extension of AS, which uses its transition rule and pheromone evaporation mechanism. Besides, as done in MMAS, BWAS always considers the systematic exploitation of local optimizers to improve the ants' solutions.

At the core of the BWAS, the three following daemon actions are found:

The BWAS pheromone trail update rule, which reinforces the edges contained in the global best solution. In addition, the update rule penalizes every connection of the worst solution generated in the current iteration, $S_{current-worst}$, that are not present in the global-best one through an additional evaporation of the pheromone trails. Hence, BWAS update rule becomes:

$$\tau_{rs} \leftarrow \tau_{rs} + \rho * f\left(C\left(S_{global-best}\right)\right), \quad \forall a_{rs} \in S_{global-best}, \qquad (22)$$

$$\tau_{rs} \leftarrow \left(1 - \rho\right) * \tau_{rs}, \ \forall a_{rs} \in S_{current-worst} \ and \ a_{rs} \notin S_{global-best} \qquad (23)$$

A pheromone trail mutation is performed to introduce diversity in the search process. To do so, the pheromone trail associated to one of the transitions starting from each node is mutated with probability P_m by considering any real-coded mutation operator. The original BWAS proposal applied an operator altering the pheromone trail of every mutated transition by adding or subtracting the same amount in each iteration. The mutation range mut(it, $\tau_{threshold}$), which depends on the average of the pheromone trails in the transitions of the global best solution, $\tau_{threshold}$ is less strong in the early stages of the algorithm and stronger in the latter ones, when the danger of stagnation is stronger:

$$\tau'_{rs} \leftarrow \begin{cases} \tau_{rs} + mut\left(it, \tau_{threshold}\right), & if \ a = 0 \\ \tau_{rs} - mut\left(it, \tau_{threshold}\right), & if \ a = 1 \end{cases} \qquad (24)$$

with a being a random value in {0,1} and it being the current iteration.

As other ACO models, BWAS considers the re-initialization of the pheromone trails when it gets stuck, which is done by setting every pheromone trail to τ_0.

2.7.2.2 Kinds of Problems Solved by ACO

ACO is one of the most recent techniques for approximate optimization. The inspiring source of ACO algorithms are real ant colonies. More specifically, ACO is inspired by the ants' foraging behavior. At the core of this behavior is the indirect communication between the ants by means of chemical pheromone trails, which enables them to find short paths between their nest and food sources. This characteristic of real ant colonies is exploited in ACO algorithms for the search of approximate solutions to discrete optimization problems, to continuous optimization problems, and to important problems in telecommunications, such as routing and load balancing (Dorigo and Stützle, 2004). Some example areas of application of ACOs are listed in Table 10.

2.7.3 Artificial Bee Colony

Artificial bee colony (ABC) algorithm was proposed by Karaboga (2005), inspired by the foraging and waggles dance behaviors of honey-bees. ABC is a relatively new member of swarm intelligence. It has received increasing interest because of its simplicity, wide applicability, and outstanding performance. The basic ABC has been compared with other evolutionary algorithms, such as GA, PSO, and differential evaluation on a limited number of test functions (Karaboğa and Baştürk, 2007a; Kang et al., 2011).

Honey bees use several mechanisms like waggle dance to optimally locate food sources and to search new ones. This makes them a good candidate for developing new intelligent search algorithms. In the ABC algorithm, the colony of artificial bees contains three groups of bees: employed bees, onlookers and scouts. A bee waiting on the dance area for making decision to choose a food source is called an onlooker and a bee going to the food source visited by itself previously is named an employed bee. A bee carrying out random search is called a scout. In the ABC algorithm, first half of the colony con-

sists of employed artificial bees and the second half constitutes the onlookers. For every food source, there is only one employed bee. In other words, the number of employed bees is equal to the number of food sources around the hive. The employed bee whose food source is exhausted by the employed and onlooker bees becomes a scout (Karaboğa and Baştürk, 2007b). The algorithm of the simulation of foraging and dance behaviors of honey bee colony adopted from Karaboğa 2005; Karaboğa and Baştürk 2007a, 2007b is given in Table 5. In the algorithm ABC, for generating an initial solution for employed bee b the Equation (25) is used.

$$x_b^j = x_{\min}^j + rand[0,1] * \left(x_{\max}^j - x_{\min}^j \right),$$
$$for\ all\ j = 1, 2, \dots, D \tag{25}$$

where, x_b^j is a parameter to be optimized for the employed bee b on the dimension j of the D-dimensional solution space, x_{max}^j and x_{min}^j are the upper and lower bounds for x_b^j, respectively. In both onlooker bee and employed bee phases, the food positions in the dimension j are obtained by the Equation (26).

$$v_b^j = x_b^j + \Phi\left(x_b^j - x_k^j \right)\ j \in \{1, 2, \dots, D\},$$
$$k \neq b\ and\ k \in \{1, 2, \dots, n\} \tag{26}$$

where, x_b^j is employed bee b, v_b^j is the new solution for x_b^j in the dimension j, x_k^j is a neighbor bee of x_b^j in employed bee population. Here $\vdots$ is a number randomly selected in the range [-1, 1], n is number of the employed bees, and $j \in \{1, 2, \dots, D\}\ and\ k \in \{1, 2, \dots, n\}$ are selected randomly. In order to generate a new food position, every onlooker bee memorizes the solution of one of n employed bees based on fitness values of the employed bees. The probability p_b of that an onlooker bee will select the selection of the

Table 10. Some example areas of application of ACOs

Application Problem	Author and Year	Application Area
Assignment	Maniezzo and Colorni, 1999	Quadratic assignment
	Fournier and Pierre, 2005	Assigning cells to switches in mobile networks
	Shyu et al., 2006	Cell assignment problem in PCS networks
	Demirel and Toksarı, 2006	Optimization of the quadratic assignment
	Yanxia et al., 2008	Weapon target assignment
	Chen et al., 2011	Wavelength assignment in WDM networks
	Stützle, 1998	Flow shop problem
Scheduling	Gagne et al., 2002	Single machine scheduling with sequence-dependent setup times
	Merkle et al., 2002	Resource constraint project scheduling
	Blum and Samples, 2004	Shop scheduling
	Blum, 2005	Open shops scheduling
	Gajpal and Rajendran, 2006	Minimizing the completion-time variance of jobs in flowshops,
	Rossi and Dini, 2007	Flexible job-shop scheduling with routing flexibility and separable setup times
	Yagmahan and Yenisey, 2008	Multi-objective flowshop scheduling
	Marimuthu et al., 2009	Scheduling m-machine flow shops with lot streaming
	Leung et al., 2010	Integrated process planning and scheduling
	Deng and Lin, 2011	Airline crew scheduling
	Gambardella and Dorigo, 1999	Vehicle routing with time windows
Vehicle routing	Bell and Mcmullen, 2004	Multiple routes of the vehicle routing
	Donati et al., 2008	Time dependent vehicle routing
	Fuellerer et al., 2010	Vehicle routing with three-dimensional loading constraints
	Yu and Yang, 2011	The period vehicle routing problem with time windows
	Simaria and Vilarinho, 2009	Balancing two-sided assembly lines
Assembly line balancing	Sabuncuoglu et al., 2009	Single model U-type assembly line balancing
	Chica et al., 2010	Time and space assembly line balancing
	Yagmahan, 2011	Mixed-model assembly line balancing
	Ozbakir et al., 2011	Parallel assembly line balancing
	Dorigo and Gambardella, 1997	Generalized traveling salesman
Traveling salesman	García-Martínez et al., 2007	Bi-criteria traveling salesman
	Yang et al., 2008	Generalized
	Ugur and Aydin, 2009	An interactive simulation and analysis software for solving traveling salesman
	Puris et al., 2010	Efficacy of a two-stage methodology for ant colony optimization: Case of study with TSP
	Chen and Chien, 2011	Solving the traveling salesman using parallelized genetic ant colony systems
Energy forecasting	Toksarı, 2009	Estimating the net electricity energy generation and demand

solution of the employed bee b is obtained as follows:

$$p_b = \frac{fit_b}{\sum_{j=1}^{D} fit_j} \qquad (27)$$

where, fit_b is the fitness value of employed bee b obtained is as follows:

$$fit_b = \begin{cases} \dfrac{1}{1+f_b} & if\ (f_b \geq 0) \\ 1 + abs(f_b) & if\ (f_b \leq 0) \end{cases} \qquad (28)$$

where, f_b is the object function. In addition, in the scout bee phase of the ABC, Equation (25) is used in order to generate new solution for the scout bee and all the onlooker bees use the Equation (26) of so as to improve the solution. The algorithm of ABC is given in Table 11.

Compared with PSO and other similar evolutionary techniques, ABC has some attractive characteristics and in numerical optimization problems proved to be more effective (Karaboğa and Baştürk, 2008). ABC has been used extensively for a variety of optimization problems and in most of these cases ABC has proven to have superior computational efficiency (Karaboğa and Akay, 2009). Some example areas of application of ABCs are listed in Table 12.

3. FINDINGS AND DISCUSSION

Meta-heuristics have been proved to be useful tools that have their own set of advantages and disadvantages. Apart from having many valuable advantages of using metaheuristics, it must be noticed that there are a number of disadvantages of using them as opposed to conventional methods. Metaheuristic methods are not function optimizers. That is, their purpose is to seek and find feasible solutions to the problem, rather than a guaranteed optimal solution. Therefore, if the model is sufficiently simple as to allow conventional methods to be able to produce an optimal solution, there seems little point in using a metaheuristic method. Other disadvantages include the fact that there exist a larger number of parameters to be set by the modeller in meta-heuristics than in conventional methods. Metaheuristics make a poor 'black box' and are more difficult to apply when only a single run of the meta-heuristic is allowed due to time or other pressures. Finally, meta-heuristic methods are known to struggle with certain tightly constrained models, although advanced constraint handling techniques and methods are now available (Goldberg, 1989).

The generic search scheme provided by meta-heuristics must be carefully adapted to the specific characteristics of the problem, e.g. by choosing an appropriate search space and effective neighborhood structures. Many well-known metaheuristics seem to converge towards a unifying framework made of a few algorithmic components. In this unifying process, new opportunities for combining the strengths of these methods will emerge, thus leading to even more powerful search models for complex real world problems.

We realize that there is an increasing trend to cooperative methods combining different approaches, parallel and distributed metaheuristics for multiobjective optimization, and software implementations. There are many advances in the area of adaptativeness in metaheuristic optimization, including hyperheuristics and self-adaptation in evolutionary algorithms, cutting edge works on adaptive, self-adaptive and multilevel metaheuristics, with application to both combinatorial and continuous optimization. The other common applications of metaheuristics are clustering, mixed-integer programming, segmentation, mapping, reducing energy consumption, allocation, and so on.

From an empirical standpoint it would be most interesting to know which algorithms perform best under various criteria for different classes

Table 11. Generic algorithm of ABC (Karaboğa and Baştürk, 2007a)

1. Initialization
For each employed bee
Generate initial solution for each employed bee by using the Equation (25)
Calculate the object function values by the equation specific for the problem
Calculate the fitness value (fit) by using Equation (28)
Reset the abandonment counter
2. Until a Termination Condition is Met
Employed Bee Phase
For each employed bee
Select a neighbor employed bee randomly
Update position of employed bee by using the Equation (26) and position of neighbor bee
Calculate the object function values by the equation specific for the problem
Calculate the fitness value (fit) by using the Equation (28)
If the fitness value of the new solution is better than the fitness value of the old solution then replace the old solution with new one and reset the abandonment counter of the new solution, else increase the abandonment counter of the old solution by Equation (25)
Onlooker Bee Phase
For each onlooker bee
Select an employed bee as neighbor randomly
Select an employed bee for improvement its solution by using the Equation (27)
Improve the solution of the employed bee by using the Equation (26) and the neighbor
Calculate the object function values by the equation specific for the problem
Calculate the fitness value (fit) by using the Equation (28)
If the fitness value of the new solution is better than the fitness value of the old solution then replace the old solution with new one and reset the abandonment counter of the new solution, else increase the abandonment counter of the old solution by Equation (25)
Scout Bee Phase
Fix the abandonment counter with the highest content
***IF** the content of the counter is higher than the predefined limit **THEN** reset the counter and by using the Equation (25) generate a new solution for the employed bee to which the counter belongs, **ELSE** continue*
3. End Until

of problems. Unfortunately, this theme is out of reach as long as we do not have any well accepted standards regarding the testing and comparison of different methods. While most papers on metaheuristics claim to provide 'high quality' results based on some sort of measure, it is still believed that there is a great deal of room for improvement in testing existing as well as new approaches from an empirical point of view (Voß, 2001).

4. CONCLUSION

This chapter provides a survey on the usage of metaheuristics in engineering. Metaheuristics techniques in engineering were outlined in detail and a literature review was provided for each technique.

Metaheuristics have become a substantial part of the heuristics stockroom with various ap-

Table 12. Some example areas of application of ABCs

Application Problem	Author and Year	Application Area
Environmental modelling	Chen et al., 2008	Modeling environmental systems
Optimization	Alatas, 2010	Global numerical optimization
	Zhu and Kwong, 2010	Numerical function optimization
	Santos de Oliveira and Schirru, 2011	Core Fuel Management Optimization
	Karaboga and Akay, 2011	Constrained optimization problems
	Sonmez, 2011	Optimization of truss structure
Vehicle routing	Szeto et al., 2011	Capacitated vehicle routing
Assigment	Tasgetiren et al., 2011	Permutation flow shops
Scheduling	Pan et al., 2011	Lot-streaming flow shop scheduling
	Ziarati et al., 2011	Resource-constrained project scheduling
	Huang and Lin, 2011	Idle-time-based filtering scheme for open shop-scheduling
Forecasting	Hsieh et al., 2011	Forecasting stock markets
	Irani and Nasimi, 2011	Hole pressure prediction in underbalanced drilling

plications in science and, even more important, in practice especially within last five years. Metaheuristics have become part of textbooks, e.g. in operations research, and a wealth of monographs is available. Specialized conferences are devoted to this topic. From a theoretical point of view, the use of most meta-heuristics has not yet been fully justified.

While convergence results regarding solution quality exist for most meta-heuristics once appropriate probabilistic assumptions are made, these turn out not to be very helpful in practice as usually a disproportionate computation time is required to achieve these results, usually convergence is achieved for the computation time tending to infinity, with a few exceptions, e.g., for the reverse elimination method within tabu search or the pilot method where optimality can be achieved with a finite, but exponential number of steps in the worst case (Voß, 2001).

Metaheuristics are powerful algorithmic approaches which have been applied with great success to many complex real world problems. Significant knowledge about the problem is required to develop a successful metaheuristic implementation.

The usage of metaheuristics in engineering problems has lately experienced a noteworthy increase. Our findings suggest an increasing awareness of motivation in metaheuristics in engineering since about 2007. Artificial neural networks and genetic algorithms are the most popular heuristic techniques. This may be since the software for these techniques is available in the market. We believe that researchers and practitioners can use the other techniques more frequently if their software is developed.

In the literature, ACO and PSO often appear in swarm intelligence Meta heuristics for scheduling. It is also evident from the literature that, the other meta heuristics like Tabu search, Simulated Annealing, Genetic Algorithms are used in integration with ACO/PSO to determine the 'near to optimal' schedule. It is also observed that the usage frequency of these hybrid approaches is increased. For the future directions, a comprehensive literature review focusing on hybrid metaheuristics is recommended.

5. FUTURE RESEARCH DIRECTIONS

As a matter of fact, metaheuristic optimization deals with optimization problems using metaheuristic algorithms. Optimization is essentially everywhere, specifically in engineering design, business, economics and finance. Metaheuristics have been used in many applications such as optimization of engineering design, business, economics and finance (Glover and Kochenberger 2003). It is an area of active research, and there is no doubt that more metaheuristic algorithms and new applications will emerge in the future. We believe that more and more metaheuristic algorithms will appear in the future.

Since resources, time, and money are always limited, the optimal utility of these available resources is essentially important. Generally, real-world optimizations are nonlinear and multimodal, under various complex constraints. Different objectives are conflicting. Even for a single objective, optimal solutions may not exist at all. In general, finding an optimal solution or even sub-optimal solutions is not an easy task. For this reason, in the future, metaheuristics will continue to be an important part of simulation methodology, too. From the perspective of the chapter focus, it is possible to say that future of the metaheuristics will continue to be developing research area by considering the effectiveness of theoretical insights.

In recent years, there is a trend to use metaheuristic techniques as providing general ideas or components of building optimization methods. Many modern metaheuristics such as Bat Algorithm, Cuckoo Search, Kangaroo Algorithm, and Firefly Algorithm use specialized heuristics to efficiently solve subproblems produced by the metaheuristic methods. Algorithmic developments in both metaheuristics and exact methods have recently drawn the two fields closely together, and combinations of metaheuristic components (usually local search) with exact methods for (mixed integer) linear programming are now common. Sometimes called matheuristics, the resulting methods often integrate existing exact procedures to solve subproblems generated by a decomposition strategy, a restriction strategy or a relaxation strategy. The results of solving these subproblems are used to guide a higher-level heuristic. Metaheuristics can be integrated with exact methods to improve the performance of the exact methods (Glover, 2005). Most metaheuristics need problem-specific design and tuning in order to achieve high performance. Since practitioners have difficulties in coding metaheuristics, user friendly and object-oriented software packages should be devoloped.

REFERENCES

Agatonovic-Kustrin, S., & Beresford, R. (2000). Basic concepts of artificial neural network (ANN) modeling and its application in pharmaceutical research. *Journal of Pharmaceutical and Biomedical Analysis*, *22*, 717–727. doi:10.1016/S0731-7085(99)00272-1

Ai, J., & Kachitvichyanukul, V. (2009). A particle swarm optimization for the vehicle routing problem with simultaneous pickup and delivery. *Computers & Operations Research*, *36*(5), 1693–1702. doi:10.1016/j.cor.2008.04.003

Alatas, B. (2010). Chaotic bee colony algorithms for global numerical optimization. *Expert Systems with Applications*, *37*(8), 5682–5687. doi:10.1016/j.eswa.2010.02.042

Anghinolfi, D., & Paolucci, M. (2009). A new discrete particle swarm optimization approach for the single-machine total weighted tardiness scheduling problem with sequence-dependent setup times. *European Journal of Operational Research*, *193*(1), 73–85. doi:10.1016/j.ejor.2007.10.044

Angira, R., & Babu, B. V. (2006). Optimization of process synthesis and design problems: A modified differential evolution approach. *Chemical Engineering Science, 61*(14), 4707–4721. doi:10.1016/j.ces.2006.03.004

Assareh, E., Behrang, M. A., Assari, M. R., & Ghanbarzadeh, A. (2010). Application of PSO and GA techniques on demand estimation of oil in Iran. *Energy, 35*, 5223–5229. doi:10.1016/j.energy.2010.07.043

Azadeh, A., Moghaddam, M., & Khakzad, M. (2011). A flexible neural network fuzzy mathematical programming algorithm for improvement of oil price estimation and forecasting. *Computers & Industrial Engineering, 62*(2). doi:doi:10.1016/j.cie.2011.06.019

Baker, B. M., & Ayechew, M. A. (2003). A genetic algorithm for the vehicle routing problem. *Computers & Operations Research, 30*, 787–800. doi:10.1016/S0305-0548(02)00051-5

Bar-Yam, Y. (Ed.). (1997). *Dynamics of complex systems*. Addison-Wesley.

Baykasoğlu, A., & Gindy, N. N. Z. (2004). Erratum to "A simulated annealing algorithm for dynamic layout problem". *Computers & Operations Research, 31*(2), 313–315. doi:10.1016/S0305-0548(03)00205-3

Bell, J. E., & McMullen, P. R. (2004). Ant colony optimization techniques for the vehicle routing problem. *Advanced Engineering Informatics, 18*, 41–48. doi:10.1016/j.aei.2004.07.001

Ben-Daya, M., & Al-Fawzan, M. (1998). A tabu search approach for the flow shop scheduling problem. *European Journal of Operational Research, 9*, 88–95. doi:10.1016/S0377-2217(97)00136-7

Bin, Y., Zhong-Zhen, Y., & Baozhen, Y. (2009). An improved ant colony optimization for vehicle routing problem. *European Journal of Operational Research, 196*, 171–176. doi:10.1016/j.ejor.2008.02.028

Blum, C. (2005). Beam-ACO-hybridizing ant colony optimization with beam search: an application to open shop scheduling. *Computers & Operations Research, 32*(6), 1565–1591. doi:10.1016/j.cor.2003.11.018

Blum, C., Puchinger, J., Raidl, G. R., & Roli, A. (2011). Hybrid metaheuristics in combinatorial optimization: A survey. *Applied Soft Computing, 11*, 4135–4151. doi:10.1016/j.asoc.2011.02.032

Blum, C., & Roli, A. (2003). Metaheuristics in combinatorial optimization: Overview and conceptual comparison. *ACM Computing Surveys, 35*(3), 268–308. doi:10.1145/937503.937505

Blum, C., Roli, A., & Sampels, M. (Eds.). (2008). Hybrid metaheuristics: An emerging approach to optimization series. *Studies in Computational Intelligence, 114*.

Blum, C., & Sampels, M. (2004). An ant colony optimization algorithm for shop scheduling problems. *Journal of Mathematical Modelling and Algorithms, 3*(3), 285–308. doi:10.1023/B:JMMA.0000038614.39977.6f

Bonabeou, E., & Meyer, C. (Eds.). (2001). *Swarm intelligence: A whole new way to think about business*. Harvard Business Review.

Bos, J. (1993). Zoning in forest management: A quadratic assignment problem solved by simulated annealing. *Journal of Environmental Management, 37*(2), 127–145. doi:10.1006/jema.1993.1010

Bouleimen, K., & Lecocq, H. (2003). A new efficient simulated annealing algorithm for the resource-constrained project scheduling problem and its multiple mode version. *European Journal of Operational Research, 149*(2), 268–281. doi:10.1016/S0377-2217(02)00761-0

Braglia, M. (1996). Optimisation of a simulated-annealing-based heuristic for single row machine layout problem by genetic algorithm. *International Transactions in Operational Research, 3*(1), 37–49. doi:10.1111/j.1475-3995.1996.tb00034.x

Brandão, J. (2004). A tabu search algorithm for the open vehicle routing problem. *European Journal of Operational Research, 157*, 552–564. doi:10.1016/S0377-2217(03)00238-8

Brandão, J. (2006). A new tabu search algorithm for the vehicle routing problem with backhauls. *European Journal of Operational Research, 173*, 540–555. doi:10.1016/j.ejor.2005.01.042

Brandão, J., & Eglese, R. (2008). A deterministic tabu search algorithm for the capacitated arc routing problem. *Computers & Operations Research, 35*, 1112–1126. doi:10.1016/j.cor.2006.07.007

Bullnheimer, B., Hartl, R. F., & Strauss, C. (1997). A new rank-based version of the ant system: A computational study. Central . *European Journal of Operational Research and Economics, 7*(1), 25–38.

Burke, E. K., & Newall, J. P. (1999). A multistage evolutionary algorithm for the timetable problem. *IEEE Transactions on Evolutionary Computation, 3*(1), 63–74. doi:10.1109/4235.752921

Cakir, B., Altiparmak, F., & Dengi, B. (2011). Multi-objective optimization of a stochastic assembly line balancing: A hybrid simulated annealing algorithm. *Computers & Industrial Engineering, 60*(3), 376–384. doi:10.1016/j.cie.2010.08.013

Cerny, V. (1985). A thermodynamical approach to the traveling salesman problem: An efficient simulation algorithm. *Journal of Optimization Theory and Applications, 45*, 41–51. doi:10.1007/BF00940812

Chau, K. W. (2006). Particle swarm optimization training algorithm for ANNs in stage prediction of Shing Mun River. *Journal of Hydrology (Amsterdam), 329*(3-4), 363–367. doi:10.1016/j.jhydrol.2006.02.025

Chen, M.-T., Lin, B. M. T., & Tseng, S.-S. (2011). Ant colony optimization for dynamic routing and wavelength assignment in WDM networks with sparse wavelength conversion. *Engineering Applications of Artificial Intelligence, 24*(2), 295–305. doi:10.1016/j.engappai.2010.05.010

Chen, R.-M. (2011). Particle swarm optimization with justification and designed mechanisms for resource-constrained project scheduling problem. *Expert Systems with Applications, 38*(6), 7102–7111. doi:10.1016/j.eswa.2010.12.059

Chen, S. H., Jakeman, A. J., & Norton, J. P. (2008). Artificial intelligence techniques: An introduction to their use for modeling environmental systems. *Mathematics and Computers in Simulation, 78*(2-3), 379–400. doi:10.1016/j.matcom.2008.01.028

Chen, S.-M., & Chien, C.-Y. (2011). Parallelized genetic ant colony systems for solving the traveling salesman problem. *Expert Systems with Applications, 38*(4), 3873–3883. doi:10.1016/j.eswa.2010.09.048

Chen, S.-M., & Chien, C.-Y. (in press). Solving the traveling salesman problem based on the genetic simulated annealing ant colony system with particle swarm optimization techniques. [in press]. *Expert Systems with Applications.*

Chen, Y., & Zhang, P. (2006). Optimized annealing of traveling salesman problem from the nth-nearest-neighbor distribution. *Physica A. Statistical and Theoretical Physics, 371*(2), 627–632. doi:10.1016/j.physa.2006.04.052

Cheng, H., Wang, X., Yang, S., & Huang, M. (2009). A multipopulation parallel genetic simulated annealing-based QoS routing and wavelength assignment integration algorithm for multicast in optical networks. *Applied Soft Computing, 9*(2), 677–684. doi:10.1016/j.asoc.2008.09.008

Chica, M., Cordon, O., Damas, S., & Bautista, J. (2009). *Adding diversity to two multiobjective constructive metaheuristics for time and space assembly line balancing. Frontiers of Assembly and Manufacturing* (pp. 211–226). Springer.

Chow, M.-Y., Sharpe, R. N., & Hung, J. C. (1993). On the application and design of artificial neural networks for motor fault detection-part I. *IEEE Transactions on Industrial Electronics, 40*(2).

Chwif, L., Barretto, M. R. P., & Moscato, L. A. (1998). A solution to the facility layout problem using simulated annealing. *Computers in Industry, 36*(1-2), 125–132. doi:10.1016/S0166-3615(97)00106-1

Cockshott, A. R., & Hartman, B. E. (2001). Improving the fermentation medium for Echinocandin B production part II: Particle swarm optimization. *Process Biochemistry, 36*(7), 661–669. doi:10.1016/S0032-9592(00)00261-2

Colorni, A., Dorigo, M., & Maniezzo, V. (1991). Distributed optimization by ant colonies. In *Proceedings of the First European Conference on Artificial Life* (pp.134-142). Paris, France: Elsevier Publishing.

Cordon, O., Fernandez de Viana, I., Herrera, F., & Moreno, L. (2000). A new ACO model integrating evolutionary computation concepts: The best-worst ant system. In M. Dorigo, M. Middendorf, & T. Stützle (Eds.), *Abstract Proceedings of ANTS2000-From Ant Colonies to Artificial Ants: A Series of International Workshops on Ant Algorithms,* (pp.22-29). IRIDIA, Universite Libre de Bruxelles, Belgium.

Da Silva, E. L., Ortiz, J. M. A., De Oliveira, G. C., & Binato, S. (2001). Transmission network expansion planning under a Tabu Search approach. *IEEE Transactions on Power Systems, 16*(1), 62–68. doi:10.1109/59.910782

Das, H., Cummings, H. P. T., & Le Van, M. D. (1990). Scheduling of serial multiproduct batch processes via simulated annealing. *Computers & Chemical Engineering, 14*(12), 1351–1362. doi:10.1016/0098-1354(90)80017-6

Das, S., Konar, A., & Chakraborty, U. K. (2005). An efficient evolutionary algorithm applied to the design of two-dimensional IIR filters. *In Proceedings of the 2005 conference on Genetic and evolutionary computation.* Washington, DC, USA.

Dawson, C. W., & Wilby, R. (1998). An artificial neural network approach to rainfall-runoff Modelling. *Hydrological Sciences—Journal—des Sciences Hydrologiques, 43*(1).

Demirel, N. Ç., & Toksarı, M. D. (2006). Optimization of the quadratic assignment problem using an ant colony algorithm. *Applied Mathematics and Computation, 183*, 427–435. doi:10.1016/j.amc.2006.05.073

Den Besten, M. L., Stutzle, T., & Dorigo, M. (2000). Ant colony optimization for the total weighted tardiness problem. In M. Schoenauer, K. Deb, G. Rudolph, X. Yao, E. Lutton, J. J. Merelo, H.-P. Schwefel (Eds.), *Proceedings of PPSNVI, Sixth Internat. Conf. on Parallel Problem Solving from Nature, Lecture Notes in Computer Science, Vol. 1917* (pp. 611–620). Berlin, Germany: Springer.

Deng, A.-M., Mao, C., & Zhou, Y.-T. (2009). Optimizing research of an improved simulated annealing algorithm to soft time windows vehicle routing problem with pick-up and delivery. *Systems Engineering - Theory & Practice, 29*(5), 186-192.

Deng, G.-F., & Lin, W.-T. (2011). Ant colony optimization-based algorithm for airline crew scheduling problem. *Expert Systems with Applications, 38*(5), 5787–5793. doi:10.1016/j.eswa.2010.10.053

Deschinkel, K., Farges, J.-L., & Delahaye, D. (2002). Optimizing and assigning price levels for air traffic management. *Transportation Research Part E, Logistics and Transportation Review, 38*(3-4), 221–237. doi:10.1016/S1366-5545(02)00007-8

Dodin, B., Elimam, A. A., & Rolland, E. (1998). Tabu search in audit scheduling. *European Journal of Operational Research, 106*(2), 373–392. doi:10.1016/S0377-2217(97)00280-4

Donati, V. A., Montemanni, R., Casagrande, N., Rizzoli, A. E., & Gambardella, L. M. (2008). Time dependent vehicle routing problem with a multi ant colony system. *European Journal of Operational Research, 185*(3), 1174–1191. doi:10.1016/j.ejor.2006.06.047

Dong, M., Wu, C., & Hou, F. (2009). Shortest path based simulated annealing algorithm for dynamic facility layout problem under dynamic business environment. *Expert Systems with Applications, 36*(8), 11221–11232. doi:10.1016/j.eswa.2009.02.091

Dorigo, M. (1992). *Optimization, learning and natural algorithms*. Unpublished doctoral dissertation, University of Politecnico di Milano, Italy.

Dorigo, M., & Gambardella, L. M. (1997a). Ant colony system: A cooperative learning approach to the traveling salesman problem. *IEEE Transactions on Evolutionary Computation, 1*, 53–66. doi:10.1109/4235.585892

Dorigo, M., & Gambardella, L. M. (1997b). Ant colonies for the travelling salesman problem. *Bio Systems, 43*, 73–81. doi:10.1016/S0303-2647(97)01708-5

Dorigo, M., Maniezzo, V., & Colorni, A. (1991). *The ant system: An autocatalytic optimizing process*. Technical Report TR91-016, Politecnico di Milano.

Dorigo, M., & Stützle, T. (Eds.). (2004). *Ant colony optimization*. Cambridge, MA: MIT Press. doi:10.1007/b99492

Eberhart, R. C., & Shi, Y. (2001). Particle swarm optimization: Developments, applications and resources. *In Proceedings of Congress on Evolutionary Computation*, Seoul, Korea. Piscataway, NJ: IEEE Service Center.

El-Bouri, A., Azizi, N., & Zolfaghari, S. (2007). A comparative study of a new heuristic based on adaptive memory programming and simulated annealing: The case of job shop scheduling. *European Journal of Operational Research, 177*(3), 1894–1910. doi:10.1016/j.ejor.2005.12.013

El-Telbany, M., & El-Karmi, F. (2008). Short-term forecasting of Jordanian electricity demand using particle swarm optimization. *Electric Power Systems Research, 78*(3), 425–433. doi:10.1016/j.epsr.2007.03.011

Farmahini-Farahani, A., Vakili, S., Fakhraie, S. M., Safari, S., & Lucas, C. (2010). Parallel scalable hardware implementation of asynchronous discrete particle swarm optimization. *Engineering Applications of Artificial Intelligence, 23*(2), 177–187. doi:10.1016/j.engappai.2009.12.001

Fogel, G. B., & Corne, D. W. (Eds.). (2002). *Evolutionary computation in bioinformatics*. Oxford, UK: Elsevier LTD, Academic Press.

Fonseca, C. M., & Fleming, P. J. (1998). Multiobjective optimization and multiple constraint handling with evolutionary algorithms – Part I: A uni□ed formulation. *IEEE Transactions on Systems, Man, and Cybernetics. Part A, Systems and Humans, 28*(1), 26–37. doi:10.1109/3468.650319

Fournier, J. R. L., & Pierre, S. (2005). Assigning cells to switches in mobile networks using an ant colony optimization heuristic. *Computer Communications, 28*, 65–73. doi:10.1016/j.comcom.2004.07.006

Fuellerer, G., Doerner, K. F., Hartl, R. F., & Iori, M. (2010). Metaheuristics for vehicle routing problems with three-dimensional loading constraints. *European Journal of Operational Research, 201*(3), 751–759. doi:10.1016/j.ejor.2009.03.046

Gagne, C., Price, W. L., & Gravel, M. (2002). Comparing an ACO algorithm with other heuristics for the single machine scheduling problem with sequence-dependent setup times. *The Journal of the Operational Research Society, 53*, 895–906. doi:10.1057/palgrave.jors.2601390

Gajpal, Y., & Rajendran, C. (2006). An ant-colony optimization algorithm for minimizing the completion-time variance of jobs in flowshops. *International Journal of Production Economics, 101*(2), 259–272. doi:10.1016/j.ijpe.2005.01.003

Gallego, R. A., Romero, R., & Monticelli, A. J. (2000). Tabu search algorithm for network synthesis. *IEEE Transactions on Power Systems, 15*(2). doi:10.1109/59.867130

Gambardella, L. M., & Dorigo, M. (1995). Ant-Q: A reinforcement learning approach to the travelling salesman problem. In *Proceedings of the Twelfth International Conference on Machine Learning*, California, USA.

Gambardella, L. M., & Dorigo, M. (1996). Solving symmetric and asymmetric TSPs by ant colonies. In *Proceedings of the IEEE Conference on Evolutionary Computation* (pp. 622-627). Nagoya, Japan.

Gambardella, L. M., & Dorigo, M. (2000). Ant colony system hybridized with a new local search for the sequential ordering problem. *INFORMS Journal on Computing, 12*(3), 237–255. doi:10.1287/ijoc.12.3.237.12636

Gambardella, L. M., Taillard, E. D., & Agazzi, G. (1999). MACS-VRPTW: A multiple ant colony system for vehicle routing problems with time windows . In Corne, D., Dorigo, M., & Glover, F. (Eds.), *New ideas in optimization* (pp. 63–76). London, UK: McGraw-Hill.

Gangadharan, R., & Rajendran, C. (1994). A simulated annealing heuristic for scheduling in a flowshop with bicriteria. *Computers & Industrial Engineering, 27*(1-4), 473–476. doi:10.1016/0360-8352(94)90337-9

García-Martínez, C., Cordón, O., & Herrera, F. (2007). A taxonomy and an empirical analysis of multiple objective ant colony optimization algorithms for the bi-criteria TSP. *European Journal of Operational Research*, *180*(1), 116–148. doi:10.1016/j.ejor.2006.03.041

Geethanjali, M., Slochanal, S. M. R., & Bhavani, R. (2008). PSO trained ANN-based differential protection scheme for power transformers. *Neurocomputing*, *71*(4-6), 904–918. doi:10.1016/j.neucom.2007.02.014

Geiger, M. J. (Ed.). (2009). *Metaheuristics in the service industry*. Berlin, Germany: Springer-Verlag.

Geng, X., Chen, Z., Yang, W., Shi, D., & Zhao, K. (2011). Solving the traveling salesman problem based on an adaptive simulated annealing algorithm with greedy search. *Applied Soft Computing*, *11*(4), 3680–3689. doi:10.1016/j.asoc.2011.01.039

Genovese, K., Lamberti, L., & Pappalettere, C. (2005). Improved global–local simulated annealing formulation for solving non-smooth engineering optimization problems. *International Journal of Solids and Structures*, *42*(1), 203–237. doi:10.1016/j.ijsolstr.2004.07.015

German, S., & German, D. (1984). Stochastic relaxation, Gibbs distributions, and the Bayesian restoration of images. *IEEE Proceedings Pattern Analysis and Machine Intelligence*, *6*(6), 721-741.

Geyik, F., & Cedimoglu, I. H. (2004). The strategies and parameters of tabu search for job-shop scheduling problem. *Journal of Intelligent Manufacturing*, *15*, 439–448. doi:10.1023/B:JIMS.0000034106.86434.46

Glover, F. (2005). Adaptive memory projection methods for integer programming . In Rego, C., & Alidaee, B. (Eds.), *Metaheuristic optimization via memory and evolution* (pp. 425–440). Kluwer Academic Publishers. doi:10.1007/0-387-23667-8_19

Glover, F., & Kochenberger, G. A. (2003). *Handbook of metaheuristics*. Springer.

Goldberg, D. (1989). *Genetic algorithms in search, optimization and machine learning*. Reading, MA: Addison-Wesley.

Hamam, Y., & Hindi, K. S. (2000). Assignment of program modules to processors: A simulated annealing approach. *European Journal of Operational Research*, *122*(2), 509–513. doi:10.1016/S0377-2217(99)00251-9

Han, K.-H., & Kim, J. H. (2002). Quantum-inspired evolutionary algorithm for a class of combinatorial optimization. *IEEE Transactions on Evolutionary Computation*, *6*(6), 580–593. doi:10.1109/TEVC.2002.804320

Handa, H., Lin, D., Chapman, L., & Yao, X. (2006). Robust solution of salting route optimisation using evolutionary algorithms. In *Proceedings of the IEEE Congress on Evolutionary Computation* (pp. 3098–3105).

Hanke, M., & Li, P. (2000). Simulated annealing for the optimization of batch distillation processes. *Computers & Chemical Engineering*, *24*(1), 1–8. doi:10.1016/S0098-1354(00)00317-3

Hasançebi, O., & Erbatur, F. (2002). Layout optimisation of trusses using simulated annealing. *Advances in Engineering Software*, *33*(7-10), 681–696. doi:10.1016/S0965-9978(02)00049-2

Hasteer, G., & Banerjee, P. (1997). Simulated annealing based parallel state assignment of finite state machines. *Journal of Parallel and Distributed Computing*, *43*(1), 21–35. doi:10.1006/jpdc.1997.1325

He, Z., Wang, N., Jia, T., & Xu, Y. (2009). Simulated annealing and tabu search for multi-mode project payment scheduling. *European Journal of Operational Research, 198*(3), 688–696. doi:10.1016/j.ejor.2008.10.005

He, Z., Yang, T., & Tiger, A. (1996). An exchange heuristic imbedded with simulated annealing for due-dates job-shop scheduling. *European Journal of Operational Research, 91*(1), 99–117. doi:10.1016/0377-2217(94)00361-0

Hertz, A., Taillard, E., & Werra, D. (2005). *A tutorial on Tabu search.* Retrieved April 14, 2005, from http://www.cs.colostate.edu/~whitley/CS640/hertz92tutorial.pdf

Hillier, F. S., & Lieberman, G. J. (2005). *Introduction to operations research* (8th ed.). New York, NY: McGraw-Hill.

Holland, J. H. (Ed.). (1975). *Adaptation in natural and artificial systems: An introductory analysis with applications to biology, control, and artificial intelligence.* Ann Arbor, MI: University of Michigan Press.

Hsieh, T.-J., Hsiao, H.-F., & Yeh, W.-C. (2011). Forecasting stock markets using wavelet transforms and recurrent neural networks: An integrated system based on artificial bee colony algorithm. *Applied Soft Computing, 11*(2), 2510–2525. doi:10.1016/j.asoc.2010.09.007

Hu, P., Cao, G.-Y., Zhu, X.-J., & Li, J. (2010). Modeling of a proton exchange membrane fuel cell based on the hybrid particle swarm optimization with Levenberg–Marquardt neural network. *Simulation Modelling Practice and Theory, 18*(5), 574–588. doi:10.1016/j.simpat.2010.01.001

Huang, Y.-M., & Lin, J.-C. (2011). A new bee colony optimization algorithm with idle-time-based filtering scheme for open shop-scheduling problems. *Expert Systems with Applications, 38*(5), 5438–5447. doi:10.1016/j.eswa.2010.10.010

Jansen, P. W., & Perez, R. E. (2011). Constrained structural design optimization via a parallel augmented Lagrangian particle swarm optimization approach. *Computers & Structures, 89*(13-14), 1352–1366. doi:10.1016/j.compstruc.2011.03.011

Jeffcoat, D. E., & Bulfin, R. L. (1993). Simulated annealing for resource-constrained scheduling. *European Journal of Operational Research, 70*(1), 43–51. doi:10.1016/0377-2217(93)90231-B

Jeong, C.-S., & Kim, M.-H. (1991). Fast parallel simulated annealing for traveling salesman problem on SIMD machines with linear interconnections. *Parallel Computing, 17*(2-3), 221–228. doi:10.1016/S0167-8191(05)80107-3

Kang, F., Li, J., & Ma, Z. (2011). Rosenbrock artificial bee colony algorithm for accurate global optimization of numerical functions. *Information Science, 181*(16), 3508–3531. doi:10.1016/j.ins.2011.04.024

Karaboğa, D. (2005). *An idea based on honeybee swarm for numerical optimization.* Technical Report TR06, Erciyes University.

Karaboga, D., & Akay, B. (2011). A modified artificial bee colony (ABC) algorithm for constrained optimization problems. *Applied Soft Computing, 11*(3), 3021–3031. doi:10.1016/j.asoc.2010.12.001

Karaboğa, D., & Akay, B. A. (2009). Comparative study of artificial bee colony algorithm. *Applied Mathematics and Computation, 214*, 108–132. doi:10.1016/j.amc.2009.03.090

Karaboğa, D., & Baştük, B. (2007b). Artificial bee colony (ABC) optimization algorithm for solving constrained optimization problems. *LNCS: Advances in Soft Computing: Foundations of Fuzzy Logic and Soft Computing, 4529*, 789–798. doi:10.1007/978-3-540-72950-1_77

Karaboğa, D., & Baştürk, B. (2007a). A powerful and efficient algorithm for numerical optimization: Artificial bee colony (ABC) algorithm. *Journal of Global Optimization, 39*(3), 459–471. doi:10.1007/s10898-007-9149-x

Karaboğa, D., & Baştürk, B. (2008). On the performance of artificial bee colony (ABC) algorithm. *Applied Soft Computing, 8*(1), 687–697. doi:10.1016/j.asoc.2007.05.007

Karaboga, D., & Ökdem, S. (2004). A simple and global optimization algorithm for engineering problems: Differential evolution algorithm. *Turkish Journal of Electrical Engineering, 12*(1).

Kariuki, B. M., Serrano-Gonzalez, H., Johnston, R. L., & Harris, K. D. M. (1997). The application of a genetic algorithm for solving crystal structures from powder diffraction data. *Chemical Physics Letters, 280*, 189–195. doi:10.1016/S0009-2614(97)01156-1

Karr, C. L., & Gentry, E. J. (1993). Fuzzy control of pH using genetic algorithms. *IEEE Transactions on Fuzzy Systems, 1*(1). doi:10.1109/TFUZZ.1993.390283

Kayhan, A. H., Ceylan, H., Ayvaz, M. T., & Gurarslan, G. (2010). PSOLVER: A new hybrid particle swarm optimization algorithm for solving continuous optimization problems. *Expert Systems with Applications, 37*(10), 6798–6808. doi:10.1016/j.eswa.2010.03.046

Kennedy, J., & Eberhart, R. (1995). Particle swarm optimization. In *Proceedings of the 1995 IEEE International Conference on Neural Networks* (pp. 1942-1948). Perth, Australia. Piscataway, NJ: IEEE Service Center.

Kim, D.-W., Kim, K.-H., Jang, W., & Chen, F. F. (2002). Unrelated parallel machine scheduling with setup times using simulated annealing. *Robotics and Computer-integrated Manufacturing, 18*(3-4), 223–231. doi:10.1016/S0736-5845(02)00013-3

Kim, H.-S., & Cho, S.-B. (2000). Application of interactive genetic algorithm to fashion design. *Engineering Applications of Artificial Intelligence, 13*, 635–644. doi:10.1016/S0952-1976(00)00045-2

Kim, J. Y., & Kim, Y. K. (2005). Multileveled symbiotic evolutionary algorithm: Application to FMS loading problems. *Applied Intelligence, 22*, 233–249. doi:10.1007/s10791-005-6621-4

Kirpatrick, S., Gelat, C. D. Jr, & Vecchi, M. P. (1983). Optimization by simulated annealing. *Science, 220*, 671–680. doi:10.1126/science.220.4598.671

Kouvelis, P., Chiang, W.-C., & Fitzsimmons, J. (1992). Simulated annealing for machine layout problems in the presence of zoning constraints. *European Journal of Operational Research, 57*(2), 203–223. doi:10.1016/0377-2217(92)90043-9

Kuo, Y. (2010). Using simulated annealing to minimize fuel consumption for the time-dependent vehicle routing problem. *Computers & Industrial Engineering, 59*(1), 157–165. doi:10.1016/j.cie.2010.03.012

Lee, I., Sikora, R., & Shaw, M. J. (1997). A genetic algorithm-based approach to flexible flow-line scheduling with variable lot sizes. *IEEE Transactions on Systems, Man, and Cybernetics. Part B, Cybernetics, 27*(1), 36–54. doi:10.1109/3477.552184

Lee, S., Ryu, J.-H., Won, J.-S., & Park, H.-J. (2004). Determination and application of the weights for landslide susceptibility mapping using an artificial neural network. *Engineering Geology, 71*, 289–302. doi:10.1016/S0013-7952(03)00142-X

Lek, S., & Guegan, J. F. (1999). Artificial neural networks as a tool in ecological modelling, an introduction. *Ecological Modelling, 120*, 65–73. doi:10.1016/S0304-3800(99)00092-7

Leung, C. W., Wong, T. N., Mak, K. L., & Fung, R. Y. K. (2010). Integrated process planning and scheduling by an agent-based ant colony optimization. *Computers & Industrial Engineering, 59*(1), 166–180. doi:10.1016/j.cie.2009.09.003

Lian, Z., Gu, X., & Jiao, B. (2006). A similar particle swarm optimization algorithm for permutation flowshop scheduling to minimize makespan. *Applied Mathematics and Computation, 175*(1), 773–785. doi:10.1016/j.amc.2005.07.042

Liang, R.-H., & Wang, Y. S. (2001). Main transformer ULTC and capacitors scheduling by simulated annealing approach. *International Journal of Electrical Power & Energy Systems, 23*(7), 531–538. doi:10.1016/S0142-0615(00)00086-7

Liao, C.-J., Tseng, C.-T., & Luarn, P. (2007). A discrete version of particle swarm optimization for flowshop scheduling problems. *Computers & Operations Research, 34*(10), 3099–3111. doi:10.1016/j.cor.2005.11.017

Lin, B., & Miller, D. C. (2004). Solving heat exchanger network synthesis problems with Tabu Search. *Computers & Chemical Engineering, 28*, 1451–1464. doi:10.1016/j.compchemeng.2003.10.004

Lin, L.-C. (2009). Optimal chiller loading by particle swarm algorithm for reducing energy consumption. *Applied Thermal Engineering, 29*(8-9), 1730–1734. doi:10.1016/j.applthermaleng.2008.08.004

Lin, S.-Y., Horng, S.-J., Kao, T.-W., Huang, D.-K., Fahn, C.-S., & Lai, J.-L. (2010). An efficient bi-objective personnel assignment algorithm based on a hybrid particle swarm optimization model. *Expert Systems with Applications, 37*(12), 7825–7830. doi:10.1016/j.eswa.2010.04.056

Lin, T.-L., Horng, S.-J., Kao, T.-W., Chen, Y.-H., Run, R.-S., & Chen, R.-J. (2010). An efficient job-shop scheduling algorithm based on particle swarm optimization. *Expert Systems with Applications, 37*(3), 2629–2636. doi:10.1016/j.eswa.2009.08.015

Liu, H., Abraham, A., & Clerc, M. (2007). Chaotic dynamic characteristics in swarm intelligence. *Applied Soft Computing, 7*(3), 1019–1026. doi:10.1016/j.asoc.2006.10.006

Liu, J., Li, G., Chen, D., Liu, W., & Wang, Y. (2010). Two-dimensional equilibrium constraint layout using simulated annealing. *Computers & Industrial Engineering, 59*(4), 530–536. doi:10.1016/j.cie.2010.06.009

Lo, Z.-P., & Bavarian, B. (1992). Optimization of job scheduling on parallel machines by simulated annealing algorithms. *Expert Systems with Applications, 4*(3), 323–328. doi:10.1016/0957-4174(92)90068-4

Low, C. (2005). Simulated annealing heuristic for flow shop scheduling problems with unrelated parallel machines. *Computers & Operations Research, 32*(8), 2013–2025. doi:10.1016/j.cor.2004.01.003

Lu, M., Lam, H.-C., & Dai, F. (2008). Resource-constrained critical path analysis based on discrete event simulation and particle swarm optimization. *Automation in Construction, 17*(6), 670–681. doi:10.1016/j.autcon.2007.11.004

Luh, G.-C., Lin, Y.-S., & Lin, C.-Y. (2011). A binary particle swarm optimization for continuum structural topology optimization. *Applied Soft Computing, 11*(2), 2833–2844. doi:10.1016/j.asoc.2010.11.013

Maniezzo, V., & Colorni, A. (1999). The ant system applied to the quadratic assignment problem. *IEEE Transaction Data Knowledge Engineering, 11*(5), 769–778. doi:10.1109/69.806935

Mariano, A. P., Costa, C. B. B., Vasco de Toledo, E. C., Melo, D. N. C., & Filho, R. M. (in press). Analysis of the particle swarm algorithm in the optimization of a three-phase slurry catalytic reactor. [in press]. *Computers & Chemical Engineering*.

Marimuthu, S., Ponnambalam, S. G., & Jawahar, N. (2009). Threshold accepting and Ant-colony optimization algorithms for scheduling m-machine flow shops with lot streaming. *Journal of Materials Processing Technology*, *209*(2), 1026–1041. doi:10.1016/j.jmatprotec.2008.03.013

Marinakis, Y., & Marinak, M. (2010). A hybrid multi-swarm particle swarm optimization algorithm for the probabilistic traveling salesman problem. *Computers & Operations Research*, *37*(3), 432–442. doi:10.1016/j.cor.2009.03.004

McKendall, A. R. Jr, Shang, J., & Kuppusamy, S. (2006). Simulated annealing heuristics for the dynamic facility layout problem. *Computers & Operations Research*, *33*(8), 2431–2444. doi:10.1016/j.cor.2005.02.021

Melouk, S., Damodaran, P., & Chang, P.-Y. (2004). Minimizing makespan for single machine batch processing with non-identical job sizes using simulated annealing. *International Journal of Production Economics*, *87*(2), 141–147. doi:10.1016/S0925-5273(03)00092-6

Merkle, D., Middendorf, M., & Schmeck, H. (2002). Ant colony optimization for resource-constrained project scheduling. *IEEE Transactions on Evolutionary Computation*, *6*(4), 333–346. doi:10.1109/TEVC.2002.802450

Metropolis, N., Rosenbluth, A., Rosenbluth, M., Teller, A., & Teller, E. (1953). Equation of state calculations by fast computing machines. *The Journal of Chemical Physics*, *21*(6), 1087–1092. doi:10.1063/1.1699114

MirHassani, S. A., & Abolghasemi, N. (2011). A particle swarm optimization algorithm for open vehicle routing problem. *Expert Systems with Applications*, *38*(9), 11547–11551. doi:10.1016/j.eswa.2011.03.032

Nearchou, A. C. (2007). Balancing large assembly lines by a new heuristic based on differential evolution method. *International Journal of Advanced Manufacturing Technology*, *34*, 1016–1029. doi:10.1007/s00170-006-0655-7

Nearchou, A. C. (2011). Maximizing production rate and workload smoothing in assembly lines using particle swarm optimization. *International Journal of Production Economics*, *129*(2), 242–250. doi:10.1016/j.ijpe.2010.10.016

Nickolay, B., Schneider, B., & Jacob, S. (1997). Parameter optimisation of an image processing system using evolutionary algorithms. In *Computer Analysis of Images and Patterns, Proceedings of the 7th International Conference, Vol. 1296. Lecture Notes in Computer Science* (pp. 637–644). Berlin, Germany: Springer.

Obayashi, S. (1998). Multidisciplinary design optimization of aircraft wing planform based on evolutionary algorithms. In *Proceedings of the 1998 IEEE International Conference on Systems, Man, and Cybernetics*. La Jolla, CA: IEEE Press.

Ogura, T., & Sato, C. (2006). A fully automatic 3D reconstruction method using simulated annealing enables accurate posterioric angular assignment of protein projections. *Journal of Structural Biology*, *156*(3), 371–386. doi:10.1016/j.jsb.2006.05.016

Oh, S.-K., Kim, W.-D., Pedrycz, W., & Park, B.-J. (2011). Polynomial-based radial basis function neural networks (P-RBF NNs) realized with the aid of particle swarm optimization. *Fuzzy Sets and Systems*, *163*(1), 54–77. doi:10.1016/j.fss.2010.08.007

Ólafsson, S. (2006). Metaheuristics . In Nelson, B. L., & Henderson, S. G. (Eds.), *Handbook on simulation, handbooks in operations research and management science VII* (pp. 633–654). Elsevier.

Oliveira, I. M. S., & Schirru, R. (2011). Swarm intelligence of artificial bees applied to in-core fuel management optimization. *Annals of Nuclear Energy*, *38*(5), 1039–1045. doi:10.1016/j.anucene.2011.01.009

Önüt, S., Tuzkaya, U. R., & Doğaç, B. (2008). A particle swarm optimization algorithm for the multiple-level warehouse layout design problem. *Computers & Industrial Engineering*, *54*, 783–799. doi:10.1016/j.cie.2007.10.012

Onwubolu, G., & Davendra, D. (2006). Scheduling flow shops using differential evolution algorithm. *European Journal of Operational Research*, *171*, 674–692. doi:10.1016/j.ejor.2004.08.043

Ozbakir, L., Baykasoglu, L. A., Gorkemli, B., & Gorkemli, L. (2011). Multiple-colony ant algorithm for parallel assembly line balancing problem. *Applied Soft Computing*, *11*(3), 3186–3198. doi:10.1016/j.asoc.2010.12.021

Özcan, U. (2010). Balancing stochastic two-sided assembly lines: A chance-constrained, piecewise-linear, mixed integer program and a simulated annealing algorithm. *European Journal of Operational Research*, *205*(1), 81–97. doi:10.1016/j.ejor.2009.11.033

Pan, Q.-K., Tasgetiren, M. F., Suganthan, P. N., & Chen, A. T.-J. (2011). A discrete artificial bee colony algorithm for the lot-streaming flow shop scheduling problem. *Information Sciences*, *181*(12), 2455–2468. doi:10.1016/j.ins.2009.12.025

Park, D. C., & El-Sharkawi, M. A., & Marks 11, R. J. (1991). Electric load forecasting using artificial neural network. *IEEE Transactions on Power Systems*, *6*(2). doi:10.1109/59.76685

Paul, G. (2010). Comparative performance of Tabu search and simulated annealing heuristics for the quadratic assignment problem. *Operations Research Letters*, *38*(6), 577–581. doi:10.1016/j.orl.2010.09.009

Peng, T., Huanchen, W., & Dongme, Z. (1996). Simulated annealing for the quadratic assignment problem: A further study. *Computers & Industrial Engineering*, *31*(3-4), 925–928. doi:10.1016/S0360-8352(96)00265-3

Perez, R. E., & Behdinan, K. (2007). Particle swarm approach for structural design optimization. *Computers & Structures*, *85*(19-20), 1579–1588. doi:10.1016/j.compstruc.2006.10.013

Pham, D. T., & Karaboga, D. (2000). *Intelligent optimisation techniques – Genetic algorithms, Tabu search, simulated annealing and neural networks*. London, UK: Springer-Verlag.

Poli, R., Kennedy, J., & Blackwell, T. (2007). Particle swarm optimization. *Swarm Intelligence*, *1*(1), 33–57. doi:10.1007/s11721-007-0002-0

Puris, A., Bello, R., & Herrera, F. (2010). Analysis of the efficacy of a two-stage methodology for ant colony optimization: Case of study with TSP and QAP. *Expert Systems with Applications*, *37*(7), 5443–5453. doi:10.1016/j.eswa.2010.02.069

Raaymakers, W. H. M., & Hoogeveen, J. A. (2000). Scheduling multipurpose batch process industries with no-wait restrictions by simulated annealing. *European Journal of Operational Research*, *126*(1), 131–151. doi:10.1016/S0377-2217(99)00285-4

Rehman, S., & Mohandes, M. (2008). Artificial neural network estimation of global solar radiation using air temperature and relative humidity. *Energy Policy*, *36*, 571–576. doi:10.1016/j.enpol.2007.09.033

Resende, M. G. C., & De Sousa, J. P. (Eds.). (2004). *Metaheuristics: Computer decision making*. Netherlands: Kluwer Academic Publishers.

Reynolds, A. P., & McKeown, G. P. (1999). Scheduling a manufacturing plant using simulated annealing and simulation. *Computers & Industrial Engineering, 37*(1-2), 63–67. doi:10.1016/S0360-8352(99)00024-8

Roh, S.-B., Ahn, T.-C., & Pedrycz, W. (2010). The design methodology of radial basis function neural networks based on fuzzy K-nearest neighbors approach. *Fuzzy Sets and Systems, 161*(13), 1803–1822. doi:10.1016/j.fss.2009.10.014

Rossi, A., & Dini, G. (2007). Flexible job-shop scheduling with routing flexibility and separable setup times using ant colony optimisation method. *Robotics and Computer-integrated Manufacturing, 23*(5), 503–516. doi:10.1016/j.rcim.2006.06.004

Sabuncuoglu, I., Erel, E., & Alp, A. (2009). Ant colony optimization for the single model U-type assembly line balancing problem. *International Journal of Production Economics, 120*(2), 287–300. doi:10.1016/j.ijpe.2008.11.017

Şahin, R. (2011). A simulated annealing algorithm for solving the bi-objective facility layout problem. *Expert Systems with Applications, 38*(4), 4460–4465. doi:10.1016/j.eswa.2010.09.117

Salleh, S., & Zomaya, A. Y. (1998). Multiprocessor scheduling using mean-field annealing. *Future Generation Computer Systems, 14*(5-6), 393–408. doi:10.1016/S0167-739X(98)00042-9

Salman, A., Ahmad, I., & Al-Mada, S. (2002). Particle swarm optimization for task assignment problem. *Microprocessors and Microsystems, 26*(8), 363–371. doi:10.1016/S0141-9331(02)00053-4

Santos de Oliveira, I. M., & Schirru, R. (2011). Swarm intelligence of artificial bees applied to in-core fuel management optimization. *Annals of Nuclear Energy, 38*(5), 1039–1045. doi:10.1016/j.anucene.2011.01.009

Saraiva, J. T., Pereira, M. L., Mendes, V. T., & Sousa, J. C. (2011). A simulated annealing based approach to solve the generator maintenance scheduling problem. *Electric Power Systems Research, 81*(7), 1283–1291. doi:10.1016/j.epsr.2011.01.013

Şenkal, O., & Kuleli, T. (2009). Estimation of solar radiation over Turkey using artificial neural network and satellite data. *Applied Energy, 86*, 1222–1228. doi:10.1016/j.apenergy.2008.06.003

Sha, D. Y., & Hsu, C.-Y. (2008). A new particle swarm optimization for the open shop scheduling problem. *Computers & Operations Research, 35*(10), 3243–3261. doi:10.1016/j.cor.2007.02.019

Shafie-Khah, M., Moghaddam, M. P., & Sheikh-El-Eslami, M. K. (2011). Price forecasting of day-ahead electricity markets using a hybrid forecast method. *Energy Conversion and Management, 52*(5), 2165–2169. doi:10.1016/j.enconman.2010.10.047

Shi, X. H., Liang, Y. C., Lee, H. P., Lu, C., & Wang, Q. X. (2007). Particle swarm optimization-based algorithms for TSP and generalized TSP. *Information Processing Letters, 103*(5), 169–176. doi:10.1016/j.ipl.2007.03.010

Shi, Y., & Eberhart, R. (1998). A modified particle swarm optimizer. *Evolutionary Computation Proceedings, IEEE World Congress on Computational Intelligence* (pp. 69-73). Anchorage, AK, USA.

Shin, K.-S., & Lee, Y.-J. (2002). A genetic algorithm application in bankruptcy prediction modeling. *Expert Systems with Applications, 23*(3), 321–328. doi:10.1016/S0957-4174(02)00051-9

Shyu, S. J., Lin, B. M. T., & Hsiao, T.-S. (2006). Ant colony optimization for the cell assignment problem in PCS networks. *Computers & Operations Research, 33*, 1713–1740. doi:10.1016/j.cor.2004.11.026

Simaria, A. S., & Vilarinho, P. M. (2009). 2-ANT-BAL: An ant colony optimisation algorithm for balancing two-sided assembly lines. *Computers & Industrial Engineering, 56*(2), 489–506. doi:10.1016/j.cie.2007.10.007

Socha, K., & Dorigo, M. (2008). Ant colony optimization for continuous domains. *European Journal of Operational Research, 185*, 1155–1173. doi:10.1016/j.ejor.2006.06.046

Sonmez, M. (2011). Artificial bee colony algorithm for optimization of truss structures. *Applied Soft Computing, 11*(2), 2406–2418. doi:10.1016/j.asoc.2010.09.003

Souilah, A. (1995). Simulated annealing for manufacturing systems layout design. *European Journal of Operational Research, 82*(3), 592–614. doi:10.1016/0377-2217(93)E0336-V

Stumberger, G., Dolinar, D., Pahner, U., & Hamayer, K. (2000). Optimization of radial active magnetic bearings using the finite element technique and differential evolution algorithm. *IEEE Transactions on Magnetics, 36*(4).

Stützle, T. (1998). An ant approach to the flow shop problem. In *Proceedings of the 6th European Congress on Intelligent Techniques and Soft Computing* (pp. 1560-1564). Aachen, Germany: Verlag Mainz.

Stützle, T., & Hoos, H. (1996). *Improving the ant system: A detailed report on the MAX-MIN ant system.* Technical Report AIDA-96-12, FG Intellektik, FN Informatik, TU Darmstadt, Germany.

Stützle, T., & Hoos, H. (2000). MAX-MIN ant system. *Future Generation Computer Systems, 16*(8), 889–904.

Suman, B., Hoda, N., & Jha, S. (2010). Orthogonal simulated annealing for multiobjective optimization. *Computers & Chemical Engineering, 34*(10), 1618–1631. doi:10.1016/j.compchemeng.2009.11.015

Sun, M., Aronson, J. E., McKeown, P. G., & Drinka, D. (1998). A tabu search heuristic procedure for the fixed charge transportation problem. *European Journal of Operational Research, 106*, 441–456. doi:10.1016/S0377-2217(97)00284-1

Sundhararajan, S., & Pahwa, A. (1994). Optimal selection of capacitors for radial distribution systems using a genetic algorithm. *IEEE Transactions on Power Systems, 9*(3), 1499–1507. doi:10.1109/59.336111

Szeto, W. Y., Wu, Y., & Ho, S. C. (2011). An artificial bee colony algorithm for the capacitated vehicle routing problem. *European Journal of Operational Research, 215*(1), 126–135. doi:10.1016/j.ejor.2011.06.006

Talbi, El-G. (Ed.). (1965). *Metaheuristics: From design to implementation.* Hoboken, NJ: John Wiley & Sons.

Tao, Q., Chang, H.-Y., Yi, Y., Gu, C.-Q., & Li, W.-J. (2011). A rotary chaotic PSO algorithm for trustworthy scheduling of a grid workflow. *Computers & Operations Research, 38*(5), 824–836. doi:10.1016/j.cor.2010.09.012

Tasgetiren, M. F., Pan, Q.-K., Suganthan, P. N., & Chen, A. H.-L. (2010). A discrete artificial bee colony algorithm for the total flowtime minimization in permutation flow shops. *Information Sciences, 181*(16), 3459–3475. doi:10.1016/j.ins.2011.04.018

Tavakkoli-Moghaddam, R., Safaei, N., & Gholipour, Y. (2006). A hybrid simulated annealing for capacitated vehicle routing problems with the independent route length. *Applied Mathematics and Computation, 176*(2), 445–454. doi:10.1016/j.amc.2005.09.040

Tavakkoli-Moghaddam, R., Safaei, N., Kah, M. M. O., & Rabbani, M. (2007). A new capacitated vehicle routing problem with split service for minimizing fleet cost by simulated annealing. *Journal of the Franklin Institute, 344*(5), 406–425. doi:10.1016/j.jfranklin.2005.12.002

Toksarı, M. D. (2009). Estimating the net electricity energy generation and demand using the ant colony optimization approach: Case of Turkey. *Energy Policy, 37*(3), 1181–1187. doi:10.1016/j.enpol.2008.11.017

Trigueros, D. E. G., Módenes, A. N., Kroumov, A. D., & Espinoza-Quiñones, F. R. (2010). Modeling of biodegradation process of BTEX compounds: Kinetic parameters estimation by using particle swarm global optimizer. *Process Biochemistry, 45*(8), 1355–1361. doi:10.1016/j.procbio.2010.05.007

Uğur, A., & Aydin, D. (2009). an interactive simulation and analysis software for solving tsp using ant colony optimization algorithms. *Advances in Engineering Software, 40*(5), 341–349. doi:10.1016/j.advengsoft.2008.05.004

Ünler, A. (2008). Improvement of energy demand forecasts using swarm intelligence: The case of Turkey with projections to 2025. *Energy Policy, 36*(6), 1937–1944. doi:10.1016/j.enpol.2008.02.018

Van Breedam, A. (1995). Improvement heuristics for the vehicle routing problem based on simulated annealing. *European Journal of Operational Research, 86*(3), 480–490. doi:10.1016/0377-2217(94)00064-J

Varadharajan, T. K., & Rajendran, C. (2005). A multi-objective simulated-annealing algorithm for scheduling in flowshops to minimize the makespan and total flowtime of jobs. *European Journal of Operational Research, 167*(3), 772–795. doi:10.1016/j.ejor.2004.07.020

Voß, S. (2001). Meta-heuristics: The state of the art. *Lecture Notes in Computer Science, 2148*, 1–23. doi:10.1007/3-540-45612-0_1

Wang, J., Cai, Y., Zhou, Y., Wang, R., & Li, C. (2011). Discrete particle swarm optimization based on estimation of distribution for terminal assignment problems. *Computers & Industrial Engineering, 60*(4), 566–575. doi:10.1016/j.cie.2010.12.014

Wang, Q. J. (1991). The genetic algorithm and its application to calibrating conceptual rainfall-runoff models. *Water Resources Research, 27*(9), 2467–2471. doi:10.1029/91WR01305

Wang, T. Y., Wu, K. B., & Liu, Y. W. (2001). A simulated annealing algorithm for facility layout problems under variable demand in cellular manufacturing systems. *Computers in Industry, 46*(2), 181–188. doi:10.1016/S0166-3615(01)00107-5

Watanabe, K., & Hashem, M. M. A. (2004). *Evolutionary computations – New algorithms and their applications to evolutionary robots. Studies in Fuzziness and Soft Computing.* Berlin, Germany: Springer.

Weile, D. S., & Michielssen, E. (1997). Genetic algorithm optimization applied to electromagnetics: A review. *IEEE Transactions on Antennas and Propagation, 45*(3). doi:10.1109/8.558650

Wilson, W. G., & Vasudevan, K. (1991). Application of the genetic algorithm to residual statics estimation. *Geophysical Research Letters, 18*(12), 2118–2184. doi:10.1029/91GL02537

Xia, W., & Wu, Z. (2005). An effective hybrid optimization approach for multi-objective flexible job-shop scheduling problems. *Computers & Industrial Engineering, 48*(2), 409–425. doi:10.1016/j.cie.2005.01.018

Xia, Y. (1996). A new neural network for solving linear programming problems and its application. *IEEE Transactions on Neural Networks, 7*(2).

Xinchao, Z. (2011). Simulated annealing algorithm with adaptive neighborhood. *Applied Soft Computing*, *11*, 1827–1836. doi:10.1016/j.asoc.2010.05.029

Yagmahan, B. (2011). Mixed-model assembly line balancing using a multi-objective ant colony optimization approach. *Expert Systems with Applications*, *38*(10), 12453–12461. doi:10.1016/j.eswa.2011.04.026

Yagmahan, B., & Yenisey, M. M. (2008). Ant colony optimization for multi-objective flow shop scheduling problem. *Computers & Industrial Engineering*, *54*(3), 411–420. doi:10.1016/j.cie.2007.08.003

Yang, J., Shi, X., Marchese, M., & Liang, Y. (2008). An ant colony optimization method for generalized TSP problem. *Progress in Natural Science*, *18*(11), 1417–1422. doi:10.1016/j.pnsc.2008.03.028

Yanxia, W., Longjun, Q., Zhi, G., & Lifeng, M. (2008). Weapon target assignment problem satisfying expected damage probabilities based on ant colony algorithm. *Journal of Systems Engineering and Electronics*, *19*(5), 939–944. doi:10.1016/S1004-4132(08)60179-6

Yaseen, S. G., & AL-Slamy, N. M. A. (2008). Ant colony optimization. *IJCSNS International Journal of Computer Science and Network Security*, *8*(6), 351-357.

Yılmaz, I., & Yuksek, A. G. (2008). An example of artificial neural network (ANN) application for indirect estimation of rock parameters. *Rock Mechanics and Rock Engineering*, *41*(5), 781–795. doi:10.1007/s00603-007-0138-7

Yin, P.-Y., Yu, S.-S., Wang, P.-P., & Wang, Y.-T. (2006). A hybrid particle swarm optimization algorithm for optimal task assignment in distributed systems. *Computer Standards & Interfaces*, *28*(4), 441–450. doi:10.1016/j.csi.2005.03.005

Yu, B., & Yang, Z. Z. (2011). An ant colony optimization model: The period vehicle routing problem with time windows. *Transportation Research Part E, Logistics and Transportation Review*, *47*(2), 166–181. doi:10.1016/j.tre.2010.09.010

Yu, V. F., Lin, S.-W., Lee, W., & Ting, C.-J. (2010). A simulated annealing heuristic for the capacitated location routing problem. *Computers & Industrial Engineering*, *58*(2), 288–299. doi:10.1016/j.cie.2009.10.007

Zarandi, M. H. F., Hemmati, A., & Davari, S. (2011). The multi-depot capacitated location-routing problem with fuzzy travel times. *Expert Systems with Applications*, *38*(8), 10075–10084. doi:10.1016/j.eswa.2011.02.006

Zegordi, S. H., Itoh, K., & Enkawa, T. (1995). Minimizing makespan for flow shop scheduling by combining simulated annealing with sequencing knowledge. *European Journal of Operational Research*, *85*(3), 515–531. doi:10.1016/0377-2217(94)00021-4

Zhang, H., Li, X., Li, H., & Huang, F. (2005). Particle swarm optimization-based schemes for resource-constrained project scheduling. *Automation in Construction*, *14*(3), 393–404. doi:10.1016/j.autcon.2004.08.006

Zhang, J.-R., Zhang, J., Lok, T.-M., & Lyu, M. R. (2007). A hybrid particle swarm optimization–back-propagation algorithm for feedforward neural network training. *Applied Mathematics and Computation*, *185*(2), 1026–1037. doi:10.1016/j.amc.2006.07.025

Zhang, R., & Wu, C. (2010). A hybrid immune simulated annealing algorithm for the job shop scheduling problem. *Applied Soft Computing*, *10*(1), 79–89. doi:10.1016/j.asoc.2009.06.008

Zhang, X., Yuan, X., & Yuan, Y. (2008). Improved hybrid simulated annealing algorithm for navigation scheduling for the two dams of the Three Gorges Project. *Computers & Mathematics with Applications (Oxford, England)*, *56*(1), 151–159. doi:10.1016/j.camwa.2007.11.041

Zhu, G., & Kwong, S. (2010). Gbest-guided artificial bee colony algorithm for numerical function optimization. *Applied Mathematics and Computation, 217*(7), 3166–3173. doi:10.1016/j.amc.2010.08.049

Ziarati, K., Akbari, R., & Zeighami, V. (2011). On the performance of bee algorithms for resource-constrained project scheduling problem. *Applied Soft Computing, 11*(4), 3720–3733. doi:10.1016/j.asoc.2011.02.002

ADDITIONAL READING

Arora, J. (1989). *Introduction to optimum design*. McGraw-Hill.

Bersini, H., & Varela, F. J. (1990). *Hints for adaptive problem solving gleaned from immune networks*. Parellel Problem Solving from Nature, PPSW1, Dortmund, FRG.

Bonabeau, E., Theraulaz, G., & Dorigo, M. (1999). *Swarm intelligence: From natural to artificial systems*. Oxford University Press.

Chung-Yuan, D., & Liang-Yuh, O. (2011). A particle swarm optimization for solving joint pricing and lot-sizing problem with fluctuating demand and trade credit financing. *Computers & Industrial Engineering, 60*(1), 127–137. doi:10.1016/j.cie.2010.10.010

Farmer, J. D., Packard, N., & Perelson, A. (1986). The immune system, adaptation and machine learning. *Physica D. Nonlinear Phenomena, 2*, 187–204. doi:10.1016/0167-2789(86)90240-X

Fortemps, P., Pirlot, M., Teghem, J., & Tuyttens, D. (1996). Using metaheuristics for solving a production scheduling problem in a chemical firm: A case study. *International Journal of Production Economics, 46–47*, 13–26. doi:10.1016/0925-5273(95)00168-9

Gediminas, V. (2006). Metaheuristics and large-scale optimization. *Technological and Economic Development of Economy, 12*(1).

Geem, Z. W., Kim, J. H., & Loganathan, G. V. (2001). A new heuristic optimization: Harmony search. *Simulation, 76*, 60–68. doi:10.1177/003754970107600201

Glover, F. (1986). Future paths for integer programming and links to artficial intelligence. *Computers & Operations Research, 13*, 533–549. doi:10.1016/0305-0548(86)90048-1

Glover, F., & Laguna, M. (1997). *Tabu search*. Boston, MA: Kluwer. doi:10.1007/978-1-4615-6089-0

Gutiahr, W. J. (2005). Two metaheuristics for multiobjective stochastic combinatorial optimization. In Lupanoy, O. B., Kasımzade, O., Chaskin, A. V., & Steinhofel, K. (Eds.), *Stochastic Algorithms: Foundations and Applications* (Vol. 3777, pp. 116–125). Proceedings. doi:10.1007/11571155_12

Helene, W., Pascale, T.-F., & Olfa, A.-K. (2007). Simulated annealing applied to test generation: Landscape characterization and stopping criteria. *Empirical Software Engineering, 12*(1), 35–63. doi:10.1007/s10664-006-7551-5

Jourdan, L., Basseur, M., & Talbi, E.-G. (2009). Hybridizing exact methods and metaheuristics: A taxonomy. *European Journal of Operational Research, 199*(3), 620–629. doi:10.1016/j.ejor.2007.07.035

Lessmann, S., Caserta, M., & Arango, I. M. (2011). Tuning metaheuristics: A data mining based approach for particle swarm optimization. *Expert Systems with Applications, 38*(10), 12826–12838. doi:10.1016/j.eswa.2011.04.075

Maniezzo, V., & Roffilli, M. (2008). Very strongly constrained problems: An ant colony optimization approach. *Cybernetics and Systems: An International Journal, 39*(4).

Moscato, P. (1986) *On evolution, search, optimization, genetic algorithms and martial arts: Towards memetic algorithms*. Caltech Concurrent Computation Program (report 826).

Parpinelli, R. S., Vargas Benitez, C. M., & Lopes, H. S. (2011). Parallel approaches for the artificial bee colony algorithm . In Panigrahi, B. K., Shi, Y. H., & Lim, M. H. (Eds.), *Handbook of swarm intelligence: Concepts, principles and applications* (*Vol. 8*, pp. 329–345). doi:10.1007/978-3-642-17390-5_14

Pellegrini, P., & Favaretto, D. (2012). Quantifying the exploration performed by metaheuristic. *Journal of Experimental & Theoretical Artificial Intelligence*, (n.d), 1–20.

Price, K., Storn, R., & Lampinen, J. (2005). *Differential evolution: A practical approach to global optimization*. Springer.

Ribeiro, C. C., Martins, L. S., & Rosseti, I. (2007). Metaheuristics for optimization problems in computer communications. *Computer Communications*, *30*(4), 656–669. doi:10.1016/j.comcom.2006.08.027

Rubinstein, R. Y. (1997). Optimization of computer simulation models with rare events. *European Journal of Operational Research*, *99*, 89–112. doi:10.1016/S0377-2217(96)00385-2

Salcedo-Sanz, S., & Su, J. (2007). Improving metaheuristics convergence properties in inductive query by example using two strategies for reducing the search space. *Computers & Operations Research*, *34*(1), 91–106. doi:10.1016/j.cor.2005.05.001

Storn, R., & Price, K. (1997). Differential evolution - A simple and efficient heuristic for global optimization over continuous spaces. *Journal of Global Optimization*, *11*, 341–359. doi:10.1023/A:1008202821328

Tangour, F., & Borne, P. (2008). Presentation of some metaheuristics for the optimization of complex systems. *Studies in Informatics and Control*, *17*(2), 169–180.

Weifeng, G., & Sanyang, L. (2011). Improved artificial bee colony algorithm for global optimization. *Information Processing Letters*, *111*(17), 871–882. doi:10.1016/j.ipl.2011.06.002

Yang, X. S. (2008). *Nature-inspired metaheuristic algorithms*. UK: Luniver Press.

Yang, X. S. (2009). Firefly algorithms for multimodal optimization. In O. Watanabe & T. Zeugmann (Eds.), *5th Symposium on Stochastic Algorithms, Foundation and Applications (SAGA 2009), LNCS, 5792*, (pp. 169–178).

Yang, X. S. (2010). *Engineering optimization: An introduction with metaheuristic applications*. John Wiley & Sons. doi:10.1002/9780470640425

Yang, X.-S. (2011). Optimization algorithms . In Kozeil, S., & Yang, X. S. (Eds.), *Computational Optimization* (*Vol. 356*, pp. 13–31). Methods and Algorithms.

Yang, X. S., & Deb, S. (2010). Engineering optimization by cuckoo search. *International Journal of Mathematical Modelling and Numerical Optimisation*, *1*(4), 330–343. doi:10.1504/IJMMNO.2010.035430

KEY TERMS AND DEFINITIONS

Ant Colony Optimization (ACO): ACO is inspired by the behavior of real ants. It is based on a parallel search over several constructive computational threads using local problem data and a dynamic memory structure containing information on the quality of previously obtained result.

Artificial Bee Colony (ABC): ABC is one of the most recently defined algorithms motivated by the intelligent behavior of honey bees. It combines local search methods, carried out by employed and onlooker bees, with global search methods, managed by onlookers and scouts, attempting to balance exploration and exploitation process.

Artificial Neural Networks (ANN): ANN is a computational technique inspired from natural neurons. ANNs connect artificial neurons in order to process information.

Differential Evolution (DE): DE is a very simple population based, stochastic function minimizer which is very powerful at the same time. It is a technique that optimizes a problem by iteratively trying to develop a candidate solution with respect to a given measure of quality.

Evolutionary Algorithm (EA): EA is a optimization technique based on the principles of natural evolution. Its algorithm uses to produce new collections of potential solutions until some stopping criterion is met.

Genetic Algorithm (GA): GA tends to thrive in an environment in which there is a very large set of candidate solutions and in which the search space is uneven and has many hills and valleys. Its algorithm creates a population of solutions and applies genetic operators such as mutation and crossover to evolve the solutions in order to find the best one(s).

Heuristics: Heuristic starts from a null solution and adds elements to build a good complete one, or a local search heuristic starting from a

complete solution and iteratively modifies some of its elements in order to achieve a better one.

Metaheuristics: A high-level general technique which guides other heuristics to search for feasible solutions in domains where the task is difficult. These are designed to tackle complex optimization problems where other optimization methods have failed to be either effective or efficient.

Particle Swarm Optimization (PSO): PSO is a population based stochastic optimization technique inspired by social behavior of bird flocking or fish schooling. The system is initialized with a population of random solutions and searches for optima by updating generations.

Simulated Annealing (SA): SA is a probabilistic technique to find the global minimum of a cost function that may possess several local minima. It works by pretending the physical process whereby a solid is slowly cooled so that when eventually its structure is frozen, this occurs at a minimum energy configuration.

Swarm Intelligence (SI): SI is defined as the emergent collective intelligence of groups of simple agents. It argues that human intelligence derives from the interactions of individuals in a social world.

Tabu Search (TS): TS is a metaheuristics that can be superimposed on other procedures to prevent them from becoming trapped at locally optimal solutions.

Chapter 17
Online Clustering and Outlier Detection

Baoying Wang
Waynesburg University, USA

Aijuan Dong
Hood College, USA

ABSTRACT

Clustering and outlier detection are important data mining areas. Online clustering and outlier detection generally work with continuous data streams generated at a rapid rate and have many practical applications, such as network instruction detection and online fraud detection. This chapter first reviews related background of online clustering and outlier detection. Then, an incremental clustering and outlier detection method for market-basket data is proposed and presented in details. This proposed method consists of two phases: weighted affinity measure clustering (WC clustering) and outlier detection. Specifically, given a data set, the WC clustering phase analyzes the data set and groups data items into clusters. Then, outlier detection phase examines each newly arrived transaction against the item clusters formed in WC clustering phase, and determines whether the new transaction is an outlier. Periodically, the newly collected transactions are analyzed using WC clustering to produce an updated set of clusters, against which transactions arrived afterwards are examined. The process is carried out continuously and incrementally. Finally, the future research trends on online data mining are explored at the end of the chapter.

DOI: 10.4018/978-1-4666-2086-5.ch017

1. INTRODUCTION

With the widespread use of network, online clustering and outlier detection as the main data mining tools have drew attention from many practical applications, especially in areas where detecting abnormal behaviors is critical, such as online fraud detection, network instruction detection, and customer behavior analysis. These applications often generate a huge amount of data at a rather rapid rate. Manual screening or checking of this massive data collection is time consuming and impractical. Because of this, online clustering and outlier detection is a promising approach for such applications. Specifically, data mining tools are used to group online activities or transactions into clusters and to detect the most suspicious entries. The clusters are used for marketing and management analysis. The most suspicious ones are investigated further to determine whether they are truly outlier.

Numerous clustering and outlier detection algorithms have been developed (Agyemang, Barker, & Alhajj, 2006; Weston, Hand, Adams, Whitrow, & Juszczak, 2008; Dorronsoro, Ginel, Sgnchez, & Cruz, 1997; Bolton & Hand, 2002; Panigrahi, 2009; He, Deng, & Xu, 2005; Wei, Qian, Zhou, Jin, & Yu, 2003; Aggarwal, Han, Wang, & Yu, 2006; Elahi, Li, Nisar, Lv, & Wang, 2008), but the majority of them are intended for continuous data. With the few approaches for categorical data (He et al., 2005; Wei et al., 2003), time efficiency and detection accuracy need to be further improved. In this chapter, we present an efficient dynamic clustering and outlier detection method for online market basket data. Market basket data are usually organized horizontally in the form of transactions, with each transaction containing a list of items bought (and/or a list of behaviors performed) by a customer during a single checkout at a (online) store. Unlike traditional data, market-basket data are known to be high dimensional, sparse, and to contain attributes of categorical nature.

Our incremental clustering and outlier detection approach consists of two phases: weighted affinity measure clustering (WC clustering) and outlier detection. First, the transaction sets are analyzed so that items are grouped using WC clustering. Then, each newly arrived transaction is examined against the item clusters that are formed in the WC clustering phase. Phase two decides whether the new transaction is an outlier. After a period of time, the newly collected transactions or data streams are analyzed using WC clustering to produce an updated item clusters, against which each newly arrived transaction afterwards is examined. The process continues incrementally. This proposed online clustering and outliner detection method has the following characteristics:

1. It is incremental. Each newly arrived transaction is examined immediately against the results from the past transactions.
2. The results of WC clustering are item clusters rather than transaction clusters so that the newly arrived transaction is examined against the item clusters rather than the whole past transactions. The number of item clusters is usually much smaller than the number of past transactions clusters.
3. The item clusters are updated periodically so that any new items and any new purchase behaviors of customers are taken into consideration to produce more accurate results for the future detection.
4. Finally, WC affinity measure, developed in our previous work, is used to improve the clustering results hence outlier detection results.

The rest of the chapter is organized as follows. Section 2 introduces background information and reviews previous research in related areas. Section 3 presents the proposed online clustering and outlier detection method in details. Section 4 concludes the research and highlights the future research trend.

2. BACKGROUND

Since the proposed method is an online clustering and outlier detection method that uses vertical data structure and weighted confidence affinity measure, we present a brief literature overview on the following aspects in this section: clustering methods, outlier detection, online data mining, affinity measure between clusters, and vertical data structures.

2.1. Clustering Methods

Clustering in data mining is a discovery process that partitions the data set into groups such that the data points in the same group are more similar to each other than the data points in other groups. Data clustering is typically considered as a form of unsupervised learning. Sometime the goal of the clustering is to arrange the clusters into a natural hierarchy. Cluster analysis can also be used as a form of descriptive data model, showing whether or not the data consists of a set of distinct subgroups.

There are many types of clustering techniques, which can be categorized in many ways (Hani & Kamber, 2001; Jain & Dubes, 1998). The categorization shown in Figure 1 is based on the structure of clusters.

As Figure 1 shows, clustering can be subdivided into partitioning clustering and hierarchical clustering. Hierarchical clustering is a nested sequence of partitions, whereas a partitioning clustering is a single partition. Hierarchical clustering methods can be further classified into agglomerative and divisive hierarchical clustering, depending on whether the hierarchical decomposition is accomplished in a bottom-up or a top-down fashion. Partitioning clustering consists of two approaches: distance-based and density-based, according to the similarity measure.

2.1.1 Partitioning Clustering Methods

Partitioning clustering methods generate a partition of the data in an attempt to recover natural groups present in the data. Partitioning clustering can be further subdivided into distance-based partitioning and density-based partitioning.

A distance-based partitioning method breaks a data set into k subsets, or clusters, such that data points in the same cluster are more similar to each other than the data points in other clusters. The most classical similarity-based partitioning methods are k-means (Hartigan & Wong, 1979) and k-medoid, where each cluster has a gravity center. The time complexity of K-means is $O(n)$ since each iteration is $O(n)$ and only a constant number of iterations is computed.

Density-based partitioning clustering has been recognized as a powerful approach for discovering arbitrary-shape clusters. In density-based clustering, clusters are dense areas of points in the data space that are separated by areas of low density

Figure 1. Categorization of clustering

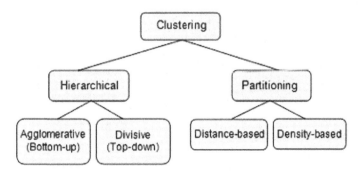

(noise). A cluster is regarded as a connected dense area of data points, which grows in any direction that density leads. Density-based clustering can usually discover clusters with arbitrary shapes without predetermining the number of clusters.

2.1.2 Hierarchical Clustering Methods

Hierarchical algorithms create a hierarchical decomposition of a data set X. The hierarchical decomposition is represented by a dendrogram, a tree that iteratively splits X into smaller subsets until each subset consists of only one object. In such a hierarchy, each level of the tree represents a clustering of X. Figure 2 shows the hierarchical decomposition process and the dendrogram of hierarchical clustering.

Hierarchical clustering methods are subdivided into agglomerative (bottom-up) approaches and divisive (top-down) approaches (Hani & Kamber, 2001). An agglomerative approach begins with each point in a distinct cluster, and successively merges clusters together until a stopping criterion is satisfied. A divisive method begins with all points in a single cluster and performs splitting until a stopping criterion is met. In our research, agglomerative hierarchical clustering is applied.

2.2. Outlier Detection

Detecting outliers is an important data mining task. From the classical view, outliers are defined as "an observation, which deviates so much from other observations as to arouse suspicions that it was generated by a different mechanism" (Hawkins, 1980). Outlier detection is used in many applications, such as credit fraud detection, network intrusion detection, cyber crime detection, customer behavior analysis, and so on. Traditional outlier detection has largely focused on univariate datasets where data follow certain known standard distributions. However, most real data are multivariate, where a data point is an outlier with respect to its neighborhood, but may not be an outlier with respect to the whole dataset (Huang & Cheung, 2002).

Outlier detection methods can be generally categorized as supervised or unsupervised (Yamanishi, Takeuchi, Williams, & Milne, 2004; Yue, Wu, Wang, Li, & Chu, 2007). In supervised methods, models are trained with labeled training data so that new data/observations can be assigned with a corresponding label given the criterion of the model. On the contrary, unsupervised methods do not need prior knowledge of outlier in a historical database, but simply detect those transactions that

Figure 2. Hierarchical decomposition and the dendrogram

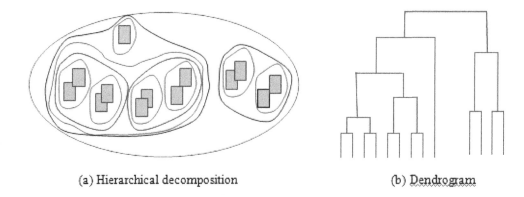

(a) Hierarchical decomposition   (b) Dendrogram

are "unusual." Many unsupervised outlier detecting methods have been developed in multivariate data, such as distance-based approaches (Ghoting, Parthasarathy, & Otey, 2008), density-based approaches (Knorr & Ng, 1998), subspace-based approaches, clustering-based approaches (Lu, Chen, & Kou, 2003), etc. However, most of them are used for continuous numerical data but not suitable for categorical data, which often appear in market-basket data.

Categorical data are those with finite unordered attribute values, such as the sex of a customer. In market-basket data, a transaction can be represented as a vector with Boolean attributes where each attribute corresponds to a single item/behavior (Guha, Rastogii, & Shim, 2000). Boolean attributes are special categorical attributes. There are a few outlier detection methods proposed for categorical data in the literature. ROCK is an agglomerative hierarchical clustering algorithm for categorical data using the links between the data points (Guha et al., 2000). The authors in (Wei et al., 2003) proposed HOT, a hypergraph partitioning algorithm to find the clusters of items/transactions of market basket data. Recently, an adherence clustering method was developed based on the taxonomy (hierarchy) of items (Yun, Chuangi, & Chen, 2006) for transactions with hierarchical items. While useful, the efficiency and accuracy of categorical outlier detection needs to be further improved.

2.3. Online Data Mining

Online data mining is mainly used for data streams. Data stream mining is concerned with extracting knowledge patterns from continuous, rapid data records. The general goal is to predict the property of new data instance based on those of previous data instances in the data stream. Applications produce streams of this type include network monitoring, telecommunication systems, customer click monitoring, stock markets, or any type of sensor system. The stream model differs from the standard relational model in the following ways (Guha, Meyerson, Mishra, Motwani, & O'Callaghan, 2003):

- The elements of a stream arrive more or less continuously.
- The order in which elements of a stream arrive are not under the control of the system.
- Data streams are potentially of unbounded size.

The above characteristics of data streams make the storage, querying and mining of such data sets highly computationally challenged. By nature, a data item in a data stream can be read only once or a small number of times using limited computing and storage capacity. Therefore, it is usually not feasible to simply store the arriving data in a traditional database management system in order to perform operations on that data later on. Rather, data streams are generally processed in an online manner.

Based on the approaches to improving processing efficiency, data stream mining can be divided into data-based and task-based. Data-based techniques refer to summarizing the whole dataset or choosing a subset of the incoming stream to be analyzed. Sampling, load shedding and sketching techniques represent the former one. Synopsis data structures and aggregation represent the later one. On the other hand, in task-based solutions, techniques from computational theory have been adopted to achieve time and space efficient solutions (Babcock, Babu, Datar, Motwani, & Widom, 2002). Specifically, existing techniques are modified and new methods are invented in order to address the computational challenges of data stream processing. Approximation algorithms, sliding window and algorithm output granularity represent this category (Babcock et al.; Safaei & Haghjoo, 2010).

There have been many researches on data stream clustering (Angiulli & Fassetti, 2010; Babcock, Babu, Datar, Motwani, & Widom, 2002;

O'Callaghan, Mishra, Meyerson, Guha, & Motwani, 2003) and data stream outlier detection (Aggarwal, Han, Wang, & Yu, 1997; Guha, Meyerson, Mishra, Motwani, & O'Callaghan, 2003; Elahi, Li, Nisar, Lv, & Wang, 2008; Phua, Gayler, Lee, & Smith-Miles, 2009). Data streams can evolve over time, thus older data may not yield much information about the current state. The online clustering methods include k-means clustering and cover tree based clustering. Clustering happens in an online manner as it takes place in the brain: each data point comes in, is processed, and then goes away. The ideal online k-means clustering is to repeat the following forever: get a new data point x and update the current set of k means. However, the method cannot store all the data it sees, because the process goes on infinitely. The online version is revised as follows (Beringeri & Hüllermeier, 2006):

1. Iterate over the set of data. For each data, find the closest mean and move the closest mean a certain distance towards the data point.
2. Repeat step 1 until termination criterion is reached.

One of the weaknesses of k-means clustering is the predefined value of k. To solve this problem, Beygelzimer, Kakade, and Langford developed a cover tree based online clustering method (Beygelzimer, Kakade, & Langford, 2006). Assume for the moment that the distances among all data points are ≤ 1. A cover tree on data points/transactions $t_1, \ldots, t_n$ is a rooted infinite tree with the following properties.

1. Each node of the tree is associated with one of the data points, t_i.
2. If a node is associated with t_i, then one of its children must also be associated with t_i.
3. All nodes at depth h are at distance at least $\frac{1}{2}h$ from each other.
4. Each node at depth h + 1 is within distance $\frac{1}{2}h$ of its parent (at depth h).

This is described as an infinite tree for simplicity of analysis, but it would not be stored as such. In practice, there is no need to duplicate a node as its own child, and so the tree would take up O(n) space. What makes cover trees especially convenient is that they can be built online, one point at a time. To insert a new point t': find the largest h such that t' is within $\frac{1}{2}h$ of some node s at depth h in the tree; and make t' a child of s. Once the tree is built, it is easy to obtain k-means clustering from it.

2.4. Affinity Measure between Clusters

A good clustering method produces high-quality clusters to ensure that data points within the same group have high similarity while being very dissimilar to points in other groups. Thus similarity/affinity measures are critical for producing high quality clustering results. Some commonly used distance measures include Euclidean distance, Manhattan distance, maximum norm, Mahalanobis distance, and Hamming distance. However, these distance measures do now work well with market-basket data clustering.

As aforementioned, market-basket data is different from traditional data. One such difference results from the categorical nature of its attributes. Therefore, traditional distance measures do not quite work effectively for such data environments. Moreover, items may not be spread in transactions evenly; in other words, some items may have much higher/lower support than the rest. Such data sets are usually described as "support-skewed" data sets.

The all-confidence measure was devised especially for data sets with skewed supports (Omiecinski, 2003; Xiong, Tan, & Kumar, 2003). Give two items I_i and I_j, all-confidence chooses the minimum value between $conf\ (\{I_i \rightarrow I_j\})$ and $conf\ (\{I_j \rightarrow I_j\})$ as the affinity measure between the two items. However, this measure is biased because it depends on the support of the larger item (i.e. has a larger support) without consideration of the other smaller item. For example, suppose $supp(\{I_1\}) = 0.5$, $supp(\{I_2\}) = 0.1$, $supp(\{I_3\}) = 0.4$, $supp(\{I_1, I_2\}) = 0.1$, and $supp(\{I_1, I_3\}) = 0.1$ where $supp(X)$ is the support of itemset X. Then the all-confidence measures for sets $\{I_1, I_2\}$ and $\{I_1, I_3\}$ will have the same value, i.e. $0.1/0.5 = 0.2$, because these two sets share the large item, I_1, regardless of the fact that the support of I_3 is much greater than the support of I_2. But according to the cosine similarity and the Jaccard measures (Han, Karypis, Kumar, & Kamber, 1998), set $\{I_1, I_2\}$ has higher affinity than $\{I_1, I_3\}$. Therefore, it should be obvious that the all-confidence affinity measure can result in many ties among item sets that involve the same large item, which can lead to inaccurate results. This motivated us to devise the weighted confidence affinity measure.

2.5. Vertical Data Structures

Vertical partition of relations has drawn a lot of attention in database, data mining, and data warehouse in the last decade. Compare to traditional horizontal partition that processes and stores data row by row, vertical approach processes and stores data column-wise.

The concept of vertical partitioning for relations and vertical mining has been well studied in data analysis fields. Wong et al. present the Bit Transposed File (BTF) model that takes advantage of encoding attribute values using a small number of bits in order to reduce the storage space in a vertically decomposed context (Wong, Liu, Olken, Rotem & Wong, 1995). The most basic vertical structure is a bitmap (Ding, Ding, & Perrizo, 2002), where every <transaction–item> intersection is represented by a bit in an index bitmap. Consequently, each item is represented by a bit vector. The AND logical operation can then be used to merge items and itemsets into larger itemset patterns. The support of an itemset is calculated by counting the number of 1-bits in the bit vector.

It has been demonstrated in the literature that vertical data approaches are very effective and usu-

ally outperform traditional horizontal approaches (Ding et al., 2002; Zakii & Hsiao, 2002). The advantage is due to the fact that logical AND or intersection operation is very efficient in calculation. For example, in Association Rule Mining (ARM), frequent item sets can be counted and irreverent transactions can be pruned via column-wise intersections. While in traditional horizontal approach, complex internal data structure, such as hash/search trees, are required. Moreover, vertical approaches can be implemented easily in parallel environments to speed up the data mining process further.

3. THE PROPOSED METHOD

In this section, we first introduce affinity function as a similarity measure, then present in details the two phases of the proposed online clustering and outlier detection method, i.e. WC clustering and outlier detection.

3.1. Affinity Function between Items

Distance or similarity measure is critical for clustering and outlier detection accuracy. Our affinity functions is applied to calculate the similarity between items and between clusters in a set of transactions $D = \{T_1, T_2, ..., T_n\}$, where n is the total number of transactions. Each transaction T_i contains a subset of the items from the item space $\{I_1, I_2, ..., I_m\}$, where m is the total number of items.

As we discussed earlier, the all-confidence measure (Omiecinski, 2003; Xiong et al., 2003) is developed to deal with skewed support. However, this measure is biased and often results in many ties among item sets and among clusters that involve the same large item, which can eventually lead to inaccurate results. To eliminate this problem while still tackling skewed-support data sets, we suggest using the weighted summation of the two confidences as the affinity measure between two items (Wang & Rahal, 2007), i.e.

$$A(I_i, I_j) = w_i * conf(\{I_i \rightarrow I_j\})$$
$$+ w_j * conf(\{I_j \rightarrow I_i\}) \quad , \qquad (1)$$

where

$$w_i = \frac{supp(\{I_i\})}{supp(\{I_i\}) + supp(\{I_j\})} \qquad (2)$$

$$w_j = \frac{supp(\{I_j\})}{supp(\{I_i\}) + supp(\{I_j\})} \qquad (3)$$

For the above definition, $A(I_i, I_j)$ is the affinity measure between item I_i and item I_j; $supp(\{I_i\})$ and $supp(\{I_j\})$ define the support of item I_i and item I_j, i.e. the proportion of transactions in the data set which contain the item I_i and item I_j respectively; $conf(\{Ii \rightarrow Ij\})$ defines the confidence of rule $Ii \rightarrow Ij$ and is calculated as $supp(\{I_i, I_j\})/supp(\{I_i\})$. For simplification, we denote $conf(\{I_i \rightarrow I_j\})$ as "the confidence from I_i's side." The equations above show that the confidences from two sides are included in the affinity measure but are weighted based on the support of each side. The higher the item support is, the more the confidence from its side contributes to the affinity measure. Consider two extreme scenarios: (1) when the two item supports are the same, the confidences from both sides are equal and contribute to the affinity equally. In this case, the affinity measure equals to one of the confidences; and (2) when the two item supports are significantly different, the contribution of the confidence from lower support side nears zero. In this case, the affinity measure approximately equals to the confidence from the higher support side.

The all-confidence measure is designed to deal with the second case above (Xiong et al., 2003). It takes the minimum confidence of the confidences from the two sides to filter out the impact of low support items. Our affinity function can still deal

with this scenario well by getting the approximate value of the confidence from the higher support side, which is the minimum confidence between the two. Therefore, our affinity function can achieve the accuracy of the all-confidence measure on skewed-support data sets while not producing misleading ties.

By replacing w_i and w_j in Equation (1) using Equations (2) and (3), replacing confidence variables with their formulas respectively, and simplifying Equation (1), we get the following affinity measure function:

$$A(I_i, I_j) = \frac{2 * supp(\{I_i, I_j\})}{supp(\{I_i\}) + supp(\{I_j\})} \qquad (4)$$

As can be observed from (4), our affinity measure function is calculated directly from supports and there are no comparisons involved. Therefore it is more efficient to compute than the all-confidence measure. The function is also very intuitive: when $supp(\{I_i, I_j\}) = supp(\{I_i\}) = supp(\{Ij\})$, $A(I_i, I_j)$ gets the maximum value of 1. This is the case where two items are always together in any transaction; in other words, if we denote the transaction set that contains I_i as $\{T(I_i)\}$, then $\{T(I_i)\} = \{T(I_j)\}$ in this case. On the other hand, if $supp(\{I_i, I_j\}) << supp(\{I_i\}) + supp(\{I_j\})$, the value of $A(I_i, I_j)$ is close to zero. That is the case where two items share very few transactions compared to their supports, i.e. $|\{T(I_i)\} \cap \{T(I_j)\}| << |\{T(I_i)\}| + |\{T(I_j)\}|$. Therefore, the range of our affinity measure between two items is (0, 1]. The higher the value of $A(I_i, I_j)$ is, the closer the two items I_i and I_j are.

3.2. Affinity Function between Clusters

During the hierarchical clustering process, not only single items are merged but, in most cases, two clusters/itemsets are also merged. We could certainly use the item affinity function defined above to calculate the affinity measure between each pair of items from two clusters and use the average value as the affinity value between the two clusters; however, this approach is time-consuming and unwarranted. Instead, we define an affinity function based on the supports of the clusters.

The support of a cluster is different from the support of an itemset in association rule mining. Instead of counting the number of transactions which contain every item of the itemset, we count the number of transactions which contain ANY item in the cluster. In another word, we use the union of the transaction set that contains each item in the cluster rather than the intersection of them. For example, if a cluster C consists of items O, P, and Q, then, the transaction set that we are after would be $\{T(O)\} \cup \{T(P)\} \cup \{T(Q)\}$ rather than $\{T(O)\} \cap \{T(P)\} \cap \{T(Q)\}$. After defining the supports of clusters, we can now define our affinity function between clusters.

Given two clusters C_i and C_j and assuming that $supp(C_i)$, $supp(C_j)$ and $supp(C_i, C_j)$ are calculated according to the above, then, the affinity function between the two clusters can be derived as follows:

$$A(C_i, C_j) = \frac{2 * supp(C_i, C_j)}{supp(C_i) + supp(C_j)} \qquad (5)$$

Comparing Equations (4) and (5), we can see that the affinity measure function between items has the same form as that between clusters. The only difference is the representation of supports. In fact, an item can be treated as the smallest cluster that contains a single item. Therefore, we can use Equation (5) to calculate affinity measures between two items, between two clusters, and even between a cluster and an item. Note that Equation (5) has the same characteristics as Equation (4) and its range of values is also [0, 1].

3.3. Overview of the Method

This section presents our incremental clustering and outlier detection method on market-basket data using vertical data structures. We adopt a two-phrase approach: WC clustering phase and outlier detection phase. First, the current transaction set is analyzed using the WC clustering method, which yields item clusters. This phase is called WC clustering. Then each newly arrived transaction is classified against the item clusters to see if the transaction is an outlier. This is the outlier detection phase. After a certain period of time, the process will go back to the WC clustering phase on newly collected transactions and then the second phase on the transactions that arrive afterwards. Thus, the two-phase process is carried on incrementally. The approach is illustrated on a sample transaction set shown in Figure 3. There are twelve transactions and seven items.

Figure 3. An example of market basket data

T_{ID}	Itemsets
T_1	I_5, I_7
T_2	I_1, I_2, I_4, I_5
T_3	I_2, I_4, I_5
T_4	I_4, I_5, I_6
T_5	I_3, I_7
T_6	I_2, I_6
T_7	I_2, I_3, I_6
T_8	I_2, I_5, I_6
T_9	I_1, I_5
T_{10}	I_2, I_3, I_7
T_{11}	I_2, I_4
T_{12}	I_4, I_6

3.4. WC Clustering

The transaction set is first transformed into an array of vertical bit vectors. Each item I_k is associated with a vector b_k. The ith bit of b_k is 1 if transaction T_i contains item I_k; it is 0 otherwise. Figure 4 shows the seven vertical bit vectors for the seven items from the sample data in Figure 3. Each vector has a size of 12. For instance, b_1 has two 1-bits in the 2nd and 9th positions because I_1 occurs in transactions T_2 and T_9.

The *WC Clustering* process starts with single-item clusters (i.e. each item is treated as a cluster initially.) The process then calculates the affinity between each pair of clusters using Equation (2) and finds the closest pair which has the highest affinity value. Henceforth, the closest cluster pairs are merged by ORing (getting the union of) the two corresponding bit vectors. The process continues calculating the affinity and merging the closest pair at next level until there is a sudden drop on the highest affinity value.

We observed that the highest affinity values for items within the same cluster stay fairly stable as the cluster grows. Therefore, this stopping rule is heuristic. On the sample data set, we stopped merging when the highest affinity value drops

from 0.627 between I_6 and C_3 at the level where I_6 is merged to the cluster $C_3 = \{I_2, I_4, I_5\}$ to 0.3 between C_4 and C_1 (See Figure 5). Thus, WC clustering ends up with item clusters: $\{I_1\}$, $\{I_2, I_4, I_5, I_6\}$, and $\{I_3, I_7\}$.

Note that the cluster $\{I1\}$ is a one item cluster. Therefore, it is not a cluster. Instead, I1 is outlier among the items. But it is not a fraud according to the definition. It is simply a unique item. As we will discuss later, it is very useful for detecting fraud transactions.

3.5. Outlier Detection

Outlier detection applies to each newly arrived transaction, T'. We treat T' as an item cluster. For example, if T' = $\{I_3, I_4, I_6\}$, then we treat it as a cluster which contains I_3, I_4 and I_6. First, affinity between T' and each of the clusters formed at WC clustering phase is calculated using Equation (6) which is derived from Equation (5), where Count(T') is the number of items in T' and Count(T', C_i) is the number of common items between T' and C_i. The affinity value is from 0-1. For example, T' = $\{I_3, I_4, I_6\}$ and $C_4 = \{I_2, I_4, I_5, I_6\}$, then A(T', C_4) = (2*2)/(3 + 4) = 0.57.

Figure 4. Vertical data representation

b_1	b_2	b_3	b_4	b_5	b_6	b_7
0	0	0	0	1	0	1
1	1	0	1	1	0	0
0	1	0	1	1	0	0
0	0	0	1	1	1	0
0	0	1	0	0	0	1
0	1	0	0	0	1	0
0	1	1	0	0	1	0
0	1	0	0	1	1	0
1	0	0	0	1	0	0
0	1	1	0	0	0	1
0	1	0	1	0	0	0
0	0	0	1	0	1	0

Figure 5. Clustering results

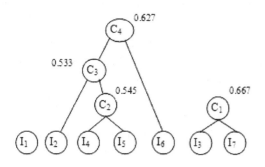

Figure 6. Newly arrived transactions

T'$_{ID}$	Itemsets
T'_1	I_2, I_3, I_7
T'_2	I_1, I_5
T'_3	I_2, I_4
T'_4	I_3, I_4, I_5, I_8
T'_5	I_3, I_4
T'_6	I_2, I_4, I_5
T'_7	I_3, I_7
T'_8	I_2, I_6

$$A(T', C_j) = \frac{2 * Count(T', Cj)}{Count(T') + Count(Cj)} \qquad (6)$$

Then, the highest affinity among the affinities between T' and all item clusters, A_{max}, is selected. If $A_{max} < \alpha$, where α is predefined threshold, T' will be identified as an outlier/outlier. For example, the transactions in Figure 6 arrive one by one after the sample transaction set in Figure 3 and assume $\alpha = 0.52$.

When T'_1 arrives, $A_{max} = (T'_1, C_1) = (2*2)/(3 + 2) = 0.8 > \alpha$. Therefore, T'_1 is not an outlier. Similarly, we calculate A_{max} for the transactions that follow and decide if any of them is an outlier or not. The results of such A_{max}-based approach are shown in Figure 7. It can be seen that one outlier, T_5', is detected in this approach.

To make the algorithm stricter, another criterion could be added: if T' contains any item outlier, such as I_1 in Figure 5, T' will be identified as an outlier no matter how large A_{max} is. In this case, there is no need to calculate an affinity between T' and any cluster. According to this stricter approach, a transaction that contains an item outlier should be immediately marked as an outlier. A_{max} is only calculated for transactions which do not have item outliers. The results of such an approach are shown in Figure 8. It can be seen that two outliers are detected in this approach. T_2' is detected as an outlier because T_2' contains an item outlier, I_1.

Figure 7. Outlier Detection Based on A$_{max}$

T'$_{ID}$	A$_{max}$	< α?	Outlier?
T'_1	0.8	N	No
T'_2	0.66	N	No
T'_3	0.66	N	No
T'_4	0.625	N	No
T'_5	0.5	Y	Yes
T'_6	0.71	N	No
T'_7	1.0	N	No
T'_8	0.66	N	No

Figure 8. A more strict approach

T'$_{ID}$	Has item outlier?	A$_{max}$	< α?	Outlier?
T'_1	N	0.8	N	No
T'_2	Y	n/a	n/a	Yes
T'_3	N	0.66	N	No
T'_4	N	0.625	N	No
T'_5	N	0.5	Y	Yes
T'_6	N	0.71	N	No
T'_7	N	1.0	N	No
T'_8	N	0.66	N	No

4. FUTURE RESEARCH DIRECTIONS

With widespread use of the Web, data stream mining has become an attractive area for researchers. The significance of this type of research lies in its many important practical applications in diverse areas, including computer network traffic, E-commerce, phone conversation, web searches, and sensor data. A data stream system constantly produces huge amount of data, which challenges researchers in many ways, including execution efficiency, storage capacity, and predication accuracy.

Data streams or online data belong to time series and sequence-based data. Mining such data involves the mining of either a sequence of data that can be referenced by time or a sequence of data which comes in a sequence. Data stream mining usually focuses on identifying data movements or data patterns in the data streams. There are many techniques that can be used on data stream mining, such as similarity mining, sequential pattern recognition, and periodicity study (Hsu, 2003).

Similarity mining is to search a pattern sequence which is close or similar to a given pattern, and this form of analysis can be broken down into two subtypes: whole sequence mining and subsequence mining. Whole sequence mining attempts to find all sequences which are similar to each other, while subsequence mining only focuses on those patterns which are similar to a specified, given sequence.

Sequential pattern recognition focuses on the identification of sequences which occur frequently in a time series or sequence of data. This is particularly useful in the analysis of customers, where certain purchase patterns could be recognized, and in the analysis of stock markets.

Periodicity study analyzes the data in order to identify patterns which repeat or recur in a time series. This type of data stream study can be further divided into full periodic, partial periodic or cyclic periodic. In general, full periodic is concerned with the situation where all of the data points in time are used to analyze the pattern of the data stream. On the other hand, partial periodicity only analyzes certain points in time to analyze the data stream pattern. Finally, cyclical periodicity relates to sets of events which occur periodically (Hsu, 2003).

There are a number of issues and challenges in data stream mining area (Khalilian & Mustapha, 2010). The following is a list of these issues:

- How to detect a change in the data streams? How to detect the changes as soon as it occurs and how to distinguish between real drift and noise?
- The algorithms required expert assistant in the form of the number of partitions expected or the expected density of clusters.
- Uncertain data: in most applications we don't have sufficient data for statistical operations so new methods are needed to manage uncertain data stream in accurate and fast fashion.
- Cluster Validity: Recent developments in data stream clustering have heightened the need for determining suitable criteria to validate results. Most outcomes of methods are depended to specific application. However, employing suitable criteria in results evaluation is one of the most important challenges in this arena.
- High dimensional data stream: There are high dimensional data sets (e.g. image processing, personal similarity, customer preferences clustering, network intrusion detection, wireless sensors network and generally time series data) which should be managed through the processing of data stream. In huge databases, data complexity can be increased by number of dimensions (Khalilian & Mustapha, 2010).
- The relationship between the proposed techniques and the needs of the real world applications is another important issue. Some of the proposed techniques try to get

to better computational complexity with some margin error without taking care to the real needs of the applications that will use the proposed approach (Gaber, Zaslavsky, & Krishnaswamy, 2005).

- The data pre-processing in the stream mining process should also be taken into consideration. That is how to design a very light-weight pre-processing techniques that can guarantee the quality of the mining results.

- The technological issue of mining data streams is also an important one. How to represent the data in such an environment in a compressed way? And which platforms are best to suit such special real-time applications?

- The formalization of real-time accuracy evaluation is another issue. That is to provide the user by a feedback by the current achieved accuracy with relation to the available resources.

- Interactive mining environment to satisfy user requirements: mining data streams is a highly application oriented field. The user requirements are considered a vital research problem to be addressed (Gaber et al., 2005).

Online clustering and fraud detection is very important with the advent of internet and online activities. Online clustering and fraud detection techniques must evolve continuously to deter criminals by adapting to their strategies.

5. CONCLUSION

The growth of data stream phenomenon and the tremendous increase of internet daily usage motivate the need for data stream mining. Although there have been a lot of researches in this area,

the research is still in its early stages. This chapter reviewed many aspects of online data clustering and outlier detection. Mainly, it proposed an incremental clustering and outlier detection method on online data streams. In the future, we will apply our approach on large scale data sets, evaluate and improve the proposed approach based on the issues mentioned above and raised by real applications. Where there are challenges, there are a great interest of researches. We are sure online data mining will continue to be an attractive research area.

REFERENCES

Aggarwal, C., Han, J., Wang, J., & Yu, P. (2005). On high dimensional projected clustering of data streams. *Data Mining and Knowledge Discovery*, *10*(3), 251–273. doi:10.1007/s10618-005-0645-7

Agyemang, M., Barker, K., & Alhajj, R. (2006). A comprehensive survey of numeric and symbolic outlier mining techniques. *Intelligent Data Analysis*, *10*(6), 521–538.

Angiulli, F., & Fassetti, F. (2010). Distance-based outlier queries in data streams: the novel task and algorithms. *Data Mining and Knowledge Discovery*, *20*(2), 290–324. doi:10.1007/s10618-009-0159-9

Babcock, B., Babu, S., Datar, M., Motwani, R., & Widom, J. (2002). Models and issues in data stream systems. In *PODS '02: Proceedings of the twenty-first ACM SIGMOD-SIGACT-SIGART Symposium on Principles of Database Systems*, (pp. 1-16). New York, NY: ACM.

Beringer, J., & Hüllermeier, E. (2006). Online clustering of parallel data streams. *Data & Knowledge Engineering*, *58*(2), 180–204. doi:10.1016/j.datak.2005.05.009

Beygelzimer, A., Kakade, S., & Langford, J. (2006). Cover trees for nearest neighbor. In *ICML '06: Proceedings of the 23rd International Conference on Machine Learning*, (pp. 97-104). New York, NY: ACM Press.

Bolton, R. J., & Hand, D. J. (2002). Unsupervised profiling methods for fraud detection. *Statistical Science*, *17*(3), 235–255.

Ding, Q., Ding, Q., & Perrizo, W. (2002). Association rule mining on remotely sensed images using p-trees. *Proceedings, PAKDD2002*, 232–238.

Dorronsoro, R., Ginel, F., Sgnchez, C., & Cruz, C. S. (1997). Neural fraud detection in credit card operations. *IEEE Transactions on Neural Networks*, *8*(4), 827–834. doi:10.1109/72.595879

Elahi, M., Li, K., Nisar, W., Lv, X., & Wang, H. (2008). Efficient clustering-based outlier detection algorithm for dynamic data stream. In *Proceedings of the 2008 Fifth International Conference on Fuzzy Systems and Knowledge Discovery - Volume 05, FSKD*, (pp. 298-304). Washington, DC: IEEE Computer Society.

Gaber, M., Zaslavsky, A., & Krishnaswamy, S. (2005). Mining data streams: A review. *SIGMOD Review*, *34*(2), 18–26. doi:10.1145/1083784.1083789

Ghoting, A., Parthasarathy, S., & Otey, M. (2008). Fast mining of distance-based outliers in high-dimensional datasets. *Data Mining and Knowledge Discovery*, *16*(3), 349–364. doi:10.1007/s10618-008-0093-2

Guha, S., Meyerson, A., Mishra, N., Motwani, R., & O'Callaghan, L. (2003). Clustering data streams: Theory and practice. *IEEE Transactions on Knowledge and Data Engineering*, *15*(3), 515–528. doi:10.1109/TKDE.2003.1198387

Guha, S., Rastogi, R., & Shim, K. (2000). Rock: A robust clustering algorithm for categorical attributes. *Information Systems*, *25*(5), 345–366. doi:10.1016/S0306-4379(00)00022-3

Han, H., Karypis, G., Kumar, V., & Mobasher, B. (1998). Hypergraph based clustering in high dimensional data sets: A summary of results. *A Quarterly Bulletin of the Computer Society of the IEEE Technical Committee on Data Engineering*, *21*(1).

Han, J., & Kamber, M. (2001). *Data mining, concepts and techniques*. Morgan Kaufmann.

Hartigan, J. A., & Wong, M. A. (1979). Algorithm as 136: A k-means clustering algorithm. *Journal of the Royal Statistical Society. Series C, Applied Statistics*, *28*(1), 100–108. doi:10.2307/2346830

Hawkins, D. (1980). *Identifications of outliers*. London, UK: Chapman and Hall.

He, Z., Deng, S., & Xu, X. (2005). An optimization model for outlier detection in categorical data. *ICIC 2005* (pp. 400-409).

Hsu, J. (2003). Critical and future trends in data mining: a review of key data mining technologies/applications. In *Data mining: Opportunities and challenges* (pp. 437–452). Hershey, PA: IGI Global. doi:10.4018/978-1-59140-051-6.ch020

Hung, E., & Cheung, D. (2002). Parallel mining of outliers in large database. *Journal of Distributed and Parallel Databases*, *12*(1), 5–26. doi:10.1023/A:1015608814486

Jain, A. K., & Dubes, R. C. (1988). *Algorithms for clustering data*. Upper Saddle River, NJ: Prentice-Hall, Inc.

Khalilian, M., & Mustapha, N. (2010). Data stream clustering: Challenges and issues. *Proceedings of the International MultiConference of Engineers and Computer Scientists,* Vol. I, IMECS 2010, March 17-19, Hong Kong.

Knorr, E. M., & Ng, R. T. (1999). Finding intensional knowledge of distance-based outliers. In *VLDB '99: Proceedings of the 25th International Conference on Very Large Data Bases*, (pp. 211-222). San Francisco, CA: Morgan Kaufmann Publishers Inc.

Lu, C. T., Chen, D., & Kou, Y. (2003). Detecting spatial outliers with multiple attributes. In *ICTAI '03: Proceedings of the 15th IEEE International Conference on Tools with Artificial Intelligence*, (pp. 122-127). Washington, DC: IEEE Computer Society.

O'Callaghan, L., Mishra, N., Meyerson, A., Guha, S., & Motwani, R. (2001). Streaming-data algorithms for high-quality clustering. In *Proceedings of IEEE International Conference on Data Engineering*.

Omiecinski, E. R. (2003). Alternative interest measures for mining associations in databases. *IEEE Transactions on Knowledge and Data Engineering*, *15*(1), 57–69. doi:10.1109/TKDE.2003.1161582

Panigrahi, S. (2009). Credit card fraud detection: A fusion approach using Dempster–Shafer theory and Bayesian learning. *Information Fusion*, *10*(4), 354–363. doi:10.1016/j.inffus.2008.04.001

Phua, C., Gayler, R., Lee, V., & Smith-Miles, K. (2009). On the communal analysis suspicion scoring for identity crime in streaming credit applications. *European Journal of Operational Research*, *195*, 595–612. doi:10.1016/j.ejor.2008.02.015

Safaei, A., & Haghjoo, M. (2010). Parallel processing of continuous queries over data streams. *Distributed and Parallel Databases*, *28*(2-3). doi:10.1007/s10619-010-7066-3

Wang, B., & Rahal, I. (2007) WC-clustering: Hierarchical clustering using the weighted confidence affinity measure. In *ICDM2007: Proceedings of the High Performance Data Mining Workshop IEEE International Conference on Data Mining*, Omaha, NE, October, (pp. 355-360).

Wei, L., Qian, W., Zhou, A., Jin, W., & Yu, J. X. (2003). HOT: Hypergraph-based outlier test for categorical data. *PAKDD 2003 . LNAI*, *2637*, 399–410.

Weston, D., Hand, D., Adams, N., Whitrow, C., & Juszczak, P. (2008). Plastic card fraud detection using peer group analysis. *Advances in Data Analysis and Classification*, *2*(1), 45–62. doi:10.1007/s11634-008-0021-8

Wong, H., Liu, H., Olken, F., Rotem, D., & Wong, L. (1995). Bit transposed files. In A Pirotte & Y. Vassiliou (Eds.), *Proceedings of the 11th Very Large Databases Conference (VLDB)*, (pp. 448-457). Morgan Kaufmann.

Xiong, H., Tan, P., & Kumar, V. (2003). Mining strong affinity association patterns in data sets with skewed support distribution. *Third IEEE International Conference on Data Mining*, Melbourne, Florida, (pp. 19–22).

Yamanishi, K., Takeuchi, J.-I., Williams, G., & Milne, P. (2004). On-line unsupervised outlier detection using finite mixtures with discounting learning algorithms. *Data Mining and Knowledge Discovery*, *8*(3), 275–300. doi:10.1023/B:DAMI.0000023676.72185.7c

Yue, D., Wu, X., Wang, Y., Li, Y., & Chu, C. (2007). A review of data mining-based financial outlier detection research. In *WiCom 2007: Proceedings of International Conference on Wireless Communications, Networking and Mobile Computing*, (pp. 5519 – 5522).

Yun, C., Chuang, K., & Chen, M. (2006). Adherence clustering: An efficient method for mining market-basket clusters. *Information Systems*, *31*(3), 170–186. doi:10.1016/j.is.2004.11.008

Zaki, M. J., & Hsiao, C. (2002). Charm: An efficient algorithm for closed itemset mining. In *SIAM International Conference on Data Mining*, (pp. 457-473).

ADDITIONAL READING

Abe, N., Zadrozny, B., & Langford, J. (2006). Outlier detection by active learning. In *KDD '06: Proceedings of the 12th ACM SIGKDD International Conference on Knowledge Discovery and Data Mining*, (pp. 504-509). New York, NY: ACM.

Aggarwal, C. C., & Yu, P. S. (2001). *Outlier detection for high dimensional data*. In SIGMOD Conference.

Andritsos, P., Tsaparas, P., Miller, R. J., & Sevcik, K. C. (2004). *Limbo: Scalable clustering of categorical data* (pp. 531-532).

Banerjee, S., Ramanathan, K., & Gupta, A. (2007). Clustering short texts using wikipedia. In *SIGIR '07: Proceedings of the 30th Annual International ACM SIGIR Conference on Research and Development in Information Retrieval*, (pp. 787-788). New York, NY: ACM.

Bansal, N., Blum, A., & Chawla, S. (2004). Correlation clustering. *Machine Learning, 56*(1), 89–113. doi:10.1023/B:MACH.0000033116.57574.95

Chandola, V., Banerjee, A., & Kumar, V. (2009). Anomaly detection: A survey. *ACM Computing Surveys, 41*(3), 1–58. doi:10.1145/1541880.1541882

Cilibrasi, R., & Vitanyi, P. M. B. (2005). Clustering by compression. *IEEE Transactions on Information Theory, 51*(4), 1523–1545. doi:10.1109/TIT.2005.844059

Davy, M., Desobry, F., Gretton, A., & Doncarli, C. (2006). An online support vector machine for abnormal events detection. *Signal Processing, 86*(8), 2009–2025. doi:10.1016/j.sigpro.2005.09.027

Dotan-Cohen, D., Melkman, A. A., & Kasif, S. (2007). Hierarchical tree snipping: clustering guided by prior knowledge. *Bioinformatics (Oxford, England), 23*(24), 3335–3342. doi:10.1093/bioinformatics/btm526

Du, K.-L. (2010). Clustering: A neural network approach. *Neural Networks, 23*(1), 89–107. doi:10.1016/j.neunet.2009.08.007

Duan, L., Xu, L., Liu, Y., & Lee, J. (2009). Cluster-based outlier detection. *Annals of Operations Research, 168*(1), 151–168. doi:10.1007/s10479-008-0371-9

Gyarmati, L., & Trinh, T. (2009). Characterizing user groups in online social networks . In Oliver, M., & Sallent, S. (Eds.), *The Internet of the Future* (*Vol. 5733*, pp. 59–68). Berlin, Germany: Springer. doi:10.1007/978-3-642-03700-9_7

Haddadi, H. (2010). Fighting online click-fraud using bluff ads. *ACM SIGCOMM Computer Communication Review, 40*(2), 21–25. doi:10.1145/1764873.1764877

Haveliwala, T. H., Gionis, A., & Indyk, P. (2000). Scalable techniques for clustering the web . In *WebDB* (pp. 129–134). Informal Proceedings.

Hodge, V., & Austin, J. (2004). A survey of outlier detection methodologies. *Artificial Intelligence Review, 22*(2), 85–126. doi:10.1023/B:AIRE.0000045502.10941.a9

Hu, J. (2008). Cancer outlier detection based on likelihood ratio test. *Bioinformatics (Oxford, England), 24*(19), 2193–2199. doi:10.1093/bioinformatics/btn372

Kerr, G., Ruskin, H. J., Crane, M., & Doolan, P. (2008). Techniques for clustering gene expression data. *Computers in Biology and Medicine, 38*(3), 283–293. doi:10.1016/j.compbiomed.2007.11.001

Kim, J., & Kim, H. (2008). Clustering of change patterns using Fourier coefficients. *Bioinformatics (Oxford, England), 24*(2), 184–191. doi:10.1093/bioinformatics/btm568

Latecki, L. J., Lazarevic, A., & Pokrajac, D. (2007). Outlier detection with kernel density functions. In *MLDM '07: Proceedings of the 5th International Conference on Machine Learning and Data Mining in Pattern Recognition*, (pp. 61-75). Berlin, Germany: Springer-Verlag.

Long, B., Zhang, Z. M., & Yu, P. S. (2007). A probabilistic framework for relational clustering. In *KDD '07: Proceedings of the 13th ACM SIGKDD International Conference on Knowledge Discovery and Data Mining*, (pp. 470-479). New York, NY: ACM.

McCallum, A., Nigam, K., & Ungar, L. H. (2000). Efficient clustering of high-dimensional data sets with application to reference matching. In *KDD '00: Proceedings of the Sixth ACM SIGKDD International Conference on Knowledge Discovery and Data Mining*, (pp. 169-178). New York, NY: ACM.

McCallum, A., Nigam, K., & Ungar, L. H. (2000). Efficient clustering of high-dimensional data sets with application to reference matching. In *KDD '00: Proceedings of the Sixth ACM SIGKDD International Conference on Knowledge Discovery and Data Mining*, (pp. 169-178). New York, NY: ACM.

Miller, R. C., & Myers, B. A. (2001). Outlier finding: Focusing user attention on possible errors. In *UIST '01: Proceedings of the 14th Annual ACM Symposium on User Interface Software and Technology*, (pp. 81-90). New York, NY: ACM.

Nock, R., & Nielsen, F. (2006). On weighting clustering. *IEEE Transactions on Pattern Analysis and Machine Intelligence, 28*(8), 1223–1235. doi:10.1109/TPAMI.2006.168

Ravi, V., Srinivas, E. R., & Kasabov, N. K. (2007). *On-line evolving fuzzy clustering. Conference on Computational Intelligence and Multimedia Applications, 2007*, Vol. 1, (pp. 347-351).

Xue, Z., Liu, S., & Qi, X. (2010). Semi-supervised outlier detection based on fuzzy rough c-means clustering. *Mathematics and Computers in Simulation, 80*(9). doi:10.1016/j.matcom.2010.02.007

Yang, J., Zhong, N., Yao, Y., & Wang, J. (2008). Local peculiarity factor and its application in outlier detection. In *KDD '08: Proceeding of the 14th ACM SIGKDD International Conference on Knowledge Discovery and Data Mining*, (pp. 776-784). New York, NY: ACM.

KEY TERMS AND DEFINITIONS

Affinity Measure: A measure to find the similarity between items in market basket data.

Clustering: A process of assigning a set of data points into groups (called clusters) so that data in the same cluster are similar based on a predefined similarity measure.

Data Streams: A sequence of digitally encoded coherent signals (packets of data or data packets) used to transmit or receive information that is in transmission.

Hierarchical Clustering: Hierarchical clustering methods create a hierarchical decomposition of a data set X. The hierarchical decomposition is represented by a dendrogram, a tree that iteratively splits X into smaller subsets until each subset consists of only one object.

Outlier Detection: A process of detecting patterns in a given data set that do not conform to an established normal behavior.

Outlier: A data instance that appears to deviate markedly from other data instances of the sample in which it occurs.

Partitioning Clustering: A process of generating a partition of the data in an attempt to recover natural groups present in the data.

Vertical Data Structures: Vertical partition of relations. Compare to traditional horizontal partition that processes and stores data row by row, vertical approach processes and stores data column-wise.

Chapter 18

Optimal Ordering of Activities of New Product Development Projects with Time and Cost Considerations

Hisham M. Abdelsalam
Cairo University, Egypt

Amany Magdy
Cairo University, Egypt

ABSTRACT

This chapter presents a Discrete Multi-objective Particle Swarm Optimization (MOPSO) algorithm that determines the optimal order of activities execution within a design project that minimizes project total iterative time and cost. Numerical Design Structure Matrix (DSM) was used to model project activities' execution order along with their interactions providing a base for calculating the objective functions. Algorithm performance was tested on a hypothetical project data and results showed its ability to reach Pareto fronts on different sets of objective functions.

INTRODUCTION

The need to reconsider traditional methods of product development and introduction has been recognized since early 1990s (Fiksel, 1991). Because products that meet the needs of customers faster than competitors grow at a rapid pace, both in

DOI: 10.4018/978-1-4666-2086-5.ch018

terms of market share and profitability, a competitive product needs to be introduced quickly without compromising product performance (Chakravarty, 2001; Kotler, 1991). The significance of time-to-market was further demonstrated by (Stalk, 1988; Blackburn, 1991; House and Price, 1991) leading to a conclusion that reduction in product development cycle time has become an essential goal (Fiksel, 1991).

In a pamphlet issued by the National Research Council (1991), four requirements for using product design as a source of competitive advantage were cited including establishing a corporate Product Realization Process (PRP) supported by top management and developing and/or adopting integrating advanced design practices into the PRP. Subsequently, planning for product evolution beyond the current design and planning concurrently for design and manufacturing were defined as means for effective PRP practice. In this spirit, the term 'Integrated Product Development' (IPD) was coined to describe a process that has been adopted by most progressive manufacturing firms, even though firms may have different names for this process (Peet and Hladik, 1989).

The motivation for adopting IPD can be further understood when the economics of product development are considered; where between 60 and 80 percent of the overall product costs are committed between the concept and preliminary design phases of the program (Armstrong, 2001). And, since only a small cumulative expenditure of funding is committed during early phases in the classical serial approach, the cost of design change increases exponentially as the development process advances as shown in Figure 1. For example, in the automotive and electronics industry, it has been shown that up to 80% of product life-cycle costs are committed during the concept and preliminary design stages, and that the cost of design changes steeply increases as a product proceeds into full-scale development and prototyping (Peet and Hladik, 1989; Port, 1990; National Research Council, 1991). Another study included in (Nevins and Whitney, 1989) showed that about 70% of the life cycle cost of a product is determined at the conceptual design stage. Furthermore, O'Grady, Ramers, and Bowen (1988) showed that design of products determines their quality and 70% to 80% of the final production cost.

Thus, the motivation for current research can be summarized as follows: (1) there is a need to reduce both product time-to-market and product development cost; (2) dealing with complex products adds more difficulty to the management of the design process within product development projects; (3) as a result, a more effective methodology – that is IPD - has to be implemented; (4) since about 80% of cost is committed at early

Figure 1. Cost impact (Source: Armstrong, 2001)

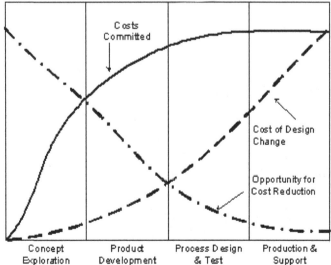

development phases, the current research focuses on improving the product design process. Figure 2 is a simple mind map of research motivation.

All dimensions of manufacturing (e.g. products, processes, markets) are becoming more complex and diverse. And, moreover, complex new products are increasingly becoming based on massive information-dominated design and manufacturing methods which require more effective and efficient methods to deal with the increasing levels of complexity. Providing tools to facilitate and manage the complexity of this information and computation intensive activities plays an important role in supporting and even enabling the complex practice of manufacturing.

The difficulties in designing complex engineering products do not only arise from their technical complexity but also from the managerial complexity necessary to coordinate interactions among various design activities, teams, and disciplines involved in the design process (Yassine, Chelst, and Falkenburg, 1999). Typically, in designing an engineering product, this product will be decomposed into possibly hundreds of activities (representing design of different components) and thousands of variable interchanges among them. The order of these activities' execution strongly affects the time and the cost needed to realize the whole project. Moreover, complexity of such projects increases given their iterative nature; some activities may need to be redone until a satisfactory solution is reached. So, a tool is needed to model these activities and their interactions, from one side, and to help re-sequence activities for efficient execution, from the other side.

Improving system performance can be achieved through efficient re-reengineering of its structure and the Design Structure Matrix (DSM) provides an effective tool for system structure understanding. The main objective of the presented research is to develop an optimization algorithm that helps guide the project manager efforts for managing the design process in complex integrated product development projects. Presented research aims toward finding an optimal activity sequence of the DSM representing a design project in terms of time and cost.

Following the introduction section, the rest of this chapter is organized as follows. Section 2 provides background on the Design Structure Matrix (DSM) and discrete MOPSO that will be used in this research. Details of the solution algorithm are presented in Section 3, followed by experimental results in Section 4. And, finally, concluding remarks are provided in Section 5.

Figure 2. Research motivation mind map

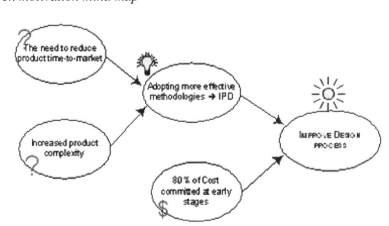

BACKGROUND

Design Structure Matrix

A product development project (PDP) fundamentally differs from a construction (or a manufacturing) project in two major aspects: (1) while the later is activity-based (i.e. an activity it to be carried out only when its predecessors are physically done), the first is information-based (activities execution and results are based mainly on information exchanged with other coupled activities); and (2) A typical PDP is characterized by its highly coupled, interdependent activities, which must converge iteratively to an acceptable design solution (Browning, 2001-a; Browning, 2001-b). There always exists a high possibility of many activities that need to be repeated before the desired specifications are met. The most common causes for such repetition (known as feedback loops in DSM terminology) are due to activities that begin work without the necessary information; the arrival of new information; change of information that leads to rework; or re-evaluated assumptions in previous activities (Browning and Eppinger, 2002; Browning, 1998; Denker, Steward, and Browning, 1999).

A project typically consists of a number of interrelated activities. For more than fifty years, a number of techniques, such as Program Evaluation and Review Technique (PERT) and Critical Path Method (CPM), have been used to handle complex projects. Unfortunately, these methods succeed only if activities are sequential and/or parallel, but fail significantly if there are iterative sub-cycles since they do not tolerate feedback relationships.

Although the idea of representing the system architectural components and relationships in the form of a matrix is not new, the term "Design Structure Matrix" (DSM) was coined by Steward (1981-a, 191-b) to denote a generic matrix-based model for project information flow analysis. Since then, the DSM is becoming a popular representation and analysis tool for system modeling, especially for purpose of decomposition and integration (Browning, 2001-b). Since its original introduction by Steward in the 1980's, the DSM has been extended to cover many application areas. Browning (2001-b) presented four main DSM applications. These applications are summarized in Table 1. This research interest is activity-based DSM.

Table 1. Summary of DSM characteristics

DSM		Representation	Application	Integration Analysis via
Category	**Type**			
Static	Component-Based or Architecture	Components in a product architecture and their relationships	System architecting, engineering, design, etc.	Clustering
	Team-Based or Organization	Individuals, groups, or teams in an organization and their relationships	Organization design, interface management, application or appropriate integration mechanisms	
Time-Based	Activity-Based or Schedule	Activities in a process and their inputs and outputs	Project scheduling, activity sequencing, cycle time reduction, risk reduction, etc.	Sequencing, Partitioning, and Tearing
	Parameter-Based	Parameters to determine a design and their relationships	Low-level process sequencing and integration	

Source: (Browning, 2001-b)

The basic DSM – Figure 3 – is a square binary matrix. As shown, activity names are placed on the left-hand side of the matrix as row headings and across the top row as column headings in the same order (order of their execution); a main DSM assumption is that activities are undertaken in the order listed from top to bottom. An off-diagonal mark (**x**) represents a coupling – an information flow or a dependency – between two activities. If an activity receives information from activity, then the matrix element (row column) contains an off diagonal mark (**x**), otherwise, the cell is empty.

Marks below the diagonal (sub-diagonal marks) are indicative of feed-forward couplings, while those above the diagonal (super-diagonal) represent feedback couplings. As they imply iterations, the latter type of couplings should be eliminated if possible or reduced to the maximum extent. If certain feedback couplings cannot be eliminated, the activities are grouped into iterative sub-cycles. For example, in Figure 2, activities (1, 2, and 3) and activities (6, 7, 8, 9, and 10) are grouped into two iterative sub-cycles.

A primary goal in basic DSM analysis is to minimize the number of feedbacks and their scope by restructuring or re-architecting the process (Browning, 2001). To achieve this goal, many algorithms/approaches were cited in the literature: partitioning and tearing approach (Steward, 1981-a; 1981-b); the Path Searching method (Gebala and Eppinger, 1991), the Reachability Matrix method (Warfield, 1973), the Triangularization algorithm (Kusiak and Wang, 1994), and the Powers of the Adjacency Matrix method (Ledet and Himmelblau, 1970); DeMaid/GA (Rogers, 1996); AGENDA (Altus, Kroo, and Gage, 1996); PSM32 (Problematics); ADePT (Austin, Baldwin, Li, and Waskett, 2000); integrated project management

Figure 3. Generic DSM

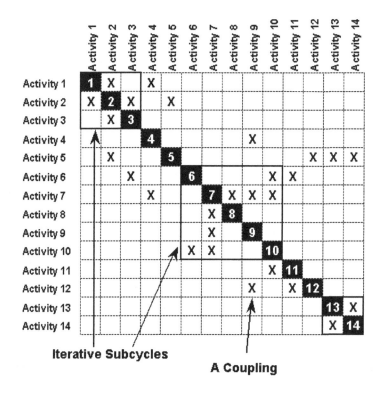

framework (Cho, 2001) ; using Simulated Annealing (Abdelsalam and Bao, 2006).

Out of these approaches only three that tried to use optimization techniques to find an optimal activities' sequence; DeMaid and AGENDA used Genetic Algorithms, and (Abdelsalam and Bao, 2006) used Simulated Annealing. Out of these approaches only three that tried to use optimization techniques to find an optimal activities' sequence; DeMaid and AGENDA used Genetic Algorithms, and (Abdelsalam and Bao, 2006) used Simulated Annealing. This chapter presents and tests a MOPSO algorithm to determine the optimal order of design projects' activities represented by DSM.

Discrete Multi-Objective Particle Swarm Optimization (MOPSO)

Particle swarm optimization (PSO) is an evolutionary computation optimization algorithm designed by Kennedy and Eberhart in 1995. PSO is a population based algorithm in which each potential solution is called a particle. Each particle moves in the problem space by defining two parameters; position and a velocity. Each particle has its own memory that keeps track of its previous best position and its corresponding fitness in it. And, among the whole swarm, the particle with greatest fitness is kept as the global best of the swarm. At each time step, each particle accelerates its personal best and global best locations with random weighted acceleration parameters.

The major difference between PSO and the other evolutionary algorithms is that PSO chooses the path of cooperation over competition; while one common characteristic of evolutionary optimization algorithms is the survival of the fittest (the best solution), the population of PSO, on the contrary, is stable and particles are not destroyed or recreated (Sharaf and El-Gammal, 2009). Particles are influenced by the best performance of their neighbours; i.e. social cooperation, allowing them to approach optimal points in the search space of

the problem. PSO does not have operators similar to crossover and mutation in Genetic Algorithm (GA), and during the run other individuals never replace with particles. Consequently, the particles in PSO have a tendency to converge to the best solution quickly compared to GA.

The applications and studies of PSO on discrete optimization problems are relatively few compared to the studies on solving continuous optimization problems (Liao, Luarn, and Tseng, 2007). In spite of the difficulties of implementation of PSO algorithm in solving combinatorial problems due to its continuous nature, the advantages of PSO motivated the researchers to do so. In 2007, Tasgetiren and others enables to overcome this problem by using the smallest position value (SPV) rule (Bean, 1994) that converts continuous position values in PSO to a discrete job permutation. Their work builds on previously effective application of the same rule in similar problems (Tasgetiren et al., 2004, 2007). Depending on the common nature of job-shop scheduling and project activities' sequencing, and the successful applications, this chapter aims towards employing PSO algorithms to obtain the optimal order of design projects' activities represented by DSM.

This research will use multi-objective PSO (or MOPSO) to solve the problem at hand. In general, a multi-objective optimization problem with -objectives to be maximized can be mathematically stated as:

$$Minimize \ f(x) = \{f_1(x), f_2(x), ..., f_k(x)\}$$

where $f_i(x)$ is the ith objective function, and $x = (x_1, x_2, ..., x_n)$ is the decision vector that belongs to the feasible region S.

The concept of Pareto dominance (Pareto optimum) was proposed by Vilfredo Pareto in 1896 and has been widely used to establish superiority between solutions in multi-objective optimization. Dominance rules that will be used in this research are defined in Table 2 (Khoi, Dario Landa-Silva and Hui, 2009).

The performance of particles in MOPSO is always compared in terms of dominance relations. The use of an external repository (archive) which stores non-dominated solutions is considered as the main characteristic of MOPSO (Mostaghim, Branke and Schmeck, 2007; Baltar and Fontane, 2006).In every generation, the particles are evaluated and the non-dominated solutions are added to the archive and the dominated solutions are pruned. In the next step, the particles are moved to new positions in the space. The particle's velocity and position are updated as below:

$$v_{ij}^t = w^{t-1}v_{ij}^{t-1} + c_1 r_1 (p_{ij}^{t-1} - x_{ij}^{t-1})$$
$$+ c_2 r_2 (g_j^{t-1} - x_{ij}^{t-1}) \quad (1)$$

$$x_{ij}^t = x_{ij}^{t-1} + v_{ij}^t \quad (2)$$

where x_i^t is position of particle i, v_i^t is velocity of particle i, p_i^t is particle personal best, g_j^t is the global best position, c_1 and c_2 are acceleration coefficients, r_1 and r_2 are uniformly distributed random numbers in [0,1], and w is the inertia weight.

The important part in MOPSO is to determine the global best particle g_j^t. In single objective PSO, it is easier to determine the global best particle by selecting the particle that has the best position. However in MOPSO, g_j^t must be selected from the updated set of non-dominated solutions stored in the archive.

PROPOSED SOLUTION ALGORITHM

The core of the presented algorithm uses the algorithm developed in (Kennedy, Eberhart, and Shi, 2001) with the addition of the inertia weight proposed by Shi and Eberhart (1998). But, as the

Table 2. Dominance rules

Rule	Definition
Pareto Dominance	A solution $x \in S$ is said to dominate a solution $x^* \in S$ $\left(x \succeq x^*\right)$ if and only if x is better than x^* in all objectives $(f_i(x) \le f_i(x^*)\forall i = 1, ..., k)$ and is accurately better than x^* in at least one objective $(f_i(x) < f_i(x^*$ for at least one $i = 1, ..., k)$.
Weak dominance	A solution x is said to weakly dominates a solution x^* $\left(x \succeq x^*\right)$ is is better than x^* in at least one objective and is as good as x^* in all other objectives.
Strong dominance	A solution x is said to strongly dominates a solution x^* $\left(x \succ x^*\right)$ if is accurately better than x^* in all objective.
Non-dominance	If x does not dominate x^* and x^* does not dominate x (weakly or strongly), then both solutions are said to be mutually non-dominated. Thus, no solution is preferred over the other.
Pareto optimal	is a solution that it is not dominated by any other solution in the solution space.
Pareto optimal set	is the set of all feasible non-dominated solution in the search space, and the corresponding objective function values in the objective space is called the *Pareto front*.

evaluation of each particle requires the order of activities (will be referred hereinafter as permutation), the smallest position value (SPV) rule applies to each particle to find its corresponding permutation (order of activities) as presented in (Tasgetiren et al., 2007).

Steps

The algorithmic steps, shown in Figure 4, encompass eight elements:

1. **Particle:** X_i^t denotes the particle in position i at iteration t and for n activities the particle will be represent as $X_i^t = (x_{i1}^t, x_{i2}^t, ..., x_{in}^t)$ where x_{ij}^t is the position value of the particle in position i with respect to the activity $j(j = 1, 2, ..., n)$. In the proposed optimization algorithm, it is required to determine the optimal sequence of project activities given that: (1) no duplication is allowed; that is two activities cannot assume the same order; and (2) the first and the last activities are known in advance; there is a starting and ending activity, thus their order will remain fixed during the optimization process. The solution representation of particle X_i^t is shown in Figure 5. Dimensions represent activities' order, thus, the number of dimensions is n, and the particle $X_i^t = (x_{i1}^t, x_{i2}^t, ..., x_{in}^t)$ corresponds to the continuous position values for the DSM activities.

2. **Population:** X^t is the set of NP particles in swarm at iteration t, i.e., $X^t = (x_1^t, x_2^t, ..., x_{NP}^t)$. The initial population of particles is constructed randomly. The continuous values of positions are established randomly using the following formula:

   a. $x_{ij}^0 = r_1$ (3)

b. Similarly, the population initial velocities are generated randomly using the following formula

c. $v_{ij}^0 = v_{min} + (v_{max} - v_{min}) * r_2$ (4)

d. where r_1 and r_2 are uniform random numbers between 0 and 1 and $v_{ij}^t[v_{min}, v_{max}] = [-4.0, 4.0]$

3. **Permutation:** To convert the continuous position values to a discrete activities permutation which enables the use of PSO in this sequencing problem, the SPV rule will be used to determine the permutation implied by the position values x_{ij}^t of particle X_i^t. A new variable Π_i^t was introduced to represent the permutation of the sequence of the activities implied by the particle X_i^t. It can be represented as $\Pi_i^t = (\Pi_{i1}^t, \Pi_{i2}^t, ..., \Pi_{in}^t)$, where Π_{ij}^t is the ID of activity j of the particle i in the permutation at iteration t (Tasgetiren et al., 2007).

a. In the solution illustrated in Figure 6, activity (4) has the smallest position value $x_{i5}^t = -2.00$, so it is assigned to be the first activity $\Pi_{i1}^t = 7$ in the permutation Π_i^t; the next activity to be executed will be (6) as it has the next smallest position value $x_{i6}^t = -1.20$; and so on. Activities, thus, are sorted according to the smallest position values x_{ij}^t to construct the permutation Π_i^t. It should be noted that, again, the first and the last activities are not considered.

4. **Particle Velocity:** V_i^t is the velocity of particle i at iteration t. It can be represented as $v_i^t = (v_{i1}^t, v_{i2}^t, ..., v_{in}^t)$, where v_{ij}^t is the velocity of particle i at iteration t with respect to the j th dimension.

5. **Inertia Weight:** To balance between the global and local direction of a particle, a parameter w^t is used. In the earlier iterations, PSO tends to widen the exploration of the

search space so a large inertia weight is used. One the other hand, as the optimization process advances, PSO tends to enhance local search so smaller inertia weight is used Acceleration coefficients: c_1 and c_2 are constants used to control the maximum step size that the particle can do.

6. **Personal Best:** P_i^t represents the best position of the particle until iteration t. the personal best is the best position associated with the best fitness value of the particle obtained so far. The personal best for each particle in the swarm can be determined and updated at each iteration t. In a maximization problem with the objective function $f(\Pi_i^t)$, the personal best is determined such that $f(\Pi_i^t) \geq f(\Pi_i^{t-1})$

7. **Global Best:** G^t denotes the best position of the globally best particle achieved so far in the whole swarm.

8. **Archive:** The best position vector of particle i, P_i^t, initialize by the initial position of particle i. in the next iteration, P_i^t is updated according to the following way: (1) if the current P_i^t dominates the new position x_i^{t+1} then $P_i^{t+1} = P_i^t$, (2) if the new position x_i^{t+1} dominates P_i^t then $P_i^{t+1} = x_i^{t+1}$

   a. In the standard PSO there is one global best position vector G^t, but in MOPSO there are several non-dominated solutions stored in the archive. In every iteration the archive is updated by adding new non-dominated solutions and removing the dominated solutions.

To generate a new population, the velocity of each particle in the population will be updated according to Equation (1). And to update the position of each particle in population, the updated velocity will be used according to Equation (2). And finally, the SPV rule will be applied to

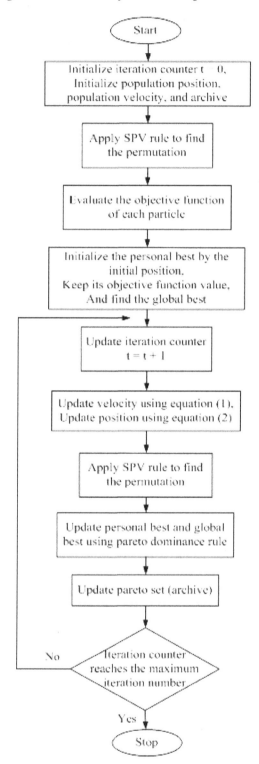

Figure 4. Flowchart of MOPSO implemented

Figure 5. Representation of one particle

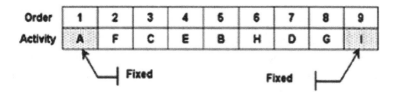

Figure 6. Permutation

	Dimension, j								
	1	2	3	4	5	6	7	8	9
x^t_{ij}		0.10	2.66	-2.00	1.30	-1.20	0.05	1.00	
v^t_{ij}									
Activities, π^t_{ij}	1	4	6	7	2	8	5	3	9

generate the permutation of each particle in the population.

Fitness Calculation

Instead of using the basic binary DSM, this research uses a multi-attribute (or numerical DSM) that allows the development of more complex DSM analysis. In the current research, the DSM used replaces coupling marks with numbers representing coupling 'iteration factor'. These iteration factors represent the number of iterations required for a certain feedback coupling to converge; the number of iterations required for a certain feedback loop to converge differs from one feedback to the other based on several factors (e.g. accuracy of original upstream activities' estimates). Although these values are supplied to the presented model directly, they can be determined through sensitivity analysis detailed in (Rogers and Bloebaum, 1994-a, 1994-b).

The model presented here assumes that an activity is fully repeated in each iteration and that learning can be accounted for, roughly, by

the appropriate choice of number of iterations (Abdelsalam and Bao, 2006). For each activity, time (duration) and associated cost are defined. And, for each feedback coupling an estimated required number of iterations for its convergence is determined ahead.

In DSM analysis, the objective of minimizing the number of feedbacks was the one used in many published studies either by using heuristics (e.g. Austin, Baldwin, Li, and Waskett, 2000; Cho, 2001) or using artificial intelligence optimization methods (Genetic Algorithm (Rogers, 1996), Simulated Annealing (Abdelsalam and Bao, 2006). Another objective function was introduced in (Altus, Kroo, and Gage, 1996) that aimed to reduce the extent of feedbacks, or, in other words, minimizing the "total length of feedbacks" of the system. In (Abdelsalam and Bao, 2006) two more objective functions were proposed: minimizing the total project time due to feedback loops or project iterative time (PIT), and minimizing the total project cost due to feedback loops or project iterative time (CIT). This research considers the four objective functions: (1) number of feedbacks;

(2) total feedback length; (3) project iterative time (PIT); and (4) project iterative cost (PIC).

To determine PIT (or CIT), this chapter follows the heuristic presented in (Abdelsalam and Bao, 2006) in which all activities contained within a feedback loop time (or cost) will be summed and multiplied by the loop's iteration factor and, then, the time (or cost) of all feedback loops are summed. To determine the iterative time (or cost) for each loop and, hence, for the whole project, this process is repeated for all feedback loops in the DSM.

EXPERIMENTAL RESULTS

To illustrate the performance of the implemented algorithm, this chapter uses the hypothetical DSM shown in Figure 7 with 20 activities and 36 couplings and each activity has its duration and associated cost and all couplings share the same strength of 1. The shown arrangement has 10 feedbacks, 26 feed-forward couplings, feedback

length of 39, PIT of 259 time units, and CIT of 2708 cost units. MOPSO parameters' values were set as: number of particles (population size) = 10; number of iterations = 100; maximum inertia = 1.2; minimum inertia = 0.4; maximum velocity = 4; minimum velocity = -4; and Pareto (archive) size = 5.

As shown in Figure 8, for each 'number of feedback' there exists a range of associated PIT indicating that minimizing the 'number of feedbacks' in a DSM does not, necessarily, guarantee minimizing the total project time. In fact, there is a trade-off between the two criteria. This case can be seen as a trade of minimizing complexity of the project (represented by the total number of feedbacks) and resource usage (represented by the total iterative time). The same situation applies to the "total feedback length as Figure 9 depicts. In the shown figure, however, the optimization algorithm succeeded to reach a point that minimizes both functions at the same time. Of course, this is a case specific and must not be taken as a general rule for other DSMs.

Figure 7. Example DSM (activities are randomly ordered)

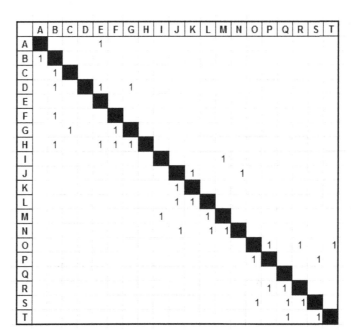

Figure 8. Pareto front – Number of feedbacks vs. PIT

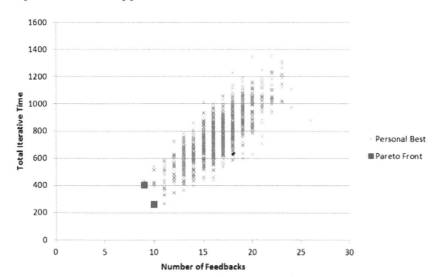

Figure 9. Pareto front – Feedback length vs. PIT

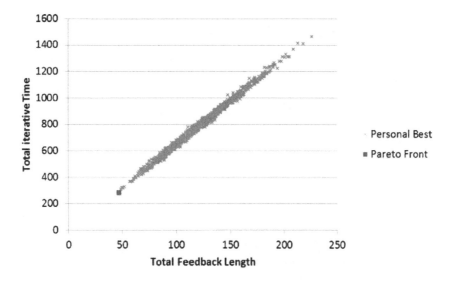

Furthermore, the results show a trade-off between the number of feedbacks and the total feedback length as shown in Figure 10. Using the number of feedbacks as an objective for simplifying a design project becomes, thus, not a wise selection.

The trade-off between PIT and PIC is shown in Figure 11. As shown, four (out of five) points of the front constituted strong-dominance and one point is considered weak dominance. Performance of the algorithm is illustrated by Figure 12 that shows the progress of Pareto fronts throughout

Figure 10. Pareto front – Number of feedbacks vs. feedback length

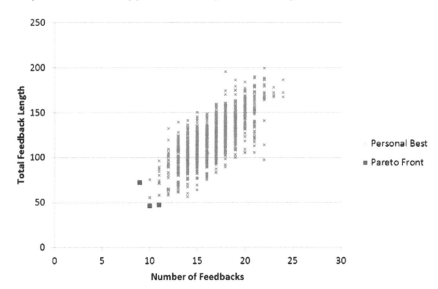

Figure 11. Pareto front – PIT vs. PIC

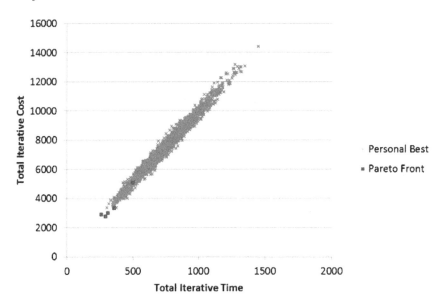

the run (100 iterations) where each graph shows the front after 10 iterations. As shown, the first front contained only one point (given that the archive starts with solution with high cost and time) followed by two concave fronts of 4 points. After that, convex fronts of four were reached until the final five point front.

FUTURE RESEARCH DIRECTIONS

Reducing time-to-market is an essential requirement for continuous competition as the effects of early introduction of new products on both market share and profitability are evident. Such understanding has led companies to adopt holistic approaches in their design department to deal

Figure 12. Pareto front progress

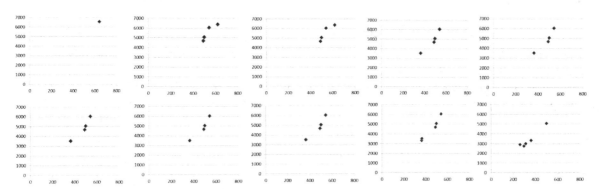

with this issue especially with the increasing complexity of products. One on these approaches is the Integrated Product Development (IPD) that aims to a framework for an effective planning and managing of engineering projects.

Within the context of IPD, the Design Structure Matrix was positioned as a tool that supports efficient analysis of the design project. This chapter used a numerical form of the DSM to determine the optimal sequence of activities' execution in an engineering design project taking into consideration the trade-off between activity time and cost.

Following the presented work, the authors suggest two areas for future research: (1) fine tuning of MPSO parameters; and (2) would include using other methods (e.g. simulation) for determining the time (and cost) of a proposed DSM order of activities.

CONCLUSION

A product development project (PDP) fundamentally differs from a construction (or a manufacturing) project in two major aspects: (1) while the later is activity-based, the first is information-based; and (2) a typical PDP is characterized by its highly coupled, interdependent activities, which must converge iteratively to an acceptable design solution. A PDP is typically a complex system. The main approach to handling such system involves: decomposing it into sub-systems and furthermore

into smaller components; and defining the relationships among these components. Following these steps, the system will be decomposed into possibly several hundreds of activities (components) and thousand of variable interchanges among these activities. The sequence of performing these activities strongly affects the time (and hence the cost) needed to realize the whole project.

The Design Structure Matrix (DSM) is a system analysis and project management tool that has received a considerable attention in literature for being able to provide a compact and clear representation of activities in product development projects and the relationships among these activities. Since its original introduction by Steward in the 1980's, the DSM has proved itself as an effective tool for analyzing and understanding system architecture especially in new product development projects and, hence, achieving improved performance.

This research aimed to determine the optimal sequence of design project activities represented by a DSM using a Discrete Multi-Objective Particle Swarm Optimization Algorithm. Optimization was done using different sets of four objective functions: number of feedbacks, total feedback length, total iterative time; and total iterative cost. Results showed that the first two objectives which were the base for basic DSM analyses in the literature do not guarantee an improved performance of project execution in terms of resources (time and cost). Time-cost trade-off, thus, is the issue that needs to be considered.

REFERENCES

Abdelsalam, H. M., & Bao, H. P. (2006). A simulation-based optimization framework for product development cycle time reduction. *IEEE Transactions on Engineering Management, 53*(1), 69–85. doi:10.1109/TEM.2005.861805

Altus, S. S., Kroo, I. M., & Gage, P. J. (1996). A genetic algorithm for scheduling and decomposition of multidisciplinary design problems. *Transactions of ASME, 118*(4), 486–489.

Armstrong, S. C. (2001). *Engineering and product development management: The holistic approach*. Cambridge University Press.

Austin, S., Baldwin, A., Li, B., & Waskett, P. (2000). Analytical design planning technique (ADePT): A dependency structure matrix tool to schedule the building design process. *Construction Management and Economics, 8*, 173–182. doi:10.1080/014461900370807

Baltar, A. M., & Fontane, D. G. (2006). A generalized multiobjective particle swarm optimization solver for spreadsheet models: Application to water quality. In *Proceedings of the Twenty Sixth Annual American Geophysical Union Hydrology Days*, 20–22 March 2006.

Bean, J. C. (1994). Genetic algorithm and random keys for sequencing and optimization. *ORSA Journal on Computing, 6*(2), 154–160. doi:10.1287/ijoc.6.2.154

Blackburn, J. D. (1991). New product development: The new time wars . In Blackburn, J. D. (Ed.), *Time-based competition*. Homewood, IL: Business One Irwin Publishers.

Browning, T. R. (1998). *Modeling and analyzing cost, schedule, and performance in complex system product development*. Ph.D. dissertation, MIT, Cambridge, MA. Browning, T. R. (2001-b). Applying the design structure matrix to system decomposition and integration problems: A review and new directions. *IEEE Transactions on Engineering Management, 48*(3), 292–306.

Browning, T. R. (2001-a). Modeling the customer value of product development processes. *Proceedings of the 11ᵗʰ Annual International Symposium of INCOSE*, Melbourne, Australia, July 1-5.

Browning, T. R., & Eppinger, S. D. (2002). Modeling impacts of process architecture on cost and schedule risk in product development. *IEEE Transactions on Engineering Management, 49*(4), 443–458. doi:10.1109/TEM.2002.806710

Chakravarty, A. K. (2001). Overlapping design and build cycles in product development. *European Journal of Operational Research, 134*, 392–424. doi:10.1016/S0377-2217(00)00264-2

Cho, S.-H. (2001). *An integrated method for managing complex engineering projects using the design structure matrix and advanced simulation*. M.S. thesis, MIT, Cambridge, MA.

Denker, S., Steward, D. V., & Browning, T. R. (1999). Planning concurrency and managing iteration in projects. *Project Management Journal, 32*(3), 31–38.

Fiksel, J. (1991). *Design for environment: Creating eco-efficient products & processes*. New York, NY: McGraw-Hill.

Gebala, D. A., & Eppinger, S. D. (1991). Methods for analyzing design procedures. In *Proceedings of ASME 3rd International Conference on Design Theory Methodology*, (pp. 227–233).

House, C. H., & Price, R. L. (1991). The return map: Tracking product teams. *Harvard Business Review*, (1): 92–100.

Kennedy, J., Eberhart, R. C., & Shi, Y. (2001). *Swarm intelligence*. San Francisco, CA: Morgan Kaufmann.

Khoi, L., Landa-Silva, D., & Li, H. (2009). An improved version of volume dominance for multiobjective optimisation . In Ehrgott, M. (Eds.), *EMO 2009, LNCS 5467* (pp. 231–245).

Kotler, P. (1991). *Marketing management: Analysis, planning, implementation and control* (7th ed.). Englewood Cliffs, NJ: Prentice-Hall.

Kusiak, N. L., & Wang, J. (1994). Reengineering of design and manufacturing processes. *Computers & Industrial Engineering, 26*(3), 521–536. doi:10.1016/0360-8352(94)90048-5

Ledet, W. P., & Himmelblau, D. M. (1970). Decomposition procedures for the solving of large scale systems. *Advances in Chemical Engineering, 8*, 185–254. doi:10.1016/S0065-2377(08)60185-4

Liao, C.-J., Tseng, C.-T., & Luarn, P. (2007). A discrete version of particle swarm optimization for flowshop scheduling problems. *Computers & Operations Research, 34*, 3099–3111. doi:10.1016/j.cor.2005.11.017

Mostaghim, S., Branke, J., & Schmeck, H. (2007). *Multi-objective particle swarm optimization on computer grids. Institute AIFB.* Germany: University of Karlsruhe.

National Research Council. (1991). *Improving engineering design: Designing for competitive advantage.* Washington, DC: National Academy Press.

Nevins, J. L., & Whitney, D. E. (Eds.). (1989). *Concurrent design of products and processes: A strategy for the next generation in manufacturing.* New York, NY: McGraw-Hill.

O'Grady, P., Ramers, D., & Bowen, J. (1988). Artificial intelligence constraint nets applied to design for economic manufacture and assembly. *Computer Integrated Manufacturing Systems, 1*(4), 204–210. doi:10.1016/0951-5240(88)90052-3

Peet, W. J., & Hladik, K. J. (1989). Organizing for global product development. *Electronic Business, 15*(5), 62–64.

Port, O. (1990, April 30). A smarter way to manufacture. *Business Week,* (pp. 110-117).

Problematics. (n.d.). *Website.* Retrieved from http://www.problematics.com

Rogers, J. L. (1996). DeMaid/GA—An enhanced design manager's aid for intelligent decomposition. *6th AIAA/USAF/NASA/OSSMO Symposium on Multidisciplinary Analysis and Optimization,* Seattle, WA, Sep. 4–6, 1996, (pp. 96-4157)

Rogers, J. L., & Bloebaum, C. L. (1994-a). Ordering design tasks based on coupling strengths. *Proceeding the 5th AIAA/USAF/NASA/ISSMO Symposium on Multidisciplinary Analysis and Optimization,* Panama City, Florida. AIAA paper No. 94-4326. Also NASA TM 109137.

Rogers, J. L., & Bloebaum, C. L. (1994-b). *Ordering design tasks based on coupling strengths.* AIAA, No. 94-4326.

Sharaf, A. M., & El-Gammal, A. A. (2009). *A multi objective multi-stage particle swarm optimization MOPSO search scheme for power quality and loss reduction on radial distribution system.* International Conference on Renewable Energies and Power Quality (ICREPQ'09)

Shi, Y., & Eberhart, R. C. (1998). A modified particle swarm optimizer. *Proceedings of the IEEE Congress on Evolutionary Computation,* (pp. 69–173). Piscataway, NJ: IEEE.

Stalk, G. (1988). Time: The next source of competitive advantage. *Harvard Business Review, 66*, 41–51.

Steward, D. V. (n,d). (1981-a). *Systems analysis and management: Structure, strategy and design.* New York, NY: Petrocelli Books Inc. Steward, D. V. (1981-b). The design structure system: A method for managing the design of complex systems. *IEEE Transactions on Engineering Management, 8*, 71–74.

Tasgetiren, M. F., Liang, Y.-C., Sevkli, M., & Gencyilmaz, G. (2004). Lecture Notes in Computer Science: *Vol. 3172. Particle swarm optimization algorithm for permutation flowshop sequencing problem* (pp. 382–390). Springer-Verlag. doi:10.1007/978-3-540-28646-2_38

Tasgetiren, M. F., Liang, Y.-C., Sevkli, M., & Gencyilmaz, G. (2007). A particle swarm optimization algorithm for makespan and total flowtime minimization in the permutation flowshop sequencing problem. *European Journal of Operational Research*, *177*, 1930–1947. doi:10.1016/j.ejor.2005.12.024

Warfield, J. N. (1973). Binary matrices in system modelling. *IEEE Transactions on Systems, Man, and Cybernetics*, *3*, 441–449. doi:10.1109/TSMC.1973.4309270

Yassine, A., Chelst, K., & Falkenburg, D. (1999). Engineering design management: An information structure approach. *International Journal of Production Research*, *37*(13), 2957–2975. doi:10.1080/002075499190374

ADDITIONAL READING

Abdelsalam, H. M., & Bao, H. P. (2007). Resequencing of design processes with activity stochastic time and cost: An optimization-simulation approach. *ASME Journal of Mechanical Design*, *129*, 150–157. doi:10.1115/1.2216730

Ariyo, O., Eckert, C. M., & Clarkson, P. J. (2006). Unpleasant surprises in the design of complex products: Why do changes propagate. *Proceedings of the 2006 ASME Design Engineering Technical Conference - 18th International Conference on Design Theory and Methodology*, Philadelphia, Pennsylvania.

Chen, W., Navin-Chandra, D., & Prinz, F. B. (1993). Product design for recyclability: A cost benefit analysis model and its application. *Proceedings of the 1993 IEEE International Symposium on Electronics and the Environment*, San Francisco, California.

Clarkson, P. J., Simons, C., & Eckert, C. (2004). Predicting change propagation in complex design. *Journal of Mechanical Design*, *126*, 788–797. doi:10.1115/1.1765117

Dahmus, J. B., Gonzalez-Zugasti, J. P., & Otto, K. N. (2001). Modular Product Architecture. *Design Studies*, *22*(5), 409–424. doi:10.1016/S0142-694X(01)00004-7

Dixon, J. R., & Poli, C. (1995). *Engineering design and design for manufacturing: A structured approach*. Conway, MA: Field Stone Publishers.

Fixson, S. K. (2003). *The multiple faces of modularity - A literature analysis of a product concept for assembled hardware products*. Ann Arbor.

Gershenson, J. K. (2005). *Design for retirement, life-cycle engineering. Class Notes*. Michigan Technological University.

Hu, D., Hu, Y., & Li, C. (2002). Mechanical product disassembly sequence and path planning based on knowledge and geometric reasoning. *International Journal of Advanced Manufacturing Technology*, *19*, 688–696. doi:10.1007/s001700200114

Ishii, K., & Kmenta, S. (2003). Introduction to design for assembly. *ME 317A Course reader, design for manufacturability: Product definition*. Stanford University Bookstore.

Lai, X., & Gershenson, J. K. (2008). DSM-based product representation for design process modularity. *Proceedings of the 2008 ASME Design Engineering Technical Conferences - 20th Interational Conference on Design Theory and Methodology (DTM)*, New York.

McCord, K. R., & Eppinger, S. D. (1993). *Managing the integration problem in concurrent engineering*. Cambridge, MA: M.I.T. Sloan School of Management.

Otto, K. N., & Wood, K. L. (2000). *Product design*. Prentice Hall.

Pahl, G., & Beitz, W. (1999). *Engineering design: A systematic approach*. New York, NY: Springer.

Pimmler, T. U., & Eppinger, S. D. (1994). Integration analysis of product decompositions. *Proceedings of the 1994 ASME Design Engineering Technical Conferences - 6th International Conference on Design Theory and Methodology*, Minneapolis, Minnesota.

Ulrich, K., & Eppinger, S. (2008). *Product design and development*. New York, NY: McGraw-Hill Higher Education.

KEY TERMS AND DEFINITIONS

Concurrent Engineering: A relatively recent term that is applied to product development, and most specifically to engineering design. This term refers to the philosophy of cross-functional cooperation and the parallelization of tasks carried out in design engineering, manufacturing engineering and other disciplines in order to create products which are better, cheaper, and more quickly brought to market.

Design Structure Matrix: Also referred to as "dependency structure matrix" – is graphical tool originally developed to model system components and relationships among these components. Later on, the tool has been used extensively if design project to model various project activities and their interdependencies as a step for improving these projects.

Multi-Objective Optimization: Also referred to multi-criteria or multi-attribute optimization – is the process of simultaneously optimizing two or more conflicting objectives subject to certain set of constraints. In such class of optimization problems, it is – usually – infeasible to identify one single solution that simultaneously optimizes all objectives; a solution is reached that, when attempting to improve an objective further, other objectives suffer as a result. Thus, algorithms used for this purpose try to identify a set of non-dominated, Pareto optimal, or Pareto efficient solutions that cannot be eliminated from consideration by replacing it with another solution which improves an objective without worsening another one.

New Product Development: The complete process of bringing a new product to market starting with 'idea generation' and ending to 'product launching'.

Particle Swarm Optimization: A population based optimization technique originally Developed by Kennedy and Eberhart in 1995. The algorithm is inspired by social behaviour of bird flocking or fish schooling in which individual swarm members can profit from the discoveries and previous experience of all other members of the school.

Trade-Off: In general, a trade-off situation involves losing one quality or aspect of something in return for gaining another quality or aspect which results in a decision to be made with full comprehension of both the upside and downside of a particular choice.

Chapter 19
Application of Meta–Heuristic Optimization Algorithms in Electric Power Systems

N.I. Voropai
Energy Systems Institute of the Siberian Branch of the Russian Academy of Sciences, Russia

A. Z. Gamm
Energy Systems Institute of the Siberian Branch of the Russian Academy of Sciences, Russia

A. M. Glazunova
Energy Systems Institute of the Siberian Branch of the Russian Academy of Sciences, Russia

P. V. Etingov
Energy Systems Institute of the Siberian Branch of the Russian Academy of Sciences, Russia

I. N. Kolosok
Energy Systems Institute of the Siberian Branch of the Russian Academy of Sciences, Russia

E. S. Korkina
Energy Systems Institute of the Siberian Branch of the Russian Academy of Sciences, Russia

V. G. Kurbatsky
Energy Systems Institute of the Siberian Branch of the Russian Academy of Sciences, Russia

D. N. Sidorov
Energy Systems Institute of the Siberian Branch of the Russian Academy of Sciences, Russia

V. A. Spiryaev
Energy Systems Institute of the Siberian Branch of the Russian Academy of Sciences, Russia

N. V. Tomin
Energy Systems Institute of the Siberian Branch of the Russian Academy of Sciences, Russia

R. A. Zaika
Energy Systems Institute of the Siberian Branch of the Russian Academy of Sciences, Russia

B. Bat-Undraal
Mongolian University of Science and Technology, Mongolia

ABSTRACT

Optimization of solutions on expansion of electric power systems (EPS) and their control plays a crucial part in ensuring efficiency of the power industry, reliability of electric power supply to consumers and power quality. Until recently, this goal was accomplished by applying classical and modern methods of linear and nonlinear programming. In some complicated cases, however, these methods turn out to be rather inefficient. Meta-heuristic optimization algorithms often make it possible to successfully cope

DOI: 10.4018/978-1-4666-2086-5.ch019

with arising difficulties. State estimation (SE) is used to calculate current operating conditions of EPS using the SCADA measurements of state variables (voltages, currents etc.). To solve the SE problem, the Energy Systems Institute of Siberian Branch of Russian Academy of Sciences (ESI of SB RAS) has devised a method based on test equations (TE), i.e. on the steady state equations that contain only measured parameters. Here, a technique for EPS SE using genetic algorithms (GA) is suggested. SE is the main tool for EPS monitoring. The quality of SE results determines largely the EPS control efficiency. An algorithm for exclusion of wrong SE calculations is described. The algorithm using artificial neural networks (ANN) is based on the analysis of results of the calculation performed solving the SE problem with different combinations of constants. The proposed procedure is checked on real data.

INTRODUCTION

Phasor measurement units (PMUs) are employed in EPS both to solve the local problems and to obtain a general picture of EPS state which is further used for solution of control problems. Placement of PMU for solution of the problems of the first group is very specific and is determined by individual features of the problems to be solved. To solve the problems of the second group, including SE problems, the universal methods are necessary to place PMUs and SCADA to provide the best properties of the SE problem, such as observability of the studied network, identifiability of bad data and accuracy of obtained estimates.

As criteria for PMU placement several criteria are used: absence of critical measurements and critical sets in the system, maximum quantity of measurements received as compared to the initial one, maximum accuracy of estimates, minimum cost of PMU placement, transformation of the network graph into tree. GA allows different PMU placement criteria to be combined. The proposed algorithm is validated by simulation.

Also the problem of PMU placement is suggested in such a way that the volume of initial information based on the SCADA and PMU measurements is sufficient to determine all the state vector components for load flow calculations without iterations. The PMU number in this case should be minimal. The problem of PMU

placement is solved by the simulated annealing (SA) method.

The problem of multi-criteria reconfiguration of distribution network with distributed generation according to the criterion of minimum power loss under normal conditions and the criterion of power supply reliability under post-emergency conditions is considered. Efficient heuristic Ant Colony algorithm is used to solve the problem. Demonstration studies have been carried out for the Central Power System of Mongolia.

To improve the accuracy of short-term forecasting two-stage intelligent approach is proposed. On the first stage the initial data is decomposed by Hilbert-Huang transform (HHT), and the second stage involves ANN model optimized with SA algorithm and Neuro-Genetic Input Selection (NGIS). To train and build the optimal structure of ANN the optimization block "NGIS-SA" is used. The results show a solid improvement in the accuracy of short-term forecast for different non-stationary processes.

To enhance transient stability in large EPSs an application of fuzzy logic power system stabilizers (FLPSS) is presented. A two-stage technology of FLPSS adaptation is considered taking into account the real conditions of a power system. Self-organizing ANN is used for clusterization of the test disturbances. GA is applied to tuning parameters of FLPSS. ANN is used on-line to adapt FLPSS to changes in operating conditions of EPS. The studies have been conducted using the models of a 14-bus multi-machine power system and regional Siberian power system as the study cases. The results obtained are presented.

Optimization of solutions on expansion of electric power systems and their control plays a crucial part in ensuring efficiency of the power industry, reliability of electric power supply to consumers and power quality.

Until recently this goal was accomplished by applying classical and modern methods of linear and nonlinear programming. In some complicated cases, however, these methods turn out to be rather inefficient. Meta-heuristic optimization algorithms often make it possible to successfully cope with arising difficulties.

The Section presents the experience of authors in applying different meta-heuristic optimization methods for solving different problems in electric power systems. Consideration is given to genetic algorithms, simulated annealing method, ant colony optimization, artificial neural networks, combination of meta-heuristic methods with fuzzy logic and artificial neural networks.

Chapter 1 deals with Genetic Algorithms application to different optimization problems. Consideration is given to the problem of power system state estimation and its specific features in terms of the use of Genetic Algorithms. The problem of PMU placement, which is an important part of the entire complex of problems related to power system state estimation, and possibilities of applying Genetic Algorithms for solving this problem are discussed. The results are illustrated with a test case study.

Comparative research showed that in some cases the Simulated Annealing method can be more effective than Genetic Algorithms for solving the optimization problem of PMU placement in EPS. Therefore, Chapter 2 presents one of the cases in detail, and the results of optimal PMU placement by the Simulated Annealing method are demonstrated by the calculations made for two test schemes.

Some problems, particular those of combinatorial character, can be effectively solved with another heuristic optimization method. This is Ant Colony Algorithm. Based on this fact Chapter 3 considers the use of Ant Colony Method for optimal reconfiguration of distribution network to determine rational points of opening loop sections according to the criterion for minimum active power losses in the network. Tests of the method on concrete electrical networks prove its effectiveness.

Chapter 4 presents two different examples of the use of Artificial Neural Network (ANN) for solving the problems of electric power systems. In the first problem ANN is employed for tuning the EPS state estimation parameters. In the second problem the optimal neural network models are applied to short-term forecasting of power system state variables. Consideration is given to the specific features of learning the Artificial Neural Networks and their use for solving the discussed problems. The results of ANN application are illustrated with test case studies.

In the end, Chapter 5 presents the use of a combination of Genetic Algorithms, Artificial Neural Network and Fuzzy Logic for optimal tuning of fuzzy PSS. The problem is solved in two stages. At the first stage for specified conditions Genetic Algorithm is used to choose a set of fuzzy PSS settings off-line. This set is then used for ANN learning. At the second stage a PSS setting that meets best the specified conditions is selected from the ANN on-line. The results are illustrated with a concrete example of fuzzy PSS.

The conclusion to the Section is formulated on the basis of the presented results describing the use of meta-heuristic methods for solving different problems of electric power systems.

1. GENETIC ALGORITHMS (GA)

1.1 Specific Features of Applying Genetic Algorithms to EPS State Estimation Problems

The state estimation (SE) problem is the most important in the set of problems of automated system of electric power system (EPS) dispatching control. The data obtained as a result of SE are applied for calculation and analysis of steady state (SS), optimization and calculation of feasible state variables, generating advices for a dispatcher, solving economic problems of EPS operation, etc. (Bartolomei & Panikovskaya, 2008). Development of market relations in electric power industry and improvement of the system of data acquisition and transmission persistently increase requirements to the efficiency of SE methods and accuracy of their results.

1.1.1 State Estimation for Energy Power Systems

The SE problem consists in calculating the EPS steady-state conditions by measurements. For this purpose the notion of state vector $x = (\delta, U)$ that comprises the magnitudes U and the phase angles δ of bus voltages is introduced. Such vector is uniquely determines all the state variables, including the measured y and unmeasured z.

The measurements used for SE include mainly the measurements received from SCADA: magnitudes of bus voltages, generation of active and reactive powers at buses, power flows in lines, sometimes - currents in lines and at buses. Pseudo measurements of loads at the buses were used to calculate bus injections in addition to the measurements:

$$\bar{y} = \{P_i, Q_i, P_{ij}, Q_{ij}, U_i, I_i, I_{ij}\} . \tag{1}$$

A mathematical statement of the SE problem is reduced to the objective function minimization

$$J = (\bar{y} - y)^T R^{-1} (\bar{y} - y) \tag{2}$$

subject to constraints in the form of steady state equations that connect measured y and unmeasured z state variables

$$w(y, z) = 0 , \tag{3}$$

here $\bar{y}$ – a vector of current measurement values; R – a diagonal matrix of weighting coefficients, whose elements are inverse to measurement variances.

A method applying Test Equations (TE) has been devised at Energy Systems Institute to solve the SE problem. The system of Equation (3) can be used to determine TEs, i.e. the equations that include only measured state variables y:

$$w_k(y) = 0. \tag{4}$$

In this case the SE problem is reduced to minimization of objective function (2) with constraints in the form of the system of TEs (4). The SE method on the basis of TEs by using the undetermined Lagrange multipliers is used in the software "OTSENKA" and described in detail in (Gamm & Kolosok, 2000).

The SE problem using the TEs is solved in two stages.

At the first stage the estimates of measured state variables included in the TEs are searched for. for this purpose calculating values of estimates which satisfy these equations and simultaneously are the most closely spaced to measurements is done.

At the second stage of algorithm application all unmeasured state variables are additionally calculated by the obtained estimates of measurements. For this purpose a basic system of measurements, i.e. a system of measurements which are least necessary for the unique determination of system state, is selected. The basis is selected by the Gaussian elimination algorithm with choice of the maximal element in the column. When introducing measurements in the basis their reliability indications are taken into account. First of all absolutely precise measurements such as zero injections at transit buses, then valid measurements and, finally, doubtful ones and pseudo measurements of bad data calculated in the program of measurement validation are placed in the basis. The possibility to retain absolutely precise measurements, for example, zero injections at transit buses is an important advantage of the SE method using TEs.

The numerical SE methods used to calculate current state variables of EPS on the basis of measurements give a reliable solution only if they do not contain bad data. Such errors cause distortion of state variables obtained in the SE procedure which leads to wrong decisions in on-line control of EPS. Therefore, detection of bad data in measurements is one of the most important problems of the SE procedure.

1.1.1.1 Bad Data Detection

The problem of critical measurements and critical sets[1] that were first defined in (Clements et al., 1983) arises when solving the SE problem for the networks with low redundancy of measurements. Bad data in such measurements cannot be detected and lead to distortion of the calculated state variables, therefore it is important to determine critical measurements (CM) and critical sets (CS) before SE problem solution. CM and CS can be easily detected on the basis of the analysis of TE structure, obtained from SCADA measurements.

For a priory detection of bad data in measurements the TE discrepancies are calculated (Gamm & Kolosok, 2000). If the measurements that enter into a TE do not contain bad data the magnitude of discrepancy should not exceed some threshold value, i.e. for each TE the condition

$$|w_k| \leq d_k \qquad (5)$$

is checked and on the basis of the check results a conclusion is made about the correctness of measurements. However, in some cases the "logical rules"[2] do not notice bad data, or incorrectly reject valid measurements or only identify the groups that include erroneous measurements.

SE problem involves some difficulties that cannot be overcome by using numerical methods. Sensitivity to bad data is the main of them that does not allow reliable estimates to be obtained, if in the snapshot there are erroneous measurements. This problem can be solved by the robust SE methods.

1.1.1.2 Robust SE Methods

After revealing the erroneous measurements the obtained estimates of measurements should be used to calculate unmeasured variables.

For this purpose the basic system of measurements y_b is chosen. It represents a set of minimum required measurements for the unique determination of state vector x. Then the following system of equations is solved

$$y_b(x) - \hat{y}_b = 0 \qquad (6)$$

When using the procedure of basis choice some special features emerge in the SE algorithm due to the necessity to take into account the validity degree of measurements when being inserted in the basis. Choice of basic measurements by the criterion of the best conditionality of the weighted Jacoby matrix does not always give an optimal solution, even if the validity degree of measurements is taken into account. This is explained by availability of errors at measurement validation. Hence, the basis can include both undetected measurements with gross errors and invalidly rejected measurements, whose values are replaced by incorrect pseudo measurements. Therefore, the robust estimation methods, i.e. the

SE methods, in which a great number of variants for basic measurements should be enumerated to determine an optimal solution, are applied and the best method that satisfies the estimation criterion should be chosen.

1.1.1.3 SE Problem Decomposition

The SE problem decomposition is a most effective way to increase the speed of solution determination. The scheme decomposition is often needed because of technical reasons (e.g. when parts of EPS belong to different owners) or for more effective application of some SE methods (e.g. use of high-precision measuring devices for SE). And if decomposition in terms of voltage level or ownership relations causes no particular difficulties, EPS decomposition by the criterion of minimum connectivity is a problem of combinatorial optimization that can be solved by experts, based on the complete enumeration of decomposition variants or heuristic methods.

1.1.2 Application of Genetic Algorithm

Hereafter the application of Genetic Algorithm and then Simulated Annealing Method for different aspects of the SE problem is suggested.

1.1.2.1 Genetic Algorithm for Bad Data Detection

In order to increase reliability of identification of measurement errors it was decided to use GAs (Zaika R.A, 2003) that allow a fuller use of the information provided by the method of TEs.

If condition (5) is met, all measurements in the i-th test equation are considered valid. Otherwise, logic rules are used to detect bad data. They are based on the exclusion of "suspicious" measurements from the system of test equations and the check of condition (5) for newly obtained equations. Calculation of large-dimension schemes noticeably complicates the logic of such a program, it requires enumeration of a large number of variants

of correct and erroneous measurements and often leads to ambiguous solutions and emergence of groups of doubtful data. Besides, when condition (5) is checked there can be errors of kind I and II, i.e. erroneous measurements are overlooked and appear in the state estimation problem or valid measurements are rejected.

Application of GAs made it possible to considerably expand the volume of initial information to be used to make a decision on validity of measurements. In the analysis we use linear combinations of TEs whose number is several times higher than the number of initial TEs. Choice of the equations that are the most sensitive to errors in measurements and neglect of equations in which errors of the first and second kinds are most probable when checking condition (5) make the validation process statistically more substantiated, which increases considerably the quality of bad data detection. The problem of validation is represented as a problem of combinatorial optimization which is solved by GA. Utility of individuals is a close analogue of the maximum likelihood criterion.

A priori preparation of data for SE on the basis of numerical methods implies not only detection of bad data but their replacement by those recalculated from other equations. Based on the experience of solving the problems described in (Zaika, 2003; Kolosok & Zaika, 2003), in (Zaika, 2008) the idea was suggested to prepare data for SE on the basis of calculated corrections of TEs. The corrections are calculated on the basis of TEs and their linear combinations for all measurements on the assumption that discrepancies of equations are only a consequence of bad data in this measurement. Since the amount of information is sufficiently large for statistical analysis we apply different filters for each measurement and thus find 1-2 most probable calculated corrections which correspond to the values of the most probable errors. Then, GA is used to solve the problem of combinatorial optimization. While solving this problem by some rules we find possible variants of measurement snapshot correction that meet the chosen criteria. The procedure is very similar to the process of basis enumeration from (Gamm, Kolosok & Zaika, 2005), however, the volume of computations is considerably smaller. The calculations show that for the snapshots consisting of 25-30 measurements the problem can be solved by complete enumeration in an acceptable time. For large schemes the application of GAs becomes obligatory. The minimum of weighted squares of TE discrepancies and measurement deviations, the maximum likelihood of measurements, and a limiting value of the maximum TE discrepancy can be used as the criterion for estimation of the best variants of correcting the measurement snapshot.

In order to encode solution in genetic algorithm each individual of the population is represented by a string of bits (0 and 1). Its length is equal to the number of measurements to be processed. While calculating fitness of an individual we use only those test equations whose non-zero coefficients correspond to "1" in the individuals. If all these test equations have a small discrepancy, fitness equals the number of such equations. If at least one of the test equations entering in this individual has a discrepancy exceeding a threshold value, this individual is assigned the minimum fitness. In the final solution zeros correspond to errone-ous measurements and unities – to correct ones. In order to process a large amount of information the identification is based on linear combinations of test equations (Figure 1).

The genetic algorithm employs a simple one-point crossover and elitist strategy, the probability of mutation in individual is 80%, in each gene of such an individual – 5%. The size of population is proportional to the number of the processed measurements. The calculation finishes if the best individual includes all test equations with small discrepancy or if the best individual does not change during a certain number of generations.

The calculations made on the basis of data on the official IEEE test scheme show that the identification of bad data in measurements on the basis of genetic algorithm is more reliable than on the basis of logic rules. However, when processing the scheme that contains more than 100 measurements the calculation takes an unacceptably long time since the time nonlinearly depends on the number of measurements. This problem can be solved by dividing the system of test equations into subsystems of smaller size. However, in most cases it is impossible to divide the system of test equations into two independent subsystems. The problem of minimizing the number of measure-

Figure 1. Coding individuals and calculation of fitness of each test equation

		1	2	3	4	5	6	7	8	9		
I		1	1	1	1	1	0	1	1	1	**Individuals**	
II		1	1	0	0	1	1	1	1	1		
III		1	1	1	0	1	1	1	1	1		
Measurements >		1	2	3	4	5	6	7	8	9		
Test Equations	**1**	1			1			1			>lim	Discrepancies of TE
	2		1		1				1	1	OK	
	3		1	1					1		OK	
	4				1		1			1	>lim	
	5	1							1		OK	
Individuals	**I**	TE with large discrepancy - 1									Fitness =	
		TE with small discrepancy — 2,3,5									1 (min)	
	II	TE with large discrepancy — no									Fitness = 2	
		TE with small discrepancy — 2,5										
	III	TE with large discrepancy — no									Fitness = 3	
		TE with small discrepancy 2,3,5										

ments that belong to both final subsystems arises. The minimization can also be done with genetic algorithm.

An individual encodes the set of test equations that enter into one or another subsystem, while the fitness function is the number of measurements that belong to both final subsystems. The lower the number, the higher the fitness of the individual. A constraint is imposed on the individuals. The constraint implies that the individuals cannot include more than 70 percent and less than 30 percent of measurements. Thus, the system of test equations is divided into two almost equal parts. The calculation stops when the certain number of iterations is exceeded or the fitness function of the obtained solution is acceptable.

If necessary, division of subsystems can be continued. Then for each obtained subsystem linear combinations are generated and the procedure of bad data identification is performed.

Table 1 shows that division of the system of test equations into 4 subsystems allows the calculation time to be decreased by an order of magnitude. Moreover, the parallel processing of the subsystems will reduce identification time even more. The calculations made have also shown inefficiency of dividing the system of test equations into too small parts.

The calculations were based on data of the IEEE 30- and 14-node test scheme for different redundancy of measurements. After steady state calculation, the normal noise from σ to 3σ, and then the gross errors from 15σ to 35σ were added to its parameters. The number of these errors was 10–25%. The calculations were performed only for active power measurements and their results are presented in Figure 2.

The data of diagram show the number of diverse identification errors that were made by using the "logic rules" and the genetic algorithm while processing the same volume of information. The number of identification errors was calculated independently of their distribution for different sets of "bad data" or other conditions. These data allow one to determine the volume of faulty information that came into the state estimation problem after initial data processing by the "logic rules" and the genetic algorithm for different scheme division variants.

The data show that gross errors are overlooked in the state estimation problem by 30–45% more seldom for the genetic algorithm than the "logic rules". The amount of false identification of true measurements is 10–70% lower. The percentage of measurement snapshots in which all errors are found correctly increases. The number of doubtful measurements is larger for the genetic algorithm at decomposition, however for the state estimation problem improvement of solution reliability is a more important factor.

When solving the problems of identification and decomposition the idea arose to apply the genetic algorithm for calculation of the estimates of state variables. In this case an individual encodes deviation of the measurement estimate from the value coming from remote control devices. For true measurements the maximum deviation is set equal to 2σ, for bad and doubtful measurements it is 45σ. Each measurement is consistent with the chromosome consisting of 6 genes (bits). This fact makes it possible to divide the deviation region into 62 parts (±31). Thus, the unit step of change for erroneous measurements equals 1.5σ, and for true measurements -0.06σ. The sum of reduced discrepancies in the test equations is applied as a fitness function. After the solution close to the optimal one is found, the maximum deviation for bad measurements is decreased to obtain more accurate estimates. Preliminary results show that the calculated estimates are close to the results obtained on the basis of the state estimation methods applied in the software "Otsenka" and flexibility and easy adjustment of the genetic algorithm make this program useful to study different aspects of the state estimation problem.

1.1.2.2 Genetic Algorithm for Robust Methods

The technique for GA application to enumerate the basis variants by the robust SE is suggested in (Gamm, Kolosok & Zaika, 2005). The main feature of GA applied to enumerate the bases is that the number of possible measurements is different for each basic variable. Individuals are coded by means of the unlimited integer alphabet. Its elements are numbers of measurements that are possible for each basic variable. Here different estimation criteria are used: smallest median, maximum likelihood, best conditionality, sum of weighted least squares. Application of algorithms for enumeration of the basis variants for SE by the TE method appreciably enhances accuracy of the estimates obtained. The best result is achieved here by the criterion of maximum likelihood of measurement residuals. Besides, in the TE method there is no need to recalculate estimation residuals with basis change. Therefore, the procedure for enumeration of basis variants does not require large volumes of calculations and can be performed with the help of GAs.

Table 1. Total time of measurement identification, s

Scheme	Complete system of test equations	System division into 2 parts	System division into 4 parts
IEEE-14 nodes (54 measurements)	20	6	3
IEEE-30 nodes (71 measurements)	30	10	5
CDO-150 nodes (234 measurements)	1900	620	130

Thus, the GAs are highly effective for the robust SE. They enable the correct result to be obtained in cases when the numerical methods do not work correctly. The reason for their high efficiency is an appropriate SE problem statement that allows the application of heuristic solution methods, on the one hand, and includes precise criteria for determination of the best solution at small volumes of calculations, on the other hand.

Figure 2. Results of measurement identification for the IEEE 30-node scheme

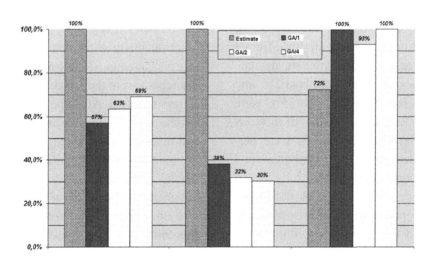

1.1.2.3 Genetic Algorithm for SE Problem Decomposition

In (Kolosok & Patsev, 2008) the EPS scheme is decomposed to determine the responsibility zones of calculated agents and places for the most efficient allocation of measuring devices. In (Zaika, 2003; Kolosok & Zaika, 2003) coefficient matrix of TEs is decomposed to accelerate the methods for bad data detection and SE. While in the first problem an expert can be involved to analyze the decomposition variants, in the problems described in (Zaika, 2003; Kolosok & Zaika, 2003) decomposition is part of internal calculations.

The procedure of decomposing the EPS scheme and coefficient matrix of TEs is described in detail in (Kolosok & Zaika, 2003). The classical GA with binary coding of individuals is applied. Unity refers the node (equation) to one subsystem, and zero – to the other. Utility is determined as an inverse value to the number of ties between subsystems and the number of measurements entering into both subsystems. Also the constraint on the size of subsystems is imposed: it is desirable that they be almost identical.

The problems of decomposition represent a class of combinatorial optimization problems in which application of GA has already become traditional.

1.2 PMU Placement for EPS State Estimation

The updating of software for EPS monitoring and control (SCADA/EMS-applications) has become possible on a qualitatively new level owing to WAMS (Wide-Area Measurement System), that allows the EPS state to be controlled synchronously and with high accuracy. The phasor measurement units (PMUs) are the main measurement equipment of these systems.

One of the applications, which will be significantly affected by the introduction of PMU, is state estimation (SE).

As compared to a standard set of measurements received from SCADA, PMU installed at the bus can measure voltage phasor at this bus and current phasors in some or all branches adjacent to this bus depending on capacity of communication channels.

To solve the state estimation problems, the universal methods are necessary to place PMU and metering devices to provide the best properties of the state estimation problem, such as observability of the considered network, identifiability of bad data and accuracy of obtained estimates (Gamm & Kolosok, 2002) These methods should be based on the observability theory that was devised to place SCADA systems (Gamm & Golub, 1990) and take into account the block character of PMU measurements. In our opinion the most effective are topological approaches based on different strategies of random search (Milosevic & Begovic, 2003; Ki-Seon Cho et al., 2001).

1.2.1 PMU Placement Criteria

A.   Improvement of Bad Data Detection

SE methods give a correct solution provided there are no bad data in the measurements and network topology, so bad data detection is a most important problem of SE. There should be quite high redundancy of measurements to reliably detect bad data and to obtain the state variables that properly reflect the EPS state.

When estimating the EPS state with a low redundancy of measurements the problem arises of validating the critical measurements (CM) and critical sets (CS). In the works on observability (Gamm & Golub, 1990; Clements et al., 1983) the non-redundant measurements whose absence leads to a loss of the considered network observability were called critical. CS are the groups of measurements in a drop-out of any measurement makes critical all the remaining measurements in the set.

Bad data in critical measurements and sets cannot be detected by the conventional methods of bad data analysis (Gamm & Kolosok, 2000; Do Couto Filho et al., 1990), and lead to distortion of the calculated operating conditions. Therefore, the reliable data acquisition systems should not contain critical measurements and critical sets.

Critical measurements can be determined when analyzing the observability of the network (Clements et al., 1983) by the diagonal elements of the sensitivity matrix, on the basis of the analysis of normalized residuals of estimation, a covariance matrix of residuals (Do Couto Filho et al., 2001)

CM and CS can be easily determined by analyzing the structure of test equation system (Gamm et al., 2005). Critical measurements are not redundant and, therefore, do not enter into the system of test equations. Thus, all the measurements not entering into the test equations are *critical measurements*. Critical sets are determined quite simply when analyzing TE obtained for a given set of measurements. Each set of such kind is formed on the basis of measurements that enter into one TE only and do not enter into any other TE. These are not necessarily all the measurements that form one TE. Part of them can belong to other test equations and, hence, do not belong to the set.

Let SCADA measurements provide observability of the network but there exist critical measurements and critical sets, i.e. the redundancy of measurements is quite low. To increase the redundancy of measurements and eliminate critical measurements and critical sets we will add PMU to the buses in the network and use GA for this purpose.

B.   Maximum Accuracy of Estimates

Irrespective of the statement and method of solving the state estimation problem the accuracy of the obtained estimates is determined by covariance matrices of erroneous estimates of the state vector $\widehat{\delta}, \widehat{U}$:

$$P_\delta = \left[\left(\frac{\partial y}{\partial \delta} \right)^T R_y^{-1} \frac{\partial y}{\partial \delta} \right]^{-1} ; \qquad (7)$$

$$P_u = \left[\left(\frac{\partial y}{\partial U} \right)^T R_y^{-1} \frac{\partial y}{\partial U} \right]^{-1} . \qquad (8)$$

When adding the measurements of magnitudes and phases of bus voltages obtained from PMU, the expressions (7, 8) are transformed into the form:

$$P_\delta = \left[\left(\frac{\partial y}{\partial \delta} \right)^T R_y^{-1} \frac{\partial y}{\partial \delta} + R_\delta^{-1} \right]^{-1} ; \qquad (9)$$

$$P_u = \left[\left(\frac{\partial y}{\partial U} \right)^T R_y^{-1} \frac{\partial y}{\partial U} + R_u^{-1} \right]^{-1} . \qquad (10)$$

Criterion

$$max \ \det\left[P_\delta, \ P_u \right], \qquad (11)$$

where P_δ, P_U are determined by (9), (10), can be used as a criterion for choosing the set of PMU placement from the viewpoint of maximum accuracy of estimates.

Diagonal matrices R_δ^{-1} and R_u^{-1} in (9), (10) make it possible:

- To essentially decrease the effect of "smearing" the errors of measured variables Δy;

- To choose a set and placement of measurements δ and U in the electric network by criterion (11);

- To provide EPS observability (nonzero values of criterion (11)) with the network topology changes due to switching;

- To maintain EPS observability when some measurements of phases are eliminated during conventional measurements of flows and injections.

- To determine what PMU is more efficient at a given stage, at a low number of PMU.

C. Transformation of the Network Graph into Tree

Placement of PMU at bus *i* allows to obtain highly accurate values of voltage magnitude and phase at this bus, that are measured with high accuracy (the accuracy of voltage magnitude measurement is of order of 0.1%, phase – 0.02). As compared to the normal SCADA measurements these measurements can be considered to be absolutely accurate and, after recording, these variables can be eliminated from the state vector and the columns corresponding to them - from the matrix H. This elimination is equivalent to the elimination of buses with PMU from the considered network.

It is known that the elimination of the buses from the considered networks leads to emergence of new ties and elimination of variables – to emergence of new non-zero elements in matrix H. In (Gamm, 1970) the author suggests the algorithm of eliminating the buses which enables one to transform the complex closed network into a tree, i.e. into the network that does not have loops.

The state estimation of such networks has some advantages: 1) the tree representation has smaller dimensionality; 2) no non-zero elements emerge when eliminating variables at triangular decomposition of matrix *H; 3)* in some cases vector *x* is calculated without iterations. All these factors reduce essentially the time of solving the SE problem.

Therefore, when solving the SE problem with the help of the algorithm (Gamm, 1970) it is expedient to place PMU at the buses whose elimination will bring the remaining part of the network to the tree representation.

D. The Maximum Number of Measurements to be Added

PMU installed at the bus can measure voltage phasor at this bus and current phasors in the branches adjacent to this bus.

The higher the connectivity of a bus and the lesser the number of SCADA measurements the bus has the larger number of additional measurements can be obtained by placing PMU at this bus.

Let us define the shortage of measurements at bus i:

$$\Delta_{meas_i} = K_{PMU_i} - K_{SCADA_i} \qquad (12)$$

as the number of measurements at bus i to be received with PMU placement at this bus minus the sum of measurements at bus i that were received from SCADA.

Any variant j of PMU placement in the network consists of k PMUs, therefore the total j-th shortage of measurements shows how many new measurements in total the network will receive depending on a specific variant of PMU placement:

$$\eta_{def_j} = \sum_{i=1}^{k} \Delta_{Meas_i} \qquad (13)$$

This criterion allows considering a block nature of PMU measurements.

1.2.2 Genetic Algorithm for PMU Placement

In (Goser et al., 2001) the method based on genetic algorithm was proposed to place metering devices in the network. Let us consider this method as applied to the problem of joint placement of SCADA and PMU. Let SCADA measurements provide observability of the network but there exist critical measurements and critical sets, i.e. the redundancy of measurements is quite low. To increase the redundancy of measurements and eliminate critical measurements and critical sets we will add PMU to the buses in the network and use GA for this purpose.

Each variant of PMU placement is set by a bit string with a length equal to the number of buses in the network. In every string 1 means presence, and 0 - absence of PMU at a bus.

The GA fitness function is determined as:

$$Fit = \frac{\eta_{def}}{\eta_{mc} + \eta_{cc} + \sum_{i=1}^{k} c_i \eta_{PMU_i} + const}, \quad (14)$$

where η_{mc} – the number of critical measurements; η_{cc}, the number of critical sets; η_{PMUi}, the number of PMUs; c_i, the installation cost of the PMU at bus I, and η_{def_j}, shortage of measurements at the j-th variant of PMU placement.

The solution is considered to be optimal if it meets the criterion *max Fit*

Before starting the genetic algorithm the shortage of measurements for each bus (η_{def}) is calculated. The other constituents of the fitness function Fit $(\eta_{PMU}, \eta_{mc}, \eta_{cc})$ are determined in the course of the GA operation.

The initial population is made up at random from the bit strings that correspond to the PMU placement variants. Fitness function (14) is calculated for each string. The full set of fitness function of all strings (individuals) is arranged in a descending order. The best individuals take part in creation of a new generation. The process of creating new generations and obtaining fitness function repeats until the optimal results in the sense of criteria *max Fit* are obtained.

In order to avoid degeneracy of solution the offspring undergo mutation. The PMU placement variants (individuals) at which the numbers of critical sets and critical measurements turn out to be zero are considered to be preferable and are transferred to the next generation without changes (elitism strategy).

It is obvious that Fit $->$ max at

$$\frac{\eta_{def} -> \max}{(\eta_{mc} + \eta_{cc} + \eta_{PMU} + 1) -> \min}.$$

Figure 3 shows a fragment of a real network in one of the regional power systems of Russia (29 SCADA measurements of active model). There are no critical measurements but there are 2 critical sets: $\{P_{13-10}, P_{10-13}\}; \{P_{12-13}, P_{12}\}$.

Table 2 presents the values of η_{def_j} (12) for the 13-bus network buses.

Figure 3. A fragment of a real network in one of the regional power systems of Russia

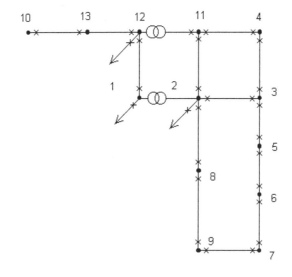

Table 2. Values for the 13-bus network buses

N°bus	1	2	3	4	5	6	7	8	9	10	11	12	13
η_{def_j}	1	1	1	1	1	1	1	1	1	1	1	1	2

According to the criterion only of tree representation PMU should be placed at buses 2. Criteria 13 and 14 PMUs should be installed at bus 13. Criterion of tree representation PMU should be placed at buses 2 and 13.

1.2.3 Several Remarks

The efficiency of the SE procedure was essentially improved by adding the PMU measurements to the conventional measurements. Choice of sites for PMU placement is of great importance when solving the SE problem. To solve it the use of GA which allows different criteria of PMU placement to be combined:

- Absence of critical measurements and critical sets in the system,
- Maximum quantity of measurements received as compared to the initial one,
- Maximum accuracy of estimates,
- Minimum cost of PMU placement,
- Transformation of the network graph into tree.

The results obtained are indicative of the fact that the optimal placement of PMU increases the accuracy of the obtained estimates and efficiency of the bad data detection algorithms.

2. SIMULATED ANNEALING METHOD (SA)

2.1 PMU Placement on the Basis of SCADA Measurements for Fast Load Flow Calculation in Electric Power Systems

The problem of steady state (SS) calculation (load flow) that is one of the first problems arisen in creation of Computer-Aided Systems of Dispatching Control plays a leading role in the complex of control problems of EPS operation and expansion and also forms a base which allows the solution of other, more sophisticated problems such as optimization of normal state of EPS, stability analysis, reliability estimation, etc.

Despite a great variety of numerous methods for load flow calculation (Stott, 1974; Krumm, 1977; Gornstein, 1981; Ayuev, 2008) the SS calculations have problems in convergence and provision of the required high-speed of algorithms. In the early 1970s development and perfection of the tools for collection, processing and transmission of measurements in EPS to calculate SS gave rise to application of the SE methods. The SE problem also consists in calculation of the voltage phasors at the buses, but on the basis of measured values of different state parameters rather than only parameters of the powers at the buses. The SE methods make it possible to construct a more accurate model of the current EPS state. However, in the case of large volume of information that is often substantially inhomogeneous due to great distinctions in measurement accuracy, they do not solve the problems of convergence and high speed of the computational algorithms, and besides aggravate them in some cases (Monticelly, 2000).

A possible way to solve these problems is to devise non-iterative or direct methods for solving the problem of SS calculation in general and the problem of SE in particular. The main idea of these methods is to apply the graph theory for reduction of the calculated scheme to the form convenient for successive calculation of the state vector components by the known SS equations and available measurement information. In this case only minimum necessary measurements are used for calculation, but not all available ones as in the traditional SE methods. Similar methods are widely applied to calculate SS and SE of distribution networks with the radial configuration (Deng, 1992; Das et al., 1995).

Here an algorithm of fast SS calculation based on the measurements of the SCADA system is presented. It applies the procedure of reducing the EPS calculated scheme to a tree and the accurate synchronized measurements of voltage magnitudes and phases at the buses that are received from the PMUs.

Measurement of these values by PMU is the most attractive way of determining all the state vector components. In practice, however, PMU placement at each bus is impossible, so the authors suggest the procedure of determining all the state vector components by the minimum possible number of PMUs with application of the SCADA

measurements and the known relations between the state variables in power systems. For example, for the available measurements shown in Figure 4 the voltage magnitudes and phases are determined in the following order. At bus j the values of δ, U are calculated through the PMU data that is installed at bus i. At bus k the values of δ, U are calculated on the basis of measurements of $\left(P_{j-k}, Q_{j-k}\right)$. To do this requires calculation of power losses and then determination of the sought values of δ_k, U_k.

2.1.1 Reduction of the Scheme to a Tree

The main idea of the algorithm for reduction of the scheme graph to a tree (Gamm, 1970) is to verify whether the scheme contains loops and if any, break them. To do this the loops are searched for on the scheme graph and the buses with the maximum number of lines are searched for in them. Such buses (see Node 3 at Figure 5 (a)) are removed from the scheme and as a result the loops are broken and the scheme is reduced to a tree and several terminal buses appear (see Nodes 2, 12, 4, 9 at Figure 5 (b)).

2.1.2 Search for the Optimal Reference Bus

The work of the algorithm for EPS scheme graph reduction to a tree may result in construction of several trees. In each tree it is necessary to find

Figure 4. Transmission line with measurements from SCADA and PMU

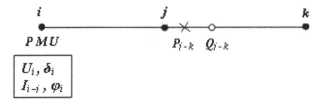

Figure 5. Fragment of real scheme: (a), start of the algorithm for scheme graph reduction to a tree; (b), continuation of the algorithm work after removal of the bus with maximum connectivity

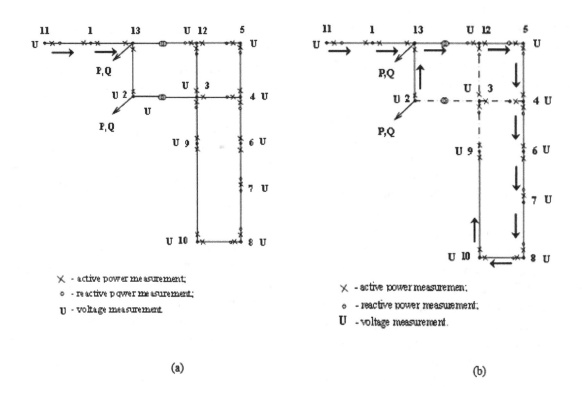

(a)   (b)

the tree vertex (the optimal reference bus) for starting calculation of the state variables. The optimal reference bus is the bus, starting from which all δ, U can be calculated with the least computer time and the minimum number of required PMUs.

Possibility of calculating δ, U at each bus is verified by transition from bus to bus along all the tree branches, provided the unknown δ, U can be calculated in addition by using different combinations of the measured and computed state variables. If δ, U cannot be determined, PMU is installed at the bus.

There are several variants for moving along the tree. Depending on location of the reference bus in the scheme the process of determining the unknown δ, U will be more successful or less successful. The successful process implies that a combination of the maximum number of measure-ments applied in calculations, the minimum number of pseudo-measurements and the mini-mum number of PMUs to be installed in the case of impossibility to determine δ, U at the consid-ered bus by using the SCADA measurements and pseudo-measurements.

2.1.3 Approaches to PMU Placement

PMU placement in the power system network is a combinatorial problem on placement of K trans-ducers at N network buses on the basis of place-ment criteria to be chosen. The problem can be solved by the complete enumeration of placement variants with the constraints, for example, not to install PMU at the terminal bus. For large-scale networks the complete enumeration requires much computer time. The logic of reasoning about the lacking need to check absolutely all the variants of

PMU placement allows elimination of the variants containing terminal buses, all the combinations of two neighboring buses, etc. from consideration and application of various heuristic approaches.

2.1.4 Getting Solution with Simulated Annealing (SA) Method

The path revealing the optimal reference bus is searched for by the simulated annealing method. The initial information is preliminarily processed to reduce the time of solving the problem. Based on the mix of measurements in the scheme the lacking pseudo-measurements for voltages, injections and power flows are calculated in addition by using the bichromatic graph (The bichromatic graph sets up a correspondence between the steady state equations and SCADA measurements in the scheme graph to calculate pseudo-measurements of state variables) (Gamm et al., 1983). A generalized list of measurements is formed based on the measurements and calculated pseudo-measurements.

The annealing method determines an optimal solution by searching for only in the direction of the objective function decrease and by avoiding the local optima on the basis of the probability of taking an incorrect decision. The objective function of the SA method (so called "energy" E) in our problem has the form:

$$\min E = \frac{K1_{PMU} + K2_{step} + K3_{double}}{K4_{success}} \qquad (15)$$

where $K1_{PMU}$, number of additionally installed PMUs; $K2_{step}$, maximum number of steps from the reference to the final bus resulting in calculation of δ, U; $K3_{double}$, number of doubling counts due to the fact that δ, U at the current bus can be calculated with the help of different measurements, and $K4_{success}$, index of successful measurements of voltage magnitudes and phases by spreading along the graph.

In turn,

$$K4_{success} = n_1\alpha_1 + n_2\alpha_2 + n_3\alpha_3 + n_4\alpha_4 + \dots,$$

with $\alpha_1 > \alpha_2 > \alpha_3 > \alpha_4 > \dots$, where α_i (are set by the researcher) represent scores for application of n_1 accurate measurements from PMU, n_2 measurements from SCADA, n_3 pseudo-measurements, n_4 pseudo-measurements obtained from the formulas containing pseudo-measurements squared.

Solution to the problem starts with the choice of an arbitrary bus considered as a reference one, assignment of PMU at it with the accurate measurements of $\delta_{PMU}, U_{PMU}, I_{ij_{PMU}}, I_{ij_{PMU}}$ and motion from it along the tree branches (count of $K4_{success}$). In this case the longer the path from the reference to the terminal bus, the greater the error accumulated during intermediate calculations. It means the necessity to choose the reference bus so that it was located approximately at an equal distance from the final buses (count of $K2_{step}$). Hence, it is more preferable to start choosing a reference bus from the more connected buses.

If the result E_{new} obtained by using (15) after the next iteration is lower than the accepted earlier optimal result $\left(E_{new} < E_{opt}\right)$, a new variant of assignment is taken $E_{opt} = E_{new}$. Otherwise, the return to the previous step or not depends on the probability value $P(\Delta E)$ of taking an incorrect decision

$$P(\Delta E) = e^{-\Delta E/(k_b T)} \qquad , \qquad (16)$$

where $\frac{\Delta E}{k_b T}$ -the Metropolis criterion that is an analog to the Boltzmann factor (Zmitrovich, 1997).

Then one of the neighboring buses is assigned as a candidate to be accepted as a reference bus. The voltage magnitudes and phases are recalculated. Thus, different buses are successively treated as candidates and the objective function value is calculated. The next more successful result is stored.

Provided on the path there is the bus, at which calculation of δ, U is impossible because of lacking measurements in the transmission lines incident to it, an additional PMU is installed there (count of $K1_{PMU}$). Then PMU with highly accurate values of δ, U, and currents in all connected lines is installed at the bus. Hence it is possible to recalculate δ, U at the ends of these lines. And if such measurements have already been obtained earlier, they are taken as doubling ones (count of $K3_{double}$).

The annealing process is controlled by the temperature T that gradually decreases to zero. The lower the T, the less probable is an incorrect decision (16). As the result the optimal solution is obtained at T that is very close to zero.

The criterion for completion of work is $\min E$.

The example of the 13-bus scheme (see Figure 6) illustrates the possibility for obtaining all the state vector components on the basis of measure-

ments from the SCADA system and the data of one PMU. Calculations were performed on the simulated and real data.

The network scheme is reduced to a tree by removal of bus 3 as the most connected one from the graph. The branches that are not included in the tree are shown by dashed lines. The use of the simulated annealing algorithm reveals that bus 13 is the optimal reference bus where PMU is installed. Additional PMUs are not required. The tree obtained has three branches.

The voltage vectors at all the buses are calculated starting with bus 13.

Point 1: A PMU is installed at bus 13. The voltage magnitudes and phases are calculated for neighboring buses 1, 2, 12 by means of PMU data by the following formulas.

$$U_j = U_i - I_{ij}(R \ \cos\phi_{ij} + X \ \sin\phi_{ij}) \qquad (17)$$

$$\delta_j = \delta_i - arctg \frac{I_{ij}(X\cos\phi - R\sin\phi)}{U_i - R\cos\phi - X\sin\phi} \qquad (18)$$

Figure 6. PMU placement: ■ *-nodes with PMU;* ▲ *-nodes with «calculated» PMU*

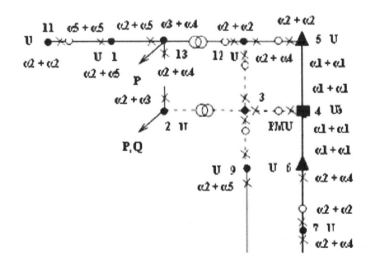

Voltage magnitudes and phases of other buses are calculated by the following measurements from the SCADA system:

Point 2: At buses 4, 6, 10 by the active and reactive power flows at the line beginning:

$$U_j = \sqrt{(U_i - \frac{P_{i-j}*R + Q_{i-j}*X}{U})^2 + (\frac{P_{i-j}*X - Q_{i-j}*R}{U})^2}$$ (19)

$$\delta_j = \delta_i - \delta_{i-j};$$

$$\delta_j = \delta_i - arctg\frac{P_{i-j}*X - Q_{i-j}*R}{U_i^2 - P_{i-j}*R - Q_{i-j}*X}$$ (20)

Point 3: At buses 11, 5, 7, 8 by the active and reactive power flows at the line end and voltage:

○ Calculation of reactive power flow at the line beginning

$$Q_{i-j} = Q_{j-i} + \frac{P_{j-i}^2 + Q_{j-i}^2}{U_j^2}*X - BU_j^2$$ (21)

○ Calculation of U_j, δ_j by Formulas (19) and (20).

Point 4: At bus 9 by all available measurements:

from $$\Delta P = P_{10-9} - P_{9-10} = \frac{P_{10-9}^2 + Q_{10-9}^2}{U_{10}^2}*R$$ (22)

the reactive power flow module is calculated at the line beginning Q_{10-9};

• Calculation of U_j by Formula (19) at different values of reactive power flows $(Q_{10-9}, -Q_{10-9})$. The choice is made of the flow, at which the obtained value of voltage magnitude corresponds to the measured one.

• Calculation of δ_j by Formula (20) at the chosen value of reactive power flow.

The components of objective function (15) for the considered scheme are calculated in the following way (see Table 3):

$K1_{PMU} = 0$, since there in no need in additional PMUs and hence, $K3_{double} = 0$. $K2_{step}$ is increased by 1 at each step from bus to bus.

Table 3. Calculation of the objective function by branch of the tree

N°	Branches	$K1_{PMU\_additional}$	$K2_{step\_max}$	$K3_{doubl}$	$K4_{success}$
1	4-5-12-13-1-11	0	5	0	$4\alpha_1 + 9\alpha_2 + 1\alpha_3 + 2\alpha_4 + 4\alpha_5$
2	4-5-12-13-2	0	4	0	$4\alpha_1 + 7\alpha_2 + 2\alpha_3 + 3\alpha_4$
3	4-6-7-8-10-9	0	5	0	$4\alpha_1 + 11\alpha_2 + 3\alpha_4 + 2\alpha_5$
					$\sum = 12\alpha_1 + 27\alpha_2 + 3\alpha_3 + 8\alpha_4 + 6\alpha_5$

Figure 7. (a). A 13-bus scheme; (b) A 5-bus scheme

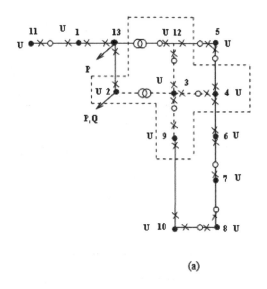

(a)

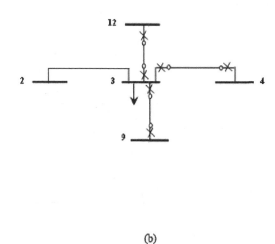

(b)

For components $K4_{success}$ the following points of calculations are applied:

n_1 - P.1 (3)-(4), n_2 - P.2 (5)-(6), n_3 - P.3 (7), n_4 -P.4 (8).

where
$\alpha_1 = 10; \alpha_2 = 5; \alpha_3 = 0.3; \alpha_4 = 0.2; \alpha_5 = 0.1$
   Finally,

$$E_{opt} = \frac{1 * C_4 + 5 + 0}{12\alpha_1 + 27\alpha_2 + 3\alpha_3 + 8\alpha_4 + 6\alpha_5}$$

$$= \frac{6}{120 + 135 + 0.9 + 1.6 + 0.6} = 0.0232$$

where C_4 is the cost of PMU (equal to 1) at the bus 4.

   Results of SA is shown in Figure 6.

   The voltage at the remote bus (see Figure 5 (b)). is calculated by separation of the 5-bus scheme from the scheme shown in Figure 7 (a).

   For the obtained scheme SE is performed by the available measurements. Voltages calculated by Formulas (17), (18), (19), (20), (21), and (22)

are taken as initial data. If the difference between the obtained voltage values and the initial data at the boundary buses of the scheme is less than some threshold, the injections in buses are adjusted.

A.   Simulation Calculation

   The SS variables $(y_{c@})$ are noised by using the random number generator. The values of measurements are calculated by the

$$y_{noise} = y_{ss} + x_{ran} * \sqrt{\sigma^2}, \tag{23}$$

where σ^2, measurement variance, $x_{ran} \rightarrow N(0,1)$.
   The voltages in the tree branches are calculated by Formulas (19) and (20). For SE of the 5-bus scheme the modeled measurements are applied as initial data. Table 4 illustrates the calculation results.

   The second column presents voltage magnitudes in the steady state. The third column shows voltage values obtained due to noise. The fourth

Table 4. Calculation results based on simulated data

N° of bus	U_{ss}	U_{noise}	U_{calc}	U_{se}
1	2	3	4	5
2	753	752	756	
3	748	748	751	*751*
4	503	503	503	*505*
5	506	509	508	*508*
6	505	508	507	
7	500	501	502	
9	502	503	504	
10	507	505	509	
11	500	499	502	*502*
12	507	505	509	
326	743	742	745	
453	502	502	504	*504*
454	*740*	*743*	*743*	

Table 5. The values of criteria ϕ

Simulated data		Real data	
SE	Non-iterative method	SE	*Non-iterative method*
6.3	*7.1*	*20.35*	*22.70*

column presents voltage values calculated by the tree branches. The fifth column illustrates voltage values obtained as a result of SE of the 5-bus scheme. The Table shows that the voltage values are calculated by the tree branches differ negligibly from the voltages of steady state.

B.   Calculation Based on Real Data

The real verified measurements and the measurements from PMU installed at bus 13 are applied as initial data. Voltages of the second column presents values of measurements. The third column shows the SE results for the 13-bus scheme. This calculation was done to determine accuracy of the results obtained by applying the suggested technique. The fourth column gives voltage values calculated by the suggested algorithm.

The criteria of quality of SE results is determined by the objective function value:

$$\phi(x) = \sum_{i=1}^{m} \frac{\left(\overline{y_i} - y_i(\hat{x})\right)^2}{\sigma_i^2} \qquad (24)$$

where $\bar{y}$, vector of measurements, $\hat{x}$ -estimates (or calculated values by the tree branches) of the state vector components.

The values of the criteria for different calculations are presented in Table 5.

The Table 4 shows that the values of criteria are approximately the same for all the calculation methods. It means that the EPS state can be calculated by the non-iterative method almost with the same accuracy as the SE method.

2.1.5 Discussion

1. The algorithm for fast SS calculation that is constructed by reduction of the calculated EPS scheme to a tree is suggested. It applies a minimum number of PMUs and an optimal set of measurements obtained from the SCADA system.
2. The algorithm for PMU placement by the SA method is worked out. The algorithm determines an optimal reference bus in the tree scheme and an optimal set of measurements that makes it possible to calculate the state vector for all the scheme buses with the minimum accumulation of calculation errors.
3. SS is calculated for a fragment of the real system based on the simulated and real data. The state vector calculated by the suggested method is shown to coincide with the results of state estimation.
4. The speed of determining EPS state by different methods is analyzed for comparison. The problem of calculating EPS state variables for the 13-bus scheme by the non-iterative method proves to be solved 0.01 s faster than the state estimation problem.

3. ANT COLONY OPTIMIZATION

Distribution networks are normally operated according to radial schemes maintained by opening the loops. The problem of distribution network

reconfiguration aimed at determining the most rational loop opening points is as a rule solved by the criteria of minimum active power losses in the network, minimum undersupplied power and minimum time for power supply restoration (Carcamo et al., 2009). The review of reconfiguration methods that include classical methods of mathematical programming and modern heuristic methods based on artificial intelligence (genetic algorithms, simulated annealing, tabu search, ant colony methods, etc.) is given in (Tavakoli et al., 2006).

In the last decade much attention has been paid to distributed generation connected to distribution network (Jenkins et al., 2000; Ackerman, 2001). Presence of distributed generation makes it easier to maintain voltage levels at nodes of distribution network, decrease active and reactive power losses in the network, provide higher level of power supply reliability by maintaining power supply from distributed generation to some consumers in the case of emergency disconnection of the main supply point in the power supply system (islanding) (Jenkins et al., 2000; Funabashi et al., 2003; Song et al., 2006).

Thus the coordination problem arises in controlling normal conditions of distribution network with distributed generation through the network reconfiguration, to provide minimum power losses and to meet the required voltage and current change limits, as well as in controlling post-emergency conditions through islanding, to provide minimum power shortage due to the loss of supply substation of main power grid (main supply point). Such multicriteria problems can not always be reduced to a one-criterion statement by introducing weighted coefficients for individual criteria. A general approach to control coordination of normal and post-emergency conditions of distribution network including distributed generation is as follows.

Under normal conditions the control aims to reconfigure the distribution network by opening loops. Here the minimum active power losses in the network are considered as the criterion

$$\sum_{l \in L} R_{lk} I_{lk}^2 \rightarrow \min, k \in K, \qquad (25)$$

where K – a set of considered normal conditions according to the load curves of consumers and loading of distributed generation plants; L – the number of branches in the network; R_{lk}, I_{lk} active resistance and current in branch l for operation conditions k.

Under post-emergency conditions if the main supply point is lost the problem of islanding arises with the islands including distributed generation plants that operate for a balanced load. The criterion of islanding is the minimum power shortage in the post-emergency conditions

$$\left(\sum_{n \in N} P_{nk} - \sum_{n* \in N*} P_{n*j} \right) \rightarrow \min, k \in K, j \in J, \qquad (26)$$

where J, a set of considered post-emergency conditions with the main supply point lost; P_{nk} the load at node n in the network under normal condition k; P_{n*j}, the load at node n^* in the post-emergency condition j of the network part including N^* nodes, that belong to all islands; N – the number of network nodes.

In control coordination of normal and post-emergency conditions of distribution network an important problem is to check whether the constraints on voltage levels at nodes and currents in network branches are met both under normal and post-emergency conditions

$$V_{nk\,\min} \leq V_{nk} \leq V_{nk\,\max,} \qquad (27)$$

$$V_{nj\,\min} \leq V_{nj} \leq V_{nj\,\max,} \qquad (28)$$

$$I_{lk} \leq I_{lk\,\max,} \qquad (29)$$

$$I_{lj} \leq I_{lj\,\max,} \qquad (30)$$

Instead of (29), (30), the values of power transmitted by the network branches can be controlled using similar inequalities.

Constraints (27), (28), (29), and (30) in the optimization of criteria (25) and (26) are checked on the basis of radial network power flow calculations. The calculations employ backward/forward sweep algorithm with respect to distributed generation plants connected to distribution network (Song et al., 2006). In order to minimize the number of such calculations the interval implementation of backward/forward sweep algorithm (Voropai & Bat-Undral, 2008) is applied which allows the ranges of voltage and current values to be obtained for groups of conditions.

There are two specific features of the problem related to islanding and determining post-emergency conditions. The first one concerns the presence of constraints (28), (30), which means different requirements for voltage levels at nodes and maximum load of network branches in the post-emergency conditions as compared to the normal conditions. The second one related to islanding is implementation of the principle of maintaining power supply, first of all, to the most important consumers at the distribution network nodes.

One of the important control coordination problems of normal and post-emergency conditions of distribution networks is minimization of switchings while passing from normal to post-emergency conditions. This is important in terms of minimizing the number of switching devices, their possible failures and personnel's errors, and predetermines consideration of problem (25), (26), (27), (28), (29), and (30) as a complex two-criterion problem. Let us consider an expedient approach to its solution.

A widely used approach is the consideration for power supply reliability through the damages due to power undersupply which allows the multi-criteria problem to be reduced to a one-criterion one (Hsiao, 2004; Hong, 2005). To this end it is necessary to have reliable estimates of specific damages due to power supply interruption for different consumers. In reality these estimates can not be obtained for all types of consumers, particularly it concerns the consumers with production processes where power supply interruptions may pose a threat to the life of people or to the environment. Therefore in a general case criteria (25) and (26) should be considered as independent and irreducible to one complex criterion.

The idea of the ant colony algorithm is rather thoroughly presented in (Dorigo & Gambardella, 1996) and given in (Jeon et al., 2003; Carpaneto & Chicco, 2006; Olamaei et al., 2007; Yiqin Xu & Jia Tian, 2008; Fu Chang Chung, 2008). Unlike (Jeon et al., 2003) here load flow is calculated in each iteration of the ant colony algorithm by the backward/forward sweep method and constraints (27) and (29) are checked. In the event that the constraints are not met the branch considered as a candidate for disconnection is excluded from consideration. In the considered problem the method of successive concessions is somewhat modified with regard to the specificity of the problem. The

modification implies that the sought solution is the point (branch) of distribution network disconnection, common for criteria (25) and (26). Criterion (25) is taken to be the most important. The procedure of the modified method of successive concessions offers a successive search for the acceptable disconnection point in terms of acceptable concession according to the first criterion with the help of island adjustment. This modified procedure will be shown in the case study in Section III.

The studied network is a simplified network of the Central Power System of Mongolia (see Figure 8 (a)). The Gusinoozyersk thermal power plant (TPP) (node 1) that is included in the Unified Power System of Russia and supplies electricity to the Central Power System of Mongolia via the 220 kV transmission line (branch 1 and 2) is conditionally taken as the main supply point. In the Central Power System of Mongolia there are 4 operating thermal power plants of a comparatively small capacity that are conditionally considered to be distributed generation sources.

Figure 8. (a) Points of electric network tripping in the normal conditions (dashed lines) and composition of islands in the post-emergency conditions (encircled); (b) Optimal points of electric network tripping in the context of requirements of the normal and post-emergency conditions

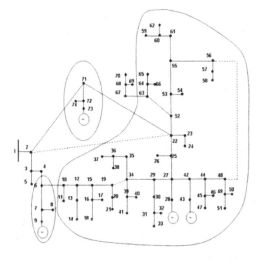 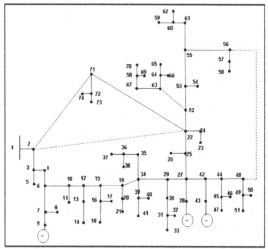

(a)   (b)

Network reconfiguration by using the criterion of minimum active power losses (25) on the basis of constraints (27), (29) allows the points of network loop disconnection to be revealed. These are branches 2-22, 19-34 and 48-56 shown in Figure 8 (a) by the dashed lines.

Then the post-emergency conditions in the Central Power System of Mongolia are studied for the case of power supply loss from the Gusinoozyersk TPP. Here the generators of the Central Power System of Mongolia cover part of the load and as a result three independent islands are formed by criterion (26). For all the islands constraints (28), (30) are met.

Comparison of the disconnection points in the normal and post-emergency conditions shows that the disconnection of branch 2-22 coincides in both cases. The disconnection of branch 48-56 is of no concern for the post-emergency conditions, since it does not influence island formation.

Consider branch 19-34. In the normal conditions this branch has to be tripped from the standpoint of minimum active power losses. Their value in this case is 14.34 MW. In the post-emergency conditions the other branch – 6 -10 is tripped. When the loop is open on this branch, in the normal conditions the power losses are 11% higher than the optimal ones. Such an increase in losses is not allowed.

Find an acceptable concession from the criterion of minimum active power losses (25) in the normal conditions by the island adjustment. Consider the variant of disconnection of branch 15-19 with the corresponding reduction of the island by excluding nodes 10, 11, 12, 13, 14, 16, 17, 18 from it. The disconnection of branch 15-19 causes an increase in losses in the normal conditions by somewhat less than 5% in comparison with the optimal value that is acceptable.

We try to expand the island by an additional concession on the basis of criterion (25). To do this, we open branch 12-15 instead of branch 15-19. In this case in the normal conditions the losses rise

by the value above 7% as compared to the optimal value, but such an increase is unacceptable.

Thus, in accordance with criteria (25) and (26) the opening of branches 2-22, 48-56 and 15-19 (see Figure 8, b) is a trade-off solution and here the concession value by criterion (25) is acceptable.

In electricity supply systems with distributed generation that is connected to the distribution electric network a complex problem of providing efficient operation of electricity supply systems in the normal conditions and reliable power supply to consumers in the post-emergency conditions at a loss of the main supply point arises. This multicriteria problem is solved here by applying the method of successive concessions. The efficiency of power system operation is studied based on the criterion of minimum active power losses by network reconfiguration that is performed by the ant colony method. In the post-emergency conditions the islanding problem is solved by using the cell formation method. The studies carried out for the Central Power System of Mongolia have shown the efficiency of the approach.

4. ARTIFICIAL NEURAL NETWORK (ANN)

4.1 ANN for Tuning the EPS State Estimation Parameters

Accurate information on state variables of electric power system (EPS) at any time instant and at any point is necessary to efficiently control the system. To filter the measurement errors and to calculate unmeasured state variables we employ a special mathematical procedure, state estimation. The SE results are used as initial information for all the online control problems. Therefore, the requirements to the quality of SE results are very high. The validity of estimation of the EPS state variables is determined by the so called vector of state X which consists of magnitudes and angles of voltage. If all voltage values are known for all nodes, it is possible to calculate all the remaining state variables.

There are two approaches to calculation of the state vector. The first approach supposes that the vector of state is a normal solution to an overdetermined system of nonlinear equations that contains all measured state variables. According to the second approach the vector of state is determined by the basic values of measurements. The basic values of measurements are a minimum set of measurements that provide EPS observability. Changing the basic set of measurements it is possible to obtain the best values of the vector of state in the sense of the criteria considered below. The choice of basic measurements was considered in (Mili et al., 1990). The quality of SE results depends largely on conditionality of the basic matrix derivatives (Holton, 1998). The matrix conditionality can be increased by equivalenting the branches with the admittances below some threshold.

Convergence of iteration process remains an important problem (Gamm, 1976). When calculating the system of equations in normalized units the rate of the iteration process convergence is higher.

State variables are converted to normalized units by the following formulae:

$$P_* = \frac{P}{S_b} \; ; \tag{31}$$

$$Q_* = \frac{Q}{S_b} \; ; \tag{32}$$

$$U_* = \frac{U}{U_b} ; \tag{33}$$

where S_b is a basic power; U_b is a basic voltage; P, Q, U are vectors of active and reactive injections, and voltage magnitude, respectively.

The algorithm for state estimation on the basis of test equations consists of 2 stages (Gamm & Kolosok, 2002).

At the first stage:

- Measured state variables are estimated;
- Basic measurements are selected;
- The basic measurements are used to determine the vector of state (U, δ).
- At the second stage:
- The obtained state vector is used to calculate all state variables (measured and unmeasured).
- The optimality of vector of state, and, as a result, the quality of SE results depends largely on how accurately the tuning parameters (constants) are selected. Each constant may take several defined values. Any of these values may turn out to be the most fitting for state estimation of one or another system.

The best results of SE, all other things being equal, (the same scheme, the same set, the same SE algorithm) can be obtained by selecting tuning parameters. By the best SE results we understand the results that satisfy the following three criteria.

Criterion 1:
- At the divergence of iteration process the tuning parameters corresponding to it are rejected. Mathematically this criterion looks as follows:

$$\|\Delta V\| < \xi, \tag{34}$$

where $\|\Delta V\|$ is the norm of deviations of estimates in the next iterations, ξ is some threshold.

Criterion 2:
- Minimum deviation of estimates obtained at first and second stages proves the correct choice of measurements to be used for calculation of the state vector. The total deviation of estimates is calculated by the formula:

$$M_{\Delta V} = \frac{\sum |(V_1 - V_2)|}{V_b}, \qquad (35)$$

where V_1 is a vector of estimates of measured parameters calculated at the first stage of SE,

V_2 is a vector of estimates of measured parameters calculated at the second stage of SE,

V_b is a basic value of measurement.

If

$$\| M_{\Delta V} \| < d, \qquad (36)$$

where d is some threshold, the obtained state vector is not rejected.

Criteri\on 3:

- The third criterion of the vector of state is closeness of the estimated parameters to measurements:

$$M_{\Delta Z} = \sqrt{\sum (V_2 - Z)^T (V_2 - Z)} \qquad (37)$$

where Z is a vector of measurements.

According to this criterion all measurements are classified into several classes using ANN (Grishin et al., 1999) more precisely - with the use of self-organizing Kohonen maps (SKM). Kohonen maps are a two-layer ANN taught without teacher. It is capable of reflecting n-dimensional vector of input variables into some region of ordered output space (Kohonen map) which, as a rule, is of an essentially lower dimensionality. SKM are self- learned on the sets of input vectors not requiring the values of output variables. In the process of SKM learning the values of weights are chosen in the way that after receiving identi-cal or at least similar input vectors the network could reflect them to the one and the same region of the output space. The process of SKM learning finishes when after receiving a new input vector the values of weights do not change.

Further the information pertaining to each class is analyzed. The measured state variables are considered to contain no errors. The closer values of estimated variables to measurements the higher quality of state estimation.

The SE process is regulated by many tuning parameters. The following parameters are studied in the work:

1. A threshold value which determines the need of branch equivalenting.
2. The way of choosing the basic measurement for the given scheme.
3. A type of calculation (normalized or non-normalized units). For calculation in normalized units the optimal basic values of voltage and power are sorted out.
4. Choice of a set of test equations.

The network of a Russian power system consisting of 194 nodes and 240 tie lines is considered as an example.

The tuning constants that lead to the best results of state estimation for a given system are sorted out for one and the same set. The set is read from Online Information Controlling System at any time instant. The maximum possible number of combinations of tuning parameters is modeled and for each of them the procedure of state estimation of the given set is started up. Table 6 shows the values of constants that are studied when solving the SE problems of the given system.

The number of combinations of constants, from which the best one is selected for the SE problem, equals $4*4*3*3*3 = 432$.

Table 6. Constants making up a combination of constants for the state estimation procedure

Constant	Possible values
Basic voltage	35,110,220 (for normalization), 1(non-normalized unit)
Basic power	100,200,500 (for normalization), 1(non-normalized unit)
Usage of test equations by loop	0(are not used), 1(are used), 1(are partially used)
Choice of a basic measurement	0(by maximum element), 1(by voltage), 2(by active injection)
A threshold to determine the necessity of line equivalent-ing	0.05, 0.1, 0.15

The results obtained are analyzed in accordance with the three criteria (Formulae (34), (35), and (37)).

Criterion 1:

- Two vectors of estimated state variables *V1*, *V2* are stored, if the iteration process converges.
  Criterion 2:

- The stored vectors *V1*, *V2* are selected by the second criterion (36), which can be written in the following form:

$$M_{\Delta V_k} = \frac{\sum_{i=1}^{nu}(U_{1i} - U_{2i})}{U_b} + \frac{\sum_{i=1}^{nq}(Q_{1i} - Q_{2i})}{S_b}$$
$$+ \frac{\sum_{i=1}^{np}(P_{1i} - P_{2i})}{S_b}$$

(38)

where U_1, U_2 are vectors of estimates of the measured voltages, that are calculated at the first and second stages, respectively;

P_1, P_2 are vectors of estimates of measured active power injections that are calculated at the first and second stages, respectively;

Q_1, Q_2 are vectors of estimates of measured reactive power injections that calculated at the first and second stages, respectively;

nu is the number of voltage measurements;

np is the number of active power measurements;

nq is the number of reactive power measurements;

k is the line number in Table 2.

Table 2 shows the results of detecting similar estimates that are arranged in order of ascending $M_{\Delta V_k}$.

Criterion 3:

Vectors V2, selected by the second criterion, are classified in accordance with (37). ANN is used for the classification. The training set is created to train the ANN. Each pattern of the set includes 200 measurements. The first pattern of the sampling is a reference pattern and represents the values of measurements in a set. The remaining patterns are made up steady state variables obtained when estimating the same set at various combinations of constants. Part of the combinations of constants is shown in Table 3. While creating the training set consideration is given to all combinations of constants at which the calculated estimates meet the second criterion. The sampling length is determined as follows:

l = n + 1,

where *n* is the number of patterns remained after verification by second criterion (36).

For the considered scheme n = 58, l = 59.

After classifying vectors *V2* into 9 classes the patterns that appeared in the class that contains the reference pattern (Table 6, in italics) are analyzed. The patterns of this class may be reclassified in order to find the vectors closer to the measurements. Each combination of constants, where these vectors are obtained, can be used to solve the SE problem.

In order to obtain the best results of state estimation for a power system at issue it is recommended to use the tuning parameters at which the vectors, that appeared in one class with the reference pattern, were calculated. Here the lesser the $M_{\Delta V_k}$ value (see Table 7) the more preferable the combination of constants.

Table 8 presents the combinations of constants, at which the SE results entered class 2 and class 1. The second class has the reference pattern.

Figure 9 shows results of classification. All patterns were classified into 9 classes using Kohonen maps. There are 59 patterns and 9 colors at the picture. In Figure 9 all patterns are painted in different colors. The patterns which have appeared in one class, have the same color. The first pattern – the reference one – has white color. The closer color of a pattern to white one, the closer the received estimations to telemeasurements.

From Figure 9 one can see, that 51, 52, 53, 55, 56 patterns are painted in white color, as well. Hence, tuning parameters that are studied when receiving these vectors, it is necessary to use for state estimation of EPS.

Analysis of the information presented in Tables 6 and 7 and the results of ANN makes it is possible to conclude that the best SE results for the given system will be at:

- A basic voltage of 220 kV,
- A basic power of 100 kW,

Table 7. Total difference between the measurements calculated at the first and second stages of the SE problem

No. of line from Tab3	Deviation of estimates			
	$\dfrac{\sum_{i=1}^{nu}(U_{1i} - U_{2i})}{U_b}$	$\dfrac{\sum_{i=1}^{nq}(Q_{1i} - Q_{2i})}{S_b}$	$\dfrac{\sum_{i=1}^{np}(P_{1i} - P_{2i})}{S_b}$	$M_{\Delta V_k}$
10	5.0	80.0	227.	312.
27	6.0	109.0	275.	390.
51	*7.0*	*81.0*	*305.*	*393.*
56	*8.0*	*81.*	*309.*	*398.*
52	*86.0*	*56.*	*270.*	*412.*
28	88.0	53.	279.	420.
25	5.0	108.	373.	486.
29	6.	108.	373.	487.
6	114.	58.	317.	489.
2	113.	58.	320.	491.
98	113.	62.	332.	507.

Table 8. Combinations with the best SE results

Combination No.	Basic power		Usage of TE	Basic measurement selection	Bus coupler circuit breaker threshold
	U	*S*			
51	*220*	*100.*	*-1*	*0*	*.15*
52	*220*	*100.*	*-1*	*2*	*.60*
53	*220*	*100.*	*-1*	*2*	*.15*
55	*220*	*100.*	*-1*	*1*	*.15*
56	*220*	*100.*	*-1*	*1*	*.60*
5	*220*	*500.*	*0*	*0*	*.60*
10	220.	500.	1	0	.15
25	220	220.	0	1	.60
26	220	220.	1	2	.15
27	220	220.	1	2	.60
28	220	220.	1	0	.15

Figure 9. Results of classification

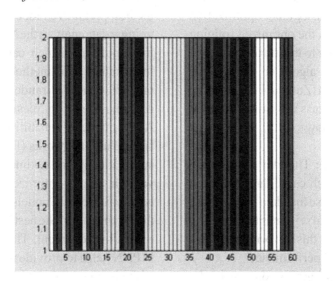

- The usage of test equations by loops partially,
- Basic measurements selected by the maximum element of the derivative matrix,
- A threshold of bus coupler circuit breaker = 0.15.

4.1.1 Several Remarks

The algorithm is introduced of selecting tuning parameters for the EPS state estimation procedure. The algorithm is based on three criteria of obtaining the best SE results. The possibility of obtaining these results is shown. Analyzing the set of SE results obtained at various combinations of tuning parameters the state vector X, at which the values will be the closest to the real data, is selected. The analysis is performed off-line.

4.2 Optimization Neural Network Models for Short-term Forecasting in Electric Power Systems

The problem of ANN training was studied in (Gorban, 1998). in terms of optimization theory. There are many publications on application of optimization algorithms for ANN training, e.g. Genetic algorithms (GAs) which are subclass of evolutionary algorithms, particle swarm optimization (PSO) which is a global optimization algorithm. For review on the optimized training of ANN readers may refer to the monograph (Osowski, 1996). Exclusion algorithm and genetic algorithm are discussed in (Zurada, 1992; Haikin, 2009). Let us briefly discuss an optimized ANN techniques presented below.

1. **Batch Elimination:** The idea is to define the input data, which cause an increase in timing, and do not use that data in the future search for the optimal set of parameters. The implementation of this algorithm allows achieving the good performance.
2. **Iterative Elimination:** In contrast to the batch exclusion, this algorithm consistently excludes the data causing the runtime increase from the starting set of data. This process is repeated with all the remaining input variables until it stops returning the negative results.

3. **Combined Elimination:** Combines the ideas of the batch and iterative algorithm exception. If the input variables have little influence on each other, the algorithm eliminates variables with a negative value, as an algorithm of group exception, otherwise, it eliminates them during the iterative process as an iterative elimination algorithm.
4. **Genetic Algorithm:** Can be employed to find a satisfactory solution to the problems which have no analytical solution. It is based on consistent selection and combination of the required parameters. It uses ideas came from biological evolution.

One of the major problems appears in ANN trainings, is the formation of an optimal input sample. An effective way of solving this problem is to use nonlinear optimization algorithms, namely simulated annealing (SA) method and neuro-genetic selection of input data (NGIS) (Haikin, 2009) which provides a procedure for selecting the best predictive model for each sample. In the training data analysis the NGIS algorithm retrieves the input data which can be discarded as less informative. This method employs optimization procedure based on random search methods, and it combines the capabilities of genetic algorithms and ANNs, namely Probabilistic and General Regression Neural Networks (PNN/GRNN) in order to automatically find optimal combinations of input variables. Such optimized GRNN-networks can be considered as models with memory because they "remember" the best results, causing the final results improvement. The radial basis functions in PNN helps to provide robustness to "bad data" in the input sample.

The method allows to analyze the properties of the SA of the original sample and to organize a "competitive" system between the different neural network predictive models as a nonlinear optimization process selects the best forecasting model. This procedure is based on competitive criteria to minimize the overall risk of ANN presented in

(Osowski, 1996). Joint optimization unit (NGIS + SA) for learning and ANN is shown in Figure 10.

Let us now consider the hybrid model for short-term forecast of parameters of expected operating conditions based on the two-stage adaptive neural network approach. The first stage involves decomposition of the time series into intrinsic modal functions and subsequent application of the Hilbert transform (Hilbert-Huang Transform, HHT, (Huang et al., 1998)). At the second stage the computed modal functions and amplitudes are employed as input functions for optimized neural networks block of our approach.

There are three main steps in our model (as shown in Figure 11) as follows:

1. The EMD algorithm is used to decompose initial non-stationary signal $x(t)$ into several IMFs. Following the Hilbert transform the corresponding instantaneous amplitude (A) and instantaneous frequency are calculated.
2. The calculated values of IMFs and As are used as input values for neural network model.

3. The optimization algorithms of neural-genetic selection and simulated annealing are used to construct the neural network model. This ANN model is learned to forecast the corresponding changes of EPS parameters on a given interval of expectation.

We apply the technique of optimization training ANN for forecasting of active power flow for a lead time interval of 1 minute in one of the power systems of Eastern Siberia (Kurbatsky et al. 2010, 2011). The results of the creating of the optimal input sample containing INF's, instantaneous amplitude *(A)* and instantaneous frequency are shown in Table 9. Employment the optimization unit (NGIS + SA) has demonstrated the advantage of RBF architecture (see Table 10).

As footnote let us conclude that optimized ANN training in combination with HHT reduces the average absolute error of 3-5% on the example of short-term forecasting of active power flows (see Table 11).

Figure 10. The optimal neural networks formation based on nonlinear optimization algorithms

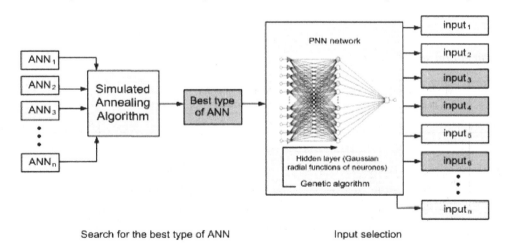

Figure 11. Optimized hybrid model construction

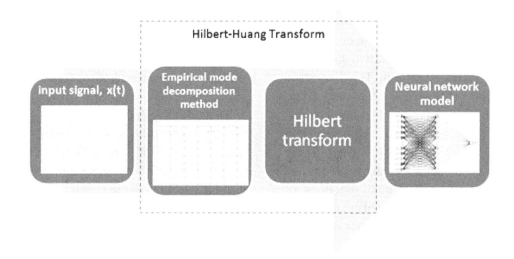

Table 9. Results of comparative studies of the dimension reduction algorithms in the short-term forecasting active power flow

Algorithm	Components of original series after HHT		
	Intrinsic mode functions, IMF	Instantaneous frequency, F	Instantaneous amplitude, A
Consistent choice with the inclusion	IMF3, IMF5-IMF8	F6	A3, A6
Consistent choice with the exception	IMF3, IMF5-IMF8	-	A2, A3, A6
Genetic algorithm	IMF3, IMF5-INF8	-	A3, A6

Table 10. Competition selection algorithm SA in the short-term forecasting active power flow

Number of SA steps	Type of forecast model	MAE, MW	Number of input neurons	Number of hidden neurons	Performance
1	MLP	7.25	9	8	0.94
2	RBF	7.23	9	11	1.02
3	RBF	7.20	9	8	0.89
4	GRNN	7.13	10	250	1.18
5	GRNN	6.27	10	250	0.88
6	GRNN	6.08	10	250	0.88
7	GRNN	5.98	10	250	0.92
8	GRNN	5.98	10	250	0.88
9	GRNN	5.93	10	250	0.91
10	**GRNN**	**5.91**	**10**	**250**	**0.88**

Table 11. Comparison of the active power flow forecasts with anticipation 1 min for different models

Period	Error	Traditional ANN model	HHT-ANN Hybrid Model
20:00 – 21:00	MAPE (%)	10.1	5.2
	MAE	6.2	1.8
	RMSE	33.1	3.1
21:00 – 22:00	MAPE (%)	9.1	4.3
	MAE	6.7	1.6
	RMSE	34.1	1.7

5. COMBINATION OF METAHEURISTIC METHODS WITH FUZZY LOGIC AND ANN

5.1 Application of Fuzzy Logic PSS to Enhance Transient Stability in Large Power Systems

The problem of power system stability improvement is very important in terms of a market environment. It is well known that power system stabilizers (PSSs) on generation units are effective tools to damp electromechanical oscillation and enhance transient stability in electric power systems.

However, the long-term operating experience has shown that conventional PSSs do not always completely use the capabilities of excitation system. The reason is a complicated selection of proper settings of controllers. Also conventional PSSs cannot provide high performance in all operating conditions, because parameters of controllers are fixed and tuned only for a specific operation point.

Recently, new approaches to designing PSSs have been proposed as a result of developing computer technologies. The most progress in the field of AI application has been made in the development of Fuzzy Logic PSSs (FLPSSs) (Zhishan, 1998; Voropai & Etingov, 2001). To date FLPSSs have evolved from mathematical modeling on simple two-machine power systems to operation in real power system (Hiyama, 1999).

A main problem of constructing a FLPSS is finding optimum parameters, such as values of scaling factors, shape of membership functions and values of rule base table. Another problem is adaptation of parameters to changing operating conditions. FLPSSs with fixed parameters have advanced robustness. Here a somewhat new view on the problem of FLPSS constructing is suggested. A GA is considered for optimal tuning of the FLPSS settings and the ANN is applied to on-line adaptation of FLPSS parameters. Besides, classification and grouping techniques are used to find operating conditions and disturbances critical for power system stability.

5.1.1 Main Idea

The commonly known structure of FLPSS is illustrated in Figure 12. Controller generally uses a scheme with two inputs (speed deviation $\Delta\omega$ and acceleration power ΔP), blocks of fuzzyfication / defuzzyfication and a decision table. The operation principle of such devices is well-known and described in many publications (Handschin, 1994; Voropai et al, 2001).

Here the GA with imposed restrictions is used that allow the well-formed rule base tables and membership functions to be received. The purpose of the proposed approach is getting near to optimal, simple and comprehensible controller.

The problem of FLPSS adaptation in a large EPS can be decomposed into two sub-problems (two stages):

Figure 12. Fuzzy logic PSS structure

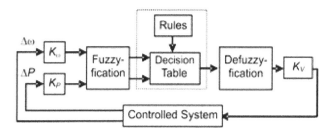

- Preliminary (off-line) tuning under various test operating conditions (including various network topologies) and disturbances;
- On-line adaptation parameters of the FLPSS to changes in the operating conditions of power system.

To solve this problem the set of disturbances that can be dangerous to transient stability is classified to identify the groups of disturbances with similar nature of transients. Thus, classification of the disturbances allows to perform the FLPSS tuning only for one selected representative from each group. A GA is used for tuning of the FLPSS settings. Optimization is carried out for several major disturbances selected on the basis of previous classification. As a result of FLPSSs tuning, the optimal values of

membership functions, rule base table and scaling factors are obtained. Simultaneously a feed-forward back-propagation ANN is trained by optimal parameters of the FLPSS obtained under different operating conditions of power system.

The second sub-problem (stage) has stringent requirements to the time limit. Therefore this sub-problem is solved using the ANN preliminarily trained at the first stage. The ANN automatically identifies power system operating conditions and adapts parameters of FLPSS in the case of operating conditions changing.

Decomposition of the problem offers possibilities to solve the fuzzy PSS adaptation problem more efficiently.

5.1.2 Stage 1(Off-Line)

5.1.2.1. Classification Technique

At the beginning operating conditions and disturbances are classified. Then, a representative selection of the studied conditions is carried out, which calls for PSSs tuning.

Consider initial conditions under which FLPSSs are preliminarily tuned, supposing that the problem of their effective location in the bulk power system is solved by one method or another.

Let $S = \{s_1, ..., s_M\}$ be a set of power system schemes (normal, post–emergency, maintenance), $Z = \{z_1, ..., z_L\}$ be a set of conditions for the studied power system which are determined by the typical points of the load curves of consumers and power plant units and $V = \{v_1, ..., v_K\}$ be a set of disturbances (short circuits, emergency tripping of generations, transmission lines and consumers etc.) which can superpose on each combination from $s_m \in S$ and $z_l \in Z$. At some combinations $\{s_m, z_l, v_k\}$, where $m = \overline{1, M}$; $l = \overline{1, L}$; $k = \overline{1, K}$, the power system stability is maintained and for some other combinations it can be violated.

Determine the conditions to be studied that represent some subset of the combinations $\{s_m, z_l, v_k\}$, for which the power system instability is possible. Here it is supposed that FLPSS adaptation to the states dangerous in terms of power system stability disturbance will also be efficient for the states which are not dangerous in terms of power system stability disturbance. Besides, it is obvious that PSS is not the only means providing power system stability, in some studied test conditions the emergency control scheme should be taken into account.

Since there are very many possible combinations $\{s_m, z_l, v_k\}$ for complex power system, the classical model of the power system dynamics with pairwise analysis of equations of mutual motion generators operate under the assumption that motion of the remaining part of the system is applied for their estimation (Agarkov et al., 1990). The elements of the square matrix $[w_{ij}]$, $i, j = \overline{1, n}$, where n is the number of generators in the power system scheme, reflect dynamic interaction of generators for the considered combinations.

One of the most objective parameters, that do not require a numerical integration, is initial mutual accelerations of generators.

The value of initial mutual accelerations of generators i and j can be calculated as:

$$\frac{d^2\delta_{ij}^{(0)}}{dt^2} = \frac{d^2\delta_i^{(0)}}{dt^2} - \frac{d^2\delta_j^{(0)}}{dt^2}, \quad (39)$$

where is an absolute value of initial acceleration of generator;

Analysis of the matrix $[w_{ij}]$ allows:

1. Identification of the combinations $\{s_m, z_l, v_k\}$ that are not dangerous in terms of stability and hence will not be studied further;
2. Classification of the combinations $\{s_m, z_l, v_k\}$ into clusters with respect to the similarity of system responses, such that for the cluster $\{s_f, z_s, v_p\}, ..., \{s_h, z_r, v_q\}$, w h e r e $f, h \in M$; $s, r \in L$; $p, q \in K$, we have $F(w_{ijfsp}) \approx F(w_{ijhrq})$, $\forall w_{ij}$, where F is some operator. Let us denote the considered cluster by G_d, $d \in D$, D is the number of clusters;

The self-organizing ANN was considered to solve this problem (see Figure 13). The matrix $[w_{ij}]$ is fed to the input layer of the ANN consisting of n(n-1)/2 neurons. The number of neurons in an output layer corresponds to the number of groups (subsets) for which the set of disturbances will be divided. Therefore, varying the number of output neurons we can vary the number of groups. After training the self-organizing ANN is able to recognize and classify groups of similar input vectors.

3. Selection of a representative combination $\{s_{md}, z_{ld}, v_{kd}\}$ for each cluster, the set of which represents the studied test conditions, under which tuning of FLPSS is required.

Figure 13. Classification of emergences by self-organizing ANN

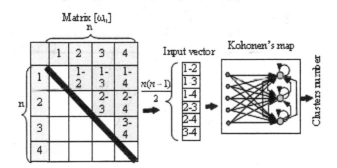

5.1.3 Tuning of Rule Base Table and Scaling Factors

Restrictions were applied to the GA to produce a well-formed rule base like in (Cheong & Lai, 2000). The value of each rule can change in a certain range relative to a value given in the default table (see Figure 13), where 1 corresponds to *NB*, 2–*NM*, 3– *NS*, 4–*ZR*, 5–*PS*, 6–*PM*, 7–*PB*. The value of the marked cells should be fixed (see Figure 14). Such measures allow us to reduce optimization time and exclude obviously incorrect rules.

Each cell (except fixed cells) may take values in the range $\pm\Delta$ of the values taken by default. The variable Δ can accept integer values in a specified range, which depends on the size of the table and amount of the output linguistic variables. The value of Δ equal to 1 is enough in the case of 25 rules. Binary values were used for chromosomes coding. Instead of coding the rule base table values, its deviations Δ from default are coded. Two bits are sufficient for each rule. In total it is necessary to adjust 22 rules, because 3 rules are fixed. Also, it is very important to correctly choose input scaling factors K_ω and K_P (see Figure 12).

5.1.4 Coding of Membership Functions

Figure 15 shows the principle of membership functions coding on the example of the FLPSS with seven fuzzy subsets and triangle membership functions. In this case, it is necessary to adjust only four parameters to produce well-formed membership functions. This kind of membership functions is characterized by the following feature: left and right corners are fixed at the points described by the apices of other triangles. The apices of extreme subsets and the apex of subset "Zero" should be fixed at the points "-1", "1" and "0". As it is shown in Figure 15, five bits are allocated on each adjustable parameter X_1, X_2, X_3, X_4.

Besides, the following constraints were used:

$$X_1 < X_2 < X_3 < X_4 \tag{40}$$

$$X_1, X_2 \in d_1, X3, X_4 \in d_2 \tag{41}$$

5.1.5 Fitness Function

A fitness function for disturbance m was chosen based on the following criterion:

Figure 14. Rule base table restriction

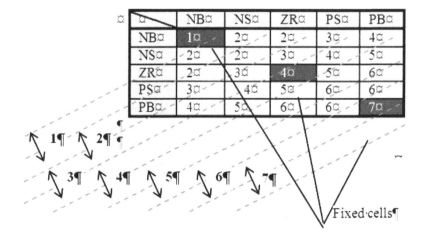

Figure 15. Membership function coding

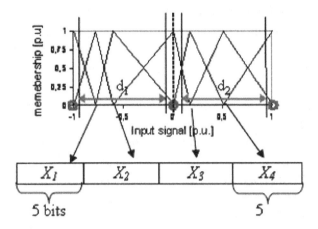

$$J_k^{(m)} = \sqrt{\frac{1}{T} \sum_{i=1}^{N} \int_{t=0}^{T} \left(\omega_0 - \omega_{i_k}^{(m)}(t) \right)^2 dt}, \qquad (42)$$

where $\omega_{i_k}^{(m)}(t)$ is a rotor speed in time interval t; ω_0 is a synchronous speed; T is time of integration; N is the number of generators; k is the index of an individual in population.

As the purpose of optimization is evaluating the influence of FLPSS on a transient process under several disturbances the following criterion was proposed:

$$J_{k_\Sigma}^j = \sqrt{\frac{1}{M} \sum_{m=1}^{M} \left(J_{k_j}^{(m)} - J_0^j \right)^2} \qquad (43)$$

where M is the quantity of disturbances; j is the index of generation; J_0 is the minimum average value in population:

$$J_0 = \min_{k=1..K} \left(\sum_{m=1}^{M} J_k^{(m)} \bigg/ M \right).$$

K is the number of individuals in population.
Application of (5) instead of simple summation allows a more exact contribution of each

disturbance to the evaluation (fitness) function to be considered.

Also scaling of the fitness function value was applied:

$$J_{scal_k}^j = J_{k_\Sigma}^j - \min_{k=1..K} \left(J_{k_\Sigma}^1 \right) \cdot \alpha, \qquad (44)$$

where α is the coefficient of correction.

5.1.6 Characteristics of GA

Hybrid initialization was used to generate the initial population of individuals. Part of population is randomly created, taking into account the above restrictions. The other part can be created based on the previous experience, expert knowledge, etc. The correct choice of the population size is very important. With a small population, there is a fast degeneration, but if the size is too big, the speed of optimization is strongly reduced. Therefore it is necessary to find a compromise decision satisfying both criteria. Obtained experimentally, the optimum size of population is about 50-100 individuals. Furthermore, the GA was updated to check "twins" in populations, in case a pair of similar individuals is detected, one of them leaves.

The one-point crossover and roulette wheel technique were used. The probability of crossover is 0.85 and the probability of mutation is 0.1.

5.1.7 Stage 2 (On-line)

The FLPSSs with fixed parameters show a good robustness to changes in the operating conditions of a power system. However, they do not always ensure the desired performance in all operating conditions. Adaptive FLPSSs do not have such a disadvantage.

We used a feed-forward back propagation network to FLPSS adaptation (see Figure 16). Parameters of operating conditions are fed for input of the net, such as values of active and reactive power of the generator units and loads. The values of FLPSS parameters are received at the network output. Thus, we have a regulator with adaptation ability and a neural network is used to store all possible kinds of FLPSS settings.

The network can be trained by any known method, for example via function approximation, pattern association or with the help of GA. The training process requires a set of examples of proper network behavior- network inputs and target outputs. Properly-trained backpropagation networks tend to give reasonable answers for the inputs they have never seen.

This generalization property makes it possible to train a network on a representative set of input/ target pairs and get good results without training the network on all possible input/ output pairs (Neural Network Toolbox, 1998). Training is off-line for the set of operating conditions. For each of them a genetic optimization is done and then the obtained optimum settings of the controller are used for training the network.

Thus, ANN application allows the new near-optimal parameters of the controller to be instantly received on-line in case of a change in operating conditions.

5.1.8 Simulation Results

5.1.8.1 Studies on the 14-Bus Power System

The special software *"PAU"* was used for calculations (Voropai et al., 2001). This program allows modeling of transient process, and also it includes special blocks for modeling fuzzy PSS and tuning by *GA*.

Figure 16. FLPSS adaptation

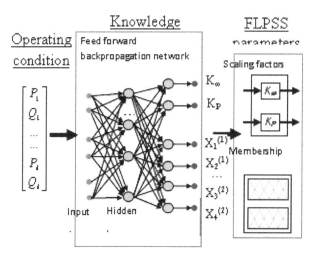

The multi-machine test power system (see Figure 17) consists of five generators. The most important generators 101,201,203 are equipped with FLPSSs. Based on irregularity of load and generation location, two areas can be separated in the network: the first one (with power shortage) is in the neighborhood of generators 1, 3 and 101, and the second one (with power surplus) is in the neighborhood of generators 201 and 203.

Two-circuit transmission lines (5–8, 8–200 and 100–202), which connect these areas, are heavily loaded even in pre-emergency conditions. Therefore disconnection of even one circuit in any of these lines is a strong disturbance which can provoke a loss of the power system transient stability.

At the first stage, the test power system was analyzed. A list of disturbances dangerous to transient stability was formed (see Table 11). Only strong disturbances were selected. Then they were classified and grouped to determine a set of the disturbances with similar nature of transients. For that purpose, initial mutual accelerations of generators were calculated for each disturbance. This information is used to train the self-organizing *ANN*.

The result of disturbances classification is given in Figure 18. The visual analysis has proved the accuracy of classification results.

5.1.9 Off-Line Simulation

Simultaneous tuning was carried out for FLPSSs installed on generators 101, 201 and 203. The controllers with five fuzzy subsets were considered. Therefore, it is necessary to adjust only two parameters of membership functions (X_1 and X_2) for each input signal. In the beginning we studied the test power system in the base (nominal) operations conditions shown in Figure 17.

Training has been done for disturbances 2, 11, 12, 14 and 15 (see Table 12).

Figure 17. The 14-bus multi-machine test power system

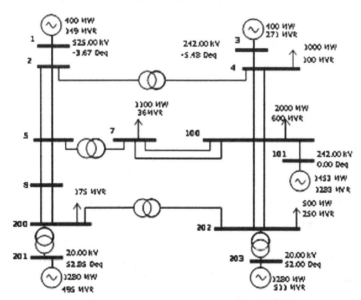

Figure 18. Disturbances classification result

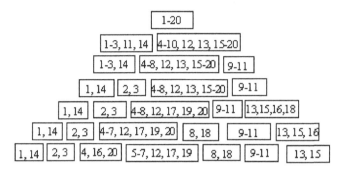

Table 12. Outage statistics and changes

Outage of double-circuit line					
Number	Branch (Node)	Number	Branch (Node)	Number	Branch (Node)
1 4	100-202 4-100	2 5	5-8 7-100	3	8-200
Outage of transformer					
6	200-202	7	2-4	8	5-7
Outage of one circuit of double-circuit line					
9 12	100-202 4-100	10	5-8	11	8-200
0,1s 3-phase short circuit in node					
13	100	14	8	15	7
Load step change					
16	100 (+25%)	17	100(-25%)		
Generator step change					
18	101	19	203	20	3
Outage of double-circuit line + autoreclosing					
21	100-202	22	5-8	23	8-200
Outage of one circuit of double-circuit line+ autoreclosing					
24	100-202	25	5-8		

As a result the optimal rule base tables, scaling factors and membership functions (Table 13 and Table 14) were obtained.

Then different kinds of disturbances were simulated to test the efficiency of the proposed optimization technique. The performance indices *J* were calculated by (42) for each test disturbance. Three cases were considered:

- Generators equipped with conventional PSSs;
- Generators equipped with FLPSS with expert settings (Zhishan et al., 1998);
- Generators equipped with FLPSS tuned by GA;
- Generators equipped with FLPSS tuned by GA.

Table 13. The rule base table for G-101, 201, 203 received after GA optimization

Speed	Acceleration power ΔP				
deviation $\Delta\omega$					
	NB	NS	ZR	PS	PB
Generator 101 (k_ω =1,1 k_p =5,7)					
NB	NB	NB	NB	NS	ZR
NS	NB	NB	NM	PS	PM
ZR	NB	NM	ZR	PS	PB
PS	NS	PS	PM	PM	PB
PB	ZR	PS	PM	PB	PB
Generator 201(203) (k_ω =1 k_p =4,1)					
NB	NB	NB	NB	NM	NS
NS	NS	NB	NS	NS	ZR
ZR	NM	NS	ZR	PM	PM
PS	NS	ZR	PM	PB	PB
PB	PS	PM	PB	PB	PB

Table 14. Membership functions parameters

Generator	Input signal ΔP		Input signal $\Delta\omega$	
	X_1	X_2	X_1	X_2
101	-0.4	0.25	-0.48	0.74
201 (203)	-0.229	0.1	-0.41	0.57

These simulations show higher efficiency of an optimized FLPSS in comparison with conventional PSS. Some examples of system response are shown for the cases with conventional PSS, expert FLPSS and FLPSS tuned by GA (see Figure 19 and Figure 20).

However, these calculations were performed for certain initial operating conditions. Therefore, the robustness of controllers was estimated.

For this test initial operating conditions have been changed according to consumer loads and power plant units twenty-four hour curves. Estimations were made for conventional PSS and GA-tuned FLPSS.

The tests have shown that FLPSS has more robust properties than the conventional PSS. The performance index of FLPSS changes a little at small and medium variations of operating conditions, but in some cases an essential deterioration of the performance has been observed. This proves the necessity to retune (adapt) the FLPSS parameters.

Figure 19. System responses for disturbance 21: (a) for conventional PSS; (b) for FLPSS with expert settings; (c) for FLPSS tuned by GA

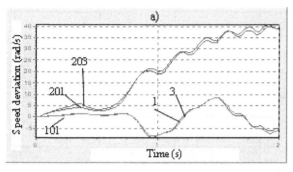

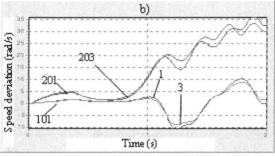

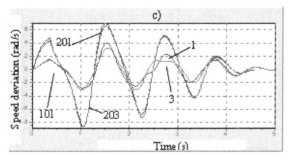

The input information should characterize current operating conditions of the power system.

Training has been carried out for various operating conditions according to winter and summer 24-hour load curves, as well as for some emergency conditions. After ANN training, the adaptive FLPSS was estimated for the same operating conditions as described in the previous section. The summary performance indices were calculated according to (43) for adaptive FLPSS, FLPSS with fixed parameters and for conventional PSS (see Figure 21). The adaptive FLPSSs have shown the best performance in all power system operating conditions.

5.1.10 Several Remarks

Here tuning and adaptation procedures for FLPSS is presented. The studies on multi-machine test power systems show that the adaptive FLPSS has better performance in comparison with conventional PSS. The following remarks can be summarized:

1. The adaptive FLPSS is the effective means to enhance transient stability in large power systems. A large number of simulations for different types of disturbances have shown

Figure 20. System responses for disturbance 18: (a) for conventional PSS; (b) for FLPSS with expert settings; (c) for FLPSS tuned by GA

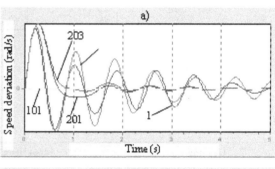

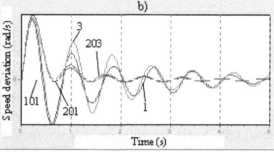

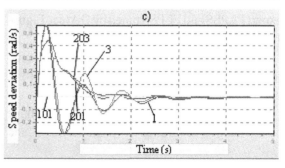

Figure 21. Comparison of performance indices for adaptive FLPSS, FLPSS and CPSS (conventional PSS)

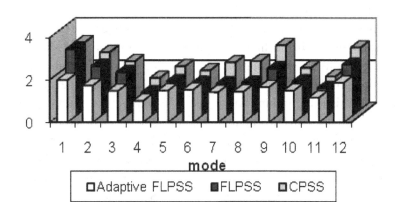

that the adaptive FLPSS prevents stability violations and damps oscillations in power system more efficiently in comparison with conventional PSS.

2. Proposed GA optimization technique is highly effective for tuning FLPSS. The studies have shown that the performance of FLPSS tuned by GA is better as compared to FLPSS with expert settings.

3. The preliminarily trained ANN applied for FLPSS adaptation allows one to maintain a high efficiency of controller in all variety of power system operating conditions and topologies.

4. Self-organized ANN allows various expected situations to be classified into the groups thus making possible to correctly select the training information for FLPSS.

6. CONCLUSION AND FUTURE RESEARCH DIRECTIONS

Recently the considered area of using meta-heuristic algorithms has attracted increasing attention of experts in different spheres, in particular in EPS. The known meta-heuristic methods of modeling and optimization are improved and the new ones are devised both in terms of specific features of concrete problems to be solved. This area is an important constituent of artificial intelligence approaches to solving important applied problems and in many cases demonstrates efficiency of the used methods as against the classical methods of mathematical programming and operations research. The results presented in this Section for EPS confirm the formulated concept.

It can be stated with assurance that the meta-heuristic methods for solving problems in electric power systems will be applied more extensively and profoundly. It is especially stimulated by active development of the Smart Grid ideology. Application of artificial intelligence methods and approaches to solve specific problems is one of its important elements. In this context there are still many problems in power generation, transmission, distribution and consumption, control of electric power systems. They are expected to be successfully solved by using meta-heuristic methods and algorithms.

There is a great variety of heuristic algorithms including the algorithms of image recognition, tabu search (TS), "greedy" algorithm, etc., that were not considered in our material. There are examples when multi-stage heuristic algorithms are created, optimization and heuristic algorithms are combined, or several heuristic algorithms are used for solving one problem. According available publications Genetic Algorithms, Swarm Particles and Simulated Annealing (SA) have been applied in the multiple period planning. Other techniques include planning with reliability criteria using SA and TS, "Niche" genetic algorithm, "genetic Chu-Beasley", constructive heuristic algorithms with classical optimization techniques and other methods. The system of heuristic methods for solving the problems, as the system of any knowledge in general, is an open type system, i.e. the development of science and technology will generate new heuristic methods.

Meta-heuristic methods have gained in popularity relatively recently and have rapidly evolved from simple concepts to complex hierarchical models reproducing organization and behavior of living and nonliving things, including human being. Generalized structure of a random meta-heuristic method supposes the use of intelligent strategy to control the problem-oriented heuristics of lower level and prevent convergence to local optimums.

The art of applying such methods is largely determined by the skill to see trends in the development of a considered area. As applied to the electric power engineering these trends concern increase in scale and complexity of network schemes, aging of equipment, at the same time development of market relations and creation of WAMS and Smart Grid technologies. Complexity of models, consideration of constraints to be imposed can require a lot of time to obtain a solution (several hours, days or even longer). Employment of the meta-heuristic methods, however, makes it possible to obtain the optimal solution.

A specific feature of the electric power engineering is the necessity to solve many problems in real time, for example the problems of electric power system state estimation, emergency control, transient dynamic analysis. Here it is necessary to maintain balance between the number of iterations and speed of calculations which should be high.

The problems of the electrical energy industry which could be solved by meta-heuristic are:

- Transmission expansion planning
- An optimal load shedding approach to enhance voltage stability
- Distributed Energy Resources planning and their optimal deployment in the radial and meshed-type distribution systems
- Optimal placement of different facilities and devices: Combined Heat and Power stations, wind turbines etc.
- System loss minimization by the feeder reconfiguration technique while considering load variations
- Grid expansion etc.

ACKNOWLEDGMENT

This study was supported by grant of Leading Scientific School of Russian Federation #1507.2012.8.

REFERENCES

Ackerman, T., Anderson, G., & Soder, L. (2001). Distributed generation: A definition. *Electric Power Systems Research*, *57*, 185–204. doi:10.1016/S0378-7796(01)00101-8

Agarkov, O. A., Voropai, N. I., Abramenkova, N. A., & Zaslavskaya, T. B. (1990). Structural analysis in power system stability studies. *Proceedings of 10th PSCC*, Graz, Austria, August 30-September 3 (pp.152-159).

Ayuev, B. I., Davydov, V. V., Erokhin, P. M., & Neuymin, V. G. (2008). *Computational models of load flow in electric power systems*. Moscow, Russia: Nauka. (in Russian)

Bartolomei, P. I., & Panikovskaya, T. Y. (2008). *Optimization of energy system operation: Teaching aid*. Ekaterinburg, Russia: UGTU – UPI. (in Russian)

Carcamo-Gallardo, A., Garcia-Santander, L., & Pezoa, J. E. (2009). Greedy reconfiguration algorithms for medium-voltage distribution networks. *IEEE Transactions on Power Delivery*, *24*, 328–337. doi:10.1109/TPWRD.2008.923997

Carpaneto, E., & Chicco, G. (2006). Distribution system minimum loss reconfiguration on the hyper-cube ant colony optimization framework. *Proceedings of the World Energy System Conference*, Torino, Italy, July 10-12 (pp.167-174).

Cheong, F., & Lai, R. (2000). Constraining the optimization of a fuzzy logic controller using an enhanced genetic algorithm. *IEEE Transactions on Systems, Man and Cybernetics . Part B*, *30*, 31–46.

Clements, K. A., Krumpholz, G. R., & Davis, P. W. (1983). Power system state estimation with measurement deficiency: An observability/measurement placement algorithm. *IEEE Transactions on Power Systems*, *102*(7), 2012–2020. doi:10.1109/TPAS.1983.318187

Das, D., Kothari, D. P., & Kalam, A. (1995). Simple and efficient method of load flow solution of radial distribution networks. *Electrical Power & Energy Systems*, *17*(5), 335–346. doi:10.1016/0142-0615(95)00050-0

Deng, Y., He, Y., & Zhang, B. (1992). A branch-estimation-based state estimation method for radial distribution systems. *IEEE Transactions on Power Delivery*, *17*(4), 1057–1062. doi:10.1109/TPWRD.2002.803800

Do Couto Filho, M. B., Leite Do Silva, A. M., & Falcao, D. M. (1990). Bibliography on power system state estimation (1968-1989). *IEEE Transactions on Power Systems*, *10*, 229–240.

Do Couto Filho, M. B., Souza, J. C. S., De Marcus, F. M. F., & Schilling, M. T. (2001). Identifying critical measurement & sets for power system state estimation. *Proceedings of IEEE Porto Power Tech Conference*.

Dorigo, M., & Gambardella, L. M. (1996). The ant system: Optimization by a colony of cooperating agents. *IEEE Transactions on Systems, Man, and Cybernetics. Part B, Cybernetics*, *26*, 132–140. doi:10.1109/3477.484436

Fu Chang, C. (2008). Reconfiguration and capacitor placement for loss reduction of distribution systems by ant colony search algorithm. *IEEE Transactions on Power Systems*, *23*, 1747–1755. doi:10.1109/TPWRS.2008.2002169

Funabashi, T., Koyanagi, K., & Yokoyama, R. (2003). A review of islanding detection methods for distributed resources. *Proceedings of the IEEE Bologna Power Tech Conference*, Bologna, Italy, 2003.

Gamm, A. Z. (1970). On bus numeration when calculating steady states of electric power systems by the Newton-Raphson method. [in Russian]. *Electrichestvo*, *2*, 59–60.

Gamm, A. Z. (1976). *Statistical methods of power system state estimation*. Moscow, Russia: Nauka. (in Russian)

Gamm, A. Z., Gerasimov, L. N., & Golub, I. I. (1983). *State estimation in electric power industry*. Moscow, Russia: Nauka. (in Russian)

Gamm, A. Z., & Golub, I. I. (1990). *Observability of electric power system*. Moscow, Russia: Nauka. (in Russian)

Gamm, A. Z., & Kolosok, I. N. (2000). *Bad data detection in measurements in electric power systems*. Novosibirsk, Russia: Nauka. (in Russian)

Gamm, A. Z., & Kolosok, I. N. (2002). *Test equations and their use for state estimation of electrical power system. Power and Electrical Engineering: Scientific Proceedings of Riga Technical University* (pp. 99–105). Riga, Latvia: RTU.

Gamm, A. Z., Kolosok, I. N., & Glazunova, A. M. (2005). Test equations for validation of critical measurements and critical sets at power system state estimation. *Proceedings of the International Conference "Power Tech 2005"*, St. Petersburg, Gamm, A. Z., Kolosok, I. N., & Zaika, R. A. (2005). Robust methods for state estimation in electric power systems and their implementation on the basis of genetic algorithm. *Elektrichestvo, 10*, 2-8. (in Russian)

Gorban, A. N. (1998). *Neural informatics*. Novosibirsk, Russia: Nauka. (in Russian)

Gornstein, V. M., Miroshnichenko, B. P., & Ponomarev, A. V. (Eds.). (1981). *Methods for optimization of power system state*. Moscow, Russia: Energiya. (in Russian)

Goser, J., Rolim, J. G., & Simoes Costa, A. J. A. (2001). Meter placement for power system state estimation: An approach based on genetic algorithms and topological observability analysis. *Proceedings of the ISAP'2001 Conference* Budapest, Hungary (pp. 15-16).

Grishin, Y. A., Kolosok, I. N., Korkina, E. S., & Em, L. V. (1999). State Estimation of electric power system for new technological systems. *Proceedings of the International Conference "Power Tech 1999"*, August 29 – September 2, Budapest.

Haikin, S. (2009). *Neural networks and learning machines*. Prentice Hall.

Handschin, E., Hoffmann, W., & Reyer, F. (1994). A new method of excitation control based on fuzzy set theory. *IEEE Transactions on Power Systems, 9*(1), 533–539. doi:10.1109/59.317569

Hiyama, T. (1999). Development of fuzzy logic power system stabilizer and further studies. *Proceedings of International Conference on Systems, Man and Cybernetics IEEE SMC'99*, Tokyo, Japan, October 12–15 (pp. 545–550).

Holton, L., Gjelsvik, A., Wu, F. F., & Liu, W. H. (1998). Comparison of different methods for state estimation. *IEEE Transactions on Power Apparatus and Systems, 3*(4), 1798–1806.

Hong, Y. Y., & Ho, S. Y. (2005). Determination of network configuration considering multiobjective in distribution system using genetic algorithms. *IEEE Transactions on Power Systems, 20*, 1062–1069. doi:10.1109/TPWRS.2005.846067

Hsiao, H. T. (2004). Multiobjective evolution programming method for feeder reconfiguration. *IEEE Transactions on Power Systems, 19*, 594–599. doi:10.1109/TPWRS.2003.821430

Huang, N. E., Zheng, S., Long, S. R., et al. (1998). The empirical mode decomposition and the Hilbert spectrum for non-linear and non-stationary time series analysis. *Proceedings of the Royal Society of London, A: Mathematics, Physics, and Engineering Sciences, 45*(1971), 903-995.

Jenkins, N., Allan, R., Crossley, P., Kirschen, D., & Strbac, G. (2000). *Embedded generation* (p. 273). London, UK: IEEE Press. doi:10.1049/PBPO031E

Jeon, Y.-J., Kim, J.-C., & Lee, S.-Y. (2003). Application of ant colony algorithm for network reconfiguration in distribution systems. *Proceedings of the IFAC Symposium on Power Plants and Power Systems Control*, Seoul, Korea, Sept. 15-19.

Ki-Seon, C., Joong-Rin, S., & Seung Ho, H. (2001). Optimal placement of PMU with GPS receiver. *Power Engineering Society Winter Meeting, IEEE*, Vol. 1, (pp.258-262).

Kolosok, I. N., & Patsev, A. S. (2008). Application of a multi-agent approach to decomposition of electric power system state estimation problem. *Proceedings of the 3rd International Scientific Conference on "Energy System: Control, Competition,* [Ekaterinburg, Russia: USTU – UPI.]. *Education, 1,* 354–359.

Kolosok, I. N., & Zaika, R. A. (2003). Study on effectiveness of genetic algorithms for validation of measurements in EPS state estimation. *Izvestia RAS* [in Russian]. *Energetika, 6,* 39–46.

Kolosok, I. N., & Zaika, R. A. (2003). Genetic algorithm as a means for enhancing the efficiency of methods for validation of information in the electric power industry. *Proceedings of the 30th International Conference on Information Technologies in Science, Education, Telecommunication, Business and Protection of Natural Resources",* Gurzuf, Ukraine (pp. 145-147). (in Russian)

Krumm, L. (1977). *The reduced gradient method for electric power system management.* Novosibirsk, Russia: Nauka. (in Russian)

Kurbatsky, V., Sidorov, D., Spiryaev, V., & Tomin, N. (2010). Using the Hilbert-Huang transform for ANN prediction of nonstationary processes. *Scientific Bulletin Electrical Engineering Faculty, 1*(12), 106–110.

Kurbatsky, V., Sidorov, D., Spiryaev, V., & Tomin, N. (2011). On the neural network approach for forecasting of nonstationary time series on the basis of the Hilbert–Huang transform. *Automation and Remote Control, 72*(7), 1405–1414. doi:10.1134/S0005117911070083

Kurbatsky, V. G., Sidorov, D. N., Spiryaev, V. A., & Tomin, N. V. (2011). The hybrid model based on Hilbert-Huang transform and neural networks for forecasting of short-term operation conditions of power system. *Proceedings of the International Conference "PowerTech'2011",* Trondheim, Norway.

MathWorks, Inc. (1998). *Neural network toolbox user's guide.*

Mili, L., Phaniraj, V., & Rousseuw, P. J. (1990). Least median of squares estimation in power system. *IEEE Transactions on Power Systems, 10,* 229–240.

Milosevic, B., & Begovic, M. (2003). Nondominated sorting genetic algorithm for optimal PMU placement. *IEEE Transactions on Power Systems, 18,* 69–75. doi:10.1109/TPWRS.2002.807064

Monticelly, A. (2000). Electric power system state estimation. *Proceedings of the IEEE, 88*(2), 262–282. doi:10.1109/5.824004

Olamaei, J., Niknam, T., Gharehpetian, G., & Jamshidpour, E. (2007). An approach based on ant colony optimization for distribution feeder reconfiguration considering distributed generation. *Proceedings of the International Conference on Electricity Distribution, CIRED,* Vienna, Austria, May 21-24.

Osowski, S. (1996). *Neural networks for information processing.* Warszawa, Poland: OWPW.

Song, J. H., Hatziargiriou, N., & Buta, A. (2006). *Electric power systems (Vol. 1,* p. 636). Bucuresti, Romania: Editura Academiei Romane.

Stott, B. (1974). Review of load-flow calculation methods. *Proceedings of the IEEE, 62,* 916–929. doi:10.1109/PROC.1974.9544

Tavakoli, M. A., Hanhifam, M. R., Lesani, H., Sanakhan, S., & Javan, E. (2006). Review on reconfiguration methods of electric distribution networks. *Proceedings of the Technical and Physical Problems in Power Engineering Conference,* Ankara, Turkey.

Voropai, N. I., & Bat-Undral, B. (2008). Load flow calculation in a radial electrical network using the interval method. [in Russian]. *Electrichestvo, 10,* 64–66.

Voropai, N. I., Efimov, D. N., Popov, D. B., & Etingov, P. V. (2001). Fuzzy logic stabilizer modeling in the transients simulation software. *Proceedings of International Conference of IEEE ISAP'2001*, Budapest, Hungary, June 18-21 (pp. 315-320).

Voropai, N. I., & Etingov, P. V. (2001). Two-stage adaptive fuzzy PSS application to power systems. *Proceedings of International Conference on Electrical Engineering ICEE'2001*, Xi'an, China, July 22-26, Vol. 1, (pp. 314-318).

Yiqin, X., & Jia, T. (2008). A new search approach in ant colony system algorithm for network reconfiguration of distribution systems. *Proceedings of International Conference on Deregulation, Restructuring, and Power Technologies (DRPT'2008),* Nanjing, China.

Zaika, R. A. (2003). Genetic algorithm for power system state estimation. *Proceedings of the International Workshop "Liberalization and Modernization of Power Systems: Congestion Management Problems",* Irkutsk, Russia (pp. 204–206).

Zaika, R. A. (2008). Electric power system state estimation on the basis of calculated corrections of test equations with the aid of genetic algorithm. *Proceedings of the 8th Baikal All-Russia Conference "Information and Mathematical Technologies in Science and Management".* Part I, – Irkutsk: ESI SB RAS (pp. 39-44). (in Russian).

Zaika, R. A. (2003). Application of genetic algorithms for electric power system state estimation. *Systemnye Issledovania v Energetike,* Papers of junior scientists at ESI SB RAS. (in Russian)

Zhishan, L., Kaigan, P., & Huaguang, Z. (1998). Robust adaptive fuzzy excitation control of multimachine electric power system. *Proceedings of POWERCON'98 Conference,* Beijing, China, August 18-22, Vol. 2 (pp. 804-808).

Zmitrovich, A. I. (1997). *Intelligence information systems.* Minsk, Belarus: TetraSystems. (in Russian)

Zurada, J. M. (1992). *Introduction to artificial neural systems.* PWS Publishing Comp.

ADDITIONAL READING

Alves da Silva, A. P., Quintana, V. H., & Pang, G. K. H. (1991). Solving data acquisition and processing problems in power systems using a pattern analysis approach. *IEE Proceedings. Part C. Generation, Transmission and Distribution, 138,* 365–376. doi:10.1049/ip-c.1991.0046

Angus, D., & Woodward, C. (2009). Multiple objective ant colony optimization. *Swarm Intelligence, 3*(1), 69–85. doi:10.1007/s11721-008-0022-4

Antonio, A. B., Torreão, J. R. A., & Couto Filho, M. B. (2001). Meter placement for power systems state estimation using simulated annealing. *Proceedings IEEE Porto Power Technology Conference.*

Bei, X., Yoon, Y., & Abur, A. (2005). Optimal placement and utilization of phasor measurements for state estimation. *Proceedings of the 15th Power Systems Computation Conference,* Liege, Belgium.

Belhadj, C. A., & Abido, M. A. (2001). Optimized voltage stability for maximum loadability using neural networks. *Proceedings of the International Conference, ISAP2001, Budapest, Hungary* (pp. 183–187).

Das, A., & Chakrabarti, B. K. (2005). *Quantum annealing and related optimization methods. Lecture Note in Physics* (*Vol. 679*). Heidelberg, Germany: Springer. doi:10.1007/11526216

Dash, P. K., Liew, A. S., & Ramakrishna, G. (1995). Power-demand forecasting using a neural network with an adaptive learning algorithm. *IEE Proceedings. Part C. Generation, Transmission and Distribution, 142*(6), 560–568. doi:10.1049/ip-gtd:19952245

El-Keib, A., & Ma, X. (1995). Application of Artificial neural networks in voltage stability assessment. *IEEE Transactions on Power Systems, 10*(4), 1890–1894. doi:10.1109/59.476054

Germond, A. J., & Nibur, D. (1993). Neural network application in Power System. *Tutorial Session Proceedings of the 11th PSCC,* Avignon, France (pp. 61–70).

Glazunova, A., Kolosok, I., & Korkina, E. (2008). Test equation method for state estimation using PMU measurements. *Proceedings of the Conference on Monitoring of Power System Dynamics Performance,* Saint Petersburg, Russia, Nº S1-18.

Iwata, A., Wakayama, K., & Sasaki, T. (1993). Electric load forecasting using a structured self-growing neural network model. *Proceedings of ANNPS,* Yokohama, Japan, (pp. 69–72).

Kab-Ju, H., Myubg-Kook, Y., & Sung-Woo, C. (1998). Daily load forecasting using the self-organizing map. *Proceedings of the International Conference on Electrical Engineering,* Vol. 2, (pp. 429-432).

Klir, G. J., Clair, S., Ute, H., & Yuan, B. (1997). *Fuzzy set theory: Foundations and applications.* Englewood Cliffs, NJ: Prentice Hall.

Klir, G. J., & Folger, T. A. (1988). *Fuzzy sets, uncertainty, and information.* Englewood Cliffs, NJ: Prentice Hall.

Kosko, B., & Isaka, S. (1993). Fuzzy logic. *Scientific American, 269*(1), 76–81. doi:10.1038/scientificamerican0793-76

Kwang-Ho, K., Hyoung-Sun, Y., & Yong-Cheol, K. (2000). Short-term load forecasting for special days in anomalous load conditions using neural networks and fuzzy inference method. *IEEE Transactions on Power Systems, 15*(2), 559–565. doi:10.1109/59.867141

Lee, K. Y., Cha, Y. T., & Park, J. H. (1992). Short-term load forecasting using an artificial neural network. *IEEE Transactions on Power Systems, 7*(1), 124–132. doi:10.1109/59.141695

Liu, Z., Bai, W., & Chen, G. (2010). Lecture Notes in Computer Science: *Vol. 6064. A new short-term load forecasting model of power system based on HHT and ANN. Proceedings of Advances in Neural Networks* (pp. 448–454). Shanghai, China.

Mao, A., Yu, J., & Guo, Z. (2005). PMU placement and data processing in WAMS that complements SCADA. *Power Engineering Society General Meeting,* Vol. 1, (pp. 780-783).

Mori, H., & Matsuzaki, O. (1999). A tabu search based approach to meter placement in static state estimation. *Proceedings of the Intelligent Systems Applied Power Systems Conference,* Rio de Janeiro, Brazil, (pp. 365–369).

Moulin, L. S., El-Sharkawi, M. A., Marks, R. J., & Alves da Silva, A. P. (2001). Automatic feature extraction for neural network based power systems dynamic security evaluation. *Proceedings of the International Conference ISAP2001,* Budapest, Hungary (pp. 41–46).

Mueller, G., Komarnicky, P., Styczynski, Z., Dzienis, C., Golub, I., & Blumchein, J. (2007). PMU placement method based on decoupled Newton power flow and sensitivity analyses. *Proceedings of International Conference on Electrical Power Quality and Utilization,* Barcelona (p. 174).

Nilanjan, S., Siddharth, S., & Ribeiro, P. F. (2007). An improved Hilbert-Huang method for analysis of time-varying waveforms in power quality. *IEEE Transactions on Power Systems, 22*(4), 1843–1850. doi:10.1109/TPWRS.2007.907542

Nuqui, R. F. (2001). *State estimation and voltage security monitoring using synchronized phasor measurement.* Dissertation, Virginia Polytechnic Institute and State University, Blacksburg, Virginia, USA. Retrieved from http://citeseer.ist.psu.edu/653208.html

Passino, K. M., & Yurkovich, S. (1998). *Fuzzy control.* Boston, MA: Addison-Wesley.

Pedrycz, W., & Gomide, F. (2007). *Fuzzy systems engineering: Toward human-centered computing.* Hoboken, NJ: Wiley-Interscience.

Piras, A. (1996). *A Multiresponse structural connectionist model for short term electrical load forecasting.* Lausanne, Switzerland: EPFL.

Press, W. H., Teukolsky, S. A., Vetterling, W. T., & Flannery, B. P. (2007). *12- Simulated annealing methods. Numerical recipes: The art of scientific computing* (3rd ed.). New York, NY: Cambridge University Press.

Riccieri, O. F., & Falcão, D. M. (1999). A meter placement method for state estimation using genetic algorithms. *Proceedings of the Intelligent Systems Applied Power Systems Conference,* Rio de Janeiro, Brazil (pp. 360–364).

Rodriguez, C., Rementeria, S., Martin, J. I., Lafuente, A., Muguerza, J., & Perez, J. (1996). Fault analysis with modular neural networks. *Electrical Power & Energy Systems, 18*(2), 99–110. doi:10.1016/0142-0615(95)00007-0

Rudnick, H., Palma, R., Cura, E., & Silva, C. (1995). Economically adapted transmission systems in open access schemes – Application of genetic algorithms. *IEEE/PES 1995 Summer Meeting,* Portland, Oregon, (pp. 1–8).

Santos, E. S. (1970). Fuzzy algorithms. *Information and Control, 17*(4), 326–339. doi:10.1016/S0019-9958(70)80032-8

Souza, J. C. S., Leite da Silva, A. M., & Alves da Silva, A. P. (1997). Data visualization and identification of anomalies in power system state estimation using artificial neural networks. *IEE Proceedings. Part C. Generation, Transmission and Distribution, 144*(5), 445–455. doi:10.1049/ip-gtd:19971168

Souza, J. C. S., Leite da Silva, A. M., & Alves da Silva, A. P. (1998). On-line topology determination and bad data suppression in power system operation using artificial neural networks. *IEEE Transactions on Power Systems, 13*(3), 796–803. doi:10.1109/59.708645

Wilkosz, K. (1981). Verification of the measurements of voltage magnitudes in electric power system. *Second International Symposium on Security Power System Operation,* Wroclaw, (pp. 1–13).

Yager, R. R., & Filev, D. P. (1994). *Essentials of fuzzy modeling and control.* New York, NY: Wiley.

Yang Yong, L. D., Rehtanz, C., & Xiu, R. (2010). Analysis of low frequency oscillations in power system based on HHT technique. *Proceedings of 9th International Conference of Environment and Electrical Engineering (EEEIC-2010),* Prague (pp. 289-296).

Zadeh, L. A. (1968). Fuzzy algorithms. *Information and Control, 12*(2), 94–102. doi:10.1016/S0019-9958(68)90211-8

Zimmermann, H. (2001). *Fuzzy set theory and its applications.* Boston, MA: Kluwer Academic Publishers. doi:10.1007/978-94-010-0646-0

KEY TERMS AND DEFINITIONS

Ant Colony: One of heuristic optimizing algorithms, that is based on the search an optimal solution by passing from one state of the problem to another, similar to the colony of ants looking for food.

Genetic Algorithm: Is a heuristic method of optimization that is based on the principles of the evolution theory in the nature. The development of genetic algorithms became particularly popular with increase in computing equipment capacity.

Simulated Annealing: A meta-heuristic probabilistic method for solving optimization problems. It searches for a good approximation to the global optimum of a given problem.

Fuzzy Logic: An approach using many valued logic; it rests on the idea that approximate is better than fixed and exact. The traditional logic theory deals with two kinds of variables (true (1) and false (0)), fuzzy logic assumes that the true values of variables can range between 0 and 1.

Short-Term Forecasting Methods: Identify underlying patterns in historical data, describe them in mathematical terms, and then extrapolate for the future short time horizon.

Hilbert-Huang Transform: An empirically based data-analysis method consisting from empirical mode decomposition (EMD) method and Hilbert transform. Its basis of expansion is adaptive, so that it can produce physically meaningful representations of data from nonlinear and non-stationary processes.

State Estimation: Electric power systems is an important procedure that allows on-line calculation of state variables for a current scheme of electric network on the basis of telemetry data. The obtained calculated model of power system is then used to solve various technological problems to effectively control electric power system.

ENDNOTES

1. In (Gamm & Golub, 1990). the non-redundant measurements whose absence leads to a loss of the calculated scheme observability were called critical (CM). Critical set (CS) are the groups of measurements in which a drop-out of any measurement makes all the remaining measurements in the critical set.

2. "Logical rules" (algorithms for validation of measurements on the basis of TEs) yield a result on the basis of statistical hypothesis test. The decision is made after checking 1-2 equations, which is the reason for low reliability of bad data detection.

Chapter 20
A Gravitational Search Algorithm Approach for Optimizing Closed-Loop Logistics Network

Abdolhossein Sadrnia
University Putra Malaysia, Malaysia

Hossein Nezamabadi-Pour
Shahid Bahonar University of Kerman, Iran

Mehrdad Nikbakht
University Putra Malaysia, Malaysia

Napsiah Ismail
University Putra Malaysia, Malaysia

ABSTRACT

Since late in the 20th century, various heuristic and metaheuristic optimization methods have been developed to obtain superior results and optimize models more efficiently. Some have been inspired by natural events and swarm behaviors. In this chapter, the authors illustrate empirical applications of the gravitational search algorithm (GSA) as a new optimization algorithm based on the law of gravity and mass interactions to optimize closed-loop logistics network. To achieve these aims, the need for a green supply chain will be discussed, and the related drivers and pressures motivate us to develop a mathematical model to optimize total cost in a closed-loop logistic for gathering automobile alternators at the end of their life cycle. Finally, optimizing total costs in a logistic network is solved using GSA in MATLAB software. To express GSA capabilities, a genetic algorithm (GA), as a common and standard metaheuristic algorithm, is compared. The obtained results confirm GSA's performance and its ability to solve complicated network problems in closed-loop supply chain and logistics.

DOI: 10.4018/978-1-4666-2086-5.ch020

1. AN INTRODUCTION TO SUPPLY CHAIN MANAGEMENT

Many descriptions for Supply Chain Management (SCM) have proposed, most commonly as roughly including a system of managing activities and facilities beginning with purchasing raw material, moving to producing goods, and finally distributing product to customers. All vendors and manufacturers, service providers, distributers, warehouses and retailers are linked in SCM. Furthermore, SCM can be considered a set of concepts used to integrate all elements in supply chain efficiently from suppliers to retailers to producing and distributing goods in the right quantities and right locations, at the best time. The main objective of SCM is minimizing costs and maximize profits simultaneously to reach service level requirements (SHEN, 2007; Simchi-Levi, Kaminsky, & Simchi-Levi, 2003).

The most important questions to consider when designing a supply chain are:

- How many raw material suppliers and partners should be selected and which ones are best?
- What kind of physical structure should be use for the supply chain?
- How many manufacturers should be included in the supply chain and where should be they established?
- How many products should be produced by each factory? When and where should those products be stored?
- What kind of logistics should we use in our supply chain?
- How many products should be transferred from one location to another location and when?
- Beyond economical figures, what other issues should be adverted in designing a supply chain?

- Are there any governmental roles based on environment issues that they should be considered?
- Which drivers may be existed entire the supply chain that can help companies to be more competitiveness?

When supply chains are being develop for a company, these questions should be answered and investigated via modeling. These models, however, might be complicated and need to use novel tools and methods to solve. In this chapter, we try to illustrate empirical applications of the gravitational search algorithm (GSA) as a new optimization algorithm to solve complicated logistics mathematical models.

The remainder of this chapter is organized as follows. Section 2 presents the basic concepts and reviews related work. Then, a mathematical model will be developed to optimize the total cost in a closed-loop logistic for gathering automobile alternators at the end of their cycle life. In section 4 metaheuristics algorithm, GSA theories and it's applications will be discussed. Finally, optimizing the total cost in a developed logistic network will be solved by using GSA in MATLAB software. To express GSA abilities and compare GSA with other algorithm, applying a genetic algorithm as common and a standard metaheuristic algorithm for optimization. Experimental results related to collecting automobile alternators is presented in Section 5. We conclude the paper in Section 6.

2. BASIC CONCEPT AND RELATED WORK

2.1 The Green Supply Chain

These days people are more cautions and careful with the environment and concerned about climate change such that businesses are taking an increasing active on in society (McWilliams & Siegel, 2000). The supply chain concept has been changed by environmental concerns so that, not only is an efficient supply chain based on economic conditions, but also interest is growing in integrating environmental issues into the entire supply chain such that they are more "green" and produce zero waste.

Literature surveys show that after the quality revolution of the 1980s and the supply chain revolution of the 1990s, Green Supply Chain Management (GrSCM) has been adverted by researchers and scientists (Srivastava, 2007). In the business world, some conflict derivers note that some theories encourage practitioners in supply chain management to "be green" and some not only do not encourage greening the supply chain, but also force and emphasis to run it throughout the supply chain . In other words, from one perspective, customers' concern for the environment leads them to be satisfied with green products and the manufacturer uses this opportunity to be agile and produce environmentally friendly products. On the other hand, the increasing severity of environmental damage such as decreases and limits in raw material resources, increases in any kind of pollutions, and overflowing landfills push practitioners to adopt a green supply chain. From this perspective, GrSCM can help companies reach a more competitive position, higher profitability, and better performance by satisfying their customers more effectively (Sarkis, 2003). Walker, Di Sisto, and McBain (2008) categorized GrSCM as either internal, requiring personal commitment from leaders, middle management, investors, and policy entrepreneurs or external, including customer pressure, legislative and regulatory requirements, competitor pressure to focus on reducing costs by minimizing waste and consuming material, and pressure from society and suppliers.

To achieve green supply chain objectives and use its ability for competitiveness, reducing costs, and protecting the environment, manufacturers try to implement various initiatives throughout

the entire in supply chain by applying a range of activities. Such activities include recycling, reusing, reworking, remanufacturing, refurbishing, reclaiming, reducing to designing reverse logistics (Srivastava, 2007) or using closed-loop logistics. In this latter case, closed-loop networks are used for re-using recycled materials along with virgin materials and can protect the environment by collecting used products and re-using them.

Industrial managers are concerned with tolerating total costs, referring to establishing reverse logistic networks and recycling plants costs. Modeling a logistic network and considering all cost aspects such as transportation, inventory carrying, and re-manufacturing, help managers find an optimum solution for balancing economic issues with recycling and the green supply chain. Many authors have attempted to develop models to optimize costs in reverse logistics; however, they question how they should solve the model and optimize its variables. In the new century, various heuristic and metaheuristic optimization methods have been developed to reach superior results and optimize models. In this chapter, we develop a mathematical model to optimize costs throughout a closed-loop logistic model for collecting, recycling, and re-manufacturing automotive alternators at the end of their life cycle. To minimize costs and find optimum variables in the model, we employ GSA as a new meta-heuristics algorithm to optimize closed-loop logistics and compare results with GA as a common and standard meta-heuristics algorithm.

Many initiatives must be considered when greening supply chains. Eltayeb et al. reviewed literature on green supply chain and categorized them into eco-design, green purchasing, supplier environmental collaboration, customer environmental collaboration, and reverse logistics (Eltayeb, Zailani, & Ramayah, 2010). Furthermore, Srivastava et al. (2007) classified the green supply chain literature into three main branches based on the problem context in supply chain design (Srivastava, 2007) as shown in Figure 1.

Figure 1. Classification based on problem context in green supply chain design

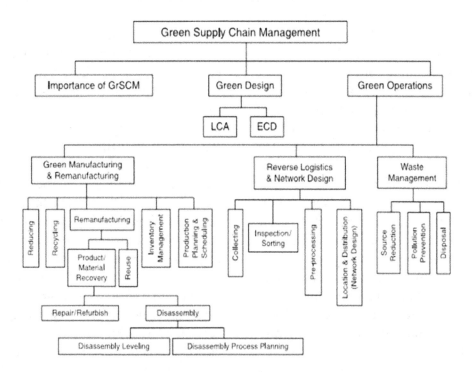

In addition to cost, which should be optimized in the supply chain, green supply chains deal with environment and ecology cancerns, waste management and optimization, green and reverse logistics, recycling, remanufacturing and green design. These issues, along with related variables and limitations, should be considered concurrently while the model and network are being developed for a green supply chain.

Regarding the variety of variables and limitations, most green supply chain problems have been known to have characteristics of being combinatorial and NP-hard. As a result, all possible combinations of decisions and variables must be explored to find the optimum solution. Notably, the time required to solve the problem becomes extremely long as the number of variables increases to more than hundreds.

2.2 Forward and Reverse Logistics

Generally, logistics involves integrating information, transportation, inventory, warehousing, material handling, and packaging. Forward logistics refers to a network of distribution facilities that is employed to procure raw material from suppliers to the manufacturer, transform these materials at the manufacturers' facilities, and finally distribute finished products to warehouses, retailers, or customers.

Traditionally, supply chains have been designed with unidirectional logistics, also called forward logistics. With the need to decrease waste and reuse products at the end of the life cycle, however, the concept of Reverse Logistics (RL) has been considered in supply chains. Currently, RL as a greening tool has become increasingly interesting to a large number of companies based on environmental concerns and regulations. The term RL has been used and defined differently by many authors. For example, some have noted that RL is the opposite of forward logistics (Fortes, 2009). Reverse logistics is a mechanism a manufacturer may use to collect products at the end of the life cycle from the point of the consumer for possible recycling and re-manufacturing. The main application of RL is to improve reclamation of products when they are at the end of the life cycle (Meade & Sarkis, 2007). Wang and Bai (2010) believed that the main task of RL could be considered collecting used products based on the balance of environment affects and cost (Z. Wang & Bai, 2010). Products that are collected using RL can be used in four forms: direct reuse, repair, recycling, and remanufacturing (Srivastava, 2007; Thierry, Salomon, Van Nunen, & Van Wassenhove, 1995).

In designing a RL process, cost is one of the significant issues to consider in the design network. For example, in the United States, more than 50% of the total value of returned goods in their end of life cycle is related to logistic costs (Yimsiri, 2009). This notable cost has forced many companies to improve the process of RL to reach optimized costs and maximum profit through the supply chain. Many scholars have studied ways to optimize the RL network for several different industries. We summarize some of these studies in Table 1.

All scholars mentioned in Table 1 tried to develop a customized model to optimize logistics network costs and examined various scenarios for special cases. They also tried to apply different tools to solve their models and minimize total supply chain costs, and extract the raw material level, manufacturing level, inventory level, and recycling level at different facilities.

2.3 Closed-Loop Network Logistics

Reverse logistics can be accomplished through the original forward channel, through a reverse channel, or through a combination that uses both the forward and reverse channels. Figure 2 illustrates a generic concept model of a reverse and forward network. It is similar to the model proposed by Wang and Bai (2010).

Collecting and transporting used products is the main task of reverse logistic The mutual relationship between the reverse and forward channels led managers and engineers to design them concurrently. Therefore, the concept of a closed-loop network or an integrated network refers to the mutual transactions between reverse logistic and forward logistic. This integration helps avoid sub-optimization results versus designing them separately. The first quantitative model for a closed-loop network in supply chain management was developed by Fleischmann, Beullens, Bloemhof-Ruwaard, and Van Wassenhove (2001), who tried to optimize forward distribution and recovery using product flow simultaneously.

3. CLOSED-LOOP SUPPLY CHAIN MODELING: AUTOMOBILE ALTERNATOR RECYCLING AS A CASE STUDY

The objective of this section is to develop a multi-tier, closed-loop network model in a supply chain to return a product at the end of its life cycle and identify which decisions should be finalized regarding material purchasing, production, distribution, recycling, and disposal.

A case study is used to illustrate the applicability of GSA in optimizing the closed-loop model. An automobile manufacturing company has

Table 1. Case studies in RL

	Scholar(s)/Year	Case study
Electric and Electronics Industrial	Bartels (1998)(Bartels, 1998)	Collection and processing of disposed batteries in EOL
	Krikke et al. (1999) (Krikke, Van Harten, & Schuur, 1999)	Copiers
	Jayaraman et al. (1999)(Jayaraman, Guide Jr, & Srivastava, 1999)	Electronic equipment remanufacturing company
	Shih (2001)(Shih, 2001)	Computers and home appliances
	Schultmann et al. (2003)(Schultmann, Engels, & Rentz, 2003)	Spent batteries
	Walther et al. (2005) (Walther & Spengler, 2005)	Waste of electrical and electronic equipment
	Nagurney et al. (2005)(Nagurney & Toyasaki, 2005)	Electronic waste
	Husumastuti et al. (2008) (Kusumastuti, Piplani, & Hian Lim, 2008)	Computer manufacturer
	Lee et al. (2008) (D. H. Lee & Dong, 2008)	EOL computer products
	Kim et al. (2009)(Kim, Yang, & Lee, 2009)	Electronic goods
	Xanthopoulos et al. (2009) (Xanthopoulos & Iakovou, 2009)	EOL electronic and electronic products
	Grunow et al. (2009)(Grunow & Gobbi, 2009)	Waste of electrical and electronic equipment
	G. Kannan et al. (2010)(Kannan, Sasikumar, & Devika, 2010)	Battery recycling
Automotive Industrial	Schultmann et al. (1999)(Schultmann, Zumkeller, & Rentz, 2006)	Automotive industry
	et al. (2008) (De La Fuente, Ros, & Cardos, 2008)	Metal-mechanic company
	Cruz-Rivera et al. (2009) (Cruz-Rivera & Ertel, 2009)	EOL vehicles
	(Cao & Zhang, 2011)(Cao & Zhang, 2011)	Automotive industry
Other Industries	Barros et al. (1998)(Barros, Dekker, & Scholten, 1998)	Sand recycling
	Louwers et al. (1999)(Louwers, Kip, Peters, Souren, & Flapper, 1999)	Carpet materials
	Ubbens (2000)	EOL metal from metal packaging materials
	Schinkel(2000)	EOL recycling of gypsum
	Van Notten (2000)	EOL recovery of glass
	Realff et al. (2004) (REALFF, AMMONS, & Newton, 2004)	Carpet recycling
	Listes et al. (2005)(Listes & Dekker, 2005)	Sand recycling
	Biehl et al. (2007) (Biehl, Prater, & Realff, 2007)	Carpet recycling
	Sheu (2008) (Sheu, 2008)	Nuclear power generation
	Pati et al. (2008)(Pati, Vrat, & Kumar, 2008)	Paper recycling
	(Wang, Lai, & Shi, 2011)(F. Wang, Lai, & Shi, 2011)	General

been selected to evaluate and test the proposed model. The chosen company was established in southeast of Asia. It produces more than 4,000 units of alternators for passenger cars. Today, the company is under great pressure to take back the used alternators at the end of the life cycle based on new governmental regulations and reduce total supply chain costs. Regarding the billing of material to produce alternators, the price of aluminum is a major cost component. The company would like to recycle the aluminum from used alternators and then use the product as raw material for producing new alternators instead of purchasing new aluminum from suppliers. This closed-loop supply chain process is used to achieve the minimum total cost.

In the case of recycling alternators, both forward and reverse logistics networks can be designed as a closed-loop network. In a forward supply chain, the major raw materials such as

Figure 2. A generic concept model of reverse and forward network

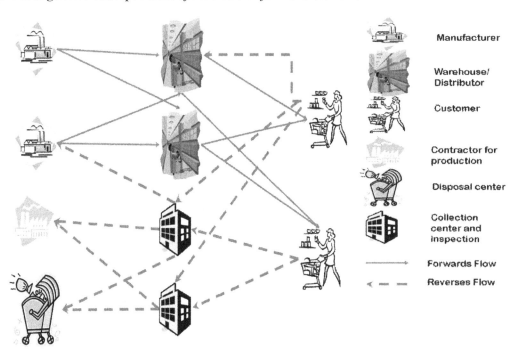

aluminum and copper wire are prepared from different suppliers to produce automobile alternators. The alternators are produced in different manufacturing plants. to the alternators must be distributed through distributors, wholesalers, retailers, and finally delivered to consumers. Figure 3 demonstrates a closed-loop supply chain for recycling alternators.

At the end of an alternator's life cycle, automobile owners leave the used alternator at the automobile service station that is normally mentioned as the same point with retailers. So, reverse logistic retailers collect used alternators and act as a collection point. The used alternator collected at the retailers should be transferred to a disassembly and recycling point. At this point, alternators disintegrate to the elements and then aluminum extract from the used materials and useless alternators should be disposed of. After cleaning and purifying the extracted aluminum, it can be reused at a manufacturing site as row material along with original materials to produce

new alternators. This is noticeable in our model, except aluminum, other component are sold to a third-party company. Besides cost benefits, environment protection is another advantage of aluminum recycling via the mention closed-loop logistics network.

The main problem here is to design a multi-tier, multi-product, closed-loop supply chain model to minimize total supply chain costs such as purchasing costs, production costs, distribution, warehousing, collection, disposal, disassembly, and recycling costs. To develop the model, the following assumptions, indices, notations, and decision variables are described as follows:

Assumptions:

- For all trips, transportation cost is fix throughout time.
- Inventory cost is fixed throughout time.
- Except aluminum, all remaining components are sold to a third party.

Figure 3. Conceptual model for forwards and reverse logistic for automobile alternator in end of life cycle

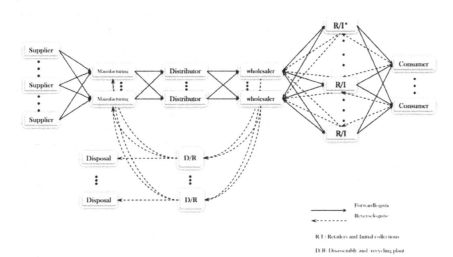

- The scraped alternators that cannot be recycled should be sent to disposal sites.
- Daily demand is deterministic and should be covered.

Indices and Sets:

- **d:** index for distributors; $d \in D$
- **i:** index for wholesalers; $i \in I$
- **j:** index for alternator retailers; $j \in J$
- **m:** index for alternator manufacturing plants; $m \in M$
- **p:** index for kind of products; $p \in P$
- **r:** index for raw materials; $r \in R$
- **s:** index for suppliers; $s \in S$
- **t:** index for time periods; $t \in T$
- **y:** index for recycling plants for alternator; $y \in Y$
- **z:** index for disposal sites; $z \in Z$

Notations:

- **TC:** Total closed-loop supply chain costs for alternator
- **PRC:** Total raw materials purchasing costs of from suppliers

- **RMIC:** Total inventory carrying costs raw material at the manufacturing plant
- **PMC:** Total processing costs in manufacturing
- **PDIC:** Total inventory carrying costs at distributor
- **DITC:** Total alternator transportation costs from distributor to wholesaler
- **PMIC:** Total alternator products inventory carrying costs
- **MDTC:** Total alternator transportation costs from manufacturing plant to distributor
- **PIIC:** Total alternator inventory carrying costs at wholesaler
- **SIIC:** Total alternator inventory carrying cost at the wholesalers for used items
- **ISTC:** Total alternator wholesalers to recycling plant transportation cost
- **IJTC:** Total alternator transportation costs from wholesaler to retailer
- **SCC:** Total alternator collection cost of the used items
- **JITC:** Total alternator retailers to the wholesalers transportation costs of the used items

- **SMC:** Total disassembly cost at the recycling plant
- **PURrst:** Purchasing cost of raw material 'r' during time period 't' from supplier 's'
- **PCMmpt:** Processing cost per product of 'p' at time period 't' at manufacturing plant 'm'
- **YRC:** Total recycling cost from the recycling plant to the third party
- **SDC:** Total disposal costs of the wastage
- **SPTC:** Total recycling plant to manufacturing plant transportation costs
- **TCDdipt:** Transportation cost per unit from distributor 'd' to wholesaler 'i' time period 't' for product 'p' at
- **TCMmdpt:** Transportation cost per unit from manufacturing plant 'm' to distributor 'd' at time period 't' for product 'p'
- **Xrp:** Amount of raw material 'r' required to produce one item of product 'p'
- **FGImpt:** Finished goods inventory of product 'p' at the manufacturing plant 'm' during the time period 't'
- **TCWijpt:** Transportation cost per unit from wholesaler 'i' to retailer 'j' for product 'p' at time period 't'
- **IRMrmt:** Raw material inventory 'r' at the manufacturing plant 'm' during the time period 't'
- **IRCrmt:** Inventory carrying cost per unit per period of raw material 'r' at the manufacturing plant 'm' during the time period 't'
- **ICFmpt:** Inventory carrying cost per unit per period for □nished goods of product 'p' at the manufacturing plant 'm' during the time period 't'
- **ICWipt:** Inventory carrying cost per unit per period of product 'p' at the wholesaler 'i' during the time period 't'
- **QHjpt:** Quantity of used items of product 'p' collected at the retailer 'j' during the time period 't'

- **CCjpt:** Collection cost per item of used products of 'p' at the retailer 'j' during the time period 't'
- **IPDdpt:** Final inventory of product 'p' at the distributor 'd' during the time period 't'
- **ICDdpt:** Inventory carrying cost per unit per period of product 'p' at the distributor 'd' during the time period 't'
- **IPWipt:** Final inventory of product 'p' at the wholesaler 'i' during the time period 't'
- **TCRjpt:** Transportation cost per unit from the retailer 'j' to the wholesaler of product 'p' at timeperiod 't'
- **CHpt:** Used products inventory of product 'p' at the wholesaler during the time period 't'
- **DCHzpt:** Disposal cost per unit of used product of 'p' to the disposal site 'z' at the time period 't'
- **TCWypt:** Transportation cost per unit of product 'p' from the wholesaler to the recycling plant 'y' at time period 't'
- **ICpt:** Inventory carrying cost per unit per period for used items of product 'p' during the time period 't'
- **QHCpt:** Quantity of used products of 'p' received during the time period 't'
- **DRpt:** Disposal rate of product 'p' at time period 't'
- **DCPypt:** Disassembly cost per unit for the used product of 'p' at the recycling plant 'y' during the time period 't'
- **RCRryt:** Recycling cost of one unit of raw material 'r' sold to the third party from the recycling plant 'y' during the time period 't'
- **Wp:** Weight of the used product 'p'
- **Yrp:** Percentage of contribution of raw material 'r' for the returned product 'p'
- **TCRrymt:** Transportation cost per ton for the required reclaimed raw material 'r' transported from the recycling plant 'y' to the manufacturing plant 'm' during the time period 't'

- **RRryt:** Recycling rate of the required raw material 'r' to be reclaimed for new production at the recycling plant 'y' during the time period 't'
- **SCRm:** Raw material storage capacity at the manufacturing plant 'm'
- **SCPm:** Finished goods storage capacity at the manufacturing plant 'm'
- **SCSs:** Supply capacity of supplier 's'
- **PTm:** Available processing time in plant 'm'
- SDPd: Storage capacity of the distributor 'd'
- **DJPjpt:** Demand at the retailer 'j' of product 'p' at time period 't'
- **CYPypt:** Capacity of the recycling plant 'y' of product 'p' at time period 't'
- **SCWi:** Storage capacity of the wholesaler 'i'
- **SCJj:** Storage capacity of the retailer 'j'
- **CZzpt:** Capacity of the disposal site 'z' for product 'p' at time period 't'

Decision Variables:

- **QPMmpt:** Product 'p' at manufacturing plant 'm' during time period 't'
- **QMDmdpt:** Quantity transported from manufacturing plant 'm' to distributor 'd' of product 'p' at time period 't'
- **RSMrsmt:** Raw material 'r' purchased from supplier 's' to the manufacturing plant 'm' during time period 't'
- **QJIzpt:** Used products of 'p' transported from the wholesaler'i' to the disposal 'z' at the time period 't'
- **QDIdipt:** Quantity transported from distributor 'd' to wholesaler 'i' of product 'p' at time period 't'
- **QIJijpt:** Quantity transported from wholesaler 'i' to retailer 'j' of product 'p' at time period 't'

- **QIYypt:** Used products of 'p' transported from the wholesaler'i' to the recycling plant 'y' at time period 't'
- **QSYypt:** Used products of 'p' recycling at the recycling plant 'y' at the time period 't'
- **QROryt:** Amount of recycled raw material 'r' from the recycling plant 'y' sold to the third party during the time period 't'
- **QRYrymt:** Required reclaimed raw material 'r' for new production transported from the recycling plant 'y' to the manufacturing plant 'm' during the time period 't'

3.1. Mathematical Formulation

As above-mentioned, the main objective is to minimize the total cost in the closed-loop logistic network and recycles used aluminum in end of life. Therefore, we can formulate objective as follows.

Minimize:

$$
\begin{aligned}
TC &= PRC + RMIC + PMC + PMIC \\
&+ MDTC + PDIC + DITC + PIIC \\
&+ IJTC + SCC + JITC + SIIC + ISTC \\
&+ SMC + YRC + SDC + SPTC
\end{aligned}
$$

$$(1)$$

where component cost can be calculated regarding to the bellow formula:

$$
PRC = \sum_{r}\sum_{s}\sum_{m}\sum_{t}(RSM_{rsmt} * PUR_{rst})
$$

$$(2)$$

$$
PMC = \sum_{m}\sum_{p}\sum_{t}\left(QPM_{mpt} * PCM_{mpt}\right)
$$

$$(3)$$

$$
MDTC = \sum_{m}\sum_{d}\sum_{p}\sum_{t}(QMD_{mdpt} * TCM_{mdpt})
$$

$$(4)$$

$$
DITC = \sum_{d}\sum_{i}\sum_{p}\sum_{t}\left(QDI_{dipt} * TCD_{dipt}\right)
$$

$$(5)$$

$$IJTC = \sum_i \sum_j \sum_p \sum_t \left(QIJ_{ijpt} * TCW_{ijpt}\right)$$

$$(6)$$

$$RMIC = \sum_r \sum_m \sum_t \left(IRM_{rmt} * IRC_{rmt}\right),$$

$$(7)$$

$$PMIC = \sum_m \sum_p \sum_t (FGI_{mpt} * ICF_{mpt})$$

$$(8)$$

$$PDIC = \sum_d \sum_p \sum_t \left(IPD_{dpt} * ICD_{dpt}\right)$$

$$(9)$$

$$PIIC = \sum_i \sum_p \sum_t (IPW_{ipt} * ICW_{ipt})$$

$$(10)$$

$$SCC = \sum_j \sum_p \sum_t \left(QH_{jpt} * CC_{jpt}\right)$$

$$(11)$$

$$JITC = \sum_j \sum_p \sum_t (QH_{jpt} * TCR_{jpt})$$

$$(12)$$

$$SDC = \sum_z \sum_p \sum_t \left(QJI_{zpt} * DCH_{zpt}\right)$$

$$(13)$$

$$ISTC = \sum_y \sum_p \sum_t (QIY_{ypt} * TCW_{ypt})$$

$$(14)$$

$$SIIC = \sum_p \sum_t (CH_{pt} * IC_{pt})$$

$$(15)$$

$$where \ CH_{pt} = CI_{p(t-1)} + QHC_{pt} - \sum_z QJI_{zpt}$$

$$- \sum_y QIY_{ypt}, \ \forall \ t \in T, p \in P.$$

$$(16)$$

$$SMC = \sum_y \sum_p \sum_t \left(QSY_{ypt} * DCP_{ypt}\right)$$

$$(17)$$

$$YRC = \sum_r \sum_y \sum_t (QRO_{ryt} * RCR_{ryt})$$

$$(18)$$

$$SPTC = \sum_r \sum_y \sum_m \sum_t (QRY_{rymt} * TCR_{rymt})$$

$$(19)$$

In addition to cost component, referring to literature there are many constrains that should be considered. As it can be seen in the following, for considering capacity of storage limitation in manufacturer plant we have formulate it in mathematic Formula (20). More, (21) refers to capacity of goods storage in manufacturer plant. Row material purchasing capacity, processing time required, quantity transportation between each point, coverage of total demand and capacity of disassembly point have been considered in rest of mathematics formula from (22), (23), (24), (25), (26), (27), (28), and (29) as bellow:

$$\sum_r \sum_s \sum_t RSM_{rsmt} \leq SCR_m \ , \ \forall m \in M.$$

$$(20)$$

$$\sum_p \sum_t QPM_{mpt} \leq SCP_m \ , \ \forall m \in M.$$

$$(21)$$

$$\sum_r \sum_m \sum_t RSM_{rsmt} \leq SCS_s \ , \ \forall s \in S.$$

$$(22)$$

$$\sum_p \sum_t QPM_{mpt} \leq PT_m \ , \ \forall m \in M.$$

$$(23)$$

$$\sum_m \sum_p \sum_t QMD_{mdpt} \leq SDP_d \ , \ \forall d \in D.$$

$$(24)$$

$$\sum_d \sum_p \sum_t QDI_{dpt} \leq SCW_i \ , \ \forall i \in I.$$

$$(25)$$

$$\sum_i \sum_p \sum_t QIJ_{ijpt} \leq SCJ_j \ , \ \forall j \in J.$$

$$(26)$$

$$\sum_{m}\sum_{p}\sum_{t}QPM_{mpt} \geq \sum_{j}\sum_{p}\sum_{t}DJP_{jpt} \qquad (27)$$

$$\sum_{j}\sum_{p}\sum_{t}QH_{jpt} \leq \sum_{y}\sum_{p}\sum_{t}CYP_{ypt} \qquad (28)$$

$$\sum_{y}\sum_{p}\sum_{t}QSY_{ypt} \leq \sum_{y}\sum_{p}\sum_{t}CYP_{ypt} \qquad (29)$$

In continuation, we are going to introduce briefly Gravitational Search Algorithm (GSA) as a novel swarm based algorithm and then try to apply it to solve closed-loop model that has been proposed here.

4. MODEL OPTIMIZATION: GRAVITATIONAL SEARCH ALGORITHM

4.1 Metaheuristic Algorithms

Heuristic algorithms have a long and distinguished track record in combinatorial optimization. Often, heuristic techniques are the only practical alternative when dealing with problem instances of realistic dimensions and characteristics. Many heuristics are improving iterative procedures that move from a given solution to a neighboring solution that is better in terms of the objective function value (or some other measure based on the solution's characteristics). Thus, at each iteration, a local search procedure identifies and evaluates solutions in the neighborhood of the current solution, selects the best one relative to given criteria, and implements the transformations required to establish the selected solution as the current one. The procedure iterates until no further improvements are possible.

Metaheuristics have been designed as strategies to guide and change other heuristics to produce solutions beyond those normally defined by local search heuristics (Glover, 1986). Compared with exact search methods, such as branch-and-bound, metaheuristics cannot generally ensure a systematic exploration of the entire solution space. Instead, they attempt to examine only parts of the solution space where, according to certain criteria, one believes good solutions may be found. Well-designed metaheuristics avoid getting trapped in local optima or sequences of visited solutions (cycling) and provide reasonable assurance that the search has not overlooked promising regions. For optimization problems, metaheuristics can be described summarily as a "walk through neighborhoods," a search trajectory through the solution domain of the problem at hand (Lourenço, 2001). Similar to classical heuristics, these iterative procedures move from a given solution to another neighboring solution. Thus, at each iteration, one evaluates moves toward solutions in the neighborhood of the current solution or in a suitably selected subset (Crainic & Toulouse, 2010).

Metaheuristics is defined as a set of algorithmic concepts that can be used to define heuristic methods that apply to a wide set of different problems. In other words, a metaheuristic can be described as a general-purpose heuristic method designed to guide an underlying problem specific heuristic such as a local search algorithm or a construction heuristic toward promising regions of the search space containing high-quality solutions. A metaheuristic is therefore a general algorithmic framework that can be applied to different optimization problems with relatively few modifications to adapt them to a specific problem.

From the practitioners' perspective, it is most important to recognize which of the many available techniques is appropriate for the model constructed. The techniques themselves fall into several categories. One recent category of techniques is often referred to as metaheuristics. The distinguishing feature of this technique is that it is one that does not guarantee that the best solution will be found; at the same time, however, it is not as complex as an optimum-seeking technique.

Although metaheuristics could include simple, commonsense, rule-of-thumb type techniques, they are typically methods that exploit specific problem features to obtain good results.

Metaheuristic optimization techniques are divided into two main categories: (i) evolutionary algorithms and (ii) algorithms based on swarm intelligence. Evolutionary algorithms are population search methods that are inspired by evolution, which leads to producing better and better approximations to a solution. In other words, the basic idea of evolutionary algorithms is to "select best, discard the rest." This means that better solutions have a better chance of surviving. Evolutionary algorithms are well suited for a wide range of combinatorial and continuous problems, although different variations are proposed: the genetic algorithm proposed by Holland (1975); evolutionary programming proposed by Fogel et al. (1966); and evolutionary strategy proposed by (1973). These algorithms differ in the main operators of evolutionary algorithms such as: selecting, recombining, mutating, or replacing.

Swarm intelligence is inspired mainly by social behavior patterns of organisms that live and interact within large groups of unsophisticated autonomous individuals. In particular, it incorporates swarming behaviors observed in flocks of birds, schools of fish, swarms of bees, colonies of ants, and even human social behavior. From such behaviors intelligence emerges (Kennedy & Eberhart, 1995), (Bonabeau, Dorigo, & Theraulaz, 1999) and (J. H. Holland, 1999). Without a central control structure, such local interactions lead to a collective, global behavior. Consequently, a swarm intelligence system can accomplish difficult tasks in dynamic and varied environments without any external guidance or control and with no central coordination. In recent years, the swarm intelligence paradigm has drawn researchers' attention, mainly as ant colony optimization and particle swarm optimization. Ant colony optimization is the first family of swarm intelligence-based search

algorithms, which was proposed by Dorigo, Maniezzo and Colorni (1999). (Dorigo, Maniezzo, & Colorni, 1991). This study modeled behavior of ants in finding the shortest path from the nest to the food source. Particle swarm optimization, proposed by Kennedy and Eberhart (1995), mimics the flocking behavior of birds and fish (Kennedy & Eberhart, 1995).

Metaheuristic algorithms (such as genetic algorithms, Tabu search, evolutionary programming, and simulated annealing), are general-purpose methods that can be applied to several different problems. These methods in particular are increasing in popularity because they are relatively simple and because increases in computing power have greatly increased the effectiveness of these techniques to reach the best solution in a shorter time and with fewer computing requirements.

Referring to the above-mentioned benefits of metaheuristics, scholars have used various metaheuristic algorithms recently to solve complicated green supply chain problems. Lourenco (2001) emphasized that supply chain problems would be an opportunity for metaheuristics that could be applied to optimize them. Table 2 illustrates many of scholars that have employed metaheuristics in any branch of green supply chain.

4.2 Gravitational Search Algorithm as a Novel Meta-Heuristics Algorithm

One of the novel heuristic optimization methods is the Gravitational Search Algorithm (GSA). It is constructed based on the law of Gravity and the notion of mass interactions. Therefore, the theory of Newtonian physics is used in the GSA algorithm (E. Rashedi, Nezamabadi-pour, & Saryazdi, 2009)

One of the novel heuristic optimization methods is the gravitational search algorithm (GSA). It is constructed based on the law of gravity and the notion of mass interactions. Therefore, the theory of Newtonian physics is used in the GSA algorithm (E. Rashedi, et al., 2009)

Table 2. Metaheuristic algorithms application in green supply chain

Author(s)/year	Subject in green supply chain	Method
(Min, Jeung Ko, & Seong Ko, 2006)	Reverse logistic	Genetic algorithm
(Schultmann, et al., 2006)	routing planning (green logistics)	Tabu search
(Farahani & Elahipanah, 2008)	Optimization in distribution planning	Genetic algorithm
(Kannan, et al., 2010)	Reverse logistic/ recycling	Genetic algorithm
(Pishvaee, Kianfar, & Karimi)	Reverse logistic	Simulated annealing
(Gambardella, et al., 2003)	logistic Optimization	Ant colony
(J. E. Lee, Rhee, & Lee, 2010)	Reverse logistics and inventory	Genetic algorithm
(Yan & Soc, 2009)	Green purchasing	Genetic algorithm
(Yanchao, Pengchao, & Litao, 2008)	Reverse logistic	Genetic algorithm
(J.E. Lee, Gen, & Rhee, 2008)	Reverse logistic	Genetic algorithm
(Farahani & Elahipanah, 2008)	Optimization in distribution	Genetic algorithm
(Yanchao, Xiaoyan, & Litao, 2008)	logistic Optimization	particle swarm optimization
(Loukil, Teghem, & Tuyttens, 2005)	Optimization scheduling plan	Review for all
(Lourenço, 2001)	logistic Optimization	Review for all

In GSA, searcher agents are a collection of masses. All these objects attract one another by gravitational force, and this force causes a global movement of all objects toward the objects with heavier masses. Hence, masses cooperate using a direct form of communication, through gravitational force. The heavy masses—which correspond to good solutions—move more slowly than lighter masses, which guarantees the exploitation step of the algorithm. Each agent has position, inertial mass, active gravitational mass, and passive gravitational mass. The position of the mass corresponds to a solution of the problem, and its gravitational and inertial masses are determined using a fitness function.

In other words, each mass presents a solution, and the algorithm is navigated by adjusting the gravitational and inertia masses properly. With the lapse of time, we expect masses to be attracted by the heaviest mass. This mass will present an optimum solution in the search space.

In this algorithm, there are N agents (masses). The position of the i th agent is defined by:

$$X_i = \left(x_i^1, \ldots, x_i^d, \ldots, x_i^n\right), \qquad i = 1, 2, \ldots, N.$$

(32)

where x_i^d presents the position of the i th agent in the d th dimension.

Based on the Newton gravitation theory, the force acting on the i th mass from the j th mass is:

$$F_{ij}^d(t) = G(t)\frac{M_i(t) \times M_j(t)}{R_{ij}(t) + \varepsilon}\left(x_j^d(t) - x_i^d(t)\right),$$

(33)

where M_i and M_j are masses of agents, $G(t)$ is the gravitational constant at time t, and R_{ij} is Euclidian distance between two agents i and j.

$$R_{ij}(t) = X_i(t), X_j(t)_2$$

(34)

For the i th agent, the randomly weighted sum of the forces exerted from other agents is expressed as:

$$F_i^d(t) = \sum_{j=1,\, j\neq 1}^{N} rand_j F_{ij}^d(t) \qquad (35)$$

Hence, based on the law motion, the acceleration of i -th agent is calculated by:

$$a_i^d(t) = \frac{F_i^d(t)}{M_{ij}(t)} \qquad (36)$$

The following equations are the next velocity and its position.

$$v_i^d(t+1) = rand_i \times v_i^d(t) + a_i^d(t) \qquad (37)$$

$$x_i^d(t+1) = x_i^d(t) + v_i^d(t+1) \qquad (38)$$

where x_i^d represents the position of i -th agent in d -th dimension, v_i^d is the velocity, a_i^d is the acceleration.

In Equations 40, 41, and 42, $best(t)$ is the best fitness of all agents at time t, and $worst(t)$ is the worst fitness of all agents:

$$best(t) = \min_{j\in\{1,\ldots,s\}} fit_j(t) \qquad (39)$$

$$worst(t) = \max_{j\in\{1,\ldots,s\}} fit_j(t) \qquad (40)$$

$$q_i(t) = \frac{fit_i(t) - worst(t)}{best(t) - worst(t)},$$

$$M_i(t) = \frac{q_i(t)}{\sum_{j=1}^{s} q_j(t)} \qquad (41)$$

$$G(t) = G(G_0, t) \qquad (42)$$

$X_i(t)$ for $i = 1, 2, \ldots, N$ Notably, gravitational constant $G(t)$ is important in determining the performance of GSA. $G(t)$ is defined to be a decreasing function of time, which is set to G_0 at the beginning and decreases exponentially toward zero as time lapses. Note that $X_i = \left(x_i^1, x_i^2, \ldots, x_i^n\right)$ indicates the position of agent i in the search space, which is a candidate solution. The pseudo code of the GSA is given by Figure 4.

4.3 Gravitational Search Algorithm Applications

Some researchers have compared the GSA algorithm with some known heuristic search methods in their papers. They confirmed the high performance of GSA in solving various nonlinear functions. As an excellent optimization algorithm, GSA has the potential to solve a broad range of optimization problems; indeed, GSA will be applied in parameter identification of a complicated nonlinear system.

Figure 4. Pseudo code of the standard GSA (SGSA)

1	Search space identification , t=0;
2	Randomized initialization $X_i(t)$ for $i = 1, 2, \ldots, N$;
3	Fitness evaluation of agents;
4	Update $G(t)$, $best(t)$, $worst(t)$ and $M_i(t)$ for $i = 1, 2, \ldots, N$;
5	Calculation of acceleration and velocity;
6	Updating agents' position to yield $X_i(t+1)$ for $i = 1, 2, \ldots, N$, $t=t+1$;
7	Repeat steps 3 to 7 until the stopping criterion is reached.

Rashedi et al. (E. Rashedi, et al., 2009) compared and evaluated the performance of the GSA with Real Genetic Algorithm (RGA), Particle Swarm Optimization (PSO), and Central Force Optimization (CFO). Particle Swarm Optimization is motivated by simulating social behavior (such as a flock of birds). This optimization approach updates the population of particles by applying an operator according to the fitness information obtained from the environment such that the population's individuals can be expected to move toward a better solution. Central Force Optimization is a deterministic multidimensional search algorithm. It models the probes that fly through the search space under the influence of gravity. At the beginning convergence, the initial probe positions are computed in a deterministic manner. The GSA algorithm could find the global optimum faster than other comparative algorithms and hence has a higher convergence rate (Li & Zhou, 2011; E. Rashedi, et al., 2009).

Thereafter Li and Zhou (Li & Zhou, 2011) introduced and Improved Gravitational Search Algorithm (IGSA) for nonlinear modeling. They compared GA, PSO, and IGSA to solve the problem. Their results showed that the GSA algorithm was more suitable for solving the problem. Yin et al. (2011) used the improved GSA for clustering data objects into sets of disjoint classes. They developed a hybrid model with GSA and K-harmonic algorithm. In their research, the authors proved that GSA could arrive at a superior result (in most cases) compared with other methods. Recently, GSA has been used in forecasting energy demand and oil consumption. The results indicate that GSA can be employed for linear and nonlinear models

in these cases (Behrang, Assareh, Ghalambaz, Assari, & Noghrehabadi, 2011).

In another paper, Rashedi et al. (2011) used gravitational search algorithm for solving the parameter estimation problem of infinite impulse response filter design. This problem is defined as a new linear and nonlinear filter modeling. They simulated the model with GA, PSO, and GSA. Thereafter, the results of some simulations were compared. The result confirmed the efficiency of the GSA method (Esmat Rashedi, et al., 2011).

5. EXPERIMENTAL RESULTS

In this section, the GSA is used to minimize the total cost of the closed-loop supply chain process. Based on data from the case of recycling alternators (see Table 3), the initial population is generated randomly. Population size is set to 50 ($N = 50$) and the maximum number of iterations is set to 200 ($T = 200$). The fitness function value is calculated without any restrictions. To consider the constrains efficiently, a penalty function is added to the objective function of Equation (1).

To evaluate the proposed method and to check its correctness, a GA is used as a common alternative approach to optimize the model. The crossover and mutation probabilities are set to $P_c = 0.9$ and $P_m = 0.05$, respectively. In GSA, G is set using the following Equation (43), where t is the current iteration:

$$G = \exp(-t / T) \qquad (43)$$

Table 3. Data of the closed-loop supply chain

No. raw materials	No. suppliers	No. products	No. manufacturing plants	No. distributors	No. wholesalers	No. retailers	No. recycling plant	No. disposal site
1	2	1	1	1	4	10	1	1

The most popular method in the heuristic search algorithm community to handle constraints is to use penalty functions that penalize infeasible solutions by reducing their fitness (increasing their cost) values in proportion to their degrees of constraint violations in maximization (minimization) problems. The penalty method transforms constrained problems into unconstrained problems by adding the term of the penalty. If a constraint is violated such that a larger term will be added to the cost function (for a minimization problem), the solution is pushed back toward to the feasible region.

A common and effective way is to penalize infeasible solutions according to its distance to feasibility. A more common and more effective penalty used in this paper includes a distance metric for each constraint and adds a penalty that becomes more severe with distance from feasibility.

Table 4. Minimization results and accuracy statistics of the GSA and GA in the closed-loop supply chain (Maximum number of iterations is 200)

Function	Results	GA	GSA	GSA-GA Unpaired t-tests
TC	Average best-so-far	177275.41	**177214.27**	*p* value < 0.0001 Extremely significant
	Average mean fitness	177823.40	**177340.64**	
	Best Fitness	177175.16	**177134.79**	
	Worst Fitness	177342.20	**177311.60**	
	STD	**37.56**	44.82	

Figure 5. Comparison of performance of GSA and GA to minimize TC. Showing the average best-so-far solution versus iteration, results represent 30 independent runs.

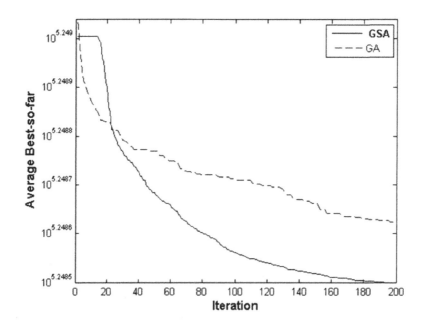

The results are averaged over 30 independent runs. The best and worst obtained fitness values, average best-so-far fitness values, average mean fitness values, and standard deviation of fitness values in last iteration of the algorithms are reported in Table 4.

As Table 3 illustrates, GSA provides better results than GA for the model. Because total cost as a main objective that should be minimize is less for the supply chain when the model is being solved by GSA comparing with GA. Table 3 also shows the results of unpaired *t* tests between the competing algorithms. The results show that the GSA is more precise in the closed-loop supply chain. This is due to the attractive power of GSA.

6. CONCLUSION AND FUTURE RESEARCH DIRECTIONS

The authors have tried to express the significant of green supply chain management and illustrated current and future trends. Evidence shows that both business and governments will be more cautious in the greening of manufacturing and supply chains. A new optimization algorithm called Gravitational Search Algorithm (GSA) was introduced. Then, to express the applications of GSA as a new metaheuristic algorithm in the supply chain, a mixed integer programming mathematical model was developed. The model aimed to optimize total costs in a closed-loop logistic for gathering automobile alternators at the end of their life cycle. Thereafter, we tried to optimize the model by using GSA in MATLAB software. To express GSA capabilities, we compared GSA with genetic algorithms as a very common and standard metaheuristic algorithm for optimization. The performance of GSA produced superior results in terms of computed final fitness values. Furthermore, the good convergence rate of GSA can be concluded from Figure 5. According to this figure, GSA tends to find the global optimum faster than GA; hence, it has a higher convergence rate.

In the future, air pollution factors, product returned collection, time responsiveness, safe inventory, social effects, and environment factors can be considered in the metaheuristic models to obtain comprehensive results.

ACKNOWLEDGMENT

We would like to sincerely thank Mr. Nasri for his continuous guidance and support as we wrote MATLAB codes. Furthermore, we are so thankful for Miss Esmat Rashedi for her suggestions as we analyzed and transcribed GSA and GA.

REFERENCES

Barros, A., Dekker, R., & Scholten, V. (1998). A two-level network for recycling sand: A case study. *European Journal of Operational Research*, *110*(2), 199–214. doi:10.1016/S0377-2217(98)00093-9

Bartels, J. J. C. (1998). Inzameling en verwerking van batterijen in Nederland - het Stibat-uitvoeringsplan . In Goor, A. R. v., Flapper, S. D. P., & Clement, C. (Eds.), *Handbook of reverse logistics (pp. F3510-3511 - F3510-3528)*. The Netherlands.

Behrang, M. A., Assareh, E., Ghalambaz, M., Assari, M. R., & Noghrehabadi, A. R. (2011). Forecasting future oil demand in Iran using GSA (Gravitational Search Algorithm). *Energy*, *36*(9), 5649–5654. doi:10.1016/j.energy.2011.07.002

Biehl, M., Prater, E., & Realff, M. J. (2007). Assessing performance and uncertainty in developing carpet reverse logistics systems. *Computers & Operations Research*, *34*(2), 443–463. doi:10.1016/j.cor.2005.03.008

Bonabeau, E., Dorigo, M., & Theraulaz, G. (1999). *Swarm intelligence: From natural to artificial systems*. USA: Oxford University Press.

Cao, S., & Zhang, K. (2011, 6-8 May 2011). *Optimization of the flow distribution of e-waste reverse logistics network based on NSGA II and TOPSIS*. Paper presented at the 2011 International Conference on E -Business and E -Government (ICEE).

Crainic, T. G., & Toulouse, M. (2010). Parallel meta-heuristics. *Handbook of metaheuristics*, (pp. 497-541).

Cruz-Rivera, R., & Ertel, J. (2009). Reverse logistics network design for the collection of end-of-life vehicles in Mexico. *European Journal of Operational Research*, *196*(3), 930–939. doi:10.1016/j.ejor.2008.04.041

De La Fuente, M., Ros, L., & Cardos, M. (2008). Integrating forward and reverse supply chains: Application to a metal-mechanic company. *International Journal of Production Economics*, *111*(2), 782–792. doi:10.1016/j.ijpe.2007.03.019

Dorigo, M., Maniezzo, V., & Colorni, A. (1991). *Positive feedback as a search strategy.*

Eltayeb, T. K., Zailani, S., & Ramayah, T. (2010). Green supply chain initiatives among certified companies in Malaysia and environmental sustainability: Investigating the outcomes. *Resources, Conservation and Recycling*, *55*(5), 495–506. doi:10.1016/j.resconrec.2010.09.003

Farahani, R. Z., & Elahipanah, M. (2008). A genetic algorithm to optimize the total cost and service level for just-in-time distribution in a supply chain. *International Journal of Production Economics*, *111*(2), 229–243. doi:10.1016/j.ijpe.2006.11.028

Fleischmann, M., Beullens, P., Bloemhof-Ruwaard, J. M., & Van Wassenhove, L. N. (2001). The impact of product recovery on logistics network design. *Production and Operations Management*, *10*(2), 156–173. doi:10.1111/j.1937-5956.2001.tb00076.x

Fogel, L. J., Owens, A. J., & Walsh, M. J. (1966). *Artificial intelligence through simulated evolution.*

Fortes, J. (2009). *Green supply chain management: A literature.*

Gambardella, L. M., Rizzoli, A. E., Oliverio, F., Casagrande, N., Donati, A., Montemanni, R., et al. (2003). *Ant colony optimization for vehicle routing in advanced logistics systems.*

Glover, F. (1986). Future paths for integer programming and links to artificial intelligence. *Computers & Operations Research*, *13*(5), 533–549. doi:10.1016/0305-0548(86)90048-1

Grunow, M., & Gobbi, C. (2009). Designing the reverse network for WEEE in Denmark. *CIRP Annals-Manufacturing Technology*, *58*(1), 391–394. doi:10.1016/j.cirp.2009.03.036

Holland, J. (1975). Adaptation in natural and artificial systems: An introductory analysis with applications to biology . In *Control and artificial intelligence*. Cambridge, MA: MIT Press.

Holland, J. H. (1999). *Emergence: From chaos to order*. Basic Books.

Jayaraman, V., Guide, V. Jr, & Srivastava, R. (1999). A closed-loop logistics model for remanufacturing. *The Journal of the Operational Research Society*, *50*(5), 497–508.

Kannan, G., Sasikumar, P., & Devika, K. (2010). A genetic algorithm approach for solving a closed loop supply chain model: A case of battery recycling. *Applied Mathematical Modelling*, *34*(3), 655–670. doi:10.1016/j.apm.2009.06.021

Kennedy, J., & Eberhart, R. (1995). *Particle swarm optimization.*

Kim, H., Yang, J., & Lee, K. D. (2009). Vehicle routing in reverse logistics for recycling end-of-life consumer electronic goods in South Korea. *Transportation Research Part D, Transport and Environment*, *14*(5), 291–299. doi:10.1016/j.trd.2009.03.001

Krikke, H., Van Harten, A., & Schuur, P. (1999). Business case Oce: Reverse logistic network redesign for copiers. *OR-Spektrum*, *21*(3), 381–409. doi:10.1007/s002910050095

Kusumastuti, R. D., Piplani, R., & Hian Lim, G. (2008). Redesigning closed-loop service network at a computer manufacturer: A case study. *International Journal of Production Economics*, *111*(2), 244–260. doi:10.1016/j.ijpe.2006.10.016

Lee, D. H., & Dong, M. (2008). A heuristic approach to logistics network design for end-of-lease computer products recovery. *Transportation Research Part E, Logistics and Transportation Review*, *44*(3), 455–474. doi:10.1016/j.tre.2006.11.003

Lee, J. E., Gen, M., & Rhee, K. G. (2008). A multi-stage reverse logistics network problem by using hybrid priority-based genetic algorithm. *IEEJ Transactions on Electronics . Information Systems*, *128*(3), 450–455.

Lee, J. E., Rhee, K. G., & Lee, H. H. (2010). *Multiobjective hybrid genetic algorithm for reverse logistics network design of inventory systems with backordering*. Paper presented at the IEEM2010 - IEEE International Conference on Industrial Engineering and Engineering Management, Macao.

Li, C., & Zhou, J. (2011). Parameters identification of hydraulic turbine governing system using improved gravitational search algorithm. *Energy Conversion and Management*, *52*(1), 374–381. doi:10.1016/j.enconman.2010.07.012

Listes, O., & Dekker, R. (2005). A stochastic approach to a case study for product recovery network design. *European Journal of Operational Research*, *160*(1), 268. doi:10.1016/j.ejor.2001.12.001

Loukil, T., Teghem, J., & Tuyttens, D. (2005). Solving multi-objective production scheduling problems using metaheuristics. *European Journal of Operational Research*, *161*(1), 42–61. doi:10.1016/j.ejor.2003.08.029

Lourenço, H. R. (2001). *Integrated logistics management: An opportunity for metaheuristics*.

Lourenco, H. R., & Empresa, U. P. F. D. d. E. i. (2001). *Supply chain management: An opportunity for metaheuristics*. Universitat Pompeu Fabra.

Louwers, D., Kip, B. J., Peters, E., Souren, F., & Flapper, S. D. P. (1999). A facility location allocation model for reusing carpet materials. *Computers & Industrial Engineering*, *36*(4), 855–869. doi:10.1016/S0360-8352(99)00168-0

McWilliams, A., & Siegel, D. (2000). Corporate social responsibility and financial performance: correlation or misspecification? *Strategic Management Journal*, *21*(5), 603–609. doi:10.1002/(SICI)1097-0266(200005)21:5<603::AID-SMJ101>3.0.CO;2-3

Meade, L., & Sarkis, J. (2007). The theory and practice of reverse logistics. *International Journal of Logistics*, *1*(3).

Min, H., Jeung Ko, H., & Seong Ko, C. (2006). A genetic algorithm approach to developing the multi-echelon reverse logistics network for product returns. *Omega*, *34*(1), 56–69. doi:10.1016/j.omega.2004.07.025

Nagurney, A., & Toyasaki, F. (2005). Reverse supply chain management and electronic waste recycling: A multitiered network equilibrium framework for e-cycling. *Transportation Research Part E, Logistics and Transportation Review, 41*(1), 1–28. doi:10.1016/j.tre.2003.12.001

Pati, R. K., Vrat, P., & Kumar, P. (2008). A goal programming model for paper recycling system. *Omega, 36*(3), 405–417. doi:10.1016/j.omega.2006.04.014

Pishvaee, M. S., Kianfar, K., & Karimi, B. (2010). Reverse logistics network design using simulated annealing. *International Journal of Advanced Manufacturing Technology, 47*(1), 269–281. doi:10.1007/s00170-009-2194-5

Rashedi, E., Nezamabadi-pour, H., & Saryazdi, S. (2009). GSA: A gravitational search algorithm. *Information Sciences, 179*(13), 2232–2248. doi:10.1016/j.ins.2009.03.004

Rashedi, E., Nezamabadi-pour, H., & Saryazdi, S. (2011). Filter modeling using gravitational search algorithm. *Engineering Applications of Artificial Intelligence, 24*(1), 117–122. doi:10.1016/j.engappai.2010.05.007

Realff, M., Ammons, J., & Newton, D. (2004). Robust reverse production system design for carpet recycling. *IIE Transactions, 36*(8), 767–776. doi:10.1080/07408170490458580

Rechenberg, I. (1973). *Evolutionsstrategie: Optimierung technischer Systeme nach Prinzipien der biologischen Evolution*. Stuttgart, Germany: Frommann-Holzbog.

Sarkis, J. (2003). A strategic decision framework for green supply chain management. *Journal of Cleaner Production, 11*(4), 397–409. doi:10.1016/S0959-6526(02)00062-8

Schinkel, H. (2000). Gipsreststoffengooi je nietweg! In van Goor, A. R., Flapper, S. D. P., & Clement, C. (Eds.), *Handboek reverse logistics*. Deventer, The Netherlands: Kluwer B.V.

Schultmann, F., Engels, B., & Rentz, O. (2003). Closed-loop supply chains for spent batteries. *Interfaces, 33*(6), 57–71. doi:10.1287/inte.33.6.57.25183

Schultmann, F., Zumkeller, M., & Rentz, O. (2006). Modeling reverse logistic tasks within closed-loop supply chains: An example from the automotive industry. *European Journal of Operational Research, 171*(3), 1033–1050. doi:10.1016/j.ejor.2005.01.016

Shen, Z. (2007). Integrated supply chain design models: A survey and future research directions. *Management, 3*(1), 1–27.

Sheu, J. B. (2008). Green supply chain management, reverse logistics and nuclear power generation. *Transportation Research Part E, Logistics and Transportation Review, 44*(1), 19–46. doi:10.1016/j.tre.2006.06.001

Shih, L. H. (2001). Reverse logistics system planning for recycling electrical appliances and computers in Taiwan. *Resources, Conservation and Recycling, 32*(1), 55–72. doi:10.1016/S0921-3449(00)00098-7

Simchi-Levi, D., Kaminsky, P., & Simchi-Levi, E. (2003). *Designing and managing the supply chain: Concepts, strategies, and case studies*. Irwin/McGraw-Hill.

Srivastava, S. K. (2007). Green supply-chain management: A state-of-the-art literature review. *International Journal of Management Reviews, 9*(1), 53–80. doi:10.1111/j.1468-2370.2007.00202.x

Thierry, M., Salomon, M., Van Nunen, J., & Van Wassenhove, L. (1995). Strategic issues in product recovery management. *California Management Review, 37*(2), 115.

Ubbens, U. M. P. (2000). De kringloop van metalenverpakkingen . In van Goor, A. R., Flapper, S. D. P., & Clement, C. (Eds.), *Handboek reverse logistics*. Deventer, The Netherlands: Kluwer B.V.

Van Notten, R. A. P. (2000). Inzameling en bewerking ten behoeve van het hergebruik van verpakkingsglas . In van Goor, A. R., Flapper, S. D. P., & Clement, C. (Eds.), *Handboek reverse logistics*. Deventer, The Netherlands: Kluwer B.V.

Walker, H., Di Sisto, L., & McBain, D. (2008). Drivers and barriers to environmental supply chain management practices: Lessons from the public and private sectors. *Journal of Purchasing and Supply Management, 14*(1), 69–85. doi:10.1016/j.pursup.2008.01.007

Walther, G., & Spengler, T. (2005). Impact of WEEE-directive on reverse logistics in Germany. *International Journal of Physical Distribution & Logistics Management, 35*(5), 337–361. doi:10.1108/09600030510607337

Wang, F., Lai, X., & Shi, N. (2011). A multi-objective optimization for green supply chain network design. *Decision Support Systems, 51*(2), 262–269. doi:10.1016/j.dss.2010.11.020

Wang, Z., & Bai, H. (2010). *Reverse logistics network: A review*. Paper presented at the IEEM2010 - IEEE International Conference on Industrial Engineering and Engineering Management, Macao.

Xanthopoulos, A., & Iakovou, E. (2009). On the optimal design of the disassembly and recovery processes. *Waste Management (New York, N.Y.), 29*(5), 1702–1711. doi:10.1016/j.wasman.2008.11.009

Yan, G., & Soc, I. C. (2009). *Research on green suppliers' evaluation based on AHP & genetic algorithm*.

Yanchao, L., Pengchao, L., & Litao, L. (2008, 6-8 April 2008). *Multi-objective optimization of reverse logistics network based on random weights and genetic algorithm*. Paper presented at IEEE International Conference on Networking, Sensing and Control, ICNSC 2008.

Yanchao, L., Xiaoyan, L., & Litao, L. (2008, 25-27 June 2008). *Multi-objective optimization of reverse logistics network based on improved particle swarm optimization*. Paper presented at the 7th World Congress on Intelligent Control and Automation, WCICA 2008.

Yimsiri, S. (2009). *Designing multi-objective reverse logistics networks using genetic algorithms*.

Yin, M., Hu, Y., Yang, F., Li, X., & Gu, W. (2011). A novel hybrid K-harmonic means and gravitational search algorithm approach for clustering. *Expert Systems with Applications, 38*(8), 9319–9324. doi:10.1016/j.eswa.2011.01.018

KEY TERM AND DEFINITIONS

Closed-Loop Logistic: Integration of forward and reverse logistic to avoid sub-optimization.

Gravitational Search Algorithm: A swarm intelligence algorithm based on the Newtonian gravity and the laws of motion.

Green Supply Chain: Supply chain that cautions systematically to environment regular, waste management, energy consumption, environment effect, recycling and product return.

Green Supply Chain: The process of using environmentally friendly inputs and transforming these inputs through change agents - whose byproducts can improve or be recycled within the existing environment. This process develops outputs that can be reclaimed and re-used at the end of their life-cycle thus, creating a sustainable supply chain.

Mixed Integer Programming: Is a mathematical method for determining a way to achieve the best outcome (such as maximum profit or lowest cost) in a given mathematical model for some list of requirements represented as linear relationships.

Reverse Logistic: A logistic network that try to collect product in end of life cycle to re-use, re-cycle and re-manufacture.

Swarm Algorithms: The algorithms mainly inspired by social behavior patterns of organisms which locate the global optimum without any central control.

Compilation of References

Aardal, K. (1998). Capacitated facility location: Separation algorithms and computational experience. *Mathematical Programming*, *81*, 149–175. doi:10.1007/BF01581103

Aardal, K., Labbe, M., Leung, J., & Queyranne, M. (1996). On the two-level uncapacitated facility location problem. *INFORMS Journal on Computing*, *8*, 289–301. doi:10.1287/ijoc.8.3.289

Aarts, E. H. L., & Korst, J. H. M. (1989). *Simulated annealing and Boltzmann machine: A stochastic approach to computing*. Chichester, UK: John Wiley and Sons.

Abdelsalam, H. M., & Bao, H. P. (2006). A simulation-based optimization framework for product development cycle time reduction. *IEEE Transactions on Engineering Management*, *53*(1), 69–85. doi:10.1109/TEM.2005.861805

Abido, M. A. (2001). Optimal power flow using particles warm optimization. *International Journal of Electrical Power & Energy Systems*, *24*(7), 563–571. doi:10.1016/S0142-0615(01)00067-9

Abou El-Ela, A. A., & Abido, M. A. (1992). Optimal operation strategy for reactive power control modelling. *Simulation and Control. Part A*, *41*(3), 19–40.

Ackermann, T., Andersson, G., & Soder, L. (2001). Distributed Generation: A definition. *International Journal of Electric Power Systems Research*, *57*(3), 195–204. doi:10.1016/S0378-7796(01)00101-8

Ackley, D. (1987). An empirical study of bit vector function optimization. *Genetic Algorithms and Simulated Annealing*, 170-215.

Adankon, M. M., & Cheriet, M. (2009). Model selection for the LSSVM. Application to handwriting recognition. *Pattern Recognition*, *42*(12), 3264–3270. doi:10.1016/j.patcog.2008.10.023

Adenso-Diaz, B., & Laguna, M. (2006). Fine-tuning of algorithms using fractional experimental designs and local search. *Operations Research*, *54*(1), 99–114. doi:10.1287/opre.1050.0243

Agarkov, O. A., Voropai, N. I., Abramenkova, N. A., & Zaslavskaya, T. B. (1990). Structural analysis in power system stability studies. *Proceedings of 10th PSCC*, Graz, Austria, August 30-September 3 (pp.152-159).

Agatonovic-Kustrin, S., & Beresford, R. (2000). Basic concepts of artificial neural network (ANN) modeling and its application in pharmaceutical research. *Journal of Pharmaceutical and Biomedical Analysis*, *22*, 717–727. doi:10.1016/S0731-7085(99)00272-1

Aggarwal, C., Han, J., Wang, J., & Yu, P. (2005). On high dimensional projected clustering of data streams. *Data Mining and Knowledge Discovery*, *10*(3), 251–273. doi:10.1007/s10618-005-0645-7

Agyemang, M., Barker, K., & Alhajj, R. (2006). A comprehensive survey of numeric and symbolic outlier mining techniques. *Intelligent Data Analysis*, *10*(6), 521–538.

Ai, J., & Kachitvichyanukul, V. (2009). A particle swarm optimization for the vehicle routing problem with simultaneous pickup and delivery. *Computers & Operations Research*, *36*(5), 1693–1702. doi:10.1016/j.cor.2008.04.003

Alatas, B. (2010). Chaotic bee colony algorithms for global numerical optimization. *Expert Systems with Applications*, *37*(8), 5682–5687. doi:10.1016/j.eswa.2010.02.042

Alaya, I., Solnon, C., & Ghedira, K. (2007). Ant colony optimization for multi-objective optimization problems. *The 19th IEEE International Conference on Tools with Artificial Intelligence,* Vol. 1, (pp. 450-457).

Alaykýran, K., Engin, O., & Döyen, A. (2007). Using ant colony optimization to solve the hybrid flow shop scheduling problems. *International Journal of Advanced Manufacturing Technology, 35*(5-6), 541–550. doi:10.1007/s00170-007-1048-2

Al-Betar, M. A., Khader, A. T., & Gani, T. A. (2008). A harmony search algorithm for university course timetabling. *7th International Conference on the Practice and Theory of Automated Timetabling* (pp. 1-12) Montreal, Canada.

Al-Betar, M., Khader, A., & Liao, I. (2010). A harmony search with multi-pitch adjusting rate for the university course timetabling. In Geem, Z. (Ed.), *Studies in computational intelligence.* Springer. doi:10.1007/978-3-642-04317-8_13

Alia, O. M., Mandava, R., & Aziz, M. E. (2010). A hybrid harmony search algorithm to MRI brain segmentation. *The 9th IEEE International Conference on Cognitive Informatics, ICCI2010* (pp. 712–719). Tsinghua University, Beijing, China: IEEE.

Alia, O. M., Mandava, R., Ramachandram, D., & Aziz, M. E. (2009a). A novel image segmentation algorithm based on harmony fuzzy search algorithm. *International Conference of Soft Computing and Pattern Recognition (SOCPAR 09)* (pp. 335–340).

Alia, O. M., Mandava, R., Ramachandram, D., & Aziz, M. E. (2009b). Harmony search-based cluster initialization for fuzzy c-means segmentation of MR images. *TENCON 2009–2009 IEEE Region 10 Conference* (pp. 1–6). Singapore.

Alia, O. M., Mandava, R., Ramachandram, D., & Aziz, M. E. (2009c). Dynamic fuzzy clustering using harmony search with application to image segmentation. *IEEE International Symposium on Signal Processing and Information Technology (ISSPIT09)* (pp. 538–543).

Alia, O. M., & Mandava, R. (2011). The variants of harmony search algorithm: an overview. *Artificial Intelligence Review, 36*(1), 49–68. doi:10.1007/s10462-010-9201-y

Aliev, A., & Aliev, R. (2002). *Soft computing and its applications.* World Scientific Publishing.

Al-Taharwa, I., Sheta, A., & Al-Weshah, M. (2008). A mobile robot path planning using genetic algorithm in static environment. *Journal of Computer Science, 4*(4), 341–344. doi:10.3844/jcssp.2008.341.344

Altiparmak, F., Gen, M., Lin, L., & Paksoy, T. (2006). A genetic algorithm approach for multi-objective optimization of supply chain networks. *Computers & Industrial Engineering, 51*, 196–215. doi:10.1016/j.cie.2006.07.011

Altroc, C. (1996). *Fuzzy logic & neurofuzzy applications in business & finance.* USA: Prentice Hall.

Altus, S. S., Kroo, I. M., & Gage, P. J. (1996). A genetic algorithm for scheduling and decomposition of multi-disciplinary design problems. *Transactions of ASME, 118*(4), 486–489.

Andres, C., & Lozano, S. (2006). A particle swarm optimization algorithm for part–machine grouping. *Robotics and Computer-integrated Manufacturing, 22*, 468–474. doi:10.1016/j.rcim.2005.11.013

Anghinolfi, D., & Paolucci, M. (2009). A new discrete particle swarm optimization approach for the single-machine total weighted tardiness scheduling problem with sequence-dependent setup times. *European Journal of Operational Research, 193*(1), 73–85. doi:10.1016/j.ejor.2007.10.044

Angira, R., & Babu, B. V. (2006). Optimization of process synthesis and design problems: A modified differential evolution approach. *Chemical Engineering Science, 61*(14), 4707–4721. doi:10.1016/j.ces.2006.03.004

Angiulli, F., & Fassetti, F. (2010). Distance-based outlier queries in data streams: the novel task and algorithms. *Data Mining and Knowledge Discovery, 20*(2), 290–324. doi:10.1007/s10618-009-0159-9

Anily, S., Glass, C. A., & Hassin, R. (1998). The scheduling of maintenance service. *Discrete Applied Mathematics, 82*, 27–42. doi:10.1016/S0166-218X(97)00119-4

Applegate, D. L., Bixby, R. E., Chvatal, V., & Cook, W. J. (2006). *The travelling salesman problem - A computational study. Princeton Series in Applied Mathematics.* Princeton University Press.

Aras, N., Ozkısacık, K. C., & Altinel, I. K. (2006). Solving the uncapacitated multi-facility Weber problem by vector quantization and self-organizing maps. *The Journal of the Operational Research Society, 57*, 82–93. doi:10.1057/palgrave.jors.2601962

Arboleya, P., Diaz, D., Guerrero, J. M., Garcia, P., Briz, F., & Gonzalez-Moran, C. (2010). An improved control scheme based in droop characteristic for microgrid converters. *Electric Power Systems Research*, (n.d), 1215–1221. doi:10.1016/j.epsr.2010.04.003

Arcus, A. (1966). COMSOAL: A computer method of sequencing operations for assembly lines. *International Journal of Production Research, 4*, 259–277. doi:10.1080/00207546508919982

Armstrong, S. C. (2001). *Engineering and product development management: The holistic approach.* Cambridge University Press.

Assareh, E., Behrang, M. A., Assari, M. R., & Ghanbarzadeh, A. (2010). Application of PSO and GA techniques on demand estimation of oil in Iran. *Energy, 35*, 5223–5229. doi:10.1016/j.energy.2010.07.043

Augerat, P., Belenguer, J. M., Benavent, E., Corber'n, A., & Naddef, D. (1998). Separating capacity constraints in the CVRP using tabu search. *European Journal of Operational Research, 106*, 546–557. doi:10.1016/S0377-2217(97)00290-7

Austin, S., Baldwin, A., Li, B., & Waskett, P. (2000). Analytical design planning technique (ADePT): A dependency structure matrix tool to schedule the building design process. *Construction Management and Economics, 8*, 173–182. doi:10.1080/014461900370807

Avella, P., & Boccia, M. (2009). A cutting plane algorithm for the capacitated facility location problem. *Computational Optimization and Applications, 43*, 39–65. doi:10.1007/s10589-007-9125-x

Avella, P., Boccia, M., & Sforza, A., A., & Vasilev, I. (2009). An effective heuristic for large-scale capacitated facility location problems. *Journal of Heuristics, 15*, 63–81. doi:10.1007/s10732-008-9078-y

Ayuev, B. I., Davydov, V. V., Erokhin, P. M., & Neuymin, V. G. (2008). *Computational models of load flow in electric power systems.* Moscow, Russia: Nauka. (in Russian)

Ayvaz, M. T. (2007). Simultaneous determination of aquifer parameters and zone structures with fuzzy c-means clustering and meta-heuristic harmony search algorithm. *Advances in Water Resources, 30*(11), 2326–2338. doi:10.1016/j.advwatres.2007.05.009

Ayvaz, M. T. (2009). Application of harmony search algorithm to the solution of groundwater management models. *Advances in Water Resources, 32*(6), 916–924. doi:10.1016/j.advwatres.2009.03.003

Azadeh, A., Moghaddam, M., & Khakzad, M. (2011). A flexible neural network fuzzy mathematical programming algorithm for improvement of oil price estimation and forecasting. *Computers & Industrial Engineering, 62*(2). doi:doi:10.1016/j.cie.2011.06.019

Azaron, A., Brown, K. N., Tarim, S. A., & Modarres, M. (2008). A multi-objective stochastic programming approach for supply chain design considering risk. *International Journal of Production Economics, 116*, 129–138. doi:10.1016/j.ijpe.2008.08.002

Azoff, E. M. (1994). *Neural network time series forecasting of financial markets.* USA: John Wiley.

Babcock, B., Babu, S., Datar, M., Motwani, R., & Widom, J. (2002). Models and issues in data stream systems. In *PODS '02: Proceedings of the twenty-first ACM SIGMOD-SIGACT-SIGART Symposium on Principles of Database Systems*, (pp. 1-16). New York, NY: ACM.

Bäck, T., Fogel, D., & Michalewicz, Z. (1997). *Handbook of evolutionary computation.* Bristol, UK: Institute of Physics Publishing Ltd.doi:10.1887/0750308958

Bai, X., Wei, H., Fujisawa, K., & Wang, Y. (2008). Semidefinite programming for optimal power flow problems. *International Journal of Electrical Power & Energy Systems, 30*(6–7), 383–392. doi:10.1016/j.ijepes.2007.12.003

Baker, B. M., & Ayechew, M. A. (2003). A genetic algorithm for the vehicle routing problem. *Computers & Operations Research, 30*, 787–800. doi:10.1016/S0305-0548(02)00051-5

Balakrishnan, N., Kanet, J., & Sridharan, S. (1999). Early/tardy scheduling with sequence dependent setups on uniform parallel machines. *Computers & Operations Research, 26*(2), 127–141. doi:10.1016/S0305-0548(98)00051-3

Balinski, M. L., & Young, H. P. (Eds.). (1982). *Fair representation*. New Haven, CT: Yale University Press.

Baltar, A. M., & Fontane, D. G. (2006). A generalized multiobjective particle swarm optimization solver for spreadsheet models: Application to water quality. In *Proceedings of the Twenty Sixth Annual American Geophysical Union Hydrology Days*, 20–22 March 2006.

Banerjee, A. (1986). A joint economic lot size model for purchaser and vendor. *Decision Sciences, 17*, 292–311. doi:10.1111/j.1540-5915.1986.tb00228.x

Banks, A., Vincent, J., & Anyakoha, C. (2007). A review of particle swarm optimization. Part I: background and development. *Natural Computing, 6*(4), 467–484. doi:10.1007/s11047-007-9049-5

Banks, A., Vincent, J., & Anyakoha, C. (2008). A review of particle swarm optimization. Part II: hybridisation, combinatorial, multicriteria and constrained optimization, and indicative applications. *Natural Computing, 7*(1), 109–124. doi:10.1007/s11047-007-9050-z

Barahona, F., & Chudak, F. (2005). Near-optimal solutions to large-scale facility location problems. *Discrete Optimization, 2*, 35–50. doi:10.1016/j.disopt.2003.03.001

Barker, P., & De Mello, R. (2001). *Determining the impact of distributed generation on power systems. I. Radial distribution systems*. Paper presented at the IEEE Power Engineering Society Summer Meeting, Seattle, WA, USA

Bar-Noy, A., Nisgav, A., & Patt-Shamir, B. (2002). Nearly optimal perfectly-periodic schedules. *Distributed Computing, 15*, 207–220. doi:10.1007/s00446-002-0085-1

Barnsley, M. F. (1993). *Fractals everywhere*. USA: Academic Press Professional.

Barros, A., Dekker, R., & Scholten, V. (1998). A two-level network for recycling sand: A case study. *European Journal of Operational Research, 110*(2), 199–214. doi:10.1016/S0377-2217(98)00093-9

Barros, A., & Labbé, M. (1994). A general model for the uncapacitated facility and depot location problem. *Location Science, 2*, 173–191.

Barr, R. S., Golden, B. L., Kelly, J., Stewart, W. R., & Resende, M. G. C. (1995). Guidelines for designing and reporting on computational experiments with heuristic methods. *Journal of Heuristics, 1*(1), 9–32. doi:10.1007/BF02430363

Bartels, J. J. C. (1998). Inzameling en verwerking van batterijen in Nederland - het Stibat-uitvoeringsplan. In Goor, A. R. v., Flapper, S. D. P., & Clement, C. (Eds.), *Handbook of reverse logistics (pp. F3510-3511 - F3510-3528)*. The Netherlands.

Bartholdi, J. J. (1993). Balancing two-sided assembly lines: A case study. *International Journal of Production Research, 31*, 2447–2461. doi:10.1080/00207549308956868

Bartholdi, J. J., Collins, R. L., Platzman, L. K., & Warden, W. H. (1983). A minimal technology routing system for meals on wheels. *Interfaces, 13*(3), 1. doi:10.1287/inte.13.3.1

Bartolomei, P. I., & Panikovskaya, T. Y. (2008). *Optimization of energy system operation: Teaching aid*. Ekaterinburg, Russia: UGTU – UPI. (in Russian)

Bar-Yam, Y. (Ed.). (1997). *Dynamics of complex systems*. Addison-Wesley.

Basak, P., Saha, A. K., Chowdhury, S., & Chowdhury, S. P. (2009). *Microgrid: Control techniques and modeling*. Paper presented at the IEEE.

Battiti, R. (1996). Reactive search: Toward self-tuning heuristics. In Rayward-Smith, I. H., Osman, I. H., Reeves, C. R., & Smith, G. D. (Eds.), *Modern heuristic search methods* (pp. 61–83). John Wiley and Sons Ltd.

Bautista, J., Companys, R., & Corominas, A. (1997). Modelling and solving the production rate variation problem (PRVP). *Top (Madrid), 5*, 221–239. doi:10.1007/BF02568551

Baykasoğlu, A., & Gindy, N. N. Z. (2004). Erratum to "A simulated annealing algorithm for dynamic layout problem". *Computers & Operations Research, 31*(2), 313–315. doi:10.1016/S0305-0548(03)00205-3

Bean, J. C. (1994). Genetic algorithms and random keys for sequencing and optimization. *ORSA Journal on Computing, 6*, 154–160. doi:10.1287/ijoc.6.2.154

Beasley, D., Bull, D. R., & Martin, R. R. (1993). An overview of genetic algorithms: Part 1, fundamentals. *University Computing, 15*, 58–69.

Beasley, J. E. (1993). *Lagrangian relaxation: Modern heuristic techniques for combinatorial problems.* New York, NY: John Wiley and Sons.

Behrang, M. A., Assareh, E., Ghalambaz, M., Assari, M. R., & Noghrehabadi, A. R. (2011). Forecasting future oil demand in Iran using GSA (Gravitational Search Algorithm). *Energy, 36*(9), 5649–5654. doi:10.1016/j.energy.2011.07.002

Bell, J. E., & McMullen, P. R. (2004). Ant colony optimization techniques for the vehicle routing problem. *Advanced Engineering Informatics, 18*, 41–48. doi:10.1016/j.aei.2004.07.001

Bellman, R. E., & Zadeh, L. A. (1970). Decision making in a fuzzy environment. *Management Science, 17*, 141–164. doi:10.1287/mnsc.17.4.B141

Ben-Daya, M., & Al-Fawzan, M. (1998). A tabu search approach for the flow shop scheduling problem. *European Journal of Operational Research, 9*, 88–95. doi:10.1016/S0377-2217(97)00136-7

Ben-Daya, M., Duffaa, O. S., & Raout, A. (Eds.). (2000). *Maintenance modeling and optimization.* Boston, MA: Springer. doi:10.1007/978-1-4615-4329-9

Beneš, O., van der Meer, J. P. M., & Konings, R. J. M. (2007). Modelling and calculation of the phase diagrams of the LiF–NaF–RbF–LaF$_3$ system. *Computer Coupling of Phase Diagrams and Thermochemistry, 31*, 209–216. doi:10.1016/j.calphad.2006.12.004

Bentley, J. J. (1992). Fast algorithms for geometric traveling salesman problems. *ORSA Journal on Computing, 4*(4), 387–411. doi:10.1287/ijoc.4.4.387

Beringer, J., & Hüllermeier, E. (2006). Online clustering of parallel data streams. *Data & Knowledge Engineering, 58*(2), 180–204. doi:10.1016/j.datak.2005.05.009

Besnard, F., Patrikssont, M., Strombergt, A. B., Wojciechowskit, A., & Bertling, L. (2009). An optimization framework for opportunistic maintenance of offshore wind power system, 2009 IEEE Bucharest *Power Technology Conference,* (pp. 1-7). Bucharest.

Beullens, P., Muyldermans, L., Cattrysse, D., & Van Oudheusden, D. (2003). A guided local search heuristic for the capacitated arc routing problem. *European Journal of Operational Research, 147*(3), 629–643. doi:10.1016/S0377-2217(02)00334-X

Bevrani, H. (2011). *Artificial neural networks.* Retrieved from http://www.bevrani.com/ANN/ANN.htm

Bevrani, H., & Hiyama, T. (April 2011). Neural network based AGC design. In *Intelligent automatic generation control.* New York, NY: CRC Press (Taylor & Francis Group).

Bevrani, H. (2009). *Robust power system frequency control.* New York, NY: Springer. doi:10.1007/978-0-387-84878-5

Beyer, H. G. (2001). *The theory of evolution strategies.* Germany: Springer.

Beygelzimer, A., Kakade, S., & Langford, J. (2006). Cover trees for nearest neighbor. In *ICML '06: Proceedings of the 23rd International Conference on Machine Learning,* (pp. 97-104). New York, NY: ACM Press.

Beynon, M. J. (2005a). A novel technique of object ranking and classification under ignorance: An application to the corporate failure risk problem. *European Journal of Operational Research, 167*, 493–517. doi:10.1016/j.ejor.2004.03.016

Beynon, M. J. (2005b). A novel approach to the credit rating problem: object classification under ignorance. *International Journal of Intelligent Systems in Accounting Finance & Management, 13*, 113–130. doi:10.1002/isaf.260

Beynon, M. J., Andrews, R. A., & Boyne, G. (2010). Evidence-based modelling of strategic fit: An introduction to RCaRBS. *European Journal of Operational Research, 207*(2), 886–896. doi:10.1016/j.ejor.2010.05.024

Bezdek, J. C. (1981). *Pattern recognition with fuzzy objective function algorithms.* New York, NY: Plenum Press Advanced Applications in Pattern Recognition. doi:10.1007/978-1-4757-0450-1

Bhattacharya, A., Abraham, A., Vasant, P., & Grosan, C. (2007). Meta-learning evolutionary artificial neural network for selecting FMS under disparate level-of-satisfaction of decision maker. *International Journal of Innovative Computing, Information and Control. Special Issue on Innovative Computing Methods of Management Engineering, 3*(1), 131–140.

Bhattacharya, A., Vasant, P., Sarkar, B., & Mukherjee, S. K. (2006). A fully fuzzified, intelligent theory-of-constraints. *Product-Mix Decision. International Journal of Production Research, 46*(3), 789–815. doi:10.1080/00207540600823187

Bianchi, L., Dorigo, M., Gambardella, L. M., & Gutjahr, W. J. (2008). A survey on metaheuristics for stochastic combinatorial optimization. *Natural Computing, 8*(2), 239–287. doi:10.1007/s11047-008-9098-4

Biehl, M., Prater, E., & Realff, M. J. (2007). Assessing performance and uncertainty in developing carpet reverse logistics systems. *Computers & Operations Research, 34*(2), 443–463. doi:10.1016/j.cor.2005.03.008

Bin, Y., Zhong-Zhen, Y., & Baozhen, Y. (2009). An improved ant colony optimization for vehicle routing problem. *European Journal of Operational Research, 196*, 171–176. doi:10.1016/j.ejor.2008.02.028

Birattari, M., Paquete, L., Stützle, T., & Varrentrapp, K. (2001). *Classification of metaheuristics and design of experiments for the analysis of components.* Technical Report AIDA-01-05, Darmstadt University of Technology, Germany.

Birbil, S. I., & Fang, S. C. (2003). An electromagnetism-like mechanism for global optimization. *Journal of Global Optimization, 25*, 263–282. doi:10.1023/A:1022452626305

Blackburn, J. D. (1991). New product development: The new time wars. In Blackburn, J. D. (Ed.), *Time-based competition*. Homewood, IL: Business One Irwin Publishers.

Blazewicz, J., Ecker, K. H., Pesch, E., & Schmidt, G. (1996). *Scheduling computer and manufacturing processes*. Berlin, Germany: Springer.

Bloemhof-Ruwaard, J. M., Salomon, M., & Van Wassenhove, L. N. (1996). The capacitated distribution and waste disposal problem. *European Journal of Operational Research, 88*, 490–503. doi:10.1016/0377-2217(94)00211-8

Blum, C. (2005). Beam-ACO-hybridizing ant colony optimization with beam search: an application to open shop scheduling. *Computers & Operations Research, 32*(6), 1565–1591. doi:10.1016/j.cor.2003.11.018

Blum, C., Puchinger, J., Raidl, G. R., & Roli, A. (2011). Hybrid metaheuristics in combinatorial optimization: A survey. *Applied Soft Computing, 11*, 4135–4151. doi:10.1016/j.asoc.2011.02.032

Blum, C., & Roli, A. (2003). Metaheuristic in combinatorial optimization: Overview and conceptual comparison. *ACM Computing Surveys, 35*(3), 268–308. doi:10.1145/937503.937505

Blum, C., Roli, A., Aguilera, M., & Sampels, M. (2008). Hybrid metaheuristics: An introduction. In *Hybrid Metaheuristics (Vol. 114*, pp. 1–30). Berlin, Germany: Springer. doi:10.1007/978-3-540-78295-7_1

Blum, C., & Sampels, M. (2004). An ant colony optimization algorithm for shop scheduling problems. *Journal of Mathematical Modelling and Algorithms, 3*(3), 285–308. doi:10.1023/B:JMMA.0000038614.39977.6f

Boardman, J. T., & Meckiff, C. C. (1985). A branch-and-bound formulation to an electricity distribution planning problem. *IEEE Transactions in Power Applications Systems, PAS-104*(8), 2112–2118. doi:10.1109/TPAS.1985.318789

Boender, C. G. E., Rinnooy, A. H. G., Stougie, L., & Timmer, G. T. (1982). A stochastic method for global optimization. *Mathematical Programming, 22*, 125–140. doi:10.1007/BF01581033

Bollapragada, S., Bussieck, M. R., & Mallik, S. (2004). Scheduling commercial videotapes in broadcast television. *Operations Research, 52*, 679–689. doi:10.1287/opre.1040.0119

Bolton, R. J., & Hand, D. J. (2002). Unsupervised profiling methods for fraud detection. *Statistical Science, 17*(3), 235–255.

Bonabeau, E., Dorigo, M., & Theraulaz, G. (1999). *Swarm intelligence: From natural to artificial systems*. New York, NY: Oxford University Press.

Bonabeou, E., & Meyer, C. (Eds.). (2001). *Swarm intelligence: A whole new way to think about business*. Harvard Business Review.

Bongartz, I., Calamai, P. H., & Conn, A. R. (1994). A projection method for l_p norm location-allocation problem. *Mathematical Programming, 66*(1-3), 283–312. doi:10.1007/BF01581151

Bose, K., & Liang, P. (1996). *Neural networks, fundamentals with graphs, algorithms and applications.* USA: McGraw-Hill.

Bos, J. (1993). Zoning in forest management: A quadratic assignment problem solved by simulated annealing. *Journal of Environmental Management, 37*(2), 127–145. doi:10.1006/jema.1993.1010

Bouleimen, K., & Lecocq, H. (2003). A new efficient simulated annealing algorithm for the resource-constrained project scheduling problem and its multiple mode version. *European Journal of Operational Research, 149*(2), 268–281. doi:10.1016/S0377-2217(02)00761-0

Bowerman, R., Hall, B., & Calamai, P. (1995). A multi-objective optimization approach to urban school bus routing: Formalation and solution method. *Transportation Research Part A, Policy and Practice, 29A*(2), 17.

Braglia, M. (1996). Optimisation of a simulated-annealing-based heuristic for single row machine layout problem by genetic algorithm. *International Transactions in Operational Research, 3*(1), 37–49. doi:10.1111/j.1475-3995.1996.tb00034.x

Brandão, J. (2004). A tabu search algorithm for the open vehicle routing problem. *European Journal of Operational Research, 157*, 552–564. doi:10.1016/S0377-2217(03)00238-8

Brandão, J. (2006). A new tabu search algorithm for the vehicle routing problem with backhauls. *European Journal of Operational Research, 173*, 540–555. doi:10.1016/j.ejor.2005.01.042

Brandão, J., & Eglese, R. (2008). A deterministic tabu search algorithm for the capacitated arc routing problem. *Computers & Operations Research, 35*, 1112–1126. doi:10.1016/j.cor.2006.07.007

Brimberg, J., Hansen, P., & Mladenovic, N. (2004). *Convergence of variable neighborhood search.* Montreal, Canada.

Brimberg, J., Hansen, P., & Mladenovic, N. (2006). Decomposition strategies for large-scale continuous location–allocation problems. *IMA Journal of Management Mathematics, 17*, 307–316. doi:10.1093/imaman/dpl002

Brimberg, J., Hansen, P., Mladenovic, N., & Salhi, S. (2008). A survey of solution methods for the continuous location-allocation problem. *International Journal of Operations Research, 5*(1), 1–12.

Brimberg, J., Hansen, P., Mladenovic, N., & Taillard, E. D. (2000). Improvements and comparison of heuristics for solving the uncapacitated multisource Weber problem. *Operations Research, 48*, 444–460. doi:10.1287/opre.48.3.444.12431

Brimberg, J., & Mladenovic, N. (1996). Solving the continuous location-allocation problem with Tabu search. *Studies in Locational Analysis, 8*, 23–32.

Brimberg, J., & Salhi, S. (2005). A continuous location-allocation problem with zone-dependent fixed cost. *Annals of Operations Research, 136*(1), 99–115. doi:10.1007/s10479-005-2041-5

Browning, T. R. (1998). *Modeling and analyzing cost, schedule, and performance in complex system product development.* Ph.D. dissertation, MIT, Cambridge, MA.

Browning, T. R. (2001-b). Applying the design structure matrix to system decomposition and integration problems: A review and new directions. *IEEE Transactions on Engineering Management, 48*(3), 292–306.

Browning, T. R. (2001-a). Modeling the customer value of product development processes. *Proceedings of the 11th Annual International Symposium of INCOSE*, Melbourne, Australia, July 1-5.

Browning, T. R., & Eppinger, S. D. (2002). Modeling impacts of process architecture on cost and schedule risk in product development. *IEEE Transactions on Engineering Management, 49*(4), 443–458. doi:10.1109/TEM.2002.806710

Brunato, M., & Battlti, R. (2008). Rash: A self-adaptive random search method. In Cotta, C., Sevaux, M., & Soerensen, K. (Eds.), *Adaptive and multilevel metaheuristics.* Berlin, Germany: Springer. doi:10.1007/978-3-540-79438-7_5

Brusco, M. J. (2008). Scheduling advertising slots for television. *The Journal of the Operational Research Society, 59*, 1363–1372. doi:10.1057/palgrave.jors.2602481

Bullnheimer, B., Hartl, R. F., & Strauss, C. (1997). A new rank-based version of the ant system: A computational study. Central. *European Journal of Operational Research and Economics, 7*(1), 25–38.

Burchett, R. C., Happ, H. H., & Vierath, D. R. (1984). Quadratically convergent optimal power flow. *IEEE Transactions on Power Apparatus and Systems, PAS-103*(11), 3267–3276. doi:10.1109/TPAS.1984.318568

Burke, E. K., & Newall, J. P. (1999). A multistage evolutionary algorithm for the timetable problem. *IEEE Transactions on Evolutionary Computation, 3*(1), 63–74. doi:10.1109/4235.752921

Burke, E., Kendall, G., Newall, J., Hart, E., Ross, P., & Schulenberg, S. (2003). Hyperheuristics: An emerging direction in modern search technology. *International Series in Operational Research & Management Science, 57*, 457–474. doi:10.1007/0-306-48056-5_16

Cai, H. R., Chung, C. Y., & Wong, K. P. (2008). Application of differential evolution algorithm for transient stability constrained optimal power flow. *IEEE Transactions on Power Systems, 23*(2), 719–728. doi:10.1109/TPWRS.2008.919241

Cakir, B., Altiparmak, F., & Dengi, B. (2011). Multi-objective optimization of a stochastic assembly line balancing: A hybrid simulated annealing algorithm. *Computers & Industrial Engineering, 60*(3), 376–384. doi:10.1016/j.cie.2010.08.013

Canongia Lopes, J. N. (2004). On the classification and representation of ternary phase diagrams: The yin and yang of a T–x approach. *Physical Chemistry Chemical Physics, 6*, 2314–2319. doi:10.1039/b315799g

Cao, S., & Zhang, K. (2011, 6-8 May 2011). *Optimization of the flow distribution of e-waste reverse logistics network based on NSGA II and TOPSIS.* Paper presented at the 2011 International Conference on E -Business and E -Government (ICEE).

Capitanescu, F., Glavic, M., Ernst, D., & Wehenkel, L. (2007). Interior-point based algorithms for the solution of optimal power flow problems. *Electric Power Systems Research, 77*(5–6), 508–517. doi:10.1016/j.epsr.2006.05.003

Carcamo-Gallardo, A., Garcia-Santander, L., & Pezoa, J. E. (2009). Greedy reconfiguration algorithms for medium-voltage distribution networks. *IEEE Transactions on Power Delivery, 24*, 328–337. doi:10.1109/TPWRD.2008.923997

Cárdenas-Barrón, L. E. (2007). Optimizing inventory decisions in a multi-stage multi-customer supply chain: A note. *Transportation Research Part E, Logistics and Transportation Review, 43*, 647–654. doi:10.1016/j.tre.2005.09.011

Cardenas-Barron, L. E. (2011). The derivation of EOQ/EPQ inventory models with two backorders costs using analytic geometry and algebra. *Applied Mathematical Modelling, 35*, 2394–2407. doi:10.1016/j.apm.2010.11.053

Carpaneto, E., & Chicco, G. (2006). Distribution system minimum loss reconfiguration on the hyper-cube ant colony optimization framework. *Proceedings of the World Energy System Conference*, Torino, Italy, July 10-12 (pp.167-174).

Caserta, M., & Quiñonez, E. (2009). A cross entropy-based metaheuristic algorithm for large-scale capacitated facility location problems. *The Journal of the Operational Research Society, 60*, 1439–1448. doi:10.1057/jors.2008.77

Cerny, V. (1985). A thermodynamical approach to the traveling salesman problem: An efficient simulation algorithm. *Journal of Optimization Theory and Applications, 45*, 41–51. doi:10.1007/BF00940812

Ceylan, H., Haldenbilen, S., & Baskan, O. (2008). Transport energy modeling with meta-heuristic harmony search algorithm, an application to Turkey. *Energy Policy, 36*(7), 2527–2535. doi:10.1016/j.enpol.2008.03.019

Chakravarty, A. K. (2001). Overlapping design and build cycles in product development. *European Journal of Operational Research, 134*, 392–424. doi:10.1016/S0377-2217(00)00264-2

Chang, C. C., & Lin, C. J. (2011). *LibSVM - A library for support vector machines.* Retrieved from http://www.csie.ntu.edu.tw/~cjlin/libsvm/.

Chang, M.-S., Lin, Y.-C., & Hsueh, C.-F. (2004). Vehicle routing and scheduling problem with time windows and stochastic demand. *Transportation Research Record, 1882*, 79–87. doi:10.3141/1882-10

Chang, P.-C., Chen, S.-H., & Fan, C.-Y. (2009). A hybrid electromagnetism-like algorithm for single machine scheduling problem. *Expert Systems with Applications, 36*, 1259–1267. doi:10.1016/j.eswa.2007.11.050

Chardaire, P., Lutton, J. L., & Sutter, A. (1999). Upper and lower bounds for the two-level simple plant location problem. *Annals of Operations Research, 86*, 117–140. doi:10.1023/A:1018942415824

Charitou, A., & Clubb, C. (1999). Earnings, cash flows and security returns over long return intervals: Analysis and UK evidence. *Journal of Business Finance & Accounting, 26*(3-4), 283–312. doi:10.1111/1468-5957.00257

Chattopadhyay, D., & Bhattacharya, K. (1995). A systems approach to least-cost maintenance scheduling for an interconnected power system. *IEEE Transactions on Power Systems, 10*(4), 2002–2007. doi:10.1109/59.476069

Chaudhuri, K. (2007, March). *Personal communication.*

Chau, K. W. (2006). Particle swarm optimization training algorithm for ANNs in stage prediction of Shing Mun River. *Journal of Hydrology (Amsterdam), 329*(3-4), 363–367. doi:10.1016/j.jhydrol.2006.02.025

Chellapilla, K. (1998). Combining mutation operators in evolutionary programming. *IEEE Transactions on Evolutionary Computation, 2*, 91–96. doi:10.1109/4235.735431

Chen, P. C., Hansen, P., Jaumard, B., & Tuy, H. (1992). *Solution of the multisource Weber and conditional Weber problems by d.c. programming.*

Chen, C. L., & Lee, W. C. (2004). Multi-objective optimization of multi-echelon supply chain networks with uncertain product demands and prices. *Computers & Chemical Engineering, 28*, 1131–1144. doi:10.1016/j.compchemeng.2003.09.014

Chen, G. (2000). *Controlling chaos and bifurcations in engineering systems.* China: CRC Press.

Cheng, C. T., Liao, S. L., Tang, Z. T., & Zhao, M. Y. (2009). Comparison of particle swarm optimization and dynamic programming for large scale hydro unit load dispatch. *Energy Conversion and Management, 50*, 3007–3014. doi:10.1016/j.enconman.2009.07.020

Cheng, H., Wang, X., Yang, S., & Huang, M. (2009). A multipopulation parallel genetic simulated annealing-based QoS routing and wavelength assignment integration algorithm for multicast in optical networks. *Applied Soft Computing, 9*(2), 677–684. doi:10.1016/j.asoc.2008.09.008

Cheng, Y. M., Li, L., Lansivaara, T., Chi, S. C., & Sun, Y. J. (2008). An improved harmony search minimization algorithm using different slip surface generation methods for slope stability analysis. *Engineering Optimization, 40*(2), 95–115. doi:10.1080/03052150701618153

Chen, L. N., & Toyoda, J. (1991). Optimal generating unit maintenance scheduling for multi area system with network constraints. *IEEE Transactions on Power Systems, 6*(3), 1168–1174. doi:10.1109/59.119262

Chen, M.-T., Lin, B. M. T., & Tseng, S.-S. (2011). Ant colony optimization for dynamic routing and wavelength assignment in WDM networks with sparse wavelength conversion. *Engineering Applications of Artificial Intelligence, 24*(2), 295–305. doi:10.1016/j.engappai.2010.05.010

Chen, P. H., & Shahandashti, S. Y. (2009). Hybrid of genetic algorithm and simulated annealing for multiple project scheduling with multiple resource constraints. *Automation in Construction, 18*, 434–443. doi:10.1016/j.autcon.2008.10.007

Chen, P., Jain, L., & Tai, C. (2005). *Computational economics: A perspective from computational intelligence.* Hershey, PA: Idea Group Publishing. doi:10.4018/978-1-59140-649-5

Chen, R.-M. (2011). Particle swarm optimization with justification and designed mechanisms for resource-constrained project scheduling problem. *Expert Systems with Applications, 38*(6), 7102–7111. doi:10.1016/j.eswa.2010.12.059

Chen, S. H., Jakeman, A. J., & Norton, J. P. (2008). Artificial intelligence techniques: An introduction to their use for modeling environmental systems. *Mathematics and Computers in Simulation, 78*(2-3), 379–400. doi:10.1016/j.matcom.2008.01.028

Chen, S.-M., & Chien, C.-Y. (2011). Parallelized genetic ant colony systems for solving the traveling salesman problem. *Expert Systems with Applications, 38*(4), 3873–3883. doi:10.1016/j.eswa.2010.09.048

Chen, S.-M., & Chien, C.-Y. (in press). Solving the traveling salesman problem based on the genetic simulated annealing ant colony system with particle swarm optimization techniques. [in press]. *Expert Systems with Applications.*

Chen, S., Wang, P., & Wen, T. (2004). *Computational intelligence in economics and finance.* New York, NY: Springer.

Chen, S., Wang, P., & Wen, T. (2007). *Computational intelligence in economics and finance (Vol. II).* New York, NY: Springer. doi:10.1007/978-3-540-72821-4

Chen, Y., & Zhang, P. (2006). Optimized annealing of traveling salesman problem from the nth-nearest-neighbor distribution. *Physica A. Statistical and Theoretical Physics, 371*(2), 627–632. doi:10.1016/j.physa.2006.04.052

Cheong, F., & Lai, R. (2000). Constraining the optimization of a fuzzy logic controller using an enhanced genetic algorithm. *IEEE Transactions on Systems, Man and Cybernetics. Part B, 30,* 31–46.

Cherkassky, V., & Ma, Y. (2004). Practical selection of SVM parameters and noise estimation for SVM regression. *Neural Networks, 17,* 113–126. doi:10.1016/S0893-6080(03)00169-2

Chern, C. C., & Hsieh, J. S. (2007). A heuristic algorithm for master planning that satisfies multiple objectives. *Computers & Operations Research, 34,* 3491–3513. doi:10.1016/j.cor.2006.02.022

Chiarandini, M., Paquete, L., Preuss, M., & Ridge, E. (2007). *Experiments on metaheuristics: Methodological overview and open issues. Technical Report DMF-2007-03-003.* Denmark: University of Copenhagen.

Chica, M., Cordon, O., Damas, S., & Bautista, J. (2009). *Adding diversity to two multiobjective constructive metaheuristics for time and space assembly line balancing. Frontiers of Assembly and Manufacturing* (pp. 211–226). Springer.

Chiong, R., Neri, F., & McKay, R. I. (2009). Nature that breeds solution. In Chiong, R. (Ed.), *Nature-inspired informatics for intelligent applications and knowledge discovery: Implications in business, science and engineering* (pp. 1–24). Hershey, PA: IGI Global. doi:10.4018/978-1-60566-705-8.ch001

Chiu, S. L. (1994). Fuzzy model identification based on cluster estimation. *Journal of Intelligent and Fuzzy Systems, 2,* 267–278.

Cho, S.-H. (2001). *An integrated method for managing complex engineering projects using the design structure matrix and advanced simulation.* M.S. thesis, MIT, Cambridge, MA.

Chopra, S., & Meindl, P. (2007). *Supply chain management strategy, planning & operation* (3rd ed.). Prentice-Hall of India.

Chowdhury, S., Chowdhury, S. P., & Crossley, P. (2009). *Microgrids and active distribution networks.* London, UK: The Institution of Engineering and Technology.

Chow, M.-Y., Sharpe, R. N., & Hung, J. C. (1993). On the application and design of artificial neural networks for motor fault detection-part I. *IEEE Transactions on Industrial Electronics, 40*(2).

Chu, S. R., Shoureshi, R., & Tenorio, M. (1990). Neural networks for system identification. *IEEE Control Systems Magazine, 10*(3), 31–35. doi:10.1109/37.55121

Chwif, L., Barretto, M. R. P., & Moscato, L. A. (1998). A solution to the facility layout problem using simulated annealing. *Computers in Industry, 36*(1-2), 125–132. doi:10.1016/S0166-3615(97)00106-1

Chyu, C., & Chang, W. (2008). Multi-exchange neighborhood search heuristics for the multi-source capacitated facility location problem. *IEMS, 8,* 29–36.

Clements, K. A., Krumpholz, G. R., & Davis, P. W. (1983). Power system state estimation with measurement deficiency: An observability/measurement placement algorithm. *IEEE Transactions on Power Systems, 102*(7), 2012–2020. doi:10.1109/TPAS.1983.318187

Clerc, M., & Kennedy, J. (2002). The particle swarm - Explosion, stability, and convergence in a multidimensional complex space. *IEEE Transactions on Evolutionary Computation, 6*(1), 58–73. doi:10.1109/4235.985692

Cockshott, A. R., & Hartman, B. E. (2001). Improving the fermentation medium for Echinocandin B production part II: Particle swarm optimization. *Process Biochemistry, 36*(7), 661–669. doi:10.1016/S0032-9592(00)00261-2

Coello, C. A. C. (2000). Use of a self-adaptive penalty approach for engineering optimization problems. *Computers in Industry, 41*, 113–127. doi:10.1016/S0166-3615(99)00046-9

Colorni, A., Dorigo, M., & Maniezzo, V. (1991). Distributed optimisation by ant colonies. *Proceedings of ECAL91-First European Conference on Artificial Life*, (pp. 134-142).

Colorni, A., Dorigo, M., & Maniezzo, V. (1994). Ant system for job-shop scheduling. *Belgian Journal of Operations Research* [JORBEL]. *Statistics and Computer Science, 34*(1), 39–53.

Conejo, A. J., Castillo, E., Mínguez, R., & García-Bertrand, R. (2006). *Decomposition techniques in mathematical programming*. Springer-Verlag.

Conover, W. (1998). *Practical nonparametric statistics*. New York, NY: Wiley.

Contaxis, G. C., Kavatza, S. D., & Vournas, C. D. (1989). An interactive package for risk evaluation and maintenance scheduling. *IEEE Transactions on Power Systems, 4*(2), 389–395. doi:10.1109/59.193807

Contreras, I. A., & Diaz, J. A. (2007). Scatter search for the single source capacitated facility location problem. *Annals of Operations Research, 157*, 73–89. doi:10.1007/s10479-007-0193-1

Cooper, L. (1963). Location-allocation problem. *Operations Research, 11*, 331–343. doi:10.1287/opre.11.3.331

Cooper, L. (1964). Heuristic methods for location-allocation problems. *SIAM Review, 6*, 37–53. doi:10.1137/1006005

Cordon, O., Fernandez de Viana, I., Herrera, F., & Moreno, L. (2000). A new ACO model integrating evolutionary computation concepts: The best-worst ant system. In M. Dorigo, M. Middendorf, & T. Stützle (Eds.), *Abstract Proceedings of ANTS2000-From Ant Colonies to Artificial Ants: A Series of International Workshops on Ant Algorithms*, (pp.22-29). IRIDIA, Universite Libre de Bruxelles, Belgium.

Cornuejols, G., Sridharan, R., & Thizy, J. M. (1991). A comparison of heuristics and relaxations for the capacitated plant location problem. *European Journal of Operational Research, 50*, 280–297. doi:10.1016/0377-2217(91)90261-S

Corominas, A., García-Villoria, A., & Pastor, R. (2009a). *Using tabu search for the response time variability problem*. Paper presented at the 3rd International Conference on Industrial Engineering and Industrial Management, Barcelona and Terrassa, Spain.

Corominas, A., García-Villoria, A., & Pastor, R. (2009b). *Resolución del response time variability problem mediante tabu search*. Paper presented at the 8th Evento Internacional de Matemática y Computación, Universidad de Matanzas, Cuba.

Corominas, A., García-Villoria, A., & Pastor, R. (2009c). *Solving the response time variable problem by means of a variable neighbourhood search algorithm*. Paper presented at the 13th IFAC Symposium of Information Control Problems in Manufacturing, Moscow, Russia.

Corominas, A., García-Villoria, A., & Pastor, R. (2009d). *Using an ant colony system to solve the response time variability problem*. Technical report IOC-DT-P-2009-06, Universitat Politècnica de Catalunya, Spain.

Corominas, A., García-Villoria, A., & Pastor, R. (2010b). *A new metaheuristic procedure for improving the solution of the response time variability problem*. Paper presented at the 4th International Conference on Industrial Engineering and Industrial Management, San Sebastián, Spain.

Corominas, A., García-Villoria, A., & Pastor, R. (2011). *Metaheuristic algorithms hybridized with variable neighbourhood search for solving the response time variability problem.* doi: 10.1007/s11750-011-0175-y

Corominas, A., García-Villoria, A., & Pastor, R. (2008). Solving the response time variability problem by means of multi-start and GRASP metaheuristics. *Frontiers in Artificial Intelligence and Applications, 184,* 128–137.

Corominas, A., Kubiak, W., & Moreno, N. (2007). Response time variability. *Journal of Scheduling, 10,* 97–110. doi:10.1007/s10951-006-0002-8

Corominas, A., Kubiak, W., & Pastor, R. (2010a). Mathematical programming modeling of the response time variability problem. *European Journal of Operational Research, 200,* 347–357. doi:10.1016/j.ejor.2009.01.014

Coy, S. P., Golden, B. L., Runger, G. C., & Wasil, E. A. (2001). Using experimental design to find effective parameter settings for heuristics. *Journal of Heuristics, 7*(1), 77–97. doi:10.1023/A:1026569813391

Crainic, T. G., & Toulouse, M. (2010). Parallel metaheuristics. *Handbook of metaheuristics,* (pp. 497-541).

Croes, G. A. (1958). A method for solving traveling salesman problems. *Operations Research, 6,* 791–812. doi:10.1287/opre.6.6.791

Cruz-Rivera, R., & Ertel, J. (2009). Reverse logistics network design for the collection of end-of-life vehicles in Mexico. *European Journal of Operational Research, 196*(3), 930–939. doi:10.1016/j.ejor.2008.04.041

Da Silva, E. L., Ortiz, J. M. A., De Oliveira, G. C., & Binato, S. (2001). Transmission network expansion planning under a Tabu Search approach. *IEEE Transactions on Power Systems, 16*(1), 62–68. doi:10.1109/59.910782

Dabbagchi, I., & Christie, R. (1993). *Power systems test case archive.* University of Washington. Retrieved February 20, 2011, from http://www.ee.washington.edu/research/pstca/

Dahal, K. P., McDonald, J. R., Burt, G. M., & Galloway, S. J. (2000). GN/SA-based hybrid techniques for the scheduling of generator maintenance in power systems. *IEEE Congress of Evolutionary Computation (CEC2000)* (pp. 567–574). San Diego.

Daniel, J. S. R., & Rajendran, C. (2005). Heuristic approaches to determine base-stock levels in a serial supply chain with a single objective and with multiple objectives. *European Journal of Operational Research, 175,* 566–592. doi:10.1016/j.ejor.2005.04.039

Daniels, R. L., Rummel, J. L., & Schantz, R. (1998). A model for warehouse order picking. *European Journal of Operational Research, 105,* 1–17. doi:10.1016/S0377-2217(97)00043-X

Das, S., Konar, A., & Chakraborty, U. K. (2005). An efficient evolutionary algorithm applied to the design of two-dimensional IIR □lters. *In Proceedings of the 2005 conference on Genetic and evolutionary computation.* Washington, DC, USA.

Das, D., Kothari, D. P., & Kalam, A. (1995). Simple and efficient method of load flow solution of radial distribution networks. *Electrical Power & Energy Systems, 17*(5), 335–346. doi:10.1016/0142-0615(95)00050-0

Das, H., Cummings, H. P. T., & Le Van, M. D. (1990). Scheduling of serial multiproduct batch processes via simulated annealing. *Computers & Chemical Engineering, 14*(12), 1351–1362. doi:10.1016/0098-1354(90)80017-6

Daskin, M., Snyder, L., & Berger, R. (2003). *Logistics systems: Design and optimization.* Springer.

Davis, L. (1985). Job shop scheduling with genetic algorithms. In *Proceedings of the 1st International Conference on Genetic Algorithms.* Lawrence Erlbaum.

Davis, L. (1991). *Handbook of genetic algorithms.* USA: Int. Thomson Com. Press.

Dawson, C. W., & Wilby, R. (1998). An artificial neural network approach to rainfall-runoff Modelling. *Hydrological Sciences—Journal—des Sciences Hydrologiques, 43*(1).

De Brabanter, K., Karsmakers, P., Ojeda, F., Alzate, C., De Brabanter, J., & Pelckmans, K. … Suykens, J. A. K. (2011). *The LS-SVMlab toolbox homepage.* Retrieved from http://www.esat.kuleuven.be/sista/lssvmlab/

De Jong, K. D. (1975). *An analysis of the behavior of a class of genetic adaptive systems.* PhD dissertation, Department of Computer and Communication Sciences, University of Michigan.

De La Fuente, M., Ros, L., & Cardos, M. (2008). Integrating forward and reverse supply chains: Application to a metal-mechanic company. *International Journal of Production Economics, 111*(2), 782–792. doi:10.1016/j.ijpe.2007.03.019

Dean, A., Dean, A., & Voss, D. (2001). *Design and analysis of experiments.* Berlin, Germany: Springer Texts in Statistics.

Debels, D., & Vanhoucke, M. (2006). The electromagnetism meta-heuristic applied to the resource-constrained project scheduling problem. *Lecture Notes in Computer Science, 3871,* 259–270. doi:10.1007/11740698_23

Deb, K. (2000). An efficient constraint handling method for genetic algorithms. *Computer Methods in Applied Mechanics and Engineering, 186,* 311–338. doi:10.1016/S0045-7825(99)00389-8

Deb, K. (2001). *Multi-objective optimization using evolutionary algorithms.* New York, NY: John Wiley & Sons.

Deep, K., & Bansal, J. C. (2009). Mean particle swarm optimization for function optimization. *International Journal of Computational Intelligence Studies, 1,* 72–92.

Deep, K., & Thakur, M. (2007a). A new crossover operator for real coded genetic algorithms. *Applied Mathematics and Computation, 188,* 895–911. doi:10.1016/j.amc.2006.10.047

Deep, K., & Thakur, M. (2007b). A new mutation operators for real coded genetic algorithms. *Applied Mathematics and Computation, 193,* 211–230. doi:10.1016/j.amc.2007.03.046

Degertekin, S. (2008). Optimum design of steel frames using harmony search algorithm. *Structural and Multidisciplinary Optimization, 36,* 393–401. doi:10.1007/s00158-007-0177-4

Dekkers, A., & Aarts, E. (1991). Global optimization and simulated annealing. *Mathematical Programming, 50,* 367–393. doi:10.1007/BF01594945

Demirel, N. Ç., & Toksarı, M. D. (2006). Optimization of the quadratic assignment problem using an ant colony algorithm. *Applied Mathematics and Computation, 183,* 427–435. doi:10.1016/j.amc.2006.05.073

Demmel, J. G., & Askin, R. G. (1992). A multiple-objective decision model for the evaluation of advanced manufacturing system technologies. *Journal of Manufacturing Systems, 11,* 179–194. doi:10.1016/0278-6125(92)90004-Y

Dempster, A. P. (1967). Upper and lower probabilities induced by a multiple valued mapping. *Annals of Mathematical Statistics, 38,* 325–339. doi:10.1214/aoms/1177698950

Den Besten, M. L., Stutzle, T., & Dorigo, M. (2000). Ant colony optimization for the total weighted tardiness problem. In M. Schoenauer, K. Deb, G. Rudolph, X. Yao, E. Lutton, J. J. Merelo, H.-P. Schwefel (Eds.), *Proceedings of PPSNVI, Sixth Internat. Conf. on Parallel Problem Solving from Nature, Lecture Notes in Computer Science, Vol. 1917* (pp. 611–620). Berlin, Germany: Springer.

Deng, A.-M., Mao, C., & Zhou, Y.-T. (2009). Optimizing research of an improved simulated annealing algorithm to soft time windows vehicle routing problem with pick-up and delivery. *Systems Engineering - Theory & Practice, 29*(5), 186-192.

Deng, G. F., & Lin, W. T. (2011). Ant colony optimization-based algorithm for airline crew scheduling problem. *Expert Systems with Applications, 38,* 5787–5793. doi:10.1016/j.eswa.2010.10.053

Deng, M., Inoue, A., & Sekiguchi, K. (2008). Lyapunov function base obstacle avoidance scheme for a two wheeled mobile robot. *Journal of Control Theory and Applications, 6*(4), 399–404. doi:10.1007/s11768-008-7017-y

Deng, Y., He, Y., & Zhang, B. (1992). A branch-estimation-based state estimation method for radial distribution systems. *IEEE Transactions on Power Delivery, 17*(4), 1057–1062. doi:10.1109/TPWRD.2002.803800

Denker, S., Steward, D. V., & Browning, T. R. (1999). Planning concurrency and managing iteration in projects. *Project Management Journal, 32*(3), 31–38.

Derrac, J., García, S., Molina, D., & Herrera, F. (2011). A practical tutorial on the use of nonparametric statistical tests as a methodology for comparing evolutionary and swarm intelligence algorithms. *Swarm and Evolutionary Computation, 1,* 3–18. doi:10.1016/j.swevo.2011.02.002

Deschinkel, K., Farges, J.-L., & Delahaye, D. (2002). Optimizing and assigning price levels for air traffic management. *Transportation Research Part E, Logistics and Transportation Review, 38*(3-4), 221–237. doi:10.1016/S1366-5545(02)00007-8

Díaz, G., González-Morán, C., Gómez-Aleixandre, J., & Diez, A. (2010). Scheduling of Droop coefficients for frequencyand voltage regulation in isolated microgrids. *IEEE Transactions on Power Systems, 25*(1). doi:10.1109/TPWRS.2009.2030425

Ding, Q., Ding, Q., & Perrizo, W. (2002). Association rule mining on remotely sensed images using p-trees. *Proceedings, PAKDD2002*, 232–238.

Dixon, W. E., Jiang, Z. P., & Dawson, D. M. (2000). Global exponential setpoint control of wheeled mobile robots: A Lyapunov approach. *Automatica, 56*(11), 1741–1746. doi:10.1016/S0005-1098(00)00099-6

Do Couto Filho, M. B., Souza, J. C. S., De Marcus, F. M. F., & Schilling, M. T. (2001). Identifying critical measurement & sets for power system state estimation. *Proceedings of IEEE Porto Power Tech Conference.*

Do Couto Filho, M. B., Leite Do Silva, A. M., & Falcao, D. M. (1990). Bibliography on power system state estimation (1968-1989). *IEEE Transactions on Power Systems, 10*, 229–240.

Dodin, B., Elimam, A. A., & Rolland, E. (1998). Tabu search in audit scheduling. *European Journal of Operational Research, 106*(2), 373–392. doi:10.1016/S0377-2217(97)00280-4

Dommel, H., & Tinny, W. (1968). Optimal power flow solution. *IEEE Transactions on Power Apparatus and Systems, PAS-87*(10), 1866–1876. doi:10.1109/TPAS.1968.292150

Donati, V. A., Montemanni, R., Casagrande, N., Rizzoli, A. E., & Gambardella, L. M. (2008). Time dependent vehicle routing problem with a multi ant colony system. *European Journal of Operational Research, 185*(3), 1174–1191. doi:10.1016/j.ejor.2006.06.047

Dong, L., Melhem, R., & Mosse, D. (1998). *Time slot allocation for real-time messages with negotiable distance constrains requirements.* Paper presented at the 4th IEEE Real-Time Technology and Applications Symposium, Denver, CO.

Dong, M., Wu, C., & Hou, F. (2009). Shortest path based simulated annealing algorithm for dynamic facility layout problem under dynamic business environment. *Expert Systems with Applications, 36*(8), 11221–11232. doi:10.1016/j.eswa.2009.02.091

Doong, S. H., Lai, C. C., & Wu, C. H. (2007). Genetic subgradient method for solving location-allocation problems. *Applied Soft Computing, 7*(1), 373–386. doi:10.1016/j.asoc.2005.06.008

Dopazo, J. F., & Merrill, H. M. (1975). Optimal generator maintenance scheduling using integer programming. *IEEE Transactions on Power Apparatus and Systems, PAS-94*(5), 1537–1545. doi:10.1109/T-PAS.1975.31996

Dorigo, M. (1992). *Optimization, learning and natural algorithms*. Ph.D. Thesis. Department of Electronics, Politecnico di Milano, Italy.

Dorigo, M., & Caro, G. D. (1999). Ant colony optimization: A new meta-heuristic. *Proceedings of the 1999 Congress on Evolutionary Computation*, (pp. 1470-1477).

Dorigo, M., Maniezzo, V., & Colorni, A. (1991). *Positive feedback as a search strategy.*

Dorigo, M., & Blum, C. (2005). Ant colony optimization theory: A survey. *Theoretical Computer Science, 344*, 243–278. doi:10.1016/j.tcs.2005.05.020

Dorigo, M., & Gambardella, L. (1997). Ant colony system: A cooperative learning approach to the traveling salesman problem. *IEEE Transactions on Evolutionary Computation, 1*(1), 53–66. doi:10.1109/4235.585892

Dorigo, M., & Gambardella, L. M. (1996). The ant system: Optimization by a colony of cooperating agents. *IEEE Transactions on Systems, Man, and Cybernetics. Part B, Cybernetics, 26*, 132–140. doi:10.1109/3477.484436

Dorigo, M., & Gambardella, L. M. (1997a). Ant colony system: A cooperative learning approach to the traveling salesman problem. *IEEE Transactions on Evolutionary Computation*, *1*, 53–66. doi:10.1109/4235.585892

Dorigo, M., & Gambardella, L. M. (1997b). Ant colonies for the travelling salesman problem. *Bio Systems*, *43*, 73–81. doi:10.1016/S0303-2647(97)01708-5

Dorigo, M., & Socha, K. (2007). An introduction to ant colony optimization. In Gonzalez, T. F. (Ed.), *Handbook of approximation algorithms and metaheuristics*.

Dorigo, M., & Stützle, T. (Eds.). (2004). *Ant colony optimization*. Cambridge, MA: MIT Press. doi:10.1007/b99492

Dorigo, M., & Stuzle, T. (2004). *Ant colony optimization*. Cambridge, MA: MIT Press. doi:10.1007/b99492

Dorronsoro, R., Ginel, F., Sgnchez, C., & Cruz, C. S. (1997). Neural fraud detection in credit card operations. *IEEE Transactions on Neural Networks*, *8*(4), 827–834. doi:10.1109/72.595879

Dostál, P. (2008). *Advanced economic analyses*. Brno, Czech Republic: VUT – FP.

Dostál, P. (2011). *Advanced decision making in business and public services*. Brno, Czech Republic: CERM.

Dowsland, K. A., & Adenso-Díaz, B. (2003). Heuristic design and fundamentals of the simulated annealing. *Inteligencia Artificial*, *19*, 93–102. doi:10.1023/A:1022188514489

Dubus, J.-P., Gonzales, C., & Perny, P. (2009). *Choquet optimization using GAI networks for multiagent/multicriteria decision-making* (pp. 377–389). Algorithmic Decision Theory, Lectures Notes in Artificial Intelligence. doi:10.1007/978-3-642-04428-1_33

Dumitrescu, D., Lazzerini, B., Jain, L. C., & Dumitrescu, A. (2000). Evolution strategies and evolutionary programming. In *Evolutionary computation* (pp. 261–281). The CRC Press International Series on Computational Intelligence.

Duval, P. E., & Poilpot, R. (1983). Determining maintenance schedule for thermal production units the KAPILA model. *IEEE Transactions on Power Apparatus and Systems*, *PAS-102*(8), 2509–2525. doi:10.1109/TPAS.1983.317751

Easton, P. D., & Harris, T. S. (1991). Earnings as an explanatory variable for returns. *Journal of Accounting Research*, *29*(1), 19–36. doi:10.2307/2491026

Eberhart, R. C., & Shi, Y. (2001). Particle swarm optimization: Developments, applications and resources. *In Proceedings of Congress on Evolutionary Computation*, Seoul, Korea. Piscataway, NJ: IEEE Service Center.

Eberhart, R. C., & Salhi, S. (2004). Special issue on particle swarm optimization. *IEEE Transactions on Evolutionary Computation*, *8*(3), 201–203. doi:10.1109/TEVC.2004.830335

Eberhat, R. C., & Shi, Y. (2001). *Particle swarm optimization: Developments, applications and resources.* Paper presented at the IEEE Congress on Evolutionary Computation.

Edwin, K. W., & Curtius, F. (1990). New maintenance scheduling method with production cast minimization via integer linear programming. *International Journal of Electrical Power & Energy Systems*, *12*(3), 165–170. doi:10.1016/0142-0615(90)90029-B

Egan, G. T., Dillon, T. S., & Morsztyn, K. (1976). An experimental method of determination of optimal maintenance schedules in power systems using branch-and-bound technique. *IEEE Transactions on Systems, Man, and Cybernetics*, *6*(8), 538–547. doi:10.1109/TSMC.1976.4309548

Ehlers, F. J. (2004). *Cybernetic analysis for stock and futures*. USA: John Wiley.

Eiben, A. E., Hinterding, R., & Michalewicz, Z. (1999). Parameter control in evolutionary algorithms. *IEEE Transactions on Evolutionary Computation*, *3*(2), 124–141. doi:10.1109/4235.771166

Eiben, A. E., & Smith, S. K. (2011). Parameter tuning for configuring and analyzing evolutionary algorithms. *Swarm and Evolutionary Computation*, *1*, 19–31. doi:10.1016/j.swevo.2011.02.001

Ekşioğlu, B., Ekşioğlu, S. D., & Pramod, J. (2008). A tabu search algorithm for the flowshop scheduling problem with changing neighborhoods. *Computers & Industrial Engineering*, *54*, 1–11. doi:10.1016/j.cie.2007.04.004

Elahi, M., Li, K., Nisar, W., Lv, X., & Wang, H. (2008). Efficient clustering-based outlier detection algorithm for dynamic data stream. In *Proceedings of the 2008 Fifth International Conference on Fuzzy Systems and Knowledge Discovery - Volume 05, FSKD*, (pp. 298-304). Washington, DC: IEEE Computer Society.

El-Bouri, A., Azizi, N., & Zolfaghari, S. (2007). A comparative study of a new heuristic based on adaptive memory programming and simulated annealing: The case of job shop scheduling. *European Journal of Operational Research*, *177*(3), 1894–1910. doi:10.1016/j.ejor.2005.12.013

El-Keib, A. A., & Ma, X. (1995). Application of artificial neural networks in voltage stability assessment. *IEEE Transactions on Power Systems*, *10*(4), 1890–1896. doi:10.1109/59.476054

Eltayeb, T. K., Zailani, S., & Ramayah, T. (2010). Green supply chain initiatives among certified companies in Malaysia and environmental sustainability: Investigating the outcomes. *Resources, Conservation and Recycling*, *55*(5), 495–506. doi:10.1016/j.resconrec.2010.09.003

El-Telbany, M., & El-Karmi, F. (2008). Short-term forecasting of Jordanian electricity demand using particle swarm optimization. *Electric Power Systems Research*, *78*(3), 425–433. doi:10.1016/j.epsr.2007.03.011

Erlenkotter, D. (1978). A dual-based procedure for uncapacitated facility location. *Operations Research*, *26*, 992–1009. doi:10.1287/opre.26.6.992

Escudero, L. F., Horton, J. M., & Scheiderich, J. E. (1980). *On maintenance scheduling for energy generators*. New York: IEEE-PES Winter Meeting.

Everitt, B. S., Landau, S., & Leese, M. (2001). *Cluster analysis*. London, UK: Arnold.

Fan, H.-Y., & Lampinen, J. A. (2003). Trigonometric mutation operation to differential evolution. *Journal of Global Optimization*, *27*, 105–129. doi:10.1023/A:1024653025686

Farahani, R. Z., & Elahipanah, M. (2008). A genetic algorithm to optimize the total cost and service level for just-in-time distribution in a supply chain. *International Journal of Production Economics*, *111*(2), 229–243. doi:10.1016/j.ijpe.2006.11.028

Farmahini-Farahani, A., Vakili, S., Fakhraie, S. M., Safari, S., & Lucas, C. (2010). Parallel scalable hardware implementation of asynchronous discrete particle swarm optimization. *Engineering Applications of Artificial Intelligence*, *23*(2), 177–187. doi:10.1016/j.engappai.2009.12.001

Fatrias, D., & Shimizu, Y. (2010). Multi-objective analysis of periodic review inventory problem with coordinated replenishment in two-echelon supply chain system through differential evolution. *Journal of Advanced Mechanical Design, Systems and Manufacturing*, *4*, 637–650. doi:10.1299/jamdsm.4.637

Fawcett, S. E., Ellram, L. M., & Ogden, J. A. (2007). *Supply chain management from vision to implementation*. New Jersey, USA: Prentice-Hall.

Feo, T. A., & Resende, M. G. C. (1989). A probabilistic heuristic for a computationally difficult set covering problem. *Operations Research Letters*, *8*, 67–81. doi:10.1016/0167-6377(89)90002-3

Fesanghary, M., Mahdavi, M., Minary Jolandan, M., & Alizadeh, Y. (2008). Hybridizing harmony search algorithm with sequential quadratic programming for engineering optimization problems. *Computer Methods in Applied Mechanics and Engineering*, *197*(33-40), pp. 3080-3091.

Fesanghary, M., Damangir, E., & Soleimani, I. (2009). Design optimization of shell and tube heat exchangers using global sensitivity analysis and harmony search algorithm. *Applied Thermal Engineering*, *29*(5–6), 1026–1031. doi:10.1016/j.applthermaleng.2008.05.018

Fiksel, J. (1991). *Design for environment: Creating eco-efficient products & processes*. New York, NY: McGraw-Hill.

Filho, V. J., & Galvão, R. D. (1998). A tabu search heuristic for the concentrator location problem. *Location Sciences*, *6*, 189–209. doi:10.1016/S0966-8349(98)00046-1

Fisher, M. L. (1985). An application oriented guide to Lagrangian relaxation. *Interfaces*, *15*, 10–21. doi:10.1287/inte.15.2.10

Fleischmann, M., Beullens, P., Bloemhof-Ruwaard, J. M., & Van Wassenhove, L. N. (2001). The impact of product recovery on logistics network design. *Production and Operations Management, 10*(2), 156–173. doi:10.1111/j.1937-5956.2001.tb00076.x

Floudas, C. A., & Pardalos, P. M. (1990). Lecture Notes in Computer Science: Vol. 455. *A collection of test problems for constrained global optimization algorithms*. Springer-Verlag.

Fogel, L. J., Owens, A. J., & Walsh, M. J. (1966). *Artificial intelligence through simulated evolution*.

Fogel, G. B., & Corne, D. W. (Eds.). (2002). *Evolutionary computation in bioinformatics*. Oxford, UK: Elsevier LTD, Academic Press.

Fonseca, C. M., & Fleming, P. J. (1998). Multiobjective optimization and multiple constraint handling with evolutionary algorithms – Part I: A unied formulation. *IEEE Transactions on Systems, Man, and Cybernetics. Part A, Systems and Humans, 28*(1), 26–37. doi:10.1109/3468.650319

Forsati, R., Mahdavi, M., Kangavari, M., & Safarkhani, B. (2008). Web page clustering using harmony search optimization. *Canadian Conference on Electrical and Computer Engineering, CCECE* (pp. 1601–1604).

Fortes, J. (2009). *Green supply chain management: A literature*.

Fournier, J. R. L., & Pierre, S. (2005). Assigning cells to switches in mobile networks using an ant colony optimization heuristic. *Computer Communications, 28*, 65–73. doi:10.1016/j.comcom.2004.07.006

Franses, P. H. (2001). *Time series models for business and economic forecasting*. UK: Cambridge University Press.

Frisch, K. V. (1976). *Bees: Their vision, chemical senses and language* (rev. ed.). Ithaca, NY: Cornell University Press.

Fu Chang, C. (2008). Reconfiguration and capacitor placement for loss reduction of distribution systems by ant colony search algorithm. *IEEE Transactions on Power Systems, 23*, 1747–1755. doi:10.1109/TPWRS.2008.2002169

Fuellerer, G., Doerner, K. F., Hartl, R. F., & Iori, M. (2010). Metaheuristics for vehicle routing problems with three-dimensional loading constraints. *European Journal of Operational Research, 201*(3), 751–759. doi:10.1016/j.ejor.2009.03.046

Fujimoto, K., Ota, T., Shimizu, Y., Ichikawa, T., Yukita, K., & Goto, Y. (2009). *Load frequency control using storage system for a micro grid*. IEEE T&D Asia. doi:10.1109/TD-ASIA.2009.5356856

Funabashi, T., Koyanagi, K., & Yokoyama, R. (2003). A review of islanding detection methods for distributed resources. *Proceedings of the IEEE Bologna Power Tech Conference*, Bologna, Italy, 2003.

Gaber, M., Zaslavsky, A., & Krishnaswamy, S. (2005). Mining data streams: A review. *SIGMOD Review, 34*(2), 18–26. doi:10.1145/1083784.1083789

Gagne, C., Price, W. L., & Gravel, M. (2002). Comparing an ACO algorithm with other heuristics for the single machine scheduling problem with sequence-dependent setup times. *The Journal of the Operational Research Society, 53*, 895–906. doi:10.1057/palgrave.jors.2601390

Gajpal, Y., & Rajendran, C. (2006). An ant-colony optimization algorithm for minimizing the completion-time variance of jobs in flowshops. *International Journal of Production Economics, 101*(2), 259–272. doi:10.1016/j.ijpe.2005.01.003

Gallego, R. A., Romero, R., & Monticelli, A. J. (2000). Tabu search algorithm for network synthesis. *IEEE Transactions on Power Systems, 15*(2). doi:10.1109/59.867130

Galvao, R. D. (2004). Uncapacitated facility location problems: Contributions. *Pesquisa Operacional, 24*, 7–38. doi:10.1590/S0101-74382004000100003

Gambardella, L. M., & Dorigo, M. (1995). Ant-Q: A reinforcement learning approach to the travelling salesman problem. In *Proceedings of the Twelfth International Conference on Machine Learning*, California, USA.

Gambardella, L. M., & Dorigo, M. (1996). Solving symmetric and asymmetric TSPs by ant colonies. In *Proceedings of the IEEE Conference on Evolutionary Computation* (pp. 622-627). Nagoya, Japan.

Gambardella, L. M., Rizzoli, A. E., Oliverio, F., Casagrande, N., Donati, A., Montemanni, R., et al. (2003). *Ant colony optimization for vehicle routing in advanced logistics systems.*

Gambardella, L. M., & Dorigo, M. (2000). Ant colony system hybridized with a new local search for the sequential ordering problem. *INFORMS Journal on Computing, 12*(3), 237–255. doi:10.1287/ijoc.12.3.237.12636

Gambardella, L. M., Taillard, E. D., & Agazzi, G. (1999). MACS-VRPTW: A multiple ant colony system for vehicle routing problems with time windows. In Corne, D., Dorigo, M., & Glover, F. (Eds.), *New ideas in optimization* (pp. 63–76). London, UK: McGraw-Hill.

Gamm, A. Z., Kolosok, I. N., & Glazunova, A. M. (2005). Test equations for validation of critical measurements and critical sets at power system state estimation. *Proceedings of the International Conference "Power Tech 2005"*, St. Petersburg.

Gamm, A. Z., Kolosok, I. N., & Zaika, R. A. (2005). Robust methods for state estimation in electric power systems and their implementation on the basis of genetic algorithm. *Elektrichestvo, 10*, 2-8. (in Russian)

Gamm, A. Z. (1970). On bus numeration when calculating steady states of electric power systems by the Newton-Raphson method. [in Russian]. *Electrichestvo, 2*, 59–60.

Gamm, A. Z. (1976). *Statistical methods of power system state estimation.* Moscow, Russia: Nauka. (in Russian)

Gamm, A. Z., Gerasimov, L. N., & Golub, I. I. (1983). *State estimation in electric power industry.* Moscow, Russia: Nauka. (in Russian)

Gamm, A. Z., & Golub, I. I. (1990). *Observability of electric power system.* Moscow, Russia: Nauka. (in Russian)

Gamm, A. Z., & Kolosok, I. N. (2000). *Bad data detection in measurements in electric power systems.* Novosibirsk, Russia: Nauka. (in Russian)

Gamm, A. Z., & Kolosok, I. N. (2002). *Test equations and their use for state estimation of electrical power system. Power and Electrical Engineering: Scientific Proceedings of Riga Technical University* (pp. 99–105). Riga, Latvia: RTU.

Gangadharan, R., & Rajendran, C. (1994). A simulated annealing heuristic for scheduling in a flowshop with bicriteria. *Computers & Industrial Engineering, 27*(1-4), 473–476. doi:10.1016/0360-8352(94)90337-9

Gao, L., & Robinson, E. P. (1994). Uncapacitated facility location: General solution procedure and computational experience. *European Journal of Operational Research, 76*, 410–427. doi:10.1016/0377-2217(94)90277-1

García, A., Pastor, R., & Corominas, A. (2006). Solving the response time variability problem by means of metaheuristics. *Frontiers in Artificial Intelligence and Applications, 146*, 187–194.

García-Martínez, C., Cordón, O., & Herrera, F. (2007). A taxonomy and an empirical analysis of multiple objective ant colony optimization algorithms for the bi-criteria TSP. *European Journal of Operational Research, 180*(1), 116–148. doi:10.1016/j.ejor.2006.03.041

García-Villoria, A., & Pastor, R. (2009). Introducing dynamic diversity in a discrete particle swarm optimization. *Computers & Operations Research, 36*, 951–966. doi:10.1016/j.cor.2007.12.001

García-Villoria, A., & Pastor, R. (2010a). Solving the response time variability problem by means of a genetic algorithm. *European Journal of Operational Research, 202*, 320–327. doi:10.1016/j.ejor.2009.05.024

García-Villoria, A., & Pastor, R. (2010b). Solving the response time variability problem by means of the electromagnetism-like mechanism. *International Journal of Production Research, 48*, 6701–6714. doi:10.1080/00207540902862545

García-Villoria, A., & Pastor, R. (2010c). Solving the response time variability problem by means of a psychoclonal approach. *Journal of Heuristics, 16*, 337–351. doi:10.1007/s10732-008-9082-2

Gaspar, A., & Collard, P. (2000). Two models of immunization for time dependent optimization. *IEEE International Conference on Systems Manufacturing and Cybernetics*, (pp. 113-118).

Gately, E. (1996). *Neural networks for financial forecasting.* USA: John Wiley.

Gebala, D. A., & Eppinger, S. D. (1991). Methods for analyzing design procedures. In *Proceedings of ASME 3rd International Conference on Design Theory Methodology*, (pp. 227–233).

Geem, Z. (2007b). Harmony search algorithm for solving sudoku. In B. Apolloni, R. J. Howlett, & L. Jain (Eds.), *11th International Conference, KES 2007 and XVII Italian Workshop on Neural Networks Conference on Knowledge-Based Intelligent Information and Engineering Systems: Part I*, (pp. 371–378). Berlin, Germany: Springer.

Geem, Z. W. (2000). *Optimal design of water distribution networks using harmony search*. Unpublished doctoral dissertation, Korea University.

Geem, Z. W., & Hwangbo, H. (2006). Application of harmony search to multi-objective optimization for satellite heat pipe design. *US-Korea Conference on Science, Technology, & Entrepreneurship (UKC 2006)* (pp. 1–3). Teaneck, NJ: Citeseer.

Geem, Z. W., & Williams, J. C. (2008). Ecological optimization using harmony search. *American Conference on Applied Mathematics*, Cambridge, Massachusetts.

Geem, Z. W. (2009a). Particle-swarm harmony search for water network design. *Engineering Optimization, 41*(4), 297–311. doi:10.1080/03052150802449227

Geem, Z. W. (Ed.). (2009b). *Harmony search algorithms for structural design optimization*. Berlin, Germany: Springer. doi:10.1007/978-3-642-03450-3

Geem, Z. W., Kim, J. H., & Loganathan, G. V. (2001). A new heuristic optimization algorithm: Harmony search. *Simulation, 76*, 60–68. doi:10.1177/003754970107600201

Geem, Z. W., Lee, K. S., & Park, Y. (2005b). Application of harmony search to vehicle routing. *American Journal of Applied Sciences, 2*(12), 1552–1557. doi:10.3844/ajassp.2005.1552.1557

Geem, Z. W., Tseng, C. L., & Park, Y. (2005a). Harmony search for generalized orienteering problem: Best touring in China. In Wang, L., Chen, K., & Ong, Y. (Eds.), *Advances in natural computation* (pp. 741–750). Berlin, Germany: Springer. doi:10.1007/11539902_91

Geem, Z., & Choi, J. Y. (2007). Music composition using harmony search algorithm. In Giacobini, M. (Ed.), *Applications of evolutionary computing* (pp. 593–600). Berlin, Germany: Springer.

Geethanjali, M., Slochanal, S. M. R., & Bhavani, R. (2008). PSO trained ANN-based differential protection scheme for power transformers. *Neurocomputing, 71*(4-6), 904–918. doi:10.1016/j.neucom.2007.02.014

Geiger, M. J. (Ed.). (2009). *Metaheuristics in the service industry*. Berlin, Germany: Springer-Verlag.

Gendreau, M., & Potvin, J.-Y. (Eds.). (2010). *Handbook of metaheuristics* (2nd ed.). New York, NY: Springer. doi:10.1007/978-1-4419-1665-5

Gendron, B., & Semet, F. (2009). Formulations and relaxations for a multi-echelon capacitated location-distribution problem. *Computers & Operations Research, 36*, 1335–1355. doi:10.1016/j.cor.2008.02.009

Geng, X., Chen, Z., Yang, W., Shi, D., & Zhao, K. (2011). Solving the traveling salesman problem based on an adaptive simulated annealing algorithm with greedy search. *Applied Soft Computing, 11*(4), 3680–3689. doi:10.1016/j.asoc.2011.01.039

Genovese, K., Lamberti, L., & Pappalettere, C. (2005). Improved global–local simulated annealing formulation for solving non-smooth engineering optimization problems. *International Journal of Solids and Structures, 42*(1), 203–237. doi:10.1016/j.ijsolstr.2004.07.015

German, S., & German, D. (1984). Stochastic relaxation, Gibbs distributions, and the Bayesian restoration of images. *IEEE Proceedings Pattern Analysis and Machine Intelligence, 6*(6), 721-741.

Ge, S. S., & Cui, Y. J. (2000). New potential functions for mobile robot path planning. *IEEE Transactions on Robotics and Automation, 16*(5), 615–620. doi:10.1109/70.880813

Ge, S. S., & Cui, Y. J. (2002). Dynamic motion planning for mobile robots using potential field method. *Autonomous Robots, 13*(3), 207–222. doi:10.1023/A:1020564024509

Geyik, F., & Cedimoglu, I. H. (2004). The strategies and parameters of tabu search for job-shop scheduling problem. *Journal of Intelligent Manufacturing, 15*, 439–448. doi:10.1023/B:JIMS.0000034106.86434.46

Ghaderi, A., Jabalameli, M. S., Barzinpour, F., & Rahmaniani, R. (2011). An efficient hybrid particle swarm optimization algorithm for solving the uncapacitated continuous location-allocation problem. *Networks and Spatial Economics*. doi:10.1007/s11067-011-9162-y

Ghedjati, F., & Portmann, M. (2009). Dynamic heuristic for the generalized job-shop scheduling problem. *IEEE International Conference on Systems, Man and Cybernetics (IEEE SMC '09)*, (pp. 2636-2641).

Ghoting, A., Parthasarathy, S., & Otey, M. (2008). Fast mining of distance-based outliers in high-dimensional datasets. *Data Mining and Knowledge Discovery*, *16*(3), 349–364. doi:10.1007/s10618-008-0093-2

Gil, N. J., & Lopes, J. A. P. (2007). *Hierarchical frequency control scheme for islanded multi-microgrids operation.* Paper presented at the PowerTech, IEEE.

Gleick, J. (1996). *Chaos.* USA: Ando Publishing.

Glover, F. (1986). Future paths for integer programming and links to artificial intelligence. *Computers & Operations Research*, *13*(5), 533–549. doi:10.1016/0305-0548(86)90048-1

Glover, F. (1990). Tabu search - Part II. *ORSA Journal on Computing*, *2*, 4–32. doi:10.1287/ijoc.2.1.4

Glover, F. (2005). Adaptive memory projection methods for integer programming. In Rego, C., & Alidaee, B. (Eds.), *Metaheuristic optimization via memory and evolution* (pp. 425–440). Kluwer Academic Publishers. doi:10.1007/0-387-23667-8_19

Glover, F., & Kochenberger, G. A. (2003). *Handbook of metaheuristics.* Springer.

Glover, F., & Kochenberger, G. A. (Eds.). (2003). *Handbook of metaheuristics.* New York, NY: Kluwer Academic Publishers.

Glover, F., & Laguna, M. (1997). *Tabu search.* Kluwer Academic Publisher. doi:10.1007/978-1-4615-6089-0

Goldberg, D. E., & Lingle, R. (1985). Alleles, loci, and the traveling salesman problem. *First International Conference on Genetic Algorithms*, (pp. 154-159).

Goldberg, D. E. (1989). *Genetic algorithms in search optimization and machine learning.* Toronto, Canada: Addison Wesley.

Gorban, A. N. (1998). *Neural informatics.* Novosibirsk, Russia: Nauka. (in Russian)

Gornstein, V. M., Miroshnichenko, B. P., & Ponomarev, A. V. (Eds.). (1981). *Methods for optimization of power system state.* Moscow, Russia: Energiya. (in Russian)

Görtz, S., & Klose, A. (2009). *A subgradient-based branch and bound algorithm for the capacitated facility location problem.* Working paper no. 2009/1, Department of Operations Research, University of Aarhus.

Goser, J., Rolim, J. G., & Simoes Costa, A. J. A. (2001). Meter placement for power system state estimation: An approach based on genetic algorithms and topological observability analysis. *Proceedings of the ISAP '2001 Conference* Budapest, Hungary (pp. 15-16).

Goyal, S. K. (1977). An integrated inventory model for a single supplier-single customer problem. *International Journal of Production Research*, *15*, 107–111. doi:10.1080/00207547708943107

Goyal, S. K. (1988). Joint economic lot size model for purchaser and vendor: A comment. *Decision Sciences*, *19*, 236–241. doi:10.1111/j.1540-5915.1988.tb00264.x

Goyal, S. K., & Gupta, Y. P. (1989). Integrated inventory models: The vendor–buyer coordination. *European Journal of Operational Research*, *41*, 261–269. doi:10.1016/0377-2217(89)90247-6

Grabisch, M. (1996). The application of fuzzy integrals in multicriteria decision-making. *European Journal of Operational Research*, *89*, 445–456. doi:10.1016/0377-2217(95)00176-X

Grabisch, M. (1997). K-ordered discrete fuzzy measures and their representation. *Fuzzy Sets and Systems*, *92*, 167–189. doi:10.1016/S0165-0114(97)00168-1

Graham, R., Lawler, E., & Rinnooy Kan, A. (1979). Optimization and approximation in deterministic sequencing and scheduling: A survey. *Annals of Discrete Mathematics*, *5*, 287–326. doi:10.1016/S0167-5060(08)70356-X

Granelli, G. P., & Montagna, M. (2000). Security-constrained economic dispatch using dual quadratic programming. *Electric Power Systems Research, 56*, 71–80. doi:10.1016/S0378-7796(00)00097-3

Gravel, M., Price, W., & Gagné, C. (2002). Scheduling continuous casting of aluminum using a multiple ant colony optimization metaheuristic. *European Journal of Operational Research, 143*, 218–229. doi:10.1016/S0377-2217(01)00329-0

Grishin, Y. A., Kolosok, I. N., Korkina, E. S., & Em, L. V. (1999). State Estimation of electric power system for new technological systems. *Proceedings of the International Conference "Power Tech 1999",* August 29 – September 2, Budapest.

Grunow, M., & Gobbi, C. (2009). Designing the reverse network for WEEE in Denmark. *CIRP Annals-Manufacturing Technology, 58*(1), 391–394. doi:10.1016/j.cirp.2009.03.036

Guha, S., Meyerson, A., Mishra, N., Motwani, R., & O'Callaghan, L. (2003). Clustering data streams: Theory and practice. *IEEE Transactions on Knowledge and Data Engineering, 15*(3), 515–528. doi:10.1109/TKDE.2003.1198387

Guha, S., Rastogi, R., & Shim, K. (2000). Rock: A robust clustering algorithm for categorical attributes. *Information Systems, 25*(5), 345–366. doi:10.1016/S0306-4379(00)00022-3

Guignard, M. (2003). Lagrangian relaxation. *Top (Madrid), 11*, 151–228. doi:10.1007/BF02579036

Gupta, M. M., et al. (2003). *Static and dynamic neural networks: From fundamentals to advanced theory.* IEEE Press & John Wiley.

Gupta, J. (1988). Two-stage hybrid flowshop scheduling problem. *The Journal of the Operational Research Society, 39*, 359–364.

Gupta, J., Krüger, K., Lauff, V., Werner, F., & Sotskov, Y. (2002). Heuristics for hybrid flow shops with controllable processing times and assignable due dates. *Computers & Operations Research, 29*, 1417–1439. doi:10.1016/S0305-0548(01)00040-5

Haenni, R. (2002). Introduction to Dempster-Shafer theory. University of Konstanz. Retrieved September 1, 2011, from http://www.iam.unibe.ch/~haenni/Homepage/TALKS/2002/ppm.pdf

Hagan, M. T. (1996). *Neural network design.* PWS.

Hagan, T., & Demuth, B. (1996). *Neural network design.* USA: PWS Publishing.

Haikin, S. (2009). *Neural networks and learning machines.* Prentice Hall.

Hamam, Y., & Hindi, K. S. (2000). Assignment of program modules to processors: A simulated annealing approach. *European Journal of Operational Research, 122*(2), 509–513. doi:10.1016/S0377-2217(99)00251-9

Han, C. C., Lin, K. J., & Hou, C. J. (1996). Distance-constrained scheduling and its applications in real-time systems. *IEEE Transactions on Computers, 45*, 814–826. doi:10.1109/12.508320

Handa, H., Lin, D., Chapman, L., & Yao, X. (2006). Robust solution of salting route optimisation using evolutionary algorithms. In *Proceedings of the IEEE Congress on Evolutionary Computation* (pp. 3098–3105).

Handschin, E., Hoffmann, W., & Reyer, F. (1994). A new method of excitation control based on fuzzy set theory. *IEEE Transactions on Power Systems, 9*(1), 533–539. doi:10.1109/59.317569

Han, H., Karypis, G., Kumar, V., & Mobasher, B. (1998). Hypergraph based clustering in high dimensional data sets: A summary of results. *A Quarterly Bulletin of the Computer Society of the IEEE Technical Committee on Data Engineering, 21*(1).

Han, J., & Kamber, M. (2001). *Data mining, concepts and techniques.* Morgan Kaufmann.

Han, K.-H., & Kim, J. H. (2002). Quantum-inspired evolutionary algorithm for a class of combinatorial optimization. *IEEE Transactions on Evolutionary Computation, 6*(6), 580–593. doi:10.1109/TEVC.2002.804320

Hanke, M., & Li, P. (2000). Simulated annealing for the optimization of batch distillation processes. *Computers & Chemical Engineering, 24*(1), 1–8. doi:10.1016/S0098-1354(00)00317-3

Hanselman, D., & Littlefield, B. (2005). *Mastering MATLAB 7*. USA: Prentice Hall.

Hansen, P., Jaumard, B., & Krau, S. (1997). *A stabilized column generation algorithm for the multisource Weber problem*. University of Montreal.

Hansen, P., & Mladenović, N. (1998). An introduction to variable neighborhood search. In Voß, S., Martello, S., Osman, I. H., & Roucairo, C. (Eds.), *Meta-heuristics: Advances and trends in local search paradigms for optimization* (pp. 433–458). New York, NY: Springer.

Hansen, P., & Mladenovic, N. (2001). Variable neighborhood search: Principles and applications. *European Journal of Operational Research*, *130*, 449–467. doi:10.1016/S0377-2217(00)00100-4

Hansen, P., Mladenovic, N., & Pérez, J. A. M. (2010). Variable neighborhood search: Methods and applications. *Annals of Operations Research*, *175*(1), 367–407. doi:10.1007/s10479-009-0657-6

Hansen, P., Mladenovic, N., & Taillard, E. D. (1998). Heuristic solution of the multisource Weber problem as a P-median problem. *Operations Research Letters*, *22*, 55–62. doi:10.1016/S0167-6377(98)00004-2

Happ, H. H., & Wirgau, K. A. (1981). A review of the optimal power flow. *Journal of the Franklin Institute*, *312*(3-4), 231–264. doi:10.1016/0016-0032(81)90063-6

Hariga, M., & Ben-Daya, M. (1999). Some stochastic inventory models with deterministic variable lead time. *European Journal of Operational Research*, *113*, 42–51. doi:10.1016/S0377-2217(97)00441-4

Harris, F. W. (1913). How many parts to make at once. *Factory, The Magazine of Management, 10*, 135–136, 152.

Hartigan, J. A., & Wong, M. A. (1979). Algorithm as 136: A k-means clustering algorithm. *Journal of the Royal Statistical Society. Series C, Applied Statistics*, *28*(1), 100–108. doi:10.2307/2346830

Hasançebi, O., & Erbatur, F. (2002). Layout optimisation of trusses using simulated annealing. *Advances in Engineering Software*, *33*(7-10), 681–696. doi:10.1016/S0965-9978(02)00049-2

Hasteer, G., & Banerjee, P. (1997). Simulated annealing based parallel state assignment of finite state machines. *Journal of Parallel and Distributed Computing*, *43*(1), 21–35. doi:10.1006/jpdc.1997.1325

Hawkins, D. (1980). *Identifications of outliers*. London, UK: Chapman and Hall.

He, Z., Deng, S., & Xu, X. (2005). An optimization model for outlier detection in categorical data. *ICIC 2005* (pp. 400-409).

Hedar, A. R., & Fukushima, M. (2004). Heuristic pattern search and its hybridization with simulated annealing for nonlinear global optimization. *Optimization Methods and Software*, *19*, 291–308. doi:10.1080/10556780310001645189

Hedar, A. R., & Fukushima, M. (2005). Derivative-free filter simulated annealing method for constrained continuous global optimization. *Journal of Global Optimization*, *35*(4).

Hendel, Y., & Sourd, F. (2007). An improved earliness-tardiness timing algorithm. *Computers & Operations Research*, *34*, 2931–2938. doi:10.1016/j.cor.2005.11.004

Herrmann, J. W. (2007). *Generating cyclic fair sequences using aggregation and stride scheduling. Technical Report*. USA: University of Maryland.

Herrmann, J. W. (2011). Using aggregation to reduce response time variability in cyclic fair sequences. *Journal of Scheduling*, *14*, 39–55. doi:10.1007/s10951-009-0127-7

Hertz, A., Taillard, E., & Werra, D. (2005). *A tutorial on Tabu search*. Retrieved April 14, 2005, from http://www.cs.colostate.edu/~whitley/CS640/hertz92tutorial.pdf

Hertz, A., & Widmer, M. (2003). Guidelines for the use of meta-heuristics in combinatorial optimization. *European Journal of Operational Research*, *151*, 247–252. doi:10.1016/S0377-2217(02)00823-8

Heydari, J., Baradaran-Kazemzadeh, R., & Chaharsooghi, S. K. (2009). A study of lead time variation impact on supply chain performance. *International Journal of Advanced Manufacturing Technology*, *40*, 1206–1215. doi:10.1007/s00170-008-1428-2

He, Z., Wang, N., Jia, T., & Xu, Y. (2009). Simulated annealing and tabu search for multi-mode project payment scheduling. *European Journal of Operational Research*, *198*(3), 688–696. doi:10.1016/j.ejor.2008.10.005

He, Z., Yang, T., & Tiger, A. (1996). An exchange heuristic imbedded with simulated annealing for due-dates job-shop scheduling. *European Journal of Operational Research*, *91*(1), 99–117. doi:10.1016/0377-2217(94)00361-0

Hillier, F. S., & Lieberman, G. J. (2005). *Introduction to operations research* (8th ed.). New York, NY: McGraw-Hill.

Hill, R. (1999). The optimal production and shipment policy for the single-vendor single-buyer integrated production–inventory problem. *International Journal of Production Research*, *37*, 2463–2475. doi:10.1080/002075499190617

Hinojosa, Y., Puerto, J., & Fernandez, F. R. (2000). A multiperiod two-echelon multicommodity capacitated plant location problem. *European Journal of Operational Research*, *123*, 271–291. doi:10.1016/S0377-2217(99)00256-8

Hiyama, T. (1999). Development of fuzzy logic power system stabilizer and further studies. *Proceedings of International Conference on Systems, Man and Cybernetics IEEE SMC'99*, Tokyo, Japan, October 12–15 (pp. 545–550).

Hiyama, T., Tokieda, M., Hubbi, W., & Andou, H. (1997). Artificial neural network based dynamic load modeling. *IEEE Transactions on Power Systems*, *12*(4), 1576–1583. doi:10.1109/59.627861

Holland, J. (1975). Adaptation in natural and artificial systems: An introductory analysis with applications to biology. In *Control and artificial intelligence*. Cambridge, MA: MIT Press.

Holland, J. H. (1975). *Adaptation in natural and artificial systems*. Ann Arbor, MI: University of Michigan Press.

Holland, J. H. (1999). *Emergence: From chaos to order*. Basic Books.

Holland, J. H. (Ed.). (1975). *Adaptation in natural and artificial systems: An introductory analysis with applications to biology, control, and artificial intelligence*. Ann Arbor, MI: University of Michigan Press.

Holton, L., Gjelsvik, A., Wu, F. F., & Liu, W. H. (1998). Comparison of different methods for state estimation. *IEEE Transactions on Power Apparatus and Systems*, *3*(4), 1798–1806.

Hong, Y. Y., & Ho, S. Y. (2005). Determination of network configuration considering multiobjective in distribution system using genetic algorithms. *IEEE Transactions on Power Systems*, *20*, 1062–1069. doi:10.1109/TPWRS.2005.846067

Hooker, J. N. (1995). Testing heuristics: We have it all wrong. *Journal of Heuristics*, *1*(1), 33–42. doi:10.1007/BF02430364

Houck, C. R., Joines, J. A., & Kay, M. G. (1996). Comparison of genetic algorithms, random restart and two-opt switching for solving large location-allocation problems. *Computers & Operations Research*, *23*(6), 587–596. doi:10.1016/0305-0548(95)00063-1

House, C. H., & Price, R. L. (1991). The return map: Tracking product teams. *Harvard Business Review*, (1): 92–100.

Hsiao, H. T. (2004). Multiobjective evolution programming method for feeder reconfiguration. *IEEE Transactions on Power Systems*, *19*, 594–599. doi:10.1109/TPWRS.2003.821430

Hsiao, J. M., & Lin, C. (2005). A buyer-vendor EOQ model with changeable lead time in supply chain. *International Journal of Advanced Manufacturing Technology*, *26*, 917–921. doi:10.1007/s00170-004-2063-1

Hsieh, C. L., & Laio, S. H. (2010). *A multi-objective evolutionary approach for an integrated location-inventory problem in vendor-managed inventory systems*. 40th International Conference on Computers and Industrial Engineering: Soft Computing Techniques for Advanced Manufacturing and Service Systems, CIE40 2010, art. no. 5668373.

Hsieh, T.-J., Hsiao, H.-F., & Yeh, W.-C. (2011). Forecasting stock markets using wavelet transforms and recurrent neural networks: An integrated system based on artificial bee colony algorithm. *Applied Soft Computing*, *11*(2), 2510–2525. doi:10.1016/j.asoc.2010.09.007

Hsu, C. T., Kang, M. S., & Chen, C. S. (2005). Design of adaptive load shedding by artificial neural networks. *IEE Proceedings. Generation, Transmission and Distribution, 152*(3), 415–421. doi:10.1049/ip-gtd:20041207

Hsu, J. (2003). Critical and future trends in data mining: a review of key data mining technologies/ applications. In *Data mining: Opportunities and challenges* (pp. 437–452). Hershey, PA: IGI Global. doi:10.4018/978-1-59140-051-6.ch020

Huang, N. E., Zheng, S., Long, S. R., et al. (1998). The empirical mode decomposition and the Hilbert spectrum for non-linear and non-stationary time series analysis. *Proceedings of the Royal Society of London, A: Mathematics, Physics, and Engineering Sciences, 45*(1971), 903-995.

Huang, C. J., Lin, C. E., & Huang, C. L. (1992). Fuzzy approach for generator maintenance scheduling. *Electric Power Systems Research, 24*(1), 31–38. doi:10.1016/0378-7796(92)90042-Y

Huang, R.-H., & Yang, C.-L. (2008). Ant colony system for job shop scheduling with time windows. *International Journal of Advanced Manufacturing Technology, 39*, 151–157. doi:10.1007/s00170-007-1203-9

Huang, Y.-M., & Lin, J.-C. (2011). A new bee colony optimization algorithm with idle-time-based filtering scheme for open shop-scheduling problems. *Expert Systems with Applications, 38*(5), 5438–5447. doi:10.1016/j.eswa.2010.10.010

Huneault, M., & Galiana, F. D. (1991). A survey of the optimal power flow literature. *IEEE Transactions on Power Systems, 6*(2), 762–770. doi:10.1109/59.76723

Hung, E., & Cheung, D. (2002). Parallel mining of outliers in large database. *Journal of Distributed and Parallel Databases, 12*(1), 5–26. doi:10.1023/A:1015608814486

Hung, K.-S., Su, S.-F., & Lee, Z.-J. (2007). Improving ant colony optimization algorithms for solving traveling salesman problems. *Journal of Advanced Computational Intelligence and Intelligent Informatics, 11*, 433–442.

Hu, P., Cao, G.-Y., Zhu, X.-J., & Li, J. (2010). Modeling of a proton exchange membrane fuel cell based on the hybrid particle swarm optimization with Levenberg–Marquardt neural network. *Simulation Modelling Practice and Theory, 18*(5), 574–588. doi:10.1016/j.simpat.2010.01.001

Hutter, F., Holger, H. H., Leyton-Brown, K., & Stuetzle, T. (2008). *Paramils: An automatic algorithm configuration framework*.

Hwang, Y. K., & Ahuja, N. (1992). A potential field approach to path planning. *IEEE Transactions on Robotics and Automation, 8*(1), 23–32. doi:10.1109/70.127236

IEEESTD (2003). *IEEE standard for interconnecting distributed resources with electric power system*s. IEEE Std 1547-2003.

Imam, S., Barker, R., & Clubb, C. (2008). The use of valuation models by UK investment analysts. *European Accounting Review, 17*(3), 503–535. doi:10.1080/09638180802016650

Inman, R. R., & Bulfin, R. L. (1991). Sequencing JIT mix-model assembly lines. *Management Science, 37*, 901–904. doi:10.1287/mnsc.37.7.901

Irnich, S. (2007). Solution of real-world problems. *European Journal of Operational Research, 190*(1), 16.

Jabalameli, M. S., & Ghaderi, A. (2008). Hybrid algorithms for the uncapacitated continuous location-allocation problem. *International Journal of Advanced Manufacturing Technology, 37*, 202–209. doi:10.1007/s00170-007-0944-9

Jain, A. K., & Dubes, R. C. (1988). *Algorithms for clustering data*. Upper Saddle River, NJ: Prentice-Hall, Inc.

Janiak, A., Kozan, E., Lichtenstein, M., & Oguz, C. (2007). Metaheuristic approaches to the hybrid flow shop scheduling problem with a cost-related criterion. *International Journal of Production Economics, 105*, 407–424. doi:10.1016/j.ijpe.2004.05.027

Jansen, P. W., & Perez, R. E. (2011). Constrained structural design optimization via a parallel augmented Lagrangian particle swarm optimization approach. *Computers & Structures, 89*(13-14), 1352–1366. doi:10.1016/j.compstruc.2011.03.011

Jayaraman, V., Guide, V. Jr, & Srivastava, R. (1999). A closed-loop logistics model for remanufacturing. *The Journal of the Operational Research Society, 50*(5), 497–508.

Jeffcoat, D. E., & Bulfin, R. L. (1993). Simulated annealing for resource-constrained scheduling. *European Journal of Operational Research*, *70*(1), 43–51. doi:10.1016/0377-2217(93)90231-B

Jenkins, N., Allan, R., Crossley, P., Kirschen, D., & Strbac, G. (2000). *Embedded generation* (p. 273). London, UK: IEEE Press. doi:10.1049/PBPO031E

Jeon, Y.-J., Kim, J.-C., & Lee, S.-Y. (2003). Application of ant colony algorithm for network reconfiguration in distribution systems. *Proceedings of the IFAC Symposium on Power Plants and Power Systems Control,* Seoul, Korea, Sept. 15-19.

Jeong, C.-S., & Kim, M.-H. (1991). Fast parallel simulated annealing for traveling salesman problem on SIMD machines with linear interconnections. *Parallel Computing*, *17*(2-3), 221–228. doi:10.1016/S0167-8191(05)80107-3

Jeong, S.-J., Kim, K.-S., & Lee, Y.-H. (2009). The efficient search method of simulated annealing using fuzzy logic controller. *Expert Systems with Applications*, *36*(3), 5. doi:10.1016/j.eswa.2008.08.020

Jia, H., Ordonez, F., & Dessouky, M. (2007). A modeling framework for facility location of medical services for large scale emergencies. *IIE Transactions*, *39*, 16–29. doi:10.1080/07408170500539113

Jimenez, F., Cadenas, J. M., Sanchez, G., Gmez-Skarmeta, A. F., & Verdegay, J. L. (2006). Multi-objective evolutionary computation and fuzzy optimization. *International Journal of Approximate Reasoning*, *43*, 59–75. doi:10.1016/j.ijar.2006.02.001

Jimenez, F., Gomez-Skarmeta, A. F., & Sanchez, G. (2004). *Nonlinear optimization with fuzzy constraints by multi-objective evolutionary algorithms* (pp. 713–722). Advances in Soft Computing, Computational Intelligence, Theory and Applications. doi:10.1007/3-540-31182-3_66

Johnson, D. S. (2002). A theoretician's guide to the experimental analysis of algorithms. In M. H. Goldwasser, D. S. Johnson, & C. C. McGeoch, (Eds.), *Data structures, near neighbor searches, and methodology: Proceedings of the 5th and 6th DIMACS Implementation Challenges*, (pp. 215-250). Providence.

Johnson, D. S., & McGeoch, L. A. (2002). *Experimental analysis of heuristics for the STSP. The traveling salesman problem and its variations*. Kluwer Academic Publishers.

Joines, J., & Houck, C. (1994). On the use of non-stationary penalty functions to solve non linear constrained optimization problems with gas. *Proceedings of the First IEEE International Conference on Evolutionary Computation* (pp. 579-584). IEEE Press.

Jourdan, L., Basseur, M., & Talbi, E. G. (2009). Hybridizing exact methods and meta-heuristics: A taxonomy. *European Journal of Operational Research*, *199*, 620–629. doi:10.1016/j.ejor.2007.07.035

Kalpic, D., Mornar, V., & Baranovic, M. (1995). Case study based on a multi period multi-criteria production planning model. *International Journal of Production Economics*, *87*, 658–669.

Kang, F., Li, J., & Ma, Z. (2011). Rosenbrock artificial bee colony algorithm for accurate global optimization of numerical functions. *Information Science*, *181*(16), 3508–3531. doi:10.1016/j.ins.2011.04.024

Kannan, G., Sasikumar, P., & Devika, K. (2010). A genetic algorithm approach for solving a closed loop supply chain model: A case of battery recycling. *Applied Mathematical Modelling*, *34*(3), 655–670. doi:10.1016/j.apm.2009.06.021

Kao, Y. T., & Zahara, E. (2008). A hybrid genetic algorithm and particle swarm optimization for multimodal functions. *Applied Soft Computing*, *8*, 849–857. doi:10.1016/j.asoc.2007.07.002

Karaboğa, D. (2005). *An idea based on honeybee swarm for numerical optimization*. Technical Report TR06, Erciyes University.

Karaboga, D., & Akay, B. (2011). A modified artificial bee colony (ABC) algorithm for constrained optimization problems. *Applied Soft Computing*, *11*(3), 3021–3031. doi:10.1016/j.asoc.2010.12.001

Karaboğa, D., & Akay, B. A. (2009). Comparative study of artificial bee colony algorithm. *Applied Mathematics and Computation*, *214*, 108–132. doi:10.1016/j.amc.2009.03.090

Karaboğa, D., & Baştük, B. (2007b). Artificial bee colony (ABC) optimization algorithm for solving constrained optimization problems. *LNCS: Advances in Soft Computing: Foundations of Fuzzy Logic and Soft Computing, 4529,* 789–798. doi:10.1007/978-3-540-72950-1_77

Karaboğa, D., & Baştürk, B. (2007a). A powerful and efficient algorithm for numerical optimization: Artificial bee colony (ABC) algorithm. *Journal of Global Optimization, 39*(3), 459–471. doi:10.1007/s10898-007-9149-x

Karaboğa, D., & Baştürk, B. (2008). On the performance of artificial bee colony (ABC) algorithm. *Applied Soft Computing, 8*(1), 687–697. doi:10.1016/j.asoc.2007.05.007

Karaboga, D., & Ökdem, S. (2004). A simple and global optimization algorithm for engineering problems: Differential evolution algorithm. *Turkish Journal of Electrical Engineering, 12*(1).

Karimi, H., Davison, E. J., & Iravani, R. (2010). Multivariable servomechanism controller for autonomous operation of a distributed generation unit: design and performance evaluation. *IEEE Transactions on Power Systems, 25*(2). doi:10.1109/TPWRS.2009.2031441

Kariuki, B. M., Serrano-Gonzalez, H., Johnston, R. L., & Harris, K. D. M. (1997). The application of a genetic algorithm for solving crystal structures from powder diffraction data. *Chemical Physics Letters, 280,* 189–195. doi:10.1016/S0009-2614(97)01156-1

Karr, C. L., & Gentry, E. J. (1993). Fuzzy control of pH using genetic algorithms. *IEEE Transactions on Fuzzy Systems, 1*(1). doi:10.1109/TFUZZ.1993.390283

Katagiri, H., Hayashida, T., Nishizaki, I., & Guo, Q. (2012). A hybrid algorithm based on tabu search and ant colony optimization for k-minimum spanning tree problems. *Expert Systems with Applications, 39,* 5681–5686. doi:10.1016/j.eswa.2011.11.103

Kayhan, A. H., Ceylan, H., Ayvaz, M. T., & Gurarslan, G. (2010). PSOLVER: A new hybrid particle swarm optimization algorithm for solving continuous optimization problems. *Expert Systems with Applications, 37*(10), 6798–6808. doi:10.1016/j.eswa.2010.03.046

Kazabov, K., & Kozma, R. (1998). *Neuro-fuzzy techniques for intelligent information systems.* Germany: Physica-Verlag.

Kazarlis, S., & Petridis, V. (1998). Varying fitness functions in genetic algorithms: studying the rate of increase in the dynamic penalty terms. *Proceedings of the 5th International Conference on Parallel Problem Solving from Nature* (pp. 211-220). Berlin, Germany: Springer Verlag.

Kennedy, J. & Eberhart, R. C. (2001). *Swarm intelligence.* Morgan Kaufmann Publisher, San Fransisco.

Kennedy, J., & Eberhart, R. (1995). Particle swarm optimization. In *Proceedings of the 1995 IEEE International Conference on Neural Networks* (pp. 1942-1948). Perth, Australia. Piscataway, NJ: IEEE Service Center.

Kennedy, J., & Eberhart, R. (2001). *Swarm intelligence.* San Diego, CA: Academic Press.

Kern, M. (2006). *Parameter adaption in heuristic search - A population-based approach.* PhD thesis, University of Essex.

Khalilian, M., & Mustapha, N. (2010). Data stream clustering: Challenges and issues. *Proceedings of the International MultiConference of Engineers and Computer Scientists,* Vol. I, IMECS 2010, March 17-19, Hong Kong.

Khalouli, S., Ghedjati, F., & Hamzaoui, A. (2008a). Method based on ant colony system for solving the hybrid flow shop scheduling problem. *7th International Conference on Modelling, Optimization and SIMulation Systems (MOSIM'08), 2,* (pp. 1407-1416).

Khalouli, S., Ghedjati, F., & Hamzaoui, A. (2008b). Ant colony optimization for solving a bi-criteria hybrid flow shop problem. *IEEE International Conference on Systems, Man and Cybernetics (SMC),* (pp. 1440-1445).

Khalouli, S., Ghedjati, F., & Hamzaoui, A. (2009). An integrated ant colony optimization algorithm for the hybrid flow shop scheduling problem. *International Conference on Computers & Industrial Engineering (CIE 2009),* (pp. 554-559).

Khalouli, S., Ghedjati, F., & Hamzaoui, A. (2010). A meta-heuristic approach to solve a JIT scheduling problem in hybrid flow shop. *Engineering Applications of Artificial Intelligence, 23*(5), 765–771. doi:10.1016/j.engappai.2010.01.008

Khan, L., Mumtaz, S., & Kamran, J. (2010). Generator maintenance scheduling using harmony search algorithm. *Journal of Engineering and Applied Sciences, 29*(1), 99–115.

Khoi, L., Landa-Silva, D., & Li, H. (2009). An improved version of volume dominance for multi-objective optimisation. In Ehrgott, M. (Eds.), *EMO 2009, LNCS 5467* (pp. 231–245).

Kim, B. I., Heragu, S. S., Graves, R. J., & Onge, A. S. (2003). Clustering-based order-picking sequence algorithm for an automated warehouse. *International Journal of Production Research, 41*(15), 3445–3460. doi:10.108 0/0020754031000120005

Kim, C. O., Jun, J., Baek, J. K., Smith, R. L., & Kim, Y. D. (2005). Adaptive inventory control models for supply chain management. *International Journal of Advanced Manufacturing Technology, 26*, 1184–1192. doi:10.1007/s00170-004-2069-8

Kim, D. (1999). Normalization methods for input and output vectors in backpropogation neural networks. *International Journal of Computer Mathematics, 71*(2), 161–171. doi:10.1080/00207169908804800

Kim, D.-W., Kim, K.-H., Jang, W., & Chen, F. F. (2002). Unrelated parallel machine scheduling with setup times using simulated annealing. *Robotics and Computer-integrated Manufacturing, 18*(3-4), 223–231. doi:10.1016/S0736-5845(02)00013-3

Kim, G. C., & Schniederjams, M. J. (1993). A multiple objective model for a just-in-time manufacturing system environment. *International Journal of Operations & Production Management, 13*, 47–61. doi:10.1108/01443579310048209

Kim, H., Hayashi, Y., & Nara, K. (1997). An algorithm for thermal unit maintenance scheduling through combined use of GA, SA and TS. *IEEE Transactions on Power Systems, 12*(1), 329–335. doi:10.1109/59.574955

Kim, H., Nara, K., & Gen, M. (1994). A method for maintenance scheduling using GA combined with SA. *Computers & Industrial Engineering, 27*(1-4), 477–480. doi:10.1016/0360-8352(94)90338-7

Kim, H.-S., & Cho, S.-B. (2000). Application of interactive genetic algorithm to fashion design. *Engineering Applications of Artificial Intelligence, 13*, 635–644. doi:10.1016/S0952-1976(00)00045-2

Kim, H., Yang, J., & Lee, K. D. (2009). Vehicle routing in reverse logistics for recycling end-of-life consumer electronic goods in South Korea. *Transportation Research Part D, Transport and Environment, 14*(5), 291–299. doi:10.1016/j.trd.2009.03.001

Kim, J. O., & Khosla, P. K. (1992). Real-time obstacle avoidance using harmonic potential functions. *IEEE Transactions on Robotics and Automation, 8*(3), 338–349. doi:10.1109/70.143352

Kim, J. Y., & Kim, Y. K. (2005). Multileveled symbiotic evolutionary algorithm: Application to FMS loading problems. *Applied Intelligence, 22*, 233–249. doi:10.1007/s10791-005-6621-4

Kim, Y. K., Kim, Y., & Kim, Y. J. (2000). Two-sided assembly line balancing: A genetic algorithm approach. *Production Planning and Control, 11*, 44–53. doi:10.1080/095372800232478

Kim, Y. K., Song, W. S., & Kim, J. H. (2009). A mathematical model and a genetic algorithm for two-sided assembly line balancing. *Computers & Operations Research, 36*(3), 853–865. doi:10.1016/j.cor.2007.11.003

Kıran, M. S., Ozceylan, E., Gunduz, M., & Paksoy, T. (2012). A novel hybrid approach based on particle swarm optimization and ant colony algorithm to forecast energy demand of Turkey. *Energy Conversion and Management, 53*, 75–83. doi:10.1016/j.enconman.2011.08.004

Kirkpatrick, S., Gelatti, C. D., & Vecchi, M. P. (1994). Optimization by simulated annealing. In H. Gutfreund & G. Tolouse (Eds.), *Advanced series in neurosciences, Vol. 3, Biology and computation: A physicist's choice*, (pp. 671–680).

Kirkpatrick, A., Gelatt, C. D. Jr, & Vechi, M. P. (1983). Optimization by simulated annealing. *Science, 220*, 671–680. doi:10.1126/science.220.4598.671

Kirkpatrick, S., Gelatt, C. D., & Vecchi, M. P. (1983). Optimization by simulated annealing. *Science, 220*, 671–680. doi:10.1126/science.220.4598.671

Ki-Seon, C., Joong-Rin, S., & Seung Ho, H. (2001). Optimal placement of PMU with GPS receiver. *Power Engineering Society Winter Meeting, IEEE,* Vol. 1, (pp.258-262).

Klepeis, J. L., Pieja, M. J., & Floudas, C. A. (2003). Hybrid global optimization algorithms for protein structure prediction: Alternating hybrids. *Biophysical Journal, 4,* 869–882. doi:10.1016/S0006-3495(03)74905-4

Klir, G. J., & Yuan, B. (1995). *Fuzzy sets and fuzzy logic, theory and applications.* New Jersey, USA: Prentice Hall.

Klose, A. (1999). An LP-based heuristic for two-stage capacitated facility location problems. *The Journal of the Operational Research Society, 50,* 157–166.

Klose, A. (2000). A Lagrangian relax and cut approach for the two-stage capacitated facility location problem. *European Journal of Operational Research, 126,* 408–421. doi:10.1016/S0377-2217(99)00300-8

Klose, A., & Drexl, A. (2005). Facility location models for distribution system design. *European Journal of Operational Research, 162*(1), 4–29. doi:10.1016/j.ejor.2003.10.031

Klose, A., & Drexl, A. (2005). Lower bounds for the capacitated facility location problem based on column generation. *Management Science, 51,* 1689–1705. doi:10.1287/mnsc.1050.0410

Knorr, E. M., & Ng, R. T. (1999). Finding intensional knowledge of distance-based outliers. In *VLDB '99: Proceedings of the 25th International Conference on Very Large Data Bases,* (pp. 211-222). San Francisco, CA: Morgan Kaufmann Publishers Inc.

Kolosok, I. N., & Zaika, R. A. (2003). Genetic algorithm as a means for enhancing the efficiency of methods for validation of information in the electric power industry. *Proceedings of the 30th International Conference on Information Technologies in Science, Education, Telecommunication, Business and Protection of Natural Resources",* Gurzuf, Ukraine (pp. 145-147). (in Russian)

Kolosok, I. N., & Patsev, A. S. (2008). Application of a multi-agent approach to decomposition of electric power system state estimation problem. *Proceedings of the 3rd International Scientific Conference on "Energy System: Control, Competition,* [Ekaterinburg, Russia: USTU – UPI.]. *Education, 1,* 354–359.

Kolosok, I. N., & Zaika, R. A. (2003). Study on effectiveness of genetic algorithms for validation of measurements in EPS state estimation. *Izvestia RAS* [in Russian]. *Energetika, 6,* 39–46.

Koren, Y., & Borenstein, J. (1991). Potential field methods and their inherent limitations for mobile robot navigation. In *Proceedings of the IEEE Conference on Robotics and Automation,* Sacramento, California, (pp. 1398-1404).

Kotb, M. F. (2008). Maintenance scheduling of generating units in electric power system. *12th International Middle-East* Power System Conference (pp. 543 – 549). Aswan.

Kotler, P. (1991). *Marketing management: Analysis, planning, implementation and control* (7th ed.). Englewood Cliffs, NJ: Prentice-Hall.

Kouvelis, P., Chiang, W.-C., & Fitzsimmons, J. (1992). Simulated annealing for machine layout problems in the presence of zoning constraints. *European Journal of Operational Research, 57*(2), 203–223. doi:10.1016/0377-2217(92)90043-9

Krarup, J., & Pruzan, P. M. (1983). The simple plant location problem: survey and synthesis. *European Journal of Operational Research, 12*(3), 36–81. doi:10.1016/0377-2217(83)90181-9

Krikke, H., Van Harten, A., & Schuur, P. (1999). Business case Oce: Reverse logistic network re-design for copiers. *OR-Spektrum, 21*(3), 381–409. doi:10.1007/s002910050095

Krumm, L. (1977). *The reduced gradient method for electric power system management.* Novosibirsk, Russia: Nauka. (in Russian)

Kubiak, W. (1993). Minimizing variation of production rates in just-in-time systems: A survey. *European Journal of Operational Research, 66,* 259–271. doi:10.1016/0377-2217(93)90215-9

Kubiak, W. (2004). Fair sequences. In Lenung, J. Y.-T. (Ed.), *Handbook of scheduling: Algorithms, models and performance analysis*. Boca Raton, FL: Chapman and Hall/CRC.

Kubiak, W. (Ed.). (2009). *Proportional optimization and fairness*. New York, NY: Springer.

Kuenne, R. E., & Soland, R. M. (1972). Exact and approximate solutions to the multisource Weber problem. *Mathematical Programming, 3*(1), 193–209. doi:10.1007/BF01584989

Kundur, P., Paserba, J., & Ajjarapu, V., Hill, Dagle, J., Stankovic, A., et al. (2004, August). Definition and classification of power system stability IEEE/CIGRE joint task force on stability terms and definitions. *IEEE Transactions on Power Systems, 19*(3), 1387–1401. doi:10.1109/TPWRS.2004.825981

Kuo, Y. (2010). Using simulated annealing to minimize fuel consumption for the time-dependent vehicle routing problem. *Computers & Industrial Engineering, 59*(1), 157–165. doi:10.1016/j.cie.2010.03.012

Kurbatsky, V. G., Sidorov, D. N., Spiryaev, V. A., & Tomin, N. V. (2011). The hybrid model based on Hilbert-Huang transform and neural networks for forecasting of short-term operation conditions of power system. *Proceedings of the International Conference "PowerTech'2011"*, Trondheim, Norway.

Kurbatsky, V., Sidorov, D., Spiryaev, V., & Tomin, N. (2010). Using the Hilbert-Huang transform for ANN prediction of nonstationary processes. *Scientific Bulletin Electrical Engineering Faculty, 1*(12), 106–110.

Kurbatsky, V., Sidorov, D., Spiryaev, V., & Tomin, N. (2011). On the neural network approach for forecasting of nonstationary time series on the basis of the Hilbert–Huang transform. *Automation and Remote Control, 72*(7), 1405–1414. doi:10.1134/S0005117911070083

Kusiak, N. L., & Wang, J. (1994). Reengineering of design and manufacturing processes. *Computers & Industrial Engineering, 26*(3), 521–536. doi:10.1016/0360-8352(94)90048-5

Kusumastuti, R. D., Piplani, R., & Hian Lim, G. (2008). Redesigning closed-loop service network at a computer manufacturer: A case study. *International Journal of Production Economics, 111*(2), 244–260. doi:10.1016/j.ijpe.2006.10.016

Kwak, N. K., Schnierderjans, M. J., & Warkentin, K. S. (1991). An application of linear goal programming to the marketing distribution. *European Journal of Operational Research, 52*, 334–344. doi:10.1016/0377-2217(91)90168-U

Lai, L. L., & Ma, J. T. (1997). Improved genetic algorithms for optimal power)ow under both normal and contingent operation states. *International Journal of Electrical Power & Energy Systems, 19*(5), 287–292. doi:10.1016/S0142-0615(96)00051-8

Landete, M., & Marín, A. (2009). New facets for the two-stage uncapacitated facility location polytope. *Computational Optimization and Applications, 44*, 487–519. doi:10.1007/s10589-008-9165-x

Lasdon, L. S. (2002). *Optimization theory for large systems*. Boston, MA: Dover Publications.

Lasseter, R. H. (2002). *MicroGrids*. Paper presented at the IEEE.

Lasseter, R. H., & Paigi, P. (2004). *Microgrid: A conceptual solution*. Paper presented at the 35th Annul IEEE Power Elecrronics Specialisrs Conference.

Lasseter, R. H., Akhil, A., Marnay, C., Stephens, J., Dagle, J., Guttromson, R., et al. (April 2002). *The CERTS microgrid concept*. White paper for transmission reliability program, Office of Power Technologies, U.S. Dept. Energy, 1.

Lasseter, R. H., Eto, J. H., Schenkman, B., Stevens, J., Vollkommer, H., & Klapp, D. (2011). CERTS microgrid laboratory test bed. *IEEE Transactions on Power Delivery, 26*(1), 325–326. doi:10.1109/TPWRD.2010.2051819

Latombe, J. C. (1991). *Robot motion planning*. Kluwer Academic Publishers.

Laumond, J. P. (1998). *Robot motion planning and control*. Springer. doi:10.1007/BFb0036069

LaValle, S. M. (2006). *Planning algorithms*. Cambridge University Press. doi:10.1017/CBO9780511546877

Ledet, W. P., & Himmelblau, D. M. (1970). Decomposition procedures for the solving of large scale systems. *Advances in Chemical Engineering, 8*, 185–254. doi:10.1016/S0065-2377(08)60185-4

Lee, J. E., Rhee, K. G., & Lee, H. H. (2010). Multi-objective hybrid genetic algorithm for reverse logistics network design of inventory systems with backordering. IEEM2010 - IEEE International Conference on Industrial Engineering and Engineering Management, art. no. 5674151, (pp. 2318-2322).

Lee, K., & El-Sharkawi, M. A. (2002). *Modern heuristic optimization techniques with applications to power systems*. IEEE Power Engineering Society (02TP160).

Lee, D. H., & Dong, M. (2008). A heuristic approach to logistics network design for end-of-lease computer products recovery. *Transportation Research Part E, Logistics and Transportation Review, 44*(3), 455–474. doi:10.1016/j.tre.2006.11.003

Lee, D.-J., & Wang, L. (2008). Small-signal stability analysis of an autonomous hybrid renewable energy power generation/energy storage system part I: time-domain simulations. *IEEE Transactions on Energy Conversion, 23*(1), 312–315. doi:10.1109/TEC.2007.914309

Lee, I., Sikora, R., & Shaw, M. J. (1997). A genetic algorithm-based approach to flexible flow-line scheduling with variable lot sizes. *IEEE Transactions on Systems, Man, and Cybernetics. Part B, Cybernetics, 27*(1), 36–54. doi:10.1109/3477.552184

Lee, J. E., Gen, M., & Rhee, K. G. (2008). A multi-stage reverse logistics network problem by using hybrid priority-based genetic algorithm. *IEEJ Transactions on Electronics. Information Systems, 128*(3), 450–455.

Lee, K. S., & Geem, Z. W. (2004). A new structural optimization method based on the harmony search algorithm. *Computers & Structures, 82*(9–10), 781–798. doi:10.1016/j.compstruc.2004.01.002

Lee, K. S., & Geem, Z. W. (2005). A new meta-heuristic algorithm for continuous engineering optimization: Harmony search theory and practice. *Computer Methods in Applied Mechanics and Engineering, 194*, 3902–3933. doi:10.1016/j.cma.2004.09.007

Lee, S. M., & Clayton, E. R. (1972). A goal programming model for academic resource allocation. *Management Science, 18*, B-395–408. doi:10.1287/mnsc.18.8.B395

Lee, S., Ryu, J.-H., Won, J.-S., & Park, H.-J. (2004). Determination and application of the weights for landslide susceptibility mapping using an artificial neural network. *Engineering Geology, 71*, 289–302. doi:10.1016/S0013-7952(03)00142-X

Lee, T. O., Kim, Y., & Kim, Y. K. (2001). Two-sided assembly line balancing to maximize work relatedness and slackness. *Computers & Industrial Engineering, 40*, 273–292. doi:10.1016/S0360-8352(01)00029-8

Lee, Z. J., Su, H. F., Chuang, C. C., & Liu, K. H. (2008). Genetic algorithm with ant colony optimization (GA-ACO) for multiple sequence alignment. *Applied Soft Computing, 8*(1), 55–78. doi:10.1016/j.asoc.2006.10.012

Lek, S., & Guegan, J. F. (1999). Artificial neural networks as a tool in ecological modelling, an introduction. *Ecological Modelling, 120*, 65–73. doi:10.1016/S0304-3800(99)00092-7

Lendasse, A., Ji, Y., Reyhani, N., & Verleysen, M. (2005). LS-SVM hyperparameter selection with a nonparametric noise estimator. *Artificial Neural Networks: Formal Models and Their Applications - ICANN 2005, 3697*, (pp. 625-630).

Lennox, C. (1999). Identifying failing companies: A re-evaluation of the Logit, Probit and DA approaches. *Journal of Economics and Business, 51*, 347–364. doi:10.1016/S0148-6195(99)00009-0

Leung, C. W., Wong, T. N., Mak, K. L., & Fung, R. Y. K. (2010). Integrated process planning and scheduling by an agent-based ant colony optimization. *Computers & Industrial Engineering, 59*(1), 166–180. doi:10.1016/j.cie.2009.09.003

Leyton-Brown, K., Nudelman, E., & Shoham, Y. (2002). Learning the empirical hardness of optimization problems: The case of combinatorial auctions. In *Principles and Practice of Constraint Programming - CP 2002*, (pp. 91 – 100).

Li, C., Zhao, H., & Chen, T. (2010). The hybrid differential evolution algorithm for optimal power flow based on simulated annealing and tabu search. *International Conference on Management and Service Science* (MASS) (pp. 1-7).

Liang, R.-H., Tsai, S.-R., Chen, Y.-T., & Tseng, W.-T. (2011). Optimal power flow by a fuzzy based hybrid particle swarm optimization approach. *Electric Power Systems Research*, *81*(7), 1466–1474. doi:10.1016/j.epsr.2011.02.011

Liang, R.-H., & Wang, Y. S. (2001). Main transformer ULTC and capacitors scheduling by simulated annealing approach. *International Journal of Electrical Power & Energy Systems*, *23*(7), 531–538. doi:10.1016/S0142-0615(00)00086-7

Liang, T. F. (2008). Interactive multi-objective transportation planning decisions using fuzzy linear programming. *Asia Pacific Journal of Operational Research*, *25*(1), 11–31. doi:10.1142/S0217595908001602

Lian, Z., Gu, X., & Jiao, B. (2006). A similar particle swarm optimization algorithm for permutation flowshop scheduling to minimize makespan. *Applied Mathematics and Computation*, *175*(1), 773–785. doi:10.1016/j.amc.2005.07.042

Liao, S. H., & Hsieh, C. L. (2010). Integrated location-inventory retail supply chain design: A multi-objective evolutionary approach. *Lecture Notes in Computer Science (including subseries Lecture Notes in Artificial Intelligence and Lecture Notes in Bioinformatics) 6457 LNCS*, (pp. 533-542).

Liao, C.-J., Tseng, C.-T., & Luarn, P. (2007). A discrete version of particle swarm optimization for flowshop scheduling problems. *Computers & Operations Research*, *34*(10), 3099–3111. doi:10.1016/j.cor.2005.11.017

Liao, K., & Diansheng, G. (2008). A clustering-based approach to the capacitated facility location problem. *Transactions in GIS*, *12*, 323–339. doi:10.1111/j.1467-9671.2008.01105.x

Li, C., & Zhou, J. (2011). Parameters identification of hydraulic turbine governing system using improved gravitational search algorithm. *Energy Conversion and Management*, *52*(1), 374–381. doi:10.1016/j.enconman.2010.07.012

Li, D. (2009). Support vector regression based image denoising. *Image and Vision Computing*, *27*(6), 623–627. doi:10.1016/j.imavis.2008.06.006

Lin, F. T. (2007, March). *Personal communication*.

Lin, B., & Miller, D. C. (2004). Solving heat exchanger network synthesis problems with Tabu Search. *Computers & Chemical Engineering*, *28*, 1451–1464. doi:10.1016/j.compchemeng.2003.10.004

Lin, C. C. (2006). A genetic algorithm for solving the two-dimensional assortment problem. *Computers & Industrial Engineering*, *50*(1-2), 175–184. doi:10.1016/j.cie.2006.03.002

Lin, C. E., Huang, C. J., Huang, C. L., & Liang, C. C. (1992). An expert system for generator maintenance scheduling using operation index. *IEEE Transactions on Power Systems*, *7*(3), 1141–1148. doi:10.1109/59.207327

Lin, L.-C. (2009). Optimal chiller loading by particle swarm algorithm for reducing energy consumption. *Applied Thermal Engineering*, *29*(8-9), 1730–1734. doi:10.1016/j.applthermaleng.2008.08.004

Lin, S. (1965). Computer solutions of the travelling salesman problem. *The Bell System Technical Journal*, *44*, 2245–2269.

Lin, S.-Y., Horng, S.-J., Kao, T.-W., Huang, D.-K., Fahn, C.-S., & Lai, J.-L. (2010). An efficient bi-objective personnel assignment algorithm based on a hybrid particle swarm optimization model. *Expert Systems with Applications*, *37*(12), 7825–7830. doi:10.1016/j.eswa.2010.04.056

Lin, T.-L., Horng, S.-J., Kao, T.-W., Chen, Y.-H., Run, R.-S., & Chen, R.-J. (2010). An efficient job-shop scheduling algorithm based on particle swarm optimization. *Expert Systems with Applications*, *37*(3), 2629–2636. doi:10.1016/j.eswa.2009.08.015

Listes, O., & Dekker, R. (2005). A stochastic approach to a case study for product recovery network design. *European Journal of Operational Research*, *160*(1), 268. doi:10.1016/j.ejor.2001.12.001

Litvinchev, I., Mata, M., Rangel, S., & Saucedo, J. (2010). Lagrangian heuristic for a class of the generalized assignment problems. *Computers & Mathematics with Applications (Oxford, England)*, *60*(4), 1115–1123. doi:10.1016/j.camwa.2010.03.070

Litvinchev, I., Rangel, S., & Saucedo, J. (2010). A Lagrangian bound for many-to-many assignment problems. *Journal of Combinatorial Optimization*, *19*(3), 241–257. doi:10.1007/s10878-008-9196-3

Liu, B. (2000). *Theory and practice of uncertainty programming*. Heidelberg, Germany: Springer-Verlag.

Liu, B. (2004). *Uncertainty theory*. Heidelberg, Germany: Springer-Verlag.

Liu, B., & Liu, Y. K. (2002). Expected value of fuzzy variable and fuzzy expected value models. *IEEE Transactions on Fuzzy Systems*, *10*, 445–450. doi:10.1109/TFUZZ.2002.800692

Liu, C. M., Kao, R. L., & Wang, A. H. (1994). Solving location-allocation problems with rectilinear distances by simulated annealing. *The Journal of the Operational Research Society*, *45*(11), 1304–1315.

Liu, G. (2010). Rough set theory based on two universal sets and its applications. *Knowledge-Based Systems*, *23*, 110–115. doi:10.1016/j.knosys.2009.06.011

Liu, H., Abraham, A., & Clerc, M. (2007). Chaotic dynamic characteristics in swarm intelligence. *Applied Soft Computing*, *7*(3), 1019–1026. doi:10.1016/j.asoc.2006.10.006

Liu, J., Li, G., Chen, D., Liu, W., & Wang, Y. (2010). Two-dimensional equilibrium constraint layout using simulated annealing. *Computers & Industrial Engineering*, *59*(4), 530–536. doi:10.1016/j.cie.2010.06.009

Liu, Y., & Zhu, X. (2007). Capacitated fuzzy two-stage location-Allocation problem. *International Journal of Innovative Computing, Information, & Control*, *3*, 987–999.

Li, Z., Halong, W. A., & Chen, G. (2006). *Integration of fuzzy logic and chaos theory*. New York, NY: Springer. doi:10.1007/3-540-32502-6

Lo, K. L., & Meng, Z. J. (2004). Newton-like method for line outage simulation. *IEE Proceedings -General Transmissions and Distributions*, *151*(2), 225-231.

Lobo, F. G., & Lima, C. F. (2005). A review of adaptive population sizing schemes in genetic algorithms. In *Proceedings of the 2005 Workshop on Parameter Setting in Genetic and Evolutionary Algorithms* (PSGEA 2005), part of GECCO 2005, Washington.

Loizou, S. G., Tanner, H. G., Kumar, V., & Kyriakopoulos, K. J. (2003). Closed loop navigation for mobile agents in dynamic environments. In *Proceedings of the IEEE/RSJ International Conference on Intelligent Robots and Systems*, Las Vegas, Nevada, (pp. 3769-3774).

Lokketangen, A. (2007). The importance of being careful. *Lecture Notes in Computer Science*, *4638*, 1–15. doi:10.1007/978-3-540-74446-7_1

Lopes, J. A. P., Moreira, C. L., & Madureira, A. G. (2006). Defining control strategies for microgrids islanded operation. *IEEE Transactions on Power Systems*, *21*(2), 919–920. doi:10.1109/TPWRS.2006.873018

Lopez-Garcia, L., & Posada-Bolivar, A. (1999). Simulator that uses Tabu search to approach the optimal solution to stochastic inventory models. *Computers & Industrial Engineering*, *37*, 215–218. doi:10.1016/S0360-8352(99)00058-3

Lorenco, H. R., Martin, O. C., & Stuetzle, T. (2002). Iterated local search. In *Handbook of metaheuristics* (pp. 321–353). Kluwer.

Lo, S.-T., Chen, R.-M., Huang, Y.-M., & Wu, C.-L. (2008). Multiprocessor system scheduling with precedence and resource constraints using an enhanced and colony system. *Expert Systems with Applications*, *34*, 2071–2081. doi:10.1016/j.eswa.2007.02.022

Loukil, T., Teghem, J., & Tuyttens, D. (2005). Solving multi-objective production scheduling problems using metaheuristics. *European Journal of Operational Research*, *161*(1), 42–61. doi:10.1016/j.ejor.2003.08.029

Lourenço, H. R. (2001). *Integrated logistics management: An opportunity for metaheuristics*.

Lourenco, H. R., & Empresa, U. P. F. D. d. E. i. (2001). *Supply chain management: An opportunity for metaheuristics*. Universitat Pompeu Fabra.

Louwers, D., Kip, B. J., Peters, E., Souren, F., & Flapper, S. D. P. (1999). A facility location allocation model for reusing carpet materials. *Computers & Industrial Engineering*, *36*(4), 855–869. doi:10.1016/S0360-8352(99)00168-0

Love, R. F., & Juel, H. (1982). Properties and solution methods for large location-allocation problems. *The Journal of the Operational Research Society*, *33*(5), 443–452.

Love, R. F., Morris, J. G., & Wesolowsky, G. O. (1988). *Facilities layout and location: Models and methods*. New York, NY: North-Holland.

Low, C. (2005). Simulated annealing heuristic for flow shop scheduling problems with unrelated parallel machines. *Computers & Operations Research*, *32*(8), 2013–2025. doi:10.1016/j.cor.2004.01.003

Lo, Z.-P., & Bavarian, B. (1992). Optimization of job scheduling on parallel machines by simulated annealing algorithms. *Expert Systems with Applications*, *4*(3), 323–328. doi:10.1016/0957-4174(92)90068-4

Lu, C. T., Chen, D., & Kou, Y. (2003). Detecting spatial outliers with multiple attributes. In *ICTAI '03: Proceedings of the 15th IEEE International Conference on Tools with Artificial Intelligence*, (pp. 122-127). Washington, DC: IEEE Computer Society.

Luh, G. C., & Liu, W. W. (2007). Motion planning for mobile robots in dynamic environments using a potential field immune network. *Proceedings of the Institution of Mechanical Engineers. Part I, Journal of Systems and Control Engineering*, *221*, 1033–1045. doi:10.1243/09596518JSCE400

Luh, G.-C., Lin, Y.-S., & Lin, C.-Y. (2011). A binary particle swarm optimization for continuum structural topology optimization. *Applied Soft Computing*, *11*(2), 2833–2844. doi:10.1016/j.asoc.2010.11.013

Luke, S. (2009). *Essentials of metaheuristics*. Lulu. Retrieved January 20th, 2012, from http://cs.gmu.edu/:sean/book/metaheuristics/

Lu, L. (1995). A one-vendor multi-buyer integrated inventory model. *European Journal of Operational Research*, *81*, 312–323. doi:10.1016/0377-2217(93)E0253-T

Lu, M., Lam, H.-C., & Dai, F. (2008). Resource-constrained critical path analysis based on discrete event simulation and particle swarm optimization. *Automation in Construction*, *17*(6), 670–681. doi:10.1016/j.autcon.2007.11.004

Lu, Z., & Bostel, N. (2005). A facility location model for logistics systems including reverse flows: The case of remanufacturing activities. *Computers & Operations Research*, *34*, 299–323. doi:10.1016/j.cor.2005.03.002

M'Hallah, R. (2007). Minimizing total earliness and tardiness on a single machine using a hybrid heuristic. *Computers & Operations Research*, *34*, 3126–3142. doi:10.1016/j.cor.2005.11.021

Mabrouk, M. H., & McInnes, C. R. (2008). Solving the potential field local minimum problem using internal agent states. *Robotics and Autonomous Systems*, *56*, 1050–1060. doi:10.1016/j.robot.2008.09.006

MacQueen, J. B. (1967). Some methods for classification and analysis of multivariate observations. In *5th Berkeley Symposium on Mathematical Statistics and Probability*, Vol. 1, (p. 281–297). Berkeley, CA: University of California Press.

Mahdavi, M., & Abolhassani, H. (2009). Harmony k-means algorithm for document clustering. *Data Mining and Knowledge Discovery*, *18*(3), 370–391. doi:10.1007/s10618-008-0123-0

Maiti, M. K. (2011). A fuzzy genetic algorithm with varying population size to solve an inventory model with credit-linked promotional demand in an imprecise planning horizon. *European Journal of Operational Research*, *213*, 96–106. doi:10.1016/j.ejor.2011.02.014

Ma, J., Lu, J., & Zhang, G. (2010). Decider: A fuzzy multi-criteria group decision support system. *Knowledge-Based Systems*, *23*, 23–31. doi:10.1016/j.knosys.2009.07.006

Majumder, R., Ledwich, A. G. G., & Zare, F. (2008, 19 March). Load sharing and power quality enhanced operation of a distributed microgrid. *IET Renewable Power Generation*, *3*(2).

Mandal, S., Maity, A. K., Maity, K., Mondal, S., & Maiti, M. (2011). Multi-item multi-period optimal production problem with variable preparation time in fuzzy stochastic environment. *Applied Mathematical Modelling, 35,* 4341–4353. doi:10.1016/j.apm.2011.03.007

Maniezzo, V., & Colorni, A. (1999). The ant system applied to the quadratic assignment problem. *IEEE Transaction Data Knowledge Engineering, 11*(5), 769–778. doi:10.1109/69.806935

Maniezzo, V., Stützle, T., & Voß, S. (Eds.). (2009). *Matheuristics: Hybridizing metaheuristics and mathematical programming.* New York, NY: Springer Annals of Information Systems.

Mariano, A. P., Costa, C. B. B., Vasco de Toledo, E. C., Melo, D. N. C., & Filho, R. M. (in press). Analysis of the particle swarm algorithm in the optimization of a three-phase slurry catalytic reactor. [in press]. *Computers & Chemical Engineering.*

Marichal, J.-L. (1998). *Agregation operators for multicreteria decision aid.* Ph.D. Thesis, University of Liege, Belgium.

Marimuthu, S., Ponnambalam, S. G., & Jawahar, N. (2009). Threshold accepting and Ant-colony optimization algorithms for scheduling m-machine flow shops with lot streaming. *Journal of Materials Processing Technology, 209*(2), 1026–1041. doi:10.1016/j.jmatprotec.2008.03.013

Marín, A. (2007). Lower bounds for the two-stage uncapacitated facility location problem. *European Journal of Operational Research, 179,* 1126–1142. doi:10.1016/j.ejor.2005.04.052

Marín, A., & Pelegrín, B. (1999). Applying Lagrangian relaxation to the solution of two-stage location problems. *Annals of Operations Research, 86,* 179–198. doi:10.1023/A:1018998500803

Marinakis, Y., & Marinaki, M. (2010). A hybrid genetic – Particle swarm optimization algorithm for the vehicle routing problem. *Expert Systems with Applications, 37,* 1446–1455. doi:10.1016/j.eswa.2009.06.085

Marinakis, Y., & Marinak, M. (2010). A hybrid multi-swarm particle swarm optimization algorithm for the probabilistic traveling salesman problem. *Computers & Operations Research, 37*(3), 432–442. doi:10.1016/j.cor.2009.03.004

Martin, R. (1999). *Large scale linear and integer optimization: A united approach.* Boston, MA: Kluwer Academic Publishers. doi:10.1007/978-1-4615-4975-8

Maslow, A. H. (1954). *Motivation and personality.* New York, NY: Harper & Bros.

MathWorks, Inc. (1998). *Neural network toolbox user's guide.*

McKendall, A. R. Jr, Shang, J., & Kuppusamy, S. (2006). Simulated annealing heuristics for the dynamic facility layout problem. *Computers & Operations Research, 33*(8), 2431–2444. doi:10.1016/j.cor.2005.02.021

McWilliams, A., & Siegel, D. (2000). Corporate social responsibility and financial performance: correlation or misspecification? *Strategic Management Journal, 21*(5), 603–609. doi:10.1002/(SICI)1097-0266(200005)21:5<603::AID-SMJ101>3.0.CO;2-3

Meade, L., & Sarkis, J. (2007). The theory and practice of reverse logistics. *International Journal of Logistics, 1*(3).

Megiddo, N., & Supowit, K. J. (1984). On the complexity of some common geometric location problems. *SIAM Journal on Computing, 13*(1), 182–196. doi:10.1137/0213014

Melo, M. T., Nickel, S., & Saldanha-da-Gama, F. (2009). Facility location and supply chain management – A review. *European Journal of Operational Research, 196*(2), 401–412. doi:10.1016/j.ejor.2008.05.007

Melo, M. T., Nickel, S., & Saldanha-da-Gama, F. (2012). A tabu search heuristic for redesigning a multi-echelon supply chain network over a planning horizon. *International Journal of Production Economics, 136,* 218–230. doi:10.1016/j.ijpe.2011.11.022

Melouk, S., Damodaran, P., & Chang, P.-Y. (2004). Minimizing makespan for single machine batch processing with non-identical job sizes using simulated annealing. *International Journal of Production Economics, 87*(2), 141–147. doi:10.1016/S0925-5273(03)00092-6

Merkle, D., & Middendorf, M. (2005). On solving permutation scheduling problems with ant colony optimization. *International Journal of Systems Science, 36*, 255–266. doi:10.1080/00207720500062306

Merkle, D., Middendorf, M., & Schmeck, H. (2002). Ant colony optimization for resource-constrained project scheduling. *IEEE Transactions on Evolutionary Computation, 6*(4), 333–346. doi:10.1109/TEVC.2002.802450

Metropolis, N., Rosenbluth, A., Rosenbluth, M., Teller, A., & Teller, E. (1953). Equation of state calculations by fast computing machines. *The Journal of Chemical Physics, 21*(6), 1087–1092. doi:10.1063/1.1699114

Michalewicz, Z. (1995). Genetic algorithms, numerical optimization, and constraints. In *Proceedings of the Sixth International Conference on Genetic Algorithms* (pp. 151–158). Morgan Kaufmann.

Michalewicz, Z. (1992). *Genetic algorithm + data structures = evolution programs*. Springer-Verlag.

Michel, L., & Van Hentenryck, P. (1997). LOCALIZER a modeling language for local search. *Principles and Practice of Constraint Programming-C, P97*, 237–251. doi:10.1007/BFb0017443

Mili, L., Phaniraj, V., & Rousseuw, P. J. (1990). Least median of squares estimation in power system. *IEEE Transactions on Power Systems, 10*, 229–240.

Milosevic, B., & Begovic, M. (2003). Nondominated sorting genetic algorithm for optimal PMU placement. *IEEE Transactions on Power Systems, 18*, 69–75. doi:10.1109/TPWRS.2002.807064

Miltenburg, J. (1989). Level schedules for mixed-model assembly lines in just-in-time production systems. *Management Science, 35*, 192–207. doi:10.1287/mnsc.35.2.192

Min, H., Jeung Ko, H., & Seong Ko, C. (2006). A genetic algorithm approach to developing the multi-echelon reverse logistics network for product returns. *Omega, 34*(1), 56–69. doi:10.1016/j.omega.2004.07.025

Minis, I., Zeimpekis, V., Dounias, G., & Ampazis, N. (2011). *Supply chain management: Advances and intelligent methods*. Hershey, PA: IGI Global.

Miranda, V., Srinivasan, D., & Proenca, L. M. (1998). Evolutionary computation in power systems. *International Journal of Electrical Power & Energy Systems, 20*(2), 89–98. doi:10.1016/S0142-0615(97)00040-9

MirHassani, S. A., & Abolghasemi, N. (2011). A particle swarm optimization algorithm for open vehicle routing problem. *Expert Systems with Applications, 38*(9), 11547–11551. doi:10.1016/j.eswa.2011.03.032

Mita, T. (2000). *Introduction to nonlinear control theory - Skill control of underactuated robots*. Shokodo Co. Ltd. (In Japanese)

Mladenovic, N., & Hansen, P. (1997). Variable neighborhood search. *Computers & Operations Research, 24*(11), 1097–1100. doi:10.1016/S0305-0548(97)00031-2

Mladenović, N., Petrović, J., Kovačević-Vujčić, V., & Čangalović, M. (2003). Solving spread spectrum radar polyphase code design problem by tabu search and variable neighbourhood search. *European Journal of Operational Research, 151*, 389–399. doi:10.1016/S0377-2217(02)00833-0

Mohammadi, T. N., Pirmoradian, M., & Hassanpour, S. B. (2008). Implicit enumeration based 0-1 integer programming for generation maintenance scheduling. *IEEE Region 8 International Conference on Computational Technologies* in *Electrical* and *Electronics Engineering* (pp. 151–154). Novosibirsk.

Mohsen, A., Khader, A., & Ramachandram, D. (2010). An optimization algorithm based on harmony search for rna secondary structure prediction. In Geem, Z. (Ed.), *Recent advances in harmony search algorithm* (pp. 163–174). Berlin, Germany: Springer. doi:10.1007/978-3-642-04317-8_14

Momoh, J. A., Adapa, R., & El-Hawary, M. E. (1999a). A review of selected optimal power flow literature to 1993-I. Nonlinear and quadratic programming approaches. *IEEE Transactions on Power Systems, 14*(1), 96–104. doi:10.1109/59.744492

Momoh, J. A., Adapa, R., & El-Hawary, M. E. (1999b). A review of selected optimal power flow literature to 1993. II. Newton, linear programming and interior point methods. *IEEE Transactions on Power Systems, 14*(1), 105–111. doi:10.1109/59.744495

Momoh, J. A., Ma, X. W., & Tomsovic, K. (1995). Overview and literature survey of fuzzy set theory in power systems. *IEEE Transactions on Power Systems*, *10*(3), 1676–1690. doi:10.1109/59.466473

Monden, Y. (Ed.). (1983). *Toyota production systems*. Norcross, GA: Engineering & Management Press.

Monticelly, A. (2000). Electric power system state estimation. *Proceedings of the IEEE*, *88*(2), 262–282. doi:10.1109/5.824004

Morales, K. A., & Quezada, C. C. (1998). A universal eclectic genetic algorithm for constrained optimization. In *Proceedings 6th European Congress on Intelligent Techniques & Soft Computing, EUFIT'98*, (pp. 518–522).

Moreira, C. L., & Lopes, J. A. P. (2007). *MicroGrids dynamic security assessment*. Paper presented at the IEEE.

Moslemi, H., & Zandieh, M. (2011). Comparisons of some improving strategies on MOPSO for multi-objective (r, Q) inventory system. *Expert Systems with Applications*, *38*, 2051–12057. doi:10.1016/j.eswa.2011.01.169

Mostaghim, S., Branke, J., & Schmeck, H. (2007). *Multi-objective particle swarm optimization on computer grids*. *Institute AIFB*. Germany: University of Karlsruhe.

Mota-Palomino, R., & Quintana, V. H. (1986). Sparse reactive power scheduling by a penalty-function linear programming technique. *IEEE Transactions on Power Systems*, *1*(3), 31–39. doi:10.1109/TPWRS.1986.4334951

Mromlinski, L. R. (1985). Transportation problem as a model for optimal schedule of maintenance outages in power systems. *International Journal of Electrical Power & Energy Systems*, *7*(3), 161–164. doi:10.1016/0142-0615(85)90045-6

Muckstadt, J. A., & Sapra, A. (2010). *Principles of inventory management* (1st ed.). New York, NY: Springer. doi:10.1007/978-0-387-68948-7

Mukerjee, R., Merrill, H. M., Erickson, B. W., Parker, J. H., & Friedman, R. E. (1991). Power plant maintenance scheduling optimizing economics and reliability. *IEEE Transactions on Power Systems*, *6*(2), 476–483. doi:10.1109/59.76689

Müller, K. R., Smola, A. J., Rätsch, G., Schölkopf, B., Kohlmorgen, J., & Vapnik, V. (1997). Predicting time series with support vector machine. In *Proceedings of 7th International Conference on Artificial Neural Networks, Springer Lecture in Computer Science 1327*, Berlin, (pp. 999-1004).

Muyldermans, L., Beullens, P., Cattrysse, D., & Van Oudheusden, D. (2005). Exploring variants of 2-and 3-opt for the general routing problem. *Operations Research*, *53*(6), 982–995. doi:10.1287/opre.1040.0205

Nagarur, N., Vrat, P., & Duongsuwan, W. (1997). Production planning and scheduling for injection mounding of pipe fittings: A case study. *International Journal of Production Economics*, *53*, 157–170. doi:10.1016/S0925-5273(97)00109-6

Nagurney, A., & Toyasaki, F. (2005). Reverse supply chain management and electronic waste recycling: A multitiered network equilibrium framework for e-cycling. *Transportation Research Part E, Logistics and Transportation Review*, *41*(1), 1–28. doi:10.1016/j.tre.2003.12.001

Nakamori, Y., & Ryoke, M. (1994). Identification of fuzzy prediction models through hyperellipsoidal clustering. *IEEE Transactions on Systems, Man, and Cybernetics*, *4*(8), 1153–1173. doi:10.1109/21.299699

Nara, K., Satoh, T., Aoki, K., & Kitagawa, M. (1991). Multi-year expansion planning for distribution systems. *IEEE Transactions on Power Systems*, *6*(3), 952–958. doi:10.1109/59.119234

National Research Council. (1991). *Improving engineering design: Designing for competitive advantage*. Washington, DC: National Academy Press.

Nearchou, A. C. (2007). Balancing large assembly lines by a new heuristic based on differential evolution method. *International Journal of Advanced Manufacturing Technology*, *34*, 1016–1029. doi:10.1007/s00170-006-0655-7

Nearchou, A. C. (2011). Maximizing production rate and workload smoothing in assembly lines using particle swarm optimization. *International Journal of Production Economics*, *129*(2), 242–250. doi:10.1016/j.ijpe.2010.10.016

Neema, M. N., Maniruzzaman, K. M., & Ohgai, A. (2011). New genetic algorithms based approaches to continuous p-median problem. *Networks and Spatial Economics*, *11*(1), 83–99. doi:10.1007/s11067-008-9084-5

Negenman, E. (2001). Local search algorithms for the multiprocessor flow shop scheduling problem. *European Journal of Operational Research*, *128*(1), 147–158. doi:10.1016/S0377-2217(99)00354-9

Negnevisky, M., & Kelareva, G. V. (1999a). Maintenance scheduling in power systems using genetic algorithms. *International conference on Electric Power Engineering* (p. 187). Budapest, Hungary.

Negnevisky, M., & Kelareva, G. V. (1999b). Genetic algorithms for maintenance scheduling in power systems. *Australasian Universities Power Engineering Conference and IEAust Electric Energy Conference* (pp. 184-189). Darwin.

Nevins, J. L., & Whitney, D. E. (Eds.). (1989). *Concurrent design of products and processes: A strategy for the next generation in manufacturing.* New York, NY: McGraw-Hill.

Nickolay, B., Schneider, B., & Jacob, S. (1997). Parameter optimisation of an image processing system using evolutionary algorithms. In *Computer Analysis of Images and Patterns, Proceedings of the 7th International Conference, Vol. 1296. Lecture Notes in Computer Science* (pp. 637–644). Berlin, Germany: Springer.

Noel, M. M. (2006). *Explorations in swarm algorithms: Hybrid particle swarm optimization and adaptive culture model algorithms.* The University Of Alabama At Birmingham.

Nwana, V., Darby-Dowman, K., & Mitra, G. (2005). A co-operative parallel heuristic for mixed zero-one linear programming: Combining simulated annealing with branch and bound. *European Journal of Operational Research*, *164*, 12–23. doi:10.1016/j.ejor.2002.12.002

O'Callaghan, L., Mishra, N., Meyerson, A., Guha, S., & Motwani, R. (2001). Streaming-data algorithms for high quality clustering. In *Proceedings of IEEE International Conference on Data Engineering.*

Obayashi, S. (1998). Multidisciplinary design optimization of aircraft wing planform based on evolutionary algorithms. In *Proceedings of the 1998 IEEE International Conference on Systems, Man, and Cybernetics.* La Jolla, CA: IEEE Press.

O'Grady, P., Ramers, D., & Bowen, J. (1988). Artificial intelligence constraint nets applied to design for economic manufacture and assembly. *Computer Integrated Manufacturing Systems*, *1*(4), 204–210. doi:10.1016/0951-5240(88)90052-3

Ogura, T., & Sato, C. (2006). A fully automatic 3D reconstruction method using simulated annealing enables accurate posterioric angular assignment of protein projections. *Journal of Structural Biology*, *156*(3), 371–386. doi:10.1016/j.jsb.2006.05.016

Ohlson, J. (1980). Financial ratios and the probabilistic prediction of bankruptcy. *Journal of Accounting Research*, *18*(1), 109–131. doi:10.2307/2490395

Oh, S.-K., Kim, W.-D., Pedrycz, W., & Park, B.-J. (2011). Polynomial-based radial basis function neural networks (P-RBF NNs) realized with the aid of particle swarm optimization. *Fuzzy Sets and Systems*, *163*(1), 54–77. doi:10.1016/j.fss.2010.08.007

Okuma, K., Urakudo, T., & Tada, Y. (2004) Lyapunov control of a two wheeled mobile robot in the presence of obstacles. In *Proceedings of 2004 Japan-USA Symposium on Flexible Automation*, Denver, Colorado, CD-ROM(JS-026).

Ólafsson, S. (2006). Metaheuristics. In Nelson, B. L., & Henderson, S. G. (Eds.), *Handbook on simulation, handbooks in operations research and management science VII* (pp. 633–654). Elsevier.

Olamaei, J., Niknam, T., Gharehpetian, G., & Jamshidpour, E. (2007). An approach based on ant colony optimization for distribution feeder reconfiguration considering distributed generation. *Proceedings of the International Conference on Electricity Distribution, CIRED,* Vienna, Austria, May 21-24.

Oliveira, I. M. S., & Schirru, R. (2011). Swarm intelligence of artificial bees applied to in-core fuel management optimization. *Annals of Nuclear Energy*, *38*(5), 1039–1045. doi:10.1016/j.anucene.2011.01.009

Omiecinski, E. R. (2003). Alternative interest measures for mining associations in databases. *IEEE Transactions on Knowledge and Data Engineering, 15*(1), 57–69. doi:10.1109/TKDE.2003.1161582

Ongsakul, W., & Bhasaputra, P. (2002). Optimal power flow with FACTS devices by hybrid TS/SA approach. *International Journal of Electrical Power & Energy Systems, 24*(10), 851–857. doi:10.1016/S0142-0615(02)00006-6

Ongsakul, W., & Tantimaporn, T. (2006). Optimal power flow by improved evolutionary programming. *Electric Power Components and Systems, 34*(1), 79–95. doi:10.1080/15325000691001458

Önüt, S., Tuzkaya, U. R., & Doğaç, B. (2008). A particle swarm optimization algorithm for the multiple-level warehouse layout design problem. *Computers & Industrial Engineering, 54*, 783–799. doi:10.1016/j.cie.2007.10.012

Onwubolu, G., & Davendra, D. (2006). Scheduling flow shops using differential evolution algorithm. *European Journal of Operational Research, 171*, 674–692. doi:10.1016/j.ejor.2004.08.043

Osman, M. S., Abo-Sinna, M. A., & Mousa, A. A. (2004). A solution to the optimal power flow using genetic algorithm. *Applied Mathematics and Computation, 155*(2), 391–405. doi:10.1016/S0096-3003(03)00785-9

Osorio, M., & Sánchez, A. (2008). A preprocessing procedure for fixing the binary variables in the capacitated facility location problem through pairing and surrogate constraint analysis. *WSEAS Transactions on Mathematics, 8*, 583–592.

Osowski, S. (1996). *Neural networks for information processing*. Warszawa, Poland: OWPW.

Ostresh, L. M. (1973). *TWAIN - Exact solutions to the two source location-allocation problem*, (pp. 29-53). Lowa city: Department of Geography, University of Lowa.

Ota, T., Yukita, K., & Nakano, H. Y. G., & Ichiyanagi, K. (2010). *Study of load frequency control for a microgrid*. IEEE.

Ow, P., & Morton, T. (1989). The single machine early/tardy problem. *Management Science, 35*(2), 177–191. doi:10.1287/mnsc.35.2.177

Ozbakir, L., Baykasoglu, L. A., Gorkemli, B., & Gorkemli, L. (2011). Multiple-colony ant algorithm for parallel assembly line balancing problem. *Applied Soft Computing, 11*(3), 3186–3198. doi:10.1016/j.asoc.2010.12.021

Özcan, U. (2010). Balancing stochastic two-sided assembly lines: A chance-constrained, piecewise-linear, mixed integer program and a simulated annealing algorithm. *European Journal of Operational Research, 205*(1), 81–97. doi:10.1016/j.ejor.2009.11.033

Ozdamar, L., & Demirhan, M. (2000). Experiments with new stochastic global optimization search techniques. *Computers and OR, 27*, 841–865. doi:10.1016/S0305-0548(99)00054-4

Palepu, K. (1986). Predicting takeover targets. *Journal of Accounting and Economics, 8*, 3–35. doi:10.1016/0165-4101(86)90008-X

Panchal, A. (2009). Harmony search in therapeutic medical physics. In Geem, Z. (Ed.), *Music-inspired Harmony search algorithm* (pp. 189–203). Berlin, Germany: Springer. doi:10.1007/978-3-642-00185-7_12

Pandya, K. S., & Joshi, S. K. (2008). A survey of optimal power flow methods. *Journal of Theoretical and Applied Information Technology, 4*(5), 450–458.

Panigrahi, S. (2009). Credit card fraud detection: A fusion approach using Dempster–Shafer theory and Bayesian learning. *Information Fusion, 10*(4), 354–363. doi:10.1016/j.inffus.2008.04.001

Pan, Q.-K., Tasgetiren, M. F., Suganthan, P. N., & Chen, A. T.-J. (2011). A discrete artificial bee colony algorithm for the lot-streaming flow shop scheduling problem. *Information Sciences, 181*(12), 2455–2468. doi:10.1016/j.ins.2009.12.025

Park, D. C., & El-Sharkawi, M. A., & Marks 11, R. J. (1991). Electric load forecasting using artificial neural network. *IEEE Transactions on Power Systems, 6*(2). doi:10.1109/59.76685

Parmee, I. C. (2003). Poor-definition, uncertainty and human factors—A case for interactive evolutionary problem reformulation. *Proceedings of the 3rd IEC Workshop of the Genetic and Evolutionary Computation Conference*.

Pasandideh, S. H. R., Niaki, S. T. A., & Tokhmehchi, N. (2011). A parameter-tuned genetic algorithm to optimize two-echelon continuous review inventory systems. *Expert Systems with Applications, 38*, 11708–11714. doi:10.1016/j.eswa.2011.03.056

Pati, R. K., Vrat, P., & Kumar, P. (2008). A goal programming model for paper recycling system. *Omega, 36*(3), 405–417. doi:10.1016/j.omega.2006.04.014

Paul, G. (2010). Comparative performance of Tabu search and simulated annealing heuristics for the quadratic assignment problem. *Operations Research Letters, 38*(6), 577–581. doi:10.1016/j.orl.2010.09.009

Pavon, R., Diaz, F., Laza, R., & Luzon, V. (2009). Automatic parameter tuning with a bayesian case-based reasoning system. a case of study. *Expert Systems with Applications, 36*(2), 3407–3420. doi:10.1016/j.eswa.2008.02.044

Pawlak, Z. (1998). Rough set theory and its applications to data analysis. *Cybernetics and Systems, 29*, 661–688. doi:10.1080/019697298125470

Peasnell, K. (1982). Some formal connections between economic values and yields and accounting numbers. *Journal of Business Finance & Accounting*, (3): 361–381. doi:10.1111/j.1468-5957.1982.tb01001.x

Peet, W. J., & Hladik, K. J. (1989). Organizing for global product development. *Electronic Business, 15*(5), 62–64.

Peng, T., Huanchen, W., & Dongme, Z. (1996). Simulated annealing for the quadratic assignment problem: A further study. *Computers & Industrial Engineering, 31*(3-4), 925–928. doi:10.1016/S0360-8352(96)00265-3

Perez, R. E., & Behdinan, K. (2007). Particle swarm approach for structural design optimization. *Computers & Structures, 85*(19-20), 1579–1588. doi:10.1016/j.compstruc.2006.10.013

Peters, E. E. (1994). *Fractal market analysis—Applying chaos theory to investment & economics*. USA: John Wiley.

Peters, E. E. (1996). *Chaos and order in the capital markets: A new view of cycles, prices*. USA: Wiley Finance Edition.

Pham, D. T., Ghanbarzadeh, A., Koç, E., Otri, S., Rahim, S., & Zaidi, M. (2009). *The bees algorithm–A novel tool for complex optimization problems*. Cardiff, UK: Intelligent Production Machines and Systems.

Pham, D. T., & Jin, G. (1995). Genetic algorithm using gradient-like reproduction operator. *Electronics Letters, 31*(18), 1558–1559. doi:10.1049/el:19951092

Pham, D. T., & Karaboga, D. (2000). *Intelligent optimisation techniques – Genetic algorithms, Tabu search, simulated annealing and neural networks*. London, UK: Springer-Verlag.

Phua, C., Gayler, R., Lee, V., & Smith-Miles, K. (2009). On the communal analysis suspicion scoring for identity crime in streaming credit applications. *European Journal of Operational Research, 195*, 595–612. doi:10.1016/j.ejor.2008.02.015

Pirayesh, M., & Yazdi, M. M. (2010). Modeling (r, Q) policy in a two-level supply chain system with fuzzy demand. *International Journal of Uncertainty. Fuzziness and Knowledge-Based Systems, 18*, 819–841. doi:10.1142/S0218488510006817

Pishvaee, M. S., Kianfar, K., & Karimi, B. (2010). Reverse logistics network design using simulated annealing. *International Journal of Advanced Manufacturing Technology, 47*(1), 269–281. doi:10.1007/s00170-009-2194-5

Poli, R., Kennedy, J., & Blackwell, T. (2007). Particle swarm optimization. *Swarm Intelligence, 1*(1), 33–57. doi:10.1007/s11721-007-0002-0

Pomerol, J.-C., & Barba-Romero, S. (2000). *Multicriterion decision making in management: Principles and practice*. Boston, MA: Kluwer.

Pope, P. F., & Walker, M. (1999). International differences in the timeliness and conservatism and classification of earnings. *Journal of Accounting Research, 37*, 53–87. doi:10.2307/2491345

Port, O. (1990, April 30). A smarter way to manufacture. *Business Week*, (pp. 110-117).

Portmann, M.-C., & Mouloua, Z. (2007). A window time negotiation approach at the scheduling level inside supply chains. In *Proceedings of the 3th Multidisciplinary International Scheduling Conference: Theory and applicAtion (MISTA 2007)*, (pp. 410-417).

Powell, M. J. D. (1983). Variable metric methods for constrained optimization. In Bachem, A., Grotschel, M., & Korte, B. (Eds.), *Mathematical programming: The state of the art* (pp. 288–311). Springer Verlag. doi:10.1007/978-3-642-68874-4_12

Problematics. (n.d.). *Website*. Retrieved from http://www.problematics.com

Pudjianto, D., Ahmed, S., & Strbac, G. (2002). Allocation of VAR support using LP and NLP based optimal power flows. *IEE Proceedings. Generation, Transmission and Distribution, 149*(4), 377–383. doi:10.1049/ip-gtd:20020200

Puris, A., Bello, R., & Herrera, F. (2010). Analysis of the efficacy of a two-stage methodology for ant colony optimization: Case of study with TSP and QAP. *Expert Systems with Applications, 37*(7), 5443–5453. doi:10.1016/j.eswa.2010.02.069

Purnomo, H. D., Wee, H. M., & Rau, H. (2011). Two-sided assembly lines balancing with assignment restrictions. *Mathematical and Computer Modelling*, in press. Retrieved from http://dx.doi.org/10.1016/j.mcm.2011.06.010

Puttgen, H., MacGregor, P., & Lambert, F. (2003). Distributed generation: Semantic type or the dawn of a new era. *IEEE Transactions on Power and Energy, 1*(1), 22–29. doi:10.1109/MPAE.2003.1180357

Raaymakers, W. H. M., & Hoogeveen, J. A. (2000). Scheduling multipurpose batch process industries with no-wait restrictions by simulated annealing. *European Journal of Operational Research, 126*(1), 131–151. doi:10.1016/S0377-2217(99)00285-4

Radhakrishnan, T., & Nandan, U. (2005). Milling force prediction using regression and neural networks. *Journal of Intelligent Manufacturing, 16*, 93–102. doi:10.1007/s10845-005-4826-4

Raidl, G. R. (2006). A unified view on hybrid metaheuristics. In Almeida, F., Blesa Aguilera, M., Blum, C., Moreno Vega, J., Pérez Pérez, M., Roli, A., & Sampels, M. (Eds.), *Hybrid metaheuristics (Vol. 4030*, pp. 1–12). Berlin, Germany: Springer. doi:10.1007/11890584_1

Raidl, G. R., Puchinger, J., & Blum, C. (2010). Metaheuristic hybrids. In Gendreau, M., & Potvin, J.-Y. (Eds.), *Handbook of metaheuristics (Vol. 146*, pp. 469–496). Springer, US. doi:10.1007/978-1-4419-1665-5_16

Rajendran, C., & Alicke, K. (2007). Dispatching in flowshops with bottleneck machines. *Computers & Industrial Engineering, 52*, 89–106. doi:10.1016/j.cie.2006.10.006

Ramik, J., & Vlach, M. (2002). Fuzzy mathematical programming: A unified approach based on fuzzy relations. *Fuzzy Optimization and Decision Making, 1*, 335–346. doi:10.1023/A:1020978428453

Ramos, M. T., & Sáenz, J. (2005). Solving capacitated facility location problems by Fenchel cutting planes. *The Journal of the Operational Research Society, 56*, 297–306. doi:10.1057/palgrave.jors.2601810

Rashedi, E., Nezamabadi-pour, H., & Saryazdi, S. (2009). GSA: A gravitational search algorithm. *Information Sciences, 179*(13), 2232–2248. doi:10.1016/j.ins.2009.03.004

Rashedi, E., Nezamabadi-pour, H., & Saryazdi, S. (2011). Filter modeling using gravitational search algorithm. *Engineering Applications of Artificial Intelligence, 24*(1), 117–122. doi:10.1016/j.engappai.2010.05.007

Rastrigin, L. A. (1974). Extremal control systems. In *Theoretical Foundations of Engineering Cybernetics Series*. Moscow, Russia: Nauka, Russian.

Ratliff, H. D., & Rosenthal, A. S. (1983). Order-picking in a rectangular warehouse: A solvable case of the traveling salesman problem. *Operations Research, 31*(3), 507–521. doi:10.1287/opre.31.3.507

Realff, M., Ammons, J., & Newton, D. (2004). Robust reverse production system design for carpet recycling. *IIE Transactions, 36*(8), 767–776. doi:10.1080/07408170490458580

Rechenberg, I. (1973). *Evolutionsstrategie: Optimierung technischer systeme nach prinzipien der biologischen evolution*. Stuttgart, Germany: Frommann-Holzboog.

Reed, J., Toombs, R., & Barricelli, N. A. (1967). Simulation of biological evolution and machine learning. *Journal of Theoretical Biology, 17*(3), 319–342. doi:10.1016/0022-5193(67)90097-5

Rehman, S., & Mohandes, M. (2008). Artificial neural network estimation of global solar radiation using air temperature and relative humidity. *Energy Policy, 36*, 571–576. doi:10.1016/j.enpol.2007.09.033

Reinelt, G. (1991). TSLIB-A traveling salesman library. *ORSA Journal on Computing, 3*, 376–384. doi:10.1287/ijoc.3.4.376

Ren, M.-L., Huang, S., & Wang, B.-M. (2010). Inventory model for major equipment maintenance companies with fuzzy and discrete spare parts demands. In Xitong, J. J. Z. (Ed.), *Computer Integrated Manufacturing Systems, CIMS, 16*, 2233-2239.

Resende, M. G. C., & De Sousa, J. P. (Eds.). (2004). *Metaheuristics: Computer decision making*. Netherlands: Kluwer Academic Publishers.

Resende, M. G. C., & Werneck, R. F. (2007). A fast swap-based local search procedure for location problems. *Annals of Operations Research, 150*(1), 205–230. doi:10.1007/s10479-006-0154-0

ReVelle, C. S., Eiselt, H. A., & Daskin, M. S. (2008). A bibliography for some fundamental problem categories in discrete location science. *European Journal of Operational Research, 184*(3), 817–848. doi:10.1016/j.ejor.2006.12.044

Reynolds, A. P., & McKeown, G. P. (1999). Scheduling a manufacturing plant using simulated annealing and simulation. *Computers & Industrial Engineering, 37*(1-2), 63–67. doi:10.1016/S0360-8352(99)00024-8

Ries, J. (2009). *Instance based flexible parameter tuning for meta-heuristics using fuzzy logic*. PhD thesis, University of Portsmouth.

Ries, J., & Beullens, P. (2011). *A semi-automated instance-based fuzzy parameter tuning strategy. Technical Report*. University of Portsmouth.

Ries, J., Beullens, P., & Salt, D. (2012). Instance-specific multi-objective parameter tuning based on fuzzy logic. *European Journal of Operational Research, 218*(2), 305–315. doi:10.1016/j.ejor.2011.10.024

Rimon, E., & Koditschek, D. E. (1992). Exact robot navigation using artificial potential functions. *IEEE Transactions on Robotics and Automation, 8*(5), 501–518. doi:10.1109/70.163777

Roa-Sepulveda, C. A., & Pavez-Lazo, B. J. (2003). A solution to the optimal power flow using simulated annealing. *International Journal of Electrical Power & Energy Systems, 25*(1), 47–57. doi:10.1016/S0142-0615(02)00020-0

Roesmer, C. (2000). Nonstandard analysis and Dempster-Shafer theory. *International Journal of Intelligent Systems, 15*, 117–127. doi:10.1002/(SICI)1098-111X(200002)15:2<117::AID-INT2>3.0.CO;2-2

Rogers, J. L. (1996). DeMaid/GA—An enhanced design manager's aid for intelligent decomposition. *6th AIAA/USAF/NASA/OSSMO Symposium on Multidisciplinary Analysis and Optimization*, Seattle, WA, Sep. 4–6, 1996, (pp. 96-4157)

Rogers, J. L., & Bloebaum, C. L. (1994-a). Ordering design tasks based on coupling strengths. *Proceeding the 5th AIAA/USAF/NASA/ISSMO Symposium on Multidisciplinary Analysis and Optimization*, Panama City, Florida. AIAA paper No. 94-4326. Also NASA TM 109137.

Rogers, J. L., & Bloebaum, C. L. (1994-b). *Ordering design tasks based on coupling strengths*. AIAA, No. 94-4326.

Roghanian, E., Sadjadi, S. J., & Aryanezhad, M. B. (2007). A probabilistic bi-level linear multi-objective programming problem to supply chain planning. *Applied Mathematics and Computation, 188*, 786–800. doi:10.1016/j.amc.2006.10.032

Roh, S.-B., Ahn, T.-C., & Pedrycz, W. (2010). The design methodology of radial basis function neural networks based on fuzzy K-nearest neighbors approach. *Fuzzy Sets and Systems, 161*(13), 1803–1822. doi:10.1016/j.fss.2009.10.014

Rosenbrock, H. H. (1960). An automatic method for finding the greatest or least value of a function. *The Computer Journal, 3*, 175–184. doi:10.1093/comjnl/3.3.175

Rosenkrantz, D. J., Stearns, R. E., & Lewis, P. M. II. (1977). An analysis of several heuristics for the traveling salesman problem. *SIAM Journal on Computing, 6*, 567–581. doi:10.1137/0206041

Rosing, K. E. (1992). An optimal method for solving the generalized multi-Weber problem. *European Journal of Operational Research, 58*(3), 414–426. doi:10.1016/0377-2217(92)90072-H

Rossi, A., & Dini, G. (2007). Flexible job-shop scheduling with routing flexibility and separable setup times using ant colony optimisation method. *Robotics and Computer-integrated Manufacturing, 23*(5), 503–516. doi:10.1016/j.rcim.2006.06.004

Roy, A., Pal, S., & Maiti, M. K. (2009). A production inventory model with stock dependent demand incorporating learning and inflationary effect in a random planning horizon: A fuzzy genetic algorithm with varying population size approach. *Computers & Industrial Engineering, 57*, 1324–1335. doi:10.1016/j.cie.2009.07.008

Saad, I., Hammadi, S., Borne, P., & Benrejeb, M. (2008). Choquet integral for criteria aggregation in the flexible job-shop scheduling problems. *Mathematics and Computers in Simulation, 76*, 447–462. doi:10.1016/j.matcom.2007.04.010

Sabri, E. H., & Beamon, B. M. (2000). A multi-objective approach to simultaneous strategic and operational planning in supply chain design. *Omega, 28*, 581–598. doi:10.1016/S0305-0483(99)00080-8

Sabuncuoglu, I., Erel, E., & Alp, A. (2009). Ant colony optimization for the single model U-type assembly line balancing problem. *International Journal of Production Economics, 120*(2), 287–300. doi:10.1016/j.ijpe.2008.11.017

Safaei, A., & Haghjoo, M. (2010). Parallel processing of continuous queries over data streams. *Distributed and Parallel Databases, 28*(2-3). doi:10.1007/s10619-010-7066-3

Safranek, R. J., Gottschlich, S., & Kak, A. C. (1990). Evidence accumulation using binary frames of discernment for verification vision. *IEEE Transactions on Robotics and Automation, 6*, 405–417. doi:10.1109/70.59366

Sahin, J., & Süral, H. (2007). A review of hierarchical facility location models. *Computers & Operations Research, 34*, 2310–2331. doi:10.1016/j.cor.2005.09.005

Şahin, R. (2011). A simulated annealing algorithm for solving the bi-objective facility layout problem. *Expert Systems with Applications, 38*(4), 4460–4465. doi:10.1016/j.eswa.2010.09.117

Sakall, U. S. (2010). A note on fuzzy multi-objective production/distribution planning decisions with multi-product and multi-time period in a supply chain. *Computers & Industrial Engineering, 59*, 1010–1012. doi:10.1016/j.cie.2010.07.008

Salhi, S., & Gamal, M. D. H. (2003). A genetic algorithm based approach for the uncapacitated continuous location allocation problem. *Annals of Operations Research, 123*(1-4), 203–222. doi:10.1023/A:1026131531250

Salleh, S., & Zomaya, A. Y. (1998). Multiprocessor scheduling using mean-field annealing. *Future Generation Computer Systems, 14*(5-6), 393–408. doi:10.1016/S0167-739X(98)00042-9

Salman, A., Ahmad, I., & Al-Mada, S. (2002). Particle swarm optimization for task assignment problem. *Microprocessors and Microsystems, 26*(8), 363–371. doi:10.1016/S0141-9331(02)00053-4

Sanchez, G., Jimenez, F., & Vasant, P. (2007). Fuzzy optimization with multi-objective evolutionary algorithms: A case study. *Proceedings of the 2007 IEEE Symposium on Computational Intelligence in Multi-criteria Decision Making* (pp. 58-64). Honolulu, Hawaii.

Santos de Oliveira, I. M., & Schirru, R. (2011). Swarm intelligence of artificial bees applied to in-core fuel management optimization. *Annals of Nuclear Energy, 38*(5), 1039–1045. doi:10.1016/j.anucene.2011.01.009

Santos, A. Jr, & da Costa, G. R. M. (1995). Optimal power flow solution by Newton's method applied to an augmented Lagrangian function. *IEE Proceedings. Generation, Transmission and Distribution, 142*(1), 33–36. doi:10.1049/ip-gtd:19951586

Santos, D., Hunsucker, J., & Deal, D. (1995). Global lower bounds for flow shops with multiple processors. *European Journal of Operational Research, 80*, 112–120. doi:10.1016/0377-2217(93)E0326-S

Sao, C. K., & Lehn, P. W. (2008). Control and power management of converter fed microgrids. *IEEE Transactions on Power Systems, 23*(3). doi:10.1109/TPWRS.2008.922232

Saraiva, J. T., Pereira, M. L., Mendes, V. T., & Sousa, J. C. (2010). Preventive generation maintenance scheduling - A simulated annealing approach to use in competitive markets. 7th Mediterranean Conference and Exhibition on *Power Generation, Transmission, Distribution and Energy Conversion* (pp. 1-8), Agia Napa.

Saraiva, J. T., Pereira, M. L., Mendes, V. T., & Sousa, J. C. (2011). A simulated annealing based approach to solve the generator maintenance scheduling problem. *Electric Power Systems Research, 81*(7), 1283–1291. doi:10.1016/j.epsr.2011.01.013

Sarangapani, J. (2006). *Neural network control of nonlinear discrete-time systems.* CRC Press. doi:10.1201/9781420015454

Sarkis, J. (2003). A strategic decision framework for green supply chain management. *Journal of Cleaner Production, 11*(4), 397–409. doi:10.1016/S0959-6526(02)00062-8

Satoh, H. (1992). A periodical maintenance scheduling of thermal and nuclear generating facilities using mixed integer programming. *Transactions of The Institute of Electrical Engineering Japan, 112-B*(1), 98–106.

Sayadi, M. K., Ramezanian, R., & Ghaffari-Nasab, N. (2010). A discrete firefly meta-heuristic with local search for makespan minimization in permutation flow shop scheduling problems. *International Journal of Industrial Engineering Computation, 1*, 1–10. doi:10.5267/j.ijiec.2010.01.001

Schauder, C., & Mehta, H. (1993, July). Vector analysis and control of advanced static VAR compensators. *Proceedings of the IEEE, 140*(Part C), 299–306.

Schinkel, H. (2000). Gipsreststoffengooi je nietweg! In van Goor, A. R., Flapper, S. D. P., & Clement, C. (Eds.), *Handboek reverse logistics.* Deventer, The Netherlands: Kluwer B.V.

Schmitting, W. (1999). *Das Traveling Salesman Problem: Anwendung und heuristische Nutzung von Voronoi-/Delaunay-Strukturen zur Loesung euklidischer, zweidimensionaler Traveling-Salesman-Probleme.* PhD thesis, University of Duesseldorf.

Schölkopf, B., Burges, C. J. C., & Smola, A. J. (1999). *Advances in kernel methods-support vector learning.* Cambridge, MA: MIT Press.

Schölkopf, B., & Smola, A. J. (2005). *Learning with kernels-support vector machines, regularization, optimization, and beyond.* London, UK: The MIT Press.

Scholköpf, B., Sung, K. K., Burges, C. J. C., Girosi, F., Niyogi, P., Poggio, T., & Vapnik, V. (1997). Comparing support vector machines with gaussian kernels to radial basis function classifiers. *IEEE Transactions on Signal Processing, 45*(11), 2758–2765. doi:10.1109/78.650102

Schubert, J. (1994). *Cluster-based specification techniques in Dempster-Shafer theory for an evidential intelligence analysis of multiple target tracks.* Department of Numerical Analysis and Computer Science Royal Institute of technology, S-100 44 Stockholm, Sweden.

Schultmann, F., Engels, B., & Rentz, O. (2003). Closed-loop supply chains for spent batteries. *Interfaces, 33*(6), 57–71. doi:10.1287/inte.33.6.57.25183

Schultmann, F., Zumkeller, M., & Rentz, O. (2006). Modeling reverse logistic tasks within closed-loop supply chains: An example from the automotive industry. *European Journal of Operational Research, 171*(3), 1033–1050. doi:10.1016/j.ejor.2005.01.016

Schwefel, H.-P. (1975). *Technical evolutionsstrategie und numerische optimierung.* Dissertation, University of Berlin.

Secrest, B. (2001). *Travelling salesman problem for surveillance mission using PSO.* PhD thesis, Air Force Institute of Technology, Ohio, USA.

Seeley, T. D. (1995). *The wisdom of the hive: The social physiology of honey bee colonies.* Cambridge, MA: Harvard University Press.

Senjyu, T., Omine, E., Tokudome, M., Yonaha, Y., Goya, T., Yona, A., et al. (2009). *Frequency control strategy for parallel operated battery systems based on Droop characteristics by applying H∞ control theory.* Paper presented at the IEEE T&d.

Şenkal, O., & Kuleli, T. (2009). Estimation of solar radiation over Turkey using artificial neural network and satellite data. *Applied Energy, 86*, 1222–1228. doi:10.1016/j.apenergy.2008.06.003

Sentz, K., & Ferson, S. (2002). *Combination of evidence in Dempster-Shafer theory. SANDIA Report (SAND2002-0835).* US: Sandia National Laboratories. doi:10.2172/800792

Sevkli, M., & Guner, A. R. (2006). *A new approach to solve uncapacitated facility location problems by particle swarm optimization.* Paper presented at the 5th International Symposium on Intelligent Manufacturing Systems.

Sha, D. Y., & Hsu, C.-Y. (2008). A new particle swarm optimization for the open shop scheduling problem. *Computers & Operations Research, 35*(10), 3243–3261. doi:10.1016/j.cor.2007.02.019

Shafer, G. A. (1976). *Mathematical theory of evidence.* Princeton, NJ: Princeton University Press.

Shafer, G., & Srivastava, R. (1990). The Bayesian and belief-function formalisms: A general perspective for auditing. In Shafer, G., & Pearl, J. (Eds.), *Readings in uncertain reasoning.* San Mateo, CA: Morgan Kaufman Publishers Inc.

Shafie-Khah, M., Moghaddam, M. P., & Sheikh-El-Eslami, M. K. (2011). Price forecasting of day-ahead electricity markets using a hybrid forecast method. *Energy Conversion and Management, 52*(5), 2165–2169. doi:10.1016/j.enconman.2010.10.047

Sharaf, A. M., & El-Gammal, A. A. (2009). *A multi objective multi-stage particle swarm optimization MOPSO search scheme for power quality and loss reduction on radial distribution system.* International Conference on Renewable Energies and Power Quality (ICREPQ'09)

Shen, Z. (2007). Integrated supply chain design models: A survey and future research directions. *Management, 3*(1), 1–27.

Sheu, J. B. (2008). Green supply chain management, reverse logistics and nuclear power generation. *Transportation Research Part E, Logistics and Transportation Review, 44*(1), 19–46. doi:10.1016/j.tre.2006.06.001

Shi, Y. H., & Eberhart, R. C. (1999). *Empirical study of particle swarm optimization.* 1999 Congress on Evolutionary Computation, Washington DC, USA, July

Shi, Y., & Eberhart, R. (1998). A modified particle swarm optimizer. *Evolutionary Computation Proceedings, IEEE World Congress on Computational Intelligence* (pp. 69-73). Anchorage, AK, USA.

Shih, L. H. (2001). Reverse logistics system planning for recycling electrical appliances and computers in Taiwan. *Resources, Conservation and Recycling, 32*(1), 55–72. doi:10.1016/S0921-3449(00)00098-7

Shimizu, Y., Wada, T., & Yamazaki, Y. (2007). Logistics optimization using hybrid metaheuristic approach under very realistic conditions. *Computer Aided Chemical Engineering, 24*, 733–738. doi:10.1016/S1570-7946(07)80145-3

Shin, K.-S., & Lee, Y.-J. (2002). A genetic algorithm application in bankruptcy prediction modeling. *Expert Systems with Applications, 23*(3), 321–328. doi:10.1016/S0957-4174(02)00051-9

Shi, X. H., Liang, Y. C., Lee, H. P., Lu, C., & Wang, L. M. (2005). An improved GA and a novel PSO-GA-based hybrid algorithm. *Information Processing Letters, 93*, 255–261. doi:10.1016/j.ipl.2004.11.003

Shi, X. H., Liang, Y. C., Lee, H. P., Lu, C., & Wang, Q. X. (2007). Particle swarm optimization-based algorithms for TSP and generalized TSP. *Information Processing Letters, 103*(5), 169–176. doi:10.1016/j.ipl.2007.03.010

Shyu, S. J., Lin, B. M. T., & Hsiao, T.-S. (2006). Ant colony optimization for the cell assignment problem in PCS networks. *Computers & Operations Research, 33*, 1713–1740. doi:10.1016/j.cor.2004.11.026

Siajadi, H., Ibrahim, R. N., & Lochert, P. B. (2006). A single-vendor multiple-buyer inventory model with a multiple-shipment policy. *International Journal of Advanced Manufacturing Technology, 27*, 1030–1037. doi:10.1007/s00170-004-2267-4

Silva, C. A., Sousa, J. M. C., Runkler, T. A., & Costa, J. M. G. (2009). Distributed supply chain management using ant colony optimization. *European Journal of Operational Research, 199*, 349–358. doi:10.1016/j.ejor.2008.11.021

Silva, E. L., Morozowski, M., Fonseca, L. G. S., Oliveira, G. C., Melo, A. C. G., & Mello, J. C. (1995). Transmission constrained maintenance scheduling of generating units a stochastic programming approach. *IEEE Transactions on Power Systems, PWRS-10*(2), 695–701. doi:10.1109/59.387905

Simaria, A. S., & Vilarinho, P. M. (2009). 2-ANTBAL: An ant colony optimisation algorithm for balancing two-sided assembly lines. *Computers & Industrial Engineering, 56*(2), 489–506. doi:10.1016/j.cie.2007.10.007

Simchi-Levi, D., Kaminsky, P., & Simchi-Levi, E. (2003). *Designing and managing the supply chain: Concepts, strategies, and case studies.* Irwin/McGraw-Hill.

Simchi-Levi, D., Kaminsky, P., & Simchi-Levi, E. (2008). *Designing and managing the supply chain concepts, strategies and case studies. New York, NY.* USA: McGraw-Hill.

Sloan, R. G. (1996). Do stock prices fully reflect information in accruals and cash flows about future earnings? *Accounting Review, 71*(3), 289–315.

Smith, J. E. (2008). Self-adaption in evolutionary aglorithms for combintorial optimisation. In Cotta, C., Sevaux, M., & Soerensen, K. (Eds.), *Adaptive and multilevel metaheuristics* (*Vol. 136*, pp. 31–57). Springer. doi:10.1007/978-3-540-79438-7_2

Smith-Miles, K., & Lopes, L. (2012). Measuring instance difficulty for combinatorial optimization problems. *Computers & Operations Research, 39*(5), 875–1194. doi:10.1016/j.cor.2011.07.006

Smola, A. J., & Scholköpf, B. (1998). *A tutorial on support vector regression.* NeuroCOLT2 Technical Report NC-TR-98-030, Royal Holloway College, University of London, UK.

Snyder, L. V. (2006). Facility location under uncertainty: A review. *IIE Transactions, 38*, 14–31. doi:10.1080/07408170500216480

Socha, K., & Dorigo, M. (2008). Ant colony optimization for continuous domains. *European Journal of Operational Research, 185*, 1155–1173. doi:10.1016/j.ejor.2006.06.046

Song, H., & Nam, K. (1999, Oct.). Dual current control scheme for PWMconverter under the unbalanced input voltage conditions. *IEEE Transactions on Industrial Electronics, 46*(5), 953–959. doi:10.1109/41.793344

Song, J. H., Hatziargiriou, N., & Buta, A. (2006). *Electric power systems* (*Vol. 1*, p. 636). Bucuresti, Romania: Editura Academiei Romane.

Sonmez, M. (2011). Artificial bee colony algorithm for optimization of truss structures. *Applied Soft Computing, 11*(2), 2406–2418. doi:10.1016/j.asoc.2010.09.003

Sorensen, K., & Glover, F. (in press). *Metaheuristics.* Retrieved January 15th, 2012, from http://www.opttek.com/sites/default/files/Metaheuristics.pdf

Sorensen, K., & Janssens, G. K. (2003). Data mining with genetic algorithms on binary trees. *European Journal of Operational Research, 151*, 253–264. doi:10.1016/S0377-2217(02)00824-X

Souilah, A. (1995). Simulated annealing for manufacturing systems layout design. *European Journal of Operational Research, 82*(3), 592–614. doi:10.1016/0377-2217(93)E0336-V

Sridharan, R. (1991). A Lagrangian heuristic for the capacitated plant location problem with side constraints. *The Journal of the Operational Research Society, 42*, 579–585.

Srinivasa, K. G., Venugopal, K. R., & Patnaik, L. M. (2007). A self-adaptive migration model genetic algorithm for data mining applications. *Information Sciences, 177*, 4295–4313. doi:10.1016/j.ins.2007.05.008

Srivastava, S. K. (2007). Green supply-chain management: A state-of-the-art literature review. *International Journal of Management Reviews, 9*(1), 53–80. doi:10.1111/j.1468-2370.2007.00202.x

Stalk, G. (1988). Time: The next source of competitive advantage. *Harvard Business Review, 66*, 41–51.

Stam, A., & Kuula, M. (1991). Selecting a flexible manufacturing system using multiple criteria analysis. *International Journal of Production Research, 29*, 803–820. doi:10.1080/00207549108930103

Steuer, R. E. (1985). *Multiple-criteria optimization: Theory, computation and application.* John Wiley and Sons.

Steward, D. V. (n,d). (1981). *Systems analysis and management: Structure, strategy and design.* New York, NY: Petrocelli Books Inc.

Steward, D. V. (1981). The design structure system: A method for managing the design of complex systems. *IEEE Transactions on Engineering Management, 8,* 71–74.

Storn, R., & Price, K. (1997). Differential evolution - A simple and efficient heuristic for global optimization over continuous spaces. *Journal of Global Optimization, 11,* 341–359. doi:10.1023/A:1008202821328

Stott, B. (1974). Review of load-flow calculation methods. *Proceedings of the IEEE, 62,* 916–929. doi:10.1109/PROC.1974.9544

Stremel, J. P. (1982). Maintenance scheduling for generating system planning. *IEEE Transactions on Power Apparatus and Systems, PAS-100*(3), 1410–1419. doi:10.1109/TPAS.1981.316616

Stuetzle, T. (1998). *Local search algorithms for combinatorial problems.* PhD thesis, Technische Universitaet Darmstadt.

Stumberger, G., Dolinar, D., Pahner, U., & Hamayer, K. (2000). Optimization of radial active magnetic bearings using the finite element technique and differential evolution algorithm. *IEEE Transactions on Magnetics, 36*(4).

Stützle, T. (1998). An ant approach to the flow shop problem. In *Proceedings of the 6th European Congress on Intelligent Techniques and Soft Computing* (pp. 1560-1564). Aachen, Germany: Verlag Mainz.

Stützle, T., & Hoos, H. (1996). *Improving the ant system: A detailed report on the MAX-MIN ant system.* Technical Report AIDA-96-12, FG Intellektik, FN Informatik, TU Darmstadt, Germany.

Stützle, T., & Hoos, H. (1997). Improvement in the ant system: Introducing min-max ant system. In *Proceedings of the International Conference on Artificial Neuronal Networks and Genetic Algorithms,* (pp. 266-274).

Stützle, T., & Hoos, H. (2000). MAX-MIN ant system. *Future Generation Computer Systems, 16*(8), 889–904.

Subbaraj, P., & Manickavasagam, K. (2007). Generation control of interconnected power systems using computational intelligence techniques. *Generation. Transmission & Distribution, IET, 1*(4), 557–563. doi:10.1049/iet-gtd:20060222

Sugeno, M. (1977). Fuzzy measures and fuzzy integrals: A survey. In Gupta, M. M., Saridis, G. N., & Gains, B. R. (Eds.), *Fuzzy automata and decision processes* (pp. 89–102).

Sugeno, M., & Yasukawa, T. (1993). A fuzzy logic based approach to qualitative modelling. *IEEE Transactions on Fuzzy Systems, 1*(1), 7–31. doi:10.1109/TFUZZ.1993.390281

Suman, B., Hoda, N., & Jha, S. (2010). Orthogonal simulated annealing for multiobjective optimization. *Computers & Chemical Engineering, 34*(10), 1618–1631. doi:10.1016/j.compchemeng.2009.11.015

Sun, M., Ducati, E., & Armentano, V. (2007). Solving capacitated facility location problem using tabu search. *Proceedings of ICM 2007* (pp. 76-81).

Sun, D. I., Ashley, B., Brewer, B., Hughes, A., & Tinney, W. F. (1984). Optimal power flow by Newton approach. *IEEE Transactions on Power Apparatus and Systems, PAS-103*(10), 2864–2875. doi:10.1109/TPAS.1984.318284

Sundaram, R. M. (1978). An application of goal programming technique in metal cutting. *International Journal of Production Research, 16,* 375–382. doi:10.1080/00207547808930029

Sundhararajan, S., & Pahwa, A. (1994). Optimal selection of capacitors for radial distribution systems using a genetic algorithm. *IEEE Transactions on Power Systems, 9*(3), 1499–1507. doi:10.1109/59.336111

Sun, M. (2008). A tabu search heuristic procedure for the capacitated facility location problem. *Journal of Heuristics, 18*(1), 1–28.

Sun, M., Aronson, J. E., McKeown, P. G., & Drinka, D. (1998). A tabu search heuristic procedure for the fixed charge transportation problem. *European Journal of Operational Research, 106,* 441–456. doi:10.1016/S0377-2217(97)00284-1

Su, S., Zhan, D., & Xu, X. (2008). An extended state task network formulation for integrated production-distribution planning in supply chain. *International Journal of Advanced Manufacturing Technology*, *37*, 1232–1249. doi:10.1007/s00170-007-1063-3

Suykens, J. A. K., Van Gestel, T., De Brabanter, J., De Moor, B., & Vandewalle, J. (2002). *Least squares support vector machines*. Singapore: World Scientific.

Suykens, J. A. K., & Vandewalle, J. (1999). Least squares support vector machine classifiers. *Neural Processing Letters*, *9*(3), 293–300. doi:10.1023/A:1018628609742

Szeto, W. Y., Wu, Y., & Ho, S. C. (2011). An artificial bee colony algorithm for the capacitated vehicle routing problem. *European Journal of Operational Research*, *215*(1), 126–135. doi:10.1016/j.ejor.2011.06.006

T'kindt, V., & Billaut, J.-C. (2002). *Multicriteria scheduling: Theory, models and algorithms*. Berlin, Germany: Srpinger.

Tabucanon, T. T. (1996). Multi objective programming for industrial engineers. In Avriel, M., & Golany, B. (Eds.), *Mathematical programming for industrial engineers* (pp. 487–542). New York, NY: Marcel Dekker, Inc.

Taillard, É. D., Waelti, P., & Zuber, J. (2008). Few statistical tests for proportions comparisons. *European Journal of Operational Research*, *185*(3), 1336–1350. doi:10.1016/j.ejor.2006.03.070

Takagi, H. (2001). Interactive evolutionary computation: Fusion of the capabilities of EC computation and human evaluations. *Proceedings of the IEEE*, *89*(9), 1275–1296. doi:10.1109/5.949485

Talbi, El-G. (Ed.). (1965). *Metaheuristics: From design to implementation*. Hoboken, NJ: John Wiley & Sons.

Talbi, E. (1999). *Métaheuristiques pour l'optimisation combinatoire multiobjectif*. Tutorial, Journées Evolutionnaires Trimestrielle.

Talbi, E.-G. (2009). *Metaheuristics, from design to implementation*. Lille, France: John Wiley & Sons.

Taleizadeh, A. A., Aryanezhad, M. B., Wee, H. M., & Jabalameli, M. S. (2011b). *Solving economic order quantity (EOQ) Model with fuzzy rough environment, quantity discount and prepayment*. Working paper.

Taleizadeh, A. A., Jolai, F., & Wee, H. M. (2011e). *Multi objective supply chain problem using a novel hybrid method of meta goal programming and firefly algorithm*. Submitted.

Taleizadeh, A. A., Aryanezhad, M. B., & Niaki, S. T. A. (2008). Optimizing multi-product multi-constraint inventory control systems with stochastic replenishment. *Journal of Applied Sciences*, *8*, 1228–1234. doi:10.3923/jas.2008.1228.1234

Taleizadeh, A. A., Barzinpour, F., & Wee, H. M. (2011c). Meta-heuristic algorithms to solve the fuzzy single period problem. *Mathematical and Computer Modelling*, *54*, 1273–1285. doi:10.1016/j.mcm.2011.03.038

Taleizadeh, A. A., Niaki, S. T. A., & Hosseini, V. (2008). The multi-product multi-constraint newsboy problem with incremental discount and batch order. *Asian Journal of Applied Sciences*, *1*, 110–122. doi:10.3923/ajaps.2008.110.122

Taleizadeh, A. A., Niaki, S. T. A., & Nikousokhan, R. (2011a). Constraint multi-product joint-replenishment inventory control problem using uncertain programming. *Applied Soft Computing*, *11*, 5143–5144. doi:10.1016/j.asoc.2011.05.045

Taleizadeh, A. A., Niaki, S. T., & Aryanezhad, M. B. (2009a). A hybrid method of pareto, TOPSIS and genetic algorithm to optimize multi-product multi-constraint inventory control systems with random fuzzy replenishments. *Mathematical and Computer Modelling*, *49*, 1044–1057. doi:10.1016/j.mcm.2008.10.013

Taleizadeh, A. A., Niaki, S. T., & Aryanezhad, M. B. (2010b). Replenish-up-to multi chance-constraint inventory control system with stochastic period lengths and total discount under fuzzy purchasing price and holding costs. *International Journal of Systems Science*, *41*, 1187–1200. doi:10.1080/00207720903171761

Taleizadeh, A. A., Niaki, S. T., & Barzinpour, F. (2011a). Multi-buyer multi-vendor multi-product multi-constraint supply chain problem with stochastic demand and variable lead time. *Applied Mathematics and Computation*, *217*, 9234–9253. doi:10.1016/j.amc.2011.04.001

Taleizadeh, A. A., Niaki, S. T., & Hosseini, V. (2009b). Optimizing multi product multi constraints bi-objective newsboy problem with discount by hybrid method of goal programming and genetic algorithm. *Engineering Optimization, 41*, 437–457. doi:10.1080/03052150802582175

Taleizadeh, A. A., Niaki, S. T., & Makui, A. (2012). Multiproduct multiple-buyer single-vendor supply chain problem with stochastic demand, variable lead-time, and multi-chance constraint. *Expert Systems with Applications, 39*, 5338–5348. doi:10.1016/j.eswa.2011.11.001

Taleizadeh, A. A., Niaki, S. T., & Seyed-Javadi, S. M. (2011). Multi-product multi-chance-constraint stochastic inventory problem with dynamic demand and partial back-ordering: A harmony search algorithm. *Journal of Manufacturing Systems, 31*(2). doi:doi:10.1016/j.jmsy.2011.05.006

Taleizadeh, A. A., Niaki, S. T., Shafii, N., Ghavamizadeh Meibodi, R., & Jabbarzadeh, A. (2010a). A particle swarm optimization approach for constraint joint single buyer single vendor inventory problem with changeable lead-time and (r,Q) policy in supply chain. *International Journal of Advanced Manufacturing Technology. International Journal of Advanced Manufacturing Technology, 51*, 1209–1223. doi:10.1007/s00170-010-2689-0

Tao, Q., Chang, H.-Y., Yi, Y., Gu, C.-Q., & Li, W.-J. (2011). A rotary chaotic PSO algorithm for trustworthy scheduling of a grid workflow. *Computers & Operations Research, 38*(5), 824–836. doi:10.1016/j.cor.2010.09.012

Tasgetiren, M. F., Liang, Y.-C., Sevkli, M., & Gencyilmaz, G. (2004). Lecture Notes in Computer Science: *Vol. 3172. Particle swarm optimization algorithm for permutation flowshop sequencing problem* (pp. 382–390). Springer-Verlag. doi:10.1007/978-3-540-28646-2_38

Tasgetiren, M. F., Liang, Y.-C., Sevkli, M., & Gencyilmaz, G. (2007). A particle swarm optimization algorithm for makespan and total flowtime minimization in the permutation flowshop sequencing problem. *European Journal of Operational Research, 177*, 1930–1947. doi:10.1016/j.ejor.2005.12.024

Tasgetiren, M. F., Pan, Q.-K., Suganthan, P. N., & Chen, A. H.-L. (2010). A discrete artificial bee colony algorithm for the total flowtime minimization in permutation flow shops. *Information Sciences, 181*(16), 3459–3475. doi:10.1016/j.ins.2011.04.018

Tavakkoli-Moghaddam, R., Safaei, N., & Gholipour, Y. (2006). A hybrid simulated annealing for capacitated vehicle routing problems with the independent route length. *Applied Mathematics and Computation, 176*(2), 445–454. doi:10.1016/j.amc.2005.09.040

Tavakkoli-Moghaddam, R., Safaei, N., Kah, M. M. O., & Rabbani, M. (2007). A new capacitated vehicle routing problem with split service for minimizing fleet cost by simulated annealing. *Journal of the Franklin Institute, 344*(5), 406–425. doi:10.1016/j.jfranklin.2005.12.002

Tavakoli, M. A., Hanhifam, M. R., Lesani, H., Sanakhan, S., & Javan, E. (2006). Review on reconfiguration methods of electric distribution networks. *Proceedings of the Technical and Physical Problems in Power Engineering Conference*, Ankara, Turkey.

Tchomté, S. K., & Gourgand, M. (2009). Particle swarm optimization: A study of particle displacement for solving continuous and combinatorial optimization problems. *International Journal of Production Economics, 121*, 57–67. doi:10.1016/j.ijpe.2008.03.015

Teitz, M. B., & Bart, P. (1968). Heuristic methods for estimating the generalized vertex median of a weighted graph. *Operations Research, 16*(5), 955–961. doi:10.1287/opre.16.5.955

Teodorovic, D. (2009). *Bees colony optimization* (pp. 39–60). Berlin, Germany: Springer.

The MathWorks. (2010a). *MATLAB – User's guide*. The MathWorks.

The MathWorks. (2010b). *MATLAB – Fuzzy logic toolbox - User's guide*. The MathWorks.

The MathWorks. (2010c). *MATLAB – Neural network toolbox - User's guide*. The MathWorks.

The MathWorks. (2010d). *MATLAB – Global optimization toolbox - User's guide*. The MathWorks.

Thierry, M., Salomon, M., Van Nunen, J., & Van Wassenhove, L. (1995). Strategic issues in product recovery management. *California Management Review, 37*(2), 115.

Tiwari, M. K., Prakash, A., Kumar, A., & Mileham, A. R. (2005). Determination of an optimal sequence using the psychoclonal algorithm. *ImechE, Part B: Journal of Engineering Manufacture, 219*, 137–149. doi:10.1243/095440505X8028

Toksarı, M. D. (2009). Estimating the net electricity energy generation and demand using the ant colony optimization approach: Case of Turkey. *Energy Policy, 37*(3), 1181–1187. doi:10.1016/j.enpol.2008.11.017

Tragantalerngsak, S., Holt, J., & Ronnqvist, M. (2000). An exact method for the two-echelon, single-source, capacitated facility location problem. *European Journal of Operational Research, 123*, 473–489. doi:10.1016/S0377-2217(99)00105-8

Trigueros, D. E. G., Módenes, A. N., Kroumov, A. D., & Espinoza-Quiñones, F. R. (2010). Modeling of biodegradation process of BTEX compounds: Kinetic parameters estimation by using particle swarm global optimizer. *Process Biochemistry, 45*(8), 1355–1361. doi:10.1016/j.procbio.2010.05.007

Trippi, R. R. (1995). *Chaos & nonlinear dynamics in the financial markets*. USA: Irwin Professional Publishing.

Tsai, J.-T., Liu, T.-K., & Chou, J.-H. (2004). Hybrid taguchi-genetic algorithm for global numerical optimization. *IEEE Transactions on Evolutionary Computation, 8*, 365–377. doi:10.1109/TEVC.2004.826895

Tsuchiya, K., Urakubo, T., & Tsujita, K. (1999). Motion control of a nonholonomic system based on the Lyapunov control method. *Journal of Guidance, Control, and Dynamics, 25*(2), 285–290. doi:10.2514/2.4880

Turabieh, H., Sheta, A., & Vasant, P. (2007). Hybrid optimization genetic algorithm (HOGA) with interactive evolution to solve constraint optimization problems for production systems. *International Journal of Computational Science, 1*(4), 395–406.

Ubbens, U. M. P. (2000). De kringloop van metalenverpakkingen. In van Goor, A. R., Flapper, S. D. P., & Clement, C. (Eds.), *Handboek reverse logistics*. Deventer, The Netherlands: Kluwer B.V.

Uehara, A., Senjyuy, T., Yonaz, A., & Funabashi, T. (2010). A frequency control method by wind farm & battery using load estimation in isolated power system. *International Journal of Emerging Electric Power Systems Research, 11*(2).

Uğur, A., & Aydin, D. (2009). an interactive simulation and analysis software for solving tsp using ant colony optimization algorithms. *Advances in Engineering Software, 40*(5), 341–349. doi:10.1016/j.advengsoft.2008.05.004

Ünler, A. (2008). Improvement of energy demand forecasts using swarm intelligence: The case of Turkey with projections to 2025. *Energy Policy, 36*(6), 1937–1944. doi:10.1016/j.enpol.2008.02.018

Vachirasricirikul, S., Ngamroo, I., Kaitwanidvilai, S., & Chaiyatham, T. (2009). *Robust frequency stabilization in a microgrid system*. IEEE T&D.doi:10.1109/TD-ASIA.2009.5356835

Valencia, L., & Rabadi, G. (2003). A multiagents approach for the job shop scheduling problem with earliness and tardiness. *IEEE International Conference on Systems, Man and Cybernetics, 2*, 1217-1222.

Valente, J., & Alves, R. (2007). Heuristics for the early/tardy scheduling problem with release dates. *International Journal of Production Economics, 106*, 261–274. doi:10.1016/j.ijpe.2006.06.006

Van Breedam, A. (1995). Improvement heuristics for the vehicle routing problem based on simulated annealing. *European Journal of Operational Research, 86*(3), 480–490. doi:10.1016/0377-2217(94)00064-J

Van Notten, R. A. P. (2000). Inzameling en bewerking ten behoeve van het hergebruik van verpakkingsglas. In van Goor, A. R., Flapper, S. D. P., & Clement, C. (Eds.), *Handboek reverse logistics*. Deventer, The Netherlands: Kluwer B.V.

Vapnik, V. N. (1995). *The nature of statistical learning theory*. New York, NY: Springer-Verlag.

Varadharajan, T. K., & Rajendran, C. (2005). A multiobjective simulated-annealing algorithm for scheduling in flowshops to minimize the makespan and total flowtime of jobs. *European Journal of Operational Research, 167*(3), 772–795. doi:10.1016/j.ejor.2004.07.020

Vasant, P. (2006). Fuzzy production planning and its application to decision making. *Journal of Intelligent Manufacturing*, *17*(1), 5–12. doi:10.1007/s10845-005-5509-x

Vasant, P. (2010). Hybrid simulated annealing and genetic algorithms for industrial production management problems. *International Journal of Computational Methods*, *7*(2), 279–297. doi:10.1142/S0219876210002209

Vasant, P., Barsoum, N., Kahraman, C., & Dimirovski, G. (2007). Application of fuzzy optimization in forecasting and planning of construction industry. In Vrakas, D., & Vlahavas, I. (Eds.), *Artificial intelligent for advanced problem solving technique* (pp. 254–265). Hershey, PA: IGI Global. doi:10.4018/978-1-59904-705-8.ch010

Vasant, P., Bhattacharya, A., Sarkar, B., & Mukherjee, S. K. (2007). Detection of level of satisfaction and fuzziness patterns for MCDM model with modified flexible S-curve MF. *Applied Soft Computing*, *7*, 1044–1054. doi:10.1016/j.asoc.2006.10.005

Vasebi, A., Fesanghary, M., & Bathaee, S. M. T. (2007). Combined heat and power economic dispatch by harmony search algorithm. *International Journal of Electrical Power & Energy Systems*, *29*(10), 713–719. doi:10.1016/j.ijepes.2007.06.006

Venditti, L., Pacciarelli, D., & Meloni, C. (2010). A tabu search algorithm for scheduling pharmaceutical packaging operations. *European Journal of Operational Research*, *202*, 538–546. doi:10.1016/j.ejor.2009.05.038

Ventura, J., & Kim, D. (2003). Parallel machine scheduling with earliness–tardiness penalties and additional resource constraints. *Computers & Operations Research*, *30*(13), 1945–1958. doi:10.1016/S0305-0548(02)00118-1

Verter, V. (2011). Uncapacitated and capacitated facility location problems. *Foundations of Location Analysis*, *155*, 25–37. doi:10.1007/978-1-4419-7572-0_2

Vesterstrom, J., & Thomsen, R. (2004). A comparative study of differential evolution, particle swarm optimization, and evolutionary algorithms on numerical benchmark problems. *Congress on Evolutionary Computation*, *2*, 1980–1987.

Villegas, J. G. (2011). *Using nonparametric test to compare the performance of metaheuristics.* [Electronic Version]. Retrieved from www-labsticc.univ-ubs.fr/or/sites/default/files/Friedman test-24062011.pdf

Von Frisch, K. (1976). *Bees: Their vision, chemical senses and language*. Ithica, NY: Cornell University Press.

Voropai, N. I., & Etingov, P. V. (2001). Two-stage adaptive fuzzy PSS application to power systems. *Proceedings of International Conference on Electrical Engineering ICEE'2001*, Xi'an, China, July 22-26, Vol. 1, (pp. 314-318).

Voropai, N. I., Efimov, D. N., Popov, D. B., & Etingov, P. V. (2001). Fuzzy logic stabilizer modeling in the transients simulation software. *Proceedings of International Conference of IEEE ISAP'2001*, Budapest, Hungary, June 18-21 (pp. 315-320).

Voropai, N. I., & Bat-Undral, B. (2008). Load flow calculation in a radial electrical network using the interval method. [in Russian]. *Electrichestvo*, *10*, 64–66.

Voß, S. (2001). Meta-heuristics: The state of the art. *Lecture Notes in Computer Science*, *2148*, 1–23. doi:10.1007/3-540-45612-0_1

Voudouris, C., & Tsang, E. (1996). *Function optimization using guided local search. Technical report*. Department of Computer Science, University of Essex.

Voudouris, C., & Tsang, E. (1999). Guided local search and its application to the traveling salesman problem. *European Journal of Operational Research*, *113*(2), 469–499. doi:10.1016/S0377-2217(98)00099-X

Wagner, H. M., & Whitin, T. M. (1958). Dynamical version of the economic lot size model. *Management Science*, *5*, 89–96. doi:10.1287/mnsc.5.1.89

Wah, B. W., & Wang, T. (2000). Tuning strategies in constrained simulated annealing for nonlinear global optimization. *International Journal of Artificial Intelligence Tools*, *9*, 3–25. doi:10.1142/S0218213000000033

Waldspurger, C. A., & Weihl, W. E. (1994). *Lottery scheduling: Flexible proportional-share resource management*. Paper presented at the 1st USENIX Symposium on Operating System Design and Implementation, Monterey, CA.

Waldspurger, C. A., & Weihl, W. E. (1995). *Stride scheduling: Deterministic proportional-share resource management*. Technical Report MIT/LCS/TM-528, Massachusetts Institute of Technology, USA.

Walker, H., Di Sisto, L., & McBain, D. (2008). Drivers and barriers to environmental supply chain management practices: Lessons from the public and private sectors. *Journal of Purchasing and Supply Management, 14*(1), 69–85. doi:10.1016/j.pursup.2008.01.007

Walther, G., & Spengler, T. (2005). Impact of WEEE-directive on reverse logistics in Germany. *International Journal of Physical Distribution & Logistics Management, 35*(5), 337–361. doi:10.1108/09600030510607337

Wang, B., & Rahal, I. (2007) WC-clustering: Hierarchical clustering using the weighted confidence affinity measure. In *ICDM2007: Proceedings of the High Performance Data Mining Workshop IEEE International Conference on Data Mining*, Omaha, NE, October, (pp. 355-360).

Wang, Z., & Bai, H. (2010). *Reverse logistics network: A review*. Paper presented at the IEEM2010 - IEEE International Conference on Industrial Engineering and Engineering Management, Macao.

Wang, F., Lai, X., & Shi, N. (2011). A multi-objective optimization for green supply chain network design. *Decision Support Systems, 51*(2), 262–269. doi:10.1016/j.dss.2010.11.020

Wang, H. F., & Hsu, H. W. (2010). A closed-loop logistic model with a spanning-tree based genetic algorithm. *Computers & Operations Research, 37*, 376–389. doi:10.1016/j.cor.2009.06.001

Wang, J. (2011). *Supply chain optimization, management and integration: Emerging applications*. Hershey, PA: IGI Global.

Wang, J., Cai, Y., Zhou, Y., Wang, R., & Li, C. (2011). Discrete particle swarm optimization based on estimation of distribution for terminal assignment problems. *Computers & Industrial Engineering, 60*(4), 566–575. doi:10.1016/j.cie.2010.12.014

Wang, M., & Liu, S. (2005). A trust region interior point algorithm for optimal power low problems. *International Journal of Electrical Power & Energy Systems, 27*(4), 293–300. doi:10.1016/j.ijepes.2004.12.001

Wang, Q. J. (1991). The genetic algorithm and its application to calibrating conceptual rainfall-runoff models. *Water Resources Research, 27*(9), 2467–2471. doi:10.1029/91WR01305

Wang, S., Watada, J., & Pedrycz, W. (2009). Value-at-risk-based two-stage fuzzy facility location problems. *IIE Transactions on Industrial Informatics, 5*, 465–482. doi:10.1109/TII.2009.2022542

Wang, T. Y., Wu, K. B., & Liu, Y. W. (2001). A simulated annealing algorithm for facility layout problems under variable demand in cellular manufacturing systems. *Computers in Industry, 46*(2), 181–188. doi:10.1016/S0166-3615(01)00107-5

Wang, Y., Liu, H., Beullens, P., & Brown, D. (2008). Travel speed predicition using fuzzy reasoning. *Lecture Notes in Artificial Intelligence, 5314*, 446–455.

Warfield, J. N. (1973). Binary matrices in system modelling. *IEEE Transactions on Systems, Man, and Cybernetics, 3*, 441–449. doi:10.1109/TSMC.1973.4309270

Watanabe, K., & Hashem, M. M. A. (2004). *Evolutionary computations – New algorithms and their applications to evolutionary robots. Studies in Fuzziness and Soft Computing*. Berlin, Germany: Springer.

Weber, A. (1909). *Uber den Standort der Industrian, (Alferd Weber's theory of the location of industries)*. University of Chicago Press.

Wee, H. M., & Yang, P. C. (2007). A mutual beneficial pricing strategy of an integrated vendor-buyers inventory system. *International Journal of Advanced Manufacturing Technology, 34*, 179–187. doi:10.1007/s00170-006-0581-8

Wei, L., Qian, W., Zhou, A., Jin, W., & Yu, J. X. (2003). HOT: Hypergraph-based outlier test for categorical data. *PAKDD 2003. LNAI, 2637*, 399–410.

Weile, D. S., & Michielssen, E. (1997). Genetic algorithm optimization applied to electromagnetics: A review. *IEEE Transactions on Antennas and Propagation, 45*(3). doi:10.1109/8.558650

Weiszfeld, E. (1937). Sur le point pour lequel la somme des distances de n points donnes est minimum. *Tohoku Mathematical Journal, 43*, 355–386.

Wei, W. D., & Liu, C. L. (1983). On a periodic maintenance problem. *Operations Research Letters*, *2*, 90–93. doi:10.1016/0167-6377(83)90044-5

Wen, J. Y., Wu, Q. H., Jiang, L., & Cheng, S. J. (2003). Pseudo-gradient based evolutionary programming. *Electronics Letters*, *39*(7), 631–632. doi:10.1049/el:20030404

Weston, D., Hand, D., Adams, N., Whitrow, C., & Juszczak, P. (2008). Plastic card fraud detection using peer group analysis. *Advances in Data Analysis and Classification*, *2*(1), 45–62. doi:10.1007/s11634-008-0021-8

Widodo, A., & Yang, B. S. (2007). Support vector machine in machine condition monitoring and fault diagnosis. *Mechanical Systems and Signal Processing*, *21*, 2560–2574. doi:10.1016/j.ymssp.2006.12.007

Wild, T. (1997). *Best practice in inventory management* (1st ed.). John Wiley & Sons, Inc.

Willis, H., & Scott, W. E. (2000). *Distributed power generation: Planning and evaluation*. New York, NY: CRC Press.

Wilson, R. H. (1934). A scientific routine for stock control. *Harvard Business Review*, *13*, 116–128.

Wilson, W. G., & Vasudevan, K. (1991). Application of the genetic algorithm to residual statics estimation. *Geophysical Research Letters*, *18*(12), 2118–2184. doi:10.1029/91GL02537

Wollenweber, J. (2008). A multi-stage facility location problem with staircase and splitting of commodities: Model, heuristic approach and application. *OR-Spektrum*, *30*, 655–673. doi:10.1007/s00291-007-0114-3

Wolpert, D. H., & Macready, W. G. (1997). No free lunch theorems for optimization. *IEEE Transactions on Evolutionary Computation*, *1*(1), 67–82. doi:10.1109/4235.585893

Wolsey, L. A. (1998). *Integer programming*. New York, NY: John Wiley and Sons.

Wong, H., Liu, H., Olken, F., Rotem, D., & Wong, L. (1995). Bit transposed files. In A Pirotte & Y. Vassiliou (Eds.), *Proceedings of the 11th Very Large Databases Conference (VLDB)*, (pp. 448-457). Morgan Kaufmann.

Wong, K. P., & Wong, S. Y. W. (1997). Hybrid genetic/simulated annealing approach to short-term multiple-fuel-constrained generation scheduling. *IEEE Transactions on Power Systems*, *12*, 776–784. doi:10.1109/59.589681

Wood, A. J., & Wollenberg, B. F. (1996). *Power generation operation and control*. New York, NY: Wiley.

Wu, Q. H., Cao, Y. J., & Wen, J. Y. (1998). Optimal reactive power dispatch using an adaptive genetic algorithm. *International Journal of Electrical Power & Energy Systems*, *20*(8), 563–569. doi:10.1016/S0142-0615(98)00016-7

Wu, Q. H., & Ma, J. T. (1995). Power system optimal reactive dispatch using evolutionary programming. *IEEE Transactions on Power Systems*, *10*(3), 1243–1249. doi:10.1109/59.466531

Wu, Z., & Weng, M. X. (2005). Multiagent scheduling method with earliness and tardiness objectives in flexible job shops. *IEEE Transactions on Systems. Man and Cybernetics-Part B*, *35*, 293–301. doi:10.1109/TSMCB.2004.842412

Xanthopoulos, A., & Iakovou, E. (2009). On the optimal design of the disassembly and recovery processes. *Waste Management (New York, N.Y.)*, *29*(5), 1702–1711. doi:10.1016/j.wasman.2008.11.009

Xia, W., & Wu, Z. (2005). An effective hybrid optimization approach for multi-objective flexible job-shop scheduling problems. *Computers & Industrial Engineering*, *48*(2), 409–425. doi:10.1016/j.cie.2005.01.018

Xia, Y. (1996). A new neural network for solving linear programming problems and its application. *IEEE Transactions on Neural Networks*, *7*(2).

Xie, C., Turnquist, M. A., & Waller, S. T. (2011). A hybrid Lagrangian relaxation and Tabu search method for interdependent-choice network design problems. In Montoya-Torres, A. J. J., Huaccho Huatuco, L., Faulin, J., & Rodriguez-Verjan, G. (Eds.), *Hybrid algorithms for service, computing and manufacturing systems: Routing and scheduling solutions* (pp. 294–324). doi:10.4018/978-1-61350-086-6.ch013

Xinchao, Z. (2011). Simulated annealing algorithm with adaptive neighborhood. *Applied Soft Computing*, *11*, 1827–1836. doi:10.1016/j.asoc.2010.05.029

Xin-She, Y. (2005). Engineering optimizations via nature-inspired virtual bee algorithms. In Jose, M., & Jose, A. (Eds.), *Artificial Intelligence and Knowledge Engineering Applications: A Bioinspired Approach* (*Vol. 3562*, pp. 317–323). Lecture Notes in Computer ScienceBerlin, Germany: Springer. doi:10.1007/11499305_33

Xiong, H., Tan, P., & Kumar, V. (2003). Mining strong affinity association patterns in data sets with skewed support distribution. *Third IEEE International Conference on Data Mining*, Melbourne, Florida, (pp. 19–22).

Xu, J., Chiu, S. Y., & Glover, F. (1998). Fine-tuning a tabu search algorithm with statistical tests. *International Transactions in Operational Research*, *5*, 233–244. doi:10.1111/j.1475-3995.1998.tb00117.x

Xu, J., Sohoni, M., McCleery, M., & Bailey, T. G. (2006). A dynamic neighbourhood based tabu search algorithm for real-world flight instructor scheduling. *European Journal of Operational Research*, *169*, 978–993. doi:10.1016/j.ejor.2004.08.023

Xu, J., & Zhao, L. (2008). A class of fuzzy rough expected value multi-objective decision making model and its application to inventory problems. *Computers & Mathematics with Applications (Oxford, England)*, *56*, 2107–2119. doi:10.1016/j.camwa.2008.03.040

Yager, R. R., & Filev, D. P. (1992). *Approximate clustering via the mountain method. Technical report.* Machine Intelligence Institute, Iona College.

Yagmahan, B. (2011). Mixed-model assembly line balancing using a multi-objective ant colony optimization approach. *Expert Systems with Applications*, *38*(10), 12453–12461. doi:10.1016/j.eswa.2011.04.026

Yagmahan, B., & Yenisey, M. (2010). Multi-objective ant colony system algorithm for flow shop scheduling problem. *Expert Systems with Applications*, *37*, 1361–1368. doi:10.1016/j.eswa.2009.06.105

Yagmahan, B., & Yenisey, M. M. (2008). Ant colony optimization for multi-objective flow shop scheduling problem. *Computers & Industrial Engineering*, *54*(3), 411–420. doi:10.1016/j.cie.2007.08.003

Yamanishi, K., Takeuchi, J.-I., Williams, G., & Milne, P. (2004). On-line unsupervised outlier detection using finite mixtures with discounting learning algorithms. *Data Mining and Knowledge Discovery*, *8*(3), 275–300. doi:10.1023/B:DAMI.0000023676.72185.7c

Yamayee, Z., & Sidenblad, K. (1983). A computationally efficient optimal maintenance scheduling method. *IEEE Transactions on Power Apparatus and Systems*, *PAS-102*(2), 330–338. doi:10.1109/TPAS.1983.317771

Yan, G., & Soc, I. C. (2009). *Research on green suppliers' evaluation based on AHP & genetic algorithm.*

Yanchao, L., Pengchao, L., & Litao, L. (2008, 6-8 April 2008). *Multi-objective optimization of reverse logistics network based on random weights and genetic algorithm.* Paper presented at IEEE International Conference on Networking, Sensing and Control, ICNSC 2008.

Yang, J., Shi, X., Marchese, M., & Liang, Y. (2008). An ant colony optimization method for generalized TSP problem. *Progress in Natural Science*, *18*(11), 1417–1422. doi:10.1016/j.pnsc.2008.03.028

Yang, X. S. (2008). *Nature-inspired meta-heuristic algorithms.* UK: Luniver Press.

Yang, X. S. (2009). Firefly algorithms for multimodal optimization. In Watanabe, O., & Zeugmann, T. (Eds.), *Stochastic algorithms: Foundations and applications SAGA* (*Vol. 5792*, pp. 169–178). Lecture Notes in Computer Science Berlin, Germany: Springer-Verlag. doi:10.1007/978-3-642-04944-6_14

Yang, X.-S. (2009). *Harmony search as a meta-heuristic algorithm. Music-inspired harmony search algorithm.* Heidelberg, Germany: Springer-Verlag Studies in Computational Intelligence.

Yan, W., Liu, F., Chung, C. Y., & Wong, K. P. (2006). A hybrid genetic algorithm–interior point method for optimal reactive power flow. *IEEE Transactions on Power Systems*, *21*(3), 1163–1169. doi:10.1109/TPWRS.2006.879262

Yan, X., & Quintana, V. H. (1999). Improving an interior point based OPF by dynamic adjustments of step sizes and tolerances. *IEEE Transactions on Power Systems*, *14*(2), 709–717. doi:10.1109/59.761902

Yanxia, W., Longjun, Q., Zhi, G., & Lifeng, M. (2008). Weapon target assignment problem satisfying expected damage probabilities based on ant colony algorithm. *Journal of Systems Engineering and Electronics, 19*(5), 939–944. doi:10.1016/S1004-4132(08)60179-6

Yao, X., Liu, Y., & Lin, G. (1999). Evolutionary programming made faster. *IEEE Transactions on Evolutionary Computation, 3*, 82–102. doi:10.1109/4235.771163

Yapicioglu, H., Smith, A. E., & Dozier, G. (2007). Solving the semi-desirable facility location problem using bi-objective particle swarm. *European Journal of Operational Research, 177*(2), 733–749. doi:10.1016/j.ejor.2005.11.020

Yare, Y., & Venayagamoorthy, G. K. (2007). Optimal scheduling of generators maintenance using modified discrete particle swarm optimization. *2007 iREP Symposium- Bulk Power System Dynamics and Control- VII, Revitalizing operational reliability* (pp. 1-8). Charleston, SC, USA.

Yare, Y., Venayagamoorthy, G. K., & Aliyu, U. O. (2008). Optimal generator maintenance scheduling using a modified discrete PSO. *IET Generation, Transmission, and Distribution, 2*(6), 834–846. doi:10.1049/iet-gtd:20080030

Yaseen, S. G., & AL-Slamy, N. M. A. (2008). Ant colony optimization. *IJCSNS International Journal of Computer Science and Network Security, 8*(6), 351-357.

Yassine, A., Chelst, K., & Falkenburg, D. (1999). Engineering design management: An information structure approach. *International Journal of Production Research, 37*(13), 2957–2975. doi:10.1080/002075499190374

Yazdani, A., & Iravani, R. (2006, July). A unified dynamic model and control for the voltage-sourced converter under unbalanced grid conditions. *IEEE Transactions in Power Delay, 21*(3), 1620–1629. doi:10.1109/TP-WRD.2006.874641

Ye, F., & Li, Y. (2011). A Stackelberg single-period supply chain inventory model with weighted possibilistic mean values under fuzzy environment. *Applied Soft Computing Journal, 11*, 5519–5527. doi:10.1016/j.asoc.2011.05.007

Yellen, J., Al-Khamis, T. M., Vemuri, S., & Lemonidis, L. (1992). Decomposition approach to unit maintenance scheduling. *IEEE Transactions on Power Systems, 7*(2), 726–733. doi:10.1109/59.141779

Yeniay, O. (2005). Penalty function methods for constrained optimization with genetic algorithms. *Mathematical and Computational Applications, 10*, 45–56.

Yılmaz, I., & Yuksek, A. G. (2008). An example of artificial neural network (ANN) application for indirect estimation of rock parameters. *Rock Mechanics and Rock Engineering, 41*(5), 781–795. doi:10.1007/s00603-007-0138-7

Yimsiri, S. (2009). *Designing multi-objective reverse logistics networks using genetic algorithms.*

Yin, M., Hu, Y., Yang, F., Li, X., & Gu, W. (2011). A novel hybrid K-harmonic means and gravitational search algorithm approach for clustering. *Expert Systems with Applications, 38*(8), 9319–9324. doi:10.1016/j.eswa.2011.01.018

Yin, P.-Y., Yu, S.-S., Wang, P.-P., & Wang, Y.-T. (2006). A hybrid particle swarm optimization algorithm for optimal task assignment in distributed systems. *Computer Standards & Interfaces, 28*(4), 441–450. doi:10.1016/j.csi.2005.03.005

Yiqin, X., & Jia, T. (2008). A new search approach in ant colony system algorithm for network reconfiguration of distribution systems. *Proceedings of International Conference on Deregulation, Restructuring, and Power Technologies (DRPT'2008),* Nanjing, China.

Yu, B., & Yang, Z. Z. (2011). An ant colony optimization model: The period vehicle routing problem with time windows. *Transportation Research Part E, Logistics and Transportation Review, 47*(2), 166–181. doi:10.1016/j.tre.2010.09.010

Yue, D., Wu, X., Wang, Y., Li, Y., & Chu, C. (2007). A review of data mining-based financial outlier detection research. In *WiCom 2007: Proceedings of International Conference on Wireless Communications, Networking and Mobile Computing,* (pp. 5519 – 5522).

Yuen, C., Oudalov, A., & Timbus, A. (2011). The provision of frequency control reserves from multiple microgrids. *IEEE Transactions on Industrial Electronics*, *58*(1). doi:10.1109/TIE.2010.2041139

Yu, H., Fang, H., Yao, P., & Yuan, Y. (2000). A combined genetic algorithm:simulated annealing algorithm for large scale system energy integration. *Computers & Chemical Engineering*, *24*, 2023–2035. doi:10.1016/S0098-1354(00)00601-3

Yun, C., Chuang, K., & Chen, M. (2006). Adherence clustering: An efficient method for mining market-basket clusters. *Information Systems*, *31*(3), 170–186. doi:10.1016/j.is.2004.11.008

Yuryevich, J., & Wong, K. P. (1999). Evolutionary programming based optimal power)ow algorithm. *IEEE Transactions on Power Systems*, *14*(4), 1245–1250. doi:10.1109/59.801880

Yu, V. F., Lin, S.-W., Lee, W., & Ting, C.-J. (2010). A simulated annealing heuristic for the capacitated location routing problem. *Computers & Industrial Engineering*, *58*(2), 288–299. doi:10.1016/j.cie.2009.10.007

Zadeh, L. (1965). Fuzzy sets. *Information and Control*, *8*, 338–353. doi:10.1016/S0019-9958(65)90241-X

Zadeh, L. A. (1965). Fuzzy sets. *Information and Control*, *8*, 338–353. doi:10.1016/S0019-9958(65)90241-X

Zahnd, U. (February 2007). *Control strategies for load-following unbalanced microgrids islanded operation*.

Zaidi, A. A., & Kupzog, F. (December 23-24,2008). *Microgrid automation - A self-configuring approach*. Paper presented at the 12th IEEE International Multitopic Conference.

Zaika, R. A. (2003). Application of genetic algorithms for electric power system state estimation. *Systemnye Issledovania v Energetike*, Papers of junior scientists at ESI SB RAS. (in Russian)

Zaika, R. A. (2003). Genetic algorithm for power system state estimation. *Proceedings of the International Workshop "Liberalization and Modernization of Power Systems: Congestion Management Problems"*, Irkutsk, Russia (pp. 204–206).

Zaika, R. A. (2008). Electric power system state estimation on the basis of calculated corrections of test equations with the aid of genetic algorithm. *Proceedings of the 8th Baikal All-Russia Conference "Information and Mathematical Technologies in Science and Management"*. Part I, – Irkutsk: ESI SB RAS (pp. 39-44). (in Russian).

Zaki, M. J., & Hsiao, C. (2002). Charm: An efficient algorithm for closed itemset mining. In *SIAM International Conference on Data Mining*, (pp. 457-473).

Zarandi, M. H. F., Hemmati, A., & Davari, S. (2011). The multi-depot capacitated location-routing problem with fuzzy travel times. *Expert Systems with Applications*, *38*(8), 10075–10084. doi:10.1016/j.eswa.2011.02.006

Zegordi, S. H., Itoh, K., & Enkawa, T. (1995). Minimizing makespan for flow shop scheduling by combining simulated annealing with sequencing knowledge. *European Journal of Operational Research*, *85*(3), 515–531. doi:10.1016/0377-2217(94)00021-4

Zhang, G., & Lu, J. (2009). A linguistic intelligent user guide for method selection in multi-objective decision support systems. *Information Science*, *179*, 2299–2308. doi:10.1016/j.ins.2009.01.043

Zhang, G., Lu, J., & Dillon, T. (2007). Decentralized multi-objective bi-level decision making with fuzzy demands. *Knowledge-Based Systems*, *20*, 495–507. doi:10.1016/j.knosys.2007.01.003

Zhang, H., Li, X., Li, H., & Huang, F. (2005). Particle swarm optimization-based schemes for resource-constrained project scheduling. *Automation in Construction*, *14*(3), 393–404. doi:10.1016/j.autcon.2004.08.006

Zhang, J.-R., Zhang, J., Lok, T.-M., & Lyu, M. R. (2007). A hybrid particle swarm optimization–back-propagation algorithm for feedforward neural network training. *Applied Mathematics and Computation*, *185*(2), 1026–1037. doi:10.1016/j.amc.2006.07.025

Zhang, R., & Wu, C. (2010). A hybrid immune simulated annealing algorithm for the job shop scheduling problem. *Applied Soft Computing*, *10*(1), 79–89. doi:10.1016/j.asoc.2009.06.008

Zhang, X., Yuan, X., & Yuan, Y. (2008). Improved hybrid simulated annealing algorithm for navigation scheduling for the two dams of the Three Gorges Project. *Computers & Mathematics with Applications (Oxford, England)*, *56*(1), 151–159. doi:10.1016/j.camwa.2007.11.041

Zhang, Y. H., Lei, F., & Zhi, Y. (2011). Optimization of cloud database route scheduling based on combination of genetic algorithm and ant colony algorithm. *Procedia Engineering*, *15*, 3341–3345. doi:10.1016/j. proeng.2011.08.626

Zhao, X., Gao, X.-S., & Hu, Z.-C. (2007). Evolutionary programming based on non-uniform mutation. *Applied Mathematics and Computation*, *192*, 1–11. doi:10.1016/j. amc.2006.06.107

Zhishan, L., Kaigan, P., & Huaguang, Z. (1998). Robust adaptive fuzzy excitation control of multi-machine electric power system. *Proceedings of POWERCON'98 Conference,* Beijing, China, August 18-22, Vol. 2 (pp. 804-808).

Zhou, L., Yang, H., & Liu, C. (2008). QPSO-Based hyper-parameters selection for LS-SVM regression. In *Proceedings of the 4th IEEE International Conference on Natural Computation*, Jinan, (pp. 130-133).

Zhou, J. L., & Tits, A. L. (1996). An SQP Algorithm for finely discretized continuous minimax problems and other minimax problems with many objective functions. *SIAM Journal on Optimization*, *6*, 461–487. doi:10.1137/0806025

Zhu, G., & Kwong, S. (2010). Gbest-guided artificial bee colony algorithm for numerical function optimization. *Applied Mathematics and Computation*, *217*(7), 3166–3173. doi:10.1016/j.amc.2010.08.049

Ziarati, K., Akbari, R., & Zeighami, V. (2011). On the performance of bee algorithms for resource-constrained project scheduling problem. *Applied Soft Computing*, *11*(4), 3720–3733. doi:10.1016/j.asoc.2011.02.002

Zimmerman, R. D., Murillo-Sánchez, C. E., & Thomas, R. J. (2011). MATPOWER steady-state operations, planning and analysis tools for power systems research and education. *IEEE Transactions on Power Systems*, *26*(1), 12–19. doi:10.1109/TPWRS.2010.2051168

Zitzler, E., & Thiele, L. (1999). Multiobjective evolutionary algorithms: A comparative case study and strength Pareto approach. *IEEE Transactions on Evolutionary Computation*, *3*(4), 257–271. doi:10.1109/4235.797969

Zmitrovich, A. I. (1997). *Intelligence information systems*. Minsk, Belarus: TetraSystems. (in Russian)

Zurada, J. M. (1992). *Introduction to artificial neural systems*. PWS Publishing Comp.

Zurn, H. H., & Quintana, V. H. (1975). Generator maintenance scheduling via successive approximations dynamic programming. *IEEE Transactions on Power Apparatus*, *94*(2), 665–671. doi:10.1109/T-PAS.1975.31894

About the Contributors

Pandian Vasant is a Senior Lecturer at Department of Fundamental & Applied Sciences, University Technology Petronas, Malaysia. He has graduated in 1986 from University of Malaya (MY) in Kuala Lumpur, obtaining his BSc Degree with Honors (II Class Upper) in Mathematics, and in 1988 also obtained a Diploma in English for Business from Cambridge Tutorial College, Cambridge, England. In the year 2002, he obtained his MSc (By Research) in Engineering Mathematics from the School of Engineering & Information Technology of University of Malaysia Sabah, Malaysia, and has a Doctoral Degree (2008) from University Putra Malaysia in Malaysia. After graduation, during 1987-88 he was Tutor in operational research at University Science Malaysia in Alor Setar, Kedah and during 1989-95 he was Tutor of Engineering Mathematics at the same university but with Engineering Campus at Tronoh, Perak. Thereafter, from 1996-2003 he became a lecturer in Advanced Calculus and Engineering Mathematics at Mara University of Technology, in Kota Kinabalu. He became Senior Lecturer of Engineering Mathematics in American Degree Program at Nilai International College (Malaysia), during 2003-2004 before taking his present position at University Teknologi Petronas in Malaysia. His main research interests are in the areas of optimization methods and applications to decision making and industrial engineering, fuzzy optimization, computational intelligence, and hybrid soft computing. Vasant has authored and co-authored 200 research papers and articles in national journals, international journals, conference proceedings, conference paper presentation, and special issues lead guest editor, lead guest editor for book chapters' project, conference abstracts, edited books, and book chapters. In the year 2009, Vasant was awarded top reviewer for the journal *Applied Soft Computing* (Elsevier). He has been Co-editor for AIP Conference Proceedings of PCO (Power Control and Optimization) conferences since 2008 and editorial board member of international journals in the area of soft computing, hybrid optimization and computer applications. Currently he's a lead managing editor for Global Journal Technology & Optimization, Editor-in-Chief of *International Journal of Energy Optimization and Engineering* (IGI Global), and organizing committee member (PCO Global) for PCO Global conferences.

* * *

Hisham M. Abdelsalam holds a Master of Science and a Ph.D. in Mechanical Engineering (Old Dominion University, Norfolk, Virginia, USA). He obtained his Bachelor's degree with honors in Mechanical Engineering from Cairo University (Cairo, Egypt). Dr. Abdelsalam is an Associate Professor in the Operations Research and Decision Support Department, Faculty of Computers and Information, Cairo University. In 2009, Dr. Abdelsalam was appointed as the Director of the Decision Support and Future Studies Center in Cairo University. Dr. Abdelsalam research focus areas are supply chain management, new product development projects, and e-government.

Rabiah Badar received her Master's degree in Electronics from Quaid-I-Azam University, Islamabad, in 2005. She did MS Computer Engineering from COMSATS Institute of Information Technology, Islamabad, in 2009. She is currently pursuing her Ph.D. degree in Electrical Engineering from COMSATS Institute of Information Technology, Abbottabad, Pakistan. Her current research interests include nonlinear adaptive control, embedded systems, artificial intelligence, facts controllers, and power system stability and control.

Leopoldo Eduardo Cárdenas-Barrón is currently a Professor at the Department of Industrial and Systems Engineering at the School of Engineering and at the Department of International Business and Marketing at the School of Business at Tecnológico de Monterrey, Campus Monterrey, México. His research areas include primarily related to inventory planning and control, logistics, and supply chain. He has published papers and technical notes in *International Journal of Production Economics, Production Planning and Control, European Journal of Operational Research, Journal of the Operational Research Society, Computers and Industrial Engineering, International Journal of Systems Science, Mathematical and Computer Modelling, Applied Mathematical Modelling, Applied Mathematics and Computation, Computers & Mathematics with Applications, Mathematical Problems in Engineering, Expert Systems with Applications, Transportation Research Part E: Logistics and Transportation Review,* among others. He has co-authored one book in the field of Simulation in Spanish. Also he is an editorial board member of several international journals.

Baasan Bat-Undraal (Eng. 1995, MSci 1997, Cand. of Sci.-PhD 2009) graduated from Mongolian University of Science and Technology, Power Engineering School in Electric Power Supply. She was as a lecture of Electric Power Supply Department in 1997-2005. She had her PhD course at Irkutsk State Technical University, Irkutsk, Russia, at Electric Power Supply Department. Her area of interests is operating conditions of electric power supply systems.

Patrick Beullens is Reader/Senior Lecturer at the Schools of Mathematics and Management, University of Southampton (UK), where he teaches on various topics in Operational Research and Management Science. His research includes the quantitative modelling of decision problems in the areas of (reverse) logistics and supply chain management, and the design of algorithms and heuristics for (combinatorial) optimisation. He also consults for companies on topics related to logistics and supply chain management. Before joining Southampton he was on the faculty at the University of Portsmouth (UK) and the University of Hasselt (Belgium), and researcher at the Erasmus University of Rotterdam (NL) and INSEAD (France).

Hassan Bevrani received PhD degree in electrical engineering from Osaka University, Osaka, Japan, in 2004. From 2004 to 2006, he was a Post-Doctoral Fellow with Kumamoto University, Kumamoto, Japan. From 2007 to 2008, he was a Senior Research Fellow with the Queensland University of Technology, Brisbane, Australia. At the time of writing this paper, he was visiting Professor with Kyushu Institute of Technology, Japan. Since 2000, he has been an Academic Member with the University of Kurdistan, Sanandaj, Iran. His current research interests include smart grids, intelligent and robust control applications in power system, and power electronic industry.

Malcolm J. Beynon is a Professor of Uncertain Reasoning at Cardiff University, UK. He gained his BSc and PhD in pure mathematics and computational mathematics, respectively, at Cardiff University. His research areas include the theoretical and application of uncertain reasoning methodologies, including Dempster-Shafer theory, fuzzy set theory, and rough set theory. Also the introduction and development of multi-criteria based decision making and classification techniques, including the classification and ranking belief simplex. He has published over 100 research articles. He is a member of the International Rough Set Society, International Operations Research Society, and the International Multi-Criteria Decision Making Society.

Mark Clatworthy is a Professor of Accounting at Cardiff University. He earned a BSc and PhD in Accounting, both from University of Wales. He teaches Financial Accounting, Research Topics in Accounting, Analysis of Financial Reporting Information, and Introduction to Stata. His research interests include financial report, audit markets, and capital markets' use of accounting information, to name a few.

Albert Corominas is a Professor of Industrial Engineering and Operations Research at the Universitat Politècnica de Catalunya (UPC), where he is a member of the Business Administration department and the ETSEIB. He has degrees in Computer Science from the Universidad Politécnica de Madrid and in Engineering from the Universidad del País Vasco (UPV); his PhD is also from the UPV. His research activities, at the Institute of Industrial and Control Engineering of the UPC, are focused on modelling and solving, by means of optimisation techniques, industrial engineering problems. He is author or co-author of books and papers that have been published in *AoOR, C&IE, C&OR, EJOR, IJFMS, IJPE, IJPR, INFOR, Interfaces, JIMO, JoSch, JORS, Omega, PP&C*, and *ORL* among other journals. Dr. Corominas is a member of ADINGOR, IIE, INFORMS, ORS, POMS, and SEIO, of the Editorial Board of the *IJPR* and of the research groups EOLI and GIOPACT, of the UPC.

Mingcong Deng received his Ph. D. degree from Kumamoto University, Japan, in 1997. He is currently a professor of Department of Electrical and Electronic Engineering, Tokyo University of Agriculture and Technology, Japan. His research interests include nonlinear system modeling and control including operator-based nonlinear control, strong stability-based control and robust parallel compensation; living body measurement.

Vo Ngoc Dieu received his B.Eng. and M.Eng. degrees in Electrical Engineering from Ho Chi Minh City University of Technology, Ho Chi Minh City, Vietnam, in 1995 and 2000, respectively and his D.Eng. degree in Energy from Asian Institute of Technology (AIT), Pathumthani, Thailand in 2007. He is Research Associate at Energy Field of Study, AIT and Lecturer at Department of Power Systems, Faculty of Electrical and Electronic Engineering, Ho Chi Minh City University of Technology, Ho Chi Minh city, Vietnam. His interests are applications of AI in power system optimization, power system operation and control, power system analysis, and power systems under deregulation.

Aijuan Dong is an Assistant Professor of Computer Science in Hood College. She received her Ph.D. in Computer Science from North Dakota State University. Her current research interests include video segmentation, annotation and access, image/video processing, data mining, and knowledge representation and inference. Dr. Dong is a member of the IEEE Woman in Engineering and the Institute of Electrical and Electronics Engineers (IEEE) society.

Pavel V. Etingov (M'05) is a Senior Researcher at the Energy Systems Institute of the Russian Academy of Sciences, Irkutsk, Russia. He was born in 1976 in Irkutsk. He graduated with honors from Irkutsk State Technical University specializing in Electrical Engineering in 1997. He was a fellow at the Swiss Federal Institute of Technology in 2000-2001. P.V. Etingov received his PhD degree in 2003 from the Energy Systems Institute of the Russian Academy of Sciences. His research interests include stability analysis of electric power systems, emergency control, FACTS devices, and application of artificial intelligence to power systems. He has been the secretary of the IEEE PES Russian Chapter since October 2005.

Petr Dostál is a Professor of Economy and Management. He teaches at Brno University of Technology, Czech Republic. His field of interest is the use of soft computing and artificial intelligence such as fuzzy logic, artificial neural networks, evolutionary algorithms, and the theory of chaos in business and public services. As an economic and organisation advisor, he has worked in private firms and institutions. He is a member of international institutions, program and organizing committees, scientific and editorial advisory boards, Berkeley Initiative in Soft Computing, Society of Computational Economics, and International Institution of Forecasters. He gives lectures at various universities at home and abroad. He has published many books and articles in international journals.

Alberto Garcia-Villoria is a Computer Engineer from the Universitat Politècnica de Catalunya (UPC) and holds a PhD in advanced automation and robotics, also by the UPC. He is a Professor of the Business Administration department. His research focuses on studying and solving scheduling problems in the field of industrial organization, along with other combinatorial optimization problems. He has participated in several research projects about the design and assembly line balancing in realistic settings and time schedule of work and production with flexible working time.

Alexander Z. Gamm graduated from the Electrotechnical Institute, Novosibirsk, Russia, where he received the PhD and D.Sc. degrees. During 1961-1962, he was a scientific worker in the Transport Power Institute, Novosibirsk. Since then, he has been with the Energy System Institute (ESI), Russian Academy of Sciences, Irkutsk. At present, he is a Chief Researcher. His special fields of interest include state estimation, optimization, and real-time control problems. Dr. Gamm is an Academician of the Russian Academy of Electrical Sciences and member of International Energy Academy.

Abdolsalam Ghaderi is Assistant Professor of Industrial Engineering at University of Kurdistan, Iran. He received his Ph.D from Iran University of Science and Technology. He also was in the University of Newcastle, Australia, for one year in 2011 as a research visitor. His research interest in operations research involves optimization and mathematical modelling for supply chain management especially in facility location and network design area. He is also interested in design and developing solution methods including exact, heuristic, and meta-heuristic algorithms.

Fatima Ghedjati is an Associate Professor in IUT of Reims, University of Reims Champagne-Ardenne, France. She received her MS degree from the University of Nancy I and PhD (1994) in computer science from the University of Paris 6, France. Her research interests are scheduling, combinatorial optimization, Multi-criteria decision, heuristics, and meta-heuristics (Genetic Algorithms, Tabu Search, Ant Colony Optimization).

Anna M. Glazunova graduated from the Irkutsk Polytechnical Institute in 1982. Since 1986 she has been working as a Researcher at Energy Systems Institute. She received the Ph.D (2002). Her research interests are: methods of state estimation of electric power systems (EPS), application of Expert Systems, and Artificial Neural Networks for on-line EPS control.

Farshid Habibi was born in Sanandaj, Iran, in 1985. He received B.S. and M.S. degrees in Electrical Engineering from University of Kurdistan, Kurdistan, Iran, in 2009 and 2012, respectively. During 2010 and 2011, he has been a Teaching Assistant for linear control systems and modern control system courses. He is currently with control laboratory of University of Kurdistan. His research area includes power electronic, intelligent and robust control methods, Micro/Smart grids, and power system dynamics and stability.

Napsiah Bt. Ismail is currently Professor of Department of Mechanical and Manufacturing Engineering, Faculty of Engineering, University of Putra Malaysia (UPM). She obtained Ph.D. from Universiti Teknologi Malaysia (UTM) in 2000 and she graduated M.Sc. in field of Mechanical from University of Leeds in UK. From 2003 to 2008, she was head of Department of Mechanical and Manufacturing Engineering in Faculty of Engineering in UPM. Prof. Napsiah has published more than 200 papers in academic books, journals, and proceedings. Her major research interest includes advanced manufacturing technology, intelligent manufacturing, automation, and sustainable manufacturing. Her papers have been presented in the several international conferences.

Lihua Jiang received her Ph. D. degree from Okayama University, Japan, in 2009. She is currently a lecturer with State Key Laboratory of Synthetical Automation for Process Industries (Northeastern University), China. She is also a vice-secretary-general of Technical Committee on Process Control, Chinese Association of Automation. Her research interests include robotics, pattern recognition, and system identification, instrumentation, and measuring.

Cengiz Kahraman is a full Professor at and the Chair of the Department of Industrial Engineering of Istanbul Technical University. His research areas include uncertain information process, computational intelligence, and fuzzy set applications in engineering economics, quality management and control, and statistical decision making. He has published over 120 journal papers, 110 conference papers, 50 book chapters, and 4 edited books. He had been a guest editor for 15 special issues in international journals.

Safa Khalouli received the MS degree in Systems' Optimization and Security (OSS) from the University of Technology Troyes-France in 2005 and the Ph.D degree in computer science from the University of Reims-Champagne-Ardenne-France, in 2010. Her current research interests include combinatorial optimization, scheduling, metaheuristics, and heuristics.

Laiq Khan received his B.Sc. (Hons) degree in Electrical Engineering from PakhtoonKwah University of Engineering and Technology, Peshawar, Pakistan in 1996 and his PhD degree (Power System Dynamics and Control) from University of Strathclyde Glasgow, UK in 2003. Before Ph.D. he worked in Siemens Pakistan as a Field Engineer for two years. He worked as an Assistant Professor in the Faculty of Electronic Engineering Ghulam Ishaq Khan Institute of Engineering Sciences and Technology, Swabi,

Pakistan from June, 2003 to Feb., 2008. Then he joined the Faculty of Electrical Engineering COMSATS Institute of IT, Abbottabad, Pakistan and worked as an Associate Professor till June, 2011. Currently he is a Professor of Power System Dynamics and Control in COMSATS IIT, Abbottbad, Pakistan. His research interests include power system stability and control using PSSs and FACTS controllers, robust control theory, intelligent control systems, nonlinear adaptive intelligent control and adaptive predictive intelligent control, power system planning, and advanced optimization techniques.

Irina N. Kolosok received hers M.Sc. degree in Electrical Engineering in 1972 at the Electromechanical Faculty of S. Peterburg Technical University. In the years 1972-85 Kolosok Irina N. has been employed at the Irkutsk Branch of the Institute "Energosetproekt" (Designing and Development of Electrical Networks). Since 1985 she has been with Energy Systems Institute (ESI) Siberian Branch of Russian Academy of Sciences, currently as a leading researcher. She received the PhD (1986) and DSc (2004) degrees. Her scientific interests are: real-time control problems, especially in the field of state estimation of electric power systems (EPS), SCADA and WAMS systems, and application of AI-methods for on-line EPS control. She is the author and co-author of about 120 publications and 5 monographs. She is senior member of IEEE PES.

Elena S. Korkina graduated from Irkutsk Polytechnic Institute on speciality of an Engineer-Economist in 1978. Since 1987 she has been working at the ESI, SB RAS in the laboratory of electric power system operation control problems. She received the Ph.D in 2009 on "Development of methods for state estimation of electric power systems based on data integration of SCADA and PMU." Her scientific interests include: real-time control problems, SCADA systems, PMU, and WAMS.

Victor G. Kurbatsky (M'08) was born on May, 27th, 1949 in Russia, PhD, Professor, Doctor of Science. He is leading researcher at the Energy Systems Institute of the Russian Academy of Sciences, Irkutsk, Russia. He received his degree of Candidate of Technical Sciences at SibNIIE (Novosibirsk) in 1984 and Doctor of Technical Sciences at the Energy Systems Institute (Irkutsk) in 1997. His research interests include: electromagnetic compatibility and power quality in electric networks, application of artificial intelligence techniques in power systems. Professor Kurbatsky is the author of several monographs and manuals and more than 230 scientific papers.

Igor Litvinchev received his M.Sc. degree from Moscow Institute of Physics and Technology (Fizteh), Moscow, Russia, and Ph.D. and Dr.Sci. degrees in Systems Modelling and Optimisation from Computing Centre, Russian Academy of Sciences, Moscow. He has held visiting positions at universities in Brazil, Mexico, as well as positions at various universities and research centres in Russia. His research focuses on large-scale system modelling, optimisation, and control. Dr. Litvinchev is a member of Russian Academy of Natural Sciences and Mexican Academy of Sciences.

Amany M. Magdy is the Assistant Director of the Decision Support and Future Studies Center (DSFS), Faculty of Computers and Information, Cairo University, Cairo, Egypt. Amany started working at DSFS in 2007 and was promoted to her current position in 2010. Amany received her B.Sc. in Operations Research and Decision Support from the Faculty of Computers & Information in 2007. She is currently working towards her M.Sc. and has published several research articles in her research focus; new product development projects.

Miguel Mata is a Professor at the postgraduate program in Logistics and Supply Chain Management at Nuevo Leon State University (UANL), México, graduated from Queretaro State University, Mexico. Obtained his M.Sc (2005) and Ph.D. (2008) degrees in Systems Engineering from the Graduate Program in Systems Engineering at UANL. His research focuses on systems modeling and optimization.

Sidra Mumtaz completed her BS and MS in Computer Engineering from COMSATS Institute of Information Technology, Abbottabad, Pakistan in 2007 and 2009, respectively. She is serving as a lecturer since 2009 to current in Electrical Engineering Department of the same university. She has been working in the field of electrical engineering for the last three years and has been involved in a number of research projects. She has published over four refereed journal papers. Her research interests include meta-heuristic paradigms, intelligent control system, power system planning, and optimization.

Hossein Nezamabadi-Pour received his B.S. degree in Electrical Engineering from Shahid Bahonar University of Kerman in 1998, and his M.S. and Ph.D. degrees in Electrical Engineering from Tarbait Moderres University, Iran, in 2000 and 2004, respectively. In 2004, he joined the Department of Electrical Engineering at Shahid Bahonar University of Kerman, Kerman, Iran, as Assistant Professor, and was promoted to Associate Professor in 2008. Dr. Nezamabadi-Pour is author and co-author of more than 200 peer reviewed journal and conference papers. His research interests include evolutionary computation, pattern recognition, soft computing, and image processing.

Mehrdad Nikbakht is Industrial Engineering Ph.D. candidate in the Department of Mechanical and Manufacturing Engineering, faculty of engineering, University of Putra Malaysia (UPM). He holds a Master of Science in the Industrial Engineering and a Bachelor of Science in the Mechanical Engineering. He has had more than 14 years experiences as a scholar and a design engineer of water facilities constructions, gas networks and senior planning and projects control in the natural gas industry and manufacturing industries. Furthermore, he has had five years experiences for teaching in courses of project planning and management, Health, Safety and Environmental (HSE) and maintenance management. His current research interests are focused on mathematical modeling and metaheuristic algorithms application in manufacturing industries, supply chain, maintenance, project, quality, and HSE management.

Lucero Ozuna is a Professor at the postgraduate program in Logistics and SupplyChain Management at Nuevo Leon State University (UANL), México, graduated from the Faculty of Physics and Mathematics at UANL. Obtained her M.Sc. (2009) and PhD (2011) degrees in Systems Engineering from the Graduate Program in Systems Engineering at UANL. Her research focuses on large scale optimization.

Rafael Pastor is a Professor of Industrial Engineering and Operations Research at the School of Industrial Engineering of Barcelona of the Universitat Politècnica de Catalunya (UPC). Previously, he worked as a product production manager for Revlon. Dr. Pastor holds a PhD in Industrial Engineering and a Master's degree in Logistics Organization. His research focuses on the use of a variety of combinatorial optimization techniques to model and solve real-world applications in production, scheduling, and manpower planning. He has published in *TOP, EJOR, JORS, IJPE, IJPR, C&OR, OMEGA, JoH, Annals of Operations Research, Ricerca Operativa, IJMTM,* and *IJSTM* among other journals.

Hindriyanto Dwi Purnomo is a Lecturer in Department of Information Technology, Satya Wacana Christian University, Indonesia. He received his B.Eng in Physic Engineering from Gadjah Mada University (INA) and Master of Information Technology from The University of Melbourne (AUS). Currently, he is a Doctoral student in Department of Industrial and Systems Engineering at Chung Yuan Christian University, Taiwan. His research interests are in the field of optimization, artificial intelligence, and application of soft computing in industrial practices. He has published several papers in journals and conferences.

Socorro Rangel received her M.Sc. degree from Campinas State University (UNICAMP), Campinas, Brazil, and Ph.D. degree from Brunel University, Uxbridge, England. She is currently an Associated Professor at the São Paulo State University(UNESP), São José do Rio Preto, Brazil. Her main research interests lies on large-scale system modelling and combinatorial optimisation.

Jana Ries is a Lecturer in Statistics and Quantitative Methods at the Business School of the University of Portsmouth. She holds an MSc in Logistics and Optimisation, and a PhD in Operational Research, both from the University of Portsmouth. Upon completing her PhD, she has worked as a post-doctoral researcher in two projects funded by the European Commission under the 7th Framework Programme: LOGMAN, on the evaluation of new Logistics and Manufacturing trends by analysing impacts on economic and environmental sustainability, and SEABILLA on the design of a decision support system for unmanned aerial vehicles in sea surveillance. Her research areas include calibration strategies for meta-heuristics, cooperative heuristic concepts, and decision support systems in transport logistics and supply chain management.

Abdolhossein Sadrnia is an Industrial Engineering PhD student in the Department of Mechanical and Manufacturing Engineering, Faculty of Engineering, University of Putra Malaysia (UPM). He holds a Master of Science in the Industrial Engineering from Sharif University of Technology, as well as more than 12 years experience in automotive supply chain, project director and project coordinator in R&D department. His current research interests are focused on green supply chain and closed-loop supply chain as well as metaheuristics algorithm application to optimize logistics network. His papers/articles have presented in the several conferences.

Jania Saucedo is a Professor at the postgraduate program in Logistics and Supply Chain Management at Nuevo Leon State University (UANL), México. Graduated from the Faculty of Physics and Mathematics at UANL. Obtained her M.Sc. (2008) and PhD (2009) degrees in Systems Engineering from the Graduate Program in Systems Engineering at UANL. Her research focuses on large scale numerical optimization.

Peter Schegner studied Electrical Power Engineering at the Darmstadt University of Technology (Germany) where he received the Dipl.-Ing. degree in 1982. After that he worked as system engineer in the field of power system control and became a member of the scientific staff at the Saarland University (Germany), receiving the Ph D degree in 1989 with a thesis on the earthfault distance protection. From 1989 until 1995 he worked as head of the development department of protection systems at AEG, Frankfurt A.M., Germany. In 1995 he became a Full Professor and head of Institute of Electrical Power Systems and High Voltage Engineering of the Dresden University of Technology (Germany).

Ozlem Senvar (M.Sc.) is a Ph.D. candidate at Marmara University, Industrial Engineering Department. She holds a Bachelor's degree in Statistics and Computer Sciences from Blacksea Technical University. She holds Master's degrees in Quality Engineering and Statistics. Ozlem Senvar's current research interests are quality engineering, statistical process control, quality management and improvement, production planning, design of experiments, data mining, et cetera.

Shoresh Shokoohi was born in Sanandaj, Iran, in 1987. He received B.Sc. (honors) and M.Sc. degrees in electrical engineering from University of Kurdistan, in 2009 and 2012, respectively. In 2010, he was with the control laboratory of University of Kurdistan, as a Lecturer. In 2009 and 2010, he was a Teaching Assistant for Linear Control Systems and Electronics courses. Currently, he is with the Instrumentation and Control Unit of IOPTC. His current research interests include voltage/frequency control of Micro/Smart Grids, robust and intelligent control theories, and applications to power systems.

Denis N. Sidorov was born on October, 30th, 1974 in Irkutsk (Russia), PhD, Associate Professor. Dr. Sidorov is Senior Researcher at the Energy Systems Institute, SB RAS In 1999 he defended his PhD thesis "Modeling of Nonlinear Dynamic Systems with Volterra Series: Theory and Applications." He was with Department of Electronic and Electrical Engineering in Trinity College Dublin (Ireland), with CNRS (Compiegne, France) involved in different DSP and NDT Projects in 2001-2005. His research interests include: DSP, pattern recognition, integral and differential equations and modeling of nonlinear dynamical systems. Dr. Sidorov is the author of 120 scientific papers.

Vadim A. Spiryaev was born on November, 9th, 1980 in Irkutsk (Russia). He works as a researcher at Energy Systems Institute. SB RAS. His research interests include: integral and differential equations, modeling of nonlinear dynamical systems. V.A. Spiryaev is the author of 27 scientific papers.

Ata Allah Taleizadeh received his B.Sc. degree in Industrial Engineering from Azad university of Qazvin and M.S. and Ph.D. degrees from Iran University of Science and Technology. His research interest areas include inventory control and management, Pricing and Revenue optimization, Supply Chain Management and Mathematical Models of Marketing. He has several publications in some journals such as *Computer and Industrial Engineering, European Journal of Industrial Engineering, Mathematical and Computer Modeling, International journal of System Sciences and Engineering Optimization, Expert Systems and with Applications, Scientia Iranica, Journal of Manufacturing Systems, Applied Soft Computing, Applied Mathematics and Computations and Journal of Computational and Applied Mathematics,* and *International Journal of Advanced Manufacturing Technology*. He has published two books in the field of Probability and Quality Control in Persian language. Also he belongs to editorial boards of some international journals.

Nikita V. Tomin (M'08) was born on December 18th in 1982, in Russia. Dr. Tomin is a Senior researcher at the Energy Systems Institute of the Russian Academy of Science, Irkutsk, Russia. In 2007 he defended his PhD thesis at the Energy Systems Institute SB RAS (Irkutsk). Dr. Tomin specializes in the field of artificial intelligence technologies in electric power systems. He is the author and co-author of more than 60 scientific papers.

Ebru Turanoglu was born in Nigde, Turkey on 13 November 1987. She graduated from Turhal Anatolian High School in 2005. Then she started to undergraduate education at Selcuk University, Engineering and Architecture Faculty, Industrial Engineering Department. In 2009, she graduated from this department and then in the same year she started Master's in Education at Selcuk University, Institute of Science, Industrial Engineering Department. She is still a Master's student and also research assistant at the same department. She researches some areas including statistical quality control and fuzzy sets theory, and metaheuristics techniques. She has one brother.

Nikolai I. Voropai (M'1996, SM'1998; F'2009) is Director of the Energy Systems Institute (Siberian Energy Institute until 1997) of the Russian Academy of Sciences, Irkutsk, Russia. He is also Head of Department at Irkutsk Technical University. He was born in Belarus in 1943. He graduated from Leningrad (St. Petersburg) Polytechnic Institute in 1966 and has been with the Siberian Energy Institute since. N.I. Voropai received his degree of Candidate of Technical Sciences at Leningrad Polytechnic Institute in 1974, and Doctor of Technical Sciences at the Siberian Energy Institute in 1990. His research interests include: modeling of power systems; operation and dynamic performance of large interconnections; reliability, security and restoration of power systems; development of national, international and intercontinental electric power grids. N.I. Voropai is a member of CIGRE, a Fellow of IEEE, and a member of PES. He is the IEEE PES Region 8 Zone East Representative.

Baoying Wang is an Associate Professor in Waynesburg University, PA, USA. She received her PhD degree in Computer Science from North Dakota State University, Master's degree from Minnesota State University of St. Cloud, and Bachelor's degree from Beijing University of Science and Technology. Her research interests include data mining, data warehouse, bioinformatics, and parallel computing. She is a member of ACM, ISCA and SIGMOD. As professional activities, she serves as a reviewer and/or a committee member of many international conferences and journals.

Yang Wang is a Lecturer in Beijing Key Laboratory of Transportation Engineering at Beijing University of Technology. He obtained his MSc and PhD from the University of York and Loughborough University in the UK in 2004 and 2007, respectively. Then, he was employed as a post-doctoral researcher at University of Portsmouth in the UK. His current research areas include traffic information engineering and control, intelligent transport systems, and traffic prediction. He has been involved in a number of researcher projects as a Principal Investigator and has published a number of peer-reviewed papers.

Hui-Ming Wee is a Professor in Department of Industrial and Systems Engineering at Chung Yuan Christian University in Taiwan. He received his BSc (Hons) in Electrical and Electronic Engineering from Strathclyde University (UK), MEng in Industrial Engineering and Management from Asian Institute of Technology (AIT) and PhD in Industrial Engineering from Cleveland State University, Ohio (USA). His research interests are in the field of production/inventory control, optimization and supply chain management. He has published more than 300 papers in refereed journals, conference papers, books and book chapters. He also serves as editorial board for a number of international journals.

Roman A. Zaika graduated from the Irkutsk Polytecnical Institute in 1999. Since 2001 he worked as scientific worker in Energy Systems Institute. He received the scientific degree in 2005. His research interests are: methods of state estimation of electric power systems and application of Genetic Algorithms for bad data identification.

Index